Smith, Hogan, and Ormerod's
TEXT, CASES, AND MATERIALS ON
CRIMINAL LAW

Twelfth edition

David Ormerod QC

Law Commissioner for England and Wales,
Professor of Criminal Justice, University College London
Bencher of Middle Temple,
Door Tenant at 18 Red Lion Court

Karl Laird

Lecturer in Law, St Edmund Hall, Oxford

OXFORD
UNIVERSITY PRESS

OXFORD
UNIVERSITY PRESS

Great Clarendon Street, Oxford, OX2 6DP,
United Kingdom

Oxford University Press is a department of the University of Oxford.
It furthers the University's objective of excellence in research, scholarship,
and education by publishing worldwide. Oxford is a registered trade mark of
Oxford University Press in the UK and in certain other countries

© Oxford University Press 2017

The moral rights of the authors have been asserted

Ninth edition 2005
Tenth edition 2009
Eleventh edition 2014

Impression: 1

Public sector information reproduced under Open Government Licence v3.0
(http://www.nationalarchives.gov.uk/doc/open-government-licence/open-government-licence.htm)

Published in the United States of America by Oxford University Press
198 Madison Avenue, New York, NY 10016, United States of America

British Library Cataloguing in Publication Data
Data available

Library of Congress Control Number: 2017939057

ISBN 978–0–19–878871–3

Printed in Great Britain by
Bell & Bain Ltd., Glasgow

Preface

In this edition of *Smith, Hogan, and Ormerod's Text, Cases, and Materials* we continue the restructuring and redesign of the book that we began in the last edition.

We intend the text to remain a single comprehensive point of reference for students and so the chapters have been thoroughly revised and restructured to ensure that they continue to reflect the typical content of the undergraduate degree syllabus for criminal law. We have also included even more case commentary and analysis to assist the reader. We maintain our belief that textbook commentary is no substitute for first-hand engagement with the relevant material. Reading source material and reflecting on its meaning and significance is crucial, not only to the development of students' analytical abilities, but ultimately for academic success and for any career in the law. To that end, we have included a sufficient number of extracts to permit students the opportunity to grapple with the relevant case law, statutory material and academic commentary themselves.

The most significant change to the content of the book has been necessitated by the judgment of the Supreme Court in *Jogee*. We have rewritten a substantial portion of the complicity chapter to take account of the changes introduced by the Supreme Court's judgment. In addition to our own commentary on the judgment, we have also included some of the criticisms that have been made by leading commentators. We hope that the chapter will give students not only the ability to state the law with confidence, but also the ability to evaluate its merits.

At OUP we have been assisted enormously by John Carroll and Sarah Stephenson who made the publication process as painless as ever. We would like to record our thanks to Joy Ruskin-Tompkins and Jonathon Price who copy-edited and proofread the entire manuscript.

The manuscript was delivered in January 2017. Annual updates will be available on the online page.

David Ormerod
Karl Laird
May 2017

New to This Edition

This edition has been comprehensively updated to take account of recent legislation and the major decisions of the appellate courts. These include:

- *Taylor* in the Supreme Court on doubly strict liability in causing death by driving unlawfully (Ch 3)
- *Golds* in the Supreme Court on diminished responsibility (Ch 8)
- *Sellu* on how bad the defendant's breach of duty must be before he will be guilty of gross negligence manslaughter (Ch 9)
- *Valujevs* on the offence of fraud by abuse of position contained in the Fraud Act 2006 (Ch 16)
- *Jogee* in the Supreme Court on complicity (Ch 19)
- *Johnson* on whether those who were convicted on the basis of 'joint enterprise' ought to be able to appeal their convictions (Ch 19)
- *HKSAR v Chan Kam Shing* in the Hong Kong Court of Final Appeal on whether the Supreme Court's judgment in *Jogee* requires a re-evaluation of the applicable law in Hong Kong (Ch 19)
- *Pace and Rogers* on the mens rea of a criminal attempt (Ch 20)
- *Serious Fraud Office v Papachristos* on the actus reus of a criminal conspiracy (Ch 21)
- *R (Collins) v Secretary of State for Justice* on how the 'householder provision' that now applies in self-defence ought to be interpreted (Ch 23)
- *Aravena* in the Ontario Court of Appeal on whether duress can be a defence to murder (Ch 23)

Outline Contents

Detailed Contents

Acknowledgements

Grateful acknowledgement is made to all the authors and publishers of copyright material that appear in this book, and in particular to the following for permission to reprint material from the sources indicated:

Extracts from Law Commission Reports, Criminal Law Review Commission Reports, Consultation Papers, and CPS Guidelines are Crown copyright material and are reproduced under Class Licence Number C01P0000148 with the permission of the Controller of OPSI and the Queen's Printer for Scotland. Parliamentary copyright material is reproduced with the permission of the Controller of Her Majesty's Stationery Office on behalf of Parliament.

Professor John Bell: extract from *Cambridge Law Journal*: Glanville Williams, 'Oblique Intention' (1987) 46 CLJ 417.

Hart Publishing Ltd: extracts from J. Horder: 'The Changing Face of the Law of Homicide' in J. Horder (ed): *Homicide Law in Comparative Perspective* (Hart, 2008).

Harvard University Press: extracts from *Thirteen Ways to Steal a Bicycle: Theft Law In The Information Age* by Stuart P. Green, Cambridge, Mass.: Harvard University Press, Copyright © 2012 by the President and Fellows of Harvard College.

Incorporated Council of Law Reporting: extracts from the *Law Reports: Court of Appeal Queen's Bench Division, House of Lords, and Supreme Court*.

Oxford University Press: extracts from S. P. Green: 'Six Senses of Strict Liability: A Plea for Formalism' in A. Simester (ed), *Appraising Strict Liability* (OUP, 2005); Andrew Ashworth: 'Belief and Intent in Criminal Liability' in J. Eekelaar and J. Bell (eds): *Oxford Essays in Jurisprudence* (OUP, 1987); extracts from A. Simester: 'On Justifications and Excuses'; B. Mitchell: 'Years of Provocation, Followed by a Loss of Control', all in L. Zedner and J. V. Roberts (eds): *Principles and Values in Criminal Law and Criminal Justice: Essays in Honour of Andrew Ashworth* (OUP, 2012); extracts from *Current Legal Problems* (CLP): D. Ormerod: 'Making Sense of Statutory Conspiracy', CLP 185 (2006); extracts from L. Farmer, 'Definitions of Crime' in P. Cane and J. Conaghen (eds) *The New Oxford Companion to Law* (2008).

Prof. Paul H. Robinson: extract from P. H. Robinson, *'Four Distinctions that Glanville Williams Did Not Make: the Practical Benefits of Examining the Interrelation Among Criminal Law Doctrines'*, in The Sanctity of Life and the Criminal Law: The Legacy of Glanville Williams, edited by D. Baker & J. Horder (CUP, 2013)

RELX (UK) Limited, trading as LexisNexis: extracts from *All England Law Reports* (All ER).

Springer: extract from A. Leipold: 'A Case for Criminal Negligence' (2010) 29 *Law and Philosophy* (Law & Phil) 455.

Sweet & Maxwell Ltd: extracts from J. C. Smith: from *Justification and Excuse in the Criminal Law* (The Hamlyn Lectures, Stevens, 1989); extracts from *Criminal Law Review*: J. Horder: 'A Critique of the Correspondence Principle in Criminal Law', Crim LR 759 (1955); J. Gobert: 'A Corporate Criminality: New Crimes for the Times', Crim LR 722 (1994); R. D. Mackay and C. Gearty: 'On Being Insane in Jersey—the Case of *Attorney General v Jason Prior*', Crim LR 560 (2001); *Sir John Smith*, Crim LR 952 (2002); Glanville Williams: 'Necessity', Crim LR 128 (1978); M. Weait, 'Knowledge, Autonomy, and Consent: R v Konzani' [2005] Crim LR

763; A. Norrie: 'The Coroners and Justice Act 2009—Partial Defences to Murder (1) Loss of Control', Crim LR 275 (2010); R. D. Mackay: 'The Coroners and Justice Act 2009—Partial Defences to Murder (2) The New Diminished Responsibility Plea', Crim LR 290 (2010); J. Horder and L. McGowan: 'Manslaughter by Causing Another's Suicide', Crim LR 1035 (2006); J. Herring: 'Mistaken Sex', Crim LR 511 (2005); H. Gross: 'Rape, Moralism and Human Rights', Crim LR 220 (2007); A. Norrie, 'After Woollin' [1999] Crim LR 532; E. J. Griew: 'Dishonesty, the Objections to *Feely* and *Ghosh*', Crim LR 341 (1985); D. Ormerod: 'Case Commentary on *Dooley*', Crim LR 544 (2006); extracts from cases reported in *Criminal Law Review*; extracts from *Law Quarterly Review*: A. Ashworth, 'Is the criminal law a lost cause?' (2000) LQR 225; A. Ashworth: 'The Scope of Criminal Liability for Omissions', 105 LQR 424 (1989); G. Williams: 'Criminal Omissions—The Conventional View', 107 LQR 86 (1991); S. Gough: 'Intoxication and Criminal Liability: The Law Commission's Proposed Reforms', 112 LQR 335 (1996); R. Goff: 'The Mental Element in the Crime of Murder', 104 LQR 30 (1988); A.P. Simester, 'Accessory liability and common unlawful purposes' (2017) LQR 73. Extracts from *Criminal Appeal Reports: R v Gibbins and Proctor*: 13 Cr App R 134, Court of Criminal Appeal (Darling, McCardie and Salter JJ) (1918); *Matthews and Alleyne*, 2 Cr App R 30, Crim LR 553, Court of Appeal, Criminal Division (Rix LJ, Crane J and Maddison HHJ) (2003); *R v Becerra and Cooper*: 62 Cr App R 212, Court of Appeal, Criminal Division (Roskill and Bridge LJJ and Kilner Brown J) (1975); *Johnson*: 89 Cr App R 148 (1989); *R v Diana Richardson*: 2 Cr App R 200, Court of Appeal, Criminal Division (Otton LJ, Turner and Dyson JJ) (1998); Also extracts from *Archbold News* (Arch Rev), *European Human Rights Law Review* (EHRLR), and *European Human Rights Reports* (EHRR).

Wiley-Blackwell: extracts from *Modern Law Review* (MLR): J. Chalmers and F. Leverick: 'Fair Labelling in Criminal Law' (2008) 71 MLR 217.

Every effort has been made to trace and contact copyright holders prior to going to press. If notified, the publisher will undertake to rectify any errors or omissions at the earliest opportunity.

Table of Statutes

References in **bold** type indicate that the text is reproduced in full.

Table of Cases

References in **bold** type indicate that the text is reproduced in full.

1

Introduction

1.1 What is a crime?

This book is concerned with the criminal law of England and Wales. There is, however, no universally accepted definition of what constitutes a crime.

L. Farmer, 'Definitions of Crime'
in P. Cane and J. Conaghan (eds), *The New Oxford Companion to Law* (2008)

There is no simple and universally accepted definition of crime in the modern criminal law, a feature that probably reflects the large and diverse range of behaviours that have been criminalized by the modern state. It is now widely accepted that crime is a category created by law—that is, a law that most actions are criminal because there is a law that declares them to be so—so this must be the starting point for any definition.

Most modern definitions of crime fall into two main categories, the moral and the procedural. Moral definitions of crime are based on the claim that there is (or should be) some intrinsic quality that is shared by all acts criminalized by the state. This quality was originally sought in the acts themselves—that all crimes were in an important sense moral wrongs, or *mala in se*—and that the law merely recognized this wrongful quality. The weakness of this approach was that is could extend to certain actions which seemed morally neutral (often referred to as *mala prohibita*), such as speeding or failing to register the birth of a child, which have been made crimes by statute. Accordingly, it is argued crimes are such because criminal law recognizes public wrongs as violations of rights or duties owed to the whole community to respect the law. This definition covers a broader range of offences, as well as recognizing the sociological fact that many acts are criminal only by virtue of being declared so by the law. The strength of this type of definition is less a description of the object of the criminal law, than as an account of the principles which should limit the proper scope of the criminal law.

Procedural definitions, by contrast, define crimes as those acts which might be prosecuted or punished under criminal procedure. The most influential definition of this type was produced by legal theorist, Glanville Williams, in 1955. He sought a purely formal definition of crime. For him, a crime is

> An act capable of being followed by criminal proceedings having a criminal outcome, and a proceeding or its outcome is criminal if it has certain characteristics which mark it as criminal.

This is undeniably circular (something is criminal if it is criminal), and seems to avoid definition of the term 'criminal' and so might appear to be of little use. However, it largely reflects more accurately the reality of the modern criminal law, where the scope of the law has extended to include large numbers of regulatory offences tried under criminal proceedings, the content of which go far beyond conduct which can easily be regarded as moral or even public wrongs. However, given the diverse range of sanctions and procedures which can be adopted, from forms of treatment or reparation to mediation or restorative justice, it is not obvious that this definition alone can help to determine what is or is not a criminal proceeding.

Not only is there no universally accepted definition of a crime, no one knows how many criminal offences actually exist in England and Wales. Unlike most jurisdictions, England and Wales has no criminal code. From very early times Parliament has created criminal offences. These have always taken effect in the context of the common law of crime, that is, the law made by the judges in the decided cases. The result is that the criminal law is spread across a huge range of statutes and decisions. It has been suggested that more offences than ever are being created.

J. Chalmers and F. Leverick, 'Tracking the Creation of Criminal Offences'
[2013] Crim LR 543

3,023 new offences?

In August 2006 it was claimed that the Labour government had created 3,023 offences since elected in May 1997. That figure has been regularly cited as evidence of the overuse of criminal law, and the Liberal Democrats made halting such overuse a commitment in their 2010 election manifesto. In due course, the *Coalition's Programme for Government*, published in May 2010, committed the government to 'introduc[ing] a new mechanism to prevent the proliferation of unnecessary new criminal offences'. In November 2010, the Ministry of Justice committed to creating 'a gateway to scrutinise all legislation containing criminal offences' and publishing annual statistics on the number of new offences.

According to the guidance contained in the resulting *Criminal Offences Gateway*, civil servants require 'Gateway clearance' if they propose to use legislation to create a new offence, repeal and re-enact an existing offence, amend an existing offence or create an enabling power in primary legislation providing for the creation or extension of criminal offences in secondary legislation or byelaws. The Secretary of State for Justice will approve proposals only if 'he is satisfied that the proposed offences are necessary': no test of necessity is set out, but there is a lengthy list of factors to be taken into account.

In December 2011, the Ministry of Justice published statistics on the creation of new criminal offences in England and Wales. According to these, 174 new criminal offences were created in the 12 months ending May 2011, compared to 712 in the 12 months ending May 2010.

At first sight, this suggests an impressive degree of success in stemming the tide of new offences. Matters are not, however, quite that simple. We have undertaken an independent research project examining the creation of offences over two time periods: the first 12 months of the New Labour government elected in 1997 and of the Coalition government elected in 2010. Our results are rather different. While the Ministry of Justice claims that 174 new offences applying to England and Wales were created in the first year of the Coalition government, our research produced a figure of 634. And while we have not ourselves examined the year prior to the Coalition government, our research demonstrates that the Ministry's own statistics do not provide an adequate factual basis for its claim that 2010–11 saw a 75.6 per cent fall in the number of offences created by legislation.

≋ *Questions*
How many offences can you think of? Dozens? Hundreds? Can you name all 9,000+ that the criminal law assumes that you and all other people over the age of 10 know? Does it matter? Is what matters that you know where to look?

The current state of affairs has led Andrew Ashworth to query whether English criminal law is a lost cause in the sense that we cannot even be clear when Parliament enacts these numerous provisions whether they are offences or not.

A. Ashworth, 'Is the Criminal Law a Lost Cause?'
(2000) 116 LQR 225 (references omitted)

I. DISTINGUISHING CRIMINAL OFFENCES BY REFERENCE TO THEIR CONTENT

The sheer bulk of English criminal law makes it highly unlikely that the substantive content of the offences conforms to a single test or set of related tests. There are probably around 8,000 offences now, mostly created over the last 150 years, under the varying influences of governments of different political hues, movements towards criminal law reform, the expansion of regulatory mechanisms, and so forth. It is therefore hardly surprising that, in his classic article on the subject, Glanville Williams concluded that there is no workable definition of a crime in English law that is content-based: only the different procedures of criminal, as distinct from civil, cases can serve as a reliable distinguishing mark. In the realm of description, then, we can affirm that the contours of English criminal law are 'historically contingent'—not the product of any principled inquiry or consistent application of certain criteria, but largely dependent on the fortunes of successive governments, on campaigns in the mass media, on the activities of various pressure groups, and so forth.

This is not to deny that there have been elements of principle in debates on criminalisation in spheres such as abortion, prostitution, homosexual acts, and now drugs. However, those debates are noteworthy for a degree of attention to the proper boundaries of the criminal law which is conspicuously absent from most other decisions to criminalise. The implementation of the Human Rights Act 1998 should bring some improvements in this respect. Indeed section 19 of the Act, already in force, requires the Minister introducing a Bill to certify that the terms of the Bill comply with the European Convention on Human Rights (or to announce that no such statement can be made). It is well known that Articles 8 to 11 of the Convention declare rights that must be respected, subject to certain exceptions—the right to respect for private and family life, the right to freedom of thought, conscience and religion, the right to freedom of expression, and the right to freedom of assembly and association. There are also other parts of the Convention that may have an impact on substantive criminal law, such as Article 2 on the justifiable use of force, Article 3 on chastisement of children, Article 5 on the insanity defence, and so on. It would be unwise to over-estimate the impact of these Convention rights on the general shape of the criminal law: they are likely to exert some influence on the substance of offences and defences, but this is unlikely to falsify the proposition that the varying content of English offences cannot be captured by any general definition of crime.

In descriptive terms, then, the contours of English criminal law are indeed historically contingent. To cast some light on this, let us examine all the statutes passed in 1997, leaving aside those applying only to Scotland or to Northern Ireland. What we find are at least 39 crimes, most of which take one of four different forms. Some 13 of them are defined so as to require the prosecution to prove either intention or recklessness, which many regard as, in principle, the most appropriate culpability standard if criminal liability is to be imposed, and certainly if a significant sanction is to be imposed. Most of these offences penalise the giving of false information. Then there are nine strict liability offences, subject to exceptions which the defendant bears the burden of proving, a familiar legislative device. Eight further offences take a somewhat similar form, except that they penalise omissions (typically, failing to comply with a statutory requirement), but they too place on the defendant the burden of establishing an excuse or exception. Finally there are six strict liability offences, some of them penalising omissions, which include no specific provision for any defences.

In terms of function, several of the offences of making false statements are designed to underpin a regulatory scheme—for example, those established by the Architects Act 1997, the Nurses, Midwives and Health Visitors Act 1997, the Sex Offenders Act 1997, the Sexual Offences (Protected Material) Act 1997, the Plant Varieties Act 1997, and the Social Security Administration (Fraud) Act 1997. The last-mentioned statute, it may be noted, also provides various strict liability offences of failing to give information as required, crimes of omission which may or may not allow the defendant to establish 'reasonable excuse' in order to avoid conviction. That statute is about the prevention and punishment of fraud, and so criminal offences would be expected. Similar expectations arise, and a similar formula is to be found, in the Firearms (Amendment) Act 1997, a statute designed to tighten the control of firearms following the shootings at Dunblane. It creates several offences of omission, some of them providing that the defendant may prove reasonable excuse or due diligence in order to avoid conviction. Lastly, the Merchant Shipping and Maritime Security Act 1997 introduces various new offences concerned with non-observance of exclusion zones by the masters or owners of ships. Again, the predominant formula is to create an offence of omission, or another strict liability offence, with the proviso that the defendant may prove reasonable excuse or due diligence.

Although 1997 was thus a year in which there were relatively few additions to the criminal law as it applies generally, the Protection from Harassment Act and the Firearms (Amendment) Act being the main exceptions, this small survey highlights some noteworthy features of the existing criminal law. First, the bulk of new offences may be described as 'regulatory', in the sense that they form part of statutory schemes for the regulation of certain spheres of social or commercial activity, and are generally enforced by the regulatory authority rather than by the police. Secondly, the bulk of new offences are characterised by three features—strict liability, omissions liability, and reverse onus provisions for exculpation. All those features lie a considerable distance from the conception of criminal laws held by many university teachers and criminal practitioners. Indeed, they are inconsistent with prominent elements of the rhetoric of English criminal law—that there is a presumption that *mens rea* is a prerequisite of criminal liability, that liability for omissions is exceptional, and that 'one golden thread' running through English criminal law is that the prosecution bears the burden of proving guilt. It would be possible to interpret this dissonance between rhetoric and reality as a deliberate part of the architecture of social control, with the judges declaiming great principles whilst Parliament continues to depart from them. The reality is probably much less orderly than that. Parliament and the judges would be unlikely bedfellows in such an enterprise, and in any event the judges themselves often qualify a principle soon after declaring it so resoundingly.

Despite the disorderly state of English criminal law, it appears that the Government does profess some principles for criminalisation. In response to a parliamentary question, Lord Williams of Mostyn has stated that offences 'should be created only when absolutely necessary', and that

'In considering whether new offences should be created, factors taken into account include whether:
- the behaviour in question is sufficiently serious to warrant intervention by the criminal law;
- the mischief could be dealt with under existing legislation or by using other remedies;
- the proposed offence is enforceable in practice;
- the proposed offence is tightly drawn and legally sound; and
- the proposed penalty is commensurate with the seriousness of the offence.

The Government also takes into account the need to ensure, as far as practicable, that there is consistency across the sentencing framework.'

We will return to these professed principles at later points in the article. For the present, it suffices to say that our brief examination of the criminal laws of 1997 confirms the 'historical contingency' thesis and suggests that the laws being enacted bear little relation to the Government's supposed principles. However, adoption of the 'historical contingency' thesis should not lead us to abandon discussion of principle, even if it warns us to scrutinise rhetoric with care. It is worth recalling the warning of Nelken that 'the corrosive force of insisting that law is no more than a social construction can also undermine objective criticism of its injustices and delegitimate attempts to shape it in supposedly more progressive directions.' With this in mind, we begin to move from the descriptive to the normative, and to consider whether it is possible to identify criteria or standards that ought to be satisfied before it is decided to criminalise certain conduct—some of which may be similar to the principles which, according to Lord Williams, inform current practice.

1.2 Principles of the criminal law

It is said by some commentators and judges that there are a number of principles that under-pin the criminal law and which the law should aspire to uphold. When considering each of the offences considered in this book, examine the extent to which these principles are adhered to.

A. Ashworth, 'Is the Criminal Law a Lost Cause?'
(2000) 116 LQR 225

VIII. THE PRINCIPLED CORE OF CRIMINAL LAW

Although I have tried in this essay to give some flavour of the proliferation of legal forms and structures for the guidance of conduct, and thereby to demonstrate a blurring of the boundaries between criminal and regulatory and between criminal and civil, the main purpose has been to develop two lines of argument.

The first is that the criminal law is indeed a lost cause, from the point of view of principle. The Government's purported criteria for creating new crimes are not followed in practice, nor have they been in the recent past. *Pace* Lord Williams, new offences have been created to penalise non-serious misbehaviour, sometimes with maximum sentences out of proportion to other maxima. The empiri-cal basis for this claim was illustrated by examples from the 1997 statute book, and particularly the offence in section 1 of the Crime and Disorder Act 1998 of breaching an anti-social behaviour order. The plain fact is that governments often take the view that the creation of a new crime sends out a symbolic message that, in blunt terms, may 'get them off a political hook'—even though the new crime fails to satisfy Lord Williams' criteria on one or more grounds.

The second line of argument is more constructive, in seeking to identify a principled core of criminal law. The core consists, it is submitted, of four interlinked principles:

The principle that the criminal law should be used, and only used, to censure persons for substantial wrongdoing. This principle recognises that the prevention of such misconduct is a reason for criminal-ising it: if serious wrongdoing can be identified, it is of social importance that its incidence be reduced. However, this should be distinguished from the less acceptable propositions (*a*) that the prevention of misconduct is a sufficient reason for criminalisation, and (*b*) that the criminal law is, either on its own or in combination with other social policies, necessarily an effective means of prevention. The tendency to over-estimate the deterrent efficacy of criminal sentencing has already been mentioned. As for crime prevention strategies, these are usually designed to minimise the risk that certain situ-ations or opportunities will come about, or that certain individuals will find it attractive to behave in particular ways. Appropriately targeted social, educational and housing policies may well have a greater preventive effect than the enactment of a criminal offence and the conviction of (what is likely to be) a relatively small proportion of offenders, a point rarely acknowledged in the political and media discussions that lead to the creation of new crimes. However, methods of crime prevention also raise questions of moral and social principle that should be kept in view.

The principle that criminal laws should be enforced with respect for equal treatment and propor-tionality. The implication is that enforcement authorities and their policies ought to be reorganised so as to reflect the relative seriousness of the wrongdoing with which they are dealing, and should not remain hidebound by traditional divisions of responsibility that fail to reflect proper assessments of the culpable wrongs involved.

The principle that persons accused of substantial wrongdoing ought to be afforded the protections appropriate to those charged with criminal offences, i.e. at least the minimum protections declared by Articles 6.2 and 6.3 of the European Convention on Human Rights. These minimum protections ought to be regarded as an inherent element of criminal procedure, and this principle as interlinked with the others. Thus, if wrongdoing is regarded as serious enough to warrant the creation of an offence, and if it is thought so serious as to require a substantial maximum sentence, it would be a violation of this principle for a government to avoid or whittle down the protections that a person facing such a charge ought to be accorded. This, it will be recalled, is one objection to the offence of failing to comply with an anti-social behaviour order contrary to section 1 of the Crime and Disorder Act 1998. A maximum penalty of five years' imprisonment has been provided for what is a strict liability offence, all the substantive issues having been determined in earlier civil proceedings without the Article 6 safeguards. Civil–criminal hybrids designed to circumvent Convention rights are wrong in principle.

The principle that maximum sentences and effective sentence levels should be proportionate to the seriousness of the wrongdoing. The implication here, as with the second principle, is that there needs to be a root-and-branch change—a thorough revision of maximum penalties and a re-assessment of sentence levels and of differentials between them.

These are put forward as core principles. It is not claimed that they should be regarded as absolute rules, and indeed at various points above some possible qualifications to them have been discussed. Derogations from them should be argued as derogations, and should be principled in themselves.

The principles also lead in other directions that cannot be examined fully in this context. At the core is the idea that, if a particular wrong is thought serious enough to justify the possibility of a custodial sentence, that wrong should be treated as a crime, with fault required and proper procedural protection for defendants. This has implications for those minor wrongs that are presently made the subject of criminal offences simply because the criminal courts offer themselves as a quick and cheap means of dealing with them: many of the 1997 offences fall into this category, as do hundreds of other strict liability offences. A fine solution would be to create a new category of 'civil violation' or 'administrative offence', which would certainly be non-imprisonable and would normally attract a financial penalty; procedures would be simplified but would preserve minimum rights for defendants, such as access to a criminal court. Another implication of the principles should be that any new criminal code for this country ought to declare the most serious offences in English law, rather than simply those traditional offences that have been the focus of textbooks over the years.

What are the prospects for thus re-structuring and restoring integrity to the criminal law? Political reality suggests that they are unpromising: in this sense, the criminal law may be a lost cause. Even governments with large parliamentary majorities, and which profess certain criteria for the creation of new offences, may either give way to the allure of media popularity or simply not care sufficiently to adhere to their own principles. In such political circumstances it is all the more necessary to re-kindle debate about the functions and characteristics that the criminal law ought to have, and to ensure that the close interconnections between criminal law, criminal procedure and sentencing are kept at the forefront of that debate.

≈ *Questions*

Consider some of the offences with which you might be familiar or have read about. Do they satisfy all of those principled bases?

What of possession of a controlled drug such as cannabis?

What of driving without a licence?

As you consider the offences in this book in detail reflect on the extent to which they can be said to be based on these fundamental principles.

1.3 Sources of criminal law

1.3.1 Statutory offences

Whether the law relating to an offence is to be found in the common law (set out in section 1.3.2) or in a statute is frequently a matter of historical accident. The offences in statutes are not collected together as a catalogue of 'criminal legislation', and many offences appear in an otherwise unrelated statute, as for example with offences in the Companies Act 2006 or the Insolvency Act 1986.

Decided cases will be important in relation to understanding statutory and common law offences. When we seek to find the law in a statutory offence, the statute must always be the starting point but statutes have to be construed by the courts. Once the statute has been construed by a higher court it is that construction which counts. If it differs from the meaning which would naturally be put upon statute by the ordinary reader, it is the construction which prevails. The reader of s 3(1) of the Theft Act 1968 must learn that the words in that section, 'the rights of an owner', mean 'a right of an owner', because the House of Lords has so decided (see section 13.3, p 346). The Law Commission pointed out years ago (Law Com Consultation Paper No 122, *Legislating the Criminal Code: Offences against the Person and General Principles* (1992), para 7.11) that the most important offences under the Offences Against the Person Act 1861 'have become in effect common law crimes, the context of which is determined by case-law and not by statute'. The words of the Act, when not positively misleading, are virtually irrelevant. That is an extreme example but, even in a relatively modern statute like the Theft Act 1968, the words of a section may be misleading to a reader who is unaware of the case law. Hence the emphasis put upon cases in this book.

1.3.1.1 Statutory interpretation

General principles of statutory interpretation will apply when considering criminal law offences. There is a long-established principle applicable specifically in criminal law: ambiguities in the definition of a criminal offence are to be construed in the defendant's favour in so far as that is compatible with the scope of definition.

> … it is a universal principle that if a penal provision is reasonably capable of two interpretations, that interpretation which is most favourable to the accused must be adopted. (per Lord Reid in *Sweet v Parsley* [1970] AC 132)

This was reiterated more recently in *Hughes* [2013] UKSC 56 in which Lords Hughes and Toulson stated:

> 26.… A penal statute falls to be construed with a degree of strictness in favour of the accused. It is undoubtedly open to Parliament to legislate to create a harsh offence or penalty, just as it is open to it to take away fundamental rights, but it is not to be assumed to have done so unless that interpretation of its statute is compelled, and compelled by the language of the statute itself. The rule of construction which applies to penal legislation, and a fortiori to legislation which carries the penalty of imprisonment, is not identical to, but is somewhat analogous to, the principle of statutory interpretation known as the principle of legality.

The courts have considered how this principle relates to the general principle that where a statute is ambiguous, it is permissible to refer to the minister's statements in the parliamentary debates to determine the intended meaning: *Pepper v Hart* [1993] AC 593, HL. The courts have concluded that it is not permissible to use *Pepper v Hart* and refer to the parliamentary debates to enlarge the scope of liability, according to *Thet v DPP* [2006] EWHC 2701 (Admin). The appellant was convicted of an offence contrary to s 2(1) of the Asylum and Immigration (Treatment of Claimants, etc) Act 2004. In the course of the judgment, construing the provision, the court stated:

> 15. I would, however, question the use of *Pepper v Hart* in the context of a criminal prosecution. [Counsel] was not able to refer the court to any case in which *Pepper v Hart* has been used in that context. If a criminal statute is ambiguous, I would question whether it is appropriate by the use of *Pepper v Hart* to extend the ambit of the statute so as to impose criminal liability upon a defendant where, in the absence of the Parliamentary material, the court would not do so. It seems to me at least arguable that if a criminal statute is ambiguous, the defendant should have the benefit of the ambiguity.

However, in *Tabnak* [2007] EWCA Crim 380, [2007] 2 Cr App R 4 at [34], a failed asylum seeker was unwilling to provide information to enable travel documentation to be obtained to facilitate his deportation. He was convicted under s 35(3) of the Asylum and Immigration (Treatment of Claimants, etc) Act 2004. The Court of Appeal upheld his conviction. Lord Phillips CJ, *obiter*, noted that what had been said in *Thet v DPP* about the inappropriateness of invoking *Pepper v Hart* by the prosecution to admit parliamentary material in a criminal case as an aid to statutory construction, may not have the same force where a defendant in a criminal case seeks to rely on parliamentary material.

Another important feature of interpretation is that since the Human Rights Act 1998 came into force, the criminal courts have been obliged to interpret offences so as to be compatible with the rights guaranteed under the European Convention on Human Rights and Fundamental Freedoms (ECHR). Under s 3 of the 1998 Act the courts must ensure that statutes 'so far as it is possible to do so, be read and given effect in a way which is compatible with the Convention rights'. Examples of the criminal courts' approach to that duty can be seen in numerous cases. Lord Bingham summarized the position in *A-G's Reference (No 4 of 2002)* [2004] UKHL 43 at [28]:

> First, the interpretative obligation under s 3 is a very strong and far reaching one, and may require the court to depart from the legislative intention of Parliament. Secondly, a Convention-compliant interpretation under s 3 is the primary remedial measure and a declaration of incompatibility under s 4 an exceptional course. Thirdly, it is to be noted that during the passage of the Bill through Parliament the promoters of the Bill told both Houses that it was envisaged that the need for a declaration of incompatibility would rarely arise. Fourthly, there is a limit beyond which a Convention-compliant interpretation is not possible, such limit being illustrated by *R (Anderson) v Secretary of State for the Home Department* [2003] 1 AC 837 and *Bellinger v Bellinger* [2003] 2 AC 467. In explaining why a Convention-compliant interpretation may not be possible, members of the committee used differing expressions: such an interpretation would be incompatible with the underlying thrust of the legislation, or would not go with the grain of it, or would call for legislative deliberation, or would change the substance of a provision completely, or would remove its pith and substance, or would violate a cardinal principle of the legislation.... All of these expressions, as I respectfully think, yield valuable insights, but none of them should be allowed to supplant the simple test enacted in the Act: 'So far as it is possible to do so ...'. While the House declined to try to formulate precise rules ... it was thought that cases in which s 3 could not be used would in practice be fairly easy to identify.

1.3.2 Common law offences

The general principles of criminal liability—principles dealing with whether someone has acted voluntarily, liability for omissions, definitions of terms of mens rea, criminal capacity, etc—are nearly all to be found in common law, not in an Act of Parliament. The great majority of crimes, however, are now defined by statute but some very important crimes are not, including murder, manslaughter and conspiracy to defraud. These are important in terms of their seriousness and number of prosecutions which occur.

Challenges have been made in recent years to some of the best established common law offences—for example, the gross negligence manslaughter offence, *Misra* [2004] EWCA Crim 2375 (dealt with in full in section 9.3.2, p 242). The defence challenge to these offences is on the basis that they lack sufficient clarity and certainty of definition to be compatible with the rule of law. The challenges to the common law offences on grounds of certainty have only rarely met with success. For example, in *Misra* the challenge to the offence of gross negligence manslaughter, was based on the fact that the offence requires the jury to decide whether the defendant's negligence was so 'gross' as to deserve to be treated as criminal. Until the jury in an individual case has returned a verdict on that matter no defendant can know whether his conduct is going to be classified as so gross as to be criminal. He might argue that he cannot know the scope of the criminal law. The Court of Appeal rejected that argument as follows:

> 63. On examination, this represents one example, among many, of problems which juries are expected to address on a daily basis. They include equally difficult questions, such as whether a defendant has acted dishonestly, by reference to contemporary standards, or whether he has acted in reasonable self-defence, or, when charged with causing death by dangerous driving, whether the standards of his driving fell far below what should be expected of a competent and careful driver. These examples represent the commonplace for juries. Each of these questions could be said to be vague and uncertain. If he made enquiries in advance, at most an individual would be told the principle of law which the jury would be directed to apply: he could not be advised what a jury would think of the individual case, and how it would be decided. That involves an element of uncertainty about the outcome of the decision-making process, but not unacceptable uncertainty about the offence itself. (per Judge LJ)

One successful challenge on rule of law grounds was in *GG* [2008] UKHL 17 where the House of Lords upheld the argument from the defence that the common law offence of conspiracy to defraud could not be used to prosecute a price-fixing arrangement in the absence of evidence of further aggravating features. The offence of conspiracy to defraud has existed for several hundred years, and had never been used to prosecute such conduct before.

The House of Lords in that case and the related appeal in *Norris v USA* [2008] UKHL 16 reiterated the importance of respect for the principle of legal certainty in common law offences (*Norris* at [52]–[62]). This echoed the comments made by Lord Bingham in *Rimmington* [2006] 1 AC 459 (below), and in *Jones* [2007] 1 AC 136. In those cases the House of Lords emphasized several principles:

> no one should be punished under a law unless it is sufficiently clear and certain to enable him to know what conduct is forbidden before he does it; and no one should be punished for any act which was not clearly and ascertainably punishable when the act was done. (at [33])

In addition, in *Jones*, Lord Bingham referred to the:

> important democratic principle in this country: that it is for those representing the people of the country in Parliament, not the executive and not the judges, to decide what conduct should be treated as lying so far outside the bounds of what is acceptable in our society as to attract criminal penalties. One would need very compelling reasons for departing from that principle. (at [29])

Even though the common law challenges have not often been successful in persuading courts to reject the application of a common law offence to given circumstances, they have encouraged the courts to acknowledge a restrictive interpretation in general. For example, in *Goldstein and Rimmington* [2005] UKHL 63 the House of Lords emphasized that the scope of a common law offence ought not to be radically enlarged. (The case involved the application of the common law offence of public nuisance (which is not dealt with in this book—for detailed analysis, see *Smith and Hogan's Criminal Law* (14th edn, 2015), Ch 32)):

> There are two guiding principles: no one should be punished under a law unless it is sufficiently clear and certain to enable him to know what conduct is forbidden before he does it; and no one should be punished for any act which was not clearly and ascertainably punishable when the act was done. If the ambit of a common law offence is to be enlarged, it 'must be done step by step on a case by case basis and not with one large leap': *Clark (Mark)* [2003] EWCA Crim 991, [2003] 2 Cr App R 363, para 13.

Common law offences are generally very broadly defined. Often they have been superseded in part by statutory offences. In *Goldstein and Rimmington*, above, the legitimacy of the common law offence of public nuisance was recognized, but Lord Bingham of Cornhill made the following observation at [30]:

> Where Parliament has defined the ingredients of an offence, perhaps stipulating what shall and shall not be a defence, and has prescribed a mode of trial and a maximum penalty, it must ordinarily be proper that conduct falling within that definition should be prosecuted for the statutory offence and not for a common law offence which may or may not provide the same defences and for which the potential penalty is unlimited…. *It cannot in the ordinary way be a reason for resorting to the common law offence that the prosecutor is freed from mandatory time limits or restrictions on penalty.* It must rather be assumed that Parliament imposed the restrictions which it did having considered and weighed up what the protection of the public reasonably demanded. I would not go to the length of holding that conduct may never be lawfully prosecuted as a generally-expressed common law crime where it falls within the terms of a specific statutory provision, but good practice and respect for the primacy of statute do in my judgment require that conduct falling within the terms of a specific statutory provision should be prosecuted under that provision unless there is good reason for doing otherwise. (Emphasis added)

Similarly, Lord Rodger of Earlsferry stated:

> 53. Here, however, according to what Mr Perry [counsel for the Crown] told the House, the Crown had deliberately chosen the common law offence in order to avoid the time-bar which Parliament had enacted and to allow the judge, if he thought fit, to impose a heavier sentence than the one permitted under statute. The issue bears some resemblance to the issue in *R v J* [2005] 1 AC 562. *There is no suggestion, of course, that the Crown acted in bad faith.* On the contrary, it is easy to understand why they did what they did. In a particular case, such as this, a time-limit which prevents prosecution once a certain time has passed since the act was committed can appear to be arbitrary and to reward an offender for concealing his offences. The sentence available under the statute may also seem inadequate to reflect the gravity of the defendant's conduct. But Parliament has deliberately chosen to intervene and to prescribe a period within which conduct of this kind can be prosecuted summarily under statute. This must be taken to reflect Parliament's judgment that, if the conduct has not been prosecuted within that time, the public interest is now against proceeding. That judgment may be based on various factors. Parliament may, for example, consider that after a certain period everyone should move on and prosecutors should turn their attention to other matters. Police and prosecution resources, it may be thought, are better spent on detecting and prosecuting recent, rather than stale, offences of this kind or recent, rather than old, incidents in a course of conduct. More serious matters should be given priority. Similarly, in the matter of sentence, Parliament has reached a view that

certain conduct is appropriately covered by an offence which can be tried only summarily and which should attract no more than a particular level of sentence. Parliament has also fixed the maximum sentence to be imposed in summary proceedings, even where the defendant is convicted of more than one charge. Again, in any particular case, the sentence available under statute may appear to the prosecutor to be inadequate. But Parliament is entitled to place an offence in what it regards as the appropriate level in the hierarchy of offences and to limit the sentencing power of a court where the accused is not tried by jury.

54. It is not for the Crown to second-guess Parliament's judgment as to any of these matters by deliberately setting out to reject the applicable statutory offences and to charge the conduct in question under common law in order to avoid the time-limits or limits on sentence which Parliament has thought appropriate. It may be that, in the light of experience, Parliament's judgment can be seen to have been flawed or to have been superseded by events. Doubtless, the prosecuting authorities have channels through which they can—and perhaps should—draw any such perceived deficiencies to the attention of the Home Secretary. It is then up to ministers and, ultimately, Parliament to decide whether the law should be changed. But, unless and until it is changed, its provisions should be respected and the Crown should not devise a strategy to avoid them. (Emphasis added)

This argument that the existence of a statutory offence precludes reliance on a common law one with which it overlaps must be kept within reasonable bounds. First, something more than mere degree of overlap is required. In *Rimmington,* there was a general offence of public nuisance which had been superseded in many instances by specific statutory wrongs. In those cases, the offence of public nuisance overlapped completely with the statutory crime. Secondly, it is worth noting the qualification of Lord Bingham (quoted previously):

I would not go to the length of holding that conduct may never be lawfully prosecuted as a generally-expressed common law crime where it falls within the terms of a specific statutory provision, but good practice and respect for the primacy of statute do in my judgment require that conduct falling within the terms of a specific statutory provision should be prosecuted under that provision unless there is good reason for doing otherwise.

If the principle is not kept within reasonable bounds, the ramifications would be staggering. It would be wrong if serious common law offences which had partial overlap with statutory offences could not be charged.

1.4 The label of an offence

As has already been pointed out, there exist thousands of offences in English law. Would it be possible or desirable for the criminal law to operate with fewer offences? For example, instead of having murder and the various manslaughter offences, would it be simpler to have a single offence of 'homicide'? One reason why this would not be desirable is that it would be contrary to the principle of fair labelling. Andrew Ashworth states that the concern of fair labelling is as follows:

to see that widely felt distinctions between kinds of offences and degrees of wrongdoing are respected and signalled by the law, and that offences are subdivided and labelled so as to represent fairly the nature and magnitude of the law-breaking.

Consider the following extract.

J. Chalmers and F. Leverick, 'Fair Labelling in Criminal Law'
(2008) 71 MLR 217

Why does labelling matter?

A further preliminary question is whether the label attached by the state to an offender's conduct matters at all. The answer to this is that labelling of criminal offences clearly does matter to some extent. We have already seen that it would be impractical to operate a purely descriptive system of criminal law whereby the offender's conduct is set out in narrative form without any attempt to categorise. At the other extreme, the criminal law could dispense with description entirely, convicting offenders merely of 'an offence', and leaving all the work to be done in sentencing, regardless of whether the conduct in question involved killing, sexual assault or shoplifting. But this would be equally impractical and no rational system of criminal law could operate in this manner. Quite apart from the fact that the severity of sentencing is a very blunt tool for assessing the level of a person's wrongdoing, it may also paint an inaccurate picture—a sentence may, for example, be substantially aggravated or mitigated as a result of factors which are unrelated to and tell us nothing about the offence itself or the offender's culpability.

Given that a criminal record has a well-documented deleterious effect on employability and earning power, it would clearly be unfair on an offender for her criminal record to misrepresent her wrongdoing. Employers likewise would seem to have a legitimate interest in knowing whether a prospective employee has a criminal record, and are surely entitled to know at least whether her crime was broadly one of dishonesty, violence, sexual misconduct, or merely a minor public order offence. Such knowledge may, indeed, be essential in order to comply with statutory obligations such as those under the Protection of Children Act 1999 [Scotland], and it is possible that the employer's knowledge might be relevant to future questions of vicarious liability. Even in this broad sense, the law sometimes fails. An example is the Scottish case of *HM Advocate v Forbes*, where the accused was alleged to have broken into a flat with the intent to rape the occupant (he had removed his clothing and was carrying a tube of cream and a garment fashioned as a hood). Although Forbes was charged initially with 'housebreaking with intent to rape', the appeal court held that no such crime was recognised by Scots law, and that the appropriate charge was one of breach of the peace.

But if we accept that labelling matters at least to some degree, what is fair labelling? How narrow does the categorisation of offences need to be in order to be 'fair'? What does fairness mean in this context? Could we, as Paul Robinson has suggested, define offences in the broadest of terms (for example 'injury to a person' or 'damage to or theft of property') and leave the majority of work to be done at the sentencing stage? Or would we lose something of importance to the criminal law by doing so?

In attempting to address some of these questions, it may be productive to start by considering in more detail why labelling matters. In his original exposition of the concept in 1982, Ashworth himself said very little about why labelling is important. He dealt with the issue only towards the end of his paper and stated that, while it might be assumed that at the time of the court hearing the police, offenders, court officials and so on will be aware of the circumstances of any offence, and will not judge it purely by its legal label:

> [O]nce the label is entered on the person's criminal record the passage of time will dim recollections of the precise nature of the offence and may result in the label being taken at face value. Both out of fairness to the individual and in order to ensure accuracy in our penal system, therefore, the legal designation of an offence should fairly represent the nature of the offender's criminality.

In *Principles of Criminal Law*, Ashworth is more expansive, noting essentially two reasons why fair labelling is important, namely 'proportionality' and 'maximum certainty'. In the section headed 'proportionality', it becomes clear during the course of the discussion that the main concern is actually fairness to offenders. The point being made under the heading 'maximum certainty' is less clear, but Ashworth touches upon the importance of legal definitions reflecting 'common patterns of thought in society' (although without really explaining why this matters) and the argument that broad labels give too much discretion to sentencers and to officials charged with enforcing the law.

≈ **Question**

Do you agree that fair labelling is important? As you study the offences in this book, consider the extent to which they conform to the principle of fair labelling.

1.5 The Human Rights Act 1998

In addition to the primary and secondary legislation of the UK Parliament, and the decisions of the English and Welsh courts, it is increasingly important to consider other legal sources which will impact on the way that English criminal law is defined and applied. Although the ECHR impact is most significant in the context of evidence and procedure, the ECHR through the Human Rights Act also has a direct impact on the operation of the substantive criminal law in many ways. The ECHR rights have relevance in many different offences. For example, in cases involving homicide issues under Article 2 and the right to life might be engaged, in sexual offences Article 8 and the right to respect for privacy may arise, in offences involving speech or protest Article 10 rights of freedom of expression might be engaged. In terms of the definition of crimes, the greatest impact might have been expected to be through Article 7, which proscribes retrospective criminalization, including a prohibition on criminal laws which are too vague and uncertain.

Article 7 provides:

(1) No one shall be held guilty of any criminal offence on account of any act or omission which did not constitute a criminal offence under national or international law at the time when it was committed. Nor shall a heavier penalty be imposed than the one that was applicable at the time the criminal offence was committed.

(2) This Article shall not prejudice the trial and punishment of any person for any act or omission which, at the time it was committed, was criminal according to the general principles of law recognised by civilised nations.

The European Court held in *Kokkinakis v Greece* (1994) 17 EHRR 397, and has reiterated many times since, that:

Article 7 is not confined to prohibiting the retrospective application of the criminal law to an accused's disadvantage: it also embodies, more generally, the principle that only the law can define a crime and prescribe a penalty (*nullum crimen, nulla poena sine lege*) and the principle that the criminal law must not be extensively construed to an accused's detriment, for instance by analogy … it follows that an offence must be clearly defined in the law. (*SW v UK* (1995) 21 EHRR 363, para 35)

The court looks to whether the individual can know from the wording of the relevant provision and, if need be, with the assistance of the courts' interpretation of it, what acts and omissions will make him criminally liable.

This is not a prohibition on the development of the common law. As the Court noted in *SW*:

> However clearly drafted a legal provision may be, in any system of law, including criminal law, there is an inevitable element of judicial interpretation. There will always be a need for elucidation of doubtful points and for adaptation to changing circumstances. Indeed, in the United Kingdom, as in the other Convention States, the progressive development of the criminal law through judicial law-making is a well entrenched and necessary part of legal tradition. Article 7 of the Convention cannot be read as outlawing the gradual clarification of the rules of criminal liability through judicial interpretation from case to case, provided that the resultant development is consistent with the essence of the offence and could reasonably be foreseen.

To date, the English courts have taken a very narrow view of the protection afforded by Article 7 and have failed to accept that crimes such as manslaughter by gross negligence (see *Misra*, section 9.3.2, p 242 and *Sellu*, section 9.3.3, p 238), public nuisance (*Goldstein* in section 1.3.2) and encouraging or assisting offences believing one or more will be committed (see *S & H*, section 22.2.3.2, p 614) are incompatible with Article 7 on the grounds of their vagueness. That is not to say that Article 7 is redundant. In *Norris v USA* [2008] UKHL 16; *GG* [2008] UKHL 17, the House of Lords relied on Article 7 in rejecting the Crown's use of conspiracy to defraud when that offence had never previously been used to prosecute the alleged wrongdoing—price-fixing. The House acknowledged (at [55]) the 'consistent message ... through cases decided from 1875 through to 1984, was that price-fixing was not of itself capable of constituting a crime.... There was no reported case, indeed, it would appear, no unreported case, no textbook, no article which suggested otherwise'. As such, it would infringe the principle of legality to impose the offence without warning. The House of Lords distinguished *SW* since in that case there was a gradual change in the law incrementally criminalizing marital rape and hence the availability of the charge had become reasonably foreseeable.

As the Human Rights Act was being implemented, leading commentators debated the likely impact the ECHR might have in producing greater certainty in the substantive criminal law. Whether Article 7 would fulfil its promise depended to a large extent on how it was interpreted and applied by the European Court of Human Rights.

C. Murphy, 'The Principle of Legality in Criminal Law under the European Convention on Human Rights'
[2010] 2 EHRLR 192

Introduction

The core of the rule of law in criminal law can be found in art.7 of the European Convention on Human Rights (ECHR) and its requirement of *nullum crimen, noella poena sine lege*. Article 7 ECHR is a non-derogable clause, and so cannot be avoided in times of national emergency. This places it alongside the prohibitions on torture and slavery as a 'higher-value' ECHR provision. The importance of the principle of legality in criminal law has been emphasised by the European Court of Human Rights. In the recent case of *Kafkaris*, the Court declared that:

> 'The guarantee enshrined in Article 7, which is *an essential element of the rule of law*, occupies a prominent place in the Convention system of protection ... It should be construed and applied, as follows from its object and purpose, in such a way as to provide effective safeguards against arbitrary prosecution, conviction and punishment.'

Similar statements concerning the rule of law had been made in previous cases. However, despite the Court's rhetoric, art.7 ECHR is in many respects the poorer relation to the better-developed art.6 ECHR (right to a fair trial). Although the 1990s saw art.7 considered for the first time, the number of cases citing the article remains low. In a survey conducted by Greer in 2006, he noted that only nine breaches of art.7 had been identified by the Court in the years 1999–2005. By way of comparison, over 2,000 breaches of art.6 were found in the same period. In academia, the article is oft-cited but little discussed. The leading textbooks on the Convention, including those by Janis, Kay and Bradley, and Jacobs and White, each only devote a handful of pages to the clause.

The article itself is similar to its equivalent (art.15) in the International Covenant of Civil and Political Rights (ICCPR). In this study, the article is described as entailing three distinct (but overlapping) rules. First, only the law can define a crime and prescribe a penalty. Secondly, conduct may not be subject to retrospective prohibition. Thirdly, conduct may not attract a higher penalty than that provided for in law when the action took place. These three prohibitions are subject to the single explicit limitation on the rule contained in art.7(2) ECHR. Each aspect is considered in turn in the following discussion.

...

Accessibility and foreseeability

In *Kafkaris*, the Court noted that the definition of both the offence and the penalty must be accessible and foreseeable. These twin requirements have consistently featured in the Court's case law, even outside the context of art.7(1) ECHR. Although frequently mentioned in art.7 judgments, it is not clear if accessibility and foreseeability are related but distinct qualities, or are one and the same. Despite inconsistencies in the language used by the Court, it is possible to distinguish two different elements. First, the law must be sufficiently clear for individuals to conduct themselves in accordance with its commands (accessibility), and secondly, where there is judicial development of the law, any changes must be predictable (foreseeability).

Accessibility and foreseeability do not prevent laws from being broadly drafted where this is necessary for the law to fulfil its role. As a result, laws concerned with offences such as proselytism and terrorism may be vague, but still compliant with art.7 ECHR. Regarding the 'clarity' of the law (accessibility in the plain meaning of the word), the Court has noted that:

> 'An individual must know from the wording of the relevant provision and, if need be, with the assistance of the courts' interpretation of it, what acts and omissions will make him criminally liable and what penalty will be imposed … a law may still satisfy the requirement … where the person concerned has to take appropriate legal advice to assess, to a degree that is reasonable in the circumstances, the consequences which a given action may entail.'

The 'thin ice' principle is relevant here. Lord Morris [in *Knuller v DPP* [1973] AC 435] described this as the idea that 'those who skate on thin ice can hardly expect to find a sign which will denote the precise spot where he [*sic*] will fall in'. Despite Ashworth's claim that the 'thin ice' principle should not 'trump' the absolute art.7(1) right, the European Court seems willing to allow it to do so. In *Coeme*, it was held that 'the applicants could not have been unaware that the conduct that they were accused of might make them liable to prosecution'. Similarly in *Custers*, the Court declared that it was predictable that 'the applicants risked being sentenced to a fine'. This reference to *risk* that criminal sanctions *might* follows counteracts the foreseeability requirement. The point was put particularly clearly in *Cantoni*. The Court declared that there are always 'grey areas at the fringes of the definition [of the law]' and art.7(1) ECHR simply requires that the law is 'sufficiently clear in the large majority of cases … the applicants must have known on the basis of their behaviour that they ran a *real risk of prosecution*'. Finally on this point, if consulting the courts is necessary for the precise meaning of the law to be determined, then art.7 ECHR must be understood as having strong links to an individual's right to legal counsel and access to justice more broadly.

The second qualitative element relates to changes to the law (foreseeability properly understood). The European Court of Human Rights has consistently held that it does not undermine the foreseeability of the law if it is adapted to reflect changing social circumstances. This change may be gradual or, in certain circumstances, may be abrupt. Gradual change is demonstrated in *SW and CR v United*

Kingdom. There, the Court held that the removal of the marital rape exception by common law development was foreseeable. It held that the House of Lords judgment:

> '... [D]id no more than continue a perceptible line of case-law development dismantling the immunity of a husband from prosecution for rape upon his wife ... there was an evident evolution, which was consistent with the very essence of the offence, of the criminal law through judicial interpretation towards treating such conduct generally as within the scope of the offence of rape. This evolution had reached a stage where judicial recognition of the absence of immunity had become a reasonably foreseeable development of the law.'

Despite the apparent foreseeability, *SW and CR* has been the subject of criticism. Beddard notes that in the unlikely event that the applicants had sought legal advice prior to committing the acts, the advice would most likely be that while reform was imminent, the exception was still valid law in the United Kingdom. Furthermore, such a profound change in the law of criminal liability should arguably be the province of the legislature, not the judiciary.

In the German reunification cases, the Court noted that changes to the law may be more dramatic. As discussed above, the Court held it legitimate for the unified German courts to convict based on GDR law, even where the organs of the former state would not have done so. The Court also commented on the foreseeability of the applicants' prosecution. It reiterated that the criminal law must be adapted to 'changing circumstances'. Whereas this usually happens gradually, the Court held it was 'wholly valid where, as in the present case, one State has succeeded another'. The reasons offered to sustain this conclusion were that (1) it was consistent with the system of the Convention, (2) the GDR Parliament has expressed such a wish, and (3) due to the 'pre-eminence' of the right to life in international human rights instruments. None of these reasons can truly justify what is, in essence, a retrospective change to an entire legal system. It is argued below that the marital rape and German reunification cases are better read as the 'balancing' of art.7 ECHR with the general spirit of the Convention. In other, more mundane circumstances, the European Court of Human Rights has held a dramatic departure from precedent to offend the requirement of foreseeability. In *Pessino*, a builder was prosecuted for carrying out construction in violation of a court order prohibiting him from doing so. Similar breaches of such court orders in the past had not attracted criminal liability. The abrupt change in approach by the French Court of Cassation resulted in a breach of art.7.

As the European Court of Human Rights itself has noted, the law must change to adapt to the facts of society it serves. When this occurs through the legislative process, there is at least the warning that process provides, and the democratic legitimacy derived from the institution. When criminal law is abruptly changed by courts, neither warning nor legitimacy are the same (no matter how many academics or official reports may have foreshadowed it). Article 7 requires that the guiding principle should always be the ability of individuals to plan their affairs in accordance with the law.

Murphy's characterization of Article 7 as the 'poorer relation' is also borne out by an examination of domestic case law. As has already been pointed out and will be examined later in greater detail the Court of Appeal has given short shrift to the proposition that gross negligence manslaughter and the offence contained in s 46 of the Serious Crime Act 2007 violate Article 7.

1.6 Codification of criminal law

It was thought that the enactment of the Human Rights Act 1998 might serve as a catalyst for the implementation of the Criminal Code.

Much effort has gone into proposals to codify our criminal law—so far, in vain. Criminal Law Commissioners worked from 1833 to 1849 (and two major Bills based on their work were introduced in 1853) but made no progress, largely because of the opposition by the judges to codification of the common law. Then a judge who was also a great criminal lawyer, Sir James Fitzjames Stephen, prepared a draft code which, he said, represented the labour of many of the best years of his life and which was introduced into Parliament in 1878 and again in 1879. Again the effort failed, probably because of opposition by the judges, especially Lord Cockburn CJ.

Modified versions of Stephen's Code became the law in Canada, New Zealand and many other jurisdictions but nothing significant happened in England until 1967 when the Home Secretary of the time, Mr Roy Jenkins, made a speech in favour of codification. Almost immediately, the Law Commission, in its second programme (1968), stated its objective of a comprehensive examination of the criminal law with a view to its codification. It established a working party which produced a series of valuable papers on the general principles of criminal law. In 1980, the Commission appointed a Criminal Code Team to consider and make proposals in relation to a code. The team reported in 1985 with a draft Criminal Code Bill covering general principles of liability and offences against the person (Law Com Report No 143, *Codification of the Criminal Law*). The generally favourable reception given to the report encouraged the Commission to proceed with the preparation of a more complete code covering, in Part I, general principles and, in Part II, the range of specific offences which would be expected in a code. A report and draft Criminal Code Bill (Law Com No 177, *A Criminal Code for England and Wales*) was published in 1989. The draft Bill is intended for the most part to be a restatement of the existing law but it also incorporates law reform proposals made by official bodies such as the Criminal Law Revision Committee and the Law Commission itself.

There followed substantial support for codification including that from very senior judges.

The Hon Mrs Justice Arden DBE, 'Criminal Law at the Crossroads: The Impact of Human Rights from the Law Commission's Perspective and the Need for a Code'
[1999] Crim LR 439

Our criminal law is a mixed system of statutory provisions and common law. The judges can within limits keep the common law up to date. Statute law, however, has to be kept up to date by Parliament. For many years there has been legislative inertia. The situation is that there is an accumulated backlog of work for Parliament leaving large areas of criminal statutes needing reform … The enactment of the Human Rights Act 1998 creates a new and pressing need for reform.

Lord Bingham CJ, 'Must We Wait for Ever?'
[1998] Crim LR 694

The arguments in favour of codification are what they have always been. First, it would bring clarity and accessibility to the law. As the Attorney-General put it in the House of Commons 130 years ago:

'Surely, it is a desirable thing that anybody who may want to know the law on a particular subject should be able to turn to a chapter of the Code, and there find the law he is in search of explained in a few intelligible and well-constructed sentences; nor would he have to enter upon a long examination of Russell on Crimes, or Archbold, and other text-books, because he would have a succinct and clear statement before him. (Hansard, HC, April 3, 1879, vol. 245 (3rd series), col. 316)'

Secondly, a code would bring coherence to this branch of the law. Sir John Smith expressed his general disbelief in codes—a disbelief which I for my part share—but he continued:

'The criminal law is entirely different. It is incoherent and inconsistent. State almost any general principle and you find one or more leading cases which contradict it. It is littered with distinctions which have no basis in reason but are mere historical accidents. I am in favour of codification of the criminal law because I see no other way of reducing a chaotic system to order, of eliminating irrational distinctions and of making the law reasonably comprehensible, accessible and certain. These are all practical objects. Irrational distinctions mean injustice. A is treated differently from B when there is no rational ground for treating him differently; and this is not justice. (Codification of the Criminal Law, Child & Co. Lecture, 1986)'

Sir John has entertained generations of students, practitioners and judges by highlighting the anomalies in our present law. As the [then] Chairman of the Law Commission has herself said [Arden J quoted above], the cure now can only be achieved by codification; it cannot be provided by the courts alone. Thirdly, a code would bring greater certainty to the law, and in this of all fields the law should be so far as possible certain. The arguments for incremental development of the law, persuasive elsewhere, have no application here. It is not just that a defendant should be held punishable for an act which would not have been thought criminal when he did it; and if he is held not liable for conduct which would at that time have been thought criminal, the almost inevitable consequence is that others have been unjustly punished. Incorporation of the ECHR reinforces the need for certainty if the principle of legality is to be observed. Even the most breathless admirer of the common law must regard it as a reproach that after 700 years of judicial decision-making our highest tribunal should have been called upon time and again in recent years to consider the mental ingredients of murder, the oldest and most serious of crimes … One hopes that parliamentary time may yet be found to achieve something that has eluded our predecessors but would, I think, come to be recognised as an important milestone in our legal and public life.

A Government paper, 'Criminal Justice: The Way Ahead' (2001, Cm 5074), included plans for 'a consolidated, modernised core criminal code'. The prospect of a single codifying statute proved unrealistic. The Law Commission did, however, begin to produce a series of Bills which could have been consolidated. The Law Commission's Report No 218, *Legislating the Criminal Code* (1993), proposed to begin with non-fatal offences against the person and contains a draft Bill covering these offences and, most importantly, some provisions governing general principles of liability which would be applicable to all offences. In February 1998, the Home Office published a Consultation Paper, 'Violence: Reforming the Offences Against the Person Act 1861' with a revised draft Bill, discussed [1998] Crim LR 317. This seemed to give real hope of a significant start on the enactment of the Code but no more was heard of the outcome and the consultation process stalled.

In more recent years, the Law Commission has moved away from a programme of implementing a single code of criminal law and opted to put forward individual law reform proposals which, incrementally, will codify the criminal law. We have seen numerous examples in the last few years including the reform of incitement in the Serious Crime Act 2007, Part 2 (see Chapter 22), the Fraud Act 2006 replacing the deception offences (see Chapter 16) and the Bribery Act 2010 replacing old statutory offences of corruption.

Provisions of the 1989 Draft Code remain useful in understanding and scrutinizing the present law and will be found at appropriate points throughout the book.

≈≈ *Questions*

If all of the offences known to English criminal law were printed in a single volume which was available at a reasonable price, who would buy it? Would it reduce the amount of crime? Would it enhance the quality of justice?

By 2017, the prospect of a criminal code for England and Wales has all but vanished. Indeed in its 10th Programme of Law Reform, the Law Commission removed mention of a codification project and introduced a new plan to simplify selected common law offences.

On the merits of codification generally, see G. de Búrca and S. Gardner, 'Codification of the Criminal Law' (1990) 10 OJLS 559.

FURTHER READING

P. Alldridge, 'Making Criminal Law Known' in S. Shute and A. Simester (eds), *Criminal Law Theory: Doctrines of the General Part* (2002)

R. A. Duff, 'Rule Violations and Wrong Doings' in S. Shute and A. Simester (eds), *Criminal Law Theory: Doctrines of the General Part* (2002)

Codification

I. H. Dennis, 'The Law Commission and the Criminal Law: Reflections on the Codification Project' in M. Dyson, J. Lee and S. Wilson Stark (eds), *Fifty Years of the Law Commissions: The Dynamics of Law Reform* (2015)

S. Gardner, 'Reiterating the Criminal Code' (1992) 55 MLR 839

I. Hare, 'A Compelling Case for the Code' (1993) 56 MLR 74

ECHR

B. Emmerson, A. Ashworth and A. MacDonald, *Human Rights and Criminal Justice* (3rd edn, 2012)

A. T. H. Smith, 'The Human Rights Act and the Criminal Lawyer: The Constitutional Context' [1999] Crim LR 25

On codification in other jurisdictions

P. R. Ferguson, 'Codifying Criminal Law: The Scots and English Draft Codes Compared' [2004] Crim LR 105

J. P. McCutcheon and K. Quinn, 'Codifying Criminal Law in Ireland' (1998) 19 Statute Law Review 131

2
The elements of a crime

> **Some of the controversies that will be examined in this chapter include:**
>
> (1) the constituents of an actus reus;
>
> (2) whether someone can be held criminally liable for an act that is involuntary;
>
> (3) the extent to which the actus reus and mens rea of an offence must coincide in time in order for a crime to be committed;
>
> (4) the liability of someone who intends to commit a crime in a certain way, but in fact commits it in some other way;
>
> (5) whether for every element of the actus reus of an offence, there *must* be a corresponding element of mens rea.

2.1 Actus reus and mens rea

2.1.1 Components of a crime

Anyone who thinks about it will readily appreciate that crimes ordinarily involve not merely blameworthy conduct, but blameworthy mental elements on the part of defendants. Suppose I take your bicycle from the space in which you have left it, ride it home and put it in my garage. Have I stolen it? The question cannot be answered without considering my state of mind at the time of the taking. Perhaps I mistook your bicycle for my own similar model which I had left in the same area. Or perhaps I mistakenly supposed that you had said I could borrow the bicycle; or, though I knew it was your bicycle and that I was taking it without your consent, I only intended to borrow it for a day. In none of these cases have I stolen it. But, if I knew it was your bicycle and I dishonestly intended to deprive you of it permanently, I am guilty of theft. The conduct is the same in every case. The difference lies in the state of mind with which the act is done.

If D, driving his car, runs V down and kills him, this will be murder if D did so intending to kill V; manslaughter if, though he did not intend to harm anyone, he was driving with such gross negligence that there was an obvious risk of death to someone and a jury thinks it deserves condemnation as that offence; causing death by careless driving if he was driving negligently; and accidental death if the collision occurred in spite of the fact that he was concentrating on what he was doing and exercising the care that a prudent and reasonably skilful driver should.

Let us take an example to explore the way the elements of offences interrelate. The offence of malicious wounding contrary to s 20 of the Offences Against the Person Act 1861 requires proof that the defendant caused a break in the victim's skin (both its inner and outer layers) and that the defendant intended to cause some kind of bodily harm or was malicious (for these purposes reckless) as to whether it was caused (ie he saw there was a risk that his conduct would cause it but went ahead and unjustifiably took the risk).

Consider D who cuts V's stomach open with a knife. D is not necessarily guilty of wounding.

- D might lack the mental element—he might not have intended or been reckless about harming V. V might have stumbled and fallen on D, a chef holding his knife about to cut a joint of beef. D would not have the mental element for the offence of wounding and would be found not guilty.

- D might have a defence. He might have cut V's stomach open and intended to do so, but have V's consent, as where D is a surgeon operating on V in hospital.

- D might also lack criminal liability if he stabbed V with intent to cause the wound but was acting in self-defence because V was running at D with a sword.

- D might have a defence where he stabbed V in the stomach with intent to do so, but was only acting in that fashion because X was pointing a gun at D's head to make him stab V. D would then plead a defence of duress.

In a case of wounding, the proscribed conduct is unlawfully causing a wound (a break in the skin) and the proscribed mental state is that the defendant intended or was reckless (malicious) about causing some bodily harm. The mental element defines the proscribed mental state that the defendant must have in relation to the proscribed conduct. In the previous example of the bicycle, the proscribed conduct is the appropriation (taking) of the property belonging to another and the proscribed mental element is that the taking was done dishonestly and with intention permanently to deprive the other of the property.

Lawyers have long found it convenient to distinguish the mental element from the other elements for the purposes of setting out the law and have called it 'mens rea'. This phrase derives from a maxim quoted by Coke in his *Institutes* (Ch 1, fo 10), '*Actus non facit reum nisi mens sit rea*': an act does not make a man guilty of a crime unless his mind also be guilty.

The use of the expression, 'actus reus', is much more recent, having apparently been coined by C. S. Kenny in the first edition of his *Outlines of Criminal Law* in 1902 (see J. Hall, *General Principles of Criminal Law* (2nd edn, 1960), p 222, fn 24). It is now an expression used throughout the common law world to designate the elements of an offence other than the mental element. The expression 'external elements' is sometimes now used to avoid reliance on Latin. The elements of the actus reus include elements of conduct, circumstances and, in some offences, consequences. For example, in the offence of rape, the proscribed conduct is penile penetration of the vagina, anus or mouth; the proscribed circumstances are that the victim was not consenting. With criminal damage, the proscribed conduct is the act which causes damage; the proscribed circumstances are that the damage was to property and that it belonged to another; and the proscribed consequences are that property was in fact damaged. It is important to realize that in many offences the actus reus may be satisfied by D omitting to act in specified ways as well as by his positive acts and for this reason we use the term 'conduct' rather than 'act'. We examine the circumstances in which an omission will suffice in Chapter 4.

Most crimes require proof of a mental element of some sort. It has to be proved with the same degree of rigour as the other elements of the crime. It is possible for the courts to dispense with mens rea in whole or in part with offences of absolute or strict liability (see Chapter 6) but, except in the anomalous case of an intoxicated offender (see section 25.7, p 739), they can never dispense with the actus reus. There are no 'thought crimes'. See D. N. Husak, 'Does Criminal Liability Require an Act?' in R. A. Duff, *Philosophy and the Criminal Law* (1998). Remember that these expressions—mens rea and actus reus—are only analytical tools: they help us to identify which elements of the offence are in dispute, etc. The only thing that matters in practice is whether the whole crime is committed.

2.2 Understanding the requirement of an act

In this section we explore what it means to do an act for the purposes of the criminal law. At this stage, it is important to emphasize that although we speak of an 'act', what we are really talking about is the conduct element of an offence. This is not as easy as it might at first appear. Reduced to its simplest terms, an act is merely a muscular movement—for example, the crooking of a finger. But this is a very narrow view. Reference to an 'act' generally includes some of the circumstances surrounding the movement, and its consequences. For instance, if, when D crooked his finger, it was gripping the trigger of a loaded gun pointing at V's heart, to say that 'D crooked his finger' would be a most incomplete and misleading way of describing what D did. We would naturally say, 'D *shot* V', taking into account the relevant circumstances and consequences. If we say, 'D *murdered V*' we take into account still more circumstances—not only the state of mind with which D pulled the trigger, but also the absence of circumstances of justification or excuse—for example, D was not a soldier in battle shooting at an enemy, V, nor was he acting in self-defence against an aggressor who was attacking D. 'Murder', unlike 'kill', connotes a particular offence and therefore an actus reus (including the absence of excuse).

Courts rarely have to address in any detail what is meant by the act involved in a crime. The next case is one of the few examples of where a court has considered this question in any detail.

Ryan v R
(1969) 121 CLR 205, High Court of Australia

(Barwick CJ, Taylor, Menzies Windeyer and Owen JJ)

Ryan entered a service station, pointed a sawn-off rifle at the attendant and demanded money. The rifle was loaded and cocked with the safety catch off. The attendant placed money on the counter. Still pointing the rifle with one hand, Ryan attempted to tie the attendant up. When the attendant moved suddenly, Ryan pressed the trigger and shot him dead. By the law of New South Wales at that time, killing in the course of committing a felony (in this case, robbery), was murder—but the act had to be a voluntary act. At his trial for murder, Ryan's defence was that he pressed the trigger involuntarily. He was convicted and his appeal to the High Court of Australia was dismissed.

[Barwick CJ, having held that a jury could not dismiss Ryan's account as incredible:]

There were therefore, in my opinion, at least four possible and distinctly different views of the discharge of the gun which, upon all the material before them, could be taken by the jury. First, the applicant's explanation could be disbelieved, and it could be concluded that he had fired the gun intentionally—that is to say, both as a voluntary act and with the intention to do the deceased harm. Second, that he fired the gun voluntarily, not intending to do any harm to the deceased but merely to frighten him as a means of self-protection. Third, that being startled, he voluntarily but in a panic, pressed the trigger but with no specific intent either to do the deceased any harm or to frighten him. Fourth, that being startled so as to move slightly off his balance, the trigger was pressed in a reflex or convulsive, unwilled movement of his hand or of its muscles. I shall later refer to these conclusions of fact as the possible views identifying each by number . . .

An occasion such as the fourth view of the evidence in the instant case (ante) would, in my opinion, be an instance of a deed not the result of a culpable exercise of the will to act. But such an occasion is in sharp contrast to the third view of those facts from which it needs carefully to be distinguished. If voluntariness is not conceded and the material to be submitted to the jury wheresoever derived provides a substantial basis for doubting whether the deed in question was a voluntary or willed act of the accused, the jury's attention must be specifically drawn to the necessity of deciding beyond all reasonable doubt that the deed charged as a crime was the voluntary or willed act of the accused. If it was not then for that reason, there being no defence of insanity, the accused must be acquitted . . . Although a claim of involuntariness is no doubt easily raised, and may involve nice distinctions, the accused, if the material adduced warrants that course, is entitled to have the issue properly put to the jury.

Windeyer J:

. . . The conduct which caused the death was of course a complex of acts all done by the applicant—loading the rifle, cocking it, presenting it, pressing the trigger. But it was the final act, pressing the trigger of the loaded and levelled rifle, which made the conduct lethal. When this was said to be a reflex action, the word 'reflex' was not used strictly in the sense it ordinarily has in neurology as denoting a specific muscular reaction to a particular stimulus of a physical character. The phrase was, as I understood the argument, used to denote rather the probable but unpredictable reaction of a man when startled. He starts. In doing so he may drop something which he is holding, or grasp it more firmly. Doctor Johnson in his Dictionary—and his definition has been in substance repeated by others—said that 'to start' means 'to feel a sudden and involuntary twitch or motion of the animal frame on the apprehension of danger'. The Oxford Dictionary speaks of a start as a 'sudden involuntary movement of the body occasioned by surprise, terror, joy or grief . . .'. But assume that the applicant's act was involuntary, in the sense in which the lexicographers use the word, would that, as a matter of law, absolve him from criminal responsibility for its consequences? I do not think so. I do not think that, for present purposes, such an act bears any true analogy to one done under duress, which, although done by an exercise of the will, is said to be involuntary because it was compelled. Neither does it, I think, bear any true analogy to an act done in convulsions or an epileptic seizure, which is said to be involuntary because by no exercise of the will could the actor refrain from doing it. Neither does it, I think, bear any true analogy to an act done by a sleep-walker or a person for some other reason rendered unconscious whose action is said to be involuntary because he knew not what he was doing.

Such phrases as 'reflex action' and 'automatic reaction' can, if used imprecisely and unscientifically, be, like 'blackout', mere excuses. They seem to me to have no real application to the case of a fully conscious man who has put himself in a situation in which he has his finger on the trigger of a loaded rifle levelled at another man. If he then presses the trigger in immediate response to a sudden threat or apprehension of danger, as is said to have occurred in this case, his doing so is, it seems to me, a consequence probable and foreseeable of a conscious apprehension of danger, and in that sense a voluntary act. The latent time is no doubt barely appreciable, and what was done might not have been done had the actor had time to think. But is an act to be called involuntary merely because the mind worked quickly and impulsively?

≋ *Questions*

Was Ryan's act: Voluntary? Blameworthy? Was Ryan in control of his actions? See for further discussion R. A. Duff, *Answering for Crime* (2007), pp 99–106.

2.2.1 Acts and automatism

Apart from the anxieties and tensions necessarily experienced by anyone taking part in an armed robbery, Ryan was not, so far as appears, suffering from an abnormality of any kind. More commonly—at least in the reported cases—the defendant who relies upon automatism claims that he had a 'blackout' and that this was due to a condition of mind or body—a tumour on the brain, arteriosclerosis (hardening of the arteries) cutting off the supply of blood to the brain, epilepsy, hyperglycaemia (high blood sugar) caused by diabetes, hypoglycaemia (low blood sugar) caused by the administration of too much insulin to control diabetes or sleep-walking; or he may say that he was suffering from concussion following a blow on the head or that he was affected by the administration by his dentist of an anaesthetic. If the defendant was indeed in a state of automatism at the time of the alleged act as a result of any of these conditions, he cannot be guilty of the crime charged; but there is a question whether he should be simply acquitted or found not guilty by reason of insanity. The importance of this categorization is that the defendant is then liable to various types of restraint (hospital orders and supervision) which the court may impose on him.

Automatism is discussed more fully in Chapter 24. What matters for present purposes is to note that offences require proof of *voluntary* conduct.

2.3 Coincidence of actus reus and mens rea

In order to constitute a crime the actus reus and the mens rea must coincide (a) in point of law and (b) in point of time. Although this is the general rule, as the following sections will demonstrate, there are a number of exceptions. When reading the following sections, consider the extent to which the exceptions have subsumed the rule.

2.3.1 Coincidence in law

All the elements of the crime charged must be proved. It is not therefore sufficient to prove that the defendant caused the actus reus of crime X with the mens rea of crime Y.

It must be remembered, however, that sometimes the same mens rea is sufficient for two or more crimes; an intention to cause grievous bodily harm is a sufficient mens rea both for the offence of causing such harm with intent contrary to s 18 of the Offences Against the Person Act 1861 and for murder. Recklessness as to grievous bodily harm is sufficient for the offence of maliciously inflicting grievous bodily harm contrary to s 20 of the Offences Against the Person Act 1861 and for manslaughter.

2.3.1.1 Transferred malice

If D, with the mens rea of a particular crime, brings about the actus reus of the same crime, he is guilty of that crime even though the victim, or object, of the offence is different from that which D intended or foresaw or ought to have foreseen. This common law doctrine is restated succinctly by the Draft Code, cl 24, and appears in the following terms in the draft Criminal Law Bill, cl 32:

32. Transferred fault and defences

(1) In determining whether a person is guilty of an offence, his intention to cause, or his awareness of a risk that he will cause, a result in relation to a person or thing capable of being the victim or subject-matter of the offence shall be treated as an intention to cause or, as the case may

be, an awareness of a risk that he will cause, that result in relation to any other person or thing affected by his conduct.

(2) Any defence on which a person might have relied on a charge of an offence in relation to a person or thing within his contemplation is open to him on a charge of the same offence in relation to a person or thing not within his contemplation.

By way of an example of the doctrine in operation, if D intends to kill A by shooting at him, but misses and kills B instead, D will be guilty of the murder of B even though killing B may have been the last thing D wanted. D's mens rea (intention to kill) is said to be transferred from A to B. The reason for this is said to be that how D caused B's death is of no legal significance. Horder calls this the 'prohibited outcome' doctrine. He states that, '[s]o long as the prohibited outcome comes about (intentional killing), it matters not how or respecting whom'. See J. Horder, 'Transferred Malice and the Remoteness of Unexpected Outcomes' [2006] Crim LR 383.

In addition, if D would have been able to plead a defence for the murder of A (eg self-defence), under the doctrine this defence transfers from A to B and so D can escape liability for the murder of B.

It is important, however, to appreciate the limitations of the doctrine. For example, if D shoots at V, intending to kill him, but misses and instead smashes the window of V's car, this will not suffice to make D guilty of criminal damage. D had an intention to kill, not to cause criminal damage. However, D would be guilty of criminal damage if he had an intention to smash V's window but instead smashes W's (or if D was reckless as to causing damage to the window of V's car).

In the relatively recent case of *Grant* [2014] EWCA Crim 143, the Court of Appeal confirmed that if D shoots into a crowd with an intention to kill X, but misses and hits Y, causing him really serious harm, D will be guilty of intentionally causing grievous bodily harm to Y. Although the harm D caused to Y was less than what he intended to cause X, an intention to kill can be taken to include an intention to cause really serious harm.

≈ *Questions*
(1) How far does the doctrine extend? D has mens rea to commit offence A and performs the actus reus of offence B. How similar must crimes A and B be?
(2) Are all forms of fault transferrable under the doctrine? What about gross negligence?
(3) Is there really a transfer of mens rea, or is the issue simply about the scope of the offence in question? For example, if D intends to shoot A but misses and kills B, can it be said that the offence of murder is committed when D intends to kill *a* person, irrespective of whether the victim is the person whose death D desired?
(4) Does *Grant* represent an extension of the doctrine, or merely the application of orthodox principles?

Courts rarely have the opportunity to consider the doctrine of transferred malice in practice. The following case is an important example of one of these rare opportunities. This case is important for two reasons. First, despite the criticisms that have been levelled at the doctrine of transferred malice over the years, the House of Lords affirmed its continued existence. Secondly, the House of Lords rejected a novel attempt to extend the application of the doctrine.

Attorney-General's Reference (No 3 of 1994)
[1997] UKHL 31, House of Lords

(Lords Goff, Mustill, Slynn, Hope and Clyde)

D stabbed his girlfriend, E, whom he knew to be pregnant. E recovered; but there was evidence that the child, V, was born prematurely as a result of the wound and, as a result of the premature birth, died after 121 days. D was charged with the murder of V. The judge directed an acquittal on the ground that no conviction of murder or manslaughter was possible in law. (A foetus is not a person in law and cannot be the victim of murder or manslaughter.) On the reference by the Attorney General, the Court of Appeal held that there was evidence that D murdered V, his intent to cause grievous bodily harm (the mens rea of murder) to E being 'transferred' to V. They also held that the foetus before birth was to be regarded as an integral part of the mother, like her arm or leg; so an intention to kill or cause grievous bodily harm to the foetus was an intention to cause grievous bodily harm to a person in being, the mother.

The House held that the foetus is not a part of the mother: the mother and the foetus are two distinct organisms, living symbiotically, not a single organism with two aspects. So an intention to kill or injure the foetus is not an intention to cause GBH to a person—it is not the mens rea of murder. It was accepted that the doctrine of transferred malice was sound law.

Lord Mustill:

The sources in more recent centuries are few. Of the two most frequently cited the earlier is *R v Pembliton* (1874) LR 2 CCR 119, [1874–80] All ER Rep 1163. In the course of a fight the defendant threw a stone at others which missed and broke a window. He was indicted for that he 'unlawfully and maliciously did commit damage, injury and spoil upon a window . . .' The jury found that he did not intend to break the window. On a case stated to the Court for Crown Cases Reserved it was argued for the prosecution that 'directly it is proved that he threw a stone . . . without just cause, the offence is established'. The ancient origins of this argument need no elaboration, and indeed the report of the argument as it developed showed that it was based on a conception of general malice. The interventions in argument are instructive. After the prosecutor had relied on the fact that the prisoner was actuated by malice, Blackburn J responded (at 120): 'But only of a particular kind, and not against the person injured.' Later, in reply to a reliance on a passage from Hale, the same judge said (at 121):

> 'Lord Coke, 3 Inst., p 56, puts the case of a man stealing deer in a park, shooting at the deer, and by the glance of the arrow killing a boy that is hidden in a bush, and calls this murder; but can any one say that ruling would be adopted now?'

This most learned of judges continued:

> 'I should have told the jury that if the prisoner knew there were windows behind, and that the probable consequence of his act would be to break one of them, that would be evidence for them of malice.'

The conviction was quashed. It is sufficient to quote briefly from the judgment of Blackburn J (at 122):

> 'We have not now to consider what would be malice aforethought to bring a given case within the common law definition of murder; here the statute says that the act must be unlawful and malicious . . . The jury might perhaps have found on this evidence that the act was malicious, because they might have found that the prisoner knew that the natural consequence of his act would be to break the glass, and although that was not his wish, yet he was reckless whether he did it or not; but the jury have not so found . . .'

This decision was distinguished in *R v Latimer* (1886) 17 QBD 359, [1886–90] All ER Rep 386. Two men quarreled in a public house. One of them struck at the other with his belt. The glancing blow bounced off and struck the prosecutrix, wounding her severely. The assailant was prosecuted and convicted for having unlawfully and maliciously wounded her, contrary to s 20 of the Offences against the Person Act 1861. Counsel for the defendant relied on *R v Pembliton*. In his judgment, Lord Coleridge CJ said ((1886) 17 QBD 359 at 361, [1886–90] All ER Rep 386 at 387):

> 'It is common knowledge that a man who has an unlawful and malicious intent against another, and, in attempting to carry it out, injures a third person, is guilty of what the law deems malice against the person injured, because the offender is doing an unlawful act, and has that which the judges call general malice, and that is enough.' . . .

My Lords, I find it hard to base a modern law of murder on these two cases. The Court in *R v Latimer* was, I believe, entirely justified in finding a distinction between their statutory backgrounds and one can well accept that the answers given, one for acquittal, the other for conviction, would be the same today. But the harking back to a concept of general malice, which amounts to no more than this, that a wrongful act displays a malevolence which can be attached to any adverse consequence, has long been out of date. And to speak of a particular malice which is 'transferred' simply disguises the problem by idiomatic language. The defendant's malice is directed at one objective, and when after the event the court treats it as directed at another object it is not recognising a 'transfer' but creating a new malice which never existed before. As Dr Glanville Williams pointed out in *Criminal Law: The General Part* (2nd edn, 1961) p 184, the doctrine is 'rather an arbitrary exception to general principles'. Like many of its kind this is useful enough to yield rough justice, in particular cases, and it can sensibly be retained notwithstanding its lack of any sound intellectual basis. But it is another matter to build a new rule upon it.

I pause to distinguish the case of indiscriminate malice from those already discussed, although even now it is sometimes confused with them. The terrorist who hides a bomb in an aircraft provides an example. This is not a case of 'general malice' where under the old law any wrongful act sufficed to prove the evil disposition which was taken to supply the necessary intent for homicide. Nor is it transferred malice, for there is no need of a transfer. The intention is already aimed directly at the class of potential victims of which the actual victim forms part. The intent and the actus reus completed by the explosion are joined from the start, even though the identity of the ultimate victim is not yet fixed. So also with the shots fired indiscriminately into a crowd. No ancient fictions are needed to make these cases of murder.

[Lord Mustill said that the question of manslaughter had caused him great anxiety, but he was persuaded by the opinion of Lord Hope.

Lord Hope, having made a detailed examination of the law of involuntary manslaughter (section 9.2, p 209) concluded:]

I think, then, that the position can be summarised in this way. The intention which must be discovered is an intention to do an act which is unlawful and dangerous. In this case the act which had to be shown to be an unlawful and dangerous act was the stabbing of the child's mother. There can be no doubt that all sober and reasonable people would regard that act, within the appropriate meaning of this term, as dangerous. It is plain that it was unlawful as it was done with the intention of causing her injury. As the defendant intended to commit that act, all the ingredients necessary for mens rea in regard to the crime of manslaughter were established, irrespective of who was the ultimate victim of it. The fact that the child whom the mother was carrying at the time was born alive and then died as a result of the stabbing is all that was needed for the offence of manslaughter when the actus reus for that crime was completed by the child's death. The question, once all the other elements are satisfied, is simply one of causation. The defendant must accept all the consequences of his act, so long as the jury are satisfied that he did what he did intentionally, that what he did was unlawful and that, applying the correct test, it was also dangerous. The death of the child was unintentional, but the nature and quality of the act which caused it was such that it was criminal and therefore punishable.

In my opinion that is sufficient for the offence of manslaughter. There is no need to look to the doctrine of transferred malice for a solution to the problem raised by this case so far as manslaughter is concerned.

[Lords Goff, Slynn and Clyde agreed with the speeches of Lords Mustill and Hope.]

≈≈ *Questions*

(1) Does the rule that an intention to cause GBH is a sufficient mens rea for murder involve a 'fiction'? No one pretends that it is an intention to kill.

(2) Does the prosecution's argument involve a 'double' transfer of intent?

(3) Ashworth states that, '[a] conviction for attempt is possible in virtually all cases which fall within the doctrine of transferred liability. D will invariably have taken the sufficient steps towards committing the offence against his intended victim for there to be the *actus reus* of an attempt, and *mens rea* will be undisputed'. See A. Ashworth, 'Transferred Malice and Punishment for Unforeseen Consequences' in P. R. Glazebrook (ed), *Reshaping the Criminal Law: Essays in Honour of Glanville Williams* (1978). Is this statement accurate? Would it have been a preferable approach to adopt in these circumstances?

The Court of Appeal in the *Attorney-General's Reference* case rejected arguments advanced based on the writings of Glanville Williams (a) that 'an unexpected difference of mode will be regarded as severing the chain of causation if it is sufficiently far removed from the intended mode', and (b) that the doctrine 'should be limited to cases where the consequence was brought about by negligence in relation to the actual victim'. These arguments were not advanced in the House of Lords.

Professor Horder argues ('Transferred Malice and the Remoteness of Unexpected Outcomes from Intentions' [2006] Crim LR 383) that the correct question should have been whether murder was a representative label for D given that there was (a) an unintended victim and (b) the death arose in a way that was not intended.

2.3.1.2 Correspondence principle

If the actus reus of an offence comprises elements A, B and C, to what extent is it necessary for the Crown to prove mens rea in relation to every element? In relation to criminal damage for example, the actus reus comprises conduct, in proscribed circumstances (property belonging to another), causing a result (damage). Is it sufficient that the Crown proves that D voluntarily threw a stone at the window or must it go further and show that D intended the damage to property and that he knew it was property of another?

Taking assault as a further example, D's conduct must cause V to apprehend immediate unlawful violence. D must have intended or been reckless whether his conduct might cause V's apprehension (the result). But D is not liable for assault unless he also has mens rea as to his conduct—he must intend to act or act voluntarily—and has mens rea as to the prohibited consequence in question (what V apprehended). There is a correspondence between all the elements of the actus reus and mens rea: there is an element of mens rea corresponding to each element of the actus reus.

As the following extract demonstrates, there are those who question the validity of the theoretical arguments that have been made to justify the existence of the correspondence principle.

J. Horder, 'A Critique of the Correspondence Principle in Criminal Law'
[1995] Crim LR 759 (references omitted)

The correspondence principle (hereinafter, the 'C' principle) concerns the relationship between actus reus and mens rea. Its definition and justification are well expressed by Ashworth and Campbell ('Recklessness in Assault—And in General?' (1991) 107 L.Q.R. 187 at p.192):

> '[I]f the offence is defined in terms of certain consequences and certain circumstances, the mental element ought to correspond with that by referring to those consequences or circumstances. If a mental element as to a lesser consequence were acceptable, this would amount to constructive criminal liability.'

. . . The C principle remains very much an ideal, if anything, rather than an accurate descriptive generalisation about crimes. Even amongst crimes requiring mens rea, not all exemplify the principle to anything like the full extent. The real problem is to decide when the C principle makes sense, even as an ideal.

In this regard, Ashworth argues that the C principle is a concrete illustration of a more abstract general principle at work within the criminal law, the principle of individual autonomy. The autonomy principle dictates that people are not to be held criminally liable unless, inter alia, they can be shown to have chosen to do, or had control over the doing of, the harm or wrong in question. At first sight, the autonomy principle's emphasis on choice and control appears to provide an attractive theoretical grounding for a subjectivist understanding of the C principle. On the subjectivist view, the C principle limits criminal liability to harms or wrongs that are intended or consciously risked; and harms or wrongs intended or consciously risked would seem to be paradigm examples of things over whose occurrence one has choice or control. On closer analysis, though, it becomes clear that the C principle cannot so easily be derived theoretically from the autonomy principle. Suppose D throws a brick from a window and, in so doing, intends to, or realises that he may, hit V. In these circumstances, if V is struck by the brick, the C principle dictates that D may be held criminally liable for the striking, because D's mens rea related to that possible outcome as an element in the actus reus. Yet, at this very point, the C principle appears to part company with the autonomy principle, as stated. When D let go of the brick, he ceased to have control over events. Since the brick would have missed V if it had been blown off course, or if V had suddenly moved, the actual fact that V was struck was as much a matter of chance as of choice or control. No doubt, D is still rightly regarded as causing the striking; but no one is in control of everything they cause to occur. So, seemingly contrary to the C principle, the autonomy principle dictates that D should be held criminally liable for no more than endangering V by throwing the brick, since that action was all that D chose to do or controlled.

See for a different view: B. Mitchell, 'In Defence of a Principle of Correspondence' [1999] Crim LR 195 and for a response see J. Horder, 'Questioning the Correspondence Principle—A Reply' [1999] Crim LR 206.

2.3.2 Coincidence in point of time

Can D be liable for an offence if he performs the actus reus at one point in time and later he forms the proscribed mental state? As the extracts in this section will demonstrate, although the general rule is that the actus reus and mens rea of the offence must coincide in point of time, the courts have taken a flexible approach to this issue. For example, in the following case the actus reus of the offence in question was characterized as a continuing act and it was sufficient for D to form the necessary mens rea during the continuance of the act.

Fagan v Metropolitan Police Commissioner
[1969] 1 QB 439, Queen's Bench Division

(Lord Parker CJ, Bridge and James JJ)

The defendant was directed by a police officer to park his car close to the kerb. He drove his car on to the officer's foot. The officer said, 'Get off, you are on my foot.' The defendant replied, 'Fuck you, you can wait', and turned off the ignition. He was convicted by the magistrates of assaulting the constable in the execution of his duty and his appeal was dismissed by Quarter Sessions who were in doubt whether the driving on to the foot was intentional or accidental but were satisfied that he 'knowingly, unnecessarily and provocatively' allowed the car to remain on the foot.

James J [with whom **Lord Parker CJ** concurred:]

. . . In our judgment, the question arising, which has been argued on general principles, falls to be decided on the facts of the particular case. An assault is any act which intentionally—or possibly recklessly—causes another person to apprehend immediate and unlawful personal violence. Although 'assault' is an independent crime and is to be treated as such, for practical purposes today 'assault' is generally synonymous with the term 'battery', and is a term used to mean the actual intended use of unlawful force to another person without his consent. On the facts of the present case, the 'assault' alleged involved a 'battery'. Where an assault involves a battery, it matters not, in our judgment, whether the battery is inflicted directly by the body of the offender or through the medium of some weapon or instrument controlled by the action of the offender. An assault may be committed by the laying of a hand upon another, and the action does not cease to be an assault if it is a stick held in the hand and not the hand itself which is laid on the person of the victim. So, for our part, we see no difference in principle between the action of stepping on to a person's toe and maintaining that position and the action of driving a car on to a person's foot and sitting in the car whilst its position on the foot is maintained.

To constitute the offence of assault, some intentional act must have been performed; a mere omission to act cannot amount to an assault. Without going into the question whether words alone can constitute an assault, it is clear that the words spoken by the appellant could not alone amount to an assault; they can only shed a light on the appellant's action. For our part, we think the crucial question is whether, in this case, the act of the appellant can be said to be complete and spent at the moment of time when the car wheel came to rest on the foot, or whether his act is to be regarded as a continuing act operating until the wheel was removed. In our judgment, a distinction is to be drawn between acts which are complete—though results may continue to flow—and those acts which are continuing. Once the act is complete, it cannot thereafter be said to be a threat to inflict unlawful force upon the victim. If the act, as distinct from the results thereof, is a continuing act, there is a continuing threat to inflict unlawful force. If the assault involves a battery and that battery continues, there is a continuing act of assault. For an assault to be committed, both the elements of actus reus and mens rea must be present at the same time. The 'actus reus' is the action causing the effect on the victim's mind: see the observations of Park[e] B, in *Regina v St George* [(1840) 9 C & P 483 at 490, 493]. The 'mens rea' is the intention to cause that effect. It is not necessary that mens rea should be present at the inception of the actus reus; it can be superimposed upon an existing act. On the other hand, the subsequent inception of mens rea cannot convert an act which has been completed without mens rea into an assault.

In our judgment, the Willesden magistrates and quarter sessions were right in law. On the facts found, the action of the appellant may have been initially unintentional, but the time came when, knowing that the wheel was on the officer's foot, the appellant (1) remained seated in the car so that his body through the medium of the car was in contact with the officer, (2) switched off the ignition of the car, (3) maintained the wheel of the car on the foot, and (4) used words indicating the intention of keeping the wheel in that position. For our part, we cannot regard such conduct as mere omission or inactivity. There was an act constituting a battery which at its inception was not criminal because there was no element of intention, but which became criminal from the moment the intention was formed to produce the apprehension which was flowing from the continuing act. The fallacy of the appellant's argument is that it seeks to equate the facts of this case with such a case as where a motorist has accidentally run over a person and, that action having been completed, fails to assist the victim with the intent that the victim should suffer.

We would dismiss this appeal.

[Bridge J delivered a dissenting judgment.]

Appeal dismissed. Leave to appeal to the House of Lords refused

The courts have struggled to maintain a strict adherence to the principle that the act and mental state must coincide *exactly* in time. In several difficult circumstances, the courts have had to treat the defendant's conduct as being a continuing state of affairs. In cases such as these, the actus reus is characterized as being part of a larger 'transaction' and the courts have accepted that D will be guilty if he forms the requisite mens rea during the course of that transaction. D will therefore be guilty even though he did not have the mens rea at the precise moment the actus reus was accomplished. The following case provides a vivid example of this approach.

Thabo Meli v R
[1954] 1 All ER 373, [1954] UKPC 1, Privy Council

(Lord Goddard CJ, Lord Reid and Mr L. M. D. da Silva)

The appellants, in accordance with a prearranged plan, took a man to a hut, gave him beer so that he was partially intoxicated and then struck him over the head. Believing him to be dead, they took his body and rolled it over a low cliff, dressing the scene to look like an accident. In fact, the man was not dead but died of exposure when unconscious at the foot of the cliff.

Lord Reid:

. . . The point of law which was raised in this case can be simply stated. It is said that two acts were done: first, the attack in the hut; and, secondly, the placing of the body outside afterwards—and that they were separate acts. It is said that, while the first act was accompanied by *mens rea*, it was not the cause of death; but that the second act, while it was the cause of death, was not accompanied by *mens rea*; and on that ground, it is said that the accused are not guilty of murder, though they may have been guilty of culpable homicide. It is said that the *mens rea* necessary to establish murder is an intention to kill, and that there could be no intention to kill when the accused thought that the man was already dead, so their original intention to kill had ceased before they did the act which caused the man's death. It appears to their Lordships impossible to divide up what was really one series of acts in this way. There is no doubt that the accused set out to do all these acts in order to achieve their plan, and as parts of their plan; and it is much too refined a ground of judgment to say that, because they were under a misapprehension at one stage and thought that their guilty purpose had been achieved before, in fact, it was achieved, therefore they are to escape the penalties of the law. Their Lordships do not think that this is a matter which is susceptible of elaboration. There appears to be no case, either in South Africa or England, or for that matter elsewhere, which resembles the present. Their

Lordships can find no difference relevant to the present case between the law of South Africa and the law of England; and they are of the opinion that by both laws there can be no separation such as that for which the accused contend. Their crime is not reduced from murder to a lesser crime merely because the accused were under some misapprehension for a time during the completion of their criminal plot.

Their Lordships must, therefore, humbly advise Her Majesty that this appeal should be dismissed.

Appeal dismissed

≋ *Question*

Arenson states that the decision in *Thabo Meli* has 'the practical effect of emasculating the doctrine of temporal coincidence beyond recognition.' Do you agree? K. Arenson, '*Thabo Meli* Revisited: The Pernicious Effects of Result-Driven Decisions' (2013) 77 J Crim L 41.

There was uncertainty after *Thabo Meli* as to the extent to which the approach adopted by the Privy Council was confined to cases in which there was a prearranged plan. In *Le Brun* [1991] 4 All ER 673, the Court of Appeal confirmed that a prearranged plan is unnecessary.

2.4 Criminal liability without an act

Being sovereign, Parliament can enact anything, even that a person commits a crime if something happens to him—for example, that he 'is found' in a particular situation. Although Parliament is sovereign, as this section will demonstrate, if it intends to create such offences, then it must make this intention explicit.

R v Larsonneur

(1933) 24 Cr App R 74, Court of Criminal Appeal

(Lord Hewart CJ, Avory and Humphreys JJ)

L was a French citizen whose entitlement to stay in the UK was restricted so as to require: 'departure from the United Kingdom not later than the 22nd March 1933'. On that date L entered the Irish Free State (which did not constitute departure from the UK under the order). The Irish authorities deported her, escorting her to Holyhead on 20 April. British police then arrested her. On 22 April she was charged under Article 18(1)(b) of the Aliens Order 1920 (below). At trial, the jury's verdict was: 'Guilty through circumstances beyond her own control'. L was sentenced to three days' imprisonment and recommended for deportation.

By the Aliens Order 1920, Article 1(3): 'Leave shall not be given to an alien to land in the United Kingdom unless he complies with the following conditions, that is to say . . . (g) he has not been prohibited from landing by the Secretary of State.' By Article 1(4), as amended: '. . . an alien who is found in the United Kingdom at any time after the expiration of the period limited by any such condition shall for the purposes of this Order be deemed to be an alien to whom leave to land has been refused . . .'. By Article 18(1)(b), as amended: 'If any alien, having landed in the United Kingdom in contravention of art 1 of this Order, is at any time found within the United Kingdom, he shall be guilty of an offence against this Order.'

Lord Hewart CJ [delivered the judgment of the court:]

In fact, the appellant went to the Irish Free State and afterwards, in circumstances which are perfectly immaterial, so far as this appeal is concerned, came back, to Holyhead. She was at Holyhead on 21 April 1933, a date after the day limited by the condition on her passport.

In these circumstances, it seems to be quite clear that art 1(4) of the Aliens Order 1920 (as amended . . .), applies. . . . The appellant was, therefore, on 21 April 1933, in the position in which she would have been if she had been prohibited from landing by the Secretary of State and, that being so, there is no reason to interfere with the finding of the jury. She was found here and was, therefore, deemed to be in the class of persons whose landing had been prohibited by the Secretary of State, by reason of the fact that she had violated the condition on her passport.

Appeal dismissed

Larsonneur was generally condemned but defended by D. J. Lanham [1976] Crim LR 276 who considered why L should have been denied the 'most readily acceptable' of all defences, physical compulsion. He concludes:

If Miss Larsonneur had been dragged kicking and screaming from France into the United Kingdom by kidnappers and the same judgment had been given by the Court of Criminal Appeal, the defence of unforeseeable compulsion would truly have been excluded and the case would be the worst blot on the pages of the modern criminal law. But she wasn't and it wasn't and it isn't.

≋ **Questions**

Did the offence consist in 'being found' or in 'landing and being found'? 'Being found' may not require a voluntary act by L, but does 'landing'?

In *Winzar v Chief Constable of Kent* (1983) The Times, 28 March, W was taken to hospital but found to be drunk and told to leave. The police were called when W remained slumped in a corridor. They took him to a police car parked in the hospital forecourt on X road. His subsequent conviction for 'being found drunk in a highway, X Road' was upheld by the Divisional Court. 'Found drunk' meant perceived to be drunk. It was enough that W was present in a highway and there perceived to be drunk. Did the police become aware of his state in the highway?

How explicit must the statute be as to whether there is a requirement of D's voluntary conduct in the offence? In *Robinson-Pierre* [2013] EWCA Crim 2396, D was convicted of offences under s 3(1) of the Dangerous Dogs Act 1991 which provided:

If a dog is dangerously out of control in a public place, the owner . . . is guilty of an offence, or if the dog while so out of control injures any person, an aggravated offence . . .

The offence occurred when police officers executing a search warrant battered down the front door of D's home and entered. D's ferocious pit bull attacked them and pursued three more officers in the street before being destroyed by armed officers called to the scene. At trial, the judge directed the jury that D was liable without proof of fault; it was enough that D was the owner of a dog that was dangerously out of control in a public place, as D's dog clearly was. D was convicted and appealed. D argued that although s 3(1) created a strict liability offence, a conviction under that section required proof that D caused or contributed to the prohibited event by his voluntary act or omission. Where acts of a third party, without D's knowledge or consent, were the sole cause of the state of affairs D was not guilty: he did not do anything to bring about the prohibited state of affairs. The Crown argued that 'how a dog ends up in the factual scenario [by] which the *actus reus* engages liability is entirely irrelevant'.

The Court of Appeal in what may be a landmark case quashed the conviction. Although s 3 was an offence of strict liability, the underlying assumption of the defence provided by s 3(2) was that someone (owner or person in charge) would be in charge of the dog. It was not therefore Parliament's intention to render the owner absolutely liable in all circumstances for the existence of the prohibited state of affairs however it arose (at [40]). The court held that there must be some causal connection between having charge of the dog and the prohibited state of affairs that has arisen.

> In our view, section 3(1) requires proof by the prosecution of an act or omission of the defendant (with or without fault) that to some (more than minimal) degree caused or permitted the prohibited state of affairs to come about. There had to be some causal connection between having charge of the dog and the prohibited state of affairs that had arisen (the danger in public).

The court relied on a wide range of authority including that from New Zealand and Canada. The court was also referred to the Supreme Court's decision in *Hughes* [2013] UKSC 56 (section 3.2.1, p 37) in relation to causing death by unlawful driving, but noted that the present offence was not cast in terms of causing a dangerous dog to be in a public place. Pitchford LJ stated at [37]:

> we do not accept that it is the law of England and Wales that Parliament cannot provide for criminal liability when there is no causative link between the act or omission of the defendant and the prohibited event. . . . To the extent that [defence counsel] seeks to derive a principle of law that even in the case of 'absolute' liability the defendant must be shown to have *caused* the prohibited state of affairs, we disagree with him. Such a conclusion would ignore the rationale for the acceptability of some offences of strict liability. The policy behind the prohibition may be regulatory; that is, it is in the public interest to place an absolute burden on the defendant to ensure that the state of affairs prohibited does not come about; alternatively, the criminal law may create an irrebuttable presumption whose effect cannot be avoided even by proof of moral rectitude.

As the court notes, in *Smith and Hogan* (13th edn, 2011) it was suggested that:

> as a matter of principle, even 'state of affairs' offences ought to require proof that D either caused the state of affairs or failed to terminate it or to act in order to do so when it was within his control and possible to do so.

The court took the view that:

> This is a view that will have many supporters. However, we have no doubt that the supremacy of Parliament embraces the power to create 'state of affairs' offences in which no causative link between the prohibited state of affairs and the defendant need be established. The legal issue is not, in our view, whether in principle such offences can be created but whether in any particular enactment Parliament intended to create one.

NB: Parliament responded by extending the offence in the Anti-social Behaviour, Crime and Policing Act 2014.

FURTHER READING

A. Ashworth, 'Defining Offences Without Harm' in A. T. H. Smith (ed), *Criminal Law: Essays in Honour of J. C. Smith* (1987)

R. A. Duff, *Answering for Crime: Responsibility and Liability in the Criminal Law* (2007), pp 202–208

S. Eldar, 'The Limits of Transferred Malice' (2012) 32 OJLS 633

P. H. Robinson, 'Should the Criminal Law Abandon the Actus Reus–Mens Rea Distinction?' in S. Shute, J. Gardner and J. Horder (eds), *Action and Value in Criminal Law* (1993)

A. T. H. Smith, 'On Actus Reus and Mens Rea' in P. Glazebrook (ed), *Reshaping the Criminal Law: Essays in Honour of Glanville Williams* (1978)

P. Westen, 'The Significance of Transferred Intent' (2013) 7 Crim L & Philosophy 321

3
Causation

Some of the controversies that will be examined in this chapter include:

(1) What should the law do where D's conduct is not the sole cause of the prohibited result? Must D be a substantial cause of the result, or does it suffice if D's contribution is more than minimal?

(2) What should the law do where there is an intervening event between D's conduct and the result—what is necessary to break the 'chain of causation'?

(3) To what extent can the actions of the victim break the chain of causation?

3.1 Introduction

Where the definition of a crime includes a result or consequence flowing from D's conduct, it must be proved that D caused that result. An act done with intent to cause the result may be an attempt to commit the crime but it will not be the full offence unless it actually causes it. Nor will it be sufficient that the *event* desired by D happens if it does not happen as a result of his act. So in *White* [1910] 2 KB 124, where D administered poison to V with intent to kill her and she died not of poison but of a heart attack, he was guilty of attempted murder but not of murder. It would have been different if the poison had brought about the heart attack. The death of V was the event which D desired to bring about but it was not the result of his act.

The discussion of causation usually occurs in the context of homicide offences, but it is an important feature in all result crimes. It is especially so in cases of strict liability where, in the absence of mens rea elements, disputes over causation become the most critical issue in determining liability. (See, for example, on environmental offences: N. Padfield, 'Clean Water and Muddy Causation' [1995] Crim LR 683.) Causation is also an important aspect of many other crimes.

Arguably, the criminal law places too much emphasis on the result occurring (which is sometimes a matter of luck) and not enough on the blameworthiness of D's conduct in seeking to bring about that result. See A. Ashworth, 'Belief Intent and Criminal Liability' in J. Eekelaar and J. Bell (eds), *Oxford Essays in Jurisprudence* (1989).

3.2 General approach to issues of causation

If confronted with a problem question that involves causation, you should consider the issues in the following order:

(1) Consider whether D's conduct is a 'but for' cause of the proscribed consequence (ask whether 'but for' D's act the result would have occurred). If D's conduct is a 'but for' cause, then consider the next question.

(2) Consider whether D's conduct is potentially a relevant legal cause of the proscribed consequence, bearing in mind the following:

  (a) D's conduct need not be the sole cause;

  (b) D's conduct must be a culpable cause;

  (c) D's conduct need not be a direct cause;

  (d) D's conduct must be more than merely *de minimis*.

(3) If D's conduct is potentially a relevant legal cause, then consider whether there is any intervening event between D's conduct and the prohibited result which breaks the chain of causation. The applicable legal principles will differ depending upon which of the following categories the case falls into:

  (a) naturally occurring events;

  (b) third party interventions;

  (c) the exceptional case of the medical profession;

  (d) victim's conduct.

The courts have commonly asserted that causation is simply a question of fact to be answered by the application of common sense. That is difficult to reconcile with the existence of a book, *Causation in the Law*, of over 500 pages with a 24-page table of cases by two eminent professors, Hart and Honoré. Given that it has been influential in the development of the law on causation, it is helpful to be familiar with their general approach. Hart and Honoré placed emphasis on giving causation its ordinary meaning. Their approach is based upon the distinction between normal and abnormal conditions. Only abnormal conditions can be categorized as causes; normal conditions cannot. Normal conditions are described as 'those conditions which are present as part of the usual state or mode of operation of the thing under enquiry'. They give as an example pervasive features of the environment. Therefore if a person lights a match near a haystack, setting it alight, the fact that there is oxygen in the air is a normal condition and therefore not a cause. However, the lighting of the match is abnormal and so it is right to classify it as a cause.

The difficulty of finding a practical approach to causation was recognized by the House of Lords in the *Empress* case, section 3.2.3.2, p 47. Whether that case helps to overcome the difficulty is a matter for debate.

3.2.1 'But for' causation

The first issue to consider is whether D is the 'but for' cause of the proscribed consequence. If D is not a 'but for' cause, then he cannot be guilty of the result crime. This is the case even if D desired the prohibited outcome, a point well illustrated by the case of *White* [1910] 2 KB 124. In short, D poisoned a drink with some cyanide. He placed it on a table for his mother to drink. The mother was found dead; she died from a heart attack. There was no evidence that the poisoned drink had accelerated her death in any way. D was charged with her murder. If we ask 'but for' D's act of poisoning the drink would she have died anyway, the answer is that she would. D's conduct was not therefore a cause of her death. He was acquitted of her murder but remained liable for attempting to murder her.

There is a danger with taking 'but for' causation too far and it leading to absurd results. If D invites V to dinner and V is run over by X and killed on the way to D's house, V would not have died 'but for' the invitation; but as a matter of common sense, no one would say 'D killed V', and D has not caused his death in law. The 'but for' test—or 'sine qua non' as it is sometimes called—serves to filter out irrelevant factors, but cannot be regarded as any more than a starting point in the causation inquiry.

The Supreme Court has recognized that 'but for' causation, if applied literally, could lead to absurd results. In *Hughes* [2013] UKSC 56 (for the facts, see section 3.2.2.2, p 39), Lords Hughes and Toulson gave the following example:

> 23. The law has frequently to confront the distinction between 'cause' in the sense of a sine qua non without which the consequence would not have occurred, and 'cause' in the sense of something which was a legally effective cause of that consequence. The former, which is often conveniently referred to as a 'but for' event, is not necessarily enough to be a legally effective cause. If it were, the woman who asked her neighbour to go to the station in his car to collect her husband would be held to have caused her husband's death if he perished in a fatal road accident on the way home. In the case law there is a well recognised distinction between conduct which sets the stage for an occurrence and conduct which on a common sense view is regarded as instrumental in bringing about the occurrence.

'But for' causation is nevertheless useful because it tells us who *cannot* be guilty. This point is demonstrated by the case of *White*. To ascertain guilt, however, is it necessary to consider whether D, who is a but for cause, is the legal cause of the proscribed consequence.

3.2.2 Legal causes

If D is a 'but for' cause of the proscribed consequence, this is not sufficient to make him guilty of a criminal offence. As the Supreme Court confirmed in *Hughes*, it is necessary also to consider whether D is a legal cause. A number of issues can arise when considering whether D is a legal cause. These will be considered in this section.

3.2.2.1 Multiple causes

A result may have more than one cause. It is sufficient for criminal liability that D's act was one of two or more causes. If the result would not have occurred as and when it did *but for* D's act that is usually enough to fix him with responsibility for it. If V is already dying of meningitis when D strikes him and the blow accelerates V's death, D is guilty of homicide. If a fatal collision occurs because two motorists are driving dangerously and a passenger is killed, both are guilty of causing death by dangerous driving. Usually it is simply a question of fact whether the act caused the result, but the matter is more complex when an act by some other person or some event intervenes between D's act and the result (see section 3.2.3, p 41).

3.2.2.2 A culpable cause?

Having identified D's act that may be a but for cause, it is necessary to consider whether that is a voluntary act and one for which D can be treated as culpable.

The case of *Dalloway* (1847) 2 Cox CC 273 illustrates that there must be a connection between the fault and the result. In this case D was driving a cart on a highway with the reins not in his hand but loose on the horse's back. A child ran into the road and was killed. Erle J directed the jury that if D could have saved the child by using the reins, he was guilty of manslaughter. If, however, the jury concluded that D could not have saved the child by using the reins, then they should acquit him. Despite the fact D was a 'but for' cause of the child's death, he could not be guilty unless the death was attributable to the culpable element in his conduct, namely his negligence in not using the reins.

In a number of recent cases, the Supreme Court has emphasized the importance of there being a connection between fault and result.

R v Hughes
[2013] UKSC 56, Supreme Court

(Lords Neuberger, Mance, Kerr, Hughes and Toulson)

D was driving along a carriageway when a vehicle driven by V travelling in the opposite direction veered across the road and collided with him. V died from his injuries. It later transpired that V was driving under the influence of heroin at the time of the fatal collision. It was accepted that the manner of D's driving was faultless. However, D was driving without a full licence and did not have insurance. D was convicted of causing the death of another person by driving a motor vehicle on a road without insurance and otherwise than in accordance with a licence, contrary to s 3ZB of the Road Traffic Act 1988. The certified question for the Supreme Court to answer was: 'Is it an offence contrary to section 3ZB of the Road Traffic Act 1988 as amended by section 21(1) of the Road Safety Act 2006 [there was further amendment in the Criminal Justice and Courts Act 2015], committed by an unlicensed, disqualified or uninsured driver, when the circumstances are that the manner of his or her driving is faultless and the deceased was (in terms of civil law) 100% responsible for causing the fatal accident or collision?'

Lords Hughes and **Toulson** delivered the judgment for a unanimous court.

25. By the test of common sense, whilst the driving by Mr Hughes created the opportunity for his car to be run into by [V], what brought about the latter's death was his own dangerous driving under the influence of drugs. It was a matter of the merest chance that what he hit when he veered onto the wrong side of the road for the last of several times was the oncoming vehicle which Mr Hughes was driving. He might just as easily have gone off the road and hit a tree, in which case nobody would suggest that his death was caused by the planting of the tree, although that too would have been a sine qua non.

. . .

28. It follows that in order to give effect to the expression 'causes . . . death . . . by driving' a defendant charged with the offence under section 3ZB must be shown to have done something other than simply putting his vehicle on the road so that it is there to be struck. It must be proved that there was something which he did or omitted to do by way of driving it which contributed in a more than minimal way to the death. The question therefore remains what can or cannot amount to such act or omission in the manner of driving.

. . .

33. Juries should thus be directed that it is not necessary for the Crown to prove careless or inconsiderate driving, but that there must be something open to proper criticism in the driving of the defendant, beyond the mere presence of the vehicle on the road, and which contributed in some more than minimal way to the death. How much this offence will in practice add to the other offences of causing death by driving will have to be worked out as factual scenarios present themselves; it may be that it will add relatively little, but this is the inevitable consequence of the language used and the principles of construction explained above.

. . .

36. For the reasons set out, inquiry into apportionment of liability in civil terms is not appropriate to a criminal trial. But it must follow from the use of the expression 'causes . . . death . . . by driving' that section 3ZB requires at least some act or omission in the control of the car, which involves some element of fault, whether amounting to careless/inconsiderate driving or not, and which contributes in some more than minimal way to the death. It is not necessary that such act or omission be the principal cause of the death. In which circumstances the offence under section 3ZB will then add to the other offences of causing death by driving must remain to be worked out as factual scenarios are presented

to the courts. In the present case the agreed facts are that there was nothing which Mr Hughes did in the manner of his driving which contributed in any way to the death. It follows that the Recorder of Newcastle was correct to rule that he had not in law caused the death by his driving. The appeal should be allowed and that ruling restored.

≋ *Question*
Does the form of words used by Parliament in the section require D to be driving in a way that is 'open to criticism'?

In the more recent case of *Taylor* [2016] UKSC 5, the Crown argued that the Supreme Court ought to depart from the reasoning in *Hughes*. The Supreme Court declined to do so, however. It now seems beyond doubt, therefore, that there must be a connection between fault and result for D to be guilty in such cases. In *Taylor*, the Crown argued that the requisite fault was present, because D was driving whilst over the drink drive limit. The Supreme Court rejected this argument, however, and held that the fault necessary for D to be guilty must have been in the manner in which he was driving the car.

3.2.2.3 Direct causes

The connection between D's culpable conduct and the proscribed result need not be direct. In *Mitchell* (1983) 76 Cr App R 293, CA, D entered a post office in which there was a lengthy queue. D tried to push in and an elderly man intervened and complained to D. D hit this man who fell back onto an 89-year-old lady who suffered a broken leg and died as a result of complications from that injury. D's conviction for manslaughter was upheld: 'We can see no reason of policy for holding that an act calculated to harm A cannot be manslaughter if, in fact it kills B. The criminality of the doer of the act is precisely the same . . .', per Staughton J at 296.

≋ *Questions*
Is there any limit to this principle? D punches X, a burly man of 20, intending to cause him serious injury. X falls onto Y who lands on V who is a newborn baby and crushes V to death. Is D liable for V's murder?

3.2.2.4 *De minimis* causes

Some factual causes are so minute that they can be ignored when considering the causation inquiry. In *Kimsey* [1996] Crim LR 35, D was convicted of causing death by dangerous driving. He had been racing another car driven by the deceased, V. D argued that the reason V crashed was because of her loss of control of the car, not because of D's collision with her car. The prosecution argued that D's conduct, by racing and/or colliding and/or driving too closely had caused V's loss of control and led to her death. The Court of Appeal confirmed that the test for whether D's conduct is a cause of the prohibited result is whether the contribution made by D's conduct to the result was 'more than minute'.

This can give rise to difficult questions of degree in cases of the killing of terminally ill individuals. The question of how much acceleration of impending death needs to be established to show that D has caused V's death raises complex and controversial issues of euthanasia. There have been a number of high-profile cases in which doctors have been prosecuted for murder, or attempted murder, where they have 'eased the passing' of a terminally ill patient, often reducing life expectancy by only hours. An example was that of Dr Cox (1992) 12 BMLR 38 ('Hard Cases Make Bad Law (Mercy Killing and Dr Cox)' (1992) 142 NLJ 1293), and a more significant one was that of Bodkin Adams, reported at [1957] Crim LR 365. See the Law Commission's Report No 304, *Murder, Manslaughter and Infanticide* (2006), Ch 7, section 7.2.3.4, p 150, on whether a defence of mercy killing ought to be introduced into English law.

3.2.3 *Novus actus interveniens* or 'breaks in the chain of causation'

If D's conduct is a 'but for' cause and is not merely *de minimis*, the question will often arise as to what impact any intervening events between D's conduct and the proscribed result have on D's liability. This commonly arises in the context of murder.

Should D remain liable for murder where he causes V some injury but before V dies:

- there is some naturally occurring event, for example lightning striking V; or
- some third party intervenes, for example D2 comes along and shoots V dead; or
- medical professionals, seeking to save V's life, blunder and accelerate his death; or
- V himself accelerates his own death?

This is a notoriously difficult area of law and the courts have struggled to produce clear principles. The diversity of factual circumstances in which interventions arise encourages the courts to distinguish cases too readily. In addition, decisions are very heavily influenced by policy considerations, particularly since most are homicide cases in which D has performed a culpable act with mens rea. The following categories of intervening event deserve consideration.

(1) Naturally occurring events.
(2) Third party interventions.
(3) The exceptional case of the medical profession.
(4) The victim's conduct.

When considering these issues in a problem question, it is important to identify which category the facts of the problem fall into. This is because the approach that ought to be adopted will differ depending upon the category of case being considered.

3.2.3.1 Natural events

According to a leading American academic writer, R. M. Perkins, if D knocks down V and leaves him unconscious on the floor of a building which collapses in a sudden earthquake and kills him, D is not guilty of homicide even if it is certain that V would not have been in the building if D had not knocked him down. But if D had struck V on the seashore and left him unconscious in the path of the incoming tide, D would be responsible for V's death by drowning. (Examples given by Perkins (1946) 36 J Cr L & Cr at 393.) The seashore example was followed in *Hallett* [1969] SASR 141, on similar facts; and the court said it would have been different if the unconscious victim had been left above the high-water mark but drowned by a wholly exceptional tidal wave (tsunami) resulting from an undersea earthquake.

≈≈ *Question*
Suppose a hospital is struck by lightning and set on fire so that everyone in it perishes. Are all the patients who were there because they had been assaulted now the victims of homicide?

3.2.3.2 Intervening acts of others

The law struggles to distinguish precisely between voluntary and involuntary actors intervening after the defendant's conduct and before the prohibited result. It is generally accepted that
where X, the intervening party, has acted in an involuntary manner, his act will not break the
chain of causation even if the act is foreseeable, and D will remain liable. On the other hand, a
free, deliberate, informed act by X will break the chain of causation, whether foreseeable or not.

Some cases had cast doubt on that principle, including the House of Lords in *Empress Car*
[1999] AC 22 where D was held liable for a pollution offence when a stranger, X, unforeseeably
damaged tanks in which D stored oil, leading a river to become polluted. We return to *Empress*
later, but before doing so discuss the leading authority *Kennedy (No 2)* [2007] UKHL 38 which
reasserted the orthodox principle that a free, deliberate, informed act by X would break the
chain of causation, whether foreseeable or not. Before discussing *Kennedy (No 2)*, however, it is
necessary to understand the circumstances which led to the House of Lords hearing that appeal.

In a succession of cases, the issue arose as to whether D who supplied V with drugs was guilty
of manslaughter where V self-injected what turned out to be a fatal overdose. In *Kennedy (No
1)* [1999] Crim LR 65, the facts were agreed: K supplied heroin to MB ('the deceased'). K prepared a 'hit' of heroin for MB and gave him the syringe ready for injection. MB injected himself
and returned the syringe to K. K left the room. The heroin resulted in MB's breathing being
affected. Although an ambulance was summoned, the injection resulted in the death of MB.
On his conviction for manslaughter (on the basis of his unlawful act of administering a noxious substances contrary to s 23 of the OAPA 1861), K appealed and the Court of Appeal upheld
his conviction ([1999] Crim LR 65) on the basis that: (a) K was a secondary party to MB's act of
self-injection (this is wrong and has now been accepted to be so by the Court of Appeal—see
section 9.2.5.2, p 222); (b) MB's act of self-injection was not a break in the chain of causation.

The idea that D (K) was a party to V's (MB's) self-injection and that V's free, informed,
deliberate act did not break the chain of causation was heretical and was subjected to very
strong criticism.

In *Kennedy (No 2)* [2005] EWCA Crim 685, because subsequent decisions of the Court
of Appeal cast doubt on the conclusion in *Kennedy (No 1)*, the case was referred back to the
Court of Appeal by the Criminal Cases Review Commission. The Court of Appeal concluded
that D remains liable if the jury considers that D was responsible for taking the action in 'joint
concert' with V to enable V to inject himself. For analysis of the Court of Appeal's decision
compare D. Ormerod and R. Fortson, 'Drugs Suppliers as Manslaughterers (Again)' [2005]
Crim LR 819 with T. Jones, 'Causation, Homicide and the Supply of Drugs' (2006) LS 139.

The Court of Appeal certified the following question of general public importance:

> When is it appropriate to find someone guilty of manslaughter where that person has been involved
> in the supply of a class A controlled drug, which is then freely and voluntarily self-administered by the
> person to whom it was supplied, and the administration of the drug then causes his death?

R v Kennedy (No 2)
[2007] UKHL 38, House of Lords

(Lords Bingham of Cornhill, Rodger of Earlsferry, Baroness Hale of Richmond, Lords Carswell and Mance)

[Lord Bingham examined the scope of s 23 of the Offences Against the Person Act 1861 and turned to
consider the issue of causation directly:]

14. The criminal law generally assumes the existence of free will. The law recognises certain exceptions, in the case of the young, those who for any reason are not fully responsible for their actions,

and the vulnerable, and it acknowledges situations of duress and necessity, as also of deception and mistake. But, generally speaking, informed adults of sound mind are treated as autonomous beings able to make their own decisions how they will act, and none of the exceptions is relied on as possibly applicable in this case. Thus D is not to be treated as causing V to act in a certain way if V makes a voluntary and informed decision to act in that way rather than another. There are many classic statements to this effect. In his article '*Finis for Novus Actus?*' (1989) 48(3) CLJ 391, 392, Professor Glanville Williams wrote:

'I may suggest reasons to you for doing something; I may urge you to do it, tell you it will pay you to do it, tell you it is your duty to do it. My efforts may perhaps make it very much more likely that you will do it. But they do not cause you to do it, in the sense in which one causes a kettle of water to boil by putting it on the stove. Your volitional act is regarded (within the doctrine of responsibility) as setting a new "chain of causation" going, irrespective of what has happened before.'

In chapter XII of *Causation in the Law*, 2nd ed (1985), p 326, Hart and Honoré wrote:

'The free, deliberate, and informed intervention of a second person, who intends to exploit the situation created by the first, but is not acting in concert with him, is normally held to relieve the first actor of criminal responsibility.'

This statement was cited by the House with approval in *R v Latif* [1996] 1 WLR 104, 115. The principle is fundamental and not controversial.

15. Questions of causation frequently arise in many areas of the law, but causation is not a single, unvarying concept to be mechanically applied without regard to the context in which the question arises. That was the point which Lord Hoffmann, with the express concurrence of three other members of the House, was at pains to make in *Environment Agency (formerly National Rivers Authority) v Empress Car Co (Abertillery) Ltd* [1999] 2 AC 22. The House was not in that decision purporting to lay down general rules governing causation in criminal law. It was construing, with reference to the facts of the case before it, a statutory provision imposing strict criminal liability on those who cause pollution of controlled waters. Lord Hoffmann made clear that (p 29E–F) common sense answers to questions of causation will differ according to the purpose for which the question is asked; that (p 31E) one cannot give a common sense answer to a question of causation for the purpose of attributing responsibility under some rule without knowing the purpose and scope of the rule; that (p 32B) strict liability was imposed in the interests of protecting controlled waters; and that (p 36A) in the situation under consideration the act of the defendant could properly be held to have caused the pollution even though an ordinary act of a third party was the immediate cause of the diesel oil flowing into the river. It is worth underlining that the relevant question was the cause of the pollution, not the cause of the third party's act.

16. The committee would not wish to throw any doubt on the correctness of *Empress Car*. But the reasoning in that case cannot be applied to the wholly different context of causing a noxious thing to be administered to or taken by another person contrary to section 23 of the 1861 Act. In *R v Finlay* [2003] EWCA Crim 3868 (8 December 2003) V was injected with heroin and died. D was tried on two counts of manslaughter, one on the basis that he had himself injected V, the second on the basis that he had prepared a syringe and handed it to V who had injected herself. The jury could not agree on the first count but convicted on the second. When rejecting an application to remove the second count from the indictment, the trial judge ruled, relying on *Empress Car*, that D had produced a situation in which V could inject herself, in which her self-injection was entirely foreseeable and in which self-injection could not be regarded as something extraordinary. He directed the jury along those lines. The Court of Appeal upheld the judge's analysis and dismissed the appeal. It was wrong to do so. Its decision conflicted with the rules on personal autonomy and informed voluntary choice to which reference has been made above. In the decision under appeal the Court of Appeal did not follow *R v Finlay* in seeking to apply *Empress Car*, and it was right not to do so.

17. In his article already cited Professor Glanville Williams pointed out (at p 398) that the doctrine of secondary liability was developed precisely because an informed voluntary choice was ordinarily regarded as a *novus actus interveniens* breaking the chain of causation:

'Principals cause, accomplices encourage (or otherwise influence) or help. If the instigator were regarded as causing the result he would be a principal, and the conceptual division between principals (or, as I prefer to call them, perpetrators) and accessories would vanish. Indeed, it was because the instigator was not regarded as causing the crime that the notion of accessories had to be developed. This is the irrefragable argument for recognising the *novus actus* principle as one of the bases of our criminal law. The final act is done by the perpetrator, and his guilt pushes the accessories, conceptually speaking, into the background. Accessorial liability is, in the traditional theory, 'derivative' from that of the perpetrator.'

18. This is a matter of some significance since, contrary to the view of the Court of Appeal when dismissing the appellant's first appeal, the deceased committed no offence when injecting himself with the fatal dose of heroin. It was so held by the Court of Appeal in *R v Dias* [2002] 2 Cr App R 96, paras 21–24, and in *R v Rogers* [2003] EWCA Crim 945, [2003] 1 WLR 1374 and is now accepted. If the conduct of the deceased was not criminal he was not a principal offender, and it of course follows that the appellant cannot be liable as a secondary party. It also follows that there is no meaningful legal sense in which the appellant can be said to have been a principal jointly with the deceased, or to have been acting in concert. The finding that the deceased freely and voluntarily administered the injection to himself, knowing what it was, is fatal to any contention that the appellant caused the heroin to be administered to the deceased or taken by him. . . .

[His lordship considered several older cases and the Court of Appeal's decision in the present case.]

25. The answer to the certified question is: 'In the case of a fully-informed and responsible adult, never'. The appeal must be allowed and the appellant's conviction for manslaughter quashed.

Appeal allowed

It is necessary to point out at this stage that in cases such as these, prosecutors have now taken to charging gross negligence manslaughter, rather than manslaughter by an unlawful and dangerous act, which is what Kennedy was charged with. The courts have been prepared to uphold convictions for that offence: see section 4.2.3.4 (see p 69) for the discussion of *Evans* [2009] EWCA Crim 650.

Although welcomed by many, the judgment of the House of Lords in *Kennedy (No 2)* has been the subject of criticism, as the following extract demonstrates:

A. Norrie, *Crime, Reason and History*
(2014), pp 184–185

From a moral, political or policy point of view, it may be right to restrict the scope of causation according to the voluntary act principle in these cases. Co-users ought not to be convicted of manslaughter where they too could have been the victim and their relationship to V was not exploitative; but was the principle under which Kennedy's conviction was overturned really so compelling? Viewed in context, it is indeed reasonable to expect that V, a drug addict, will self-inject when presented with a loaded syringe. Nor is it implausible to see the preparation of a loaded syringe and its presentation to V as part of a joint, concerted action, as in the Court of Appeal's discussion in this case of two nurses preparing an injection for a patient, where only one actually injects and the other prepares the syringe and applies the plaster. There are defensible moral grounds for arguing for culpability in such cases, as occurs in Scotland and in some US jurisdictions. On the other hand, there is something irreducibly individual in human agency that is observed in the final act of the user pushing the syringe into the arm and operating the plunger. It is this that the orthodox English approach associated with Hart and Honoré rests upon. Thus, depending on how one contextualises or decontextualizes the final act, the facts in *Kennedy (No 2)* could come out as involving a new intervening voluntary act—or not. Hence the resolute application of principle that is 'fundamental and not controversial' ultimately appears underdetermined morally by the facts of the case. The fundamental principle is so malleable that the case could have gone either way, and one is left to reflect that the judges may be deploying the principle in order to achieve the moral and policy result they approve, rather than for its own sake. The principle is not determinative, even when it is followed.

If the act of the third party is not voluntary, then it will not break the chain of causation and D will still be liable. The following case is an extreme example of that principle in operation.

R v Pagett

[1983] EWCA Crim 1, Court of Appeal, Criminal Division

(Robert Goff LJ, Cantley and Farquharson JJ)

Pagett (P), armed with a shotgun, took a girl, Gail Kinchen (K), who was six months' pregnant by him, from the home of her mother and stepfather by force, wounding the stepfather, and violently assaulting her mother. P took K to a block of flats, pursued by the police. The police called on P to come out. Eventually he did so, holding K in front of him as a shield. He approached two police officers and fired the shotgun. The officers fired back instinctively not taking any particular aim. K was struck by three bullets and died. P was convicted of, *inter alia*, manslaughter. He appealed on the ground that the judge had misdirected the jury that, on these facts, he had caused K's death.

[Robert Goff LJ delivered the judgment of the court:]

. . . [T]he whole subject of causation in the law has been the subject of a well-known and most distinguished treatise by Professors Hart and Honoré, *Causation in the Law*. Passages from this book were cited to the learned judge, and were plainly relied upon by him; we, too, wish to express our indebtedness to it. It would be quite wrong for us to consider in this judgment the wider issues discussed in that work. But, for present purposes, the passage which is of most immediate relevance is to be found in Chapter XII, in which the learned authors consider the circumstances in which the intervention of a third person, not acting in concert with the accused, may have the effect of relieving the accused of criminal responsibility. The criterion which they suggest should be applied in such circumstances is whether the intervention is voluntary, ie whether it is 'free, deliberate and informed.' We resist the temptation of expressing the judicial opinion whether we find ourselves in complete agreement with that definition; though we certainly consider it to be broadly correct and supported by authority. Among the examples which the authors give of non-voluntary conduct, which is not effective to relieve the accused of responsibility, are two which are germane to the present case, viz a reasonable act performed for the purpose of self-preservation, and an act done in performance of a legal duty.

There can, we consider, be no doubt that a reasonable act performed for the purpose of self-preservation, being of course itself an act caused by the accused's own act, does not operate as a *novus actus interveniens*. If authority is needed for this almost self-evident proposition, it is to be found in such cases as *Pitts* (1842) Car & M 284, and *Curley* (1909) 2 Cr App R 96. In both these cases, the act performed for the purpose of self-preservation consisted of an act by the victim in attempting to escape from the violence of the accused, which in fact resulted in the victim's death. In each case it was held as a matter of law that, if the victim acted in a reasonable attempt to escape the violence of the accused, the death of the victim was caused by the act of the accused. Now one form of self-preservation is self-defence; for present purposes, we can see no distinction in principle between an attempt to escape the consequences of the accused's act, and a response which takes the form of self-defence. Furthermore, in our judgment, if a reasonable act of self-defence against the act of the accused causes the death of a third party, we can see no reason in principle why the act of self-defence, being an involuntary act caused by the act of the accused, should relieve the accused from criminal responsibility for the death of the third party. Of course, it does not necessarily follow that the accused will be guilty of the murder, or even of the manslaughter, of the third party; though in the majority of cases he is likely to be guilty at least of manslaughter. Whether he is guilty of murder or manslaughter will depend upon the question whether all the ingredients of the relevant offence have been proved; in particular, on a charge of murder, it will be necessary that the accused had the necessary intent. . . .

No English authority was cited to us, nor we think to the learned judge, in support of the proposition that an act done in the execution of a legal duty, again of course being an act itself caused by the act of the accused, does not operate as a novus actus interveniens. . . . Even so, we agree with the learned judge that the proposition is sound in law, because as a matter of principle such an act cannot be regarded as a voluntary act independent of the wrongful act of the accused. A parallel may be drawn with the so-called 'rescue' cases in the law of negligence, where a wrongdoer may be held liable in negligence to a third party who suffers injury in going to the rescue of a person who has been put in danger by the defendant's negligent act. Where, for example, a police officer in the execution of his duty acts to prevent a crime, or to apprehend a person suspected of a crime, the case is surely *a fortiori*. Of course, it is inherent in the requirement that the police officer, or other person, must be acting in the execution of his duty that his act should be reasonable in all the circumstances: see section 3 of the Criminal Law Act 1967. Furthermore, once again we are only considering the issue of causation. If intervention by a third party in the execution of a legal duty, caused by the act of the accused, results in the death of the victim, the question whether the accused is guilty of the murder or manslaughter of the victim must depend on whether the necessary ingredients of the relevant offence have been proved against the accused, including in particular, in the case of murder, whether the accused had the necessary intent.

The principles which we have stated are principles of law. This is plain from, for example, the case of *Pitts* (1842) Car & M 284, to which we have already referred. It follows that where, in any particular case, there is an issue concerned with what we have for convenience called *novus actus interveniens*, it will be appropriate for the judge to direct the jury in accordance with these principles. It does not however follow that it is accurate to state broadly that causation is a question of law. On the contrary, generally speaking causation is a question of fact for the jury. Thus in, for example, *Towers* (1874) 12 Cox CC 530, the accused struck a woman; she screamed loudly, and a child whom she was then nursing turned black in the face, and from that day until it died suffered from convulsions. The question whether the death of the child was caused by the act of the accused was left by the judge to the jury to decide as a question of fact. But that does not mean that there are no principles of law relating to causation, so that no directions on law are ever to be given to a jury on the question of causation. On the contrary, we have already pointed out one familiar direction which is given on causation, which is that the accused's act need not be the sole, or even the main, cause of the victim's death for his act to be held to have caused the death.

Appeal dismissed

≈≈≈ *Questions*

In what way were the police officers' acts capable of being described as 'involuntary'? What is the purpose of firearms training if officers are going to fire their weapons involuntarily?

As noted, the House of Lords in a case called *Empress* had previously adopted a very different approach to causation than the one adopted in *Kennedy (No 2)*.

Empress Car Co v National Rivers Authority
[1998] UKHL 5, House Lords

(Lords Browne-Wilkinson, Lloyd, Nolan, Hoffmann and Clyde)

The question was whether the company had caused the pollution of a river, contrary to what was then an offence under s 85(1) of the Water Resources Act 1991, by installing a tank of diesel oil in a position where, if the tap was turned on, the oil would flow into the river, and by omitting to provide a proper lock or other protection against misuse. The tap was turned on by a person unknown and the entire contents flowed into the river. The House upheld the conviction of the company.

Lord Hoffmann [having remarked on the many cases in which justices who have attempted to apply their common sense to the issue of causation have been reversed by the Divisional Court, went on to offer some guidance:]

The first point to emphasise is that commonsense answers to questions of causation will differ according to the purpose for which the question is asked. Questions of causation often arise for the purpose of attributing responsibility to someone, for example, so as to blame him for something which has happened or to make him guilty of an offence or liable in damages. In such cases, the answer will depend upon the rule by which responsibility is being attributed. Take, for example, the case of the man who forgets to take the radio out of his car and during the night someone breaks the quarterlight [ie side window], enters the car and steals it. What caused the damage? If the thief is on trial, so that the question is whether he is criminally responsible, then obviously the answer is that he caused the damage. It is no answer for him to say that it was caused by the owner carelessly leaving the radio inside. On the other hand, the owner's wife, irritated at the third such occurrence in a year, might well say that it was his fault. In the context of an inquiry into the owner's blameworthiness under a non-legal, commonsense duty to take reasonable care of one's own possessions, one would say that his carelessness caused the loss of the radio.

Not only may there be different answers to questions about causation when attributing responsibility to different people under different rules (in the above example, criminal responsibility of the thief, commonsense responsibility of the owner) but there may be different answers when attributing responsibility to different people under the same rule. In *National Rivers Authority v Yorkshire Water Services Ltd* [1995] 1 All ER 225, [1995] 1 AC 444 the defendant was a sewerage undertaker. It received sewage, treated it in filter beds and discharged the treated liquid into the river. One night someone unlawfully discharged a solvent called iso-octanol into the sewer. It passed through the sewage works and entered the river. The question was whether the defendant had caused the consequent pollution. Lord Mackay of Clashfern LC, with whom the other members of the House agreed, said ([1995] 1 All ER 225 at 231, [1995] 1 AC 444 at 452):

'. . . I am of opinion that Yorkshire Water Services having set up a system for gathering effluent into their sewers and thence into their sewage works there to be treated, with an arrangement deliberately intended to carry the results of that treatment into controlled waters, the special circumstances surrounding the entry of iso-octanol into their sewers and works do not preclude the conclusion that Yorkshire Water Services caused the resulting poisonous, noxious and polluting matter to enter the controlled waters, notwithstanding that the constitution of the effluent so entering was affected by the presence of iso-octanol.'

So in the context of attributing responsibility to Yorkshire Water Services under s 85(1) (then s 107(1)(a) of the Water Act 1989), it had caused the pollution. On the other hand, if the person who put the iso-octanol into the sewer had been prosecuted under the same subsection, it would undoubtedly have been held that he caused the pollution. . . .

I turn next to the question of third parties and natural forces. In answering questions of causation for the purposes of holding someone responsible, both the law and common sense normally attach great significance to deliberate human acts and extraordinary natural events. A factory owner carelessly leaves a drum containing highly inflammable vapour in a place where it could easily be accidentally ignited. If a workman, thinking it is only an empty drum, throws in a cigarette butt and causes an explosion, one would have no difficulty in saying that the negligence of the owner caused the explosion. On the other hand, if the workman, knowing exactly what the drum contains, lights a match and ignites it, one would have equally little difficulty in saying that he had caused the explosion and that the carelessness of the owner had merely provided him with an occasion for what he did. One would probably say the same if the drum was struck by lightning. In both cases one would say that although the vapour-filled drum was a necessary condition for the explosion to happen, it was not caused by the owner's negligence. One might add by way of further explanation that the presence of an arsonist workman or lightning happening to strike at that time and place was a coincidence. . . .

I would also wish to avoid the language of foreseeability in relation to the inquiry into causation. In deciding whether some particular factor has played so important a part that any activity by the defendant should be seen as entirely superseded as a causative element, it is not a consideration of the foreseeability, or reasonable foreseeability, of the extraneous factor which seems to me to be appropriate, but rather its unnatural, extraordinary or unusual character. Matters of fault or negligence are not of immediate relevance in the present context and the concepts particularly related to those matters should best be avoided.

In *Empress*, the House decided only that the justices were *entitled to find*, on the evidence, that Empress caused the pollution. But the facts were not in dispute. Could the justices have properly decided that Empress did *not* cause the pollution? Should not *the law* say either that this was the offence, or that it was not? If the factory owner does not cause the explosion where the workman deliberately drops his match into the oil drum, why did Empress cause the pollution when the unknown person turned on the tap? Can you see any difference? In both cases the intervention was 'free, deliberate and informed'. Bear in mind what was held in *Pagett*. Could it be that the outcome in *Empress* resulted from the current concern to prevent pollution? Although far from conclusive, in *Natural England v Day* [2014] EWCA Crim 2683 Lord Thomas CJ made the following observation (at [23]):

we see strong arguments for following the approach in *Empress Car* in relation to the [Wildlife and Countryside Act 1981], if the issue ever arises on the facts of any properly developed case.

If a different approach to causation does continue to apply in the environmental context, this lends weight to Lord Hoffmann's suggestion that causation is not a single, unvarying concept.

~~~ *Questions*
(1) If a swimmer had swallowed the oil-polluted water and died, or a passer-by had been killed by the exploding drum, could the owner have been guilty of manslaughter by gross negligence?
(2) What is the status of *Empress* after the House of Lords' decision in *Kennedy (No 2)* and the more recent judgments of the Supreme Court in *Hughes* and *Taylor* (discussed earlier)?

3.2.3.3 Intervening medical treatment

It has been noted that many of the difficult issues on causation arise in cases of homicide. In those cases a common problem is that following the defendant's infliction of injury on V, V is treated by medical professionals in a less than perfect manner. In what circumstances will the medical intervention break the chain of causation? Bear in mind that the judgments in these cases are laden with policy considerations—the courts do not want to be 'letting off' D who has, with mens rea, culpably caused some injury particularly when the medical profession are compelled to treat V, frequently in under-resourced circumstances.

It is also important to remember that the question to focus on is whether the defendant is liable for V's death or whether there is a break in the chain of causation. The question is not whether the medical professional is criminally liable. That is a separate inquiry. There is nothing to prevent two people being independent causes of V's death and each being criminally liable. (Assassin D1 shoots V in the head and at the same time assassin D2, acting independently of D1, shoots V in the heart. Each bullet would have been sufficient to kill V. Both D1 and D2 are guilty of murder.)

In *Jordan* (1956) 40 Cr App R 152, D stabbed V. V was taken to hospital, where the wound had almost healed when a doctor administered a drug to which V was allergic. V died. The Court of Criminal Appeal held that the medical treatment and not D's act had caused the death of V. This seems to have been because the wound had virtually healed by the time V died and the treatment provided by the hospital was 'palpably wrong'. However, this case is generally thought of as exceptional. The position of the law now seems to be that medical intervention will not break the chain of causation as long as D's original act remains a significant and operative cause of V's death. This was clarified in the following case.

R v Cheshire
[1991] 1 WLR 844, Court of Appeal, Criminal Division

(Beldam LJ, Boreham and Auld JJ)

During an argument in a fish and chip shop at about midnight on 9/10 December 1987 D produced a handgun and shot V in the thigh and stomach. During his treatment in hospital V developed respiratory problems and a tracheotomy tube was placed in his windpipe. He died in hospital on 15 February 1988. At the post-mortem it was found that V's windpipe had become obstructed due to narrowing near the site of the tracheotomy scar.

D was charged with murder. The pathologist who conducted the post-mortem gave evidence that the immediate cause of death was cardio-respiratory arrest 'due to a condition which was produced as a result of treatment to provide an artificial airway in the treatment of gunshot wounds of the abdomen and leg.' And he said, 'In other words, I give as the cause of death cardio-respiratory arrest due to gunshot wounds of the abdomen and leg.' For the appellant it was conceded that the sequence of events which had led to the deceased's death was not that described by the pathologist but a consultant surgeon, Mr Eadie, gave it as his opinion that by 8 February 1988 the wounds of the thigh and the abdomen no longer threatened the life of the deceased and his chances of survival were good. In his view, 'The cause of his death was the failure to recognise the reason for his sudden onset and continued breathlessness after the 8th February [and the] severe respiratory obstruction, including the presence of stridor [on 14 February] . . .'

Mr Eadie said that V would not have died if his condition had been diagnosed and properly treated. The doctors had been negligent and this was the cause of death; but they had not, in his opinion, been grossly negligent or reckless.

Judge Lowry QC directed the jury that 'the bullets caused the death, even if the treatment was incompetent, negligent. For you to find that the chain was broken, the medical treatment or lack of medical treatment must be reckless . . . Reckless conduct is where somebody could not care less. He acts or fails to act careless of the consequences, careless of the comfort or safety of another person . . .' D was convicted of murder.

[Beldam LJ, having quoted from the judgment of Robert Goff LJ in *Pagett*, in section 3.2.3.2, p 45 and his expression of indebtedness to Hart and Honoré, continued:]

Whilst medical treatment unsuccessfully given to prevent the death of a victim with the care and skill of a competent medical practitioner will not amount to an intervening cause, it does not follow that treatment which falls below that standard of care and skill will amount to such a cause. As Professors Hart and Honore comment, treatment which falls short of the standard expected of the competent medical practitioner is unfortunately only too frequent in human experience for it to be considered abnormal in the sense of extraordinary. Acts or omissions of a doctor treating the victim for injuries he has received at the hands of a defendant may conceivably be so extraordinary as to be capable of being regarded as acts independent of the conduct of the defendant but it is most unlikely that they will be.

We have not been referred to any English authority in which the terms of the direction which should be given to a jury in such a case have been considered. We were referred to *Reg. v Jordan* (1956) 40 Cr.App.R. 152 in which the appellant who had been convicted of murder sought leave to call further evidence about the cause of the victim's death. The application was granted and evidence was received by the court that the stab wound from which the victim died eight days later was not the cause of the victim's death. The deceased had died from the effects of sensitivity to Terramycin which had been given to him after his intolerance to it was established and in abnormal quantity. The court considered that the introduction into the system of the victim of a substance shown to be poisonous to him and in quantities which were so great as to result in pulmonary oedema leading to pneumonia were factors which ought to have been before the jury and which in all probability would have affected their decision.

Jordan's case was described in the later case of *Reg. v. Smith* [1959] 2 Q.B. 35 as a very particular case dependent upon its exact facts. The appellant in *Smith* had been convicted at court-martial of the murder of another soldier by stabbing him. The victim had been dropped twice while being taken to the medical reception station and was subsequently given treatment which was said to be incorrect and harmful. Lord Parker C.J., giving the judgment of the court-martial appeal court, rejected a contention that his death did not result from the stab wound. He said, at pp. 42–43:

'It seems to the court that if at the time of death the original wound is still an operating cause and a substantial cause, then the death can properly be said to be the result of the wound, albeit that some other cause of death is also operating. Only if it can be said that the original wounding is merely the setting in which another cause operates can it be said that the death does not result from the wound. Putting it in another way, only if the second cause is so overwhelming as to make the original wound merely part of the history can it be said that the death does not flow from the wound.'

Both these cases were considered by this court in *Reg. v. Malcherek* [1981] 1 W.L.R. 690, in which it had been argued that the act of a doctor in disconnecting a life support machine had intervened to cause the death of the victim to the exclusion of injuries inflicted by the appellants. In rejecting this submission Lord Lane C.J., after considering *Reg. v. Jordan*, 40 Cr.App.R. 152 and *Reg. v. Smith* [1959] 2 Q.B. 35, said [1981] 1 W.L.R. 690, 696:

'In the view of this court, if a choice has to be made between the decision in *Reg. v. Jordan*, 40 Cr.App.R. 152 and that in *Reg. v. Smith* [1959] 2 Q.B. 35, which we do not believe it does (*Reg. v. Jordan* being a very exceptional case), then the decision in *Reg. v. Smith* is to be preferred.'

Later in the same judgment Lord Lane C.J., said, at pp. 696–697:

'There may be occasions, although they will be rare, when the original injury has ceased to operate as a cause at all, but in the ordinary case if the treatment is given bona fide by competent and careful medical practitioners, then evidence will not be admissible to show that the treatment would not have been administered in the same way by other medical practitioners. In other words, the fact that the victim has died, despite or because of medical treatment for the initial injury given by careful and skilled medical practitioners, will not exonerate the original assailant from responsibility for the death.'

In those two cases it was not suggested that the actions of the doctors in disconnecting the life support machines were other than competent and careful. The court did not have to consider the effect of medical treatment which fell short of the standard of care to be expected of competent medical practitioners.

[Having considered passages from the judgments of the Supreme Court of Victoria in *R v Evans and Gardiner (No 2)* VR 523, Beldam LJ continued:]

It seems to us that these two passages demonstrate the difficulties in formulating and explaining a general concept of causation but what we think does emerge from this and the other cases is that when the victim of a criminal attack is treated for wounds or injuries by doctors or other medical staff attempting to repair the harm done, it will only be in the most extraordinary and unusual case that such treatment can be said to be so independent of the acts of the defendant that it could be regarded in law as the cause of the victim's death to the exclusion of the defendant's acts.

Where the law requires proof of the relationship between an act and its consequences as an element of responsibility, a simple and sufficient explanation of the basis of such relationship has proved notoriously elusive.

In a case in which the jury have to consider whether negligence in the treatment of injuries inflicted by the defendant was the cause of death we think it is sufficient for the judge to tell the jury that they must be satisfied that the Crown have proved that the acts of the defendant caused the death of the deceased adding that the defendant's acts need not be the sole cause or even the main cause of death it being sufficient that his acts contributed significantly to that result. Even though negligence in the treatment of the victim was the immediate cause of his death, the jury should not regard it as excluding the responsibility of the defendant unless the negligent treatment was so independent of his acts, and in itself so potent in causing death, that they regard the contribution made by his acts as insignificant.

It is not the function of the jury to evaluate competing causes or to choose which is dominant provided they are satisfied that the defendant's acts can fairly be said to have made a significant contribution to the victim's death. We think the word 'significant' conveys the necessary substance of a contribution made to the death which is more than negligible.

… Although for reasons we have stated we think that the judge erred when he invited the jury to consider the degree of fault in the medical treatment rather than its consequences, we consider that no miscarriage of justice has actually occurred. Even if more experienced doctors than those who attended the deceased would have recognised the rare complication in time to have prevented the deceased's death, that complication was a direct consequence of the appellant's acts which remained a significant cause of his death. We cannot conceive that, on the evidence given, any jury would have found otherwise.

Accordingly, we dismiss the appeal.

Appeal dismissed

The intervening medical treatment which D alleges constitutes a break in the chain of causation may involve an omission. In *McKechnie* (1992) 94 Cr App R 51, DD beat up an elderly man, V, who suffered very serious head injuries and remained unconscious for weeks. Doctors discovered that V had a duodenal ulcer but decided that it would be too dangerous to operate because he was still unconscious from his beating. V died as a result of the ulcer bursting. DD were convicted and appealed, *inter alia*, on the direction as to causation. The Court of Appeal upheld the conviction: 'The Recorder's statement of the question of the intervening events—the doctor's decision not to operate on the duodenal ulcer because [V's] head injuries made such an operation dangerous—properly directed the jury, not to the correctness of the medical decision, but to its reasonableness', per Auld J at 58.

3.2.3.4 The victim's conduct as a break in the chain of causation

This is, again, an area in which the courts have struggled to define any clear principles. A number of difficult issues arise.

- To what extent does it matter that V 'acts' and exacerbates his position rather than 'omits to save himself'?
- If there is a principle that D 'takes his victim as he finds him' does this extend beyond taking V's physical infirmities (eg egg shell skull) to include also V's psychological idiosyncrasies (eg refusal to seek medical attention)?
- To what extent does D take only V's pre-existing conditions as found?
- Is the question whether V's conduct breaks the chain of causation if it is unforeseeable or if it is outwith a range of reasonable actions?

It is a well-known principle of the civil law that D takes the victim of his wrongdoing as he finds him. D cannot complain if, unbeknownst to him, V is a haemophiliac who dies from the pin prick D inflicted. In the following case, the court confirmed that in the criminal law as in the civil law, D must 'take his victim as he finds him'. An issue arose, however, as to whether this principle was confined to V's physiological idiosyncrasies, or whether D must take his victim as he finds him in a more holistic sense—encompassing the victim's *mind* as well as his body.

R v Blaue
[1975] EWCA Crim 3, Court of Appeal, Criminal Division

(Lawton LJ, Thompson and Shaw JJ)

The appellant was convicted of manslaughter on the ground of diminished responsibility. He had inflicted four serious stab wounds on the deceased, one of which pierced a lung. The deceased, a Jehovah's Witness, refused to have a blood transfusion because it was contrary to her religious beliefs, and acknowledged this refusal in writing, despite the surgeon's advice that without the transfusion she would die. The Crown conceded at the trial that had she had the blood transfusion she would not have died. Blaue appealed on the ground, *inter alia*, that Mocatta J, following *Holland* (1841) 2 Mood & R 351, in effect directed the jury to find causation proved.

[Lawton LJ delivered the judgment of the court:]

. . . In *Holland* [(1841) 2 Mood & R 351] the defendant, in the course of a violent assault, had injured one of his victim's fingers. A surgeon had advised amputation because of danger to life through complications developing. The advice was rejected. A fortnight later the victim died of lockjaw: '. . . the real question is', said Maule J [2 Mood & R 351 at 352], 'whether in the end the wound inflicted by the prisoner was the cause of death?' That distinguished judge left the jury to decide that question as did the judge in this case. They had to decide it as juries always do, by pooling their experience of life and using their common sense. They would not have been handicapped by a lack of training in dialectics or moral theology.

Maule J's direction to the jury reflected the common law's answer to the problem. He who inflicted an injury which resulted in death could not excuse himself by pleading that his victim could have avoided death by taking greater care of himself: see Hale [*Pleas of the Crown* (1800), pp 427, 428]. The common law in Sir Matthew Hale's time probably was in line with contemporary concepts of ethics. A man who did a wrongful act was deemed *morally* responsible for the natural and probable consequences of that act. Counsel for the appellant asked us to remember that since Sir Matthew Hale's day the rigour of the law relating to homicide has been eased in favour of the accused. It has been—but this has come about through the development of the concept of intent, not by reason of a different view of causation. Well known practitioner's textbooks, such as *Halsbury's Laws* [3rd edn, vol 10, p 706] and *Russell on Crime* [(12th edn, 1964), vol 1, p 30], continue to reflect the common law approach. Textbooks intended for students or as studies in jurisprudence have queried the common law rule. See Hart and Honoré, *Causation in the Law* [(1959), pp 320, 321], and *Smith and Hogan* [*Criminal Law* (3rd edn, 1973), p 214].

The physical cause of death in this case was the bleeding into the pleural cavity arising from the penetration of the lung. This had not been brought about by any decision made by the deceased girl but by the stab wound.

Counsel for the appellant tried to overcome this line of reasoning by submitting that the jury should have been directed that if they thought the girl's decision not to have a blood transfusion was an unreasonable one, then the chain of causation would have been broken. At once the question arises—reasonable by whose standards? Those of Jehovah's Witnesses? Humanists? Roman Catholics? Protestants of Anglo-Saxon descent? The man on the Clapham omnibus? But he might well be an admirer of Eleazar who suffered death rather than eat the flesh of swine [see 2 Maccabees, ch 6, vv 18–31] or of Sir Thomas More who, unlike nearly all his contemporaries, was unwilling to accept Henry VIII as Head of the Church in England. Those brought up in the Hebraic and Christian traditions would probably be reluctant to accept that these martyrs caused their own deaths.

As was pointed out to counsel for the appellant in the course of argument, two cases, each rais-ing the same issue of reasonableness because of religious beliefs, could produce different verdicts depending on where the cases were tried. A jury drawn from Preston, sometimes said to be the most Catholic town in England, might have different views about martyrdom to one drawn from the inner suburbs of London. Counsel for the appellant accepted that this might be so; it was, he said, inherent in trial by jury. It is not inherent in the common law as expounded by Sir Matthew Hale and Maule J. It has long been the policy of the law that those who use violence on other people must take their vic-tims as they find them. This in our judgment means the whole man, not just the physical man. It does not lie in the mouth of the assailant to say that his victim's religious beliefs which inhibited him from accepting certain kinds of treatment were unreasonable. The question for decision is what caused her death. The answer is the stab wound. The fact that the victim refused to stop this end coming about did not break the causal connection between the act and death . . .

Appeal dismissed

≈≈ *Questions*

(1) Was not the wound a substantial and operating cause (*Smith*, section 3.2.3.3, p 50) of death? If so, did it matter whether the victim's rejection of the blood transfusion was also a cause of death?

(2) Suppose that D's victim had been a child who was then abducted by her parents so as to avoid the transfusion and had died. Would the defendant still have been guilty of man-slaughter? Would the parents also have been guilty? See *Re S* [1993] 1 FLR 376.

(3) Would it have made a difference if V's objection to the treatment was based upon an irra-tional fear of doctors?

How far does the principle enunciated in *Blaue* extend? Does D remain liable even if V does something completely unreasonable? In *Dear* [1996] Crim LR 595, D stabbed V with a Stanley knife after allegations that V had sexually abused D's 12-year-old daughter. V died. D claimed that V had broken the chain of causation by either reopening the wounds (suicide) or if the wounds had reopened naturally, by failing to stop the bleeding. The Court of Appeal held there was no need to inquire whether V had behaved negligently or grossly negligently:

. . . the cause of the deceased's death was bleeding from the artery which the defendant had sev-ered. Whether or not the resumption or continuation of that bleeding was deliberately caused by the deceased, the jury were entitled to find that the [defendant's] conduct made an operative and signifi-cant contribution to the death.

In the case of *D* [2006] EWCA Crim 1139, D had struck his partner a minor blow on the fore-head and she had then committed suicide. This was against a lengthy background of domes-tic abuse amounting to psychological but not psychiatric injury by D. It was held that the infliction of mere psychological harm would not suffice to construct a manslaughter charge. However, in an *obiter dictum*, the Court of Appeal left open the possibility that a manslaugh-ter conviction might be available:

where a decision to commit suicide has been triggered by a physical assault which represents the cul-mination of a course of abusive conduct, it would be possible . . . to argue that the final assault played a significant part in causing the victim's death.

In terms of causation, even if D's conduct in causing psychological injury was treated as a sufficient, unlawful and dangerous act, could it ever be a sufficient cause in law? There may be little doubt that in fact it operated as a cause of the suicide, but will V's actions in choosing to commit suicide break the chain of causation? Could causation have been established had the Crown relied on the unlawful act of assault? Surely there is an implicit requirement that the causation question focuses only on the unlawful act relied on by the Crown as the one that is dangerous?

Can D ever be liable for manslaughter where V has committed suicide and D's act is not at that moment a continuing and operative cause of death? Is it sufficient that V fears D's immediate attack in physical terms? Is it sufficient that V fears D's continued psychological abuse? Can suicide ever be a reasonably foreseeable response to violence or further psychological harm? Can suicide ever be within a range of reasonable responses to a threat of such harm? To what extent must D take his victim as found 'psychologically' as well as physically? Is a charge of gross negligence manslaughter preferable in these cases? See J. Horder and L. McGowan, 'Manslaughter by Causing Another's Suicide' [2006] Crim LR 1035.

Compare the approach taken in the so-called 'fright and flight' cases where V seeks to escape from D and in doing so suffers a fatal injury. In *Pitts* (1842) Car & M 284, it was held (at 284) that:

> If a person, being attacked, should form an apprehension of immediate violence, an apprehension which must be well grounded and justified by the circumstances, throw himself for escape into a river, and be drowned, the person attacking him is guilty of murder.

In none of the reported 'flight' cases does it appear that the victims have chosen to commit suicide; rather, they have behaved in a dangerous fashion, being aware that their choice of escape may expose them to danger of injury or death.

In *Williams* (1992) 95 Cr App R 1, V, a hitch-hiker, leapt from a moving car and died from his injuries. The other occupants of the car were convicted of V's manslaughter, and robbery of V. On the question as to whether V had broken the chain of causation between the unlawful act of robbery and his death, the Court of Appeal (per Stuart-Smith LJ at 8) held:

> The jury should consider . . . whether the deceased's reaction in jumping from the moving car was within the range of responses which might be expected from a victim placed in the situation which he was. The jury should bear in mind any particular characteristic of the victim and the fact that in the agony of the moment he may act without thought and deliberation.

⁓ Question
Is the correct test to apply that from *Williams* (was V's act 'daft') or that from *Blaue*?

This issue was considered more recently in *Lewis* [2010] EWCA Crim 151. D had been driving in the early hours of the morning when some students crossed the road in front of him and one struck his car. D got out of the car and on the Crown's case D then pushed one of the women students. Her brother, V, intervened. D chased V into the road, where V was hit and killed by an oncoming car. D was convicted of unlawful act manslaughter and appealed. In relation to whether V's act broke the chain of causation, Pitchford LJ stated that the judge was not bound to use the precise language of *Williams* and direct the jury to consider whether V's act was 'proportionate' or 'daft' to reinforce to them that not every flight response ought to be regarded as a foreseeable consequence of an unlawful act. It was enough that the judge had directed the jury to consider whether V's response 'might have been expected' as a result of D's act and, if it was, then it was caused by D.

3.3 Criticisms and reform

Any law that exists on the question of causation in the criminal law is common law. Clause 17 of the Draft Criminal Code is an attempt to restate the common law principles. Whether it does so successfully is disputed but its principal critic, Glanville Williams, remarks ((1989) 48 CLJ at 405–406) that 'it concentrates the mind wonderfully' and it at least provides a basis for discussion. Clause 17 provides:

17. Causation

(1) Subject to subsections (2) and (3), a person causes a result which is an element of an offence when—

   (a) he does an act which makes a more than negligible contribution to its occurrence; or

   (b) he omits to do an act which might prevent its occurrence and which he is under a duty to do according to the law relating to the offence.

(2) A person does not cause a result where, after he does such an act or makes such an omission, an act or event occurs—

   (a) which is the immediate and sufficient cause of the result;

   (b) which he did not foresee; and

   (c) which could not in the circumstances reasonably have been foreseen.

(3) A person who procures, assists or encourages another to cause a result that is an element of an offence does not himself cause that result so as to be guilty of the offence as a principal except when—

   (a) section 26(1)(c) [procuring an act by an innocent agent] applies; or

   (b) the offence itself consists in the procuring, assisting or encouraging another to cause the result.

The exemption that would be created by this subsection is criticized by Glanville Williams ('*Finis* for *Novus Actus*' (1989) 48 CLJ 391) as being both too wide and too narrow.

≈≈ *Question*

Does the Draft Code, cl 17, provide a clearer statement of the law than presently exists?

FURTHER READING

A. Ashworth, 'Defining Offences Without Harm' in P. F. Smith (ed), *Criminal Law: Essays in Honour of J. C. Smith* (1987)

R. Heaton, 'Dealing in Death' [2003] Crim LR 497

K. Laird, 'The Decline of Criminal Law Causation Without Limits' (2016) 132 LQR 566

A. Norrie, 'A Critique of Criminal Causation' (1991) 54 MLR 685

A. Norrie, *Crime Reason and History* (3rd edn, 2014), Ch 7

S. Shute, 'Causation: Foreseeability v Natural Consequences' (1992) 55 MLR 584

J. Stannard, 'Criminal Causation and the Careless Doctor' (1992) 55 MLR 577

G. R. Sullivan and A. P. Simester, 'Causation Without Limits: Causing Death While Driving Without a Licence, While Disqualified, or Without Insurance' [2012] Crim LR 753

V. Tadros, *Criminal Responsibility* (2005), pp 159–185

4
Omissions

Some of the controversies that will be examined in this chapter include:

(1) the difficulty in drawing distinctions between positive acts causing a prohibited result and failures to prevent a prohibited result;

(2) the circumstances in which the law regards it as appropriate to place a person under a duty to act on pain of criminal sanction for failure to do so; and

(3) issues surrounding establishing how D's failure to act can have *caused* the prohibited result.

4.1 Introduction

The criminal sanction is, as we have noted, the most serious censure the State can impose on an individual and the imposition of the criminal sanction for doing nothing therefore sounds bizarre. In this chapter we examine the circumstances in which a person can be held criminally liable for not acting as well as for acting. In fact, the defendant's failure to act might not always be so easily described as 'doing nothing', and there are many situations in which the imposition of the criminal sanction is considered to be appropriate.

Many statutes make it a specific offence to omit to do something, for example a motorist who fails to give his name and address after an accident or a company which fails to make a prescribed return under the relevant Companies Acts may be guilty of an offence. These offences, despite ascribing criminal liability to D for an omission, are uncontroversial. Most of them are of a regulatory nature. They seem to respect the principles of fair labelling and fair warning since the conviction attaches explicitly to the failure to act and not to its consequences. The controversial question is how the criminal law should deal with omissions in cases other than those where the offence is created in terms of 'failing to do x'.

How should the criminal law impose liability for omissions in relation to general offences such as murder, manslaughter and assault? The debate is a long-standing one, raising fundamental questions about the extent to which the criminal law should infringe upon the autonomy of the individual.

At *common law*, criminal liability for pure omissions is exceptional. The generally accepted definitions of most offences include a verb like 'kill', 'assault', 'damage' or 'take' which (at first sight, at least) requires an action of some kind. There are exceptions. In *Dytham* [1979] 3 All ER 641, a police officer, D, was on duty at 1 am when he saw a man, V, being ejected from a nightclub and being kicked and beaten by a number of bouncers. D took no steps to intervene. V died. D was charged with misconduct whilst acting as an officer of justice in that he deliberately failed to carry out his duties as a police constable by wilfully omitting to take any steps to preserve the peace or to protect V or to arrest or otherwise bring to justice the assailants. The conviction was upheld.

4.2 The present law

The courts' approach to the imposition of liability for omissions requires consideration of four issues.

(1) Is D's conduct properly categorized as an omission, or as an act? If it can possibly be categorized as an act, the courts are likely to seek to do so to avoid complication.

(2) If the conduct of the accused is regarded as an 'omission' it is necessary to ask whether the particular offence is one for which an omission will be capable of grounding liability.

(3) If an omission is a basis for liability under the offence, the question is whether D was under a duty to act. In result crimes, the result has occurred, so no one prevented it from occurring but, clearly, not everyone in the jurisdiction of the court (ie England and Wales for most offences) is liable for failing to do so. What are the criteria for identifying what it is that makes D liable but not the whole population?

(4) Where the definition of the crime requires proof that D 'caused' a certain result, can he be said to have caused that result by doing nothing?

4.2.1 Act or omission?

Although the difference between an act and an omission may seem obvious, as many of the cases in this chapter reveal, the distinction between acts and omissions is often tenuous and arguably too fine to bear the strain of distinguishing between circumstances in which there is no criminal liability and where there is liability in full measure. Some of the most striking examples of the difficulty in distinguishing acts and omissions arise in the medical context, as the next section will demonstrate.

4.2.1.1 Act or omission—killing for failing to continue to keep alive?

In order to understand why the distinction between an act and an omission matters in this context, it is necessary to appreciate two things. First, a doctor must not force treatment upon a patient who is competent and who refuses it. This remains the case even if the patient would die without the treatment in question. Secondly, if a patient is unable to express his wishes because, for example, he is in a persistent vegetative state, the doctor must act in the best interests of the patient. This does not mean, however, that a doctor is under a duty to keep that patient alive at all costs. On the contrary, sometimes it may be in the patient's interest no longer to continue to receive treatment if to do so would prolong his suffering. This does not mean, however, that a doctor can act to end a patient's life. These issues were considered by the House of Lords in the following case.

Airedale National Health Service Trust v Bland
[1992] UKHL 5, House of Lords

(Lords Keith of Kinkel, Goff of Chieveley, Lowry, Browne-Wilkinson and Mustill)

In 1989, Anthony Bland, then aged 17, was injured in the Hillsborough Stadium disaster. He suffered irreversible brain damage and thereafter was in a persistent vegetative state (PVS)— no cognitive function, no sight, hearing, capacity to feel pain, move his limbs or communicate in any way. Being unable to swallow, he was fed by naso-gastric tube. Repeated infections were treated by antibiotics. The consensus of medical opinion was that there was no hope of his improvement or recovery.

On the application (with the support of Bland's parents) of the Airedale NHS Trust, in whose hospital Bland was a patient, Sir Stephen Brown P granted a declaration that the Trust might lawfully (a) discontinue all life-sustaining treatment including ventilation, nutrition and hydration by artificial means and (b) discontinue medical treatment except for the purpose of enabling Bland to die peacefully with the greatest dignity and least distress. The Court of Appeal (Bingham MR, Butler-Sloss and Hoffmann LJJ) dismissed an appeal by the Official Solicitor, who then appealed to the House of Lords. He submitted that the withdrawal of artificial feeding would constitute murder. The House, though accepting that their decision in this civil action would not be legally binding on a criminal court, unanimously dismissed the appeal.

[Lord Keith made a speech dismissing the appeal.]

Lord Goff:

Why is it that the doctor who gives his patient a lethal injection which kills him commits an unlawful act and indeed is guilty of murder, whereas a doctor who, by discontinuing life support, allows his patient to die may not act unlawfully and will not do so if he commits no breach of duty to his patient? Professor Glanville Williams has suggested (see *Textbook of Criminal Law* (2nd edn, 1983) p 282) that the reason is that what the doctor does when he switches off a life support machine 'is in substance not an act but an omission to struggle' and that the 'omission is not a breach of duty by the doctor, because he is not obliged to continue in a hopeless case'.

I agree that the doctor's conduct in discontinuing life support can properly be categorised as an omission. It is true that it may be difficult to describe what the doctor actually does as an omission, for example where he takes some positive step to bring the life support to an end. But discontinuation of life support is, for present purposes, no different from not initiating life support in the first place. In each case, the doctor is simply allowing his patient to die in the sense that he is desisting from taking a step which might, in certain circumstances, prevent his patient from dying as a result of his pre-existing condition: and as a matter of general principle an omission such as this will not be unlawful unless it constitutes a breach of duty to the patient. I also agree that the doctor's conduct is to be differentiated from that of, for example, an interloper who maliciously switches off a life support machine because, although the interloper may perform exactly the same act as the doctor who discontinues life support, his doing so constitutes interference with the life-prolonging treatment then being administered by the doctor. Accordingly, whereas the doctor, in discontinuing life support, is simply allowing his patient to die of his pre-existing condition, the interloper is actively intervening to stop the doctor from prolonging the patient's life, and such conduct cannot possibly be categorized as an omission . . . If the justification for treating a patient who lacks the capacity to consent lies in the fact that the treatment is provided in his best interests, it must follow that the treatment may, and indeed ultimately should, be discontinued where it is no longer in his best interests to provide it. The question which lies at the heart of the present case is, as I see it, whether on that principle the doctors responsible for the treatment and care of Anthony Bland can justifiably discontinue the process of artificial feeding upon which the prolongation of his life depends.

It is crucial for the understanding of this question that the question itself should be correctly formulated. The question is not whether the doctor should take a course which will kill his patient, or even take a course which has the effect of accelerating his death. The question is whether the doctor should or should not continue to provide his patient with medical treatment or care which, if continued, will prolong his patient's life. The question is sometimes put in striking or emotional terms, which can be misleading. For example, in the case of a life support system, it is sometimes asked: should a doctor be entitled to switch it off, or to pull the plug? And then it is asked: can it be in the best interests of the patient that a doctor should be able to switch the life support system off, when this will inevitably result in the patient's death? Such an approach has rightly been criticized as misleading, for example by Professor Ian Kennedy (in his paper in *Treat Me Right, Essays in Medical Law and Ethics* (1988)), and by Thomas J in *Auckland Area Health Board v A-G* [1993] 1 NZLR 235 at 247. This is because the question is not whether it is in the best interests of the patient that he should die. The question is whether it is in the best interests of the patient that his life should be prolonged by the continuance of this form of medical treatment or care.

The correct formulation of the question is of particular importance in a case such as the present, where the patient is totally unconscious and where there is no hope whatsoever of any amelioration of his condition. In circumstances such as these, it may be difficult to say that it is in his best interests that the treatment should be ended. But, if the question is asked, as in my opinion it should be, whether it is in his best interests that treatment which has the effect of artificially prolonging his life should be continued, that question can sensibly be answered to the effect that it is not in his best interests to do so.

[Lords **Lowry** and **Browne-Wilkinson** made speeches dismissing the appeal.]

Lord Mustill:

After much expression of negative opinions I turn to an argument which in my judgment is logically defensible and consistent with the existing law. In essence it turns the previous argument on its head by directing the inquiry to the interests of the patient, not in the termination of life but in the continuation of his treatment. It runs as follows. (i) The cessation of nourishment and hydration is an omission not an act. (ii) Accordingly, the cessation will not be a criminal act unless the doctors are under a present duty to continue the regime. (iii) At the time when Anthony Bland came into the care of the doctors decisions had to be made about his care which he was unable to make for himself. In accordance with *F v West Berkshire Health Authority* [1989] 2 All ER 545, [1990] 2 AC 1 these decisions were to be made in his best interests. Since the possibility that he might recover still existed his best interests required that he should be supported in the hope that this would happen. These best interests justified the application of the necessary regime without his consent. (iv) All hope of recovery has now been abandoned. Thus, although the termination of his life is not in the best interests of Anthony Bland, his best interests in being kept alive have also disappeared, taking with them the justification for the non-consensual regime and the correlative duty to keep it in being. (v) Since there is no longer a duty to provide nourishment and hydration a failure to do so cannot be a criminal offence.

My Lords, I must recognise at once that this chain of reasoning makes an unpromising start by transferring the morally and intellectually dubious distinction between acts and omissions into a context where the ethical foundations of the law are already open to question. The opportunity for anomaly and excessively fine distinctions, often depending more on the way in which the problem happens to be stated than on any real distinguishing features, has been exposed by many commentators, including in England the authors above-mentioned, together with Smith and Hogan *Criminal Law* (6th edn, 1988) p 51, Beynon 'Doctors as murderers' [1982] Crim LR 17 and Gunn and Smith '*Arthur's* case and the right to life of a Down's syndrome child' [1985] Crim LR 705. All this being granted, we are still forced to take the law as we find it and try to make it work. Moreover, although in cases near the borderline the categorisation of conduct will be exceedingly hard, I believe that nearer the periphery there will be many instances which fall quite clearly into one category rather than the other. In my opinion the present is such a case, and in company with Compton J in *Barber v Superior Court of Los Angeles County* 147 Cal App 3d 1006 at 1017 (1983) amongst others I consider that the proposed conduct will fall into the category of omissions.

I therefore consider the argument to be soundly based. Now that the time has come when Anthony Bland has no further interest in being kept alive, the necessity to do so, created by his inability to make a choice, has gone; and the justification for the invasive care and treatment together with the duty to provide it have also gone. Absent a duty, the omission to perform what had previously been a duty will no longer be a breach of the criminal law.

> ≋ *Questions*
> (1) Is there really a difference between the questions:
>   (a) 'is it in the best interests of the patient that he should die?' and
>   (b) 'is it in the best interests of the patient that his life should be prolonged by this treatment?'
> (2) 'How can it be lawful to allow a patient to die slowly, though painlessly, over a period of weeks from lack of food but unlawful to produce his immediate death by a lethal injection, thereby saving his family from yet another ordeal to add to the tragedy that has already struck them?'—per Lord Browne-Wilkinson—who thought this was 'undoubtedly the law'. Have you an answer?

In *Re A (children)* [2001] Fam 147, the case of the conjoined twins (section 23.5, p 651), Johnson J, the trial judge, held that the reasoning in *Bland* could be applied to that case. He thought that the course proposed by the doctors—to separate the twins and allow only Jodie to live—was not 'a positive act but merely the withdrawal of Mary's blood supply'. It was as if Jodie stood in the same relation to Mary as the various machines did in relation to Bland. But none of the judges in the Court of Appeal agreed—though Robert Walker LJ did say at one point that, following separation, Mary 'would die because tragically her own body, on its own, is not and never has been viable'. Ward LJ went as far as to say that the distinction between act and omission was irrelevant: 'It is important to stress that it makes no difference whether the killing is by act or by omission. That is a distinction without a difference.' He referred to the speeches of Lords Lowry, Browne-Wilkinson and Mustill in *Bland*. But was not the distinction between act and omission the foundation of the decision in *Bland*, unhappy though their lordships were with it? If Mary were not being kept alive by Jodie, it seems clear that it would not have been unlawful to omit to take steps which might briefly have prolonged her life. Yet Johnson J's conclusion was rejected by the CA. *Bland* was held to be materially different. This was not a case of discontinuing treatment. Mary was not receiving treatment. The operation would be a positive act. It would involve the use of the scalpel and 'a number of invasions of Mary's body . . . before the positive step was taken of clamping the aorta and bringing about Mary's death'.

4.2.2 Offences capable of being committed by omission

If the conduct of the defendant is regarded as an omission, the next question that arises is whether the offence with which he is charged is one for which a conviction can be secured on the basis of an omission rather than an act. This requires careful statutory interpretation of the offence or analysis of the elements of the offence if it is a common law crime. Some offences would appear not to be capable of commission by omission, as, for example, with attempted offences discussed in the next section.

4.2.2.1 Statutory interpretation

One striking example of a statutory offence turning on the word 'act' is in relation to attempts (section 20.4, p 546). The Criminal Attempts Act 1981 makes it an offence to do 'an act more than merely preparatory' to the commission of the full offence. It seems strange then to contemplate an offence of attempt by omission. In *Nevard* [2006] EWCA Crim 2896, D seriously injured his wife by striking her with an axe and a knife. He then forced her to abandon her attempt to dial 999 to call for assistance. The emergency services rang back on the number she had used, but D took the call and told them that his grandchildren must have been fooling around with the phone. The police remained suspicious so attended the scene and found D's wife, whose injuries were not fatal. D was charged with wounding with intent and with attempted murder. He pleaded guilty to the wounding. Having been directed by the judge as to the elements of attempted murder, the jury asked: 'Can you clarify whether an attempt to withhold care/emergency services constitutes attempted murder, knowing he has pleaded guilty to wounding with intent.' The trial judge's answer was:

> Obviously if a person comes across somebody who is seriously injured in the street and fails to call the emergency services, they could not be charged with attempted murder . . . the straight answer to the question is 'yes' and it is necessary for me to elaborate upon that. To be sure of attempted murder you must be sure that he did an act or acts with the intention of killing Mrs Nevard . . . The Crown's case is that he struck the blows with the axe or the axe handle. When that did not work he went and got a knife and stabbed her with that kitchen knife . . . and also that he slashed her arms with a Stanley knife and that when he did those acts, his intention was that she should die. Now, where the withholding of the emergency services may help you is as to what his intention was . . . In other words, by seeing what he did after the event you may get an insight as to what his intention was.

Nevard appealed against conviction. The Court of Appeal upheld the conviction, but suggested that the judge should have made explicit to the jury that attempting to divert the emergency services could not in itself constitute attempted murder.

≈ **Questions**

Was not D's conduct in taking the return call and lying a sufficient act? He took positive steps to prevent the emergency services responding to his wife's call. If V dies because D prevents the emergency services from reaching him, or from helping him if they do arrive (eg by keeping them away at gunpoint), that must make D a substantial cause of V's death, even if D was not the one who inflicted the original injuries. If D takes such positive measures to prevent the emergency services arriving, but despite his best efforts V lives, D must surely have attempted to cause V's death. Why should D not be guilty of attempted murder?

The language of the Criminal Attempts Act may seem clear, but with other offences the position is less clear cut. Professor Glanville Williams suggested that a criminal code should state that enactments creating offences in words primarily referring to 'acts' are not to be interpreted to include mere omissions unless the enactment expressly so provides. If Parliament wishes to penalize omissions it must direct its mind to the subject and make its meaning clear. (See (1987) 7 LS 92 at 97, 'What Should the Code Do About Omissions?'.) Professor Williams concedes that 'some words can legitimately be held to "specify" both acts and omissions, even though they refer expressly to neither', instancing the word 'neglect' (at 97).

≈ **Questions**

Some words certainly do describe conduct which can be performed by act or omission, as, for example, with 'obstruct'. If I am standing in a narrow passage blocking your way, and I refuse to move, does not my omission 'obstruct' you? And is not 'obstruction' a result crime, rather than a conduct crime?

Homicide

At common law it is established that there can be liability for murder and gross negligence manslaughter by an omission: *Gibbins and Proctor* (1918) 13 Cr App R 134 in section 4.2.3.3 (murder); *Stone and Dobinson* in section 4.2.3.3 (manslaughter).

4.2.3 Who is under a duty to act?

Though an offence is capable of being committed by omission, it does not follow that everyone is under a duty to act. The courts have recognized a number of categories in which a duty to act arises, each of which is discussed in the following sections (4.2.3.1–4.2.3.4). These categories are:

(1) Duties arising out of a contractual relationship.

(2) Duties arising as a result of a voluntary undertaking.

(3) Duties arising as a result of a special relationship between D and V.

(4) Duties arising from the fact that D has created (or possibly only contributed to) a dangerous situation.

4.2.3.1 Contract

In *Pittwood* (1902) 19 TLR 37, D, a gatekeeper on a railway line, had a contractual duty to his employer to keep the gate closed. D opened the gate and forgot to close it. V, assuming that the way was safe as the gate was open was then killed by a passing train. D's counsel argued that D only owed a duty to his employers under his contract, but the court held that a man might incur criminal liability arising from such a contract.

≋ *Questions*

(1) What types of contract will give rise to such a duty? Is it only contracts involving a protective or 'health and safety'-based purpose?

(2) Aside from the difficulty of which contracts are sufficient to establish a duty, there is the question of the content and scope of the duty. If D is a lifeguard employed by the council, does his duty to save a drowning stranger in the council's pool apply when D has formally clocked off work for the day? Does D's liability under contract depend on V's knowledge that D is under contract with X (eg the council or the railway company)?

4.2.3.2 Voluntary undertakings

In some cases, it may be the case that D has voluntarily assumed a duty towards V. In *Instan* [1893] 1 QB 450, for example, D lived with and maintained V, her aunt aged 73. For the final few days before her death V was completely incapacitated. D bought food with her aunt's money, but failed to give her any. Nor did D summon medical help. Death ensued from exhaustion and gangrene. D was convicted of manslaughter. The court affirmed her conviction. Coleridge LCJ concluded that a there was a duty—a 'legal common law duty is nothing else than the enforcing by law of that which is a moral obligation without legal enforcement'.

See further G. Mead, 'Contracting into Crime: A Theory of Criminal Omissions' (1991) 11 OJLS 147 at 168, arguing that a person who has voluntarily undertaken responsibility ought to be under a duty because:

First he is more likely to be aware that a person may be in a position of peril and in need of assistance. He will know of the vulnerability of the victim in a way that others may not. Second, he may be more capable of carrying out the required task than will a third party. We might assume that, in most cases where D undertakes to do a particular thing, he feels he has the ability to do it, whereas a third party, who has not given such an undertaking will not necessarily possess the required skills to do what is needed in order to avert danger to V. The third point is that if other people are aware of the undertaking they might feel it unproductive for them to get involved as well. They might reasonably think that they would be simply getting in the way and hinder the completion of the task in question.

~~~ *Questions*
(1) Was D's duty in *Instan* a result of her voluntary undertaking? Her relationship? Her cohabitation? Her being paid by her aunt?
(2) Is the existence of a moral duty a sufficient basis for the imposition of criminal liability?
(3) If D assumes some responsibility for V, it seems less objectionable for the law to impose liability for his subsequent omissions. But what of the objections based on principles of fair labelling and fair warning? Is the scope of the duty and its content sufficiently clearly prescribed to satisfy these principled concerns?

4.2.3.3 Special relationships

Many of the cases involving relationships also involve a voluntary undertaking by the party, and it is unclear to what extent the courts would impose a duty on the basis of a relationship per se. There are some cases, however, in which the court has imposed a duty upon D, despite the fact it cannot necessarily be said that D has voluntarily assumed it.

The most obvious type of relationship in which it has been held that a duty to act arises is that between parent and child. This is supported by statutory obligations such as s 1 of the Children and Young Persons Act 1933. The failure of parents to feed and care for their children has given rise to liability for manslaughter and even in one case for murder, as the following extract demonstrates.

R v Gibbins and Proctor
(1918) 13 Cr App R 134, Court of Criminal Appeal

(Darling, McCardie and Salter JJ)

Walter Gibbins and Edith Proctor were living together with Gibbins' daughter, Nelly, aged 7, and other children. The children were healthy except for Nelly, who was kept upstairs apart from the others and was starved to death. There was evidence that Proctor hated Nelly and cursed and hit her, from which the jury could infer that she had a very strong interest in Nelly's death. Gibbins was in regular employment, earning good wages, all of which he gave to Proctor. According to Gibbins's counsel, it was his duty to provide the money; it was Proctor's to provide the food. When Nelly died, Proctor told Gibbins to bury her out of sight which he did, in the brickyard where he worked. Gibbins and Proctor were tried together and convicted of murder of Nelly. They appealed, *inter alia*, on the ground of misdirection.

[Darling J delivering the judgment of the court:]

. . . the misdirection here complained of is on a crucial matter, where [the judge] told the jury what they must find in order to convict either prisoner of murder. He said, 'The charge against the prisoners is, in the first place, that they killed this child Nelly, or caused her death, by malice aforethought. That means they intended she should die and acted so as to produce that result.' If that is a misdirection it is one in favour of the prisoners . . . 'If you think that one or other of those prisoners wilfully and intentionally withheld food from that child so as to cause her to weaken and to cause her grievous bodily injury, as the result of which she died, it is not necessary for you to find that she intended or he intended to kill the child then and there. It is enough if you find that he or she intended to set up such a set of facts by withholding food or anything as would in the ordinary course of nature lead gradually but surely to her death.' In our opinion that direction amply fulfils the conditions which a judge should observe in directing the jury in such a case as this. . . .

'If the omission to provide necessary food or raiment was accompanied with an intention to cause the death of the child, or to cause some serious bodily injury to it, then it would be malicious in the sense imputed by this indictment, and in a case of this kind it is difficult, if not impossible, to understand how a person who contemplated doing serious bodily injury to the child by the deprivation of food, could have meditated anything else than causing its death.' The word used is 'contemplated', but what has to be proved is an intention to do grievous bodily injury. In our opinion the judge left the question correctly to the jury, and there is no ground for interfering with the convictions for those reasons.

It has been said that there ought not to have been a finding of guilty of murder against Gibbins. The court agrees that the evidence was less against Gibbins than Proctor, Gibbins gave her money, and as far as we can see it was sufficient to provide for the wants of themselves and all the children. But he lived in the house and the child was his own, a little girl of seven, and he grossly neglected the child. He must have known what her condition was if he saw her, for she was little more than a skeleton. He is in this dilemma; if he did not see her the jury might well infer that he did not care if she died; if he did he must have known what was going on. The question is whether there was evidence that he so conducted himself as to shew that he desired that grievous bodily injury should be done to the child. He cannot pretend that he shewed any solicitude for her. He knew that Proctor hated her, knew that she was ill and that no doctor had been called in, and the jury may have come to the conclusion that he was so infatuated with Proctor, and so afraid of offending her, that he preferred that the child should starve to death rather than that he should be exposed to any injury or unpleasantness from Proctor. It is unnecessary to say more than that there was evidence that Gibbins did desire that grievous bodily harm should be done to the child; he did not interfere in what was being done, and he comes within the definition which I have read, and is therefore guilty of murder.

The case of Proctor is plainer. She had charge of the child. She was under no obligation to do so or to live with Gibbins, but she did so, and receiving money, as it is admitted she did, for the purpose of supplying food, her duty was to see that the child was properly fed and looked after, and to see that she had medical attention if necessary. We agree with what Lord Coleridge CJ said in *Instan* [1893] 1 QB 450: 'There is no case directly in point, but it would be a slur upon, and a discredit to the administration of, justice in this country if there were any doubt as to the legal principle, or as to the present case being within it. The prisoner was under a moral obligation to the deceased from which arose a legal duty towards her; that legal duty the prisoner has wilfully and deliberately left unperformed, with the consequence that there has been an acceleration of the death of the deceased owing to the non-performance of that legal duty.' Here Proctor took upon herself the moral obligation of looking after the children; she was *de facto*, though not *de jure*, the wife of Gibbins and had excluded the child's own mother. She neglected the child undoubtedly, and the evidence shews that as a result the child died . . .

Appeals dismissed

Beyond what may be described as these 'core categories of relationship', it remains unclear which other relationships will give rise to a duty which might trigger D's liability. In *Stone and Dobinson* [1977] QB 354, [1977] 2 All ER 341, CA, S and D—S's mistress—allowed S's sister, Fanny, to lodge with them. The sister became infirm while lodging with them and died of tox-aemia from infected bed sores and prolonged immobilization. S and D had made only half-hearted and wholly ineffectual attempts to secure medical attention for the sister. Upholding the convictions of S and D for manslaughter, the court said:

There is no dispute, broadly speaking, as to the matters on which the jury must be satisfied before they can convict of manslaughter in circumstances such as the present. They are: (1) that the defend-ant undertook the care of a person who by reason of age or infirmity was unable to care for himself; (2) that the defendant was grossly negligent in regard to his duty of care; (3) that by reason of such negligence the person died. It is submitted on behalf of the appellants that the judge's direction to the jury with regard to the first two items was incorrect.

At the close of the prosecution's case submissions were made to the judge that there was no, or no sufficient, evidence that the appellants, or either of them, had chosen to undertake the care of Fanny.

That contention was advanced by Mr. Coles [counsel for the appellant] before this court as his first ground of appeal. He amplified the ground somewhat by submitting that the evidence which the judge had suggested to the jury might support the assumption of a duty by the appel-lants does not, when examined, succeed in doing so. He suggests that the situation here is unlike any reported case. Fanny came to this house as a lodger. Largely, if not entirely due to her own eccentricity and failure to look after herself or feed herself properly, she became increasingly infirm and immobile and eventually unable to look after herself. Is it to be said, asks Mr. Coles rhetorically, that by the mere fact of becoming infirm and helpless in these circumstances, she casts a duty on her brother and the appellant Dobinson to take steps to have her looked after or taken to hospital? The suggestion is that, heartless though it may seem, this is one of those situations where the appellants were entitled to do nothing; where no duty was cast upon them to help, any more than it is cast upon a man to rescue a stranger from drowning, however easy such a rescue might be.

This court rejects that proposition. Whether Fanny was a lodger or not she was a blood relation of the appellant Stone; she was occupying a room in his house; the appellant Dobinson had undertaken the duty of trying to wash her, of taking such food to her as she required. There was ample evidence that each appellant was aware of the poor condition she was in by mid-July. It was not disputed that no effort was made to summon an ambulance or the social services or the police despite the entreat-ies of [neighbours]. A social worker used to visit [Stone]. No word was spoken to him. All these were matters which the jury were entitled to take into account when considering whether the necessary assumption of a duty to care for Fanny had been proved.

This was *not* a situation analogous to the drowning stranger. They *did* make efforts to care. They tried to get a doctor; they tried to discover the previous doctor. The appellant Dobinson helped with the washing and the provision of food. All these matters were put before the jury in terms which we find it impossible to fault. The jury were entitled to find that the duty had been assumed. They were entitled to conclude that once Fanny became helplessly infirm, as she had by July 19, the appellants were, in the circumstances, obliged either to summon help or else to care for Fanny themselves . . .

≈≈≈ *Questions*
> ≈≈≈ *Questions*
> Is the duty imposed because of the cohabitation? The relationship? The decision by D and S to assist Fanny? All of these? Given the limited capacity of the defendants, were their ineffectual efforts not enough to satisfy any duty that arose?

Marriage is a sufficient basis for a duty (*Hood* [2004] 1 Cr App R (S) 431), so the question surely cannot be based on blood relationships. Is the true basis of the relationship duty one of mutual interdependence? The case law on this issue is inconsistent. In *Evans* [2009] EWCA Crim 650 (section 4.2.3.4, p 69), the Court of Appeal framed the question it had to consider—about the liability of a half-sister for her sibling's death—in the following way:

> . . . notwithstanding that their relationship lacked the features of familial duty or responsibility which marked her mother's relationship with the deceased, [D] was under a duty to take reasonable steps for the safety of the deceased once she appreciated that the heroin she procured for her was having a potentially fatal impact on her health.

So it seems that half-sisters do not owe each other a duty. What about siblings that share both parents? In *Barrass* [2011] EWCA Crim 2629, D and V were siblings. V had a mild learning disorder and suffered from various physical ailments, she died in her room after a long period of self-neglect. D was convicted of gross negligence manslaughter on the following basis:

> [D] was the only person who could have alerted the authorities to her condition and he had been grossly negligent in failing to provide for her basic needs of care, warmth and clothing and to summon assistance when her condition deteriorated. As the judge was to remark in his sentencing remarks, the appellant must have entered her room every day because he had provided food to her, but the only other care he had given her, until calling for the emergency services when it was too late, was to reposition her television set.

What was D's duty founded on in this case? Was it the fact of their familial relationship or was it because there was simply no one else to care for V and alert the authorities to her condition? As has already been mentioned, it has been suggested that the duty is founded upon a settled relationship of mutual interdependence between D and V.

A. Ashworth, 'Manslaughter by Omission and the Rule of Law'
[2015] Crim LR 563

> What does our present enquiry reveal about the significance of family or other relationships? Apart from parent-child (and, perhaps, married couples or civil partners living together) it does not seem profitable to focus on the nature of the relationship between the defendant and the deceased, D and V. The strongest criterion is D's assumption of responsibility for V's welfare, combined with the requirement that D be aware, or ought reasonably to be aware, that V is in a life-threatening condition. The assumption of responsibility can derive from an explicit statement or agreement, or it can be inferred from a settled relationship of mutual interdependence. There are obvious problems of certainty here, since there can be no clear indicator of the quantum of mutual interdependence necessary to fulfil the requirement. Acts of assistance should not be sufficient on their own, except insofar as they can be said to provide evidence of a longer-term assumption of responsibility for V's welfare. However, acts of assistance that involve seclusion (i.e. taking V away from a more public place to a more private place) might be said to amount to an assumption of responsibility for the other's welfare, even by someone who has not otherwise assumed responsibility for V. Yet unless the

concept of assumption of responsibility can be explained in greater detail, preferably with widely-publicized statutory illustrations to inform people about the types of situation in which the concept applies, there must be grave doubts about whether it is a suitable foundation for such a serious offence as manslaughter.

≈ Questions

(1) Do you agree with Ashworth's assessment that the current law does not provide a suitable foundation for such a serious offence as manslaughter? Would it be preferable to have a specific statutory offence, which would be less serious, of 'failing to discharge a duty'?

(2) What is the extent of a duty imposed by relationships? Is it a duty to do what is reasonable? What D believes to be reasonable? That which is necessary to avert the danger from V?

(3) Should a strong 14-year-old owe a duty to his ailing mother? Should a duty extend between siblings? Does a student D owe a duty to his anorexic flatmate, V, to call for medical treatment for her? Does he owe a duty to feed her?

4.2.3.4 Creation of a dangerous situation or 'supervening fault'

Where D creates a dangerous situation, the law may impose a duty upon him to act to prevent harm resulting. The principle for determining liability where D creates a dangerous situation was pronounced by the House of Lords in the following case.

R v Miller
[1982] UKHL 6, House of Lords

(Lords Diplock, Keith, Bridge, Brandon and Brightman)

The defendant lay on a mattress in a house in which he was a squatter and lit a cigarette. He fell asleep and woke to find the mattress on fire. He went into the next room and fell asleep. The house caught fire and £800 worth of damage was done. He was charged with arson, contrary to s 1(1) and (3) of the Criminal Damage Act 1971, in that he 'damaged by fire a house . . . intending to do damage to such property or recklessly as to whether such property would be damaged'. He was convicted and his appeal to the Court of Appeal was dismissed. He appealed to the House of Lords. Note that at the time of this decision the mens rea for the offence was governed by the test of recklessness in *Caldwell* (section 5.3.1, p 98).

Lord Diplock:

The first question is a pure question of causation; it is one of fact to be decided by the jury in a trial on indictment. It should be answered No if, in relation to the fire during the period starting immediately before its ignition and ending with its extinction, the role of the accused was at no time more than that of a passive bystander. In such a case the subsequent questions to which I shall be turning would not arise. The conduct of the parabolical priest and Levite on the road to Jericho may have been indeed deplorable, but English law has not so far developed to the stage of treating it as criminal; and if it ever were to do so there would be difficulties in defining what should be the limits of the offence.

If, on the other hand the question, which I now confine to: 'Did a physical act of the accused start the fire which spread and damaged property belonging to another?', is answered 'Yes', as it was by the Jury in the instant case, then for the purpose of the further questions the answers to which are determinative of his guilt of the offence of arson, the conduct of the accused, throughout the period from immediately before the moment of ignition to the completion of the damage to the property by the fire, is relevant; so is his state of mind throughout that period.

Since arson is a result-crime the period may be considerable, and during it the conduct of the accused that is causative of the result may consist not only of his doing physical acts which cause the fire to start or spread but also of his failing to take measures that lie within his power to counteract the danger that he has himself created. And if his conduct, active or passive, varies in the course of the period, so may his state of mind at the time of each piece of conduct. If, at the time of any particular piece of conduct by the accused that is causative of the result, the state of mind that actuates his conduct falls within the description of one or other of the states of mind that are made a necessary ingredient of the offence of arson by s 1(1) of the Criminal Damage Act 1971 (ie intending to damage property belonging to another or being reckless whether such property would be damaged), I know of no principle of English criminal law that would prevent his being guilty of the offence created by that subsection. Likewise I see no rational ground for excluding from conduct capable of giving rise to criminal liability conduct which consists of failing to take measures that lie within one's power to counteract a danger that one has oneself created, if at the time of such conduct one's state of mind is such as constitutes a necessary ingredient of the offence. I venture to think that the habit of lawyers to talk of 'actus reus', suggestive as it is of action rather than inaction, is responsible for any erroneous notion that failure to act cannot give rise to criminal liability in English law.

No one has been bold enough to suggest that if, in the instant case, the accused had been aware at the time that he dropped the cigarette that it would probably set fire to his mattress and yet had taken no steps to extinguish it he would not have been guilty of the offence of arson, since he would have damaged property of another being reckless whether any such property would be damaged.

I cannot see any good reason why, so far as liability under criminal law is concerned, it should matter at what point of time before the resultant damage is complete a person becomes aware that he has done a physical act which, whether or not he appreciated that it would at the time when he did it, does in fact create a risk that property of another will be damaged, provided that, at the moment of awareness, it lies within his power to take steps, either himself or by calling for the assistance of the fire brigade if this be necessary, to prevent or minimise the damage to the property at risk . . .

My Lords, in the instant case the prosecution did not rely on the state of mind of the accused as being reckless during that part of his conduct that consisted of his lighting and smoking a cigarette while lying on his mattress and falling asleep without extinguishing it. So the jury were not invited to make any finding as to this. What the prosecution did rely on as being reckless was his state of mind during that part of his conduct after he awoke to find that he had set his mattress on fire and that it was smouldering, but did not then take any steps either to try to extinguish it himself or to send for the fire brigade, but simply went into the other room to resume his slumbers, leaving the fire from the already smouldering mattress to spread and to damage that part of the house in which the mattress was.

The recorder, in his lucid summing up to the jury (they took 22 minutes only to reach their verdict), told them that the accused, having by his own act started a fire in the mattress which, when he became aware of its existence, presented an obvious risk of damaging the house, became under a duty to take some action to put it out. The Court of Appeal upheld the conviction, but its ratio decidendi appears to be somewhat different from that of the recorder. As I understand the judgment, in effect it treats the whole course of conduct of the accused, from the moment at which he fell asleep and dropped the cigarette onto the mattress until the time the damage to the house by fire was complete, as a continuous act of the accused, and holds that it is sufficient to constitute the statutory offence of arson if at any stage in that course of conduct the state of mind of the accused, when he fails to try to prevent or minimize the damage which will result from his initial act, although it lies within his power to do so, is that of being reckless whether property belonging to another would be damaged: . . .

My Lords, these alternative ways of analysing the legal theory that justifies decision which has received nothing but commendation for its accord with common sense and justice have, since the publication of the judgment of the Court of Appeal in the instant case, provoked academic controversy.

Each theory has distinguished support. Professor J C Smith espouses the 'duty theory' (see [1982] Crim LR 526 at 528); Professor Glanville Williams who, after the decision of the Divisional Court in *Fagan v Metropolitan Police Comr* [set out in section 2.3.2, p 29] appears to have been attracted by the duty theory, now prefers that of the continuous act (see [1982] Crim LR 773). When applied to cases where a person has unknowingly done an act which sets in train events that, when he becomes aware of them, present an obvious risk that property belonging to another will be damaged, both theories lead to an identical result; and, since what your Lordships are concerned with is to give guidance to trial judges in their task of summing up to juries, I would for this purpose adopt the duty theory as being the easier to explain to a jury; though I would commend the use of the word 'responsibility', rather than 'duty' which is more appropriate to civil than to criminal law since it suggests an obligation owed to another person, ie the person to whom the endangered property belongs, whereas a criminal statute defines combinations of conduct and state of mind which render a person liable to punishment by the state itself.

[Lords Keith, Bridge, Brandon and Brightman agreed.]

Appeal dismissed

≋ **Questions**
(1) Was the defendant held liable for damaging the house by falling asleep while smoking? Or for damaging the house by failing to take reasonable steps to put out the burning bed?
(2) What if the defendant's fellow squatter had (a) sustained grievous bodily harm or (b) died in the fire?

Compare the approach taken by the Divisional Court in *Fagan v Metropolitan Police Commissioner* [1969] 1 QB 439. In that case, set out in section 2.3.2, p 29, D had driven onto a police officer's foot and when told of that fact by the officer had delayed in moving his car. He was convicted by the magistrates of assaulting the constable in the execution of his duty. In the Divisional Court, it was held that:

. . . On the facts found, the action of the appellant may have been initially unintentional, but the time came when, knowing that the wheel was on the officer's foot, the appellant (i) remained seated in the car so that his body through the medium of the car was in contact with the officer, (ii) switched off the ignition of the car, (iii) maintained the wheel of the car on the foot, and (iv) used words indicating the intention of keeping the wheel in that position. For our part, we cannot regard such conduct as mere omission or inactivity. There was an act constituting a battery which at its inception was not criminal because there was no element of intention, but which became criminal from the moment the intention was formed to produce the apprehension which was flowing from the continuing act. The fallacy of the appellant's argument is that it seeks to equate the facts of this case with such a case as where a motorist has accidentally run over a person and, that action having been completed, fails to assist the victim with the intent that the victim should suffer.

Bridge J dissented, holding that:

after the wheel of the appellant's car had accidentally come to rest on the constable's foot, what was it that the appellant *did* which constituted the act of assault? However the question is approached, the answer which I feel obliged to give is: precisely nothing. The car rested on the foot by its own weight and remained stationary by its own inertia. The appellant's fault was that he omitted to manipulate the controls to set it in motion again.

> ≋ *Question*
> Was there a 'continuing act' in *Miller* or in *Fagan*?

In *Santana-Bermudez* [2003] EWHC 2908 (Admin), S-B, a drug user, had assured a police officer about to search him that he was carrying no 'sharps'. The officer stabbed her finger on a syringe needle in his pocket during the search. Applying *Miller*, Maurice Kay J said:

> . . . where someone (by act or word or a combination of the two) creates a danger and thereby exposes another to a reasonably foreseeable risk of injury which materialises, there is an evidential basis for the actus reus of an assault occasioning actual bodily harm. It remains necessary for the prosecution to prove an intention to assault or appropriate recklessness.

In *Miller*, it was undoubtedly the case that the dangerous situation that arose was solely attributable to D. What would be the position if D was a contributory cause, but not the sole cause, of the dangerous situation? In *Evans* [2009] EWCA Crim 650, D supplied heroin to her half-sister, V. Having self-injected the heroin, it became clear that V was suffering from the symptoms of an overdose. Instead of summoning medical assistance, D stayed with V through the night in the hope that she would recover. V died. D was found guilty of gross negligence manslaughter. The Court of Appeal stated that D's duty to summon medical assistance did not arise from her status as V's half-sister, nor from the fact that she supplied V with the heroin. Rather, the Court of Appeal relied on the principle first propounded in *Miller* to find that D was under a duty to summon medical assistance and had breached that duty by failing to do so. However, it could be said that these facts are distinguishable from *Miller* on the basis that V also contributed to the creation of a dangerous situation by virtue of her choice to inject the heroin. The Court of Appeal held that:

> The duty necessary to found gross negligence manslaughter is plainly not confined to cases of a familial or professional relationship between the defendant and the deceased. In our judgment, consistently with *R v Adomako* [1995] 1 AC 171 and the link between civil and criminal liability for negligence, for the purposes of gross negligence manslaughter, when a person has created or contributed to the creation of a state of affairs which he knows, or ought reasonably to know, has become life threatening, a consequent duty on him to act by taking reasonable steps to save the other's life will normally arise.

It is important to appreciate that the inclusion of the phrase 'or contributes to' arguably represents an extension of the *Miller* principle. What will remain for subsequent courts to decide is how much of a contribution D must make before the duty to act crystallizes. This issue has not yet been considered by a court, however.

4.3 A general duty of rescue?

One of the most controversial issues in this area of law is whether there ought to be a general duty of rescue. Proposals have often been made for the imposition of a general duty, particularly to save others from death or serious injury. Consider which of the competing views represented by the following extracts you find most convincing.

Andrew Ashworth, 'The Scope of Criminal Liability for Omissions'
(1989) 105 LQR 424

Although the paradigm of criminal liability is a prohibition on the culpable doing of a certain act, all systems of criminal law seem to include offences of omission. Some will have been drafted expressly so as to penalise an omission, e.g. 'failing to . . . ,' usually in the context of an undertaking or activity such as running a business or driving a motor vehicle. There may be other offences worded in a way which leaves open the possibility that they may be committed by omission as well as by acts. References to omissions should not, of course, be taken to imply that we may be said to omit to do everything that we do not do each day. The term 'omission' is properly applied only to failure to do things which there is some kind of duty to do, or at least things which it is reasonable to expect a person to do (on the basis of some relationship or role).

What the scope of such duties should be is therefore a major question for the legislature when considering criminal law reform and for the courts when developing the common law or interpreting statutes. Two contrasting positions may be identified, the 'conventional view' and the 'social responsibility view.' They are not polar opposites, and in a practical sense the difference between them is a matter of the extent of the duties recognised. But the two views do proceed from different theoretical foundations, and these are important when considering reasons for and against particular instances of criminal liability for omissions. What it is proposed to call the 'conventional view'—though one cannot be sure how settled or how prevalent it is—maintains that the criminal law should be reluctant to impose liability for omissions except in clear and serious cases. It is accepted that there are many activities in modern society which must, to some extent, be regulated by criminal offences, of which some will properly be offences of omission; it is also accepted that citizens have duties to support the collective good by paying taxes, etc., and that such duties may be reinforced by offences of omission; but the distinctive argument is that our duties towards other individuals should be confined to duties towards those for whom we have voluntarily undertaken some responsibility. Whereas we owe negative duties (e.g. not to kill or injure) to all people, it is right that we should owe positive duties (e.g. to render assistance, to support) only to a circumscribed group of people with whom there exists a special relationship. When supporters of the conventional view are pressed to justify this limitation, they might tend to argue that there is moral distinction between acts and omissions, maintaining that failure to perform an act with foreseen bad consequences is morally less bad than performing an act with the identical foreseen bad consequences.

. . . Adherents to the 'social responsibility view' would draw attention to the co-operative elements in social life, and would argue that it may be fair to place citizens under obligations to render assistance to other individuals in certain situations. This does not commit them to the view that the criminal law should enforce general duties to help all persons at all times. But it leads them to doubt whether the existence of some relationship or voluntary undertaking should be regarded as a precondition of criminal omissions liability. And it may also lead them to attack the argument that there is a general moral distinction between failing to perform an act with foreseen bad consequences and performing an act with identical bad consequences. All types of offence vary in their seriousness, of course, and even if it were true that on the whole omissions are less culpable than acts, it would not follow that omissions are less suitable for criminal prohibition than acts. On the 'social responsibility view,' then, there is no reason to accept the limitation imposed on omissions liability by the 'conventional view.'

. . . The conventional view embodies a minimalist stance on criminal liability for omissions. It accepts that criminal law is the sharpest end of a legal structure which aims to ensure both that respect for social values is enforced and that essential social needs are provided for. It therefore accepts criminal liability for such omissions as non-payment of taxes. But it regards it as exceptional, and as requiring special justification, for the criminal law to impose duties to assist other individuals. Apart from special relationships (such as parent-child) and other voluntarily undertaken duties, there should be no criminally enforceable duties to assist others or to perform socially useful acts.

The main buttress is an argument from individual autonomy and liberty. Each person is regarded as an autonomous being, responsible for his or her own conduct. One aim of the law is to maximise individual liberty, so as to allow each individual to pursue a conception of the good life with as few constraints as possible. Constraints there must be, of course, in modern society: but freedom of action should be curtailed only so far as is necessary to restrain individuals from causing injury or loss to others. Setting these outer limits to freedom of action is, however, much more acceptable than requiring certain actions of a citizen, especially at times and in circumstances which may be inconvenient and may conflict with one's pursuit of one's personal goals. To impose a duty to do X at a certain time prevents the citizen from doing anything else at that time, whereas the conventional prohibitions of the criminal law leave the citizen free to do whatever else is wanted apart from the prohibited conduct. Moreover, the criminal law should recognise an individual's choices rather than allowing liability to be governed by chance, and the obligation to assist someone in peril may be thrust upon a chance passer-by, who may well prefer not to become involved at all. If I am driving to a concert 50 miles away which is to feature a soloist who is being heard for the last time in this country, should I be obliged to stop and render assistance to the victims of a road accident in which I was not involved, at the risk of missing part or the whole of the concert? It is no argument to say that such a journey is always open to the possibility of chance happenings, such as engine failure in the car, a road blocked by a fallen tree, and so on, because in the case of the accident victims I am physically free to drive on to my destination whereas the other happenings amount to physical prevention, and render me incapable of reaching my destination on time. Thus it is no argument to say that all arrangements are vulnerable to chance, since the law can strive to minimise its effect and to keep individual choice as wide as possible. There is a choice whether to stop and offer assistance or to continue on my way to the concert, but an offence requiring a citizen to stop and render assistance would effectively foreclose that choice, coercing me to sacrifice the pursuit of my own interests in favour of alleviating the misfortunes of others to whom I have not voluntarily assumed any duty. By its 'chance' nature, the incidence of such a duty reduces the predictability of one's obligations and impinges on the liberty to pursue one's conception of the good life. On the conventional view, then, I deserve moral praise if I stop to assist the accident victims and thereby lose the opportunity to attend the (whole) concert, but it does not follow that I deserve blame if I do not stop. Praise may be appropriate for an act of 'saintliness' going beyond duty, whereas the duties themselves require only the basic conditions of peaceful co-existence. Stopping to help is part of the morality of aspiration, not the morality of duty.

In thus equating individual autonomy with negative liberty (i.e. liberty not to do certain acts), the conventional view rejects broad duties to others as paternalistic, and as failing to respect each individual's right to self-determination. Any obligation to help others in peril begs the question of who is to decide what 'peril' is. Individuals may choose to engage in amateur boxing or in motor cycle racing, knowing of the high risk of injury but deciding that it is worth the risk in order to enjoy the excitement of the sport. Are these boxers or motor cyclists 'in peril'? Few would extend a citizen's obligation to intervene (where it exists) to these cases, probably because the individual's decision to engage in the sport may be assumed to be an informed and settled decision. Self-determination, a value closely entwined with individual autonomy, would be impaired by the intervention of others. But what about the person who decides to commit suicide and jumps from a bridge into the River Thames? Should the passing citizen be obliged to alert the emergency services or, if the conditions are favourable, to mount a rescue attempt? The passing citizen is unlikely to know about the potential suicide's state of mind. It is known that some attempts at suicide proceed from an unbalanced state of mind, and some are merely attempts to draw attention to the person's problems rather than to relinquish life. On the conventional view these possibilities for paternalistic intervention should not be made the basis of any legal duty. If a citizen sees what appears to be an attempted suicide, the citizen's freedom from non-voluntary obligations together with the potential suicide's right to self-determination are sufficient to conclude the case against a duty to intervene.

A third argument looks to the social consequences of the opposite, 'social responsibility' view. Its effect in requiring each citizen to offer assistance to others in peril might on the one hand reduce the autonomy and privacy of others in pursuing their own objectives and enjoyment, however dangerous it may appear to others, and might on the other hand make citizens into busybodies who believe that they must be constantly advising others to avoid risk and danger. In other words, it might be too intrusive and too onerous—both tendencies which go against the maximisation of liberty which is the keynote of the conventional view.

Fourthly, there is the argument that the 'social responsibility' view is unpractical because it would require each of us to avert or alleviate large numbers of situations which we know about. One strand of this argument calls attention to the problem of setting limits to the individuals duties on the social responsibility view: must I sell my car and my house, live at subsistence level and devote all my surplus earnings and time to preventing so many people from 'sleeping rough' in London, or to provide towards the relief of starvation in Africa? In what way do perils of these kinds differ materially from the accident victims or the person who jumps into the River Thames? A second strand of the argument is that the 'social responsibility' view may lead to the inculpation of large numbers of people, e.g. all the members of a crowd who witness someone being beaten up by others. It is excesses of this nature, in the depth and breadth of the obligations imposed, which are seen as sufficient to condemn the 'social responsibility' view as an unworkable moral or legal standard.

A fifth argument draws strength from the principle of legality: it maintains that citizens are so unaccustomed to thinking in terms of legal duties to act (as distinct from the well-known prohibitions) that it is unfair to impose such burdens except in circumstances which are well-defined and well-publicised. Protagonists might add that few provisions on general liability for omissions attain these standards, and that the obligation to take reasonable steps to assist a person in peril is much too uncertain to meet these standards. The social consequence is likely to be that ignorance of the law is a frequent occurrence, which cannot be good either for society or for the individuals concerned. Wide conceptions of social responsibility must therefore be rejected as a basis for criminal legislation: the conventional view, with its few well-known and voluntarily assumed duties to others, is the preferable approach.

The individualism of the conventional view doubted

The arguments for the conventional view may appear strong and practical, but they depend on a narrow, individualistic conception of human life which should be rejected as a basis for morality and (although this raises further issues) as a basis for criminal liability. Let us look again at the arguments, in turn.

The first argument, based on individual autonomy and freedom, is altogether too pure. To the extent that the conventional view relies on 'social fact' for some of its justifications, it is worth pointing out that rarely is individual autonomy promoted as a supreme value throughout a moral or legal system. For example, paternalistic considerations are taken to outweigh it when imposing a duty to wear a seat belt in the front seat of a car: this restricts individual liberty and self-determination, and it may be justified by reference to the known dangers of travelling without a seat-belt, combined with the relatively large benefit (in the social costs of health care) reaped from such a comparatively minor infringement of freedom of action. Systems of criminal law typically include a wide range of offences which impose duties to act, in relation to taxation, motoring and business activities . . .

The second and third arguments for the conventional view establish, however, that limits must be set to the obligations to others if the ideal of individual autonomy is not to be submerged beneath a welter of duties imposed on each person. The resolution of these conflicts of theory and practice is no easy matter, but the 'social responsibility' view would at least start from the assumption that duties to others are not necessarily alien to individual autonomy, and would have to reconcile this with the desirability of individuals safeguarding their own interests too. This dilemma, which also underlies the fourth argument for the conventional view, demonstrates the need for principled debate about the extent of social co-operation necessary to realise individual autonomy. Those who advocate 'social responsibility' bear the heavy burden of formulating defensible and workable criteria for the imposition of duties to act. Indeed, as the fifth argument showed, attention is also necessary to the promulgation of such rules. In so far as it is true that people do not consider that they have legal duties to assist others, any legislation to introduce such duties must be phrased as precisely as possible, and must be supported by a programme of education and information. These represent considerable challenges for the 'social responsibility' view on criminal liability for omissions.

. . . On the 'social responsibility' view there are arguments for imposing certain obligations on individuals as citizens. These arguments are not founded on a simple benefit/burden calculation, that whoever takes the benefits of living in a certain society must in fairness expect to have to submit to its burdens. Such an approach leaves many unanswered questions about the quantum of burden which must be borne in order to have access to certain benefits. The reasoning is rather that the imposition of certain minimal duties shows a concern for the rights of other members of the community and therefore for the community itself, and so tends to promote the maximisation of liberty. However, the idea of maximum liberty relates to each individual as a member of the community rather than to each individual in isolation. Thus an apparent diminution of the freedom of one citizen (by requiring that citizen to take reasonable steps to prevent a harm or to call the emergency services) may be justifiable by reference to the augmentation of the freedom of another citizen (who is under attack or otherwise in danger), and such justification is in the context of striving towards a community in which the liberty of each and all can be maximised.

Once the case for imposing some citizenship duties is made out, there remain difficult questions about the proper extent and scope of these duties. Duties towards the collective good such as the duty to pay taxes may be established fairly easily, but duties towards other individuals who are strangers require further justification. It is thought that the arguments above establish the case for a duty to take steps to save other citizens in peril. It is true that this duty must be hedged about with qualifications, so as to ensure that the obligations are neither too dangerous nor too onerous for the citizen upon whom they fall. . . .

≈≈ *Questions*
(1) Do you agree that there should be a general offence of failing to save citizens in peril?
(2) V is sleeping in a shop doorway. It is a bitterly cold night and V looks very pale. D is walking past the doorway and notices V. D eyes the empty vodka bottle at V's side, fears an angry and violent response if he gets involved so decides to walk by. Should D be guilty of a criminal offence if V dies? If so, of what offence? Manslaughter? An offence of failing to assist?

Glanville Williams, 'Criminal Omissions—The Conventional View' (1991) 107 LQR 86

. . . Ashworth says that there is no moral difference between (i) a positive act and (ii) an omission when a duty is established. But even if this is so, he has already conceded a difference between the two when he says that an omission is culpable only when there is duty to act. The duty requirement sometimes involves considerations that are irrelevant to crimes of commission. Of course, every crime is a breach of legal duty not to commit the crime, but this is part of the meaning of the word 'crime.'

The point is that no requirement of a particular duty not to act (over and above the specification of the crime) applies to wrongs of commission.

. . . First, . . . omissions liability should be exceptional, and needs to be adequately justified in each instance. Secondly, when it is imposed this should be done by clear statutory language. Verbs primarily denoting (and forbidding) active conduct should not be construed to include omissions except when the statute contains a genuine implication to this effect—not the perfunctory and fictitious implication that judges use when they are on the law-path instead of the purely judge-path. Thirdly, maximum penalties applied to active wrongdoing should not automatically be transferred to corresponding omissions; penalties for omissions should be rethought in each case.

The case for the conventional view

The arguments for this philosophy may be briefly stated. (I would have thought them too obvious to need statement.) First, society's most urgent task is the repression of active wrongdoing. Bringing the ignorant or lethargic up to scratch is very much a secondary endeavour, for which the criminal process is not necessarily the best suited.

Secondly, our attitudes to wrongful action and wrongful inaction differ. There may be instances where our blood boils at the same temperature on account of both, but these are very exceptional. The only likely instance that comes to my mind is that of parents who are charged with killing their baby (i) by smothering it or (ii) by starving it to death. In this instance we are likely to feel more angry and sad about the slow starvation (an omission) than about the comparatively merciful infliction of death with a pillow. But on other occasions we almost always perceive a moral distinction between (for example) killing a person and failing to save his life (the former being the worse); and similarly between other acts and corresponding omissions.

This moral distinction, which we express in our language, reflects differences in our psychological approach to our own acts and omissions. We have much stronger inhibitions against active wrongdoing than against wrongfully omitting. This again is coupled with the fact that it is in every way easier not to do something (personal needs apart) than to do it. Also, a requirement to do something presupposes the ability to do it (the physical ability, and often the financial and educational ability as well), whereas almost everyone has the ability to refrain from ordinary physical acts.

Thirdly, serious crimes of commission can usually be formulated merely by stating the forbidden conduct, but laws creating crimes of omission are rarely directed against the whole world. They are intended to operate only against particular classes of person (and sometimes only for the protection of particular classes), in which case these persons must be singled out in the statement of the crime. To take an example: the courts can, in theory, punish everyone (with exceptions) who knowingly kills, but they cannot punish everyone who fails to save life, without some minimum specification of whose lives are to be saved. I cannot be made criminally responsible when I knowingly fail to save (and do not even try to save) the lives of unfortunate inhabitants of the Ganges delta who are drowned in floods; yet I could do something to help them by selling my house and giving the money to a suitable charity. Ashworth meets the point by saying that the requirement of duty 'establishes moral responsibility and delineates in time and space the number of people who may be said to have omitted'. . . . Very well, but this looks like translating law into morals rather than morals into law. Anyway, Ashworth does not propose that everything that may be regarded as a moral duty should automatically become a legal duty. So when we propose to punish omissions we are left with the problem of defining the scope of legal duty.

Fourthly, when crimes are expressed with the use of verbs implying action, it is a breach of the principle of legality to convict people of them when they have not acted; and it is unfair 'labelling' (Ashworth's expression) to convict non-doers of acts under the name of doers.

Fifthly, and perhaps most important of all, the law enforcement agencies (including the courts) have their work cut out to deal with people who offend by active conduct. The prisons, it is scarcely necessary to recall, are packed with them. To extend the campaign by attempting to punish all (or large groups of) those who contribute to the evil result by failing to co-operate in the great endeavour of producing a happier world would exceed the bounds of possibility.

Ashworth says of the conventional view that the supporting arguments 'depend on a narrow, individualistic conception of human life which should be rejected as a basis for morality and (although this raises further issues) as a basis for criminal liability' . . . I leave it to the reader to judge whether the arguments as I have formulated them deserve this stricture.

In justifying the conventional view I have made no reference to the philosophy of individualism or to the autonomy principle, both of which Ashworth (erroneously I think) regards as the foundation of the conventional view. How far the State should provide financial succour and social services for those in need has nothing to do with the question whether individuals should be criminally punishable for not providing others with these advantages. To bring these considerations based on general social policy into the discussion simply muddies the waters. The same remark applies to Ashworth's support for legislation requiring the wearing of seat-belts, support which is now platitudinous, as well as being irrelevant to his attack on 'the conventional view.' The argument against treating omissions in the same way as positive acts does not go to the extent of saying that omissions running contrary to the public interest should never be punishable. Those who oppose seat belt legislation (among whom I am not to be counted) do so on the ground that it unjustifiably restricts bodily liberty, not on the ground that it wrongly punishes omissions. The legislation forbids one to drive in a car without belting up, and the forbidden conduct is a hybrid act/omission, which is legally classified as an act, not an omission.

≈≈ *Question*

Do you find Williams' view more convincing than Ashworth's?

4.4 Omissions and causation

Assuming that the offence in question is one which can be interpreted so as to be committed by omission and that there is a relevant category of duty, the question remains: how can D cause any harm by omission?

It has been argued (Brian Hogan, 'Omissions and the Duty Myth' in P. F. Smith (ed), *Criminal Law: Essays in Honour of J. C. Smith* (1987), p 85) that it is not true that results can be 'caused' by omission and that it ought to follow that no one should be liable for a 'result crime' because of a mere omission.

If grandma's skirts are ignited by her careless proximity to the gas oven, the delinquent grandson cannot be said to have killed her by his failure to dowse her. No sensible doctor would enter as the cause of her death, say, failure to telephone the fire brigade. . . . [Professor Hogan continues:]

If any proposition is self-evident (and, arguably, none is) it is that a person cannot be held to have caused an event which he did not cause. Hence my delinquent child cannot sensibly be said to have caused the death of his grandmother simply by a failure to take steps (which may or may not have been successful anyway) to prevent that death. To say to the child, 'You have killed your grandmother' would simply be untrue.

This is not to say that I am against liability for omissions. There would be nothing in principle objectionable in Parliament enacting a law which made it an offence for a member of a household to fail to take steps reasonably available to him to prevent or minimize harm to other members of the household. There are of course numerous instances where Parliament (and a handful where the common law) has penalised omissions but what is noteworthy is that the defendant is penalised for the omission but not visited with liability for the consequences of that omission. . . .

So in no sense am I against liability for omission. I would ask only two conditions of a law punishing omissions. One is that it be clearly articulated and the other is that it seeks to punish the defendant for his dereliction and does not artificially treat him as a cause of the event he has not brought about by his conduct. . . .

Thus far I have discussed cases where by no stretch of the imagination can it be said that the defendant has caused a result by his inaction. The question then arises whether a result may ever be caused by inaction. My answer is: No. On the other hand a result may be caused by the defendant's *conduct* and the totality of the defendant's conduct causing a result may properly include what he has not done as well as done. In such cases I doubt whether it is very, or at all, helpful to analyze each phase of the defendant's conduct as one of omission or commission. The question is simply: did the defendant's *conduct* cause the result?

Take a simple example. X, driving his car, sees Y beginning to cross the road ahead. X realizes that unless he takes some action, such as removing his foot from the accelerator to the brake or turning to left or right, he will run down Y. In fact he takes no action whatsoever and runs down Y. Charged with an offence in relation to the harm done to Y, X would surely be laughed out of court if he said: I did not do anything to cause harm to Y. We would not have the slightest difficulty in saying that X ran down Y and was the cause of the harm to Y. *R v Miller* [section 4.2.3.4, p 69] holds, and with respect rightly, that one who inadvertently (or otherwise faultlessly, presumably) starts a chain of events causing harm may be properly held liable if, having become aware that he was the cause, he fails to take steps reasonably available to him to prevent or minimize the damage that will ensue. A fortiori the driver X. There is nothing inadvertent about his causing of harm to Y. X chooses to stay with a course of conduct which he knows will cause harm to Y.

This view is not universally held, however. The contrary view has been expressed (see A. Leavens, 'A Causation Approach to Criminal Omissions' (1988) 76 Cal LR 547) in the following terms:

Such a view of causation is flawed because its inquiry is too limited. It depends on a definition of the status quo as the existing physical state of affairs at the precise time of the omission . . . Our everyday notions of causation, however, are not so limited because we understand that the status quo encompasses more than the physical state of affairs at a given time. Indeed, in everyday usage the status quo is taken to include expected patterns of conduct, including actions designed to avert certain unwanted results. When, for example, a driver parks a car on a steep hill, it is normal to set the parking brake and put the car in gear. If the driver forgets to do so and the car subsequently rolls down the hill, smashing into another car, we would say that the failure to park properly was a departure from the status quo. This failure, not the visibly steep hill or the predicate act of pulling the car to the curb, was the cause of the collision. Once we realize that a particular undesirable state of affairs can be avoided by taking certain precautions, we usually incorporate these precautions into what we see as the normal or at rest state of affairs. A failure to engage in the preventative conduct in these cases can thus be seen as an intervention that disturbs the status quo. When such a failure to act is a necessary condition (a 'but for' cause) of a particular harm, then that failure fairly can be said to cause that harm. In the above example, the driver's failure to park the car in a proper manner caused the accident as surely as if he had actually driven his car into the other . . .

Despite the existence of this theoretical disagreement, the courts have accepted that it is possible to commit a result crime by omission. The rules on causation, which were discussed in the previous chapter, will therefore be applicable. For D to be guilty, it must be established that it was D's breach of duty that caused the prohibited result. For example, in the case of *Miller*,

D was guilty of arson because his failure to call the fire brigade caused damage to property belonging to another. If, on the other hand, D's failure to call the fire brigade made no difference to whether the property was damaged, then it could not be said that he caused it and he would not have been guilty.

FURTHER READING

L. Alexander, 'Criminal Liability for Omissions: An Inventory of Issues' in S. Shute and A. Simester (eds), *Criminal Law Theory: Doctrines of the General Part* (2002)

A. Ashworth, *Positive Obligations in Criminal Law* (2013)

P. Glazebrook, 'Criminal Omissions: The Duty Requirements in Offences Against the Person' (1960) 76 LQR 386

J. Glover, 'Not Striving to Keep Alive' in J. Glover, *Causing Death and Saving Lives* (1977)

B. Hogan, 'Omissions and the Duty Myth' in P. F. Smith (ed), *Criminal Law: Essays in Honour of J. C. Smith* (1987)

G. Hughes, 'Criminal Omissions' (1958) 67 Yale LJ 590

I. Kennedy, 'Switching Off Life Support Machines: The Legal Implications' [1977] Crim LR 443

J. Keown, 'Beyond *Bland*: A Critique of the BMA Guidance on Withholding and Withdrawing Medical Treatment' (2000) 20 LS 66

A. Simester, 'Why Omissions are Special' (1995) 1 Legal Theory 311

J. C. Smith, 'Liability for Omissions in Criminal Law' (1984) 4 LS 88

5
Fault

> **Some of the controversies that will be examined in this chapter include:**
>
> (1) How intention is defined and in particular:
>
>   • how judges ought to direct juries in instances when it was not D's purpose to cause the prohibited outcome;
>
>   • precisely when a jury is entitled to find intention when D foresaw an outcome as virtually certain and whether it is obligated to do so;
>
>   • the extent to which it can be said that 'oblique' intention is a form of intention at all.
>
> (2) How recklessness should be defined and in particular:
>
>   • whether recklessness ought to be a subjective or an objective concept;
>
>   • whether there should there be a different conception of recklessness that is dependent upon whether the offence in question is a result or conduct crime.
>
> (3) The appropriateness of criminalizing instances of negligence.

5.1 Introduction

There are some offences, not always minor ones, called 'offences of strict liability', where a person may be convicted although he was not at fault. Generally, however, the law requires proof of fault of some kind. Offences of strict liability are considered in Chapter 6. We saw at the outset in Chapter 2 that criminal offences generally involve a mental element (mens rea). In offences which require proof of a result which is forbidden by the criminal law, the 'fault' or mens rea is usually the state of mind the defendant had about whether that *result* would be caused. Some offences may require proof of some proscribed *circumstance*, and the mens rea or fault is usually the state of mind the defendant had about whether that circumstance exists at the time (as with rape where D's conduct must occur in circumstances where V is not consenting and D has no reasonable belief that V is consenting).

In the present chapter we consider the different types of fault which the criminal law requires. When examining an unfamiliar offence these are usually relatively easy to identify as the same forms of mens rea are routinely included by Parliament in offences: intention, knowledge, belief, recklessness, etc. Historically Parliament used other terms such as maliciously, wilfully, etc. Although arcane sounding, they are also easy to identify when looking at the offence.

There are degrees of fault. The most blameworthy mental element is an *intention* to bring about the forbidden result or *knowledge* that a circumstance exists. Also blameworthy, but less so, is *recklessness* whether a result be caused or a circumstance exists. So, intentional killing is murder and reckless killing is manslaughter. 'Intentionally' and 'recklessly' are ordinary words of the English language but experience shows that they are capable of different meanings. The ordinary people who sit on juries, as well as philosophers, may well differ as to whether a particular state of mind constitutes intention, or recklessness, or neither of these. Many of the most important and difficult cases in recent years have been concerned with the meaning of these terms.

Sometimes the fault which must be proved is not intention or recklessness but guilty knowledge of some sort. For example, when a person is found in possession of stolen goods, say a car, he commits a crime only if he knew or believed that the car was stolen. If he bought it in perfect good faith, it is his misfortune, not his fault. He may be guilty of the tort of conversion because the car still belongs to its original owner. The tort requires no fault. He may have to return the car or account to the owner for its value and may have lost the price he paid. But the innocent buyer of stolen goods commits no crime. If, however, he knew or believed the car was stolen when he bought it, he is guilty of the crime of handling stolen goods.

What matters is whether the fault that is specified in the offence is proved. It is not a question of whether D was morally blameworthy but whether he had intention, knowledge or recklessness etc as the offence requires.

Fault is not limited to states of mind. A person who did not foresee a harmful result of his conduct obviously did not intend it but it may be that he *ought* to have foreseen the risk of causing it and avoided doing so, as a reasonably prudent person would. For some crimes, this is sufficient fault. The prosecution have to prove only that the defendant did not behave in the way a reasonable person would and, in the case of a result crime, thereby caused the proscribed result. This is negligence. There may be degrees of negligence. Any deviation from the standard of care to be expected of a reasonable person is sufficient for civil liability in the tort of negligence; but if the criminal law imposes liability for negligence, it sometimes requires 'gross' negligence—a very serious deviation from the required standard.

5.2 Intention

The word 'intention' and the phrase 'with intent to' are commonly found in the definition of offences. It is important to appreciate at the outset that if a bodily movement is voluntary, it could then be said that it is intended. The concern of this chapter is whether D intended the *consequences* of a particular act. Taking criminal damage as an example, it is necessary for D's conduct to have caused damage and for D to have done so intentionally or recklessly. As with many crimes there is also a mens rea requirement as to the circumstances: in criminal damage the property damaged must belong to another and D must have intended or been reckless as to whether it did.

A number of problems arise in the application of intention, in particular: (1) how is it to be defined; (2) can D be held to have intended result A when he sought only to achieve result B (which would almost inevitably result also in A)?

The current state of the law is:

(1) a result is intended when it is the actor's purpose to cause it;

(2) a court or jury *may also find* that a result is intended, though it is not the actor's purpose to cause it, when:

    (a) the result is a virtually certain consequence of that act, and

    (b) the actor knows that it is a virtually certain consequence.

There has been much controversy as to the proper legal meaning of intention. A variety of interpretations is possible. One of the reasons that there is still so much controversy is because the definition is central to serious offences such as murder. The courts struggle to define the boundaries of what types of behaviour they want that offence to include.

Two core definitions are debated. We could accept that D 'intends' a result only if:

the proscribed result is the 'purpose' or 'aim', that is, a *direct intention* of the accused;

or, in addition,

the proscribed result is foreseen by the accused as 'virtually certain' to occur or even just 'highly probable' to occur. This is called *oblique intention*.

With direct intention the focus is on D's purpose, not his desire or wish as to the consequences. D can intend by having a result as his purpose without desiring it, as where D gives V a lethal injection to put him out of his pain, but wishes he did not have to. Note also that the definition of intention is wider than 'premeditation' where that term is used to denote planning or calculated acts. Intention extends beyond those cases to include spontaneous conduct. Professor Duff has suggested that a way of testing whether D intended the outcome is to ask: would he regard himself as having failed if he did not achieve the result that he is alleged to have intended (eg death or GBH in murder)? (R. A. Duff, *Intention, Agency and Criminal Liability* (1990), p 61.) Another way of deciding whether D had direct intention might be to ask whether D acted *in order to bring about* the result.

With oblique intent, the idea is that a result is intended where it is not D's *purpose* but is foreseen by him as a *probable* result of his act. This raises several problems: should it be sufficient that D foresees the result as probable? If so, how probable must it be?

A majority of the House of Lords in *Hyam v DPP* [1975] AC 55 appeared to accept that it was sufficient to convict someone of murder (which requires proof of intent to kill or cause serious harm), if D saw either of those results as 'probable'.

In *Hyam*, D had poured petrol through her rival's letterbox in an effort to get her to leave the area so that D would have the undivided attentions of her lover. D claimed that she thought that the house was empty. It was not and children inside died. At the trial Ackner J directed the jury that a person has the mens rea of murder if, when he does the act which kills, he knows that it is highly probable that he will cause death or grievous bodily harm. His direction was held by the majority of the House of Lords to be correct as a definition of the mens rea for murder. However, the House did not provide a definition of intention. The speeches of the House of Lords are confusing. Lord Hailsham, one of the majority, emphatically said that this definition of the mens rea for murder was not the test of intention. Viscount Dilhorne and Lord Cross, though disposed to think that it did amount to intention, decided only that it was a sufficient mens rea for murder. The minority thought that mens rea for murder should extend to cases where D saw it as probable that he would cause death (but not where he saw only serious harm as probable). Lord Diplock (one of the minority), however, took a view of the *ratio decidendi* different from that stated above because he said in *Whitehouse; Lemon* [1979] AC 617 at 638:

What *R v Hyam* [*Hyam v DPP*] [1975] AC 55 confirmed is that the legal definition of intention includes two states of mind (1) where D did an act because he desired it to produce that particular result and (2) D who, when he did the act, was aware that it was likely to produce that result but was prepared to take the risk that it might do so, in order to achieve some other purpose which provided his motive for doing what he did.

In the next case, *Moloney*, the House began with the assumption that the mens rea of murder is an intention to kill or to cause grievous bodily harm. Consequently, the question in issue *was* the meaning of intention. The House of Lords held that the 'golden rule' is that the judge should avoid any elaboration on what is meant by intention, instead leaving the interpretation to the jury's good sense. The House of Lords was also keen to distinguish between the definition of intention as a matter of substantive criminal law and the evidence of such intention, which is a matter of proof. The court considered previous case law and the impact of s 8 of the Criminal Justice Act 1967:

A court or jury, in determining whether a person has committed an offence,—(a) shall not be bound in law to infer that he intended or foresaw a result of his actions by reasons only of its being a natural and probable consequence of those actions; but (b) shall decide whether he did intend or foresee that result by reference to all the evidence, drawing such inferences from the evidence as appear proper in the circumstances.

R v Moloney
[1984] UKHL 4, House of Lords

(Lord Hailsham LC, Lords Fraser, Edmund-Davies, Keith and Bridge)

The appellant (M) and his stepfather (S) drank heavily at a wedding anniversary party. After the rest of the family had gone to bed, M and S remained and were heard laughing and talking in an apparently friendly way until nearly 4 am when a shot rang out. M telephoned the police, saying, 'I've just murdered my father.' He stated that they had had a disagreement as to who was quicker at loading and firing a shotgun. At S's request he got two shotguns and cartridges. M was first to load. S said 'I didn't think you'd got the guts, but if you have pull the trigger.' M stated 'I didn't aim the gun. I just pulled the trigger and he was dead.'

M was convicted of murder and his appeal was dismissed by the Court of Appeal. He appealed to the House of Lords.

Lord Hailsham LC and Lords Fraser, Edmund-Davies and Keith said that they agreed with the speech of Lord Bridge.

[**Lord Bridge**, having held that the direction given by the trial judge, Stephen Brown J, was unsatisfactory and potentially misleading, continued:]

The golden rule should be that, when directing a jury on the mental element necessary in a crime of specific intent, the judge should avoid any elaboration or paraphrase of what is meant by intent, and leave it to the jury's good sense to decide whether the accused acted with the necessary intent, unless the judge is convinced that, on the facts and having regard to the way the case has been presented to the jury in evidence and argument, some further explanation or elaboration is strictly necessary to avoid misunderstanding. In trials for murder or wounding with intent, I find it very difficult to visualise a case where any such explanation or elaboration could be required, if the offence consisted of a direct attack on the victim with a weapon, except possibly the case where the accused shot at A and killed B, which any first year law student could explain to a jury in the simplest of terms. Even where the death results indirectly from the act of the accused, I believe the cases that will call for a direction by reference to foresight of consequences will be of extremely rare occurrence. I am in full agreement with the view expressed by Viscount Dilhorne that, in [*Hyam v DPP*] [1975] AC 55, 82 itself, if the issue of intent had been left without elaboration, no reasonable jury could have failed to convict.

I do not, of course, by what I have said in the foregoing paragraph, mean to question the necessity, which frequently arises, to explain to a jury that intention is something quite distinct from motive or desire. But this can normally be quite simply explained by reference to the case before the court or, if necessary, by some homely example. A man who, at London airport, boards a plane which he knows to be bound for Manchester, clearly intends to travel to Manchester, even though Manchester is the last place he wants to be and his motive for boarding the plane is simply to escape pursuit. The possibility that the plane may have engine trouble and be diverted to Luton does not affect the matter. By boarding the Manchester plane, the man conclusively demonstrates his intention to go there, because it is a moral certainty that that is where he will arrive . . .

[Rejecting the suggestion in *DPP v Smith* that the Act, to amount to murder, must be 'aimed at' someone, Lord Bridge continued:]

But what of the terrorist who plants a time bomb in a public building and gives timely warning to enable the public to be evacuated? Assume that he knows that, following evacuation, it is virtually certain that a bomb disposal squad will attempt to defuse the bomb. In the event the bomb explodes and kills a bomb disposal expert. In our present troubled times, this is an all too tragically realistic illustration. Can it, however, be said that in this case the bomb was 'aimed' at the bomb disposal expert? . . .

Starting from the proposition established by *R v Vickers* [1957] 2 All ER 741, [1957] 2 QB 664, as modified by *DPP v Smith* [1961] AC 290 that the mental element in murder requires proof of an intention to kill or cause really serious injury, the first fundamental question to be answered is whether there is any rule of substantive law that foresight by the accused of one of those eventualities as a probable consequence of his voluntary act, where the probability can be defined as exceeding a certain degree, is equivalent or alternative to the necessary intention. I would answer this question in the negative. . . .

I am firmly of opinion [*sic*] that foresight of consequences, as an element bearing on the issue of intention in murder, or indeed any other crime of specific intent, belongs, not to the substantive law, but to the law of evidence. Here again I am happy to find myself aligned with my noble and learned friend, Lord Hailsham of St Marylebone LC, in [*Hyam v DPP*] [1974] 2 All ER 41, [1975] AC 55, where he said, at p 65: 'Knowledge or foresight is at the best material which entitles or compels a jury to draw the necessary inference as to intention.' A rule of evidence which judges for more than a century found of the utmost utility in directing juries was expressed in the maxim: 'A man is presumed to intend the natural and probable consequences of his acts.' In *DPP v Smith* [1961] AC 290 your Lordships' House, by treating this rule of evidence as creating an irrebuttable presumption and thus elevating it, in effect, to the status of a rule of substantive law, predictably provoked the intervention of Parliament by section 8 of the Criminal Justice Act 1967 [this is set out earlier] to put the issue of intention back where it belonged, viz, in the hands of the jury, 'drawing such inferences from the evidence as appear proper in the circumstances.' I do not by any means take the conjunction of the verbs 'intended or foresaw' and 'intend or foresee' in that section as an indication that Parliament treated them as synonymous; on the contrary, two verbs were needed to connote two different states of mind.

I think we should now no longer speak of presumptions in this context but rather of inferences. In the old presumption that a man intends the natural and probable consequences of his acts the important word is 'natural'. This word conveys the idea that in the ordinary course of events a certain act will lead to a certain consequence unless something unexpected supervenes to prevent it. One might almost say that, if a consequence is natural, it is really otiose to speak of it as also being probable.

Section 8 of the Criminal Justice Act 1967 leaves us at liberty to go back to the decisions before that of this House in *DPP v Smith* [1961] AC 290 and it is here, I believe, that we can find a sure, clear, intelligible and simple guide to the kind of direction that should be given to a jury in the exceptional case where it is necessary to give guidance as to how, on the evidence, they should approach the issue of intent.

I know of no clearer exposition of the law than that in the judgment of the Court of Criminal Appeal (Lord Goddard CJ, Atkinson and Cassels JJ) delivered by Lord Goddard CJ in *R v Steane* [1947] KB 997 where he said, at p 1004:

> 'No doubt, if the prosecution prove an act the natural consequence of which would be a certain result and no evidence or explanation is given, then a jury may, on a proper direction, find that the prisoner is guilty of doing the act with the intent alleged, but if on the totality of the evidence there is room for more than one view as to the intent of the prisoner, the jury should be directed that it is for the prosecution to prove the intent to the jury's satisfaction, and if, on a review of the whole evidence, they either think that the intent did not exist or they are left in doubt as to the intent, the prisoner is entitled to be acquitted.'

In the rare cases in which it is necessary to direct a jury by reference to foresight of consequences, I do not believe it is necessary for the judge to do more than invite the jury to consider two questions. First, was death or really serious injury in a murder case (or whatever relevant consequence must be proved to have been intended in any other case) a natural consequence of the defendant's voluntary act? Secondly, did the defendant foresee that consequence as being a natural consequence of his act? The jury should then be told that if they answer yes to both questions it is a proper inference for them to draw that he intended that consequence.

Appeal allowed

≈≈ *Question*

Is Lord Bridge correct that the individual at London airport who boards the plane for Manchester intends to travel to Manchester even though it might be the last place he wants to be? Does the example elucidate the meaning of intention? Consider this question in light of the following extract.

R. Buxton, 'Some Simple Thoughts on Intention'
[1988] Crim LR 484

This example has attracted a good deal of criticism: the traveller can be said to desire to travel to Manchester (in order to escape his pursuers) just as much as to intend to travel there; the traveller wanted in one sense to go to Manchester rather than remain where he was; the traveller may, consistently with Lord Bridge's account, simply have boarded the first available plane, which raises difficulties about saying that he intended to travel to *Manchester*. The first two of these complaints may turn principally on the shifting meaning of the words 'desire' and 'want,' to which we have drawn attention above; but the real trouble about the example . . . is that, because it does not deal with any specifically criminal conduct, it does not focus on any defined consequence of the agent's actions as the subject of the description of his mental attitude.

Where the same events can be categorised under a series of equally valid descriptions (taking a flight; travelling to Manchester; escaping pursuit) the layman's difficulty, raised by Lord Bridge's example, of deciding which of those descriptions relates to the agent's intention and which to his motive is solved for the criminal lawyer by the definition of the crime with which the agent is charged. If, as Dr. Williams suggests [at (1987) 46 CLJ 433] in this context, one were dealing with an offence of taking a plane ticket with intent to travel to Manchester, it would be clear that the question was whether the agent's intention (purpose) in buying the ticket was to travel to Manchester, and equally clear that it would be no defence to such a charge that his reason or motive for that travel was to escape pursuit. But that, in itself, tells us nothing about the difference between intention and desire. What does illuminate that difference is the fact that intention in the law is confined to cases of the production by the agent of consequences specified in the definition of the crime with which he is charged, to which event or activity the language of purpose is appropriate but the language of desire may not be.

5.2.1 The extended definition of intention

Moloney tells us that in most cases the jury will need no explanation of 'intention'. However, in some cases an explanation will be needed and it is important that the law can provide a clear definition of what constitutes intention for those hard cases. We can now turn to consider the extended meaning of intention.

First, a result which is desired is intended, even though the actor knows that the chances of achieving it are remote. Because D *wants* to kill V, he takes great care in aiming a gun at him and pulling the trigger; but V is half a mile away and he knows his chances of hitting him are remote. Surely, he intends to kill V.

Secondly, a result which is known to be an inevitable concomitant of the desired result must also be intended. A much used illustration is that of D who plants a bomb in a plane, timed to explode in mid-Atlantic and destroy the cargo in order to enable him to obtain the insurance money. D wishes the crew no ill—he would be delighted if they should, by some miracle, escape—but he knows that, if his plan succeeds, their deaths are, for all practical purposes, inevitable. It is generally agreed that D intends to kill the crew. Suppose, however, that D knows that this particular type of bomb has a 50 per cent failure rate. There is an even chance that the bomb will not go off. He still intends to destroy the cargo because that is his purpose. Does it not follow that he also intends to kill the crew? This is neither a certain result nor a desired result but it appears to be enough that it is the inevitable concomitant of a desired result. Lord Bridge's terrorist of course wants the bomb to go off. If he wants it to go off at a time when he knows the bomb squad will be attempting to defuse it the case is indistinguishable from that of the bomb in the plane; but if he is merely indifferent as to whether the squad will be working on the bomb at the time, it is difficult to see that he intends to kill or injure them.

Although it is clear that those two instances fall within the extended definition of intention, the more general question of how that concept should be defined at the boundary with recklessness has remained problematic for the courts. The next case in the unravelling saga of the meaning of intention is *Hancock and Shankland* [1985] UKHL 9 in which the House of Lords sought to qualify and clarify what was said in *Moloney* about the extended definition of intention. Hancock (H) and Shankland (S) were miners on strike from work as part of a national strike of miners which led to numerous incidents of serious violence. They objected to a miner (X) going to work. X was going to work in a taxi driven by the deceased, Wilkie (W). H and S pushed a concrete block weighing 46 lb and a concrete post weighing 65 lb from a bridge over the road along which X was being driven by W with a police escort. The block struck the taxi's windscreen and killed W. H and S were prepared to plead guilty to manslaughter but the Crown decided to pursue the charge of murder. The defence was that H and S intended to block the road but not to kill or do serious bodily harm to anyone. Mann J directed the jury in accordance with the *Moloney* 'guidelines' (see section 5.2, p 84). H and S were convicted of murder. The Court of Appeal quashed their conviction. The Crown appealed to the House of Lords. Delivering a judgment with which the other Law Lords agreed, Lord Scarman held that the guidelines enunciated in *Moloney* were unsafe and misleading because they did not make reference to probability. This was a problem for the following reason:

> The greater the probability of a consequence the more likely it is that the consequence was foreseen and … if that consequence was foreseen the greater the probability is that the consequence was also intended … [T]he probability, however high, of a consequence is only a factor.

Lord Scarman also emphasized that juries needed to be reminded that the decision is theirs and must be reached upon consideration of all the evidence.

The next decisive step in the interpretation of the concept followed swiftly from the Court of Appeal as the Lord Chief Justice sought to clarify the meaning of intention for the assistance and guidance of the trial judges who must deal with these offences on a daily basis. The guidance is more practical than that provided by the House of Lords.

R v Nedrick
[1986] EWCA Crim 2, Court of Appeal, Criminal Division

(Lord Lane CJ, Leggatt and Kennedy JJ)

Nedrick, having threatened to 'burn out' a woman against whom he bore a grudge, poured paraffin through the letterbox of her house and set it alight. The woman's child died in the fire. Nedrick was charged with murder. The direction was given to the jury before the publication of the speeches in *Moloney*.

> **Lord Lane CJ:**
>
> We have endeavoured to crystallise the effect of their Lordships' speeches in *R v Moloney* and *R v Hancock* in a way which we hope may be helpful to judges who have to handle this type of case.
>
> It may be advisable first of all to explain to the jury that a man may intend to achieve a certain result whilst at the same time not desiring it to come about . . . [Lord Lane discussed Lord Bridge's illustration of the man boarding a plane at London Airport, section 5.2, p 85 and Lord Scarman's criticism of the *Moloney* guidelines in *Hancock*.]
>
> Where the charge is murder and in the rare cases where the simple direction is not enough, the jury should be directed that they are not entitled to infer the necessary intention unless they feel sure that death or serious bodily harm was a virtual certainty (barring some unforeseen intervention) as a result of the defendant's actions and that the defendant appreciated that such was the case.
>
> Where a man realises that it is for all practical purposes inevitable that his actions will result in death or serious harm, the inference may be irresistible that he intended that result, however little he may have desired or wished it to happen. The decision is one for the jury to be reached on a consideration of all the evidence.
>
> *Appeal allowed*

Glanville Williams was critical of the direction proposed by the Court of Appeal in *Nedrick* and identified a number of problems with it.

G. Williams, 'Oblique Intention'
(1987) 46 CLJ 417

> The practice proposed in one case by the Court of Appeal (referring to *Nedrick*), acting in the dim and delusive light of *Moloney*, was to tell the jury that a person may intend to achieve a certain result whilst

at the same time not desiring it to come about; they must not find that he intended the result merely because he foresaw it as probable; and if he thought that the risk of its happening was very slight, then it may be easy for them to conclude that he did not intend it; they are not entitled to infer the necessary intention unless they feel sure that the result was a virtual certainty (barring some unforeseen intervention) and the defendant appreciated this. Although this mode of instruction perhaps 'works' well enough, there are several objections to it.

(1) It unnecessarily mystifies the concept of intention (as Professor J. C. Smith has pointed out). The instruction leaves the legal notion of intention unexplained, telling the jury what the definition is not, without telling them what it is. The jury are instructed that they may infer this undefined and apparently unknowable entity from given facts, without informing them what is the thing that they are supposed to be inferring.

(2) This mystery-making occurs because the instruction fails to state that intention normally involves desire (alternatively expressed as purpose), the only exception being the case of realisation of virtual certainty. This exception apart, the test is: would the defendant have felt that he failed in his purpose if the expected result did not happen?

(3) The jury, having been told (i) that they 'must not' find intention merely because the defendant foresaw the result as probable, will be puzzled when they are then told (ii) that if the defendant foresaw a very slight risk of the result 'it may be easy' for them to conclude that he did not intend it. Proposition (ii) is merely a weaker case of (i), and in the absence of other clues to intent proposition (ii) should follow a *fortiori* from (i); they *must not.*

(4) The instruction misleadingly states that intention cannot be inferred unless the defendant appreciated that the result would be a virtual certainty. On the contrary, whenever it can be inferred from the evidence as a whole that the defendant desired the result to follow from his acts, this means that he intended it, whether he foresaw it as a virtual certainty or as any degree of probability down to an outside chance. The judges disable themselves from giving the jury this clear instruction because for obscure reasons they balk at acknowledging the significance of desire (or purpose) in the concept of intention.

The approach in *Nedrick* was finally endorsed with some minor alteration by the House of Lords to provide us with the latest and most authoritative judicial explanation of the meaning of intention.

R v Woollin
[1998] UKHL 28, House of Lords

(Lords Browne-Wilkinson, Nolan, Steyn, Hoffmann and Hope of Craighead)

W lost his temper and threw his three-month-old son on to a hard surface, killing him. It was not alleged that W intended to kill; the issue was as to intention to cause serious harm. The appellant denied that he had any such intention.

Giving the judgment of the Court of Appeal, Roch LJ observed about *Nedrick* that:

although the use of the phrase 'a virtual certainty' may be desirable and may be necessary, it is only necessary where the evidence of intent is limited to the admitted actions of the accused and the consequences of those actions. It is not obligatory to use that phrase or one that means the same thing in cases such as the present where there is other evidence for the jury to consider.

Lord Steyn delivered the principal speech with which Lords Nolan and Hope agreed. Lords Browne-Wilkinson and Hoffmann also agreed that the appeal should be allowed.

Lord Steyn reviewed the cases leading up to the decision in *Nedrick*:]

The direct attack on *Nedrick*

It is now possible to consider the Crown's direct challenge to the correctness of *R v Nedrick*. First, the Crown argued that *R v Nedrick* prevents the jury from considering all the evidence in the case relevant to intention. The argument is that this is contrary to the provisions of s 8 of the 1967 Act. [His lordship quoted the provisions of the Act set out in section 5.2, p 84.]

Paragraph (a) is an instruction to the judge and is not relevant to the issues on this appeal. The Crown's argument relied on para (b), which is concerned with the function of the jury. It is no more than a legislative instruction that in considering their findings on intention or foresight the jury must take into account all relevant evidence: see Professor Edward Griew 'States of mind, presumptions and inferences' in *Criminal Law: Essays in Honour of J C Smith* (1987) pp 68, 76–77. *R v Nedrick* is undoubtedly concerned with the mental element which is sufficient for murder. So, for that matter, in their different ways were *Smith, Hyam, Moloney* and *Hancock*. But, as Lord Lane CJ emphasised in the last sentence of *R v Nedrick* [1986] 3 All ER 1 at 4: 'The decision is one for the jury to be reached on a consideration of all the evidence.' *R v Nedrick* does not prevent a jury from considering all the evidence: it merely stated what state of mind (in the absence of a purpose to kill or to cause serious harm) is sufficient for murder. I would therefore reject the Crown's first argument.

In the second place the Crown submitted that *R v Nedrick* is in conflict with the decision of the House in *R v Hancock*. Counsel argued that in order to bring some coherence to the process of determining intention Lord Lane CJ specified a minimum level of foresight, namely virtual certainty. But that is not in conflict with the decision in *R v Hancock*, which, apart from disapproving Lord Bridge's 'natural consequence' model direction, approved *R v Moloney* in all other respects. And in *R v Moloney* [1985] 1 All ER 1025 at 1036 Lord Bridge said that if a person foresees the probability of a consequence as little short of overwhelming this 'will suffice to *establish* the necessary intent' (my emphasis). Nor did the House in *R v Hancock* rule out the framing of model directions by the Court of Appeal for the assistance of trial judges. I would therefore reject the argument that the guidance given in *R v Nedrick* was in conflict with the decision of the House in *R v Hancock*.

The Crown did not argue that as a matter of policy foresight of a virtual certainty is too narrow a test in murder. Subject to minor qualifications, the decision in *R v Nedrick* was widely welcomed by distinguished academic writers: see Professor J C Smith QC's commentary on *R v Nedrick* [1986] Crim LR 742 at 743–744, Glanville Williams 'The mens rea for murder: leave it alone' (1989) 105 LQR 387, J R Spencer 'Murder in the dark: a glimmer of light?' [1986] CLJ 366–367 and Ashworth *Principles of Criminal Law* (2nd edn, 1995) p 172. It is also of interest that it is very similar to the threshold of being aware that it *will* occur 'in the ordinary course of events' in the Law Commission's draft Criminal Code (see *Criminal Law: Legislating the Criminal Code: Offences against the Person and General Principles* (Law Com No 218 (1993) (Cm 2370), App A (Draft Criminal Law Bill with Explanatory Notes) pp 90–91): cf also Professor J C Smith QC 'A note on "intention" ' [1990] Crim LR 85 at 86. Moreover, over a period of 12 years since *R v Nedrick* the test of foresight of virtual certainty has apparently caused no practical difficulties. It is simple and clear. It is true that it may exclude a conviction of murder in the often cited terrorist example where a member of the bomb disposal team is killed. In such a case it may realistically be said that the terrorist did not foresee the killing of a member of the bomb disposal team as a virtual certainty. That may be a consequence of not framing the principle in terms of risk-taking. Such cases ought to cause no substantial difficulty since immediately below murder there is available a verdict of manslaughter which may attract in the discretion of the court a life sentence. In any event, as Lord Lane eloquently argued in a debate in the House of Lords, to frame a principle for particular difficulties regarding terrorism 'would produce corresponding injustices which would be very hard to eradicate' (see 512 HL Official Report (5th series) col 480). I am satisfied that the *Nedrick* test, which was squarely based on the decision of the House in *R v Moloney*, is pitched at the right level of foresight.

The argument that *Nedrick* has limited application

The Court of Appeal ([1997] 1 Cr App R 97 at 107) held that the phrase 'a virtual certainty' should be confined to cases where the evidence of intent is limited to admitted actions of the accused and the consequences of those actions. It is not obligatory where there is other evidence to consider. The Crown's alternative submission on the appeal was to the same effect. This distinction would introduce yet another complication into a branch of the criminal law where simplicity is of supreme importance. The distinction is dependent on the vagaries of the evidence in particular cases. Moreover, a jury may reject the other evidence to which the Court of Appeal refers. And in preparing his summing up a judge could not ignore this possibility. If the Court of Appeal's view is right, it might compel a judge to pose different tests depending on what evidence the jury accepts. For my part, and with the greatest respect, I have to say that this distinction would be likely to produce great practical difficulties. But, most importantly, the distinction is not based on any principled view regarding the mental element in murder. Contrary to the view of the Court of Appeal, I would also hold that s 8(b) of the 1967 Act does not compel such a result.

In my view the ruling of the Court of Appeal was wrong. It may be appropriate to give a direction in accordance with *R v Nedrick* in any case in which the defendant may not have desired the result of his act. But I accept that the trial judge is best placed to decide what direction is required by the circumstances of the case.

[Lord Steyn said that the conviction of murder was unsafe and must be quashed.]

The status of *Nedrick*

In my view Lord Lane CJ's judgment in *R v Nedrick* provided valuable assistance to trial judges. The model direction is by now a tried and tested formula. Trial judges ought to continue to use it. On matters of detail I have three observations, which can best be understood if I set out again the relevant part of Lord Lane CJ's judgment. It was:

'(A) When determining whether the defendant had the necessary intent, it may therefore be helpful for a jury to ask themselves two questions. (1) How probable was the consequence which resulted from the defendant's voluntary act? (2) Did he foresee that consequence? If he did not appreciate that death or serious harm was likely to result from his act, he cannot have intended to bring it about. If he did, but thought that the risk to which he was exposing the person killed was only slight, then it may be easy for the jury to conclude that he did not intend to bring about that result. On the other hand, if the jury are satisfied that at the material time the defendant recognised that death or serious harm would be virtually certain (barring some unforeseen intervention) to result from his voluntary act, then that is a fact from which they may find it easy to infer that he intended to kill or do serious bodily harm, even though he may not have had any desire to achieve that result . . . (B) Where the charge is murder and in the rare cases where the simple direction is not enough, the jury should be directed that they are not entitled to infer the necessary intention unless they feel sure that death or serious bodily harm was a virtual certainty (barring some unforeseen intervention) as a result of the defendant's actions and that the defendant appreciated that such was the case. (C) Where a man realises that it is for all practical purposes inevitable that his actions will result in death or serious harm, the inference may be irresistible that he intended that result, however little he may have desired or wished it to happen. The decision is one for the jury to be reached on a consideration of all the evidence.' (See [1986] 3 All ER 1 at 3–4.)

First, I am persuaded by the speech of my noble and learned friend Lord Hope of Craighead that it is unlikely, if ever, to be helpful to direct the jury in terms of the two questions set out in (A). I agree that these questions may detract from the clarity of the critical direction in (B). Secondly, in their writings previously cited Glanville Williams, Professor Smith and Andrew Ashworth observed that the use of the words 'to infer' in (B) may detract from the clarity of the model direction. I agree. I would substitute the words 'to find'. Thirdly, the first sentence of (C) does not form part of the model direction. But it would always be right for the just to say, as Lord Lane CJ put it, that the decision is for the jury upon a consideration of all the evidence in the case.

≈ *Questions*
(1) The House rejects 'infer' in favour of 'find'. Is there any difference?
(2) Has the House of Lords defined intention as a matter of criminal law? If so, what is the test that must be applied?
(3) Did the House simply allow 'intention' to go undefined but accept that as a matter of evidence it can be inferred from foresight?

5.2.2 Inferring intention from foresight

The notion that intention can be inferred from foresight goes back at least to Lord Hailsham's speech in *Hyam*. In *Moloney* (section 5.2, p 84), Lord Bridge seemed to think that the notion derived support from s 8 of the Criminal Justice Act 1967. What the section says is that the court or jury must decide whether D 'did intend or foresee that result, drawing such inferences from the evidence as appear proper in the circumstances'.

'The evidence', it seems, is the nature of the act done by D and the relevant circumstances in which it was done—all objective facts. Depending on the nature of those facts, a court or jury might conclude that:

(1) D wanted to cause that result—it was his aim, object or purpose; or

(2) though he did not want to cause that result:

   (a) he foresaw that he would do so—it was certain or virtually certain to happen; or

   (b) he foresaw that he might—it was (i) highly probable, or (ii) probable, or at least (iii) possible.

None of these alternatives involves inferring one state of mind from another—a notion which some regard as impossible. The question in practice is whether the legal definition of intention should be limited to (1) and (2)(a) or extends to (2)(b)(i) or (ii) or (iii).

At one point in his speech Lord Steyn said 'The effect of the critical direction [in *Nedrick*] is that a result foreseen as virtually certain *is* an intended result' (emphasis in original). Is this what intention means in the non-legal context? There are some who argue that the plain meaning of intention has been distorted in order to ensure those who intuition tells us ought to be guilty of murder are in fact guilty of that offence, as the following extract explains.

R. Goff, 'The Mental Element in the Crime of Murder'
(1988) 104 LQR 30

The narrowing down of the mental element in murder to the concept of 'intention' has generally been welcomed by jurists. But they are discovering that some cases, which they *feel* ought to be embraced within the crime of murder, do not quite fit within the concept of intention; and so they are embarking on the enterprise of illegitimately expanding the concept of intention to include these cases. The classic example of this technique is to be found in the idea of 'oblique' intent as expounded by Professor Glanville Williams in his *Textbook of Criminal Law*.

. . .

Now I have to confess that, as soon as somebody starts using an expression like 'oblique intention,' I become suspicious; because I suspect that it is only necessary to use the rather mysterious adjective 'oblique' to bring within 'intention' something which is not intention at all. And that is exactly what is happening here. For the trouble with this kind of approach is that it has distorted the plain meaning of the word. To the [example of the plane bomber]—did the defendant mean to destroy the parcel? The answer is, of course, yes, he did. But to the question—did the defendant mean to kill the pilot? The answer is, no, he didn't. Indeed, if he saw the pilot safely descending by parachute, he would no doubt be delighted; and so it is absurd to say that he meant to kill him. Of course, if the pilot is killed by the explosion, I share Professor Glanville Williams' *feeling* that the defendant can properly be called a murderer; but I do not think that that result can be achieved by artificially expanding the meaning of the word 'intention.' Quite apart from anything else, it can only lead to difficulties in directing juries. In a jury system, it is far better, if you can, to use a word in its plain and ordinary meaning. And you do not intend something merely because you know that it is virtually certain to happen.

Following the decision in *Woollin* there remained uncertainty over whether the House of Lords had defined intention as a matter of law or merely provided guidance on what was sufficient evidence from which to infer that state of mind. This distinction is important. If the House of Lords merely provided guidance, then a jury would not be bound to find that D intended the prohibited consequence, even though he might have appreciated that it was virtually certain. In the following case, the Court of Appeal clarified this aspect of the law.

Matthews and Alleyne

[2003] 2 Cr App R 30, [2003] Crim LR 553, Court of Appeal, Criminal Division

(Rix LJ, Crane J and Maddison HHJ)

M and A were convicted of the robbery, kidnapping and murder of Jonathan (J). J was attacked on leaving a club in the early hours of the morning, and ultimately thrown off a bridge 25 feet high into a river 64 feet wide. J could not swim and drowned. A co-accused gave evidence that J had said he could not swim. One ground of appeal was that the judge had directed the jury that foresight of virtual certainty of consequences *was* intention.

Rix LJ [His lordship reviewed the facts and positions taken by the various co-defendants:]

25. The essential ground of appeal argued on behalf of both Alleyne and Matthews is that the judges' direction on intent was a misdirection, and that in consequence their convictions for murder are unsafe. . . .

. . .

39. Mr Coker for the Crown on this appeal submits that in *Woollin* the House of Lords has finally moved away from a rule of evidence to a rule of substantive law. In this connection he drew attention to a sentence in Lord Steyn's speech at pp.17 and 93F where he says, immediately after setting out Lord Lane's observations in *Nedrick*, that the effect of the critical direction is that a result foreseen as virtually certain is an intended result.

40. We also relies on what Professor Sir John Smith has to say in his note on *R. v Woollin* [1998] Crim LR 890 and in Smith and Hogan, *Criminal Law*, 10th edition [2002], at 70ff. Thus in the former, Professor Smith said this:

'A jury might still fairly ask: We are all quite sure that D knew that it was virtually certain that his act would cause death. You tell us we are entitled to find that he intended it. Are we bound to find that? Some of us want to and some do not. How should we decide? The implication appears to be that, even now, they are not so bound. But why not? At one point Lord Steyn says of *Nedrick* "The effect of the critical direction is that a result foreseen as virtually certain is an intended result". If that is right, the only question for the jury is, Did the defendant foresee the result as virtually certain? If he did, he intended it. That, it is submitted is what the law should be; and it now seems that we have at last moved substantially in that direction. The *Nedrick* formula, however, even as modified (entitled to find), involves some ambiguity with the hint of the existence of some ineffable, undefinable, notion of intent, locked in the breasts of the jurors.'

41. Moreover, in the latter treatise (at 72) Professor Smith cites Lord Lane speaking in the debate on the report of the House of Lords Select Committee on Murder (HL Paper, 78-I, 1989) as follows:

'in *Nedrick* the court was obliged to phrase matters as it did because of earlier decisions in your Lordships House by which it was bound. We had to tread very gingerly indeed in order not to tread on your Lordships toes. As a result, *Nedrick* was not as clear as it should have been. However, I agree with the conclusions of the committee that intention should be defined in the terms set out in para.195 of the report on p.50. That seems to me to express clearly what in Nedrick we failed properly to explain.'

42. The definition referred to, as *Smith and Hogan* goes on to explain, is that stated in cl.18(b) of the Draft Code (itself referred to by Lord Steyn in *Woollin*) as follows:

'A person acts intentionally with respect to a result when he acts either in order to bring it about or being aware that it will occur in the ordinary course of events.'

43. In our judgment, however, the law has not yet reached a definition of intent in murder in terms of appreciation of a virtual certainty. Lord Lane was speaking not of what was decided in *Nedrick* (or in the other cases which preceded it) nor of what was thereafter to be decided in *Woollin*, but of what the law in his opinion should be, as represented by the cl.18(b) definition. Similarly, although the law has progressively moved closer to what Professor Smith has been advocating (see his commentaries in the Criminal Law Review on the various cases discussed above), we do not regard *Woollin* as yet reaching or laying down a substantive rule of law. On the contrary, it is clear from the discussion in *Woollin* as a whole that *Nedrick* was derived from the existing law, at that time ending in *Moloney and Hancock*, and that the critical direction in *Nedrick* was approved, subject to the change of one word.

44. In these circumstances we think that the judge did go further than the law as it stands at present permitted him to go in redrafting the *Nedrick/Woollin* direction into a form where, as Mr Coker accepts (although we have some doubt about this), the jury were directed to find the necessary intent proved provided they were satisfied in the case of any defendant that there was appreciation of the virtual certainty of death. This is to be contrasted with the form of the approved direction which is in terms of not entitled to find the necessary intention, unless.

45. Having said that, however, we think that, once what is required is an appreciation of virtual certainty of death, and not some lesser foresight of merely probable consequences, there is very little to choose between a rule of evidence and one of substantive law. It is probably this thought that led Lord Steyn to say that a result foreseen as virtually certain is an intended result. Lord Bridge had reflected the same thought when he had said, in *R. v Moloney* (1985) 81 Cr.App.R. 93, 101, [1985] AC 905, 920C, that if the defendant there had had present to his mind, when he pulled the trigger, that his gun was pointing at his stepfathers head at a distance of six feet and its inevitable consequence, then the inference was inescapable, using words in their ordinary, everyday meaning, that he intended to kill his stepfather. Lord Lane had also spoken in *Nedrick* of an irresistible inference.

46. We also think that on the particular facts of this case, reflected in the judges directions, the question of the appellants [*sic*] intentions to save Jonathan from drowning highlight the irresistible nature of the inference or finding of intent to kill, once the jury were sure both that the defendants appreciated the virtual certainty of death (barring some attempt to save him) and that at the time of

throwing Jonathan from the bridge they then had no intentions of saving him. If the jury were sure that the appellants appreciated the virtual certainty of Jonathan's death when they threw him from the bridge and also that they then had no intention of saving him from such death, it is impossible to see how the jury could not have found that the appellants intended Jonathan to die. . . .

Appeal dismissed

In *MD* [2004] EWCA Crim 1391 (at [29]), the Court of Appeal described oblique intention as:

designed to help the prosecution fill a gap in the rare circumstances in which a defendant does an act which caused death without the purpose of killing or causing serious injury, but in circumstances where death or serious bodily harm had been a virtual certainty (barring some unforeseen intervention) as a result of the defendant's action and the defendant had appreciated that such was the case. *Woollin* is not designed to make the prosecution's task more difficult. Many murderers whose purpose was to kill or cause serious injury would escape conviction if the jury was only given a *Woollin* direction. The man who kills another with a gun would be able to escape liability for murder if he could show [this seems to be an error and the court can be presumed to mean the prosecution show] that he was such a bad shot that death or serious bodily harm was not a virtual certainty or that the defendant had thought that death or serious bodily harm was not a virtual certainty.

In *Allen* [2005] EWCA Crim 1344, the Court of Appeal emphasized (at [63]) that it 'is only in an exceptional case that the extended direction by reference to foresight becomes necessary'. The further explanation must be provided only where the judge thinks it necessary to avoid misunderstanding.

When the oblique intention direction is delivered, what should a judge say to a jury who ask—'what are we seeking to "find" which may turn this state of mind of foresight of virtual certainty into one of intention?' Is the answer that they should look for some indefinable moral aspect to the state of mind?

In *Stringer* [2008] EWCA Crim 1222, M, aged 14, was alleged to have started a fire in his family home early one morning and walked off, knowing that five occupants were asleep upstairs. The issue at trial was as to the admissibility of interviews with him in which he was asked about whether he realized it was certain that people would die or be seriously injured if there was a fire started in the hallway when they were asleep. The Court of Appeal upheld the conviction:

if the jury were satisfied (as they must have been) that M started the fire after putting accelerant at the foot of the stairs, that he watched it take hold and then walked away, there could be only one answer to the question whether in fact it was a virtual certainty that somebody in the house would suffer really serious harm or death from M's actions. It would be wholly unrealistic to imagine all the occupants escaping from the house by jumping from the upstairs windows without any of them suffering any serious harm. This must have been obvious to any ordinary person at the time. Even taking account of M's age and the fact that his IQ was low/average, the inference that he must have appreciated it on that morning was also overwhelming. On the facts as the jury must have found them, the conclusion that M had the necessary intent was bound to follow.

~~~ **Question**

Dan plants a bomb in a public space and sets it to detonate. He rings the local police and gives them a 15-minute warning to clear the building in which the bomb is planted. The police clear the building in 10 minutes and Victor, a bomb disposal expert, enters the building immediately to defuse the device. It explodes four minutes earlier than D had designed. The blast kills Victor and Fred, a homeless man who had been asleep under one of the seating areas in the building and who was unaware of the evacuation. How would you direct the jury on the matter of intention at Dan's trial for the murder of Victor and Fred?

5.2.3 Cases in which intention is aligned with purpose

Despite the fact that we have just been discussing how the meaning of 'intent' in the criminal law has been accepted by the highest courts on numerous occasions to be broader than purpose, in some cases the definition or application of the concept of intention has been aligned with purpose. In such cases, D's conviction has been quashed because it was not his purpose to cause the prohibited outcome even though it was virtually certain and D knew this to be the case. In *R v Steane* [1947] 1 All ER 813, for example, D made radio broadcasts for the enemy and was convicted of doing acts likely to assist the enemy with intent to assist the enemy. He did so because he was threatened that if he did not he and his family would be sent to a concentration camp. D claimed he had no intention of assisting the enemy and what he did was done to save his wife and children. The Court of Criminal Appeal quashed D's conviction even though D knew that his purpose, ensuring he and his family were spared being sent to a concentration camp, could only be achieved by making the radio broadcasts.

Steane is by no means the only case in which 'intent' is construed to mean, in effect, purpose. In *Burke* [1988] Crim LR 839, CA, it was held that a person commits an offence under s 1(3) of the Protection from Eviction Act 1977 when he does an act with intent to cause a residential occupier to give up the occupation of premises although the act (storage of furniture in a bathroom), when done without any such intention, is an act which he is perfectly entitled to do. The act must be one which is 'calculated'—meaning 'likely'—to interfere with the peace or comfort of the residential occupier, but that is the sole requirement of the actus reus. The essence of the offence is the intent with which the act is done.

To take a more recent example, in *R (Nicklinson) v Ministry of Justice* [2014] UKSC 38, Lord Neuberger stated that, 'a doctor commits no offence when treating a patient in a way which hastens death, if the purpose of the treatment is to relieve pain and suffering'. This remains the case despite the fact the treatment will inevitably hasten death.

5.2.4 Reform of the law concerning intention

Since *Nedrick* the law concerning intention has been considered on numerous occasions by various bodies. The Law Commission Report on Codification (April 1989) proposed a definition which would apply, unless the context otherwise requires, to all code offences which require proof of intention. A Select Committee of the House of Lords on Murder and Life Imprisonment (Nathan Committee, HL Paper 78–1, 24 July 1989) recommended that, for the purposes of the law of murder (the only offence within the Committee's terms of reference), intention should be defined on the lines proposed in the Codification Report. The Law Commission returned to the topic in its Report No 304 on *Murder, Manslaughter and Infanticide* (2006).

The Law Commission's homicide review led it to consider a number of proposals in relation to intention. In Consultation Paper No 177, *A New Homicide Act for England and Wales* (2006), Chs 3 and 4, the Commission offered two models for consideration, one based on the clauses above, and one seeking to codify the common law position as set out in *Woollin* (section 5.2.1). The proposal to provide a definition of 'intentionally' for the offence of murder, was as follows:

> Subject to the proviso set out below:
> a person acts 'intentionally' with respect to a result when he or she acts either:
>
> (1) in order to bring it about, or
>
> (2) knowing that it will be virtually certain to occur; or
>
> (3) knowing that it would be virtually certain to occur if he or she were to succeed in his or her purpose of causing some other result.
>
> Proviso: a person is not to be deemed to have intended any result, which it was his or her specific purpose to avoid.

This proposal was criticized by commentators including Alan Norrie, 'Between Orthodox Subjectivism and Moral Contextualism' [2006] Crim LR 486 who argued that it included a concealed defence of necessity. Following consultation the Law Commission provisionally rejected the proposal to define, preferring to retain the flexibility inherent in the present law (in the moral elbow room it provides).

The Law Commission finally settled on the following recommendation (Law Com Report No 304, Ch 4):

> We recommend that the existing law governing the meaning of intention is codified as follows:
>
> (1) A person should be taken to intend a result if he or she acts in order to bring it about.
>
> (2) In cases where the judge believes that justice may not be done unless an expanded understanding of intention is given, the jury should be directed as follows: an intention to bring about a result may be found if it is shown that the defendant thought that the result was a virtually certain consequence of his or her action.

This definition removes the unnecessary requirement that the result was a virtual certainty.

5.3 Recklessness

Recklessness is a form of mens rea which is generally considered less blameworthy than intention. It usually describes the state of mind of someone who has seen a risk of the proscribed result arising and has gone on, unreasonably, to take the risk.

For most of the last century the law seemed settled. The leading case was *Cunningham* [1957] QB 396, in which Byrne J held that recklessness meant that, 'the accused has foreseen that the particular kind of harm might be done and yet has gone on to take the risk of it'. This definition confirmed that the test for establishing recklessness had two important features. First, the test was subjective. D could only be reckless if he foresaw the risk. If D did not foresee the risk, he could not be reckless, no matter how obvious it might have been to others. Secondly, to be reckless, D need only foresee the existence of *a* risk. The risk did not need to be highly likely to occur.

In the last 30 years, recklessness has become one of the most hotly debated issues in criminal law in England and Wales. As this section will demonstrate, the orthodox understanding of recklessness has been challenged in the years since *Cunningham* was decided.

5.3.1 The rise and fall of objective recklessness

Despite the court confirming in *Cunningham* that recklessness connotes a subjective standard, the majority of the House of Lords in *Caldwell* [1982] AC 341 ruled:

> a person charged with an offence under s 1(1) of the 1971 Act is 'reckless as to whether or not any property would be destroyed or damaged' if (1) he does an act which in fact creates an obvious risk that property will be destroyed or damaged and (2) when he does the act he either has not given any thought to the possibility of there being any such risk or has recognised that there was some risk involved and has none the less gone on to do it.

The direction in *Caldwell* represented a significant departure from the test for recklessness that was enunciated in *Cunningham*. This is because, applying *Caldwell*, a person could be reckless despite the fact he did not foresee the existence of the risk. The law shifted from a subjective to an objective test. An individual could therefore be guilty so long as a reasonable person would have foreseen the risk, despite the fact D himself did not. The potential unfairness of this test is acutely demonstrated by the case of *Elliott v C* [1983] 2 All ER 1005. D, a 14-year-old girl with learning difficulties, set fire to a shed by lighting white spirit. The court confirmed that, applying *Caldwell*, D was guilty because the question that needed to be asked was not whether D foresaw the risk of damage to the shed, but whether a reasonable person would have foreseen the risk. As D failed to consider the risk, and it would have been obvious to a reasonable person, she was guilty. This is particularly unfair, given that D's age and learning difficulties may have meant that she was incapable of appreciating the risk. D was therefore being punished for failing to foresee a risk that she may have been incapable of foreseeing.

The House of Lords in *G* [2003] UKHL 50, a landmark decision, overturned *Caldwell* and set the law back on its subjective path.

R v G and another
[2003] UKHL 50, House of Lords

(Lords Bingham of Cornhill, Browne-Wilkinson, Steyn, Hutton and Rodger of Earlsferry)

G and R, aged 11 and 12, went camping without their parents' permission. During the night they set fire to newspapers in the yard at the back of a shop and threw the lit newspapers under a wheelie bin. They left without putting out the fire. The fire spread to the wheelie bin and to the shop causing £1m worth of damage. The boys' case was that they expected the newspapers to burn themselves out on the concrete floor. Neither appreciated the risk of the fire spreading as it did. They were charged with arson contrary to s 1(1) and (3) of the 1971 Act. The judge directed the jury in accordance with *Caldwell* [1982] AC 341, expressing reservations about that being a harsh test. The Court of Appeal upheld the convictions stating that *Caldwell* had been rightly applied and certified the issue of recklessness as one of general public importance.

Lord Bingham of Cornhill:

1. My Lords, the point of law of general public importance certified by the Court of Appeal to be involved in its decision in the present case is expressed in this way:

> 'Can a defendant properly be convicted under s 1 of the Criminal Damage Act 1971 on the basis that he was reckless as to whether property was destroyed or damaged when he gave no thought to the risk but, by reason of his age and/or personal characteristics, the risk would not have been obvious to him, even if he had thought about it?'

The appeal turns on the meaning of 'reckless' in that section. This is a question on which the House ruled in *R v Caldwell* [1981] 1 All ER 961, [1982] AC 341, a ruling affirmed by the House in later decisions. The House is again asked to reconsider that ruling.

[His lordship referred to the facts, the trial judge's direction on the law and then examined the historical background to the 1971 Act.]

14. Enactment of the 1971 Act did not at once affect the courts' approach to the causing of unintentional damage. In *R v Briggs* [1977] 1 All ER 475, [1977] 1 WLR 605 the defendant had been charged under s 1(1) of the 1971 Act as a result of damage caused to a car and the appeal turned on the trial judge's direction on the meaning of 'reckless'. The appeal succeeded since the judge had not adequately explained that the test to be applied was that of the defendant's state of mind. The Court of Appeal (James LJ, Kenneth Jones and Peter Pain JJ) ruled ([1977] 1 All ER 475 at 477–478, [1977] 1 WLR 605 at 608):

'A man is reckless in the sense required when he carries out a deliberate act knowing that there is some risk of damage resulting from that act but nevertheless continues in the performance of that act.'

This definition was adopted but modified in *R v Parker* [1977] 2 All ER 37, [1977] 1 WLR 600 where the defendant in a fit of temper had broken a telephone by smashing the handset violently down on to the telephone unit and had been convicted under s 1(1) of the 1971 Act. The court (Scarman and Geoffrey Lane LJJ and Kenneth Jones J) ([1977] 2 All ER 37 at 39–40, [1977] 1 WLR 600 at 603–604) readily followed *R v Briggs* but held that the defendant had been fully aware of all the circumstances and that if—

'he did not know, as he said he did not, that there was some risk of damage, he was, in effect, deliberately closing his mind to the obvious-the obvious being that damage in these circumstances was inevitable.'

The court accordingly modified the *R v Briggs* definition in this way:

'A man is reckless in the sense required when he carries out a deliberate act knowing or closing his mind to the obvious fact that there is some risk of damage resulting from that act but nevertheless continuing in the performance of that act.'

This modification made no inroad into the concept of recklessness as then understood since, as pointed out by Professor Glanville Williams *Textbook of Criminal Law* (1st edn, 1978) p 79, cited by Lord Edmund-Davies in his dissenting opinion in *R v Caldwell* [1981] 1 All ER 961 at 970, [1982] AC 341 at 358:

'A person cannot, in any intelligible meaning of the words, close his mind to a risk unless he first realises that there is a risk; and if he realises that there is a risk, that is the end of the matter.'

15. The meaning of 'reckless' in s 1(1) of the 1971 Act was again considered by the Court of Appeal (Geoffrey Lane LJ, Ackner and Watkins JJ) in *R v Stephenson* [1979] 2 All ER 1198, [1979] QB 695. The defendant had tried to go to sleep in a hollow he had made in the side of a haystack. Feeling cold, he had lit a fire in the hollow which had set fire to the stack and damaged property worth £3,500. He had been charged and convicted under s 1(1) and (3) of the 1971 Act. The defendant however had a long history of schizophrenia and expert evidence at trial suggested that he may not have had the same ability to foresee or appreciate risks as the mentally normal person. Giving the reserved judgment of the court, Geoffrey Lane LJ ([1979] 2 All ER 1198 at 1201–1203, [1979] QB 695 at 700–703) reviewed the definition of recklessness in the Law Commission's Working Paper No 31, the acceptance of that definition by the leading academic authorities and the House of Lords' adoption of a subjective meaning of recklessness in tort in *British Railways Board v Herrington* [1972] 1 All ER 749, [1972] AC 877. The

court thought it fair to assume that those who were responsible for drafting the 1971 Act were intending to preserve its legal meaning as described in Kenny and expressly approved in *R v Cunningham*. The court then continued:

'What then must the prosecution prove in order to bring home the charge of arson in circumstances such as the present? They must prove that (1) the defendant deliberately committed some act which caused the damage to property alleged or part of such damage; (2) the defendant had no lawful excuse for causing the damage (these two requirements will in the ordinary case not be in issue); (3) the defendant either (a) intended to cause the damage to the property, or (b) was reckless whether the property was damaged or not. A man is reckless when he carries out the deliberate act appreciating that there is a risk that damage to property may result from his act. It is however not the taking of every risk which could properly be classed as reckless. The risk must be one which it is in all the circumstances unreasonable for him to take. Proof of the requisite knowledge in the mind of the defendant will in most cases present little difficulty. The fact that the risk of some damage would have been obvious to anyone in his right mind in the position of the defendant is not conclusive proof of the defendant's knowledge, but it may well be, and in many cases doubtless will be, a matter which will drive the jury to the conclusion that the defendant himself must have appreciated the risk.'

The appeal was accordingly allowed. But the court recognised that what it called the subjective definition of recklessness produced difficulties. One of these was where a person by self-induced intoxication deprived himself of the ability to foresee the risks involved in his actions. The court suggested that a distinction was to be drawn between crimes requiring proof of specific intent and those, such as offences under s 1(1) of the 1971 Act, involving no specific intent ([1979] 2 All ER 1198 at 1204, [1979] QB 695 at 704) [see Chapter 25]:

'Accordingly it is no defence under the 1971 Act for a person to say that he was deprived by self-induced intoxication of the ability to foresee or appreciate an obvious risk.'

≈≈ *Questions*

Was Stephenson capable of appreciating the risk of the harm he caused? Was Briggs? Was Parker?

[His lordship continued by discussing *R v Caldwell* [1982] UKHL 1:]

17. *R v Caldwell* [1981] 1 All ER 961, [1982] AC 341 was a case of self-induced intoxication. The defendant, having a grievance against the owner of the hotel where he worked, got very drunk and set fire to the hotel where guests were living at the time. He was indicted upon two counts of arson. The first and more serious count was laid under s 1(2) of the 1971 Act, the second count under s 1(1). He pleaded guilty to the second count but contested the first on the ground that he had been so drunk at the time that the thought there might be people in the hotel had never crossed his mind. His conviction on count 1 was set aside by the Court of Appeal which certified the following question ([1981] 1 All ER 961 at 964, [1982] AC 341 at 344):

'Whether evidence of self-induced intoxication can be relevant to the following questions-(a) Whether the defendant intended to endanger the life of another; and (b) Whether the defendant was reckless as to whether the life of another would be endangered, within the meaning of Section 1(2)(b) of the Criminal Damage Act 1971.'

In submitting that the two questions should be answered (a) Yes and (b) No, counsel for the Crown did not challenge the correctness of *R v Briggs* or *R v Stephenson*.

18. In a leading opinion with which Lord Keith of Kinkel and Lord Roskill agreed, but from which Lord Wilberforce and Lord Edmund-Davies dissented, Lord Diplock discounted ([1981] 1 All ER 961 at 964–965, [1982] AC 341 at 351) Professor Kenny's statement of the law approved in *R v Cunningham* as directed to the meaning of 'maliciously' in the Malicious Damage Act 1861 and having no bearing on the meaning of 'reckless' in the 1971 Act. It was, he held, no less blameworthy for a man whose mind was affected by rage or excitement or drink to fail to give his mind to the risk of damaging property than for a man whose mind was so affected to appreciate that there was a risk of damage to property but not to appreciate the seriousness of the risk or to trust that good luck would prevent the risk occurring. He observed ([1981] 1 All ER 961 at 965, [1982] AC 341 at 352):

'My Lords, I can see no reason why Parliament when it decided to revise the law as to offences of damage to property should go out of its way to perpetuate fine and impracticable distinctions such as these, between one mental state and another. One would think that the sooner they were got rid of the better.'

Reference was made to *R v Briggs, R v Parker* and *R v Stephenson*, but Lord Diplock saw no warrant for assuming that the 1971 Act, whose declared purpose was to revise the law of damage to property, intended 'reckless' to be interpreted as 'maliciously' had been ([1981] 1 All ER 961 at 966, [1982] AC 341 at 353). He preferred the ordinary meaning of 'reckless' which—

'surely includes not only deciding to ignore a risk of harmful consequences resulting from one's acts that one has recognised as existing, but also failing to give any thought to whether or not there is any such risk in circumstances where, if any thought were given to the matter, it would be obvious that there was. If one is attaching labels, the latter state of mind is neither more nor less "subjective" than the first. But the label solves nothing. It is a statement of the obvious; mens rea is, by definition, a state of mind of the accused himself at the time he did the physical act that constitutes the actus reus of the offence; it cannot be the mental state of some non-existent hypothetical person.'

To decide whether a person had been reckless whether harmful consequences of a particular kind would result from his act it was necessary to consider the mind of 'the ordinary prudent individual' ([1981] 1 All ER 961 at 966, [1982] AC 341 at 354). In a passage which has since been taken to encapsulate the law on this point, and which has founded many jury directions (including that in the present case) Lord Diplock then said ([1981] 1 All ER 961 at 967, [1982] AC 341 at 354):

'In my opinion, a person charged with an offence under s 1(1) of the 1971 Act is "reckless as to whether or not any property would be destroyed or damaged" if (1) he does an act which in fact creates an obvious risk that property will be destroyed or damaged and (2) when he does the act he either has not given any thought to the possibility of there being any such risk or has recognised that there was some risk involved and has none the less gone on to do it. That would be a proper direction to the jury; cases in the Court of Appeal which held otherwise should be regarded as overruled.'

On the facts Lord Diplock concluded ([1981] 1 All ER 961 at 967, [1982] AC 341 at 355) that the defendant's unawareness, owing to his self-induced intoxication, of the risk of endangering the lives of hotel residents was no defence if that risk would have been obvious to him had he been sober. He held ([1981] 1 All ER 961 at 967, [1982] AC 341 at 356) that evidence of self-induced intoxication was relevant to a charge under s 1(2) based on intention but not to one based on recklessness.

19. In his dissenting opinion Lord Edmund-Davies expressed ([1981] 1 All ER 961 at 969, [1982] AC 341 at 357) 'respectful, but profound, disagreement' with Lord Diplock's dismissal of Professor Kenny's statement which was—

'accurate not only in respect of the law as it stood in 1902 but also as it has been applied in countless cases ever since, both in the United Kingdom and in other countries where the common law prevails . . .'

Lord Edmund-Davies drew attention to the Law Commission's preparation of the 1971 Act and its definition of recklessness in Working Paper No 31 and continued:

> 'It was surely with this contemporaneous definition and the much respected decision of *R v Cunningham* in mind that the draftsman proceeded to his task of drafting the 1971 Act.'

He observed ([1981] 1 All ER 961 at 970, [1982] AC 341 at 358):

> 'In the absence of exculpatory factors, the defendant's state of mind is therefore all-important where recklessness is an element in the offence charged, and s 8 of the Criminal Justice Act 1967 has laid down that: "A court or jury, in determining whether a person has committed an offence,—(a) shall not be bound in law to infer that he intended *or foresaw* a result of his actions by reason only of its being a natural and probable consequence of those actions; but (b) shall decide whether he did intend *or foresee* that result by reference to all the evidence, drawing such inferences from the evidence as appear proper in the circumstances."' (Emphasis added.)

Lord Edmund-Davies differed from the majority on the relevance of evidence of self-induced intoxication: in his opinion ([1981] 1 All ER 961 at 972, [1982] AC 341 at 361) such evidence was relevant to a charge under s 1(2) whether the charge was based on intention or recklessness.

R v Lawrence

20. Judgment was given by the House in *R v Lawrence* [1981] 1 All ER 974, [1982] AC 510 on the same day as *R v Caldwell*, although only two members (Lord Diplock and Lord Roskill) were party to both decisions. The defendant had ridden a motor cycle along an urban street after nightfall and had collided with and killed a pedestrian. He had been charged and convicted under s 1 of the Road Traffic Act 1972 which made it an offence to cause the death of another person by driving a motor vehicle on a road recklessly. His appeal had succeeded on the ground of an inadequate direction to the jury. The issue on appeal to the House concerned the mental element in a charge of reckless driving.

21. Lord Hailsham of St Marylebone LC ([1981] 1 All ER 974 at 975, 978, [1982] AC 510 at 516, 520, 521), agreeing with Lord Diplock and with the majority in *R v Caldwell*, understood recklessness to evince 'a state of mind stopping short of deliberate intention, and going beyond mere inadvertence . . .' Lord Diplock ([1981] 1 All ER 974 at 982, [1982] AC 510 at 526) rehearsed the history of motoring offences based on recklessness beginning with s 1 of the Motor Car Act 1903 and applied essentially the same test as laid down in *R v Caldwell*, by reference to the 'ordinary prudent individual'. He formulated an appropriate jury direction to the same effect, mutatis mutandis, as that in *R v Caldwell*. But he added ([1981] 1 All ER 974 at 982, [1982] AC 510 at 527):

> 'It is for the jury to decide whether the risk created by the manner in which the vehicle was being driven was both obvious and serious and, in deciding this, they may apply the standard of the ordinary prudent motorist as represented by themselves. If satisfied that an obvious and serious risk was created by the manner of the defendant's driving, the jury are entitled to infer that he was in one or other of the states of mind required to constitute the offence and will probably do so; but regard must be given to any explanation he gives as to his state of mind which may displace the inference.'

Lord Fraser of Tullybelton, Lord Roskill and Lord Bridge of Harwich agreed with Lord Hailsham of St Marylebone LC and Lord Diplock.

Later cases

22. The decisions in *R v Caldwell* and *R v Lawrence* were applied by the House (Lord Diplock, Lord Keith of Kinkel, Lord Bridge of Harwich, Lord Brandon of Oakbrook and Lord Brightman) in *R v Miller* [1983] 1 All ER 978, [1983] 2 AC 161 [section 4.2.3.4, p 69], although subject to a qualification

germane to the facts of that case but not to the facts of the present case ([1983] 1 All ER 978 at 983, [1983] 2 AC 161 at 179).

23. In *Elliott v C (a minor)* [1983] 2 All ER 1005, [1983] 1 WLR 939 the defendant was a 14-year-old girl of low intelligence who had entered a shed in the early morning, poured white spirit on the floor and set it alight. The resulting fire had flared up and she had left the shed, which had been destroyed. She was charged under s 1(1) of the 1971 Act and at her trial before justices the prosecution made plain that the charge was based not on intention but on recklessness. The justices sought to apply the test laid down in *R v Caldwell* [1981] 1 All ER 961, [1982] AC 341 but inferred that in his reference to 'an obvious risk' Lord Diplock had meant a risk which was obvious to the particular defendant. The justices acquitted the defendant because they found that the defendant had given no thought at the time to the possibility of there being a risk that the shed and contents would be destroyed, and this risk would not have been obvious to her or appreciated by her if she had thought about the matter ([1983] 2 All ER 1005 at 1007–1008, [1983] 1 WLR 939 at 945). The prosecutor's appeal was allowed. Glidewell J, giving the first judgment, accepted the submission that—

> 'if the risk is one which would have been obvious to a reasonably prudent person, once it has also been proved that the particular defendant gave no thought to the possibility of there being such a risk, it is not a defence that because of limited intelligence or exhaustion she would not have appreciated the risk even if she had thought about it.'

Robert Goff LJ felt constrained by the decisions of the House in *R v Caldwell*, *R v Lawrence* and *R v Miller* to agree, but he expressed his unhappiness in doing so and plainly did not consider the outcome to be just. A petition for leave to appeal against this decision was dismissed by an appeal committee.

24. The defendant in *R v Stephen Malcolm R* (1984) 79 Cr App R 334 had thrown petrol bombs at the outside wall of the bedroom of a girl who he believed had informed on him in relation to a series of burglaries. He had admitted throwing the bombs but claimed he had done so to frighten the girl and without realising that if a bomb had gone through the window it might have killed her. He was charged with arson under s 1(2) of the 1971 Act, on the basis of recklessness. At trial, it was submitted on the defendant's behalf that when considering recklessness the jury could only convict him if he did an act which created a risk to life obvious to someone of his age and with such of his characteristics as would affect his appreciation of the risk (at 337). On the trial judge ruling against that submission the defendant changed his plea and the issue in the Court of Appeal (Ackner LJ, Bristow and Popplewell JJ) was whether the ruling had been correct. The court held that it had: if the House had wished to modify the *Caldwell* principle to take account of, for instance, the age of the defendant, the opportunity had existed in *Elliott's* case and it had not been taken. Although concerned at the principle it was required to apply, the court had little doubt that on the facts of the case the answer would have been the same even if the jury had been able to draw a comparison with what a boy of the defendant's age would have appreciated.

[His lordship referred to the appeal in the driving case of *R v Reid* [1992] 3 All ER 673, [1992] 1 WLR 793.]

26. In *R v Coles* [1995] 1 Cr App R 157 a 15-year-old defendant convicted under s 1(2) of the 1971 Act on the basis of recklessness again challenged, unsuccessfully, the rule laid down by Lord Diplock in *R v Caldwell*. Since recklessness was to be judged by the standard of the reasonable, prudent man, it followed that expert evidence of the defendant's capacity to foresee the risks which would arise from his setting fire to hay in a barn had been rightly rejected.

27. In the present case the Court of Appeal (Dyson LJ, Silber J and Judge Beaumont QC) reviewed the authorities ([2002] EWCA Crim 1992 at [18], [2003] 3 All ER 206 at [18]) but was in no doubt that the *Caldwell* test had been rightly applied. It acknowledged (at [23]) that the *Caldwell* test had been criticised and had not been applied in a number of Commonwealth jurisdictions and saw great force in these criticisms but held that it was not open to the Court of Appeal to depart from it.

Conclusions

28. The task confronting the House in this appeal is, first of all, one of statutory construction: what did Parliament mean when it used the word 'reckless' in s 1(1) and (2) of the 1971 Act? In so expressing the question I mean to make it as plain as I can that I am not addressing the meaning of 'reckless' in any other statutory or common law context. In particular, but perhaps needlessly since 'recklessly' has now been banished from the lexicon of driving offences, I would wish to throw no doubt on the decisions of the House in *R v Lawrence and R v Reid*.

29. Since a statute is always speaking, the context or application of a statutory expression may change over time, but the meaning of the expression itself cannot change. So the starting point is to ascertain what Parliament meant by 'reckless' in 1971. As noted above, s 1 as enacted followed, subject to an immaterial addition, the draft proposed by the Law Commission. It cannot be supposed that by 'reckless' Parliament meant anything different from the Law Commission. The Law Commission's meaning was made plain both in its report (Law Com No 29) and in Working Paper No 23 which preceded it. These materials (not, it would seem, placed before the House in *R v Caldwell*) reveal a very plain intention to replace the old-fashioned and misleading expression 'maliciously' by the more familiar expression 'reckless' but to give the latter expression the meaning which *R v Cunningham* [1957] 2 All ER 412, [1957] 2 QB 396 and Professor Kenny had given to the former. In treating this authority as irrelevant to the construction of 'reckless' the majority fell into understandable but clearly demonstrable error. No relevant change in the mens rea necessary for proof of the offence was intended, and in holding otherwise the majority misconstrued section 1 of the Act.

30. What conclusion is by no means determinative of this appeal. For the decision in *R v Caldwell* was made more than 20 years ago. Its essential reasoning was unanimously approved by the House in *R v Lawrence*. Invitations to reconsider that reasoning have been rejected. The principles laid down have been applied on many occasions, by Crown Court judges and, even more frequently, by justices. In the submission of the Crown, the ruling of the House works well and causes no injustice in practice. If Parliament had wished to give effect to the intention of the Law Commission it has had many opportunities, which it has not taken, to do so. Despite its power under *Practice Statement (Judicial Precedent)* [1966] 3 All ER 77, [1966] 1 WLR 1234 to depart from its earlier decisions, the House should be very slow to do so, not least in a context such as this.

31. These are formidable arguments, deployed by Mr Perry with his habitual skill and erudition. But I am persuaded by Mr Newman QC for the appellants that they should be rejected. I reach this conclusion for four reasons, taken together.

32. First, it is a salutary principle that conviction of serious crime should depend on proof not simply that the defendant caused (by act or omission) an injurious result to another but that his state of mind when so acting was culpable. This, after all, is the meaning of the familiar rule *actus non facit reum nisi mens sit rea*. The most obviously culpable state of mind is no doubt an intention to cause the injurious result, but knowing disregard of an appreciated and unacceptable risk of causing an injurious result or a deliberate closing of the mind to such risk would be readily accepted as culpable also. It is clearly blameworthy to take an obvious and significant risk of causing injury to another. But it is not clearly blameworthy to do something involving a risk of injury to another if (for reasons other than self-induced intoxication (see *DPP v Majewski* [1976] 2 All ER 142, [1977] AC 443)) one genuinely does not perceive the risk. Such a person may fairly be accused of stupidity or lack of imagination, but neither of those failings should expose him to conviction of serious crime or the risk of punishment.

33. Secondly, the present case shows, more clearly than any other reported case since *R v Caldwell* [1981] 1 All ER 961, [1982] AC 341, that the model direction formulated by Lord Diplock (see [18], above) is capable of leading to obvious unfairness. As the excerpts quoted above reveal, the trial judge regretted the direction he (quite rightly) felt compelled to give, and it is evident that this direction offended the jury's sense of fairness. The sense of fairness of 12 representative citizens sitting as a jury (or of a smaller group of lay justices sitting as a bench of magistrates) is the bedrock

on which the administration of criminal justice in this country is built. A law which runs counter to that sense must cause concern. Here, the appellants could have been charged under s 1(1) of the 1971 Act with recklessly damaging one or both of the wheelie-bins, and they would have had little defence. As it was, the jury might have inferred that boys of the appellants' age would have appreciated the risk to the building of what they did, but it seems clear that such was not their conclusion (nor, it would appear, the judge's either). On that basis the jury thought it unfair to convict them. I share their sense of unease. It is neither moral nor just to convict a defendant (least of all a child) on the strength of what someone else would have apprehended if the defendant himself had no such apprehension. Nor, the defendant having been convicted, is the problem cured by imposition of a nominal penalty.

34. Thirdly, I do not think the criticism of *R v Caldwell* expressed by academics, judges and practitioners should be ignored. A decision is not, of course, to be overruled or departed from simply because it meets with disfavour in the learned journals. But a decision which attracts reasoned and outspoken criticism by the leading scholars of the day, respected as authorities in the field, must command attention. One need only cite (among many other examples) the observations of Professor John Smith [1981] Crim LR 392 at 393–396 and Professor Glanville Williams 'Recklessness Redefined' (1981) 40 CLJ 252. This criticism carries greater weight when voiced also by judges as authoritative as Lord Edmund-Davies and Lord Wilberforce in *R v Caldwell* itself, Robert Goff LJ in *Elliott v C (a minor)* [1983] 2 All ER 1005, [1983] 1 WLR 939 and Ackner LJ in *R v Stephen Malcolm R* (1984) 79 Cr App R 334. The reservations expressed by the trial judge in the present case are widely shared. The shop floor response to *R v Caldwell* may be gauged from the editors' commentary, to be found in *Archbold's Pleading, Evidence and Practice in Criminal Cases* (41st edn, 1982) pp 1009–1010 (para 17–25). The editors suggested that remedial legislation was urgently required.

35. Fourthly, the majority's interpretation of 'reckless' in s 1 of the 1971 Act was, as already shown, a misinterpretation. If it were a misinterpretation that offended no principle and gave rise to no injustice there would be strong grounds for adhering to the misinterpretation and leaving Parliament to correct it if it chose. But this misinterpretation is offensive to principle and is apt to cause injustice. That being so, the need to correct the misinterpretation is compelling.

36. It is perhaps unfortunate that the question at issue in this appeal fell to be answered in a case of self-induced intoxication. For one instinctively recoils from the notion that a defendant can escape the criminal consequences of his injurious conduct by drinking himself into a state where he is blind to the risk he is causing to others. In *R v Caldwell* it seems to have been assumed (see [18], above) that the risk would have been obvious to the defendant had he been sober. Further, the context did not require the House to give close consideration to the liability of those (such as the very young and the mentally handicapped) who were not normal, reasonable adults. The overruling by the majority of *R v Stephenson* [1979] 2 All ER 1198, [1979] QB 695 does however make it questionable whether such consideration would have led to a different result.

37. In the course of argument before the House it was suggested that the rule in *R v Caldwell* might be modified, in cases involving children, by requiring comparison not with normal, reasonable adults but with normal, reasonable children of the same age. This is a suggestion with some attractions but it is open to four compelling objections. First, even this modification would offend the principle that conviction should depend on proving the state of mind of the individual defendant to be culpable. Second, if the rule were modified in relation to children on grounds of their immaturity it would be anomalous if it were not also modified in relation to the mentally handicapped on grounds of their limited understanding. Third, any modification along these lines would open the door to difficult and contentious argument concerning the qualities and characteristics to be taken into account for purposes of the comparison. Fourth, to adopt this modification would be to substitute one misinterpretation of s 1 for another. There is no warrant in the Act or in the *travaux preparatoires* which preceded it for such an interpretation.

38. A further refinement, advanced by Professor Glanville Williams (1981) 40 CLJ 252 at 270–271, adopted by the justices in *Elliott's* case and commented upon by Robert Goff LJ in that case is that a defendant should only be regarded as having acted recklessly by virtue of his failure to give any thought to an obvious risk that property would be destroyed or damaged, where such risk would have been obvious to him if he had given any thought to the matter. This refinement also has attractions, although it does not meet the objection of principle and does not represent a correct interpretation of the section. It is, in my opinion, open to the further objection of over-complicating the task of the jury (or bench of justices). It is one thing to decide whether a defendant can be believed when he says that the thought of a given risk never crossed his mind. It is another, and much more speculative, task to decide whether the risk would have been obvious to him if the thought had crossed his mind. The simpler the jury's task, the more likely is its verdict to be reliable. Robert Goff LJ's reason for rejecting this refinement ([1983] 2 All ER 1005 at 1011–1012, [1983] 1 WLR 939 at 950) was somewhat similar.

39. I cannot accept that restoration of the law as understood before *R v Caldwell* would lead to the acquittal of those whom public policy would require to be convicted. There is nothing to suggest that this was seen as a problem before *R v Caldwell*, or before the 1971 Act. There is no reason to doubt the common sense which tribunals of fact bring to their task. In a contested case based on intention, the defendant rarely admits intending the injurious result in question, but the tribunal of fact will readily infer such an intention, in a proper case, from all the circumstances and probabilities and evidence of what the defendant did and said at the time. Similarly with recklessness: it is not to be supposed that the tribunal of fact will accept a defendant's assertion that he never thought of a certain risk when all the circumstances and probabilities and evidence of what he did and said at the time show that he did or must have done.

40. In his printed case, Mr Newman advanced the contention that the law as declared in *R v Caldwell* was incompatible with art 6 of the European Convention for the Protection of Human Rights and Fundamental Freedoms 1950 (as set out in Sch 1 to the Human Rights Act 1998). While making no concession, he forbore to address legal argument on the point. I need say no more about it.

41. For the reasons I have given I would allow this appeal and quash the appellants' convictions. I would answer the certified question obliquely, basing myself on cl 18(c) of the Criminal Code Bill annexed by the Law Commission to its report *A Criminal Code for England and Wales* (1989) (Law Com no 177) vol 1, Report and Draft Criminal Code Bill):

> '[A] person acts . . . "recklessly" [within the meaning of s 1 of the 1971 Act] with respect to—
> (i) a circumstance when he is aware of a risk that it exists or will exist; (ii) a result when he is aware of a risk that it will occur; and it is, in the circumstances known to him, unreasonable to take the risk . . .'

Lord Steyn: . . .

45. In my view the very high threshold for departing from a previous decision of the House has been satisfied in this particular case. In summary I would reduce my reasons to three propositions. First, in *R v Caldwell* the majority should have accepted without equivocation that before the passing of the 1971 Act foresight of consequences was an essential element in recklessness in the context of damage to property under s 51 of the Malicious Damage Act 1861. Secondly, the matrix of the immediately preceding Law Commission recommendations shows convincingly that the purpose of s 1 of the 1971 Act was to replace the out of date language of 'maliciously' causing damage by more modern language while not changing the substance of the mental element in any way. Foresight of consequences was to remain an ingredient of recklessness in regard to damage to property. Thirdly, experience has shown that by bringing within the reach of s 1(1) cases of inadvertent recklessness the decision in *R v Caldwell* became a source of serious potential injustice which cannot possibly be justified on policy grounds. . . .

52. In the case before the House the two boys were 11 and 12 respectively. Their escapade of camping overnight without their parents' permission was something that many children have undertaken. But by throwing lit newspapers under a plastic wheelie-bin they caused £1m of damage to a shop. It is, however, an agreed fact on this appeal that the boys thought there was no risk of the fire spreading in the way it eventually did. What happened at trial is highly significant. The jury were perplexed by the *Caldwell* directions which compelled them to treat the boys as adults and to convict them. The judge plainly thought this approach was contrary to common sense but loyally applied the law as laid down in *R v Caldwell*. The view of the jurors and the judge would be widely shared by reasonable people who pause to consider the matter. The only answer of the Crown is that where unjust convictions occur the judge can impose a lenient sentence. This will not do in a modern criminal justice system. Parliament certainly did not authorise such a cynical strategy.

53. Ignoring the special position of children in the criminal justice system is not acceptable in a modern civil society. In 1990 the United Kingdom ratified the United Nations *Convention on the Rights of the Child* (New York, 20 November 1989; TS 44 (1992); Cm 1976) (the UN convention) which entered into force on 15 January 1992. Article 40(1) provides:

> 'States Parties recognize the right of every child alleged as, accused of, or recognized as having infringed the penal law to be treated in a manner consistent with the promotion of the child's sense of dignity and worth, which reinforces the child's respect for the human rights and fundamental freedoms of others and which takes into account the child's age and the desirability of promoting the child's reintegration and the child's assuming a constructive role in society.' (My emphasis.)

This provision imposes both procedural and substantive obligations on state parties to protect the special position of children in the criminal justice system. For example, it would plainly be contrary to art 40(1) for a state to set the age of criminal responsibility of children at, say, five years. Similarly, it is contrary to art 40(1) to ignore in a crime punishable by life imprisonment, or detention during Her Majesty's pleasure, the age of a child in judging whether the mental element has been satisfied. It is true that the UN convention became binding on the United Kingdom after *R v Caldwell* was decided. But the House cannot ignore the norm created by the UN convention. This factor on its own justified a reappraisal of *R v Caldwell*.

≈ *Questions*

Is there a strong argument for having a special test of recklessness for children? What about adults with mental or physical incapacity?

---

54. If it is wrong to ignore the special characteristics of children in the context of recklessness under s 1 of the 1971 Act, an adult who suffers from a lack of mental capacity or a relevant personality disorder may be entitled to the same standard of justice. Recognising the special characteristics of children and mentally disabled people goes some way towards reducing the scope of s 1 of the 1971 Act for producing unjust results which are inherent in the objective mould into which the *Caldwell* analysis forced recklessness. It does not, however, restore the correct interpretation of s 1 of the 1971 Act. The accepted meaning of recklessness involved foresight of consequences. This subjective state of mind is to be inferred 'by reference to all the evidence, drawing such inferences from the evidence as appear proper in the circumstances' (per Lord Edmund-Davies [1981] 1 All ER 961 at 970, [1982] AC 341 at 358, citing s 8 of the Criminal Justice Act 1967). That is what Parliament intended by implementing the Law Commission proposals.

55. This interpretation of s 1 of the 1971 Act would fit in with the general tendency in modern times of our criminal law. The shift is towards adopting a subjective approach. It is generally necessary to

look at the matter in the light of how it would have appeared to the defendant. Like Lord Edmund-Davies I regard s 8 of the 1967 Act, as of central importance. There is, however, also a congruence of analysis appearing from decisions of the House. In *Director of Public Prosecutions v Morgan* [1975] 2 All ER 347, [1976] AC 182 [[1975] UKHL 3] the House ruled that a defence of mistake must be honestly rather than reasonably held. In *Beckford v R* [1987] 3 All ER 425 at 432, [1988] AC 130 at 145 per Lord Griffiths [section 23.6.1, p 661], the House held that self-defence permits a defendant to use such force as is reasonable in the circumstances as he honestly believed them to be. *B (a minor) v Director of Public Prosecutions* [2000] 1 All ER 833, [2000] 2 AC 428 concerned the offence contrary to s 1(1) of the Children Act 1961 [see section 6.3.1, p 125]. The House held that the accused's honest belief that a girl was over 14 need not be based on reasonable grounds. Lord Nicholls of Birkenhead observed ([2000] 1 All ER 833 at 837, [2000] 2 AC 428 at 462):

> 'Considered as a matter of principle, the honest belief approach must be preferable. By defini-
> tion the mental element in a crime is concerned with a subjective state of mind, such as intent
> or belief.'

To same effect is *R v K* [2001] UKHL 41, [2001] 3 All ER 897, [2002] 1 AC 462 [section 6.3.1, p 126] where it was held that while a girl under the age of 16 cannot in law consent to an indecent assault, it is a defence if the defendant honestly believed she was over 16. It is true that the general picture is not entirely harmonious. Duress requires reasonable belief (see Lord Lane CJ in *R v Graham* [1982] 1 All ER 801 at 806, [1982] 1 WLR 294 at 300, approved by the House of Lords in *R v Howe* [1987] 1 All ER 771, [1987] AC 417; *R v Martin* [1989] 1 All ER 652). Duress is a notoriously difficult corner of the law. However, in *R v Graham* [1982] 1 All ER 801 at 806, [1982] 1 WLR 294 at 300 [section 23.3.3, p 634] Lord Lane CJ stated that in judging the accused's response the test is:

> '. . . have the prosecution made the jury sure that a sober person of reasonable firmness, shar-
> ing the characteristics of the defendant, would not have responded to whatever he reasonably
> believed [the threatener] said or did by taking part in the [offence].' (My emphasis.)

The age and sex of the defendant (but possibly no other characteristics) are relevant to the cogency of the threat (see *R v Bowen* [1996] 4 All ER 837, [1997] 1 WLR 372). In regard to provocation a wider view of the impact on defendant has prevailed (see *R v Smith* [2000] 4 All ER 289, [2001] 1 AC 146 (by a three to two majority)) [see now Chapter 8].

56. These developments show that what Lord Diplock described in *R v Caldwell* [1981] 1 All ER 961 at 966, [1982] AC 341 at 353 as an 'esoteric meaning' of recklessness was also consistent with the general trend of the criminal law.

Conclusion on *Caldwell*

57. The surest test of a new legal rule is not whether it satisfies a team of logicians but how it performs in the real world. With the benefit of hindsight the verdict must be that the rule laid down by the majority in *R v Caldwell* failed this test. It was severely criticised by academic lawyers of distinction. It did not command respect among practitioners and judges. Jurors found it difficult to understand: it also sometimes offended their sense of justice. Experience suggests that in *R v Caldwell* the law took a wrong turn.

58. That brings me to the question whether the subjective interpretation of recklessness might allow wrongdoers who ought to be convicted of serious crime to escape conviction. Experience before *R v Caldwell* did not warrant such a conclusion. In any event, as Lord Edmund-Davies explained ([1981] 1 All ER 961 at 970, [1982] AC 341 at 358), if a defendant closes his mind to a risk he must realise that there is a risk and, on the evidence, that will usually be decisive. One can trust the realism of trial judges, who direct juries, to guide juries to sensible verdicts and juries can in turn be relied on to apply robust common sense to the evaluation of ridiculous defences. Moreover, the endorsement

by Parliament of the Law Commission proposals could not seriously have been regarded as a charter for the acquittal of wrongdoers.

59. In my view the case for departing from *R v Caldwell* has been shown to be irresistible.

60. I agree with the reasons given by Lord Bingham of Cornhill. I have nothing to add to his observations on self-induced intoxication.

Appeal allowed

The House of Lords in *G* made clear that the principle espoused in *Caldwell* was unacceptable for serious crimes (see in particular Lord Bingham at [32]). In this respect, the House of Lords was endorsing its commitment to subjectivism (oddly enough it has done so at a time when Parliament keeps creating serious offences based on objective fault elements, as in sexual offences).

The law is returned to what it was intended to be. Recklessness in criminal damage is to be construed in a subjective sense—by looking to the state of mind of the individual defendant.

Although *G* was a unanimous decision, Lord Rodger was clearly not as committed to the subjectivist approach to recklessness as his brethren:

Lord Rodger of Earlsferry:

65. It is no secret that, for a long time, many of the leading academic writers on English criminal law have been 'subjectivists'. By that I mean, at the risk of gross over-simplification, that they have believed that the criminal law should punish people only for those consequences of their acts which they foresaw at the relevant time. Those who subscribe to that philosophy will tend to approve the concept of recklessness in *R v Cunningham* [1957] 2 All ER 412, [1957] 2 QB 396. The late Professor Glanville Williams and the late Professor John Smith, who were members of the influential Criminal Law Revision Committee, were two of the most distinguished proponents of such views. . . .

68. It is equally clear that other views are not only possible but have actually been adopted by English judges at different times over the centuries. Their judgments reveal many strands of thinking (see J Horder 'Two Histories and Four Hidden Principles of Mens Rea' (1997) 113 LQR 95). There is therefore no reason to treat the concept of recklessness expounded in *R v Cunningham* either as being the quintessence of the historic English criminal law on the point or as necessarily providing the best solution in all circumstances. Indeed in *R v Stephenson* [1979] 2 All ER 1198, [1979] QB 695, a case on s 1(1) of the 1971 Act, Geoffrey Lane LJ recognised that the subjective approach was problematical in certain situations. Having made it quite clear that in his view the test of recklessness under the 1971 Act remained subjective and that the knowledge or appreciation of risk of some damage must have entered the defendant's mind, he commented ([1979] 2 All ER 1198 at 1204, [1979] QB 695 at 704):

> 'There is no doubt that the subjective definition of "recklessness" does produce difficulties. One of them which is particularly likely to occur in practice is the case of the person who by self-induced intoxication by drink or drugs deprives himself of the ability to foresee the risks involved in his actions. Assuming that by reason of his intoxication he is not proved to have foreseen the relevant risk, can he be said to have been "reckless"? Plainly not, unless cases of self-induced intoxication are an exception to the general rule. In our judgment the decision of the House of Lords in *Director of Public Prosecutions v Majewski* ([1976] 2 All ER 142, [1977] AC 443) makes it clear that they are such an exception.'

In *R v Caldwell* just the kind of problem envisaged by Geoffrey Lane LJ arose: the defendant said that he was so drunk that it did not occur to him that there might be people in the hotel whose lives might be endangered if he set fire to it. Part of what Lord Diplock did to confront the kind of difficulty identified by Geoffrey Lane LJ was to adopt a wider definition of recklessness that covered culpable inadvertence. In so doing, as the House now holds, he misconstrued the terms of the 1971 Act.

69. It does not follow, however, that Lord Diplock's broader concept of recklessness was undesirable in terms of legal policy. On the contrary, there is much to be said for the view that, if the law is to operate with the concept of recklessness, then it may properly treat as reckless the man who acts without even troubling to give his mind to a risk that would have been obvious to him if he had thought about it. This approach may be better suited to some offences than to others. For example, in the context of reckless driving the House endorsed and re-endorsed a more stringent version (see *R v Lawrence* [1981] 1 All ER 974, [1982] AC 510; *R v Reid* [1992] 3 All ER 673, [1992] 1 WLR 793). I refer in particular to the discussion of the policy issues by Lord Goff of Chieveley in *R v Reid* [1992] 3 All ER 673 at 686–689, [1992] 1 WLR 793 at 808–812. Moreover, the opposing view, that only advertent risk-taking should ever be included within the concept of recklessness in criminal law, seems to be based, at least in part, on the kind of thinking that the late Professor Hart demolished in his classic essay, 'Negligence, Mens Rea and Criminal Responsibility' (1961), reprinted in HLA Hart *Punishment and Responsibility* (1968) pp 136–157.

70. Because the decision in *R v Caldwell* involved this legitimate choice between two legal policies, I was initially doubtful whether it would be appropriate for the House to overrule it. An alternative way to allow the appeal by reanalysing Lord Diplock's speech and overruling *Elliott v C (a minor)* [1983] 2 All ER 1005, [1983] 1 WLR 939 might well have been found. But, for the reasons that I have already indicated, I have come to share your Lordships' view that we should indeed overrule *R v Caldwell* and set the law back on the track that Parliament originally intended it to follow. If Parliament now thinks it preferable for the 1971 Act to cover culpably inadvertent as well as advertent wrongdoers, it can so enact. The Law Commission recognised that, if codifying the law, Parliament might wish to adopt that approach (see A Criminal Code for England and Wales (1989) (Law Com no 177) vol 2, Commentary on Draft Criminal Code Bill, p 366 (para 8.21), pp 446–447 (para 17.6)).

≋ *Questions*

Do you agree that 'there is much to be said for the view that, if the law is to operate with the concept of recklessness, then it may properly treat as reckless the person who acts without even troubling to turn *his or her* mind to a risk that would have been obvious if they had thought about it'?

See the excellent article by J. Horder, 'Two Histories and Four Hidden Principles of *Mens Rea*' (1997) 113 LQR 95.

Was the House of Lords right to reject a modified position of the *Caldwell* approach to deal only with cases involving children? Why should the law tolerate a child's incapacities any more than those of an adult with a relevant disability? On recklessness and *G*, see the excellent discussion by H. Keating, 'Reckless Children' [2007] Crim LR 546. Professor Keating conducted empirical work, based on hypothetical scenarios similar to those in *G*. These revealed that 69 per cent of members of the public *do* regard behaviour such as that of the boys as criminally blameworthy. Most of those believed that boys of that age (11 and 12) were old enough to have realized the risks involved. Do you agree?

In overturning *Caldwell* and adopting a subjective approach to the concept in English law once again, Lord Bingham in *G* did recognize that this would entail having to rely upon juries to, 'apply robust common sense to the evaluation of ridiculous defences'. The question remains whether a subjective standard of recklessness makes it too easy for defendants to avoid liability by claiming that they did not foresee the existence of the risk in question. In *Seray-Wurie v DPP* [2012] EWHC 208 (Admin), for example, D was charged with criminal damage after using black marker pen to write on two parking notices placed by the management company in the residential estate where he lived. On appeal from the magistrates' court, the Crown Court directed itself that when it comes to recklessness D must be aware that there is a risk of a certain result occurring and that in those circumstances it was unreasonable to take that risk. It found that D was aware that there was a risk that his writing on the notices would cause damage to them. The basis for this was that D was an intelligent man and that he must have appreciated it because any normal person would have done so. D appealed his conviction by way of case stated to the Divisional Court and argued that although he accepted writing on the parking notices with a black marker pen, he did not intend to cause damage to them, nor was he reckless as to whether damage would be caused. In upholding D's conviction, Lloyd Jones J held as follows (at [21]):

> I accept that if the Crown Court had concluded that the requirement of recklessness was satisfied because the risk would have been obvious to a reasonable person that would have been the application of an objective test and would, after G, be wrong in law. However, it is clear from the transcript of the judgment that the Crown Court did not fall into that error. On the contrary, in deciding whether the appellant was aware of the risk of damage the Crown Court took into account the circumstances known to the appellant and found that the evidence led it to the sure conclusion that, despite his assertion to the contrary, he did appreciate that there was a risk of damage. The Crown Court did not make a finding of objective recklessness, that is, it did not conclude that damage was not foreseen but that it ought to have been foreseen. It concluded that it was sure that the appellant appreciated that damage was likely to result. The court made a finding as to the subjective state of mind of the appellant. In coming to that conclusion it was entitled to consider how obvious was the risk. As [counsel for the Crown] puts it, the more obvious the risk the less inclined a tribunal will be to accept that a defendant was not aware of it, absent any characteristics of a defendant that would affect his ability to appreciate the risk. However, the test applied remains the subjective test.

Does the subjective approach place too much reliance on jurors' ability to identify and disregard specious claims by defendants that they did not appreciate the existence of the risk? How are juries to distinguish between genuine and false denials in circumstances other than when D is a child or suffers from some kind of objectively identifiable cognitive incapacity? To get round this, does the approach of the Divisional Court seem to reverse the burden of proof?

5.3.1.1 Subjective recklessness of general application

Although explicitly a decision on the criminal damage offences, G is, it seems, being accepted as providing the correct test for recklessness in any offence for which that state of mind suffices as the fault element. In *A-G's Reference (No 3 of 2003)* [2004] EWCA Crim 868, [2004] 2 Cr App R 23, the defendant police officers had arrested V who had been injured in a fight and had become abusive and aggressive towards hospital staff when receiving treatment. Following medical confirmation that V was fit to be detained, he was placed partially face down wearing handcuffs in the custody suite but developed breathing difficulties and died. The officers were charged with gross negligence manslaughter and misconduct in a public office. They were acquitted on the judge's direction because (a) there was a lack of causation on the gross negligence counts, and (b) there was insufficient evidence of recklessness for a conviction for misconduct. On the reference by the Attorney General, the court considered the subjective approach to recklessness pronounced in G. The Crown sought to restrict the impact of G in two ways. First, it was argued that the House of Lords expressly limited its conclusions on recklessness to criminal damage. It was argued that in conduct crimes such as misconduct in public office, the issue of recklessness ought to be focused on the misconduct itself, not on the likelihood of any result being caused. The Crown argued that the prosecution ought to succeed on proof that there has been misconduct by the defendant and he was *'indifferent'* as to whether the acts or omissions constituting the misconduct may have any consequences. The court rejected any such limitation on the subjective approach in *G*. Secondly, the Crown argued that in crimes in which liability arises because of a duty situation, an objective test of recklessness ought to apply so that those who do not advert to the risk of harm to particular individuals ought to be found reckless. The Court of Appeal rejected the argument. The court considered the House of Lords' interpretation of 'wilful neglect' in the case of duty as in *Sheppard* [1981] AC 394 (dealing with child neglect), and emphasized that in its view *Sheppard* imposed a subjective test in which the characteristics of the individual defendant were to be taken into consideration. The Court of Appeal's conclusion was (at [7]) that *Sheppard* 'did not impose a lower duty on the prosecution than *G*'. For the purposes of wilful neglect or misconduct it was necessary for the offender to have subjective awareness of the duty to act or a subjective recklessness as to the existence of the duty.

5.3.2 Foresight of 'a' risk

As we discussed earlier, in *Cunningham* Byrne J held that it sufficed for D to have foreseen the existence of *a* risk. In *Brady* [2006] EWCA Crim 2413, D was drunk when he climbed on railings at a nightclub and fell onto the dance floor below causing serious injuries to V who was dancing there. Directing the jury as to recklessness, the judge had said, 'where there is no issue of intoxication [see section 25.3, p 717] the test requires that the defendant should be aware of a risk and go on to take it, the risk being of injury'. He then directed the jury on recklessness in the context of voluntary intoxication, saying, 'if the defendant had been sober and in good mental shape would he have realised that some injury . . . might result from his actions in what he was doing in the condition he was in that night'. D's first ground of appeal was that the effect of the decision in *G and another* [2003] UKHL 50 required the jury to be directed that the Crown had to establish that D had foreseen 'an obvious and significant risk' of injury to another by his actions, or else that he would have done so had he been sober. The Court of Appeal held *G* does not require proof that D had foreseen 'an obvious and significant risk' in order to establish that he had acted recklessly; and it followed that there was no need for a trial judge directing a jury as to recklessness to qualify the word 'risk' by the words 'obvious and significant'. However, the Court of Appeal allowed the appeal, because the judge had failed to direct the jury as to recklessness in sufficiently clear and careful terms. The judge had directed the jury that the only issue for them was one of recklessness, when in fact it had been necessary for him to direct the jury as to recklessness in the different contexts of whether the appellant had deliberately jumped from the railings or whether he had accidentally fallen. Further, it was not sufficiently clear from the judge's directions that the test of recklessness was not an objective one.

See also *Booth* [2006] EWHC 192 (Admin), where D damaged V's car when he was knocked down by V. D was convicted of criminal damage since he was reckless as to the damage having seen a risk of being knocked down and closed his mind to that risk.

≈≈≈ ***Question***

Must D be aware of a risk of causing the exact harm that the law prohibits, or is it sufficient if D has a general sense that his conduct is risky?

5.4 Malice

Many old statutes use the word 'maliciously' to describe the mental element required. 'Malice' was not given its natural meaning of 'spitefully' or 'with ill-will'. Professor C. S. Kenny in his *Outlines of Criminal Law* (1947) stated the general proposition that:

> in any statutory definition of a crime, 'malice' must . . . be taken—not in its vague common law sense as 'wickedness' in general, but—as requiring an actual intention to do the particular kind of harm that in fact was done (or at least a recklessness as to doing it). (15th edn, p 189)

In the famous case of *Cunningham* [1957] 2 All ER 412, which was discussed earlier, D, in order to steal money from a gas meter, ripped the meter away from the supply pipes and released a cloud of noxious coal gas into the house next door. D was charged with *maliciously* administering a noxious substance (the gas) to the neighbour so as thereby to endanger her life, contrary to s 23 of the Offences Against the Person Act 1861. The Court of Criminal Appeal referring to Kenny stated that:

> in any statutory definition of a crime 'malice' must be taken not in the old vague sense of 'wickedness' in general, but as requiring either (1) an actual intention to do the particular *kind* of harm that in fact was done, or (2) recklessness as to whether such harm should occur or not (i.e. the accused has foreseen that the particular kind of harm might be done, and yet has gone on to take the risk of it). (*Outlines of Criminal Law*, 1902)

The House of Lords confirmed that interpretation in *Savage; Parmenter* [1991] 4 All ER 698. Malice is therefore a form of subjective fault. D must personally 'foresee a risk', but it is unclear whether it also requires proof that taking the foreseen risk was *unjustified*. See further section 10.4.2.1.

5.5 Knowledge

Some of the cases discussed previously raise a more general problem about knowledge in the criminal law: at what point must D know the risk and must it be at the forefront of his mind before he can be said to know it? Does a person 'know' a fact which is not present to his mind at the relevant moment, though he is quite capable of recalling it? Professor Glanville Williams at one time thought he does. The following passage in the first edition of his *Textbook of Criminal Law* (1978), p 79, does not appear in the second edition but it is not clear whether he changed his mind. He was discussing *Parker* (discussed in Lord Bingham's speech in *G* see section 5.3.1, p 98). D, in a telephone kiosk, being frustrated by his inability to get through, twice slammed the telephone down on to its cradle. On the second occasion he smashed it. Charged with criminal damage, he said that he did not realize at the time he acted that he was likely to break the telephone. The Court of Appeal held he was rightly convicted because 'a man is reckless when he carried out the deliberate act knowing or closing his mind to the obvious fact that there is some risk of damage resulting from that act, but nevertheless continued the performance of that act.'

The case was such a paradigm of recklessness that the appeal might well have been dismissed on the ground that no miscarriage of justice had actually occurred, even if the direction was regarded as misleading. Parker must have slammed the receiver down extremely hard to break the plastic, and it is impossible to believe that he did not know the risk of damaging it.

It is a misunderstanding of the legal requirement to suppose that this knowledge of risk must be a matter of conscious awareness at the moment of the act. We grow up in a world in which we come to know, from the earliest age, that things are broken by rough treatment. Some things are more resistant than others: one could, in a temper, kick a farm tractor or the wheel of a lorry without doing damage. But is there anyone who does not know that a telephone receiver can be damaged by being violently slammed down? The fact that it is slammed down because of a feeling of frustration is nothing to the purpose.

If this is right, what was all the fuss over *DPP v Smith* (section 7.3.1, p 153) about? Smith, rightly suspected by a police officer of having stolen goods in his car, drove off at speed with the officer hanging on to the car and pursued an erratic course until he was thrown off in the path of an oncoming vehicle and killed. The whole incident lasted about ten seconds: [1961] AC at 298 and 302. The Court of Criminal Appeal, whose judgment seems now to be rehabilitated (section 7.3.1, p 153), thought the relevant question was as to the state of mind of the defendant during those ten seconds of panic. But if when Smith was sitting quietly at home, relaxed in his armchair, someone had said to him, 'Jim, if you were to drive off in your car at top speed in a busy street with a copper clinging to the bonnet, do you think it is likely that he would suffer serious injury?' would not his reply have been an unprintable affirmative? The Court of Criminal Appeal in that case, however, thought that the relevant question was what Smith thought in a moment of panic and the ten seconds which the whole episode occupied.

In some offences, knowledge appears as the explicit mens rea requirement. The definition of the term was subjected to scrutiny in the House of Lords in two cases dealing with money laundering and conspiracies to launder money. The judicial view is clear: knowledge is true belief and one cannot know something or a circumstance that has yet to occur. As the Canadian Supreme Court explained in *USA v Dynar* [1997] 2 SCR 462:

> In the Western legal tradition, knowledge is defined as *true* belief: 'The word "know" refers exclusively to true knowledge; we are not said to "know" something that is not so'.

This view was endorsed in the House of Lords in two more recent cases. In *Montila* [2004] 1 WLR 3141, the House accepted (at [27]) that:

> A person cannot know that something is A when in fact it is B. The proposition that a person knows that something is A is based on the premise that it is true that it is A. The fact that the property is A provides the starting point. Then there is the question whether the person knows that the property is A.

Subsequently, in *Saik* [2006] UKHL 18, the House of Lords concluded:

> the word 'know' should be interpreted strictly and not watered down. In this context knowledge means true belief.

See, generally, S. Shute, 'Knowledge and Belief in the Criminal Law' in S. Shute and A. Simester (eds), *Criminal Law Theory: Doctrines of the General Part* (2002), Ch 8 and see G. R. Sullivan, 'Knowledge, Belief and Culpability', ibid, Ch 9.

5.5.1 'Wilful blindness'

A requirement of knowledge has frequently been held to be satisfied by proof of what is sometimes called 'wilful blindness'.

It has indeed been stated in the House of Lords, in *Westminster City Council v Croyalgrange Ltd* [1986] 2 All ER 353 at 359, that:

> it is always open to the tribunal of fact, when knowledge on the part of a defendant is required to be proved, to base a finding of knowledge on evidence that the defendant had deliberately shut his eyes to the obvious or refrained from inquiry because he suspected the truth but did not want to have his suspicions confirmed.

In so far as this states a universal rule, it goes too far. In handling stolen goods a person is not taken to 'know' that the goods are stolen merely because he suspects that they may be stolen and asks no questions because he prefers not to know.

In the seminal case on the subject, *Roper v Taylor's Garage* [1951] 2 TLR 284 at 288, Devlin J emphasized:

> a vast distinction between a state of mind which consists of deliberately refraining from making inquiries, the result of which a person does not care to have [wilful blindness], and a state of mind which is merely neglecting to make such inquiries as a reasonable and prudent person would make [constructive knowledge].

See M. Wasik and M. P. Thompson, 'Turning a Blind Eye as Constituting Mens Rea' (1981) 32 NILQ 324 at 337–341. Glanville Williams described it in terms of suspicion '*plus*' a deliberate omission to inquire: *Criminal Law: The General Part* (1953), p 127, para 41.

Wilful blindness is distinct from recklessness because, while recklessness involves knowledge of a danger *or risk* and persistence in a course of conduct which creates *a risk* that the prohibited result will occur, wilful blindness arises where a person who has become aware of the need for some inquiry declines to make the inquiry because he does not wish to know the truth. He would prefer to remain ignorant.

Wilful blindness does not include negligence: *Flintshire County Council v Reynolds* [2006] EWHC 195 (Admin) confirmed that negligence is not a form of 'knowledge'. In *Flintshire* (at [17]), it was emphasized that a person who has 'constructive notice' may be negligent as to the relevant facts, but is not to be taken to have knowledge of them.

5.5.2 Knowledge distinguished from belief

According to the Court of Appeal in *Hall* (1985) 81 Cr App R 260 at 264, [1985] Crim LR 377:

> Belief, of course, is something short of knowledge. It may be said to be the state of mind of a person who says to himself: 'I cannot say I know for certain that [the circumstance exists] but there can be no other reasonable conclusion in the light of all the circumstances, in the light of all that I have heard and seen'.

In *Moys* (1984) 79 Cr App R 72, the court suggested simply that the question whether D knew or believed that the proscribed circumstance existed is a subjective one and that suspicion, even coupled with the fact that D shut his eyes to the circumstances, is not enough.

5.5.3 Knowledge distinguished from suspicion/reasonable grounds to suspect

There are many serious offences with low-level mens rea requirements such as 'suspicion' and 'having reasonable grounds to suspect'. The money laundering offences in the Proceeds of

Crime Act 2002 and offences in the Terrorism Acts are some of the clearest examples. In the mens rea hierarchy, suspicion comes below belief (which is below knowledge).

5.5.3.1 Suspicion

In *Da Silva* [2006] EWCA Crim 1654, 'suspicion' was held to impose a subjective test: D's suspicion need not be based on 'reasonable grounds'. D must think that there is a possibility, which is more than fanciful, that the relevant facts exist. Use of words like 'fleeting thought' and 'inkling' is apt to mislead. The court held (at [16]) that the:

> essential element in the word 'suspect' and its affiliates, in this context, is that the defendant must think that there is a possibility, which is more than fanciful, that the relevant facts exist. A vague feeling of unease would not suffice. But the statute does not require the suspicion to be 'clear' or 'firmly grounded and targeted on specific facts', or based upon 'reasonable grounds'.

The court adopted the dictionary definitions, which are consistent with the previous judicial interpretations of the concept of suspicion in the related field of criminal procedure such as that of Lord Devlin in *Hussien v Chang Fook Kam* [1970] AC 942 at 948:

> Suspicion in its ordinary meaning is a state of conjecture or surmise where proof is lacking: 'I suspect but I cannot prove'. Suspicion arises at or near the starting point of an investigation of which the obtaining of prima facie proof is the end.

5.5.3.2 Reasonable grounds to suspect

In *Saik* [2006] UKHL 18 (a case on former offences of money laundering), the House of Lords held that the mens rea element 'reasonable grounds to suspect', also found in many of the current money laundering offences, includes a requirement that the defendant had actual suspicion. Lord Hope concluded at [52]–[55] that:

> the first requirement contains both a subjective part—that the person suspects—and an objective part—that there are reasonable grounds for the suspicion.

It had previously been widely assumed that this mens rea element was a purely objective one, requiring proof only that the reasonable person would have formed the suspicion on the facts available, irrespective of whether the individual defendant formed such suspicion himself. In *R v AB* [2017] EWCA Crim 129, the Court of Appeal distinguished *Saik*. The test of reasonable grounds to suspect in Terrorism Act offences is an objective one.

〰 *Question*
Should 'suspicion' be a sufficient basis of fault for serious offences?

5.6 Negligence

Recklessness is the conscious taking of an unjustifiable risk, while negligence is the inadvertent taking of an unjustifiable risk. If D is aware of the risk and decides to take it, he is reckless; if he is unaware of the risk, but ought to have been aware of it, he is negligent. Where D did consider whether or not there was a risk and concluded, wrongly and unreasonably, that there was no risk, or so small a risk that it would have been justifiable to take it, he is negligent.

Before *Caldwell*, and now under the present law since *G* overruled *Caldwell*, a clear line is drawn by judges between recklessness and negligence. Recklessness is advertent risk-taking. Negligence is inadvertent risk-taking. In both cases the risk is an unreasonable risk that a prudent person would not take. The reckless person is aware of the risk, while the negligent person ought to have been aware of it but is not. Thus for Jerome Hall (GPCL 114–115):

> Recklessness is like [intentionality] in that the actor is conscious of a forbidden harm, he realizes that his conduct increases the risk of its occurrence, and he has decided to create that risk;
>
> whereas—
>
> . . . negligence implies inadvertence, ie that the defendant was completely unaware of the dangerousness of his behaviour although actually it was unreasonably increasing the risk of the occurrence of an injury.

Similarly, for Dr J. W. C. Turner (writing as editor of *Russell on Crime* (12th edn, 1964), pp 41–42) a reckless person is one who:

> acts with full knowledge that he is taking the chance that this secondary result will follow . . . His precise mental attitude will be one of two kinds (a) he would prefer that the harmful result should not occur, or (b) he is indifferent as to whether it does or does not occur. Whichever it may be the common law makes no distinction in his liability.

Whereas (p 43):

> Negligence . . . in this connection connotes *inadvertence* . . .

Glanville Williams (*Criminal Law: The General Part* (2nd edn, 1961), p 100) wrote:

> Responsibility for some crimes may be incurred by the mere neglect to exercise due caution, where the mind is not actively but negatively or passively at fault. This is inadvertent negligence. Since advertent negligence has a special name (recklessness) it is convenient to use 'negligence' generally to mean inadvertent negligence.

While *Caldwell* was a binding authority, this distinction between advertent and inadvertent risk-taking was no longer synonymous with the distinction between recklessness and negligence. Inadvertent risk-taking arising from a failure to give thought to the existence of a risk amounted to *Caldwell* recklessness. The only distinction between *Caldwell* recklessness and negligence lay in the existence of the so-called 'lacuna': if D had personally thought about the risk and failed to see the obvious risk he would not fall within the definition of recklessness set out by Lord Diplock in *Caldwell*.

Given the importance of whether a defendant is reckless or negligent, it might be thought that there would exist a sophisticated body of literature on the distinction between the two. This does not appear to be the case; a lacuna that Douglas Husak has described as 'scandalous'.

Although negligence is undoubtedly recognized as a form of mens rea, there are those who believe that it does not demonstrate sufficient culpability to justify the imposition of criminal sanction.

L. Alexander and K. Kessler Ferzan with S. Morse, *Crime and Culpability:*
A Theory of Criminal Law
(2009), p 70

I. Why Negligence Is Not Culpable

Essentially, those who deem negligence to be culpable argue that failure to advert to a risk that one had a fair chance to perceive (had one tried) is culpable, even though it does not entail a conscious choice to produce or to unreasonably risk harm.

We disagree. The world is full of risks to which we are oblivious. Or, more accurately, because risk is an epistemic, not ontic, notion, [meaning that it is one contingent upon knowledge rather than one based upon factual existence] we frequently believe we are creating a certain level of risk when someone in an epistemically superior position to ours would assess the risk to be higher or lower than we have estimated. Sometimes the epistemically superior position is the product of better information: for example the doctor knows that what we believe is just a mole is in fact a life-threatening melanoma. At other times, we have failed to notice something that another might have noticed, or we have forgotten sometime that another might have remembered. Once in a while, our lack of information, failure to notice, failure to make proper inferences from what information we do have, or forgetfulness results in our underestimating the riskiness of our conduct and causing harm.

We are not morally culpable for taking risks of which we are unaware. At any point in time we are failing to notice a great many things, we have forgotten a great many things, and we are misinformed or uninformed about many things. An injunction to notice, remember, and be fully informed about anything that bears on risks to others is an injunction no human being can comply with, so violating this injunction reflects no moral defect. Even those most concerned with the well-being of others will violate this injunction constantly.

The argument the authors make is that people can and often do make momentary mistakes, and that acts of clumsiness or stupidity hardly seem like the sort of things for which people should be held criminally liable. Consider, however, the following response.

A. Leipold, 'A Case for Criminal Negligence'
(2010) 29 Law & Phil 455

Let's begin with the strong argument. A claim that negligence isn't enough starts at the bottom of a large hill, because our willingness to impose serious sanctions on a negligent actor is deeply rooted. We do not think it especially unfair to fire someone from their job, drive them out of business, or make them pay huge sums of money (including punitive damages) for gross inattention to detail. And of course descriptively, criminal liability has always been, and often still is, based on negligent behavior. So at the outset there is nothing intuitively shocking about treating someone as a criminal when they engage in a 'gross deviation from the standard of care that a reasonable person would observe in the actor's situation'.

The authors respond that whatever the criminal law is doing now with negligence is flawed, because it is not based on truly blameworthy acts. The core problem with negligence, they say, is that 'an injunction to notice . . . and to be fully informed about *everything* that bears on risks to others is an injunction no human can comply with, so violating this injunction reflects no moral defect'. And apparently we are all sinners, because 'even those most concerned with the well being of others will violate this injunction constantly'.

I would agree that *if* the negligence standard really required us to be fully informed about everything that bears on the risk of harm to others, it should have no place in the criminal law (or maybe the civil law, for that matter). But it doesn't, and as a result, I do not think that negligence requires an impossible degree of attentiveness, nor do I think people are constantly violating its commands.

As Eric Johnson and others have nicely pointed out, the Model Penal Code does not require me to know *everything* on pain of being found negligent, but instead, asks (a) what things did I know at the time I acted? and (b) within that universe of facts, was my failure to perceive a risk a gross departure from what a reasonable person would perceive? This is the plain import of the requirement that we evaluate the actor's riskcreating behavior 'under the circumstances known to him'. Consider the case of the pedestrian talking on a cell phone who blindly steps off the curb, causing the oncoming driver to swerve and nearly crash. The pedestrian is surely acting carelessly and stupidly, but nothing in the negligence standard makes him liable for negligent homicide simply because he was not fully informed that the swerving driver was rushing a sick friend to the hospital, and the near-accident so unnerved the driver that he drove too slowly and failed to get medical attention in time.

Stated differently, nothing in the negligence standard requires unrealistic perceptiveness or care. Nor is criminal negligence, properly defined, so widespread that everyone is routinely exceeding its limits, making it unfair to sanction the few unlucky souls who happen to get caught. Criminal negligence is explicitly relative—it only reaches those departures from the attentiveness that an ordinary person would observe. (The authors, of course, offer sharp and valid criticisms of the reasonable person standard, but that is a different point.) We know that ordinary people sometimes forget to lock up the cleaning supplies, sometimes take their eye off the road for just a moment, and do not always rotate their tires every 5,000 miles to prevent uneven tread wear that can lead to a blowout. On the other hand, those who take these behaviors to extreme degrees—taking your eye off the road for 40 seconds to send a text message—have so far departed from a reasonable standard of care that a jury can justifiably characterize it as a moral defect.

≈≈ *Questions*

Should negligence be a sufficient fault for criminal offences? If so, should it constitute the mens rea for only those crimes that are of least seriousness?

There is also uncertainty as to what extent it is necessary in an evaluation of negligence to take account of the defendant's characteristics.

In *RSPCA v C* [2006] EWHC 1069 (Admin), it was held that the question whether a juvenile (aged 15) was negligent in not taking an injured cat to the vet should be judged by the standards of a reasonable girl of *her* age. Cf *Price* [2014] EWCA Crim 229 (negligence in the military).

≈≈ *Questions*

Which other characteristics ought to be taken into account? Is age a unique factor?

In *C* [2001] Crim LR 845, the defendant, who was a paranoid schizophrenic, had performed the conduct for the offence of stalking by sending offensive letters to his MP, on at least two occasions. He was convicted and appealed on the basis that the judge should have directed the jury to consider his mental disorder as a relevant condition of the hypothetical reasonable person in s 1(2) of the Protection from Harassment Act 1997. The Protection from Harassment Act 1997, s 1(1)(b) read with s 1(2), imposes a requirement that the course of conduct (which is alleged to amount to harassment) must be one which D knew *or ought to have known* amounts to harassment. That is a statutory crime of negligence. The test of whether he knew or ought to have known is, under s 1, whether a reasonable person *in possession of the same informa-tion* as D would think the course of conduct did amount to harassment. The Court of Appeal held that s 1(2) involved a purely objective test relating to the reasonable person and reason-able conduct. D's illness was not relevant to that question. Section 1(2) seeks to endow the reasonable person with knowledge of circumstances that would render otherwise seemingly innocuous conduct harassing.

≈≈ **Question**

D1 knows that previous advances towards V have been rejected and continues to send gifts. D2 who suffers from schizophrenia has previously been rebuffed in his advances to V but con-tinues to send her flowers. Are D1 and D2 guilty of harassment?

See more generally on negligence as an element of harassment, under the Protection from Harassment Act 1997, E. Finch, 'Stalking the Perfect Stalking Law: An Evaluation of the Efficacy of the Protection from Harassment Act 1997' [2002] Crim LR 703 at 714.

Section 2A of the Road Traffic Act 1991 contains the offence of dangerous driving. The offence contains two limbs. First, D's driving must have fallen far below what would be expected of a competent and careful driver and, secondly, it would have been obvious to the competent and careful driver that driving in this way would be dangerous. This is a statutory offence of negligence. Section 2A(3) states: 'in determining for the purposes of those subsec-tions what would be expected of, or obvious to, a competent and careful driver in a particu-lar case, regard shall be had not only to the circumstances of which he could be expected to be aware but also to any circumstances shown to have been within the knowledge of the accused.' In *Bannister* [2009] EWCA Crim 1571, D was an advanced police driver who was convicted of dangerous driving after losing control of his car and crashing it into a copse of trees having driven at 113 mph in wet conditions. On appeal D contended that, by virtue of s 2A(3), the jury should have been directed that they could take into account his advanced driv-ing skills in evaluating whether he was driving dangerously. The Court of Appeal rejected this argument and held that such an interpretation of s 2A would detract from its objective nature.

≈≈ **Question**

Does s 2A(3) necessarily import a subjective element into the offence? Would this be consist-ent with how negligence has been interpreted outside the context of dangerous driving?

FURTHER READING

Intention

R. A. Duff, 'The Obscure Intentions of the House of Lords' [1986] Crim LR 771

J. Horder, 'Intention in the Criminal Law—A Rejoinder' (1995) MLR 678

I. Kugler, *Direct and Oblique Intention in the Criminal Law* (2002)

N. Lacey, 'A Clear Concept of Intention' (1993) 56 MLR 621

N. Lacey, 'In(de)terminable Intentions' (1995) 58 MLR 692

A. W. Norrie, 'Oblique Intention and Legal Politics' [1989] Crim LR 793

A. Pedain, 'Intention and the Terrorist Example' [2003] Crim LR 579

J. C. Smith, 'Intention in Criminal Law' (1974) 27 CLP 93

J. C. Smith, 'A Note on Intention' [1990] Crim LR 85

V. Tadros, *Criminal Responsibility* (2005), Ch 8

G. Williams, 'The Mens Rea for Murder—Leave it Alone' (1989) 105 LQR 387

Recklessness

J. Brady, 'Recklessness, Negligence, Indifference and Awareness' (1980) 43 MLR 381

D. Kimel, 'Inadvertent Recklessness in Criminal Law' (2004) 120 LQR 548

V. Tadros, 'Recklessness and the Duty to Take Care' in S. Shute and A. Simester (eds), *Criminal Law Theory: Doctrines of the General Part* (2002)

Knowledge

E. Griew, 'Consistency, Communication and Codification—Reflections on Two Mens Rea Words' in P. R. Glazebrook (ed), *Reshaping the Criminal Law* (1978), p 57

S. Shute, 'Knowledge and Belief in the Criminal Law' in S. Shute and A. Simester (eds), *Criminal Law Theory: Doctrines of the General Part* (2002), p 171

G. R. Sullivan, 'Knowledge, Belief and Culpability' in S. Shute and A. Simester (eds), *Criminal Law Theory: Doctrines of the General Part* (2002), p 207

Negligence

H. L. A. Hart, 'Negligence, *Mens Rea* and Criminal Responsibility' in *Punishment and Responsibility* (1968)

A. P. Simester, 'Can Negligence be Culpable?' in J. Horder (ed), *Oxford Essays in Jurisprudence* (2000)

6
Strict liability

Some of the controversies that will be examined in this chapter include:

(1) the presumption of mens rea—that is, unless Parliament has indicated otherwise, a mental element is taken to be an unexpressed ingredient of every statutory offence;

(2) how to ascertain whether an offence is in fact one of strict liability;

(3) whether strict liability infringes Article 6 of the European Convention on Human Rights (ECHR);

(4) the merits of strict liability offences.

6.1 Introduction

A crime is one of strict liability if there is any one or more of the elements of the actus reus which do not require proof of fault—intention, knowledge, recklessness, belief, suspicion or even negligence. The imposition of strict liability is seen as a direct conflict with the primacy of the requirement of fault—mens rea—in criminal offences. Although the courts have recently reaffirmed the significance of the mens rea principle, there are now so many strict liability offences in English criminal law that in practical terms strict liability is of enormous importance.

This chapter focuses on identifying the circumstances in which an offence will be construed as one of strict liability—that is, where the Crown will not have to establish mens rea in relation to every element of the actus reus. It may be surprising to find that offences of great seriousness carrying heavy penalties and with serious social stigma have been interpreted as ones of strict liability. For example, the House of Lords has held that in sexual offences involving children under 13, liability as to age is strict. D aged 14 has sexual intercourse with V aged 12. V consents to the act. V has told D that she is 13. D has no reason to disbelieve her. He is guilty of an offence under s 5 of the Sexual Offences Act 2003 of having sex with a child under 13 carrying a maximum sentence of life imprisonment even though he had no idea V was under 13. See *G*, section 6.5.1, p 135.

6.2 What does strict liability mean?

There is a degree of confusion over the meaning of strict liability, which is both disappointing and surprising. It is commonly said that, in offences of strict liability, 'no mens rea' need be proved. Indeed, it was held in *Sandhu* [1997] Crim LR 288, that mens rea not only need not, but must not, be proved. As the cases in this chapter will show, strict liability usually means that no mens rea need be proved with respect to one or more elements of the offence. It does not mean that no mental element whatever need be proved. Lord Edmund-Davies in *Whitehouse; Lemon* [1979] 1 All ER 898 at 920 cited the statement in *Smith and Hogan* (see 9th edn, 1999, p 98) that 'an offence is regarded—and properly regarded—as one of strict liability if no mens rea need be proved as to a single element in the actus reus'. Care has to be taken with the definition. The single element to which no mens rea attaches is usually one of crucial importance so the effect is that a person with no moral culpability may be convicted.

S. P. Green, 'Six Senses of Strict Liability: A Plea for Formalism'
in A. Simester (ed), *Appraising Strict Liability* (2005) (references omitted)

1. Six Senses of Strict Criminal Liability

In this section, I consider the various ways in which the term 'strict liability' has been used in the criminal law literature. Six different senses of the term will be identified: (1) offences that contain at least one material element for which there is no corresponding *mens rea* element; (2) statutory schemes that bar the use of one or more *mens-rea*-negating defences; (3) procedural devices that require a defendant's intent to be presumed from other facts; (4) offences that require a less serious form of *mens rea* than has traditionally been required by the criminal law; (5) offences that require a less serious form of harmfulness than has traditionally been required by the criminal law; and (6) offences that require a less serious form of wrongfulness than has traditionally been required by the criminal law.

Offences Omitting Requirement of Mens Rea

The most common use of the term 'strict liability' in the criminal law—and the only one, ultimately, that I can recommend—is to refer to offences that contain at least one material element for which there is no corresponding *mens rea* requirement. By *mens rea*, I mean the requirement that a defendant perform a voluntary physical act with intent, purpose, knowledge, belief, recklessness, negligence, or some other prescribed mental state. Thus, strict liability in this first sense is simply criminal liability in the absence of intent, purpose, knowledge, and the like. . . . [Within this category] several clarifications are in order. First, we can distinguish between offences for which no *mens rea* is required with respect to any material element (referred to here as 'pure' strict liability), and offences for which no *mens rea* is required with respect to at least one element but is required with respect to at least one other element (referred to as 'impure' strict liability). [See *Larsonneur*, section 2.4, p 32.]

. . . [S]tatutory rape is properly viewed as a strict liability offence because, although the defendant must be shown to have engaged intentionally in sexual intercourse with an under-age person, the offence does not require that the defendant know that the victim was under age [see the Sexual Offences Act 2003, s 5, section 6.5.1, p 135]. That is, a defendant may be convicted of statutory rape even though he reasonably but mistakenly believed that the victim was old enough to consent to intercourse. Secondly, within the category of impure strict liability, we can distinguish between 'constructive' and 'non-constructive' strict liability. [Unlawful act manslaughter involves constructive strict liability in that what must usually be proved is *mens rea* as to some crime—ie the intentional commission of an offence but no mens rea as to death, see section 9.2.1.1, p 210.] The *mens rea* required for non-constructive forms of strict liability (such as statutory rape) is not *mens rea* as to a crime. Indeed, it is not *mens rea* as to any form of wrongdoing. Rather, it is simply *mens rea* as to some defining element, such as, in the case of selling adulterated food or drugs, knowledge that one has sold food or drugs. Thus, once we consider non-constructive forms of strict liability, we can see how much broader the class of impure strict liability is than the class of pure strict liability. Thirdly, there are some offences that, while they do not require proof of *mens rea*, do allow the defendant to offer a defence of 'due diligence' [see section 6.7.2, p 142]. Because such offences omit the requirement of *mens rea*, they should be regarded as imposing strict liability in this first sense identified; although, as we shall see below, they might not satisfy the requirements of so-called 'substantive' strict liability. Fourthly, we can distinguish between offences that do not require a showing of *mens rea*, but do allow the assertion of affirmative defences such as mistake of fact; and offences that not only do not require a showing of *mens rea* but also prohibit the assertion of affirmative defences (this latter kind of strict liability is usually referred to as 'absolute liability').

In addition, following the Model Penal Code's culpability scheme, we can distinguish among strict liability with respect to a (1) conduct element, (2) result element, and (3) attendant circumstance element. Driving an automobile above the speed limit is an example of an offence that typically imposes strict liability with respect to the defendant's conduct. The prosecution need not prove that the defendant intended to drive above the speed limit, or even that he believed that he was driving in such a manner, in order for liability to be imposed. [Unlawful act manslaughter] is an example of an offence that imposes strict liability with respect to a result element. The defendant need not intend, or even believe, that his conduct might result in death in order for liability to be imposed. Statutory rape imposes strict liability with respect to an attendant circumstance—namely, the circumstance of whether the . . . victim is below the statutory age. Once again, the defendant need not be aware that the attendant circumstance existed. . . .

[Green describes each of the other five uses of the term strict liability and continues:]

Formal versus Substantive Strict Liability

A number of commentators have distinguished broadly between two different senses of the term 'strict liability': (1) 'formal' strict liability (also referred to as 'narrow', 'legal', or 'elemental' strict liability); and (2) 'substantive' strict liability (also referred to as 'broad' or 'moral' strict liability). In order to determine whether a statute involves strict liability in the substantive sense, we need to apply a normative test; that is, we need to ask whether, under such a regime, a defendant can be convicted without a showing of moral 'fault'. By contrast, determining whether a criminal statute involves strict liability in the formal sense can supposedly be determined by a 'mechanical' test without consideration of the statute's deeper moral content, simply by asking whether the offence requires a showing of some form of mental element.

Of the six kinds of strict liability identified in the previous section, only the first—omission of the *mens rea* requirement—qualifies as formal. The other five—barring *mens-rea*-negating defences; presuming intent; and reducing the level of required culpability, harmfulness, or wrongfulness—are all substantive. Thus, the position that I am advocating in this chapter can be reframed as follows: The term 'strict liability' should be used solely in its formal or legal sense, and not in its substantive or moral sense . . .

[Green offers:] five reasons for eschewing the substantive senses of strict liability and adhering strictly to its formal sense: First, moving away from the substantive sense of strict liability and towards a formalistic approach is consistent with an important parallel trend in the criminal law away from the broad, 'blameworthiness' sense of *mens rea* and towards its narrow, 'elemental' sense. Secondly, there are significant, perhaps irresoluble, difficulties in determining whether an offence entails substantive strict liability. Thirdly, talking about strict liability in the substantive sense contributes to a mistaken impression of moral equivalence among different forms of what I shall refer to as 'moral deficiency' in the criminal law. Fourthly, talking about strict liability in the substantive sense creates confusion in determining whether a statute should be interpreted as omitting *mens rea*. Finally, talk of substantive strict liability leads to a miscalculation of the extent of the overcriminalization problem.

6.3 When will strict liability be imposed?

Most offences are now defined by statute. It is therefore a question of statutory construction whether the external elements of the offence require proof of mental elements and, if so, what each mental element is. Often the definition uses a word or a phrase—'knowingly', 'with intent to', 'recklessly', 'wilfully', 'dishonestly', and so on—which gives guidance to the court. Often the definition uses a verb or noun which imports a mental element of some kind—'permits' and 'possesses', are examples—so that there cannot be an actus reus without that mental element.

However, it does not follow that, simply because Parliament has not used a word or phrase importing a mental element, the court will necessarily find that mens rea is not required. On the contrary, the courts have frequently asserted that there is a presumption in favour of mens rea which must be rebutted by the prosecution; but the application of this presumption has been far from consistent.

All earlier cases must now be reconsidered in the light of the two leading cases, *B (a minor) v DPP* [2000] UKHL 13 and *K* [2002] 1 AC 642, which follow. The presumption of mens rea is reasserted with particular emphasis. It applies to all statutory offences, unless excluded expressly or by necessary implication. According to Lord Steyn, 'It can only be displaced by specific language, ie, an express provision or a necessary implication.' What distinguishes these from earlier pronouncements is not only the fact that they are two unanimous decisions of the House of Lords but also the fact that they effectively overrule *Prince* (1875) LR 2 CCR 154, regarded as the leading case on strict liability for 125 years, and many cases which applied it. (Prince was convicted of taking a girl under 16 out of the possession of her parents although he believed on reasonable grounds that she was 18. Liability as to her age was held to be strict.) The principles stated by the House are not limited to age-related elements of the actus reus; there is a presumption of mens rea in respect of every element of the actus reus unless displaced.

6.3.1 The presumption of mens rea as a constitutional principle

The first question in determining whether an offence is one of strict liability is to consider whether the statute imposes a requirement of mens rea expressly or by necessary implication. The House of Lords reasserted the primacy of the presumption of mens rea in two important cases: *B v DPP* and *R v K*. In *B v DPP*, D, who was 15, met V, who was under the age of 14, on a bus and incited her to commit a sexual act on him. D was charged with inciting a girl under the age of 14 to commit an act of gross indecency, contrary to s 1(1) of the Indecency with Children Act 1960. An issue arose as to whether D should be acquitted if D genuinely believed that V was over the age of 14. At first instance, it was held that the offence D was charged with was one of strict liability and that a mistaken belief as to the age of the victim was no defence. The Divisional Court agreed with this interpretation of the law and held that the purpose of s 1(1) was to offer protection to children under the age of 14, irrespective of whether the defendant knew the age of the victim. D appealed to the House of Lords. The House of Lords, in quashing D's conviction, held that because the offence in s 1(1) made no mention of mens rea, the starting point for a court was the common law presumption that mens rea was an essential ingredient unless Parliament had indicated a contrary intention either expressly or by necessary implication. The House of Lords observed that there was no agreement that strict liability was necessary to the enforcement of the law in sexual matters. After examining the relevant authorities, the House of Lords concluded that there was no unequivocal intention to displace the common law presumption. Therefore, it was necessary for the prosecution to prove the absence of a genuine belief on the part of the accused that the victim was 14 or over.

The judgment in *B v DPP* proved to be controversial. There were some who thought the House of Lords, if presented with the opportunity, would deviate from the unequivocal approach it had taken. As the next case demonstrates, however, this prediction proved to be inaccurate.

R v K
[2001] UKHL 41, House of Lords

(Lords Bingham, Nicholls, Steyn, Hobhouse and Millett)

K, aged 26, was charged with indecent assault on a girl C, aged 14, contrary to the Sexual Offences Act 1956, s 14(1) [see now the offence of sexual assault under the Sexual Offences Act 2003, s 3, section 12.2.3, p 332]. K claimed that C consented and that she had told him she was 16 and that he had had no reason to disbelieve her. At trial it was argued that the prosecution had to prove that at the time of the incident K did not honestly believe that C was 16 or over. The Court of Appeal certified the following point of law of general public importance:

(a) Is a defendant entitled to be acquitted of the offence of indecent assault on a complainant under the age of 16 years, contrary to s 14(1) of the 1956 Act, if he may hold an honest belief that the complainant in question was aged 16 years or over?

(b) If yes, must the belief be held on reasonable grounds?

Lord Bingham of Cornhill:

Section 14 of the 1956 Act is in these terms:

'(1) It is an offence, subject to the exception mentioned in subsection (3) of this section, for a person to make an indecent assault on a woman.

(2) A girl under the age of sixteen cannot in law give any consent which would prevent an act being an assault for the purposes of this section.

(3) Where a marriage is invalid under section two of the Marriage Act 1949, or section one of the Age of Marriage Act 1929 (the wife being a girl under the age of sixteen), the invalidity does not make the husband guilty of any offence under this section by reason of her incapacity to consent while under that age, if he believes her to be his wife and has reasonable cause for the belief.

(4) A woman who is a defective cannot in law give any consent which would prevent an act being an assault for the purposes of this section, but a person is only to be treated as guilty of an indecent assault on a defective by reason of that incapacity to consent, if that person knew or had reason to suspect her to be a defective.'

This section is matched by a parallel section, s 15, which makes it an offence for a person to make an indecent assault on a man. Subsections (2) and (3) of s 15 are to the same effect, in relation to men, as sub-ss (2) and (4) in relation to women.

If the provisions of s 14 were part of a single, coherent legislative scheme and were read without reference to any overriding presumption of statutory interpretation, there would be great force in the simple submission which Mr Scrivener, resisting this appeal on behalf of the Crown, based upon them: sub-ss (3) and (4) define circumstances in which a defendant's belief, knowledge or suspicion exonerate a defendant from liability for what would otherwise be an indecent assault; if it had been intended to exonerate a defendant who believed a complainant to be 16 or over, this ground of exoneration would have been expressed in sub-s (2); the omission of such a provision makes plain that no such ground of exoneration was intended.

It is, however, plain that s 14 was not part of a single, coherent legislative scheme. The 1956 Act was a consolidation Act. Its provisions derived from diverse sources. The rag-bag nature of the 1956 Act and its predecessor statutes has been the subject of repeated comment: see, for example, the observations of the draftsman of the Offences Against the Person Act 1861 Act quoted in *B (a minor) v DPP* [2000] 1 All ER 833 at 848, [2000] 2 AC 428 at 473; the criticisms of Lord Nicholls of Birkenhead in the same case (see [2000] 1 All ER 833 at 841, [2000] 2 AC 428 at 465); the description of the Act by Professor Lacey as 'a patchwork of pre-existing offences' in 'Beset by Boundaries: The Home Office Review of Sex Offences' [2001] Crim LR 3; the recognition of the Home Office in 'Setting the Boundaries: Reforming the law on sex offences; Vol 1, p 35, para 3.2.3 (July 2000) that the present legislation 'does not form a coherent code'.

[His lordship then referred to the offences under the old legislation and how they were criticized on the basis that they did not afford adequate protection to children]

Neither in s 14 nor elsewhere in the 1956 Act is there any express exclusion of the need to prove an absence of genuine belief on the part of a defendant as to the age of an underage victim. Had it been intended to exclude that element of mens rea it could very conveniently have been so provided in or following sub-s (2).

For reasons already given, significance cannot be attached to the inclusion of grounds of exoneration in sub-ss (3) and (4) and the omission of such a ground from sub-s (2), although sub-ss (3) and (4) do reflect parliamentary recognition that a defendant should not be criminally liable if he misapprehends a factual matter on which his criminal liability depends. There is nothing in the language of this statute which justifies, as a matter of necessary implication, the conclusion that Parliament must have intended to exclude this ingredient of mens rea in s 14 any more than in s 1. If the effect of the presumption is read into s 14, with reference to the defendant's belief as to the age of the victim, no absurdity results. With the wisdom of hindsight it can be seen that Avory J was right to hold, in *R v Forde*, that the statutory defence in s 2 of the 1922 Act could not be read into s 1 of that Act, but he was wrong in failing to apply to s 1 of the 1922 Act the overriding presumption referred to in [17] above. He may, no doubt, have been misled by the now discredited authority of *R v Prince* (1875) LR 2 CCR 154, [1874–80] All ER Rep 881, which although not apparently cited will have been very familiar to him.

I consider that [the trial judge] reached the right conclusion. The Court of Appeal gave more weight to the re-enactment of the relevant provisions in 1956 than was appropriate for a consolidation Act.

I would accordingly give an affirmative answer to the first certified question. It is common ground that a negative answer should be given to the second question. In giving those answers I would make the following concluding points: (1) Nothing in this opinion has any bearing on a case in which the victim does not in fact consent. While s 14(2) provides that a girl under the age of 16 cannot in law give any consent which would prevent an act being an assault, she may in fact (although not in law) consent. If it is shown that she did not consent, and that the defendant did not genuinely believe that she consented, any belief by the defendant concerning her age is irrelevant, since her age is relevant only to her capacity to consent. (2) While a defendant's belief need not be reasonable provided it is honest and genuine, the reasonableness or unreasonableness of the belief is by no means irrelevant. The more unreasonable the belief, the less likely it is to be accepted as genuine (see *R v Gladstone Williams* [1987] 3 All ER 411 at 415.) (3) Although properly applied to s 1 of the 1960 Act and s 14 of the 1956 Act, the presumption cannot be applied to ss 5 and 6 of the 1956 Act. Those sections as a pair derive directly from corresponding sections in the 1871 Act, as demonstrated above. The statutory or young man's defence was introduced into what is now s 6. Its omission from what is now s 5 is plainly deliberate. A genuine belief that a child three years under the age of consent was over that age would in any event defy credulity. Section 6(3) of the 1956 Act plainly defines the state of knowledge which will exonerate a defendant accused under that section, and this express provision necessarily excludes the more general presumption. (4) Nothing in this opinion should be taken to minimise the potential seriousness of the offence of indecent assault. While some instances of the offence may be relatively minor, others may be scarcely less serious than rape itself. This is reflected in the maximum penalty, now increased to ten years' imprisonment, and the mandatory requirement that those convicted be subject to the notification requirements of the Sex Offenders Act 1997. These considerations make it more rather than less important that, in any forthcoming recasting of the law on sexual offences, the *mens rea* requirement should be defined with extreme care and precision. Parliament is sovereign and has the responsibility to decide where the boundaries of criminal activity should be drawn. . . . I would allow this appeal.

[Lord Nicholls agreed, Lords Steyn and Hobhouse made concurring speeches.]

Lord Millett:

My Lords, I have had the advantage of reading in draft the speech of my noble and learned friend Lord Bingham of Cornhill, with which I agree. For the reasons he gives I would allow the appeal and answer the certified questions as he proposes.

I do so without reluctance but with some misgiving, for I have little doubt that we shall be failing to give effect to the intention of Parliament and will reduce s 14 of the Sexual Offence Act 1956 to incoherence. The section creates a single offence of indecent assault. It is intended for the protection of women. Subsection (2) and the first part of sub-s (4) extend the scope of the section. They are intended to protect women who are particularly vulnerable and who by reason of age or mental infirmity may be prevailed upon to give their consent to what would otherwise be an indecent assault. Subsection (3) and the proviso to sub-s (4) afford the defendant a limited defence based on the defendant's state of mind.

The need for such a defence in the case of a woman with impaired mental faculties is obvious. Her mental state may well not be apparent, and it would be manifestly unjust to deny a defence where the defendant believed that she was normal and had no reason to suspect that she was not. The absence of a similar proviso to sub-s (2), while suggesting that no similar defence is intended in the case of underage girls, does not lead inevitably to that conclusion. But sub-s (3) is a different matter. Introduced when the age of marriage was raised to 16, its policy is self-evident. There is no need to extend the scope of the section, designed to protect women from assault and young girls from exploitation, to a girl whom the defendant believes he has married. In such a case the defendant has not taken advantage of her age for his own sexual gratification. On the contrary, he is labouring under the belief that he has undertaken a lifelong responsibility towards her.

Yet sub-s (3) requires the defendant's mistaken belief in the subsistence of a valid marriage to be reasonable as well as honest. To afford a defendant who has not married the girl a more generous defence than one who believes he has is grotesque. It cannot have been the intention of Parliament, either in 1929 when it introduced the sub-s (3) defence, or when it consolidated the law in 1956. Parliament must have known that it was a commonplace for men to be convicted of the offence despite their genuine belief that the girl was over 16, a matter which went to mitigation but not defence. Parliament not only viewed this state of affairs with equanimity, but on the earlier occasion at least legislated on a basis which made no sense unless this was the law.

But the age of consent has long since ceased to reflect ordinary life, and in this respect Parliament has signally failed to discharge its responsibility for keeping the criminal law in touch with the needs of

> society. I am persuaded that the piecemeal introduction of the various elements of s 14, coupled with the persistent failure of Parliament to rationalise this branch of the law even to the extent of removing absurdities which the courts have identified, means that we ought not to strain after internal coherence even in a single offence. Injustice is too high a price to pay for consistency.
>
> *Appeal allowed*

Lord Bingham observes that a man who has sexual intercourse with a girl aged 12 is unlikely to be able plausibly to assert that he believed her to be 16 but (a) it is not impossible, (b) that does not affect the principle, and (c) the 'man'—who may be a boy—may easily have believed her to be 13 or 14. See the discussion, section 6.5.1, p 135, of the mens rea in relation to the corresponding offences under the Sexual Offences Act 2003.

≈ **Questions**

Did not Lord Millett acknowledge the truth—that the House, having lost patience with Parliament, was ignoring its plain intention? Can this be justified? Is it a breach of the constitutional principle that Parliament is sovereign?

In *Kumar* [2005] Crim LR 470, [2004] EWCA Crim 3207, K's conviction for buggery, contrary to s 12 of the Sexual Offences Act 1956, following consensual anal intercourse with the 14-year-old complainant was quashed by the Court of Appeal. It was held that the mental element had not been excluded expressly from s 12 by any compellingly clear or truly necessary implication, and that such a construction did not give rise to any internal inconsistency. Buggery stemmed from a common law offence and was unlike the age-based offences in the 1956 Act.

The cases of *B* and *K* met with warm approval from some (Sir John Smith at [2000] Crim LR 403 and [2001] Crim LR 993), and harsh criticism from others (eg P. Glazebrook, 'How Old Did *You* Think She Was?' (2001) 60 CLJ 26).

6.3.1.1 Application of *B v DPP* and *K*

The offences in issue in *B v DPP* [2000] UKHL 13 and *K* [2002] 1 AC 642 have been replaced by those in the Sexual Offences Act 2003, which itself contains numerous strict liability offences (see Chapter 12). The cases remain important authorities on the presumption of mens rea generally. It would be misleading, however, to think that since *B* and *K* the courts have consistently rejected strict liability; far from it. There are numerous instances of provisions being interpreted as imposing strict liability, see, for example, *Mohammed* [2002] EWCA Crim 1856, 2 WLR 1050 (materially contributing to insolvency by gambling carrying two years' imprisonment) and *Matudi* [2004] EWCA Crim 697 (importing prohibited animal products). In *Jackson* [2006] EWCA Crim 2380, the Court of Appeal held that the offence of unlawful low flying contrary to s 51 of the Air Force Act 1955, was one of strict liability. In *Deyemi* [2007] EWCA Crim 2060, possession of an electronic stun gun was held to constitute possession of a firearm where D was unaware it was a weapon: liability was strict. In those cases, the court had found the presumption rebutted by necessary implication having regard to well-established criteria: the words of the statute, seriousness of the offence, stigma attaching, legislative purpose, statutory context, ease of proof, etc. These are all discussed in the next section.

What *B* and *K* should do is cause the courts to revisit decisions in which particular statutes and words in statutes were previously found to impose strict liability. In *Cambridgeshire CC v Associated Lead Mills Ltd* [2005] EWHC 1627 (Admin), although Kennedy LJ was prepared to uphold a conviction based on a strict interpretation of the term 'use' on the basis of previous case law, Walker J, having regard to the discussion of the 'revitalised presumption' in *B* and *K* questioned whether even the offence based on 'use' is to be construed as one of strict liability.

More recently in *Brown* [2013] UKSC 43, the Supreme Court held that the offence of having unlawful carnal knowledge of a girl under the age of 14 years contrary to s 4 of the Criminal Law Amendment Acts (Northern Ireland) 1885–1923 was an offence of strict liability. Lord Kerr stated that the same policy considerations which were at issue in *G* [2008] UKHL 37 applied to the facts of this case, namely protecting young girls. See section 6.5.1, p 135.

6.3.2 Factors relevant to determining strict liability

The identification of offences of strict liability, or, more precisely, the identification of the element or elements in the offence which will attract strict liability remains a difficult problem.

The factors commonly cited as influencing the decision whether the presumption of mens rea is rebutted in any case include:

(1) the use of verbs and adverbs importing a mental element—knowingly, wilfully, etc;

(2) the social context of the crime:

   (a) whether it is a 'real crime' or a quasi-crime or regulatory offence;

   (b) whether the crime is one of general or special prohibition—the latter making it more likely that the presumption will be rebutted;

   (c) the ease with which those affected by the regulation might comply;

   (d) the social danger involved;

(3) the severity of the punishment.

In *Gammon (Hong Kong) Ltd v A-G of Hong Kong* [1984] UKPC 17, Lord Scarman attempted to give some guidance by listing five criteria:

(1) there is a presumption of law that mens rea is required before a person can be held guilty of a criminal offence; (2) the presumption is particularly strong where the offence is 'truly criminal' in character; (3) the presumption applies to statutory offences, and can be displaced only if this is clearly or by necessary implication the effect of the statute; (4) the only situation in which the presumption can be displaced is where the statute is concerned with an issue of social concern; public safety is such an issue; (5) even where a statute is concerned with such an issue, the presumption of mens rea stands unless it can be shown that the creation of strict liability will be effective to promote the objects of the statute by encouraging greater vigilance to prevent the commission of the prohibited act.

This must now be read in the light of *B* and *K*.

Lord Scarman says that the presumption which always favours mens rea is particularly strong where the offence is truly criminal. The presumption can only be displaced where the statute is concerned with an issue of social concern. Even here the presumption in favour of mens rea remains unless it can be shown that the creation of strict liability will be effective to promote the objects of the statute by creating greater vigilance. Can all this be reconciled with the assertion by Lord Steyn in *K* that the presumption 'can only be displaced by specific language, ie, an express provision or a necessary implication'? Up to an uncertain point it is possible to identify offences, or elements in offences, which were, and perhaps still are, likely to attract strict liability. Usually, though by no means invariably, the offence is one created in a statute which seeks to regulate the activities of a particular class of persons such as licensees, or the sellers of food and drugs, or employers in industry and commerce. Hence the expression 'regulatory offences', namely, offences which are meant to regulate the carrying on of particular activities. It might be convenient, it would certainly be simpler, if all such offences could be classified as offences of strict liability but it is not as straightforward as that. Parliament is (or the parliamentary draftsmen are) unhelpful in that the use of a mens rea word (eg 'knowingly' or 'permitting') in one provision and its absence in another provision (or sometimes in the same provision) appears to be haphazard and without any underlying rationale.

The importance of the distinction between 'regulatory offences' and 'true crimes' was emphasized recently by Lord Sumption in *Taylor* [2016] UKSC 5. His lordship characterized the offence in issue in that case, namely aggravated vehicle taking contrary to s 12A of the Theft Act 1968, as a serious crime that was in no sense a regulatory or 'quasi-criminal' enactment. After citing the judgment of the House of Lords in *Sweet v Parsley*, Lord Sumption offered some guidance on how 'true crimes' may be distinguished from mere 'regulatory offences'.

26. The rule [ie that mens rea is an essential ingredient of every offence] was never absolute, even in late Victorian England, when *R v Tolson* 23 QBD 168 was decided. But in general a criminal offence will require proof of mens rea unless strict liability is either required by the clear language of the act or necessary for the achievement of its purpose. Cases in the latter category usually involve regulatory statutes. Wills J, immediately after the passage which I have quoted, gave as examples 'byelaws ... regulating the width of thoroughfares, the height of buildings, the thickness of walls, and a variety of other matters necessary for the general welfare, health, or convenience'. Such legislation generally has two characteristic features. The first is that its requirements are founded on collective convenience rather than moral imperatives. Lord Reid in *Sweet v Parsley* [1970] AC 132 called such offences 'quasi-criminal'. But, as he observed at p 149, where the offence carries a significant moral stigma, it is necessary to consider 'whether, in a case of this gravity, the public interest really requires that an innocent person should be prevented from proving his innocence in order that fewer guilty men may escape'. The second characteristic feature of offences of strict liability is that, although fault in the actual commission of the offence may be unnecessary, there are none the less positive steps that the prospect of criminal liability may cause people to take in order to prevent the offence from occurring.

≋ *Question*

Do you think the distinction between 'true crimes' and 'quasi-crimes' is sufficiently clear for it to act as the determinant of whether an offence is one of strict liability? See K. Laird, 'The Decline of Criminal Law Causation Without Limits' (2016) 132 LQR 566.

Despite the fact that the courts regularly cite the features listed earlier in this section in *Gammon* as being important in determining whether an offence is one of strict liability, it remains difficult to discern from the cases to what extent, if at all, the courts openly express one dominant feature (statutory construction, real or quasi-crime, social context, penalty, etc) as the basis for imposing or refusing to impose strict liability.

Some famous examples of the courts addressing whether the offence before them was one of strict liability include the following.

Cundy v Le Cocq [1884] 13 QBD 207, Queen's Bench Division: the court held that the offence under s 13 of the Licensing Act 1872 was one of strict liability. D, being the keeper of licensed premises, unlawfully sold intoxicating liquor to a drunken person. It was proved that there had been a sale of intoxicating liquor and that the person served was drunk. Neither D nor his servants had noticed that the person served was drunk; that person had been quiet and had done nothing to indicate insobriety.

Alphacell Ltd v Woodward [1972] UKHL 4: D was a company that caused large quantities of polluted material to flow into a river. The pumps that D had installed at his plant to prevent this failed to work on the day in question because they were blocked by debris. D had regularly inspected the mechanism and no debris had been in them when the pumps were inspected a few days before the overflow. D was found guilty of the offence under the Rivers (Prevention of Pollution) Act 1951 which criminalized a person who 'causes or knowingly permits to enter a stream any poisonous, noxious or polluting matter'. The House of Lords upheld the conviction. There was no mens rea as to the form of the offence based on 'causing' pollution.

〰 **Question**

Was the case then, one of strict liability? But could this be said of the *Empress Car* case [1999] 2 AC 22, section 3.2.3.2, p 47?

See further G. Richardson, 'Strict Liability for Regulatory Crime: The Empirical Research' [1987] Crim LR 295, who reports that 'the majority of enforcement officers regard [strict liability] with favour and urge its retention' (at 303). In regulatory offences this claim that 'negotiated compliance' by a regulatory authority is more efficient is often advanced. See J. Rowan-Robinson, P. Q. Watchman and C. R. Barker, 'Crime and Regulation' [1988] Crim LR 211.

Warner v Metropolitan Police Commissioner [1968] 2 All ER 356, House of Lords: D was convicted of possessing drugs. He was found in possession of two boxes. One box contained perfume (which D was in the habit of selling), the other 20,000 tablets containing a prohibited drug. D claimed he thought both boxes contained perfume and he had not looked inside them. Lord Guest concluded: 'There are therefore, three requisites of possession. First, there must be actual or potential physical control, secondly physical control is not possession, unless accompanied by intention, hence, if a thing is put into a hand of a sleeping person, he had not possession of it. Thirdly, the possibility and intention must be visible or evidenced by external signs, for if the thing shows no signs of being under the control of anyone, it is not possessed'. A person must know he is in possession of the thing but there is no need to prove awareness that it is a drug. See now s 28 of the Misuse of Drugs Act 1971.

〰 **Questions**

(1) Why does the offence of possession of these articles need to be interpreted so strictly?

(2) D is found carrying a sealed package which contains heroin. How would the judges have dealt with him if he believed: (a) the box was empty; (b) the box contained aspirin, or sweets, or jewellery, or stolen jewellery, or explosives, or something, but he had no idea what?

6.4 Strict liability and defences

If an offence is one of strict liability it might be thought that it is not therefore possible to plead a defence, either originating in statute or common law, to negate liability. However this is not the case, as liability is not 'absolute'. For example, the Divisional Court accepted in *Santos v CPS* [2013] EWHC 550 (Admin) that necessity could be pleaded as a defence to the strict liability offences of riding a motorcycle without insurance and protective headgear. In addition, it was explicitly stated in the earlier case of *Martin* [1988] EWCA Crim 2 that duress can be pleaded as a defence to a crime of strict liability.

The relationship between strict liability defences was considered by the Court of Appeal in more detail in *Gregory* [2011] EWCA Crim 1712. G was convicted of possessing an altered firearm (sawn-off shotgun) without a firearm certificate and of possessing a firearm when prohibited. G and his mother had been observed going into a wood and on emerging an hour later when their car was stopped, a sawn-off shotgun was found in the boot. G claimed that he had found a package whilst walking in the woods. He realized it was a firearm and had taken it back to the car intending to keep it. However, his mother persuaded him to hand it into the police and they were on their way to the local police station when they were stopped. At trial for the possession offences, the judge ruled that s 1(1) of the Firearms Act 1968 created an absolute offence (ie one with no mens rea and no defences: see section 6.4, and that G's mental state was irrelevant. There being no defence to the charge, G thereupon pleaded guilty. The judge considered G's version of events at a Newton hearing (a hearing of facts to determine sentence) and found that G had not come across the gun by chance and that he had not proposed immediately to take it to the police. G appealed arguing that the judge was wrong to conclude that s 1(1) created an absolute offence and, in the alternative, that the guilty plea was entered on a flawed basis since the defence of duress of circumstances should have been available to him. The Court of Appeal upheld the conviction. The offence was one of 'strict' liability rather than one of 'absolute' liability. As the Lord Chief Justice stated at [10]:

> it was wrong for him [ie the judge] to describe the offence as one of absolute liability. To be in possession of a firearm without a firearm certificate is an offence of strict liability. The authorities are consistent and numerous. They are conveniently summarised in *R v Zahid* [2010] EWCA Crim 2158, adopting *R v Deyemi and Edwards* [2008] 1 Cr App R 25.

There does seem to be uncertainty over whether insanity is available as a defence, however. In *DPP v H* [1997] 1 WLR 1406, McGowan LJ doubted whether the defence was available because, 'the [insanity] defence is based on an absence of mens rea but none is required for the offence of driving with an excess of alcohol'. However, the insanity defence is not predicated upon a denial of mens rea but rather a denial of moral responsibility for committing the actus reus of the offence, so the validity of this authority seems to be rather questionable. See section 24.4, p 693.

6.5 Strict liability offences and the ECHR

The arguments relating to the relationship between the burden of proof and the imposition of strict liability were clearly fuelled by the arrival of the Human Rights Act. It has been argued that the imposition of strict liability might engage, for example:

- Article 3 (freedom from inhuman or degrading treatment). Was the criminal trial for sexual offending degrading treatment in *R v K*, section 6.3.1.1?

- Article 8 (respect for privacy). Are the Article 8 rights of a 15-year-old who has sex with a consenting 12-year-old who told him she was 13 infringed when he is sent to prison for up to a maximum of life imprisonment? See *G* in the following section, p 135.

See G. R. Sullivan, 'Strict Liability for Criminal Offences in England and Wales following Incorporation into English Law of the ECHR' in A. Simester (ed), *Appraising Strict Liability* (2005), p 206.

Since the Human Rights Act does not empower courts to 'strike down' statutes, the challenge is not of the same magnitude as that in, for example, the United States, where it is possible for some strict liability offences to be held to be unconstitutional (R. A. Duff, 'Strict Liability, Legal Presumptions and the Presumption of Innocence' in A Simester (ed), *Appraising Strict Liability* (2005), p 125).

6.5.1 Strict liability and Article 6

A major controversy has been whether strict liability offences infringe the presumption of innocence guaranteed under Article 6(2) of the European Convention. Some commentators argued that strict liability offences may offend against Article 6(2) because once the prohibited act is proved, D is 'presumed' to be liable. See, for example, V. Tadros and S. Tierney, 'The Presumption of Innocence and the Human Rights Act' (2004) 67 MLR 402. Some commentators argued that the effect of the presumption and the imposition of strict liability is the same, but this functional equivalence was keenly disputed by others (see P. Roberts, 'Strict Liability and the Presumption of Innocence' in A. Simester (ed), *Appraising Strict Liability* (2005), p 151). Most commentators regarded the argument based on Article 6(2) as a weak one. As Professor Ashworth explained:

> it is wrong to convict people of serious offences without proof of culpability, and that is a separate argument from the presumption of innocence. It is not an argument about evidence and procedure at all but an argument about the proper preconditions of criminal liability. (A. Ashworth, 'Four Threats to the Presumption of Innocence' (2006) E & P 241 at 252–253)

The English courts agreed, drawing a distinction between the protection afforded under Article 6(2) which was procedural and the imposition of strict liability in substantive criminal law, and holding, in cases such as *Barnfather v Islington LBC* [2003] EWHC 418 (Admin), that Article 6(2) is restricted to providing procedural protection and does not render the imposition of strict liability incompatible with Article 6(2). As Lord Bingham stated in *Sheldrake* [2005] 1 AC 246 at [21] (emphasis added):

> The overriding concern is that a trial should be fair, and the presumption of innocence is a fundamental right directed to that end. The Convention does not outlaw presumptions of fact or law but requires that these should be kept within reasonable limits and should not be arbitrary. *It is open to states to define the constituent elements of a criminal offence, excluding the requirement of mens rea.* But the substance and effect of any presumption adverse to a defendant must be examined, and must be reasonable. Relevant to any judgment on reasonableness or proportionality will be the opportunity given to the defendant to rebut the presumption, maintenance of the rights of the defence, flexibility in application of the presumption, retention by the court of a power to assess the evidence, the importance of what is at stake and the difficulty which a prosecutor may face in the absence of a presumption.

The issue came before the House of Lords for direct consideration in the case of *G*.

R v G and another
[2008] UKHL 37, House of Lords

(Lords Hoffmann, Hope, Carswell, Baroness Hale and Lord Mance)

G, who was aged 15, pleaded guilty to rape of a child under 13 (Sexual Offences Act 2003, s 5). Section 5 of the Sexual Offences Act 2003 provides:

(1) A person commits an offence if —

    (a) he intentionally penetrates the vagina, anus or mouth of another person with his penis; and

    (b) the other person is under 13.

(2) A person guilty of an offence under this section is liable, on conviction on indictment, to imprisonment for life.

G's basis of plea was that V consented and that he reasonably believed her to be older than 13, because she had so informed him. The Court of Appeal upheld his conviction and confirmed that s 5 creates an offence of strict liability to which belief in consent or the age of the victim has no application. The actus reus of the offence is vaginal, anal or oral sexual intercourse with a victim under 13, whether the victim consented or not. Section 5 created an offence even where the defendant reasonably believed that the child was 16 or over. The presumption of mens rea was negatived by necessary implication, arising from the contrast of the express references to reasonable belief that a child was 16 or over, in other sections—s 9 of the 2003 Act—and the absence of any such reference in relation to children under 13. G appealed. The Court of Appeal dismissed the appeal against conviction but allowed an appeal against sentence and substituted a conditional discharge. It certified two questions as being of general public importance:

(1) May a criminal offence of strict liability violate article 6(1) and/or 6(2) . . . ?

(2) Is it compatible with a child's rights under article 8 . . . to convict him of rape contrary to section 5 . . . in circumstances where the agreed basis of plea establishes that his offence fell properly within the ambit of section 13 . . . ?

G appealed to the House of Lords.

[Lord Hoffmann stated the facts and continued:]

3. The mental element of the offence under section 5, as the language and structure of the section makes clear, is that penetration must be intentional but there is no requirement that the accused must have known that the other person was under 13. The policy of the legislation is to protect children. If you have sex with someone who is on any view a child or young person, you take your chance on exactly how old they are. To that extent the offence is one of strict liability and it is no defence that the accused believed the other person to be 13 or over.

4. Article 6(1) provides that in the determination of his civil rights or any criminal charge, everyone is entitled to a 'fair and public hearing' and article 6(2) provides that everyone charged with a criminal offence 'shall be presumed innocent until proved guilty according to law'. It is settled law that Article 6(1) guarantees fair procedure and the observance of the principle of the separation of powers but not that either the civil or criminal law will have any particular substantive content: see *Matthews v Ministry of Defence* [2003] UKHL 4; [2003] 1 AC 1163. Likewise, article 6(2) requires him to be presumed innocent of the offence but does not say anything about what the mental or other elements of the offence should be. In the case of civil law, this was established (after a moment of aberration) by

Z v United Kingdom (2002) 34 EHRR 3. There is no reason why the reasoning should not apply equally to the substantive content of the criminal law. In *R v Gemmell* [2002] EWCA Crim 1992; [2003] 1 Cr App R 343, 356, para 33 Dyson LJ said:

> 'The position is quite clear. So far as Article 6 is concerned, the fairness of the provisions of the substantive law of the Contracting States is not a matter for investigation. The content and interpretation of domestic substantive law is not engaged by Article 6.'

5. The only authority which is said to cast any doubt upon this proposition is the decision of the Strasbourg court in *Salabiaku v France* (1988) 13 EHRR 379 and in particular a statement in paragraph 28 (at p.388) that 'presumptions of fact or of law' in criminal proceedings should be confined 'within reasonable limits'. No one has yet discovered what this paragraph means but your Lordships were referred to a wealth of academic learning which tries to solve the riddle.

6. My Lords, I think that judges and academic writers have picked over the carcass of this unfortunate case so many times in attempts to find some intelligible meat on its bones that the time has come to call a halt. The Strasbourg court, uninhibited by a doctrine of precedent or the need to find a ratio decidendi, seems to have ignored it. It is not mentioned in *Z v United Kingdom* (2002) 34 EHRR 3. I would recommend your Lordships to do likewise. For my part, I would simply endorse the remarks of Dyson LJ in *R v Gemmell* [2003] 1 Cr App R 343, 356 . . .

[His lordship dismissed the Article 8 argument.]

Lord Hope of Craighead:

. . .

Article 6(2)

24. Mr Owen's primary submission was that the offence which section 5 creates, interpreted as one of strict liability, is incompatible with article 6(2) of the Convention, which provides that everyone charged with a criminal offence shall be presumed innocent until proved guilty according to law. He sought support for this argument in the observations of the European Court in *Salabiaku v France* (1988) 13 EHRR 379. In paras 27–28 of its judgment the court said:

> '27. As the Government and the Commission have pointed out, in principle the Contracting States remain free to apply the criminal law to an act where it is not carried out in the normal exercise of one of the rights protected under the Convention and, accordingly, to define the constituent elements of the resulting offence. In particular, and again in principle, the Contracting States may, under certain conditions, penalise a simple or objective fact as such, irrespective of whether it results from criminal intent or from negligence. Examples of such offences may be found in the laws of the Contracting States.
>
> . . . 28 . . . Presumptions of fact or of law operate in every legal system. Clearly, the Convention does not prohibit such presumptions in principle. It does, however, require the Contracting States to remain within certain limits in this respect as regards criminal law. . . .
>
> Article 6(2) does not therefore regard presumptions of fact or of law provided for in the criminal law with indifference. It requires States to confine them within reasonable limits which take into account the importance of what is at stake and maintain the rights of the defence.'

25. Mr Owen sought to apply what he described as the reasonable limits test to the offence that section 5 creates. The effect of any offence of strict liability, he said, was to create a presumption that the accused had done something of which he was innocent. So the creation of strict criminal liability will always engage a consideration of compatibility with the presumption of innocence in article 6(2). The conduct to which the appellant had pleaded guilty in this case was morally blameless, as the complainant willingly agreed to have sexual intercourse with him. It was difficult to distil from *Salabiaku* a clear principle that strict criminal liability was always free from regulation under article 6(2). The

European Court said in para 27 that the Contracting States could penalise a simple or objective fact as such irrespective of whether there was criminal intent. But it had made it clear that it could only do so under certain conditions. This was to be read as applying not just to matters of procedure. The substance of an offence could be examined too, and it would violate article 6(2) if it failed properly to recognise that the accused is to be presumed innocent until proven guilty of the conduct which it was intended to deter.

. . .

27. This argument seems me to read far too much into the wording of article 6(2) and to the Court's reasoning in *Salabiaku*. Article 6(2), like article 6(3), must be read in the context of article 6(1). The article as a whole is concerned essentially with procedural guarantees to ensure that there is a fair trial, not with the substantive elements of the offence with which the person has been charged. As has been said many times, article 6 does not guarantee any particular content of the individual's civil rights. It is concerned with the procedural fairness of the system for the administration of justice in the contracting states, not with the substantive content of domestic law: *Matthews v Ministry of Defence* [2003] 1 AC 1163, para 3, per Lord Bingham of Cornhill, paras 30–35 per Lord Hoffmann, para 142, per Lord Walker of Gestingthorpe; *R (Kehoe) v Secretary of State for Work and Pensions* [2005] UKHL 48; [2006] 1 AC 42, para 41. The approach which the article takes to the criminal law is the same. Close attention is paid to the requirements of a fair trial. But it is a matter for the contracting states to define the essential elements of the offence with which the person has been charged. So when article 6(2) uses the words 'innocent' and 'guilty' it is dealing with the burden of proof regarding the elements of the offence and any defences to it. It is not dealing with what those elements are or what defences to the offence ought to be available.

28. The observations in paras 27–28 of *Salabiaku* are not inconsistent with this analysis. As the Court of Appeal noted in para 31 of its decision, that case was decided, in accordance with the practice of the Strasbourg court, on its own facts. The principles which it was seeking to enunciate are set out in rather general terms, which that court has not so far attempted to enlarge upon. But the key to a proper understanding of the passage as a whole is to be found in the first sentence of para 27. It contains a clear affirmation of the principle that the contracting states are free to apply the criminal law to any act, so long as it is not one which is carried out in the exercise of one of the rights protected under the Convention. Accordingly they are free to define the constituent elements of the offence that results from that act. So when the court said in the next sentence that the contracting states may 'under certain conditions' penalise a simple or objective fact as such, irrespective of whether it results from criminal intent or negligence, it was reaffirming the same principle. As in the previous sentence, the certain conditions that are referred to indicate that objection could be taken if the offence was incompatible with other articles of the Convention. But they have no wider significance. If there is no such incompatibility, the definition of the constituents of the offence is a matter for domestic law.

29. *Salabiaku* is not easy to construe, as my noble and learned friend Lord Hoffmann points out. But I do not agree with him that we should simply ignore it. Read in the way I have indicated, it continues to offer guidance about the extent of the guarantee that is afforded by article 6(2). Dyson LJ's remarks in *R v Gemmell* [2003] 1 Cr App R, 343, 356, para 33 with which I too agree, are consistent with that guidance. The substantive content of the criminal law does not raise issues of fairness of the kind to which that article is directed.

30. I would therefore respectfully endorse the conclusion which the Court of Appeal drew from the reasoning in *Salabiaku*. It said in para 33:

'An absolute offence may subject a defendant to conviction in circumstances where he has done nothing blameworthy. Prosecution for such an offence and the imposition of sanctions under it may well infringe articles of the Convention other than article 6. The legislation will not, however, render the trial under which it is enforced unfair, let alone infringe the presumption of innocence under article 6(2).'

It follows that I would not attach the significance to the decision in *Hansen v Denmark* that Mr Owen sought to attach to it. The offence in that case was one of strict liability. But, as the court noted, the burden of proof of all its elements was throughout on the prosecution. As it said, there was nothing to indicate that the courts in fulfilling their functions started from the assumption that the applicant was liable. This passage in its judgment is consistent with the view that article 6(2) does not proscribe offences of strict liability, so long as the prosecution bears the burden of proof of all the elements that constitute the offence.

31. That requirement is plainly met in this case. So I would hold that section 5 of the 2003 Act is not incompatible with article 6(2) of the Convention and that the prosecutor's act in prosecuting the appellant under that section was not unlawful in that respect.

[**Lord Mance** and **Baroness Hale** concurred with Lords Hoffmann and Hope on the Article 6 issues. **Lord Carswell** addressed only the Article 8 issue.]

≈≈ *Questions*
(1) Was G blameworthy?
(2) Did G deserve the label 'statutory rapist'?
(3) What differences are there in legislating to provide:
    (a) it is an offence to touch a person under 13 sexually even if the defendant is unaware that the person is under 13; and
    (b) if a person under 13 is touched sexually by the defendant, he is presumed to have known that she was under 13 unless he proves the contrary.

G applied to have his case heard by the European Court of Human Rights. In *G v UK* (2011) 53 EHRR SE25, it was held that the complaint was inadmissible and so the case never reached the Court for a full hearing. In dismissing the case, the Court held that there was no potential violation of Article 6.

28. The Court notes that Parliament created the offence under s.5 of the 2003 Act in order to protect children from sexual abuse. As the domestic courts confirmed, the objective element (actus reus) of the offence is penile penetration, by any person old enough for criminal responsibility, of the vagina, anus or mouth of a child aged 12 or under. The subjective element (mens rea) is intention to penetrate. Knowledge of, or recklessness as to, the age of the child or as to the child's unwillingness to take part in the sexual activity are not elements of the offence.

29. In the instant case, the prosecution was required to prove all the elements of the offence beyond reasonable doubt. The Court does not consider that Parliament's decision not to make available a defence based on reasonable belief that the complainant was aged 13 or over can give rise to any issue under art.6(1) or (2) of the Convention. Section 5 of the 2003 does not provide for presumptions of fact or law to be drawn from elements proved by the prosecution. The principle considered in *Salabiaku* therefore has no application here.

It was held that Article 8 was engaged but that it was inarguable that there was an infringement of the right to respect for private and family life.

37. It remains for the Court to determine whether the continued prosecution, conviction and sentencing of the applicant were 'necessary in a democratic society' within the meaning of the second paragraph of art.8. The Court recalls that, according to its established case law, the notion of necessity

implies that the interference corresponds to a pressing social need and, in particular, that it is proportionate to the legitimate aim pursued. In determining whether an interference is 'necessary in a democratic society', the Court will take into account that a margin of appreciation is left to the national authorities (see, among many authorities, *Laskey* at [42]).

38. The scope of this margin of appreciation is not identical in each case and will vary according to the context. Thus, where the activities at stake involve an intimate aspect of private life, the margin allowed to the state is generally narrow (see, *mutatis mutandis, Dudgeon* at [52]; and *ADT v United Kingdom* (2001) 31 E.H.R.R. 33 at [37]). On the other hand, in this case the countervailing public interest was the need to protect the complainant and other children in her position against premature sexual activity, exploitation and abuse. As the domestic courts pointed out, the state is under a positive obligation under art.8 to protect vulnerable individuals from sexual abuse (*X v Netherlands*; compare *KA v Belgium*). The Court has found that the contracting states enjoy a wide margin of appreciation as regards the means to ensure adequate protection against rape (*MC v Bulgaria* (2005) 40 E.H.R.R. 20 at [154]). Given the nature of the public interest at stake, the Court concludes that the state authorities' margin of appreciation in the present case must be wide.

39. As Baroness Hale observed, the consequences of penetrative sex for a child of 12 or under may be very harmful. The Court does not consider that the national authorities can be said to have exceeded the margin of appreciation available to them by creating a criminal offence which is called 'rape' and which does not allow for any defence based either on apparent consent by the child or on the accused's mistaken belief about the child's age. Nor does the Court consider that the authorities exceeded their margin of appreciation by deciding to prosecute the applicant for this offence, particularly since the legislation permitted for a broad range of sentences and the mitigating circumstances in the applicant's case were taken into account by the Court of Appeal.

6.6 The merits of strict liability

The potential merits of imposing strict liability have long been debated. For a collection of essays considering the topic, see A. Simester, *Appraising Strict Liability* (2005). In the following extract taken from that collection of essays, Andrew Simester sets out the moral objections to strict liability in the following terms.

Andrew Simester, 'Is Strict Liability Always Wrong?'
in A. Simester, *Appraising Strict Liability* (2005) (references omitted)

3. Intrinsic Objections to Strict Liability

It is, in short, arguable that there are instrumental benefits to be gained from the device of strict liability, although their scope and extent is uncertain. However, assuming they exist, those benefits must be weighed against the intrinsic moral objections to strict liability set out below. In the context of stigmatic crimes, it seems to me that these objections are decisive.

Objections Specific to Paradigm (Stigmatic) Crimes

Suppose that the state were to create a crime of 'homicide', defined as a strict liability offence of causing death. Objections to crimes of this type depend, in turn, on the nature of the criminal law. Without dwelling on the familiar analysis, there seem to me to be certain paradigm features associated with the criminalization of xing. Ex ante, μing is prohibited and declared to be wrong: citizens are not merely requested but instructed not to μ. Ex post, where D is found to have transgressed, he is convicted of xing and liable to punishment which may be substantial, perhaps including imprisonment. The conviction and the punishment also express censure, to D, V, and the public at large. As well as suffering hard treatment, D is labelled as a particular sort of criminal (a 'μer'), a labelling that conveys a public implication of culpable wrongdoing.

These paradigm features of the criminal law imply certain objections to making xing a strict liability crime, at least where strict liability leads to conviction of blameless defendants. (The subset of cases where strict liability does not lead to conviction of blameless defendants is considered in § 4.)

Wrongful Censure

The main objection to strict liability in stigmatic crimes law is that it involves the conviction and punishment of persons who are not at fault. Morally speaking, it is wrong to convict the innocent. If a person does not deserve to be convicted then he has a right not to be; and his conviction cannot be justified by such consequential considerations as deterrence.

Since both are censorious, this objection applies to both conviction and punishment. The imposition of punishment is, *qua* punishment, justified only when D deserves it, in virtue of culpably having done wrong. Indeed, the imposition of hard treatment cannot count as punishment unless it conveys this message. But in the context of strict liability, the state does not rely on the proposition that D is culpable as a precondition of imposing punishment. So the state cannot claim to be punishing D in accordance with D's desert; it is simply imposing hard treatment in virtue of the fact that xing (an *actus reus*) has occurred.

This criticism may be evaded, in part. Even if xing is a strict liability offence, the quantum of punishment imposed for transgressions might still be related to desert in a criminal legal system that required *sentences* to take account of D's level of culpability, with fault being a post-conviction matter for consideration during sentencing.

However, the same get-out is not available with regard to the conviction itself. Independently of the sanction imposed, the conviction also conveys censure. A conviction for μ-ing has the effect of naming D a criminal (in respect of that particular offence), a branding which is communicated to society as well as to D. Assuming that, if imposed on a strict liability basis, the label 'criminal-μ,' continues to retain its stigmatic quality, this amounts to systematic moral defamation by the state. Given the public understanding of that designation, when it labels him a criminal the state is no longer telling the public the truth about D. People have a right not to be censured falsely as criminals, a right that is violated when one is convicted and punished for a stigmatic crime without proof of culpable wrongdoing.

That falsehood is no ordinary lie. There is something especially troubling when wrongful censure is imposed by the state. In ordinary defamation cases, the attack is characteristically private; it may affect D, and even harm D's interests, but it lacks the authoritative voice of the state and normally does not undermine his membership of the community. An act of defamation may bring D into conflict with P, but it normally does not alienate D from society. By contrast, convictions are official. They condemn D on behalf of society as a whole. To say that D has a criminal record is to say that he has been labelled as a reprehensible wrongdoer; that the state has made a formal adverse statement about *him*. Moreover, the statement marks D out in such a way that it becomes appropriate, within the community, for the regard in which he is held to be affected. Certain exclusions, both social and professional, may legitimately follow. As such, the criminal record becomes part of the material that frames D's engagement with his community, with adverse implications for D's ability to live his life— a life that is, in part, defined in terms of D's interactions within, and membership of, his society. The conviction (and indeed the punishment, in its censorious facet) tends not only to censure D for the particular act that is proscribed, but also to undermine D's participation in the society itself.

Censure and Stigma

We can elaborate this concern by distinguishing between censure, which the state expresses through its action of convicting (and punishing) the defendant, and the effect of that action, in terms of the stigma that attaches to D and his conduct. Of course, as the foregoing discussion has suggested, one reason why the state ought not falsely to censure D for a serious crime is supplied by the consequences for D's life. But the two do not always go together, and D has a right to be neither falsely censured nor falsely stigmatized. Even if D suffers no stigma, the state should not purport to censure him without believing him to be culpable. Telling lies is wrong in itself and not merely because of the consequences.

Consider, on the other hand, an argument that the state is not *really* censuring D, since both the state and D know that fault has not been proved when D is convicted of a strict liability offence. The problem with this 'private colloquy' reasoning is that the state should not ignore the significance of its actions for others. When labelling D guilty of a stigmatic crime, the state is bound by the public meaning of the words it uses. Thus, for example, Parliament cannot legitimately enact an offence of 'paedophilia', defined as 'parking for more than one hour on a central London street'. It cannot do so because that is not what paedophilia means. Even if D understands that the label is a technical usage, the state may not disregard the rest of its audience, and the effect that such a label will have on D's life.

Treating a conviction for 'paedophilia' as highly stigmatic is, of course, a reasonable public response. A more difficult case would arise if the reaction of the public, in terms of stigmatizing D, is unreasonable and far exceeds what is deserved in light of the state's censure. Suppose that, in the public mind, parking offenders (labelled as such) came to be regarded like paedophiles. In that event, a strict liability parking conviction, although not intended as censorious, would be highly stigmatic. Even in this sort of case, at least where the stigma is predictable, it seems to me that the state should take account of the consequences of a conviction for defendants. The offence should no longer involve strict liability.

Rights and Instrumental Reasons

Of course, some error in the criminal justice system is unavoidable. When the state convicts a person of a stigmatic offence, it generally requires that guilt be proved beyond reasonable doubt. Inevitably, this leaves open the possibility that a particular defendant, properly convicted on that standard of proof, is not in fact guilty. The defamation and wrongful punishment of such persons is none the less justified. Moreover, it is justified by consequential reasons: in particular, by the need to set an achievable standard of proof if society is to have a practicable criminal justice system at all. It might be thought that an analogy can be drawn between these instrumental considerations, which permit wrongful convictions whenever the criminal proof standard is met, and those set out in § 2, which support convictions on the basis of strict liability.

But the analogy strikes me as false. Where guilt is proved beyond reasonable doubt in stigmatic crimes, the state convicts in good faith—D is believed to be culpable. Further, although error is systemic it remains unsystematic: the distribution of error is unknown, and we cannot predict the likelihood that any particular conviction is a mistake. By contrast, where strict liability is employed in a stigmatic crime, the state consistently labels D as a culpable wrongdoer without believing this to be true. Moreover, defamation is predictable—there are reasons for thinking that the state is particularly likely to censure and punish D wrongly in that class of cases. Hence, while instrumental considerations of an institutional nature may sometimes be relied upon to justify the risk of good-faith erroneous convictions, arguments of this type seem inadequate to justify strict liability for stigmatic crimes.

6.7 Compromise positions on strict liability

6.7.1 The 'halfway house'

Many common law countries have developed a so-called 'halfway house' between strict liability and a full mens rea requirement. It takes various forms but, in general, the effect is that the prosecution has to prove the commission of the actus reus but then the onus shifts to the defendant to prove, on the balance of probabilities, that he did not have mens rea and was not negligent. Sometimes it does not go so far but imposes a merely evidential burden on the defendant. See, for example, *City of Sault Ste Marie* (1978) 85 DLR 3d 161 at 181, where the Canadian Supreme Court acknowledged a defence for the defendant to:

> avoid liability by proving that he took all reasonable care. This involves consideration of what a reasonable man would have done in the circumstances. The defence would be available if the accused reasonably believed in a mistaken set of facts which, if true, would render the act or omission innocent, or if he took all reasonable steps to avoid the particular event.

Lord Cooke, a distinguished New Zealand judge who sees merit in the halfway house, noted in his Hamlyn lectures that the doctrine had made no headway in England. Subsequently, the theory was rejected in *B (a minor) v DPP* and not referred to in *K*. It seems that it has no future in England unless included in the statute in question.

Hostility to statutory reverse onuses, following the enactment of the Human Rights Act 1998 (cf *Lambert* [2001] UKHL 37) makes it even less likely that the courts will depart from the *Woolmington* principle unless statute requires, and the European Convention permits, them to do so.

See also the comparative study by J. Spencer and A. Pedain, 'Approaches to Strict and Constructive Liability in Continental Criminal Law' in A. Simester (ed), *Appraising Strict Liability* (2005) noting that a reason for continental systems avoiding strict liability is that their procedures allow for proof more easily than the strict adversarial system in England.

6.7.2 Due diligence defences

It is common for the drastic effect of a statute imposing strict liability to be mitigated by the provision of a statutory 'due diligence' defence. Such defences usually impose on the defendant a burden of proving both that he had no mens rea and that he took all reasonable precautions and exercised all due diligence to avoid the commission of an offence. Such provisions are a distinct advance on unmitigated strict liability; but they are still a deviation from the fundamental principle that the prosecution must prove the whole of their case.

See for discussion, D. Parry, 'Judicial Approaches to Due Diligence' [1995] Crim LR 695; C. Manchester, 'Knowledge Due Diligence and Strict Liability in Regulatory Offences' [2006] Crim LR 213.

In some recent cases the courts have held that although liability is strict as to an element of the offence, so mens rea is irrelevant in that sense, it can be relevant when considering the due diligence defence.

An example is the case of *Unah* [2011] EWCA Crim 1837. U was convicted of possession of a false identity document contrary to s 25(5) of the Identity Cards Act 2006.

Section 25(5) of the Identity Cards Act 2006 (now replaced by the Identity Documents Act 2010) provided:

> (5) It is an offence for a person to have in his possession or under his control, without reasonable excuse—
>
>   (a) an identity document that is false;
>
>   (b) an identity document that was improperly obtained;
>
>   (c) an identity document that relates to someone else . . .

U was a Nigerian national with indefinite leave to remain in the UK. U had presented documents at a job centre interview including her current Nigerian passport, an expired Nigerian passport and a document evidencing her indefinite leave to remain. The expired passport was a false one. U's current Nigerian passport was legitimate. U claimed that she had believed that the false passport was a legitimate one. She had obtained that passport, now acknowledged to be false, by completing the appropriate forms and paying the appropriate fee, and had done so with the help of a friend who regularly travelled to the UK. At trial, U accepted that she had had the passport in her possession and that the biographical page was counterfeit, but claimed that she had not known or believed that the identity document was false and, therefore, she had a reasonable excuse. As a preliminary matter, the judge ruled that the offence under s 25(5) was one of strict liability and that the defendant had no defence in law to the charge. The trial judge ruled that the defence of 'reasonable excuse' applied where a defendant could justify his or her possession or control of the false document, for example where a person found a document and took it to the police to be handed in, or where a police officer confiscated the document. It was not possible for U to claim that her lack of knowledge of the falsity of the document was a 'reasonable excuse'. U pleaded guilty on re-arraignment and appealed against conviction. The Court of Appeal allowed the appeal. In determining whether an excuse was reasonable, reference to the circumstances in which a document had been obtained, which had caused a defendant to believe it was genuine, were relevant to the jury's consideration.

A belief that a document is genuine might, for example, explain why it has not been thrown away or handed in to the police. It is capable of providing an explanation for the possession of the document. Of course, there may be circumstances where the explanation as to why the defendant has the document in his or her possession is simply not believed by the jury, or it may be that the jury accepts the explanation advanced but does not consider that it is reasonable in all the circumstances. But the concept of reasonable excuse is potentially a broad one, and we do not see why the circumstances in which the document was obtained, and which may cause the defendant to believe that it was genuine, should be ignored when considering whether an excuse for possessing it is reasonable or not. (at [5])

The court had regard to the other offences created under s 25 as an aid to the construction of subs (5). Section 25(5) does not contain the words 'with the requisite intention' as found in s 25(1). That suggested that the fact that a defendant did not have the knowledge or belief that a document was false was not in itself an excuse. The Court of Appeal accepted that there was no justification to imply those words into the s 25(5) offence: it is not necessary for the Crown to prove that D knew he had the document or that he knew it was false. However, the reasonable excuse defence could apply where a defendant denied either knowing possession and/or knowledge of the falsity of the document. The defence would not, however, be satisfied by a defendant merely claiming a lack of knowledge; something more was required.

Note that the Identity Documents Act 2010 repealed the Identity Cards Act 2006, although ss 25 and 26 (possession of false identity documents etc) and s 38 of the 2006 Act are replaced by very similar (but not identical) provisions contained in ss 4 to 10 of that Act.

See also the similar approach to defences based on reasonable excuse in *JB v CPS* [2012] EWHC 72 (Admin).

6.8 Reform

The Law Commission suggested in its draft Criminal Code Bill, cl 20:

(1) Every offence requires a fault element of recklessness with respect to each of its elements other than fault elements, unless otherwise provided.

(2) Subsection 1 does not apply to pre-Code offences. . . .

The recklessness referred to is *Cunningham*, not *Caldwell*, recklessness.

The Law Commission considered a suggestion that the presumption in favour of mens rea should be displaceable only by an *express* provision requiring some fault other than recklessness, or stating that no fault is required. But, said the Commission, 'We do not think that this would be appropriate. We are mindful of the constitutional platitude pointed out by Lord Ackner in *Hunt* [1987] AC 352 at 380, that the courts must give effect to what Parliament has provided not only expressly but also by necessary implication. If the terms of a future enactment creating an offence plainly implied an intention to displace the presumption created by clause 20(1), the courts would no doubt feel obliged to give effect to that intention even if the present clause were to require express provision for the purpose.'

In 2010, the Law Commission published a consultation paper *Criminal Liability in Regulatory Contexts* (Law Com Consultation Paper No 195) in which it considered the use of criminal offences against business enterprises. As part of its examination of this branch of the criminal law, consideration was given to the prevalence of strict liability in so-called 'regulatory offences'. The Law Commission made the following proposals and posed the following questions.

CONCLUSION

6.92 In an ideal world, criminal offences created by statute would always indicate when fault need not be proved, or if it needs to be proved what kind of fault (or defence) is involved. Since there are so many criminal offences under statute that fall short of the ideal, we believe that, subject to some possible exceptions, the courts should be given the power to apply a defence of due diligence in all the circumstances to statutory offences that would otherwise involve strict liability with no adequate defence. This approach has the advantage of leaving the strict basis of liability in the relevant provision intact. That means the courts will no longer need to search for what may be non-existent Parliamentary intention respecting fault requirements and will no longer need to decide whether a presumption that fault must be proved applies, and if so, whether the presumption has been displaced.

6.93 Clearly, the courts would not apply the defence of due diligence where to do so would defeat the purpose of the statute. A related point is that we would expect the courts not to apply it if, despite the absence of a requirement for proof of a positive fault requirement, there are specific defences applicable to the offence that mean the fairness objective has been met. Even where the courts did apply it, the burden of proof, on the balance of probabilities, would be on the defendant to establish that due diligence in the circumstances had been shown.

6.94 We believe that the introduction of the power to apply the defence has the potential to secure the fairness objective in a greater range of cases than at present. Moreover, unlike the presumption that fault must be proved, it can secure the fairness objective in a way that is sensitive to the differences between the capacities and resources of defendants to organise their affairs in such a way that offences are not committed in the course of business.

PROPOSALS AND QUESTIONS

6.95 We provisionally propose that:

Proposal 14: The courts should be given a power to apply a due diligence defence to any statutory offence that does not require proof that the defendant was at fault in engaging in the wrongful conduct. The burden of proof should be on the defendant to establish the defence.

6.96 If proposal 14 is accepted, we also provisionally propose that:

Proposal 15: The defence of due diligence should take the form of showing that due diligence was exercised in all the circumstances to avoid the commission of the offence.

6.97 However, we recognise that consultees may prefer this defence to have the same wording and to impose the same standards as the most commonly encountered statutory form of the defence. Accordingly, we ask following question:

Question 1: Were it to be introduced, should the due diligence defence take the stricter form already found in some statutes, namely, did the defendant take all reasonable precautions and exercise all due diligence to avoid commission of the offence?

6.98 We ask the further question:

Question 2: If the power to apply a due diligence defence is introduced, should Parliament prevent or restrict its application to certain statutes, and if so which statutes?

FURTHER READING

A. Ashworth, 'Should Strict Criminal Liability be Removed from All Imprisonable Offences?' in A. Ashworth, *Positive Obligations in Criminal Law* (2013)

P. Brett, 'Strict Responsibility: Possible Solutions' (1974) 37 MLR 417

J. Horder, 'Strict Liability, Statutory Construction and the Spirit of Liberty' (2002) 118 LQR 458

L. H. Leigh, *Strict and Vicarious Liability* (1982)

A. Simester (ed), *Appraising Strict Liability* (2005)

7
Murder

> **Murder:**
>
> Murder is committed when a person unlawfully causes the death of a human being under the Queen's Peace with intention to kill or cause serious injury.
>
> **Some of the controversies that will be examined in this chapter include:**
>
> (1) when does life begin and end for the purposes of the law of murder;
>
> (2) should an intention to cause really serious harm suffice as the mens rea for murder;
>
> (3) how might this area of the law be reformed so as to reflect generally recognized principles of the criminal law?

7.1 Introduction

The classic definition of the offence, still in use today, derives from a book from the seventeenth century. That definition provided by Coke is:

> Murder is when a man of sound memory, and of the age of discretion, unlawfully killeth within any county of the realm any reasonable creature *in rerum natura* under the king's peace, with malice aforethought, either expressed by the party or implied by law, [so as the party wounded, or hurt, etc die of the wound or hurt, etc within a year and a day after the same]. (Coke 3 Inst 47)

The Law Commission has described the law of murder as a 'rickety structure set upon shaky foundations': Law Commission Consultation Paper No 177, *A New Homicide Act for England and Wales* (2005), para 1.4. See section 7.4.1, p 160.

Murder carries a mandatory sentence of life imprisonment; it has the most serious stigma of any offence and yet it is still defined only at common law. It is no surprise then that the Law Commission proposed reform. See Law Commission Consultation Paper No 177 and Law Commission Report No 304, *Murder Manslaughter and Infanticide* (2006); section 7.4.2, p 161. Reform is no easy task. One of the reasons that the offence is so difficult to define satisfactorily is that the offence must deal with such fundamental questions.

7.2 The actus reus of murder

The actus reus of murder and manslaughter is generally the same. It is the unlawful killing of any person 'under the Queen's Peace'. Each word merits close attention.

7.2.1 Causing death

It must be proved that the defendant caused the death of the deceased person. Most of the problems in relation to causation arise in the context of homicide. The leading cases have been considered in Chapter 3, and reference may be made to these.

In homicide, it is important not to lose sight of the fact that what must be caused is some acceleration of death: everyone must die sooner or later. It follows that every killing is merely an acceleration of death; and it makes no difference for this purpose that the victim is already suffering from a fatal disease or injury (or historically was under sentence of death).

7.2.2 Year and a day rule

At common law, homicide was committed only if the death occurred within a year and a day of the act causing death (see D. Yale, 'A Year and A Day in Homicide' (1989) 48 CLJ 202, and on the reform see Law Commission Consultation Paper No 136, *The Year and a Day Rule in Homicide* (1994)). That rule was abolished by the Law Reform (Year and a Day Rule) Act 1996. If an act can be shown to be the cause of death, it may now be murder, or any other homicide offence, or suicide, however much time has elapsed between the act and the death. In some cases, for example where three years or more separate D's act and V's death, the consent of the Attorney General is needed to prosecute for murder.

7.2.3 A person 'in being'

The victim of homicide must have been born and not have died before the defendant's act took effect. Although this principle is discussed here exclusively in connection with homicide, it is probably applicable to offences against the person generally.

7.2.3.1 Birth

If the child has 'an existence independent of its mother' it is capable of being murdered. To have such an existence the child must have been wholly expelled from its mother's body and be alive. The cord and afterbirth need not have been expelled from the mother nor severed from the child. The tests of independent existence which the courts have accepted are that the child should have an independent circulation, and that it should have breathed after birth. But there are difficulties about both these tests. There are very few modern cases on the point.

In *Re A (children) (conjoined twins: surgical separation)* [2000] EWCA Civ 254, the court was satisfied that one of the conjoined twins, Mary, was 'a reasonable creature in being', having an existence independent of her mother, although she was wholly dependent on Jodie, the other twin, for her continued existence. Mary thus came under the protection of the law of murder.

> Brooke LJ:
>
> Advances in medical treatment of deformed neonates suggest that the criminal law's protection should be as wide as possible, and a conclusion that a creature in being was not reasonable would be confined only to the most extreme cases of which this is not an example. Whatever might have been thought of as [mere 'monsters'] by Bracton, Coke, Blackstone, Locke and Hobbes, different considerations would apply today. This proposition might be tested in this way: suppose an intruder broke into the hospital and stabbed twin M causing her death. Clearly it could not be said that his actions would be outside the limit of the law of homicide.
>
> Modern English statute law has mitigated the prospective burden that might otherwise fall on the parents of severely handicapped children and their families if they are willing to avail themselves of

its protection at any time up to the time the child (or children) is born. [His lordship considered the Abortion Act 1967, s 1(1)(d), as substituted by the Human Fertilisation and Embryology Act 1990, s 37(1), and continued:] Once a seriously handicapped child is born alive, the position changes, and it is as much entitled to the protection of the criminal law as any other human being.

7.2.3.2 Killing or injuring the foetus

There is, predictably, great controversy about defining the point at which a foetus becomes a human or, in this particular context, about defining the point at which the foetus deserves the protection of the criminal law of homicide.

- It is not murder to kill a foetus in the womb or in the process of leaving the womb.
- If the foetus is not capable of being born alive, the offence of destruction under s 58 of the Offences Against the Person Act 1861 (OAPA) may have been committed.
- Where the foetus is capable of being born alive and is killed, it is an offence under the Infant Life (Preservation) Act 1929.

≈≈ *Question*

Should it be murder to destroy a foetus with intent to do so? From what point in gestation? From conception? From the point at which the foetus is *capable* of living an independent existence, that is, is viable?

In *A-G's Reference (No 3 of 1994)* [1997] UKHL 31, D stabbed his pregnant girlfriend. At that point in time it was not appreciated that the stab wound had penetrated the abdomen of the foetus. D pleaded guilty to the offence of wounding. The girlfriend gave birth to a 'grossly premature' daughter. The stabbing had in fact injured the foetus. The daughter survived for 120 days; her death was attributable to her being grossly premature. The defendant was charged with murder. The trial judge ruled that there could be no conviction for either murder or manslaughter. The Attorney General referred the issue to the Court of Appeal which held that since the foetus was a part of the mother, the defendant's intent to cause at least serious injury to the mother was sufficient to found liability for murder in respect of the child. On appeal to the House of Lords, Lord Mustill regarded the following as established rules:

Lord Mustill:

. . . 1. it is sufficient to raise a prima facie case of murder (subject to entire or partial excuses such as self-defence or provocation [now loss of control]) for it to be proved that the defendant did the act which caused the death intending to kill the victim or to cause him at least grievous bodily harm. Although it will be necessary to look at the reasoning which founded this rule, it is undeniably a part of English law: see *R v Vickers* [1957] 2 All ER 741, [1957] 2 QB 664; *Hyam v DPP* [1974] 2 All ER 41, [1975] AC 55 and *R v Cunningham* [1981] 2 All ER 863, [1982] AC 566. Thus, if M had died as a result of the injuries received B would have been guilty of murdering her, even though in the everyday sense he did not intend her death.

2. If the defendant does an act with the intention of causing a particular kind of harm to X, and unintentionally does that kind of harm to Y, then the intent to harm X may be added to the harm actually done to Y in deciding whether the defendant has committed a crime towards Y. This rule is usually referred to as the doctrine of 'transferred malice', a misleading label but one which is too firmly entrenched to be discarded. Nor would it be possible now to question the rule itself, for although the

same handful of authorities are called up repeatedly in the texts they are constantly cited without disapproval . . . [See section 2.3.1.1, p 24.]

3. Except under statute an embryo or foetus *in utero* cannot be the victim of a crime of violence. In particular, violence to the foetus which causes its death *in utero* is not a murder. The foundation authority is the definition by Sir Edward Coke of murder by reference to the killing of 'a reasonable creature, in *rerum natura*' (see 3 Co Inst (1680) 50). The proposition was developed by the same writer into examples of prenatal injuries as follows:

> 'If a woman be quick with childe, and by a potion or otherwise killeth it in her wombe; or if a man beat her, whereby the child dieth in her body, and she is delivered of a dead childe; this is a great misprision, and no murder . . .'

It is unnecessary to look behind this statement to the earlier authorities, for its correctness as a general principle, as distinct from its application to babies expiring in the course of delivery or very shortly thereafter, has never been controverted. It can, for example, be found in 4 Bl Com (1830) 198, *Stephen Digest of the Criminal Law* (1877) p 138, *Smith and Hogan Criminal Law* (8th edn, 1996) p 338 and in many other places over the years.

4. The existence of an interval of time between the doing of an act by the defendant with the necessary wrongful intent and its impact on the victim in a manner which leads to death does not in itself prevent the intent, the act and the death from together amounting to murder, so long as there is an unbroken causal connection between the act and the death.

5. Violence towards a foetus which results in harm suffered after the baby has been born alive can give rise to criminal responsibility even if the harm would not have been criminal (apart from statute) if it had been suffered *in utero*. Once again, the rule founds on a statement of Coke, following immediately after the passage above quoted:

> '. . . if the childe be born alive, and dieth of the potion, battery, or other cause, this is murder: for in law it is accounted a reasonable creature, *in rerum natura*, when it is born alive.' (See 3 Co Inst 50.)

This view did not at first command universal acceptance, largely on the practical ground that medical science did not then permit a clear proof of causal connection, but it was adopted in early Victorian times by the *Fourth Report of the Commissioners on Criminal Law* (1839), British Parliamentary Papers (1839) vol 19, pp 235, 266 and the Second Report of the Commissioners for Revising and Consolidating Criminal Law (1846), British Parliamentary Papers (1846) vol 24, pp 107, 127 and never substantially doubted since. In *R v West* (1848) 2 Car & Kir 784, 175 ER 329, a case to which I must briefly return, the rule was extended to a situation such as the present where the assault caused the death, not through injury to the child, but by causing the child to be born prematurely. In *R v Senior* (1832) 1 Mood CC 346, 168 ER 1298 the principle was applied to manslaughter, where death resulted from gross negligence by a midwife before the child had been fully born. Since the principle is not disputed I will not cite the numerous references to it by institutional writers during the past three centuries . . .

≈≈≈ *Questions*

(1) D intended to stab the girlfriend. He intended to cause her at least GBH. If he had missed and stabbed V standing next to the girlfriend and V had died, would D have been guilty of murder?

(2) Should D be guilty of murdering the child which was born and died as a result of the injury D inflicted?

7.2.3.3 Article 2 and the right to life

The European Court of Human Rights (ECtHR) has declined to decide directly whether the foetus is protected by the right to life in Article 2. In *Vo v France* [2004] 2 FCR 577, a doctor negligently caused fatal injury to a viable foetus after mistaking the mother's identity for that of another patient. The French Criminal Court acquitted him on the basis that the foetus was not a human being for the purposes of the offence. On application to the ECtHR, the Court ruled that the issue of life's commencement and its protection by criminal law was within the margin of appreciation extended to the Member States. The Court acknowledged (at [80]) that in:

> the circumstances examined to date by the Convention institutions—that is, in the various laws on abortion—the unborn child is not regarded as a 'person' directly protected by Article 2 of the Convention and that if the unborn do have a 'right' to 'life', it is implicitly limited by the mother's rights and interests. The Convention institutions have not, however, ruled out the possibility that in certain circumstances safeguards may be extended to the unborn child . . . It is also clear from an examination of these cases that the issue has always been determined by weighing up various, and sometimes conflicting, rights or freedoms claimed by a woman, a mother or a father in relation to one another or vis-à-vis an unborn child.

The Grand Chamber of the ECtHR in *A, B and C v Ireland* (2011) 53 EHRR 13 confirmed (at [222]) that:

> it was neither desirable nor possible to answer the question of whether the unborn was a person for the purposes of Article 2 of the Convention, so that it would be equally legitimate for a State to choose to consider the unborn to be such a person and to aim to protect that life.

7.2.3.4 Death

Defining the point in time at which life ends so that the person is no longer the subject of the protection of the law of homicide is also difficult.

Criminal Law Revision Committee, Fourteenth Report, *Offences Against the Person*
(1980), Cmnd 7844

> 37. We have considered whether there should be a statutory definition of death. A memorandum issued by the honorary secretary of the Conference of Medical Royal Colleges and Faculties in the United Kingdom on 15 January 1979 refers to an earlier report of the Conference which expressed their unanimous opinion that 'brain death' could be diagnosed with certainty. The memorandum states that the report published by the Conference has been widely accepted and says that the identification of brain death means that a patient is truly dead, whether or not the function of some organs, such as a heart beat, is still maintained by artificial means. Brain death is said to be when all the functions of the brain have permanently and irreversibly ceased. We are however extremely hesitant about embodying in a statute (which is not always susceptible of speedy amendment) an expression of present medical opinion and knowledge derived from a field of science which is continually progressing and inevitably altering its opinions in the light of new information. If a statutory definition of death were to be enacted there would, in our opinion, be a risk that further knowledge would cause it to lose the assent of the majority of the medical profession. In that event, far from assisting the medical profession, for example in cases of organ transplants, the definition might be a hindrance to them. Moreover, while there might be agreement that the statutory definition was defective, there might be differences of view about the proper content of any new definition. An additional reason for not recommending a definition of death is that such definition would have wide repercussions

outside offences against the person and the criminal law. A legal definition of death would also have to be applicable in the civil law. It would be undesirable to have a statutory definition confined only to offences against the person, which is the extent of our present remit. For these reasons therefore we are not recommending the enactment of a definition of death.

≈ Question

The Criminal Law Revision Committee (CLRC) was unwilling to recommend any definition because, to put the matter simply, medical advances cause the goalposts to be shifted. This is, perhaps, a convincing argument against a statutory definition of death. But who defines death in a case where it is relevant?

The following case illustrates how medical advances, which mean that seriously injured people can potentially be kept alive artificially for an indefinite period of time, impact upon established principles of the criminal law.

Airedale NHS Trust v Bland
[1992] UKHL 5, House of Lords

(Lords Keith of Kinkel, Goff of Chieveley, Lowry, Browne-Wilkinson and Mustill)

B was very seriously injured in the Hillsborough disaster. He suffered irreversible brain damage which left him in a persistent vegetative state. All medical opinion was that there was no hope of recovery or improvement. The Health Authority sought a declaration that it would be lawful to discontinue all life-sustaining treatment including all medical and nutritional support except so as to allow B to die peacefully with the least pain. The House of Lords held that it would be lawful to discontinue the treatment even though in this case there was no consent by B. As the time had come when B had no further interest in being kept alive, the necessity for the treatment had gone and it would not be unlawful to omit to perform what had previously been a duty.

Lord Keith of Kinkel:

Where one individual has assumed responsibility for the care of another who cannot look after himself or herself, whether as a medical practitioner or otherwise, that responsibility cannot lawfully be shed unless arrangements are made for the responsibility to be taken over by someone else. . . . [I]t is of course true that in general it would not be lawful for a medical practitioner who assumed responsibility for the care of the unconscious patient simply to give up treatment in circumstances where continuance of it would confer some benefit on the patient.

See section 4.2.1.1, p 59, for the discussion in relation to failures to keep alive and positive acts terminating life.

Section 4 of the Mental Capacity Act 2005 deals with the circumstances in which treatment or its withdrawal is in the best interests of the patient. It is stipulated in s 4(5) that where the determination of what is in the best interests of the person relates to life-sustaining treatment, the person making the decision 'must not in considering whether the treatment is in the best interests of the person concerned, be motivated by a desire to bring about his death'.

In its review of the homicide offences, the Law Commission declined to engage in reform of mercy killings and euthanasia, preferring to see that as part of a free-standing review: Law Com Report No 304, para 1.6.

The Court of Appeal reiterated in *Inglis* [2010] EWCA Crim 2637 that mercy killings constitute murder. This is not altered by the D's purported benevolent motives for the killing. V was involved in an accident and suffered catastrophic head injuries, which left him in a vegetative state. D, his mother, injected him with a fatal dose of heroin, as she believed she needed to relieve her son of his suffering. Her first attempt at doing this failed and D was charged with attempted murder, but she succeeded on her second attempt and was found guilty of murder. The Lord Chief Justice stated:

37. On any view this case is a tragedy, not only for the appellant, who has lost a precious and loved son, but for the father and brothers of the deceased and the extended family. There is a wider public interest in the case because the issues to which it gives rise are immensely sensitive and difficult, and they have attracted an increasing measure of public interest and concern. Therefore we must underline that the law of murder does not distinguish between murder committed for malevolent reasons and murder motivated by familial love. Subject to well established partial defences, like provocation or diminished responsibility, mercy killing is murder. The offences of which the appellant was convicted, and for which she fell to be sentenced, were attempted murder and murder. The sentence on conviction for murder is mandatory. The judge had no alternative but to order imprisonment for life. He then had to assess the length of the minimum period to be served before the possibility of release from prison on licence could arise for consideration. In making that assessment he was obliged to have regard to the statutory provisions in schedule 21 [Criminal Justice Act 2003 in relation to sentencing for murder].

38. We must also emphasise that the law does not recognise the concept implicit in the defence statement that [V] was 'already dead in all but a small physical degree'. The fact is that he was alive, a person in being. However brief the time left for him, that life could not lawfully be extinguished. Similarly, however disabled [V] might have been, a disabled life, even a life lived at the extremes of disability, is not one jot less precious than the life of an able-bodied person. [V's] condition made him especially vulnerable, and for that among other reasons, whether or not he might have died within a few months anyway, his life was protected by the law, and no one, not even his mother, could lawfully step in and bring it to a premature conclusion. Until Parliament decides otherwise, the law recognises a distinction between the withdrawal of treatment supporting life, which, subject to stringent conditions, may be lawful, and the active termination of life, which is unlawful.

39. We cannot decide the case on the basis of whichever of the contradictory strands of public opinion in this extremely sensitive area happens to coincide with our own views, assuming that is, that if we had allowed our personal feelings to impinge on our discussions, that there would be any coincidence of views. How the problems of mercy killing, euthanasia, and assisting suicide should be addressed must be decided by Parliament, which, for this purpose at any rate, should be reflective of the conscience of the nation. In this appeal we are constrained to apply the law as we find it to be. We cannot amend it, or ignore it.

≈ *Questions*
(1) V has been in a serious road traffic accident and his heart has stopped beating. He is in the emergency room at the hospital and the surgeon is about to start working on him. The surgeon is very confident that V will be capable of being revived. A colleague goes outside to tell D, V's wife, the prognosis. D is very disappointed. She hates V. D dashes into the emergency room and stabs V with a scalpel before the surgeons can resuscitate V. Is D guilty of murder? If not, of what?
(2) Should there be a partial defence of 'compassionate killing'? See H. Keating and J. Bridgeman, 'Compassionate Killings: The Case for a Partial Defence' (2012) 75 MLR 697.

7.2.4 The Queen's Peace

'Alien enemies' who are actually engaged in hostile operations against the Crown will not be within the Queen's Peace. Their killing will not, therefore, amount to murder: *Page* [1954] 1 QB 170. An argument that an Egyptian national who had been murdered in an Egyptian village by a British soldier serving there was not within the Queen's Peace, was rejected. Killings by armed forces personnel of enemy forces will be criminal if the enemy agents have already surrendered. Note that murder committed by a British citizen outside England can still be tried by English courts: OAPA, s 9. (See further P. Rowe, 'Murder and the Law of War' (1991) 42 NILQ 216.) Note that the civilian criminal law applies to police and armed forces using lethal force on citizens. (See cases discussed on self-defence, in particular see *Clegg* [1995] 1 AC 482.) M. Hirst, 'Murder Under the Queen's Peace' [2008] Crim LR 541, argues that 'The killing must be committed by a person to whom, and in circumstances to which, the English law of murder applies. One could perhaps say, instead, that it must be committed under (or against) the Queen's peace.' For an interesting discussion of the domestic criminal legality of drone strikes, see S. Gardner, 'The Domestic Criminal Legality of the RAF Drone Strike in Syria in August 2015' [2015] Crim LR 35. Somewhat surprisingly, the argument was not advanced in *Blackman* [2017] EWCA Crim 190.

7.3 Mens rea

The mens rea for murder is that D must have malice aforethought. In modern language this means that D must have intended to kill or cause grievous bodily harm.

7.3.1 Subjective nature of test

The prosecution have to satisfy the jury so as to make them sure that the accused had the requisite state of mind, whatever it is, when he did the fatal act. This was not always clear. In *DPP v Smith* [1960] 3 All ER 161, [1961] AC 290, D, fearing that V, a police officer, was about to discover stolen goods in his car, drove off at high speed with V clinging on to the bonnet. D drove at increasing speed for 130 yards, during which time his car struck three oncoming vehicles, until V was finally thrown off into the path of another vehicle and killed. Restoring D's conviction for murder, Viscount Kilmuir LC, with whom all their lordships concurred, said (at 167):

The jury must, of course, in such a case as the present make up their minds on the evidence whether the accused was unlawfully and voluntarily doing something to someone. The unlawful and voluntary act must clearly be aimed at someone in order to eliminate cases of negligence or of careless or dangerous driving. Once, however, the jury are satisfied as to that, it matters not what the accused in fact contemplated as the probable result or whether he ever contemplated at all, provided he was in law responsible and accountable for his actions, that is, was a man capable of forming an intent, not insane within the M'Naghten Rules and not suffering from diminished responsibility. On the assumption that he is so accountable for his actions, the sole question is whether the unlawful and voluntary act was of such a kind that grievous bodily harm was the natural and probable result. The only test available for this is what the ordinary responsible man would, in all the circumstances of the case, have contemplated as the natural and probable result.

Few cases can have attracted such a barrage of hostile criticism from the commentators. It was considered in, though not formally overruled by, *Hyam, Moloney* and *Hancock*. Lord Diplock did say in *Hyam* [1974] UKHL 2 that it was wrongly decided, and Lord Bridge in

Moloney [1984] UKHL 4 and Lord Scarman in *Hancock* [1985] UKHL 9 said that in so far as it laid down an objective test it did not represent the common law. Another view expressed (by Lord Hailsham in *Hyam* among others) was that there was no need to overrule it because its effect had been modified by s 8 of the Criminal Justice Act 1967 (section 5.2, p 84). As we have seen, however, s 8, properly construed, does not affect the mens rea required for any crime. The section is concerned with how intention or foresight must be proved, not when they must be proved.

The issue had to be met, as it were, head on, in *Frankland and Moore* [1987] UKPC 3. The appellants had been convicted on a *Smith* direction on the Isle of Man at a time when the Isle of Man had no provision equivalent to s 8. Since the common law is the same in this matter as the common law of England, it was necessary to decide whether *Smith* correctly stated the common law. It was forthrightly held by five Law Lords that it did not. While decisions of the Privy Council cannot overrule decisions of the House of Lords, it seems safe to assume that the decision in *Smith* is not, and never was, the law of England.

7.3.2 Definition of mens rea for murder

The current law is that the definition of malice aforethought is satisfied by proof of an intention (direct or oblique) to kill or cause really serious harm.

The mental element required for the crime of murder, as for the crime of manslaughter, has varied over the centuries. Prior to s 1 of the Homicide Act 1957 a person who killed in the course of committing a felony involving violence (eg robbery) was guilty of murder. The abolition of that doctrine of constructive malice must be the starting point of a discussion of the mental element in murder though it tells us more about what the mental element for murder is not than what it is. Section 1 provides:

1. Abolition of 'constructive malice'

(1) Where a person kills another in the course or furtherance of some other offence, the killing shall not amount to murder unless done with the same malice aforethought (express or implied) as is required for a killing to amount to murder when not done in the course or furtherance of another offence.

(2) For the purposes of the foregoing subsection, a killing done in the course or for the purpose of resisting an officer of justice, or of resisting or avoiding or preventing a lawful arrest, or of effecting or assisting an escape or rescue from legal custody, shall be treated as a killing in the course or furtherance of an offence.

The section uses the expression 'malice aforethought' to describe the mens rea of murder. Traditionally the mens rea of murder was always described as malice aforethought but the term is unhelpful: 'malice' does not mean ill will and 'aforethought' tells us no more than that the mens rea must not come as an afterthought. It is simply a label used to refer to those mental states (whatever they are) that suffice for murder.

7.3.3 Intention to kill or cause really serious harm

Section 1 refers to two kinds of malice aforethought: 'express' and 'implied'. 'Express' malice must be a reference to whatever was considered as express malice at common law. What that was has nowhere been judicially defined nor has there been any explanation of it in the case law since the Homicide Act. What did Parliament (or the draftsman) have in mind when it was enacted that express malice sufficed for murder? The term was used by the institutional writers to denote those whose conduct was intentional. The earlier writers (Hale, Hawkins) did not restrict the term to those who intentionally caused death, but it now appears that the term 'express malice' means 'with intent to kill', and 'implied malice' means 'with intent to do serious bodily harm'. The House of Lords confirmed in *Cunningham* [1981] 2 All ER 863 that an intention to cause really serious harm is also a sufficient mens rea for murder.

There are two significant problems with this aspect of the law:

(A) the absence of a clear definition of the meaning of intention;

(B) the fact that murder is committed even if D intended that only GBH and not death should be caused.

(A) What is the definition of intention in murder?

As a result of decades of judicial development, the defendant will have the mens rea for murder if either of the following is satisfied:

(a) it was D's purpose to kill or to cause really serious harm—that is, D would have considered his act a failure if he did not cause death or really serious harm. Another way of expressing this test is to consider whether D acted *in order to bring about* death or really serious harm; or

(b) the jury will be entitled to find that the defendant intended to kill or to cause really serious harm if death or really serious harm was a virtually consequence of his act, barring some unforeseen intervention, and D appreciated that this was the case.

Although the mens rea for murder can now be stated with relative ease, there are those who are critical of the fact intention encompasses both indirect as well as direct intention, as the following extract demonstrates.

A. Norrie, 'After *Woollin*'
[1999] Crim LR 532

There has always been a deep-seated problem in the murder cases because what they have given with one hand, a narrow foresight of virtual certainty test, they have taken back with the other, through a broader foresight of probability approach in the guidelines. The guidelines in *Moloney* proved a Trojan Horse by virtue of which *Hyam* recklessness remained a part of the mens rea of murder. While declaring an orthodox subjectivist principle to be at the core of the law, the appeal courts undercut it by what they said judges should tell juries. It is not surprising, given the passage quoted [in *Woollin*] from *Nedrick*, that the trial judge in *Woollin* instructed his jury according to foresight of virtual certainty one day and according to foresight of substantial risk the next, because *Hancock* and *Shankland* and *Nedrick* sanction both approaches. . . .

In *Woollin*, Lord Steyn declares that the words 'entitled to infer' in the model *Nedrick* direction should be replaced with the clearer 'entitled to find'. Professor Smith applauds the move, but wonders if the change in wording will remove one problem with the original formulation. If indirect intention is a species of intention, then to identify foresight of a virtual certainty in the accused's mind is to identify that she intended the crime. The use of the word 'entitled' however suggests that the jury may so identify intention, but, alternatively may not do so. 'Entitled' is permissive rather than obligatory, so that the formulation 'involves some ambiguity with the hint of the existence of some ineffable, undefinable, notion of intent, locked in the breasts of the jurors' . . .

I have previously argued that the idea of a mysterious gap between the law of intention and a factual finding of foresight of a virtual certainty owed its initial existence to some loose talk in *Moloney* about the place of foresight in the law of indirect intention. Lord Bridge wanted to distinguish recklessness from indirect intention, but he did so by suggesting that 'intend' and 'foresee' 'connote two different states of mind'. What he should have said, to be consistent with his analysis of indirect intention, was that the relevant distinction was between the mental states of 'foresight of a moral certainty' and 'foresight of a consequence within the range of probability'. Having said what he said, however, he then had to deal with the question of how the accused's foresight could be relevant to the law of (indirect) intention. His answer was that it played an evidential role so that indirect intention could be inferred from it. How this was logically possible given Lord Bridge's initial premise was never made clear, but the result of his argument was the idea of a gap between evidence of foresight of moral certainty and the law of indirect intention such that the former may, but need not, lead to a finding (previously an inference) of intention. This idea has remained an idée fixe of the law ever since, despite Professor Smith's best efforts to disabuse the judges of it. . . .

A narrow account of th[e] law makes *Woollin* and *Moloney* manslaughterers, a broad account makes them murderers, but neither the broad nor the narrow account actually captures the moral essence of the judgment that lies behind, but is mediated through, the law. . . .

In *Hyam*, the judges opted for the broad approach, but while the test of foresight of probable or highly probable consequence covered Mrs Hyam, it did not catch the essence of her moral wrongdoing. While 'foresight of a probable consequence of death or serious injury' carries moral information, it is still a relatively neutral way of describing the reckless animus with which Mrs Hyam addressed her victims. Still, unlike 'foresight of moral certainty', the lesser degree of risk enables her conviction. Again the test reflects the desired moral conclusion, but does not embody it. . . .

[T]he broader spirit of *Hyam* has always lurked within the indirect intention cases even when they have denied it, and this is as true of *Woollin* as the others. The case law contains both foresight of virtual certainty and foresight of (high) probability elements precisely because neither approach adequately embodies the moral judgments required by the murder label. For the same reason *mutatis mutandis*, the cases also leave the door ajar to a narrower, direct intention only, interpretation of the law in the manner of *Steane*.

Foresight of virtual certainty, even if it is not 'intention', is a condition precedent to liability where D does not have direct intent; and foreseeing that the result was highly probable is materially different from foreseeing that it was virtually certain. But Professor Norrie's article suggests that the present formula leaves open the possibility of the addition of a further ingredient in the mens rea.

≋ *Question*
What is the judge to say if the jury tell him they are unanimous that D foresaw that the result was virtually certain, but are divided as to whether he intended it, and seek guidance as to how they should decide?

The best practical advice to the judge is probably to fudge the issue: 'Members of the jury, intention is an ordinary word of the English language. It is a matter for you, applying your common sense and knowledge of the world.' This tells the jury nothing but it may result in a verdict. Would a more honest instruction to the jury be: 'If, in the light of all the evidence you have heard, you are satisfied D deserves to be convicted of murder, call his state of mind intention and convict. Otherwise acquit him of murder and convict him of manslaughter.' It may be that is how the jury do it anyway. And Professor Norrie's article suggests—in effect—that this may be the right answer.

It is already the law (section 9.3, p 227) in gross negligence that the test is whether the negligence is 'bad enough' to be condemned as criminal. This direction makes sense if it is treated as bad enough to be manslaughter (section 9.3.3, p 238). That approach has long been heavily criticized on the ground that it leaves a question of law to be determined by the jury (cf *Misra* [2004] EWCA Crim 2375; *Sellu* [2016] EWCA Crim 1716, section 9.3.2, p 237). But if we are to have a law of manslaughter by gross negligence—and we do—there is probably no other way. There is no logical compulsion for a similar principle in murder; but should it be adopted as a matter of policy where it is not alleged that it was D's purpose to cause death or GBH? Should the judge be required to tell the jury in all such cases—not waiting to be asked: 'If you are sure that D knew the result was virtually certain, then, and only then, are you entitled to convict him of [murder]. But you will do so only if you are sure that, in the light of all the evidence, his conduct in causing death was bad enough to deserve condemnation as murder'?

This would explain the judges' strange reluctance to treat foresight of virtual certainty as intention in murder cases and insist that it is only evidence; but would it be fair to allow this escape route for hard cases where it is not D's purpose to kill, while excluding any escape route for D where death or GBH is his purpose? The mercy killer acts with the purpose of causing death, and his is perhaps the hardest case of all. The surgeons in *Re A (children) (conjoined twins)* were not guilty of murder, not simply because of their impeccable motives, but because the killing of Mary was necessary to defend the life of Jodie or was justified by a more general defence of necessity.

(B) Intention to commit GBH is sufficient mens rea for murder

In addition to the criticisms that are made of the fact virtual certainty can be equated with intention, there are those who argue that it is anomalous for an intention to cause really serious harm to be sufficient mens rea for murder. For example, in *A-G's Reference (No 3 of 1994)* [1997] UKHL 31, [1997] Crim LR 829, in *Powell & Daniels and English* [1997] UKHL 57 and in *Woollin* [1998] UKHL 28, [1998] Crim LR 890, HL, Lords Mustill and Steyn criticized what Lord Mustill called the 'conspicuous anomaly', that an intention to cause GBH is the mens rea of murder, as an instance of 'constructive crime'—that is, where the mens rea of a lesser offence is sufficient to ground liability for a greater: 'The fault element does not correspond to the conduct leading to the charge, ie the causing of death. A person is liable to conviction for a more serious crime than he foresaw . . .' '. . . a defendant may be convicted of murder who is in no ordinary sense a murderer.'

'Anomaly' implies something irregular or exceptional. In the context of offences against the person, the murder rule is hardly an anomaly. The law of offences against the person abounds in constructive crime—it appears to be the general rule. Under s 20 of the OAPA, unlawfully and maliciously inflicting GBH, it is enough that D foresaw some harm, not necessarily grievous harm: *DPP v Parmenter* [1992] UKHL 1. Under s 47, assault occasioning ABH, it is not necessary to prove that D foresaw any harm—the mens rea of common assault, a mere summary offence, is enough.

The Select Committee of the House of Lords on Murder and Life Imprisonment (1989, HL Paper 78-1) stated:

52. Two main criticisms have been made of the present definition of murder. The first is that it is too broad in so far as it requires the conviction of murder of a person who kills, intending to cause serious bodily harm but not to kill and who may not even foresee the possibility of death occurring . . .

53. The second criticism is that the definition is too narrow in that it does not cover the killer who displays outrageous recklessness; for example the terrorist who kills by an act done with intent to cause fear of death or injury, but does not intend to cause death or serious, or indeed any, bodily harm.

The Committee recommended that the first criticism be met by implementing the definition of murder proposed by the Law Commission (following the CLRC) in the Draft Code.

After considering much evidence, including the argument by Lord Goff of Chieveley in favour of the Scottish concept of 'wicked recklessness' ('The Mental Element in the Crime of Murder' (1988) 104 LQR 30, below and the reply by Glanville Williams, 'The Mens Rea for Murder: Leave it Alone' (1989) 105 LQR 387), the Committee concluded that the proper place for reckless killings in English law was in the law of manslaughter. The principle of the Code definition should not be distorted to deal with the reckless terrorist and other wickedly reckless killers, who will in any event be liable to imprisonment for life (para 76).

Robert Goff, 'The Mental Element in the Crime of Murder'
(1988) 104 LQR 30

. . . I turn from intention to kill to intention to cause grievous bodily harm. In *Hyam* Lord Diplock, in a dissenting speech, suggested that the historical basis for the existence of this alternative form of the mental element in murder was unsound; he considered that, if the defendant did not intend to kill, he 'must have intended or foreseen as a likely consequence of his act that human life would be endangered.' But Lord Diplock's historical interpretation was emphatically rejected by the House of Lords in the later case of *Cunningham*. It is now settled by that case, for the time being at least, that this alternative form of the mental element, i.e. intention to cause grievous bodily harm, does indeed exist in English law, and further that (following a statement to the like effect by Viscount Kilmuir in *Smith*) grievous bodily harm means, quite simply, really serious bodily harm.

But the most serious objections exist to this as a form of the mental element in the crime of murder. The most fundamental objection is that the crime of murder is concerned with unlawful killing of a particularly serious kind; and it seems very strange that a man should be called a murderer even though not only did he not intend to kill the victim, but he may even have intended that he should not die. There are cases known to occur where the defendant does indeed intend not to kill but only to cause serious injury—as, for example, in the case of terrorists who punish traitors from their ranks by 'knee-capping' them—shooting them in the knee with a gun. This they do with a positive intent not to kill but to leave the victim maimed, *pour encourager les autres*. If a man so injured were to die in consequence, perhaps because he contracted an infection from his wound, the man who 'knee-capped' him would, in English law, be held to have murdered him, even though he positively intended not to kill him.

In case the point may be thought to be fanciful, let me give an example from my own practical experience. In certain areas of England there is a horrible practice called 'glassing.' A man takes a pint-size beer glass, knocks the top off on the edge of a table leaving a jagged edge, and then rams the jagged edge into the face of his victim—obviously causing dreadful cuts and scarring to his face. I found myself trying a young man for murder at Nottingham. He had gone out to a local public house with his uncle. They both had too much to drink. Another young man was there, who was regarded as an enemy. 'Glass him!' said the uncle to his nephew, and the boy proceeded to do so. But for some reason—perhaps the victim moved slightly—he caught not his face but the side of his neck, and severed his jugular vein. The victim staggered outside, covered with blood, and died shortly afterwards. The assailant and his uncle were both charged with murder. The facts were beyond dispute. The two defendants were ready to plead guilty to manslaughter; but the prosecution was not prepared to accept the plea, and the trial proceeded on the charge of murder. I summed up to the jury, as was my duty, on the basis that, if the jury were sure that the assailant had intended to kill his victim, or to cause him really serious bodily harm, then they should convict him of murder. The jury acquitted the defendants of murder but convicted them of manslaughter, and I sentenced them accordingly. Now it was plain to me, and must have been plain to the jury, that the assailant did indeed intend to cause the victim really serious bodily harm; yet they could not bring themselves to call him a murderer. This was a feeling with which I entirely sympathised, for the simple reason that, not merely could it never have crossed the assailant's mind that there was any risk of causing death to his victim, but he was horrified when he died. It may interest you to know that a colleague of mine on the English Bench had exactly the same experience in another case involving glassing.

The truth is that, for the reasons I have given, an intent to cause really serious harm should not be of itself sufficient to constitute the mental element in the crime of murder. Considerations such as these have led some law reformers to propose that a gloss should be placed upon this form of mental element. Such was the recommendation of the Criminal Law Revision Committee in its 14th Report (1980), to which I have already referred. I think it right that I should at this stage set out their recommendation in full:

'We therefore conclude that it should be murder:

(a) if a person, with intent to kill, causes death and

(b) if a person causes death by an unlawful act intended to cause serious injury and known by him to involve a risk of causing death.'

In addition, the Committee proposed a third possible category (to meet fears expressed about terrorism) as follows:

'That it should be murder if a person causes death by an unlawful act intended to cause fear (of death or serious injury) and known to the defendant to involve a risk of causing death.'

It is of course with recommendation (b) that we are at present concerned. To me there are two serious objections to this formulation. The first is that it is restricted to cases where there is an intention to cause serious injury. But why is it so limited? If a defendant does an unlawful act known by him to involve the risk of causing death, it would appear that (on this formulation) it is the knowledge of that risk which renders him a murderer. So what of the case where he only intends to cause a slight injury, or indeed no injury at all, but knows that his action involves a risk of causing death? Why should that be any different? For example, a nick in the skin of a haemophiliac could be as dangerous to life as a more serious wound to a normal man. Again, a man may project some missile in the vicinity of another, not intending harm but realising that there is a risk that, if it strikes some vital part, the other man may die; on the Committee's approach, if the victim was so struck, and died, that could not be murder. The formulation reeks, therefore, of a gloss upon an old but objectionable formula, rather than being a reformulation of the requisite intent. But there is a second objection, that as well as being too narrow (in the sense I have indicated) it is also, in another sense, too wide. The criterion chosen is that the defendant's act is known by him to involve a risk of causing death. But is that enough? For one may recognise a risk, and discount it as unrealistic; one may recognise a risk, and hope to avoid it. If a man does so, should he be called a murderer? For myself, I doubt it. Something more is, I think, required.

The additional suggestion, chosen to meet fears about terrorism, appears to me to be subject to the same objections. Indeed, it leads to the startling consequence that if a terrorist, not intending to cause fear of death or serious injury, but realising that his action involves a risk of causing death, blows up a national monument in order to publicise his cause and thereby kills the night watchman, then that cannot be murder. But I feel that this proposed category should not in any event constitute a separate category; and I also feel that, if one could look deep under the skin of category (b), it might be possible to discern a reformulation which would, on a more satisfactory basis, embrace both category (b) and the additional category designed to deal with terrorist.

[In Scots law] 'when death results from the perpetration of any serious or dangerous crime, murder may have been committed, although the specific intent to kill be absent. This is so where the crime perpetrated involves either wilful intent to do grave personal injury, or the wilful use of dangerous means implying wicked disregard of consequences to life.'

If this approach is right, then both English and Scots law should abandon intention to cause grievous bodily harm or grave personal injury as constituting of itself a sufficient mental element for the crime of murder, if indeed this be Scots law.

> ≈≈ *Questions*
>
> Can the GBH rule be defended as (a) reflecting a general principle that the law imposes an obligation on an attacker to take the unforeseen consequences of his actions (J. Horder, 'Two Histories and Four Hidden Principles of Mens Rea' (1997) 113 LQR 9)?
>
> Or (b) as an appropriate response in cases of death caused by an 'attack' (W. Wilson, 'Murder and the Structure of Homicide' in A. Ashworth and B. Mitchell (eds), *Rethinking English Homicide Law* (2000), pp 44–46)?

7.4 Reform

> ≈≈ *Question*
>
> Given the difficulty in defining the core elements, should murder and manslaughter be abolished and replaced with a crime of unlawful killing?

The Law Commission, in its Report No 290, *Partial Defences to Murder* (2004) urged the Government to permit a review of the law of murder. Part 2 of that Report provided a useful summary of the defects in the present law.

The Commission concluded that:

2.74 The present law of murder in England and Wales is a mess. There is both a great need to review the law of murder and every reason to believe that a comprehensive consideration of the offence and the sentencing regime could yield rational and sensible conclusions about a number of issues. These could include the elements which should comprise the substantive offence; what elements, if any, should elevate or reduce the level of culpability; and what should be the appropriate sentencing regime. We recommend that the Law Commission be asked to conduct a review of the law of murder with a view to:

(1) considering the definition of the offence, together with any specific complete or partial defences which may seem appropriate.

(2) considering whether the offence of murder should be further categorised on grounds of aggravation and/or mitigation and if so what those categories should comprise.

(3) in the light of (1) and (2), considering the application of a mandatory life sentence to the offence of murder or to any specific categories of murder.

(4) Examining how each of (1), (2) and (3) may differently be addressed where the offender is a child.

7.4.1 Law Commission Consultation Paper No 177, *A New Homicide Act for England and Wales*

The Law Commission published Consultation Paper No 177 (2006), which proposed a radical restructuring of the offences.

'First degree murder' (mandatory life penalty):

(1) intentional killing.

'Second degree murder' (discretionary life maximum penalty):

(1) killing where the offender did not intend to kill but did intend to do serious harm.

(2) recklessly indifferent killing, where the offender realised that his or her conduct involved an unjustified risk of killing, but pressed on with that conduct without caring whether or not death would result.

(3) cases in which there is a partial defence to what would otherwise be 'first degree murder'.

'Manslaughter' (fixed term of years maximum penalty):

(1) killing through gross negligence;

(2) killing through an intentional act intended to cause injury or involving recklessness as to causing injury.

'Other offences':

(1) infanticide; complicity in suicide.

Defences reducing 'first degree murder' to 'second degree murder'

(1) provocation (gross provocation or fear of serious violence).

(2) diminished responsibility.

(3) duress (threat of death or of life-threatening injury).

On the Commission's proposals, see: W. Wilson, 'The Structure of Criminal Homicide' [2006] Crim LR 471; A. Norrie, 'Between Orthodox Subjectivism and Moral Contextualism: Intention and the Consultation Paper' [2006] Crim LR 486; G. R. Sullivan, 'Complicity for First Degree Murder and Complicity in an Unlawful Killing' [2006] Crim LR 502; C. Wells and O. Quick, 'Getting Tough with Defences' [2006] Crim LR 514; V. Tadros, 'The Homicide Ladder' (2006) 69 MLR 601; J. Rogers, 'The Law Commission's Proposed Restructuring of Homicide' (2006) 70 J Crim L 223.

7.4.2 Law Commission Report No 304, *Murder, Manslaughter and Infanticide*

In its final recommendations in Report No 304 (2006), the Law Commission made some significant changes to the provisional proposals. Most significantly, the Law Commission extended the proposed offences:

(1) **First degree murder** (mandatory life penalty)

(a) Killing intentionally.

(b) Killing where there was an intention to do serious injury, coupled with an awareness of a serious risk of causing death.

(2) **Second degree murder** (discretionary life maximum penalty)

(a) Killing where the offender intended to do serious injury.

(b) Killing where the offender intended to cause some injury or a fear or risk of injury, and was aware of a serious risk of causing death.

(c) Killing in which there is a partial defence to what would otherwise be first degree murder.

(3) **Manslaughter** (discretionary life maximum penalty)

    (a) Killing through gross negligence as to a risk of causing death.

    (b) Killing through a criminal act:

        (i) intended to cause injury; or

        (ii) where there was an awareness that the act involved a serious risk of causing injury.

    (c) Participating in a joint criminal venture in the course of which another participant commits first or second degree murder, in circumstances where it should have been obvious that first or second degree murder might be committed by another participant.

J. Horder, 'The Changing Face of the Law of Homicide'
in J. Horder (ed), *Homicide Law in Comparative Perspective* (2008)

2. The Fault Element for First Degree Murder

Under the Commission's proposals, first degree murder will be committed when someone kills intentionally, or kills with an intention to do serious injury, in the awareness that there is a serious risk of causing death. This involves a change from the provisional proposals in the Consultation Paper, where the proposal was that first degree murder should be confined to intentional killing. There was considerable support amongst the Commission's consultees for confining first degree murder (and, hence, the mandatory life sentence) to intentional killing. That said, the Commission decided that to confine it so closely would have meant that some killings morally just as heinous as intentional killings would have escaped categorisation as first degree murder. An example might be the person who tortures his victim in hideous ways over a prolonged period, but the victim dies of a resulting heart attack before the torturer has forced the information from him. In such a case, the desire to continue the application of the torture is inconsistent with an intention to kill through the act of torture, as such, but there are compelling grounds for regarding the torturer as guilty of murder. The torturer has intentionally inflicted serious injury. Further, in cases of prolonged and severe torture he or she is bound to be aware of a serious risk that the victim will die in the course of the torture whether or not the information demanded has yet been revealed. Under the expanded definition of first degree murder the Law Commission is now recommending, the torturer in such cases will therefore be guilty of first degree murder. In more commonplace cases the expanded definition also gives greater reassurance that a charge of first degree murder is appropriate. If, say, D shoots or stabs V in the head or heart, then, in the absence of any special explanation about his intentions, D can readily be found to have had the fault element for first degree murder.

    The recommended definition of first degree murder does little more than update the proposal made for reform of the law of murder in England and Wales in the Draft Criminal Code of 1989. What are different are the recommendations for the new middle-tier offence of second degree murder. Second degree murder is made to do a great deal of work under the Commission's recommendations. It functions both as a free-standing offence in two different situations and as the crime to which first degree murder is reduced when a plea of provocation [now loss of self control], diminished responsibility or half-completed suicide pact is successful on a first degree murder charge. I shall be concerned here with its function as a free-standing offence.

3. Second Degree Murder: Cases of Intending Serious Injury

The first situation in which second degree murder is committed, as a freestanding offence, is when someone kills having intended to do serious injury, even if they were *un*aware of a serious risk of causing death (compare first degree murder, above). Under the current law, killing in these circumstances is murder. Broadly speaking, that reflects the position in jurisdictions in, or influenced by, the English-speaking world, although in mainland European jurisdictions killing in such circumstances would commonly be a lesser offence. The current position in English law can lead to injustice, because it means that the mandatory sentence of life imprisonment must be passed on someone who may have had no idea that his or her actions might cause death. Such a person should not fall within the highest category of homicide, as is recognised by those jurisdictions that treat it as second degree murder or as some other offence. Under the draft code of 1989, someone who killed having intended to do injury regarded as serious by the jury would have been guilty of manslaughter. The Commission does not now regard this as a satisfactory solution. Manslaughter is widely considered to be an over-broad crime even at it stands. It would have become still wider with the inclusion of killing where there was an intention to do serious injury. This would have been a serious matter, because it is likely that a large proportion of killings currently categorised as murder take place when there is an intention to do serious injury but no intention to kill. Moreover, there are sound moral reasons for thinking that killing with intent to do serious injury should be treated as a crime of murder, even if not as first degree murder. The nature of the harm intentionally done will in many cases mean that the defendant has made death a foreseeable consequence of his or her action. To launch an attack of that severity against another person demonstrates a disregard for the vital interests of others deserving of the label 'murderous', even if it would not be right to regard the crime as one of first degree murder. Liability for second degree murder is justified by the fact that when death occurs, albeit unforeseen, D is not being held responsible for harm done out of all proportion to the harm intended. Consequently, there is no need to add, as the 1878–9 Bill does, the further restriction that the intentional infliction of serious injury must have been for the purpose facilitating the commission of a range of specified offences. The history of such 'felony murder' provisions has not been a happy one although, as indicated above, many jurisdictions have retained them and they have a small band of spirited and ingenious contemporary defenders. Such provisions lead to the drawing of arbitrary distinctions between offenders. They entail secondary litigation, often leading to further complexity and arbitrariness, over the meaning of terms such as 'for the purpose of facilitating'. We are better off without them.

4. Second Degree Murder: Tackling Reckless Killing

Under the Commission's recommendations, the second situation in which second degree murder is committed as a substantive offence will be when D intends to cause some injury, or a fear or risk of injury, in the awareness that he or she is posing a serious risk of causing death. [T]he Commission's recommendation now eschews use of the term 'recklessness'. . . . The first kind of reckless killer meant to fall within second degree murder is (in general terms) the kind regarded under the old law as acting out of malice aforethought, and hence guilty of murder, but currently falling outside the scope of murder because there is no actual intent to kill or to inflict serious injury:

Recklessness Case 1: D injects V with an illegal drug, realising that the drug may amount to an overdose or contain potentially lethal impurities. The drug is an overdose or does contain such impurities, and V dies in consequence.

Recklessness Case 2: D sets fire to V's house where V is asleep, intending to cause V to run in terror from the house, but knowing that V may be killed if he or she does not escape. V fails to escape and is killed.

In both cases, D's potentially harmful act is aimed at V in the knowledge that the act poses a risk of death. Under the Commission's provisional proposals, in both cases D could be regarded as acting with 'reckless indifference'. The question was to be whether D's attitude towards injecting V was 'if this causes V's death, so be it', or 'so what?'.

The second kind of killer meant to be caught by the provisional proposal was one who, without aiming any potentially harmful act at V, none the less acted with such a high degree of recklessness that his or her attitude could be regarded as one of indifference:

Recklessness Case 3: D overloads a lorry with people hoping to obtain entry to Britain illegally. Although (as D knows) there is no way of ensuring that fresh air enters the locked compartments where the people are hidden, D completes a long journey into Britain without stopping to check on the people's condition, in order more quickly to obtain his payment. A number of people in the compartments are suffocated to death.

In this example, likewise, it seems plausible to suppose that D's attitude is 'if death is caused, so be it'. That would make him recklessly indifferent, and hence guilty of second degree murder even though no act of his was aimed at causing injury or the fear or risk of injury. The insistence that a lethal act manifest reckless *indifference*, if it is to amount to second degree murder, was meant to ensure that not all killing by advertent risk-taking became second degree murder:

Recklessness Case 4: D is an electrician. D has installed wiring that he or she knows does not meet official safety standards, because he or she is highly sceptical about the value of the 'officious meddling' involved in setting standards. The poor quality of the wiring leads to V being electrocuted and killed.

In this case, it seems unlikely that D could fairly be said to be manifesting a callous attitude towards potential victims, although his or her conduct is reprehensible and in a basic sense 'reckless'. D's misplaced distrust in officialdom explains his or her actions better than a disregard for the safety of electricity users. D could be found guilty of manslaughter by gross negligence, but should not (at least on these facts) be guilty of second degree murder. Commentators on the Commission's provisional proposals were sharply critical of 'reckless indifference' as a test of liability, principally on the grounds that it was too vague or left too much unstructured discretion to the jury. There would certainly be no improvement on the present law if a whole series of cases had to be taken to the appeal courts to determine meaning of 'reckless indifference'. Consequently, in its final recommendations, the Commission has the reckless indifference term and substituted a test with clearer language, the test of whether D 'intended to cause injury, or a fear or a risk of injury, and was aware of a serious risk of causing death'. The question is whether that test fulfils the same function as the test of reckless indifference. How does it apply to the recklessness cases 1–4 above? In case 1, D can be found guilty of second degree murder under the Law Commission's recommendations because D intended to cause injury (in the shape of the injection) and was aware of a serious risk of causing death. . . . [T]he Law Commission's recommendations for second degree murder extend to cases in which D intends to cause a *fear or risk* of injury, in the awareness that a serious risk of death is being posed. There is good reason for extending the mental element in this way, and it is illustrated by case 2. . . . D intended that V should fear injury, and hence D falls within the scope of second degree murder because D was also aware of a serious risk that V might be killed. The Commission further extends the scope of second degree murder . . . to cover cases where D intends to create a risk of injury, aware that there is a serious risk of causing death. What kinds of cases does this extension cover?

Recklessness Case 5: D intends to play 'Russian roulette' with V. D puts a single bullet into a revolver, spins the barrel and points the gun at V's head while V is not looking. Without checking to see whether the gun will actually fire, D pulls the trigger. The gun goes off, killing V.

Here, D intends to subject V to a risk of injury and is aware that in so doing there is a serious risk of causing V's death. If the Commission's recommendations had stopped short at intending to cause a *fear* of injury, then whether D was guilty of second degree murder in this kind of example would have turned on whether or not V was sufficiently aware of what D was about to do to fear injury. The boundary between homicide offences ought not to turn on such an issue.

The Law Commission's Report on Homicide is also considered in A. Ashworth, 'Principles, Pragmatism and the Law Commission's Recommendations on Homicide Law Reform' [2007] Crim LR 333.

The Law Commission proposals on the redefinition of murder were not all incorporated in the Coroners and Justice Bill 2009 which became the Coroners and Justice Act 2009. The Government decided only to implement the Law Commission's proposed reforms to provocation and diminished responsibility. The other reforms to homicide remain unimplemented. The reformed partial defences to murder are considered in full in Chapter 8.

More recently, in *Homicide and the Politics of Law Reform* (2012) Professor Horder has questioned the aspiration for enacting a fully codified law of homicide in a single statute, preferring more piecemeal reform. He also argues that the citizenry has become dispossessed in debates over reforms of the law of homicide, as the public's opinion has become largely irrelevant in the law reform process. He states that this is especially pernicious in the context of murder and manslaughter as they are forms of 'violative' offence, meaning that they violate the victim him or herself, rather than merely that person's rights. Without consulting the public on the law of homicide, it will lack the necessary moral authority. To combat this, Horder states that any proposals for reform must contain a mechanism whereby the views of the citizenry can be ascertained on a periodic basis. He recommends that the merits of morally controversial legal reforms ought to be automatically subjected to periodic review every 15 to 20 years. Do you think this is a good idea?

FURTHER READING

H. Briggs, *Euthanasia, Death with Dignity and the Law* (2002)

A. du Bois-Pedain, 'The Duty to Preserve Life and its Limits in English Criminal Law' in J. Horder and D. Baker (eds), *The Sanctity of Life and the Criminal Law* (2013)

B. Mitchell, 'Culpably Indifferent Murder' (1996) 25 Anglo Am LR 64

B. Mitchell, 'Public Perceptions of Homicide and Criminal Justice' (1998) 38 British J Criminology 453

B. Mitchell, 'Further Evidence of the Relationship Between Legal and Public Opinion on the Homicide Law' [2000] Crim LR 814

J. Munby, 'Medicine and the Law of Homicide: A Case for Reform?' (2012) 23 KCLJ 207

J. Temkin, 'Pre-natal Injury, Homicide and the Draft Criminal Code' (1986) 45 CLJ 414

W. Wilson, 'Murder and the Structure of Homicide' in A. Ashworth and B. Mitchell (eds), *Rethinking English Homicide Law* (2000)

8
Voluntary manslaughter

Voluntary manslaughter:

Voluntary manslaughter is committed where a defendant satisfies the elements of the offence of murder but successfully pleads a partial defence to murder. Three partial defences to murder exist:

(1) where D kills with the mens rea for murder but he has lost his self-control and the other conditions of the partial defence are satisfied (governed by ss 54 to 56 of the Coroners and Justice Act 2009);

(2) where D kills with the mens rea for murder but qualifies for the partial defence of diminished responsibility (under s 52 of the 2009 Act);

(3) where D kills in pursuance of a suicide pact.

Some of the controversies that will be examined in this chapter include:

(1) the extent to which the deceased's alleged sexual infidelity is relevant if D pleads that he lost his self-control at the time of the killing;

(2) whether the loss of control defence is capable of being pleaded by victims of domestic violence;

(3) whether loss of control can be characterized as an excusatory or a justificatory defence;

(4) what constitutes a recognized medical condition for the purposes of diminished responsibility.

8.1 Introduction

Manslaughter is a complex crime and exists in numerous forms. There are two principal categories: voluntary manslaughter and involuntary manslaughter. Voluntary manslaughter comprises three types all of which deal with the situations where the defendant kills with the fault required for murder but, because of the presence of a particular extenuating circumstance recognized by law, the offence is reduced to manslaughter. The other category—'involuntary manslaughter'—consists of killings committed with a fault element less than that required for murder but recognized by the common law as sufficient to found liability for manslaughter. These are dealt with in the next chapter. The statutory offence of corporate manslaughter is dealt with in Chapter 26.

It should be emphasized that regardless of the categories there is only one offence of manslaughter. Whether the defendant is guilty of the voluntary or the involuntary variety, the verdict is simply manslaughter. The only qualification to this is that, where diminished responsibility has been left to the jury, it is the practice for some judges to invite the jury to specify when giving their verdict whether, if it is one of manslaughter, it is a finding of diminished responsibility.

A life sentence is mandatory for murder but for manslaughter the maximum is life and there is no minimum. It is an offence which may be committed with a wide variety of culpability and sometimes may be properly dealt with by a fine or a conditional or absolute discharge.

The law in relation to voluntary manslaughter was altered significantly as a result of reforms introduced by the Coroners and Justice Act 2009. The new law has been in force since October 2010. Although this chapter will focus on the new law, at times it will also be necessary to examine what it replaced. This is helpful not only to assist in understanding the proper interpretation of the new provisions but also to evaluate whether they have achieved the aims intended of them.

8.2 Loss of control

The common law recognized a defence of provocation for centuries. The most authoritative statement of the common law defence was found in *Duffy* [1949] 1 All ER 932 in which Devlin J stated that murder was reduced to manslaughter where D killed with the mens rea for murder provided that at the time of the killing he had been subjected to:

some act, or series of acts, done by the dead man to the accused, which would cause in any reasonable man, and actually causes in the accused, a sudden and temporary loss of self-control, rendering the accused so subject to passion as to make him or her for the moment not master of his mind.

The common law defence was modified by s 3 of the Homicide Act 1957. The three elements of provocation as stipulated in the Act were that if D, when he killed, had the mens rea for murder, he would be guilty of manslaughter if:

(1) things said or done provoked him;

(2) he suffered a sudden and temporary loss of self-control; and

(3) the provocation was enough to make a reasonable man do as D did (with the reasonable man sharing those of D's characteristics that would affect the gravity of the provocation but not those which affected his ability to exercise self-control).

The defence was extremely controversial. One of the most powerful criticisms made of the defence was that it operated in a discriminatory fashion. Individuals who killed their abusive partners had to adduce evidence that they suffered from a 'sudden and temporary loss of control'. This was often difficult for women to demonstrate. Owing to a relative lack of physical strength, it is uncommon for women to lash out in this way. For example, in *Ahluwalia* [1992] 4 All ER 889 D suffered years of physical and psychological abuse at the hands of V, her husband. After he threatened to beat her again, D waited until V had gone to bed before pouring petrol on him and setting him alight. V died from his injuries six days later. There was evidence that the killing was premeditated. D was convicted of murder. The Court of Appeal mitigated the harshness of the 'sudden and temporary loss of control' requirement by stating that the partial defence could arise as a result of a 'slow burn' reaction rather than an immediate loss of control. Nevertheless, female victims of domestic abuse who killed their abusers were often forced to rely on diminished responsibility to avoid conviction for murder, which many thought unfairly stigmatized them.

The serious problems with the provocation defence prompted calls for reform. Law Commission papers examined numerous options for reform, including abolition of the partial defence altogether. The Law Commission summarized the problems with the defence in Report 290.

Law Commission Report No 290, *Partial Defences to Murder* (2004)

3.20 There was widespread dissatisfaction among consultees both with the theoretical underpinning of the defence of provocation and with its various component parts. It is not underpinned by any clear rationale. There is widespread agreement that the concept of provocation has become far too loose, so that a judge may be obliged to leave the issue to the jury when the conduct and/or the words in question are trivial. The concept of loss of self-control has proved to be very troublesome. The supposed requirement of a sudden and temporary loss of self-control has given rise to serious problems, especially in the 'slow burn' type of case. There is much controversy about the supposed objective test (that the provocation was enough to make a reasonable person do as the defendant did), which has been interpreted by the majority of the House of Lords in *Smith (Morgan)* in a way that may enable a defendant to rely on personal idiosyncrasies which make him or her more short tempered than other people . . .

3.36 Powerful arguments can be advanced for and against the abolition of provocation as a defence. Abolitionists argue that a person who is sane and who kills another person unlawfully, with the intent required for murder, ought to be guilty of murder however great the provocation may have been. Provocation may be a mitigating circumstance which should be taken into account in passing sentence, but not in defining the offence. Assessing sentence requires a balanced appraisal of all the circumstances of the case (aggravating as well as mitigating), and this is a judicial rather than a jury function. Not only is it inappropriate that provocation should be singled out among other possible mitigating circumstances as providing a special partial defence, but there are great difficulties in trying to define what may amount to provocation and how serious it has to be in order to amount to a partial defence.

3.37 Those who argue for the retention of some form of provocation defence, whether or not the mandatory sentence is retained, say that there are moral and practical reasons for doing so. Where the defendant's conduct was precipitated by really serious provocation, it is morally right that this should be reflected in the way that society labels and sentences the defendant; and it is desirable that the factual and evaluative question whether the defendant was provoked in that sense should be taken by the jury. A short sentence (or even in some circumstances a non-custodial sentence) for a provoked killing will be more understandable by, and acceptable to, the public if it results from a conviction by a jury of an offence not carrying the title of murder, than a decision by a judge after a conviction for murder. The existence of such a partial defence is justifiable in the law of murder, although there is no similar partial defence to non-fatal offences of violence, not only because the sentence for murder is fixed by law but also because of the unique gravity and stigma attached to murder. The real problem with provocation is not the underlying concept, but the way it has developed. It needs to be reshaped.

For criticism, see R. D. Mackay and B. Mitchell, 'But is this Provocation? Some Thoughts on Law Commission Report No 290' [2005] Crim LR 44.

The final provisions as enacted derive from Law Commission Report No 304, *Murder, Manslaughter and Infanticide* (2006). However, there are significant differences between the Law Commission's recommendations and what was finally enacted in ss 54 to 56 of the Coroners and Justice Act 2009, which states as follows.

Coroners and Justice Act 2009

54. Partial defence to murder: loss of control

(1) Where a person ('D') kills or is a party to the killing of another ('V'), D is not to be convicted of murder if—

(a) D's acts and omissions in doing or being a party to the killing resulted from D's loss of self-control,

(b) the loss of self-control had a qualifying trigger, and

(c) a person of D's sex and age, with a normal degree of tolerance and self restraint and in the circumstances of D, might have reacted in the same or in a similar way to D.

(2) For the purposes of subsection (1)(a), it does not matter whether or not the loss of control was sudden.

(3) In subsection (1)(c) the reference to 'the circumstances of D' is a reference to all of D's circumstances other than those whose only relevance to D's conduct is that they bear on D's general capacity for tolerance or self-restraint.

(4) Subsection (1) does not apply if, in doing or being a party to the killing, D acted in a considered desire for revenge.

(5) On a charge of murder, if sufficient evidence is adduced to raise an issue with respect to the defence under subsection (1), the jury must assume that the defence is satisfied unless the prosecution proves beyond reasonable doubt that it is not.

(6) For the purposes of subsection (5), sufficient evidence is adduced to raise an issue with respect to the defence if evidence is adduced on which, in the opinion of the trial judge, a jury, properly directed, could reasonably conclude that the defence might apply.

(7) A person who, but for this section, would be liable to be convicted of murder is liable instead to be convicted of manslaughter.

55. Meaning of 'qualifying trigger'

(1) This section applies for the purposes of section 54.

(2) A loss of self-control had a qualifying trigger if subsection (3), (4) or (5) applies.

(3) This subsection applies if D's loss of self-control was attributable to D's fear of serious violence from V against D or another identified person.

(4) This subsection applies if D's loss of self-control was attributable to a thing or things done or said (or both) which—

(a) constituted circumstances of an extremely grave character, and

(b) caused D to have a justifiable sense of being seriously wronged.

(5) This subsection applies if D's loss of self-control was attributable to a combination of the matters mentioned in subsections (3) and (4).

(6) In determining whether a loss of self-control had a qualifying trigger—

(a) D's fear of serious violence is to be disregarded to the extent that it was caused by a thing which D incited to be done or said for the purpose of providing an excuse to use violence;

(b) a sense of being seriously wronged by a thing done or said is not justifiable if D incited the thing to be done or said for the purpose of providing an excuse to use violence;

(c) the fact that a thing done or said constituted sexual infidelity is to be disregarded.

(7) In this section references to 'D' and 'V' are to be construed in accordance with section 54.

(8) The fact that one party to a killing is by virtue of this section not liable to be convicted of murder does not affect the question whether the killing amounted to murder in the case of any other party to it.

Provocation has therefore been abolished and replaced with loss of control. The partial defence comprises three main elements. There must be:

(1) A loss of self-control (not necessarily sudden).

(2) D's loss of control must have been attributable to one or both of two specified 'qualifying triggers':

    (a) D's fear of serious violence from V against D or another identified person; and/or

    (b) things done or said (or both) which:

        (i) constitute circumstances of an extremely grave character, and

        (ii) cause D to have a justifiable sense of being seriously wronged.

(3) A person of D's sex and age, with a normal degree of tolerance and self-restraint and in the circumstances of D, might have reacted in the same or a similar way to D.

Each of these elements will be examined in turn, in addition to some other features of the defence.

8.2.1 No considered desire for revenge

The best place to start when considering loss of control is s 54(4) which states:

(4) Subsection (1) does not apply if, in doing or being a party to the killing, D acted in a considered desire for revenge.

The reason why it is best to start by considering this element is because, even if all the other elements of the defence are otherwise present, the defence cannot apply if D acted in a considered desire to revenge. In *Clinton* [2012] EWCA Crim 2 (discussed more fully in section 8.2.6.2), Lord Judge CJ observed that the greater the level of deliberation, the less likely it will be that the killing followed a true loss of self-control. The Lord Chief Justice explained:

10. In the broad context of the legislative structure, there does not appear to be very much room for any 'considered' deliberation. In reality, the greater the level of deliberation, the less likely it will be that the killing followed a true loss of self control.

However, there is no guidance in the statute as to what is meant by 'considered'. To illustrate the difficulty in identifying whether there is a considered desire for revenge when D has lost control, it is useful to consider examples from the old law. There was held to be sufficient evidence of provocation to go to the jury in *Thornton* [1992] 1 All ER 306 where a wife had previously declared an intention to kill her brutally abusive husband, and after a fresh provocation she went to the kitchen, took and sharpened a carving knife and returned to another room where she fatally stabbed him. Is that a considered desire for revenge? Similarly, under the old law, in *Pearson* [1992] Crim LR 193, although DD had armed themselves in advance with the fatal weapon and the killing was a joint enterprise, provocation was left. Is arming oneself evidence of a considered desire for revenge? In *Baillie* [1995] Crim LR 739, where D, being greatly enraged, fetched a gun from an attic and drove his car to V's house (stopping for petrol on the way) before shooting him, provocation was also left to the jury. Would this be regarded as a considered desire for revenge? Although there is no guidance in the Act as to what is meant by 'considered desire for revenge', the minister did state the following in the course of Parliamentary debates on the Bill.

> the expression 'considered desire for revenge' achieves the right balance in ensuring that thought-out revenge killings are excluded without automatically barring every case where revenge may be part of a complex range of motivations.

≈≈≈ *Questions*

Does the inclusion of this restriction have the potential to undermine one of the aims in replacing provocation with loss of control, namely to ensure that women who are the victims of domestic abuse can plead loss of control if they kill their abusers? Would the defendant in *Ahluwalia* have been able to plead loss of control?

8.2.2 A loss of control

This element of the defence marks a significant departure from the Law Commission's proposals. The Law Commission had proposed abandoning the requirement that there be a loss of control. This was ultimately rejected by the Government. It was feared that omitting the requirement that D killed as a result of a loss of control would result in those who committed so-called 'honour' and gang-related killings would be able to avoid liability for murder by successfully pleading loss of control. As will be seen, there are those who argue that the reintroduction of this requirement has undermined the aims of the defence and rendered it conceptually incoherent. There is no definition in the legislation of the term 'loss of control'. In *Jewell* [2014] EWCA Crim 414, Rafferty LJ observed that this term had been defined in *Smith and Hogan's Criminal Law* (13th edn, 2011) as 'a loss of the ability to act in accordance with considered judgement or a loss of normal powers of reasoning'. Her ladyship accepted that definition. In the subsequent case of *Gurpinar* [2015] EWCA Crim 178, however, the Court of Appeal declined to offer further guidance on how the term 'loss of control' ought to be understood. One of the matters the court declined to offer further guidance upon is whether there has to be a total loss of control. Lord Thomas CJ preferred not to express a view on these matters and stated that they would have to await a case where they arise.

Although this element of loss of control is similar to provocation, it differs in that s 54(2) explicitly states that:

> (2) For the purposes of subsection (1)(a), it does not matter whether or not the loss of control was sudden.

However, it might be wondered how the jury will be able to determine whether D in fact lost her self-control if her reaction was not sudden. Indeed, Edwards argues that habituated gender thinking will continue to impress on the construction of this, as well as other, elements of the defence. Given that anger is typically regarded as signifying that someone has lost his or her self-control, the jury might be inclined to believe that D was acting out of a considered desire for revenge if her reaction does not conform to this societal stereotype. It is argued that this has the potential to undermine one of the central aims of the new defence. See S. Edwards, 'Loss of Self-Control: Why His Anger is Worth More Than Her Fear' in A. Reed and M. Bohlander (eds), *Loss of Control and Diminished Responsibility: Domestic, Comparative and International Perspectives* (2011).

In *Dawes* [2013] EWCA Crim 322, in a series of three conjoined appeals, the Court of Appeal sought to clarify a number of points in relation to the loss of control defence. Two of the appeals concerned the refusal to leave loss of control to the jury. In the third case the appellant argued that the judge had failed adequately to direct the jury fully as to loss of control and that his summing-up failed to deal with both sides fairly. Dawes was alleged to have stabbed a man in the neck having found him with D's wife on their sofa in the early hours (D claimed to be acting in self-defence). The second appellant, Hatter, stabbed his partner in the neck and claimed to have done so in a bizarre accident—the evidence was he had taken the knife to the scene and was angry as she was about to leave him. The third appellant, Bowyer, burgled a house and tortured and killed the occupant (a man he was competing with for the affections of a local prostitute).

The Lord Chief Justice stated that whether there was a loss of control is a question of the subjective state of mind of D. His lordship went on to observe that:

> Provided there was a loss of control, it does not matter whether the loss was sudden or not. A reaction to circumstances of extreme gravity may be delayed. Different individuals in different situations do not react identically, nor respond immediately. Thus for the purposes of the new defence, the loss of control may follow from the cumulative impact of earlier events. For the purposes of this first ingredient, the response to what used to be described as 'cumulative provocation' requires consideration in the same way as it does in relation to cases in which the loss of control is said to have arisen suddenly. Given the changed description of this defence, perhaps 'cumulative impact' is the better phrase to describe this particular feature of the first requirement.

≋ *Questions*

(1) Does this explanation help? If the members of the jury assume they know what a loss of control looks like, and this assumption is based upon the male stereotype, might they be inclined to find that D's act was one of premeditated murder if her reaction does not conform to this stereotype?

(2) Carol Withey suggests that if a loss of control is deemed to be central to the defence, then it would have been better to formulate a separate defence for domestic abuse cases where there would be no loss of control requirement. Do you agree? See C. Withey, 'Loss of Control, Loss of Opportunity?' [2011] Crim LR 263.

It has also been argued that the requirement that there be a loss of control has rendered the defence conceptually incoherent. Remember that the Government decided to retain the Law Commission's proposals in relation to the qualifying triggers but then also added the loss of control element. The following extract explains how this came about and also what the implications might be from a philosophical perspective.

A. Norrie, 'The Coroners and Justice Act 2009—Partial Defences to Murder (1) Loss of Control'
[2010] Crim LR 275

Loss of Control

The story of the law's reform away from and then back to loss of control is slightly complex. It begins with a concern of the Law Commission to exclude unmeritorious cases while admitting others. The problem was to permit the inclusion of, say, the abused woman who kills, but who acts with some apparent degree of premeditation, and to exclude other cases such as those of 'honour killing' or a case like *Baillie* [see section 8.2.1], in both of which there is a strong motive of revenge. In light of this worry about the unworthy case of revenge creeping in under cover of the moral approach, the Law Commission proposed what became s.54(4) on 'considered desire for revenge', but also considered alternatives to strengthen the position, including that the defendant should have acted out of 'extreme emotional disturbance' or 'immediately' following the provocation.

The problem was that a person should be able to claim the defence who has acted out of a justifiable sense of being seriously wronged, in response to a grave provocation, but not in a situation where they have converted their justifiable anger into a cold calculation for revenge. What is required is that the person act out of anger 'in the moment'. The example of honour killing is slightly beside the point here, because it would be excluded on the basis that there was no justifiable sense of being seriously wronged. *Baillie* is perhaps nearer the mark, where the defendant drove to a drug dealer's house and killed him, acting as 'self-appointed judge, jury and executioner'. The Law Commission accordingly, in addition to the no 'considered desire for revenge' requirement, sought a marker for the 'in the moment' nature of the anger. This could be indicated either by a defendant's 'extreme emotional disturbance', or by immediacy in point of time between the provocation and response. The former would, however, add a different, jarring, element to the new moral basis for the defence. As well as acting out of justified anger, one would need to be emotionally disturbed. This involved bringing loss of self-control back into the picture, and was therefore inconsistent with the new rationale of the defence as stated by the Commission. The latter was perhaps more promising, since it linked the reaction to the time when 'the blood was up'. However, the problem with this approach was that it was thought that it could not apply equally to the fear trigger—why is not stated, but it may be that there was a worry that in the case of the abused woman, bringing in an immediacy requirement would undermine the core idea that the partial defence could be used in cases of non-imminence or improper pre-emption. Still, one might have thought that the clear stipulation that the person not have acted out of considered revenge would have been enough to indicate the moral scope of the new law in relation to either the anger or fear triggers, and this was in fact where the Law Commission left the matter.

Not so with the Government. When we come to the new law, we find that it is concerned that there is a risk of the partial defence being used inappropriately, in honour killing and also gang-related cases, and even in appropriate cases such as those of the abused woman who kills. Even there, there,

> 'is still a fundamental problem . . . where a defendant has killed while basically in full possession of his or her senses, even if he or she is frightened . . .'.

At this point, the Government jumps tracks on the Law Commission's approach, for under it, the angry or fearful defendant *is* in control of their senses, albeit acting out of anger or fear. The Law Commission relied on judges and juries (in terms of ss.54(4) and (6)) to distinguish acting out of justified anger or serious fear from killing in cold-blooded revenge, but it opened the door to this departure from its proposals by acknowledging that the stipulation against revenge might be insufficient. If it is right that the immediacy requirement was rejected because it would counteract the fear trigger in cases of pre-emptive violence, that only left 'extreme emotional disturbance' as a means of checking revengeful violence. That however, as I have said, is only a hop and a skip away from loss of self-control. Hence, the Government, picking up the Law Commission's hesitancy, reintroduced loss of self-control into the defence, and, indeed, even called it that.

What will be the practical effect of this change? We need to consider its impact on the two modes of provocation under the new and old law. The first is imperfect justification. Here, the defendant acts out of fear of serious violence or where something that has been said or done is extremely grave and causes a justifiable sense of being seriously wronged. These are the qualifying triggers which permit, under the new law, a loss of self-control. That loss, however, must not be in conditions where the defendant acted from a considered desire for revenge. In addition, that person must have lost their self-control, though this need not be 'sudden'. What does this add to the law? On the one hand, it may make no substantial difference to an actual case, since it might be thought that any person who kills out of anger *must*, at some level, have lost their self-control—why else would they have killed? That the killing could not take place out of revenge already means that that problem is covered. A loss of self-control may just become another way for the jury to test that the person did not act in revenge. On the other hand, however, the idea of loss of self-control must have some substance, and though the removal of the 'sudden' requirement may help where the defendant's provoked reaction is delayed or gradual, there can now still be an argument as to whether there was a loss of self-control. In the case of the abused woman who acts after a time delay, will this not take the law back into disputes about whether there was a loss of self-control, and from there, into questions of suddenness, for, it might be thought, a test for and constitutive feature of any loss of self control in anger is that it have an element of suddenness? How else does one identify a loss of control, except as a moment of departure from being in control? The concern may be that, with both the anger and the fear triggers, the reintroduced requirement for loss of control will work against the new understanding that killing out of anger or fear represents a form of imperfectly justified action. Now, as well as a legitimately grounded sense of anger or fear, the defendant must also show a loss of self-control. Will that not work against the core logic of the new defence? Will it return defendants to the difficulty in pleading both reasonable self defence and a mitigatory defence based on loss of control?

≈≈ *Questions*

Was it a mistake for the Government to include the requirement that D must have lost self-control? What might this element have been replaced with? Consider the following extract and evaluate whether 'provoked extreme emotional disturbance' would be preferable to loss of self-control.

B. Mitchell, 'Years of Provocation, Followed by a Loss of Control'
in L. Zedner and J. Roberts (eds), *Principles and Values in Criminal Law and Criminal Justice: Essays in Honour of Andrew Ashworth* (2012)

The loss of self-control requirement

At the heart of the new law there remains the need for a loss of self-control, and it is difficult to avoid the conclusion that this will necessarily prevent much of the reform and improvement in the law which had been sought. The Law Commission was worried that a loss of self-control requirement would inevitably favour men over women and thought that there was no overriding need to replace it with some other form of subjective requirement; rather, it would be sufficient to stipulate that the provocation had not been triggered by a considered desire for revenge, that the defendant should not have 'engineered' or incited it, and that either judges could exclude undeserving cases or that juries could be trusted to do so. Ashworth though criticized that Commission's approach [see A. Ashworth, *Principles of Criminal Law* (2009)] on theoretical rather than practical grounds—it 'seeks to detach the provocation defence from one of its true rationales, which is that a good reason for partially excusing such defendants is that they acted during a distinct emotional disturbance resulting from what was done to them'. Ashworth's concern is not with the proposal to abolish the loss of self-control requirement but with the suggestion that there should be nothing put in its place. Interestingly, Horder had earlier floated the idea [see J. Horder, 'Reshaping the Subjective Element in the Provocation Defence' (2005) 25 OJLS 123] of what he called 'provoked extreme emotional disturbance' as a substitute for the subjective requirement. Indeed various alternatives to the loss of self-control element have been offered, some of which also seek to put emotional disturbance at the core of the subjective test. Such suggestions have been criticized for their uncertainty. Regrettably, though, the government's preferred condition, that there must be a loss of self-control, remains undefined and vague and there is no apparent reason to assume that the case law on it will be any more consistent that it was under the old common law.

. . .

The paradigmatic provocation case under the old common law was based on the idea that the defendant 'exploded' with anger (and lashed out with fatal violence), and the anger then subsided. But whether the new law will be noticeably different in this respect from the common law is open to doubt. It has already been suggested that this distinction between the old and the new law ought not in fact to make much difference. A loss of self-control can only occur 'as a moment of departure from being in control'. Moreover, the decision to admit evidence of cumulative provocation over a lengthy period, so as to provide the context in which the final incident (which may have been relatively trivial) occurred, effectively undermined the element of suddenness. Conversely, as has already been indicated, the new plea will automatically fail if the defendant acted in a considered desire for revenge, and the longer the time gap between the trigger and the fatal assault, the greater is the risk that the court will infer that the killing was vengeful.

Thus it has elsewhere been suggested that rather than focus on the physical nature of the defendant's reaction, the law should concentrate on the impact of the trigger (provocation) on his mind— after all, the defendant receives and processes the trigger in his mind; the physical response flows from that and is merely (ambiguous) evidence of the impact of the trigger. Arguably, therefore, the law should instead put some form of mental or emotional disturbance at the heart of the plea. One consequence of this would be the avoidance of the problem in both the old and the new law satisfactorily reconciling the loss of self-control requirement with acceptance of a time lapse before the fatal assault.

As has already been pointed out, whether there was a loss of control is a subjective question. However, in *Dawes* the Lord Chief Justice made the following observation which could be interpreted as injecting an element of objectivity into the first stage of the defence.

For the individual with normal capacity of self-restraint and tolerance, unless the circumstances are extremely grave, normal irritation, and even serious anger do not often cross the threshold into loss of control.

Might this have the potential to make it more difficult for women who are the victims of domestic abuse to plead the defence?

8.2.3 The qualifying triggers

There are two potential qualifying triggers and the statute makes clear that D can rely on them individually or in combination.

(1) D's *fear of serious violence* from V against D or another identified person; and/or

(2) *things done or said* (or both) which:

    (a) constitute circumstances of an *extremely grave character*; and

    (b) cause D to have a justifiable sense of being seriously wronged.

The words 'attributable to' connote a causal requirement, however the statute does not provide any further clarification on this issue. As a preliminary matter of interpretation, it is important to bear in mind that Lord Judge CJ in *Dawes* [2013] EWCA Crim 322 stated that the circumstances in which the qualifying triggers will apply is much narrower than under the equivalent provisions in the former defence of provocation. Also, in *Clinton* [2012] EWCA Crim 2, it was held that each of the elements in the respective qualifying triggers requires objective evaluation.

8.2.4 Qualifying trigger 1: D's fear of serious violence

The inclusion of this qualifying trigger was one of the Law Commission's proposals and marks a significant departure from the old law. The purpose of including this element of the defence was for the benefit of women who suffer domestic abuse and kill their abuser. Section 55(3) provides:

> This subsection applies if D's loss of self-control was attributable to D's fear of serious violence from V against D or another identified person.

It is important to appreciate at the outset the constraints placed upon this qualifying trigger. D must fear *serious violence* from the individual he then goes on to kill. It will not suffice if she fears anything less than this. The fear of serious violence must be against D himself or an *identified* third party. Thus D will not be able to establish the existence of this trigger if he fears serious violence from V against an amorphous class of people. Finally, the fear must emanate from an attack V, no one else.

This first limb may be one relied on well beyond the domestic violence setting, including in cases of householders who kill using excessive force and those who kill using excessive force in bar brawls. There is scope for the defence to be used in a very broad range of killings that were previously classed as murder and which previously attracted no defence. For example, D who stabs V in a fight in the pub might claim that he stabbed V having feared that V was going to stab him first. Even if D has used excessive force given the threat he thought he faced, and even if D has made an unreasonable mistake about the need for any force at all, he will, if the jury believe his story may be true and that he lost control, be convicted only of manslaughter. This is a significant change in the law.

Judges are not obliged to leave the defence to the jury in the way that they were with provocation: s 54(6). The defence must be left if 'sufficient evidence is adduced to raise an issue with respect to the defence' and this is when 'evidence is adduced on which, in the *opinion* of the trial judge, a jury, properly directed, could reasonably conclude that the defence might apply'. This remedies one of the problems with the provocation defence, namely that judges were obliged to leave the defence to the jury in every case in which there was some evidence of provocation even if the defence was not pleaded by D (and even if it ran counter to D's interests as where D was really wanting to suggest he was acting in self-defence and was in a controlled frame of mind).

In *Dawes* [2013] EWCA Crim 322, the Lord Chief Justice gave important guidance as to how 'opinion' in this context ought to be interpreted. His lordship stated that 'opinion' means the opinion of the court and is not used in the sense that different judges may reasonably form different opinions about the way in which the discretion should be exercised. What the section requires is a judgement, which may be right or wrong. On appeal, it will be for the Court of Appeal to determine whether the defence should have been left to the jury, bearing in mind the advantage that the judge will have from having heard the evidence. If the trial judge's judgement was wrong, the defendant will have been denied his entitlement to the jury's verdict and so his conviction will be quashed.

It is also necessary to appreciate that the first qualifying trigger of the defence encroaches upon the territory normally occupied by self-defence. See Chapter 23. There are, however, important distinctions between loss of control and self-defence.

- loss of control is only available on a charge of murder, whether as a principal or secondary participant. Self-defence is available as a defence to any charge;
- if D successfully pleads self-defence it leads to a full acquittal, whereas if D successfully pleads loss of control, his liability is merely reduced from murder to manslaughter;
- self-defence is available if D believes in a threat to him or others of *any* violence. Loss of control is only available if D believes himself or an identified other to be at risk of *serious* violence;
- if the degree of force used by D is, viewed objectively, excessive, that will deprive D of a defence of self-defence, but will not automatically deprive D of this defence. This is because it suffices if a person with a normal degree of tolerance and self-restraint *might* have acted in the same or a similar way as D did;
- if D seeks to plead self-defence, he must be reacting to an imminent attack. Imminence is not necessary with loss of control, provided that there is a fear of serious violence.

In *Dawes* [2013] EWCA Crim 322, the Lord Chief Justice observed that:

59. The loss of control defence is not self-defence, but there will often be a factual overlap between them. It will be argued on the defendant's behalf that the violence which resulted in the death of the deceased was, on grounds of self-defence, not unlawful. This defence is now governed by s.76 of the Criminal Justice and Immigration Act 2008. In the context of violence used by the defendant there are obvious differences between the two defences and they should not be elided. These are summarised in *Smith and Hogan, 13th Edition* [2011], at p 135. The circumstances in which the defendant, who has lost control of himself, will nevertheless be able to argue that he used reasonable force in response to the violence he feared, or to which he was subjected, are likely to be limited. But even if the defendant may have lost his self-control, provided his violent response in self-defence was not unreasonable in the circumstances, he would be entitled to rely on self defence as a complete defence. S.55(3) is focussed on the defendant's fear of *serious* violence. We underline the distinction between the terms of the qualifying trigger in the context of loss of control with self-defence, which is concerned with the threat of violence in any form. Obviously, if the defendant genuinely fears serious violence then, in the context of self-defence, his own response may legitimately be more extreme. Weighing these considerations, it is likely that in the forensic process those acting for the defendant will advance self-defence as a complete answer to the murder charge, and on occasions, make little or nothing of the defendant's response in the context of the loss of control defence. As we have already indicated, the decision taken on forensic grounds (whether the judge believes it to be wise or not) is not binding on the judge and, provided the statutory conditions obtain, loss of control should be left to the jury. Almost always, we suggest, the practical course, if the defence is to be left, is to leave it for the consideration of the jury after it has rejected self-defence.

In addition to the potential confusion between this qualifying trigger and self-defence, there are a significant number of ambiguities in the legislation itself. For example, what constitutes 'serious violence'? Does psychological abuse fall within this category? Further, must the fear be a reasonable one, or does it suffice that it is genuinely held? For example, what of D who hears her husband coming home from work and putting his key in the front door, signalling to D that further physical abuse is potentially imminent? To anyone not in D's situation, it would be perceived as an overreaction if she then goes on to lose her self-control and kill V. However, it could be argued that D has a heightened perception of her future safety that is incomprehensible to someone who has not been the victim of domestic abuse. See S. Edwards, 'Loss of Self-Control: Why His Anger is Worth More Than Her Fear' in A. Reed and M. Bohlander (eds), *Loss of Control and Diminished Responsibility: Domestic, Comparative and International Perspectives* (2011).

When considering the relationship between this qualifying trigger and s 55(6)(a), it should be borne in mind what Lord Judge CJ stated in *Dawes*, namely that an individual who is out to incite violence would be unlikely to 'fear' serious violence and if this is the case the trigger will not be present. This restriction is considered in section 8.2.6.

8.2.5 Qualifying trigger 2: things said or done . . .

This qualifying trigger bears the closest resemblance to the old law of provocation, however there are a number of differences. Section 55(4) provides:

> (4) This subsection applies if D's loss of self-control was attributable to a thing or things done or said (or both) which—
>
>   (a) constituted circumstances of an extremely grave character, and
>
>   (b) caused D to have a justifiable sense of being seriously wronged.

D must raise evidence both that the thing done or said constituted circumstances of an extremely grave character *and* that they caused D to have a justifiable sense of being seriously wronged. Although it was intended that victims of domestic abuse would primarily rely on the fear of serious violence qualifying trigger, it has been suggested that they ought to rely on this trigger. If domestic abuse is understood as a form of coercive control and a breach of trust, then why should victims not rely on this qualifying trigger? See J. Herring, 'The Serious Wrong of Domestic Abuse and the Loss of Control Defence' in A. Reed and M. Bohlander (eds), *Loss of Control and Diminished Responsibility: Domestic, Comparative and International Perspectives* (2011).

At the outset it is important to point out that there must be a thing said or done by someone; mere circumstances, such as a traffic jam, will not suffice. In this respect the new defence mirrors the old. Under the 1957 Act the source of the provocation was limited to acts of human agency. This limitation is open to criticism. For example, Mitchell cogently argues that the insistence that the loss of control stems from human conduct makes the resultant killing resemble a form of revenge and so undermines the justificatory aspect of it. See B. Mitchell, 'Loss of Self Control Under the Coroners and Justice Act 2009: Oh No!' in A. Reed and M. Bohlander (eds), *Loss of Control and Diminished Responsibility: Domestic, Comparative and International Perspectives* (2011).

8.2.5.1 'circumstances of an extremely grave character'

For the purposes of this second qualifying trigger, the threshold is that things said and/or done must constitute circumstances of an 'extremely grave character.' The intention is to restrict the scope of the defence. This element renders the defence much narrower than the previous law. It is intended to be an objective test but in assessing the gravity of the situation some subjective assessment of D's circumstances may be relevant. As Lord Judge commented in *Clinton* [2012] EWCA Crim 2:

> the question whether the circumstances were extremely grave and whether the defendants sense of grievance was justifiable require objective evaluation.

This was reiterated in *Dawes* [2013] EWCA Crim 322, in which the Lord Chief Justice stated that whether a circumstance is of an *extremely* grave character and that it leads to a *justifiable* sense of being seriously wronged requires objective assessment by the judge at the end of the evidence. The existence of a qualifying trigger is *not* defined solely on the defendant's say so.

8.2.5.2 'justifiable sense of being seriously wronged'

The defendant must have been caused by the things done or said to have a 'justifiable sense of being seriously wronged'. This obviously imports an objective evaluation of the thing said or done and is intended significantly to limit the scope of the defence. As an example of how this aspect of the defence might work, consider some scenarios from the old law. In *Doughty* (1986) 83 Cr App R 319, it was assumed that the crying of a newborn baby could constitute a provocative act. D was thus able to escape liability for murder when he suffocated the baby to get it to stop crying. Under the new law, even if it was accepted that the baby's incessant crying constituted circumstances of an extremely grave character, the jury would not find that it caused D to have a justifiable sense of being seriously wronged. In *Mohammed* [2005] EWCA Crim 1880, D sought unsuccessfully to plead provocation when he killed his unmarried daughter after finding her having sex, which was against his religious beliefs. This would clearly not fall within this limb of the defence as it could not cause D to have a justifiable sense of being seriously wronged. Although D may argue that he felt seriously wronged, such is not sufficient to establish that this is justified.

Once again, this aspect of the defence contains a number of ambiguities. For example, must the things said or done be directed at D or does it suffice that they are directed at a third party and cause D to have a justifiable sense of being seriously wronged?

8.2.6 Other limitations on the defences

8.2.6.1 No defence if either trigger is self-induced

Section 55(6) places constraints on what can constitute a qualifying trigger. The first constraint is contained in s 55(6)(a) and (b), which states:

> (6) In determining whether a loss of self-control had a qualifying trigger—
>
>   (a) D's fear of serious violence is to be disregarded to the extent that it was caused by a thing which D incited to be done or said for the purpose of providing an excuse to use violence;
>
>   (b) a sense of being seriously wronged by a thing done or said is not justifiable if D incited the thing to be done or said for the purpose of providing an excuse to use violence;

It is unclear whether this alters the law or is a codification of the common law. The ambiguity is caused by the requirement that it must have been D's *purpose* to provide an excuse to use violence. Need it be his sole purpose? Compare the position in self-defence in section 25.7, p 739 and the case of *Hatton*.

The leading case under the old law of provocation was *Johnson* (1989) 89 Cr App R 148. In *Johnson*, J and R had been drinking at a nightclub. J made threats of violence to R's female friend and to R himself. A struggle developed between J and R. J was carrying a flick knife. He stabbed R and killed him. He was convicted of murder and appealed on the ground that the judge ought to have, but did not, direct the jury on provocation.

Watkins LJ:

There was undoubtedly evidence to suggest that, if the appellant had lost his self-control, it was his own behaviour which caused others to react towards him in the way we have described.

We were referred to the decision of the Privy Council in *Edwards v R* [1973] AC 648. In that case the trial Judge had directed the jury thus:

'In my view the defence of provocation cannot be of any avail to the accused in this case . . . it ill befits the accused, having gone there with the deliberate purpose of blackmailing this man—you may well think it ill befits him to say out of his own mouth that he was provoked by any attack. In my view the defence of provocation is not one which you need consider in this case.'

The full Court in Hong Kong held that this direction was erroneous. The Privy Council agreed with the full Court. On the particular facts of the case Lord Pearson, giving the judgment of the Board, said (page 658): 'On principle it seems reasonable to say that (1) a blackmailer cannot rely on the predictable results of his own blackmailing conduct as constituting provocation . . . and the predictable results may include a considerable degree of hostile reaction by the person sought to be blackmailed; (2) but if the hostile reaction by the person sought to be blackmailed goes to extreme lengths it might constitute sufficient provocation even for the blackmailer; (3) there would in many cases be a question of degree to be decided by the jury.' Those words cannot, we think, be understood to mean, as was suggested to us, that provocation which is 'self-induced' ceases to be provocation for the purposes of section 3.

The relevant statutory provision being considered by the Privy Council was in similar terms to section 3. In view of the express wording of section 3, as interpreted in *Camplin*, which was decided after *Edwards*, we find it impossible to accept that the mere fact that a defendant caused a reaction in others, which in turn led him to lose his self-control, should result in the issue of provocation being kept outside a jury's consideration. Section 3 clearly provides that the question is whether things done or said or both provoked the defendant to lose his self-control. If there is any evidence that it may have done, the issue must be left to the jury. The jury would then have to consider all the circumstances of the incident, including all the relevant behaviour of the defendant, in deciding (a) whether he was in fact provoked and (b) whether the provocation was enough to make a reasonable man do what the defendant did.

Accordingly, whether or not there were elements in the appellant's conduct which justified the conclusion that he had started the trouble and induced others, including the deceased, to react in the way they did, we are firmly of the view that the defence of provocation should have been left to the jury.

Conviction for murder quashed. Conviction for manslaughter substituted

The Court of Appeal in *Dawes* [2013] EWCA Crim 322 offered guidance on the continuing validity of *Johnson*. Lord Judge CJ held that, for the purposes of loss of control, the impact of *Johnson* has been diminished, but not wholly extinguished by the legislative provisions in ss 54 to 56 of the Criminal Justice Act 2009. His lordship stated that:

One may wonder (and the judge would have to consider) how often a defendant who is out to incite violence could be said to 'fear' serious violence; often he may be welcoming it. Similarly, one may wonder how such a defendant may have a justifiable sense of being seriously wronged if he successfully incites someone else to use violence towards him. Those are legitimate issues for consideration, but as a matter of statutory construction, the mere fact that in some general way the defendant was behaving badly and looking for and provoking trouble does not of itself lead to the disapplication of the qualifying triggers based on s.55(3)(4) and (5) unless his actions were intended to provide him with the excuse or opportunity to use violence.

8.2.6.2 Sexual infidelity

In a case involving the second qualifying trigger, s 55(6)(c) provides that:

> the fact that a thing done or said constituted sexual infidelity is to be disregarded.

This provision was not contained within the Law Commission's proposals, but was added by the Government. The following reason for its addition was given by the minister.

> The history of the partial defence of provocation has led to a commonly held belief that that defence can be abused by men who kill their wives out of sexual jealousy and revenge over infidelity. That erodes the confidence of the public in the fairness of the criminal justice system . . . we want to make it clear that it is unacceptable for a defendant who has killed an unfaithful partner to seek to blame the victim for what occurred. (Hansard HC, Public Bill Committee, 3 March 2009, col 439 (Maria Eagle))

The provision was designed to demonstrate a clear shift in policy. The Ministry of Justice in its summary of proposals stated that:

> It is quite unacceptable for a defendant who has killed an unfaithful partner to seek to blame the victim for what occurred. We want to make it absolutely clear that sexual infidelity on the part of the victim can never justify reducing a murder charge to manslaughter.

The inclusion of this provision proved to be extremely controversial and in fact was defeated in the House of Lords but was then reinstated in the Commons.

The provision gives rise to a number of issues.

- What constitutes sexual infidelity, in particular what types of relationship are encompassed by that term?
- Can words constitute sexual infidelity? For example, what if D is told by X that his wife, V, is having an affair.
- Can sexual infidelity be considered by the jury as part of the context in which D killed V?

The Court of Appeal gave guidance on a number of issues in the following case.

R v Clinton
[2012] EWCA Crim 2, Court of Appeal, Criminal Division

(Lord Judge CJ, Henriques and Gloster JJ)

There were three conjoined appeals against convictions for murder, but it was only the facts of *Clinton*'s case that raised the issue of the proper interpretation of the sexual infidelity clause. D and V had been married for a number of years. D and V were in financial difficulties. In addition, V had developed a relationship with another man she had met on a social networking site. V left the family home for a trial separation two weeks before being murdered. D showed signs of a suicidal ideation. V visited the family home and it was D's evidence that she told him in graphic detail about the affairs that she had been having with various men. In addition, D stated that V had taunted him about his intention to commit suicide, saying that he did not have the courage to go through with it. Finally, D stated that V had threatened to leave him to care for their children alone. D stated that he then lost his control and strangled V to death. It was the Crown's case that the murder of V was an act of revenge, evinced by the fact that D had previously set fire to V's car and had written what appeared to be a murder/suicide note prior to the fatal attack. D sought to plead loss of control but the judge refused to leave the defence to the jury on the basis that there was no evidence that there was a loss of control attributable to one of the qualifying triggers. This ruling was based on the fact that the judge disregarded what V had told D about the extent of her infidelity. It was this ruling that D appealed.

[In ruling that the defence ought to have been left to the jury and ordering a retrial, Lord Judge CJ stated:]

16. We immediately acknowledge that the exclusion of sexual infidelity as a potential qualifying trigger is consistent with the concept of the autonomy of each individual. Of course, whatever the position may have been in times past, it is now clearly understood, and in the present context the law underlines, that no one (male or female) owns or possesses his or her spouse or partner. Nevertheless daily experience in both criminal and family courts demonstrates that the breakdown of relationships, whenever they occur, and for whatever reason, is always fraught with tension and difficulty, with the possibility of misunderstanding and the potential for apparently irrational fury. Meanwhile experience over many generations has shown that, however it may become apparent, when it does, sexual infidelity has the potential to create a highly emotional situation or to exacerbate a fraught situation, and to produce a completely unpredictable, and sometimes violent response. This may have nothing to do with any notional 'rights' that the one may believe that he or she has over the other, and often stems from a sense of betrayal and heartbreak, and crushed dreams.

17. [Counsel for D] drew attention to and adopted much of the illuminating and critical commentary by Professor Ormerod at pp.520–522 in Smith and Hogan's *Criminal Law* [13th edn, 2011]. To begin with, there is no definition of 'sexual infidelity'. Who and what is embraced in this concept? Is sexual infidelity to be construed narrowly so as to refer only to conduct which is related directly and exclusively to sexual activity? Only the words and acts constituting sexual activity are to be disregarded: on one construction, therefore, the effects are not. What acts relating to infidelity, but distinguishable from it on the basis that they are not 'sexual', may be taken into account? Is the provision directly concerned with sexual infidelity, or with envy and jealousy and possessiveness, the sort of obsession that leads to violence against the victim on the basis expressed in the sadly familiar language, 'if I cannot have him/her, then no one else will/can'? The notion of infidelity appears to involve a relationship between the two people to which one party may be unfaithful. Is a one-night-stand sufficient for this purpose?

18. Take a case like *R v Stingel* [1990] 171 CLR 312, an Australian case where a jealous stalker, who stabbed his quarry when he found her, on his account, having sexual intercourse. He does not face any difficulty with this element of the offence, just because, so far as the stalker was concerned, there was no sexual infidelity by his victim at all. Is the jealous spouse to be excluded when the stalker is not? In *R v Tabeel Lewis* . . . an 18 year old Jehovah's Witness killed his lover, a 63 year old co-religionist, because on one view, he was ashamed of the consequences, if she carried out her threat to reveal their affair to the community. She was not sexually unfaithful to him, but he killed her because he feared that she would betray him, not sexually, but by revealing their secret. [Counsel for D] asked rhetorically, why should the law exclude one kind of betrayal by a lover but not another?

19. [Counsel for the Crown] agreed that 'sexual infidelity' is not defined. He suggested that its ambit is not confined to 'adultery' and that no marriage or civil partnership ceremony or any formal arrangement is required to render the violent reaction of the defendant to the sexual infidelity of the deceased impermissible for the purposes of a qualifying trigger. He suggested however that the concept of 'infidelity' involves a breach of mutual understanding which is to be inferred within the relationship, as well as any of the more obvious expressions of fidelity, such as those to be found in the marriage vows. Notwithstanding their force, these considerations do not quite address the specific requirement that the infidelity to be disregarded must be 'sexual' infidelity. The problem was illustrated when [counsel for the Crown] postulated the example of a female victim who decided to end a relationship and made clear to her former partner that it was at an end, and whether expressly or by implication, that she regarded herself as free to have sexual intercourse with whomsoever she wanted. After the end of the

relationship, any such sexual activity could not sensibly be called 'infidelity'. If so, for the purposes of any qualifying trigger, it would not be caught by the prohibition in section 55(6)(c). In such a case the exercise of what [counsel for the Crown] described as her sexual freedom might possibly be taken into account in support of the defence, if she was killed by her former partner, whereas, if notwithstanding her disillusionment with it, she had attempted to keep the relationship going, while from time to time having intercourse with others, it could not.

20. [Counsel for D] and [counsel for the Crown] could readily have identified a large number of situations arising in the real world which, as a result of the statutory provision, would be productive of surprising anomalies. We cannot resolve them in advance. Whatever the anomalies to which it may give rise, the statutory provision is unequivocal: loss of control triggered by sexual infidelity cannot, on its own, qualify as a trigger for the purposes of the second component of this defence. This is the clear effect of the legislation.

21. The question however is whether it is a consequence of the legislation that sexual infidelity is similarly excluded when it may arise for consideration in the context of another or a number of other features of the case which are said to constitute an appropriate permissible qualifying trigger. The issue is complex.

22. To assist in its resolution, [counsel for the Crown] drew attention to the formal guidance issued by the Crown Prosecution Service on this issue. This provides that 'it is the issue of sexual infidelity that falls to be disregarded under sub-section (6)(c). However certain parts of the case may still amount to a defence under section 55(4)'. The example is given of the defendant who kills her husband because he has raped her sister (an act of sexual infidelity). In such a case the act of sexual infidelity may be disregarded and her actions may constitute a qualifying trigger under section 55(4).

23. This example is interesting as far as it goes, and we understand it to mean that the context in which sexual infidelity may arise may be relevant to the existence of a qualifying trigger, but in truth it is too easy. Any individual who witnesses a rape may well suffer temporary loss of control in circumstances in which a qualifying trigger might well be deemed to be present, although in the case of a rape of a stranger, insufficient to cause the defendant to have a sense of being seriously wronged personally. A much more formidable and difficult example would be the defendant who kills her husband when she suddenly finds him having enthusiastic, consensual sexual intercourse with her sister. Taken on its own, the effect of the legislation is that any loss of control consequent on such a gross betrayal would be totally excluded from consideration as a qualifying trigger. Let us for the purposes of argument take the same example a little further. The defendant returns home unexpectedly and finds her spouse or partner having consensual sexual intercourse with her sister (or indeed with anyone else), and entirely reasonably, but vehemently, complains about what has suddenly confronted her. The response by the unfaithful spouse or partner, and/or his or her new sexual companion, is to justify what he had been doing, by shouting and screaming, mercilessly taunting and deliberately using hurtful language which implies that she, not he, is responsible for his infidelity. The taunts and distressing words, which do not themselves constitute sexual infidelity, would fall to be considered as a possible qualifying trigger. The idea that, in the search for a qualifying trigger, the context in which such words are used should be ignored represents an artificiality which the administration of criminal justice should do without. And if the taunts by the unfaithful partner suggested that the sexual activity which had just been taking place was infinitely more gratifying than any earlier sexual relationship with the defendant, are those insults—in effect using sexual infidelity to cause deliberate distress—to be ignored? On the view of the legislation advanced for our consideration by [counsel for the Crown], they must be. Yet, in most criminal cases, as our recent judgment in the context of the riots and public order demonstrates, context is critical.

24. We considered the example of the wife who has been physically abused over a long period, and whose loss of self control was attributable to yet another beating by her husband, but also, for the first time, during the final beating, taunts of his sexual activities with another woman or other women.

And so, after putting up with years of violent ill-treatment, what in reality finally caused the defend-ant's loss of control was hurtful language boasting of his sexual infidelity. Those words were the final straw. [Counsel for the Crown] invited us to consider (he did not support the contention) whether, on a narrow interpretation of the statutory structure, if evidence to that effect were elicited (as it might, in cross-examination), there would then be no sufficient qualifying trigger at all. Although the persistent beating might in a different case fall within the provisions for qualifying triggers in section 55(4)(a) and (b), in the case we are considering, the wife had endured the violence and would have continued to endure it but for the sudden discovery of her husband's infidelity. On this basis the earlier history of violence, as well as the violence on the instant occasion, would not, without reference to the claims of sexual infidelity, carry sufficient weight to constitute a qualifying trigger. Yet in the real world the husband's conduct over the years, and the impact of what he said on the particular occasion when he was killed, should surely be considered as a whole.

25. We addressed the same issue in discussion about the impact of the words 'things said' within subsection 55(6)(c). Everyone can understand how a thing done may constitute sexual infidelity, but this argument revolved around finding something 'said' which 'constituted' sexual infidelity. [Counsel for the Crown] accepted that no utterance, as such, could constitute sexual infidelity, at any rate as narrowly construed. Professor Ormerod suggests the example of a defendant hearing a wife say to her lover, 'I love you'. On close examination, this may or may not provide evidence of *sexual* infidelity. However it does not necessarily 'constitute' it, and whether it does or not depends on the relation-ship between the parties, and the person by whom and to whom and the circumstances in which the endearment is spoken. It may constitute a betrayal without any sexual contact or intention. [Counsel for D] raised another question. He pointed out that in the case of *Clinton*, Mrs Clinton confessed to having had an affair on the day before she was killed, but earlier she boasted that she had had sex with five men. If the boast, intended to hurt, was simply untrue, how could those words 'constitute' infidelity?

26. We are required to make sense of this provision. It would be illogical for a defendant to be able to rely on an untrue statement about the victim's sexual infidelity as a qualifying trigger in support of the defence, but not on a truthful one. Equally, it would be quite unrealistic to limit its ambit to words spoken to his or her lover by the unfaithful spouse or partner during sexual activity. In our judgment things 'said' includes admissions of sexual infidelity (even if untrue) as well as reports (by others) of sexual infidelity. Such admissions or reports will rarely if ever be uttered without a context, and almost certainly a painful one. In short, the words will almost invariably be spoken as part of a highly charged discussion in which many disturbing comments will be uttered, often on both sides.

27. We must briefly return to the second example suggested by Professor Ormerod, that is the defendant telling his spouse or partner that he or she loves someone else. As we have said, this may or may not provide evidence of *sexual* infidelity. But it is entirely reasonable to assume that, faced with such an assertion, the defendant will ask who it is, and is likely to go on to ask whether they have already had an affair. If the answer is 'no' there would not appear to be any sexual infidelity. If the answer is 'yes', then obviously there has been. If the answer is 'no', but it is perfectly obvious that the departing spouse intends to begin a full relationship with the new partner, would that constitute sexual infidelity? And is there a relevant distinction between the defendant who believes that a sexual relationship has already developed, and one who believes that it has not, but that in due course it will. Situations arising from overhearing the other party to a relationship saying 'I love you', or saying to the defendant, 'I love someone else', simple enough words, will give rise to manifold difficulties in the context of the prohibition on sexual infidelity as a qualifying trigger.

28. This discussion of the impact of the statutory prohibition in section 55(6)(c) arises, we empha-sise, in the context, not of an academic symposium, but a trial process in which the defendant will be entitled to give evidence. There is no prohibition on the defendant telling the whole story about the relevant events, including the fact and impact of sexual infidelity. To the contrary: this evidence will

have to be considered and evaluated by the jury. That is because notwithstanding that sexual infidelity must be disregarded for the purposes of the second component if it stands alone as a qualifying trigger, for the reasons which follow it is plainly relevant to any questions which arise in the context of the third component, and indeed to one of the alternative defences to murder, as amended in the 2009 Act, diminished responsibility.

29. We shall return to the question whether, notwithstanding that it must be disregarded if it is the only qualifying trigger, a thing done or said which constitutes sexual infidelity is properly available for consideration in the course of evaluating any qualifying trigger which is not otherwise prohibited by the legislation.

. . .

Sexual infidelity—conclusion

34. We must now address the full extent of the prohibition against 'sexual infidelity' as a qualifying trigger for the purposes of the loss of control defence. The question is whether or not sexual infidelity is wholly excluded from consideration in the context of features of the individual case which constitute a permissible qualifying trigger or triggers within section 55(3) and (4).

35. We have examined the legislative structure as a whole. The legislation was designed to prohibit the misuse of sexual infidelity as a potential trigger for loss of control in circumstances in which it was thought to have been misused in the former defence of provocation. Where there is no other potential trigger, the prohibition must, notwithstanding the difficulties identified earlier in the judgment, be applied.

36. The starting point is that it has been recognised for centuries that sexual infidelity may produce a loss of control in men, and, more recently in women as well as men who are confronted with sexual infidelity. The exclusion created by section 55(6) cannot and does not eradicate the fact that on occasions sexual infidelity and loss of control are linked, often with the one followed immediately by the other. Indeed on one view if it did not recognise the existence of this link, the policy decision expressly to exclude sexual infidelity as a qualifying trigger would be unnecessary.

37. In section 54(1)(c) and (3) the legislation further acknowledges the impact of sexual infidelity as a potential ingredient of the third component of the defence, when all the defendant's circumstances fall for consideration, and when, although express provision is made for the exclusion of some features of the defendant's situation, the fact that he/she has been sexually betrayed is not. In short, sexual infidelity is not subject to a blanket exclusion when the loss of control defence is under consideration. Evidence of these matters may be deployed by the defendant and therefore the legislation proceeds on the basis that sexual infidelity is a permissible feature of the loss of control defence.

38. The ambit of section 55(3) and (4)—the second component, the qualifying triggers—is clearly defined. Any qualifying trigger is subject to clear statutory criteria. Dealing with it broadly, to qualify as a trigger for the defendant's loss of control, the circumstances must be extremely grave and the defendant must be subject to a justifiable sense of having been seriously wronged. These are fact specific questions requiring careful assessment, not least to ensure that the loss of control defence does not have the effect of minimising the seriousness of the infliction of fatal injury. Objective evaluation is required and a judgment must be made about the gravity of the circumstances and the extent to which the defendant was seriously wronged, and whether he had a justifiable sense that he had been seriously wronged.

39. Our approach has, as the judgment shows, been influenced by the simple reality that in relation to the day to day working of the criminal justice system events cannot be isolated from their context. We have provided a number of examples in the judgment. Perhaps expressed most simply, the man who admits, 'I killed him accidentally', is never to be treated as if he had said 'I killed him'. That would be absurd. It may not be unduly burdensome to compartmentalise sexual infidelity where it is the only element relied on in support of a qualifying trigger, and, having compartmentalised it in this

way, to disregard it. Whether this is so or not, the legislation imposes that exclusionary obligation on the court. However, to seek to compartmentalise sexual infidelity and exclude it when it is integral to the facts as a whole is not only much more difficult, but is unrealistic and carries with it the potential for injustice. In the examples we have given earlier in this judgment, we do not see how any sensible evaluation of the gravity of the circumstances or their impact on the defendant could be made if the jury, having, in accordance with the legislation, heard the evidence, were then to be directed to excise from their evaluation of the qualifying trigger the matters said to constitute sexual infidelity, and to put them into distinct compartments to be disregarded. In our judgment, where sexual infidelity is integral to and forms an essential part of the context in which to make a just evaluation whether a qualifying trigger properly falls within the ambit of subsections 55(3) and (4), the prohibition in section 55(6)(c) does not operate to exclude it.

40. We have proceeded on the assumption that legislation is not enacted with the intent or purpose that the criminal justice system should operate so as to create injustice. We are fortified in this view by the fact that, although the material did not assist in the construction of section 55(6)(c), our conclusion is consistent not only with the views expressed in Parliament by those who were opposed in principle to the enactment of section 55(6)(c) but also with the observations of ministers who supported this limb of the legislation.

[Lord Judge found support for this approach in the statements made by ministers as the Bill was proceeding through Parliament.]

44. Our approach to the legislative structure is entirely consistent with these responses.

≋ *Questions*

(1) Does permitting sexual infidelity to be considered as part of the context undermine the policy rationale for the prohibition or does it mitigate an otherwise unfair aspect of the legislation?

(2) Should each qualifying trigger be compartmentalized, so that it has to stand or fall on its own merit? For this argument, see D. Baker and L. Zhao, 'Contributory Qualifying and Non-Qualifying Triggers in the Loss of Control Defence: A Wrong Turn on Sexual Infidelity' (2012) 76 J Crim L 254.

8.2.7 Mistakes in relation to either trigger

What if D honestly, but mistakenly, believes that V is going to inflict serious violence on him? Similarly, what if D mistakenly believes things were said or done, but in fact they were not? This might arise, for example, if D mistakenly thinks that V has directed a racial slur at him. The question is whether D can still plead loss of control despite his mistaken belief? The legislation is silent on this particular issue. In relation to the first qualifying trigger, self-defence is available if D holds a genuine though mistaken (even if unreasonable) belief of the threat to him of *any* violence. Arguably therefore, the new defence should be available if D genuinely believes himself to be at risk of *serious* violence. In relation to the second qualifying trigger, if D honestly believes that things were said or done which, when *viewed objectively* (see *Dawes*, section 8.2.2, p 167) constituted circumstances of an extremely grave character and caused him to have a justifiable sense of being seriously wronged, he ought to be able to plead the defence. This was the position the Law Commission adopted. Of course, it might be difficult for the jury to believe that D had a *justifiable* sense of being seriously wronged if he was unreasonably mistaken about the thing being said or done.

8.2.8 Combined triggers

The legislation explicitly states that D can rely on one or both of the qualifying triggers—that he killed having lost control because he was in fear of serious violence and had a justifiable sense of being seriously wronged. The two limbs might be relied on by the woman who kills her abusive partner after years of torment when she lost control fearing another violent attack by him. In *Dawes* [2013] EWCA Crim 322, the Lord Chief Justice alluded to the possibility that the defendant will often seek to rely on the existence of more than one qualifying trigger, so that this scenario will become the norm rather than the exception. His lordship went on to make the point that, as the legislation recognizes in s 55(5), there are unlikely to be many cases where the only feature of the evidence relating to the qualifying trigger that deals with fear of serious violence will be something completely isolated from things done or said within s 55(4). Therefore, in most cases, the qualifying trigger based on a fear of violence will almost inevitably include consideration of things said and done: a combination of the features identified in s 55(3) and (4).

≋ *Questions*

What if D seeks to rely on both qualifying triggers and there is insufficient evidence of each limb in isolation but a combination would satisfy s 54(5)? Should the judge leave the defence to the jury?

8.2.9 Degree of tolerance and self-restraint

In addition to the loss of control and the existence of a qualifying trigger, the final limb of the defence imports a requirement of an additional objective requirement. Section 54(1)(c) provides:

> (c) a person of D's sex and age, with a normal degree of tolerance and self restraint and in the circumstances of D, might have reacted in the same or in a similar way to D.

Further clarification is offered in s 54(3):

> (3) In subsection (1)(c) the reference to 'the circumstances of D' is a reference to all of D's circumstances other than those whose only relevance to D's conduct is that they bear on D's general capacity for tolerance or self-restraint.

In order to understand this element of the defence, it is necessary to have some knowledge of what it replaced. Under the 1957 Act, the courts struggled to reach a clear position on the extent to which it was necessary or desirable to take into account the characteristics of the particular defendant when assessing the likely response of the reasonable person to the provocation. There were numerous visits to the House of Lords on this issue with a worrying lack of consistency in the answers provided. In deciding that D's age and gender was relevant, the House of Lords in *Camplin* [1978] 2 All ER 168 stated that:

> Although it is now for the jury to apply the 'reasonable man' test, it still remains for the judge to direct them what, in the new context of the section, is the meaning of this apparently inapt expression, since powers of ratiocination bear no obvious relationship to powers of self-control. Apart from this the judge is entitled, if he thinks it helpful, to suggest considerations which may influence the jury in forming their own opinions as to whether the test is satisfied; but he should make it clear that these are not

instructions which they are required to follow: it is for them and no one else to decide what weight, if any, ought to be given to them.

As I have already pointed out, for the purposes of the law of provocation the 'reasonable man' has never been confined to the adult male. It means an ordinary person of either sex, not exceptionally excitable or pugnacious, but possessed of such powers of self-control as everyone is entitled to expect that his fellow citizens will exercise in society as it is today. A crucial factor in the defence of provocation from earliest times has been the relationship between the gravity of provocation and the way in which the accused retaliated, both being judged by the social standards of the day.

The House of Lords in *Smith* [1998] 4 All ER 387 went on to expand the type of characteristics that could be included for consideration to encompass those that impacted upon D's capacity to exercise self-control irrespective of whether they were also relevant to the gravity of the provocation. This left the jury with no benchmark against which to assess D's conduct in killing when out of control. In *A-G for Jersey v Holley* [2005] UKPC 23, a specially convened nine-member Board of the Privy Council concluded by a majority that *Smith* was wrongly decided. The majority held that within the objective limb of provocation a distinction should be drawn between characteristics of D that were to be taken into account because they affected the gravity of the provocation he faced and those relating to the ability to exercise self-control. The latter were not to be taken into account in assessing the defence.

On one interpretation, the provisions in the Coroners and Justice Act 2009 might be seen as simply codifying the decisions in *Camplin* and *Holley*. However, there are a number of features of the third limb of loss of control that are important and which make it quite different from the law it replaced.

- Unlike the former law, reference is made to 'tolerance' in addition to self-restraint. Tolerance and self-restraint are two distinct qualities. This element was included in the Law Commission's drafts to reflect the idea that in addition to a comparison with a person of normal self-control, the defendant's conduct should be compared to that of a person who is not 'a bigot'. It excludes from the defence the person with unacceptable attitudes as well as those with an unacceptable temper. See R. Taylor, 'The Model of Tolerance and Self-Restraint' in A. Reed and M. Bohlander (eds), *Loss of Control and Diminished Responsibility: Domestic, Comparative and International Perspectives* (2011).

- The words that a person '*might* have reacted in the same or similar way to D' is more generous to D than the requirement in s 3 of the 1957 Act which was that 'the provocation is enough *to make* reasonable man do as he did'. In this respect, loss of control is arguably more generous than provocation. The word 'reacted' is not defined.

- The words 'in the circumstances of D' may enable a jury to adopt a more generous approach when judging D's response than might have been possible under s 3 as interpreted in *Holley*. It is important to note that s 54(3) clarifies s 54(1)(c) so that the reference to 'the circumstances of D' includes '*all* of D's circumstances' except those which bear on D's 'general capacity for tolerance and self-restraint' (eg a propensity to violent outbursts). This opens up a broader range of subjective considerations than under the *Holley* test. However, Mitchell argues that this reproduces the law after the decision in *Holley* so that the individual characteristics of D will only be attributable to the 'person with normal tolerance and self-restraint' if they are relevant to the triggering event. See B. Mitchell, 'Years of Provocation, Followed by a Loss of Control' in L. Zedner and J. Roberts (eds), *Principles and Values in Criminal Law and Criminal Justice* (2012).

- Section 54(3) excludes circumstances 'whose only relevance to D's conduct is that they bear on D's general capacity for tolerance or self restraint'. That restriction is similar to the old law in *excluding* certain features. However, there is now no positive requirement that D's individual circumstances have to affect the gravity of the triggering conduct in order for them to be *included* in the jury's assessment of what the person of D's age and sex might have done. This represents a reversal of the *Camplin* test, which focused expressly on whether D's characteristics affected the gravity. *Any* circumstances are now relevant unless their only relevance bears on the general capacity for tolerance and self-restraint.

≈≈ **Questions**

Why were age and sex singled out as opposed to other attributes, such as race? Are these not superfluous since these attributes would fall to be considered as a 'circumstance'?

8.2.9.1 Can voluntary intoxication constitute a relevant 'circumstance'?

A question arose as to whether voluntary intoxication could constitute a relevant circumstance for the purposes of the partial defence. In *Asmelash* [2013] EWCA Crim 157, D and V had spent the day together drinking alcohol. D claimed that V had been verbally abusive towards him and had tried to sexually assault him when they returned to the hostel in which they both resided. D took a knife, intending to scare V, but swung the knife at V when he began to advance towards him. The knife entered V's back, killing him. D pleaded loss of control. In directing the jury as to the elements of the defence, the judge directed the jury that they should disregard the fact that D was voluntarily intoxicated. D was convicted and appealed. The Court of Appeal held that the judge was right to direct the jury as he did. Lord Judge CJ stated:

> 22. It has of course been long understood that the consumption of alcohol, or indeed the taking of drugs, may diminish the ability of an individual to control or restrain himself, so that, in drink, or affected by drugs, he may behave in a way in which he would not have behaved when sober or drug free. Although it may sometimes impact on the question whether the constituent elements of a crime, in particular in relation to the required intent, have been proved, self-induced intoxication does not provide a defence to a criminal charge. This principle was applied to the defence of provocation in *McCarthy* [1954] 2 QB 105, and in the context of the law of Jersey which corresponded with s.3 of the Homicide Act 1957, underlined in *Attorney General for Jersey v Holley* [2005] [2 AC] 580. Indeed for several decades now, judicial directions to the jury considering the provocation defence in the context of the voluntary consumption of alcohol, referred to the reasonable sober person in the position of the defendant. If [counsel for D]'s submission is correct, a remarkably benign development to the issue of alcohol has been adopted as part of the statutory ingredients of the loss of control defence when, simultaneously, the defence itself is in many ways much more restrictive than the former provocation defence. In *Dowds*, after a valuable analysis of the policy reasons underlining the approach of the criminal law to the issue of self-induced intoxication, headed *Voluntary Drunkenness in English Criminal Law*, the court observed:
>
> > 'The exception which prevents a defendant from relying on his voluntary intoxication, save upon the limited question of whether a "specific intent" has been formed, is well entrenched and formed the unspoken backdrop for the new statutory formula. There has been no hint of any dissatisfaction with that rule of law. If Parliament had meant to alter it, or depart from it, it would undoubtedly have made its intention explicit.'
>
> 23. As Hughes LJ explained in *Dowds* [see section 8.3.2.2], on occasions when recasting a defence in statutory form, express provision is made about the approach to self-induced drunkenness (see s.75(5) of the Criminal Justice and Immigration Act 2008 which put the law of self-defence into

statutory form). On other occasions, however, a new statute simply proceeded on the basis of the well established principles of law, and specific legislative provision was unnecessary.

24. In essence, therefore, [counsel for D]'s submission proceeds on the basis that in the absence of any express statutory provision, in the context of 'loss of control', a new approach to the issue of voluntary drunkenness is required. We disagree. We can find nothing in the 'loss of control' defence to suggest that Parliament intended, somehow, that the normal rules which apply to voluntary intoxication should not apply. If that had been the intention of Parliament, it would have been spelled out in unequivocal language. Moreover, faced with the compelling reasoning of this court in *Dowds* in the context of diminished responsibility, it is inconceivable that different criteria should govern the approach to the issue of voluntary drunkenness, depending on whether the partial defence under consideration is diminished responsibility or loss of control. Indeed, given that in a fair proportion of cases, both defences are canvassed before the jury, the potential for uncertainty and confusion which would follow the necessarily very different directions on the issue of intoxication depending on which partial defence was under consideration, does not bear contemplation.

25. Our conclusion does not bear the dire consequences suggested by [counsel for D]. It does not mean that the defendant who has been drinking is deprived of any possible loss of control defence: it simply means, as the judge explained, that the loss of control defence must be approached without reference to the defendant's voluntary intoxication. If a sober individual in the defendant's circumstances, with normal levels of tolerance and self-restraint might have behaved in the same way as the defendant confronted by the relevant qualifying trigger, he would not be deprived of the loss of control defence just because he was not sober. And different considerations would arise if, a defendant with a severe problem with alcohol or drugs was mercilessly taunted about the condition, to the extent that it constituted a qualifying trigger, the alcohol or drug problem would then form part of the circumstances for consideration.

26. In our judgment the judge was right to direct the jury as he did. This ground of appeal fails.

8.2.10 The underlying philosophy

As a concluding matter it is worth considering how the defence fits into the typical excuse/ justification dichotomy. Norrie explains the new defence in the following terms:

A. Norrie, 'The Coroners and Justice Act 2009—Partial Defences to Murder (1) Loss of Control'
[2010] Crim LR 275

In their first report, the Law Commission distinguished two approaches to provocation, one with a justificatory, the other with an excusatory basis. While acknowledging that this was problematic, the Commission felt it did produce helpful arguments, and the distinction between the two operates to identify two different philosophies of provocation. What are these? The first is that of what I shall call *imperfect justification*, and it is this which informs the Law Commission's own thinking. In this view, anger is not a morally impermissible emotion, for it reveals a normal and, at one level, appropriate, even perhaps virtuous, response to certain forms of words or action. How this insight fits with the law is complex and operates at two different levels. Some would argue that 'anger cannot ethically afford any ground for mitigating the gravity of deliberately violent action', but the counter-argument is that it 'can be an ethically appropriate emotion and that . . . it may be a sign of moral weakness or human coldness not to feel strong anger'. Even in this view, however, anger cannot justify outright a violent response, certainly not a killing. Nevertheless,

'a killing in anger produced by serious wrongdoing is ethically less wicked, and therefore deserving of a lesser punishment, than, say, killing out of greed, lust, jealousy or for political reasons'.

Where a 'belief that the provoked [person] has been wronged by the provoker . . . is justified, it does not justify the provoked person in giving vent to his or her emotions by resorting to unlawful violence, however great the provocation. Two wrongs do not make a right. However, . . . there is a distinction in moral blameworthiness between over reaction to grave provocation and unprovoked use of violence.'

This idea of responding by way of an action that requires a nuanced and complex judgment of *both* its particular rightfulness *and* its overall wrongness I seek to catch by the term 'imperfect justification'. Note that in this approach, no reference need be made to a loss of self-control, for on this account, it is the way that anger righteously informs action, albeit in a context of overall wrongness, that provides the element of justification to set against the overall sense of a wrongdoing. On this model, it would be inappropriate to require a loss of self-control as a part of the defence. The defendant need not be out of control, though he or she acted when the 'blood was up'. Indeed to be out of control might take the moral edge off what has been done in righteous, but sanctionable, anger. Note also that what is true of anger is also true of fear, for fear too may be an appropriate and justified, if overall wrongful, emotional response. With both anger and fear, 'there is a common element namely a response to unjust conduct'.

If this is the approach of the Law Commission, how does it compare with the previous law and its underlying theoretical approach? As the Law Commission point out, the approach informing the 1957 Act was not one of justification but one based on excuse. Though they do not elaborate it, I would call it one of *compassionate excuse*. This reflects the fact that the person is held to have lost self-control, so that their act is intrinsically marked from the first as wrong. It is (arguably) one thing to act out of morally appropriate anger, remaining in control of one's actions, the new approach. It can never be right at any level to lose one's control, for this entails a defect in one's rationality, the sine qua non of moral action. Loss of self-control, hijacking reason, is a problem from the start. At the same time, it can in appropriate circumstances be understood, sympathised with, and therefore be partially condoned or excused. The law condemns the act both for the wrong done *and* the loss of control, but still extends a compassionate hand to the actor. This is the basis for the idea that provocation is a concession to human frailty, for the loss of self-control and its consequence is condemned, but the weakness it represents is viewed with sympathy. Note in this, by the way, the crucial rider 'in appropriate circumstances', for it is not every loss of self-control that will produce sympathy. Much will depend on the moral quality of the provocation to which there was a reaction, as well as to the particular human circumstances of the defendant. What was it about both the provocation and the provoked defendant that caused her to lose self-control, and is the 'ordinary person' sympathetic to their plight? Is their weakness something that can be condoned on a 'there but for the grace of God go I' basis? In sum, if the moral mark of the new Law Commission approach is that conduct is imperfectly rightful, and therefore both condemned and partially vindicated, the mark of the old law was that conduct was partially excused, both wrongful and partially condoned on ground of compassion. This, as we shall see, marks out two different territories for the old law of provocation and the new law of loss of control. I now return to the core problems that led to change in the law.

8.3 Diminished responsibility

Section 2 of the Homicide Act 1957 introduced a new defence to murder: 'diminished responsibility'. The defence has been substituted with one of the same name contained in s 52 of the Coroners and Justice Act 2009. The new provisions have been in force since October 2010. Unlike provocation, the defence of diminished responsibility was a relatively recent import into English law and in fact originated in Scotland in the middle of the nineteenth century. As with loss of control, diminished responsibility is only a defence to a charge of murder and if successfully pleaded it reduces murder to manslaughter. By s 2(2) of the 1957 Act, the burden of proof is on D. This is in contrast to loss of control, where the burden of proof is on the Crown to disprove that D lost his control if he adduces sufficient evidence to raise it as an issue. In *Foye* [2013] EWCA Crim 475, this reverse burden was upheld as being compatible with Article 6 of the European Convention on Human Rights (ECHR). Lord Hughes rationalized the different approach of the two defences in the following terms:

> In particular, it is plain beyond a peradventure that the reverse onus is applied by Parliamentary statute to diminished responsibility and not to loss of control. That is deliberate and entirely comprehensible. Diminished responsibility depends on the internal mental condition of the defendant. Loss of control depends on an objective judgment of his actions as a reaction to external circumstances.

This was confirmed recently in *Wilcocks* [2016] EWCA Crim 2043.

Before the changes introduced by the 2009 Act, diminished responsibility comprised the following four elements:

(1) an abnormality of mind;

(2) which arose from one of the specified conditions set out in the Act;

(3) which substantially impaired;

(4) D's mental responsibility.

None of these elements was defined with any precision and it was often said that the courts colluded with psychiatrists to keep the elements of the defence as vague as possible so that the mandatory life sentence for murder could be avoided in deserving cases where it would otherwise apply. There were numerous calls for reform. In its Report No 290, *Partial Defences to Murder* (2004), the Law Commission concluded that there was 'overwhelming support' for reform. The Law Commission recommended that reforms to the law of diminished responsibility be postponed until after the implementation of its proposed reforms to murder. The Government decided, however, to enact the reforms to diminished responsibility without making the recommended reforms to murder. See L. Kennefick, 'Introducing a New Diminished Responsibility Defence for England and Wales' (2011) 74 MLR 750.

The defence is now as substituted by s 52 of the Coroners and Justice Act 2009 which provides:

> (1) In section 2 of the Homicide Act 1957 (c. 11) (persons suffering from diminished responsibility), for subsection (1) substitute—
>
> '(1) A person ("D") who kills or is a party to the killing of another is not to be convicted of murder if D was suffering from an abnormality of mental functioning which—
>
> (a) arose from a recognised medical condition,
>
> (b) substantially impaired D's ability to do one or more of the things mentioned in subsection (1A), and
>
> (c) provides an explanation for D's acts and omissions in doing or being a party to the killing.
>
> (1A) Those things are—
>
> (a) to understand the nature of D's conduct;
>
> (b) to form a rational judgment;
>
> (c) to exercise self-control.
>
> (1B) For the purposes of subsection (1)(c), an abnormality of mental functioning provides an explanation for D's conduct if it causes, or is a significant contributory factor in causing, D to carry out that conduct.'

> (2) In section 6 of the Criminal Procedure (Insanity) Act 1964 (c. 84) (evidence by prosecution of insanity or diminished responsibility), in paragraph (b) for 'mind' substitute 'mental functioning'.

Section 2(2) to (4) of the Homicide Act 1957 remains unaffected by the 2009 Act:

> (2) On a charge of murder, it shall be for the defence to prove that the person charged is by virtue of this section not liable to be convicted of murder.
>
> (3) A person who but for this section would be liable, whether as principal or as accessory, to be convicted of murder shall be liable instead to be convicted of manslaughter.
>
> (4) The fact that one party to a killing is by virtue of this section not liable to be convicted of murder shall not affect the question whether the killing amounted to murder in the case of any other party to it.

The four elements of the defence are now as follows:

(1) an 'abnormality of mental functioning';

(2) the abnormality must arise from a 'recognised medical condition';

(3) D's 'mental responsibility' must be substantially impaired. This means that his ability to do one of more of the three things in s 2(1A) must be substantially impaired. The three things are:

   (a) to understand the nature of D's conduct;

   (b) to form a rational judgement;

   (c) to exercise self-control;

(4) the abnormality of mental functioning from a 'recognised medical condition' must be a cause or a contributory cause of D's conduct in killing.

What should immediately be clear is that although the defence retains the title 'diminished responsibility' it no longer requires an evaluation of D's responsibility for killing. Indeed, the term 'responsibility' is to be found nowhere in the new provisions. Might this be a problem when the principle of fair labelling is considered?

Each of the elements of the new defence will be examined in turn.

8.3.1 An 'abnormality of mental functioning'

Under the old s 2 test (of 'abnormality of mind') the determination of 'abnormality' could be left to the jury as was explained by Lord Parker CJ in *Byrne* [1960] 2 QB 396 in the following terms:

> 'Abnormality of mind,' which has to be contrasted with the time-honoured expression in the M'Naughten Rules 'defect of reason,' means a state of mind so different from that of ordinary human beings that the reasonable man would term it abnormal. It appears to us to be wide enough to cover the mind's activities in all its aspects, not only the perception of physical acts and matters, and the ability to form a rational judgment as to whether an act is right or wrong, but also the ability to exercise will power to control physical acts in accordance with that rational judgment. The expression 'mental responsibility for his acts' points to a consideration of the extent to which the accused's mind is answerable for his physical acts which must include a consideration of the extent of his ability to exercise will power to control his physical acts.

This formula was appropriate under the old law, when the jury had to consider a concept as loose and general as the 'mind' and were being asked to evaluate whether D's mind deviated from the norm. However, the new provision is much stricter and more reliance will be placed upon expert evidence. As such, it may be wondered whether there is much for the jury to do in this respect. In *Bunch* [2013] EWCA Crim 2498, the court held that the new defence did not diminish the authority of cases under the old defence which held that medical evidence, though not formally required by the Act was a 'practical necessity' if the defence was to succeed: *Dix* (1982) 74 Cr App R 306.

8.3.2 'recognised medical condition'

The abnormality of mental functioning must arise 'from a recognised medical condition'. This is designed to be wider than the familiar list of bracketed causes in the original definition in s 2 of the 1957 Act. It is intended to produce clearer expert evidence from psychiatrists and psychologists and to allow sufficient flexibility for the new defence to develop in line with medical understanding and practice. Two obvious questions arise when considering this element of the defence: what kind(s) of medical condition; recognized by whom?

8.3.2.1 'medical condition'

This new element of the definition was intended to provide a clearer foundation for the defence. As the Royal College of Psychiatrists explained, it will:

> encourage reference within expert evidence to diagnosis in terms of one or two of the accepted internationally classificatory systems of mental conditions (i.e. the World Health Organisation: International Classification of Diseases (ICD-10); and the American Psychiatric Association: Diagnostic and Statistical Manual of Mental Disorders (DSM-IV [now V]); see CP 19/08 fn 13) without explicitly writing those systems into the legislation.

It should be noted that *any* medical condition will suffice. This will include physiological conditions in addition to those of a psychological and psychiatric nature. A recent study conducted by Professors Mackay and Mitchell demonstrates that the most common medical conditions suffered by those who plead diminished responsibility are schizophrenia, depression, personality disorder and psychosis. See R. Mackay and B. Mitchell, 'The New Diminished Responsibility Plea in Operation: Some Initial Findings' [2017] Crim LR 18.

8.3.2.2 'recognised'

It is important to note that whether the condition that D was suffering from at the time he committed the killing is a 'recognised medical condition' is a question of law. Just because a condition is recognized by the medical community does not mean it will fall within the terms of the Act. The Court of Appeal clarified this point in the following case.

R v Dowds
[2012] EWCA Crim 281, Court of Appeal, Criminal Division

(Hughes LJ, Simon and Lang JJ)

D was convicted of murdering his partner, V, by stabbing her 60 times. Their relationship had been a violent one. D and V engaged in binge drinking, and on the night of the killing they had consumed 2 litres of vodka. At trial, D claimed that he had no recollection of the attack and that he lacked mens rea and also relied on the partial defences of diminished responsibility and loss of self-control. D sought to rely on diminished responsibility by claiming to have an abnormality of mental functioning arising from his 'recognised medical condition', namely 'acute intoxication' (which is listed in ICD-10), and that substantially impaired his capacity as defined in the section.

The trial judge refused to accept that 'acute intoxication' was a 'recognised medical condition' for the purposes of the defence: (a) on the grounds of policy because the Law Commission and Parliament could not have intended with the new formulation of the defence to allow voluntary intoxication to qualify for the defence and (b) because the state of acute intoxication was temporary.

[Dismissing D's appeal and upholding his conviction, **Hughes LJ** stated:]

10. It was established in 1975 in *R v Fenton* (1975) 61 Cr App R 261 that the effect on the mind of voluntary intoxication could not give rise to diminished responsibility. The defendant, who had shot four people in two different locations, had a number of other conditions, including paranoid psychopathy, which did raise the possibility of diminished responsibility, although the jury had rejected that defence. The trial judge had directed the jury to consider those but to leave out of account the defendant's heavy intoxication. This court held that the judge had been correct. The reasoning of Lord Widgery CJ, at pp 263–264, was brief:

'We recognise that cases may arise hereafter where the accused proves such a craving for drink or drugs as to produce in itself an abnormality of mind; but that is not proved in this case. The defendant did not give evidence and we do not see how self-induced intoxication can of itself produce an abnormality of mind due to inherent causes.'

It is perhaps significant that counsel for the defendant had felt able to argue his case only on the basis that a craving for, or an inability to resist the temptations of, drink was a feature of psychopathy, and thus became relevant to diminished responsibility indirectly. No one suggested that simple drunkenness could found a defence of diminished responsibility, and on the facts of the case a craving for, or inability to resist the need of, drink was not shown.

11. The law as explained in *R v Fenton* was never significantly questioned. It was in due course endorsed by the House of Lords in *R v Dietschmann* [2003] 1 AC 1209. That case resolved an uncertainty about how to approach the case of a defendant who *both* suffered from a mental abnormality and was also intoxicated. The House of Lords held that the correct approach was for the jury to ignore the effects of intoxication and to ask whether, leaving out the drink, the defendant's other condition(s) of mental abnormality substantially impaired his responsibility for the killing. It was treated as axiomatic that simple voluntary drunkenness was incapable of founding a plea of diminished responsibility.

12. As foreshadowed in *R v Fenton* the courts also had to deal with cases where the defendants' condition went beyond simple drunkenness into physical or psychological addiction such as, arguably, to amount to a mental abnormality. In dealing with such cases it was once again treated as axiomatic that simple voluntary drunkenness without such additional condition was incapable of founding the plea of diminished responsibility. See, most recently, *R v Wood* [2009] 1 WLR 496, 507—in particular para 23—and *R v Stewart* [2009] 1 WLR 2507, in particular paras 26 and 29.

13. This court's judgment in *R v Wood* usefully explains what is very clearly the case. The axiomatic rule that simple voluntary drunkenness, without more, cannot found diminished responsibility, is not a rule special to the partial defence. It is but one example of the general approach of English criminal law to voluntary drunkenness. Sir Igor Judge P, as he then was, put it in this way in *R v Wood*, para 23:

'Dealing with the point very broadly, the consumption of alcohol before a defendant acts with murderous intent and kills cannot, without more, bring his actions within the concept of diminished responsibility. On its own, voluntary intoxication falls outside the ambit of the defence. This is consistent with the general approach of the law that, save in the context of offences of specific intent, and proof of that intent, criminal acts committed under the influence of self induced intoxication are not for that reason excused. Public policy proceeds on the basis that a defendant who voluntarily takes alcohol and behaves in a way which he might not have behaved when sober is not normally entitled to be excused from the consequences of his actions.'

14. It is true that in the particular case of diminished responsibility under the original form of section 2 of the 1957 Act, there was an additional reason why simple voluntary drunkenness could not found the defence. That was because it could not readily be brought within the expression 'inherent cause' and clearly had none of the other sources listed in the bracketed clause in the section. But there can be no doubt that independently of the particular statutory language, the general principle to which Sir Igor Judge P referred in *R v Wood* does indeed underlie English criminal law.

[His lordship then set out the general approach that the criminal law of England and Wales adopts towards voluntary intoxication, namely that it is not a defence but merely one way of negating mens rea in the case of crimes of specific intent.]

Amending section 2 of the Homicide Act 1957

[His lordship then discussed the background to the Law Commission report leading to the 2009 Act.]

26. The report contains no further discussion at all of the law relating to voluntary intoxication. We infer that that was because nothing had changed since 2004 when the existing law had been so clearly commended [in *Dietschmann*]; there had so far as we are aware been no significant discussion about it in any public quarter. The Commission did slightly amend its formulation of diminished responsibility into what was substantially the form adopted by the Coroners and Justice Act 2009. (There was a suggested addition of developmental immaturity which was not adopted by Parliament but that is irrelevant to the present issue.) For present purposes the significant change in formulation was to move from 'an abnormality of mental functioning *arising from an underlying condition*' (2004) to 'an abnormality of mental functioning *arising from a recognised medical condition*' (2006) (our emphasis).

27. The Commission explained the reasons for this slightly altered formulation in paras 5.114–5.120. They were: (i) the law ought no longer to be constrained by a fixed set of causes of mental malfunction but should be responsive to developments in medicine and psychiatry; and (ii) the altered formulation would help to make clearer the relationship between the role of the medical expert and the role of the jury.

28. As to the first of those, the Commission quoted at length from, and endorsed, evidence given to it by the Royal College of Psychiatrists. The college was concerned to establish that the partial defence should be grounded in valid medical diagnosis, rather than in imaginative or idiosyncratic fringe opinion. In that context the college had said this, at para 5.114:

'It would also encourage reference within expert evidence to diagnosis in terms of one or two of the accepted internationally classificatory systems of mental conditions (WHO ICD 10 and AMA DSM) without explicitly writing those systems into the legislation . . . Such an approach would also avoid individual doctors offering idiosyncratic "diagnoses" . . .'

It is apparent from this, and from the total silence in the 2006 report on the subject of voluntary intoxication, that the altered formulation owed nothing whatever to any intention in any quarter to alter the law on that topic.

. . .

41. If we had concluded that the defence of diminished responsibility ought to have been left to the jury, we should have been unable to accept the Crown's invitation to hold that it could not have succeeded in any event because of what must have been the findings of the jury. We agree that the jury must have rejected the defendant's assertion that he had been so drunk as to be unable to form the intention to kill or to do serious bodily harm. We agree that his use of the telephone in the immediate

aftermath of the killing tends quite strongly to suggest that he was in much better control of himself than was suggested. We agree that there were good grounds on which it may well be that the jury rejected also his assertion that he had no recollection of events. We agree that the jury rejected the argument that he had lost self-control in circumstances in which a reasonable man might have done as he did. But if it had been the law that voluntary acute intoxication could found diminished responsibility, the level of drunkenness involved would not necessarily have to reach inability to form an intent, nor would the loss of self-control necessarily have to be such as might have led a reasonable man to do as the defendant did. On our very clear conclusions, however, these considerations do not arise. Voluntary acute intoxication, whether from alcohol or other substance, is not capable of founding diminished responsibility.

≋ *Questions*

(1) If not all the conditions 'recognised' by psychiatrists in DSM-V and ICD-10 are 'recognised' in law for the purposes of the new defence, which ones are? How is the judge to decide?

(2) Hughes LJ stated: 'It is enough to say that it is quite clear that the re-formulation of the statutory conditions for diminished responsibility was not intended to reverse the well established rule that voluntary acute intoxication is not capable of being relied upon to found diminished responsibility. That remains the law. *The presence of a "recognised medical condition" is a necessary, but not always a sufficient, condition to raise the issue of diminished responsibility*' (emphasis added). So what is the missing element that makes a condition in DSM-V 'sufficient' to qualify?

The DSM and ICD manuals contain thousands of medical conditions. If it was sufficient that any one would suffice for this element of the new defence it would render it available to an enormous range of people. The manuals contain some striking examples of conditions such as 'unhappiness' (R45.2), 'irritability and anger' (R45.4), 'suspiciousness and marked evasiveness' (R46.5), 'pyromania' (F63.1), 'paedophilia' (F65.4), 'sado-masochism' (F65.5) and 'kleptomania' (F63.2). DSM-V includes similar conditions such as 'exhibitionism', 'sexual sadism' and 'intermittent explosive disorder'. The Government expressed the view that the legislation must be sufficiently flexible to cater for emerging medical conditions. However, there are those who argue that this element of the defence will deprive it of sufficient flexibility that was one of the benefits of the former law.

In *R v Lindo* [2016] EWCA Crim 1940, L appealed his conviction for murder, relying on fresh evidence from psychiatrists that L had, since being imprisoned, shown symptoms of schizophrenia which may not have been fully appreciated at trial. The court dismissed the appeal. Significantly, the court commented on the availability of the defence of diminished responsibility where the abnormality of mental functioning relied on by the accused was a drug-induced psychosis. As was well established following *Dowds* [2012] EWCA Crim 281, voluntary intoxication will not constitute a 'recognised medical condition' for the purposes of the defence. Although voluntary intoxication might lead to a state of acute intoxication which is recognized in medicine as a 'condition', that does not mean that as a matter of law it qualifies as a 'recognised medical condition'. The court noted at [59]:

59. We have our doubts therefore as to whether there was evidence of a recognised medical condition fit to be left to the jury. Drug-induced psychosis standing alone would not suffice and a drug induced psychosis combined with a prodromal state does not seem to us to be sufficient to trigger the operation of the section.

It is no surprise that the court follows *Dowds* in relation to drug-induced psychoses. The question that remains is what principles or policies dictate when a 'condition' recognized in medicine will not be a 'recognised medical condition' under s 2. The answer seems to be that it will be a policy decision made on a case-by-case basis.

R. D. Mackay, 'The Coroners and Justice Act 2009—Partial Defences to Murder (2) The New Diminished Responsibility Plea'
[2010] Crim LR 290

Recognised medical condition

The concept of a recognised medical condition is of itself nothing new. For example, it has been the subject of judicial comment within the context of disability litigation. However, its introduction as a requirement for a diminished responsibility plea is novel—but viewed as necessary by the MOJ,

> 'to accommodate future developments in diagnostic practice and encourage defences to be grounded in a valid medical diagnosis linked to the accepted classificatory systems which together encompass the recognised physical, psychiatric and psychological conditions'.

The relevant classificatory systems referred to by the MOJ are the two cited above by Baroness Murphy. However, while the phrase 'recognised medical condition' will clearly encompass all relevant mental disorders which fall within ICD-10 and DSM-IV, it is not restricted to these, and, as the MOJ concedes, must cover both 'psychological' and 'physical' conditions. Clearly, therefore, it is not limited to recognised mental disorders and must include conditions like epilepsy, sleep disorders and diabetes. In short, this is a concept which is capable of covering any and all medical conditions and as such is wider than the bracketed causes in s.2(1) of the 1957 Act which it replaces. These bracketed causes were open to criticism in that they were not psychiatrically recognised and their meaning had taxed the courts. However, it was clear that to succeed in a plea under s.2(1) the abnormality of mind had to fall within one or more of these bracketed causes, thus restricting the plea's availability. There is no such restriction relating to the scope of 'recognised medical condition' in s.52 of the Coroners and Justice Act 2009, so it is to the new plea's other requirements which one must turn for this. Before doing so, however, three additional remarks may be made about 'recognised medical condition'.

First, although it has been suggested above that this concept is wider than its counterpart in the original s.2(1) of the 1957 Act, there is ironically a danger that—because it focuses exclusively on the need for a defined and demonstrable condition which is medically recognised—it may fail to include those 'mercy killing' cases which currently qualify for a diminished responsibility plea. The reason for this is that because the wording of the current plea is so obscure, the court and the experts are sometimes able to enter into a benevolent conspiracy, thus permitting the psychiatric evidence to be stretched so as 'to produce a greater range of exemption from liability for murder than its terms really justify'. In short, therefore—having regard to the difficulty which psychiatrists experienced in bringing such cases within 'abnormality of mind' under the original s.2 of the 1957 Act—the concept of 'recognised medical condition' may exacerbate this difficulty. Secondly, in his article on the new loss of control plea, Alan Norrie makes it clear that as this new plea is narrower than the provocation plea which it replaces, cases such as *Humphreys* (emotional immaturity) and *Acott* (low intelligence) are unlikely to fall within its scope. And the same is likely to be true in relation to s.52 of the Coroners and Justice Act 2009, as its requirements—including the need for a 'recognised medical condition'— lack the flexibility of the original s.2 of the 1957 Act, which it turn often permitted both pleas to be combined; a defence strategy which is now much less likely to succeed owing to the fact that both new pleas are drafted in a manner which militates against possible overlap. Finally, by whom does the condition need to be recognised? Most of us can 'recognise' certain conditions of a medical nature. Presumably, however, what is meant here is that in order to fall within s.52 of the Coroners and Justice

Act 2009, it must be a professionally accepted medical condition; although such recognition it seems will no longer be restricted to those with psychiatric expertise but will include, where relevant, all other branches of the medical profession and psychologists.

8.3.3 A 'substantial impairment of mental ability'

Whereas under the old s 2 of the 1957 Act the matter that had to be substantially impaired was D's *mental responsibility* for acting as he did, the matter that now has to be shown to be substantially impaired is D's *ability to do* any of the things mentioned in the new s 2(1A). Therefore, what was a test of moral responsibility for the jury's determination under the former regime has become a medical one which will require expert evidence to resolve.

Recently, in *Golds* [2016] UKSC 61, the Supreme Court gave guidance on how the term 'substantial' ought to be understood. G appealed against a decision of the Court of Appeal dismissing his appeal against his conviction for murder. G had admitted killing V and at trial he sought to rely on the defence of diminished responsibility. The psychiatric evidence was to the effect that G suffered from an abnormality of mental functioning arising from a recognized medical condition. The issue was whether, for the purposes of s 2 of the Homicide Act 1957 as amended, that abnormality had 'substantially' impaired his ability to understand the nature of his conduct, form a rational judgement or exercise self-control. The trial judge directed the jury that 'substantially' was an everyday word which did not require elucidation. G was convicted of murder. The Court of Appeal endorsed the judge's direction. The court rejected G's argument that a line of authority established that the 'substantially impaired' test would be met if the impairment was 'more than merely trivial'. The Supreme Court agreed and gave the following guidance on how 'substantially' ought to be understood:

(1) Ordinarily in a murder trial where diminished responsibility is in issue the judge need not direct the jury beyond the terms of the statute and should not attempt to define the meaning of 'substantially'. Experience has shown that the issue of its correct interpretation is unlikely to arise in many cases. The jury should normally be given to understand that the expression is an ordinary English word, that it imports a question of degree, and that whether in the case before it the impairment can properly be described as substantial is for it to resolve.

(2) If, however, the jury has been introduced to the question of whether *any* impairment beyond the merely trivial will suffice, or if it has been introduced to the concept of a spectrum between the greater than trivial and the total, the judge should explain that whilst the impairment must indeed pass the merely trivial before it need be considered, it is not the law that *any* impairment beyond the trivial will suffice. The judge should likewise make this clear if a risk arises that the jury might misunderstand the import of the expression; whether this risk arises or not is a judgment to be arrived at by the trial judge who is charged with overseeing the dynamics of the trial. Diminished responsibility involves an impairment of one or more of the abilities listed in the statute to an extent which the jury judges to be substantial, and which it is satisfied significantly contributed to his committing the offence. Illustrative expressions of the sense of the word may be employed so long as the jury is given clearly to understand that no single synonym is to be substituted for the statutory word ...

Is the word substantial an ordinary English word if the court also accepts it has a further, more refined meaning? Why not apply that in all cases from the outset?

8.3.3.1 'to understand the nature of D's conduct'

This is similar to the first limb of the insanity plea. An example provided by the Law Commission of how this element might be satisfied was of a 10-year-old boy with a recognized medical condition (amended to reflect the provision as enacted):

who has been left to play very violent video games for hours on end for much of his life, loses his temper and kills another child when the child attempts to take a game from him. When interviewed, he shows no real understanding that, when a person is killed they cannot simply be later revived, as happens in the games he has been continually playing.

It has been observed that defining the expression 'nature of D's conduct' could prove to be a 'judicial nightmare'. What aspects of D's conduct bear upon the 'nature' of it? See R. Fortson, 'The Modern Partial Defence of Diminished Responsibility' in A. Reed and M. Bohlander (eds), *Loss of Control and Diminished Responsibility: Domestic, Comparative and International Perspectives* (2011).

8.3.3.2 'to form a rational judgement'

Although the Act states that the thing that must be impaired is D's ability to form a rational judgement, strictly speaking this is not the proper way to express this aspect of the defence. It is more accurate to say that it is D's ability to rationally form a judgement which must be impaired. What matters is the ability, not the outcome.

The Law Commission gave the following examples (some of which have been amended for these purposes):

(1) a woman who has been diagnosed as being in a state of learned helplessness, consequent upon violent abuse suffered at her husband's hands, comes to believe that only burning her husband to death will rid the world of his sins;

(2) a mentally subnormal boy believes that he must follow his older brother's instructions, even when they involve taking take part in a killing. He says, 'I wouldn't dream of disobeying my brother and he would never tell me to do something if it was really wrong';

(3) a depressed man who has been caring for many years for a terminally ill spouse, kills her, at her request. He says that he had found it progressively more difficult to stop her repeated requests dominating his thoughts to the exclusion of all else, so that 'I felt I would never think straight again until I had given her what she wanted.'

8.3.3.3 The 'ability to exercise control'

This is a significant change and if construed widely could render the defence available in a broader range of circumstances than either (1) or (2).

8.3.4 An explanation (or cause) of the killing

The defence is narrowed further by the requirement that the abnormality of mental functioning, arising from a recognized medical condition substantially impairing the defendant's ability in a relevant manner, must also 'explain' his acts in killing. By s 2(1B) 'an explanation' for D's conduct is provided 'if it causes, or is a significant contributory factor in causing, D to carry out that conduct'. The issue that immediately arises is whether this provision imports a strict causal requirement. Section 2(1B) does not say that for the defence to succeed a sufficient explanation can only be provided if the abnormality of mental functioning is a cause. On this basis, a causal link is just one of the ways in which the killing might be 'explained'. There may be cases where the abnormality provides an explanation sufficient to mitigate the conduct to manslaughter even if there is no causal link. However, the language in debates was clearly envisaging a causal link. In debates, the minister stated that:

> We do not believe that the partial defence should succeed where random coincidence has brought together the activity of the person and the recognised medical condition . . . there must have been at least a significant contributory factor in causing the defendant to act as he did. We do not require the defence to prove that it was the only cause or the main cause or the most important factor, but there must be something that is more than a merely trivial factor. (Hansard HC, Public Bill Committee, 4 March 2009, col 416)

The need for any causal requirement has been challenged by some.

R. D. Mackay, 'The Coroners and Justice Act 2009—Partial Defences to Murder (2) The New Diminished Responsibility Plea'
[2010] Crim LR 290

Provides an explanation for D's acts and omissions in doing or being a party to the killing

This provision follows the recommendation of the Law Commission. Initially the Commission recommended a stronger causal provision which was as follows,

> 'the abnormality was a significant cause of the defendant's conduct in carrying out or taking part in the killing'.

However, after consultation the Commission decided that such a requirement might be problematical and instead opted for the provision (which now appears in subs.(1)(c) of the 1957 Act as amended) stating,

> 'we have framed the issue in these terms: the abnormality of mind, or developmental immaturity, or both, must be shown to be 'an explanation' for D's conduct. This ensures that there is an appropriate connection (that is, one that grounds a case for mitigation of the offence) between the abnormality of mental functioning or developmental immaturity and the killing. It leaves open the possibility, however, that other causes or explanations (like provocation) may be admitted to have been at work, without prejudicing the case for mitigation.'

Both the MOJ and government ministers have repeatedly opined that a stronger causal requirement is necessary. As a result subs.(1B) of the 1957 Act as amended provides:

> 'For the purposes of subsection (1)(c), an abnormality of mental functioning provides an explanation for D's conduct if it causes, or is a significant contributory factor in causing, D to carry out that conduct.'

The MOJ has been adamant that, 'there must be some connection between the condition and the killing for the partial defence to be justified'. In its response to its consultation exercise the MOJ further opined:

> 'With regard to the link between the impairment and the defendant's conduct, we have carefully thought through the various comments made but have concluded that it is right to maintain the position set out in the consultation paper. We are satisfied that it is right that, while it need not be the sole cause of the defendant's behaviour, it should be a significant contributory factor in causing the conduct—that is, more than a merely trivial factor. The partial defence should certainly not succeed where the jury believes that the impairment made no difference to the defendant's behaviour—he would have killed anyway.'

The Attorney General explained this further during debate on the Bill in the House of Lords saying:

'The Government consider it is necessary to spell out what connection between the abnormality of mental functioning and the killing is required for the partial defence to succeed. Otherwise a random coincidence would suffice. It need not be the sole cause or even the most important factor in causing the behaviour but it must be more than merely a trivial factor. We believe this gets the balance about right.'

The reference to 'random coincidence' seems strange. How—it may be asked—can this be possible if the defendant is able to prove that his abnormality of mental functioning gave rise to a substantial impairment of one or more of the abilities specified in subs.(1A) of the 1957 Act as amended? Surely, if such is the case then the killing cannot have been a 'random coincidence'. In any event, why, if the defendant proves that this is so, is this not enough? On possible line of argument is that subs.(1B) of the 1957 Act as amended is merely making express provision for what is already impliedly provided for in the original s.2(1). Two sources might be used to support this approach. The first is the following remark made by Lord Hutton in *Dietchschmann* [*sic*]:

'I think that in referring to substantial impairment of mental responsibility the subsection does not require the abnormality of mind to be the *sole cause* of the defendant's acts in doing the killing. In my opinion, even if the defendant would not have killed if he had not taken drink, the *causative effect of the drink* does not necessarily prevent an abnormality of mind suffered by the defendant from substantially impairing his mental responsibility for his fatal acts.'

The second is the Judicial Studies Board Specimen Direction on diminished responsibility which states:

'Substantially impaired means just that. You must conclude that his abnormality of mind was *a real cause* of the defendant's conduct. The defendant need not prove that his condition was the sole cause of it, but he must show that it was more than merely a trivial one [which did not make any real/appreciable difference to his ability to control himself].'

The following points can be made about these sources. First, Lord Hutton's reference to 'sole cause' has to be read in the context of the facts of the case, namely the causative relationship between the effect of alcohol and abnormality of mind. There is no suggestion in *Dietchschmann* that his Lordship was seeking to express an opinion on the need for some more general causal requirement in s.2(1) of the 1957 Act. Secondly, the reference in the Specimen Direction to 'real cause' is nowhere to be found in Lord Hutton's judgment. Despite this the Specimen Direction was used by Maria Eagle MP, the Parliamentary Under-Secretary of State, to support her conclusion that:

'While there is no reference to causation in [the] statute, we believe that the existing requirement that the abnormality substantially impairs mental responsibility for the killing implies a causative connection and that in practice the law is applied in this way. We therefore do not consider that the approach we are taking here represents any real departure from current law and practice or indeed from the Law Commission proposal.'

However, such a conclusion seems highly contentious for, as is mentioned above, there is no real support for such a strict causal requirement within the original s.2(1) of the 1957 Act. Not only that, no other diminished responsibility plea contains any such express requirement. In particular, none is to be found in the New South Wales revised plea upon which s.52 of the 2009 Act is modelled. Finally, it seems worth in this connection turning to the insanity defence. The *M'Naghten Rules* do not contain any such similar causal requirement. All the Rules require is 'a defect of reason, from disease of the mind'. What is necessary is that a 'disease of the mind' cause 'a defect of reason'. There is no additional need to prove that the 'disease of the mind' *caused or was a significant contributory factor in causing, D to carry out his conduct.* As a result one is compelled to ask whether it will not now be easier for a defendant whose mental state at the time of the offence satisfies all the elements of both pleas (with the exception of this causal requirement) to prove insanity within the *M'Naghten Rules* rather than the new diminished responsibility plea.

There are those who argue that the problems arising from the causal requirement are more illusory than real. Rudi Fortson QC gives the following three reasons:

(1) the abnormality need not be the sole cause of D's conduct;

(2) the provision arguably just gives legislative effect to what was the existing law as expounded in *Dietschmann*; and

(3) since *Walton v The Queen* [1978] AC 788, the jury must consider all the evidence that is relevant to the question of whether the partial defence is made out.

See R. Fortson, 'The Modern Partial Defence of Diminished Responsibility' in A. Reed and M. Bohlander (eds), *Loss of Control and Diminished Responsibility: Domestic, Comparative and International Perspectives* (2011).

The Supreme Court in *Golds* (above) also commented, *obiter*, on the circumstances in which a judge should withdraw murder from the jury where there is uncontradicted medical evidence of diminished responsibility. The case of *Brennan* [2014] EWCA Crim 2387 had suggested that in a case where there was uncontradicted medical evidence a judge should withdraw the charge of murder if no reasonable jury could convict. The Supreme Court offered valuable advice:

50. It may be agreed that the ordinary principles of *R v Galbraith* are capable of being applied in a trial where the sole issue is diminished responsibility. A court ought, however, to be cautious about doing so, and for several reasons. First, a murder trial is a particularly sensitive event. If the issue is diminished responsibility, a killing with murderous intent must, *ex hypothesi*, have been carried out. If a trial is contested, it is of considerable importance that the verdict be that of the jury. Second, the onus of proof in relation to diminished responsibility lies on the defendant, albeit on the balance of probabilities rather than to the ordinary criminal standard. The *Galbraith* process is generally a conclusion that no jury, properly directed, could be satisfied that the Crown has proved the relevant offence so that it is sure. In the context of diminished responsibility, murder can only be withdrawn from the jury if the judge is satisfied that no jury could fail to find that the defendant has proved it. Thirdly, a finding of diminished responsibility is not a single-issue matter; it requires the defendant to prove that the answer to each of the four questions set out in para 8 above is 'yes'. Whilst the effect of the changes in the law has certainly been to emphasise the importance of medical evidence, causation (question 4) is essentially a jury question. So, for the reasons explained above, is question 3: whether the impairment of relevant ability(ies) was substantial. That the judge may entertain little doubt about what he thinks the right verdict ought to be is not sufficient reason in this context, any more than in any other, for withdrawing from the jury issues which are properly theirs to decide.

Where, however, in a diminished responsibility trial the medical evidence supports the plea and is uncontradicted, the judge needs to ensure that the Crown explains the basis on which it is inviting the jury to reject that evidence. He needs to ensure that the basis advanced is one which the jury can properly adopt. If the facts of the case give rise to it, he needs to warn the jury that brutal killings may be the product of disordered minds and that planning, whilst it may be relevant to self-control, may well be consistent with disordered thinking. While he needs to make it clear to the jury that, if there is a proper basis for rejecting the expert evidence, the decision is theirs — that trial is by jury and not by expert—it will also ordinarily be wise to advise the jury against attempting to make themselves amateur psychiatrists, and that if there is undisputed expert evidence the jury will probably wish to accept it, unless there is some identified reason for not doing so. To this extent, the approach of the court in *Brennan* is to be endorsed.

8.3.5 Intoxicated defendants

Two situations need to be considered:

(1) D who is acutely intoxicated, but not alcoholic (see section 8.3.2);

(2) D who has a recognized medical condition (including alcoholic dependency syndrome) and is drunk.

(1) In *Dowds* (section 8.3.2.2), Hughes LJ stated that acute voluntary intoxication is not a 'recognised medical condition' for the purposes of the defence.

(2) If D suffers from some 'recognised medical condition' and also happens to be intoxicated at the time he kills V. In *Dietschmann* [2003] UKHL 10, Lord Hutton held that:

> even if the defendant would not have killed if he had not taken drink, the causative effect of the drink does not necessarily prevent an abnormality of mind suffered by the defendant from substantially impairing his mental responsibility for his fatal acts.

So in this situation, the question under the new law seems to be whether, *ignoring the intoxication*, there was an abnormality of mental functioning arising from a recognized medical condition. If so, whether that abnormality of mental functioning substantially impaired D's ability in a relevant way and, if so, whether that abnormality of mental functioning was a cause of the conduct by which D killed. D should be entitled to the defence even if D might not have killed had he not been drunk, provided the abnormality of mental functioning arising from the recognized medical condition nevertheless explains his conduct in killing. If D would have killed even if he had not been suffering from an abnormality of mental functioning, whether D can plead the partial defence depends on whether s 2(1A) is interpreted as importing a causal requirement. See further, M. Gibson, 'Intoxicants and Diminished Responsibility: The Impact of the Coroners and Justice Act 2009' [2011] Crim LR 909.

8.4 Suicide pacts and assisting suicide

A further partial defence to murder is provided by s 4 of the Homicide Act 1957. The defence is only partial, as with diminished responsibility and loss of control, and the successful plea will result in a conviction for manslaughter.

Homicide Act 1957, s 4

> (1) It shall be manslaughter, and shall not be murder, for a person acting in pursuance of a suicide pact between him and another to kill the other or be a party to the other . . . being killed by a third person.
>
> (2) Where it is shown that a person charged with the murder of another killed the other or was a party to his . . . being killed, it shall be for the defence to prove that the person charged was acting in pursuance of a suicide pact between him and the other.
>
> (3) For the purposes of this section 'suicide pact' means a common agreement between two or more persons having for its object the death of all of them, whether or not each is to take his own life, but nothing done by a person who enters into a suicide pact shall be treated as done by him in pursuance of the pact unless it is done while he has the settled intention of dying in pursuance of the pact.

The provision in s 4 must be read alongside the Suicide Act 1961, which deals with those cases in which D does not cause V's death but assists or tries to help V to commit suicide.

Suicide Act 1961, s 1

The rule of law whereby it is a crime for a person to commit suicide is hereby abrogated.

Coroners and Justice Act 2009, s 59, amending Suicide Act 1961, s 2

(2) In section 2 (criminal liability for complicity in another's suicide), for subsection (1) substitute—

'(1) A person ("D") commits an offence if—

    (a) D does an act capable of encouraging or assisting the suicide or attempted suicide of another person, and

    (b) D's act was intended to encourage or assist suicide or an attempt at suicide.

(1A) The person referred to in subsection (1)(a) need not be a specific person (or class of persons) known to, or identified by, D.

(1B) D may commit an offence under this section whether or not a suicide, or an attempt at suicide, occurs.

(1C) An offence under this section is triable on indictment and a person convicted of such an offence is liable to imprisonment for a term not exceeding 14 years.'

(3) In subsection (2) of that section, for 'it' to the end substitute 'of a person it is proved that the deceased person committed suicide, and the accused committed an offence under subsection (1) in relation to that suicide, the jury may find the accused guilty of the offence under subsection (1).'

(4) After that section insert—

'2A Acts capable of encouraging or assisting

(1) If D arranges for a person ("D2") to do an act that is capable of encouraging or assisting the suicide or attempted suicide of another person and D2 does that act, D is also to be treated for the purposes of this Act as having done it.

(2) Where the facts are such that an act is not capable of encouraging or assisting suicide or attempted suicide, for the purposes of this Act it is to be treated as so capable if the act would have been so capable had the facts been as D believed them to be at the time of the act or had subsequent events happened in the manner D believed they would happen (or both).

(3) A reference in this Act to a person ("P") doing an act that is capable of encouraging the suicide or attempted suicide of another person includes a reference to P doing so by threatening another person or otherwise putting pressure on another person to commit or attempt suicide.

2B Course of conduct

A reference in this Act to an act includes a reference to a course of conduct, and a reference to doing an act is to be read accordingly.'

8.4.1 Assisted suicide

There have been recent attempts to clarify when an individual who assists someone who would otherwise be unable to commit suicide will be prosecuted. In the landmark case of *R (Purdy) v DPP* [2009] UKHL 45, P challenged the lawfulness of the failure of the DPP to issue a crime-specific policy identifying the facts and circumstances that would be taken into account when deciding whether to prosecute an individual for assisting suicide. The House of Lords agreed that P's rights under Article 8(1) of the ECHR were engaged and that the failure to promulgate a crime-specific policy meant that the infringement was not justified under Article 8(2). As a result of the judgment, the DPP published the policy mandated by the House of Lords. More recently in *R (Nicklinson) v Ministry of Justice* [2013] EWCA Civ 961 the Court of Appeal held that the DPP's blanket prohibition on assisting suicide was not a disproportionate interference with Article 8. However, the court went on to find that the guidelines in relation to medical professionals who assist their patients to commit suicide were not sufficiently clear to satisfy the requirements of Article 8(2); some indication of the weight that the DPP accorded to the fact that the helper was acting in his capacity as a health-care professional and the victim was in his care was necessary. The case was appealed unsuccessfully to the Supreme Court: [2014] UKSC 38. See further F. Stark, 'Necessity and *Nicklinson*' [2013] Crim LR 949.

8.4.2 Reform

In its Consultation Paper No 173, *Partial Defences to Murder* (2003), the Law Commission recommended abolishing the partial defence of assisted suicide. In its Report No 304, *Murder, Manslaughter and Infanticide* (2006), Part 7, the Commission examined the defence in the context of mercy killing and reliance on the suicide defence by those caring for terminally ill individuals. It recommended retention of the defence.

Joint suicide and complicity in suicide

7.42 Section 4 of the Homicide Act 1957 enables D to be convicted of manslaughter rather than murder if D kills V pursuant to a suicide pact. Section 2(1) of the Suicide Act 1961 [as it then was] provides that a person who 'aids, abets, counsels or procures' V to commit suicide is guilty of an offence ('complicity in suicide') punishable with a term of imprisonment not exceeding 14 years. Section 2(2) provides that a person may be convicted of the section 2(1) offence on a charge of murder or manslaughter.

7.43 In some suicide pacts where the intention of D and V is that each should die together, D kills V by setting in train a series of events that results in V's death. In such cases a verdict of manslaughter under section 4 is available but a verdict of complicity in suicide under section 2(1) is not.

7.44 In the CP, we queried whether this was fair given that in 'die together' suicide pacts there may well have been mutual assistance and support in the acts leading up to the attempt to commit suicide together. The verdict of complicity in suicide is not available because, perhaps by chance, the survivor was the one who performed what is taken to be the key conduct which caused V's death.

7.45 We invited views on whether on an indictment for murder or manslaughter, it ought to be possible for D to be convicted of complicity in suicide if the conduct that killed V was meant by D and V to end both their lives. The views of consultees were fairly evenly divided. In the absence of strong support for such a change, we are not minded to recommend it.

Final thoughts and recommendations

7.46 Although we are not making any recommendations for an offence or partial defence of 'mercy' killing, we make the following observations.

7.47 First, Professor Mitchell's surveys suggest that public opinion is generally not unsympathetic to those who believe that they are killing as an act of mercy, particularly if V has expressed a wish to be killed. The surveys reveal very little support for the imposition of a mandatory sentence of life imprisonment in genuine cases of 'mercy' killing. In addition, there is no clear evidence of a majority favouring no kind of prosecution in such cases.

7.48 Secondly, Parliament has already afforded statutory recognition to killings committed as acts of mercy. It has identified killing out of mercy as a potentially mitigating factor in fixing the length of the minimum term following a conviction for murder. There are three reasons why it is arguable that it would be more satisfactory if, in cases of rational 'mercy' killing, Parliament were to make 'mercy' killing a partial defence rather than purely a matter going to mitigation of the minimum term. First, for a genuine 'mercy' killer, a life long licence seems neither necessary nor appropriate. Secondly, if there is a dispute of fact as to D's motive for killing V, it might be thought better that the jury, rather than the trial judge, should decide the issue. Thirdly, a partial defence would avoid the need for the practice, which concerns some of our consultees, of dressing up rational 'mercy' killing cases as ones of diminished responsibility by means of a sympathetic report from a pliant psychiatrist which the court and prosecution are content not to challenge.

7.49 We recommend that the Government should undertake a public consultation on whether and, if so, to what extent the law should recognise either an offence of 'mercy' killing or a partial defence of 'mercy' killing.

7.50 We recommend that, pending the outcome of any public consultation, section 4 of the Homicide Act 1957 should be retained.

FURTHER READING

Diminished responsibility

R. D. Mackay, 'Diminished Responsibility and Mentally Disordered Killers' in A. Ashworth and B. Mitchell (eds), *Rethinking English Homicide Law* (2000)

E. Tennant, *The Future of the Diminished Responsibility Defence to Murder* (2001)

Loss of control

A. Ashworth, 'The Doctrine of Provocation' (1976) 35 CLJ 292

J. Horder, *Provocation and Responsibility* (1992)

J. Horder, *Homicide and the Politics of Law Reform* (2012), Ch 8

A. Howe, '"Red Mist" Homicide: Sexual Infidelity and the English Law of Murder (Glossing Titus Andronicus)' (2013) 33 LS 407

B. J. Mitchell, R. D. Mackay and W. J. Brookbanks, 'Pleading for Provoked Killers: In Defence of *Morgan Smith*' (2008) 124 LQR 675

V. Norse, 'Passion's Progress: Modern Law Reform and the Provocation Defense' (1997) 106 Yale LJ 1331

Suicide

K. Wheat, 'The Law's Treatment of the Suicidal' [2000] Med L Rev 182

9
Involuntary manslaughter

Involuntary manslaughter:

A person is guilty of involuntary manslaughter where:

(1) he is not guilty of murder by reason only of the fact that, because of voluntary intoxication, he lacked the fault required (Chapter 25); or

(2) he kills another:

  (a) by an unlawful and dangerous act; or

  (b) being grossly negligent as to death; or

  (c) being reckless (in the *Cunningham* sense) as to death or serious bodily harm.

Some of the controversies that will be examined in this chapter include:

(1) whether the unlawful act manslaughter offence is too wide because the offence is constructive and has minimal subjective fault;

(2) whether the unlawful act manslaughter offence is too vague;

(3) whether a supplier of drugs can be liable for manslaughter if V, the person he supplied them to, dies from having taken them;

(4) whether gross negligence manslaughter infringes the European Convention on Human Rights (ECHR).

9.1 Introduction

The previous chapter examined those categories of manslaughter in which the defendant killed with the mens rea for murder, but qualified for one of the partial defences which reduced his crime to one of voluntary manslaughter. In this chapter we examine those types of manslaughter committed where the defendant lacks the mens rea for murder—called involuntary manslaughter. There are various forms of the offence and the culpability involved can range from just short of murder to just worse than accident—sometimes it may even be properly dealt with by a fine or a conditional or absolute discharge.

In recent years, Parliament has also introduced a range of statutory crimes of homicide. These include many driving-related offences and the offence under s 5 of the Domestic Violence, Crime and Victims Act 2004, relating to causing or allowing the death of a child or vulnerable adult in the household. On the merits of specific statutory offences as opposed to common law manslaughter offences, see A. Ashworth, 'Manslaughter Generic or Nominate Offences' in C. Clarkson and S. Cunningham (eds), *Criminal Liability for Non-Aggressive Death* (2008). The offence of corporate manslaughter is examined in

Chapter 26. That offence cannot be committed by a human actor, either as a principal or as an accessory.

Throughout the chapter we will be considering whether the types of involuntary manslaughter, each of which results in a conviction bearing the same label, share a similar degree of blameworthiness. It should be noted from the outset that there are difficulties in definition. In part, this stems from the common law status of the offence, and in part because it must be a flexible offence capable of covering all unlawful killings (other than murder and cases caught by specific statutory provisions). The Law Commission concluded that the offence of manslaughter was at risk of being devalued by being left as a 'residual amorphous, catch all homicide offence' (Law Com Report No 304, *Murder, Manslaughter and Infanticide* (2006), para 2.19).

The difficulties of defining involuntary manslaughter were described by Lord Atkin in *Andrews v DPP* [1937] AC 576, [1937] 2 All ER 552 in the following terms:

> My Lords, of all crimes manslaughter appears to afford most difficulties of definition, for it concerns homicide in so many and so varying conditions. From the early days, when any homicide involved penalty, the law has gradually evolved 'through successive differentiations and integrations' until it recognises murder on the one hand, based mainly, though not exclusively, on an intention to kill, and manslaughter on the other hand, based mainly, though not exclusively, on the absence of intention to kill, but the presence of an element of 'unlawfulness' which is the elusive factor.

9.2 'Unlawful act' manslaughter

The doctrine of constructive murder, now abolished, was mentioned previously in Ch 7. That led to a murder conviction where D killed in the course of a felony. There existed a similar doctrine of constructive manslaughter where death was caused during the commission of an 'unlawful' act (any offence that was not as serious as a felony). The doctrine of constructive murder was narrowed down by the judges before being abolished by the Homicide Act 1957. Somewhat similarly, the doctrine of constructive manslaughter has been narrowed down but, despite recommendations of the Criminal Law Revision Committee and the Law Commission (section 9.5, p 247), has not been abolished.

The current law is that D is guilty of manslaughter if he causes V's death by an unlawful and dangerous act. The only mens rea required is an intention to do that act and any fault required to render it unlawful. Provided that a reasonable person would have been aware of the circumstances making the conduct dangerous, it is irrelevant that D is unaware that it is unlawful or that it is dangerous, or that he is unaware of the circumstances which make it dangerous, or whether D himself ought to have been aware of those circumstances.

The elements of the offence are:

- an unlawful act,
- which is performed intentionally,
- which is dangerous in the eyes of a sober and reasonable person, and
- which causes death.

The crime of manslaughter is 'constructed' on the fact that D is committing an unlawful and dangerous act. This explains why the offence is sometimes known as 'constructive manslaughter'. Identifying that base crime on which manslaughter is constructed is essential. In all cases it is useful to ask: what would be charged against D if no one had died? By way of example, if D throws a brick at a greenhouse knowing that V is standing nearby, if V dies when a shard of glass enters his eye, D may be guilty of unlawful act manslaughter. The base offence would be criminal damage: that is, what would have been charged had no one died.

9.2.1 An 'unlawful' act

Simply stating that the law requires the Crown to prove that D performed an 'unlawful' act opens up a whole raft of questions: must the 'unlawful' act be more than a mere tort or breach of contract? Must it involve the commission of a crime? If so, must all elements of the crime be proved? Will any type of crime suffice or must it be an offence of violence against the person? Is it sufficient that the crime is one of strict liability? Can unlawful act manslaughter be committed by omission?

9.2.1.1 Requirement that D commits a crime

Historically, the offence of unlawful act manslaughter was committed where D killed someone in the course of committing a tort. For example, in *Fenton* (1830) 1 Lew CC 179, Tindal CJ directed the jury that throwing stones down a mine shaft was a trespass and therefore it followed that the defendant was guilty of manslaughter where, as a result of his throwing a stone down the shaft, some scaffolding broke, a corf overturned and miners were killed. However, in *Franklin* (1883) 15 Cox CC 163, Sussex Assizes, it was settled that the unlawful act must amount to a criminal offence committed by the defendant before there can be an unlawful act manslaughter conviction. In that case, Field J stated that 'the mere fact of a civil wrong committed by one person against another ought not to be used as an incident which is a necessary step in a criminal case. I have a great abhorrence of constructive crime'. This decision had the obvious effect of narrowing the scope of the offence somewhat. As will be seen, at various stages in history judges have sought to contract and expand the scope of unlawful act manslaughter, thereby demonstrating what an amorphous offence it is.

In the following case the Court of Appeal clarified certain aspects of the offence, in particular that the unlawful act amounts to a criminal offence.

R v Lamb
[1967] 2 All ER 1282, Court of Appeal, Criminal Division

(Sachs LJ, Lyell and Geoffrey Lane JJ)

As a joke, Lamb pointed at his best friend a revolver with five chambers. It had bullets in two of the chambers but neither of these was opposite the barrel. He therefore thought it was safe to pull the trigger. His friend was also treating the matter as a joke. Lamb pulled the trigger and shot his friend dead. The revolver functioned in such a way that, when the trigger was pulled, the chambers rotated, bringing the loaded chamber opposite the barrel, before the firing pin struck. Lamb was charged with manslaughter and set up the defence of accident. The judge directed that the pointing of the revolver and pulling of the trigger was an unlawful act even if there was no intent to injure or alarm and that the jury did not need to consider whether the pointing of the gun was an assault.

[Sachs LJ, reading the judgment of the court:]

Counsel for the Crown, however, had at all times put forward the correct view that for the act to be unlawful it must constitute at least what he then termed 'a technical assault'. In this court, moreover, he rightly conceded that there was no evidence to go to the jury of any assault of any kind. Nor did he feel able to submit that the acts of the appellant were on any other ground unlawful in the criminal sense of that word. Indeed no such submission could in law be made: if, for instance, the pulling of the trigger had had no effect because the striking mechanism or the ammunition had been defective no offence would have been committed by the appellant. Another way of putting it is that mens rea being now an essential ingredient in manslaughter (compare *Andrews v DPP* [[1937] AC 576 at 582, [1937] 2 All ER 552 at 555, 556; section 9.3, p 227] and *Church* [[1965] 2 All ER 72 at 76, [1966] 1QB 59 at 70; section 9.2.3, p 213] this could not in the present case be established in relation to the first ground except by proving that element of intent without which there can be no assault. It is perhaps as well to mention that when using the phrase 'unlawful in the criminal sense of that word' the court has in mind that it is long settled that it is not in point to consider whether an act is unlawful merely from the angle of civil liabilities. That was first made clear in *Franklin* [(1883) 15 Cox CC 163]. The relevant extracts from this and from later judgments are collected in *Russell on Crime* (11th edn, 1958), pp 651–658. The whole of that part of the summing-up which concerned the first ground was thus vitiated by misdirections based on an erroneous concept of the law; and the strength with which that ground was put to the jury no doubt stemmed from the firm view of the trial judge, expressed more than once in the course of the discussion on law in relation to the undisputed facts: 'How can there be a defence to the charge of manslaughter? Manslaughter requires no intent.' . . . [His lordship discussed the judge's direction on criminal negligence.] The general effect of the summing-up was thus to withdraw from the jury the defence put forward on behalf of the appellant. When the gravamen of a charge is criminal negligence—often referred to as recklessness—of an accused, the jury have to consider amongst other matters the state of his mind, and that includes the question of whether or not he thought that that which he was doing was safe. In the present case it would, of course, have been fully open to a jury, if properly directed, to find the accused guilty because they considered his view as to there being no danger was formed in a criminally negligent way. But he was entitled to a direction that the jury should take into account the fact that he had indisputably formed this view and that there was expert evidence as to this being an understandable view. Strong though the evidence of criminal negligence was, the appellant was entitled as of right to have his defence considered but he was not accorded this right and the jury was left without a direction on an essential matter. Those defects of themselves are such that the verdict cannot stand . . .

Appeal allowed

≈≈ *Questions*

(1) Could Lamb, in the view of the court, be guilty though he believed his conduct was perfectly safe?

(2) What would have been the position if:

   (a) Lamb had intended to alarm his friend by pointing the gun but the friend was not alarmed?

   (b) Lamb did not intend to alarm his friend, or foresee that he might be alarmed, but the friend was in fact alarmed?

In *Scarlett* [1993] 4 All ER 629, D, a licensee, killed a trespasser by using excessive force while lawfully expelling him from his pub. D's conviction for manslaughter was quashed because the judge had directed that D was guilty if he had used unnecessary and unreasonable force—which would have been the tort of battery. To be guilty of manslaughter it was necessary to prove that D committed the crime of battery, not just the tort. That meant proving that D's use of force was excessive in the circumstances *which D believed to exist—Gladstone Williams*, section 23.6.1.1, p 660.

In assessing whether a base crime has been committed on which the unlawful act manslaughter charge might be constructed, it is important to have regard to whether all the elements of that offence can be proved and any defences disproved. In *Slingsby* [1995] Crim LR 570, D had vaginal and anal sex with V with her consent. Then, also with her consent, he penetrated her vagina and rectum with his hand. V suffered cuts caused by a signet ring on D's hand. She did not realize for some time that the injuries were potentially very serious. Eventually she was admitted to hospital but died from septicaemia. D was charged with manslaughter by an unlawful and dangerous act. Judge J, as he then was, ruled that, putting the Crown's case at its highest, there was no manslaughter. The injuries were suffered as a result of vigorous sexual activity with V's consent. In other words, V consented to the battery and the sexual acts. There was no base crime committed on which manslaughter could be constructed. It would, in Judge J's judgement, be contrary to principle to treat as criminal activity that which would not otherwise amount to an assault merely because in the course of that activity an injury occurred. The Crown offered no evidence and a verdict of not guilty was returned.

The acts done by D to V in *Slingsby* would plainly have been assaults or batteries if V had not consented to them. Since in law it is possible for V to consent to assault and in fact she did so, there was no crime. In *Meachen* [2006] EWCA Crim 2414, the level of injury caused by D inserting his fingers into V's anus was serious. The question for the court was whether D had a defence of consent to that injury (GBH under the Offences Against the Person Act 1961, s 20). D did have a defence provided (a) V consented to it in fact or D believed she did, and (b) the law was prepared to recognize that that level of injury could be consented to in the performance of vigorous sex (see section 11.4.2, p 288). The Court of Appeal quashed D's conviction. He had a genuine belief in her consent. The case is instructive for present purposes although it did not involve death.

In *A* [2005] 69 J Crim L 394, D's post-exam celebrations included pushing V into a river where he drowned. D claimed that he was entitled to a defence of belief in consent, his actions being mere horseplay. The Court of Appeal confirmed that if D had caused V to fall in the river by a non-accidental act and D did not have a genuine belief in V's consent to the assault, D would be liable for manslaughter if all sober and reasonable people realized it was dangerous in the sense discussed below. It is vital to check that D has committed the base crime.

9.2.2 An intentional act

What mens rea must D have in the commission of the unlawful act or 'base crime'? Is it sufficient that he performs a voluntary act that is in fact unlawful? Is it necessary for the Crown to prove that D had the mens rea that is required by the terms of the base crime?

In the *A-G's Reference (No 3 of 1994)* [1997] UKHL 31, D had stabbed his pregnant girlfriend in the abdomen and the foetus was injured. The foetus was born alive but died from injuries sustained in the womb. The trial judge ruled that there was no offence of murder on such facts, and the Attorney General referred the case to the Court of Appeal and ultimately to the House of Lords. In the course of the discussion of murder and transferred intention, the House of Lords also addressed the possible application of unlawful act manslaughter to such facts:

The first point to be made here is that to require the prosecutor to prove beyond reasonable doubt that it was reasonably foreseeable that an unlawful act such as that which was committed in this case would result in the risk of injury to the child some time after being born would make it very difficult in practice for him to obtain a conviction.

The intention which must be discovered is an intention to do an act which is unlawful and dangerous. In this case, the act which had to be shown to be an unlawful and dangerous act was the stabbing of the child's mother. There can be no doubt that all sober and reasonable people would regard that act, within the appropriate meaning of this term, as dangerous. It is plain that it was unlawful as it was done with the intention of causing her injury. As the defendant intended to commit that act, all the ingredients necessary for mens rea in regard to the crime of manslaughter were established, irrespective of who was the ultimate victim of it. The fact that the child whom the mother was carrying at the time was born alive and then died as a result of the stabbing is all that was needed for the offence of manslaughter when the actus reus for that crime was completed by the child's death. The question, once all the other elements are satisfied, is simply one of causation. The defendant must accept all the consequences of his act, so long as the jury are satisfied that he did what he did intentionally, that what he did was unlawful and that, applying the correct test, it was also dangerous (per Lord Hope of Craighead at 958).

Remember it is helpful to ask when considering this element of the offence what crime D would be convicted of had no one died. All elements of the so-called base crime must be proved in full. In addition to proving the mens rea and actus reus of the base offence, the prosecution must disprove any defences to the base offence raised by D.

9.2.3 Dangerousness

In relation to the test for dangerousness, is it sufficient that the reasonable person considers it dangerous? What amounts to danger? A risk of death? A risk of some lesser injury? As the following case will demonstrate, the test is an objective one and sets a very low threshold for what constitutes a dangerous act.

R v Church
[1965] EWCA Crim 1, Court of Criminal Appeal

(Edmund Davies, Marshall and Widgery JJ)

The appellant, according to his account, took a woman, Mrs Nott, to his van for sex. He was unable to satisfy her. She reproached him and slapped his face. They had a fight and he knocked her unconscious. He tried unsuccessfully for about half an hour to wake her, panicked, dragged her out of the van and put her in the river. Mrs Nott drowned.

At the trial, the appellant said for the first time that he thought she was dead when he put her in the water. The judge directed the jury that if Mrs Nott in fact was alive when thrown into the river, whether the appellant knew it or not, that was manslaughter. The jury convicted him of manslaughter.

[Edmund Davies J having cited the judge's direction on this issue:]

Such a direction is not lacking in authority; see, for example, *Shoukatallie v R* [[1962] AC 81, [1961] 3 All ER 996], in Lord Denning's opinion [[1962] AC 81 at 86, 92, [1961] 3 All ER 996 at 998, 1001], and Dr Glanville Williams' *Criminal Law* (2nd edn) at p 173. Nevertheless, in the judgment of this court it was misdirection. It amounted to telling the jury that, whenever any unlawful act is committed in relation to a human being which resulted in death there must be, at least, a conviction for manslaughter. This might at one time have been regarded as good law: see, for example, *Fenton* [(1830) 1 Lew CC 179]. It appears to this court, however, that the passage of years has achieved a transformation in this branch of the law and, even in relation to manslaughter, a degree of mens rea has become recognised as essential. To define it is a difficult task, and in *Andrews v DPP* [[1937] AC 576 at 582, [1937] 2 All ER 552 at 555; section 9.3, p 227] Lord Atkin spoke of the element of ' "unlawfulness" which is the elusive factor'. Stressing that we are here leaving entirely out of account those ingredients of homicide which might justify a verdict of manslaughter on the grounds of (a) criminal negligence, or (b) provocation or (c) diminished responsibility, the conclusion of this court is that an unlawful act causing the death of another cannot, simply because it is an unlawful act, render a manslaughter verdict inevitable. For such a verdict inexorably to follow, the unlawful act must be such as all sober and reasonable people would inevitably recognise must subject the other person to, at least, the risk of some harm resulting therefrom, albeit not serious harm . . .

If such be the test, as we adjudge it to be, then it follows that, in our view, it was a misdirection to tell the jury *simpliciter* that it mattered nothing for manslaughter whether or not the appellant believed Mrs Nott to be dead when he threw her in the river . . .

[The court dismissed the appeal on the ground that judge's direction on criminal negligence was an adequate one and, quite apart from that, the principle of *Thabo Meli*, section 2.3.2, p 31, applied to manslaughter (following Glanville Williams, *Criminal Law* (2nd edn), p 174) and the jury were entitled to regard the appellant's conduct as a series of acts which culminated in her death.]

Appeal dismissed

≈ *Questions*

(1) What was the crime with which Church could have been charged had no one died?

(2) What does 'at least, the risk of some harm resulting therefrom, albeit not serious harm . . .' mean? What type of risk? What degree of harm?

(3) D, aged 11, is throwing stones at a tin can he has perched on the edge of a bridge over a canal. One stone thrown misses the can and lands on a passing barge beneath, hitting V, aged 2, who is killed. Is D liable for manslaughter? What further information do you require to determine his liability?

(4) Professor Horder argues that in most cases the additional requirement that the act be dangerous is superfluous as danger is inherent in the unlawful act itself. Do you agree? See J. Horder, *Homicide and the Politics of Law Reform* (2012).

See further R. A. Duff, 'Whose Luck is it Anyway?' in C. Clarkson and S. Cunningham (eds), *Criminal Liability for Non Aggressive Death* (2008).

In the *A-G's Reference* case (section 9.2.2, p 212) involving the stabbing of the pregnant woman, Lord Mustill stated (at 950):

All that is needed, once causation is established, is an act creating a risk to *anyone*; and such a risk is obviously established in the case of any violent assault by the risk to the person of the victim herself (or himself). In a case such as the present, therefore, responsibility for manslaughter would automatically be established, once causation has been shown simply by proving a violent attack even if (which cannot have been the case here) the attacker had no idea that the woman was pregnant. On a broader canvas, the proposition involves that manslaughter can be established against someone who does any wrongful act leading to death in circumstances where it was foreseeable that it might hurt anyone at all; and that this is so even if the victim does not fall into any category of persons whom a reasonable person in the position of the defendant might have envisaged as being within the area of potential risk.

Difficulty arises in cases where the victim has some characteristic that makes D's act dangerous in circumstances where it would not be so if V did not have the characteristic. The rule is that the characteristic is only relevant if it would have been known to the sober and reasonable observer of the event (ie the commission of the base crime), even if it was not known to D. For example, in *Watson* [1989] 2 All ER 865 D burgled V's house. V was a frail, 87-year-old man. It was held that the base crime of burglary became 'dangerous' as soon as V's frailty and age would have been obvious to the reasonable observer. The unlawful act continued through the 'whole of the burglarious intrusion' so that when V died of a heart attack that was caused by D's continuing in the burglary after it had become dangerous, he was guilty of manslaughter. This can be contrasted with *Dawson* (1985) 81 Cr App R 150 in which V had a weak heart and died during an attempted robbery. V was standing behind armour-plated glass and D was brandishing a replica firearm. It was held that D was not guilty of manslaughter because the reasonable observer would not, at any point in the continuance of the base crime—robbery—have known of V's peculiar susceptibility. Therefore that act of robbery was not 'dangerous' in the *Church* sense.

However, there remains uncertainty over the extent to which the reasonable bystander is endowed with the knowledge of the accused. For example, D intends to rob a bank but does not wish to harm anyone. For this reason he buys what he has been told is a replica shotgun. Unbeknownst to D, the shotgun is in fact real. When D points the gun at V and pulls the trigger the gun fires and kills him. Would the reasonable bystander have the same knowledge as D that the gun was a replica? In *Dawson,* Watkins LJ stated:

> this test [ie the dangerousness test] can only be undertaken upon the basis of the knowledge gained by a sober and reasonable man as though he were present at the scene of and watched the unlawful act being performed . . . he has the same knowledge as the man attempting to rob and no more.

This could indicate that the reasonable bystander would also think the gun a replica.

However, this was doubted in *Ball* [1989] Crim LR 730 in which it was observed that:

> . . . *Dawson's* case goes no further than showing that the sober and reasonable man must look at the unlawful act to see if it is dangerous and not at the peculiarities of the victim.

Ball can, however, be distinguished from *Dawson* on its facts. In that case D took a shotgun and loaded it with cartridges from his pocket. The pocket contained both live and blank cartridges and D had no way of knowing what he had loaded his shotgun with. The reasonable bystander would surely have thought there was the risk of some harm, given that it was just as likely that D had loaded the shotgun with live cartridges as with blanks. In his comment on the case, Professor Smith stated:

> The sober and reasonable man cannot be treated as having come on the scene at the moment of the fatal act with no knowledge of any earlier events. His knowledge must surely include awareness of the preparatory acts done by the defendant—in the present case his taking up a handful of cartridges from a pocket which he knew to contain both live ones and blanks. It was this act which made the subsequent pulling of the trigger dangerous and the sober and reasonable person would have recognised it as such.

In the more recent case of *JF and NE* [2015] EWCA Crim 351, the Court of Appeal confirmed that *Dawson* continues to represent the correct approach and held that there is no need for the defendant to foresee a risk of death. The Lord Chief Justice agreed with the following criticism that has been made by Professor Ashworth:

> In the longer term, common law manslaughter ought to be revisited by the Law Commission, since its most recent review of homicide law was focused on other matters and consequently treated this form of manslaughter rather cursorily: Law Com. No.304, *Murder, Manslaughter and Infanticide* (2006), pp.61–64.   [I]t is more appropriate that there be wide consultation on detailed questions about the ambit of any such offence than that these issues be resolved piecemeal by the courts, without clear parameters to guide them. ([2013] Crim LR 335)

It was held that whether there ought to be a change in the law is a matter for Parliament.

9.2.4 Can there be manslaughter by an unlawful and dangerous omission?

In *Khan and Khan* [1998] Crim LR 830, the court said that manslaughter by omission is no more than an example of manslaughter arising from a grossly negligent breach of duty. Certainly the fault alleged in omission cases will usually be gross negligence. But is gross negligence the only form of manslaughter available for omissions? There can be a murder conviction based on an omission in breach of a duty to act, with intent to cause grievous bodily harm: *Gibbins and Proctor* (1918) 13 Cr App R 134, section 4.2.3.3, p 65, and it seems logical that, if the intent was to cause some lesser degree of harm, the offence should be manslaughter. This falls into the 'constructive' category rather than that of gross negligence. However, there is authority saying that a criminal omission can never be an 'unlawful act' for the purposes of constructive manslaughter: *Lowe* [1973] 1 All ER 805, [1973] QB 702 (Glanville Williams, *Textbook of Criminal Law* (2nd edn, 1983), p 276). However, that case was forcefully and cogently criticized by the Ashworth in [1976] Crim LR 529: 'In the absence of strong and clear arguments in favour of treating homicide by neglect as less serious than other forms of homicide, the distinction set out in *Lowe* can only be based on superstition.'

9.2.5 Causing death

The unlawful, intentional, dangerous act by D must cause V's death. The ordinary principles of causation discussed in Chapter 3 apply here. In some cases, the causal link between the unlawful act and the death can be very difficult to establish.

The next case illustrates how difficult the offence of unlawful act manslaughter can be, with issues as to the unlawfulness, dangerousness and causation all arising. The extract is a relatively long one to allow for examination of each of these problems in a complex case.

R v Carey
[2006] EWCA Crim 17, Court of Appeal, Criminal Division

(Dyson LJ, Tomlinson and Andrew-Smith JJ)

The victim, Aimee Wellock (aged 15), and three friends were walking in a park area. The three defendants had spent the afternoon there drinking alcohol. When Aimee and her group met Carey's group by chance, Carey and her group began to abuse Aimee's group verbally. Carey struck one of Aimee's group, James, from behind and he moved away from both groups. Carey then punched another of Aimee's group, Shelley, in the face three times, causing her to fall over. Carey carried on the assault by kicking her on the nose, mouth and top of the right arm while she was down. Carey finally attacked Aimee, who was about 10 metres away from where Shelley had been assaulted. The attack on Aimee and her friends lasted about one minute. Aimee ran off, covering a distance of 109 metres over rough grass and up a slight slope. Aimee felt faint, collapsed and died that same night. The post-mortem revealed that the immediate cause of death was ventricular fibrillation (dysrhythmia). Aimee suffered from a severely diseased heart. Even the doctors who had treated her for certain other medical conditions were unaware of it. Aimee appeared physically fit and participated in dancing and other physical activities. The experts found that Aimee might not have died if she had not run 109 metres. Both experts accepted that the event 'most proximate to the collapse and therefore most likely to have been the precipitating factor which led to Aimee's death was her running away from the incident'.

The unlawful act (base crime) alleged against Carey was an affray contrary to s 3 of the Public Order Act 1986:

> (1) A person is guilty of affray if he uses or threatens unlawful violence towards another and his conduct is such as would cause a person of reasonable firmness present at the scene to fear for his personal safety.
>
> (2) Where 2 or more persons use or threaten the unlawful violence, it is the conduct of them taken together that must be considered for the purposes of sub-section (1).
>
> (3) For the purposes of this section a threat cannot be made by the use of words alone.

Carey was convicted of unlawful act manslaughter and appealed.

> **Dyson LJ** [dealt with the facts, and issues relating to the appeal against conviction for affray]:
>
> 26. This being a case of alleged unlawful act manslaughter, it is not in issue that the Crown had to prove three elements, namely (i) that there was an unlawful act, (ii) which was dangerous in the sense that the unlawful act subjected Aimee to the risk of physical harm, and (iii) that the unlawful act caused her death.
>
> 27. At the close of the Crown case, Mr Harrison submitted that count 1 should be withdrawn from the jury. He contended that causation was not made out because (i) there was no evidence that the affray caused Aimee to run away (and thereby suffer the ventricular fibrillation), and (ii) in any event, there was no evidence that anyone would have recognised that running as she did would subject Aimee to the risk of harm. The judge rejected both arguments. He held that causation was a question of fact for the jury. As regards the second argument, he said that 'the necessity of establishing at least a risk of physical harm is a self-contained requirement that has nothing to do with causation, but is concerned only with the dangerousness of the unlawful act. If the act was unlawful and dangerous in the *R v Church* sense and caused the deceased's death, unlawful act manslaughter will be made out.'
>
> 28. The unlawful act relied on in this case is affray. It is important to emphasise at the outset that the Crown chose not to rely on C's assault on Aimee as the unlawful act in question. They could have attempted to secure convictions for manslaughter against C on the basis that she was Aimee's direct assailant and against the other defendants on the basis of joint enterprise liability for that assault.

> ∼∼ *Question*
>
> Could a conviction be secured on the basis that Carey caused Aimee to apprehend unlawful violence (base crime of assault) and that in reasonable response Aimee fled and died as a result?

> [His lordship continued:]
>
> The second element of the offence of unlawful act manslaughter is that of dangerousness. The act must be recognisably dangerous. This is a relatively recent limitation on unlawful act manslaughter and was clearly articulated in those terms by the Court of Appeal in *Larkin* [1943] 1 All ER 217. [His lordship referred to *Larkin* and then to *Church*.]
>
> 31. The *Church* test was subsequently approved by Lord Salmon in *Newbury* [1977] AC 500, 507C E saying that he was sure that in *Church* the court did not intend to differ from or qualify anything that had been said in *Larkin*. We are inclined to agree with Mr Harrison that, *pace* Lord Salmon, there is a difference between the tests for dangerousness set out in these two cases. *Larkin* requires that the act is likely to injure another; *Church* only requires a risk of some harm resulting. As Mr Harrison points

out, as a matter of ordinary language, there is a difference between foresight that an act is likely to injure another, and foresight that there is a risk of some harm resulting. But the difference is not material in the present case. We propose to adopt the *Church* formulation on the grounds that it is more recent, was expressly approved in *Newbury* and is more satisfactory . . .

34. In later cases, the Court of Appeal explained both the type of harm which should have been foreseen, and the knowledge and attributes which could be ascribed to the reasonable person by whose response it is determined whether the act was dangerous. Two cases are of particular relevance to the present appeal. [His lordship referred to *Dawson* and *Watson* [section 9.2.3, p 215] . . .

35. Thus, in considering whether the unlawful act is dangerous in the context of manslaughter, it may be relevant to have regard to the attributes of the victim. Of course, a punch which causes a person to fall will almost inevitably satisfy the test of dangerousness. That is why a defendant who punches a victim who falls and suffers a fatal head injury as a result is guilty of manslaughter. It is foreseeable that the victim is at risk of suffering some physical harm from such a punch (albeit not serious harm), and that is sufficient. Physical harm includes shock. The reason why the death resulting from the attempted robbery of the 60 year old petrol station attendant was not manslaughter was that the attempted robbery was not dangerous in the relevant sense. It was not foreseeable that an apparently healthy 60 year old man would suffer shock and a heart attack as a result of such an attempted robbery. On the other hand, the jury properly found that it was foreseeable that an obviously frail and very old man was at risk of suffering shock leading to a heart attack as a result of a burglary committed at his home late at night.

36. . . . Mr Harrison rightly conceded that there may be circumstances in which a verdict of unlawful act manslaughter can properly be entered where the alleged unlawful act is affray. Suppose that a very old and obviously frail man is the victim of an affray in which a number of youths participate; and suppose further that he is not physically assaulted, but each of the youths uses and/or threatens violence (but not by words alone) such that a person of reasonable firmness present at the scene would fear for his personal safety; and finally suppose that, as a result of the incident, the man suffers a heart attack from which he dies. On such facts, the jury might well conclude that the affray would be dangerous in the sense of being an act which sober and reasonable people would recognise subjected the old man at least to the risk of some harm resulting from it (shock), and so could properly find the youths guilty of manslaughter. The case would be analogous to *Watson*.

37. But, in our view quite rightly, the judge declined to leave the manslaughter charge to the jury on the basis that the affray had caused Aimee to suffer shock leading to her heart attack. In his summing up, the judge explained to the jury that they should 'take shock out of this case' because the difference between emotional upset, which is not physical harm, and shock, which is, is a 'grey area'. We agree with this observation, but would go further. Even if the affray had caused Aimee to suffer shock as opposed to emotional upset, the affray lacked the quality of dangerousness in the relevant sense. This is because it would not have been recognised by a sober and reasonable bystander that an apparently healthy 15 year old (or indeed anyone else present) was at risk of suffering shock as a result of this affray. In our view, this affray was less dangerous in the relevant sense than the attempted robbery of the 60 year old petrol station attendant in *Dawson*. The risk of that victim suffering shock leading to a heart attack would have been recognised by a sober and reasonable person as more likely than the risk of Aimee suffering shock leading to a heart attack as a result of the affray.

38. But the judge did accept the submission of Mr Myerson [counsel for the Crown] that it was sufficient that, in determining whether the affray subjected Aimee to the risk of at least some physical harm, it was legitimate to aggregate the infliction of violence on her two friends to the violence on herself, and to decide that that aggregated violence satisfied the test of dangerousness. The only remaining question was whether that aggregated violence was a cause of death. That this was the judge's view appears more clearly in his summing up than in the judgment that he gave when he

ruled on the submission at the close of the Crown case . . . [His lordship quoted from the judge's summing-up.]

41. Thus, in deciding whether any appellant had committed an unlawful act against Aimee which was dangerous in the relevant sense, the jury could take into account the violence inflicted on all three of the victims and not just that inflicted on Aimee. It followed that the jury did not have to be sure that the assault on her by C was a cause of Aimee's death; it was sufficient if the violence by all defendants on all three victims was causative of death.

[His lordship considered the offence of affray.] . . .

46. In the present case, the only dangerous act in the relevant sense was the assault by C on Aimee. A punch to the face is a dangerous unlawful act. If Aimee had fallen against a hard surface and suffered an injury from which she had died, C would have been guilty of manslaughter on a straightforward application of *Church* principles. But in the circumstances of this case, Aimee's death was not caused by injuries that were a foreseeable result of the assault in the sense that the risk of such injuries would have been recognised by a sober or reasonable person having the knowledge that the appellants had. As we understand it, Mr Myerson accepts this. The slight injuries caused by the assault cannot be said to have been a cause of her death. That is why the judge did not direct the jury that it was necessary for them to be sure that the physical harm actually inflicted was a cause of her death before they could convict of manslaughter.

47. It follows from the fact that (a) the only dangerous act perpetrated on Aimee (C's punch) did not cause her death, and (b) the other acts and threats of violence used in the course of the affray were not dangerous in the relevant sense as against Aimee, that none of the appellants was guilty of manslaughter.

48. By way of postscript, we should say a word about 'escape'. There are circumstances where the *actus reus* of a crime is completed by the act of the victim rather than that of the offender. Thus, where the victim injures himself in a fall whilst attempting to escape from an attack by the offender, the latter may be regarded as having caused that injury. Or take the case of the defendant convicted of assault occasioning actual bodily harm to his victim who was injured jumping from his moving car after he had assaulted her in that car: *Roberts* (1971) 56 Cr App R 95.

49. In his summing up, the judge directed the jury: 'if, however, you conclude that Aimee was still reasonably in fear of being attacked and that running away was a reasonable thing to do, you may conclude that the affray was a significant cause of death.' Mr Harrison and Mr Watson both submit that there was no evidence that Aimee was running away in order to escape from the possibility of further attack, rather than because she wanted to get home as quickly as possible. They say that the judge should not have left that issue to the jury, since it was impossible for the jury to decide why she ran away. Indeed, they say that there was no evidence that she was running away from her assailants: they were heading in the opposite direction and there was no actual or threatened violence present at the time when Aimee ran.

50. Mr Myerson did not rely on the death caused by the running away as analogous to the injury caused during the attempted escape in *Roberts*. He did not advance the case as an 'escape' case in that sense. He does not submit that Aimee ran off in fear of being attacked or threatened with violence. Rather, he submits that the running away was part of 'one overall incident which comprises the necessary crime antecedent to the death. Escape was not relied on. It was simply part of the overall picture which the jury had to consider because the case involved the run uphill and that was the last thing Aimee did.' . . . Viewed in that light, it seems to us that the running away does not require any modification of what we have already said. We do not understand Mr Myerson to submit that, if we reject his other arguments, the manslaughter conviction should be upheld by reason of the running away point . . .

53. For the reasons that we have given, to hold these appellants liable for the death of Aimee in circumstances such as occurred in this case would involve an unwarranted extension of the law. In our

view, such an extension would come close to saying that if X commits an unlawful act but for which Y would not have died, X is criminally liable for the death of Y. That is not our law. Our law requires that X commits an unlawful act which is dangerous in the sense that it is recognised by sober and reasonable persons as subjecting Y to the risk of some physical harm which in turn causes the death. The only act committed against Aimee which was dangerous in that sense was C's assault on her, but physical harm resulting from the assault itself did not cause Aimee's death. It must follow that none of the appellants was guilty of manslaughter.

Appeal against the conviction for manslaughter allowed

In relation to what the court has to say about those cases where V dies in the course of fleeing from D, the later case of *Lewis* [2010] EWCA Crim 151 is instructive. Here, the Court of Appeal upheld the judge's direction to the jury that they should consider whether V running away from D was one of the responses which might reasonably be expected from someone who found himself in V's situation. If it was, D would remain liable. In cases of death during flight from an unlawful act, it is necessary to show that but for the unlawful act, flight and therefore death would not have occurred.

These are not isolated examples: see also *MJ* [2012] EWCA Crim 2293.

≈≈ *Questions*

(1) What was the unlawful act committed by Carey? Why did the Crown not rely on the assault on Aimee and the flight by her to avoid that assault? Cf *Roberts* (1971) 56 Cr App R 95.

(2) Was the act dangerous? Was it only dangerous when viewed in combination with the acts of others?

(3) Is the court right in its analysis of aggregating the conduct of many? If D1 is waving a machete around and D2 is shaking his fist at V, their affray comprises their combined conduct. Likewise, the dangerousness of the acts is properly assessed by looking at the combination of their conduct. It is submitted that there is no problem in aggregating the conduct of D1, D2 and D3 towards V1 and V2. Take a case where in the course of a robbery D1 issues serious threats against V1 and D2 issues threats to V2, and the obviously frail V2 died from a heart attack induced by the shock. It is submitted that the actions of D1 and D2 could be aggregated in determining whether the conduct was sufficiently 'dangerous' in the sense required by *Church*.

(4) Did the unlawful and dangerous act cause Aimee's death? If not, what did?

9.2.5.1 Problem cases of causation in unlawful act manslaughter: (1) suicide

The courts have faced numerous difficult cases in which the boundaries of unlawful act manslaughter have been challenged in relation to causation.

R v D

[2006] EWCA Crim 1139, Court of Appeal, Criminal Division

(Sir Igor Judge P, Henriques and Fulford JJ)

D had struck his partner a minor blow on the forehead and she had then committed suicide. This was against a lengthy background of domestic abuse by D amounting to psychological but not psychiatric injury of V. D was charged with manslaughter. Issues arose as to whether his single act of striking her was a sufficient unlawful act. The problem was that the victim's suicide was a free, deliberate and informed act; it broke the chain of causation. The alternative of treating the whole of D's abusive course of conduct to V as the unlawful act was problematic because the acts did not amount to anything other than psychological harm falling short of a recognized psychiatric injury which would amount to actual or grievous bodily harm (see section 10.2.1.1, p 251). The trial judge held that the infliction of mere psychological harm would not suffice to construct a manslaughter charge. However, in an *obiter dictum*, the Court of Appeal left open the possibility that a manslaughter conviction might be available:

where a decision to commit suicide has been triggered by a physical assault which represents the culmination of a course of abusive conduct, it would be possible . . . to argue that the final assault played a significant part in causing the victim's death.

J. Horder and L. McGowan, 'Manslaughter by Causing Another's Suicide'
[2006] Crim LR 1035

. . . A cause of death is still cause, in law, even if it is only one of a number of operating causes. So, the fact that the defendant's final assault could only be understood as playing a minor causal role in the victim's suicide, does not prevent that final assault being a cause of her suicide. That being so, what is then the legal significance of the preceding years of abuse causing the psychological trauma? It is that evidence of years of abuse bolsters the case for saying that the final assault was indeed, in law, a cause of the victim's suicide. In that regard, we need to distinguish two kinds of case. In the first kind of case . . . there is an assault shortly before the suicide that triggers the suicide, whereas in the second kind of case . . . there is no such assault.

[Direct assault cases]

. . . if, a blow causes someone to commit suicide, so long as the blow is still regarded as an operating and substantial cause of V's death (even if not the only or main cause) manslaughter is committed. Suppose that D assaults V on a single occasion, for the first time in the relationship. V, perhaps moved by mixed motives of shame and fear, commits suicide in consequence. Can D be straightforwardly regarded as the cause of V's death, in such a case?

There have been cases in which it is the victim's own reaction—typically, in seeking to escape an impending assault—that explains the harm the victim suffered. In such cases, there is authority for the view that if the defendant's conduct is to be regarded as one of the causes of the victim's reaction, that reaction must have been within a range of responses that might reasonably have been expected in the situation in question. According to the Court of Appeal in *Mackie* [(1973) 57 Cr App R 453 at 460 (per Stephenson LJ)], if it is still to be regarded as caused by the defendant's conduct the victim's reaction must be: 'the natural consequence of the assault charged, not something which could not be expected, but something which any reasonable and responsible man in the assailant's shoes would have foreseen.'

. . . in a case where the victim's reaction is one of deliberate self-harm (something not at issue in *Mackie*) it might seem difficult to satisfy the *Mackie* test when it is a first-time assault by D that has led to V's suicide. In a case like *Dhaliwal*, however, it might seem easier to satisfy the test. The final assault is the latest episode in a history of abuse. So, the fact that the victim has been subject to such abuse makes it more likely that a jury will accept that her reaction in committing suicide was within the range of what might be considered 'natural'. To this must be added the fact that cultural and religious influences on the victim made self-harm a more likely (a more natural) response in the longer term to the defendant's ongoing abuse.

. . .

[Indirect cases]

In many cases, there will be no final assault of a 'back-breaking straw' kind, that leads the victim to commit suicide. Suppose that D, who has subjected V to years of abuse, has been away abroad for some weeks on business, but is due to return shortly. Unable to face the prospect of resuming their abusive relationship, V commits suicide before D's return. Has D caused V to commit suicide? In such a case, the prosecution's argument will be that the cumulative effect of abuse for, inter alia, of non-fatal offences committed over a period of time, readily explains the victim's decision to commit suicide. This brings her suicide within the range of natural (i.e. not wholly unnatural) reactions to the abuse. There can be no doubt that, in some circumstances, the law does permit the effect of blows, or other wrongs, to be aggregated or assessed cumulatively so that the whole is regarded as, in law, greater than the sum of the parts. Individual injuries forming a part of a single attack can, for example, be aggregated for the purpose of judging whether the bodily harm done was 'grievous'. Individual actions can also be assessed cumulatively in deciding whether they amount to a course of 'harassment'. By analogy, it may be argued that (at least in some cases) the persistence of abuse, if not any one violent incident, is what establishes a causal link between that abuse and a consequent suicide. As has already been pointed out, moreover, it ought to be all the easier to establish such a link when suicide is much more likely to have been perceived by a victim of abuse as 'the only way out' for reasons such as religious and cultural background.

. . . When a relationship is characterised by persistent domestic abuse (especially in the kind of cultural and religious context to be found in *Dhaliwal*), the experience of living with the abuse is liable to affect the victim's decision-making processes, and to influence the range and character of actions she regards as legitimate, inevitable or natural. Through the way in which it shapes her world and her self-perception, the abuse may establish a controlling influence over how the victim understands and responds to her situation. . . .

It might be that a decision on the part of a victim of abuse to commit suicide is best explained, in straightforward causal terms, by a depressive condition induced by the abuse. In that event, the defendant will be liable for manslaughter on the basis that his abuse triggered the operation of a special vulnerability of the victim. On our account, however, the causal link between the abuse and the suicide can be (lack of) freedom-based, and need not be based on a victim's special vulnerability. An abuse-based controlling influence can, in this context, make a decision to commit suicide something that the victim was not truly free to avoid, because other avoiding actions were in practical terms ruled out by the effect of that influence. In that regard, the nature and degree of abuse suffered before the decision to commit suicide was taken should be an influential but not a decisive factor in establishing a casual connection between the abuse and the suicide. The understandable development of a suicidal state of mind may be as much a product of the very fact that domineering control has been established and maintained over a long period, as by the direct effects of the abuse that underpins that control.

≈≈ *Question*

Do you agree that someone like Dhaliwal has caused his wife's death?

9.2.5.2 Problem cases of causation in unlawful act manslaughter: (2) drug misuse cases

In a series of cases since the 1990s, the Court of Appeal struggled with the situation where D supplies V with drugs, V self-injects what turns out to be a fatal overdose and D is prosecuted for manslaughter. On a charge of unlawful act manslaughter, requiring proof of an unlawful, intentional and dangerous act causing death, there is a requirement to prove that D committed an unlawful act (the base crime). The Crown repeatedly relied on two options: (a) that D administered a noxious substance contrary to s 23 of the Offences Against the Person Act 1861, or (b) that D was an accessory to V's injection. Both were fundamentally flawed. D was not guilty of administering since V himself administered the drugs. V's act, if it was free and informed, broke the chain of causation. Nor could D be liable as a secondary party—V committed no offence to which D could be an accessory. It is not an offence to inject drugs or to kill oneself.

The principal problem with the decisions was that they ran contrary to the orthodox principle of causation: V's free, voluntary, deliberate, informed act should, on well-established grounds, break the chain of causation. As Glanville Williams explained:

> The new intervening act (*novus actus interveniens*) of a responsible actor, who had full knowledge of what he is doing, and is not subject to mistake or pressure, will normally operate to relieve the defendant of liability for a further consequence, because it makes the consequence too remote . . . What a person does (if he has reached adult years, is of sound mind and is not acting under mistake, intimidation or other similar pressure) is his own responsibility, and is not regarded as having been caused by other people. (*Textbook of Criminal Law* (2nd edn, 1983), p 391)

Despite the very basic nature of these propositions, the Court of Appeal in a series of cases created enormous confusion. In *Kennedy (No 1)* [1999] Crim LR 65, it had been held that D was a party to V's self-injection and that V's free, informed, deliberate act did not break the chain of causation. This was plainly wrong. In *Dias* [2000] 2 Cr App R 96, it was recognized that D could not be a secondary party in these circumstances since V commits no crime in which D can assist. That was correct. In *Rogers* [2003] 2 Cr App R 160, [2003] Crim LR 555, *Dias* was distinguished where D held the tourniquet for V while he injected; in those circumstances it was held that D was playing a part in the mechanics of the injection as a principal. That has now been held to be wrong (see the House of Lords' decision in *Kennedy (No 2)* in the following extract). In *Finlay* [2003] EWCA Crim 3868, the Court of Appeal suggested that D could be liable provided he was a factual cause of V's death unless V's act of self-injection was extraordinary. That too was plainly wrong. See also *Richards* [2002] EWCA Crim 3175. Because of the decision in *Dias*, Kennedy brought a second appeal against his conviction, arguing that the decision in *Kennedy (No 1)* had subsequently been undermined by decisions such as *Dias*. In *Kennedy (No 2)* [2005] EWCA Crim 785, the court reviewed the many controversial and often inconsistent decisions on this issue but managed only to perpetuate the errors. The Court of Appeal in *Kennedy (No 2)* (at [42]) sought to create an exception to the general principle that V's free, informed, voluntary act breaks the chain of causation where D is acting in 'joint concert' with V:

> . . . if a defendant is acting in concert with the deceased, what the deceased does in concert with the defendant will not break the chain of causation, even though the general principles as to causation have to be applied. This was recognised by Lord Steyn when he qualified the general position when saying in *R v Latif & Others* [1996] 2 Cr. App. R. 92 at p 104: 'The free, deliberate and informed intervention of a second person, who intends to exploit the situation created by the first, *but is not acting in concert with him* is held to relieve the first actor of criminal responsibility.' (emphasis added)

This reasoning was fundamentally flawed. See section 3.2.3.2, p 42. See D. Ormerod and R. Fortson, 'Drug Suppliers Manslaughter (Again)' [2005] Crim LR 819.

R v Kennedy (No 2)
[2007] UKHL 38, House of Lords

(Lords Bingham of Cornhill, Rodger of Earlsferry, Baroness Hale of Richmond, Lords Carswell and Mance)

Kennedy lived in a hostel with Marco Bosque and Andrew Cody, who shared a room. On 10 September 1996, Kennedy visited their room. Bosque was drinking with Cody. According to Cody, Bosque told the appellant that he wanted 'a bit to make him sleep' and Kennedy told Bosque to take care that he did not go to sleep permanently. Kennedy prepared a dose of heroin for Bosque and gave him a syringe ready for injection. Bosque then injected himself and returned the empty syringe to Kennedy who left the room. Bosque then appeared to stop breathing. An ambulance was called and he was taken to hospital, where he was pronounced dead. The cause of death was inhalation of gastric contents while acutely intoxicated by opiates and alcohol. Kennedy appealed against the decision of the Court of Appeal's decision in his second appeal to uphold his conviction. The question certified by the Court of Appeal Criminal Division for the opinion of the House of Lords was:

> When is it appropriate to find someone guilty of manslaughter where that person has been involved in the supply of a class A controlled drug, which is then freely and voluntarily self-administered by the person to whom it was supplied, and the administration of the drug then causes his death?

Lord Bingham [stated the facts and continued:]

Manslaughter

6. It is well-established and not in any way controversial that a charge of manslaughter may be founded either on the unlawful act of the defendant ('unlawful act manslaughter') or on the gross negligence of the defendant. This appeal is concerned only with unlawful act manslaughter and nothing in this opinion should be understood as applying to manslaughter caused by gross negligence.

7. To establish the crime of unlawful act manslaughter it must be shown, among other things not relevant to this appeal,

(1) That the defendant committed an unlawful act;

(2) That such unlawful act was a crime (*R v Franklin* (1883) 15 Cox CC 163; *R v Lamb* [1967] 2 QB 981, 988; *R v Dias* [2001] EWCA Crim 2986, [2002] 2 Cr App R 96, para 9); and

(3) That the defendant's unlawful act was a significant cause of the death of the deceased (*R v Cato* [1976] 1 WLR 110, 116–117).

There is now, as already noted, no doubt but that the appellant committed an unlawful (and criminal) act by supplying the heroin to the deceased. But the act of supplying, without more, could not harm the deceased in any physical way, let alone cause his death. As the Court of Appeal observed in *R v Dalby* [1982] 1 WLR 425, 429, 'the supply of drugs would itself have caused no harm unless the deceased had subsequently used the drugs in a form and quantity which was dangerous'. So, as the parties agree, the charge of unlawful act manslaughter cannot be founded on the act of supplying the heroin alone.

8. The parties are further agreed that an unlawful act of the appellant on the present facts must be found, if at all, in a breach of section 23 of the Offences against the Person Act 1861 . . .

9. As it now effectively reads, section 23 of the 1861 Act provides:

> **'Maliciously administering poison, etc, so as to endanger life or inflict grievous bodily harm**
>
> Whosoever shall unlawfully and maliciously administer to or cause to be administered to or taken by any other person any poison or other destructive or noxious thing, so as thereby to endanger

the life of such person, or so as thereby to inflict upon such person any grievous bodily harm, shall be guilty of [an offence] and being convicted thereof shall be liable . . . to [imprisonment] for any term not exceeding ten years . . .'

The opening and closing words of the section raise no question relevant to this appeal. The substance of the section creates three distinct offences: (1) administering a noxious thing to any other person; (2) causing a noxious thing to be administered to any other person; and (3) causing a noxious thing to be taken by any other person. It is not in doubt that heroin is a noxious thing, and the contrary was not contended.

10. The factual situations covered by (1), (2) and (3) are clear. Offence (1) is committed where D administers the noxious thing directly to V, as by injecting V with the noxious thing, holding a glass containing the noxious thing to V's lips, or (as in *R v Gillard* (1988) 87 Cr App R 189) spraying the noxious thing in V's face.

11. Offence (2) is typically committed where D does not directly administer the noxious thing to V but causes an innocent third party TP to administer it to V. If D, knowing a syringe to be filled with poison instructs TP to inject V, TP believing the syringe to contain a legitimate therapeutic substance, D would commit this offence.

12. Offence (3) covers the situation where the noxious thing is not administered to V but taken by him, provided D causes the noxious thing to be taken by V and V does not make a voluntary and informed decision to take it. If D puts a noxious thing in food which V is about to eat and V, ignorant of the presence of the noxious thing, eats it, D commits offence (3).

13. In the course of his accurate and well-judged submissions on behalf of the Crown, Mr David Perry QC accepted that if he could not show that the appellant had committed offence (1) as the unlawful act necessary to found the count of manslaughter he could not hope to show the commission of offences (2) or (3). This concession was rightly made, but the committee heard considerable argument addressed to the concept of causation, which has been misapplied in some of the authorities, and it is desirable that it should be clear why the concession is rightly made. . . .

18. The criminal law generally assumes the existence of free will. The law recognises certain exceptions, in the case of the young, those who for any reason are not fully responsible for their actions, and the vulnerable, and it acknowledges situations of duress and necessity, as also of deception and mistake. But, generally speaking, informed adults of sound mind are treated as autonomous beings able to make their own decisions how they will act, and none of the exceptions is relied on as possibly applicable in this case. Thus D is not to be treated as causing V to act in a certain way if V makes a voluntary and informed decision to act in that way rather than another. There are many classic statements to this effect.

[His lordship dismissed the argument based on causation, holding that the victim's free voluntary act broke the chain of causation between D's act of supply and the death of V. Nor was it possible to argue that D caused V to take or caused to be administered to V since V's act broke the chain of causation, see section 3.2.3.2, p 42.]

19. The sole argument open to the Crown was, therefore, that the appellant administered the injection to the deceased. It was argued that the term 'administer' should not be narrowly interpreted. Reliance was placed on the steps taken by the appellant to facilitate the injection and on the trial judge's direction to the jury that they had to be satisfied that the appellant handed the syringe to the deceased 'for immediate injection'. But section 23 draws a very clear contrast between a noxious thing administered to another person and a noxious thing taken by another person. It cannot ordinarily be both. In this case the heroin is described as 'freely and voluntarily self-administered' by the deceased. This, on the facts, is an inevitable finding. The appellant supplied the heroin and prepared the syringe. But the deceased had a choice whether to inject himself or not. He chose to do so, knowing what he was doing. It was his act.

20. In resisting this conclusion Mr Perry relied on *R v Rogers* [2003] 1 WLR 1374. In that case the defendant pleaded guilty, following a legal ruling, to a count of administering poison contrary to section 23 of the 1861 Act and a count of manslaughter. The relevant finding was that the defendant physically assisted the deceased by holding his belt round the deceased's arm as a tourniquet, so as to raise a vein in which the deceased could insert a syringe, while the deceased injected himself. It was argued in support of his appeal to the Court of Appeal that the defendant had committed no unlawful act for purposes of either count. This contention was rejected. The court held (para 7) that it was unreal and artificial to separate the tourniquet from the injection. By applying and holding the tourniquet the defendant had played a part in the mechanics of the injection which had caused the death. There is, clearly, a difficult borderline between contributory acts which may properly be regarded as administering a noxious thing and acts which may not. But the crucial question is not whether the defendant facilitated or contributed to administration of the noxious thing but whether he went further and administered it. What matters, in a case such as *R v Rogers* and the present, is whether the injection itself was the result of a voluntary and informed decision by the person injecting himself. In *R v Rogers*, as in the present case, it was. That case was, therefore, wrongly decided.

21. It is unnecessary to review the case law on this subject in any detail. In *R v Cato* [1976] 1 WLR 110 the defendant had injected the deceased with heroin and the present problem did not arise. In *R v Dalby* [1982] 1 WLR 425 the deceased had died following the consumption of drugs which the defendant had supplied but the deceased had injected. There was apparently no discussion of section 23, but it was held that the supply could not support a conviction of manslaughter. At the trial of the present appellant there was no consideration of section 23 and the trial judge effectively stopped defence counsel submitting to the jury that the appellant had not caused the death of the deceased. In dismissing his first appeal the Court of Appeal said:

> 'We can see no reason why, on the facts alleged by the Crown, the appellant in the instant case might not have been guilty of an offence under section 23 of the Offences against the Person Act 1861. Perhaps more relevantly, the injection of the heroin into himself by Bosque was itself an unlawful act, and if the appellant assisted in and wilfully encouraged that unlawful conduct, he would himself be acting unlawfully.'

But the court gave no detailed consideration to the terms of section 23, and it is now accepted that the deceased's injection of himself was not an unlawful act.

22. In *R v Dias* [2002] 2 Cr App R 96 the defendant had been convicted of manslaughter. He had prepared a syringe charged with heroin which he had handed to the deceased, who had injected himself. The court recognised that the chain of causation had probably been broken by the free and informed decision of the deceased, and noted the error in the decision on the appellant's first appeal as to the unlawfulness of the deceased's injection of himself.

[His lordship referred to the Court of Appeal's suggestion that the liability might rest on a principle of joint administration.]

24. It is possible to imagine factual scenarios in which two people could properly be regarded as acting together to administer an injection. But nothing of the kind was the case here. As in *R v Dalby* and *R v Dias* the appellant supplied the drug to the deceased, who then had a choice, knowing the facts, whether to inject himself or not. The heroin was, as the certified question correctly recognises, self-administered, not jointly administered. The appellant did not administer the drug. Nor, for reasons already given, did the appellant cause the drug to be administered to or taken by the deceased.

25. The answer to the certified question is: 'In the case of a fully-informed and responsible adult, never'. The appeal must be allowed and the appellant's conviction for manslaughter quashed. The appellant must have his costs, here and below, out of central funds.

26. Much of the difficulty and doubt which have dogged the present question has flowed from a failure, at the outset, to identify the unlawful act on which the manslaughter count is founded. It

matters little whether the act is identified by a separate count or counts under section 23, or by particularisation of the manslaughter count itself. But it would focus attention on the correct question, and promote accurate analysis of the real issues, if those who formulate, defend and rule on serious charges of this kind were obliged to consider how exactly, in law, the accusation is put.

Appeal allowed

≋ *Questions*

(1) Was V's act really a free act if he was a heroin addict and D had heroin to offer?

(2) Lord Bingham stated that 'informed' adults are treated by the law as autonomous beings. Does this impose a threshold of knowledge that V must possess and if he does not the supplier could be guilty of manslaughter if V dies from taking the drug? For example, what if, unbeknownst to V, the heroin was of a higher purity than he was accustomed to and D did not inform him of this fact?

(3) Should 'using' prohibited drugs be an offence? If so, V would have committed an offence and D would have aided and abetted that offence. There would be an unlawful act on which to base D's liability for manslaughter if V died.

In *Burgess* [2008] EWCA Crim 516, the Court of Appeal subsequently suggested that had the matter fallen for consideration (on the facts D had pleaded on a basis that could not stand in the light of the House of Lords' decision), D raising the vein for V would suffice as an act of administering. It was held that 'if a defendant may be convicted on the basis that the fatal dose was jointly administered then it follows that he is not automatically entitled to be acquitted if the deceased rather than the defendant physically operated the plunger'. There is obviously a difficult borderline between contributory acts which might properly be regarded as administering a noxious thing and acts which might not. The evidence is likely to be patchy: one participant is dead and the other, the defendant, likely to have been heavily intoxicated. *Burgess* might therefore serve as an example falling just the other side of the line from *Rogers*. Whether the necessary proximity existed between the actions of D and V is for the jury to determine. Liability for manslaughter will exist where D has provided the drugs to V whose act of self-administration was not free and voluntary.

See further W. Wilson, 'Dealing with Drug Induced Homicide' in C. Clarkson and S. Cunningham (eds), *Criminal Liability for Non-Aggressive Deaths* (2008). Cf the approach in the case of *HM Advocate v McAngus* (2009), High Court of Justiciary, which decided not to follow *Kennedy (No 2)*.

It is important to point out that while there cannot be liability for unlawful act manslaughter in the drug misuse cases (subject to the caveats mentioned earlier), that is not to say that D is therefore not guilty of any offence. D may be guilty of gross negligence manslaughter. This issue will be considered in the next section.

9.3 Manslaughter by gross negligence

The elements of the offence are now established to be:

- a duty of care owed by the defendant;
- a gross breach of that duty which created a risk of death;
- breach of which duty caused death.

The House of Lords sought to clarify what the elements of this offence are in the case of *Adomako*.

R v Adomako
[1995] AC 171, House of Lords

(Lord Mackay of Clashfern LC, Lords Keith of Kinkel, Goff of Chieveley, Browne-Wilkinson and Woolf)

During an operation at which the appellant was assisting as anaesthetist, the tube carrying oxygen from the ventilator to the patient became disconnected. The appellant failed to notice the disconnection and some six minutes later the patient suffered a cardiac arrest from which, despite efforts at resuscitation, he died. At no stage did the appellant check the integrity of the equipment. The case against the appellant was that he had been grossly negligent in failing to notice or respond appropriately to obvious signs that a disconnection had occurred and that the patient had ceased to breathe.

Lord Mackay of Clashfern, LC:

. . . On behalf of the appellant it was conceded at his trial that he had been negligent. The issue was therefore whether his conduct was criminal. . . .

The jury convicted the appellant of manslaughter by a majority of 11 to 1. The Court of Appeal, Criminal Division dismissed the appellant's appeal against conviction but certified that a point of law of general public importance was involved in the decision to dismiss the appeal, namely:

'In cases of manslaughter by criminal negligence not involving driving but involving a breach of duty is it a sufficient direction to the jury to adopt the gross negligence test set out by the Court of Appeal in the present case following *R v Bateman* (1925) 19 Cr App Rep 8 and *Andrews v DPP* [1937] 2 All ER 552, [1937] AC 576 without reference to the test of recklessness as defined in *R v Lawrence* [1981] 1 All ER 974, [1982] AC 510 or as adapted to the circumstances of the case?'

The decision of the Court of Appeal is reported at [1993] 4 All ER 935, [1994] QB 302 along with a number of other cases involving similar questions of law. The Court of Appeal held that except in cases of motor manslaughter the ingredients which had to be proved to establish an offence of involuntary manslaughter by breach of duty were the existence of the duty, a breach of the duty which had caused death and gross negligence which the jury considered to justify a criminal conviction; the jury might properly find gross negligence on proof of indifference to an obvious risk of injury to health or of actual foresight of the risk coupled either with a determination nevertheless to run it or with an intention to avoid it but involving such a high degree of negligence in the attempted avoidance as the jury considered justified conviction or of inattention or failure to advert to a serious risk of going beyond mere inadvertence in respect of an obvious and important matter which the defendant's duty demanded he should address; and that, in the circumstances, the appeals of the two junior doctors and the electrician would be allowed and the appeal of the anaesthetist, namely Dr Adomako, would be dismissed. The reason that the Court of Appeal excepted the cases of motor manslaughter and their formulation of the law was the decision of this House in *R v Seymour* [1983] 2 All ER 1058, [1983] 2 AC 493 in which it was held that where manslaughter was charged and the circumstances were that the victim was killed as a result of the reckless driving of the defendant on a public highway, the trial judge should give the jury the direction which had been suggested in *R v Lawrence* [1981] 1 All ER 974, [1982] AC 510 but that it was appropriate also to point out that in order to constitute the offence of manslaughter the risk of death being caused by the manner of the defendant's driving must be very high.

In opening his very cogent argument for the appellant before your Lordships, counsel submitted that the law in this area should have the characteristics of clarity, certainty, intellectual coherence and general applicability and acceptability. For these reasons he said the law applying to involuntary manslaughter generally should involve a universal test and that test should be the test already applied in this House to motor manslaughter. He criticised the concept of gross negligence which was the basis of the judgment of the Court of Appeal submitting that its formulation involved circularity, the jury being told in effect to convict of a crime if they thought a crime had been committed and that accordingly using gross negligence as the conceptual basis for the crime of involuntary manslaughter was unsatisfactory and the court should apply the law laid down in *R v Seymour* [1983] 2 All ER 1058, [1983] 2 AC 493 generally to all cases of involuntary manslaughter or at least use this as the basis for providing general applicability and acceptability.

Like the Court of Appeal your Lordships were treated to a considerable review of authority. I begin with *R v Bateman* (1925) 19 Cr App Rep 8 and the opinion of Lord Hewart CJ, where he said (at 10–12):

[Lord Mackay quoted extensively from Lord Hewart's judgment, pp 10–13, concluding:]

'The foregoing observations deal with civil liability. To support an indictment for manslaughter the prosecution must prove the matters necessary to establish civil liability (except pecuniary loss), and, in addition, must satisfy the jury that the negligence or incompetence of the accused went beyond a mere matter of compensation and showed such disregard for the life and safety of others as to amount to a crime against the State and conduct deserving punishment.'

Next I turn to *Andrews v DPP*, which was a case of manslaughter through the dangerous driving of a motor car. In a speech with which all the other members of this House who sat agreed, Lord Atkin said at pp. 581–582:

'of all crimes manslaughter appears to afford most difficulties of definition, for it concerns homicide in so many and so varying conditions. From the early days when any homicide involved penalty the law has gradually evolved "through successive differentiations and integrations" until it recognises murder on the one hand, based mainly, though not exclusively, on an intention to kill, and manslaughter on the other hand, based mainly, though not exclusively, on the absence of intention to kill but with the presence of an element of "unlawfulness" which is the elusive factor. In the present case it is only necessary to consider manslaughter from the point of view of an unintentional killing caused by negligence, that is, the omission of a duty to take care. I do not propose to discuss the development of this branch of the subject as treated in the successive treatises of Coke, Hale, Foster and East and in the judgments of the courts to be found either in directions to juries by individual judges or in the more considered pronouncements of the body of judges which preceded the formal Court of Crown Cases Reserved. Expressions will be found which indicate that to cause death by any lack of due care will amount to manslaughter; but as manners softened and the law became more humane a narrower criterion appeared. After all, manslaughter is a felony, and was capital, and men shrank from attaching the serious consequences of a conviction for felony to results produced by mere inadvertence. The stricter view became apparent in prosecutions of medical men or men who professed medical or surgical skill for manslaughter by reason of negligence. As an instance I will cite *Rex v. Williamson* (1807) 3 C. & P. 635 where a man who practised as an accoucheur [a male midwife], owing to a mistake in his observation of the actual symptoms, inflicted on a patient terrible injuries from which she died. "To substantiate that charge"—namely, manslaughter—Lord Ellenborough said, "the prisoner must have been guilty of criminal misconduct, arising either from the grossest ignorance or the most criminal inattention." The word "criminal" in any attempt to define a crime is perhaps not the most helpful: but it is plain that the Lord Chief Justice meant to indicate to the jury a high degree of negligence. So at a much later date in *Rex v. Bateman*, 19 Cr.App.R. 8 a charge of manslaughter was made against a qualified medical practitioner in similar circumstances to those of *Williamson's* case.'

Lord Atkin then referred to the judgment of Lord Hewart C.J. from which I have already quoted and went on, at p. 583:

'Here again I think with respect that the expressions used are not, indeed they were probably not intended to be, a precise definition of the crime. I do not myself find the connotations of mens rea helpful in distinguishing between degrees of negligence, nor do the ideas of crime and punishment in themselves carry a jury much further in deciding whether in a particular case the degree of negligence shown is a crime and deserves punishment. But the substance of the judgment is most valuable, and in my opinion is correct. In practice it has generally been adopted by judges in charging juries in all cases of manslaughter by negligence, whether in driving vehicles or otherwise. The principle to be observed is that cases of manslaughter in driving motor cars are but instances of a general rule applicable to all charges of homicide by negligence. Simple lack of care such as will constitute civil liability is not enough: for purposes of the criminal law there are degrees of negligence: and a very high degree of negligence is required to be proved before the felony is established. Probably of all the epithets that can be applied "reckless" most nearly covers the case. It is difficult to visualise a case of death caused by reckless driving in the connotation of that term in ordinary speech which would not justify a conviction for manslaughter: but it is probably not all-embracing, for "reckless" suggests an indifference to risk whereas the accused may have appreciated the risk and intended to avoid it and yet shown such a high degree of negligence in the means adopted to avoid the risk as would justify a conviction. If the principle of *Bateman's* case, 19 Cr.App.R. 8 is observed it will appear that the law of manslaughter has not changed by the introduction of motor vehicles on the road. Death caused by their negligent driving, though unhappily much more frequent, is to be treated in law as death caused by any other form of negligence: and juries should be directed accordingly.'

In my opinion the law as stated in these two authorities is satisfactory as providing a proper basis for describing the crime of involuntary manslaughter. Since the decision in *Andrews v DPP* [1937] 2 All ER 552, [1937] AC 576 was a decision of your Lordships' House, it remains the most authoritative statement of the present law which I have been able to find and although its relationship to *R v Seymour* [1983] 2 All ER 1058, [1983] 2 AC 493 is a matter to which I shall have to return, it is a decision which has not been departed from. On this basis in my opinion the ordinary principles of the law of negligence apply to ascertain whether or not the defendant has been in breach of a duty of care towards the victim who has died. If such breach of duty is established the next question is whether that breach of duty caused the death of the victim. If so, the jury must go on to consider whether that breach of duty should be characterised as gross negligence and therefore as a crime. This will depend on the seriousness of the breach of duty committed by the defendant in all the circumstances in which the defendant was placed when it occurred. The jury will have to consider whether the extent to which the defendant's conduct departed from the proper standard of care incumbent upon him, involving as it must have done a risk of death to the patient, was such that it should be judged criminal.

It is true that to a certain extent this involves an element of circularity, but in this branch of the law I do not believe that is fatal to its being correct as a test of how far conduct must depart from accepted standards to be characterised as criminal. This is necessarily a question of degree and an attempt to specify that degree more closely is I think likely to achieve only a spurious precision. The essence of the matter, which is supremely a jury question, is whether, having regard to the risk of death involved, the conduct of the defendant was so bad in all the circumstances as to amount in their judgment to a criminal act or omission.

My Lords the view which I have stated of the correct basis in law for the crime of involuntary manslaughter accords I consider with the criteria stated by counsel although I have not reached the degree of precision in definition which he required, but in my opinion it has been reached so far as practicable and with a result which leaves the matter properly stated for a jury's determination.

My Lords in my view the law as stated in *R v Seymour* [1983] 2 All ER 1058, [1983] 2 AC 493 should no longer apply since the underlying statutory provisions on which it rested have now been repealed by the Road Traffic Act 1991. It may be that cases of involuntary motor manslaughter will as a result become rare but I consider it unsatisfactory that there should be any exception to the generality of the statement which I have made, since such exception, in my view, gives rise to unnecessary complexity. For example, in *Kong Cheuk Kwan v R* (1985) 82 Cr App Rep 18, it would give rise to unnecessary differences between the law applicable to those navigating vessels and the lookouts on the vessels.

I consider it perfectly appropriate that the word 'reckless' should be used in cases of involuntary manslaughter, but as Lord Atkin put it 'in the ordinary connotation of that word'. Examples in which this was done, to my mind, with complete accuracy are *R v Stone, R v Dobinson* [1977] 2 All ER 341, [1977] QB 354 and *R v West London Coroner, ex p Gray* [1987] 2 All ER 129, [1988] QB 467.

…

In my view the summing up of the learned judge in the present case was a model of clarity in analysis of the facts and in setting out the law in a manner which was readily comprehensible by the jury. The summing up was criticised in respect of the inclusion of the following passage:

'Of course you will understand it is not for every humble man of the profession to have all that great skill of the great men in Harley Street but, on the other hand, they are not allowed to practise medicine in this country unless they have acquired a certain amount of skill. They are bound to show a reasonable amount of skill according to the circumstances of the case, and you have to judge them on the basis that they are skilled men, but not necessarily so skilled as more skilful men in the profession, and you can only convict them criminally if, in your judgment, they fall below the standard of skill which is the least qualification which any doctor should have. You should only convict a doctor of causing a death by negligence if you think he did something which no reasonably skilled doctor should have done.'

The criticism was particularly of the latter part of this quotation in that it was open to the meaning that if the defendant did what no reasonably skilled doctor should have done it was open to the jury to convict him of causing death by negligence. Strictly speaking this passage is concerned with the statement of a necessary condition for a conviction by preventing a conviction unless that condition is satisfied. It is incorrect to treat it as stating a sufficient condition for conviction. In any event I consider that this passage in the context was making the point forcefully that the defendant in this case was not to be judged by the standard of more skilled doctors but by the standard of a reasonably competent doctor. There were many other passages in the summing up which emphasised the need for a high degree of negligence if the jury were to convict and read in that context I consider that the summing up cannot be faulted.

For these reasons I am of the opinion that this appeal should be dismissed and that the certified question should be answered by saying:

'In cases of manslaughter by criminal negligence involving a breach of duty, it is a sufficient direction to the jury to adopt the gross negligence test set out by the Court of Appeal in the present case following *R v Bateman* (1925) 19 Cr App Rep 8 and *Andrews v DPP* [1937] 2 All ER 552, [1937] AC 576 and it is not necessary to refer to the definition of recklessness in *R v Lawrence* [1981] 1 All ER 974, [1982] AC 510, although it is perfectly open to the trial judge to use the word "reckless" in its ordinary meaning as part of his exposition of the law if he deems it appropriate in the circumstances of the particular case.'

We have been referred to the consultation paper by the Law Commission, *Criminal Law, Involuntary Manslaughter An Overview* (Law Com no 135 [1994]), and we have also been referred to a number of standard textbooks. I have also had the opportunity of considering the note by Sir John Smith in [1994] Crim LR 292 since the hearing was completed. While I have not referred to these in detail I have derived considerable help in seeking to formulate my view as a result of studying them.

I have reached the same conclusion on the basic law to be applied in this case as did the Court of Appeal. Personally I would not wish to state the law more elaborately than I have done. In particular I think it is difficult to take expressions used in particular cases out of the context of the cases in which they were used and enunciate them as if applying generally. This can I think lead to ambiguity and perhaps unnecessary complexity. The task of trial judges in setting out for the jury the issues of fact and the relevant law in cases of this class is a difficult and demanding one. I believe that the supreme test that should be satisfied in such directions is that they are comprehensible to an ordinary member of the public who is called to sit on a jury and who has no particular prior acquaintance with the law. To make it obligatory on trial judges to give directions in law which are so elaborate that the ordinary member of the jury will have great difficulty in following them, and even greater difficulty in retaining them in his memory for the purpose of application in the jury room, is no service to the cause of justice. The experienced counsel who assisted your Lordships in this appeal indicated that as a practical matter there was a danger in over-elaboration of definition of the word 'reckless'. While therefore I have said in my view it is perfectly open to a trial judge to use the word 'reckless' if it appears appropriate in the circumstances of a particular case as indicating the extent to which a defendant's conduct must deviate from that of a proper standard of care, I do not think it right to require that this should be done and certainly not right that it should incorporate the full detail required in *R v Lawrence* [1981] 1 All ER 974, [1982] AC 510.

[Lords Keith of Kinkel, Goff of Chieveley, Browne-Wilkinson and Woolf agreed.]

Appeal dismissed

≈ **Question**
Does the test operate unfairly against doctors given that they have little control over whether they deal with circumstances which pose a risk of death?

9.3.1 A duty of care: a civil standard of negligence?

Although gross negligence manslaughter requires an examination of whether the defendant owed the victim a duty of care, that is not to say that the offence incorporates all the principles of the civil law.

In *Wacker* [2002] EWCA Crim 1944, the defendant used his HGV to transport 60 illegal immigrants into the UK via Dover. The only ventilation to the container on the HGV was a small vent. The vent was shut and remained closed for over five hours. Fifty-eight of the people hidden in the container suffocated. The defendant was convicted of 58 offences of manslaughter. At his trial the Crown accepted the general proposition that the principle of *ex turpi causa non oritur actio* applied in determining whether there was a duty of care in considering a charge of manslaughter by gross negligence, just as it did in determining whether a civil claim for damages for negligence could succeed.

The judge held that a proper distinction could be drawn between those criminal activities for which the passengers were solely responsible, those for which there was a shared responsibility and those for which the defendant and others were solely responsible. He ruled that the defendant's failure to ensure that the concealed illegal immigrants had sufficient air was incidental to their role but critical to the defendant's own role so that, in establishing the necessary duty of care, since the immigrants would be 'relying' on a matter incidental to their criminality, they would not be 'relying' upon their own unlawful conduct. The defendant appealed against the manslaughter convictions contending that no duty of care could be said to have been owed by him to the illegal immigrants because they shared the same joint illegal purpose; and that the judge had been wrong in his directions to the jury as to the circumstances in which a duty of care would arise. He also appealed against sentence. The Attorney General referred to the court the sentences for manslaughter as being unduly lenient, although he did not contend that the total sentence should be increased but only to the way in which the total of 14 years had been made up.

It was held that as a matter of public policy there was no justification for concluding that the criminal law should decline to hold a person as criminally responsible for the death of another simply because the two were engaged in some joint unlawful activity at the time or because there might have been an element of acceptance of a degree of risk by the victim in order to further the joint unlawful enterprise. Nor could the duty to take care be permitted to be affected by the countervailing demands of the criminal enterprise. It was not necessary to examine whether the distinction between matters for which the immigrants were responsible and those incidental to their illegality was a proper one; how matters might have been characterized in a civil claim had no relevance to the issue that the jury had to decide. Accordingly, the approach taken in the court below had been too favourable to the defendant. In every other respect, the necessary ingredients of the offence of manslaughter had been properly left to the jury and there were no reasons to doubt the safety of those convictions.

How is D to know what duties of civil law will be sufficient to trigger potential criminal liability? In *Yaqoob* [2005] EWCA Crim 1269, the defendant was a manager of a minicab firm and he had failed to inspect the tyres of a minibus involved in a fatal accident. It was held that it was open to the jury to find that there was a duty to inspect and maintain beyond that required for a MOT test, council inspections and other duties imposed by regulation. Moreover, the jury did not require expert evidence to assess that duty.

There are established categories where a duty of care has been recognized to exist in the context of gross negligence manslaughter, such as between husband and wife (*Meeking* [2012] EWCA Crim 641); parent and child (*Evans* [2009] EWCA Crim 650); when one stores materials of an extremely hazardous nature on one's premises (*Winter and Winter* [2010] EWCA Crim 1474); and when a duty is voluntarily assumed (*C* [2011] EWCA Crim 3272). However, as the next section shows, there are more difficult categories on the periphery.

9.3.1.1 Gross negligence manslaughter: drug misuse cases

In *Kennedy (No 2),* the House of Lords stated emphatically that a supplier of drugs cannot be guilty of unlawful act manslaughter if the person to whom he supplies the drugs dies from having taken them, as long as that person is a fully informed and responsible adult and chooses to take the drugs voluntarily. However, a different approach is taken in the context of gross negligence manslaughter. As the following case demonstrates, the supplier of drugs can be guilty of gross negligence manslaughter and the fact that V self-administered them does not break the chain of causation. By extending the doctrine that was first propounded in *Miller* [1982] UKHL 6 (section 4.2.3.4, p 69) a five-member Court of Appeal based D's liability for gross negligence manslaughter on her having created *or contributed to* a dangerous situation. The duty arose when D realized or ought to have realized that V was suffering from a life-threatening reaction to the heroin she had supplied.

R v Evans

[2009] EWCA Crim 650, Court of Appeal, Criminal Division

(Lord Judge CJ, Moore-Bick LJ, Calvert-Smith, Christopher Clark and Holroyde JJ)

D supplied V, her 16-year-old half-sister, with heroin. After V self-injected the heroin, she developed symptoms that D recognized as being consistent with an overdose. D and her mother, X, who was also in the house, believed that they were responsible for V but did not seek medical assistance as they feared getting into trouble. V was put to bed but was found dead the next morning. The cause of death was heroin poisoning. X was convicted of gross negligence manslaughter on the basis that she owed V a duty of care, as she was her mother. The Crown based D's duty of care towards V not on the fact of their familial relationship, but on the fact that D did not seek medical attention when it became apparent that V was having a life-threatening adverse reaction to the drug that D had supplied her. In essence, this was a case of liability arising from an omission. D appealed her conviction, arguing that the judge had been wrong to conclude that D owed V a duty of care.

Lord Judge CJ:

20. The question in this appeal is not whether the appellant may be guilty of manslaughter for having been concerned in the supply of the heroin which caused the deceased's death. It is whether, notwithstanding that their relationship lacked the features of familial duty or responsibility which marked her mother's relationship with the deceased, she was under a duty to take reasonable steps for the safety of the deceased once she appreciated that the heroin she procured for her was having a potentially fatal impact on her health.

21. When omission or failure to act are in issue two aspects of manslaughter are engaged. Both are governed by decisions of the House of Lords. The first is manslaughter arising from the defendant's gross negligence: *R v Adomako* [1995] 1 AC 171. The second arises when the defendant has created a dangerous situation and when, notwithstanding his appreciation of the consequent risks, he fails to take any reasonable preventative steps: *R v Miller* [1983] 2 AC 161. Gross negligence manslaughter and unlawful act manslaughter are not necessarily mutually exclusive: *R v Willoughby* [2005] 1 WLR 1880. The same applies to the aspects of manslaughter presently under consideration. Indeed care needs to be taken to avoid the risk of allowing the convenience of addressing the different circumstances in which manslaughter may arise to be converted into a compartmentalised, mutually isolated series of offences each inconveniently described by the same word, 'manslaughter'.

22. Miller's duty to act arose after he fell asleep in a squat while holding a lighted cigarette. He woke up and found that his mattress was smouldering. He left the room in which he had been asleep and went back to sleep in an adjoining room. He wholly ignored the smouldering mattress. The house caught fire. He was convicted of arson. In the House of Lords argument ranged over whether his omission to act engaged what was described as the 'duty theory' espoused by Professor J C Smith or whether his reckless omission to rectify the consequences of his earlier unintended act attracted the 'continuing act theory' supported by Professor Glanville Williams. It was submitted that there was no liability in criminal law for an omission unless there was a legal duty to act imposed by common law or by statute, and that no statutory provision imposed a duty neglect of which involved criminal liability, and no common law duty to extinguish an accidental fire or fire innocently started had previously been 'declared'.

23. The decision of the House of Lords was expressed in the single opinion of Lord Diplock. Both theories, he said, led to an identical result. The 'continuing act' basis for liability was not disavowed, but the duty theory was adopted only on the basis that it was easier to explain to a jury, provided the word 'responsibility' rather than 'duty' was used. In fact, the issue has continued to be addressed in the context of 'duty' rather than responsibility, and we shall continue to do so. More important, however, Lord Diplock observed, at p 176, that he could see

'no rational ground for excluding from conduct capable of giving rise to criminal liability, conduct which consists of failing to take measures that lie within one's power to counteract a danger that one has oneself created, if at the time of such conduct one's state of mind is such as constitutes a necessary ingredient of the offence . . . I cannot see any good reason why, so far as liability under criminal law is concerned, it should matter at what point of time before the resultant damage is complete a person becomes aware that he has done a physical act which, whether or not he appreciated that it would at the time when he did it, does in fact create a risk that property of another will be damaged; provided that, at the moment of awareness, it lies within his power to take steps, either himself or by calling for the assistance of the fire brigade if this be necessary, to prevent or minimise the damage to the property at risk.'

24. The mens rea necessary for arson was, and thereafter the analysis focussed on, recklessness. But the reasoning in the decision does not exclude liability where a different mens rea is required. And if, for example, the result of the fire in *R v Miller* had included the death of a fellow squatter, it appears to us that Miller would properly have been convicted of manslaughter by gross negligence as well as arson: *R v Willoughby* [2005] 1 WLR 1880.

25. Adomako was an anaesthetist and the deceased was his patient. He plainly owed him a duty of care. Lord Mackay of Clashfern LC in the only speech, expressed the opinion that [1995] 1 AC 171, 187: 'the ordinary principles of the law of negligence apply to ascertain whether or not the defendant has been in breach of a duty of care towards the victim who has died.' He answered the certified question, at p 188: 'In cases of manslaughter by criminal negligence involving a breach of duty, it is a sufficient direction to the jury to adopt the gross negligence test set out by the Court of Appeal in the present case . . .'

26. Our attention was drawn to a number of subsequent authorities. In *R v Khan (Rungzabe)* [1998] Crim LR 830 a young woman was supplied by the appellants with heroin. This was probably the first occasion on which she had used heroin. She took ten times the recommended therapeutic dosage and twice the amount likely to be taken even by an experienced user of heroin. She became 'obviously very ill'. She needed medical attention. The appellants, who were drug dealers, left her where she was and did nothing to assist. On the next day they returned and found that she was dead. If she had received medical attention she would probably have survived.

27. The jury was directed that they could consider a manslaughter verdict on the basis of omission. This could arise only if the appellants had set in train 'a chain of events' which gave rise to a risk of harm to the deceased. The relevant act was the supply of heroin to her. The second necessary ingredient was knowledge or awareness of the obvious risk that, having taken the heroin, the deceased would or might be harmed, and that they deliberately took no steps to rectify it. The effect of the direction was 'to extend the duty to summon medical assistance to a drug dealer who supplies heroin to a person who subsequently dies'. This court held that that might be correct (*sed quaere* today, in the light of *R v Kennedy (No 2)* [2008] AC 269), but the issue needed to be closely addressed with the jury. The summing up in relation to manslaughter by omission was flawed. The convictions were quashed. The issue which arises in the present appeal was not directly addressed, although impliedly at any rate it appears that the court would not have rejected criminal liability on this basis.

28. *R v Sinclair, Johnson and Smith* (1998) 148 NLJ 1353 raised similar issues. For these purposes the detailed facts need no narrative. Johnson's conviction for manslaughter was quashed on the basis that his conduct had not demonstrated a 'voluntary assumption of a legal duty of care'. What he had done was rather 'a desultory attempt to be of assistance'. The facts were not capable of giving rise to a legal duty of care in his case. Sinclair, however, was in a different position. He was a close friend of the deceased. They lived together, almost like brothers. Sinclair paid for and supplied the deceased with the first dose of methadone and helped him to obtain the second dose. He knew that the deceased was not an addict. He remained with the deceased throughout the period of his unconsciousness. For a long time he was the only person who was with him. On this basis there was material on which the jury, properly directed, could have found that Sinclair owed the deceased a legal duty of care. That accords with the present case.

29. In *R v Willoughby* [2005] 1 WLR 1880 the appellant was convicted of manslaughter on the basis of arson. He owned some premises which he decided to destroy by fire. He recruited a man called Drury to help him set fire to the premises. In an explosion the premises collapsed and Mr Drury died. The court accepted that a duty to look after the deceased did not arise merely because the appellant owned the premises which collapsed and in which he was killed. But that fact, taken together with the additional facts that the destruction of the premises was for his financial benefit, that he enlisted the deceased to take part, and that his role was to spread petrol inside the premises, were sufficient, 'in conjunction' to be capable of giving rise to a duty of care: para 20.

30. In *R v Wacker* [2003] QB 1207 the appellant's convictions for manslaughter arose from the horrific deaths of 58 illegal immigrants hiding in a container loaded on to a trailer. The appellant was the lorry driver. It was suggested that he owed no duty of care to any of the deceased because they were parties to the same illegal purpose. The court, at para 38, had 'no difficulty in concluding that . . . the [appellant] did voluntarily assume the duty of care [for those in the container]', and he was aware that 'no one's actions other than his own could realistically prevent [them] from suffocating to death'. The appeal was dismissed on the basis that, once the jury decided that the appellant knew about those travelling in the container, it was a very plain case of gross negligence manslaughter.

31. These authorities are consistent with our analysis. None involved what could sensibly be described as manslaughter by mere omission and in each it was an essential requirement of any potential basis for conviction that the defendant should have failed to act when he was under a duty to do so. The duty necessary to found gross negligence manslaughter is plainly not confined to cases of a familial or professional relationship between the defendant and the deceased. In our judgment, consistently with *R v Adomako* [1995] 1 AC 171 and the link between civil and criminal liability for negligence, for the purposes of gross negligence manslaughter, when a person has created or contributed to the creation of a state of affairs which he knows, or ought reasonably to know, has become life threatening, a consequent duty on him to act by taking reasonable steps to save the other's life will normally arise.

[The Court of Appeal also made clear that whether a duty of care exists between D and V is a question of law not fact and is for the judge to determine. The jury are to be directed on what the law is—ie whether a duty of care existed—if they find certain facts to be established.]

45. In some cases, such as those arising from a doctor/patient relationship where the existence of the duty is not in dispute, the judge may well direct the jury that a duty of care exists. Such a direction would be proper. But if, for example, the doctor were on holiday at the material time, and the deceased asked a casual question over a drink, it may very well be that the question whether a doctor/patient relationship existed, and accordingly whether a duty of care arose, would be in dispute. In any cases where the issue is in dispute, and therefore in more complex cases, and assuming that the judge has found that it would be open to the jury to find that there was a duty of care, or a duty to act, the jury should be directed that if facts a + b and/or c or d are established, then in law a duty will arise, but if facts x or y or z were present, the duty would be negatived. In this sense, of course, the jury is deciding whether the duty situation has been established. In our judgment this is the way in which *R v Willoughby* should be understood and, understood in this way, no potential problems arising from article 6 and article 7 of the Convention are engaged.

≋ *Questions*

(1) Why did V's self-injection not break the chain of causation? Is *Evans* inconsistent with *Kennedy (No 2)*? See D. Baker, 'Omissions Liability for Homicide Offences: Reconciling *R v Kennedy* with *R v Evans*' (2010) 74 J Crim L 310.

(2) How much of a 'contribution' to a dangerous situation must D make before the duty of care crystallizes?

(3) Could D have avoided liability by quickly leaving the scene after handing over the heroin so that she would have been unaware of whether V had had an adverse reaction or not? If so, does this possibility mean that prosecutions in cases such as *Evans* will be rare?

(4) Would D have been liable if the circumstances were the same but it had been X who supplied the heroin? Consider *Phillips* [2013] EWCA Crim 358 where the allegations against D were as follows:

i) having supplied [V] with a quantity of diarmorphine [*sic*] (heroin), a controlled drug of Class A, [D] owed him a duty of care;

ii) in breach of that duty and knowing that the state of affairs had become life-threatening, [D] failed to take reasonable steps to ensure that [V] received appropriate medical treatment;

iii) that breach of duty amounted to gross negligence;

iv) that negligence was a substantial cause of the death of [V].

Is it the supply of drugs that gives rise to the duty of care? Is that what was decided in *Evans*? Does the supply of heroin (or any drug) necessarily create or contribute to a dangerous situation?

9.3.2 Risk of death

Though Lord Mackay refers to a risk of death, it was not completely clear whether if D created a risk of causing serious bodily harm to V that would be sufficient. But in *Gurphal Singh* [1999] Crim LR 582, the judge directed: 'The circumstances must be such that a reasonably prudent person would have foreseen a serious and obvious risk not merely of injury or even serious injury but of death.' The Court of Appeal has now confirmed in *Misra* that a risk of death is required.

R v Misra and Srivastava
[2004] EWCA Crim 2375, Court of Appeal, Criminal Division

(Judge LJ, Deputy Chief Justice of England and Wales, Treacy and Bean JJ)

M and S were doctors who, on duty in a hospital, failed to recognize that a knee-surgery patient had developed toxic shock syndrome. The poison built up in his body and he died. The prosecution relied not on M and S's failure to diagnose the precise condition, since that was a rare one and failure to identify it may well not have amounted to negligence at all. The Crown relied on their failure to appreciate that the patient was seriously ill, despite his showing persistent signs of infection and notwithstanding suggestions by other members of the medical team. M and S did not obtain the blood results that someone had ordered nor did either make any inquiry about the results. They did not seek help from senior colleagues. An expert for the prosecution testified that if he were examining a third- or fourth-year medical student, and the student failed to diagnose infection in such circumstances, he would have thought of failing the student on that basis alone.

49. No issue arises whether both appellants owed a duty of care to the deceased, or were negligently in breach of it. There was however helpful argument about the nature of the relevant risk. Was it, as the judge directed the jury in the present case 'serious risk to life', or was it much broader, extending to serious risk to safety as well as life? In its original formulation in *Bateman*, Lord Hewitt CJ referred to 'disregard to the life and safety of others' in the sense of serious injury. In *Seymour*, the risk was confined to the risk of death. In *Stone* [1977] QB 554 and *West London Coroner, ex parte Grey* [1988] QB 467, [1987] 2 All ER 129 reference was made to risks in broader terms, extending to health and welfare. Although Lord Mackay spoke in approving terms of these decisions in a different context, it is clear that his approval was directed to the deployment of the word 'reckless'. He was

not addressing, and it would have been inconsistent with his own analysis of the legal principles if he were approving, the wider basis for identifying risk described in *Stone* and *West London Coroner ex parte Grey*. It is also striking that Lord Mackay did not expressly adopt or approve the broader formulation of risk made by Lord Taylor CJ in *Prentice*. Since *Adomako*, this issue has been addressed in this court, in *R (on the application of Gurphal) v Singh* [1999] CLR 582 and the Divisional Court in *Lewin v CPS*, unreported, 24 May 2002. In *Gurphal Singh*, this court strongly approved the trial judge's direction in a case of manslaughter by gross negligence that 'the circumstances must be such that a reasonably prudent person would have foreseen a serious and obvious risk not merely of injury, even serious injury, but of death'. In *Lewin*, the Divisional Court applied that direction.

50. Mr David Perry, on behalf of the Attorney General, informed us that, as a matter of policy, when making a decision whether to prosecute for this offence in cases like the present, the Director of Public Prosecutions looks for evidence of an obvious risk of death, and that, if the extent of the risk were limited to the obvious risk of serious injury, and no more, prosecution would not follow.

51. The editors of *Blackstone's Criminal Practice* suggest that the law needs clarification, and that, if it were clarified, some 'degree of symmetry' between murder and manslaughter would be achieved if, for the purposes of gross negligence manslaughter, the risk should extend to grievous bodily harm. Professor Smith took the contrary view, suggesting that 'if we are to have an offence of homicide by gross negligence at all, it seems right that it should be . . . limited. The circumstances must be such that a reasonably prudent person would have foreseen a serious risk, not merely of injury, even serious injury, but of death.'

52. There will, of course, be numerous occasions when these distinctions are entirely theoretical. From time to time, however, they will be of great significance, not only to the decision whether to prosecute, but also to the risk of conviction of manslaughter. In our judgment, where the issue of risk is engaged, *Adomako* demonstrates, and it is now clearly established, that it relates to the risk of death, and is not sufficiently satisfied by the risk of bodily injury or injury to health. In short, the offence requires gross negligence in circumstances where what is at risk is the life of an individual to whom the defendant owes a duty of care. As such it serves to protect his or her right to life.

≈ **Question**
D performs an act which is lawful (therefore not unlawful act manslaughter) and which does not objectively pose a risk of death, but his action causes V's death. Can D be charged with manslaughter? See section 9.4, p 244.

9.3.3 Grossness of the breach

This aspect of the test has been very heavily criticized. The question is whether the negligence was bad enough to amount to a crime and conduct deserving of punishment. This is easy enough to state, but difficult to apply. Consider driving as an example; every instance of driving without due care and attention is a crime and it can scarcely be the law that every such case would be manslaughter if the driving happened to cause death. How bad does the negligence have to be to be gross? As *Andrews* decided, even causing death by *dangerous* driving is not *necessarily* manslaughter. In the recent case of *Sellu* [2016] EWCA Crim 1716, the Court of Appeal quashed D's conviction because the trial judge had failed to assist the jury in approaching their task of identifying the line that separates even serious or very serious mistakes or lapses from conduct which is so bad that it ought to be criminal. The threshold is therefore a high one.

One of the criticisms that is made of the law is that the test for establishing whether the breach was gross is circular. In *Misra*, the Court of Appeal addressed these concerns.

Judge LJ [reading the judgment of the court:]

28. Mr Michael Gledhill QC on behalf of Dr Misra submitted that manslaughter by gross negligence is an offence which lacks certainty. As presently understood, it requires the trial judge to direct the jury that the defendant should be convicted of manslaughter by gross negligence if they are satisfied that his conduct was 'criminal'. Indeed, the effect of his argument was that it is a separate additional ingredient of this offence that the jury has to decide whether the defendant's conduct amounted to a crime. Relying in particular on the Law Commission paper on Involuntary Manslaughter (Law Com. No. 237 [1996]) as a convenient summary of a good deal of the debate by distinguished academic commentators, he suggested that the current test is 'circular'. It is this circularity which leads to uncertainty. Mr Gledhill drew attention to, and adopted for the purposes for his argument, the way in which the Law Commission identified the potential problems arising from linking the civil and the criminal law concepts of negligence where the allegation against the defendant arose from omission. This was such a case. 'It is by no means certain that the scope of liability for negligent omissions is the same in criminal law as it is in tort.' The principles were 'so unclear' that it is difficult to tell whether 'the law as currently understood represents a change, and if so, what the implications might be.' The relevant part of the Law Commission paper ends, 'It is possible that the law in this area fails to meet the standard of certainty required by the European Convention on Human Rights (ECHR).' In Mr Gledhill's submission this is an understatement: the standard of certainty is not met.

29. To develop his argument on uncertainty, Mr Gledhill focussed our attention on art 7 of the ECHR, entitled 'No punishment without law', which provides:

'7(1) No-one shall be held guilty of any criminal offence on account of any act or omission which did not constitute a criminal offence under national or international law at the time when it was committed nor shall a heavier penalty be imposed than the one that was applicable at the time the criminal offence was committed.'

In our view the essential thrust of this Article is to prohibit the creation of offences, whether by legislation or the incremental development of the common law, which have retrospective application. It reflects a well-understood principle of domestic law, that conduct which did not contravene the criminal law at the time when it took place should not retrospectively be stigmatised as criminal, or expose the perpetrator to punishment. As Lord Reid explained in *Waddington v Miah* [1974] 2 All ER 377, [1974] 59 Cr App R 149 at p. 150 and 151,

'There has for a very long time been a strong feeling against making legislation, and particularly criminal legislation, retrospective. . . . I use retrospective in the sense of authorising people being punished for what they did before the Act came into force.'

[His lordship reviewed English common law authorities for the principle of legality.]

34. . . . In summary, it is not to be supposed that prior to the implementation of the Human Rights Act 1998, either this Court, or the House of Lords, would have been indifferent to or unaware of the need for the criminal law in particular to be predictable and certain. Vague laws which purport to create criminal liability are undesirable, and in extreme cases, where it occurs, their very vagueness may make it impossible to identify the conduct which is prohibited by a criminal sanction. If the court is forced to guess at the ingredients of a purported crime any conviction for it would be unsafe. That said, however, the requirement is for sufficient rather than absolute certainty.

[His lordship referred to the ECHR case law on the requirement of certainty and continued:]

37. Since the implementation of the Human Rights Act, the issue of uncertainty has also been addressed on a number of occasions in this court. It has been decided that the offence of making

indecent photographs of children was sufficiently certain to satisfy arts 8 and 10 of the Convention (*R v Smethurst* [2001] EWCA Crim 772, [2002] 1 Cr App Rep 50, 165 JP 377); that the offence of publishing an obscene article satisfies the requirements of art 7 of the Convention (*R v Perrin* [2002] EWCA Crim 747); and that the offence of causing a public nuisance, by sending an envelope through the post containing salt, which was suspected to be anthrax, contrary to common law, was also sufficiently certain to satisfy the requirements of art 7, 8 and 10 of the Convention (*R v Goldstein* [2003] EWCA Crim 3450, [2004] 1 Cr App R 388). In each case the uncertainty argument was rejected. In *Goldstein* itself, at p. 395, Latham LJ commented:

'The elements of the offence are sufficiently clear to enable a person, with appropriate legal advice if necessary, to regulate his behaviour. . . . A citizen, appropriately advised, could foresee that the conduct identified was capable of amounting to a public nuisance.'

In our judgment, the incorporation of the ECHR, while providing a salutary reminder, has not effected any significant extension of or change to the 'certainty' principle as long understood at common law.

[His lordship dealt with the issues of recklessness and gross negligence discussed later in the chapter.]

58. We can now return to the argument based on circularity and uncertainty, and the application of arts 6 and 7 of the ECHR. The most important passages in the speech of Lord Mackay on the issue of circularity read:

'. . . The jury must go on to consider whether that breach of duty should be characterised as gross negligence and therefore as a crime. This will depend on the seriousness of the breach of duty committed by the defendant in all the circumstances in which the defendant was placed when it occurred. The jury will have to consider whether the extent to which the defendant's conduct departed from the proper standard of care incumbent upon him, involving as it must have done a risk of death to the patient, was such that it should be judged criminal.

It is true that, to a certain extent, this involves an element of circularity, but in this branch of the law I do not believe that is fatal to its being correct as a test of how far conduct must depart from accepted standards to be characterised as criminal . . . The essence of the matter which is supremely a jury question is whether, having regard to the risk of death involved, the conduct of the defendant was so bad in all the circumstances as to amount in their judgment to a criminal act or omission.'

59. Mr Gledhill suggested that this passage demonstrated that an additional specific ingredient of this offence was that the jury had to decide whether the defendant's conduct amounted to a crime. If the jury could, or was required to, define the offence for itself, and accordingly might do so on some unaccountable or unprincipled or unexplained basis, to adopt Bacon, the sound given by the law would indeed be uncertain, and would then strike without warning. Mr Gledhill's argument then would be compelling.

60. Looking at the authorities since *Bateman*, the purpose of referring to the differences between civil and criminal liability, whether in the passage in Lord Mackay's speech to which we have just referred, or in directions to the jury, is to highlight that the burden on the prosecution goes beyond proof of negligence for which compensation would be payable. Negligence of that degree could not lead to a conviction for manslaughter. The negligence must be so bad, 'gross', that if all the other ingredients of the offence are proved, then it amounts to a crime and is punishable as such.

61. This point was addressed by Lord Atkin in *Andrews* at p. 582, when he referred to *Williamson* (1807) 3 C&P 635:

'. . . where a man who practiced as an accoucheur, owing to a mistake in his observation of the actual symptoms, inflicted on a patient terrible injuries from which she died.'

To substantiate that charge—namely, manslaughter—Lord Ellenborough said, 'The prisoner must have been guilty of criminal misconduct, arising either from the grossest ignorance or the most criminal inattention.' The word 'criminal' in any attempt to define a crime is perhaps not the most helpful: but it is plain that the Lord Chief Justice meant to indicate to the jury a high degree of negligence. So at a much later date in *Bateman* (1925) 18 Cr. App. R 8 a charge of manslaughter was made against a qualified medical practitioner in similar circumstances to those of *Williamson's* case . . . I think with respect that the expressions used are not, indeed they were probably not intended to be, a precise definition of the crime.

62. Accordingly, the value of references to the criminal law in this context is that they avoid the danger that the jury may equate what we may describe as 'simple' negligence, which in relation to manslaughter would not be a crime at all, with negligence which involves a criminal offence. In short, by bringing home to the jury the extent of the burden on the prosecution, they ensure that the defendant whose negligence does not fall within the ambit of the criminal law is not convicted of a crime. They do not alter the essential ingredients of this offence. A conviction cannot be returned if the negligent conduct is or may be less than gross. If however the defendant is found by the jury to have been grossly negligent, then, if the jury is to act in accordance with its duty, he must be convicted. This is precisely what Lord Mackay indicated when, in the passage already cited, he said, '. . . The jury must go on to consider whether that breach of duty should be characterised as gross negligence and therefore as a crime' (our emphasis). The decision whether the conduct was criminal is described not as 'the' test, but as 'a' test as to how far the conduct in question must depart from accepted standards to be 'characterised as criminal'. On proper analysis, therefore, the jury is not deciding whether the particular defendant ought to be convicted on some unprincipled basis. The question for the jury is not whether the defendant's negligence was gross, and whether, additionally, it was a crime, but whether his behaviour was grossly negligent and consequently criminal. This is not a question of law, but one of fact, for decision in the individual case.

63. On examination, this represents one example, among many, of problems which juries are expected to address on a daily basis. They include equally difficult questions, such as whether a defendant has acted dishonestly, by reference to contemporary standards, or whether he has acted in reasonable self-defence, or, when charged with causing death by dangerous driving, whether the standards of his driving fell far below what should be expected of a competent and careful driver. These examples represent the commonplace for juries. Each of these questions could be said to be vague and uncertain. If he made enquiries in advance, at most an individual would be told the principle of law which the jury would be directed to apply: he could not be advised what a jury would think of the individual case, and how it would be decided. That involves an element of uncertainty about the outcome of the decision-making process, but not unacceptable uncertainty about the offence itself.

64. In our judgment the law is clear. The ingredients of the offence have been clearly defined, and the principles decided in the House of Lords in *Adomako*. They involve no uncertainty. The hypothetical citizen, seeking to know his position, would be advised that, assuming he owed a duty of care to the deceased which he had negligently broken, and that death resulted, he would be liable to conviction for manslaughter if, on the available evidence, the jury was satisfied that his negligence was gross. A doctor would be told that grossly negligent treatment of a patient which exposed him or her to the risk of death, and caused it, would constitute manslaughter.

65. After Lord Williams' sustained criticism of the offence of manslaughter by gross negligence, the House of Lords in *Adomako* clarified the relevant principles and the ingredients of this offence. Although, to a limited extent, Lord Mackay accepted that there was an element of circularity in the process by which the jury would arrive at its verdict, the element of circularity which he identified did not then and does not now result in uncertainty which offends against Article 7, nor if we may say so, any principle of common law. Gross negligence manslaughter is not incompatible with the ECHR. Accordingly the appeal arising from the question certified by the trial judge must be dismissed.

[His lordship reviewed the facts.]

Appeals dismissed

≈≈ *Questions*

(1) How will a defendant know with certainty whether the conduct he is engaged in performing negligently will be regarded as being so grossly negligent as to constitute the offence of manslaughter?

(2) The court explains that 'a doctor would be told that grossly negligent treatment of a patient which exposed him or her to the risk of death, and caused it, would constitute manslaughter' (at [64]). What should the response be when the doctor then asks how gross his negligent conduct has to be in order to be convicted? How can the relevant standard be described to the doctor otherwise than by reference to whether the jury thinks that it is criminal?

(3) Should gross negligence manslaughter be abolished? See O. Quick, 'Medicine, Mistakes and Manslaughter: A Criminal Combination?' (2010) 69 CLJ 186.

For further criticisms of the test, see V. Tadros, 'The Limits of Manslaughter' in C. Clarkson and S. Cunningham (eds), *Criminal Liability for Non Aggressive Death* (2008).

9.3.4 Gross negligence and mens rea

In *Misra*, the appellants also argued that in the light of the decision of the House of Lords in *G* the gross negligence manslaughter formulation should be abandoned in favour of a test of subjective reckless manslaughter. The Court of Appeal rejected this ground of appeal.

39. After he had fully considered the recent decision of the House of Lords in *R v G and Another* [2003] UKHL 50, [2004] 1 AC 1034, [section 5.3, p 98] Mr Gledhill deployed an additional argument which was not before Langley J. In essence, he submitted that with the exception of causing death by dangerous driving, no serious criminal offence could be committed without mens rea. He relied on what Lord Bingham, at para 32, described as a 'salutary principle that conviction of serious crime should depend on proof not simply that the defendant caused (by act or omission) an injurious result to another but that his state of mind when so acting was culpable'. Unless some element of mens rea, such, for example, as recklessness, was a necessary ingredient of manslaughter by gross negligence, this essential principle was contravened. . . .

55. It is convenient now to address the argument that the decision in *R v G and Another* should lead us to reassess whether gross negligence manslaughter should now be replaced by and confined to reckless manslaughter. As we have shown, precisely this argument by Lord Williams of Mostyn was rejected in *Adomako*. We also note, first, that Parliament has not given effect to possible reforms on this topic discussed by the Law Commission and, second, notwithstanding that *Adomako* was cited in argument in *R v G and Another*, it was not subjected to any reservations or criticisms. Indeed in his speech Lord Bingham of Cornhill emphasised that in *R v G* he was not addressing the meaning of 'reckless' in any other statutory or common law context than s 1(1) and (2) of the Criminal Damage Act 1971. In these circumstances, although we gave leave to Mr Gledhill to amend his grounds of appeal to enable him to deploy the argument, we reject it.

56. We can now reflect on Mr Gledhill's associated contention that if recklessness is not a necessary ingredient of this offence, the decision in *Attorney General's Reference (No. 2 of 1999)* [2000] QB 796, [2000] 3 All ER 182 led to the unacceptable conclusion that manslaughter by gross negligence did not require proof of any specific state of mind, and that the defendant's state of mind was irrelevant. In our judgment the submission is based on a narrow reading of the decision that a defendant may properly be convicted of gross negligence manslaughter in the absence of evidence as to his state of

mind. However when it is available, such evidence is not irrelevant to the issue of gross negligence. It will often be a critical factor in the decision (see *R (on the application of Rowley) v DPP* [2003] EWHC 693). In *Adomako* itself, Lord Mackay directed attention to 'all' of the circumstances in which the defendant was placed: he did not adopt, or endorse, or attempt to redefine the list of states of mind to which Lord Taylor CJ referred in *Prentice*, which was not in any event 'exhaustive' of possible relevant states of mind. It is therefore clear that the defendant is not to be convicted without fair considera- tion of all the relevant circumstances in which his breach of duty occurred. In each case, of course, the circumstances are fact-specific.

57. Mr Gledhill nevertheless contended that even so, the problem of mens rea remains. This, he argued was a necessary, but absent ingredient of the offence. We have reflected, of course, that if the defendant intends death or really serious harm, and acts in such a way to cause either, and death results, he would be guilty of murder. If he intends limited injury, and causes death, he would be guilty of manslaughter in any event. We are here concerned with the defendant who does not intend injury, but who in all the contemporaneous circumstances is grossly negligent. As a matter of strict language, 'mens rea' is concerned with an individual defendant's state of mind. Speaking generally, negligence is concerned with his failure to behave in accordance with the standards required of the reasonable man. Looked at in this way, the two concepts are distinct. However the term 'mens rea' is also used to describe the ingredient of fault or culpability required before criminal liability for the defendant's actions may be established. In *Sweet v Parsley* [1970] AC 132, [1969] 1 All ER 347, Lord Reid explained that there were occasions when gross negligence provided the 'necessary mental element' for a seri- ous crime. Manslaughter by gross negligence is not an absolute offence. The requirement for gross negligence provides the necessary element of culpability.

More recently, in *S* [2015] EWCA Crim 558, the Court of Appeal confirmed that in the context of gross negligence manslaughter there is no requirement for the prosecution to prove any mens rea. The court expressed the applicable test in these terms: 'whether a reasonable and prudent person of the applicant's age and experience would have foreseen a serious risk of death and, if so, whether the applicant's conduct fell so far below the standard of care required that it was grossly negligent such that it constituted a crime'.

≋ **Question**

Is the gross negligence formula more favourable to the defendant than the *Caldwell* reckless- ness form of mens rea?

A difference between recklessness and gross negligence is that the recklessness test did not include the requirement that the jury must be satisfied that D's conduct was bad enough to be a crime. A direction in *Caldwell* terms deprived D of the chance of acquittal on that ground. In *Prentice*, for example, there were many strongly mitigating factors in the doctors' conduct, which were irrelevant if the jury were concerned only with what was foreseeable, but highly relevant to the question whether their behaviour was bad enough to deserve condemnation as manslaughter.

Like Lord Atkin in *Andrews*, Lord Mackay in *Adomako* considers it 'perfectly appropriate' that the word 'reckless' should be used in cases of manslaughter but, again agreeing with Lord Atkin, 'in the ordinary connotation of that word' But what is the 'ordinary connotation of that word' which Lord Atkin and Lord Mackay had in mind?

Lord Mackay in *Adomako* gives as an example of where recklessness was used 'with com- plete accuracy' the case of *Stone and Dobinson* [1977] 2 All ER 341, [1977] QB 354, CA. There S and D, S's mistress, allowed S's sister to lodge with them. The sister became infirm while lodging with them and died of toxaemia from infected bed sores and prolonged immobiliza-tion. S and D had made only half-hearted and wholly ineffectual attempts to secure medical attention for the sister. Upholding the convictions of S and D for manslaughter, the court said (at 347):

> The duty which a defendant has undertaken is a duty of caring for the health and welfare of the infirm person. What the Crown has to prove is a breach of that duty in such circumstances that the jury feel convinced that the defendant's conduct can properly be described as reckless. That is to say a reckless disregard of danger to the health and welfare of the infirm person. Mere inadvertence is not enough. The defendant must be proved to have been indifferent to an obvious risk of injury to health, or actu-ally to have foreseen the risk but to have determined nevertheless to run it.

≈ *Questions*

(1) Is this statement entirely clear? Does it suggest, with its contrasting tests of indifference *or* foresight, that D may be accounted indifferent without actual foresight of the risk?

(2) The risk as to which it is stated D must be reckless, is a risk not of death but merely of 'health and welfare'. What does that mean? Is it now the law that if on a charge of man-slaughter the case against D proceeds on the basis of gross negligence, the prosecution must prove that the reasonable man would have foreseen that the conduct in question involved a risk of death, but if it proceeds on recklessness it is enough to prove that D was indifferent to or foresaw some risk much less than death? If so, is this defensible?

9.4 Reckless manslaughter

Manslaughter by advertent recklessness, that is, conscious risk-taking, still survives as a sepa-rate head of manslaughter.

It is necessary for this offence to exist in order to deal with cases where D kills, but has not performed an unlawful dangerous *act* (that form of manslaughter applies only to acts) and his conduct is such that it does not satisfy the test of gross negligence because, for example, it does not pose a risk of death. As we have seen, where D killed by an act (not unlawful apart from the fact that it is done recklessly) knowing that it was highly probable that he would cause serious bodily harm, before the decision in *Moloney* this would have been murder (*Hyam*). It must still be manslaughter. Where death is so caused, the jury do not have to decide whether it is 'bad enough' to amount to a crime. That question is appropriate only when we are concerned with degrees of negligence. The jury are not asked this question in non-fatal offences against the person which may be committed recklessly, so it would be quite inconsistent if it applied when death is caused. What is uncertain is whether there is a sufficient fault:

(1) when D's awareness of an unreasonable risk is of less than high probability; or

(2) where the risk he foresees is of bodily harm, less than serious bodily harm.

It is submitted that the better view is that reckless manslaughter includes (1) but not (2). Arguably, it should include (1) because a distinction based solely on the degree of probabil-ity is unsatisfactory since that is only one of many factors which may determine whether conduct is properly characterized as reckless. It should not include (2) because, by analogy with murder, manslaughter should be limited to cases where the known risk is of serious bodily harm.

R v Lidar (Narinder Singh)

(1999) Court of Appeal, Criminal Division (unreported)

(Evans LJ, Alliott and Jackson JJ)

The deceased, Kully, was killed when he was hanging on to a car, with half his body through the car window, fighting with the appellant who was driving. He was carried about 225 metres when his feet caught in the nearside rear wheel and he fell to the ground and was run over, suffering fatal crush injuries.

Evans LJ [his lordship reviewed the facts and the evidence:]

The relevant direction of law as regards manslaughter was this:

'In order for manslaughter to be proved in this case, the Crown have to prove that the defendant acted recklessly. Recklessly in this context means that the defendant foresaw that some physical harm, however slight, might result to Kully from driving the car as he did and yet ignoring that risk he nevertheless went on to drive as he did. Mere inadvertence is not enough. The defendant must have been proved to have been indifferent to an obvious risk of injury to health or actually to have foreseen the risk but to have determined nevertheless to run it. If you are sure that the defendant acted recklessly you find him guilty of manslaughter. If you are not sure you find him not guilty'.

[His lordship reviewed the grounds of appeal.]

Mr Beckman applied for leave to add a further ground, which is to the effect that the judge ought to have directed the jury that this was a case of 'gross negligence' manslaughter which they should approach in accordance with the House of Lords' judgment in *Adomako* [1995] 1 AC 171. Whether the submission was that the 'gross negligence' direction should be given in addition to or in substitution for the 'recklessness' direction in fact given was not made entirely clear, but there was no complaint about the terms in which the direction was given, if 'recklessness' was appropriate. The application to add this ground of appeal was not opposed by Mr Milmo QC for the prosecution, and we gave leave because of the connection which must exist between the proper definition of the offence of manslaughter and the relevance of the suggested defences of self-defence and necessity to it . . .

[His lordship dealt with the issue of self-defence.] . . .

In *Adomako* the House of Lords affirmed the characteristics of 'gross negligence' manslaughter and further held that there is no distinction in principle between motor manslaughter and other cases where gross negligence is the basis of criminal liability. The House of Lords also held that juries might properly be directed in terms of recklessness although the precise definition derived from *Seymour* [1983] 2 AC 493 should no longer be used (188A). Lord Mackay LC said this:

'I consider it perfectly appropriate that the word "reckless" be used in cases of involuntary manslaughter, but as Lord Atkin put it "in the ordinary connotation of that word." Examples in which this was done, in my mind with complete accuracy are *Reg v Stone* [1977] QB 354 and *Reg v West London Coroner ex parte Gray* [1988] QB 467 . . . I entirely agree with the view that the circumstances to which a charge of involuntary manslaughter may apply are so various that it is unwise to attempt to categorise or detail specimen directions. For my part I would not wish to go beyond the description of the basis in law which I have already given' (187H–188B).

Nothing here suggests that for the future 'recklessness' could no longer be a basis for proving the offence of manslaughter: rather, the opposite. *Smith & Hogan* records that 'For many years the courts have used the terms "recklessness" and "gross negligence" to describe the fault required for involuntary manslaughter . . . without any clear definition of either term. It was not clear whether these terms were merely two ways of describing the same thing, or whether they represented two distinct conditions of fault' (page 375). After referring to *Adomako*, the learned author continues

> '*Reckless manslaughter*. Gross negligence is a sufficient, but not necessarily the only fault for manslaughter. To some extent manslaughter by overt recklessness, conscious risk-taking still survives' (p.377).

He goes on to ask whether it is necessary for the offence of reckless manslaughter that the risk foreseen is of serious, rather than non-serious, bodily harm.

In our judgment, the judge was correct in his view that this was a case of 'reckless' manslaughter and to direct the jury accordingly. We reject the alternative submission that he was wrong not to direct the jury as to gross negligence manslaughter, whether in place of or in substitution for the direction as to recklessness. Indeed, in a case such as the present, we find it difficult to understand how the point of criminal liability can be reached, where gross negligence is alleged, without identifying the point by reference to the concept of recklessness as it is commonly understood: that is to say, whether the driver of the motor vehicle was aware of the necessary degree of risk of serious injury to the victim and nevertheless chose to disregard it, or was indifferent to it. If the gross negligence direction had been given, the recklessness direction would still have been necessary. The recklessness direction in fact given made the gross negligence direction superfluous and unnecessary.

. . .

Recklessness

The direction given by the judge might be said to be open to criticism for failing to specify, first, that there had to be a high probability of physical harm to Kully, and secondly, that the risk was of serious injury rather than, as the judge put it, 'injury to health' and 'some physical harm, however slight'. This criticism was not advanced as a ground of appeal, but we should nevertheless consider what force there might be in it. In our judgment, there is none, because in the circumstances of this case both requirements undoubtedly were satisfied. The risk of harm to Kully, of which the jury has found that the appellant was aware, was clearly and unarguably a high degree of risk of serious injury to him. In the circumstances, therefore, we are satisfied that the verdict could not be considered unsafe if there was a mis-direction in this respect.

Appeal dismissed

There is a great difference between subjective recklessness and a case of inadvertent negligence, like *Adomako*. Adomako was quite unaware of the risk his failure was causing to the life of the patient but in some cases the prosecution's case is based on a defendant's personal appreciation of the obvious and serious risk of death to someone. In those cases, the fault involved—subjective recklessness—is different, not merely in degree, but in kind, from the neglect which satisfies some regulatory offence, so the question of reconciling the two does not, or should not, arise.

The significance of the reckless manslaughter category may become more obvious in the light of the changes following the Supreme Court's landmark decision in *Jogee* [2016] UKSC 8 on joint enterprise. Under the law prior to that decision dealing with joint enterprise, D would be liable for murder where he participated with P in a joint criminal venture with a common purpose and P murdered V in the course of that and D foresaw that P might intentionally kill or do GBH. Post-*Jogee*, in such a case D would be convicted of manslaughter, D's liability might best be described as a form of reckless manslaughter. He has foreseen a risk of death or GBH. That may affect the likely sentence he receives. A reckless manslaughter where D has set out with P to commit a violent crime will be much more serious than many unlawful act manslaughters where no subjective mens rea needs to be proved.

9.5 Reform

9.5.1 Law Com No 237

The Law Commission (Law Com Report No 237, *Involuntary Manslaughter* (1996)) recommended the abolition of the common law offence of involuntary manslaughter and its replacement by two offences as follows:

1.—(1) A person who by his conduct causes the death of another is guilty of reckless killing if—

    (a) he is aware of a risk that his conduct will cause death or serious injury; and

    (b) it is unreasonable for him to take that risk having regard to the circumstances as he knows or believes them to be.

(2) A person guilty of reckless killing is liable on conviction on indictment to imprisonment for life.

2.—(1) A person who by his conduct causes the death of another is guilty of killing by gross carelessness if—

    (a) a risk that his conduct will cause death or serious injury would be obvious to a reasonable person in his position;

    (b) he is capable of appreciating that risk at the material time; and

    (c) either—

        (i) his conduct falls far below what can reasonably be expected of him in the circumstances; or

        (ii) he intends by his conduct to cause some injury or is aware of, and unreasonably takes, the risk that it may do so.

(2) There shall be attributed to the person referred to in subsection (1)(a) above—

    (a) knowledge of any relevant facts which the accused is shown to have at the material time; and

    (b) any skill or experience professed by him.

(3) In determining for the purposes of subsection (1)(c)(i) above what can reasonably be expected of the accused regard shall be had to the circumstances of which he can be expected to be aware, to any circumstances shown to be within his knowledge and to any other matter relevant for assessing his conduct at the material time.

(4) Subsection (1)(c)(ii) above applies only if the conduct causing, or intended to cause, the injury constitutes an offence.

(5) A person guilty of killing by gross carelessness is liable on conviction on indictment to imprisonment for a term not exceeding [ ] years.

9.5.2 Law Com No 304

In relation to unlawful act manslaughter, the Law Commission's latest recommendation (in Law Com Report No 304, *Murder, Manslaughter and Infanticide* (2006)) is that the offence will be recast as killing another person:

(a) through the commission of a criminal act intended by the defendant to cause injury, or

(b) through the commission of a criminal act that the defendant was aware involved a serious risk of causing some injury ('criminal act manslaughter').

The Law Commission's latest recommendations on gross negligence as part of the *Murder, Manslaughter and Infanticide* Report are that the offence be recast as follows:

A person is guilty of gross negligence manslaughter if:

(1) a person by his or her conduct causes the death of another;

(2) a risk that his or her conduct will cause death . . . would be obvious to a reasonable person in his or her position;

(3) he or she is capable of appreciating that risk at the material time; and

(4) . . . his or her conduct falls far below what can reasonably be expected of him or her in the circumstances.

The Law Commission recommends abolition of reckless manslaughter. The Commission suggests that all cases will now be adequately catered for in either (a) the new second degree murder offence where D realizes there is a serious risk of death from his conduct and intends to cause injury, or (b) the new version of gross negligence proposed above. The Commission has overstated the case here. Consider D who engages in an activity which 'because of his specialist knowledge' he realizes carries a risk of injury. That risk is not of a type that a reasonable person would appreciate. D kills V in the course of his activity. D cannot be liable for gross negligence: even though D's mental state can be considered by the jury in evaluating whether his conduct is grossly negligent, there is no objective risk of death. Nor is D guilty of second degree murder unless he sees a risk of death.

FURTHER READING

Unlawful act manslaughter

C. Clarkson and S. Cunningham (eds), *Criminal Liability for Non-Aggressive Death* (2008)

B. Mitchell, 'Minding the Gap in Unlawful and Dangerous Act Manslaughter: A Moral Defence for One-Punch Killers' (2008) 72 J Crim L 537

B. Mitchell, 'More Thoughts About Unlawful and Dangerous Act Manslaughter and the One-Punch Killer' [2009] Crim LR 502

B. Mitchell and R. D. Mackay, 'Investigating Involuntary Manslaughter: An Empirical Study of 127 Cases' (2011) 31 OJLS 165

W. Wilson, 'Dealing with Drug Induced Homicide' in C. Clarkson and S. Cunningham (eds), *Criminal Liability for Non-Aggressive Deaths* (2008)

Gross negligence manslaughter

S. Gardner, 'Manslaughter by Gross Negligence' (1995) 111 LQR 22

Law Commission Report No 237, *Involuntary Manslaughter* (1996), Part III

J. Stannard, 'From Andrews to Seymour and Back Again' (1996) 47 NILQ 1

G. Williams, 'Gross Negligence Manslaughter and Duty of Care in "Drugs" Cases: *R v Evans*' [2009] Crim LR 631

Reform

J. Horder, *Homicide and the Politics of Law Reform* (2012)

H. Keating, 'The Restoration of a Serious Crime' [1996] Crim LR 535

M. Wasik, 'Form and Function in the Law of Involuntary Manslaughter' [1994] Crim LR 883

10

Non-fatal offences against the person

Offences:

This chapter examines the non-fatal (non-sexual) offences against the person:

- assault at common law: any act by which D, intentionally or recklessly, causes V to apprehend immediate unlawful personal violence;

- battery at common law: any act by which D, intentionally or recklessly, inflicts unlawful personal violence upon V;

- assault occasioning actual bodily harm (ABH) (s 47 of the Offences Against the Person Act 1861 (OAPA)): intentional or reckless assault or battery which causes some bodily harm;

- maliciously wounding or inflicting grievous bodily harm (s 20 OAPA): unlawfully maliciously wounding or causing serious injury to another;

- causing grievous bodily harm with intent (s 18 OAPA);

- poisoning-type offences:

  - (s 23 OAPA) unlawfully and maliciously administering to or causing to be administered to or be taken by any other person any poison or other destructive or noxious thing, so as thereby to endanger the life of such person, or so as thereby to inflict upon such person any grievous bodily harm;

  - (s 24 OAPA) unlawfully and maliciously administering to or causing to be administered to or be taken by any other person any poison or other destructive or noxious thing, with intent to injure, aggrieve or annoy such person.

Some of the controversies that will be examined in this chapter include:

(1) whether psychiatric illness can amount to an offence against the person;

(2) what level of harm constitutes 'actual' bodily harm as opposed to 'grievous' bodily harm;

(3) whether actual bodily harm must be 'inflicted' or merely caused.

10.1 Introduction

The conduct examined in this chapter ranges from a trivial tap on the shoulder to levels of harm threatening life itself. The relevant offences are archaic in their definition and lacking in any coherent structure. They are, however, extremely important. Not only are they frequently prosecuted, but they also give rise to interesting questions on issues central to the criminal law, such as how the autonomy of the individual should be respected.

Although there is no formal ladder or hierarchy of offences something which has recently been criticized by the Law Commission (Consultation Paper No 217, *Reform of Offences Against the Person—A Scoping Consultation Paper* (2014) and Report No 361, *Offences Against the Person* (2015); see section 10.4.2.3, p 261 for discussion), it is traditional to begin with the two offences which involve the least harm.

It is important to bear in mind that these offences are not the only ones that criminalize those who cause another to suffer some form of harm. For example, ss 20 to 22 of the Criminal Justice and Courts Act 2015 criminalize care workers who ill-treat or wilfully neglect those in their care. This chapter will be solely concerned with the relevant common law offences and those contained in the Offences Against the Person Act 1861, however.

10.2 Assault and battery

An assault is any act by which D, intentionally or recklessly, causes V to apprehend immediate unlawful personal violence. A battery is any act by which D, intentionally or recklessly, inflicts unlawful personal violence upon V. But 'violence' here includes any unlawful touching of another, however slight.

Assault and battery are two separate offences, and each is also a core element of more serious aggravated offences—for example, assaulting a police officer in the execution of his duty, assault occasioning actual bodily harm, etc. Understanding the offences of assault and battery is therefore extremely important. It is also important to appreciate that an allegation of battery does not also include an allegation of assault. The Court of Appeal made this clear in *Nelson* [2013] EWCA Crim 30. Keith J stated that:

> 7. As we have said, the offence of common assault is committed when the defendant does something of a physical kind which causes someone else to apprehend that they are about to be struck. It follows that an ingredient of the offence of common assault is that that has to have been apprehended by the person who is alleged to have been the victim of that assault. Such an apprehension, however, is not required for the offence of assault by beating. As *Smith & Hogan's Criminal Law* (2011), 13th ed, says at p 623:
>
>> 'It used to be said that every battery involves an assault; but that is plainly not so, for in battery there need be no apprehension of the impending violence. A blow from behind is not any less a battery because [the victim] was unaware that it was coming.'
>
> It follows that because one of the ingredients of the offence of common assault is not among the ingredients of the offence of [battery] an allegation of [battery] does not amount to or include, whether expressly or by implication, an allegation of common assault.

Criminal Justice Act 1988, s 39

> Common assault and battery shall be summary offences and a person guilty of either of them shall be liable to [an unlimited] fine, to imprisonment for a term not exceeding six months, or to both.

The CPS charging standards advise that the appropriate charge is assault or battery (rather than aggravated assaults) where the injuries sustained amount to no more than: grazes, scratches, abrasions, minor bruising, swellings, reddening of the skin, superficial cuts or a 'black eye'.

10.2.1 The elements of assault and battery

10.2.1.1 Apprehending/suffering unlawful violence

In assault the victim must apprehend (ie anticipate rather than be in fear of) immediate unlawful violence; in battery he must suffer such violence. In *Collins v Wilcock* [1984] 3 All ER 374, the Divisional Court confirmed that, 'The fundamental principle, plain and incontestable, is that every person's body is inviolate. It has long been established that any touching of another person, however slight, may amount to a battery.' The court clarified that not every touching will constitute a battery, however.

Generally speaking, consent is a defence to battery; and most of the physical contacts of ordinary life are not actionable because they are impliedly consented to by all who move in society and so expose themselves to the risk of bodily contact. So nobody can complain of the jostling which is inevitable from his presence in, for example, a supermarket, an underground station or a busy street; nor can a person who attends a party complain if his hand is seized in friendship, or even if his back is (within reason) slapped (see *Tubervell v Savage* (1669) 1 Mod Rep 3, 86 ER 684). Although such cases are regarded as examples of implied consent, it is more common nowadays to treat them as falling within a general exception embracing all physical contact which is generally acceptable in the ordinary conduct of daily life.

Robert Goff LJ said in delivering the judgment of the court that, 'The law draws a distinction, in terms more easily understood by philologists than by ordinary citizens, between assault and battery.' However difficult it may be for the ordinary citizen to understand the distinction, it is essential for lawyers to do so. Assault and battery are distinct crimes with distinctive features. The distinction between the two has become blurred partly because the word 'assault' is commonly used (the *Oxford English Dictionary* so uses it) to include a battery, and partly because one and the same act (a punch on the nose, a kick on the shin) commonly amounts to both an assault and a battery. But, as Robert Goff LJ goes on to explain, a battery involves an unlawful and unwanted contact with the body of another while assault involves causing another to apprehend an unlawful unwanted contact.

≈≈≈ *Questions*

What offences does D commit in the following circumstances:

(1) he sneaks up on V and strikes V on the back of the head with a blunt instrument;

(2) he sneaks up on V intending to strike V on the back of the head, swings his weapon but misses;

(3) he aims a gun, which he knows to be unloaded, at V's face and threatens to shoot V and V believes the gun is loaded;

(4) he aims a gun at V which he knows to be unloaded and threatens to shoot V and V also knows the gun is unloaded;

(5) he aims a gun at V which he believes to be unloaded and threatens to shoot V and V also believes the gun to be unloaded but, unknown to both, the gun is in fact loaded and when D pulls the trigger V is shot and injured?

One very controversial question which had been debated for centuries was whether there could be an assault by words alone—can D cause V to apprehend immediate unlawful violence as much by shouting at V as by shaking his fist at V? The House of Lords considered these issues in the next case.

R v Ireland; R v Burstow

[1997] UKHL 34, House of Lords

(Lords Goff, Slynn, Steyn, Hope and Hutton)

Ireland made repeated silent telephone calls, mostly at night, to three women who consequently suffered psychiatric illness. His conviction on three counts of assault occasioning
actual bodily harm (s 47) (section 10.4, p 256) was upheld by the Court of Appeal, holding that
since repeated telephone calls could cause the victim to apprehend immediate and unlawful
violence, his conduct was capable of amounting to assault and that psychiatric injury could
amount to actual bodily harm.

Burstow had conducted an eight-month campaign of harassment against a woman, including both silent and abusive telephone calls. She was fearful of personal violence and a psychiatrist testified that she was suffering from a severe depressive illness. B's appeal against
conviction on one count of unlawfully and maliciously inflicting grievous bodily harm contrary to s 20 of the 1861 Act (section 10.4, p 256) was dismissed by the Court of Appeal on the
ground that psychiatric injury could amount to GBH under s 20. At the time the Protection
from Harassment Act 1997 was not in force.

[Lord Goff and Lord Slynn said they agreed with the speech of Lord Steyn.]

Lord Steyn:

My Lords, it is easy to understand the terrifying effect of a campaign of telephone calls at night by a
silent caller to a woman living on her own. It would be natural for the victim to regard the calls as menacing. What may heighten her fear is that she will not know what the caller may do next. The spectre
of the caller arriving at her doorstep bent on inflicting personal violence on her may come to dominate
her thinking. After all, as a matter of common sense, what else would she be terrified about? The victim may suffer psychiatric illness such as anxiety neurosis or acute depression. Harassment of women
by repeated silent telephone calls, accompanied on occasions by heavy breathing, is apparently a
significant social problem. That the criminal law should be able to deal with this problem, and so far as
is practicable, afford effective protection to victims is self-evident.

From the point of view, however, of the general policy of our law towards the imposition of
criminal responsibility, three specific features of the problem must be faced squarely. First, the
medium used by the caller is the telephone: arguably it differs qualitatively from a face-to-face offer
of violence to a sufficient extent to make a difference. Secondly, ex hypothesi the caller remains
silent: arguably a caller may avoid the reach of the criminal law by remaining silent however menacing the context may be. Thirdly, it is arguable that the criminal law does not take into account 'mere'
psychiatric illnesses.

[His lordship considered the use of offences under the Telecommunications Act (now the
Communications Act 2003, s 127) and the offences under the Protection from Harassment Act 1997.]

It is now necessary to consider whether the making of silent telephone calls causing psychiatric
injury is capable of constituting an assault under section 47. The Court of Appeal, as constituted in
Ireland, answered that question in the affirmative. There has been substantial academic criticism
of the conclusion and reasoning in *Ireland*: see *Archbold News*, Issue 6, 12 July 1996, *Archbold's
Criminal Pleading, Evidence & Practice* (1995), Supplement No 4 (1996) pp 345–347, Smith and
Hogan *Criminal Law*, 8th ed. [1996] 413, Herring 'Assault by Telephone' [1997] C.L.J. 11, and 'Assault'
by Jonathan Herring [1997] Crim L.R. 434, 435–436. Counsel's arguments, broadly speaking, challenged the [Court of Appeal] decision in *Ireland* on very similar lines. Having carefully considered

the literature and counsel's arguments, I have come to the conclusion that the appeal ought to be dismissed.

The starting point must be that an assault is an ingredient of the offence under section 47. It is necessary to consider the two forms which an assault may take. The first is battery, which involves the unlawful application of force by the defendant upon the victim. Usually, section 47 is used to prosecute in cases of this kind. The second form of assault is an act causing the victim to apprehend an imminent application of force upon her: see *Fagan v Metropolitan Police Commissioner* [1969] 1 Q.B. 439, 444D–E).

One point can be disposed of, quite briefly. The Court of Appeal was not asked to consider whether silent telephone calls resulting in psychiatric injury is capable of constituting a battery. But encouraged by some academic comment it was raised before your Lordships' House. Counsel for Ireland was most economical in his argument on the point. I will try to match his economy of words. In my view it is not feasible to enlarge the generally accepted legal meaning of what is a battery to include the circumstances of a silent caller who causes psychiatric injury.

It is to assault in the form of an act causing the victim to fear an immediate application of force to her that I must turn. Counsel argued that as a matter of law an assault can never be committed by words alone and therefore it cannot be committed by silence. The premise depends on the slenderest authority, namely an observation by Holroyd J to a jury that 'no words or singing are equivalent to an assault': see *Meade's and Belt's Case* (1823) 1 Lew C.C. 184. The proposition that a gesture may amount to an assault, but that words can never suffice, is unrealistic and indefensible. A thing said is also a thing done. There is no reason why something said should be incapable of causing an apprehension of immediate personal violence, eg a man accosting a woman in a dark alley saying 'come with me or I will stab you'. I would, therefore, reject the proposition that an assault can never be committed by words.

That brings me to the critical question whether a silent caller may be guilty of an assault. The answer to this question seems to me to be 'yes, depending on the facts'. It involves questions of fact within the province of the jury. After all, there is no reason why a telephone caller who says to a woman in a menacing way 'I will be at your door in a minute or two' may not be guilty of an assault if he causes his victim to apprehend immediate personal violence. Take now the case of the silent caller. He intends by his silence to cause fear and he is so understood. The victim is assailed by uncertainty about his intentions. Fear may dominate her emotions, and it may be the fear that the caller's arrival at her door may be imminent. She may fear the *possibility* of immediate personal violence. As a matter of law the caller may be guilty of an assault: whether he is or not will depend on the circumstance and in particular on the impact of the caller's potentially menacing call or calls on the victim. Such a prosecution case under section 47 may be fit to leave to the jury. And a trial judge may, depending on the circumstances, put a common sense consideration before [the] jury, namely what, if not the possibility of imminent personal violence, was the victim terrified about?

I conclude that an assault may be committed in the particular factual circumstances which I have envisaged. For this reason I reject the submission that as a matter of law a silent telephone caller cannot ever be guilty of an offence under section 47. In these circumstances no useful purpose would be served by answering the vague certified question in *Ireland*.

Having concluded that the legal arguments advanced on behalf of Ireland on section 47 must fail, I nevertheless accept that the concept of an assault involving immediate personal violence as an ingredient of the section 47 offence is a considerable complicating factor in bringing prosecutions under it in respect of silent telephone callers and stalkers. That the least serious of the ladder of offences is difficult to apply in such cases is unfortunate.

10.2.1.2 Immediacy

Earlier cases showed a tendency to take a generous view of 'immediacy'. In *Lewis* [1970] Crim LR 647, D was uttering threats from another room. In *Logdon v DPP* [1976] Crim LR 121, it was held that D committed an assault by showing V a pistol in a drawer and declaring that he would hold her hostage. In *Smith v Chief Superintendent of Woking Police Station* (1983) 76 Cr App R 234, [1983] Crim LR 323 (assault by looking through the window of a bed-sitting room at V in her nightclothes with intent to frighten her), Kerr LJ limited his decision to a case where D 'is immediately adjacent, albeit on the other side of a window' and distinguished, without dissenting from, the opinion in the fourth edition of *Smith and Hogan* (1978) that 'there can be no assault if it is obvious to V that D is unable to carry out his threat, as where D shakes his fist at V who is safely locked inside his car'. There may be an assault although D has no means of carrying out the threat. The question is whether he intends to cause V to believe that he can and will carry it out and whether V does so believe. This is consistent with offences against the person being result crimes rather than conduct crimes.

In *Ireland*, the House of Lords did no more than reject the submission that a silent telephone caller can *never* be guilty of assault. Lords Slynn and Hutton made it clear that the House was not deciding how the concept of immediacy should be applied or whether it was satisfied in *Ireland*. If the caller says, 'There's a bomb under your house which I am about to detonate' there would seem to be a clear case of assault. What about Lord Steyn's suggestion of the caller who says, 'I will be at your door in a minute or two'? Notice that it is not enough that the victim is immediately alarmed. He must anticipate that something is going to happen *immediately*. In *Constanza* [1997] 2 Cr App R 492, [1997] Crim LR 576, D made numerous silent telephone calls, sent over 800 letters to V, repeatedly drove past her home and on three occasions wrote offensive words on her front door. She received two letters on 4 and 12 June which she interpreted as clear threats. D's conviction of assault occasioning actual bodily harm was upheld. It is easy to accept that V was immediately put in fear but did she really apprehend *immediate* violence when she read letters at the breakfast table? See also *Cox* [1998] Crim LR 810 and commentary. Is the offence of assault fitted to deal with an ongoing campaign of this kind?

Lord Hope in *Ireland* says that, in the case of a telephone call, the silence conveys a message to V and that it is, perhaps, otherwise where the parties are in the same room. The caller does something more than remain silent; he rings up. What if he is present and merely gives a hard stare, or glowers? Is the question for the jury simply 'Are you sure that D's conduct caused V to apprehend immediate violence and that D intended that it should, or knew that it might?' Is there any difference in principle between a gesture (which can certainly be an assault) and a glare?

10.2.1.3 Mens rea

For assault, the defendant must intend or be subjectively reckless as to whether the victim apprehends immediate unlawful violence. For battery, the defendant must intend or be reckless as to whether he causes unlawful personal violence to the victim. These principles were confirmed by the Court of Appeal in *Venna* [1975] 3 All ER 788.

The reference to recklessness in *Venna* is clearly a reference to *Cunningham* recklessness, that is, requiring foresight by the defendant of the risk of the physical contact to another which occurs (battery) or the apprehension by another of physical contact (assault) and going on to take that risk. Since *G* [2003] UKHL 50 (section 5.3, p 98) there can be no suggestion that *Caldwell*-type recklessness has any part to play in offences against the person.

Hostility

Robert Goff LJ addresses the issue of hostility in *Collins v Wilcock*, section 10.2.1.1, p 251, and appears to conclude that hostility is not an ingredient of assault and battery. His lordship says that nobody can complain of the jostling which is inevitable in a supermarket, underground station or a busy street. It is not unknown, for example, for numbers of football supporters returning from a game to dash through shopping precincts, shouting obscenities and rudely pushing shoppers aside. Do they commit a battery? If so, is this because their jostling is accompanied by rudeness or hostility or for some other reason?

In *Brown*, section 11.4.2, p 288, the case of sadomasochists injuring each other, Lord Jauncey appears to accept that hostility is an ingredient of assault but concludes, 'If the appellants' activities in relation to the receivers [of the painful injury] were unlawful they were also hostile and a necessary ingredient of assault was present.' But if the act is unlawful, as it must be to constitute an assault or battery, does it add anything to the ingredients of the crimes to say that it is therefore hostile? In *B* [2013] EWCA Crim 3, in which D was charged with common assault for force-feeding V, the Court of Appeal stated *obiter* that:

> The element of assault frequently and usefully described as hostility is a means of conveying to the jury that some non-hostile contact is an ordinary incident of life to which we all impliedly consent.

~~~ *Questions*

D pats V, a complete stranger, on the back in an exuberant fashion at V's birthday party. Why is D not guilty of battery? Is it because there is no hostility? Is it because he has a genuine belief in the consent of V to that action?

10.2.1.4 Unlawfulness

The physical contact which D must cause V to apprehend in assault and actually cause in a battery must be unlawful violence. In *Blackburn v Bowering* [1994] 3 All ER 380, the Court of Appeal emphasized that the judge was wrong to rule that it was irrelevant to D's liability that he thought that he was acting lawfully.

10.3 Consent and assault

The subject of consent to offences against the person is dealt with in detail in the next chapter. For present purposes it is sufficient to note that consent will only be valid if:

(1) V has (or D believes that V has) given true consent—not therefore where, for example, V has been deceived or acts under threats or duress; and

(2) the level of harm consented to (or which D believes V has consented to) is assault or battery or a greater level of harm arising in an exceptional activity (surgery, sports, etc).

The courts have not resolved expressly whether consent is an element of actus reus or a defence, as the next chapter will discuss in greater detail.

10.4 Occasioning actual bodily harm, wounding, inflicting GBH and causing GBH

Three closely related offences under the Offences Against the Person Act 1861 (OAPA) require consideration. They are, in ascending order of gravity:

Section 47

Whoever shall be convicted upon an indictment of any assault occasioning actual bodily harm shall be liable [to imprisonment for five years] . . .

Section 20

Whoever shall unlawfully and maliciously wound or inflict any grievous bodily harm upon any other person either with or without any weapon or instrument, shall be guilty . . . [of an offence and liable to imprisonment for five years].

Section 18

Whosoever shall unlawfully and maliciously by any means whatsoever wound or cause any grievous bodily harm to any person . . . with intent . . . to do some grievous bodily harm to any person, or with intent to resist or prevent the lawful apprehension of any person, shall be guilty . . . [of an offence and liable to imprisonment for life].

CPS charging standards recommend charging s 47 where there is a loss or breakage of teeth, loss of consciousness, extensive or multiple bruising, displaced broken nose, minor fractures, minor non-superficial cuts or psychiatric injury. By comparison, examples of what would usually amount to s 20 include: injury resulting in permanent disability or permanent loss of sensory function; injury which results in more than minor permanent, visible disfigurement; broken or displaced limbs or bones, including fractured skull; compound fractures, broken cheek bone, jaw, ribs, etc; injuries which cause substantial loss of blood, usually necessitating a transfusion; injuries resulting in lengthy treatment or incapacity; psychiatric injury (CPS Charging Standard http://www.cps.gov.uk/legal/l_to_o/offences_against_the_person/index.html#a15).

10.4.1 Section 47: occasioning actual bodily harm

The offence under s 47 can be committed by D assaulting V or battering V and causing V a level of injury amounting to actual bodily harm. D's mens rea need only be an intention or subjective recklessness as to the assault or battery. It is not necessary to prove that D intended or was reckless as to causing any actual bodily harm. It is a constructive crime.

In *DPP v Smith* [2006] EWHC 94 (Admin), D sat on top of V and cut off the pony tail at the back of her head, without her consent. The victim accepted that there were no cuts to her scalp or other breaks of the skin caused while her hair was being cut. D submitted that there was no actual bodily harm and the critical ingredient of the offence had not been established. The justices acceded to that submission. The prosecution appealed by way of case stated. The Divisional Court held, allowing the prosecutor's appeal, that having regard to the dictionary definitions, in ordinary language 'harm' was not limited to 'injury' and extended to 'hurt' or 'damage'. 'Bodily', whether used as an adjective or adverb, was 'concerned with the body'. It was settled law that evidence of external bodily injury, or a break in or bruise to the surface of the skin, was not required for there to be an assault occasioning actual bodily harm. It applied to all parts of the body including the victim's organs, his nervous system and his brain. Furthermore, an assault occasioning actual bodily harm might be committed by words or gestures alone, without the need for any physical contact between the assailant and the body of the victim. Therefore, physical pain consequent on an assault was not a necessary ingredient of the offence. It followed that the respondent's actions in cutting off a substantial part of the victim's hair in the course of an assault on her, was capable of amounting to an assault which occasioned actual bodily harm. Whether it was alive beneath the surface of the skin or dead tissue above the surface of the skin, the hair was an attribute and part of the human body. It was intrinsic to each individual and to the identity of each individual. Previous authority establishes that actual bodily harm comprises 'any hurt or injury calculated to interfere with the health or comfort of the victim': *Donovan* [1934] 2 KB 498.

Smith is authority *only* for the proposition that on these facts the magistrates would be entitled to find that cutting off a *substantial* amount of a person's hair without consent is *capable* of amounting to actual bodily harm.

It has been accepted by the House of Lords in *Ireland* that actual bodily harm can include either physical injury or psychiatric injury.

R v Ireland; R v Burstow
(section 10.2.1.1, p 252)

Lord Steyn:

It will now be convenient to consider the question which is common to the two appeals, namely whether psychiatric illness is capable of amounting to bodily harm in terms of sections 18, 20 and 47 of the Act of 1861. The answer must be the same for the three sections . . .

. . . [C]ourts of law can only act on the best scientific understanding of the day. Some elementary distinctions can be made. The appeals under consideration do not involve structural injuries to the brain such as might require the intervention of a neurologist. One is also not considering either psychotic illness or personality disorders. The victims in the two appeals suffered from no such conditions. As a result of the behaviour of the appellants they did not develop psychotic or psychoneurotic conditions. The case was that they developed mental disturbances of a lesser order, namely neurotic disorders. For present purposes the relevant forms of neurosis are anxiety disorders and depressive disorders. Neuroses must be distinguished from simple states of fear, or problems in coping with everyday life. Where the line is to be drawn must be a matter of psychiatric judgment. But for present purposes it is important to note that modern psychiatry treats neuroses as recognisable psychiatric illnesses: see *Liability for Psychiatric Illness*, Law Commission Consultation Paper No 137 (1995) Part III (The Medical Background) and Mullany and Handford *Tort Liability for Psychiatric Damage* (1993), discussion on 'A medical perspective' pp 24–42, and particular at 30, footnote 88). Moreover, it is essential to bear in mind that neurotic illnesses affect the central nervous system of the body, because emotions such as fear and anxiety are brain functions. . . .

[His lordship referred to developments in the civil law.]

The criminal law has been slow to follow this path. But in *Reg v Chan-Fook* [1994] 1 WLR 689 the Court of Appeal squarely addressed the question whether psychiatric injury may amount to bodily harm under section 47 of the Act of 1861. The issue arose in a case where the defendant had aggressively questioned and locked in a suspected thief. There was a dispute as to whether the defendant had physically assaulted the victim. But the prosecution also alleged that even if the victim had suffered no physical injury, he had been reduced to a mental state which amounted to actual bodily harm under section 47. No psychiatric evidence was given. The judge directed the jury that an assault which caused an hysterical and nervous condition was an assault occasioning actual bodily harm. The defendant was convicted. Upon appeal the conviction was quashed on the ground of misdirections in the summing up and the absence of psychiatric evidence to support the prosecution's alternative case. The interest of the decision lies in the reasoning on psychiatric injury in the context of section 47. In a detailed and careful judgment given on behalf of the court Hobhouse L.J. said (at p695G–H:

> 'The first question on the present appeal is whether the inclusion of the word "bodily" in the phrase "actual bodily harm" limits harm to harm to the skin, flesh and bones of the victim . . . The body of the victim includes all parts of his body, including his organs, his nervous system and his brain. Bodily injury therefore may include injury to any of those parts of his body responsible for his mental and other faculties.'

In concluding that 'actual bodily harm' is capable of including psychiatric injury Hobhouse L.J. emphasised (at p. 696C) that—

> 'it does not include mere emotions such as fear or distress nor panic nor does it include, as such, states of mind that are not themselves evidence of some identifiable clinical condition.'

He observed that in the absence of psychiatric evidence a question whether or not an assault occasioned psychiatric injury should not be left to the jury. . . .

The proposition that the Victorian legislator when enacting sections 18, 20 and 47 of the Act of 1861, would not have had in mind psychiatric illness is no doubt correct. Psychiatry was in its infancy in 1861. But the subjective intention of the draftsman is immaterial. The only relevant inquiry is as to the sense of the words in the context in which they are used. Moreover the Act of 1861 is a statute of the 'always speaking' type: the statute must be interpreted in the light of the best current scientific appreciation of the link between the body and psychiatric injury.

For these reasons I would, therefore, reject the challenge to the correctness of *Chan-Fook* [1994] 1 WLR 689. In my view the ruling in that case was based on principled and cogent reasoning and it marked a sound and essential clarification of the law. I would hold that 'bodily harm' in sections 18, 20 and 47 must be interpreted so as to include recognizable psychiatric illness . . .

Expert evidence is required to prove a 'recognizable psychiatric illness'. Even where V can give evidence of headaches and physical pain, capable of being abh and occurring after the assault (*stricto sensu*—not a battery), there must be expert evidence to prove that these were caused by psychiatric injury: *Morris* [1998] 1 Cr App R 386. Serious psychiatric injury is gbh.

≈≈≈ *Questions*

Does the expert or the jury decide whether it is 'serious'? Is it really feasible to prove that the defendant foresaw that he would or might cause (a) a condition that the expert witness subsequently diagnoses as a recognizable psychiatric injury, (b) a condition which a judge and jury is not competent to recognize?

In *D* [2006] EWCA Crim 1139, in the course of its discussion of manslaughter, the Court of Appeal held that psychological injury, not amounting to an identified or recognized psychological condition, could not amount to 'bodily harm'. *Chan-Fook* (1994) 99 Cr App R 147 drew a clear distinction between psychiatric illness on the one hand and other psychological harm or states of mind on the other. The distinction drawn in *Chan-Fook* (upheld in *Ireland; Burstow* [1998] AC 147) was consistent with authority in the civil law, where it had been applied in claims for personal injury. In *D*, the Crown argued that 'bodily harm' encompassed psychological harm other than a recognized psychiatric illness or condition. This amounted to an argument that the clear line in *Chan-Fook* should be blurred, or a degree of elasticity should be introduced to it. To do so, although easy in theory, would go beyond the well-understood principles by which the common law developed incrementally and logically. The extension sought by the Crown would introduce a significant element of uncertainty about the true ambit of the relevant legal principles to which the concept of 'bodily harm' in the 1861 Act applied, which would be compounded by the inevitable problems of conflicting medical opinion in what was a constantly developing area of practice. By adhering to the principle of recognizable psychiatric illness, although some medical experts might be concerned with the way in which the definitions were arrived at, the issue required to be addressed could be clearly understood and those responsible for advising the prosecution and defence could approach their cases with a degree of certainty. In *Golding* [2014] EWCA Crim 889, the Court of Appeal confirmed again that the ambit of bodily harm is restricted to recognizable psychiatric illness and does not encompass psychological disturbance. In that case, there was no evidence that V was suffering from a recognizable psychiatric illness, merely her account of how she felt about having been infected with genital herpes. This was insufficient, the court observed, to constitute bodily harm.

When considering the extent to which *psychological* harm is criminalized, it is important to bear in mind the new offence contained in s 76 of the Serious Crime Act 2015. This provision creates an offence of controlling or coercive behaviour in an intimate or family relationship. On indictment, this offence carries a maximum sentence of five years' imprisonment, which is the same maximum sentence available under ss 47 and 20 OAPA. By virtue of this provision, D commits an offence if he:

(1) repeatedly or continuously engages in behaviour towards another person ('V') that is controlling or coercive;

(2) at the time of the behaviour, D and the other person are personally connected;

(3) the behaviour has a serious effect on the other person; and

(4) D knows or ought to know that the behaviour will have a serious effect on the other person.

There are a number of important features to bear in mind when considering this offence. First, D and V must be 'personally connected', which is defined in the statute as being or having previously been in an intimate personal relationship or living together as members of the same family. Secondly, D's behaviour will have a 'serious effect' on V if it causes V to fear, on at least two occasions, that violence will be used against him or her or it causes V serious alarm or distress which has a substantial adverse effect on V's usual day-to-day activities. Thirdly, D cannot avoid liability by arguing that he did not know his behaviour would have a serious effect on V, as it will suffice that he ought to have known that it would have had such an effect. Finally, it is a defence for D to show that he believed he was acting in V's best interests and his behaviour was in all the circumstances reasonable. The offence is intended to deal with domestic abuse before it escalates into physical harm, but as it is still relatively new, whether it has been successful remains to be seen. For discussion, see V. Bettinson, 'Criminalising Coercive Control in Domestic Violence Cases: Should Scotland Follow the Path of England and Wales?' [2016] Crim LR 165.

10.4.2 Section 20

Section 20 creates two offences: malicious wounding and maliciously inflicting grievous bodily harm.

10.4.2.1 Malicious wounding

Malice is interpreted to mean subjective recklessness. In *Brady* [2006] EWCA Crim 2413, the Court of Appeal held that *G* on subjective recklessness does not require proof that D had foreseen 'an obvious and significant risk' in order to establish that he had acted recklessly. D was drunk when he climbed on railings at a nightclub and fell onto the dance floor below causing serious injuries to V. The court allowed the appeal, because the judge had failed to direct the jury as to recklessness in sufficiently clear and careful terms. It is unclear whether malice is identical to recklessness. Both require foresight of a risk of the harm, recklessness also requires proof of an unjustified taking of that risk, but it is not clear that malice also requires proof of that second element.

In order to constitute a wound, the continuity of the whole skin must be broken. Where a pellet fired by an air pistol hit V in the eye but caused only an internal rupturing of blood vessels and not a break in the skin, there was no wound: *C (a minor) v Eisenhower* [1984] QB 331. It is not enough that the cuticle or outer skin be broken if the inner skin remains intact. Where V was treated with such violence that his collarbone was broken, it was held that there was no wound if his skin was intact: *Wood* (1830) 1 Mood CC 278. It was held to be a wound, however, where the lining membrane of the urethra was ruptured and bled, evidence being given that the membrane is precisely the same in character as that which lines the cheek and the external skin of the lip.

≋ **Question**

Why should the criminal law provide a specific offence labelled as 'wounding' rather than treat such cases as grievous or actual bodily harm as necessary? See on the significance of appropriate labelling to reflect the moral differences in harms caused, J. Gardner, 'Rationality and the Rule of Law in Offences Against the Person' (1994) 53 CLJ 520.

10.4.2.2 Maliciously inflicting grievous bodily harm: s 20

'Grievous bodily harm' was formerly interpreted to include any harm which seriously interferes with health or comfort; but in *DPP v Smith*, section 5.2, p 85, the House of Lords said that there was no warrant for giving the words a meaning other than that which they convey in their ordinary and natural meaning. Grievous bodily harm may cover cases where there is no wounding as, for instance, the broken collarbone in *Wood*. Conversely, there might be a technical 'wounding' which could not be said to amount to grievous bodily harm (see previous section). Psychiatric injury is sufficient for an offence under s 20 (*Ireland* (section 10.2.1.1, p 251)). In *Golding* [2014] EWCA Crim 889, the Court of Appeal confirmed that the phrase 'grievous bodily harm' means really serious harm, but that it is not necessary for the harm to be either permanent or dangerous. The court elaborated as follows:

It is not a precondition that the victim should require treatment or that the harm should have lasting consequences. In assessing whether the particular harm was grievous, account has to be taken of the effect on and the circumstances of the particular victim. Ultimately, the assessment of harm done in an individual case in a contested trial will be a matter for the jury, applying contemporary social standards.

Whereas s 18 uses the word 'cause', s 20 uses 'inflict'. In a series of cases from 1861 to 1983 it was held or assumed that the words 'inflict' and 'wound' both imply an 'assault'. The effect was that D could be convicted of an offence under s 20 only if it was proved that he wounded or caused grievous bodily harm by committing an assault. The House of Lords in *Wilson* [1984] AC 242 at 260, resolved the matter by deciding, following the Australian case of *Salisbury* [1976] VR 452 at 461, that 'inflict' does not, after all, imply an assault. Arguably, the case decided no more than that; but Lord Roskill cited the opinion of the Australian court that 'inflict' has a narrower meaning than 'cause' and requires 'force being violently applied to the body of the victim'. The leading case was *Clarence*, but in the conjoined case of *Ireland; Burstow* the House of Lords held that there was 'no radical divergence' between the terms 'cause' and 'inflict'. For practical purposes, the two are now treated as being synonymous. In that case Lord Hope suggested: 'the word "inflict" implies that the consequence of the act is something which the victim is likely to find unpleasant or harmful.' But what about *Brown* [1993] 2 All ER 75, [1994] 1 AC 212, HL, section 11.4.2, p 288 Everyone was having a jolly good time. If grievous bodily harm had been proved (it was not), would the House really have held that, though there was an unlawful wounding contrary to s 20, there was no unlawful 'inflicting' contrary to that section?

10.4.2.3 Disease transmission

In the case of *Clarence* (1888) 22 QBD 23, D was charged with committing offences contrary to the OAPA after he infected his wife with gonorrhoea. It was held, however, that the transmission of disease did not fall within the scope of the 1861 Act because it could not be said that D 'inflicted' the harm upon his wife given that she consented to the sexual intercourse by which it was transmitted. This issue arose again in *Dica* [2004] EWCA Crim 1103 in which D, knowing he was HIV positive, recklessly infected a number of his sexual partners with HIV. Judge LJ in the Court of Appeal upheld D's conviction on the basis that if the case of *Clarence* were to be decided today, his conviction would be upheld. Therefore, the Court of Appeal in *Dica* confirmed that the transmission of disease, in that case HIV, is capable of constituting a criminal offence.

In the years since *Dica* was decided there have been a handful of cases in which the transmission of various sexually transmitted diseases has been criminalized. In *Golding* [2014] EWCA Crim 889, for example, D's conviction for an offence contrary to s 18 of the 1861 Act was upheld after he infected his sexual partner with genital herpes. This has proved to be a controversial development, as the following extract demonstrates.

M. Weait, 'Criminal Law and the Sexual Transmission of HIV: *R v Dica*'
(2005) 68 MLR 121

Much of the difficulty in *Dica* stems from the fact that he was charged and convicted under s 20 of the OAPA 1861. This is not a provision that was designed to deal with the transmission of disease, let alone the complexities associated with the transmission of disease in the context of intimate sexual relations. The very fact that the critical issue has been identified as consent, which is not included as an element of the offence, demonstrates this. In the absence of any clear legislative strategy or political will to address the deficiencies of the law in this area people who infect others will continue to be prosecuted selectively and convicted on the basis of inevitably subjective evaluations by juries about whether the relationship they had with their partner was one in which consent to the risk of infection was likely. The potential for discrimination against certain categories of people the Black African refugee, the gay or bisexual man, the IV drug user will also remain unless some definite action is taken, and soon. People who infect others with serious diseases they know they have may lack any moral capital; but the same charge may be leveled at a legal framework which fails adequately to acknowledge our shared responsibility for reducing the incidence and spread of HIV and STIs, and which reinforces social stigma against those who, though they may have infected others, are also people who have themselves been infected.

So far, criminalization in England and Wales has been limited to the reckless or intentional transmission of sexually transmitted diseases. There have been no recorded prosecutions for the transmission of non-sexually transmitted diseases. For discussion of this issue, see K. Laird, 'Criminalising Contagion—Questioning the Paradigm' in C. Stanton and H. Quirk (eds), *Criminalising Contagion: Legal and Ethical Challenges of Disease Transmission and the Criminal Law* (2016).

As the next chapter will discuss in greater detail, an individual who knows he or she is infected with a sexually transmitted disease can avoid liability by disclosing this fact to their uninfected sexual partner and, before engaging in intercourse, obtaining their consent to taking the risk of the disease being transmitted. If the other party contracts the disease in question, the case of *Konzani* [2005] EWCA Crim 706 confirms that their consent will constitute a valid defence.

Criminalizing the transmission of sexually transmitted diseases has proved to be controversial. The implications of criminalization upon autonomy and public health objectives have been the subject of particular scrutiny, as the following extract demonstrates.

M. Weait, 'Knowledge, Autonomy and Consent: *R v Konzani*'
[2005] Crim LR 763 (references omitted)

Autonomy

Given the importance of the principles at stake, the judgment of the Court of Appeal in *Konzani* is disappointing in its exploration of the justifications for the conclusion reached. Such principled justification as exists is to be found in one critical passage, referred to above, where it explains that a complainant's 'personal autonomy is not enhanced if [the defendant] is exculpated when he recklessly transmits the HIV virus to her through consensual sexual intercourse'. What might this mean, and what merit does it have as a justification for imposing criminal liability *via* the denial of a defence based on honest belief in consent?

Autonomy means, literally, self-government. In the context of law generally, and in the context of the law as it relates to sexual offences and offences against the person in particular, it suggests the right of a person to be free from unwarranted and unwanted physical interference. Thus the essence of rape law, in which the absence of consent is definitional of the *actus reus,* is that no legal wrong is done if consent exists, because the partner with whom a person has sexual intercourse is exercising his or her autonomy rather than having it infringed or violated; and where consent operates as a defence to a charge of assault, or causing bodily harm, it reflects the law's recognition that there exists a sphere (albeit one circumscribed by public policy considerations) in which people should be entitled to freedom from liability because to hold otherwise would result in a significant and unjustified diminution of essential human freedoms. It is of critical importance to recognise the distinction. In the former (rape) example the reason why the law does not criminalise the putative defendant is that there is no legally recognised harm committed. However in the latter (assault) example the law protects a putative defendant from criminal liability not on the basis that no recognisable harm has been caused, but because of the context in which it has taken place. It follows that in such circumstances the law is not, at least *prima facie*, concerned with protecting, or indeed 'enhancing' the autonomy of the person harmed, but rather with protecting the person who harms from the imposition of unjustified liability. Put simply, it is his autonomy (in the sense of his right to be free from unwarranted interference and condemnation by the state) that the law is concerned to protect.

If the principles underpinning this argument are sound then any departure from them demands strong and careful justification. With respect, the Court of Appeal in *Konzani* not only departs from them but fails to provide any such justification. The court indicates that a complainant's autonomy is not enhanced by exculpating a person who recklessly harms her by transmitting HIV (and, by implication, that it is enhanced by denying such a defendant the right to assert an honest belief in her consent to the risk of such harm). In so doing it starts from the premise that, in the context of non-fatal offences against the person at least, it is the autonomy of the person harmed that it is the law's function to protect. However, if this were so then those who recklessly harm people should be denied the defence of consent on the basis of honest belief or otherwise, irrespective of the context in which such harm occurs; and yet case law demonstrates that this is not the case. Without explicitly acknowledging this difficulty, the court identifies the failure of a person to disclose his known HIV positive status, and the deception that is thereby practised on a partner to whom he transmits HIV, as the basis for making the distinction. The nondiscloser may not assert an honest belief in his partner's consent, because the fact of non-disclosure renders her 'consent' uninformed, legally nugatory, and therefore not one on which he is, or should be, entitled to rely. This line of reasoning is emphasised in the court's second reference to the autonomy of a complainant, when it states that this is

> 'not normally protected by allowing a defendant who knows that he is suffering from the HIV virus which he deliberately conceals, to assert an honest belief in his partner's informed consent to the risk of the transmission of the HIV virus. Silence in these circumstances is incongruous with honesty, or with a genuine belief that there is an informed consent. Accordingly, in such circumstances the issue either of informed consent, or honest belief in it will only rarely arise: in reality, in most cases, the contention would be wholly artificial.'

What is to be made of the court's deployment of autonomy in this way? While it no doubt has a certain intuitive appeal, it is submitted that the consequences of this line of reasoning are such that it should be rejected.

The court recognised in *Dica* that people should be entitled in principle to consent to the risks associated with sexual intercourse because to deny them this right (and the correlative defence such a right provides to those who expose them to such risks) would amount to an infringement of autonomy that only Parliament should sanction. In *Konzani*, however, the court has made clear that only an informed consent, grounded in knowledge gained from direct or indirect disclosure of a partner's HIV positive status, amounts to consent for these purposes. In effect, therefore, the cumulative *ratio* of the two cases is not that a person should be entitled to consent to the risks associated with sexual intercourse, but that she should be entitled to consent to such risks as have been directly or indirectly disclosed to her. It is only in the latter context that a defendant's claim of honest belief in consent can, and should, be legally recognised. If this is indeed the *ratio,* a number of consequences follow.

First, in emphasising that it is only in the most exceptional of cases that nondisclosure to a sexual partner by an HIV positive person will be 'congruent' with an honest belief, the court has, in effect, imposed a standard of reasonable belief in cases where there has been an absence of disclosure. This may be consistent with legislative developments in the law of rape, but if such is the trajectory the law should follow then it is submitted that this should be for Parliament to decide, not—with respect— the Court of Appeal. Secondly, the court has also, in effect, imposed a positive duty of disclosure on people who know they are HIV positive (and who wish to avoid potential criminal liability) before they have sex which carries the risk of transmission. Since there is no reason in principle why this positive duty should be limited to HIV (which is, for those able to access treatment at least, a manageable if life-limiting condition), it should be assumed that it applies to all those who are aware that they are suffering from a serious STI. Given that chlamydia may, if untreated in a woman, lead to infertility, that hepatitis B can lead to severe liver damage, and that syphilis—if untreated—can result in significant mental and physical impairment, it is presumably safer to assume that this positive duty now applies to all those who have been diagnosed with these, and other potentially serious, diseases who wish to avoid the possibility of prosecution and imprisonment. Thirdly, in the absence of any indication to the contrary by the court, disclosure as a precautionary principle ought presumably to be adopted by those that are infected with serious or potentially serious contagious diseases. A passenger with SARS or 'flu' may very well be aware that on a transatlantic 747 flight there could be elderly people or others with impaired immune systems (including people living with HIV). Such people's autonomy is certainly not 'enhanced' if the passenger is able to assert that he honestly believed they would consent to being infected by a virus that results in their developing pneumonia; nor is it 'normally protected', where, knowing that he is suffering from a condition that can cause such an effect, he conceals this information. These consequences of the court's reasoning may be thought more or less fanciful; but the point is, surely, that in using the language of autonomy so loosely, and in failing to specify precisely what the justification for, and scope of, the decision in *Konzani* is, the Court of Appeal has delivered a judgment that fails abjectly to deal with the core issues which its subject matter raises.

Concluding remarks: public health and criminal law

It is a perfectly legitimate question to ask whether, and if so in what circumstances, a person should be held criminally liable for the transmission of serious disease. The problem is that our answer to that question will inevitably depend on the assumptions we make about the role of the criminal law and the values and principles that inform it. If we start, as is commonplace, within the liberal legal tradition that emphasises autonomy, choice, individual responsibility and rationality, which treats causation as unidirectional and a matter of 'common sense', and which resorts to 'public policy' when confronted with hard cases, it is no wonder that the transmission of HIV by people who fail to disclose their HIV positive status to partners who are subsequently infected is constructed as a wrong that should be punished. It is also inevitable, given that criminal trials are concerned only with the finding of facts in, and the application of existing law to, the individual case, and that criminal appeals deal only with the discrete point(s) of law at issue, that the broader context of transmission is occluded and the wider social and epidemiological implications of criminalisation ignored.

Some concrete examples should serve to illustrate why the current approach of the law to the transmission of HIV is a problem. As a result of *Dica* and *Konzani* a person who, knowing his own HIV positive status, recklessly transmits HIV to a sexual partner, commits a criminal offence. He may only escape liability where the person to whom he transmits the virus gave an informed consent to the risk of transmission. The Court of Appeal in *Konzani* has indicated that such consent will, essentially, arise only where there has been prior disclosure. A number of potentially adverse consequences for public health may follow from this. First, by treating recklessness in this context simply as conscious unjustifiable risk-taking, but without clarifying whether the appropriate use of condoms negates recklessness as a matter of law, the Court of Appeal has provided no clear guidance as to whether their use will preclude the possibility of a conviction. It would be useful if such clarification could be provided so that people living with HIV understand the scope of any duty they might have. Secondly, the requirement that a person knows his HIV positive status before he can be treated as reckless may have the effect of dissuading some people from having an HIV test and so accessing available medical care, advice and treatment. While it is to be welcomed that, as a matter of general principle, no liability should be incurred by people who are in fact unaware that they may transmit HIV to their partner(s), and that the alternative (of imposing liability on those who are aware (or ought to be aware) that they may be HIV positive) would cast the net of liability too widely, the courts should recognise, and deal explicitly with, the potential public health consequences of applying the *mens rea* requirement in this way. Third, by in effect imposing a duty to disclose known HIV status prior to sex which carries the risk of transmission (which, even if prophylaxis is used, remains a possibility) the courts appear to be working on the assumption, implicitly at least, that those who are HIV positive and know this will in fact (if they behave in the rational manner upon which criminal law and the justification for punishment are premised) disclose their status to partners in order to avoid criminal liability. Moreover, as a direct result of this people may assume that sexual partners who do *not* disclose their HIV positive status are in fact HIV negative—why would they risk a criminal conviction for a serious offence by not doing so? Finally, where an HIV positive person has not disclosed prior to sex, and where transmission may have occurred, that person may be dissuaded from informing his partner of the possibility thereby preventing that partner from accessing post-exposure prophylaxis (*i.e.* intensive drug treatment that may prevent the virus taking hold) because to do so would in effect amount to confessing the commission of a serious criminal offence.

These consequences demonstrate that if we start from a set of *a priori* assumptions about the function(s) of criminal law in this context, and treat incidents of HIV transmission simply as an opportunity to apply the principles which have traditionally informed the law relating to non-fatal offences against the person, we risk doing more harm than good. UNAIDS, and many other national and international organisations have—since the early years of the HIV/AIDS pandemic—emphasised the importance of dealing with the spread of HIV as first and foremost a public health issue in which we are all implicated, and for which we are all ultimately responsible. If legislators, courts, prosecutors and police, resisted the immediate temptation to treat alleged cases of HIV transmission as individualised, momentary and (potentially) blameworthy incidents; if they were willing to acknowledge and treat seriously the mass of sound empirical research which explains the reasons why people fail to disclose their HIV positive status to significant others; and if they were to recognise that the use of the criminal law may serve not only to perpetuate people's anxieties about HIV, but also, critically, to have a negative public health impact, this would—I believe—better serve the public interest in the longer term.

In its scoping consultation paper on reforming offences against the person (Law Com No 217, *Reform of Offences Against the Person—A Scoping Consultation Paper* (2014)), the Law Commission considered whether, under a revised statute governing offences against the person, there should be liability for the transmission of disease. In its final report (Law Com Report No 361, *Offences Against the Person* (2015)) the Commission recommended that in any new statute governing offences against the person, which would be based upon the draft Home Office bill from 1998, the offences of causing serious injury should be capable of including the intentional or (as the case may be) reckless transmission of disease; accordingly disease should fall within the definition of injury. The Commission also recommended that, if it is desired to pursue further the possibility of excluding criminal liability for the reckless transmission of disease, or of creating special offences for such transmission, this should follow a wider review.

≋ **Questions**
(1) Should only the *intentional* transmission of disease be criminalized?
(2) To what extent does the current law fail to respect individual autonomy?

10.4.3 Section 18: grievous bodily harm with intent

Each of the elements has been considered earlier in this chapter. Note that the offence carries a maximum of life imprisonment.

In every case the Crown must establish an ulterior intent which may be either intent to do grievous bodily harm or intent to resist or prevent the lawful apprehension or detainer of *any* person. Recklessness is not enough. Where the allegation is of intentionally causing GBH, it is sufficient that D intended to cause the harm he did, irrespective of whether he would regard that as really serious harm. Where, under s 18, the charge is of causing grievous bodily harm with intent to do grievous bodily harm, the word 'maliciously' obviously has no part to play. Any mens rea which that word might import is comprehended within the ulterior intent.

Where the charge is of malicious wounding or causing grievous bodily harm with intent to resist lawful apprehension, the word 'maliciously' is important and that mens rea must be proved according to its usual definition: *Morrison* (1989) 89 Cr App R 17 (D, seized by a police woman as she was arresting him, dived through a window pane and the officer was dragged with him suffering serious facial injury. D clearly *intended* to resist arrest. The Court of Appeal held he must also be subjectively (*Cunningham*) reckless as to the grievous bodily harm). A mere intent to resist lawful apprehension should not found liability for a charge of wounding or causing grievous bodily harm. It is submitted that the Court of Appeal went too far in *Mowatt* [1968] 1 QB 421 at 426–427, in saying that 'In section 18 the word maliciously adds nothing.' In cases such as *Morrison* it clearly does.

Research has suggested that the moral distinction between the s 18 and s 20 offences has been eroded by the availability of the alternative verdicts and the frequency with which they are returned. In one study, albeit some years ago, only 23 per cent of those indicted for s 18 were convicted of that offence, whilst 53 per cent were convicted of s 20 and only one in ten of the contested s 18 trials led to an outright acquittal: E. Genders, 'Reform of the Law of the Offences Against the Person: Lessons from the Law in Action' [1999] Crim LR 689.

10.5 Racially aggravated assaults

The Crime and Disorder Act 1998 created a new category of racially aggravated crimes and in the wake of 9/11, the Anti-terrorism, Crime and Security Act 2001 extended these to include religiously aggravated offences. (See E. Burney, 'Using the Law of Racially Aggravated Offences' [2003] Crim LR 28. See generally, M. Malik, 'Racist Crime: Racially Aggravated Offences in the Crime and Disorder Act 1998' (1999) 62 MLR 409; M. Idriss, 'Religion and the Anti-terrorism, Crime and Security Act 2001' [2002] Crim LR 890.)

Crime and Disorder Act 1998, s 28

28. Meaning of 'racially or religiously aggravated'

(1) An offence is racially or religiously aggravated for the purposes of sections 29 to 32 below if—

(a) at the time of committing the offence, or immediately before or after doing so, the offender demonstrates towards the victim of the offence hostility based on the victims membership (or presumed membership) of a racial or religious group; or

(b) the offence is motivated (wholly or partly) by hostility towards members of a racial or religious group based on their membership of that group.

(2) In subsection (1)(a) above—

'membership', in relation to a racial or religious group, includes association with members of that group;

'presumed' means presumed by the offender.

(3) It is immaterial for the purposes of paragraph (a) or (b) of subsection (1) above whether or not the offenders hostility is also based, to any extent, on any other factor not mentioned in that paragraph.

(4) In this section 'racial group' means a group of persons defined by reference to race, colour, nationality (including citizenship) or ethnic or national origins.

(5) In this section 'religious group' means a group of persons defined by reference to religious belief or lack of religious belief.

A person commits an offence under s 29 of the 1998 Act if he commits an offence:

(1) under s 20 OAPA (malicious wounding or grievous bodily harm, section 10.4, p 256); or

(2) s 47 of that Act (section 10.4, p 256); or

(3) a common assault (section 10.2, p 250)

which is 'racially or religiously aggravated' for the purposes of s 29.

Offences (1) and (2) are punishable on indictment with seven years' imprisonment (compared with five years for the basic, non-aggravated offence) and offence (3) with two years, the basic offence being triable only summarily. In cases where offence (1) or (2) is charged, a jury could convict of the basic offence if they were satisfied that it had been committed, but were not satisfied that aggravation was proved. A jury could not, however, convict of a common assault because that is triable only summarily.

'Race' is widely defined to include colour, nationality (including citizenship) or ethnic or national origins. It has been held that 'African' does not denote an ethnic, but does denote a racial group (*White* [2001] Crim LR 576). The courts have taken an extremely wide view of what constitutes a race and racial group. It has been accepted that the terms are satisfied by non-inclusive expressions as where D demonstrates hostility to V by calling him 'non-white' or 'foreign'. It has been said, *obiter*, that a racially aggravated assault might be committed by one white person on another if the former were, for example, to call the latter 'nigger lover': *DPP v Pal* [2000] Crim LR 756.

'Religious group' means a group of persons defined by reference to religious belief or lack of religious belief. The Act gives no further guidance. Given the broad interpretation in Article 9 of the European Convention on Human Rights (ECHR), it would seem likely that the domestic courts will interpret the offence as affording protection to a religion as widely understood. By analogy with the interpretation of race, non-inclusive terms will suffice, for example 'gentile': *DPP v M* [2004] EWHC 1453 (Admin). In *Rogers* [2007] UKHL 8, the House of Lords held that using the words 'bloody foreigners' and 'get back to your own country' were capable of constituting the aggravated offence.

≈ *Questions*

(1) Is there a danger of every trivial dispute with an assault or public order offence or criminal damage becoming a racially aggravated offence if D calls V some racial or religious name in the process? Should such prosecutions be used for the racially aggravated offences so as to deter the use of racist slurs?

(2) Lord Monson in the debates on the Crime and Disorder Bill anticipated this problem and described the section as Orwellian in that it seeks to police people's emotions (Hansard HL, 12 February 1998, col 1266). Do you agree?

(3) Why are these particular offences (only) capable of being aggravated? Why not theft or robbery or rape?

(4) At present, only insults relating to religion and race are criminalized in this way. Should the law extend the aggravated offences to include hostility on the basis of disability, sexual orientation or transgender identity? See the Law Commission Report No 348, *Hate Crime: Should the Current Offences be Extended?* (2014).

It is important to appreciate the difference between cases under s 28(1)(a) and those under s 28(1)(b).

10.5.1 Section 28(1)(a): demonstration of hostility

Cases under s 28(1)(a) involve proof that D demonstrated hostility (an objective test). It is irrelevant what his motivations were and whether he had multiple reasons for demonstrating the hostility. It is also sufficient that D has demonstrated hostility based on V's presumed membership of a racial or religious group. So, for example, D calling V a 'Paki' would be sufficient even if V was in fact from India not Pakistan. Under s 28(1)(a), a raft of cases makes it clear that the offence extends to cases which may have a racially neutral gravamen but in the course of which there is hostility demonstrated towards the victim based on his presumed race. (See Maurice Kay J in *Woods* [2002] EWHC 85 (Admin) at [11].) In *Johnson v DPP* [2008]

EWHC 509 (Admin), J appealed by way of case stated against the trial judge's decision in the Crown Court to uphold his conviction for a racially aggravated public order offence. J, who was black, had been involved in an argument with two white parking attendants in the course of which J told them 'This is our patch not yours' and 'You don't belong here' and in particular J said 'Why don't you [go and deal with] your white uncles and aunties'. J was convicted of the racially aggravated form of s 5 of the Public Order Act 1986. J argued that the mere fact that reference was made to the colour of the parking attendants and to leaving the black community alone was not sufficient to constitute racial hostility. The Crown Court dismissed his appeal as did the Divisional Court, concluding that it was reasonably open to the court to conclude that the words used by J had demonstrated a racial hostility at least in part. It was clear from the language that J had been talking in racial terms.

In *Johnson,* it did not matter whether the hostility displayed was partly racial and partly directed at a general class of individuals, namely parking attendants.

10.5.2 Section 28(1)(b): motivated by hostility

Under s 28(1)(b), the prosecution must prove that D was motivated by hostility on grounds of race or religion. That is a subjective test. In addition, it does not matter whether D presumed anything about V's race or religion.

In *DPP v Howard* [2008] EWHC 608 (Admin), H chanted 'I'd rather be a Paki than a cop' at his neighbours who were police officers. H was convicted of using threatening, abusive or insulting words or behaviour within the hearing or sight of a person likely to be caused harassment, alarm or distress contrary to the Public Order Act 1986, s 5, but the magistrates concluded that there was insufficient evidence on which they could be satisfied that the racially aggravated offence under s 28 of the Crime and Disorder Act had been made out. They found that the evidence showed that H's hostility was motivated *only* by his intense dislike of X and not even as a result of his intense dislike of the police. The prosecution appealed by way of case stated, arguing that no reasonable magistrate, properly directed, could conclude that this was not racially aggravated. The Divisional Court dismissed the appeal, concluding that the magistrates were entitled to come to the conclusion they did: there was an abundance of evidence that the *sole* motivation for H's chanting was his hostility toward X personally. Moses LJ suggested (at [12]) that:

> prosecutors should be careful not to deploy [s 28(1)(b)] where offensive words have been used, but in themselves have not in any way been the motivation for the particular offence with which a defendant is charged. It diminishes the gravity of this offence to use it in circumstances where it is unnecessary to do so and where plainly it cannot be proved.

In terms of the broader social objective of the legislation, the section may well be regarded as a success if it deters individuals from using racist language in *any* context. Whether this will be the effect or whether those convicted will bear such resentment at the stigma as to become more racist is debatable. See generally Law Commission Report No 348, *Hate Crime: Should the Current Offences be Extended?* (2014).

10.6 Administering poison, etc

Offences Against the Person Act 1861, s 23

> Whosoever shall unlawfully and maliciously administer to or cause to be administered to or taken by any other person any poison or other destructive or noxious thing, so as thereby to endanger the life

of such person, or so as thereby to inflict upon such person any grievous bodily harm shall be guilty of [an offence], and being convicted thereof shall be liable . . . to [imprisonment] for any term not exceeding ten years . . .

Offences Against the Person Act 1861, s 24

Whosoever shall unlawfully and maliciously administer to or cause to be administered to or taken by any other person any poison or other destructive or noxious thing, with intent to injure, aggrieve, or annoy such person, shall be guilty of [an offence], and being . . . convicted thereof shall be liable to [imprisonment for a term not exceeding five years].

10.6.1 A poison or noxious thing

Sections 23 and 24 both speak of 'any poison or other destructive or noxious thing' which suggests a common definition. But the definition appears to have reference, under s 23, to the effect it is required to have and, under s 24, to the intentions of D. Thus if D, intending to kill, places a small amount of cyanide in his victim's glass of milk (cf *White*, section 3.1, p 36) he is guilty of attempted murder but not of the offence under s 23 if the amount was so small that the victim was in no danger of suffering death or grievous bodily harm. D would, however, commit the offence under s 24 because he has administered a noxious substance and his intent to kill is more than enough to satisfy an intent to injure, aggrieve or annoy. Cyanide remains a noxious thing though administered in an amount too small to cause harm. It was held in *Marcus* [1981] 2 All ER 833, [1981] 1 WLR 774, CA, that a thing which would not ordinarily be described as noxious (in that case it was a sedative but it would embrace many proprietary medicines) was noxious if administered in a sufficient amount to injure, aggrieve or annoy. In *Cato* [1976] 1 All ER 260, the Court of Appeal held that heroin could constitute a noxious thing. Recently, in *CP* [2015] QB 459, Lord Dyson MR set out the elements of the offence in the following terms:

The actus reus of an offence contrary to section 23 requires (i) the administering of a poison to a person, (ii) the infliction on such person of grievous bodily harm and (iii) a causal link between (i) and (ii). An essential ingredient of the offence, therefore, is the infliction of grievous bodily harm on a person. Grievous bodily harm to a foetus will not suffice. On the facts of this case, the harm caused to CP by reason of [her mother's] excessive consumption of alcohol was caused *before* her birth. Tragically, the harm was the brain damage with which CP was born. She was born with limited growth potential as she had symmetrical intrauterine growth retardation. All the suffering that CP has endured and will continue to endure during her life is the consequence of the harm that was inflicted on her when she was in her mother's womb. The distinction between (i) harm or injury caused by an act and (ii) the consequences of the harm or injury is critical. An offence contrary to section 23 is complete if D, with the requisite mens rea, inflicts grievous bodily harm on V. If V suffers further harm *as a result of* the grievous bodily harm, that does not give rise to a further offence. The further harm is simply a consequence of the grievous bodily harm. It may well be relevant to an assessment of the gravity of the offence that has been committed, but it is not part of the actus reus of the offence itself.

10.6.2 Administer, cause to be administered or cause to be taken

To complete the offence D must 'administer or cause to be administered to or taken by' the victim the poison or other destructive or noxious thing. In *Gillard* (1988) 87 Cr App R 189,

[1988] Crim LR 531, CA, D was convicted of conspiring to commit an offence (the offence being that of administering a noxious thing contrary to s 24) contrary to s 1(1) of the Criminal Law Act 1977 in agreeing with others to spray CS gas (a potent eye, throat and skin irritant) into the faces of P and others. Delivering the judgment of the court, McNeill J said:

> Where . . . the learned recorder was in error was in holding that 'administering' and 'taking' were to be treated effectively as synonymous or as conjunctive words in the section: on the contrary, the repeated use of the word 'or' makes it clear that they are disjunctive. The word 'takes' postulates some 'ingestion' by the victim: 'administer' must have some other meaning and there is no difficulty in including in that meaning such conduct as spraying the victim with noxious fluid or vapour, whether from a device such as a gas canister or, for example, hosing down with effluent. There is no necessity when the word 'administer' is used to postulate any form of entry into the victim's body, whether through any orifice or by absorption. [T]he proper construction of 'administer' in s24 includes conduct which not being the application of direct force to the victim nevertheless brings the noxious thing into contact with his body.

R v Kennedy (No 2)
[2007] UKHL 38, House of Lords

(Lords Bingham of Cornhill, Rodger of Earlsferry, Baroness Hale of Richmond, Lords Carswell and Mance)

The appeal arose from a manslaughter conviction where K prepared a syringe of heroin and handed it to V who self-injected and died from the effects (see Chapter 9). The certified question for the House of Lords was:

> When is it appropriate to find someone guilty of manslaughter where that person has been involved in the supply of a class A controlled drug, which is then freely and voluntarily self-administered by the person to whom it was supplied, and the administration of the drug then causes his death?

The Committee in a remarkably short unanimous judgment delivered by Lord Bingham, concluded that the Court of Appeal had been in error.

> **Lord Bingham** [his lordship stated the facts and discussed the manslaughter offence—see section 9.2.5.2, p 224:]
>
> 8. The parties are further agreed that an unlawful act of the appellant on the present facts must be found, if at all, in a breach of section 23 of the Offences against the Person Act 1861. Although the death of the deceased was the tragic outcome of the injection on 10 September 1996 the death is legally irrelevant to the criminality of the appellant's conduct under the section: he either was or was not guilty of an offence under section 23 irrespective of the death.
>
> [His lordship referred to s 23.]
>
> 9. The opening and closing words of the section raise no question relevant to this appeal. The substance of the section creates three distinct offences: (1) administering a noxious thing to any other person; (2) causing a noxious thing to be administered to any other person; and (3) causing a noxious thing to be taken by any other person. It is not in doubt that heroin is a noxious thing, and the contrary was not contended.
>
> 10. The factual situations covered by (1), (2) and (3) are clear. Offence (1) is committed where D administers the noxious thing directly to V, as by injecting V with the noxious thing, holding a glass containing the noxious thing to V's lips, or (as in *R v Gillard* (1988) 87 Cr App R 189) spraying the noxious thing in V's face.
>
> 11. Offence (2) is typically committed where D does not directly administer the noxious thing to V but causes an innocent third party TP to administer it to V. If D, knowing a syringe to be filled with

poison instructs TP to inject V, TP believing the syringe to contain a legitimate therapeutic substance, D would commit this offence.

12. Offence (3) covers the situation where the noxious thing is not administered to V but taken by him, provided D causes the noxious thing to be taken by V and V does not make a voluntary and informed decision to take it. If D puts a noxious thing in food which V is about to eat and V, ignorant of the presence of the noxious thing, eats it, D commits offence (3).

13. In the course of his accurate and well-judged submissions on behalf of the Crown, Mr David Perry QC accepted that if he could not show that the appellant had committed offence (1) as the unlawful act necessary to found the count of manslaughter he could not hope to show the commission of offences (2) or (3). This concession was rightly made, but the committee heard considerable argument addressed to the concept of causation, which has been misapplied in some of the authorities, and it is desirable that it should be clear why the concession is rightly made.

. . .

19. The sole argument open to the Crown was, therefore, that the appellant administered the injection to the deceased. It was argued that the term 'administer' should not be narrowly interpreted. Reliance was placed on the steps taken by the appellant to facilitate the injection and on the trial judge's direction to the jury that they had to be satisfied that the appellant handed the syringe to the deceased 'for immediate injection'. But section 23 draws a very clear contrast between a noxious thing administered to another person and a noxious thing taken by another person. It cannot ordinarily be both. In this case the heroin is described as 'freely and voluntarily self-administered' by the deceased. This, on the facts, is an inevitable finding. The appellant supplied the heroin and prepared the syringe. But the deceased had a choice whether to inject himself or not. He chose to do so, knowing what he was doing. It was his act.

20. In resisting this conclusion Mr Perry relied on *R v Rogers* [2003] 1 WLR 1374. In that case the defendant pleaded guilty, following a legal ruling, to a count of administering poison contrary to section 23 of the 1861 Act and a count of manslaughter. The relevant finding was that the defendant physically assisted the deceased by holding his belt round the deceased's arm as a tourniquet, so as to raise a vein in which the deceased could insert a syringe, while the deceased injected himself. It was argued in support of his appeal to the Court of Appeal that the defendant had committed no unlawful act for purposes of either count. This contention was rejected. The court held (para 7) that it was unreal and artificial to separate the tourniquet from the injection. By applying and holding the tourniquet the defendant had played a part in the mechanics of the injection which had caused the death. There is, clearly, a difficult borderline between contributory acts which may properly be regarded as administering a noxious thing and acts which may not. But the crucial question is not whether the defendant facilitated or contributed to administration of the noxious thing but whether he went further and administered it. What matters, in a case such as *R v Rogers* and the present, is whether the injection itself was the result of a voluntary and informed decision by the person injecting himself. In *R v Rogers*, as in the present case, it was. That case was, therefore, wrongly decided.

21. It is unnecessary to review the case law on this subject in any detail. In *R v Cato* [1976] 1 WLR 110 the defendant had injected the deceased with heroin and the present problem did not arise. In *R v Dalby* [1982] 1 WLR 425 the deceased had died following the consumption of drugs which the defendant had supplied but the deceased had injected. There was apparently no discussion of section 23, but it was held that the supply could not support a conviction of manslaughter. At the trial of the present appellant there was no consideration of section 23 and the trial judge effectively stopped defence counsel submitting to the jury that the appellant had not caused the death of the deceased. In dismissing his first appeal the Court of Appeal said:

> 'We can see no reason why, on the facts alleged by the Crown, the appellant in the instant case might not have been guilty of an offence under section 23 of the Offences against the Person Act 1861. Perhaps more relevantly, the injection of the heroin into himself by Bosque was itself an unlawful act, and if the appellant assisted in and wilfully encouraged that unlawful conduct, he would himself be acting unlawfully.'

But the court gave no detailed consideration to the terms of section 23, and it is now accepted that the deceased's injection of himself was not an unlawful act.

22. In *R v Dias* [2002] 2 Cr App R 96 the defendant had been convicted of manslaughter. He had prepared a syringe charged with heroin which he had handed to the deceased, who had injected himself. The court recognised that the chain of causation had probably been broken by the free and informed decision of the deceased, and noted the error in the decision on the appellant's first appeal as to the unlawfulness of the deceased's injection of himself.

. . .

24. It is possible to imagine factual scenarios in which two people could properly be regarded as acting together to administer an injection. But nothing of the kind was the case here. As in *R v Dalby* and *R v Dias* the appellant supplied the drug to the deceased, who then had a choice, knowing the facts, whether to inject himself or not. The heroin was, as the certified question correctly recognises, self-administered, not jointly administered. The appellant did not administer the drug. Nor, for reasons already given, did the appellant cause the drug to be administered to or taken by the deceased.

Appeal allowed

In *Burgess* [2008] EWCA Crim 516, the Court of Appeal subsequently suggested that had the matter fallen for consideration, D's act of raising V's vein would make him responsible for the administration. It was held that 'if a defendant may be convicted on the basis that the fatal dose was jointly administered then it follows that he is not automatically entitled to be acquitted if the deceased rather than the defendant physically operated the plunger'.

≈≈ *Question*

Consider D's liability if:

(1) he puts cyanide in V's tea and hands V the tea;

(2) he puts cyanide in V's tea and leaves the cup by V's bedside;

(3) he puts cyanide in V's tea and gets X, V's 9-year-old child, to take it to him.

What difference does it make in each of these examples if V knows that the tea contains cyanide?

10.6.3 Maliciously

R v Cunningham
[1957] 2 All ER 412, Court of Criminal Appeal

The case is set out in section 5.3, p 97, where the meaning of this term was considered. It will be recalled that the term 'maliciously' is now treated as being synonymous with 'recklessly' (but see the discussion of *Brady* at p 260).

10.7 Reform of the law of offences against the person

The Home Office Consultation Document, *Violence: Reforming the Offences Against the Person Act 1861* (February 1998) acknowledged that, 'That Act was itself not a coherent statement of the law but a consolidation of much older law. It is therefore not surprising that the law has been widely criticised as archaic and unclear and that it is now in urgent need of reform.' Lord Ackner has agreed with the blunter criticism that the Act is a ragbag of offences brought together from a wide variety of sources with no attempt, as the draftsman frankly acknowledged, to introduce consistency as to substance or as to form: *Savage* [1991] 4 All ER 698 at 721. But, notwithstanding the admitted urgency, nothing more has been heard (as at February 2017) from the Home Office since February 1998, so lawyers and students must continue to grapple with the archaic and unclear law.

The Home Office Consultation Document included a draft Bill. The Bill is based on the recommendations first made by the Criminal Law Revision Committee, Fourteenth Report, *Offences Against the Person* (1980), Cmnd 7844, adopted in the Law Commission Draft Code and then, in a modified form, in Law Commission Report No 218 (1993).

The law in this area is far from satisfactory, for a variety of reasons. The Law Commission commented that it 'was defective on grounds both of effectiveness and of justice' (Consultation Paper No 122, *Legislating the Criminal Code: Offences Against the Person and General Principles* (1992)). It is an area of law which is very clearly in need of reform. Law Commission Report No 218 contained recommendations, but these have been superseded by those in the Home Office, *Consultation Paper on Violence* (1998), on which see J. C. Smith, 'Offences Against The Person: The Home Office Consultation Paper' [1998] Crim LR 317.

The Law Commission has considered this issue again more recently (Consultation Paper No 217, *Reform of Offences against the Person—A Scoping Consultation Paper* (2014)). In this consultation paper, the Commission considered that there would be benefit in pursuing reform of the law of offences against the person in the form of a modern statute that would replace all or most of the Offences Against the Person Act 1861. The Commission identified the following problems with the law.

(1) there is some incoherence in the classification of the offences, for example:

   (a) some offences relate to narrowly specialised situations, or include complex lists of situations, rather than setting out a clear principle;

   (b) the offences are not clearly classified in order of seriousness;

(2) the mental element of some offences is not clearly expressed, and does not reflect the external elements of those offences;

(3) the language is often archaic and obscure;

(4) there are redundancies in the drafting, such as the use of 'maliciously' together with a more clearly defined requirement of intent;

(5) there are references to obsolete legal concepts and procedures, which are only resolved by interpretation provisions in other statutes.

The comprehensive reform described by the Commission would largely be modelled upon the Home Office 1998 draft Bill.

In its final report (Report No 361, *Reform of Offences against the Person* (2015)) the Law Commission recommended using the hierarchy of injury offences in the 1998 draft Bill, which distinguishes between serious or severe injuries and injury in general. Unlike the current law, the offence of recklessly causing serious injury would only be committed if D was aware of the risk that his conduct would cause serious injury. This would ensure the offences adhere to the correspondence principle. The reforms would ensure a clearer distinction between each offence, whilst also modernizing the language used to describe the offences. See Table 10.1.

Table 10.1 Table of existing and Law Commission's proposed new offences

Section (of OAPA 1861 unless otherwise stated)	Existing offences			Law Commission's proposed new offences		
	Description	Mode of trial and sentence		Clause (of 1998 draft Bill unless otherwise stated)	Description	Mode of trial and sentence
18	Wounding or causing grievous bodily harm with intent to cause grievous bodily harm	Crown Court; life		1	Intentionally causing serious injury *Note: wounding is not included unless the wound is a serious injury.*	Crown Court; life
20	Malicious wounding or infliction of grievous bodily harm *Note: the defendant must intend or be reckless about some harm; not necessarily about a wound or grievous bodily harm.*	Either way; 5 years		2	Recklessly causing serious injury *Note: D must be reckless about the risk of serious injury; wounding is not included unless the wound is a serious injury.*	Either way; 7 years
47	Assault occasioning actual bodily harm *Note: this includes every assault or battery which in fact causes injury, whether or not the defendant intended or was reckless about injury.*	Either way; 5 years		3	Intentionally or recklessly causing injury (whether or not by assault) *Note: D must intend or be reckless about the risk of some injury.*	Either way; 5 years

Common law	Battery	Magistrates; 6 months	Recommended in report but not in 1998 draft Bill	Aggravated assault	Magistrates; 12 months
	Note: this means actual physical violence, including any unlawful touching however slight. At present, this offence is sometimes used for cases of low-level injuries.			*Note: includes every physical or threatened assault which in fact causes injury, whether or not D intended or was reckless about injury.*	
Common law	Assault	Magistrates; 6 months	4 (modified)	Physical assault	Magistrates; 6 months
	Note: this means causing a person to apprehend physical violence, in the same sense as above.			*Note: should not be used for cases of low-level injury, as these may be charged as aggravated assault.*	
23	Administering noxious substance to endanger life or inflict grievous bodily harm	Crown Court; 10 years	4 (modified)	Threatened assault	Magistrates; 6 months
24	Administering noxious substance with intent to injure or annoy	Crown Court; 5 years	11	Administering a substance capable of causing injury	Either way; 5 years
				Note: where injury caused, offences under clauses 1 to 3 may also apply. There is also an offence of using a stupefying substance to enable sexual activity, with a maximum sentence of 10 years: Sexual Offences Act 2003, s 61.	

In its report, the Law Commission concluded as follows:

SUMMARY

4.172. There is overwhelming support for using the 1998 draft Bill as the basis for reform, and we recommend doing so. We also recommend maintaining the principal features of the draft Bill, namely:

(1) creating general offences of causing injury by whatever means, rather than specific offences distinguishing the type of injury or the means by which it was caused;

(2) distinguishing offences of causing serious harm from offences of causing harm;

(3) in each offence, making the level of injury that must be intended or foreseen correspond to the level of injury that must occur;

(4) creating separate offences of intentionally causing serious injury and recklessly causing serious injury, but a single offence of intentionally or recklessly causing injury.

4.173. On points of detail, we recommend:

(1) that the main injury offences should be defined in terms of 'conduct', and not distinguish between acts and omissions;

(2) that injury should be defined as in the existing law, so that mental injury is confined to recognised psychiatric conditions;

(3) that there should be no statutory definition of intention or recklessness;

(4) that there should be no explicit provision about jurisdiction in cases where the conduct or the harm caused by it occurs outside England and Wales;

(5) that there should be specific provisions about consent in the offences replacing assault and in any offence concerning low level injuries;

(6) that the mode of trial of the three main injury offences should be as stated in the draft Bill, namely that the offence under clause 1 should be triable on indictment only and the offences under clauses 2 and 3 should be triable either way.

FURTHER READING

On assault and battery

M. Hirst, 'Assault, Battery and Indirect Violence' [1999] Crim LR 557

J. Horder, 'Reconsidering Psychic Assault' [1998] Crim LR 392

J. E. Stannard, 'Sticks, Stones and Words: Emotional Harm and the English Criminal Law' (2010) 74 J Crim L 533

On HIV transmission

S. H. Bronitt, 'Spreading Disease and the Criminal Law' [1994] Crim LR 21

D. Ormerod and M. J. Gunn, 'Criminal Liability for the Transmission of HIV' [1996] 1 Web JCLI

J. Slater, 'HIV, Trust and the Criminal Law' (2011) 75 J Crim L 309

K. J. M. Smith, 'Sexual Etiquette, Public Interest and the Criminal Law' (1991) 42 NILQ 309

On racially and religiously aggravated assaults

M. A. Walters, 'Conceptualizing "Hostility" for Hate Crime Law: Minding "the Minutiae" when Interpreting Section 28(1)(a) of the Crime and Disorder Act 1998' (2014) 34 OJLS 47

Reform

S. Demetriou, 'Not Giving up the Fight: A Review of the Law Commission's Scoping Report on Non-Fatal Offences Against the Person' (2016) 80 J Crim L 188

M. Gibson, 'Getting Their "Act" Together? Implementing Statutory Reform of Offences Against the Person' [2016] Crim LR 597

11
Consent and offences against the person

In offences against the person, the question of consent to the harm or risk of harm is vitally important. In deciding whether D can be liable, it is important to have regard to two general questions:

(1) has V given true consent (or does D believe V has); and

(2) what level of harm has V consented to (or does D believe V has consented to)?

Some of the controversies that will be examined in this chapter include:

(1) the threshold of harm to which consent can be lawfully given—should V be permitted to consent to any level of harm or only to minor harms;

(2) whether a person should be permitted to consent to different levels of harm in relation to certain activities: surgery, boxing, horseplay, etc;

(3) whether the transmission or risk of transmission of diseases or infections can be consented to;

(4) what constitutes 'true' consent.

11.1 Introduction

In the previous chapter we examined the range of offences against the person. In this chapter we examine the controversial question of whether and, if so, when a sane adult should be permitted to consent to harm to himself or to the risk of harm to himself.

The law in this area is heavily influenced by policy considerations, as in the case of *Barnes* [2004] EWCA Crim 3246 (an injury caused in the course of an amateur football match). In that case, Lord Woolf CJ stated that, 'the exceptions to the rule that a person cannot consent to his being caused actual harm, are based on public policy'. One of the issues to consider throughout this chapter is the extent to which the law is too heavily influenced by policy.

11.2 How to approach the issue of consent

It is necessary to address two different problems:

(1) situations in which V cannot be said to have given true consent—where, for example, V has been deceived or acts under threats or duress; and

(2) cases where V gives factual consent but this is treated as a matter of policy as being ineffective in the eyes of the law.

By way of introduction, it must be emphasized that the law is far from straightforward. The most logical approach, it is suggested, is to:

(1) Ascertain whether V has consented in fact:
   (a) V's apparent consent may have been vitiated by fraud or force;
   (b) if V has not consented consider whether D has a genuine belief in V's consent.

(2) Consider the level of harm inflicted:
   (a) if the level of harm is:
   (i) one to which V may in law consent (assault or battery) and either V may have consented ((1)(a) above), or
   (ii) D may have a genuine belief in V's consent to that harm ((1)(b) above),
       D is entitled to be acquitted;
   (b) if the level of harm is such that V may not generally consent in law (ABH, wounding, GBH, etc) D will be guilty even if V consented in fact unless either:
   (i) the conduct in question represents an exceptional category in which V's consent will be recognized (sports, surgery, boxing, etc) and D has V's consent or a genuine belief in it, or
   (ii) D intended only to cause a level of harm to which V's factual consent would be legally recognized (assault or battery) and V had consented to that lower level of harm, or if V had not, D nevertheless genuinely believed that V had.

11.3 Factual consent

The Crown must establish that V was not consenting.

In *H v CPS* [2010] EWHC 1374 (Admin), the Divisional Court sought to emphasize that consent ordinarily cannot be implied. V was a teacher at a school for children with emotional, behavioural and social needs. D committed battery on V and sought to argue that V, by accepting employment at a school specializing in the education of children with emotional and behavioural issues, had accepted that there would be incidents where relatively minor violence would be used against him by pupils, and that they would have to use physical force to restrain pupils. In rejecting this argument, Cranston J stated that implied consent was limited to cases in which the injury arose in sports and should not be extended to encompass such situations.

11.3.1 Apparent consent vitiated by force or fraud: (1)(a)

V's apparently factual consent may be vitiated by force, or fraud as to the nature of the act or the identity of the actor. Factual consent is used here in the sense that V agreed to the infliction of the force in question, be it a slight touching or force of a more grievous nature.

R v Diana Richardson

[1998] 2 Cr App R 200, Court of Appeal, Criminal Division

(Otton LJ, Turner and Dyson JJ)

R was a dentist. She was suspended from practice by the General Dental Council. She continued to practise as a dentist and treated patients including performing drilling of teeth and fixing of fillings, etc.

In the Crown Court at Nottingham, before HHJ Matthewman QC, following a ruling by the judge the appellant changed her pleas to guilty on six counts of assault occasioning actual bodily harm. She appealed her conviction.

Otton LJ:

The agreed basis upon which the plea of guilty was tendered was that the appellant had practised while suspended, that the treatment was of a reasonable standard and was carried out on willing patients who had presented themselves for such treatment, and that all of the complainants had been treated by her before her suspension, without complaint.

Miss Caroline Bradley on behalf of the appellant now concentrates her argument on the issue of consent. She acknowledges that without consent the surgical procedures carried out were capable of amounting to an assault in law.

The general proposition which underlies this area of the law is that the human body is inviolate but there are circumstances which the law recognises where consent may operate to prevent conduct which would otherwise be classified as an assault from being so treated. Reasonable surgical interference is clearly such an exception. Counsel relies upon the *dicta* of Lord Lane CJ in *A-G's Reference (No 6 of 1980)* (1981) 73 Cr App Rep 63, [1981] QB 715 where it was held that an assailant was not guilty of assault if the victim consented to it but that an exception to that principle existed where the public interest required. Lord Lane said at p 66 and p 719:

'Nothing which we have said is intended to cast doubt upon the accepted legality of . . . lawful chastisement . . . reasonable surgical interference . . . etc. The apparent exceptions can be justified as involving the exercise of a legal right, in the case, of chastisement . . . or as needed in the public interest, in other cases.'

Thus it can be accepted that a person may give lawful consent to the infliction of actual bodily harm upon himself and is justifiable as being in the public interest where reasonable surgical treatment is concerned. But the question then arises, what is the effect on the validity of consent, if any, if the complainant has had concealed from them the true nature of the status of the person who, in the guise of performing a reasonable surgical procedure, subsequently inflicts bodily harm.

Professor J C Smith QC, in Smith and Hogan *Criminal Law* (8th ed [1996]), at p 420 states:

'Fraud does not necessarily negative consent. It does so only if it deceives P as to the identity of the person or the nature of the act.'

This statement of principle is derived from *Clarence* (1888) 22 QBD 23 where the victim [D's wife] consented to sexual intercourse with the accused and although she would not have consented had she been aware of the disease from which D knew he was suffering, this was no assault. Wills J stated at p 7:

'That consent obtained by fraud is no consent at all is not true as a general proposition either in fact or in law.'

Stephen J stated at p 44:

'. . . The only sorts of fraud that so far destroy the effect of a woman's consent as to convert a connection consented to in fact into a rape are frauds as to the nature of the act itself, or as to the identity of the person who does the act.'

There is a clear line of authority concerning fraud and the nature of the act. In *Williams* [1923] 1 KB 340 the appellant, a choir master, had sexual intercourse with a girl of sixteen years of age under the pretence that her breathing was not quite right and that he had to perform an operation to enable her to produce her voice properly. The girl submitted to what was done under the belief, wilfully and fraudulently induced by the appellant, that she was being medically and surgically treated by the appellant and not with any intention that she should have intercourse with him. The Court of Criminal Appeal held that the appellant was properly convicted of rape. Lord Hewart CJ referred to *Case* (1850) 4 Cox CC 220 where a medical practitioner had sexual connection with a girl of fourteen years of age upon the pretence that he was treating her medically and the girl made no resistance owing to a bona fide belief that she was being medically treated. It was held that he was properly convicted of an assault and might have been convicted of rape. The Lord Chief Justice also referred with approval to the *dicta* of Branson J in *Dicken* (1877) 14 Cox CC 8:

> 'The law has laid it down that where a girl's consent is procured by the means which the girl says this prisoner adopted, that is to say, where she is persuaded that what is being done to her is not the ordinary act of sexual intercourse but is some medical or surgical operation in order to give her relief from some disability from which she is suffering, then that is rape although the actual thing that is done was done with her consent, because she never consented to the act of sexual intercourse. She was persuaded to consent to what he did because she thought it was not sexual intercourse and because she thought it was a surgical operation.'

In *Harms* (1944) 2 DLR 61 the Supreme Court of Canada considered s 298 of the Canadian Criminal Code which established that in order to vitiate consent the false or fraudulent misrepresentation had to be as to the nature and quality of the act. Harms had falsely represented himself to be a medical doctor. Although the complainant knew that he was proposing sexual intercourse she consented thereto because of his representations that the intercourse was in the nature of a medical treatment necessitated by a condition which he said he had diagnosed. Harms was not a medical man at all. The court held that a jury was entitled to conclude that the nature and quality of the act as far as the complainant was concerned was therapeutic and not carnal. In other words, the complainant had consented to a therapeutic act, which it was not, and had not consented to a carnal act which it was. The consent induced by the fraudulent representation was held to have been vitiated.

The later case of *Bolduc and Bird v R* (1967) 63 DLR (2d) 82 was held to be on the other side of the line. The Supreme Court of Canada considered the case of a doctor who falsely represented that his colleague was a medical student and obtained the complainant's consent to the colleague's presence at a vaginal examination. It was held that there was no indecent assault because the fraud was not as to the nature and quality of what was to be done. It was observed that the defendant's conduct was 'unethical and reprehensible', but did not have the effect of vitiating the consent.

In *Papadimitropoulos* (1957) 98 CLR 249 the High Court of Australia considered the case of a complainant who had sexual relations with a man whom she believed to be her husband. Unknown to her no valid marriage ceremony had ever taken place. The complainant had consented to sexual intercourse under the belief, fraudulently induced, that she had contracted a valid marriage to the man whom she believed to be her husband. It was held that in these circumstances this did not support a conviction for rape. [His lordship referred to the Australian court's findings.]

This result is not altogether surprising, for otherwise every bigamist would be guilty of rape.

The Law Commission in their Consultation Paper No 139 'Consent in the Criminal Law', having considered fraud and consent generally proposed a lesser offence of obtaining consent by deception and stated (at para 6.27) that:

> 'consent should not in general be *nullified* by deception as to any circumstances other than the nature of the act and the identity of the person doing it, but that deception as to other circumstances should give rise to liability for a lesser offence than that of non-consensual conduct. Where the defendant is aware that the other person is or may be mistaken about the nature of the

act or the defendant's identity, we think that the other person's consent should be nullified as if the mistake by fraud . . . If a deception as to circumstances in question would give rise to liability *only* for our proposed offence of obtaining consent by deception, as distinct from the more serious offence of acting without any consent at all, liability for taking advantage of a self-induced mistake as to that circumstance could at *most* be for the lesser offence.'

It is, thus, unremarkable that neither counsel has been able to cite any authority in which the complainant in a sexual case has been deceived as to the identity of the assailant and her apparent consent has held to have been vitiated by fraud. . . .

Miss Bradley who argued the case ably contends that the complainants were deceived neither as to the nature or quality of the act nor as to the identity of the person carrying out the act. The statutory offence was created to punish such conduct as took place here.

Both before the judge and before this Court the respondent expressly disavowed reliance upon the nature or quality of the act. Mr Peter Walmsley succinctly submitted that the patients were deceived into consenting to treatment by the representation that the defendant was a qualified and practising dentist and not one who had been disqualified. He further submitted that the evidence of the patients was unequivocal: had they known that the defendant had been suspended they would not have consented to any treatment. If the treatment had been given by a person impersonating a dentist it would have been an assault. There was no distinction to be drawn between the unqualified dentist and one who is suspended. On this basis there was a mistake as to the true identity of the defendant.

We are unable to accept that argument. There is no basis for the proposition that the rules which determine the circumstances in which consent is vitiated can be different according to whether the case is one of sexual assault or one where the assault is non-sexual [see now s 76 of the Sexual Offences Act 2003 in relation to sexual cases]. The common element in both these cases is that they involve an assault, and the question is whether consent has been negatived. It is nowhere suggested that the common law draws such a distinction. The common law is not concerned with the question whether the mistaken consent has been induced by fraud on the part of the accused or has been self induced. It is the nature of the mistake that is relevant, and not the reason why the mistake has been made. In summary, either there is consent to actions on the part of a person in the mistaken belief that he or they are other than they truly are, in which case it is assault or, short of this, there is no assault.

In essence the Crown contended that the concept of the 'identity of the person' should be extended to cover the qualifications or attributes of the dentist on the basis that the patients consented to treatment by a qualified dentist and not a suspended one. We must reject that submission. In all the charges brought against the appellant the complainants were fully aware of the identity of the appellant. To accede to the submission would be to strain or distort the every day meaning of the word identity, the dictionary definition of which is 'the condition of being the same'.

It was suggested in argument that we might be assisted by the civil law of consent, where such expressions as 'real' or 'informed' consent prevail. In this regard the criminal and the civil law do not run along the same track. The concept of informed consent has no place in the criminal law. It would also be a mistake, in our view, to introduce the concept of a duty to communicate information to a patient about the risk of an activity before consent to an act can be treated as valid. The gravamen of the appellant's conduct in the instant case was that the complainants consented to treatment from her although their consent had been procured by her failure to inform them that she was no longer qualified to practice. This was clearly reprehensible and may well found the basis of a civil claim for damages. But we are quite satisfied that it is not a basis for finding criminal liability in the field of offences against the person.

We have arrived at this conclusion without any real difficulty. It is our considered view that the common law has developed as far as it can without the intervention of the legislature. For the better part of a century, the common law concept of consent in the criminal law has been certain and clearly delineated. It is not for this Court to attempt to unwrite the law which has been settled for so long. This is an area in which it is to be hoped that the proposals of the Law Commission will be given an early opportunity for implementation.

Finally, we feel obliged to observe that we are left with a state of unease at the procedure which was adopted in this case. We are concerned about the wisdom of the Crown being prepared to accept 'reasonable surgical intervention' as the factual basis of the plea. If the allegations of assault occasioning actual bodily harm had been persisted in and proved in accordance with the committal statements there would have been little or no room for the defence of consent. The nature of the dental treatment (if proved) would have gone far beyond the treatment that was either contemplated or consented to by the patients or their parents.

Accordingly, we must allow the appeal and quash the convictions.

Appeal allowed. Convictions quashed

≈≈ *Questions*

How could the prosecution both (a) agree that the treatment was of a reasonable standard and (b) allege that it constituted actual bodily harm? Is a dentist properly drilling a diseased tooth (or a surgeon properly amputating a limb to save life) causing 'harm'? If consent had been vitiated—for example, there had been a misrepresentation of identity—there would have been an assault but, if the treatment was necessary and competently done, would it have been an assault occasioning actual bodily harm? In the circumstances of *Richardson*, would it have been an assault occasioning actual bodily harm if the treatment had been harmful? Does V's consent to proper treatment negative D's assault if the treatment by D is improper? What if the treatment amounts to *grievous* bodily harm?

Section 76 of the Sexual Offences Act 2003 provides that it shall be conclusively presumed that V was not consenting where D has deceived V as to the nature or purpose of his acts or as to his identity. As the next chapter will examine, however, as a result of judicial interpretation of the Sexual Offences Act 2003, potentially any deception is capable of negating consent in the context of sexual offences. In relation to non-sexual offences, the question remains whether a deception as to the quality or purpose of the act, as opposed to its nature, will vitiate consent. See section 12.2.1.7, p 320.

R v Dica

[2004] EWCA Crim 1103, Court of Appeal, Criminal Division

(Lord Woolf CJ, Judge LJ and Forbes J)

D was charged with two offences under s 20 of the Offences Against the Person Act 1861 where, knowing that he was HIV positive, he had unprotected intercourse with two sexual partners causing each to be infected with the virus. He did not disclose his HIV status to either partner. He was convicted and appealed on the basis that (a) the trial judge had, notwithstanding *Clarence* (1889) 22 QB 23, held that it was open to the jury to convict D, and (b) the trial judge had ruled that whether or not the complainants knew of D's condition, their consent, if any, was irrelevant and provided no defence (this issue is dealt with in section 12.2.1.7, p 320).

Lord Justice Judge [his lordship stated the facts and continued]:

10. It is perhaps important to emphasise at the outset that the prosecution did not allege that the appellant had either raped or deliberately set out to infect the complainants with disease. Rather, it

was alleged that when he had consensual sexual intercourse with them, knowing that he himself was suffering from HIV, he was reckless whether they might become infected. Thus, in the language of the counts in the indictment, he 'inflicted grievous bodily harm' on them both.

11. It was not in dispute that at least on the majority of occasions, and with both complainants, sexual intercourse was unprotected. Recklessness, as such, was not in issue. If protective measures had been taken by the appellant that would have provided material relevant to the jury's decision whether, in all the circumstances, recklessness was proved.

12. Although both women were willing to have sexual intercourse with the appellant, the prosecution's case was that their agreement would never have been given if they had known of the appellant's condition. The appellant would have contended that he told both women of his condition, and that they were nonetheless willing to have sexual intercourse with him, a case which in the light of the judge's ruling, he did not support in evidence. The suggestion would have been strongly disputed by them both.

. . .

(a) The Crown's case

Concealment of the truth by the appellant

33. The judgments of the majority in *Clarence* included considerable discussion about the issue of fraud (in the sense of concealment), and the consequences if consent were vitiated. Again, however, the observations have to be put into the context of the perceived requirement that in the absence of an assault Clarence could not be guilty of the s.20 offence, and the deemed consent of the wife to have sexual intercourse with her husband. . . .

36. Clarence did not face a charge of rape or indecent assault, yet the concept of his wife's notional consent to the act of sexual intercourse was inextricably linked with the quashing of his convictions for offences of violence. He was not charged with an offence under s 3(2) of the Criminal Law Amendment Act 1885, until recently, s.3 of the Sexual Offences Act 1956, and now in slightly different terms, s.4 of the Sexual Offences Act 2003. . . .

37. The present case is concerned with and confined to s.20 offences alone, without the burdensome fiction of deemed consent to sexual intercourse. The question for decision is whether the victims' consent to sexual intercourse, which as a result of his alleged concealment was given in ignorance of the facts of the appellant's condition, *necessarily amounted to consent to the risk of being infected by him* (emphasis added). If that question must be answered 'Yes', the concept of consent in relation to s.20 is devoid of real meaning.

38. The position here is analogous to that considered in *R v Tabassum* [2000] 2 CAR 328. The appellant was convicted of indecently assaulting women who allowed him to examine their breasts in the mistaken belief that he was medically qualified. Rose LJ considered *Clarence*, and pointed out that in relation to the infection suffered by the wife, this was an additional, unexpected, consequence of sexual intercourse, which was irrelevant to her consent to sexual intercourse with her husband. Rejecting the argument that an 'undoubted consent' could only be negatived if the victim had been deceived or mistaken about the nature and quality of the act, and that consent was not negatived 'merely because the victim would not have agreed to the act if he or she had known all the facts', Rose LJ observed, in forthright terms, 'there was no true consent'. Again, in *R v Cort* [2003] 3 WLR 1300, a case of kidnapping, the complainants had consented to taking a ride in a motor car, but not to being kidnapped. They wanted transport, not kidnapping. Kidnapping may be established by carrying away by fraud.

> 'It is difficult to see how one could ever consent to that once fraud was indeed established. The "nature" of the act here is therefore taking the complainant away by fraud. The complainant did not consent to that event. All that she consented to was a ride in the car, which in itself is irrelevant to the offence and a different thing from that with which Mr Cort is charged.'

39. In our view, on the assumed fact now being considered, the answer is entirely straightforward. These victims consented to sexual intercourse. Accordingly, the appellant was not guilty of rape. Given the long-term nature of the relationships, if the appellant concealed the truth about his condition from them, and therefore kept them in ignorance of it, there was no reason for them to think that they were running any risk of infection, and they were not consenting to it. On this basis, there would be no consent sufficient in law to provide the appellant with a defence to the charge under s.20.

. . .

In *Dica*, the victims had been defrauded as to the risk of infection (and hence had not consented to bodily harm), but had not been defrauded as to the nature of the act of sexual intercourse (and hence had not been raped). The next chapter will consider whether, had D actively deceived the victims about his HIV-positive status, he could also be guilty of rape.

The Court of Appeal finally lays to rest that aspect of *Clarence* relating to implied consent. Thus, where V is unaware of D's infected state, by consenting to the act of unprotected sexual intercourse she cannot be said to have impliedly consented to the risk of infection from that intercourse. In principle, this aspect of the decision is welcome. True consent is based on an informed choice being made only when V has *all* 'information' relevant to the decision. The decision respects the principle.

> ≈≈ *Questions*
> (1) To what extent is D obliged to inform his sexual partners where D merely suspects that he is HIV positive?
> (2) Does D have a right not to know what his own HIV status is? Cf V. Tadros, *Criminal Responsibility* (2006), p 247.

John Spencer has written that:

To infect an unsuspecting person with a grave disease you know you have, *or may have*, by behaviour that you know involves a risk of transmission, and that you know you could easily modify to reduce or eliminate the risk, is to harm another in a way that is both needless and callous. For that reason, criminal liability is justified unless there are strong countervailing reasons. In my view there are not. (J. Spencer, 'Liability for Reckless Infection: Part 2' (2004) 154 NLJ 385, 448)

In contrast, M. Weait ('Criminal Law and the Sexual Transmission of HIV: *R v Dica*' (2005) 68 MLR 121) writes:

While it may be right and proper to affirm that consent to intercourse itself should not be taken to imply consent to the risk of resultant harm, it is arguable that *Dica* does not—at least so far as its interpretation of *Clarence* is concerned—mean that consent to intercourse will necessarily imply an absence of consent to harm where other conditions are met—i.e. where the defendant is ignorant of his HIV positive status or where he knows and his partner is aware of the fact. If it were otherwise, *Dica* would mean that a person who was ignorant of his HIV positive status could not lawfully have unprotected consensual intercourse with anyone, nor could a person who knew of a partner's HIV positive status give a legally recognised consent to intercourse with them. If such a couple were to have sexual intercourse it seems counter-intuitive to suggest that they are not having consensual intercourse, but are instead having non-consensual intercourse in respect of which there has been consent to the risk of HIV transmission. Such an interpretation would render the distinction between conduct of this kind and rape so fine as to be unsustainable—a conclusion which the Court of Appeal was keen to preclude.

See further M. Weait, *Intimacy and Responsibility: The Criminalisation of HIV Transmission* (2006); M. Weait, 'Knowledge, Autonomy, Consent: *R v Konzani*' [2005] Crim LR 763. On whether the mens rea for an offence of transmission following *Dica* and *Konzani* involves D's knowledge that he is infected, see S. Ryan, 'Reckless Transmission of HIV: Knowledge and Culpability' [2006] Crim LR 981.

Note that the CPS has a special policy on prosecuting sexually transmitted infection cases: http://www.cps.gov.uk/publications/prosecution/sti.html.

R v Konzani
[2005] EWCA Crim 706, Court of Appeal, Criminal Division

(Judge LJ, Grigson J and Radford HHJ)

K had been informed that he was HIV positive, and he subsequently had unprotected sexual intercourse with three complainants, having not revealed to any of them that he was HIV positive. Each of the three contracted HIV. K was charged with inflicting grievous bodily harm on each of them contrary to s 20 of the Offences Against the Person Act 1861 (OAPA). K argued that by consenting to the intercourse, each consented to the risks associated with sexual intercourse. The judge directed the jury that the consent of the complainant might provide the defendant with a defence only if that consent was an informed and willing consent to the risk of contracting HIV. The jury convicted. The defendant appealed on the basis that (a) the judge had failed to leave to the jury the issue whether the defendant might honestly, even if unreasonably, have believed that the complainants had consented to the risk of contracting the HIV virus; and (b) that the judge had misdirected the jury on the issue of consent.

Judge LJ:

... 5. Notwithstanding their evidence that he withheld vital information about his condition from them, and that each complainant expressly denied that she consented to the risk of catching the HIV virus from him, counsel on his behalf addressed the jury on the basis that by consenting to unprotected sexual intercourse with him, they were impliedly consenting to all the risks associated with sexual intercourse. He argued that as infection with the HIV virus may be one possible consequence of unprotected sexual intercourse, the complainants had consented to the risk of contracting the HIV virus from him. Accordingly he should be acquitted. By their verdicts, the jury found that none of the complainants consented to the risk of contracting the HIV virus.

...

Consent

34. Referring to HIV, the judge directed the jury that they had to be sure that the complainant in each individual case:

'... did not willingly consent to the risk of suffering that infection. Note that I use the phrase "to the risk of suffering that infection" and not merely just "to suffering it". That is an important point which Mr Roberts rightly drew to your attention in his speech to you this morning. He put it this way, it is whether she consented to that risk, not consented to being given the disease which is, as he put it graphically, a mile away from the former. That is right, but note that I use the word "willingly" in the phrase "willingly consent", and I did that to highlight that the sort of consent I am talking about means consciously.'

He returned to the clear and important distinction between 'running a risk on one hand and consenting to run that risk on the other', pointing out that the prosecution had to establish that the complainant 'did not willingly consent to the risk of suffering the infection in the sense of her having consciously thought about it at the time and decided to run it'. He added that the appellant should be acquitted, if, in relation to any complainant, she had thought of the risk of getting HIV, and nevertheless decided to take the risk. In answer to a question from the jury, he returned to emphasise that before the appellant could be convicted, the prosecution had to prove that she 'did not willingly consent to the risk of suffering that infection', and he repeated that for the purposes of his direction, 'willingly' meant 'consciously'. He again repeated the distinction between 'running a risk on the one hand and consenting to run that risk on the other', adding that the 'willing' consent involved knowing the implications of infection with the HIV virus.

35. In short, the judge explained that before the consent of the complainant could provide the appellant with a defence, it was required to be an informed and willing consent to the risk of contracting HIV . . .

42. The recognition in *R v Dica* of informed consent as a defence was based on 'but limited by' potentially conflicting public policy considerations. In the public interest, so far as possible, the spread of catastrophic illness must be avoided or prevented. On the other hand, the public interest also requires that the principle of personal autonomy in the context of adult non-violent sexual relationships should be maintained. If an individual who knows that he is suffering from the HIV virus conceals this stark fact from his sexual partner, the principle of her personal autonomy is not enhanced if he is exculpated when he recklessly transmits the HIV virus to her through consensual sexual intercourse. On any view, the concealment of this fact from her almost inevitably means that she is deceived. Her consent is not properly informed, and she cannot give an informed consent to something of which she is ignorant. Equally, her personal autonomy is not normally protected by allowing a defendant who knows that he is suffering from the HIV virus which he deliberately conceals, to assert an honest belief in his partner's informed consent to the risk of the transmission of the HIV virus. Silence in these circumstances is incongruous with honesty, or with a genuine belief that there is an informed consent. Accordingly, in such circumstances the issue either of informed consent, or honest belief in it will only rarely arise: in reality, in most cases, the contention would be wholly artificial.

43. This is not unduly burdensome. The defendant is not to be convicted of this offence unless it is proved that he was reckless. If so, the necessary *mens rea* will be established. Recklessness is a question of fact, to be proved by the prosecution. Equally the defendant is not to be convicted if there was, or may have been an informed consent by his sexual partner to the risk that he would transfer the HIV virus to her. In many cases, as in *Dica* itself, provided recklessness is established, the critical factual area of dispute will address what, if anything, was said between the two individuals involved, one of whom knows, and the other of whom does not know, that one of them is suffering the HIV virus. In the final analysis, the question of consent, like the issue of recklessness is fact-specific.

44. In deference to Mr Roberts' submission, we accept that there may be circumstances in which it would be open to the jury to infer that, notwithstanding that the defendant was reckless and concealed his condition from the complainant, she may nevertheless have given an informed consent to the risk of contracting the HIV virus. By way of example, an individual with HIV may develop a sexual relationship with someone who knew him while he was in hospital, receiving treatment for the condition. If so, her informed consent, if it were indeed informed, would remain a defence, to be disproved by the prosecution, even if the defendant had not personally informed her of his condition. Even if she did not in fact consent, this example would illustrate the basis for an argument that he honestly believed in her informed consent. Alternatively, he may honestly believe that his new sexual partner was told of his condition by someone known to them both. Cases like these, not too remote to be fanciful, may arise. If they do, no doubt they will be explored with the complainant in cross-examination. Her answers may demonstrate an informed consent. Nothing remotely like that was suggested here. In a different case, perhaps supported by the defendant's

own evidence, material like this may provide a basis for suggesting that he honestly believed that she was giving an informed consent. He may provide an account of the incident, or the affair, which leads the jury to conclude that even if she did not give an informed consent, he may honestly have believed that she did. Acknowledging these possibilities in different cases does not, we believe, conflict with the public policy considerations identified in *R v Dica*. That said, they did not arise in the present case.

45. Why not? In essence because the jury found that the complainants did not give a willing or informed consent to the risks of contracting the HIV virus from the appellant. We recognise that where consent does provide a defence to an offence against the person, it is generally speaking correct that the defendant's honest belief in the alleged victim's consent would also provide a defence. However for this purpose, the defendant's honest belief must be concomitant with the consent which provides a defence. Unless the consent would provide a defence, an honest belief in it would not assist the defendant. This follows logically from *R v Brown* [see section 11.4.2]. For it to do so here, what was required was some evidence of an honest belief that the complainants, or any one of them, were consenting to the risk that they might be infected with the HIV virus by him. There is not the slightest evidence, direct or indirect, from which a jury could begin to infer that the appellant honestly believed that any complainant consented to that specific risk. As there was no such evidence, the judge's ruling about 'honest belief' was correct. In fact, the honest truth was that the appellant deceived them.

46. In our judgment, the judge's directions to the jury sufficiently explained the proper implications to the case of the consensual participation by each of the complainants to sexual intercourse with the appellant. The jury concluded, in the case of each complainant, that she did not willingly or consciously consent to the risk of suffering the HIV virus.

Appeal against conviction dismissed

11.3.2 D genuinely but mistakenly believes V has consented to an assault or battery: (1)(b)

Consistent with the decisions in *Kimber* [1983] 3 All ER 316, and *Gladstone Williams* (1987) 78 Cr App R 276, section 23.6.1.1, p 660, it was held in *Jones* (1986) 83 Cr App R 375, [1987] Crim LR 123, CA, that there is no assault where D genuinely believes in the other's consent, and it is irrelevant whether that belief is reasonably held or not.

≈≈≈ *Questions*

D has unprotected sex with V. What is D's liability for an offence against the person if:

(1) D knows he is HIV positive and he believes that V knows this but he has not told her himself?

(2) D suspects he may be HIV positive and he believes that V is aware that he, D, may be, but he has not discussed it with her?

11.4 Consent recognized in law

11.4.1 Level of harm capable of being consented to in law: (2)(a)

On the level of harm to which V may in law consent see *Brown* in the following extract.

11.4.2 V may give valid factual consent to assault or battery and higher levels of harm in exceptional categories of conduct: (2)(b)

Beyond assault and battery, the *general* rule is that V may not give valid consent. Only in exceptional cases (surgery, sport, etc) may V consent to the infliction or risk of infliction of more serious injury than assault and battery. This is a controversial approach.

R v Brown
[1992] UKHL 7, House of Lords

(Lords Templeman, Jauncey of Tullichettle, Lowry, Mustill and Slynn of Hadley)

The appellants belonged to a group of sadomasochists who willingly cooperated in the commission of acts of violence against each other for sexual pleasure. Their activities included whipping and caning on the bare buttocks, branding, the application of stinging nettles to the genital area and inserting map pins or fish hooks into the penis. There was no permanent injury done, no infection of the wounds and no evidence that any of the men had sought medical treatment. Their actions were carried out in private and there was no complaint made to the police who found out about these activities by chance when they were investigating other matters. The appellants were convicted of assault occasioning actual bodily harm contrary to s 47, and, in three cases, of malicious wounding contrary to s 20 OAPA.

These convictions were upheld by the Court of Appeal which certified the following point of law of general public importance:

> Where A wounds or assaults B occasioning him actual bodily harm in the course of a sado-masochistic encounter, does the prosecution have to prove lack of consent on the part of B before they can establish A's guilt under section 20 and section 47 of the 1861, Offences Against the Person Act?

Lord Templeman:

Three of the appellants pleaded guilty to charges under section 20 when the trial judge ruled that the consent of the victim afforded no defence.

In the present case each of the appellants intentionally inflicted violence upon another (to whom I refer as 'the victim') with the consent of the victim and thereby occasioned actual bodily harm or in some cases wounding or grievous bodily harm. Each appellant was therefore guilty of an offence under section 47 or section 20 of the Act of 1861 unless the consent of the victim was effective to prevent the commission of the offence or effective to constitute a defence to the charge.

In some circumstances violence is not punishable under the criminal law. When no actual bodily harm is caused, the consent of the person affected precludes him from complaining. There can be no conviction for the summary offence of common assault if the victim has consented to the assault. Even when violence is intentionally inflicted and results in actual bodily harm, wounding or serious bodily harm the accused is entitled to be acquitted if the injury was a foreseeable incident of a lawful activity in which the person injured was participating. Surgery involves intentional violence resulting in actual or sometimes serious bodily harm but surgery is a lawful activity. Other activities carried on with consent by or on behalf of the injured person have been accepted as lawful notwithstanding that they involve actual bodily harm or may cause serious bodily harm. Ritual circumcision, tattooing, ear-piercing and violent sports including boxing are lawful activities.

In earlier days some other forms of violence were lawful and when they ceased to be lawful they were tolerated until well into the 19th century. Duelling and fighting were at first lawful and then tolerated provided the protagonists were voluntary participants. But where the results of these activities was the maiming of one of the participants, the defence of consent never availed the aggressor; see *Hawkins Pleas of the Crown* (1824), 8th edn, chapter 15. A maim was bodily harm whereby a man was deprived of the use of any member of his body which he needed to use in order to fight but a bodily injury was not a maim merely because it was a disfigurement. The act of maim was unlawful because the King was deprived of the services of an able-bodied citizen for the defence of the realm. Violence which maimed was unlawful despite consent to the activity which produced the maiming. In these days there is no difference between maiming on the one hand and wounding or causing grievous bodily harm on the other hand except with regard to sentence.

When duelling became unlawful, juries remained unwilling to convict but the judges insisted that persons guilty of causing death or bodily injury should be convicted despite the consent of the victim.

Similarly, in the old days, fighting was lawful provided the protagonists consented because it was thought that fighting inculcated bravery and skill and physical fitness. The brutality of knuckle fighting however caused the courts to declare that such fights were unlawful even if the protagonists consented. Rightly or wrongly the courts accepted that boxing is a lawful activity.

In *R v Coney* (1882) 8 QBD 534, the court held that a prize-fight in public was unlawful . . .

The conclusion is that a prize-fight being unlawful, actual bodily harm or serious bodily harm inflicted in the course of a prize-fight is unlawful notwithstanding the consent of the protagonists.

In *R v Donovan* [1934] 2 KB 498 the appellant in private beat a girl of seventeen for purposes of sexual gratification, it was said with her consent. Swift J said, at 507 that:

'It is an unlawful act to beat another person with such a degree of violence that the infliction of bodily harm is a probable consequence, and when such an act is proved, consent is immaterial.'

In *A-G's Reference (No 6 of 1980)* [1981] 2 All ER 1057, [1981] QB 715 where two men quarrelled and fought with bare fists Lord Lane CJ, delivering the judgment of the Court of Appeal, said at 719:

'. . . It is not in the public interest that people should try to cause, or should cause, each other bodily harm for no good reason. Minor struggles are another matter. So, in our judgment, it is immaterial whether the act occurs in private or in public; it is an assault if actual bodily harm is intended and/or caused. This means that most fights will be unlawful regardless of consent. Nothing which we have said is intended to cast doubt upon the accepted legality of properly conducted games and sports, lawful chastisement or correction, reasonable surgical interference, dangerous exhibitions, etc. These apparent exceptions can be justified as involving the exercise of a legal right, in the case of chastisement or correction, or as needed in the public interest, in the other cases.' [Cf *Slingsby*, section 9.2.1.1, p 210.]

Duelling and fighting are both unlawful and the consent of the protagonists affords no defence to charges of causing actual bodily harm, wounding or grievous bodily harm in the course of an unlawful activity.

The appellants and their victims in the present case were engaged in consensual homosexual activities. The attitude of the public towards homosexual practices changed in the second half of this century. Change in public attitudes led to a change in the law . . . . [Lord Templeman referred to the Wolfenden Report and subsequent legislation.]

My Lords, the authorities dealing with the intentional infliction of bodily harm do not establish that consent is a defence to a charge under the Act of 1861. They establish that the courts have accepted that consent is a defence to the infliction of bodily harm in the course of some lawful activities. The question is whether the defence should be extended to the infliction of bodily harm in the course of sado-masochistic encounters. The Wolfenden Committee did not make any recommendations about sado-masochism and Parliament did not deal with violence in 1967. The Act of 1967 is of no assistance for present purposes because the present problem was not under consideration.

The question whether the defence of consent should be extended to the consequences of sado-masochistic encounters can only be decided by consideration of policy and public interest. Parliament can call on the advice of doctors, psychiatrists, criminologists, sociologists and other experts and can also sound and take into account public opinion. But the question must at this stage be decided by this House in its judicial capacity in order to determine whether the convictions of the appellants should be upheld or quashed.

Counsel for some of the appellants argued that the defence of consent should be extended to the offence of occasioning actual bodily harm under section 47 of the Act of 1861 but should not be available to charges of serious wounding and the inflicting of serious bodily harm under section 20. I do not consider that this solution is practicable. Sado-masochistic participants have no way of foretelling the degree of bodily harm which will result from their encounters. The differences between actual bodily harm and serious bodily harm cannot be satisfactorily applied by a jury in order to determine acquittal or conviction.

Counsel for the appellants argued that consent should provide a defence to charges under both section 20 and section 47 because, it was said, every person has a right to deal with his body as he pleases. I do not consider that this slogan provides a sufficient guide to the policy decision which must now be made. It is an offence for a person to abuse his own body and mind by taking drugs. Although the law is often broken, the criminal law restrains a practice which is regarded as dangerous and injurious to individuals and which if allowed and extended is harmful to society generally. In any event the appellants in this case did not mutilate their own bodies. They inflicted bodily harm on willing victims. Suicide is no longer an offence but a person who assists another to commit suicide is guilty of murder or manslaughter. [NB: his lordship is wrong on this. See section 8.4, p 204.]

The assertion was made on behalf of the appellants that the sexual appetites of sadists and masochists can only be satisfied by the infliction of bodily harm and that the law should not punish the consensual achievement of sexual satisfaction. There was no evidence to support the assertion that sado-masochist activities are essential to the happiness of the appellants or any other participants but the argument would be acceptable if sado-masochism were only concerned with sex, as the appellants contend. In my opinion sado-masochism is not only concerned with sex. Sado-masochism is also concerned with violence. The evidence discloses that the practices of the appellants were unpredictably dangerous and degrading to body and mind and were developed with increasing barbarity and taught to persons whose consents were dubious or worthless.

A sadist draws pleasure from inflicting or watching cruelty. A masochist derives pleasure from his own pain or humiliation. The appellants are middle-aged men. The victims were youths some of whom were introduced to sado-masochism before they attained the age of 21 [then the age of consent for men to have sex with men]. In his judgment in the Court of Appeal, Lord Lane CJ said that two members of the group of which the appellants formed part, namely one Cadman and the appellant Laskey:

'. . . were responsible in part for the corruption of a youth K . . . It is some comfort at least to be told, as we were, that K has now it seems settled into a normal heterosexual relationship. Cadman had befriended K when the boy was 15 years old. He met him in a cafeteria and, so he says, found out that the boy was interested in homosexual activities. He introduced and encouraged K in "bondage affairs". He was interested in viewing and recording on videotape K and other teenage boys in homosexual scenes . . . One cannot overlook the danger that the gravity of the assaults and injuries in this type of case may escalate to even more unacceptable heights.'

[His lordship referred to various of the sadomasochistic acts which had been performed, that while the appellants had not contracted AIDS, two members of the group had died from AIDS, that the assertion that the instruments were sterile could not remove the risk of infection, that cruelty to humans had been supplemented by cruelty to animals in the form of bestiality, and that, given the nature of the acts, it was not surprising there had been no complaint to the police.]

In principle there is a difference between violence which is incidental and violence which is inflicted for the indulgence of cruelty. The violence of sado-masochistic encounters involves the indulgence of cruelty by sadists and the degradation of victims. Such violence is injurious to the participants and unpredictably dangerous. I am not prepared to invent a defence of consent for sado-masochistic encounters which breed and glorify cruelty and result in offences under sections 47 and 20 of the Act of 1861 . . .

≋ *Questions*

(1) Were the defendants engaged in violence or sexual activity?

(2) Counsel for some of the appellants argued that consent should be a defence to a charge under s 47 but not to serious wounding or serious bodily harm under s 20. Lord Templeman rejected this because 'differences between actual bodily harm and serious bodily harm cannot be satisfactorily applied by a jury in order to determine acquittal or conviction'. But is this not a distinction which juries are regularly called upon to make?

Lord Jauncey of Tullichettle:

. . . It was accepted by all the appellants that a line had to be drawn somewhere between those injuries to which a person could consent to infliction upon himself and those which were so serious that consent was immaterial. They all agreed that assaults occasioning actual bodily harm should be below the line but there was disagreement as to whether all offences against section 20 of the Act of 1861 should be above the line or only those resulting in grievous bodily harm. The four English cases to which I have referred were not concerned with the distinction between the various types of assault and did not therefore have to address the problem raised in these appeals. However it does appear that in *Donovan; A-G's Reference (No 6 of 1980)*, and *Boyea* (1992) 156 JP 505, [1992] Crim LR 574, the infliction of actual bodily harm was considered to be sufficient to negative any consent. Indeed in *Donovan* and *Boyea* such injuries as were sustained by the two women could not have been described as in any way serious. Cave J in *Coney* also appeared to take the same view. On the other hand, Stephen J in Coney appeared to consider that it required serious danger to life and limb to negative consent, a view which broadly accords with the passage in his digest to which I have already referred. A similar view was expressed by McInerney J in the Supreme Court of Victoria in *Pallante v Stadiums Property Ltd* [1976] VR 331.

I prefer the reasoning of Cave J in *Coney* and of the Court of Appeal in the later three English cases which I consider to have been correctly decided. In my view the line properly falls to be drawn between assault at common law and the offence of assault occasioning actual bodily harm created by section 47 of the Offences Against the Person Act 1861, with the result that consent of the victim is no answer to anyone charged with the latter offence or with a contravention of section 20 unless the circumstances fall within one of the well known exceptions such as organised sporting contests and games, parental chastisement or reasonable surgery. There is nothing in sections 20 and 47 of the Act of 1861 to suggest that consent is either an essential ingredient of the offences or a defence thereto . . .

[I]n considering the public interest it would be wrong to look only at the activities of the appellants alone, there being no suggestion that they and their associates are the only practitioners of homosexual sado-masochism in England and Wales. This House must therefore consider the possibility that these activities are practised by others and by others who are not so controlled or responsible as the appellants are claimed to be. Without going into details of all the rather curious activities in which the appellants engaged it would appear to be good luck rather than good judgment which has prevented serious injury from occurring. Wounds can easily become septic if not properly treated, the free flow of blood from a person who is HIV positive or who has AIDS can infect another and an inflicter who is carried away by sexual excitement or by drink or drugs could very easily inflict pain and injury beyond the level to which the receiver had consented. Your Lordships have no information as to whether such situations have occurred in relation to other sado-masochistic practitioners. It was no doubt these dangers which caused Lady Mallalieu to restrict her propositions in relation to the public interest to the actual rather than the potential result of the activity. In my view such a restriction is quite unjustified. When considering the public interest potential for harm is just as relevant as actual harm. As Mathew J said in *Coney* (1882) 8 QBD 534, 547:

> 'There is however abundant authority for saying that no consent can render that innocent which is in fact dangerous.'

Furthermore, the possibility of proselytisation and corruption of young men is a real danger even in the case of these appellants and the taking of video recordings of such activities suggest that secrecy may not be as strict as the appellants claimed to your Lordships. If the only purpose of the activity is the sexual gratification of one or both of the participants what then is the need of a video recording?

My Lords I have no doubt that it would not be in the public interest that deliberate infliction of actual bodily harm during the course of homosexual sado-masochistic activities should be held to be lawful. In reaching this conclusion I have regard to the information available in these appeals and of such inferences as may be drawn therefrom. I appreciate that there may be a great deal of information relevant to these activities which is not available to your Lordships. When Parliament passed the Sexual Offences Act 1967 which made buggery and acts of gross indecency between consenting males lawful it had available the Wolfenden Report (1957) (Cmnd 247) which was the product of an exhaustive research into the problem. If it is to be decided that such activities as the nailing by A of B's foreskin or scrotum to a board or the insertion of hot wax into C's urethra followed by the burning of his penis with a candle or the incising of D's scrotum with a scalpel to the effusion of blood are injurious neither to B, C and D nor to the public interest then it is for Parliament with its accumulated wisdom and sources of information to declare them to be lawful.

There was argument as to whether consent, where available, was a necessary ingredient of the offence of assault or merely a defence. There are conflicting data as to its effect. In Coney Stephen J referred to consent as 'being no defence', whereas in *A-G's Reference (No 6 of 1980)* [1981] 2 All ER 1057, [1981] QB 715 Lord Lane CJ referred to the onus being on the prosecution to negative consent. In *Collins v Wilcock* [1984] 1 WLR 1172, 1177F Goff LJ referred to consent being a defence to a battery. If it were necessary, which it is not, in this appeal to decide which argument was correct I would hold that consent was a defence to but not a necessary ingredient in assault. . . .

I would . . . dismiss the appeals.

[**Lord Lowry** made a speech dismissing the appeals.]

Lord Mustill:

. . . I ask myself not whether as a result of the decision in this appeal, activities such as those of the appellants should *cease* to be criminal, but rather whether the Act of 1861 (a statute which I venture to repeat once again was clearly intended to penalise conduct of a quite different nature) should in this new situation be interpreted so as to *make* it criminal. Why should this step be taken? Leaving aside repugnance and moral objection, both of which are entirely natural but neither of which are in my opinion grounds upon which the court could properly create a new crime, I can visualise only the following reasons:

1. Some of the practices obviously created a risk of genito-urinary infection, and others of septi-caemia. These might indeed have been grave in former times, but the risk of serious harm must surely have been greatly reduced by modern medical science.

2. The possibility that matters might get out of hand, with grave results. . . . If this happened, those responsible would be punished according to the ordinary law, in the same way as those who kill or injure in the course of more ordinary sexual activities are regularly punished. But to penalise the

appellants' conduct even if the extreme consequences do not ensue, just because they might have done so would require an assessment of the degree of risk, and the balance of this risk against the interests of individual freedom. Such a balancing is in my opinion for Parliament, not the courts. . . .

3. I would give the same answer to the suggestion that these activities involved a risk of accelerating the spread of auto-immune deficiency syndrome, and that they should be brought within the Act of 1861 in the interests of public health. The consequence would be strange, since what is currently the principal cause for the transmission of this scourge, namely consenting buggery between males, is now legal. Nevertheless, I would have been compelled to give this proposition the most anxious consideration if there had been any evidence to support it. But there is none, since the case for the respondent was advanced on an entirely different ground.

4. There remains an argument to which I have given much greater weight. As the evidence in the present case has shown, there is a risk that strangers (and especially young strangers) may be drawn into these activities at an early age and will then become established in them for life. This is indeed a disturbing prospect, but I have come to the conclusion that it is not a sufficient ground for declaring these activities to be criminal under the Act of 1861. The element of the corruption of youth is already catered for by the existing legislation; and if there is a gap in it which needs to be filled the remedy surely lies in the hands of Parliament, not in the application of a statute which is aimed at other forms of wrong-doing.

Leaving aside the logic of this answer, which seems to me impregnable, plain humanity demands that a court addressing the criminality of conduct such as that of the present should recognise and respond to the profound dismay which all members of the community share about the apparent increase of cruel and senseless crimes against the defenceless. Whilst doing so I must repeat for the last time that in the answer which I propose I do not advocate the decriminalisation of conduct which has hitherto been a crime: nor do I rebut a submission that a new crime should be created, penalising this conduct, for Mr Purnell has rightly not invited the House to take this course. The only question is whether these consensual private acts are offences against the existing law of violence. To this question I return a negative response. I would allow these appeals.

[**Lord Slynn** made a speech and said that he would allow the appeals.]

Appeals dismissed

≋ *Questions*
(1) How should Parliament define the limits of consent to injury or physical harm (or the risk thereof) in criminal law? See P. Roberts, 'The Philosophical Foundations of Consent in the Criminal Law' (1997) 17 OJLS 389.
(2) Is the level of harm to which one is permitted to consent clearly defined?

The judges in *Brown* seem to agree that consent is a complete defence to common assault and (except for persons under 16 and those with mental illness) that it would have been a defence to the charge of indecent assault (now repealed, see Sexual Offences Act 2003); yet in *Donovan*, where V consented to being caned, it was held that, but for misdirection, D's convictions for common and indecent assault would have been upheld; and that view seems to have been generally accepted. Lord Lowry, however, [1993] 2 All ER at 97, finds this aspect of *Donovan* hard to follow: 'If the jury, properly directed, had found that consent was not disproved, they must have acquitted the appellant of the only charges brought against him. How, then, could they have convicted the appellant of either of those charges or of the offence of assault, occasioning actual bodily harm, with which he was *not* charged?'

11.4.3 Is D's conduct in causing the impermissible level of harm within an 'exceptional' category? (2)(b)

D will not be liable if the conduct in question represents an exceptional category in which V's consent will be recognized (sports, surgery, boxing, etc) and D has V's consent or a genuine belief in it.

What are the exceptional categories listed in *Brown*?

≈≈ *Questions*

(1) What do the following activities have in common: surgery, sports, boxing, horseplay, tattooing, ritual male circumcision? Are they all likely to result in the same level of harm? Do they all necessarily involve the infliction of harm, or merely the risk of the infliction of harm? Are they all accepted by society generally to be beneficial to the person on whom the resulting injury is inflicted?

(2) Does this list of exceptions based on policy grounds reflect a coherent and desirable approach to the limits of consent? See Law Commission Consultation Paper No 139, *Consent in the Criminal Law* (1995).

In *Wilson* [1996] 2 Cr App R 241, [1996] Crim LR 573, D branded his initials with a hot knife on his wife's buttocks. She had wanted his initials to be tattooed thereon, but, as he did not know how to do that, she had agreed to the branding instead. D was charged with assault occasioning actual bodily harm, contrary to s 47. The judge held that he was bound by *Brown* to direct the jury to convict. The Court of Appeal quashed D's conviction, saying that they shared the trial judge's disquiet that the proceedings should have been brought. *Brown* was not authority for the proposition that consent was no defence to a charge under s 47 in all circumstances. *Brown* concerned sadomasochism involving torture, danger of serious physical injury and blood infection. The act in *Donovan* was done for the purposes of sexual gratification and had an aggressive element. There was no aggressive element on D's part. D was assisting W to acquire a physical adornment, not logically different from a tattoo. The court asked itself, did public policy and the public interest demand that D's activity should be visited by the sanctions of the criminal law—that is, should the *offence* be extended, and answered, no. In *Brown*, Lord Templeman thought that the question was whether the *defence* of consent should be extended to the consequences of sadomasochistic activity; and answered, no. Compare the approach of Lord Mustill in *Brown*. May the result then depend on how the court poses the question?

≈≈ *Questions*

Is the effect of *Wilson* that bottom-branding is to be added to a list of exceptions—manly sports, male circumcision, ear-piercing, tattooing, etc—where consent is a defence to a charge under s 47 or s 20? Or does it mean that consent is, after all, a defence to those charges—*except* where public policy demands it should not be? Would the result have been different if Wilson had admitted that he derived sexual gratification from the performance of the operation? Should it be different?

In *Emmett* (1999) The Times, 15 October, E participated in sadomasochistic practices with his partner, which included igniting lighter fuel poured over her breasts and applying ligatures to her neck. E was convicted under s 47 OAPA. The Court of Appeal upheld the conviction, distinguishing *Wilson* on the basis that a s 47 offence had not been committed, there was no evidence of significant harm in that case and the parties had been married (in the present case the parties had only married since the incident). Is this a convincing basis for distinction? Is it a distinction that would withstand challenge under Article 8 and Article 14 of the European Convention on Human Rights (ECHR)? See section 11.5, p 298.

R v Dica
(section 11.3.1, p 282)

[The court referred to the cases of *Brown, Boyea, Donovan*, etc.]

46. These authorities demonstrate that violent conduct involving the deliberate and intentional infliction of bodily harm is and remains unlawful notwithstanding that its purpose is the sexual gratification of one or both participants. Notwithstanding their sexual overtones, these cases were concerned with violent crime, and the sexual overtones did not alter the fact that both parties were consenting to the deliberate infliction of serious harm or bodily injury on one participant by the other. To date, as a matter of public policy, it has not been thought appropriate for such violent conduct to be excused merely because there is a private consensual sexual element to it. The same public policy reason would prohibit the deliberate spreading of disease, including sexual disease.

47. In our judgement the impact of the authorities dealing with sexual gratification can too readily be misunderstood. It does not follow from them, and they do not suggest, that consensual acts of sexual intercourse are unlawful merely because there may be a known risk to the health of one or other participant. These participants are not intent on spreading or becoming infected with disease through sexual intercourse. They are not indulging in serious violence for the purposes of sexual gratification. They are simply prepared, knowingly, to run the risk—not the certainty—of infection, as well as all the other risks inherent in and possible consequences of sexual intercourse, such as, and despite the most careful precautions, an unintended pregnancy. At one extreme there is casual sex between complete strangers, sometimes protected, sometimes not, when the attendant risks are known to be higher, and at the other, there is sexual intercourse between couples in a long-term and loving, and trusting relationship, which may from time to time also carry risks.

48. The first of these categories is self-explanatory and needs no amplification. By way of illustration we shall provide two examples of cases which would fall within the second.

49. In the first, one of a couple suffers from HIV. It may be the man: it may be the woman. The circumstances in which HIV was contracted are irrelevant. They could result from a contaminated blood transfusion, or an earlier relationship with a previous sexual partner, who unknown to the sufferer with whom we are concerned, was himself or herself infected with HIV. The parties are Roman Catholics. They are conscientiously unable to use artificial contraception. They both know of the risk that the healthy partner may become infected with HIV. Our second example is that of a young couple, desperate for a family, who are advised that if the wife were to become pregnant and give birth, her long-term health, indeed her life itself, would be at risk. Together the couple decide to run that risk, and she becomes pregnant. She may be advised that the foetus should be aborted, on the grounds of her health, yet, nevertheless, decide to bring her baby to term. If she does, and suffers ill health, is the male partner to be criminally liable for having sexual intercourse with her, notwithstanding that he knew of the risk to her health? If he is liable to be prosecuted, was she not a party to whatever crime was committed? And should the law interfere with the Roman Catholic couple, and require them, at the peril of criminal sanctions, to choose between bringing their sexual relationship to an end or violating their consciences by using contraception?

50. These, and similar risks, have always been taken by adults consenting to sexual intercourse. Different situations, no less potentially fraught, have to be addressed by them. Modern society has not thought to criminalise those who have willingly accepted the risks, and we know of no cases where one or other of the consenting adults has been prosecuted, let alone convicted, for the consequences of doing so.

51. The problems of criminalising the consensual taking of risks like these include the sheer impracticability of enforcement and the haphazard nature of its impact. The process would undermine the general understanding of the community that sexual relationships are pre-eminently private and essentially personal to the individuals involved in them. And if adults were to be liable to prosecution for the consequences of taking known risks with their health, it would seem odd that this should be confined to risks taken in the context of sexual intercourse, while they are nevertheless permitted to take the risks inherent in so many other aspects of everyday life, including, again for example, the mother or father of a child suffering a serious contagious illness, who holds the child's hand, and comforts or kisses him or her goodnight.

52. In our judgement, interference of this kind with personal autonomy, and its level and extent, may only be made by Parliament. . . .

60. In view of our conclusion that the trial judge should not have withdrawn the issue of consent from the jury, the appeal is allowed. . . .

R v Konzani
(section 11.3.1, p 285)

Judge LJ:

. . . 35. In short, the judge explained that before the consent of the complainant could provide the appellant with a defence, it was required to be an informed and willing consent to the risk of contracting HIV. . . .

40. *R v Dica* represented what Lord Mustill in *R v Brown* described as a 'new challenge', and confirmed that in specific circumstances the ambit of the criminal law extended to consensual sexual intercourse between adults which involved a risk of the most extreme kind to the physical health of one participant. In the context of direct physical injury, he pointed out that cases involving the '. . . consensual infliction of violence are special. They have been in the past, and will continue to be in the future, the subject of special treatment by the law'. In his subsequent detailed examination of the 'situations in which the recipient consents or is deemed to consent to the infliction of violence upon him', activity of the kind currently under consideration did not remotely fall within any of the ten categories which he was able to identify. *Brown* itself emphatically established the clear principle that the consent of the injured person does not form a kind of all purpose species of defence to an offence of violence contrary to s 20 of the 1861 Act.

41. We are concerned with the risk of and the actual transmission of a potentially fatal disease through or in the course of consensual sexual relations which did not in themselves involve unlawful violence of the kind prohibited in *R v Brown*. The prosecution did not seek to prove that the disease was deliberately transmitted, with the intention required by s 18 of the 1861 Act. The allegation was that the appellant behaved recklessly on the basis that knowing that he was suffering from the HIV virus, and its consequences, and knowing the risks of its transmission to a sexual partner, he concealed his condition from the complainants, leaving them ignorant of it. When sexual intercourse occurred these complainants were ignorant of his condition. So although they consented to sexual intercourse, they did not consent to the transmission of the HIV virus.

~~~ *Questions*
(1) Why should V be permitted to consent to the *risk* of a potentially fatal infection of HIV by sex, but not to the *risk* of infection from the use of implements in genital torture?
(2) Are the categories of exceptional conduct clearly defined?

In relation to injury or the risk of injury in sport, a number of categories need to be separated.

First, if the rules of the sport permit an unacceptably dangerous act, the law need not recognize the validity of V's factual consent. That is a matter of public policy. Boxing continues to be lawful despite potentially life-threatening injury and the participants' intention to cause grievous bodily harm. See J. Anderson, *The Legality of Boxing: A Punch Drunk Love?* (2007).

Secondly, where unlike boxing and martial arts, playing within the rules of the particular sport does not *necessarily* involve D causing actual bodily harm, but D intentionally inflicts actual bodily harm or worse, V's consent is irrelevant and D commits the offence: *Bradshaw* (1878) Cox CC 83.

Thirdly, and most difficult in practical terms to apply, if in playing such a sport D was reckless only as to the causing of the injury the question will be whether V impliedly consented to the risk of that level of injury in the context in which it was inflicted. The question of whether the conduct was within the rules of the game is not the sole determinant of liability. It would be too simplistic to suggest that V's consent is only valid within the rules of the game. V may well, as a matter of fact, impliedly consent to the *risk* of injury occurring in conduct outside the rules as in a late tackle in football, or an illegitimate bouncer in cricket: *Moore* (1898) 14 TLR 229. It is therefore necessary to look to a broader range of factors. In *Barnes* [2005] EWCA Crim 3246, the Court of Appeal preferred to adopt an objective evaluation of these circumstances as in Canada (see *Ciccarelli* (1989) 54 CCC (3d) 121) and advocated by Law Commission Consultation Paper No 134, *Consent and Offences Against the Person* (1994). That approach was criticized by S. Gardner, 'The Law and the Sportsfield' [1994] Crim LR 513, but received generally favourable responses: Law Commission Consultation Paper 139, *Consent in Criminal Law* (1995), paras 12.6–12.23. Although one important factor will be whether the injury was inflicted when D was acting outside the rules of the game, it is submitted that this may require qualification so as to emphasize that only rules designed to protect against injury are considered: it should not, for example, be relevant that the impugned tackle occurred when D was breaking the offside rule.

For an analysis questioning the objective approach to consent in sports, but denying the need for a uniform approach throughout the criminal law, see B. Livings, 'A Different Ball Game' (2007) 71 J Crim L 534, cf C. Elliott and C. de Than, 'The Case for a Rational Reconstruction of Consent in Criminal Law' (2007) 70 MLR 225.

11.4.4 The level of harm caused is impermissible, but D intended only to cause consensual permissible harm or harm within an exceptional category with consent (2)(b)

D is not guilty if he intended only to cause a level of harm/harm in a context in which V's factual consent would be legally recognized and V had consented to that type of harm, or if V had not, D nevertheless genuinely believed that V had.

In *Meachen* [2006] EWCA Crim 2414, D administered a date rape drug to V. There was a dispute between the Crown and defence whether V consented to taking the drugs. D's case was that he penetrated her anus with several fingers while she was straddled on top of him bouncing up and down, as a result of which she suffered permanent and very serious injuries to her anus. D claimed that V had consented to anal penetration by his fingers and that he had not intended or foreseen injury to her. The Court of Appeal held that liability under s 20 requires proof that D intended to cause injury or was subjectively reckless as to whether he might cause injury. In this case, although the level of injury was GBH and therefore V could not in law consent to it, D was entitled to be acquitted if he intended only to inflict a battery on V by penetrating her anus (or was reckless about doing so) and he had her consent to that activity or he genuinely believed he had her consent to that activity. The decision clarifies the law substantially over the previous explanations offered by the Court of Appeal.

The problems had derived from an overbroad statement in the *A-G's Reference (No 6 of 1980)* [1981] QB 715, where two youths aged 18 and 17 settled an argument by a fist fight and one sustained a bleeding nose and bruises to his face and it was held that the other was guilty of assault occasioning actual bodily harm. 'It is not in the public interest that people should try to cause or should cause each other actual bodily harm for no good reason. Minor struggles are another matter. So, in our judgment, it is immaterial whether the act occurs in private or in public; it is an assault if actual bodily harm is *intended and/or caused*. This means that most fights will be unlawful regardless of consent.' This should now be read subject to *Meachen*.

≈≈ *Questions*

D (an adult) spanks V (an adult) with her consent. Is D guilty of an offence if:

(1) he intended to inflict bodily harm, as V desired, but was too timid in his delivery and inflicted only a battery;

(2) he intended to cause only a minor battery (as V desired), but he misjudged his strength and inflicted actual bodily harm?

11.5 Consent and the ECHR

In *Laskey v UK* (1997) 24 EHRR 39, the European Court of Human Rights heard an application made by the defendants in *Brown* alleging breaches of Article 8—the right to respect for private life. The European Court held unanimously there was no violation:

36. The Court observes that not every sexual activity carried out behind closed doors necessarily falls within the scope of Article 8. In the present case, the applicants were involved in consensual sado-masochistic activities for purposes of sexual gratification. There can be no doubt that sexual orientation and activity concern an intimate aspect of private life (see, *mutatis mutandis*, the *Dudgeon v the United Kingdom* judgment of 22 October 1981, Series A no. 45, p. 21, § 52). However, a considerable number of people were involved in the activities in question which included, *inter alia*, the recruitment of new 'members', the provision of several specially-equipped 'chambers', and the shooting of many video-tapes which were distributed among the 'members' . . . It may thus be open to question whether the sexual activities of the applicants fell entirely within the notion of 'private life' in the particular circumstances of the case.

However, since this point has not been disputed by those appearing before it, the Court sees no reason to examine it of its own motion in the present case. Assuming, therefore, that the prosecution and conviction of the applicants amounted to an interference with their private life, the question arises whether such an interference was 'necessary in a democratic society' within the meaning of the second paragraph of Article 8. . . .

38. In support of their submission, the applicants alleged that all those involved in the sado-masochistic encounters were willing adult participants; that participation in the acts complained of was carefully restricted and controlled and was limited to persons with like-minded sado-masochistic proclivities; that the acts were not witnessed by the public at large and that there was no danger or likelihood that they would ever be so witnessed; that no serious or permanent injury had been sustained, no infection had been caused to the wounds, and that no medical treatment had been required. Furthermore, no complaint was ever made to the police—who learnt about the applicants' activities by chance. . . .

39. The applicants submitted that their case should be viewed as one involving matters of sexual expression, rather than violence. With due regard to this consideration, the line beyond which consent is no defence to physical injury should only be drawn at the level of intentional or reckless causing of serious disabling injury.

40. For the Government, the State was entitled to punish acts of violence, such as those for which the applicants were convicted, that could not be considered of a trifling or transient nature, irrespective of the consent of the victim. In fact, in the present case, some of these acts could well be compared to 'genital torture' and a Contracting State could not be said to have an obligation to tolerate acts of torture because they are committed in the context of a consenting sexual relationship. The State was moreover entitled to prohibit activities because of their potential danger.

The Government further contended that the criminal law should seek to deter certain forms of behaviour on public health grounds but also for broader moral reasons. In this respect, acts of torture—such as those at issue in the present case—may be banned also on the ground that they undermine the respect which human beings should confer upon each other. In any event, the whole issue of the role of consent in the criminal law is of great complexity and the Contracting States should enjoy a wide margin of appreciation to consider all the public policy options. . . .

43. The Court considers that one of the roles which the State is unquestionably entitled to undertake is to seek to regulate, through the operation of the criminal law, activities which involve the infliction of physical harm. This is so whether the activities in question occur in the course of sexual conduct or otherwise.

44. The determination of the level of harm that should be tolerated by the law in situations where the victim consents is in the first instance a matter for the State concerned since what is at stake is related, on the one hand, to public health considerations and to the general deterrent effect of the criminal law, and, on the other, to the personal autonomy of the individual.

45. The applicants have contended that, in the circumstances of the case, the behaviour in question formed part of private morality which is not the State's business to regulate. In their submission the matters for which they were prosecuted and convicted concerned only private sexual behaviour.

The Court is not persuaded by this submission. It is evident from the facts established by the national courts that the applicants' sado-masochistic activities involved a significant degree of injury or wounding which could not be characterised as trifling or transient. This, in itself, suffices to distinguish the present case from those applications which have previously been examined by the Court concerning consensual homosexual behaviour in private between adults where no such feature was present (see the *Dudgeon v the United Kingdom* judgment cited above, the *Norris v Ireland* judgment of 26 October 1988, Series A no. 142, and the *Modinos v Cyprus* judgment of 22 April 1993, Series A no. 259).

46. Nor does the Court accept the applicants' submission that no prosecution should have been brought against them since their injuries were not severe and since no medical treatment had been required.

In deciding whether or not to prosecute, the State authorities were entitled to have regard not only to the actual seriousness of the harm caused—which as noted above was considered to be significant—but also, as stated by Lord Jauncey of Tullichettle . . . , to the potential for harm inherent in the acts in question. In this respect it is recalled that the activities were considered by Lord Templeman to be 'unpredictably dangerous' . . .

≈≈≈ *Questions*

Do you agree that the English law is sufficiently certain? Do you agree that criminalization is necessary and proportionate so as to fall within Article 8(2)?

FURTHER READING

M. Allen, 'Consent and Assault' (1994) 58 J Crim Law 183

N. Bamforth, 'Sadomasochism and Consent' [1994] Crim LR 661

M. Giles, 'Consensual Harm and the Public Interest' (1994) 57 MLR 101

D. Kell, 'Social Disutility and Consent' (1994) 14 OJLS 121

Law Commission Consultation Paper No 134, *Consent and Offences against the Person* (1994)

Law Commission Consultation Paper No 139, *Consent in Criminal Law* (1995)

D. Ormerod, 'Consent and Offences Against the Person: Law Commission Consultation Paper No 134' (1994) 57 MLR 928

D. Ormerod and M. J. Gunn, 'Consent—A Second Bash' [1996] Crim LR 694

P. Roberts, 'The Philosophical Foundations of Consent in the Criminal Law' (1997) 17 OJLS 389

S. Shute, 'Something Old, Something New, Something Borrowed—Three Aspects of the Consent Project' [1996] Crim LR 684

J. Tolmie, 'Consent to Harmful Assaults: The Case for Moving Away from Category Based Decision Making' [2012] Crim LR 656

12

Sexual offences

Sexual Offences Act 2003—the main offences:

Rape—s 1: The defendant, A, commits rape if he intentionally penetrates the vagina, anus or mouth of another person (B) with his penis, B does not consent to the penetration, and A does not reasonably believe that B consents.

Sexual penetration—s 2: The defendant, A, commits an offence if he intentionally sexually penetrates the vagina or anus of another person (B) with a part of his body or anything else without consent and A does not reasonably believe that B consents.

Sexual assault—s 3: The defendant, A, commits an offence if he intentionally sexually touches another person (B), the touching is sexual, B does not consent to the touching and A does not reasonably believe that B consents.

Causing a person to engage in sexual activity—s 4: The defendant, A, commits an offence if he intentionally causes another person (B) to engage in a sexual activity, B does not consent to engaging in the activity and A does not reasonably believe that B consents.

Some of the controversies that will be examined in this chapter include:

(1) Parliament's failure to define core elements of the offences, such as 'consent' and 'sexual' and the attempts by the courts to fill these lacunae;

(2) the overly wide breadth of some of the offences;

(3) whether a deception perpetrated by the defendant necessarily vitiates the complainant's consent;

(4) the effect of voluntary alcohol consumption on the complainant's ability to consent to sexual acts;

(5) the normative underpinning of the offences, that is, whether the rationale for their enactment is the protection of autonomy or some other value;

(6) the excessive use of strict liability.

12.1 The background to the Sexual Offences Act 2003

The law governing sexual offences is now found in the Sexual Offences Act 2003. The 2003 Act provisions are based on research from the Home Office consultation paper, *Setting the Boundaries, Reforming the Law on Sexual Offences* (see N. Lacey, 'Beset by Boundaries' [2001] Crim LR 3). See also, for an interesting comparison, Scottish Law Commission Discussion Paper No 131, *Rape and Other Offences* (2006).

The Act was prompted by calls for urgent reform due to concern over attrition rates (ie the proportion of those cases reported as sexual assaults which did not lead to a successful conviction) rising dramatically in the 1980s and 1990s. See HM Crown Prosecution Service Inspectorate, *Report of the Joint Investigation into the Investigation and Prosecution of Cases Involving Allegations of Rape* (2002). See further J. Temkin and B. Krahe, *The Justice Gap* (2008).

For detailed criticism of the old law, see J. Temkin, *Rape and the Legal Process* (2nd edn, 2002). Most of the relevant law was contained in the Sexual Offences Act 1956, but that was itself merely a consolidation of various statutes dating back to the late nineteenth century. The law was widely regarded as: incoherent; discriminatory; failing to reflect the morality, prevalent sexual attitudes and practices of the twenty-first century; and providing inadequate protection for the vulnerable, while also failing to respect the sexual autonomy of those capable of making informed choices about their sexual behaviour. Many aspects of the old law were so discriminatory as to be incompatible with European Convention on Human Rights (ECHR) obligations: for example, offences such as gross indecency between males breached Article 8: *ADT v UK* (2000) 31 EHRR 803. The Government review in *Setting the Boundaries* set out to produce coherent and clear offences which protect individuals, especially children and the more vulnerable, from abuse and exploitation. It also aimed to enable more appropriate punishment of abusers, and to create a statutory framework which would be fair and non-discriminatory in accordance with the ECHR and the Human Rights Act 1998.

The 2003 Act redefines many of the offences found in the old legislation, but introduces a great number of new offences. It has been subjected to stringent and cogent criticism: see especially J. Temkin and A. Ashworth, 'Rape, Sexual Assaults and the Problems of Consent' [2004] Crim LR 328. It is impossible to deal with all of the offences in this chapter. The focus is on the non-consensual offences.

12.2 Non-consensual offences

12.2.1 Rape

Sexual Offences Act 2003, s 1

> (1) A person (A) commits an offence if—
>   (a) he intentionally penetrates the vagina, anus or mouth of another person (B) with his penis,
>   (b) B does not consent to the penetration, and
>   (c) A does not reasonably believe that B consents.
> (2) Whether a belief is reasonable is to be determined having regard to all the circumstances, including any steps A has taken to ascertain whether B consents.

Note that the Act adopts an odd style, with the offender always referred to as 'A' and the complainant or victim as 'B'. We follow that approach in this chapter.

12.2.1.1 The actus reus

For the first time in England and Wales, the 2003 Act extended rape to include non-consensual oral sex. It was argued by some that this inclusion devalues 'real' rape. Prosecutors should specify which orifice is alleged to have been penetrated, but there is only one offence: *K* [2009] 1 Cr App R 131. The offence can be committed as a principal offender only by a man. Note that s 2 (section 12.2.2) provides a new offence of sexual penetration by objects other than the penis. Section 79(3) makes clear that surgically reconstructed body parts are included as parts of the 'body'. A, with his surgically reconstructed penis, can rape B with her surgically reconstructed vagina. This closes a loophole under the old law: see M. Hicks and G. Branston, 'Transsexual Rape—A Loophole Closed?' [1997] Crim LR 565.

Under the 1956 Act, it was held that sexual intercourse was a continuing act, and if B withdrew consent at any time during the act, A would commit the actus reus of rape: *Kaitamaki v R* [1985] AC 147, PC. Rape is now defined in terms of 'penetration' rather than 'sexual intercourse', and s 79(2) provides that penetration is a continuing act. Section 44 of the 1956 Sexual Offences Act (now repealed) provided that it was not necessary to prove the completion of intercourse by the 'emission of seed'. There is no such provision in the 2003 Act.

≋ **Question**

Should all acts of sexual penetration by whatever object be classified as rape?

12.2.1.2 Consent

The crucial element of rape (and the other non-consensual offences discussed in this chapter) is the absence of consent. Without that, penile penetration is not criminal. Sections 74 to 76 of the 2003 Act seek to provide a clear definition of consent that can be applied consistently. These sections create three separate routes by which the prosecution may seek to establish absence of consent:

- s 74: general definition of consent;
- s 75: rebuttable presumptions; and
- s 76: conclusive (ie irrebuttable) presumptions.

Despite this purported clarification, defining consent remains problematic.

≋ **Questions**

(1) Is it possible to define 'consent' in statutory language in a way that can be applied in practice?

(2) Why is the absence of consent an element of the actus reus? Could it be a defence?

(3) Is the act of sexual intercourse prima facie 'wrong'? Should the penetrator need to justify his action of penetration in every case? Cf the argument by M. Madden Dempsey and J. Herring, 'Why Sexual Penetration Requires Justification' (2007) 27 OJLS 467.

12.2.1.3 Section 74

Section 74 provides that:

a person consents if he agrees by choice, and has the freedom and capacity to make that choice.

This definition, based on 'free agreement', is intended to emphasize that the absence of B's protest, resistance or injury does not necessarily signify B's consent. Although the Act is silent as to the precise moment at which B's consent or agreement must be present, it is clear that the relevant time is that of the alleged sexual wrongdoing.

J. Temkin and A. Ashworth ([2004] Crim LR 328) point out that freedom is only used to rule out the suggestion of some or all of its antitheses (see at 336, citing J. Austin, 'A Plea for Excuses' in H. Morris (ed), *Freedom and Responsibility* (1961), p 8).

The interpretation of s 74 has been considered in a number of cases and it is clear that the question of whether or not B consented to sexual activity is highly context-dependent. The difficulty lies in deciding whether conduct by A can be sufficient in law and fact to vitiate B's freedom to choose whether to engage in sexual activity. It is important to appreciate the fact that consent is not the same as submission. The necessity of distinguishing between the two sometimes arises in cases involving grooming. In *Ali* [2015] EWCA Crim 1279, for example, Fulford LJ made the following observation:

> … grooming does not necessarily vitiate consent, it starkly raises the possibility that a vulnerable or immature individual may have been placed in a position in which he or she is led merely to acquiesce rather than to give proper or real consent. One of the consequences of grooming is that it has a tendency to limit or subvert the alleged victim's capacity to make free decisions, and it creates the risk that he or she simply submitted because of the environment of dependency created by those responsible for treating the alleged victim in this way. Indeed, the individual may have been manipulated to the extent that he or she is unaware of, or confused about, the distinction between acquiescence and genuine agreement at the time the incident occurred.

In cases such as this, his lordship held that the question of whether real or proper consent was given will usually be for the jury, unless the evidence clearly indicates that a proper consent was given.

12.2.1.4 Deception and consent

When the legislation was first enacted, there was disagreement as to whether only those deceptions perpetrated by A listed in s 76 (as to identity, nature and purpose) can ever negate B's consent or whether a deception that does not fall within s 76 can nevertheless vitiate consent if the jury finds that it denies B freedom to choose within s 74. The courts seem to have accepted that there are forms of deception that will negate consent because they fall within s 74 even though they are not listed within s 76. A literal textual analysis of the Act might conclude that once it has been held that the deception perpetrated on B falls outside the limited scope of s 76, it is no longer relevant. One way of explaining the courts' approach is to say that deception may negate B's agreement, capacity or freedom and this explains why deception might fall to be considered in s 74 even though it is not listed as a factor in that section. As the following cases demonstrate, difficulties arise in delineating what types of deception by A ought to fall within s 74.

R (F) v Director of Public Prosecutions
[2013] EWHC 945 (Admin), Divisional Court

(Lord Judge CJ, Fulford and Sweeney JJ)

This case was an application for judicial review of a decision not to initiate a prosecution for rape. A and B were a married couple. A (referred to as the 'intervener' in the extract below as this is a judicial review case) displayed a domineering attitude towards B and was physically and verbally aggressive when they had sex. In addition, A would often demand sex from B. B was adamant that she did not want to have any more children, but was unable to use the contraceptive pill for medical reasons. Although they sometimes used a condom, A did not like doing so, and therefore their preferred method of contraception was withdrawal. B did not object to having intercourse in this manner, provided that A withdrew before he ejaculated. One afternoon, B agreed to have intercourse with A, but he failed to withdraw before he ejaculated. The issue was whether ejaculation without consent could transform consensual intercourse into rape. The CPS decided not to prosecute A for rape. The DPP's senior legal adviser conducted a review of this decision and agreed with it.

[In directing the CPS to reconsider whether to prosecute, **Lord Judge CJ** stated:]

22. At the time when the review was written [counsel for the CPS] did not have the advantage of the judgment of the Divisional Court in *Assange v Swedish Prosecution Authority* [2011] EWHC 2849 (Admin). It was submitted to the Divisional Court that as the complainant had consented to sexual intercourse only on the basis that Assange would use a condom, even if he did not, that fact was or would be irrelevant. She had consented to intercourse. Sir John Thomas, President of the Queen's Bench Division, explained, at para 86:

> 'The question of consent in the present case is to be determined by reference to s.74. The allegation is clear and covers the alternative; it is not an allegation that the condom came off accidentally or was damaged accidentally. It would plainly be open to a jury to hold that, if (the complainant) had made clear that she would only consent to sexual intercourse if Mr Assange used a condom, then there would be no consent if, without her consent, he did not use a condom, or removed or tore the condom without her consent. His conduct in having sexual intercourse without a condom in circumstances where she had made clear she would only have sexual intercourse if he used a condom would therefore amount to an offence under the Sexual Offences Act 2003, whatever the position may have been prior to that Act.'

23. Having reached that conclusion, the Divisional Court addressed the question whether Mr Assange's conduct in having sexual intercourse without a condom, or in continuing with it after removing, damaging or tearing the condom was 'deceptive'. The point did not require a firm conclusion, but it was accepted that 'it could be argued that sexual intercourse without a condom was different to sexual intercourse with a condom, given the presence of a physical barrier, a perceived difference in the threat in the degree of intimacy, the risks of disease and the prevention of a pregnancy; moreover the editors of *Smith and Hogan* (12th Edition [2008] at p.866) commented that it had been argued that unprotected sexual intercourse should be treated as being different in nature to protected sexual intercourse'. However, the court was not inclined to accept this approach, noting that the editors of *Smith and Hogan* approached the possible deception in relation to the use of a condom as 'likely to be held to remove any purported free agreement by the complainant under s.74'. The court further noted a view to similar effect expressed in the well known text book *Rook and Ward on Sexual Offences* (4th edition at paragraph 1.216.)

24. We must emphasise that we are not addressing the situation in which sexual intercourse occurs consensually when the man, intending to withdraw in accordance with his partner's wishes, or their understanding, nevertheless ejaculates prematurely, or accidentally, within rather than outside his partner's vagina. These things happen. They always have and they always will, and no offence is committed when they do. They underline why withdrawal is not a safe method of contraception. Equally we are not addressing the many fluctuating ways in which sexual relationships may develop, as couples discover and renew their own levels of understanding and tolerance, their codes of communication, express or understood, and mutual give and take, experimentation and excitement. These are intensely private matters, personal to the couple in question.

25. The facts suggested by the evidence in this case are quite different. It is inappropriate to examine the incident of sexual intercourse in February 2010 in isolation from the well evidenced history (including his own admissions) of the intervener's sexual dominance of the claimant and her unenthusiastic acquiescence to his demands. Given that essential background, the evidence about the incident in February 2010 is reasonably open to this analysis. Consensual penetration occurred. The claimant consented on the clear understanding that the intervener would not ejaculate within her vagina. She believed that he intended and agreed to withdraw before ejaculation. The intervener knew and understood that this was the only basis on which she was prepared to have sexual intercourse with him. There is evidence from the history of the relationship, as well as what he said when

sexual intercourse was taking place, and his observations to the claimant afterwards, that although he never disclosed his intention to her (because if she had known he knew that she would have never have consented), either from the outset of penetration, or after penetration had begun, he intended that this occasion of sexual intercourse would culminate in ejaculation within her vagina, whatever her wishes and their understanding. In short, there is evidence that he deliberately ignored the basis of her consent to penetration as a manifestation of his control over her.

26. In law, the question which arises is whether this factual structure can give rise to a conviction for rape. Did the claimant consent to this penetration? She did so, provided, in the language of s.74 of the 2003 Act, she agreed by choice, when she had the freedom and capacity to make the choice. What Assange underlines is that 'choice' is crucial to the issue of 'consent', and indeed we underline that the statutory definition of consent provided in s.74 applies equally to s.1(1)(c) as it does to s.1(1)(b). The evidence relating to 'choice' and the 'freedom' to make any particular choice must be approached in a broad commonsense way. If before penetration began the intervener had made up his mind that he would penetrate and ejaculate within the claimant's vagina, or even, because 'penetration is a continuing act from entry to withdrawal' (see s.79(2) of the 2003 Act) he decided that he would not withdraw at all, just because he deemed the claimant subservient to his control, she was deprived of choice relating to the crucial feature on which her original consent to sexual intercourse was based. Accordingly her consent was negated. Contrary to her wishes, and knowing that she would not have consented, and did not consent to penetration or the continuation of penetration if she had any inkling of his intention, he deliberately ejaculated within her vagina. In law, this combination of circumstances falls within the statutory definition of rape.

≋ Question

Rogers states that in a case such as this one there should be no liability for a non-consensual sexual offence as the offences in the 2003 Act are designed to protect a person's sexual autonomy, not their sexual health or their desire not to have a baby. Do you agree? See J. Rogers, 'The Effect of "Deception" in the Sexual Offences Act 2003' [2013] 4 Arch Rev 7.

In *R v EB* [2006] EWCA Crim 2495, the defendant had had unprotected sexual intercourse with the complainant without disclosing that he was HIV-positive. The question arose whether evidence of his HIV status was admissible. The Court of Appeal held that:

17. Where one party to sexual activity has a sexually transmissible disease which is not disclosed to the other party any consent that may have been given to that activity by the other party is not thereby vitiated. The act remains a consensual act. However, the party suffering from the sexual transmissible disease will not have any defence to any charge which may result from harm created by that sexual activity, merely by virtue of that consent, because such consent did not include consent to infection by the disease.

. . . as a matter of law, the fact that the appellant may not have disclosed his HIV status is not a matter which could in any way be relevant to the issue of consent under section 74 in relation to the sexual activity in this case.

≋ Questions

(1) In *Assange*, it was argued that the reason why the defendant in *EB* was not liable was because he had not lied to the complainant about his being HIV-positive; she had just never asked. Should this make a difference? For critique, see A. Sharpe, 'Expanding

> Liability for Sexual Fraud Through the Concept of "Active Deception": A Flawed Approach' (2016) 80 J Crim L 28.
>
> (2) In the last chapter we discussed the fact that D will be guilty of an offence against the person if he fails to disclose to V the fact he is HIV-positive and transmits the virus to her. In the context of sexual offences, however, D will only be guilty if V asks him about his HIV status and he actively deceives her about it. Would it be preferable for the law to adopt a consistent approach in sexual and other violence offences as to when deception is capable of negating consent?

The issue of whether B's consent has been vitiated due to her having been deprived of 'choice' has been considered in a number of rather unusual circumstances, as the following case illustrates.

R v McNally

[2013] EWCA Crim 1051, Court of Appeal, Criminal Division

(Leveson LJ and Kenneth Parker and Stewart JJ)

A, aged 17, was a transgender man, having been born female. When aged 13, A started an online relationship with B who was a similar age. A did not tell B that he had been born female and B claimed that she remained ignorant of that fact. After a number of years A and B met in person, on four occasions. On each occasion A penetrated B's vagina, both orally and digitally. B purchased condoms so that they could have full intercourse, but A declined. A was eventually confronted by B's mother and confirmed that he had been born a female. A complaint was made to the police and A subsequently pleaded guilty to committing assault by penetration, contrary to s 2 of the Sexual Offences Act 2003.

[In upholding A's conviction, **Leveson LJ** made the following comments in relation to s 74:]

23. The case for the Crown was that [B]'s consent was obtained by fraudulent deception that the appellant was a male and that had she known the truth, she would not have consented to acts of vaginal penetration. [Counsel for A] argues that deception as to gender cannot vitiate consent; in the same way deception as to age, marital status, wealth or, following *EB*, HIV status being deceptions as to qualities or attributes cannot vitiate consent. Thus, he submits that *Assange* and *R(F)* can be distinguished as the deceptions in those cases were not deceptions as to qualities or attributes but as to the features of the act itself.

24. We reject this analysis. First and foremost, *EB* was not saying that HIV status could not vitiate consent if, for example, the complainant had been positively assured that the defendant was not HIV positive: it left the issue open. As [counsel for the Crown contends], the argument that in *Assange* and *R(F)* the deceptions were as to the features of the act is not sustainable: the wearing of a condom and ejaculation are irrelevant to the definition of rape and are not 'features' of the offence and no such rationale is suggested. In the last two cases, it was alleged that the victim had consented on the basis of a premise that, at the time of the consent, was false (namely, in one case, that her partner would wear a condom and, in the second, that he would ejaculate outside her body).

25. In reality, some deceptions (such as, for example, in relation to wealth) will obviously not be sufficient to vitiate consent. In our judgment, Lord Judge's observation that 'the evidence relating to "choice" and the "freedom" to make any particular choice must be approached in a broad common-sense way' identifies the route through the dilemma.

26. Thus while, in a physical sense, the acts of assault by penetration of the vagina are the same whether perpetrated by a male or a female, the sexual nature of the acts is, on any common sense

view, different where the complainant is deliberately deceived by a defendant into believing that the latter is a male. Assuming the facts to be proved as alleged, [B] chose to have sexual encounters with a boy and her preference (her freedom to choose whether or not to have a sexual encounter with a girl) was removed by the appellant's deception.

27. It follows from the foregoing analysis that we conclude that, depending on the circumstances, deception as to gender can vitiate consent . . .

≈≈ *Questions*

(1) If A tells B that he is very wealthy and knows that this is the only reason B will ever have sex with him, why (per Leveson LJ) does this deception not nullify B's freedom to only have sexual intercourse with wealthy men, thus making A guilty of rape?

(2) Why does deception as to some attributes negate consent, while for others it does not? Applying a 'broad commonsense' approach, how are we to decide?

(3) B is vehemently anti-Semitic and tells A that she will not have sex with anyone of Jewish descent. A is in fact Jewish, but does not disclose this to B and he proceeds to have sexual intercourse with her anyway. Should the law protect B's freedom to practise her anti-Semitism, thus making A guilty of rape? See A. Sharpe, 'Criminalising Sexual Intimacy: Transgender Defendants and the Legal Construction of Non-Consent' [2014] Crim LR 207.

(4) Is *McNally* distinguishable from *EB* (earlier in this section)? What is the difference between A actively deceiving B and A not disabusing B of a false assumption he knows that B has made?

Although the courts now seem to have accepted that active deception can negate consent for the purposes of s 74, there is disagreement over what forms of deception ought to be capable of negating consent, as the following extracts demonstrate.

J. Herring, 'Mistaken Sex'
[2005] Crim LR 511

Throughout history people have used all manner of deceptions to persuade others to have sex with them. And some things never change. . . . Yet the law has traditionally been reluctant to criminalise the use of deception in sexual relationships. Consider this: Ted tells Mary he loves her and would like to marry her. As a result she buys him presents and lends him money. They also engage in sexual relationships. In fact Ted is a rogue. He has no feelings towards Mary and is known to have behaved in this way towards many women. If the facts could be proved there would be little difficulty in obtaining a conviction for obtaining property by deception. But it is generally thought that there would be no sexual offence; nor should there be. But why not? Is the law willing to protect property to a greater extent than sexual autonomy? . . .

The traditional approach asks whether the victim's mistake is sufficient to negate her consent. The proper question should be: is the defendant's act that to which the victim has consented? . . .

We could formulate a legal rule that would look something like this:

If at the time of the sexual activity a person:

(i) is mistaken as to a fact; and

(ii) had s/he known the truth about that fact would not have consented to it

then s/he did not consent to the sexual activity. If the defendant knows (or ought to know) that s/he did not consent (in the sense just described) then s/he is guilty of an offence.

Included within the word 'fact', in this test, would be the state of mind of the defendant. The mistake need not be to an issue which would be regarded as material to the reasonable person, if it was a pre-requisite to consent for the particular victim. Nor is there a need for the defendant to have caused the victim's mistake by a deception. So if A does not disclose his criminal past to his sexual partner, B, where B would not have consented to the activity had she known of it, B should be taken to have not consented. For A to engage in sexual activities with B knowing that B would not be consenting if A revealed facts about himself amounts to a fundamental lack of respect for B's sexual autonomy. Of course many people will be uninterested in their partner's past and that will not be relevant to a decision as to whether or not to consent to sexual relations. Further the mens rea requirement ensures that defendants will not be prosecuted when they did not (or should not have) realised that their partners would regard a particular fact as fundamental to their consent.

. . . The proposal is straightforward and explicable to juries. The Sexual Offences Act 2003 provides the courts with an opportunity to consider again the meaning of consent and to develop it along the lines proposed in this article. . . .

Not everyone agrees with the approach advocated by Herring. Although the argument below is framed in terms of s 76, it applies with equal force to s 74.

H. Gross, 'Rape, Moralism and Human Rights'
[2007] Crim LR 220

Jonathan Herring has proposed that the law of rape be extended to cover cases in which a man has deceived a woman about his feelings for her and about his intention to marry her in order to get her to have sex with him. If the man is right about the importance to her of love and marriage and is successful in seducing her through his deception he can be charged with rape. Herring's proposal rests on certain innovative ideas about consent. He suggests more generally that a woman is entitled to be informed about any facts that would make a difference to her decision to have sex. Any deception regarding such a fact would nullify her consent. His proposal does not stop there. If the man knew, or ought to have known, that the woman was mistaken about something that would make a difference to her decision, he is criminally liable since there was not valid consent to having sex.

This is an ambitious proposal. The law places strict limits on the kinds of deception that nullify consent. If the woman is deceived about what is going on, or about who she is doing it with, any consent she may have given is a nullity. If she is duped into thinking it is a medical procedure rather than intercourse, or deceived into thinking that the man in the darkened room is her boyfriend rather than someone else at the party, the man has had sex without valid consent. The law does not require the man to tell the woman the truth about whatever might be of concern to her in deciding whether to have sex.

Herring, however, is encouraged by s.76 of the Sexual Offences Act 2003 which provides that intentional deception as to the purpose of the act creates a conclusive presumption both that the woman did not consent to the act and that the man did not reasonably believe she did. In the Sexual Offences Act 2003 deception as to the purpose of the act is presumably meant to cover with greater precision of language than the common law provided the sort of case where a singing teacher told his student he needed to make an air passage to assist her in her singing and proceeded to have intercourse with her. Herring, however, argues that the purpose of the act should be extended to include what the parties understood the act of sexual intercourse to be about. If the man deceives the woman about his feelings and his intentions, under this enlarged conception of purpose he would be deceiving her about the purpose of the act. He is falsely representing the act as a way of expressing his feelings and expectations for the future. Having deceived her about the purpose of the act, he has vitiated any consent she may have given.

. . .

The first thing to be said is that s.76 is not on the books to punish men's deception, but to provide women with the protection they need when sex for a purpose is proposed. Consent to sex, like consent to other activities, may be strictly qualified, and the interests of the woman which the law protects by requiring consent remain protected against violation outside the bounds of the consent that is given. When a woman consents to engaging in intercourse for a particular purpose her consent is limited to sexual activity for that purpose. The purpose of an activity is determined by what the person engaging in it intends to accomplish by it. If it is a joint activity, as sex is, the two people engaging in it must both intend to accomplish the same thing for the activity to have that thing as its purpose. If it is not the man's intention to accomplish through intercourse what the woman intends to accomplish, their intercourse is not for the purpose that the woman supposes and so she has not consented to the intercourse they have. The singing teacher did not in fact intend to improve the singing ability of his gullible student by having sex with her, as he said, and so there was not consent to the sex they had. Had he truly believed the sex would open her air passages and help her singing their sex would be for the purpose he said and so her consent would be effective. Cases such as this are cases of sex for an ulterior purpose, an instrumental activity prompted by something to be achieved that marks its success. Such sex stands in stark contrast to the commonplace recreational activity that sex usually is. Sex simply for the pleasures of sex is not consented to conditionally, and though in deciding to have such sex a woman may well have made certain assumptions and may entertain certain expectations her willingness will not be conditional upon those expectations being pursued through the sex.

Herring's proposal for extending rape liability amounts to giving certain moral strictures legal effect. The proposed obligation not to deceive in obtaining consent comes down simply to making the telling of lies to get sex a punishable offence, at least when what is lied about is important to the woman. Placing the sex act on an elevated moral plane is an essential part of the argument. For Herring, prevailing social attitudes are a disappointment, and public education to change them would be needed once the law of rape is extended as he suggests. What now are regarded as gambits in a game of seduction would be seen as fraudulent misrepresentations that corrupt a high-minded activity in which the participants are entitled to rely on mutual respect and honesty. On this view, in deciding to engage in sexual intercourse the woman is putting at risk her sexual autonomy and the preservation inviolate of the most intimate part of her person. Surely she is entitled to be protected by the law against the ignoble designs of some trickster.

See also J. Herring's spirited response, 'Human Rights and Rape: A Reply to Hyman Gross' [2007] Crim LR 228.

Herring's approach has recently been subject to fresh criticism on the basis that it has a disproportionate impact on transgender people.

A. Sharpe, 'Criminalising Sexual Intimacy: Transgender Defendants and the Legal Construction of Non-Consent'
[2014] Crim LR 207

In opposition to this first claim is the view that gender history is a material fact that sexual partners ought to know if their consent is to be considered valid. This view is premised on the value of sexual autonomy and it almost certainly enjoys considerable weight in normative terms. The argument is, as already noted, put most forcefully by Jonathan Herring. While recognising that total transparency would place an undue burden on individuals, Herring insists that, if consent is to be valid, facts must be disclosed where considered 'material'. This amounts to a claim that the right to sexual autonomy trumps the right to privacy. Indeed, Herring renders this claim explicit in relation to transgender-cisgender sexual relations. I find this claim unpersuasive. However, before articulating my argument that consent should not be viewed as vitiated even in circumstances where gender history is considered a material fact, I want to put in issue precisely the claim that gender history ought to be considered a material fact. The claim that gender history ought to be considered a material fact serving to vitiate consent is grounded either in general normative terms, which amounts to a claim that such a view enjoys widespread support, or focuses more specifically on the importance of this historical information to a sexual partner. Herring makes the latter claim.

In my view, gender history ought *not* to be considered a material fact for the purposes of criminal prosecution. To treat it as such is to cast doubt on the authenticity of the gender identities of transgender people. As argued earlier, transgender people are not engaged in some form of pretence or masquerade. Typically, their gender identities manifest early in life and, as already noted, the phenomenon of transgenderism is recognised by the medical community and the state provides both public funding for treatment and provision for gender recognition. Further, and while it is not my contention that the legitimacy of prosecution should turn on whether gender claims have been legally recognised, the fact of legal recognition appears to introduce a further objection to prosecution. While the transgender defendants in the cases under consideration have not, as yet, received a [gender recognition certificate], a fact perhaps due to their tender age, possession of a certificate signifies legal recognition of 'acquired' gender 'for all legal purposes'. Further, while non-disclosure of gender history constitutes a ground for nullity proceedings under the Matrimonial Causes Act 1973, the Gender Recognition Act (GRA) 2004 did not introduce or amend any criminal legislation to produce the same effect. For example, non-disclosure might have been added to the list of conclusive or evidential presumptions contained within the SOA. Accordingly, in the context of legally recognised transgender people, criminal prosecution might be viewed as a denial of the recognition conferred and contrary to the GRA. However, suppose we were to concede that gender history is a material fact, would this then clinch the argument in favour of criminalisation of non-disclosure? I argue that it does not. For the justification of a disclosure requirement depends not merely on establishing gender history as a material fact, but on demonstrating that a right to know in such circumstances is *not* trumped by other considerations.

12.2.1.5 Capacity and consent

One of the elements central to s 74 is that of the victim's 'capacity'. That term is not further defined. Is what matters whether B has the *mental* capacity to choose to perform the specified act with A on the occasion in question? It is unclear to what extent B must have the capacity to understand the consequences of the action as well as its nature. For example, must B understand the risks of disease and pregnancy from unprotected intercourse in cases of penile penetration? No further clarification, indeed only obfuscation, is generated by cross-referring to the offences protecting those with a mental disorder in s 30(2) whereby:

(a) he lacks the capacity to choose whether to agree to the touching (whether because he lacks sufficient understanding of the nature or reasonably foreseeable consequences of what is being done, or for any other reason), or

(b) he is unable to communicate such a choice to A.

In *C* [2009] UKHL 42, B was a 28-year-old woman with a history of serious mental disorders. Her mental disorders could manifest themselves in episodes of impulsive and aggressive behaviour, delusions, hallucinations, depression or manic episodes. At the time of the offences she was living in supervised accommodation. She developed irrational concerns for her safety if she remained in the area, and so she left her accommodation. She met A who had offered to help her. A gave her crack cocaine and made her perform oral sex on him and a co-defendant. In interview B said that she had performed the acts out of fear of violence.

A was convicted of an offence of sexual activity with a person with a mental disorder impeding choice contrary to s 30(1) of the Sexual Offences Act 2003. The Court of Appeal allowed A's appeal against conviction and certified the following question of general public importance:

> Whether the decision of the Court of Appeal . . . has unduly limited the scope of section 30(1) of the Sexual Offences Act beyond that which Parliament intended. Specifically (a) in holding that a lack of capacity to choose cannot be person or situation specific; (b) in holding that an irrational fear that prevents the exercise of choice cannot be equated with a lack of capacity to choose; (c) in holding that to fall within section 30(2)(b) a complainant must be physically unable to communicate by reason of his mental disorder.

The House of Lords allowed the appeal, reinstated A's conviction and in doing so answered the three certified question in the affirmative. Baroness Hale, speaking for a unanimous House, clarified a number of points in relation to the section. First, whether an individual has the capacity to consent is both person- and circumstance-specific. Secondly, the section is interpreted as being able to encompass a wide range of circumstances, including an irrational fear, as was the case here. It is sufficient if B has an irrational fear and it is this irrational fear that leads her to acquiesce to the sexual contact. Finally, an inability to communicate is not limited to those cases where B is physically unable to communicate. Rather, s 30 is wide enough to encompass cases where B's inability is attributable to a mental disorder.

~~~ *Questions*
(1) Does the 2003 Act provide a clear workable set of definitions of consent and capacity that can be applied?
(2) B has a mental disorder and an irrational fear of men with Welsh accents. A, from Wales, is unaware of that. He makes sexual advances to B and she is too afraid to resist. Is A guilty of rape? Or an offence under s 30?
(3) C. Elliott and C. De Than, 'The Case for a Rational Reconstruction of Consent in Criminal Law' (2007) 70 MLR 225 argue that the test of capacity under s 74 should be based on whether B was capable of understanding at the material time the nature and reasonably foreseeable consequences of the act and able to communicate her consent effectively (at 242). Is this preferable to the court's approach?
(4) Given that the definition of rape now encompasses oral penetration, in *C* above why was A not charged with the rape of B? Baroness Hale gave two reasons why a charge under s 30 might be preferable. First, because 'the prosecution has only to prove the inability to refuse rather than that the complainant actually did not consent'. Secondly, because the mens rea under s 30 is easier to prove than that required for rape. The reason for this is that all that needs to be shown to make D guilty under s 30 is that the defendant knew the complainant had a mental disorder and therefore is likely to be unable to refuse. Do you find either of these explanations convincing?

Intoxicated consent

A very practical problem is at what point self-induced intoxication vitiates consent. Under the 1956 Act, if a complainant, through alcohol or drugs, was not capable of exercising a judgement on consent, she was not consenting—that was a matter of law. The Government rejected a suggestion for a provision in the 2003 Act that 'someone who is inebriated could claim they were unable to give consent—as opposed to someone who was unconscious for whatever reason, including because of alcohol' on the ground that it would give rise to 'mischievous accusations'.

In *Dougal* (2005) Swansea Crown Court (discussed in *Bree* below), the trial judge directed the jury to enter a 'not guilty' verdict when the prosecutor informed the judge that he did not propose to proceed further because the prosecution were unable to prove that the complainant had not given consent because of her level of intoxication. The decision was controversial since all that B had said was that she 'could not remember'. Following the furore over that case, the Government raised the issue in a Consultation Paper, *Convicting Rapists and Protecting Victims* (2006) asking 'Does the law on capacity need to be changed. Should there be a statutory definition of capacity?' Subsequently, the Court of Appeal has sought to pre-empt the need for legislative intervention by encouraging trial judges to leave the issue to the common sense of the jury where there is evidence that B might not have been consenting owing to intoxication. On jury attitudes to intoxicated rape complainants, see also E. Finch and V. Munro, 'Breaking Boundaries: Sexual Consent in the Jury Room' (2006) 26 LS 303.

R v Bree
[2007] EWCA Crim 256, Court of Appeal, Criminal Division

(Sir Igor Judge P, Hallett LJ and Gloster J)

D, aged 25, and M, aged 19, had been drinking together. Both had voluntarily consumed large amounts of alcohol. M and D returned to M's student flat. M accepted her account of events was 'very patchy'. She agreed that she did not say 'no' to sexual intercourse, although she did remember saying 'no' when asked if she had a condom. D testified that he was 'absolutely positive' that she was awake and conscious throughout. She had removed her own pyjamas and responded to his touching positively by moaning quietly, and rolling on to her back and opening her legs. It was agreed that they had 'brief sex'. D was convicted of rape.

[Sir Igor Judge P delivered the judgment of the court. His lordship set out the facts and s 74.]

One of the objectives of the Sexual Offences Act 2003, which came into force on 1 May 2004, was to bring coherence and clarity to the meaning of consent. The provisions relating to consent represented the result of substantial discussion and Parliamentary debate about the principles which should apply to the acutely sensitive and intensely personal area of sexual relationships, whether they arise in the context of a long established marriage, or partnership, or a casual sexual encounter between total strangers. Arguments about consent abound just because consent to sexual intercourse extends from passionate enthusiasm to reluctant or bored acquiescence, and its absence includes quiet submission or surrender as well as determined physical resistance against an attacker which might expose the victim to injury, and sometimes death. The declared objective of the White Paper, *Protecting the Public* (Cm. 5668, 2002) was to produce statutory provisions relating to consent which would be 'clear and unambiguous'. As enacted, the legislation on this topic has not commanded totally uncritical enthusiasm. For some it goes too far, and for others not far enough. The law in the area, and our decision, must be governed by the definition of consent in section 74.

Neither 'freedom', nor 'capacity', are further defined or explained within section 74 itself, nor indeed in sections 75 and 76, which create evidential presumptions relating to consent. We note the analysis in the illuminating article, *The Sexual Offences Act 2003, Rape, Sexual Assault and the Problems of Consent*, (2004) CLR 328 by Professor Temkin and Professor Ashworth, that 'it might be thought that "freedom" and "choice" are ideas which raise philosophical issues of such complexity as to be ill-suited to the needs of criminal justice—clearly those words do not refer to total freedom or choice, so all the questions about how much liberty of action satisfies the "definition" remains at large'. Notwithstanding these philosophical difficulties, it is clear that for the purposes of the 2003 Act 'capacity' is integral to the concept of 'choice', and therefore to 'consent'.

Section 75 and section 76 of the 2003 Act [see sections 12.2.1.6 and 12.2.1.7] address the issue of consent in practical situations which arise from time to time in cases of alleged sexual offences including rape. They are not, however, exhaustive. The presumptions in section 75 are evidential and rebuttable, whereas those in section 76 are irrebuttable and conclusive. In this appeal we are not concerned with either of the conclusive presumptions relating to consent specified in section 76. The common characteristic of the particular situations covered by the evidential presumptions in section 75 is that they are concerned with situations in which the complainant is involuntarily at a disadvantage. Section 75(2)(f) is plainly adequate to deal with the situation when a drink is 'spiked', but unless productive of a state of near unconsciousness, or incapacity, this paragraph does not address seductive blandishments to have 'just one more' drink. Section 75(2)(d) repeats well established common law principles, and acknowledges plain good sense, that, if the complainant is unconscious as a result of her voluntary consumption of alcohol, the starting point is to presume that she is not consenting to intercourse. Beyond that, the Act is silent about the impact of excessive but voluntary alcohol consumption on the ability to give consent to intercourse, or indeed to consent generally.

It is perhaps helpful to identify a number of features of the law relating to consent which although obvious are sometimes overlooked. On any view, both parties to the act of sexual intercourse with which this case is concerned were the worse for drink. Both were adults. Neither acted unlawfully in drinking to excess. They were both free to choose how much to drink, and with whom. Both were free, if they wished, to have intercourse with each other. There is nothing abnormal, surprising, or even unusual about men and women having consensual intercourse when one, or other, or both have voluntarily consumed a great deal of alcohol. Provided intercourse is indeed consensual, it is not rape.

In cases which are said to arise after voluntary consumption of alcohol the question is not whether the alcohol made either or both less inhibited than they would have been if sober, nor whether either or both might afterwards have regretted what had happened, and indeed wished that it had not. If the complainant consents, her consent cannot be revoked. Moreover it is not a question whether either or both may have had very poor recollection of precisely what had happened. That may be relevant to the reliability of their evidence. Finally, and certainly, it is not a question whether either or both was behaving irresponsibly. As they were both autonomous adults, the essential question for decision is, as it always is, whether the evidence proved that the appellant had sexual intercourse with the complainant without her consent.

Before the 2003 Act, it was not difficult to identify the relevant legal principles, and for a judge to explain the law relating to the voluntary consumption of alcohol (or drugs) by a complainant. Thus, for example, in *R v Malone* [1998] 2 CAR 447 the Court of Appeal upheld the direction:

> 'She does not claim to have physically resisted nor to have verbally protested. She says the drink has disabled her from doing either . . . she has told you she did not consent . . . you must be sure that the act of sexual intercourse occurred without (her) consent. Submitting to an act of sexual intercourse, because through drink she was unable physically to resist though she wished to, is not consent. If she submits to intercourse because of the drink she cannot physically resist, that, of course, is not consent. No right thinking person would say that in those circumstances she was genuinely consenting to what occurred. What occurred . . . not wishing to have intercourse but being physically unable to do anything about it . . . would plainly, as a matter of common sense be against her will. It would be without her consent'.

We record this direction as illustrative of what was regarded as an appropriate direction in the circumstances of an individual case to a particular jury, rather than a learned disquisition of the law of consent as applied to rape. We should however highlight *R v Lang* [1976] 62 CAR 50 which summarised the relevant principle. The jury sought guidance from the judge on the question of whether the complainant's alcohol consumption may have vitiated her consent to sexual intercourse. The court observed

'. . . there is no special rule applicable to drink and rape. If the issue be, as here, did the woman consent? The critical question is not how she came to take the drink, but whether she understood her situation and was capable of making up her mind. In *Howard* [1965] 50 CAR 56 the Court of Criminal Appeal had to consider the case of a girl under 16. Lord Parker CJ . . . said: . . . "in the case of a girl under 16 the prosecution . . . must prove either that she physically resisted, or, if she did not, that her understanding and knowledge was such that she was not in a position to decide whether to consent or resist". In our view these words are of general application whenever there is present some factor, be it permanent or transient, suggesting the absence of such understanding or knowledge . . . None of this was explained to the jury. Their attention was focussed by the judge upon how she came to take drink, not upon the state of her understanding and her capacity to exercise judgment in the circumstances.'

In the context of the statutory provision in section 74, it is noteworthy that *Lang* decided thirty years or so ago, directly focussed on the 'capacity' of the complainant to decide whether to consent to intercourse or not. These are the concepts with which the 2003 Act itself is concerned.

We are not aware of any reported decisions which deal with this aspect of the new legislation. We should however refer to the much publicised case of *R v Dougal*, heard in Swansea Crown Court, in November 2005. Having heard the evidence of the complainant, the Crown decided to offer no further evidence. Before the jury counsel for the Crown explained:

'the prosecution are conscious of the fact that a drunken consent is still a consent and that in the answer, in cross examination, she said, in terms, that she could not remember giving her consent and that is fatal to the prosecution's case. In those circumstances the prosecution will have no further evidence on the issue of consent. This is a case of the word of the defendant against that of the complainant on that feature It is fatal to the prosecution's case . . .'

The judge (Roderick Evans J) directed the jury that as the prosecution was no longer seeking a guilty verdict, there was only one verdict which could be returned, and that was an acquittal. He added that he agreed with the course the prosecution had taken.

Without knowing all the details of the case, and focusing exclusively on the observations of counsel for the Crown in *Dougal*, it would be open to question whether the inability of the complainant to remember whether she gave her consent or not might on further reflection be approached rather differently. Prosecuting counsel may wish he had expressed himself more felicitously. That said, one of the most familiar directions of law provided to juries who are being asked to conclude that the voluntary consumption of alcohol by a defendant should lead to the conclusion that he was too drunk to form the intention required for proof of the crime alleged against him, is that a drunken intent is still an intent. (*R v Sheehan and Moore* [1975] 60 CAR 308 at 312). So it is, and that we suspect is the source of the phrase that a 'drunken consent is still consent'. In the context of consent to intercourse, the phrase lacks delicacy, but, properly understood, it provides a useful shorthand accurately encapsulating the legal position. We note in passing that it also acts as a reminder that a drunken man who intends to commit rape, and does so, is not excused by the fact that his intention is a drunken intention.

Some of the hugely critical discussion arising after *Dougal* missed the essential point. Neither counsel for the Crown, nor for that matter the judge, was saying or coming anywhere near saying, either that a complainant who through drink is incapable of consenting to intercourse must nevertheless be deemed to have consented to it, or that a man is at liberty to have sexual intercourse with a woman who happens to be drunk, on the basis that her drunkenness deprives her of her right to choose whether to have intercourse or not. Such ideas are wrong in law, and indeed, offensive. All that was being said in *Dougal* was that when someone who has had a lot to drink is in fact consenting to intercourse, then that is what she is doing, consenting: equally, if after taking drink, she is not consenting, then by definition intercourse is taking place without her consent. This is unexceptionable.

In our judgment, the proper construction of section 74 of the 2003 Act, as applied to the problem now under discussion, leads to clear conclusions. If, through drink (or for any other reason) the complainant has temporarily lost her capacity to choose whether to have intercourse on the relevant occasion, she is not consenting, and subject to questions about the defendant's state of mind, if intercourse takes place, this would be rape. However, where the complainant has voluntarily consumed even substantial quantities of alcohol, but nevertheless remains capable of choosing whether or not to have intercourse, and in drink agrees to do so, this would not be rape. We should perhaps underline that, as a matter of practical reality, capacity to consent may evaporate well before a complainant becomes unconscious. Whether this is so or not, however, is fact specific, or more accurately, depends on the actual state of mind of the individuals involved on the particular occasion.

Considerations like these underline the fact that it would be unrealistic to endeavour to create some kind of grid system which would enable the answer to these questions to be related to some prescribed level of alcohol consumption. Experience shows that different individuals have a greater or lesser capacity to cope with alcohol than others, and indeed the ability of a single individual to do so may vary from day to day. The practical reality is that there are some areas of human behaviour which are inapt for detailed legislative structures. In this context, provisions intended to protect women from sexual assaults might very well be conflated into a system which would provide patronising interference with the right of autonomous adults to make personal decisions for themselves.

For these reasons, notwithstanding criticisms of the statutory provisions, in our view the 2003 Act provides a clear definition of 'consent' for the purposes of the law of rape, and by defining it with reference to 'capacity to make that choice', sufficiently addresses the issue of consent in the context of voluntary consumption of alcohol by the complainant. The problems do not arise from the legal principles. They lie with infinite circumstances of human behaviour, usually taking place in private without independent evidence, and the consequent difficulties of proving this very serious offence. The jury were rightly directed that an essential requirement before the appellant could be convicted was that M did not consent to intercourse. They were told that 'a person consents if he agrees by choice and has the freedom and capacity to make that choice'. The statutory definition having been read, no further elucidation was given. Our attention was drawn to *R v Olugboga* [1981] 73 CAR 344, decided after the enactment of the Sexual Offences (Amendment) Act 1976. As Professor Temkin and Professor Ashworth explain, the report *Setting the Boundaries: Reforming the Law on Sexual Offences* (2000) which echoed a much earlier report by an advisory group chaired by Heilbron J in November 1975, suggested that the broad approach to consent and submission adopted in *Olugboga* should be abandoned. In our view, even if these criticisms are justified, the judgment contains passages of continuing value. The court rejected the submission on behalf of the Crown that a trial judge was required 'merely to leave the issue of consent to a jury in a similar way to that in which the issue of dishonesty is left in trials for offences under the Theft Act'. Because of the myriad circumstances in which the issue of consent may arise, the judgment continued, 'We do not think that the issue of consent should be left to a jury without some further direction. What this should be will depend on the circumstances of each case.'

In this case the jury should have been given some assistance with the meaning of 'capacity' in circumstances where the complainant was affected by her own voluntarily induced intoxication, and also whether, and to what extent they could take that into account in deciding whether she had consented. Moreover, the judge did not address the changed way in which the prosecution put its case against the appellant. There is a significant difference between an allegation that the complainant was unconscious and for that reason not consenting to intercourse, and an allegation that, although she was capable of giving consent, despite her state, she was not in fact consenting to intercourse and was giving clear indications that she was rejecting the appellant. The potential for confusion was compounded by the fact that the complainant herself asserted, more than once, that she was unconscious at different stages of the encounter. At the same time the Crown conceded that what she believed to be and said were periods of unconsciousness should for the purposes of the trial be treated as moments of memory deficit caused by drink. Of course if the Crown was not contending that she was unconscious, that at least was consistent with the appellant's case that she was indeed conscious throughout. . . .

Appeal allowed

〰 *Questions*
(1) Do you agree with the court that the definition of consent is clear?
(2) Should the Court of Appeal have focused more on B's lack of capacity to consent, rather than whether or not she 'actually' consented? See G. Firth, 'Not an Invitation to Rape: The Sexual Offences Act 2003, Consent and the Case of the "Drunken" Victim' (2011) 62 NILQ 99.

In *Hysa* [2007] EWCA Crim 2056, a 16-year-old girl on a New Year's Eve celebration in London became separated from her friends and after drinking half a bottle of vodka, and taking cannabis, ended up in a car with three strangers. One allegedly raped her and digitally penetrated her vagina. She confirmed in her evidence that she did not want to have sex with the man, that she did not think that she did so willingly and she did not think that she would have consented. She said she could not remember what she had said to the man because she was drunk. When pressed in cross-examination, she said she could not recall what she was thinking or saying. Counsel for the Crown argued that it was clear that the complainant meant she could not say whether she had actually said 'yes' or 'no'. The Court of Appeal concluded that the judge erred in withdrawing the case:

It was for the jury, not the judge, to decide, on the basis of the evidence called, whether, on these facts, in this case, the complainant had the capacity to consent and/or in fact consented to intercourse or not. . . . Issues of consent and capacity to consent to intercourse in cases of alleged rape should normally be left to the jury to determine. It would be a rare case indeed where it would be appropriate for a judge to stop a case in which, on one view, a 16 year old girl, alone at night and vulnerable through drink, is picked up by a stranger who has sex with her within minutes of meeting her and she says repeatedly she would not have consented to sex in these circumstances.

More recently, in *Kamki* [2013] EWCA Crim 2335, the Court of Appeal approved of the following guidance that was given to the jury:

  a. A person consents if he or she agrees by choice and has the freedom and capacity to make that choice,

  b. When a person is unconscious, there is no such freedom or capacity to choose,

  c. Where a person has not reached a state of unconsciousness and experiences some degree of consciousness, further considerations must be applied,

  d. A person can still have the capacity to make a choice and have sex even when they have had a lot to drink (thereby consenting to the act),

  e. Alcohol can make people less inhibited than when they are sober and everybody has the choice whether or not to have sex,

f. If through drink a woman has temporarily lost the capacity to choose to have sexual intercourse, she would not be consenting,

g. Before a complete loss of consciousness arises, a state of incapacity to consent can nevertheless
be reached. Consideration has to be given to the degree of consciousness or otherwise in order
to determine the issue of capacity,

h. In this particular case, the jury would have to consider the evidence of M to determine what her
state of consciousness or unconsciousness was and to determine what effect this would have
on her capacity to consent,

i. If it is determined that the complainant did have the capacity to make a choice, it would then
have to be considered whether she did or may have consented to sexual intercourse.

≈≈≈ *Questions*

(1) B is drunk. A knows that B has been drinking but is unsure how much. A penetrates B
with his penis. B does not resist or give positive encouragement. What must the prosecution show in order to secure a conviction for rape?

(2) What should the jury be told in such a case?

12.2.1.6 Section 75: evidential presumptions

If A is proved to have performed the relevant act to which s 75 applies (in the case of rape that
is penile penetration), and it is proved that any of the circumstances listed in s 75(2) exists and
A knows it exists, the complainant is taken not to have consented and A not to have a reasonable belief in her consent unless sufficient evidence is adduced to raise the issue.

The circumstances in s 75(2) and (3) are:

(2) . . .

(a) any person was, at the time of the relevant act or immediately before it began, using violence against the complainant or causing the complainant to fear that immediate violence
would be used against him;

(b) any person was, at the time of the relevant act or immediately before it began, causing the
complainant to fear that violence was being used, or that immediate violence would be
used, against another person;

(c) the complainant was, and the defendant was not, unlawfully detained at the time of the
relevant act;

(d) the complainant was asleep or otherwise unconscious at the time of the relevant act;

(e) because of the complainant's physical disability, the complainant would not have been able
at the time of the relevant act to communicate to the defendant whether the complainant
consented;

(f) any person had administered to or caused to be taken by the complainant, without the
complainant's consent, a substance which, having regard to when it was administered or
taken, was capable of causing or enabling the complainant to be stupefied or overpowered
at the time of the relevant act.

(3) In subsection (2)(a) and (b), the reference to the time immediately before the relevant act began
is, in the case of an act which is one of a continuous series of sexual activities, a reference to the
time immediately before the first sexual activity began.

In Parliament, Baroness Scotland of Asthal explained:

In order for these presumptions not to apply, the defendant will need to satisfy the judge from the evidence that there is a real issue about consent that is worth putting to the jury. The evidence relied on may be, for example, evidence that the defendant himself gives in the witness box, or evidence given on his behalf by a defence witness, or evidence given by the complainant during cross-examination. If the judge is satisfied that there is sufficient evidence to justify putting the issue of consent to the jury, then the issues will have to be proved by the prosecution in the normal way. If the judge does not think the evidence relied on by the defendant meets the threshold, he will direct the jury to find the defendant guilty. (Hansard HL, 17 June 2003, col 670)

Any one of the circumstances must be 'proved' before the presumption bites. A has to *know* that 'those circumstances existed' (s 75(1)(c)). But the requirement is only that any *one* circumstance is proved (s 75(1)(b)). The presumption only applies in the first place if three issues are proved by the prosecution—the sexual act (in rape that is penile penetration), the specified circumstance and A's awareness of it.

A problem stems from the fact that there is no direct match between the issues proved by the prosecution in s 75(1) and the issues about which A is obliged to raise evidence. The prosecution are establishing the act, the circumstance and the awareness of the circumstance. A is not required to rebut those directly. He has to rebut the presumed legal consequences of the elements that have been proved by the prosecution—A rebuts consent/reasonable belief in consent. For example, the prosecution prove that A had sex and that the circumstance existed—B was unconscious and produced some evidence that A was aware of that circumstance. A then raises an issue that although he was aware of the unconsciousness, he reasonably believed in B's consent but does not challenge that sex occurred nor that she was unconscious. It seems that the presumption still applies in relation to the absence of consent. The prosecution might prove absence of consent merely by proving the three initial elements of the presumption in s 75(1). Is it for the judge to decide whether or not A's evidential burden is discharged?

If the trial judge decides that there is sufficient evidence to raise an issue as to whether the complainant consented and/or the accused reasonably believed the complainant was consenting, then the judge will put the issues to the jury and s 75 has no part to play. In the relatively rare cases where the judge decides that there is not sufficient evidence on one or both of the issues, a s 75 direction must be given on that issue. See *White* [2010] EWCA Crim 1929 at [10].

As to what is necessary before A discharges the evidential burden, Lord Judge CJ in *Ciccarelli* [2011] EWCA Crim 2665 stated that there must be some evidence that A's belief was reasonable. In that case, the reasonableness of A's belief was based on a single flirtatious advance that B denied had occurred. The Court of Appeal held that the trial judge was correct to hold that this was insufficient to raise any issue for the consideration of the jury. In *Mba* [2012] EWCA Crim 2773, the Court of Appeal held that because the jury had found A guilty of committing grievous bodily harm with intent on B, this negated any question as to consent on the part of B or reasonable belief in her consent and so therefore A's conviction was safe despite the deficiencies in the judge's summing-up.

Threats of violence

The threat of/actual violence in s 75(2)(a) and (b) need not emanate from A. The 2003 Act has no section to replace s 2 of the Sexual Offences Act 1956 (procuring sexual intercourse by threats). A question arises as to why the element in s 75(2)(a) should be one of immediate violence. What if A threatens B that he will get her 'one day' unless she has sex with him now? This aspect of the provision could be considered problematic.

Unconscious victims

It seems uncontroversial that when B is unconscious she cannot consent to sexual acts. This is, however, a rebuttable presumption.

≋ *Questions*

(1) A and B agree that they will have sex later that evening when they return from the party they are both attending. By the time they leave the party, B is so heavily intoxicated that she cannot walk and A carries her home. He has sex with her while she is unconscious. Rape?

(2) A touches B sexually (note that the presumption applies to offences of touching and not just penetrative acts) as she sleeps. This is a gesture of intimacy to wake her. Is A presumed to have acted without her consent? What would A have to show to rebut the presumption?

See also *Bree*, section 12.2.1.5, p 313, on intoxication and unconsciousness.

Stupefying complainants

This provision was introduced late in the Bill's progress as a response to the growing concern over 'drug-assisted rape'. See E. Finch and V. Munro, 'Intoxicated Consent and the Boundaries of Drug Assisted Rape' [2003] Crim LR 773; 'The Sexual Offences Act 2003: Intoxicated Consent and Drug Assisted Rape Revisited' [2004] Crim LR 789. Under the old law there was a much narrower offence under s 4(1) of the 1956 Act applicable to administering drugs to women with intent to stupefy or overpower in order only to facilitate intercourse. The new presumption of non-consent applies to complainants of both sexes and to sexual acts other than vaginal intercourse.

Although targeted at drugs which induce states of incapacity such as Rohypnol and GHB (gamma hydroxyl butyrate acid), there is no statutory limitation on the type of substance which will trigger the presumption. Alcohol is certainly capable of satisfying the definition, so A who surreptitiously laces B's soft drink with spirits will be caught. If B's consumption is purely voluntary and fully informed, the presumption does not apply. The section does not apply to the 'seductive blandishments to have "just one more drink"' per Igor Judge P in *Bree*, at [24] (section 12.2.1.5, p 313).

12.2.1.7 Section 76: conclusive presumptions

If A performed the relevant act (in the case of rape that is penetration—it will differ as between the other non-consensual offences) and any one of the circumstances specified in s 76(2) existed, it is to be *conclusively presumed* that the complainant did not consent to the relevant act, and that A did not believe that the complainant consented. The circumstances in s 76(2) are:

(a) the defendant intentionally deceived the complainant as to the nature or purpose of the relevant act;

(b) the defendant intentionally induced the complainant to consent to the relevant act by impersonating a person known personally to the complainant.

Section 76(2)(a): nature or purpose

The 2003 Act changes the law quite significantly in respect of frauds vitiating consent. It is important to distinguish between frauds as to the nature of the act, frauds as to the purpose of the act and frauds as to peripheral issues.

Under the 1956 Act, frauds by A as to the nature of the act would vitiate B's consent. In *Flattery* (1877) 2 QBD 410 (approved in *Williams* [1923] 1 KB 340), A told B, aged 19, that he could cure her of her fits by performing a surgical operation upon her. She allowed him to have intercourse with her, believing that the act was a surgical one.

≋ *Questions*

If in this case B did not understand what sexual intercourse was (ie she had no sexual education at all), would this be an offence under s 76(2)(a)? What if B knew what sexual intercourse involved (ie the mechanics of the act), but not the social implications of having sex?

It has been held that a defendant's failure to disclose his HIV status did not affect the issue of consent in rape where there were no allegations that A had deceived B, rather that he had forcibly attacked B. The evidence of his HIV status should have been excluded: *EB* [2006] EWCA Crim 2945 (section 12.2.1.4). There was an argument that although under the old law a deception as to HIV-infected status was only a deception as to an attribute, and not the nature of the act, there could be no rape, the new law might prompt the courts to take a different view. In *EB*, the Court of Appeal rejected this idea. If A has not disclosed his HIV-positive status to B, he will be at risk of conviction under s 20 of the Offences Against the Person Act 1861 (section 10.4, p 261). The courts' view is that he has defrauded B as to the risk of infection, but he has not defrauded B as to the nature of the act of sexual intercourse. As a result of more recent case law, however, had B asked A about his HIV status and he actively deceived her, a jury could conclude that this deprived B of the freedom to choose whether to have sex with A within the meaning of s 74.

Frauds as to the purpose of the Act are much more difficult to deal with under the old law. In *Linekar* [1994] EWCA Crim 2, [1995] Crim LR 321, A was charged with raping a prostitute, B. A approached B and she agreed to have intercourse with him for £25. Having had intercourse A left without paying. Was that a fraud as to the purpose? Is it the purpose of the act or the actor that matters? This issue was considered in the next case.

R v Jheeta

[2007] EWCA Crim 1699, Court of Appeal, Criminal Division

(Sir Igor Judge P, Simon J and HHJ Goldsack QC)

The victim, B, was a student who had had a sexual relationship with A. She started receiving text messages and telephone calls of a threatening nature, for example 'We are going to kidnap you'; 'We are going to convert you'; 'We are going to kill you'. She told A. He was responsible for all the messages, but hid this fact from her and offered to arrange protection for her. He claimed to have alerted the police on her behalf and sent her text messages purporting to be from a police officer: PC Ken. Regular text messages were sent to B asking her for details of the phone calls and messages she had received, and requiring her to submit statements by text. 'PC Ken' told B that A would be able to watch her house and arrange for security including undercover protection at a cost of £1,000 annually. She paid. PC Bob took over from PC Ken—he too was a fiction created by A. PC Thomas was created and he sent more messages. Whenever she sought to break off with A, she would receive text messages from the different police officers, telling her that A had tried to kill himself and that she should do her duty and take care of him. She was told that she should sleep with A, and that she would be liable to a fine if she did not. She received something like 50 such demands over a four-year period. On each occasion B had intercourse with A in a hotel room. But for the messages from the fictitious police officers, she would not have done so. Eventually A's subterfuge was uncovered.

[Sir Igor Judge P reviewed the facts and A's response in police interview.]

In answer to the direct question, 'when you had sex with [B] on those occasions, did you have true consent?', he responded 'No'. He admitted that she had intercourse with him because of the texts. She would have been content with intercourse from time to time, but he wanted greater frequency. These admissions assume considerable significance when the basis of plea is examined. . . .

[His lordship referred to the indictment and the possible pleas that had been considered and then to ss 74 to 76 of the Act.]

Our particular concern is with section 76(2)(a), the 'nature and purpose' of the 'relevant act'. For the purposes of sections 75 and 76, relevant act is defined by section 77. In the context of rape the relevant act is 'the defendant intentionally penetrating, with his penis, . . . another person ("the complainant")'. The provisions relating to consent are not confined to rape, but do not at present require further examination. Perhaps more important, the offence of procuring a woman to have sexual intercourse by false pretences ceased to exist when the 2003 Act came into force. . . .

This consideration provided part of the foundation for the submission by [counsel for the Crown] that a statute which brought together all the offences of a sexual nature cannot have been intended to decriminalise deliberate conduct designed to deceive a woman into having sexual intercourse. Here, the appellant's purpose was to deceive the complainant into having sexual intercourse with him in order to alleviate or remove the problems which she, having been deceived by him, believed she faced. The result was that she submitted to intercourse because of those extraneous pressures. These submissions broadened from the narrow consideration of section 76(2)(a) of the Act into the wider question of consent as defined in section 74. The appellant's actions deprived the complainant of her freedom to choose whether or not to have intercourse with him. He pleaded guilty on the basis that at least on some occasions her freedom to choose was constrained by his actions. For the moment we shall confine our attention to the irrebuttable presumption in section 76(2)(a).

[Counsel for the appellant] submitted that the Act incorporated the common law on these issues into statute, and created the irrebuttable evidential presumptions. The fact that the presumptions in section 76 are conclusive reinforced the need for circumspection about an extended interpretation of the 'nature or purpose' of the relevant act. The deception, within the limits described in the basis of plea, is conceded, but it was not a deception about the nature or purpose of the relevant act. The complainant was sexually experienced. She was aware of the nature and purpose of intercourse, and the identity of the applicant. The advice given to the appellant was incorrect in law. There was no deception operating on the mind of the complainant about the nature or purpose of the Act. The conclusive presumptions could not be established. The plea was tendered after legal advice which did not accurately reflect the statutory provisions. Therefore the convictions are unsafe.

Our approach is to address the ambit of section 76 in the context of the creation of an irrebuttable evidential presumption, with wide application to effectively every incident of sexual touching. Professor Temkin and Professor Ashworth explained one possible consequences of a wide interpretation of 76 in their valuable article, *The Sexual Offences Act 2003 (1) Rape Sexual Assault and the Problems of Consent* (2004) CLR 328 at 338.

'Those who are uncomfortable with the full implications of sexual autonomy may not share the view that a conclusive presumption of absence of consent should apply where D has sex with C who is asleep at the time. The provisions of the Act on consent apply not only to rape and assault by penetration but also to touching which falls within sexual assault or causing sexual activity. A conclusive presumption of absence of consent and absence of reasonable belief in consent, if applied to all situations where C was asleep at the time, would render D liable for sexual assault if he sexually touched his partner C while C was asleep even though D was in the habit of doing so and C had not objected to this in the past'.

The writers point out that a complaint, and subsequent prosecution, would be unlikely. However it would seem pretty surprising to couples sharing a bed to be told that the law prohibited either of them from intimately touching the other while asleep, and that they would be potentially liable to prosecution and punishment, for a sexual touch of the sleeping partner as a preliminary to possible sexual activity which the sleeping partner, on awakening, might welcome. The article also addresses 'the problem' of the repeal of the offence of procuring sexual intercourse by false representations. It explains that convictions for this offence were rare, adding that 'in the unusual case where this issue occurs, the vague terms of section 74 now assume a heightened importance'.

The starting point in our analysis is to acknowledge that in most cases, the absence of consent, and the appropriate state of the defendant's mind, will be proved without reference to evidential or conclusive presumptions. When they do apply, section 75 and section 76 are directed to the process of proving the absence of consent to whichever sexual act is alleged. They are concerned with presumptions about rather than the definition of consent. The evidential presumptions in section 75 continue to require the prosecution to disprove consent if, in the circumstances defined in the section, there is sufficient evidence to raise the issue. These presumptions are not conclusive, merely evidential. However section 76 raises presumptions conclusive of the issue of consent, and thus where intercourse is proved, conclusive of guilt. They therefore require the most stringent scrutiny.

In our judgment the ambit of section 76 is limited to the 'act' to which it is said to apply. In rape cases the 'act' is vaginal, anal or oral intercourse. Provided this consideration is constantly borne in mind, it will be seen that section 76(2)(a) is relevant only to the comparatively rare cases where the defendant deliberately deceives the complainant about the *nature or purpose* of one or other form of intercourse. No conclusive presumptions arise merely because the complainant was deceived in some way or other by disingenuous blandishments of or common or garden lies by the defendant. These may well be deceptive and persuasive, but they will rarely go to the nature or purpose of intercourse. Beyond this limited type of case, and assuming that, as here, section 75 has no application, the issue of consent must be addressed in the context of section 74.

It may be helpful to reinforce these observations by reference to a number of cases at common law which provide examples of deceptions as to the nature or purpose of the act of intercourse.

[His lordship referred to *Flattery* and *Williams*, section 12.2.1.7, p 321.]

Deception as to purpose is sometimes said to be exemplified in *R v Tabassum* [2000] 2 CAR 328, a decision described by the late Professor Sir John Smith as a 'doubtful case'. A number of women agreed to participate in a breast cancer research programme at the behest of the appellant when, as a result of what he said or did, or both, they wrongly believed that he was medically qualified or trained. They consented to a medical examination, not to sexual touching by a stranger. 'There was consent to the nature of the act, but not to its quality'. However section 76(2)(a) does not address the 'quality' of the act, but confines itself to its 'purpose'. In the latest edition of *Smith and Hogan Criminal Law*, (11th edition [2005]) Professor David Ormerod identifies a better example, *R v Green* [2002] EWCA Crim 1501. Bogus medical examinations of young men were carried out by a qualified doctor, in the course of which they were wired up to monitors while they masturbated. The purported object was to assess their potential for impotence. Although the experiment did not involve any form of intercourse, it illustrates the practice of a deception as to the 'purpose' of the physical act.

These examples demonstrate the likely rarity of occasions when the conclusive presumption in section 76(2)(a) will apply. For example, *R v Linekar* [[1994] EWCA Crim 2]] would not fall within its ambit. The appellant promised to pay a prostitute £25 if she had intercourse with him. It was a promise he never intended to keep. On this aspect of the case, that is, that the defendant tricked the prostitute into having intercourse with him, the judge left it to the jury to consider whether his fraud vitiated her consent which was given on the basis that he would pay. The conviction was quashed. The consent given by the complainant was a real consent, which was not destroyed by the appellant's false pretence. If anything, he was guilty of an offence under section 3 of the 1956 Act, that is an offence identical to the offence alleged in counts one and two of the present indictment. Linekar deceived the prostitute about his intentions. He undoubtedly lied to her. However she was undeceived about either the nature or the purpose of the act, that is intercourse. Accordingly the conclusive presumptions in section 76 would have no application.

With these considerations in mind, we must return to the present case. On the written basis of plea the appellant undoubtedly deceived the complainant. He created a bizarre and fictitious fantasy which, because it was real enough to her, pressurised her to have intercourse with him more frequently than she otherwise would have done. She was not deceived as to the nature or purpose of intercourse, but deceived as to the situation in which she found herself. In our judgment the conclusive presumption in section 76(2)(a) had no application, and counsel for the appellant below were wrong to advise on the basis that it did. . . .

Appeal against conviction dismissed

≋ *Questions*

(1) About what, if anything, had B been deceived in this case? Did she understand the physical nature of the acts? Was she deceived about with whom she was doing them?

(2) What of A, a doctor, who tells B, accurately, that an intimate medical examination is necessary. She allows this to happen. X, A's friend, derives sexual gratification from watching covertly (cf *Bolduc & Bird* (1967) 63 DLR (2d) 82). Is there a deception as to 'the purpose' of the acts?

In *Piper* [2007] EWCA Crim 2151, A invited young women who were 'willing to flaunt it' to attend interviews for 'modelling work'. They had to strip to their underwear and A secretly video-recorded them. A measured them for bikinis and 'was more careless with his hands than one might have expected him to be if he were doing it with any sense of appropriateness'. He pleaded guilty to sexual assault and 'acknowledged that the women would not have consented to allow themselves to be measured or take their clothes off if they had appreciated that it was a charade'.

A more bizarre twist on this problem arose in *Devonald* [2008] EWCA Crim 527. The complainant was a 16-year-old boy who had been in a relationship with A's daughter. The relationship had broken down and, believing B to have treated his daughter badly, A sought to teach him a lesson by deliberately embarrassing him. A set up a fake email account pretending to be a young woman. A then corresponded with B over the internet and persuaded B to masturbate in front of a webcam. A was convicted of an offence of causing a person to engage in sexual activity without consent, having changed his plea to guilty following a ruling by the judge. The trial judge ruled that s 76(2)(a) of the Sexual Offences Act 2003 would apply. The Court of Appeal dismissed an application for leave to appeal. It was open to the jury to conclude that B had been deceived as to the purpose of the masturbation.

≋ *Questions*

(1) Has B been deceived as to the nature of the act of masturbation? Was B deceived as to A's purpose in getting him to masturbate? Under s 4 it is arguable that it is this latter act which is the one about which B must be deceived—see s 77 of the Act which defines the

'relevant act' about which B must be deceived as being 'the defendant intentionally causing another person to engage in the activity where the activity is sexual'.

(2) A tells B that his sexual technique is guaranteed to give her an orgasm. Because of this B has sex with him. A's performance is totally disappointing and B fails to have an orgasm. Has A raped B?

On one interpretation, it could be said that the decisions in *Jheeta* and *Devonald* conflict. The Court of Appeal resolved this conflict in *B* [2013] EWCA Crim 832 and held that, to the extent that there is any inconsistency between the two cases, *Jheeta* ought to be followed. In doing so, Hallett LJ stated that because s 76 contains a conclusive presumption, it ought to be narrowly interpreted and will only apply in rare cases.

R v B
[2013] EWCA Crim 832, Court of Appeal, Criminal Division

(Hallett LJ, Bean J and HHJ Pert QC)

B had been in a sexual relationship with A for five years. A contacted B on Facebook using the false name 'Grant'. B developed an online relationship with Grant, to the extent that she sent him pictures of herself posing topless. Grant then threatened B that if she did not engage in various sexual acts over the internet, he would send the compromising pictures to her employer and post them on the internet. B obeyed. B eventually confided to A about what Grant was making her do. A told B that she should lure Grant to a secluded place so that he could put the blackmail to an end. A subsequently told B that he had killed Grant and showed her a picture of a man with a gun to his head. A few weeks later, B was contacted on Facebook by A, who was now posing as 'Chad'. Chad told B that he was a friend of Grant's and knew what he had done. Chad claimed to be in possession of the topless photographs and told B he would send them to her employer if she did not do as he demanded. As a result of this, B carried out further acts involving penetration of her vagina and anus with objects. Eventually B contacted the police who discovered that it was A who had been posing as Grant and Chad. A denied that he believed that B was not consenting. A was found guilty of causing a person to engage in sexual activity without consent, contrary to s 4 of the Sexual Offences Act 2003.

Hallett LJ [gave the following guidance on the interpretation of s 76]:

9. Miss Kidd for the prosecution relied heavily upon a decision of this court in *R v Devonald* [2008] EWCA Crim 527. Devonald was a renewed application for leave to appeal against conviction on the basis the judge wrongly allowed reliance upon section 76.

[Her Ladyship set out the facts of *Devonald* and continued:]

10. Here, Miss Kidd observed, the complainant was led to believe that she was performing sexual acts for one or two complete strangers, under threat that if she failed to comply her place of work would be informed and the intimate pictures distributed. Thus, the deceit was threefold: as to the identity of the recipients of the web feed, the motivation of the recipients and the consequences of the failure to submit to the demands. Miss Kidd argued it would be artificial to divorce one of those facts from another. They should be looked at in the round and if so together they amounted to a clear case of deceit as to *purpose* of the relevant act.

11. Mr Bindloss for the defence submitted that section 76 did not apply. He preferred to rely upon the decision in *R v Jheeta* [2007] 2 Cr App R 34 in which the Court considered a full appeal against conviction as opposed to an application for leave.

[Her Ladyship then set out the facts of *Jheeta*, quoting the extract earlier in this section, and also of *Assange* before continuing:]

15. Nevertheless the judge chose to follow *Devonald*. He noted that the conclusive presumptions under section 76 should only apply in a very limited number of cases but was persuaded by Miss Kidd's arguments that the facts of the present case were very similar to those of *Devonald*. If, therefore, section 76 was applicable in *Devonald*, it was applicable in this case. He rejected Mr Bindloss' argument that the cases of *Jheeta* and *Devonald* conflicted and that *Jheeta* ought to be followed. He decided he would leave the issue of whether the complainant had been deceived as to purpose of the acts to the jury, but direct them that if they found deceit proved, the conclusive presumptions applied. He directed the jury in these terms (page 4G):

> 'The remaining issues in the case are to do with consent or reasonable belief in consent. Before I deal with consent and reasonable belief in consent in more detail, let me refer you to a question that Miss Kidd asked you Mr Bindloss took a different view about it. Miss Kidd said, "Did the defendant deceive Miss X?" Mr Bindloss said rightly, "That is not the right question." The question is not, "Did the defendant deceive Miss X?" It is accepted that he did deceive her as to who was sending messages. The question you have to ask yourselves in fact is did the defendant deceive Miss X as to the purpose of the acts? What the prosecution say is that she was deceived by the defendant by him pretending that he was one of two complete strangers whom she had never met, by threatening to tell her work what she had been doing on the internet or to publish pictures or footage of her on websites if she did not do as he told her, whereas in fact the reality was that he wasn't one of two complete strangers. He was her boyfriend. He was doing it for his own gratification or perhaps to get back at her for using Facebook, or to test loyalty, or to teach her to say no. This were various things that were raised by him during the course of his interviews. He said that since he was her boyfriend, he would never have published anything which harmed her.
>
> So the question, members of the jury, is: has the prosecution made you sure that he deceived her as to the purpose of the acts? By deceiving her as to who it was and making all the threats, was he deceiving her to the purpose of the acts? If you are sure that he did deceive her as to the purpose of the various acts then, members of the jury, as a matter of law you must find that she did not consent to those acts and that the defendant did not believe that she consented to those acts. So if you are sure that he deceived her as to the purposes of the acts, you do not need to go on in detail the question of whether the prosecution has proved she was not consenting or whether they had proved that the defendant did not reasonably believe she was consenting.
>
> It is only if the prosecution has not proved that she was deceived as to the purpose of the acts, only then would you have to go on to consider consent or reasonable belief in consent.'

Throughout the remainder of the summing-up the judge repeatedly referred to whether or not there had been 'deceit as to purpose' with no further explanation of what that meant. In his explanation of the route to verdict, he confirmed that if the jury was satisfied that the complainant had been 'deceived as to the purpose of the act', that was the end of the matter; their verdicts must be guilty.

16. There is but one ground of appeal and that was that the judge was wrong in law so to rule and so to direct. Mr Bindloss maintained his argument before us that there was here no 'deceit as to *purpose*'. He provided a dictionary definition of the word '*purpose*' namely: 'the reason for doing something' or the 'objective in doing something'. Taking those as the definitions of *purpose* he was prepared to accept that the decision in *Devonald* was correct because the applicant Devonald plainly misled the complainant as to his purpose for the sexual act. His true purpose was the complainant's humiliation not, as the complainant thought, sexual gratification.

17. Here, Mr Bindloss argued that the motive was clearly sexual gratification. That was the Crown's own case. The complainant was never asked as to what she understood the purpose or the motive of the person at the end of the webcam to be. One presumes she would have assumed the motive was sexual gratification; if so she was not misled as to the purpose.

18. In any event, Mr Bindloss argued the judge failed to give the jury an adequate direction on the application of section 76. It was incumbent upon him to give the jury clear directions as to the limited extent of the meaning of the word *purpose* and to identify the relevant evidence going to that issue. In reality, he simply adopted the prosecution approach of a global summary of the evidence coupled with the question: 'was the complainant thereby deceived as to purpose?'. He rolled up the various deceitful elements of the appellant's conduct. At no time did he direct the jury that deceit as to identity or deceit as to consequences would not be enough standing alone (see *Jheeta*).

19. There is no definition of the word *purpose* in the Act. It is a perfectly ordinary English word and one might have hoped it would not be necessary to provide a definition. It has been left to the courts and academics to struggle with its meaning in the context of a sexual act. We say 'struggle' advisedly because it may not be straightforward to ascertain the *purpose* of a sexual act. Those engaging in a sexual act may have a number of reasons or objectives and each party may have a different objective or reason. The Act does not specify whose *purpose* is under consideration. There is, therefore, a great danger in attempting any definition of the word *purpose* and in defining it too widely. A wide definition could bring within the remit of section 76 situations never contemplated by Parliament.

20. We shall, therefore, simply apply the normal rules of statutory construction and echo what was said in *Jheeta*. Where, as here, a statutory provision effectively removes from an accused his only line of defence to a serious criminal charge it must be strictly construed. We respectfully adopt the approach of the court in *Jheeta*. If there is any conflict between the decisions in *Jheeta* and *Devonald*, we would unhesitatingly follow *Jheeta*. Thus, it will be a rare case in which section 76 should be applied.

21. Is this one of those rare cases? Miss Kidd reminded the court of the extent of the deception and the affect upon the complainant. It was not unlike the extent and effect of the deception in *Jheeta*. Just as in *Jheeta*, this appellant undoubtedly deceived his girlfriend in a cruel and despicable way. However, the fact that there was a catalogue of deception of an unpleasant kind begs the question as to whether it was deception as to *purpose* so as to trigger the operation of section 76. We have our doubts.

22. The complainant was never asked what her purpose or understanding of the purpose of the act was and the appellant's purpose seems far from clear. His accounts varied but the most likely explanation, as the prosecution argued, was some kind of perverted sexual gratification. The complainant knew full well what she was being asked to do and what she did in fact do, namely perform a sexual act for the benefit of the camera. She could have been in no doubt that the motive was at least in part sexual gratification. If so, on one view, even if one were to extend the definition of *purpose* to include the appellant's intention, as has been suggested, there is here no evidence going to the issue of deceit as to his purpose.

23. Further, we see force in Mr Bindloss's submission that if reliance was to be placed on section 76, which effectively withdrew the accused's only line of defence, it was incumbent upon the judge to identify the evidence which went to the issue of 'deceit as to purpose'. Here there was no such analysis, and the jury were never directed that the word had a restricted meaning—see *Jheeta*. They were not informed that deceit as to what some commentators have called 'peripheral matters' was not enough.

24. For those reasons we are troubled by the way in which the prosecution put their case and by the way in which it was left to the jury. We understand how prosecuting counsel and the judge may have thought that the decision in *Devonald* applied and appeared to support reliance on section 76. However, as we have indicated, reliance upon section 76 in this case, on these facts and this evidence, was misplaced. The prosecution needed to look no further than the provisions of Section 74. It provides that 'a person consents if he agrees by choice and has the freedom and capacity to make that choice'. If the complainant only complied because she was being blackmailed, the prosecution might argue forcefully she did not agree by choice.

25. We turn to the question of safety. Miss Kidd argued there was ample evidence here to establish guilt. The complainant was a compelling witness and her distress obvious to all concerned. Miss Kidd submitted there cannot in truth have been any defence on actual consent or even reasonable belief in consent. Had the jury been directed solely by reference to section 74 she submitted the verdict would have been the same.

26. We see considerable force in the submission that the complainant was a compelling witness and was dreadfully distressed by the appellant's behaviour. However, whatever one thinks of him, he was entitled to a fair trial. He had only one avenue of defence, and given the admitted level of his deceit, that defence was effectively taken from him. Reluctantly, therefore, we feel we have no option but to declare the conviction unsafe.

≈≈≈ *Question*

(1) Has s 76 now been rendered obsolete? In what circumstances might it apply?

(2) Section 76 deals with cases in which there is a deception as to identity only where A was impersonating someone known to B. Was Grant 'known' to B?

Section 76(2)(b)

By virtue of s 142(3) of the Criminal Justice and Public Order Act 1994, it was rape for a man to induce a woman to have intercourse with him by impersonating her husband. At common law, this was extended to include impersonation of long-term (heterosexual) partnerships: *Elbekkay* [1994] EWCA Crim 1. Section 76(2)(b) extends the law beyond any particular category or duration of relationship, it also extends beyond the offence of rape to other acts of penetration and sexual activity. See also R. Williams, 'Deception Mistake and the Vitiation of the Victim's Consent' (2008) 124 LQR 132.

≈≈≈ *Question*

In s 76(2)(b) are all people B has ever met 'known personally to' B? Is it only those with whom B has had some greater degree of intimacy? Can B be known personally to a person by email correspondence? Consider the couple who arrange to meet after internet dating. A gets cold feet and decides he cannot face meeting B. X, his friend, steps in and assumes A's name. Is there a conclusive presumption that B was not consenting to any subsequent sexual activity?

12.2.1.8 The mens rea of rape

The current test of mens rea as set out in s 1 of the 2003 Act (section 12.2.1, p 312) is markedly different from that proposed by the House of Lords in one of the most controversial decisions in the last few decades: *DPP v Morgan* [1975] 2 All ER 347, HL. There must be mens rea as to the penetration and also as to whether B is consenting. Despite the use of the word 'intention', in *Grewal* [2010] EWCA Crim 2448, relying upon *Heard* [2007] EWCA Crim 125, the Court of Appeal confirmed that rape is a crime of basic intent.

After *Morgan* and following the Heilbron Report (Cmnd 6352, 1975), rape was redefined in s 1(1) of the Sexual Offences (Amendment) Act 1976 to include the case where the defendant was reckless as to whether the victim consents. The courts defined the mens rea as a state where A was reckless in the sense that he 'couldn't care less' whether B consented. The test was subjective. Someone cannot be said not to care less about something unless he has realized that there is a risk of it, and carried on. It might be that he has not in fact thought about it and if he had he would not have cared less, but that was not the test. It remained the case that A's unreasonable beliefs that B was consenting, if believed by the jury, would lead to an acquittal. There was little categorical evidence that *Morgan* defences were successfully run, so jurors were presumably not readily believing defendants' spurious claims. Nevertheless, the plea was easy to run and difficult to disprove, and sent an undesirable message—that it is acceptable to take unreasonable risks as to someone's consent to sexual conduct. See J. Horder, 'Cognition, Emotion and Criminal Culpability' (1990) 106 LQR 469 at 477; T. Pickard, 'Culpable Mistakes' (1980) 30 U Toronto LJ 75; C. Wells, 'Swatting the Subjectivist Bug' [1982] Crim LR 209.

One of the most significant effects of the 2003 Act is to reverse *Morgan*: a genuine but unreasonable belief in consent will be a sufficient mens rea for the offences in ss 1 to 4.

The mens rea in rape and the other non-consensual offences (ss 1 to 4) is that A does not reasonably believe B consents. Assessing whether a belief is reasonable is to be determined having regard to all the circumstances, including any steps A has taken to ascertain whether B consents.

Several issues remain controversial.

- Complexity—there are in effect two reasonableness elements. D's belief must be reasonable and, in assessing that, the process by which he came to that belief must be reasonable.

- Lack of a purely objective test—the question is whether A has a reasonable belief in consent. This must relate to A's personal capacity to evaluate whether B is consenting. A who does not think about B's consent is guilty, as is A who considers and wrongly concludes that B is consenting—unless that mistake is reasonable. The possibility of a purely objective test—whether the reasonable person would have believed B was consenting—was considered, but rejected in favour of this test which pays some heed to A's physical and mental capabilities. See for discussion of alternatives, H. Power, 'Towards a Redefinition of the *Mens Rea* of Rape' (2003) 23 OJLS 379.

- Ambiguity over how s 1(2) applies—is the correct question as to (a) A's purely subjective belief about consent measured against a standard of reasonableness applied by the jury or magistrate, or (b) A's assessment that his own belief as to consent was reasonable?

- Is *Morgan* successfully abolished? Can A who is of limited mental capacity, who genuinely but unreasonably holds the belief that B is consenting, still run the defence that *he* made such efforts as *he* considered reasonable?

- Uncertainty over which of A's characteristics are to be considered when assessing whether it was reasonable for him to hold that belief in B's consent. The Government's view was that 'it is for the jury to decide whether any of the attributes of the defendant are relevant to their deliberations, subject to directions from the judge where necessary'. 'All the circumstances' would appear to include all circumstances that might be relevant to whether a belief is reasonable. Ministerial statements in Parliament have made it clear that 'circumstances' are not limited to surrounding facts: Lord Falconer of Thoroton, Hansard HL, 2 June 2003, vol 648, col 1076. Furthermore, in response to concerns expressed in Parliament that the New Zealand approach (where the reasonableness of D's belief is assessed wholly objectively, without any heed to his capacity or state of mind) might be adopted, Baroness Scotland of Asthal provided reassurance, ibid, 17 June 2003, vol 649, col 678:

We fully expect that characteristics such as mental incapacity and extreme youth will be taken into account in line with existing case law in such issues. We would not expect our courts to follow the New Zealand approach. We believe we can rely principally on case law as regards reasonableness.

The Court of Appeal in *B* [2013] EWCA Crim 3 considered the issue of whether a belief that B was consenting that was based upon A's delusional state of mind brought about by metal disorder was reasonable. Hughes LJ stated that:

Unless the state of mind amounted to insanity in law, beliefs in consent arising from conditions such as delusional psychotic illness or personality disorders had to be judged by objective standards of reasonableness and not by taking into account a mental disorder that induced a belief which could not reasonably arise without it.

Therefore the trial judge was correct to direct the jury that they should leave A's mental illness out of the equation when asking whether any belief that he may have had in consent was reasonable, but that if there might, independently of the illness, have been a reasonable belief, that would result in a verdict of not guilty. The court did recognize, however, that there may be cases in which A's personality or abilities might be relevant to whether his positive belief in consent was reasonable, but that was an issue for determination on specific facts. So, for example, a defendant with Asperger's might not understand subtle and non-verbal cues to desist. Such beliefs would not be so irrational as to be ignored under the Act. This obviously leaves scope for some fine distinctions to be drawn in future cases.

> ≋ *Questions*
> Will A's lack of sexual experience be relevant? His learning disability? His extreme youth and lack of understanding of sexual mores? Surely not his voluntarily intoxication through alcohol or drugs? What of A's knowledge of B's previous sexual history?

Mistakes and consent

What of A who claims that he thought on reasonable grounds X would be consenting to the sexual penetration which he then mistakenly performed on B? Can A claim he has a reasonable belief in consent? In *Whitta* [2006] EWCA Crim 2626, A had agreed with X that they would have sex later after the party they were both attending. Both A and X were adults but drunk. A, having removed his glasses, later entered a bedroom and digitally penetrated B, the sleeping 51-year-old mother of the party host. B was also very drunk. A desisted as soon as he realized his mistake. The trial judge ruled that mistake as to the identity in this context was irrelevant—liability was strict.

> ≋ *Question*
> A had penetrated the vagina of another, B. Is that enough? Does the express statutory reference to a specific person '(B)' rather than use of the words 'of another' itself alter things? Is the question then whether A has reasonable grounds for believing the person that he did penetrate would be consenting or whether he can rely on the reasonable belief in the consent of the person he thought he was penetrating?

The trial judge ruled that:

Are the jury entitled to consider mistaken identity as a relevant circumstance in assessing reasonable belief or is the phrase 'having regard to all the circumstances' limited to whatever took place between the defendant and the complainant named in the indictment?

In my view, it is the narrow view which must be adopted in that the wording of the section and of the indictment clearly relate to a named complainant in section 1(1) and the requirement in subsection (2) cannot widen the scope of such consideration so as to allow for the defendant's state of mind in relation to any third party.

It is therefore not the jury in this case to be allowed to consider the circumstances which may have prevailed had the person whose vagina he penetrate been some person other than the complainant.

The Court of Appeal, in a sentencing appeal referred by the Attorney General, noted that:

We disagree with this analysis of the ruling. The effect of the judge's ruling is that it is not a defence to a charge under sections 1 or 2 of the SOA if the defendant has made a mistake, however reasonable, as to the identity of the person to whom the sexual activity is directed. In his ruling the judge did not decide that the offender's belief was not reasonable or that he had omitted to take the necessary care. He decided that the offender's belief was irrelevant because he did not believe that C consented.

If the ruling is right, then the three offences are offences of strict responsibility *as far as and only as far as* the identity of the complainant is concerned. This being so, the judge must determine the level of the defendant's culpability, if any, in order to determine the appropriate sentence.

We note in passing that a possible alternative way of dealing with this very rare set of circumstances would be to hold that the offence is committed if a reasonable (and therefore sober) person would have realised that the person being penetrated or sexually touched was not the person whom the defendant thought he was consensually penetrating or touching.

> ≈≈≈ **Question**
> A is on holiday with his partner, X. He falls asleep on the sunbed with X snoozing in the sunbed next to his. He half awakes, reaches out his hand and pats the bottom of the person lying on the next sunbed assuming it is X. It is not X, but B a 12-year-old girl who has occupied the sunbed when X went for a swim. What offences has A committed?

12.2.2 Assault by penetration

Sexual Offences Act 2003, s 2

(1) A person (A) commits an offence if—

    (a) he intentionally penetrates the vagina or anus of another person (B) with a part of his body or anything else,

    (b) the penetration is sexual,

    (c) B does not consent to the penetration, and

    (d) A does not reasonably believe that B consents.

(2) Whether a belief is reasonable is to be determined having regard to all the circumstances, including any steps A has taken to ascertain whether B consents.

Penetration with fingers and inanimate objects such as knives and bottles is caught by this section. The issues of consent and mens rea are as discussed previously in relation to rape. The act of penetration is regarded as continuing until withdrawal. Since the degree of penetration need only be slight, and 'vagina' includes 'vulva', oral sex performed on a woman is caught by s 2.

It seems doubtful that there is an element of mens rea as to the 'sexual' nature of the penetration. As a matter of principle, each element of the actus reus ought to have a corresponding element of mens rea. (Cf the view of Lord Hope in *G* [2008] UKHL 37, section 6.5.1, p 135.) Penetration must be 'sexual' as defined in the following section.

≋ *Questions*

(1) Is A who forcibly penetrates B with an object solely as an act of violence and humiliation guilty under s 2?

(2) A penetrates B's anus with his fingers in the course of an intimate search of B who is under arrest for drugs offences. Does A commit an offence? What if A secretly derives sexual pleasure from doing so?

12.2.2.1 Sexual

'Sexual' is defined in s 78:

> Penetration, touching or any other activity is sexual if a reasonable person would consider that—
>
> (a) whatever its circumstances or any person's purpose in relation to it, it is because of its nature sexual, or
>
> (b) because of its nature it may be sexual and because of its circumstances or the purpose of any person in relation to it (or both) it is sexual.

See *H* (section 12.2.3, p 333).

The penetration must be intentional; there is no crime of reckless sexual penetration. However, following *Heard* [2007] EWCA Crim 125 (section 25.3, p 722), the voluntarily intoxicated defendant cannot rely on his intoxicated state to support his claim that his penetration of B with an object/part of his body was not intentional.

12.2.3 Sexual assault

Sexual Offences Act 2003, s 3

> (1) A person (A) commits an offence if—
>
> (a) he intentionally touches another person (B),
>
> (b) the touching is sexual,
>
> (c) B does not consent to the touching, and
>
> (d) A does not reasonably believe that B consents.
>
> (2) Whether a belief is reasonable is to be determined having regard to all the circumstances, including any steps A has taken to ascertain whether B consents.

Sexual is defined as in section 12.2.2.1.

'Touching' is defined in s 79(8):

> Touching includes touching—
>
> (a) with any part of the body,
>
> (b) with anything else,
>
> (c) through anything,
>
> and in particular includes touching amounting to penetration.

The 2003 Act focuses not on 'assault' as under the old law but on 'touching'. This may be significant. No hostility is required. Sexual words do not constitute a touching (but might have been assaults). D, who walks towards someone with his penis exposed, commits no touching, but this would have been indecent assault—*Rolfe* (1952) 36 Cr App R 4.

R v H

[2005] EWCA Crim 732, Court of Appeal, Criminal Division

(Lord Woolf CJ, Davis and Field JJ)

A approached B, a stranger, at 10 pm as she walked across a field and said to her 'Do you fancy a shag?' B ignored him whereon A grabbed B's tracksuit bottoms by the fabric, attempted to pull her towards him and attempted unsuccessfully to put his hand over her mouth. B escaped. A was convicted of sexual assault, contrary to s 3 of the Sexual Offences Act 2003. Two issues had arisen at trial:

(1) whether the touching of B's tracksuit bottoms alone amounted to the 'touching' of another person within the meaning of s 79(8) of the 2003 Act; and

(2) whether anything which had occurred amounted to what a reasonable person might regard as being 'sexual' within the meaning of s 78 of the Act, which provides:

. . . penetration, touching, or any other activity is sexual if a reasonable person would consider that:

(a) whatever its circumstances or any person's purpose in relation to it, it is because of its nature sexual, or

(b) because of its nature it may be sexual and because of its circumstances or the purpose of any person in relation to it (or both) it is sexual.

The Lord Chief Justice [his lordship referred to Temkin and Ashworth [2004] Crim LR 328 (section 12.1), and to the relevant statutory provisions:]

8. In this case we are concerned with section 78(b). Miss Egerton who appears on behalf of the Crown accepts that (a) has no application. The nature of the touching with which we are concerned was not inevitably sexual. It is important to note that there are two requirements in section 78(b). First, there is the requirement that the touching because of its nature may be sexual; and secondly, there is the requirement that the touching because of its circumstances or the purpose of any person in relation to it (or both) is sexual.

9. Miss Egerton agreed with the view of the court expressed in argument that if there were not two requirements in (b), the opening words 'because of its nature it may be sexual' would be surplus. If it was not intended by the legislature that effect should be given to those opening words, it would be sufficient to create an offence by looking at the touching and deciding whether because of its circumstances it was sexual. In other words, there is not one comprehensive test. It is necessary for both halves of section 78(b) to be complied with.

10. It is no doubt because of this aspect of section 78(b) and the article in the Criminal Law Review that Mr West who appears on behalf of the appellant referred to *R v Court*. That case dealt with an alleged indecent assault. An assistant in a shop struck a 12 year old girl visitor twelve times, for no apparent reason, outside her shorts on her buttocks. The assistant was convicted. Both this court and the House of Lords dismissed the assistant's appeal. At pages 42B–43E of his speech Lord Ackner set out his general approach. On reading that passage it is understandable why the article should have made the comment to which we referred. It is quite clear to the court that the staged approach which we have observed in section 78 is reflected in Lord Ackner's speech. The only difficulty that we have with applying Lord Ackner's approach is that he referred to *R v George* [1956] Crim LR 52. In that case

the prosecution relied on the fact that on a number of occasions the defendant had removed a shoe from a girl's foot. He had done so, as he admitted, because it gave him a perverted sexual gratification. Streatfeild J ruled that an assault became indecent only if it was accompanied by circumstances of indecency towards the person alleged to have been assaulted and that none of the assaults in that case (namely the removal or attempted removal of the shoes) could possibly amount to an indecent assault.

11. We would express reservations as to whether or not it would be possible for the removal of shoes in that way, because of the nature of the act that took place, to be sexual as sexual is defined now in section 78. That in our judgment may well be a question that it would be necessary for a jury to determine.

12. The fact that in section 78(b) there are two different questions which we have sought to identify complicates the task of the judge and that of the jury. If there is a submission of 'no case' the judge may have to ask himself whether there is a case to be left to the jury. He will answer that question by determining whether it would be appropriate for a reasonable person to consider that the touching because of its nature may be sexual. Equally, the judge will have to consider whether it would be possible for a reasonable person to conclude, because of the circumstances of the touching or the purpose of any person in relation to the touching (or both), that it is sexual. If he comes to the conclusion that a reasonable person could possibly answer those questions adversely to the defendant, then the matter would have to be left to the jury.

13. We would suggest that in that situation the judge would regard it as desirable to identify two distinct questions for the jury. First, would they, as twelve reasonable people (as the section requires), consider that because of its nature the touching that took place in the particular case before them could be sexual? If the answer to that question was 'No', the jury would find the defendant not guilty. If 'Yes', they would have to go on to ask themselves (again as twelve reasonable people) whether in view of the circumstances and/or the purpose of any person in relation to the touching (or both), the touching was in fact sexual. If they were satisfied that it was, then they would find the defendant guilty. If they were not satisfied, they would find the defendant not guilty.

14. In that suggested approach the reference to the nature of the touching in the first half refers to the actual touching that took place in that case. In answering the first question, the jury would not be concerned with the circumstances before or after the touching took place, or any evidence as to the purpose of any person in relation to the touching.

[His lordship referred to s 62, 'Committing an offence with intent to commit a sexual offence' and outlined the facts revealed by the evidence in the present case.]

24. . . . Where a person is wearing clothing we consider that touching of the clothing constitutes touching for the purpose of the section 3 offence.

25. As against that approach Mr West relied on section 79(8) (set out above). He submits that under section 79(8)(c) touching through anything (through clothing), if pressure in some form is not brought against the body of the person concerned, there cannot be touching; there has to be some form of touching of the body of the individual who is alleged to have been assaulted, even if it be through clothing. Mr West submits that, having regard to the complainant's evidence in this case, there was no such touching.

26. It is important to note that the opening words of section 79(8) are 'touching includes touching' and in particular 'through anything'. Subsection (8) is not a definition section. We have no doubt that it was not Parliament's intention by the use of that language to make it impossible to regard as a sexual assault touching which took place by touching what the victim was wearing at the time.

27. The second unsuccessful submission made by Mr West for the case to be withdrawn from the jury was as to whether anything occurred which a reasonable person could regard as sexual within the meaning of the Act. The judge's view was that there were here clearly circumstances in which the offence was alleged to have occurred, including the words alleged to have been spoken beforehand, which could make the actions which took place properly to be regarded as being sexual. In his approach at that time, and indeed in his summing-up, the judge did not take a two stage approach to section 78(b). He looked at the matter as a whole. The problem about that approach is that in a borderline case a person's intention

or other circumstances may appear to show that what happened was sexual, although their nature might not have been sexual. For the reasons we have already given that approach is not one which we regard as appropriate, although we recognise that in the great majority of cases the answer will be the same whether the two stage approach is adopted or the position is looked at as a whole.

[His lordship dealt with other grounds of appeal.]

Appeal dismissed

In *Court* [1989] AC 28, A, an assistant in a shop, pulled a girl aged 12, who was in the shop, across his knee and spanked her clothed bottom. When asked why he did it, he said 'Buttock fetish'. The House held (Lord Goff dissenting) that because it was ambiguous whether the act was indecent it was legitimate to refer to A's motive. In circumstances where the act was unambiguously indecent there was no need to refer to A's motive. In cases where the act was unambiguously not indecent, A's indecent motive could not make it such.

~~~ *Questions*
Would Court be convicted under s 3? What if Court had pulled the girl's shorts down and spanked her, and done so in the belief that this was an appropriate punishment because he believed her to be shoplifting? Would the jury even be entitled to consider his motive or would his act be caught by s 78(a)?

In *H*, Lord Woolf CJ referred to the Temkin and Ashworth article which states that:

. . . as under the *Court* test, conduct, which on the face of it is not sexual, cannot be brought within that description by pointing to its circumstances and/or purpose. The *Court* test and its application have been criticised as 'vague' and unclear, but a superior alternative remains to be found. In practice, in most cases, it will not be difficult to apply the test in section 78(a). It will be in unusual cases only that section 78(b) will be brought into play. Whilst section 78 might require some fine-tuning, it was wise to have included a provision of this kind. In Canada a decision to exclude any such provision from the legislation has led to a costly proliferation of cases in which courts have been called upon to rule in what circumstances a particular assault may be described as sexual.

His lordship stated that 'the expectation indicated in that part of the article that it will only be in unusual cases that section 78(b) will be brought into play is probably over-optimistic, as the facts of this case indicate'.

~~~ *Questions*
(1) Fetishes include such conduct as stroking shoes, touching hair. Is there any conduct that a reasonable person would conclude may *not* be sexual?
(2) In *H*, the defendant touched only B's clothes. How can that be a touching of the 'person' as s 3 requires? What if A touches only the hem of B's skirt? Is that distinguishable from touching B's bikini-clad buttock? Would soaking B's flimsy T-shirt be a sexual touching? Does A have to be holding the implement that touches B where it is alleged that he touched with something?

The touching must be intentional. What then of A, who is drunk at the office party, and who gropes B and claims that any contact was 'accidental'? In *Heard* [2007] EWCA Crim 125 (section 25.3, p 722), the Court of Appeal held that although it had a requirement for intentional touching, the offence should be treated as one of basic intent: it is no excuse for A to rely on his voluntary intoxication that he intended to touch the complainant in a sexual manner. On policy grounds the court was clearly entitled to assume that Parliament had not intended to change the law (although it should be noted that under the pre-2003 law, the offence of indecent assault was not always a basic intent crime).

Lord Justice Hughes states that:

> To flail about, stumble or barge around in an unco-ordinated manner which results in an unintended touching, objectively sexual, is not this offence. If to do so when sober is not this offence, then nor is it this offence to do so when intoxicated. It is also possible that such an action would not be judged by the jury to be objectively sexual, on the basis that it was clearly accidental, but whether that is so or not, we are satisfied that in such a case this offence is not committed. The intoxication, in such a situation, has not impacted on intention. Intention is simply not in question. What is in question is impairment of control of the limbs. . . . '[A] drunken intent is still an intent', the corollary [is] that 'a drunken accident is still an accident'.

≈≈≈ *Questions*

(1) A takes LSD. He thinks he is at the centre of the earth stroking a strange mammal. He is in fact stroking B's breast. Is he guilty under s 3?

(2) A is out drinking with his mates. He is drunk and showing off. As B, the barmaid, bends over to collect glasses nearby, A pretends to grope her from behind. He intends to miss but get a laugh from his mates. He misjudges and makes contact with her bottom. Is he guilty of an offence under s 3? Is the touching accidental or reckless?

12.2.4 Intentionally causing someone to engage in sexual activity

Sexual Offences Act 2003, s 4

(1) A person (A) commits an offence if—

   (a) he intentionally causes another person (B) to engage in an activity,

   (b) the activity is sexual,

   (c) B does not consent to engaging in the activity, and

   (d) A does not reasonably believe that B consents.

(2) Whether a belief is reasonable is to be determined having regard to all the circumstances, including any steps A has taken to ascertain whether B consents.

This is potentially a very useful offence, which has as one of its purposes criminalizing the actions of women who force men to penetrate them. Other examples of the offence would include A requiring B to masturbate A, or to masturbate B, or A requiring B to masturbate C, etc. The offence can be committed by words alone. See *Devonald* [2008] EWCA Crim 527 (section 12.2.1.7, p 324). It is commonly prosecuted for indecent text messaging where A incites B to have sex with him: for example, *A* [2006] EWCA Crim 2103; *Hinton-Smith* [2005] EWCA Crim 2575.

Sexual is as defined in section 12.2.2.1; touching is as defined in section 12.2.3. Sections 74 to 76 (consent and presumptions discussed in sections 12.2.1.3 to 12.2.1.7) apply.

Section 4(4) elevates the crime to an indictable offence with a maximum sentence of life imprisonment if it involves: penetration of B's anus or vagina; penetration of B's mouth with a person's penis; penetration of a person's anus or vagina by B with his body or otherwise; penetration of a person's mouth with B's penis.

Since A must 'cause' the action, it can be assumed that it is sufficient for A to be *a* cause without being the sole cause (see section 3.2.1, p 37).

≈ *Questions*

A, aged 18, texts B, aged 18, to whom he has taken a fancy. He asks her to come round to his flat for sex that night. B has never shown any interest in A in a sexual manner. Is A guilty of the offence under s 4? What if B decides to go round anyway because she really likes A?

12.3 Offences against children

[...] some of the most heavily criticized offences in the Act, in par- [...]alization and undue reliance on prosecutorial discretion. The [...] to distinguish between exploitative sexual activity against a [...]lder individuals or not) and that of informed consensual sexual [...]ldren under that age.

[...]ces Act 2003 (2) Child and Family Offences'

[...]pen to two obvious criticisms: complexity and obscurity, and 'legisla-[...]eed for this, because behind the specific crimes of consensual sex with [...]e of crimes that punish every form of non-consensual sex. So it would [...]ple to exclude from the offences of consensual sex with minors, any [...]s of the same or similar age. . . .

[...]ial over-criminalization was countered with the responses that [...]priate discretion. But, as the Joint Parliamentary Committee on

Creating catch all offences and then relying on the prosecutor's discretion to sort things out satisfactorily undermines [the rule of law]. It leaves prosecutors to do the job that Parliament should be doing, and gives them discretion to prosecute (or not to prosecute) people who ought never to have been within the scope of criminal liability in the first place. (12th Report 2002–3 *Scrutiny of Bills: Further Progress Report* 2003 (HL 119; HC 765))

12.3.1 Children under 13

Sections 5 to 8 create offences against children under 13.

- Section 5 makes it an offence carrying maximum life imprisonment for A intentionally to penetrate the vagina, anus or mouth of a person under 13 with his penis. Liability as to age is strict (see *G* [2008] UKHL 37, section 6.5.1, p 135). Lord Hoffmann stated:

The mental element of the offence under section 5, as the language and structure of the section makes clear, is that penetration must be intentional but there is no requirement that the accused must have known that the other person was under 13. The policy of the legislation is to protect children. If you have sex with someone who is on any view a child or young person, you take your chance on exactly how old they are. To that extent the offence is one of strict liability and it is no defence that the accused believed the other person to be 13 or over.

Note that A is guilty of this offence even if B was consenting or indeed initiated the conduct. B, 12 years old, who willingly performs fellatio on A, her 12-year-old boyfriend, thereby renders him a rapist. Is X, A's friend, who tells A that he should ask B to perform oral sex guilty of assisting or encouraging rape?

Baroness Hale, in *G*, stated:

Every male has a choice about where he puts his penis. It may be difficult for him to restrain himself when aroused but he has a choice. There is nothing unjust or irrational about a law which says that if he chooses to put his penis inside a child who turns out to be under 13 he has committed an offence (although the state of his mind may again be relevant to sentence). He also commits an offence if he behaves in the same way towards a child of 13 but under 16, albeit only if he does not reasonably believe that the child is 16 or over. So in principle sex with a child under 16 is not allowed. When the child is under 13, three years younger than that, he takes the risk that she may be younger than he thinks she is. The object is to make him take responsibility for what he chooses to do with what is capable of being, not only an instrument of great pleasure, but also a weapon of great danger.

Do you agree that there is nothing unjust in this? Is prosecutorial discretion enough to prevent this offence being misused?

- Section 6 creates an offence of penetration of the anus or the vagina. Consent is irrelevant. Liability is strict as to the age of the victim. The maximum sentence is life imprisonment. The penetration must be sexual so, for example, a vaginal examination of a girl under 13 performed by a medical professional is not caught by the offence.

- Section 7 creates an offence of intentional sexual touching of a child under 13. 'Touching' and 'sexual' are defined at sections 12.2.2.1 and 12.2.3, above. The maximum sentence is 14 years on indictment; six months summarily. Is liability as to the 'sexual' nature of the touching strict? Does the law's denial of the factual consent of the under 13-year-old to engage in sexual touching clash with the law's willingness to accept such a child's capacity to consent to, for example, invasive medical procedures? What proportion of the population do you think might have committed this offence?

- Section 8 creates an offence where A intentionally causes or incites another person (B) to engage in an activity and B is under 13. Liability as to age is strict. Consent is irrelevant. The maximum sentence is life imprisonment if the act involved penetration. How many offences are created? See *Grout* [2011] EWCA Crim 299. Andrew, aged 14, asks Britney, aged 12, to give him a 'shiner' (see *B v DPP* [2000] UKHL 13 (section 6.3.1, p 125)), meaning for her to perform oral sex on him. In her naivety Britney mistakenly believes that Andrew wants her to give him a black eye, so she hits Andrew and causes him severe facial bruising. Consider the criminal liability of Andrew and Britney.

Note that there is no liability for aiding and abetting or counselling rape of a child under 13 if the actor's purpose is to protect the child from STD/pregnancy or to protect his or her physical safety or promote his or her emotional well-being, unless the actor's purpose is to gain sexual gratification or to cause or encourage the relevant sexual act: s 73. The doctor who provides contraceptives to the 12-year-old girl to protect her in her consensual sexual acts with her partner will not be aiding and abetting her 'rape'. What of the parent who takes the view that he would rather his daughter had sex with her boyfriend in the safety of her bedroom than, say, the local bus shelter?

12.3.2 Children aged 13 to 15 inclusive

Sections 9 to 12 deal with cases where B is aged 13 to 15 inclusive. Each section creates offences for the defendant aged over 18. Section 13 also makes these offences available (with different sentences) where the defendant is under 18, in which case the sentence is one of six months summarily, five years on indictment: s 13.

The group of offences dealing with conduct towards children aged 13 to 15 inclusive demonstrates the unnecessary complexity and overlapping nature of the provisions in the 2003 Act.

- Section 9 creates an offence for A intentionally to touch B sexually, where B is aged under 16. If B is aged 13 to 15, A is not guilty if he has a reasonable belief that B is 16. The offence is indictable only and carries a maximum sentence of 14 years' imprisonment if the activity involves penetration. Consent is irrelevant. A, 18, who kisses or touches his consenting 15-year-old girlfriend is guilty of the offence if that is a 'sexual touching'—of course that falls to be decided by the jury. A, 18, who kisses his 12-year-old consenting girlfriend is guilty, even if she said she was 16. There is no defence for couples under 16, lawfully married in another country and visiting England or Wales. Does the section reflect the reality of sexual conduct of under 16-year-olds in the twenty-first century? During the debates in Parliament the Home Secretary offered champagne to anyone who could provide a more suitable code of offences. How might a better form of offences have been drafted?

- Section 10 creates an offence where A intentionally causes or incites another person (B) to engage in a sexual activity. If B is aged over 12 and under 16, A is not guilty if he has a reasonable belief that B is 16. Note that the offence is indictable only and carries a maximum sentence of 14 years' imprisonment if the activity involves penetration. The offence can also be committed by a person under 18; if so, the maximum sentence is one of six months summarily, five years on indictment: s 13.

- Section 11 creates an offence for A intentionally to engage in a sexual activity for the purpose of obtaining sexual gratification, where he engages in it when another person (B) is present or can observe it, and A knows or believes that B is aware, or intends that B should be aware, that he is engaging in it. If B is aged over 12 and under 16, A is not guilty if he has a reasonable belief that B is 16. The maximum sentence is ten years on indictment, six months summarily. The offence can also be committed by a person under 18; if so, the sentence is one of six months summarily, five years on indictment: s 13. This is designed to tackle the paedophile who performs sexual acts in a child's presence to gain sexual gratification. Note that there must be a person under 16 who is able to see the act. An undercover officer alone witnessing the event will not suffice.

- Section 12 creates an offence where A, for the purpose of obtaining sexual gratification, intentionally causes B, aged under 16, to watch a third person engaging in a sexual activity, or to look at an image of any person engaging in an activity. If B is aged over 12 and under 16, A is not guilty if he has a reasonable belief that B is 16. The maximum sentence is ten years on indictment, six months summarily. The offence can also be committed by a person under 18; if so, the sentence is one of six months summarily, five years on indictment: s 13. The offence was included to deal with paedophiles who use pornography as part of their grooming process. They show pornographic images to children in an attempt to break down the child's inhibitions about engaging in sexual conduct. In *Abdullahi* [2006] EWCA Crim 2060, the Court of Appeal held that it was sufficient that A showed the images for the purpose of obtaining sexual gratification, either by enjoying seeing the complainant looking at the images or with a view to putting the complainant in the mood to provide sexual gratification to A later.

- Section 14 creates an offence for A intentionally to arrange or facilitate something that he intends to do, intends another person to do or believes that another person will do, in any part of the world, where doing it will involve the commission of an offence under any of ss 9 to 13. The section is subject to defences for child protection (protecting the child from sexually transmitted infection; the physical safety of the child; preventing the child from becoming pregnant; or promoting the child's emotional well-being by the giving of advice). The maximum sentences are 14 years on indictment, six months summarily. In *R* [2008] EWCA Crim 619, the court gave a wide interpretation to s 14. It was acknowledged to be wider than attempt because it does not require proof of any act that is 'more than merely preparatory' to one of the relevant child sex offences. The court held that it does not require any 'agreement'. A asked the prostitute to arrange a child prostitute but she did not do so and therefore A could not be said to have done more than attempt to commit the s 14 offence.

- Section 15 provides an offence commonly known as 'grooming'. It is an offence if A has met or communicated with B, aged under 16, on one occasion, and (a) subsequently A intentionally meets B, or A travels with the intention of meeting B in any part of the world or arranges to meet B in any part of the world, or B travels with the intention of meeting A in any part of the world, *and* (b) A intends to do anything to or in respect of B, during or after the meeting which if done will involve the commission by A of a relevant offence. If B is aged over 12 and under 16, A is not guilty if he has a reasonable belief that B is 16. The maximum sentence is ten years on indictment, six months summarily. A, aged 18, writes a love letter to B, aged 15, arranging to meet at the local club. A hopes that the evening will end in sexual activity. Is A guilty of the offence? In *G* [2010] EWCA Crim 1693, the Court of Appeal held that A can be guilty of grooming even though there was no communication or contact of a sexual nature on the two occasions before he met B to engage in conduct which would amount to an offence.

- Section 67 of the Serious Crime Act 2015, inserts a new s 15A into the Sexual Offences Act 2003. This provision makes it an offence for A, who is over the age of 18, to communicate with B, who is under the age of 16, where the communication is sexual or intended to encourage B to make a sexual communication. A must be acting for sexual gratification in sending the message and must not reasonably believe that B is aged 16 or over.

- Section 69 of the Serious Crime Act 2015 makes it an offence to be in possession of what is termed a 'paedophile manual'. This is described in the legislation as an item that contains advice or guidance about abusing children sexually. Various defences exist for legitimate reasons for possession, not having viewed the items, them having been sent unsolicited and deleted promptly.

≈ *Question*

The Act is supposed to modernize the law and to reflect the sexual mores of the twenty-first century. Having regard to the offences involving children, do you think it does?

12.4 Other sexual offences

12.4.1 Abuse of trust

The Sexual Offences (Amendment) Act 2000 created new offences of abuse of a position of trust. The 2003 Act replaces them with four offences where A (aged over 18) who is in a position of trust to B (under 18):

(1) sexually touches B (s 16);

(2) causes or incites B to engage in sexual activity (s 17);

(3) engages in sexual activity in B's presence for the purpose of sexual gratification (s 18);

(4) causes B to watch a sexual image or activity for the purpose of obtaining sexual gratification.

The most notable feature of the sections is that the offences criminalize consensual conduct with those under 18. Although 16- and 17-year-olds may consent to sexual activity in other circumstances, they cannot do so with those who 'look after' them (see ss 21 and 22). No offence is committed where A has a reasonable belief that B is aged over 18 (unless B is under 13). There is a defence for A to prove that he was lawfully married to B (aged 16) or that immediately before the position of trust arose there existed a lawful sexual relationship between them. This covers cases where, for example, A and B had a sexual relationship before A became a trainee teacher at B's school.

12.4.2 Family offences

The 2003 Act creates two sets of offences to deal with offences within the family. In relation to children, ss 25 and 26 criminalize the same forms of activity as ss 9 and 12 (above):

- sexual touching and
- causing a child to engage in sexual activity.

Sections 25 and 26 differ from ss 9 and 12 in two important respects: B must be under 18 and A must be a family member. Family membership is defined in very broad terms in the Act, extending well beyond blood relationships to reflect the diverse structures of modern life. Family members include:

- blood and adoptive relationships (parents, current or former foster parents, grandparents, brothers, sisters, half-brothers, half-sisters, aunts and uncles);
- wider family members who live, or have lived, in the same household as the child or who are, or have been, regularly involved in caring for, training or supervising or being in sole charge of the child (step-parents, cousins, step-siblings, current or former foster siblings);
- others who are living in the same household as the child and who hold a position of trust or authority in relation to the child at the time of the alleged offence. This offence will not be committed if A has a lawful sexual relationship with the child after the familial relationship has ceased, even where the child is under 18.

The breadth of the extended family caught by the Act reflects the shift in emphasis in the legislation from a blood relationship-based offence of heterosexual intercourse (incest based on eugenics arguments) to one based on gender-neutral exploitation of sexual vulnerability in the home environment. There are defences in s 28 where A is lawfully married to B at the time of engaging in the sexual activity, and under s 29 where A proves that a lawful sexual relationship existed between A and B immediately before the familial relationship arose.

12.4.3 Offences involving mental disorder

The Act provides three specific groups of offences to protect those with a mental disorder. In each category the types of behaviour criminalized are roughly the same as those in relation to children. In short, the activities prohibited are:

- sexual touching of B;
- causing or inciting sexual activity by B;
- engaging in sexual activity in B's presence;
- causing B to watch sexual activity.

When these activities arise in an exploitative context they are criminalized. The three contexts are:

- ss 30 to 33 where B is mentally disordered and 'unable to refuse';
- ss 34 to 37 where B is mentally disordered and the activity is caused by 'threats or deception or inducement' (which need not vitiate consent under s 74);
- ss 38 to 41 where B is mentally disordered and A is 'in a relationship as a carer'.

There are numerous general improvements in the new scheme. Creating specific offences produces much fairer labelling—defendants are convicted of offences that better describe their actions. The language has been modernized, and gender specificity has been removed. This is not mere window dressing: for example, one result is that mentally disordered men are protected against heterosexual abuse. The offensive terminology of the 1956 Act has been replaced by the appropriate (but technical) language of the Mental Health Acts. However, as with the Act in general, there is tremendous complexity.

See *C* [2009] UKHL 42 (section 12.2.1.5, p 312) on the meaning of 'capacity'.

12.4.4 Preliminary and other offences

The Act also introduces offences of:

- intentional administration of a substance/causing it to be taken by B without consent with intent to stupefy/overpower to enable any person to engage in sex with B: s 61;
- committing an offence with intent to commit a sexual offence: s 62;
- trespass with intent to commit a sexual offence: s 63; see Chapter 15;
- intentionally exposing one's genitals with the intention that another person will see them and be caused alarm or distress: s 66;
- for the purposes of sexual gratification, observing another person doing a 'private act' (or recording or installing equipment to record that) in the knowledge that the other person does not consent to being observed for that purpose: s 67. Section 68 defines 'private act' as 'an act done in a place and in circumstances where the person would reasonably expect privacy and either the person's genitals, buttocks or breasts are exposed or covered only by underwear, or the person is using a lavatory or the person is doing a sexual act that is not of a kind ordinarily done in public';
- bestiality: s 69;
- necrophilia: s 70;
- engaging in sexual activity in a public lavatory: s 71.

FURTHER READING

CPS guidance: http://www.cps.gov.uk/legal/p_to_r/rape_and_sexual_offences

E. B. Freedman, *Redefining Rape* (2013)

H. Reece, 'Rape Myths: Is Elite Opinion Right and Popular Opinion Wrong?' (2013) 33 OJLS 1

J Stannard, 'The Emotional Dynamics of Consent' (2015) 79 J Crim L 422.

J. Stanton-Ife, 'Mental Disorder and Sexual Consent: *Williams* and After' in J. Horder and D. Baker (eds), *The Sanctity of Life and the Criminal Law* (2013)

S. Wallerstein, '"A Drunken Consent Is Still Consent"—Or Is It? A Critical Analysis of the Law on a Drunken Consent to Sex Following *Bree*' (2009) 73 J Crim L 582

13
Theft

> **Theft:**
>
> D commits theft if he dishonestly appropriates property belonging to another with the intention of permanently depriving the other of it: s 1 of the Theft Act 1968.
>
> **Some of the controversies that will be examined in this chapter include:**
>
> (1) the extent to which the criminal law of theft conflicts with civil law concepts of property;
> (2) whether it is possible to steal property that belongs to oneself;
> (3) the types of property that may be stolen;
> (4) the extent to which it is possible to provide a definition of 'dishonestly'.

13.1 Introduction

The law governing theft and related offences is to be found in the Theft Act 1968. That Act was supplemented by offences introduced in the Theft Act 1978 and the Theft (Amendment) Act 1996. Significant sections of these latter Acts were repealed and replaced by the Fraud Act 2006 (see Chapter 16).

The law of theft as defined in England and Wales may appear to be unduly technical. Since the offence is designed to protect rights in relation to property, ownership, possession, etc which are concepts defined in civil law, the offence must necessarily rely on the civil law definitions of these concepts, and these tend to be complex ones. There is a tension between a general moral understanding of stealing and the technical definition in the offence.

> To steal something is to violate in some fundamental way another's right of ownership. Note that this is different from saying that stealing is merely a violation of some particular set of laws concerning property. To be sure, in modern, liberal societies, we tend to think of rights of ownership in legalistic terms, and the law of property certainly plays a significant role in shaping and informing our understanding of what it means to own things and to have them stolen. But the concept of stealing itself seems to be in some fundamental way pre-legal. Small children and primitive man both have a sense of what it means to own things and they undoubtedly have a sense that having such things involuntarily taken from them in some way constitutes a 'wrong'. (S. P. Green, *Lying, Cheating and Stealing: A Moral Theory of White Collar Crime* (2005), pp 89–90)

13.1.1 Interpreting the 1968 Act

The 1968 Act constitutes the authoritative, comprehensive and exclusive source of the law of theft. But, of course, a law of theft assumes the existence of laws relating to property and ownership. As we will see, s 5 of the Theft Act 1968 states when property is to be treated as belonging to another for the purposes of theft, and it is immediately apparent that in order fully to determine key terms under that section (such as whether there is another with a 'proprietary right or interest' or whether property is 'subject to a trust') reference must be made to civil cases, whether decided before or after the coming into force of the Theft Act. These provide authoritative explanations of these concepts. Hence, whether D is guilty of theft may involve a consideration of the law of contract, the Sale of Goods Acts or principles of equity.

Aside from necessary reference to definitions of general application and to civil law concepts, the Theft Act represents a clean break with the past. In their interpretation, the courts have aimed to give words and expressions their ordinary meaning so as to avoid undue technicality and subtlety. There is nothing wrong with that, of course, as a general precept of statutory interpretation but it led to a practice, endorsed by the House of Lords in *Brutus v Cozens* [1972] 2 All ER 1297, [1973] AC 854, of leaving the interpretation, at least of 'ordinary' words and expressions to be determined by a jury or magistrates as a matter of fact. This can be problematic as it is sometimes difficult to discern precisely what the 'ordinary' meaning of certain words is.

Consider throughout the chapter:

- to what extent the appellate courts are content to uphold the conviction of those who have been found to have acted dishonestly, even if the conviction for the offence charged is technically flawed;
- to what extent theft is treated as a 'dishonesty' rather than a 'property'-based offence?

The law is technical and complex. Some have questioned whether the time has come for a redefinition which would simplify the law of theft, as has now occurred with the deception offences being replaced by the broad and non-technical fraud offences in the Fraud Act 2006.

In examining the courts' interpretation of the theft offence which was designed as part of a new code, it is worth considering the extent to which a more radical approach would be desirable in any new codification of the law. The pressure for reform is increased by the fact that, in some instances, the Act has been overtaken by technological advances.

13.2 Basic definition of theft

Theft Act 1968, s 1(1)

A person is guilty of theft if he dishonestly appropriates property belonging to another with the intention of permanently depriving the other of it; and 'thief' and 'steal' shall be construed accordingly.

The Sentencing Council issued a new Guideline, *Theft Offences*, in 2016.

Theft Act 1968, s 7

7. Theft

A person guilty of theft shall on conviction on indictment be liable to imprisonment for a term not exceeding seven years.

Theft therefore comprises five elements: (a) appropriating (b) property (c) belonging to another (d) dishonestly (e) with an intention permanently to deprive the other of the property. Each requires detailed consideration.

13.3 Appropriation

Theft Act 1968, s 3

3. 'Appropriates'

(1) Any assumption by a person of the rights of an owner amounts to an appropriation, and this includes, where he has come by the property (innocently or not) without stealing it, any later assumption of a right to it by keeping or dealing with it as owner.

(2) Where property or a right or interest in property is or purports to be transferred for value to a person acting in good faith, no later assumption by him of rights which he believed himself to be acquiring shall, by reason of any defect in the transferor's title, amount to theft of the property.

The meaning of 'appropriation' is fundamental in the law of theft and has been the subject of extensive litigation.

Three issues created problems of interpretation:

(1) whether s 3 requires that D appropriated *all* of the rights of the owner over the item of property;

(2) whether D acting with V's consent in relation to the property could be held to be appropriating it (eg where V consents to D taking the property because D has tricked V);

(3) whether D could appropriate property in which he obtained the entire proprietary interest by the transfer from V (eg where V makes D a gift of the property so that D has 'indefeasible title').

As the law now stands, there is an appropriation if D has assumed a right of the owner. There is no need for the Crown to establish that he has assumed *all* the rights. In addition, D can be guilty of theft even when he has an indefeasible title to the property in question, such as by way of gift.

All three issues were resolved by the House of Lords' cases of *Morris* [1984] UKHL 1, *Gomez* [1992] UKHL 4 and *Hinks* [2000] UKHL 53. *Morris* and *Gomez* were examined by the House of Lords in the controversial case of *Hinks* which follows.

It is important to bear in mind that the question whether D has appropriated property belonging to another is not the same as whether he is guilty of theft. Only if he has the dishonest intent permanently to deprive will he be a thief. When reading the following extract, consider whether the House of Lords has interpreted the elements of theft in such a way as to render it a 'thought crime' too heavily dependent on mens rea.

R v Hinks
[2000] UKHL 53, House of Lords

(Lords Slynn, Jauncey, Steyn, Hutton and Hobhouse)

Hinks (H), a 38-year-old woman, was friendly with John Dolphin (JD). She described herself as JD's main carer. There was evidence that JD was extremely naive and gullible. It would be easy to take advantage of him. But he understood the concept of ownership and was quite capable of making a gift. In a period of a few months, he withdrew about £60,000 from his building society account. The money was deposited in H's account. JD also gave H a television set. H was convicted of theft of money and the television. The question left to the jury was

'Was [JD] so mentally incapable that the defendant herself realised that ordinary and decent people would regard it as dishonest to accept a gift from him?' On appeal it was argued that, if the gift from JD to H was valid, the acceptance of it could not be theft. Rose LJ, dismissing the appeal, ruled:

. . . in relation to theft, one of the ingredients for a jury to consider is not whether there has been a gift, valid or otherwise, but whether there has been an appropriation. A gift may be clear evidence of appropriation. But a jury should not, in our view, be asked to consider whether a gift has been validly made.

H appealed.

[Lord Jauncey said he would dismiss the appeal for the reasons given by Lord Steyn.]

Lord Steyn:

Since the enactment of the Theft Act 1968 the House of Lords has on three occasions considered the meaning of the word 'appropriates' in s 1(1) of the 1968 Act, namely in *Lawrence v Comr of Police for the Metropolis* [1971] 2 All ER 1253, [1972] AC 626; in *R v Morris; Anderton v Burnside* [1983] 3 All ER 288, [1984] AC 320; and in *R v Gomez* [1993] 1 All ER 1, [1993] AC 442. The law as explained in *Lawrence's* case and *R v Gomez*, and applied by the Court of Appeal in the present case ([2000] 1 Cr App Rep 1) has attracted strong criticism from distinguished academic lawyers: see for example, JC Smith [1993] Crim LR 304 and [1998] Crim LR 904; Edward Griew *The Theft Acts* (7th edn, 1995) pp 41–59; ATH Smith 'Gifts and the Law of Theft' [1999] CLJ 10. These views have however been challenged by equally distinguished academic writers: PR Glazebrook 'Revising the Theft Acts' [1993] CLJ 191–194 [Peter Glazebrook's article does not in fact 'challenge' these views and the reference to it is omitted in [2001] 2 AC 241 at 244]; Simon Gardner 'Property and Theft' [1998] Crim LR 35. The academic criticism of *R v Gomez* provided in substantial measure the springboard for the present appeal. The certified question before the House is as follows: 'Whether the acquisition of an indefeasible title to property is capable of amounting to an appropriation of property belonging to another for the purposes of s 1(1) of the Theft Act 1968'. In other words, the question is whether a person can 'appropriate' property belonging to another where the other person makes him an indefeasible gift of property, retaining no proprietary interest or any right to resume or recover any proprietary interest in the property.

Before the enactment of the 1968 Act English law required a taking and carrying away of the property as the actus reus of the offence. In 1968 Parliament chose to broaden the reach of the law of theft by requiring merely an appropriation. The relevant sections of the Act are as follows:

[Lord Steyn set out the relevant provisions of the Theft Act and the facts of the case, and quoted from the trial judge's summing-up and the judgment of the Court of Appeal; and continued:]

My Lords, counsel for the appellant has not expressly asked the House to depart from the previous decisions of the House. He did, however, submit with the aid of the writings of Sir John Smith that the conviction of a donee for receiving a perfectly valid gift is a completely new departure. Relying on the academic criticism of the earlier decisions of the House counsel submitted that their reach should not be extended. . . .

V

The starting point must be the words of the statute as interpreted by the House in its previous decisions. The first case in the trilogy is *R v Lawrence* [1971] 2 All ER 1253, [1972] AC 626. The defendant, a taxi driver, had without objection on the part of an Italian student asked for a fare of £6 for a journey for which the correct lawful fare was 10s 6d. The taxi driver was convicted of theft. On appeal the main contention was that the student had consented to pay the fare. But it was clear that the appellant had not told the student what the lawful fare was. With the agreement of all the Law Lords hearing the case Viscount Dilhorne observed:

> 'Prior to the passage of the Theft Act 1968, which made radical changes in and greatly simplified the law relating to theft and some other offences, it was necessary to prove that the property alleged to have been stolen was taken "without the consent of the owner" (Larceny Act 1916, s 1(1)). These words are not included in s 1(1) of the Theft Act 1968, but the appellant contended that the subsection should be construed as if they were, as if they appeared after the word "appropriates". Section 1(1) provides: "A person is guilty of theft if he dishonestly appropriates property belonging to another with the intention of permanently depriving the other of it; and 'thief' and 'steal' shall be construed accordingly." I see no ground for concluding that the omission of the words "without the consent of the owner" was inadvertent and not deliberate, and to read the subsection as if they were included is, in my opinion, wholly unwarranted. Parliament by the omission of these words has relieved the prosecution of the burden of establishing that the taking was without the owner's consent. That is no longer an ingredient of the offence. Megaw LJ, delivering the judgment of the Court of Appeal ([1970] 3 All ER at 935, [1971] 1 QB at 376), said that the offence created by s 1(1) involved four elements: "(i) a dishonest (ii) appropriation (iii) of property belonging to another (iv) with the intention of permanently depriving the owner of it." I agree. That there was appropriation in this case is clear. Section 3(1) states that any assumption by a person of the rights of an owner amounts to an appropriation. Here there was clearly such an assumption. That an appropriation was dishonest may be proved in a number of ways. In this case it was not contended that the appellant had not acted dishonestly.' (See [1971] 2 All ER 1253 at 1254–1255, [1972] AC 626 at 631–632.)

Viscount Dilhorne expressly added that belief that the passenger gave informed consent (ie knowing that he was paying in excess of the fare) 'is relevant to the issue of dishonesty, not to the question whether or not there has been an appropriation' (see [1971] 2 All ER 1253 at 1255, [1972] AC 626 at 632). The appeal was dismissed. The *ratio decidendi* of *Lawrence's* case, namely that in a prosecution for theft it is unnecessary to prove that the taking was without the owner's consent, goes to the heart of the certified question in the present case.

The second decision of the House was *R v Morris; Anderton v Burnside* [1983] 3 All ER 288, [1984] AC 320, in 1983, a consolidated appeal involving two cases in each of which the defendant attached a price label to goods in a supermarket which showed a price lower than that which was properly payable for the goods. The defendant intended to pay the lower price at the checkout. In the first case the defendant's deception was detected at the checkout point and in the second he paid the lower prices at the checkout. He was convicted of theft in both cases. The House concluded that the defendant had been rightly convicted of theft on both counts. In each case the certified question was the rolled-up one whether there had been a 'dishonest appropriation' of goods. These questions were answered in the affirmative. However, in the single substantive judgment Lord Roskill made an observation, which was in conflict with the ratio of *Lawrence's* case and had to be corrected in *R v Gomez*. Lord Roskill said:

> 'If one postulates an honest customer taking goods from a shelf to put in his or her trolley to take to the check-point there to pay the proper price, I am unable to see that any of these actions involves any assumption by the shopper of the rights of the supermarket. In the context of s 3(1), the concept of appropriation in my view involves not an act expressly or impliedly authorised by the owner but an act by way of adverse interference with or usurpation of those rights.' (See [1983] 3 All ER 288 at 293, [1984] AC 320 at 332.)

It will be observed that this observation was not necessary for the decision of the case: absent this observation the House would still have held that there had been an appropriation. Lord Roskill took the view that he was following the decision in *Lawrence's* case. It is clear, however, that his observation (as opposed to the decision in *R v Morris*) cannot stand with the ratio of *Lawrence's* case. And as his observation, cast in terms of 'the honest customer', shows Lord Roskill conflated the ingredients of appropriation and dishonesty contrary to the holding in *Lawrence's* case.

The third decision of the House was in *R v Gomez* [1993] 1 All ER 1, [1993] AC 442, in 1992. The defendant was employed as an assistant shop manager. He agreed with two accomplices that goods would be supplied by the shop in return for cheques which he knew to be stolen. He told the manager of the shop that the cheques were as good as cash. The Court of Appeal held that there was a voidable contract between the owner of the shop and the dishonest receivers of the goods; that the transfer was with the consent of the owner; and that accordingly there was no appropriation. The Court of Appeal quashed the conviction arising from a plea of guilty. The following question was certified:

> 'When theft is alleged and that which is alleged to be stolen passes to the defendant with the consent of the owner, but that consent has been obtained by a false representation, has, a) an appropriation within the meaning of s. 1(1) of the Theft Act 1968 taken place, or, b) must such a passing of property necessarily involve an element of adverse [interference] with or usurpation of some right of the owner?' (see [1993] 1 All ER 1 at 4, [1993] AC 442 at 444.)

By a majority (Lord Lowry dissenting) the House answered branch (a) of the certified question in the affirmative and branch (b) in the negative. In crystalline terms Lord Keith of Kinkel speaking for all the numbers of the majority ruled the following ([1993] 1 All ER 1 at 12, [1993] AC 442 at 464). (1) The meaning of the relevant provisions must be determined by construing the statutory language without reference to the report which preceded it, namely the eighth report of the Criminal Law Revision Committee on *Theft and Related Offences* (Cmnd 2977 (1966)). (2) The observations of Lord Roskill in *R v Morris* were unnecessary for the decision of that case; that they were in clear conflict with the ratio of *Lawrence's* case; and that they were wrong. (3) *Lawrence's* case must be accepted as authoritative and correct, and 'there is no question of it now being right to depart from it'. At the same time Lord Keith ([1993] 1 All ER 1 at 12, [1993] AC 442 at 463), endorsed the judgment of Parker LJ in the civil case of *Dobson v General Accident Fire and Life Assurance Corp plc* [1989] 3 All ER 927, [1990] 1 QB 274 where Parker LJ highlighted the conflict between *Lawrence's* case and *R v Morris* and chose to follow *Lawrence's* case. (4) Any act may be an appropriation notwithstanding that it was done with the consent or authorisation of the owner. In *R v Gomez* [1993] 1 All ER 1, [1993] AC 442 at 448 the House was expressly invited to hold that 'there is no appropriation where the entire proprietary interest passes'. That submission was rejected. The leading judgment in *R v Gomez* was therefore in terms which unambiguously rule out the submission that s 3(1) does not apply to a case of a gift duly carried out because in such a case the entire proprietary interest will have passed. In a separate judgment (with which Lord Jauncey of Tullichettle expressed agreement) Lord Browne-Wilkinson observed:

> 'I regard the word "appropriation" in isolation as being an objective description of the act done irrespective of the mental state of either the owner or the accused. It is impossible to reconcile the decision in *Lawrence* (that the question of consent is irrelevant in considering whether this has been an appropriation) with the views expressed in *Morris*, which latter views in my judgment were incorrect.' (See [1993] 1 All ER 1 at 39, [1993] AC 442 at 495–496.)

In other words it is immaterial whether the act was done with the owner's consent or authority. It is true of course that the certified question in *R v Gomez* referred to the situation where consent had been obtained by fraud. But the majority judgments do not differentiate between cases of consent induced by fraud and consent given in any other circumstances. The ratio involves a proposition of general application. *R v Gomez* therefore gives effect to s 3(1) of the 1968 Act by treating 'appropriation' as a neutral word comprehending 'any assumption by a person of the rights of an owner'. If the law is as held in *R v Gomez*, it destroys the argument advanced on the present appeal, namely that an indefeasible gift of property cannot amount to an appropriation.

VI

Counsel for the appellant submitted in the first place that the law as expounded in *R v Gomez* and *Lawrence's* case must be qualified to say that there can be no appropriation unless the other party (the owner) retains some proprietary interest, or the right to resume or recover some proprietary interest, in the property. Alternatively, counsel argued that 'appropriates' should be interpreted as if the word 'unlawfully' preceded it. Counsel said that the effect of the decisions in *Lawrence's* case and *R v Gomez* is to reduce the actus reus of theft to 'vanishing point' (see Smith and Hogan *Criminal Law* (9th edn, 1999) p 505). He argued that the result is to bring the criminal law 'into conflict' with the civil law. Moreover, he argued that the decisions in *Lawrence's* case and *R v Gomez* may produce absurd and grotesque results. He argued that the mental requirements of dishonesty and intention of permanently depriving the owner of property are insufficient to filter out some cases of conduct which should not sensibly be regarded as theft. He did not suggest that the appellant's dishonest and repellent conduct came within such a category. Instead he deployed four examples for this purpose, namely the following. (1) S makes a handsome gift to D because he believes that D has obtained a First. D has not and knows that S is acting under that misapprehension. He makes a gift. There is here a motivational mistake which, it is submitted, does not avoid the transaction. (Glanville Williams *Textbook of Criminal Law* (1978) p 788). (2) P sees D's painting and, thinking he is getting a bargain, offers D £100,000 for it. D realises that P thinks the painting is a Constable, but knows that it was painted by his sister and is worth no more than £100. He accepts P's offer. D has made an enforceable contract and is entitled to recover and retain the purchase price (*Smith and Hogan* pp 507–508). (3) A buys a roadside garage business from B, abutting on a public thoroughfare; unknown to A but known to B, it has already been decided to construct a bypass road which will divert substantially the whole of the traffic from passing A's garage. There is an enforceable contract and A is entitled to recover and retain the purchase price. The same would be true if B *knew* that A was unaware of the intended plan to construct a bypass road. (Compare Lord Atkin in *Bell v Lever Bros Ltd* [1932] AC 161 at 224, [1931] All ER Rep 1 at 30.) (4) An employee agrees to retire before the end of his contract of employment, receiving a sum of money by way of compensation from his employer. Unknown to the employer, the employee has committed serious breaches of contract which would have enabled the employer to dismiss him without compensation. Assuming that the employee's failure to reveal his defaults does not affect the validity of the contract, so that the employee is entitled to sue for the promised compensation, is the employee liable to be arrested for the theft the moment he receives the money? (Glanville Williams 'Theft and Voidable Title' [1981] Crim LR 666 at 672).

My Lords, at first glance these are rather telling examples. They may conceivably have justified a more restricted meaning of s 3(1) than prevailed in *Lawrence's* case and *R v Gomez*. The House ruled otherwise and I am quite unpersuaded that the House overlooked the consequences of its decision. On the facts set out in the examples a jury could possibly find that the acceptance of the transfer took place in the belief that the transferee had the right in law to deprive the other of it within the meaning of s 2(1)(a) of the 1968 Act. Moreover, in such cases a prosecution is hardly likely and, if mounted, is likely to founder on the basis that the jury will not be persuaded that there was dishonesty in the required sense. And one must retain a sense of perspective. At the extremity of the application of legal rules there are sometimes results which may seem strange. A matter of judgment is then involved. The rule may have to be recast. Sir John Smith has eloquently argued that the rule in question ought to be recast. I am unpersuaded. If the law is restated by adopting a narrower definition of appropriation, the outcome is likely to place beyond the reach of the criminal law dishonest persons who should be found guilty of theft. The suggested revisions would unwarrantably restrict the scope of the law of theft and complicate the fair and effective prosecution of theft. In my view the law as settled in *Lawrence's* case and *R v Gomez* does not demand the suggested revision.

Those decisions can be applied by judges and juries in a way which, absent human error, does not result in injustice.

Counsel for the appellant further pointed out that the law as stated in *Lawrence's* case and *R v Gomez* creates a tension between the civil and the criminal law. In other words, conduct which is not wrongful in a civil law sense may constitute the crime of theft. Undoubtedly, this is so. The question whether the civil claim to title by a convicted thief, who committed no civil wrong, may be defeated by the principle that nobody may benefit from his own civil *or* criminal wrong does not arise for decision. Nevertheless there is a more general point, namely that the interaction between criminal law and civil law can cause problems: compare Beatson and Simester 'Stealing One's Own Property' (1999) 115 LQR 372. The purposes of the civil law and the criminal law are somewhat different. In theory the two systems *should* be in perfect harmony. In a practical world there will sometimes be some disharmony between the two systems. In any event, it would be wrong to assume on a priori grounds that the criminal law rather than the civil law is defective. Given the jury's conclusions, one is entitled to observe that the appellant's conduct should constitute theft, the only available charge. The tension between the civil and the criminal law is therefore not in my view a factor which justifies a departure from the law as stated in *Lawrence's* case and *R v Gomez*. Moreover, these decisions of the House have a marked beneficial consequence. While in some contexts of the law of theft a judge cannot avoid explaining civil law concepts to a jury (eg in respect of s 2(1)(a)), the decisions of the House of Lords eliminate the need for such explanations in respect of appropriation. That is a great advantage in an overly complex corner of the law.

VII

My Lords, if it had been demonstrated that in practice *Lawrence* and *Gomez* were calculated to produce injustice that would have been a compelling reason to revisit the merits of the holdings in those decisions. That is however, not the case. In practice the mental requirements of theft are an adequate protection against injustice. In these circumstances I would not be willing to depart from the clear decisions of the House in *Lawrence* and *Gomez*. This brings me back to counsels' principal submission, namely that a person does not appropriate property unless the other (the owner) retains, beyond the instant of the alleged theft, some proprietary interest or the right to resume or recover some proprietary interest. This submission is directly contrary to the holdings in *Lawrence's* case and *R v Gomez*. It must be rejected. The alternative submission is that the word 'appropriates' should be interpreted as if the word 'unlawfully' preceded it so that only an act which is unlawful under the general law can be an appropriation. This submission is an invitation to interpolate a word in the carefully crafted language of the 1968 Act. It runs counter to the decisions in *Lawrence's* case and *R v Gomez* and must also be rejected. It follows that the certified question must be answered in the affirmative . . .

[**Lord Hutton** made a speech giving reasons why he would allow the appeal and quash the convictions.]

≋ *Questions*
(1) Was it unjust to convict Hinks of theft? Was she better described as a thief or a deceiver? Does it really matter?
(2) Lord Steyn states that: 'Given the jury's conclusions, one is entitled to observe that the appellant's conduct should constitute theft, the only available charge.' Does this put the cart before the horse? Just because D 'should' be guilty of theft does not necessarily mean all the elements of the offence are present.

Lord Hobhouse:

Rose LJ said ([2000] 1 Cr App Rep 1 at 9):

> 'In our judgment, in relation to theft, one of the ingredients for a jury to consider is not whether there has been a gift, valid or otherwise, but whether there has been appropriation. *A gift may be clear evidence of appropriation.* But a jury should not, in our view, be asked to consider whether a gift has been validly made . . .' (My emphasis.)

The dismissiveness of this reasoning is in itself remarkable but the proposition which needs particularly to be examined is that which I have emphasised bearing in mind that the Court of Appeal draws no distinction between a fully effective gift and one which is vitiated by incapacity, fraud or some other feature which would lead both the man in the street and the law to say that the transfer was not a true gift resulting from an actual intention of the donor to give. Another aspect of the Court of Appeal's reasoning which also has to be examined is the relationship of that proposition to the concept of dishonesty. It is explicit in the Court of Appeal judgment that the relevant definition of the crime of theft is to be found in the element of dishonesty and *R v Ghosh* [1982] 2 All ER 689, [1982] QB 1053 and that this is to receive no greater definition than consciously falling below the standards of an ordinary and decent person and may include anything which such a person would think was morally reprehensible. It may be no more than a moral judgment.

The reasoning of the Court of Appeal therefore depends upon the disturbing acceptance that a criminal conviction and the imposition of custodial sanctions may be based upon conduct which involves no inherent illegality and may only be capable of being criticised on grounds of lack of morality. This approach itself raises fundamental questions. An essential function of the criminal law is to define the boundary between what conduct is criminal and what merely immoral. Both are the subject of the disapprobation of ordinary right-thinking citizens and the distinction is liable to be arbitrary or at least strongly influenced by considerations subjective to the individual members of the tribunal. To treat otherwise lawful conduct as criminal merely because it is open to such disapprobation would be contrary to principle and open to the objection that it fails to achieve the objective and transparent certainty required of the criminal law by the principles basic to human rights.

I stress once more that it is not my view that the resort to such reasoning was necessary for the decision of the present case. I would be reluctant to think that those of your Lordships who favour dismissing this appeal have fallen into the trap of believing that, without adopting the reasoning of the Court of Appeal in this case, otherwise guilty defendants will escape justice. The facts of the present case do not justify such a conclusion nor do the facts of any other case which has been cited on this appeal.

[Lord Hobhouse examined ss 1 to 6 of the 1968 Act, and continued:]

Section 5 and, particularly, s 5(4) demonstrate that the 1968 Act has been drafted so as to take account of and require reference to the civil law of property, contract and restitution. The same applies to many other sections of the 1968 Act. For example, s 6 is drafted by reference to the phrase 'regardless of the other's rights'—that is to say rights under the civil law. Section 28, dealing with the restoration of stolen goods, clearly can only work if the law of theft recognises and respects transfers of property valid under the civil law, otherwise it would be giving the criminal courts the power to deprive citizens of their property otherwise than in accordance with the law.

Section 5 shows that the state of mind of the transferor at the time of transfer may be relevant and critical. Similarly, the degree of the transferee's knowledge will be relevant to the s 5 question quite independently of any question under s 2. For instance, where there has been a mistake on the part of the transferor, the position under s 5(4) can be different depending on whether or not the transferee was aware of the mistake.

Further, it will be appreciated that the situations to which s 5 is relevant can embrace gifts as well as other transactions such as transfers for value. The prosecution must be able to prove that, at the time of the alleged appropriation, the relevant property belonged to another within the meaning given to that phrase by s 5. Where the defendant has been validly given the property he can no longer appropriate property belonging to another. The Court of Appeal does not seem to have had their attention directed to s 5. The question certified on the grant of leave to appeal is self-contradictory [see [1998] Crim LR at 906. The House of Lords amended the question; see earlier in this section, p 347]. The direction of the trial judge approved by the Court of Appeal is inadequate. There is no law against appropriating your own property as defined by s 5.

[Lord Hobhouse examined s 2(1) of the 1968 Act and continued:]

Although s 2 is headed 'Dishonestly', this quotation shows that it is as much involved with the application of the concepts 'appropriation' and 'property belonging to another'. Paragraph (a) contemplates that the defendant believes that he has the right to appropriate the property and (b) his belief that he would have the consent of the person to whom the property belongs to appropriate it. If belief in such a right or such consent can prevent the defendant's conduct from amounting to theft (whatever the jury may think of it), how can it be said that his knowledge that he has such a right or the actual consent of the person to whom the property belongs is irrelevant? How can it be said that the right of the defendant to accept a gift is irrelevant—or the fact that the transferor has actually and validly consented to the defendant having the relevant property? Yet it is precisely these things which the judgment of the Court of Appeal would wholly exclude.

Section 2(1) is cutting down the classes of conduct which the jury are at liberty to treat as dishonest. They qualify the *R v Ghosh* approach and show that in any given case the court must consider whether it is adequate to give an unqualified *R v Ghosh* direction as the Court of Appeal held to be sufficient in the present case.

Gifts

The discussion in the present case has been marked by a failure to consider the law of gift. Perhaps most remarkable is the statement of the Court of Appeal that 'a gift may be clear evidence of appropriation'. The making of a gift is the act of the donor. It involves the donor in forming the intention to give and then acting on that intention by doing whatever it is necessary for him to do to transfer the relevant property to the donee. Where the gift is the gift of a chattel, the act required to complete the gift will normally be either delivery to the donee or to a person who is to hold the chattel as the bailee of the donee; money can be transferred by having it credited to the donee's bank account—and so on. Unless the gift was conditional, in which case the condition must be satisfied before the gift can take effect, the making of the gift is complete once the donor has carried out this step. The gift has become the property of the donee. It is not necessary for the donee to know of the gift. The donee, on becoming aware of the gift, has the right to refuse (or reject) the gift in which case it revests in the donor with resolutive effect. (See 20 *Halsbury Laws* (4th edn. reissue) paras 48–49 and the cases cited.)

What consequences does this have for the law of theft? Once the donor has done his part in transferring the property to the defendant, the property, subject to the special situations identified in the subsections of s 5, ceases to be 'property belonging to another'. However wide a meaning one were to give to 'appropriates', there cannot be a theft. For it to be possible for there to be a theft there will have to be something more, like an absence of a capacity to give or a mistake satisfying s 5(4). Similarly, where the donee himself performs the act necessary to transfer the property to himself, as he would if he himself took the chattel out of the possession of the donor or, himself, gave the instructions to the donor's bank, s 5(1) would apply and mean that that constituent of the crime of theft would at that time have been satisfied.

If one treats the 'acceptance' of the gift as an appropriation, and this was the approach of the judge and is implicit in the judgment of the Court of Appeal (despite their choice of words), there are immediate difficulties with s 2(1)(a). The defendant did have the right to deprive the donor of the property.

The donor did consent to the appropriation; indeed, he intended it. There are also difficulties with s 6 as she was not acting regardless of the donor's rights; the donor has already surrendered his rights. The only way that these conclusions can be displaced is by showing that the gift was not valid. There are even difficulties with s 3 itself. The donee is not 'assuming the rights of an owner': she has them already.

My Lords, the relevant law is contained in ss 1 to 6 of the 1968 Act. They should be construed as a whole and applied in a manner which presents a consistent scheme both internally and with the remainder of the 1968 Act. The phrase 'dishonestly appropriates' should be construed as a composite phrase. It does not include acts done in relation to the relevant property which are done in accordance with the actual wishes or actual authority of the person to whom the property belongs. This is because such acts do not involve any assumption of the rights of that person within s 3(1) or because, by necessary implication from s 2(1), they are not to be regarded as dishonest appropriations of property belonging to another.

Actual authority, wishes, consent (or similar words) mean, both as a matter of language and on the authority of the three House of Lords cases, authorisation not obtained by fraud or misrepresentation. The definition of theft therefore embraces cases where the property has come to the defendant by the mistake of the person to whom it belongs and there would be an obligation to restore it—s5(4)—or property in which the other still has an equitable proprietary interest—s 5(1). This would also embrace property obtained by undue influence or other cases coming within the classes of invalid transfer recognised in *Re Beaney (decd)* [1978] 2 All ER 595, [1978] 1 WLR 770.

In cases of alleged gift, the criteria to be applied are the same. But additional care may need to be taken to see that the transaction is properly explained to the jury. It is unlikely that a charge of theft will be brought where there is not clear evidence of at least some conduct of the defendant which includes an element of fraud or overt dishonesty or some undue influence or knowledge of the deficient capacity of the alleged donor. This was the basis upon which the prosecution of the appellant was originally brought in the present case. On this basis there is no difficulty in explaining to the jury the relevant parts of s 5 and s 2(1) and the effect of the phrase 'assumption of the rights of an owner'. . . .

I would answer the certified question in the negative. But, in any event, I would allow the appeal and quash the conviction because the summing-up failed to direct the jury adequately upon the other essential elements of theft, not just appropriation.

Appeal dismissed

≋ **Questions**
Do you find Lord Hobhouse's reasoning more compelling than that of the majority? Is he right that there was there no inherent illegality in what D did and, if so, does this necessarily preclude criminalization?

13.3.1 All or any of the rights of an owner?

The owner of property has the right to do as he will with it in terms of using it, selling it, offering to sell it, hiring it, destroying it, doing nothing with it, etc. The owner has all of those rights over his property. In *Morris*, discussed in *Hinks*, section 13.3, p 348, Lord Roskill rejected an argument that in s 3, section 13.3, 'the rights of an owner' means *all* those rights, saying that the later words 'any assumption of a right' in s 3(1) and 'no later assumption by him of rights' in s 3(2) militated strongly against that view: it was sufficient that D assumed one such right, for example labelling goods. In *Gomez*, Lord Keith said that Lord

Roskill was 'undoubtedly right'. See also E. Melissaris, 'The Concept of Appropriation and the Offence of Theft' (2007) 70 MLR 581, who also concludes that Lord Roskill is right in this interpretation.

~~~ **Questions**

Do you agree that this was a correct, or possible, interpretation of s 3? Does not 'a right *to it*' (italicized words omitted by Lord Roskill) mean all the rights?

Note that Morris would now be guilty of an offence under the Fraud Act (see section 16.2, p 417).

13.3.2 Gifts and theft

It was generally accepted prior to *Hinks* that Parliament had intended the 1968 Act to be construed in such a way that there could be no theft where the conduct alleged to be an appropriation was something D was within his civil law rights to do. Thus, if D was made a gift of some property by V, it was his to retain and the civil law would protect that right. It was thought impossible for there to be an appropriation and theft for D to retain the gift in accordance with that civil law right, but *Hinks* holds that it can be theft.

For further critical discussion of *Hinks*, see [2001] Crim LR 263; A. T. H. Smith, 'Theft or Sharp Practice: Who Cares Now?' (2001) 60 CLJ 21; and for a defence of the decision, S. Shute, 'Appropriation and the Law of Theft' [2002] Crim LR 445. Shute suggests that dishonest conduct such as that in *Hinks*, although it might not constitute a civil law wrong, 'may nonetheless have a tendency to undermine property rights either directly by attacking the interests that they protect, or indirectly by weakening an established system of property rights and so threatening the public good that the system represents'.

~~~ **Questions**

(1) Hinks was ordered to pay £19,000 compensation to Dolphin. Compensation for what? For keeping a gift which she was entitled to keep as a matter of civil law? The jury's verdict did not decide that she did not have an *indefeasible* title to the property.

(2) To what extent does *Hinks* promote the use of theft as an offence criminalizing the exploitation of the vulnerable rather than the infringement of property rights? Should that be a concern *for the law of theft* (as opposed to fraud or some other form of statutory protection)? See A. L. Bogg and J. Stanton-Ife, 'Protecting the Vulnerable: Legality, Harm and Theft' (2003) 23 LS 402.

Not all commentators agree that the House of Lords has interpreted the law in an undesirable fashion. Consider the following extract.

S. P. Green, *13 Ways to Steal a Bicycle*
(2012), pp 105–107

Unfortunately, though lack of consent clearly plays a significant role in defining the moral structure of theft, there is a danger in putting too much weight solely on that concept. For a start, it is clear that lack of consent does not *sufficiently* describe the wrongfulness of stealing, since there are many cases in which property taken without the consent of the owner does not constitute stealing, such as where the taker acts under a claim of right or (if the taker is the government) pursuant to its power of eminent domain, forfeiture or taxation.

The more difficult question is whether lack of consent should be regarded as a *necessary* condition for stealing. A trio of post-Theft Act cases in England might be thought to raise doubt about this contention.

[Green then describes the facts and outcomes of *Lawrence*, *Gomez* and *Hinks* before continuing:]

Do these cases really establish the proposition that lack of consent should no longer be regarded as a necessary element of theft? To understand why they do not, it is necessary to look more clearly into what is meant by *consent*. The problem is that consent (or lack of it) means different things in different contexts. Thus, those cases that at first seem to have eliminated lack of one form of consent as an element of theft may in fact still require lack of consent in a different form.

A good place to begin this inquiry is with the work of Peter Westen, who, though focusing primarily on the offence of rape, has provided insight into how we conceive of consent more generally. Westen describes four basic senses in which to talk about the concept, but for present purposes the key distinction is between factual attitudinal consent, factual expressive consent, and prescriptive consent. *Factual attitudinal consent* reflects the consenter's state of mind at the time she consents; it occurs when the consenter's 'all things considered' desire is to acquiesce in the requested conduct. Thus, a person who agrees to have sex or surrender property to avoid threatened physical injury can be said to have consented in the factual attitudinal sense of the term because, all things considered, she prefers to submit rather than to suffer the threatened harm. With *factual expressive consent*, the consenter not only acquiesces mentally to the proposed action, but also makes her acquiescence known to others. Factual attitudinal or expressive consent is involuntary if it is made under the pressure of coercion; it is unknowing if it is obtained through deception; and it is incomplete if it is given by one who is incapable of understanding that to which she consents. Such forms of consent are to be contrasted with *prescriptive consent*, which to be recognized by law as consent must be made voluntarily, knowingly, and competently.

Westen's framework is helpful for understanding the role that lack of consent plays in defining the moral content of theft crimes. Consider again the three House of Lords decisions discussed above. In each case, an argument can be made that, though the defendant gave his factual expressive consent, he did not give his prescriptive consent: In *Lawrence*, the victim taxi passenger's English was poor, he apparently did not understand how much the taxi fare should have cost, and he was presumably nervous and intimidated; in *Gomez*, the victim employer was deceived by the defendant into believing that the checks were 'good as cash'; and then in *Hinks* the victim was of low intelligence and was essentially under the coercive influence of the defendant. Thus, when the Law Lords said in each case that lack of consent was no longer an element of the offense, what they really meant is that lack of *factual expressive* consent is no longer an element of the offense, not that lack of *prescriptive* consent is no longer an element. Had the victims of *Lawrence*, *Gomez*, and *Hinks* not been duped or coerced into giving up the money that they did, the outcome of the cases would surely have been different.

≈≈ *Question*

If Green is correct about the proper interpretation of the cases, does this not suggest that the more appropriate offence to have charged D with was fraud rather than theft?

13.3.3 Appropriation by keeping

D borrows V's lawnmower for a week, and at the end of the week D resolves that he will keep it. At the end of the week D leaves the mower where it is in his garage hoping that V will forget about it and intending to keep it. Is this an appropriation? Is this theft? See the words of s 3— an appropriation includes 'where he has come by the property (innocently or not) without stealing it, any later assumption of a right to it by keeping or dealing with it as owner.'

13.3.4 Where does the appropriation occur?

Although the House of Lords' interpretation of s 3 has made the law easier for prosecutors by extending the scope of the meaning of appropriation, it still leaves problems, and arguably creates more problems, in identifying when the appropriation occurred. The appropriation and the mens rea must coincide in time for there to be a theft.

In *Atakpu* [1993] 4 All ER 215, [1994] QB 69, CA, the convictions of the defendants for conspiracy to steal were quashed where they hired cars in Germany and Belgium with the intention of shipping them to England, altering their identity and selling them to unsuspecting purchasers. On the *Gomez* (and now *Hinks*) view, the cars were stolen in Germany and Belgium and the defendants could not steal again in England property which they had already stolen abroad. Cf G. R. Sullivan and C. Warbrick [1994] Crim LR 650.

13.3.5 Continuing appropriation?

It is often important to know how long a particular theft continued. For example, D may be guilty of a theft by aiding and abetting it while it is being committed by P, but D cannot aid and abet once the theft by P is over. When it finished is crucial. Similarly, D may be guilty of robbery if he uses force while theft is being committed but not by using force when the theft is at an end. See G. Williams, 'Appropriation: A Single or Continuous Act' [1978] Crim LR 69.

13.3.6 Section 3(2)

Section 3(2) provides:

> Where property or a right or interest in property is or purports to be transferred for value to a person acting in good faith, no later assumption by him of rights which he believed himself to be acquiring shall, by reason of any defect in the transferor's title, amount to theft of the property.

The Criminal Law Revision Committee (CLRC), in its Eighth Report on which the Theft Act was based, observed (*Theft and Related Offences* (1966), Cmnd 2977, para 37):

> A person may buy something in good faith, but may find out afterwards that the seller had no title to it. . . . If the buyer nevertheless keeps the thing or otherwise deals with it as owner, he could, on the principles stated above, be guilty of theft. It is arguable that this would be right; but on the whole it seems to us that, whatever view is taken on the buyer's moral duty, the law would be too strict if it made him guilty of theft.

In *Adams* (1993) 15 Cr App R (S) 466, [1993] Crim LR 72, CA, D, in good faith, purchased motorcycle parts but did not suspect they were stolen until two or three days later. D's conviction for stealing the parts was quashed. At the time of the acquisition of the parts—the relevant time under s 3(2)—he believed he had become their owner and by thereafter exercising an owner's rights he could not be guilty of theft even though he realized that he had no title to the parts.

~~~ **Question**

Suppose Adams, after discovering the parts are stolen, sells them to V, an innocent purchaser, for £100. May Adams be convicted of (a) stealing the parts; (b) stealing the £100?

13.4 Property

Theft Act 1968, s 4

4. 'Property'

(1) 'Property' includes money and all other property, real or personal, including things in action and other intangible property.

(2) A person cannot steal land, or things forming part of land and severed from it by him or by his directions, except in the following cases, that is to say—

(a) when he is a trustee or personal representative, or is authorised by power of attorney, or as liquidator of a company, or otherwise, to sell or dispose of land belonging to another, and he appropriates the land or anything forming part of it by dealing with it in breach of the confidence reposed in him; or

(b) when he is not in possession of the land and appropriates anything forming part of the land by severing it or causing it to be severed, or after it has been severed; or

(c) when, being in possession of the land under a tenancy, he appropriates the whole or part of any fixture or structure let to be used with the land.

For purposes of this subsection 'land' does not include incorporeal hereditaments; 'tenancy' means a tenancy for years or less period and includes an agreement for such a tenancy, but a person who after the end of a tenancy remains in possession as statutory tenant or otherwise is to be treated as having possession under the tenancy, and 'let' shall be construed accordingly.

(3) A person who picks mushrooms growing wild on any land, or who picks flowers, fruit or foliage from a plant growing wild on any land, does not (although not in possession of the land) steal what he picks, unless he does it for reward or for sale or other commercial purpose.

For purposes of this subsection 'mushroom' includes any fungus, and 'plant' includes any shrub or tree.

(4) Wild creatures, tamed or untamed, shall be regarded as property; but a person cannot steal a wild creature not tamed nor ordinarily kept in captivity, or the carcase of any such creature, unless either it has been reduced into possession by or on behalf of another person and possession of it has not since been lost or abandoned, or another person is in course of reducing it into possession.

Almost anything may be 'property' and, if it is possessed or owned by someone, it 'belongs to' him. While s 4 identifies certain kinds of property which cannot be stolen, it does not otherwise provide a definition of property, whether tangible or intangible, which is capable of being stolen. To determine what is property for this purpose, recourse has to be made to the civil law. Merely because something has a value does not mean that it constitutes property. For example, a wifi signal does not constitute property under this definition should it?

In summary, s 4(1) treats as property: money (ie coins and banknotes); all other property (eg DVD players, iPhones, handbags, etc); things in action (types of property which can only be enforced by bringing a legal action—not things which can be taken physically, eg bank credits) see, for example, *Kohn* (1979) 69 Cr App R 395, *Hilton* [1997] EWCA Crim 661, [1997] Crim LR

761; other intangible property (eg export quotas (*A-G of Hong Kong v Nai Keung* [1987] 1 WLR 1339), patents (Patents Act 1977, s 30), copyright (Copyright, Designs and Patents Act 1988, s 213)). In addition, it was held in *Smith* [2011] EWCA Crim 66 that the definition of property includes items that it is unlawful to possess, in this instance drugs.

13.4.1 Intangible property

Intangible property includes such things as debts, copyright or shares in a company. The most common forms of intangible property that are stolen are 'things in action', that is, types of property that can only be enforced by bringing a legal action, for example a debt.

The main difficulties lie not in determining what constitutes intangible property but in determining how such property is appropriated and the owner permanently deprived of it. Suppose that D without permission publishes V's poems. This is a breach of copyright but is the copyright stolen? Since D does not intend to deprive V *of the copyright* the case would seem to be analogous to a dishonest use by D of V's car which is not theft in the absence of intention permanently to deprive. So how does D set about stealing V's copyright?

13.4.1.1 Bank accounts

One case where it is easy to see how intangible property is appropriated is where D causes V's bank account to be debited and his own credited. See *Chan Man-sin v A-G of Hong Kong* [1988] 1 WLR 196, [1988] 1 All ER 1, PC. Where a bank account is in credit, the relationship between banker and customer is that of a debtor and creditor. In law, the customer, V, does not have 'money in the bank'; there is no specific pile of money that is designated as his. The property that he has is a 'thing in action', a right to payment by the bank of the sum of money it owes him. If D dishonestly causes a bank to debit V's account, D does not appropriate V's money, he appropriates a thing in action belonging to V (V's right to payment of that sum from the bank) and is guilty of theft of that property. If V has an authorized overdraft with the bank, V has a right to payment from the bank of the sum up to the limit of that agreed overdraft, and that is property—a thing in action—that D may steal by dishonestly causing the bank to debit V's account. For example, in *Kohn* (1979) 69 Cr App R 395, D, an accountant, drew cheques on the company's account for his own personal items. He was convicted of theft of the company's thing in action (ie the company's right to sue the bank for £x had now been diminished). See E. J. Griew, 'Stealing and Obtaining Bank Credits' [1986] Crim LR 356 and R. Heaton, 'Cheques and Balances' [2005] Crim LR 747 (both written before the deception offences in the Theft Act 1968 were replaced by the Fraud Act 2006).

13.4.2 Stealing cheques

Where V writes a cheque payable to D (or in more formal language 'draws a cheque in his favour') in what circumstances can D be guilty of theft, and of what? As a matter of banking law, a cheque is a piece of paper which, if given for consideration, creates a thing in action—a right for D to sue V for the amount stated. When V writes a cheque payable to D, D obtains two items of property:

(1) the piece of paper which previously belonged to V (or the bank). The Court of Appeal, in *Clark* [2001] Crim LR 572, [2001] EWCA Crim 884, held following *Preddy* [1996] UKHL 13 in the House of Lords that a cheque cannot be stolen. For criticism, see the commentary at [2001] Crim LR 572. In *Roach* [2011] EWCA Crim 918, Elias LJ considered *Preddy* and held that the decision did not preclude a conviction for the theft of the physical cheque in circumstances where D had no intention ever to cash it, for example when the cheque was signed by someone famous;

At first sight it is a perfectly obvious proposition that a person may steal only the property of another and, equally, that he cannot steal his own property. Usually the issue is clear-cut. So D is guilty of theft if, with mens rea, he snatches V's handbag; the handbag being owned and possessed by V and D having no proprietary interest in it whatever. Conversely, if D arranges for the 'disappearance' of his own property in order to perpetrate a fraud on insurers it may be that D will commit other offences but it is plain that he cannot be convicted of theft.

But property may 'belong to' more than one person. V may have some interest in the property less than ownership. The handbag snatched from V might have been lent by O (the owner) to P (who thereby acquired possession) and P has in turn asked V to hold it while P unlocks her car door. Here V has mere custody of the handbag but this suffices under s 5(1) and the handbag is stolen from her by D who takes it. It is also stolen from O and P but it is equally stolen from V.

There is nothing odd in extending theft to an appropriation of property from someone who is not the exclusive owner of the property. Nor is there any oddity in holding that a person may be guilty of theft though he himself has a proprietary right or interest in the property. If, in the illustration concerning the handbag, P (the possessor) dishonestly intending to keep it for herself, tells O (the owner) that it was stolen from her by D, then both in law and good sense it can be said that P has stolen it from O.

Even a person who is the owner in the strict sense may steal the property if there is another 'owner'. So in *Bonner* [1970] 2 All ER 97n, [1970] 1 WLR 838, CA, it was held that where property is held by a partnership, one partner, even though he is a joint owner of all partnership property, may steal partnership property if he appropriates it to himself intending to defeat the interests of the other partners. The essential idea is that D may be guilty of theft where in respect of particular property he acts so as to usurp the interests that *any* others have in that property.

It should be noted that s 5 encompasses both legal and equitable interests. Where property is subject to a trust, it belongs to both the trustee (legal interest) and the beneficiary (equitable interest) and it may be stolen from either.

The following sections will examine some instances where it is difficult to discern whether the property in question 'belonged to another'.

13.5.1 What constitutes possession or control by V?

One difficulty arises when the defendant alleges that the property he has appropriated was abandoned or 'ownerless'. In *Woodman* [1974] EWCA Crim 1, the Court of Appeal held that the key question is whether someone else was in control of the property in question. In this case, D had taken a significant quantity of scrap metal from a disused factory that belonged to English China Clays. D was convicted but argued that the metal was ownerless. The Court of Appeal disagreed, however, holding that, 'there was evidence of English China Clays being in control of the site and prima facie in control of articles on the site as well. The fact that it could not be shown that they were conscious of the existence of this or any particular scrap iron does not destroy the general principle that control of a site by excluding others from it is prima facie control of articles on the site as well.'

Generally, possession or control is shown by some measure of control in fact accompanied by an intention to exclude others. Obviously, a householder retains possession or control (indeed, he retains ownership) of 'unwanted' items which he consigns to his attic or cellar even though he cannot itemize them. Even household rubbish consigned to the dustbin remains in his disposition for he would certainly not want any Tom, Dick or Harry (or tabloid journalist) looking for items of value in his dustbin. In *R (Rickets) v Basildon Magistrates' Court*

[2010] EWHC 2358 (Admin), D was observed taking bags of clothes that had been left outside the front of one charity shop (British Heart Foundation) and also those that had been left in bins behind another (Oxfam). He was charged with theft. In dismissing D's claim for judicial review of the decision to commit him to the Crown Court for trial, Wyn Williams J stated that it could not be inferred that the property had been abandoned:

10. I deal first with what I shall call the British Heart Foundation charge. In my judgment, the following inferences were open to the court. First, that persons unknown had deposited the items outside the shop with the intention of giving the items to the British Heart Foundation. Second, it was a permissible inference that the British Heart Foundation would have been willing either to keep the items with a view to resale in its shop or to dispose of them. In either event, of course, at some stage the items would have become within the possession or control of the British Heart Foundation and it would have had a proprietary right in the items.

11. It does not seem to me, however, that it was open to the court to infer that at the moment in time when the appropriation took place the British Heart Foundation had acquired a proprietary interest in, or had taken possession or control of, the items.

12. In my judgment it cannot be said that the British Heart Foundation acquired possession of the items or assumed control of them or even acquired a proprietary interest in them simply by virtue of the fact that they were left in close proximity to the shop.

13. However, it is clearly the case, in my judgment, that it was open to the court to infer that the items had not been abandoned. The obvious inference on the bare facts before the justices was that persons unknown had intended the goods to be a gift to the British Heart Foundation. Those persons had an intention to give; they had also attempted to effect delivery. Delivery would be complete, however, only when the British Heart Foundation took possession of the items. Until that time, although the unknown would-be donor had divested himself of possession of the items, he had not given up his ownership of the items. I accept that it would have been more appropriate to lay a charge of stealing property belonging to persons unknown, though as I have said it is not material to the resolution of this case that the claimant was charged with appropriating items belonging to the British Heart Foundation.

14. In my judgment the above analysis shows that it was open to the court to conclude that there was evidence from which a court could properly determine that the property belonged to another at the time of appropriation by the claimant. That being the case, in my judgment, the claimant was properly committed on that charge for trial. It will obviously be a matter for the prosecution to consider how best to frame the indictment when the claimant is actually indicted in the Crown Court.

15. I turn to the charge alleging theft from Oxfam since it is somewhat different on the facts. The claimant admits that the items taken from Oxfam were items which had been placed in bins in close proximity to the rear of the shop. In my judgment, it would be open to a court to infer either that would-be donors had placed the items in the bins for receipt by Oxfam or that employees of Oxfam had placed the items in the bins for onward disposal by the local authority. This analysis assumes of course that the bins belonged to or were controlled by Oxfam, which is not presently disputed.

16. Upon that assumption it would be open to a court to infer that Oxfam had taken delivery of the items once placed within the bins. Alternatively, it could infer that Oxfam had taken possession of the items and had then placed them in the bins for disposal. Either way, Oxfam were in possession of the items at the time of the appropriation by the claimant.

17. I am also of the view that it would be open to the court to conclude that the bins were controlled by Oxfam even if this is disputed. The bins were in close proximity to the rear of the premises. That of itself, in my judgment, raises a permissible inference, in the absence of any other evidence, that the bins were under the control of Oxfam. In any event, if the prosecutor so chooses he or she can allege in the indictment in the Crown Court that the property belongs to a person unknown. That cannot be objectionable for the reasons I have given earlier in this judgment.

(1) D and E are refuse operatives working for the local authority. They separate out anything they consider might be valuable from the 'rubbish' left by householders before placing the other material in their employer's vehicle. Would they be guilty of stealing from their employer or from the householder or both?

(2) Do 'freegans' (those who take food from supermarket refuse areas when it has been discarded because it has passed its sell-by date) commit theft? See S. Thomas, 'Do Freegans Commit Theft?' (2010) 30 LS 98.

13.5.2 Property belonging to another and bank transfers

If D induces V to transfer money electronically from V's account to D's account, what item of property is D alleged to have obtained? The House of Lords answered this question in *Preddy* [1996] UKHL 13, in which it was held that D had not appropriated property belonging to another. As a matter of civil law the House of Lords held that the property which D has obtained is the new chose in action constituted by the debt now owed to him by his bank, and represented by the credit entry in his own bank account. This item of property did not come into existence until the debt so created was owed to him by his bank, and therefore that new item of property never belonged to anyone else. As D cannot be guilty of theft, there was potentially a lacuna in the law. This was addressed by the hasty enactment of the offence of obtaining a money transfer by deception, which was contained in the Theft (Amendment) Act 1996. See now s 1 of the Fraud Act 2006, section 16.1, p 414.

13.5.3 In what circumstances can D steal property in which he himself has a proprietary interest?

We have seen that a number of people might simultaneously have an interest in property, but can D be guilty of stealing his own property? In *Turner (No 2)* [1971] 2 All ER 441, Turner took his car to Brown's garage for repairs. Mr Brown claims that he did those repairs and then parked the car around the corner 10 to 20 yards from the garage. Brown kept the ignition key which Turner gave him. Turner called at the garage and asked if the car was ready. On being told that it was ready subject to being tuned, Turner said that he would return on the next day to collect it and pay. A few hours later, however, Mr Brown found that the car had gone. Whoever had taken it had had a key, because the key that Mr Brown had was still on his garage keyboard. He reported the matter to the police. Brown went round the neighbouring streets to see if he could find the car, and eventually several days later he found it parked in a street near to Turner's flat. Brown took the car back to his garage, took out the engine and then towed it back less the engine to the place from which he had taken it. The Court of Appeal held that Turner could be guilty of stealing the car. Applied correctly, this principle is uncontroversial. Although Turner was the owner of the car, the garage had a proprietary interest in it, known as a lien, until Turner paid the bill for the work that was undertaken. The car therefore was 'property belonging to another' because, in the language of s 5(1), the garage had a proprietary right or interest in it. The issue with the case, however, is that the jury were never directed to consider whether the garage had a lien over the car.

13.5.4 Equitable interests

Despite the breadth of s 5(1), it would not be sufficient to offer protection in all circumstances. Section 5 provides additional protection by deeming someone other than D to have a proprietary right or interest in specified circumstances.

Section 5(2) deals with cases where the alleged theft is of trust property by a trustee. If special provision were not made, the trustee thief might argue that he had exclusive legal right to the property. It provides:

> Where property is subject to a trust, the persons to whom it belongs shall be regarded as including any person having a right to enforce the trust, and an intention to defeat the trust shall be regarded accordingly as an intention to deprive of the property any person having that right.

13.5.5 Property received by D to retain and deal with

A circumstance in which s 5(1) would not be sufficient to offer protection is the case where D obtains property from V and is under an obligation to deal with it in a particular way. For example, V gives D, her flatmate, money on the understanding that D will use it to pay the gas bill. V (probably) has no proprietary right or interest in the money once it has passed and if D spent the money on herself rather than the gas she would not commit theft. Section 5(3) provides a solution to such problems.

Section 5(3) provides:

> Where a person receives property from or on account of another, and is under an obligation to the other to retain and deal with that property or its proceeds in a particular way, the property or proceeds shall be regarded (as against him) as belonging to the other.

13.5.5.1 An obligation to retain and deal

This crucial element of the section was examined in *Hall* [1972] 2 All ER 1009. H had been running a travel agency in the course of which he took deposits from customers for future travel. H was prosecuted for theft when, in several cases, no flights materialized, no refund was made and H accepted that he was unable to make any repayment. H claimed to have paid into the firm's general trading account all the sums received by him. He claimed there could be no theft because the money became his own property and had been applied by him in the conduct of the firm's business. Edmund Davies LJ in the Court of Appeal held that H's conviction had to be quashed because the prosecution failed to establish (a) that the clients expected H to retain and deal with the money in a particular way and (b) that H had made such an undertaking.

Section 5(3) requires careful consideration to be given to the precise terms of the obligation it is alleged D is under. *Foster* [2011] EWCA Crim 1192 demonstrates how complex an investigation into whether s 5(3) applies can be. F ran a scheme whereby work colleagues invested sums with him expecting him to pool the sums and place large bets on football and other sports. The funds invested were used by F for his own purposes. The trial judge allowed the counts of theft to be left to the jury based on s 5(3). The defendant claimed that not all the property that he obtained from investors had been subject to an obligation to retain or deal in that particular way and that he had made clear to investors that funds could be used at his discretion. The Court of Appeal quashed the conviction for theft. The prosecution failed to establish that all the investors expected the money to be dealt with in the manner alleged. If only some investors held such an expectation, given that their property was amalgamated with that of those who did not and it is money from this 'mixed fund' that D was alleged to have used for his own purposes, D could not be guilty. This is because it was impossible on the facts to tell whether D had utilized property that constituted restricted funds or whether he used property that was not subject to the restriction.

13.5.6 Property got by another's mistake

Like s 5(2) and (3), s 5(4) provides a deeming provision (ie a provision inserted into the legislation to clarify how something is to be treated or regarded) where as against D, property will be treated as belonging to another provided certain criteria are satisfied. In s 5(4), in addition to the property having been got by mistake, there must be a legal obligation to make restoration of the property or its value.

Section 5(4) provides:

> Where a person gets property by another's mistake, and is under an obligation to make restoration (in whole or in part) of the property or its proceeds or of the value thereof, then to the extent of that obligation the property or proceeds shall be regarded (as against him) as belonging to the person entitled to restoration, and an intention not to make restoration shall be regarded accordingly as an intention to deprive that person of the property or proceeds.

Of all the provisions in s 5, s 5(4) certainly appears to be the most complicated. As a simple example of the way in which s 5(4) was designed to operate, consider *A-G's Reference (No 1 of 1983)* [1984] 3 All ER 369, [1985] QB 182. D, a police officer, received her pay from her employer by way of direct debit. On one occasion she was overpaid by £74.74 but when she became aware of this she decided to take no action though she did not subsequently withdraw any of this money. At her trial for theft, the trial judge directed an acquittal. Lord Lane CJ, on behalf of the court, held that he was wrong to do so. Referring to s 5(4), Lord Lane said that D was under no obligation to restore the money or its proceeds but was under an obligation to restore the value thereof. But there is another point of interest in this case. D had not spent the overpayment; it remained in her bank account.

In *Chase Manhattan Bank NA v Israel-British Bank (London) Ltd* [1979] 3 All ER 1025, [1981] Ch 105, it was held by Goulding J that a person who pays money (or, presumably, delivers any property) to another under a mistake of fact retains an equitable interest in the money and the conscience of the recipient is subject to a fiduciary duty to respect his proprietary right. In *Shadrokh-Cigari* [1988] Crim LR 465, CA, a bank in the United States in error credited the account of a child at an English bank with £286,000 instead of £286. D, the child's guardian, got the child to sign banker's drafts and when D was arrested only £21,000 remained in the account. Upholding D's conviction for theft from the English bank, the court said that the drafts belonged to the bank and although legal ownership passed to D by delivery, the bank retained an equitable interest by virtue of the principle in *Chase Manhattan*. It was accordingly not necessary to rely on s 5(4) though the subsection provided an alternative route to conviction.

13.6 Dishonesty

The mens rea of the offence comprises two elements: dishonesty and an intention permanently to deprive the other of the property.

Dishonesty is the element of mens rea in offences under the Theft Act 1968, the Fraud Act 2006 and at common law (eg conspiracy to defraud). It is surprising that it remains undefined by Parliament.

In theft, the principal element of mens rea in the offence of theft is that D was acting dishonestly in appropriating the property. Section 2 of the Act provides:

Theft Act 1968, s 2

2. 'Dishonestly'

(1) A person's appropriation of property belonging to another is not to be regarded as dishonest—

  (a) if he appropriates the property in the belief that he has in law the right to deprive the other of it, on behalf of himself or of a third person; or

  (b) if he appropriates the property in the belief that he would have the other's consent if the other knew of the appropriation and the circumstances of it; or

  (c) (except where the property came to him as trustee or personal representative) if he appropriates the property in the belief that the person to whom the property belongs cannot be discovered by taking reasonable steps.

(2) A person's appropriation of property belonging to another may be dishonest notwithstanding that he is willing to pay for the property.

Section 2 does not define dishonesty. It merely tells us that three specified beliefs negative dishonesty and that the intention specified in s 2(2) does not necessarily do so. But s 2 makes it clear that where it applies D's *belief* is of paramount importance. If D believes he has a legal right to property he should not be convicted of theft, however unreasonable his belief may be. If he believes that V would have consented to the appropriation he cannot be accounted dishonest, though only a fool (which D is) could have believed that V would give consent. If D finds and appropriates property in circumstances in which any person who gave thought to it would realize the owner could be traced by taking reasonable steps, D is not dishonest if this thought does not occur to him. But the definition in s 2 is only partial. In the absence of a full statutory definition, the courts have had to step in. The leading case remains *Ghosh* [1982] EWCA Crim 2.

R v Ghosh
[1982] EWCA Crim 2, Court of Appeal, Criminal Division

(Lord Lane CJ, Lloyd and Eastham JJ)

The defendant was a doctor who, it was alleged, had treated private patients using NHS facilities and claimed money for doing so. The court discussed the use of dishonesty as a concept across the Theft Act (including in relation to offences that have since been abolished) and at common law.

[Lord Lane CJ read the following judgment of the court:]

The grounds of appeal are simply that the judge misdirected the jury as to the meaning of dishonesty.

. . . The law on this branch of the Theft Act 1968 is in a complicated state and we embark on an examination of the authorities with great diffidence.

When *R v McIvor* [1982] 1 All ER 491, [1982] 1 WLR 409 came before the Court of Appeal, there were two conflicting lines of authority. On the one hand there were cases which decided that the test of dishonesty for the purposes of the Theft Act 1968 is, what we venture to call, subjective, that is to say, the jury should be directed to look into the mind of the defendant and determine whether he knew he was acting dishonestly: see *R v Landy* [1981] 1 All ER 1172 at 1181, [1981] 1 WLR 355 at 365 where Lawton LJ, giving the reserved judgment of the Court of Appeal said:

> 'An assertion by a defendant that throughout a transaction he acted honestly does not have to be accepted but has to be weighed like any other piece of evidence. If that was the defendant's state of mind, or may have been, he is entitled to be acquitted. But if the jury, applying their own notions of what is honest and what is not, conclude that he could not have believed he was acting honestly, then the element of dishonesty will have been established. What a jury must not do is to say to themselves: "If we had been in his place we would have known we were acting dishonestly, so he must have known he was."'

On the other hand there were cases which decided that the test of dishonesty is objective. Thus in *R v Greenstein; R v Green* [1976] 1 All ER 1 at 6, [1975] 1 WLR 1353 at 1359 the judge in the court below had directed the jury:

> '. . . The question you have to decide and what this case is all about is whether these defendants, or either of them, carried out their stagging operations [a share-purchasing scheme] in a dishonest way. To that question you apply your own standards of dishonesty. It is no good, you see, applying the standards of anyone accused of dishonesty otherwise everybody accused of dishonesty, if he were to be tested by his own standards, would be acquitted automatically, you may think. The question is essentially one for a jury to decide and it is essentially one which the jury must decide by applying its own standards.'

The Court of Appeal, in a reserved judgment, approved that direction.

In *R v McIvor* [1982] 1 All ER 491 at 497, [1982] 1 WLR 409 at 417 the Court of Appeal sought to reconcile these conflicting lines of authority. They did so on the basis that the subjective test is appropriate where the charge is conspiracy to defraud, but in the case of theft the test should be objective. [His lordship referred to that passage and other judgments on conspiracy to defraud referred to therein.] In *Scott v Comr of Police for the Metropolis* [1974] 3 All ER 1032, [1975] AC 819 Viscount Dilhorne stated as follows ([1974] 3 All ER 1032 at 1036, [1975] AC 819 at 836–837):

> 'The Criminal Law Revision Committee in their eighth report on "Theft and Related Offences" (Cmnd 2977 (1966)) in para 33 expressed the view that the important element of larceny, embezzlement and fraudulent conversion was "undoubtedly the dishonest appropriation of another person's property"; in para 35 that the words "dishonestly appropriates" meant the same as "fraudulently converts to his own use or benefit, or the use or benefit of any other person", and in para 39 that "dishonestly" seemed to them a better word than "fraudulently". Parliament endorsed these views in the Theft Act 1968, which by s 1(1) defined theft as the dishonest appropriation of property belonging to another with the intention of permanently depriving the other of it. Section 17 of that Act replaces ss82 and 83 of the Larceny Act 1861 and the Falsification of Accounts Act 1875. The offences created by those sections and by that Act made it necessary to prove that there had been an "intent to defraud". Section 17 of the Theft Act 1968 substitutes the words "dishonestly with a view to gain for himself or another or with intent to cause loss to another" for the words "intent to defraud". If "fraudulently" in relation to larceny meant "dishonestly" and "intent to defraud" in relation to falsification of accounts is equivalent to the words now contained in s 17 of the Theft Act 1968 which I have quoted, it would indeed be odd if "defraud" in the phrase "conspiracy to defraud" has a different meaning and means only a conspiracy which is to be carried out by deceit.'

Later on in the same speech Viscount Dilhorne continued as follows ([1974] 3 All ER 1032 at 1038, [1975] AC 819 at 839):

> 'As I have said, words take colour from the context in which they are used, but the words "fraudulently" and "defraud" must ordinarily have a very similar meaning. If, as I think, and as the

Criminal Law Revision Committee appears to have thought, "fraudulently" means "dishonestly", then "to defraud" ordinarily means, in my opinion, to deprive a person dishonestly of something which is his or of something to which he is or would or might but for the perpetration of the fraud be entitled.'

In *Scott* the House of Lords were only concerned with the question whether deceit is an essential ingredient in cases of conspiracy to defraud; and they held not. As Lord Diplock said ([1974] 3 All ER 1032 at 1040, [1975] AC 819 at 841), 'dishonesty of any kind is enough'. But there is nothing in *Scott* which supports the view that, so far as the element of dishonesty is concerned, 'theft is in a different category from conspiracy to defraud'. On the contrary the analogy drawn by Viscount Dilhorne between the two offences, and indeed the whole tenor of his speech, suggests the precise opposite.

Nor is there anything in *R v Landy* itself which justifies putting theft and conspiracy to defraud into different categories. Indeed the court went out of its way to stress that the test for dishonesty, whatever it might be, should be the same whether the offence charged be theft or conspiracy to defraud. This is clear from the reference to *R v Feely* [1973] 1 All ER 341, [1973] QB 530, which was a case under s 1 of the Theft Act 1968. Having set out what we have for convenience called the subjective test, the court in *R v Landy* [1981] 1 All ER 1172 to 1181, [1981] 1 WLR 355 at 365 continued:

'In our judgment this is the way *R v Feely* should be applied in cases where the issue of dishonesty arises. It is also the way in which the jury should have been directed in this case.'

In support of the distinction it is said that in conspiracy to defraud the question arises in relation to an agreement. But we cannot see that this makes any difference. If A and B agree to deprive a person dishonestly of his goods, they are guilty of conspiracy to defraud: see *Scott*'s case. If they dishonestly and with the necessary intent deprive him of his goods, they are presumably guilty of theft. Why, one asks respectfully, should the test be objective in the case of simple theft, but subjective where they have agreed to commit a theft?

[The court considered the implications of the dishonesty test in the offences of deception.]

We feel, with the greatest respect, that in seeking to reconcile the two lines of authority in the way we have mentioned, the Court of Appeal in *McIvor* was seeking to reconcile the irreconcilable. It therefore falls to us now either to choose between the two lines of authority or to propose some other solution.

In the current supplement to *Archbold's, Pleading, Evidence and Practice in Criminal Cases* (40th edn, 1979) para 1460, the editors suggest that the observations on dishonesty by the Court of Appeal in *R v Landy* can be disregarded 'in view of the wealth of authority to the contrary'. The matter, we feel, is not as simple as that.

In *R v Waterfall* [1969] 3 All ER 1048, [1970] 1 QB 148 the defendant was charged under s 16 of the 1968 Act with dishonestly obtaining a pecuniary advantage from a taxi driver. Lord Parker CJ, giving the judgment of the Court of Appeal, said ([1969] 3 All ER 1048 at 1049–1050, [1970] 1 QB 148 at 150–151):

'The sole question as it seems to me in this case revolves round the third ingredient, namely, whether that what was done was done dishonestly. In regard to that the deputy recorder directed the jury in this way: ". . . if on reflection and deliberation you came to the conclusion that [the appellant] never did have any genuine belief that [the appellant's accountant] would pay the taxi fare, then you would be entitled to convict him . . ." In other words, in that passage the deputy recorder is telling the jury they had to consider what was in this particular appellant's mind; had he a genuine belief that the accountant would provide the money? That, as it seems to this court, is a perfectly proper direction subject to this, that it would be right to tell the jury that they can use as a test, although not a conclusive test, whether there were any reasonable grounds for that belief. Unfortunately, however, just before the jury retired, in two passages of the transcript the deputy recorder, as it seems to this court, was saying that one cannot hold that the appellant had a genuine belief unless he had reasonable grounds for that belief.'

Lord Parker CJ then sets out the passages in question and continues:

'. . . the court is quite satisfied that those directions cannot be justified. The test here is a subjective test, whether the appellant had an honest belief, and of course whereas the absence of reasonable ground may point strongly to the fact that that belief is not genuine, it is at the end of the day for the jury to say whether or not in the case of this particular man he did have that genuine belief.'

That decision was criticised by academic writers. But it was followed shortly afterwards in *R v Royle* [1971] 3 All ER 1359, [1971] 1 WLR 1764, another case under s 16 of the 1968 Act. Edmund Davies LJ, giving the judgment of the court, said ([1971] 3 All ER 1359 at 1365, [1971] 1 WLR 1764 at 1769–1770):

'The charges being that debts had been dishonestly "evaded" by deception, contrary to s 16(2) (a), it was incumbent on the commissioner to direct the jury on the fundamental ingredient of dishonesty. In accordance with *R v Waterfall* they should have been told that the test is whether the accused had an honest belief and that, whereas the absence of reasonable ground might point strongly to the conclusion that he entertained no genuine belief in the truth of his representation, it was for them to say whether or not it had been established that the appellant had no such genuine belief.'

It is to be noted that the court in that case treated the 'fundamental ingredient of dishonesty' as being the same as whether the defendant had a genuine belief in the truth of the representation.

In *R v Gilks* [1972] 3 All ER 280, [1972] 1 WLR 1341, which was decided by the Court of Appeal the following year, the appellant had been convicted of theft contrary to s 1 of the 1968 Act. The facts were that he had been overpaid by a bookmaker. He knew that the bookmaker had made a mistake, and that he was not entitled to the money. But he kept it. The case for the defence was that 'bookmakers are a race apart'. It would be dishonest if your grocer gave you too much change and you kept it, knowing that he had made a mistake. But it was not dishonest in the case of a bookmaker.

The deputy chairman of the court below directed the jury as follows:

'Well, it is a matter for you to consider, members of the jury, but try and place yourselves in [the appellant's] position at that time and answer the question whether in your view he thought he was acting honestly or dishonestly.'

(See [1972] 3 All ER 280 at 283, [1972] 1 WLR 1341 at 1345.)

Cairns LJ, giving the judgment of the Court of Appeal held that that was, in the circumstances of the case, a proper and sufficient direction on the matter of dishonesty. He continued ([1972] 3 All ER 280 at 283, [1972] 1 WLR 1341 at 1345):

'On the face of it the appellant's conduct was dishonest; the only possible basis on which the jury could find that the prosecution had not established dishonesty would be if they thought it possible that the appellant did have the belief which he claimed to have.'

A little later *R v Feely* came before a court of five judges. The case is often treated as having laid down an objective test of dishonesty for the purpose of s 1 of the 1968 Act. But what it actually decided was (i) that it is for the jury to determine whether the defendant acted dishonestly and not for the judge, (ii) that the word 'dishonestly' can only relate to the defendant's own state of mind, and (iii) that it is unnecessary and undesirable for judges to define what is meant by 'dishonestly'.

It is true that the court said ([1973] 1 All ER 341 at 345, [1973] QB 530 at 537–538):

'Jurors when deciding whether an appropriation was dishonest can be reasonably expected to, and should, apply the current standards of ordinary decent people.'

It is that sentence which is usually taken as laying down the objective test. But the passage goes on:

'In their own lives they have to decide what is and what is not dishonest. We can see no reason why, when in a jury box, they should require the help of a judge to tell them what amounts to dishonesty.'

The sentence requiring the jury to apply current standards leads up to the prohibition of judges from applying *their* standards. That is the context in which the sentence appears. It seems to be reading too much into that sentence to treat it as authority for the view that 'dishonesty can be established independently of the knowledge or belief of the defendant'. If it could, then any reference to the state of mind of the defendant would be beside the point.

This brings us to the heart of the problem. Is 'dishonestly' in s 1 of the 1968 Act intended to characterise a course of conduct? Or is it intended to describe a state of mind? If the former, then we can well understand that it could be established independently of the knowledge or belief of the accused. But if, as we think, it is the latter, then the knowledge and belief of the accused are at the root of the problem.

Take for example a man who comes from a country where public transport is free. On his first day here he travels on a bus. He gets off without paying. He never had any intention of paying. His mind is clearly honest; but his conduct, judged objectively by what he had done, is dishonest. It seems to us that, in using the word 'dishonestly' in the 1968 Act, Parliament cannot have intended to catch dishonest conduct in that sense, that is to say conduct to which no moral obloquy could possibly attach.

This is sufficiently established by the partial definition in s 2 of the Theft Act 1968 itself. All the matters covered by s2(1) relate to the belief of the accused. Section 2(2) relates to his willingness to pay. A man's belief and his willingness to pay are things which can only be established subjectively. It is difficult to see how a partially subjective definition can be made to work in harness with the test which in all other respects is wholly objective.

If we are right that dishonesty is something in the mind of the accused (what Professor Glanville Williams calls 'a special mental state'), then if the mind of the accused is honest, it cannot be deemed dishonest merely because members of the jury would have regarded it as dishonest to embark on that course of conduct.

So we would reject the simple uncomplicated approach that the test is purely objective, however attractive from the practical point of view that solution may be.

There remains the objection that to adopt a subjective test is to abandon all standards but that of the accused himself, and to bring about a state of affairs in which 'Robin Hood would be no robber' (see *R v Greenstein*). This objection misunderstands the nature of the subjective test. It is no defence for a man to say, 'I knew that what I was doing is generally regarded as dishonest; but I do not regard it as dishonest myself. Therefore I am not guilty.' What he is, however, entitled to say is, 'I did not know that anybody would regard what I was doing as dishonest.' He may not be believed; just as he may not be believed if he sets up 'a claim of right' under s2(1) of the 1968 Act, or asserts that he believed in the truth of a misrepresentation under s 15 of the 1968 Act [the deception offence that has now been repealed]. But if he is believed, or raises a real doubt about the matter, the jury cannot be sure that he was dishonest.

In determining whether the prosecution has proved that the defendant was acting dishonestly, a jury must first of all decide whether according to the ordinary standards of reasonable and honest people what was done was dishonest. If it was not dishonest by those standards, that is the end of the matter and the prosecution fails. If it was dishonest by those standards, then the jury must consider whether the defendant himself must have realised that what he was doing was by those standards dishonest. In most cases, where the actions are obviously dishonest by ordinary standards, there will be no doubt about it. It will be obvious that the defendant himself knew that he was acting dishonestly. It is dishonest for a defendant to act in a way which he knows ordinary people consider to be dishonest, even if he asserts or genuinely believes that he is morally justified in acting as he did.

For example, Robin Hood or those ardent anti-vivisectionists who remove animals from vivisection laboratories are acting dishonestly, even though they may consider themselves to be morally justified in doing what they do, because they know that ordinary people would consider these actions to be dishonest.

Cases which might be described as borderline, such as *Boggeln v Williams* [1978] 2 All ER 1061, [1978] 1 WLR 873, will depend on the view taken by the jury whether the defendant may have believed what he was doing was in accordance with the ordinary man's idea of honesty. A jury might have come to the conclusion that the defendant in that case was disobedient or impudent, but not dishonest in what he did.

So far as the present case is concerned, it seems to us that once the jury had rejected the defendant's account in respect of each count in the indictment (as they plainly did), the finding of dishonesty was inevitable, whichever of the tests of dishonesty was applied. If the judge had asked the jury to determine whether the defendant might have believed that what he did was in accordance with the ordinary man's idea of honesty, there could have only been one answer, and that is No, once the jury had rejected the defendant's explanation of what happened.

In so far as there was a misdirection on the meaning of dishonesty, it is plainly a case for the application of the proviso to s2(1) of the Criminal Appeal Act 1968 [a power the Court of Appeal previously held to uphold a conviction despite finding errors at trial].

This appeal is accordingly dismissed.

Appeal dismissed

Ghosh clarifies the earlier law in some respects—it confirms that the test is subjective—but it still leaves the jury to determine as a matter of fact (a) whether D's conduct would be regarded as dishonest by the ordinary standards of reasonable and honest people; and (b) whether D was aware that it would be regarded as dishonest by those standards (not by his own standards).

The Court of Appeal considered the concept of dishonesty in the relatively recent case of *Hayes* [2015] EWCA Crim 1944. D was a trader in an investment bank who was convicted of committing conspiracy to defraud for manipulating the LIBOR rate, which is the interest which banks can charge on commercial loans. As already mentioned, one of the elements of the offence of conspiracy to defraud is dishonesty, which is defined with reference to the test described in *Ghosh*. D appealed his conviction. It was argued on D's behalf that the trial judge had misdirected the jury in relation to the first (objective) limb of the *Ghosh* test. More specifically, it was argued that the trial judge was wrong to direct the jury, when considering whether D's actions would be considered dishonest according to the ordinary standards of reasonable and honest people, to disregard the evidence that was adduced of the market practice that prevailed in banks at the time of D's conduct. In rejecting this argument and upholding the validity of the trial judge's direction, the Court of Appeal held that:

29. The first limb sets out the objective standard or the standards of ordinary and reasonable people. The submission made on behalf of the appellant was that although there was no dispute that an objective standard had to be determined, it was right that it should be determined by taking into account the standards of the market. It is clear therefore in our view that the only purpose of arguing that the evidence to which we have referred was relevant, was that the jury would be asked to set an objective standard for a market or a group of traders (whatever that standard might be) and not the ordinary standards of honest and reasonable people.

...

32. Not only is there is no authority for the proposition that objective standards of honesty are to be set by a market, but such a principle would gravely affect the proper conduct of business. The history of the markets have shown that, from time to time, markets adopt patterns of behaviour which are dishonest by the standards of honest and reasonable people; in such cases, the market has simply abandoned ordinary standards of honesty. Each of the members of this court has seen

such cases and the damage caused when a market determines its own standards of honesty in this way. Therefore to depart from the view that standards of honesty are determined by the standards of ordinary reasonable and honest people is not only unsupported by authority, but would undermine the maintenance of ordinary standards of honesty and integrity that are essential to the conduct of business and markets.

By confirming the validity of the trial judge's direction in relation to the first limb, it has been argued that the court has curtailed the discretion *Ghosh* was intended to afford juries.

N. Dent and A. Kervick, '*Ghosh*: A Change in Direction?'
[2016] Crim LR 553

The concern is that where prosecutions for dishonesty offences are brought against members of a particular trade, industry or profession and where the defendant asserts that they did not consider that what they were doing was dishonest (because it was common practice within their field), the court may be invited by the prosecution to give a modified *Ghosh* direction, as the trial judge did in *Hayes*. By judicially indicating what must not be taken into account when formulating a test on dishonesty, the jury are potentially placed in a straightjacket, devoid of the very latitude that they have hitherto been expected to exercise. This contrasts with the usual assumption that juries are inherently better placed to reach this determination on moral issues than the bench.

≋ **Question**

Should juries have regard to the common practices of a certain trade, industry or profession when considering the objective limb of the *Ghosh* test?

K. Campbell, 'The Test of Dishonesty in *Ghosh*' (1994) 43 CLJ 349, cogently argues that the second limb of the *Ghosh* test is superfluous if under the first limb the jury is properly directed to take account of all the circumstances. Taking the oft-quoted example of D who fails to pay a travel fare because he is new to the country and is accustomed to free public transport, it should not be necessary to rely on the second limb to conclude that D is not dishonest. A properly directed jury would so conclude under the first limb. Campbell suggests that if the aim is to provide this hybrid test it should be: whether a reasonable jury, applying ordinary standards of honesty, is prepared to excuse D's failure to recognize that his own behaviour would be regarded as dishonest by the standards of ordinary people.

≋ **Question**

Would Campbell's suggestion be an improvement on *Ghosh*?

In *Peters v R* [1998] HCA 7, D was convicted of conspiracy to defraud and the High Court of Australia, the highest court in Australia, had to decide whether the trial judge was correct to direct the jury in accordance with the *Ghosh* test. The *Ghosh* test had earlier been rejected by the Supreme Court of Victoria in the case of *Salvo* [1980] VR 401. In that case, the court held that dishonesty meant that D had obtained the property 'without any belief that he has in law the right to deprive the other of it'. D's contention was that the jury ought to have been directed in accordance with that subjective test. In rejecting the *Ghosh* test, Toohey and Gaudron JJ stated:

Dishonesty

15. There is a degree of incongruity in the notion that dishonesty is to be determined by reference to the current standards of ordinary, honest persons and the requirement that it be determined by asking whether the act in question was dishonest by those standards and, if so, whether the accused must have known that that was so. That incongruity comes about because ordinary, honest person determine whether a person's act is dishonest by reference to that person's knowledge or belief as to some fact relevant to the act in question or the intention with which the act was done. They do not ask whether he or she must be taken to have realised that the act was dishonest by the standards of ordinary, honest persons. Thus, for example, the ordinary person considers it dishonest to assert as true something that is known to be false. And the ordinary person does so simply because the person making the statement knows it to be false, not because he or she must be taken to have realised that it was dishonest by the current standards or ordinary, honest persons.

16. There are also practical difficulties involved in the *Ghosh* test. Those difficulties arise because, in most cases where honesty is in issue, the real question is whether an act was done with knowledge or belief of some specific thing or with some specific intent, not whether it is properly characterised as dishonest. To take a simple example: there is ordinarily no question whether the making of a false statement with intent to deprive another of his property is dishonest. Rather, the question is usually whether the statement was made with knowledge of its falsity and with intent to deprive. Of course, there may be unusual cases in which there is a question whether an act done with knowledge of some matter or with some particular intention is dishonest. Thus, for example, there may be a real question whether it is dishonest, in the ordinary sense, for a person to make a false statement with intent to obtain stolen property from a thief and return it to its true owner.

17. The practical difficulties with the *Ghosh* test arise both in the ordinary case where the question is whether an act was done with knowledge or belief of some specific matter or with some specific intent and in the unusual case where the question is whether an act done with some particular knowledge, belief or intent is to be characterised as dishonest. In the ordinary case, the *Ghosh* test distracts from the true factual issue to be determined; in the unusual case, it conflates what really are two separate questions, namely, whether they are satisfied beyond reasonable doubt that the accused had the knowledge, belief or intention which the prosecution alleges and, if so, whether, on that account, the act is to be characterised as dishonest. In either case, the test is likely to confuse rather than assist in deciding whether an act was or was not done dishonestly.

A *Ghosh* direction on dishonesty is not necessary in every case. If D claims that his appropriation of property was not dishonest because he believed that he had in law the right to deprive the other of it, or because he believed the owner would consent, or he believed the owner could not be traced by taking reasonable steps (these are all cases falling within the partial definition in s 2), then the only issue for the jury or magistrates is whether he did so genuinely believe. Or D may claim that he took the goods (a book from a bookshop, say) absent-mindedly and had no intention to steal. In such cases a *Ghosh* direction would be inapt and, indeed, misleading.

The Criminal Law Revision Committee, the body responsible for the Theft Act 1968, said that dishonesty is 'something which laymen can easily recognize when they see it'.

≋ *Questions*
(1) Can you easily recognize dishonesty when you see it? Do you think that you would always agree with your friends on what is and what is not dishonest? If not, is it satisfactory to settle the matter by vote after discussion which is presumably what a jury would do where opinions differ?
(2) Is dishonesty really an element of mens rea or a defence?

The Law Commission in Consultation Paper No 155, *Legislating the Criminal Code: Fraud and Deception* (1999) provisionally took the view that a Home Secretary could not safely be advised to make a statement of compatibility in relation to a Bill creating a general dishonesty offence. The Commission resiled from that view in its Report No 276, *Fraud* (2002).

The present law under *Ghosh* has its critics (see eg E. J. Griew, *Dishonesty and the Jury* (1974) and 'Dishonesty, the Objections to *Feely* and *Ghosh*' [1985] Crim LR 341; and D. W. Elliott, 'Dishonesty in Theft: A Dispensable Concept' [1982] Crim LR 395); but it also has its defenders (see A. Samuels's book review of *Dishonesty and the Jury* [1974] Crim LR 493; R. Tur, 'Dishonesty and the Jury Question' in A. Phillips Griffiths (ed), *Philosophy and Practice* (1985).

E. J. Griew, 'Dishonesty, the Objections to *Feely* and *Ghosh*'
[1985] Crim LR 341

A1. More, longer and more difficult trials

If the law is right in principle, so be it; the fact that it tends to multiply and prolong trials cannot be a decisive objection. But as an addition to other objections it is of such practical importance that it should have pride of place. There are several distinct points.

(a) The question tends to increase the number of trials. Whereas a different approach to the dishonesty issue might make clear that given conduct was dishonest as a matter of law and therefore constituted an offence, the *Feely* question leaves the issue open. It may be worth a defendant's while to take his chance with the jury. . . . Defences such as these provide ground for a contest where, before *Feely*, the defendants might have felt constrained to plead guilty.

(b) The question tends to complicate and lengthen contested cases. For it is difficult to say of any evidence relating to the defendant's state of mind or to the special circumstances in which he acted that it is irrelevant to the *Feely* issue. Moreover, it must be in the interests of some defendants to extend and complicate trials in order to obfuscate the issue. This point is shortly stated but is surely of considerable importance.

(c) At the end of a trial the jury may have to be asked not simply whether the defendant acted with the state of mind he claims to have had, or in other circumstances that, as he suggests, may have rendered his act not dishonest, but also (if he may have done so) whether his act with that state of mind, or in those circumstances, was dishonest according to ordinary standards. If these matters are not kept separate the jury may be seriously misled. But their careful separation shows the complexity of the direction that the *Feely* question will dictate in some cases. Nor can that question be avoided even if a conclusion on it adverse to the defendant is the only one that a jury acting reasonably can reach. The matter must be left to the jury to determine. . . .

(d) The separate matters just referred to, that may need to figure in the judge's direction, must then be handled by the jury in their deliberations. They may find them hard to keep separate. The issues we present to juries should be as simple as possible; jury service, after all, imposes tasks on ordinary people that they are not accustomed to discharge. The *Feely* question involves complications that we are not justified in supposing that all jurors are competent to handle.

A2. Inconsistent decisions

The *Feely* question carries an unacceptable risk of inconsistency of decision. This objection has been voiced by many critics. The problem of inconsistency is likely, of course, to affect only a small proportion of cases. In most cases the issue is one as to the facts: what did D do? what was his state of mind? Once the facts are found there will usually be only one plausible answer to the *Feely* question. It is only in a minority of cases that the matter will truly admit of argument. But within this crucial marginal group different juries, as the presumptive embodiment of ordinary decent standards, may take different views of essentially indistinguishable cases. The law of the relevant offence will then vary as between different defendants. This must be unacceptable.

A3. Fiction of community norms

The *Feely* question implies the existence of a relevant community norm. In doing so it glosses over differences of age, class and cultural background which combine to give the character of fiction to the idea of a generally shared sense of the boundary between honesty and dishonesty. This is the more obvious in a society with the range of cultural groups that ours now has; and it is the more relevant since jury service was extended to the generality of electors between 18 and 65. [Note this has since been extended further.] It is simply naive to suppose—surely no one does suppose—that there is, in respect of the dishonesty question, any such single thing as 'the standards of ordinary decent people.' Although most people will unite in condemning, or in tolerating, some forms of behaviour, there are others as to which considerable divergence of view will exist. How juries cope with this obvious difficulty we do not know. Presumably some acquittals derive from the triumph of the most relaxed standard represented on the jury. The present objection is not to outcomes, however, but to the illegitimacy of the stated test as resting disreputably on a reference to a fictitious category.

A4. 'Dishonestly' as an 'ordinary word'

The foregoing objection to the *Feely* question is closely related to another. The jury are to consult their sense of ordinary standards because the word 'dishonestly' is 'in common use.' Jurors in their own lives 'have to decide what is and what is not dishonest'; they do not 'require the help of a judge to tell them what amounts to dishonesty.' For 'the meaning of an ordinary word of the English language is not a question of law.' This is the heart of the reasoning in *Feely*. The premise is that the issue is a semantic one; whether the defendant acted 'dishonestly' depends upon what 'dishonestly' means.

The conclusion is that the issue requires the application of ordinary 'standards.' Between the premise and the conclusion lies the proposition that the meaning of the word 'dishonestly' will be found by a reference to standards. This silent step in the argument is itself interesting but is not of present concern. What must be expressed here is a doubt about the 'ordinary word.' It simply does not follow from the truth that a word such as 'dishonestly' is an ordinary word that all speakers of the language share the same sense of its application or non-application in particular contexts. Once again, it is to the marginal case, where the issue is live and crucial, that this common sense objection particularly applies. Even judges, a relatively homogeneous group of uniformly high linguistic competence, have been known to differ on the application of the epithet 'dishonest' in a marginal case. It is not acceptable that the meaning of 'dishonestly' should be 'whatever in a particular case it conveys to the mind or minds of the tribunal of fact without any instruction as to the meaning . . .'

A5. Specialised cases

The *Feely* question is in any case unsuitable where the context of the case is a specialised one, involving intricate financial activities or dealings in a specialised market. It is neither reasonable nor rational to expect ordinary people to judge as 'dishonest' or 'not dishonest' conduct of which, for want of relevant experience, they cannot appreciate the contextual flavour. Their answer to the *Feely* question ought sometimes to be that ordinary people have no standards in relation to the conduct in question. Juries do not reply in this rebellious way. Again, we do not know how they cope. Perhaps in some cases they take their cue from the fact of prosecution ('the prosecution are sure it was dishonest; of course the defendant says it was not!') or from the evidence of witnesses who do understand the context; but then they are not applying the *Feely* test. Perhaps in others they acquit because, perforce, they are not satisfied that the arcane activities of which they have heard offend against 'ordinary' standards; and then the test may produce a pernicious result.

A6. Ordinary dishonest jurors

The general understanding is that the jury may be taken to represent the 'ordinary decent people' to whom the *Feely* question refers. That is why, without incurring the disapproval of the Court of Appeal either in his own case or in *Ghosh*, the trial judge in *Greenstein* spoke to the jury of their 'applying [their] own standards.' Yet a vast number of what must surely be theft, handling and minor fraud offences are committed by 'ordinary,' even 'ordinary decent,' people such as serve upon juries: theft at work ('perks'), handling stolen goods being offered in the neighbourhood ('from off the back of a lorry'), inflation of expenses claims, inaccuracy or concealment in the income tax return. These ordinary people, as jurors, will either apply their own standards, as being the prevalent standards of which they know; or they will demand of their defendants higher standards than they themselves attain. To the extent (if at all) that the former occurs, the Court of Appeal in *Feely* and *Ghosh* will have achieved a reduction in the scope of dishonesty offences which it certainly did not intend. We ought not, on the other hand, to view the latter, presumably more common, occurrence with complacency. It is perfectly acceptable for the law to require a jury to apply a standard higher than its own; it is not acceptable that the law should invite a jury to impose such a standard by an act of creative hypocrisy. The law in effect expects many jurors, in relation to very common kinds of offences, to have one conception of ordinary standards outside court and another conception inside. This is disreputable.

A7. 'Anarchic' verdicts

The *Feely* question, offered without qualification to the jury, is 'a question of moral estimation without guidelines' and permits ' "anarchic" verdicts which are not technically perverse'. A jury without stars or compass cannot be accused of bad navigation. The direction it takes may be deplorable but cannot be wrong. A consequence of this, it has been pointed out, is that members of unpopular groups may receive inadequate protection from the law. Nothing, in any case, can prevent a jury from refusing to convict where the victim of the theft or obtaining alleged is someone whom they regard as 'fair game.' Such a disregard of property rights is easier to achieve, however, if it does not involve rebellion against a judicial direction but can pass as the performance of the jury's own evaluative function.

A8. What is 'dishonest' should be a matter of law

Whether an individual defendant was dishonest is, of course, a question for the jury. But it should be so only in the sense that the jury will find the facts upon the strength of which, applying legal principles, they will be able to say whether the defendant acted dishonestly. Whether the facts that they find constitute a case of 'dishonesty' within the meaning of that word in the particular legal context is a matter of legal principle upon which they should be able to turn to the law for clear guidance.

. . .

A9. Dishonesty and defences

Leaving the dishonesty issue to the untutored application of community standards allows the issue a potentially unlimited function. The jury may be unwilling to condemn a defendant's conduct as 'dishonest' because they sympathise with his motive or are inclined to excuse what he did in the difficult circumstances in which he found himself; they may be still less willing if they are prepared to say that his conduct was justified in the circumstances. Thus the jury may create for their defendant a defence of necessity greater than any known to the law or a defence of pressure of circumstances where the law knows only a plea in mitigation. But the law of defences should develop in a disciplined way under judicial control, save indeed to the extent that it is statutorily defined.

The preceding paragraph assumes that a jury response such as sympathy with the defendant's motive or with his dilemma in an emergency is capable of affecting their judgment of his conduct as 'honest' or 'dishonest.' Similarly, a familiar objection to the *Ghosh* question (B5 below) assumes that it allows a defendant to claim that he did not know that his conduct would be regarded as 'dishonest' because he thought that right-thinking people would approve of it on moral grounds. These assumptions can be challenged. It may be said that sympathy with a motive, or an inclination to condone what is done in an emergency, has nothing to do with a judgment about honesty; that the question 'was it honest according to ordinary standards?' is a narrower question than 'was it justifiable or praise-worthy by ordinary standards?' That would, indeed, be a way of slightly limiting the mischief of *Feely* and *Ghosh*. The difficulty with it is that it would require an explanation to the jury of what is meant by 'dishonest' in the *Feely* question itself. But the jury do not need such an explanation; they know what the word means!

. . .

B. Objections to the *Ghosh* question

The second question is: Must the defendant have known that what he was doing was dishonest according to the standards of ordinary decent people?

B1. More, longer and more difficult trials

Compare objection A1. The *Ghosh* question (a) creates an additional ground for contested trials; (b) justifies the introduction of additional evidence; (c) further complicates the judge's direction; and (d) adds further to the complexity of the jury's task. There is no need to labour these points.

. . .

B3. Inept correction of error

Two cases after *Feely* had introduced reference to the question whether the defendant knew or believed that he was acting dishonestly (*Boggeln v Williams* [1978] 2 All ER 1061; *Landy* [1981] 1 All ER 1172). . . . *Ghosh* was an attempt to reintroduce order into a subject that had become inconsistent and confused. But the job was ineptly performed.

All that needed to be done was to point out that reference to the defendant's belief in the honesty of his own conduct was an inappropriate way of taking into account his 'state of mind.' It is true that, as the Court of Appeal has repeatedly asserted, proof of dishonesty requires reference to the defendant's state of mind. But it does so only in the sense that there must first be a finding as to whether he acted (or may have acted) with a belief (e.g. a claim of right), an intention (e.g. to take the valuable goods he has found to the police station) or an expectation (e.g. of an immediate power to repay) that is relevant under section 2(1) of the Theft Act 1968 or may be regarded by the jury as relevant to the *Feely* question. Once a relevant state of mind has been found, the only question remaining to be answered is whether section 2(1) or the jury's sense of ordinary decent standards makes the defendant's conduct with that state of mind dishonest. This is a question, not as to what state of mind the defendant had, but as to how that state of mind is to be characterised.

The confusion on this point in the *Ghosh* judgment is clear to see in the treatment of the hypothetical of a visitor from a foreign country where public transport is free. He travels on a bus without paying. Does he do so dishonestly? The court says that 'his conduct, judged objectively by what he has done, is dishonest.' The error enters the argument at this point. It cannot be right, as the structure of the court's argument plainly implies, that the visitor's conduct would be regarded as dishonest by ordinary decent standards. If the jury knew that he believed public transport to be free, they would say that, according to ordinary standards, he had not behaved dishonestly. There is no need to go further; his 'state of mind' has already been taken into account. But the court, having declared him dishonest when 'judged objectively,' has to introduce a further 'subjective' element to rescue him. That leads to the question: 'Did he know it was dishonest?'—an entirely unnecessary question.

B4. Mistake of law

The *Ghosh* question 'allows something like a mistake of law to be a defence.' The question is a mere addendum to the *Feely* question; it is the answer to the latter that determines the view to be taken of the defendant's conduct as in principle criminal. The jury's apprehension of current standards makes law for the case; the defendant's misapprehension of those standards is indeed 'something like a mistake of law.' It is not strictly one, of course; his failure to realise that ordinary people would call his conduct dishonest means (taking *Ghosh* literally) that it is not dishonest.

B5. The 'Robin Hood defence'

A person may defend his attack on another's property by reference to a moral or political conviction so passionately held that he believed (so he claims) that 'ordinary decent' members of society would regard his conduct as proper, even laudable. If the asserted belief is treated as a claim to have been ignorant that the conduct was 'dishonest' by ordinary standards (and it has been assumed that it might be so treated, and if the jury think (as exceptionally they might) that the belief may have been held, *Ghosh* produces an acquittal. The result is remarkable. Robin Hood must be a thief even if he thinks the whole of the right-thinking world is on his side.

B6. A further threat to standards

A person reared or moving in an environment in which it is generally regarded as legitimate to take advantage of certain classes of people—perhaps bookmakers or employers—may plausibly claim that he did not realise that his conduct, of which a member of such a class was a victim, was generally regarded as dishonest. It is not acceptable that a claim of that sort should be capable even of being advanced. It has been said that 'the [*Ghosh*] question presents an even greater threat to the standard of honesty than the [*Feely* question].'

≈ **Questions**

Do you find these criticisms convincing? Are there reported instances of juries struggling with the concept? If not, why not?

13.6.1 Reform of dishonesty

Would it be possible and desirable to enact an exhaustive definition of dishonesty? Suppose the partial definition in the 1968 Act had been made an exhaustive definition; would this adequately meet the case? Alternatively, consider a provision that a person appropriating property belonging to another *is* to be regarded as dishonest unless one of the three present exceptions applies—

or, (d) he intends to replace the property with an equivalent, having no doubt that no detriment whatever will be caused to the owner by the appropriation.

This would exempt the person who takes money from his employer's till, knowing that he is forbidden to do so, but intending, and having no doubt that he will be able, to replace it before it is missed. *Should* he be exempted from liability for theft?

A. Halpin, 'The Test for Dishonesty' [1996] Crim LR 283 at 294 suggests the following redefinition:

1. The treatment by a person of the property of another is to be regarded as dishonest where it is done without a belief that the other would consent to that treatment if he knew of all the circumstances, unless the person believes that the law permits that treatment of the property. 2. The treatment by a person of the property of another is not to be regarded as dishonest if done (otherwise than by a trustee or personal representative) in the belief that the person to whom the property belongs is unlikely to be discovered by taking reasonable steps.

More radically, D. W. Elliott ('Dishonesty in Theft: A Dispensable Concept' [1982] Crim LR 395 at 398) proposes dispensing with the word 'dishonestly' altogether and adding a new s 2(3): 'No appropriation of property belonging to another which is not detrimental to the interests of the other in a significant practical way shall amount to theft of the property.'

≋ *Questions*
Is this any improvement? D takes £20 from David Beckham's wallet. Theft? Would it matter if it was the only £20 in the wallet and Beckham could not get to an ATM?

Ghosh is not followed in most other common law jurisdictions. For example, when the Irish Law Reform Commission examined options for reforming the law it recommended defining dishonestly as, 'without a claim of right made in good faith'. The rationale for defining dishonestly was as follows: 'To by-pass the judge and leave the definition of fundamental legal concepts to the jury would be an unwarranted exercise in misguided populism.' Do you agree?

13.6.2 No requirement of intention to gain

Section 1(2) of the 1968 Act provides:

> It is immaterial whether the appropriation is made with a view to gain, or is made for the thief's own benefit.

This section is designed to deal with cases such as:

(1) D who takes V's original art work, leaving V the catalogue valuation price in cash. The fact that D paid is not determinative of his dishonesty;

(2) D the shop worker who charges his friend, E, for only some of the goods in E's trolley. The fact that the gain was for E does not prevent D being a thief; and

(3) D who throws V's iPhone off a cliff. D is guilty of theft notwithstanding the fact that he intends only to cause loss to V and not gain for himself or anyone else.

In *Wheatley and Penn v Commissioner of Police of the British Virgin Islands* [2006] UKPC 24, Lord Bingham observed that:

> It is certainly true that in most cases of theft there will be an original owner of money or goods who will be poorer because of the defendant's conduct. But in one of the two cases in *R v Morris* the defendant was arrested before paying the reduced price for the goods, so that the supermarket suffered no loss [section 13.3, p 348], and in *R (on the application of A) v Snaresbrook Crown Court* [2001] All ER (D) 123, para 25, it was accepted that the alleged theft was carried out for a purpose which could financially benefit the company. In providing that an appropriation may be dishonest even where there is a willingness to pay, [the section] shows that the prospect of loss is not determinative of dishonesty.

13.7 Intention permanently to deprive

The offence of theft can be committed irrespective of whether V is permanently deprived of his property. What matters is not that there is a permanent deprivation, but that D *intends* that V will be permanently deprived of the property.

In the ordinary run of cases the issue presents no problems. If D takes V's book he is a thief if he intends to keep it but guilty of no offence if he intends to restore it to V.

But some cases are not quite so ordinary. Several problematical situations had arisen under the old law and the 1968 Act sought to provide for them:

(1) cases where D borrowed V's property in such circumstances as to amount to a permanent deprivation;

(2) cases in which D took V's property and offered to sell it back to V;

(3) cases in which D took V's property and provided him with a means of recovering it (eg sending him the pawn ticket); and

(4) cases where D returned the property to V with all its goodness gone (eg returning V's batteries once flat).

The CLRC was firm in its view that, special instances apart, dishonest borrowing should not in general be an offence and accordingly retained in the definition of theft the requirement for an intention permanently to deprive as had always been the case with its predecessor, the offence of larceny. The CLRC, however, proposed no elaboration of the words 'with the intention of permanently depriving the other of it' and seems to have assumed that the expression would be interpreted as it had been under the earlier law. But someone always knows, or claims to know, better and s 6 was added to the CLRC's Bill.

Theft Act 1968, s 6

6. 'With the intention of permanently depriving the other of it'

(1) A person appropriating property belonging to another without meaning the other permanently to lose the thing itself is nevertheless to be regarded as having the intention of permanently depriving the other of it if his intention is to treat the thing as his own to dispose of regardless of the other's rights; and a borrowing or lending of it may amount to so treating it if, but only if, the borrowing or lending is for a period and in circumstances making it equivalent to an outright taking or disposal.

(2) Without prejudice to the generality of subsection (1) above, where a person, having possession or control (lawfully or not) of property belonging to another, parts with the property under a condition as to its return which he may not be able to perform, this (if done for purposes of his own and without the other's authority) amounts to treating the property as his own to dispose of regardless of the other's rights.

See on s 6 generally, J. R. Spencer, 'The Metamorphosis of Section 6 of the Theft Act' [1977] Crim LR 653.

13.7.1 Interpreting s 6

Academic analysis of the section was highly critical, regarding it as confusing and obscure. The courts soon came to agree.

R v Lloyd

[1985] EWCA Crim 1, Court of Appeal, Criminal Division

(Lord Lane CJ, Farquharson and Tudor Price JJ)

The appellant, a projectionist at a cinema, removed films which were to be shown at the cinema and took them to his accomplices who made a master videotape from which they were able to reproduce large numbers of copies. The films were out of the possession of the owners for only a few hours. The aim was to sell the copies to the great advantage of the accomplices and financial detriment of the owners. The appellant was convicted of conspiracy to steal.

Lord Lane CJ:

The trial judge issued his certificate by posing the following question:

> 'Whether the offence of conspiracy to steal is committed when persons dishonestly agree to take a film from a cinema without authority intending it should be returned within a few hours but knowing that many hundreds of copies will be subsequently made and that the value of the film so returned will thereby be substantially reduced?'

The complaint by the appellants is this, that the judge misdirected the jury first of all in leaving the question for them to decide whether the removal of a film in these circumstances could amount to theft, and secondly, in allowing them to consider s6(1) of the Theft Act 1968 as being relevant at all in the circumstances of this case.

The point is a short one. It is not a simple one. It is not without wider importance, because if the judge was wrong in leaving the matter in the way in which he did for the jury to consider, it might mean, as we understand it, that the only offence of which a person in these circumstances could be convicted would be a conspiracy to commit a breach of the Copyright Act 1956. At the time when this particular case was being tried, the maximum penalties available for the substantive offence under the Copyright Act were minimal. Those penalties have now been increased by the provisions of the Copyright (Amendment) Act 1983, and in the light of that Act it can be said that, although Parliament perhaps has not entirely caught up with this type of prevalent pirating offence, it is at least gaining on it. [NB: the copyright offences have since been substituted in more recent legislation.]

We turn now to the provisions of the Theft Act 1968, the conspiracy alleged being a breach of that particular Act. Section 1(1) of the 1968 Act provides:

[His lordship read s 1(1). See section 13.2, p 345.]

On that wording alone these appellants were not guilty of theft or of conspiracy to steal. The success of their scheme and their ability to act with impunity in a similar fashion in the future, depended, as we have already said, on their ability to return the film to its rightful place in the hands of the Odeon cinema at Barking as rapidly as possible, so that its absence should not be noticed. Therefore the intention of the appellants could more accurately be described as an intention temporarily to deprive the owner of the film and was indeed the opposite of an intention permanently to deprive.

What then was the basis of the prosecution case and the basis of the judge's direction to the jury? It is said that s 6(1) of the Theft Act 1968 brings such actions as the appellants performed here within the provisions of s 1. The judge left the matter to the jury on the basis that they had to decide whether the words of s6(1) were satisfied by the prosecution or not. Section 6(1) reads as follows:

> 'A person appropriating property belonging to another without meaning the other permanently to lose the thing itself is nevertheless to be regarded as having the intention of permanently depriving the other of it if his intention is to treat the thing as his own to dispose of regardless of the other's rights; and a borrowing or lending of it may amount to so treating it if, but only if, the borrowing or lending is for a period.'

That section has been described by J. R. Spencer in 'The Metamorphosis of Section 6 of the Theft Act' [1977] Crim LR 653 as a section which 'sprouts obscurities at every phrase', and we are inclined to agree with him. It is abstruse. But it must mean, if nothing else, that there are circumstances in which a defendant may be deemed to have the intention permanently to deprive, even though he may intend the owner eventually to get back the object which has been taken . . .

[Counsel for D referred to a number of past authorities.]

In general we take the same view as Professor Griew in his book *The Theft Acts 1968 and 1978* (4th edn, 1982) para 2-73, namely that s 6 should be referred to in exceptional cases only. In the vast majority of cases it need not be referred to or considered at all.

Deriving assistance from another distinguished academic writer, namely Professor Glanville Williams, we would like to cite with approval the following passage from his *Textbook of Criminal Law* (2nd edn, 1983) p 719:

'In view of the grave difficulties of interpretation presented by section 6, a trial judge would be well advised not to introduce it to the jury unless he reaches the conclusion that it will assist them, and even then (it may be suggested) the question he leaves to the jury should not be worded in terms of the generalities of the subsection but should reflect those generalities as applied to the alleged facts. For example, the question might be: "Did the defendant take the article, intending that the owner should have it back only on making a payment? If so, you would be justified as a matter of law in finding that he intended to deprive the owner permanently of his article, because the taking of the article with that intention is equivalent to an outright taking."'

Bearing in mind the observations of Edmund Davies LJ in *R v Warner* (1970) 55 Cr App R 93, [1971] Crim LR 114, we would try to interpret s 6 in such a way as to ensure that nothing is construed as an intention permanently to deprive which would not prior to the 1968 Act have been so construed. Thus the first part of s 6(1) seems to us to be aimed at the sort of case where a defendant takes things and then offers them back to the owner for the owner to buy if he wishes. If the taker intends to return them to the owner only on such payment, then, on the wording of s 6(1), that is deemed to amount to the necessary intention permanently to deprive: see for instance *R v Hall* (1849) 1 Den 381, 169 ER 291, where the defendant took fat from a candlemaker and then offered it for sale to the owner. His conviction for larceny was affirmed. There are other cases of similar intent. For instance. I have taken your valuable painting. You can have it back on payment to me of £X,000. If you are not prepared to make that payment, then you are not going to get your painting back.

It seems to us that in this case we are concerned with the second part of s 6(1), namely the words after the semi-colon: 'and a borrowing or lending of it may amount to so treating it if, but only if, the borrowing or lending is for a period and in circumstances making it equivalent to an outright taking or disposal.'

These films, it could be said, were borrowed by Lloyd from his employers in order to enable him and the others to carry out their 'piracy' exercise.

Borrowing is ex hypothesi not something which is done with an intention permanently to deprive. This half of the subsection, we believe, is intended to make it clear that a mere borrowing is never enough to constitute the necessary guilty mind unless the intention is to return the 'thing' in such a changed state that it can truly be said that all its goodness or virtue has gone. For example *R v Beecham* (1851) 5 Cox CC 181, where the defendant stole railway tickets intending that they should be returned to the railway company in the usual way only after the journeys had been completed. He was convicted of larceny. The judge in the present case gave another example, namely the taking of a torch battery with intention of returning it only when its power is exhausted.

That being the case, we turn to inquire whether the feature films in this case can fall within this category. Our view is that they cannot. The goodness, the virtue, the practical value of the films to the owners has not gone out of the article. The film could still be projected to paying audiences, and, had everything gone according to the conspirators' plans, would have been projected in the ordinary way to audiences at the Odeon cinema, Barking, who would have paid for their seats. Our view is that those particular films which were the subject of this alleged conspiracy had not themselves diminished in value at all. What had happened was that the borrowed film had been used or was going to be used to perpetrate a copyright swindle on the owners whereby their commercial interests were grossly and adversely affected in the way that we have endeavoured to describe at the outset of this judgment. The borrowing, it seems to us, was not for a period, or in such circumstances, as made it equivalent to an outright taking or disposal. There was still virtue in the film.

For those reasons we think that the submissions of counsel for the appellants on this aspect of the case are well founded. Accordingly, the way in which the trial judge directed the jury was mistaken, and accordingly this conviction of conspiracy to steal must be quashed . . .

Appeals allowed. Convictions quashed

In *Warner* (referred to in *Lloyd*), D removed a toolbox from V's workshop next door and when questioned by the police denied that he had taken it. There had been some ill-feeling between D and V concerning the parking of cars and D later said that it was his intention to return the toolbox and that he told lies to the police because he had panicked. It was held that the trial judge had misdirected the jury in saying that D could be convicted of theft if his intention was that V should lose the use of his tools indefinitely.

≈≈≈ **Question**
Consider *Oxford v Moss*, section 13.4.2, p 360. Was not the borrowing of the paper equivalent to an outright taking in that the examination paper, once its contents were disclosed, was valueless to the university?

In *Bagshaw* [1988] Crim LR 321, CA, D was charged with the theft of gas cylinders and claimed that he had borrowed them. His conviction for stealing the cylinders was quashed because the trial judge had not properly explained to the jury that D could be convicted only if he intended to retain the cylinders until all their 'goodness' had gone. But was all their goodness gone by the use of the gas they contained? D was not charged with the theft of the gas (and to such a charge he would appear to have had no defence) but with stealing the cylinders. If the cylinders could be refilled with gas, was all—or any—of their goodness gone?

A person borrows property when he intends to return that property. This is not the same thing as restoring its equivalent. D, short of money to buy his lunch, 'borrows' money from the petty cash float in his employer's office which he intends to repay with an equivalent amount at a later stage. D may have a defence to a charge of theft in that he is not acting dishonestly but he cannot claim that he has not deprived his employer permanently of the money (ie those pound coins) which he has taken: *Velumyl* [1989] Crim LR 299, CA.

In *Marshall* [2000] EWCA Crim 3530, [1999] Crim LR 317, the defendants were observed obtaining underground tickets or travel cards from members of the public passing through the barriers, and reselling them to other potential customers. Mantell LJ said at 287:

It is submitted [s 6(1)] . . . is to be construed narrowly and confined to the sort of case of which Lord Lane gave an example and of which the present is not one. However, this Court had to consider a similar situation in the case of *Fernandes* [1996] 1 Cr App Rep 175 where at p 188 Auld LJ giving the judgment of the Court said this:

'In our view section 6(1), which is expressed in general terms, is not limited in its application to the illustrations given by Lord Lane CJ in *Lloyd*. Nor in saying that in most cases it would be unnecessary to refer to the provision, did Lord Lane suggest it should be so limited. The critical notion, stated expressly in the first limb and incorporated by reference in the second is, whether a defendant intended to "treat the thing as his own to dispose of regardless of the other's rights." The second limb of subsection (1) and also subsection (2) are merely specific illustrations of the application of that notion. We consider that section 6 may apply to a person in possession or

> control of another's property who, dishonestly and for his own purpose, deals with that property in such a manner that he knows he is risking its loss.'
>
> In our judgment and following *Fernandes* the subsection is not to be given the restricted interpretation for which the appellants contend.
>
> The principal submission put forward on behalf of the appellants is that the issuing of the ticket is analogous to the drawing of a cheque in that in each instance a *chose in action* is created which in the first case belongs to the customer and in the second to the payee. So by parity of reasoning with that advanced by Lord Goff in *R v Preddy* [section 13.5.2, p 364], the property acquired belonged to the customer and not London Underground Limited and there can have been no intention on the part of the appellant to deprive London Underground Limited of the ticket which would in due course be returned to the possession of London Underground Limited. Attractive though the submission appears at first blush we do not think that it can possibly be correct.
>
> 'A "*chose in action*" is a known legal expression used to describe all personal rights of property which can only be claimed or enforced by action, and not by taking physical possession.' (See *Torkington v Magee* [1902] 2 KB 427, per Channell J at p 430.) On the issuing of an underground ticket a contract is created between London Underground Limited and the purchaser. Under that contract each party has rights and obligations. Theoretically those rights are enforceable by action. Therefore, it is arguable, we suppose, that by the transaction each party has acquired a *chose in action*. On the side of the purchaser it is represented by a right to use the ticket to the extent which it allows travel on the underground system. On the side of London Underground Limited it encompasses the right to insist that the ticket is used by no one other than the purchaser. It is that right which is disregarded when the ticket is acquired by the appellant and sold on. But here the charges were in relation to the tickets and travel cards themselves and a ticket form or travel card and, dare we say, a cheque form is not a *chose in action*. The fact that the ticket form or travel card may find its way back into the possession of London Underground Limited, albeit with its usefulness or 'virtue' exhausted, is nothing to the point. Section 6(1) prevails for the reasons we have given.

Preddy decided that, because the thing in action represented by the cheque never belonged to anyone but the defendant, *the cheque* could not be stolen or obtained by him. Was the court right to reject the argument that the same principle must apply to the tickets? The cheque and the ticket are both pieces of paper which, when given for consideration, create and represent a thing in action: the right to receive the amount of money for which the cheque is drawn and the right to travel to the named destination, or to enjoy some other service. In both cases, the thing in action belongs not to the drawer or supplier, V, but to the recipient, D. In neither case can D be guilty of the offence of obtaining *the thing in action* from V, or stealing it from him for that thing never is, nor could be, property belonging to V. The court did not explain what is the difference between the two pieces of paper. One possible difference is that the ticket continues (because an operative condition on it so provides) to belong to the company, V, throughout, whereas the cheque form belongs to the payee, D, when it is delivered to him. D can lawfully burn it or tear it up if he wants to. But is that a material difference? In the cheque case envisaged in *Preddy*, the cheque form belonged to V at the critical moment—the instant before it was delivered to D. The instant of delivery is the time when theft is committed. The paper on which both the cheque and the ticket are printed is considered to be the property of V at the moment of the alleged theft.

≈≈ *Questions*

What then is the material difference, if any, between the cheque and the ticket? If the cheque is not stolen, as *Preddy* decides, is the ticket?

13.7.2 Intention

D must *intend* permanent deprivation. Suppose D takes V's car in London which he later abandons in Leeds. D realizes that the car may be restored to V but it is a matter of indifference to him whether it is or not. Does D *intend* permanently to deprive V? (Might he be said to be reckless?) Can it be said that he has treated the car as his own 'to dispose of regardless of the other's rights' and this is 'in circumstances making it equivalent to an outright taking or disposal'? As the next case demonstrates, ascertaining whether D intended to deprive V *permanently* of the property can prove difficult.

R v Mitchell
[2008] EWCA Crim 850, Court of Appeal, Criminal Division

(Rix LJ, David Clarke J and HHJ Stewart QC)

Mrs Davis, who was sitting in her husband's BMW late at night in a country lane in Essex, was physically attacked and thrown out of the car by a group of men who were in a car being pursued by the police. Mr Davis's BMW was driven off and was subsequently found an hour-and-three-quarters later, a few miles away with its hazard lights flashing. The men then took a Vauxhall Cavalier which they later left abandoned and burnt out. M, one of the four men involved, was convicted of robbery. He appealed against conviction.

[Rix LJ stated the facts and continued:]

11. . . . The question in this case was whether the facts laid by the prosecution established a case to go before the jury of violence in the pursuit of theft. Had there been an intention permanently to deprive Mr or Mrs Davis of ownership of the BMW?

[His lordship recited s 6 and continued:]

13. There has been some discussion in cases, as will be seen, as to whether s 6 waters down or extends or only exemplifies the underlying requirement for theft of an intention permanently to deprive. Taking the wording of s 6(1) by itself without regard to authority it would seem that there is the possibility of a s 6 intention, that is to say an intention to treat the thing as his own to dispose of regardless of the other's rights, as somewhat extending the intention permanently to deprive, because the section begins with the hypothesis that property belonging to another has been taken 'without meaning the other permanently to lose the thing itself'. Although those words carefully avoid the word 'intention', since the word 'meaning' is used instead, or the word 'deprived' since the word 'lose' is used instead, nevertheless it would appear that the purpose of the section is to render a Defendant to be regarded or deemed as having the necessary s 1 intention of permanently depriving the owner of his property if the s 6(1) intention is established. Having said that, we observe that the jurisprudence discusses the extent to which s 6 goes beyond the essential underlying intention of permanently depriving the owner of his property.

[His lordship referred to *R v Warner* (1970) 135 JP 199, 55 Cr App Rep 93, [1971] Crim LR 114 (section 13.7.1, p 384); *R v Lloyd and others* [1985] QB 829, [1985] 2 All ER 661, 149 JP 634 (section 13.7.1, p 381) and continued:]

21. The next case is *R v Coffey* [1987] Crim LR 498. That concerned the obtaining of machinery by a worthless cheque. The Defendant had obtained the machinery in order to put pressure upon someone with whom he had a dispute. The appeal was again allowed because the summing-up was defective but in the course of this court's judgment it was observed that this was one of those rare cases where s 6(1) could usefully be deployed before the jury, but the jury should have been invited to consider whether the taking of the machinery in the circumstances obtaining in that case was equivalent to an outright taking or disposal.

22. In *R v Cahill* [1993] Crim LR 141 a package of newspapers had been taken by the Defendant and, he said, put outside the front door of a friend of his as a joke. Section 6(1) had been brought into play at the trial but in summing up the matter to the jury the recorder in that case had dropped from his directions the statutory words in their place 'to dispose of'. That was held to be a misdirection because this court approved what Professor Smith had said of those words in his book on *The Law of Theft* as follows:

'The attribution of an ordinary meaning to the language of section 6 presents some difficulties. It is submitted, however, that an intention merely to use the thing as one's own is not enough and that 'dispose of' is not used in the sense in which a general might 'dispose of' his forces but rather in the meaning given by the Shorter Oxford dictionary: To deal with definitely; to get rid of; to get done with, finish. To make over by way of sale or bargain, sell.'

So that appeal was allowed as well. A note by Professor Smith followed the extract of that report by way of commentary. Professor Smith pointed out that that case could have been dealt with without mentioning s 6 at all since the question was 'Did the Defendant intend the package of newspapers to be lost to the newsagent forever?'— as might well have been the case where that package had disappeared to some strange doorstep. If, however, s 6 was to be invoked at all, the question would be whether the virtue had gone out of the thing, even if the Defendant had believed that the newsagent would get his papers back the following day, but at a time when they would be quite useless to him. So upon that basis s 6 might have been correctly deployed.

23. Finally, in *R v Fernandes* [1996] 1 Cr App Rep 175 this jurisprudence was revisited in the context of a case where a solicitor had invested client's money at his disposal in his colleague's back street money-lending business where it was lost. It was argued that s 6 should not have been deployed in that case. But in his judgment Auld LJ accepted that this was a case of proper use of it, saying at 188E:

'We consider that section 6 may apply to a person in possession or control of another's property who, dishonestly and for his own purpose, deals with that property in such a manner that he knows he is risking its loss.

In the circumstances alleged here, an alleged dishonest disposal of someone else's money on an obviously insecure investment, we consider that the judge was justified in referring to section 6. His direction, looked at as a whole, did not water down the requirement that the jury should be sure of an intention permanently to deprive as illustrated by that provision.'

24. It is in the light of that jurisprudence that we have to consider the ruling of the judge on the application of no case to answer. What was said to the judge was that in the circumstances of this case there was no intention permanently to deprive Mr or Mrs Davis of their BMW, nor was there an intention within s 6, which the prosecution also relied upon, to treat the thing as the Defendant's own to dispose of regardless of the owner's rights. The car had only been driven for a few miles before being abandoned. The fact of abandonment showed that there was no intention permanently to deprive the owners of it or to dispose of it irrespective of the owner's rights. The judge, however, considered that there was either in the taking or in the use or in the abandonment of the vehicle evidence capable of amounting to a disposal under s 6(1). Of those three matters—the taking, the use and the abandonment—the judge in particular had emphasised the abandonment where he said 'It appears to me that abandonment in those circumstances might amount to a disposal. That is a matter which in my judgment should be decided by a jury.'

25. In our judgment the judge erred in these considerations. So far as the abandonment itself of the car was concerned, a matter which on this appeal Mr Jackson on behalf of the Crown has not relied upon, that of course operated as a factor in favour of the defence. Moreover, the fact that its hazard lights were left on emphasized that there was no intention to avoid drawing attention to the car. So far as the use of the vehicle is concerned, again a matter not relied upon on this appeal by Mr Jackson, its use amounted to being driven just a few miles before its abandonment. So far as the taking is

concerned, that was the one matter which Mr Jackson stressed in his submissions to the court. Those submissions proceeded in this way. When he was asked whether the red Fiesta, which was the car into which Mrs Davis' assailants had decamped from the BMW later that night, had been stolen Mr Jackson answered that question with the answer 'No'. He was then asked to state what the difference was between the taking of the Fiesta and the taking of the BMW. His first response was to say that the difference was the removal of Mrs Davis by force from the BMW and also the breaking of its windows. Subsequently in his submissions he abandoned the breaking of the windows as being a critical difference. Ultimately he took his stand upon the removal of Mrs Davis by force. This for him was the critical and distinguishing feature. This was the feature which showed that her assailants intended to treat the car as their own to dispose of regardless of the other's rights.

26. At some point during his submissions Mr Jackson, before being reminded of the words 'to dispose of', which Professor Smith had emphasised in his *Law of Theft* (see above) and which this court similarly picked up in *Cahill*, omitted those words and emphasised, as we can well understand him saying, that the treatment of Mrs Davis showed an intention to treat the BMW as the Defendant's own regardless of the other's rights (but omitting the words 'to dispose of'). Of course, everything about the taking and use of the BMW, like any car taken away without the owner's authority, indicates an intention to treat such a car regardless of the owner's rights. That is the test of conversion in the civil law. But not every conversion is a theft. Theft requires the additional intention of permanently depriving the owner or the substituted intention under s 6(1). The fact that the taking becomes more violent, thereby setting up a case of robbery, if there is an underlying case of theft, does not in itself turn what would be a robbery, if there was a theft, into a case of robbery without theft. The theft has to be there without the violence which would turn the theft into robbery.

27. Turning to the Vauxhall Cavalier which was destroyed at the end of the day because it was set on fire, Mr Jackson accepted that even there was nothing about the circumstances of that case which would entitle the case of theft of the Cavalier to be left to a jury. We are not so sure of that. If it were the case that a car was taken for the purposes of destroying it, that would be a case of theft, and where another's car has been set on fire that may be some evidence on which an intention permanently to deprive or a s 6(1) intention may be inferred. It seems to us, however, that in considering that the cases of both the Fiesta and the Cavalier could not support, and indeed, as he told us, would not be prosecuted, as a case of theft, Mr Jackson was going far to demonstrate that the case of the taking of the BMW cannot be regarded as a case of theft (or therefore robbery) either. In effect, subject to Mr Jackson's necessary concession regarding the Fiesta, Mr Jackson's submissions would run the danger of turning every case of taking and driving away without authority under s 12 of the Theft Act [see Chapter 17] into a case of theft, whereas of course the whole point of s 12 is to get round the problem that a car which is taken and driven away for a ride, only to be abandoned, is not easily found to be a case of theft.

28. In our judgment the facts of this case simply do not support a case to go before a jury of theft and therefore robbery of the BMW. The BMW was plainly taken for the purposes of a getaway. There was nothing about its use or subsequent abandonment to suggest otherwise. Indeed, its brief use and subsequent abandonment show very clearly what was the obvious *prima facie* inference to be drawn from its taking which was that the occupants of the Subaru needed another conveyance that evening. We therefore consider that the judge erred in being beguiled by s 6 into leaving this count of robbery to the jury.

29. . . . We think that the factors for the jury to consider were put before the jury but of course the recorder never directed them, for the purposes of s 6(1) and the jurisprudence which we have considered, to ask themselves whether those factors amounted to such an outright taking or disposal or an intention within the words of s 6(1) as to amount to the equivalence of an intention permanently to deprive. We consider that the authorities which we have reviewed in this judgment show that the purpose of s 6 is not greatly to widen the requirement of s 1's intention permanently to deprive. A slightly

broader definition of that intention is there provided in order to deal with a small number of difficult cases which had either arisen in the past under the common law or might arise in the future where, although it might be hard to put the matter strictly in terms of an intention permanently to deprive, in the sense of meaning the owner permanently to lose the thing itself, nevertheless something equivalent to that could be obtained through the intention to treat the thing as his own to dispose of, regardless of the other's rights, remembering Professor Smith's Oxford English dictionary use of the words 'to dispose of'. Thus, the newspaper taken but only returned on the next day when it is out of date, or a ticket which had been used, or a cheque which is paid, or something which has been substantially used up or destroyed, or something which would only be returned to its owner subject to a condition, all these are the sorts of examples to be found in the jurisprudence which discusses s 6. All of these cases are of ready equivalence to an intention permanently to deprive. None of them go any way towards extending the scope of s 6 to a case, however violent, of the taking of a car for the purposes of its brief use before being abandoned with its lights on. It must be remembered of course that a car with its licence plates on, left on the road, is utterly unlike a bundle of newspapers which have disappeared from a newsagents shop to a place where they would not be found. . . .

Appeal allowed

> ≈≈ **Question**
> Could Mitchell have been charged with robbery of the petrol in the BMW?

See also *Raphael* [2008] EWCA Crim 1014, where R had been convicted of conspiracy to rob V by forcibly taking his car and then inviting him to pay for its safe return. The court held that such conduct could indeed amount to robbery. Sir Igor Judge P said:

47. The express language of section 6 specifies that the subjective element necessary to establish the mens rea for theft includes an intention on the part of the taker 'to treat the thing as his own to dispose of regardless of the other's rights'. In our judgment it is hard to find a better example of such an intention than an offer, not to return [V's] car to him in exactly the same condition it was when it was removed from his possession and control, but to sell his own property back to him, and to make its return subject to a condition or conditions inconsistent with his right to possession of his own property.

48. This is not a case in which the vehicle was taken for what is sometimes inaccurately described as a 'joy ride'. Section 12 of the Theft Act has no application to it. It was only 'abandoned' after the purpose of the robbery had been frustrated and its possible usefulness to the robbers dissipated. Equally the appropriation of the car was not conditional in the sense described in *Easom* (1971) 55 Cr App R 410, where it was held that theft was not established if the intention of the appropriator of the property was 'merely to deprive the owner of such of his property as, on examination, proves worth taking and then, on finding that the booty is to him valueless, leaves it ready at hand to be re-possessed by the owner'.

Failure to explain correctly to the jury how they ought to approach the question of whether D had an intention permanently to deprive can render a conviction unsafe. In the case of *Waters* [2015] EWCA Crim 402, the Court of Appeal reiterated that if the condition attached to the return of the item is one which would not be fulfilled or not be fulfilled in the foreseeable future, then the circumstances may well amount to an intention permanently to deprive. On the other hand, if the condition can readily be fulfilled and may be fulfilled in the near future, the jury may well conclude that intention to deprive has not been made out. It is incumbent upon the judge to explain the difference between these two scenarios to the jury. In this case,

D made return of the property in question conditional upon DH being persuaded to come and talk to her. The Court of Appeal quashed D's conviction on the basis that the jury might have thought that even if DH could be found in the near future and therefore it was likely that the property would rapidly be returned to its owner, nevertheless there was an intention to permanently to deprive the owner of the property. Such a conclusion was held to be incorrect.

FURTHER READING

Appropriation

J. Beatson and A. Simester, 'Stealing One's Own Property' (1999) 115 LQR 372

A. L. Bogg and J. Stanton-Ife, 'Protecting the Vulnerable: Legality, Harm and Theft' (2003) 23 LS 402

S. Gardner, 'Property and Theft' [1998] Crim LR 35

P. R. Glazebrook, 'Revising the Theft Acts' (1993) 52 CLJ 191

S. Green, 'Theft and Conversion—Tangibly Different?' (2012) 128 LQR 564

S. Shute, 'Appropriation and the Law of Theft' [2002] Crim LR 445

J. C. Smith, 'The Sad Fate of the Theft Act 1968' in W. Swadling and G. Jones (eds), *The Search for Principle: Essays in Honour of Lord Goff of Chieveley* (1999), p 97

Property

R. Cross, 'Protecting Confidential Information under the Criminal Law of Theft and Fraud' (1991) 11 OJLS 264

R. Hammond, 'Theft of Information' (1984) 100 LQR 252

J. Hull, 'Stealing Secrets: A Review of the Law Commission Consultation Paper' [1998] Crim LR 246

J. C. Smith, 'Obtaining Cheques by Deception or Theft' [1997] Crim LR 396

J. C. Smith, 'Stealing Tickets' [1998] Crim LR 723

Belonging to another

D. W. Elliott, 'Directors' Thefts and Dishonesty' [1991] Crim LR 732

Dishonesty

K. Campbell, 'The Test of Dishonesty in *Ghosh*' (1994) 43 CLJ 349

D. W. Elliott, 'Dishonesty in Theft: A Dispensable Concept' [1982] Crim LR 395

E. J. Griew, 'Dishonesty, the Objections to *Feely* and *Ghosh*' [1985] Crim LR 341

A. Halpin, 'The Test for Dishonesty' [1996] Crim LR 283

A. Samuels, 'Dishonesty and the Jury' [1974] Crim LR 493

A. Steele, 'The Meanings of Dishonesty in Theft' (2009) 38 Common Law World Rev 103

R. Tur, 'Dishonesty and the Jury Question' in A. Phillips Griffiths (ed), *Philosophy and Practice* (1985)

Intention permanently to deprive

J. R. Spencer, 'The Metamorphosis of Section 6 of the Theft Act' [1977] Crim LR 653

G. Williams, 'Temporary Appropriation Should be Theft' [1981] Crim LR 129

14
Robbery

Robbery defined:

A person is guilty of robbery if he commits theft and immediately before or at the time of doing so, and in order to do so, he uses force on any person or puts or seeks to put any person in fear of being then and there subjected to force.

Some of the controversies that will be explored in this chapter include:

(1) the level of contact that is necessary before it can be said that 'force' was applied to V thereby turning what would be theft into robbery;

(2) the fact that it is not sufficient that the use of force was gratuitous. D must use force *in order to* commit theft.

14.1 Introduction

Robbery is one of the most serious offences in English law and certainly one of the most serious in the Theft Act 1968. It carries a maximum sentence of life imprisonment, and can only be tried in the Crown Court. The reason it is regarded so seriously is clear once the basic ingredients of the offence are considered: stealing with the use or threat of force. This is a hybrid offence with elements of offences against the person and dishonesty.

14.2 Elements of the offence

Theft Act 1968, s 8

(1) A person is guilty of robbery if he steals, and immediately before or at the time of doing so, and in order to do so, he uses force on any person or puts or seeks to put any person in fear of being then and there subjected to force.

(2) A person guilty of robbery, or of an assault with intent to rob, shall on conviction on indictment be liable to imprisonment for life.

14.2.1 Theft

Robbery is essentially a form of aggravated stealing (synonymous with theft) so proof of theft is essential to a conviction. All of the elements of theft must be established.

14.2.1.1 Appropriation

The robbery is complete when the theft is complete, that is, when the appropriation takes place. So in *Corcoran v Anderton* (1980) 71 Cr App R 104, [1980] Crim LR 385, DC, where D and E sought to take V's handbag by force, it was held the theft was complete when D snatched the handbag from V's grasp though it then fell from D's hands and the defendants made off without it. Their argument that this was only an attempt was rejected since the snatching of the handbag from V constituted an appropriation.

In *Hale* (1978) 68 Cr App R 415, [1979] Crim LR 596, CA, D and E entered V's house and while D was upstairs stealing a jewellery box, E was downstairs tying up V. The Court of Appeal declined to quash their convictions for robbery even though D might have appropriated the jewellery box before the force was used. The court said (at 418):

> the act of appropriation does not suddenly cease. It is a continuous act and it is a matter for the jury to decide whether or not the act of appropriation has finished. Moreover, it is quite clear that the intention to deprive the owner permanently, which accompanied the assumption of the owner's rights was a continuing one at all material times. This Court therefore rejects the contention that the theft had ceased by the time [V] was tied up. As a matter of common sense [E] was in the course of committing theft; he was stealing.

14.2.1.2 Property belonging to another

The requirement that the property belongs to another is unlikely to present difficulties in a robbery case. There will be few cases in which D uses force to obtain an item of intangible property from V, or in which some other problematical form of property is appropriated. However, there might be an issue in circumstances where D believes that he is retrieving property that belongs to himself, even though it is currently in V's possession.

> ≋ **Question**
> D in London telephones V in his office in the bank HQ in Halifax and threatens to detonate a bomb under V's desk unless V makes an electronic transfer of funds into D's account. Is this robbery?

14.2.1.3 Dishonesty

The *Ghosh* test applies, see section 13.6, p 367. In *Robinson* [1977] Crim LR 173, CA, D ran a saving club to which V's wife owed £7. Meeting V, D and others threatened him and in the fight which followed £5 fell from V's pocket which D took, claiming he was still owed £2. Quashing D's conviction for robbery, it was held that all D had to raise was an honest belief in entitlement to the money and not that he honestly believed that he was entitled to take it in the way he did.

> ≋ **Question**
> Should a belief in a right to the property also entitle D to use force to obtain it?

14.2.1.4 Intention permanently to deprive

In *Raphael* [2008] EWCA Crim 1014, R had been convicted of conspiracy to rob V by forcibly taking his car and then offering V the opportunity to buy it back. The Court of Appeal referred to s 6 of the Theft Act 1968 (section 13.7, p 380), and concluded that this was clearly capable of amounting to robbery. See section 13.7, p 380.

Difficulties can arise in distinguishing between the requirement that there be both an appropriation and also an intention permanently to deprive. Remember that each must be established and must occur at the same point in time. In *Vinall* [2011] EWCA Crim 2652, two young men were cycling along a cycle path when they came across a group of three young men. The allegation was that V was punched from his bicycle and was chased away. The group of three then walked away with the bicycle. The bicycle was subsequently found abandoned 50 yards away from where it had been taken from its owner. The Court of Appeal held that it was open to the judge to direct the jury to consider whether the later abandonment of V's bicycle was evidence from which they could infer that defendants intended *at the time of the taking* (ie when the force was used) to treat the bicycle as their own to dispose of regardless of V's rights. If that was the way the judge had chosen to leave the issue of intent to the jury, an explicit direction would have been required explaining that an intention formed only upon abandonment of the bicycle 50 yards away was inconsistent with and fatal to the allegation of robbery. A similar issue arose in the subsequent case of *Zerei* [2012] EWCA Crim 1114. D and another man approached V in a car park. D told V that he was going to take his car. When V refused, a struggle broke out during which D punched V and took out a knife. V's car keys were taken from him and D drove off with his car. The car was found abandoned a while later. D was convicted of robbery and argued that the judge had given the jury the impression that the forcible taking of the car itself might amount to proof of an intention permanently to deprive. He argued that the judge in his summing-up had not made it clear that taking a car by violence, irrespective of the rights of the owner, was completely different to an intention permanently to deprive. In quashing the conviction, the Court of Appeal found three issues with the judge's directions to the jury. First, the judge did indeed give the jury the false impression that the forcible taking of the car was sufficient to constitute an intention permanently to deprive. The court made clear that it is not. Secondly, the distinction between an intention permanently to deprive and taking of possession which merely defeated the rights of the owner for a short period of time was not made sufficiently clear. Finally, the judge should have pointed out to the jury that the abandonment of the car a short period of time after it was appropriated was relevant to the issue of whether there was an intention permanently to deprive. See also the discussion of *Waters* in Chapter 13 at p. 389.

14.2.2 Force

A person is guilty of robbery contrary to s 8 of the Theft Act 1968 if he steals, and immediately before or at the time of doing so, and in order to do so, *he [a] uses force on any person or [b] puts or [c] seeks to put any person in fear of being then and there subjected to force.*

Few difficulties arise in cases where it is alleged that D uses force. This could be a push, a punch, etc. However, there are marginal cases which are much more difficult. The High Court considered what constitutes force in the following case.

Director of Public Prosecutions v RP
[2012] EWHC 1657 (Admin), Divisional Court

(Mitting J)

DD walked past V and asked her for a cigarette. V replied that she did not have a spare one. In response to this, D1 snatched the cigarette that V had in her hand. At no point did D1's hand ever make contact with V's. Although V was pushed after the incident, the prosecution did not put the case as a continuing act. DD were found guilty of robbery and appealed.

4. . . . The case raised, therefore, a single and very narrow issue: does the snatching of a cigarette from between the fingers of a person smoking it, without physical contact between the snatcher and the person smoking it, amount to robbery, provided, of course, that the elements of theft are present? . . .

5. Under the law as it existed before the enactment of the Theft Act 1968, the answer would unquestionably have been no. What the old law required was that greater force than was merely required to take an object was required to be applied before the offence became an offence of robbery. Section 8 of the Theft Act 1968 provides:

[His lordship recited s 8 of the Theft Act 1968.]

. . .

6. As a matter of language, it is important to note that the statute requires the use of 'force on any person' or putting 'any person in fear of being then and there subjected to force'. Although the old distinctions under the Larceny Act 1916 have gone, there remains a basic requirement for the commission of the offence that force is used on a person.

7. Ms Zentler-Munro, for the appellants, accepts that the snatching of a handbag from a woman holding it on her shoulder or in her hand will ordinarily amount to robbery because by the very act of pulling on the handbag force will inevitably be applied to the person of the woman from whom the handbag is snatched. Her concession is a proper and inevitable one in the light of the case law as it has developed since the enactment of the Theft Act 1968.

8. The starting point is *R. v Dawson and James* (1977) 64 Cr. App. R. 170. The facts were that at Liverpool Pier Head a sailor on shore leave waiting for the ferry was surrounded by two men, one standing on either side of him, who nudged him on the shoulder, causing him to lose his balance. While trying to keep his balance, a third man got his hand into the sailor's pocket and took his wallet. It was contended before the trial court that that did not amount to the offence of robbery. The judge left the offence to the jury, who convicted him. In giving the judgment of the court, Lawson L.J. said the following at 172:

> 'The choice of the word "force" is not without interest because under the Larceny Act 1916 the word "violence" had been used, but Parliament deliberately on the advice of the Criminal Law Revision Committee changed that word to "force". Whether there is any difference between "violence" or "force" is not relevant for the purposes of this case; but the word is "force". It is a word in ordinary use. It is a word which juries understand. The learned judge left it to the jury to say whether jostling a man in the way which the victim described to such an extent that he had difficulty in keeping his balance could be said to be the use of force. The learned judge, because of the argument put forward by [counsel for the appellant], went out of his way to explain to the jury that force in these sort of circumstances must be substantial to justify a verdict.
>
> Whether it was right for him to put that adjective before the word "force" when Parliament had not done so we will not discuss for the purposes of this case. It was a matter for the jury. They were there to use their common sense and knowledge of the world. We cannot say that their decision as to whether force was used was wrong. They were entitled to the view that force was used.'

The force there used, although not substantial on one view, was nonetheless direct force applied to the person of the sailor.

9. The next case in point is *R. v Clouden*, only reported, as far as I know, in the *Criminal Law Review* for 1987, p.56. The appellant approached a woman who was carrying a shopping basket in her left hand from behind and wrenched it down and out of her grasp with both hands and ran off with it. He was convicted of robbery. In dismissing his appeal, the court observed (see holding at [1987] Crim. L.R. 56) that:

> 'The old cases distinguished between force on the actual person and force on the property which in fact causes force on the person but, following *Dawson* and *James* . . ., the court should direct attention to the words of the statute without referring to the old authorities. The old distinctions

have gone. Whether the defendant used force on any person in order to steal is an issue that should be left to the jury. The judge's direction to the jury was adequate. He told the jury quite clearly at the outset what the statutory definition was, though thereafter he merely used the word "force" and did not use the expression "on the person".'

10. It seems to me from that brief report of the decision that the court in *Clouden* had in mind the need for the prosecution to prove the use of 'force on any person' and not merely 'force', but concluded that despite the lack of repeated reference to 'force on any person' in the summing-up, it was nonetheless adequate because the judge had drawn attention to the statutory definition at some part of his summing-up. That decision attracted an interesting commentary from Professor Smith (the author of *The Law of Theft*) [1987] Crim. L.R. 56:

> 'Robbery at common law and under the Larceny Acts was governed by the principle stated by Garrow B in *Gnosil* (1824) 1 Car. & P. 304: "The mere act of taking being forcible will not make this offence highway robbery; to constitute the crime of highway robbery the force used must be either before or at the time of taking and must be of such a nature to show it was intended to overpower the party robbed and prevent his resisting, and not merely to get possession of the property stolen . . ." According to this statement, it would appear there was no evidence in the present case of robbery as it was before the Theft Act 1968 came into effect.
>
> As the present court was aware, the Criminal Law Revision Committee did not intend that the draft bill which became the Theft Act 1968 should affect this rule. In their *Eighth Report* (Cmnd. 2997 [1966]) para.65, the Committee stated: "We should not regard mere snatching of property such as a handbag, from an unresisting owner as using force for the purpose of the definition, though it might be so if the owner resisted." The present decision and Dawson and James, which foreshadowed it, show that the Committee would have been wise to state the principle in *Gnosil* in order to preserve it because the wording of the section left open the construction now put upon it. It is a warning to the codifier that, if he intends the refinements of the law he is codifying to be observed, he should state them. Opinions will of course differ on where lines should be drawn; but it may well be thought that conduct such as that in the present case is more akin to that of the pickpocket than the bank robber and is quite adequately dealt with by the offence of theft which is, after all, punishable with a maximum of ten years' imprisonment.'

The force of those comments is not reduced by the fact that the maximum sentence has now been reduced to seven years.

11. Other more recent authorities have been cited to me but they do no more than make passing observations and do not contain statements forming part of the decision of the court which bind me.

12. I refer finally to an extract from a work bearing Professor Smith's name but in fact now written by Professor Ormerod. If it is not Professor Ormerod's words that I am quoting, it shows that Professor Smith must have changed his mind. In para.7.08 of *Smith's Law of Theft*, 9th edn, the author observes:

> 'Force
>
> The term "force" was preferred by the CLRC to "violence", which was used in the Larceny Act 1916 to designate an aggravated form of robbery. Though the difference, if any, between the words is an elusive one, it is probable that "force" is a slightly wider term. Thus it might be argued that simply to hold a person down is not violence but it certainly involves the use of force against the person. Force denotes any exercise of physical strength against another whereas violence seems to signify a dynamic exercise of strength as by striking a blow. In *Dawson*, it was held that, where D nudges V so as to cause him to lose his balance and enable D to steal, it is a question of fact for the jury whether the nudge amounts to "force". It is submitted that it would be better if the law gave an answer to the question—preferably in the affirmative. It is submitted that no jury could reasonably find that the slight physical contact that might be involved where D picks V's pocket would amount to a use of force.'

13. I agree with those observations. This case sits neatly in between the two paradigm examples given by the author. There was, on the facts found by the court, no physical contact between the hand of RP and the hand of [V]. The court was invited to consider the case on the basis that the mere snatching of a cigarette from between the fingers of [V] was sufficient to amount to the use of force on her person. I remind myself that borderline questions, such as a question of what amounts to the use of force on a person when the force used is minimal, are questions for the court at first instance and that it is not for an appellate court to put a gloss on the words in s.8 of the Theft Act 1968.

14. However, in the stated case, the court did not find as a fact that RP used force on [V]. What the court found clearly was that a cigarette was snatched, on the prosecution case, without there being contact with [V], that that amounted to the use of force by RP and that the force was used in order to steal the cigarette. Those findings were clearly all open to the court but they do not amount to a finding that force was used on the person of [V], unless the mere removal of a cigarette from between her fingers itself is capable of amounting to the use of force upon her person.

15. In my judgment, it is not. This case falls squarely on the side of pickpocketing and such like, in which there is no direct physical contact between thief and victim. It cannot be said that the minimal use of force required to remove a cigarette from between the fingers of a person suffices to amount to the use of force on that person. It cannot cause any pain unless, perhaps, the person resists strongly, in which case one would expect inevitably that there would be direct physical contact between the thief and victim as well. The unexpected removal of a cigarette from between the fingers of a person is no more the use of force on that person than would be the removal of an item from her pocket. This offence is properly categorised as simple theft.

16. I therefore allow the appeal of the three appellants against their conviction for robbery, substitute convictions for theft and leave the sentence undisturbed.

≋ *Questions*

(1) D pumps a noxious gas into a bank causing the occupants to be overcome by the fumes and D then steals from them while they are incapacitated. Has he robbed them?

(2) Altering the facts of *DPP v RP*, what if the cigarette had been lit and when RP tried to snatch it from V it made contact with her hand? Would this suffice to constitute force?

In cases where D puts or seeks to put V in fear of force, rather than actually using force, the position is slightly more complicated, but the courts have glossed over the potential problems. The Divisional Court confirmed in *DPP v R* [2007] EWHC 739 (Admin), that robbery does not require proof that V was actually put in fear. It is submitted that this must be correct, otherwise the commission of the offence would turn on the courage of the victim. That case does not, however, answer the question whether it is necessary for the victim to *apprehend* that force will be used. Where the allegation is that D *put any person in fear of being then and there subjected to force*, in that form of the offence, it would seem to be a necessary element. Support for that proposition is derived from *Grant v CPS* (10 March 2000, unreported), QBD, although the court in *DPP v R* cast doubt on that case. Where D *seeks to put* V in fear of force there is no need for V to be in fear in fact, nor it seems for V to apprehend force; the offence turns solely on D's intention. It is important to emphasize that it is sufficient that D's intent is to produce a state of mind where V apprehends force; it is enough that D intends to put V in fear. *Tennant* [1976] Crim LR 133, Nottingham Crown Court, makes clear that D may threaten to use force and satisfy the requirement of the offence of robbery although V is not made to apprehend the immediate infliction of force on him which is necessary to constitute an assault.

14.2.2.1 In order to steal

Force must be used 'in order to' steal. If D knocks V senseless in a fight and then decides to make off with V's watch which has fallen from his wrist pocket, it would not be robbery; it would be assault and theft. Conversely, if D steals property without using force but subsequently uses or threatens force to retain it or in effecting an escape, it would not be robbery.

Under the pre-1968 law it was not sufficient that force was used in the taking of the property: the force had to be used to overpower the person or prevent resistance from him. This was examined in *RP* in section 14.2.2.

≈≈≈ **Question**

D is about to go out one day to steal a new suit from a shop. He tells his wife of his plan and she threatens to telephone the police. D pushes her into the bathroom and locks the door and does not free her until he returns later wearing his new suit. Is this robbery?

14.2.2.2 Force on any person

The force may be on *any* person. In *Smith v Desmond* [1965] AC 960, [1965] 1 All ER 976, HL, D and E were held to have robbed V and X, night watchman and maintenance engineer respectively, in a bakery, where force was used on them in order to steal from an office some distance away on the premises. V and X's employer's property was in their immediate care and protection. The case is obviously within the terms of s 8 which extends to any case in which force is used on any person in order to steal. The threat of force may similarly be made to any person; but the offence is committed only if D seeks to put that person in fear of being subjected to force. It is not sufficient that he seeks to cause that person to fear that someone else will be subjected to force: *Taylor (Richard)* [1996] CLY 1518 (D handing to V, a bank cashier, a note saying that D had a gun pointed at a customer).

14.2.3 Reform

Ashworth ('Robbery Reassessed' [2002] Crim LR 851) questions whether the offence is necessary:

> Robbery is an amalgamated offence. Like burglary, it combines two separate wrongs. Unlike burglary, the two wrongs in robbery are both crimes. The offence combines theft of property with the use or threat of force. It is not specified which wrong should be regarded as more important, but surely the amount of violence should be given the greater significance, on the ground that violence is generally a much greater attack on an individual's well-being. It is possible to conceive of a case where an enormous sum of money is taken by using a small amount of (threatened) force, but even then we should bear in mind that the maximum sentence for theft is seven years. In most cases of street robberies and robberies at building society branches, off-licences and so forth, the robber only sets out to obtain a modest sum and does so, and therefore the theft component of the sentence should be small and well below the maximum for that crime. More significant, surely, is the amount of force. . . . The law of offences against the person reflects the relative seriousness of violence and threats in a rather unsatisfactory way. If we had a reformed law on violence, it would distinguish the various offences according to the degree of harm and the degree of culpability, and would assign graduated penalties from the least serious up to the most serious. Robbery should mirror this, or have at least two degrees of seriousness.

A more radical proposal would be to abolish the offence of robbery. It would then be left to prosecutors to charge the components of theft and violence separately, which would focus the court's attention on those two elements, separately and then (for sentencing purposes) in combination. The principal difficulty with this is the absence from English law of an offence of threatening injury: between the summary offence of assault by posing a threat of force, and the serious offence of making a threat to kill, there is no intermediate crime. This gap ought to be closed; and, if it were, there would be a strong argument that the crime of robbery would be unnecessary.

≋ *Question*

Do you agree that a crime of robbery ought to be unnecessary or is there something distinctive about force or the threat of force being used to commit theft? Consider this question in the light of the following extract.

S. P. Green, *13 Ways To Steal A Bicycle*
(2012)

Robbery was probably the first form of theft to be criminalized. It has a strong claim to being the most morally wrongful and socially harmful form of theft and, indeed, the empirical study described in Chapter 1 indicated that it occupied a class by itself in terms of blameworthiness. Little elaboration is presumably needed to explain why it is morally wrong to inflict unjustified pain or fear on others. Any theory of morality, whether consequentialist or non-consequentialist, will regard such acts as among the most wrongful. The seriousness with which robbery was viewed by the criminal law—Coke called it 'amongst the most heinous [of] felonies'—is evidenced by the fact that the penalties for robbery are invariably higher than for other forms of theft. In this, the law of robbery parallels the law of sexual assault, which normally treats forcible rape as a more serious crime than rape by deception or coercion. At the same time, it is worth nothing that despite the fear and loathing with which robbery is normally viewed, there are nevertheless cases in which robbing bandits are celebrated as heroes who (whether they intend to or not) serve an important societal function.

The secondary wrong in robbery is so significant that it tends to overshadow the primary wrong of misappropriation. As the [Model Penal Code] commentary puts it:

> The violent petty thief operating in the streets and alleys of big cities—the 'mugger'—is one of the main sources of insecurity and concern in the population at large. There is a special element of terror on this kind of depredation. The ordinary citizen does not feel particularly threatened by surreptitious larceny, embezzlement, or fraud. But there is understandable abhorrence of the robber who accosts on the streets and who menaces his victims with actual or threatened violence against which there is a general sense of helplessness.

At the same time, it is important not to underestimate the way in which the wrongfulness of robbery is colored by the element of property misappropriation. Consider the most recent legal debacle involving O.J. Simpson. In September 2007, Simpson and several associates burst into a room at a Las Vegas hotel, several of them brandishing guns, and seized various mementos, including many items previously autographed by Simpson. In his subsequent trial, Simpson maintained that he had been conducting a 'sting operation' to recover property that, he claimed, had been stolen from him years earlier by a former agent. Assuming for the moment that his factual contention was true, could the fact that Simpson owned the property legitimately serve as a defense to robbery? Interestingly the law varies. A handful or courts—such as the Nevada court in which Simpson was ultimately convicted—have said that the proper charge was robbery regardless of who owned the property. However, I believe that the better view is that the proper charge was not robbery, but rather assault, since, assuming Simpson actually did have a right to recover the goods, he would not have been attempting to violate anyone's rights to property.

It is also worth considering how robbery should be distinguished from mere larceny [ie theft] particularly in cases of pick pocketing. Jewish law takes a subjective approach: if the victim is aware of the physical taking from his person, the act is robbery, if not, the act is considered larceny. Anglo-American law takes a contrasting, objective approach. Simply having physical contact with the victim is not enough to merit charges of robbery, even if the victim is aware of the contact. For there to be robbery, there must be some objective violence or intimidation.

Unfortunately, the line between robbery and larceny is not always clear. Even relatively light force, such as barging into someone or tugging at a handbag in such a way that the owner's hand is pulled downwards, has been held to constitute force sufficient to constitute robbery. Yet, as Andrew Ashworth has suggested [in the article previously extracted], such cases are troubling. 'It is difficult', he says, 'to draw the line between sufficient and insufficient force, but if robbery is to continue to be regarded as a serious offence, triable only on indictment and punishable with life imprisonment, surely something more than a bump, a push, or a pull, should be required.' Indeed, as Ashworth points out, the law surrounding robbery, at least in England, is much less finely graded than that surrounding assault. Because of this, he argues that robbery, in its current form, plainly breaches the principle of fair labeling. He therefore recommends a statutory scheme that would reflect the moral distinctions between theft by means of a 'mere push' and theft by means of 'serious violence'.

I assume that Ashworth would prefer something like the approach to robbery taken in the United States. Under the [Model Penal Code], only those thefts involving the infliction or threat of immediate 'serious bodily injury' are treated as robbery and subject to heightened punishment. If the theft involves only minimal force, the [Model Penal Code] treats it as 'ordinary theft'. Many states have an even more finely graded robbery offence scheme, which distinguishes among offences such as simple robbery, armed robbery, first degree robbery, second degree robbery, purse snatching and car jacking. In general, the more aggravated forms of robbery tend to be those in which the offender uses a weapon or inflicts or threatens serious physical injury.

≈≈ *Questions*

(1) If O. J. Simpson had burst into a hotel room in England in the way described, would he have committed robbery?

(2) Does English law's approach to robbery contravene the principle of fair labelling?

(3) Is the approach taken in the United States to robbery more satisfactory than English law? What might be the downside of the scheme Green sets out?

FURTHER READING

D. Ormerod and K. Laird, *Smith and Hogan's Criminal Law* (14th edn, 2015), Ch 20 and references therein

D. Ormerod and D. H. Williams, *Smith's Law of Theft* (9th edn, 2007), Ch 7

15

Burglary and related offences

> **Burglary:**
>
> A person is guilty of burglary if he enters any building or part of a building as a trespasser and with intent to commit one of a list of offences (theft, GBH, criminal damage) or having entered as a trespasser he commits theft or GBH or attempts one or more of those offences.
>
> An offence of aggravated burglary applies where D commits burglary with a weapon.
>
> **Some of the controversies that will be explored in this chapter include:**
>
> (1) the disagreement as to the rationale for the existence of burglary as an offence distinct from theft;
>
> (2) the increasingly technical nature of burglary as an offence and the conflict with cases substantiating the requirements of certain elements of it;
>
> (3) the problems that can arise from reliance on the notion of 'trespass' (a civil law concept) when D has been invited to enter for a particular purpose or by a person in the household who is not the owner.
>
> (4) the need for an offence of aggravated burglary with a statutory maximum sentence of life imprisonment.
>
> Within the offence are a number of important distinctions, depending on which form of the offence D would have committed.

15.1 Burglary

Burglary involves D either (a) entering a building as a trespasser with intent to commit certain specified offences or (b) having entered a building as a trespasser committing one of a list of specified offences.

15.1.1 Introduction

Burglary is an offence that has existed for centuries, but was only codified in statute relatively recently. Although the non-legal understanding is that burglary consists of 'breaking and entering', the offence is no longer defined in that manner.

Under the Theft Act 1968 burglary can now be committed in one of four ways and it is important to appreciate the distinctions between each variation, given how technical they have become. The elements of the various forms of the offence are:

(1) D enters (a) a building or part of a building (b) as a trespasser (c) with intent (d) to commit an offence of theft, criminal damage or GBH; or

(2) D enters (a) a building or part of a building (b) as a trespasser and (c) once in the building D steals or inflicts GBH on a person therein or attempts either of those things; or

(3) D enters (a) a dwelling or part of a dwelling (b) as a trespasser (c) with intent (d) to commit an offence of theft, criminal damage or grievous bodily harm; or

(4) D enters (a) a dwelling or part of a dwelling (b) as a trespasser and (c) once in the building D steals or inflicts GBH on a person therein or attempts either of those things.

Burglary is one of the most serious offences contained in the 1968 Act, as reflected by the statutory maximum sentence of ten years' imprisonment upon conviction, or 14 years if the building is a dwelling. In addition, it is also one of the most prevalent offences that is committed in England and Wales each year. Given its seriousness and the frequency with which it is committed, it is surprising that it remains unclear precisely what harm the offence of burglary is designed to protect against. Is it: the invasion of private space and the associated sense of violation; the risk of violent confrontation; or aggravated forms of theft or violence? (See G. R. Sullivan and A. P. Simester, 'On the Nature and Rationale of Property Offences' in R. A. Duff and S. P. Green (eds), *Defining Crimes* (2005), pp 168, 192.) Perhaps it would be better to abandon the search for a single, overarching justification for the offence? For example, Stuart Green argues that the offence involves the primary wrong of theft, GBH, etc in addition to a secondary wrong, consisting of the violation of the victim's sense of security. (See S. P. Green, *13 Way To Steal A Bicycle* (2012), pp 122–123.)

15.1.2 The external elements

Theft Act 1968, s 9

(1) A person is guilty of burglary if—

   (a) he enters any building or part of a building as a trespasser and with intent to commit any such offence as is mentioned in subsection (2) below; or

   (b) having entered any building or part of a building as a trespasser he steals or attempts to steal anything in the building or that part of it or inflicts or attempts to inflict on any person therein any grievous bodily harm.

(2) The offences referred to in subsection (1)(a) above are offences of stealing anything in the building or part of a building in question, of inflicting on any person therein any grievous bodily harm . . ., and of doing unlawful damage to the building or anything therein.

(3) A person guilty of burglary shall on conviction on indictment be liable to imprisonment for a term not exceeding—

   (a) where the offence was committed in respect of a building or part of a building which is a dwelling, fourteen years;

   (b) in any other case, ten years.

(4) References in subsections (1) and (2) above to a building, and the reference in subsection (3) above to a building which is a dwelling, shall apply also to an inhabited vehicle or vessel, and shall apply to any such vehicle or vessel at times when the person having a habitation in it is not there as well as at times when he is.

Note that burglary included entering a building as a trespasser with intent to rape a person therein, until this element of the offence was replaced by s 63 of the Sexual Offences Act 2003—trespassing with intent to commit a sexual offence (see section 15.3, p 411).

15.1.2.1 Entry

At common law the insertion of any part of D's body, however small—a finger through an opening—was a sufficient entry. It seems that Parliament assumed when passing the Theft Act 1968 that the common law would continue to apply (see Hansard HL, vol 290, cols 85 and 86). The courts have not done what was expected. In *Collins* [1972] 2 All ER 1105 (in the next extract), Edmund Davies LJ appears to suggest that the law changed so that it now requires a 'substantial and effective' entry. In *Brown* [1985] Crim LR 212, however, it was held there was a sufficient entry where D's feet were on the ground outside a shop and the top half of his body was inside the broken shop window, as if he was rummaging for goods displayed there. The court said that the word 'substantial' did not materially assist but the entry must be 'effective' and in that case it was. Perhaps D was already in a position to steal? Similarly, in *Ryan* [1996] Crim LR 320, D became trapped by the neck with only his head and right arm inside the window. His argument that his act was not capable of constituting an entry because he could not have stolen anything was rejected. These latter cases seem to undermine the assertion of Edmund Davies LJ in *Collins* that entry must be 'substantial and effective'.

> ≋ *Question*
> In what sense could Ryan's entry be said to be 'effective'?

Parliament cannot have intended that D must have got so far into the building as to be able to accomplish his unlawful purpose, as this would arguably undermine the rationale for the offence. D who enters intending to cause GBH to V is surely guilty of burglary when he enters through the ground-floor window though V is on the fourth floor. Thus it is hard to see that there is any requirement that the act be either an 'effective' or a 'substantial' entry. *Ryan* decided only that there was evidence on which a jury could find that D had entered. This suggests that it is open to a jury to find D had not entered. It is unsatisfactory in principle that it should be open to a jury to find that there is no entry when such facts are established. Is the best course to accept the continued existence of the common law rule? It at least has the benefit of being a relatively certain test and one that is easy to apply.

> ≋ *Questions*
> Has D 'entered' when he: (a) uses his 9-year-old child to climb through the window to steal; (b) uses a trained animal to do so; (c) pokes a telescopic grab handle through the letterbox to seize property inside the building; (d) sends a letter bomb to V's house through the post?

15.1.2.2 As a trespasser
R v Collins
[1972] EWCA Crim 1, Court of Appeal, Criminal Division

(Edmund Davies and Stephenson LJJ, Boreham J)

The facts of this case are memorable given how extraordinary they are. The appellant, Stephen Collins, was convicted of burglary with intent to commit rape. (At that time the burglary offence included entering as a trespasser with intent to rape. That offence has been replaced with one discussed at section 15.3, p 411. For the purposes of the discussion of trespass, the case remains good law.) The complainant went to bed one evening with her bedroom window open; the bed being located somewhere near the open window. In the early hours of the morning, the complainant awoke to find the appellant standing naked (except for his socks) in her window with an erect penis. Importantly, the complainant was unable to remember whether the appellant was standing on the outside of the windowsill, or on that part of the sill which was inside the room. Thinking that the figure in the window was her boyfriend, the complainant sat up in bed. The appellant then descended from the window and the pair had sex. When the complainant realized that the man with whom she had had sex was not her boyfriend, she slapped him and he promptly left. The appellant told the police that he had been drinking at the time and that he had climbed the ladder to the complainant's bedroom with the intention of trying to have sex with her.

[Edmund Davies LJ delivered the judgment of the court.]

Now, one feature of the case which remained at the conclusion of the evidence in great obscurity is where exactly Collins was at the moment when, according to him, the girl manifested that she was welcoming him. Was he kneeling on the sill outside the window or was he already inside the room, having climbed through the window frame, and kneeling upon the inner sill? It was a crucial matter, for there were certainly three ingredients that it was incumbent upon the Crown to establish. Under section 9 of the Theft Act of 1968, which renders a person guilty of burglary if he enters any building or part of a building as a trespasser and with the intention of committing rape [note that this version of the offence has been repealed by the Sexual Offences Act 2003], the entry of the accused into the building must first be proved. Well, there is no doubt about that, for it is common ground that he did enter this girl's bedroom. Secondly, it must be proved that he entered as a trespasser. We will develop that point a little later. Thirdly it must be proved that he entered as a trespasser with intent at the time of entry to commit rape therein.

The second ingredient of the offence—the entry must be as a trespasser—is one which has not, to the best of our knowledge, been previously canvassed in the courts. Views as to its ambit have naturally been canvassed by the textbook writers, and it is perhaps not wholly irrelevant to recall that those who were advising the Home Secretary before the Theft Bill was presented to Parliament had it in mind to get rid of some of the frequently absurd technical rules which had been built up in relation to the old requirement in burglary of a 'breaking and entering'. The cases are legion as to what this did or did not amount to, and happily it is not now necessary for us to consider them. But it was in order to get rid of those technical rules that a new test was introduced, namely that the entry must be 'as a trespasser'.

What does that involve? According to the learned editors of *Archbold* [*Criminal Pleading, Evidence and Practice* (37th edn, 1969), p 572, para 1505]:

'Any intentional, reckless or negligent entry into a building will, it would appear, constitute a trespass if the building is in the possession of another person who does not consent to the entry. Nor will it make any difference that the entry was the result of a reasonable mistake on the part of the defendant, so far as trespass is concerned.'

If that be right, then it would be no defence for this man to say (and even were he believed in saying), 'Well, I honestly thought that this girl was welcoming me into the room and I therefore entered, fully believing that I had her consent to go in'. If *Archbold* is right, he would nevertheless be a trespasser, since the apparent consent of the girl was unreal, she being mistaken as to who was at her window. We disagree. We hold that, for the purposes of section 9 of the Theft Act [1968], a person entering a building is not guilty of trespass if he enters without knowledge that he is trespassing or at least without acting recklessly as to whether or not he is unlawfully entering.

A view contrary to that of the learned editors of *Archbold* was expressed in Professor Smith's book on '*The Law of Theft*' [then in its first edition (1968), pp 123, 124, para 462], where, having given an illustration of an entry into premises, the learned author comments:

'It is submitted that . . . D should be acquitted on the ground of lack of mens rea. Though, under the civil law, he entered as a trespasser, it is submitted that he cannot be convicted of the criminal offence unless he knew of the facts which caused him to be a trespasser or, at least, was reckless.'

The matter has also been dealt with by Professor Griew [then in its first edition *The Theft Act 1968*, pp 52, 53, para 4-05] who in his work on the Theft Act [1968] has this passage:

'What if D wrongly believes that he is not trespassing? His belief may rest on facts which, if true, would mean that he was not trespassing: for instance, he may enter a building by mistake, thinking that it is the one he has been invited to enter. Or his belief may be based on a false view of the legal effect of the known facts: for instance, he may misunderstand the effect of a contract granting him a right of passage through a building. Neither kind of mistake will protect him from tort liability for trespass. In either case, then, D satisfies the literal terms of section 9(1): he "enters . . . as a trespasser". But for the purposes of criminal liability a man should be judged on the basis of the facts as he believed them to be, and this should include making allowances for a mistake as to rights under the civil law. This is another way of saying that a serious offence like burglary should be held to require mens rea in the fullest sense of the phrase: D should be liable for burglary only if he knowingly trespasses or is reckless as to whether he trespasses or not. Unhappily it is common for Parliament to omit to make clear whether mens rea is intended to be an element in a statutory offence. It is also, though not equally, common for the courts to supply the mental element by construction of the statute.'

We prefer the view expressed by Professor Smith and Professor Griew to that of the learned editors of *Archbold*. In the judgment of this Court, there cannot be a conviction for entering premises 'as a trespasser' within the meaning of section 9 of the Theft Act 1968 unless the person entering does so knowing that he is a trespasser and nevertheless deliberately enters, or, at the very least, is reckless as to whether or not he is entering the premises of another without the other party's consent.

Having so held, the pivotal point of this appeal is whether the Crown established that this Appellant at the moment that he entered the bedroom knew perfectly well that he was not welcome there or, being reckless as to whether he was welcome or not, was nevertheless determined to enter. That in turn involves consideration as to where he was at the time that the complainant indicated that she was welcoming him into her bedroom. If, to take an example that was put in the course of argument, her bed had not been near the window but was on the other side of the bedroom, and he (being determined to have her sexually even against her will) climbed through the window and crossed the bedroom to reach her bed, then the offence charged would have been established. But in this case, as we have related, the layout of the room was different, and it became a point of nicety which had to be conclusively established by the Crown as to where he was when the girl made welcoming signs, as she unquestionably at some stage did.

How did the learned Judge deal with this matter? We have to say regretfully that there was a flaw in his treatment of it. Referring to section 9, the learned Judge said:

'. . . There are three ingredients. First is the question of entry. Did he enter into that house? Did he enter as a trespasser? That is to say, did he—was the entry, if you are satisfied there was an entry, intentional or reckless? And, finally, and you may think this is the crux of the case as opened to you by [counsel for the Crown], if you are satisfied that he entered as a trespasser, did he have the intention to rape this girl?'

The learned judge then went on to deal in turn with each of these three ingredients. He first explained what was involved in 'entry' into a building. He then dealt with the second ingredient. But the learned Judge here unfortunately repeated his earlier observation that the question of entry as a trespasser depended on 'was the entry intentional or reckless?' We have to say that this was putting the matter inaccurately. This mistake may have been derived from a passage in the speech of Crown counsel when replying to the submission of 'No case'. [Counsel for the Crown] at one stage said:

'Therefore, the first thing that the Crown have got to prove, my Lord, is that there has been a trespass which may be an intentional trespass, or it may be a reckless trespass.'

Unfortunately the trial judge regarded the matter as though the second ingredient in the burglary charged was whether there had been an intentional or reckless entry, and when he came to develop this topic in his summing-up that error was unfortunately perpetuated. The learned Judge told the jury:

'He had no right to be in that house, as you know, certainly from the point of view of [the girl's mother], but if you are satisfied about entry, did he enter intentionally or recklessly? What the Prosecution say about that is, you do not really have to consider recklessness because when you consider his own evidence he intended to enter that house, and if you accept the evidence I have just pointed out to you, he, in fact, did so. So, at least, you may think, it was intentional. At the least, you may think it was reckless because as he told you he did not know whether the girl would accept him.'

We are compelled to say that we do not think the learned Judge by these observations made it sufficiently clear to the jury the nature of the second test about which they had to be satisfied before this young man [the appellant] could be convicted of the offence charged. There was no doubt that his entry into the bedroom was 'intentional'. But what the accused had said was, 'She knelt on the bed, she put her arms around me and then I went in'. If the jury thought he might be truthful in that assertion, they would need to consider whether or not, although entirely surprised by such a reception being accorded to him, this young man might not have been entitled reasonably to regard her action as amounting to an invitation to him to enter. If she in fact appeared to be welcoming him, the Crown do not suggest that he should have realised or even suspected that she was so behaving because, despite the moonlight, she thought he was someone else. Unless the jury were entirely satisfied that the Appellant made an effective and substantial entry into the bedroom without the complainant doing or saying anything to cause him to believe that she was consenting to his entering it, he ought not to be convicted of the offence charged. The point is a narrow one, as narrow maybe as the window sill which is crucial to this case. But this is a criminal charge of gravity and, even though one may suspect that his intention was to commit the offence charged, unless the facts show with clarity that he in fact committed it he ought not to remain convicted.

Some question arose as to whether or not Collins [the appellant] can be regarded as a trespasser ab initio. But we are entirely in agreement with the view expressed in *Archbold* [*Criminal Pleading, Evidence and Practice* (37th edn, 1969) p 572, para 1505] that the common law doctrine of trespass ab initio has no application to burglary under the Theft Act 1968. One further matter that was canvassed ought perhaps to be mentioned. The point was raised that, the complainant not being the tenant or occupier of the dwelling-house and her mother being apparently in occupation, this girl herself could not in any event have extended an effective invitation to enter, so that even if she had expressly and with full knowledge of all material facts invited Collins in, he would nevertheless be a trespasser. Whatever be the position in the law of tort, to accept such a proposition as acceptable in the criminal law would be unthinkable.

We have to say that this appeal must be allowed on the basis that the jury were never invited to consider the vital question as to whether this young man did enter the premises as a trespasser, that is to say knowing perfectly well that he had no invitation to enter or reckless of whether or not his entry was with permission. The certificate of the learned Judge, as we have already said, demonstrated that he felt there were points involved calling for further consideration. That consideration we have given to the best of our ability. For the reasons we have stated, the outcome of the appeal is that this young man must be acquitted of the charge preferred against him. The appeal is accordingly allowed and his conviction quashed.

Appeal allowed. Conviction quashed

> ≋ **Questions**
> (1) When did Collins enter the building? At that time what intention did he have?
> (2) When did Collins make a 'substantial' entry into the building? For what purpose was that entry also 'effective'?
> (3) Was the daughter's permission to enter the building enough to prevent Collins being a trespasser?

In the subsequent case of *Jones; Smith* [1976] 3 All ER 54, the Court of Appeal clarified that a person is a trespasser for the purposes of the offences of burglary if either:

(1) he enters premises of another knowing that he is entering in excess of the permission that has been given to him, or

(2) being reckless whether he is entering in excess of the permission that has been given to him to enter,

providing the facts are known to the accused which enable him to realize that he is acting in excess of the permission given or that he is acting recklessly as to whether he exceeds that permission. In that case D entered his father's property with intent to steal—the father having given him general permission to enter.

> ≋ **Question**
> Glanville Williams argued that the decision in *Jones and Smith* contradicts that in *Collins*, since in that case 'it must have been held . . . that the defendant was not a trespasser although, since he intended to commit rape if necessary, he knew that his intention was "in excess of the permission"' (*Textbook of Criminal Law* (2nd edn, 1983), p 849). The court in *Jones and Smith* evidently did not consider this aspect of it. If *Jones and Smith* is right, *Collins* should have been convicted of burglary. Do you agree?

Where it is open to the prosecution to do so the prosecution will normally rely on s 9(1)(b) rather than s 9(1)(a) (eg where the burglar steals or attempts to steal in the building). The reason for that is that under s 9(1)(b) it is not necessary to prove that D entered with the relevant intent. But, whichever limb is relied on, the prosecution must prove that D entered as a trespasser. It is not enough that D becomes a trespasser, for example by hiding in a store until after closing time: *Laing* [1995] Crim LR 395, CA. D who does so may, of course, thereafter commit burglary by entering another 'part' of the store as a trespasser.

15.1.2.3 Building or part of a building

In *Stevens v Gourley* (1859) 7 CBNS 99, a question arose whether a wooden structure measuring 16 by 13 feet and intended to be used as a shop was a building for the purposes of the Metropolitan Building Act 1855, though it was without foundations and merely rested on timbers laid on the surface. Byles J observed that a building must be 'intended to be permanent, or at least to endure for a considerable time'. So what of the portable cabins placed at building sites to provide eating and toilet facilities for those working on the site? Would it make any difference that the works are planned to take months or only a matter of days? In *B and S v Leathley* [1979] Crim LR 314, Carlisle Crown Court, a freezer container had been placed in a farmyard for goods storage. For some two or three years it had been resting on sleepers, was connected to the mains electricity and the doors were equipped with locks. It was held to be a building. Cf *Norfolk Constabulary v Seekings and Gould* [1986] Crim LR 167,

Norwich Crown Court. Needing extra storage space, a supermarket had two lorry trailers towed to the site. There they were unhitched, left standing on their wheeled chassis and connected to the mains electricity. Steps were provided for access and entry was made by unlocking the trailer shutters. They had been in use for a year when D and E tried to effect an entry. It was held that the trailers remained vehicles and had not become buildings. What if their tyres had been removed to prevent anyone taking them from the site?

In considering the appropriate interpretation of 'building' in s 2 of the Cremation Act 1902, Lord Neuberger MR in *R (Ghai) v Newcastle City Council* [2010] EWCA Civ 59, stated that if one approaches the issue of what 'building' means by making a preliminary assumption, it would be incorrect to take a somewhat artificially narrow meaning of the word and then see whether the context justifies a more expansive meaning. It is more appropriate to take the word's more natural, wider, meaning and then consider whether, and if so to what extent, that meaning is cut down by the statutory context in which the word is used.

It is important to remember that s 9(4) of the Theft Act 1968 confirms that 'building' encompasses inhabited vehicles and vessels, including when they are unoccupied.

≋ *Questions*

(1) Would a wedding marquee set up on the lawn of the house of the bride's parents be capable of being burgled?

(2) Why should it matter that the trespass is to a building? Does the inclusion of this element provide an indication as to what harm the offence is intended to protect against?

The issue of a 'part of a building' was addressed in *Walkington* [1979] 2 All ER 716, [1979] 1 WLR 1169, CA. D entered the 'counter area' (a rectangle made up from movable counters which housed a till and which was reserved to staff) of a department store and was seen to open and shut the till drawer. It was held, upholding D's conviction for burglary, that whether the counter area was sufficient to amount to an area from which the public were excluded was a matter for the jury; there was ample evidence from which the jury could conclude that it was such an area and that D knew it.

≋ *Questions*

Does Dan, a law student, commit burglary in any of the following cases?

(1) He enters an old telephone kiosk with intent to break open the coin box and steal its contents.

(2) He enters the law library and, seeing that no one is around, he goes behind the library counter and steals a bottle of juice that the library assistant had brought for her lunch.

(3) He enters the departmental secretary's room intending to pass through into the office of the head of department in order to steal an examination paper, but is stopped by the secretary before he reaches the office.

(4) He enters a hall of residence, intending to enter any room that might have been left unlocked, in order to steal therein.

(5) He falls asleep in a cinema and wakes to find the building closed. On his way out through the foyer he helps himself to some sweets from the kiosk which stands near the entrance.

(6) He enters the Law Department's computing facility intending to use a computer to order goods over the internet using an unauthorized credit card as payment for them.

15.1.3 Mens rea

The mens rea involves two elements: (a) as to the trespassory entry and (b) as to the ulterior offence.

15.1.3.1 Mens rea as to trespassory status

Collins (section 15.1.2, p 402) shows that D must be proved to know (or be subjectively reckless as to) the facts which make him a trespasser.

15.1.3.2 Mens rea as to the ulterior offence

It must be shown that D either:

- in respect of s 9(1)(a), entered with intent to steal, or to inflict GBH, or to do unlawful damage to the building or anything therein; or
- in respect of s 9(1)(b), entered and committed, or attempted to commit, the offence of stealing or of inflicting GBH.

It is not immediately apparent why D, if he enters a building as a trespasser without intent to commit any offence, is not a burglar if he thereafter decides to set it alight but is a burglar if he steals some trinket.

15.1.4 The ulterior offences

15.1.4.1 Theft

Stealing clearly means theft contrary to s 1 of the 1968 Act.

≋ Questions
(1) In *Morris* (section 13.3, p 348), was the defendant a burglar? Are all shoplifters?
(2) What of D, a plumber, who on arriving at V's house in response to a call-out realizes she is vulnerable and confused. He decides to lie to her as to the extent of the repair necessary. When, if at all, does he become a burglar?

In *Downer* [2009] EWCA Crim 1361, D was convicted of aggravated burglary against V. D claimed that V was a drug dealer who had taken his money but failed to supply the drugs, and that D had gone to V's house to get either the drugs or his money back.

≋ Questions
Can D be guilty of burglary if he enters a building as a trespasser with the genuinely held belief that he is retrieving property that belongs to him? Would such an argument constitute a true defence or does it negate an element of the offence? Note that in *Lopatta* (1983) 35 SASR 101, it was held that D's belief as to the law or facts does not have to be soundly based, provided it is genuinely held.

15.1.4.2 Grievous bodily harm

Grievous bodily harm must extend to those offences where the infliction of GBH is an offence (viz the Offences Against the Person Act 1861, ss 20 and 23). Following the decision in *Mandair*

[1995] 1 AC 208 (removing the distinction between causes and inflicts), it surely extends to the s 18 offence which uses 'causes' rather than 'inflicts'. Whether it extends to murder is undecided but it would certainly be surprising if it did not do so: the greater may be taken to include the less. It is important to note that there are differences depending on whether reliance is placed on s 9(1)(a) or s 9(1)(b):

- in respect of s 9(1)(a), intent must be proved, and thus the offence must be that under s 18 (GBH with intent to do GBH);

- in respect of s 9(1)(b), offences of s 18, 20 or 23 of the Offences Against the Person Act 1861 would suffice.

Under s 9(1)(b), another distinction seems to be suggested by *Jenkins* [1983] 1 All ER 1000, CA. It will be noticed that while s 9(1)(a) refers to 'offences of . . . inflicting on any person therein any grievous bodily harm', s 9(1)(b) merely refers to the infliction (or attempt to inflict) any grievous bodily harm without specifying that it must be an offence. This led the Court of Appeal in *Jenkins* to give the following example (at 1004):

> An intruder gains access to the house without breaking in (where there is an open window for instance). He is on the premises as a trespasser and his intrusion is observed by someone in the house of whom he may not even be aware, and as a result that person suffers a severe shock with a resulting stroke . . .

The House of Lords allowed the appeal in *Jenkins* [1984] AC 242, [1983] 3 All ER 448, without expressing any opinion on this matter.

15.1.5 Burglary in respect of a dwelling

Since the Criminal Justice Act 1991, burglary of a dwelling is a separate offence carrying a maximum sentence of 14 years' imprisonment. In addition, s 111 of the Powers of Criminal Courts (Sentencing) Act 2000 requires a judge to impose a minimum three-year custodial sentence upon conviction of a third 'domestic' burglary. Neither 'dwelling' nor 'domestic' is defined; however, s 9(4) of the Theft Act 1968 does state that references to dwelling encompass inhabited vehicles and vessels, including when they are unoccupied. In *Flack* [2013] EWCA Crim 115, [2103] Crim LR 521, the Court of Appeal declined to give guidance as to how dwelling ought to be interpreted, instead holding that it is a question of fact to be decided by the jury in each case. However, when considering whether an empty house undergoing renovations was a dwelling, Macduff J in *Sticklen* [2013] EWCA Crim 615 stated that, 'the justification for treating a dwelling as being different from other properties (and the judge mentioned a shed or a factory) is the very fact that it is someone's home, occupied, with personal and sentimental property within it. . . . Those factors do not apply here: there were no occupants, there were no personal objects, this was not someone's home with personal space being violated—indeed, no new tenant or purchaser had yet been identified. The premises were not only unoccupied, they had been empty for many months and were bare and unfurnished.' (See K. Laird, 'Conceptualising the Interpretation of "Dwelling" in s 9 of the Theft Act 1968' [2013] Crim LR 656.)

As 'dwelling' is an aggravating element in the offence warranting a higher maximum sentence of imprisonment, it should, in principle, import a requirement of mens rea.

15.2 Aggravated burglary

Theft Act 1968, s 10

> (1) A person is guilty of aggravated burglary if he commits any burglary and at the time has with him any firearm or imitation firearm, any weapon of offence, or any explosive; and for this purpose—
>
> (a) 'firearm' includes an airgun or air pistol, and 'imitation firearm' means anything which has the appearance of being a firearm, whether capable of being discharged or not; and
>
> (b) 'weapon of offence' means any article made or adapted for use for causing injury to or incapacitating a person, or intended by the person having it with him for such use; and
>
> (c) 'explosive' means any article manufactured for the purpose of producing a practical effect by explosion, or intended by the person having it with him for that purpose.
>
> (2) A person guilty of aggravated burglary shall on conviction on indictment be liable to imprisonment for life.

15.2.1 Articles of aggravation

These include (a) articles made for causing injury to a person; (b) articles adapted for causing injury to a person; (c) articles which D has with him for that purpose; (d) any article made for incapacitating a person; (e) any article adapted for incapacitating a person; and (f) any article which D has with him for that purpose.

15.2.2 At the time of the burglary

It must be proved that D had the article of aggravation with him at the time of the commission of the burglary. Where the charge is one of entry with intent (s 9(1)(a)) this is the time of the entry; where it is one of committing a specified offence, having entered, etc (s 9(1)(b)), it is the time of commission of the specified offence. In *Francis* [1982] Crim LR 363, CA, the Ds who were armed with sticks were allowed by V to enter after they noisily demanded entry. They then discarded their sticks and subsequently stole articles in the house. Their convictions for aggravated burglary were quashed; they may have entered with weapons of offence but there was no evidence that at the point of entry they intended to steal. But in *O'Leary* (1986) 82 Cr App R 341, CA, D's conviction for aggravated burglary was upheld where, having entered as a trespasser, he took a knife from the kitchen, went upstairs and forced the occupants to part with property at knifepoint. At the time of committing the offence under s 9(1)(b) he had with him the weapon of offence.

Importantly, in *Wiggins* [2012] EWCA Crim 885, Pitchford LJ confirmed that where the principal in an offence of burglary does not have with him at the time of the commission of the offence an article of aggravation, but a secondary party does, neither party can be guilty of aggravated burglary.

15.2.2.1 Has with him

'Has with him' has been interpreted to require knowledge by D that he has the article with him since what aggravates the burglary, and attracts the higher penalty, must be D's decision to have the article of aggravation with him: *Stones* (1989) 89 Cr App R 26, CA.

Under s 10, what appears to aggravate the burglary is not the use of the firearm, weapon of offence or explosive, but the *possession* of any of these articles at the time of the commission of the burglary. If at the time of commission D 'has with him' a firearm or a kilo of explosive it can be no defence that D did not use it in the course of the burglary and never intended to do so: *Klass* [1998] 1 Cr App R 453.

With 'weapon of offence' the position is slightly more complicated. Two categories must be distinguished:

(1) if the article is one made or adapted for use for causing injury or for incapacitating, D may be convicted of aggravated burglary though he neither uses nor intends to use the weapon in the course of the burglary;

(2) if the article is intended by D for use for causing injury or for incapacitating, D may be convicted of aggravated burglary only if he had it with him for such use. But if D does have the article with him for such use, he may be convicted of aggravated burglary though he does not intend to use the article for such use during the course of the burglary. So D's conviction for aggravated burglary was upheld in *Stones* even though, as he claimed, he carried a knife in case he was attacked by a rival gang and had no intention of using it during the burglary. The mischief aimed at by s 10, the court said, included the case where the weapon was carried to injure a person unconnected with the burglary because D, if challenged, might use it during the burglary.

But the section requires that D 'has with him' the firearm, etc at the time of the commission of the offence. In *O'Leary*, D, it may fairly be said, 'has with him' a weapon, the kitchen knife, at the time he threatened the householders since he had possession of it for some moments.

≈≈≈ *Question*

Suppose D is in the kitchen in the course of stealing the food processor when he is surprised by the householder. D seizes a rolling pin and threatens the householder with this. Is this aggravated burglary? Cf *Kelly* (1992) 97 Cr App R 295, [1993] Crim LR 763, CA, and commentary.

15.3 Trespass with intent to commit a sexual offence

Sexual Offences Act 2003, s 63

63. Trespass with intent to commit a sexual offence

(1) A person commits an offence if—

(a) he is a trespasser on any premises,

(b) he intends to commit a relevant sexual offence on the premises, and

(c) he knows that, or is reckless as to whether, he is a trespasser.

(2) In this section—

'premises' includes a structure or part of a structure;

'relevant sexual offence' [is all those in that Part of the Act];

'structure' includes a tent, vehicle or vessel or other temporary or movable structure.

Note the significant differences from burglary: (a) the offence is wider, since any trespass is sufficient and there is no need to prove a trespassory entry; (b) the trespass relates to 'premises', which is wider than the concept of a building or part of a building; (c) the concept of 'structure' is widely defined; (d) as with s 9(1)(a) there is no need for the ulterior offence to occur; (e) the ulterior offences are all those in Part 1 of the Sexual Offences Act 2003. In *Pacurar* [2016] EWCA Crim 569, the Court of Appeal held that the prosecution does not need to specify on the indictment the particular sexual offence that D may have intended to commit on the premises.

≋ *Questions*

(1) Was the creation of this offence necessary? Consider this question in the light of *Heeney* [2009] EWCA Crim 1393. In that case D entered a woman's flat at 2 am and made his way to her bedroom where he pounced on her, pushed her onto the bed and then began to touch her sexually. The court observed that those facts arguably gave rise to a charge under s 63 or s 3 of the 2003 Act, D having originally been charged with attempted rape.

(2) Would Collins have committed the s 63 offence?

15.4 Going equipped with housebreaking implements

Section 25 of the Theft Act 1968 makes it an offence for a person to have in his possession when not in his abode any article for use in the course of or in connection with any burglary or theft. The offence is described as 'going equipped'. Cf s 6 of the Fraud Act 2006, section 16.6, p 440.

FURTHER READING

P. J. Pace, 'Burglarious Trespass' [1985] Crim LR 716

16
Fraud

Fraud:

A person is guilty of fraud

- under s 2 if he dishonestly makes a false representation with intent to gain or cause loss or expose another to a risk of loss;
- under s 3 if he dishonestly fails to disclose information which he is under a legal duty to disclose with intent to gain or cause loss or expose another to a risk of loss;
- under s 4 if he abuses a position he occupies in which he is expected to safeguard the financial interests of another or not to act against them with intent to gain or cause loss or expose another to a risk of loss.

Section 11 of the Fraud Act:

D commits an offence if, by a dishonest act, he obtains services for which payment is or will become due and knowing that the services are or might have to be paid for, with intent to avoid payment in whole or in part, D fails to pay.

Section 6 of the Fraud Act:

D commits an offence if he possesses or has under his control any article for use in the course of or in connection with any fraud.

Section 7 of the Fraud Act:

D is guilty of an offence if he makes, adapts, supplies or offers to supply any article knowing that it is designed or adapted for use in the course of or in connection with fraud, or intending it to be used to commit, or assist in the commission of, fraud.

Some of the controversies that will be examined in this chapter include:

(1) whether the general fraud offence extends the scope of liability too far;

(2) the extent to which an individual can commit a criminal offence in circumstances where his conduct would not give rise to civil liability;

(3) the fact that, unlike the Theft Act 1968, under the Fraud Act 2006 there is no guarantee of an acquittal where D thinks he has a right in law to act as he did;

(4) given the width of the actus reus of the general fraud offence, whether the effect of the Fraud Act 2006 is to criminalize lying.

16.1 Introduction

This chapter is concerned with the offence of fraud. It is a statutory offence that can be committed in one of three ways: by making a false representation, by failing to disclose information and by abuse of position. Each has a different actus reus and mens rea, but for the most part liability turns on whether D was dishonest. In addition, this chapter examines the related offences of obtaining services dishonestly, possession of articles for fraud and making or supplying articles for use in frauds.

16.1.1 The general fraud offence under the 2006 Act

The principal offence is the general fraud offence created by s 1 in the following terms:

> (1) A person is guilty of fraud if he is in breach of any of the sections listed in subsection (2) (which provide for different ways of committing the offence).
>
> (2) The sections are—
>
>   (a) section 2 (fraud by false representation),
>
>   (b) section 3 (fraud by failing to disclose information), and
>
>   (c) section 4 (fraud by abuse of position).

Each form of the offence is based on dishonest conduct against property interests, and carries a maximum ten-year sentence on indictment. Fraud is an incredibly wide offence, deliberately drafted to avoid technicality.

16.1.2 Background

The Fraud Act 2006 came into force on 15 January 2007. The immediate history of the Act can be traced to the Law Commission Consultation Paper No 155, *Legislating the Criminal Code: Fraud and Deception* (1999), the subsequent Law Commission Report No 276, *Fraud* (2002) and the Home Office Consultation Paper, *Fraud Law Reform* (2004) which developed the Law Commission's proposals. However, calls for reform of the dishonesty offences, and in particular those based on deception, have been circulating for many years.

The Fraud Act 2006 abolished all the deception offences in the Theft Acts 1968 and 1978 (including one inserted by the Theft (Amendment) Act 1996). It replaced the deception offences with a basic fraud offence with emphasis on the defendant's conduct rather than the actions or beliefs of the victim. It introduced very wide-reaching preliminary offences of possessing/making equipment to commit frauds. The offence of obtaining services by deception was replaced by obtaining services dishonestly. Controversially, conspiracy to defraud remains, but whether it can be safely abolished without leaving serious gaps in the law will be kept under review. Guidance has been issued by the Attorney General on when it is appropriate for prosecutors to rely on that charge.

16.1.2.1 The merits of a general fraud offence

The Fraud Act 2006 was enacted to remedy the defects in the various deception offences that it replaced. Some academic commentators argued that the only way of meeting the difficulties created by these offences was to reject them in favour of a general fraud offence. The merits of general fraud offences have been debated for decades. The core advantage offered is by shifting the focus of the offence from whether D made false representations that were believed by V and caused a specific result, to whether D's dishonest conduct was sufficiently fraudulent to give rise to criminal liability. See further G. R. Sullivan, 'Framing an Acceptable General Offence of Fraud' (1989) 53 J Crim L 92.

Over the years, proponents of a general fraud offence argued for a model requiring not only that the prosecution prove that the defendant behaved dishonestly and with intent to gain/cause loss but also that there were economic interests actually imperilled by the conduct. This would certainly pose fewer problems than the model on which the Fraud Act is based, where there is no requirement of proof of the conduct having the potential to imperil economic interests or of D having caused the victim to believe any representation.

When considering the matter, most commentators doubted, however, whether a general fraud offence could ever be drafted which does not extend potential criminal liability too far (see J. C. Smith, 'Fraud and The Criminal Law' in P. Birks (ed), *Criminal Justice and Human Rights—Pressing Problems in the Law* (1995), Vol 1, p 49). By the end of the chapter you will be able to assess for yourself how accurate their belief was.

The Fraud Act is based on recommendations of the Law Commission set out in its Report No 276, *Fraud* (2002):

1.6 In asking us to consider the law of fraud, the former Home Secretary was particularly interested in whether the introduction of a general fraud offence would improve the criminal law. We have now come to the conclusion that it would. We consider that it would improve the law in each of the respects raised by the former Home Secretary:

(1) It should make the law more comprehensible to juries, especially in serious fraud trials. The charges which are currently employed in such trials are numerous, and none of them adequately describe or encapsulate the meaning of 'fraud'. The statutory offences are too specific to offer a general description of fraud; while the common law offence of conspiracy to defraud is so wide that it offers little guidance on the difference between fraudulent and lawful conduct. Thus, at present, juries are not given a straightforward definition of fraud. If they were, and if that were the key to the indictment, it should enable them to focus more closely on whether the facts of the case fit the crimes as charged.

(2) A general offence of fraud would be a useful tool in effective prosecutions. Specific offences are sometimes wrongly charged, in circumstances when another offence would have been more suitable. This can result in unjustified acquittals and costly appeals. Furthermore, it is possible that excessively broad crimes, such as conspiracy to defraud, may result in prosecutors wasting resources on those who should never have been charged at all. A generalised crime which nonetheless provides a clear definition of fraudulent behaviour may assist prosecutors to weigh up whether they have a realistic chance of securing a conviction.

(3) Introducing a single crime of fraud would dramatically simplify the law of fraud. Clear, simple law is fairer than complicated, inaccessible law. If a citizen is contemplating activities which could amount to a crime, a clear, simple law gives better guidance on whether the conduct is criminal, and fairer warning of what could happen if it is. Furthermore, when a defendant is charged with a clear, simple law, they will be better able to understand their options when pleading to the charge; and, if pleading not guilty, they will be better able to conduct their defence.

(4) A general offence of fraud would be aimed at encompassing fraud in all its forms. It would not focus on particular ways or means of committing frauds. Thus it should be better able to keep pace with developing technology.

1.7 In line with these conclusions, we recommend that the eight offences of deception created by the Theft Acts 1968–96 should be repealed, and that the common law crime of conspiracy to defraud should be abolished. In their place we recommend the creation of two new statutory offences—one of fraud, and one of obtaining services dishonestly.

Although the Fraud Act 2006 does make it easier to prosecute instances of fraud, the pitfalls of a general fraud offence are not to be underestimated. Consider the following passage.

D. Ormerod, 'Criminalising Lying' [2007] Crim LR 193, concludes at 218:

> General fraud offences offer many practical advantages including the clearer expression of large scale criminality in one charge; the ability to render complex schemes more readily understood by jurors; the avoidance of fragmenting factual chronologies to meet technical requirements of specific counts on the indictment; the removal of the risk of duplicity or of overloading the indictment; and the ease of cross-admissibility of evidence. These practical advantages must not, however, be allowed to produce a general offence that is overbroad, based too heavily on the ill-defined concept of dishonesty, too vague to meet the obligation under Art.7 of the ECHR, and otherwise deficient in principle. It is certainly questionable whether the Act has secured these practical advantages at the cost of undermining important principles. The offences are so wide that they provoke the kind of astonishment that Professor Green expresses when considering the lowest common denominator of the moral content of fraud: 'if fraud really were to encompass not just stealing by deceit, but also deceptive and non-deceptive breaches of trust, conflicts of interest, nondisclosure of material facts, exploitation, taking unfair advantage, non-performance of contractual obligations, and misuse of corporate assets, it would be virtually impossible to distinguish between different offenses in terms of their nature and seriousness, and even to know whether and when one had committed a crime.'

(See further S. P. Green, *Lying, Cheating and Stealing: A Moral Theory of White Collar Crime* (2005), p 151 and Ch 14 generally.)

What is important to appreciate about the Fraud Act 2006 before proceeding any further is that it is an offence drafted in the inchoate mode; D can be guilty of fraud without ever having caused any loss or having gained anything. In this respect, it is similar to other inchoate offences, such as attempts and conspiracy. Andrew Ashworth explains the new approach in the following way, with reference to the offence of fraud by making a false representation.

A. Ashworth, 'The Criminal Law's Ambivalence About Outcomes'
in R. Cruft, M. H. Kramer and M. R. Reiff (eds), *Crime, Punishment, and Responsibility: The Jurisprudence of Antony Duff* (2011)

> It seems that what happened in 2006 was that the law relating to fraud moved from an objectivist model, in which the causing of a particular outcome by particular means was prohibited, to a broadly subjectivist model, focused on the defendant's culpability and on what the defendant intended to achieve . . . What is interesting about the impact of the 2006 Act is that the new, broader, subjectivist definition of fraud includes 'those that fail as well as those that succeed' in the substantive offence. Indeed, by dint of the new definition, they have not failed, because all that needs to be proved is that they tried—that they made the false representation. In effect, the new offence of fraud has moved into the space that was previously occupied by attempt to defraud . . .

16.2 Section 2: fraud by false representation

The offence created by s 1(2)(a) of the Act is incredibly broad. The offence is described in s 2, which provides:

> (1) A person is in breach of this section if he—
>
>   (a) dishonestly makes a false representation, and

(b) intends, by making the representation—

    (i) to make a gain for himself or another, or

    (ii) to cause loss to another or to expose another to a risk of loss.

(2) A representation is false if—

    (a) it is untrue or misleading, and

    (b) the person making it knows that it is, or might be, untrue or misleading.

(3) 'Representation' means any representation as to fact or law, including a representation as to the state of mind of—

    (a) the person making the representation, or

    (b) any other person.

(4) A representation may be express or implied.

(5) For the purposes of this section a representation may be regarded as made if it (or anything implying it) is submitted in any form to any system or device designed to receive, convey or respond to communications (with or without human intervention).

Section 1 provides that the maximum sentence on indictment is ten years.

The actus reus requires proof that D made a false representation; and the mens rea requires proof that D knew the representation was or knew that it might be false, and acted dishonestly, and with intent to gain, or cause loss. Contrast the offence with those of deception under the old law: it had to be proved that D's conduct actually deceived V and caused him to do whatever act was appropriate to the offence charged—transferring property, executing a valuable security, etc. Under s 2, there is no need to prove: a result of any kind; that the alleged victim or indeed any person believed any representation; that any person acted on it; or that the accused succeeded in making a gain or causing a loss by the representation.

≈ *Questions*

Under the s 2 offence can D be liable in the following cases?

(1) D tells V that the T-shirt he is selling was worn by David Beckham. V knows that the statement is untrue, but likes the T-shirt so buys it anyway;

(2) D tells V that he is authorized to use the credit card (with D's father's name on it). V does not care whether that is true or not and takes payment from the card;

(3) D sends an email to V (and 10,000 others) offering to sell them a guaranteed way to make money on the stock market which would never fail and net them 100 per cent returns in a week. V does not read or even see the false statement as his email provider deletes it as spam;

(4) D sends the email as in (3), but his ISP automatically deletes it as spam before it is sent to anyone;

(5) D visits a self-service fuel station and, having filled his car, tells the cashier that he has an arrangement with the manager so that he does not need to pay;

(6) D decides to fake his own death and claim the insurance money. He sets out in his canoe intending to fake an accident at sea. He paddles out and then abandons the canoe, swimming safely to shore. He then hides away with the help of his accomplice wife who makes the demand to the insurance company. After six months the company pay out to the wife; and

(7) in order to ensure that his son is offered a place at the best local school, D provides his sister's address on the application form instead of his own, as it is within the school's catchment area.

In each case, consider also at what point in time D would have completed the offence under s 2.

16.2.1 Making a false representation

16.2.1.1 Making

A false representation can be 'made' by speech, writing or conduct. D satisfies this element of the offence as much by saying to a customer: 'this is a genuine Renoir I have for sale' as by describing the painting in those terms in his sale catalogue. Forms of physical conduct other than speech or writing will suffice, as where D nods assent in response to the question 'Is this a genuine Renoir?' Classic examples will be false representations on mortgage application forms or loan application forms. The s 2 form of the offence is also specifically designed to criminalize 'phishing' on the internet. D who posts on the internet a website purporting to be that of a bank or financial institution, encouraging account holders to reveal their passwords and confidential information, will commit the offence. It does not matter that the website is ignored by everyone; the making of the false representation suffices.

It is arguable that the representation is made either (a) as soon as D articulates it, (b) only if it is also addressed to something, (c) only when it is actually perceived as such by a person, that is, when it is communicated. It is submitted that under s 2 of the Fraud Act 2006 there need not be a completed communication in the sense that a person must read or hear or see D's statement in order for it to constitute a representation. A representation would seem to be 'made' as soon as articulated, but in accordance with the ordinary use of the word, a representation must be made 'to' someone or something. Cf C. Withey, 'The Fraud Act 2006' (2007) 71 J Crim L 220, suggesting that the offence is not committed unless a communication is completed. This is difficult to square with the statutory wording and Parliament's intent.

The false representation element of the offence is so ill-defined that it is unclear whether D can be liable for the s 2 offence when he omits to rectify a belief V has formed. Section 3 of the Act expressly provides for an offence of fraud by failing to disclose (section 16.3, p 431). A broad reading of s 2 would overlap significantly with that section. However, s 3 is limited to cases in which the defendant is under *a legal duty* to disclose information. The position seems to be:

- if D makes a false representation he can be liable under s 2;

- if D makes a false representation, but at the time he makes it, he believes it to be true—it is submitted that if D discovers that the statement is false and thereafter does not seek to rectify any misunderstanding, he should be liable under s 2;

- if D makes a statement which is true, but which V misunderstands and on V's misunderstanding would render the statement false, D is not liable at the time he makes the statement. If D realizes that V has misunderstood him:

  – D is liable under s 3 if D is under a legal duty to inform V; but

  – if D is not under a legal duty to inform V, D's only liability may be under s 2; and

- if D makes a true statement, but circumstances change so that the statement becomes inaccurate and D realizes this, D may be liable under s 2. D will be liable under s 3 if he is under a legal duty to correct his statement. As the *Allen* case, later in this section, p 419, demonstrates, liability will turn on the facts.

In *DPP v Ray* [1974] AC 370, Lord Pearson referred to there being a 'continuing representation' in the 1968 Act deception offences: 'By continuing representation I mean in this case not a continuing effect of an initial representation, but a representation which is being made by conduct at every moment throughout that course of conduct . . .' Lord Hodson held that under the deception offences, while a party may be under a duty to communicate a relevant change of circumstances before the contract is made, he does not deceive the seller by failing to communicate such a change after the contract has been entered into.

In *Rai* [2000] 1 Cr App R 242, [2000] Crim LR 192, D obtained a grant from the city council to provide a bathroom for his disabled mother. Before it was installed, she died. D did not inform the council and allowed the work to proceed. He was convicted of obtaining services by deception. Rai argued that he had no legal or contractual duty to inform the council of his mother's death. The Court of Appeal rejected this argument and held that positive acquiescence could amount to deception.

This issue was considered more recently and with explicit reference to the Fraud Act 2006 in *Government of UAE v Allen* [2012] EWHC 1712 (Admin). A was a British national who obtained a mortgage from a bank in the United Arab Emirates. The mortgage was to be paid over a period of 20 years and the funds were to come from A's credit card account, which was held with the bank. A supplied the bank with an undated cheque made out for the amount of the loan as security in case she defaulted on the payments. Some 20 months later, A defaulted on her mortgage payments and the bank sought to cash the cheque, but it was dishonoured as A did not have sufficient funds in her account to cover the amount. A returned to the UK and was convicted in her absence in the UAE of an offence of issuing an uncovered cheque and was sentenced to three years' imprisonment. The UAE sought A's extradition and the issue for the Divisional Court to consider was whether the requirement of dual criminality was made out, that is, whether A would on those facts have committed an offence in the UK.

Toulson LJ referred to the cases mentioned previously and found that A would not have committed an offence in the UK.

> There are some circumstances recognised in the case law in which a person who has made a true representation will be under a duty to inform the representee if there is a significant change in the circumstances, as previously represented, before the representation has been acted upon. In particular, where a representation is made in the course of negotiations, it will be readily understood as intended to subsist up to the conclusion of the negotiations, so that if it becomes incorrect before it has been acted upon by the representee the representor will be guilty of misrepresentation by remaining silent.

On the facts of the case it was held that A gave her bank no undertaking that she would provide it with information about any later change in her circumstances. Further, Toulson LJ concluded that there was no principled basis for construing an implied continuing representation into the loan agreement. The court observed that implied representations are legal constructs intended to give effect to what honest parties involved in a transaction would reasonably read into each others' conduct.

It is said by commentators that the overriding principle should be that the criminal law ought to take its lead from the civil law; the maxim *caveat emptor* ought to operate to restrict the scope of liability. The issue was debated in the early parliamentary stages of the Bill and the Attorney General accepted that there are occasions when:

> something that most of us naturally might think of as a non-disclosure is transformed by a fiction of the law into an implicit misrepresentation. But it is a fiction; it is not how people think about it. People will frequently say, 'I was not misled because I understand that he was implicitly making this representation to me. He just did not disclose something; he was dishonest in not disclosing it;

and the purpose of that was to make a gain or to do something else'. One can think of many other examples where that would be the true basis on which a charge would be laid. (Hansard HL, 19 July 2005, cols 1411–1412)

However, remember that in *Hinks* [2000] UKHL 53, [2001] Crim LR 162 (see section 13.3, p 346) the House of Lords was willing to find criminal liability in circumstances were there was no civil liability.

≋ *Questions*

(1) Do you agree with Toulson LJ's example that failure to bring to the other side's attention a change of circumstances when conducting a negotiation warrants criminalization? If there is to be any liability at all, should it not be for a contractual misrepresentation or the tort of deceit?

(2) D establishes a website asking people to sponsor him to do the London Marathon in a year's time. D's training does not go so well and six months before the marathon he decides not to run it, but still intends to collect money for charity. Fraud? What if D had never intended to run the marathon?

16.2.1.2 'Attempted' false representation

Since the s 2 offence can be committed as soon as D has made a false representation, there is only limited scope for a charge of attempt. Possible examples include where D, having prepared documents containing false statements, is apprehended en route to post those to V or where D unwittingly tells the truth. In *Deller* (1952) 36 Cr App R 184 (see Chapter 20), D induced V to purchase his car by representing, *inter alia*, that it was free from encumbrances, that is, that D had ownership and was free to sell it. In fact, D had previously executed a document that purported to mortgage the car to a finance company and, no doubt, he thought he was telling a lie. He was charged with a deception-based offence. However, the document by which the transaction had been effected was probably void in law for the technical reason that it was as an unregistered bill of sale. If the document was void the car *was* free from encumbrances—'. . . quite accidentally and, strange as it may sound, dishonestly, the appellant had told the truth'. D's conviction was therefore quashed by the Court of Criminal Appeal, for, though he had mens rea, no actus reus had been established. The Court of Appeal considered *Deller* in *Cornelius* [2012] EWCA Crim 500. D made a number of representations on various mortgage application forms that he thought were false but which turned out to be true. D's convictions were therefore quashed, as he had made no false representations. The Court of Appeal declined to substitute a conviction for attempted fraud as, contrary to the defendant in *Deller*, the court could not conclude that the jury were sure that Cornelius had intended to be dishonest in respect of these very technical representations. There was no evidence that he had turned his mind to the veracity or otherwise of the statements on the mortgage application forms.

≋ *Questions*

(1) Given how widely the offence is drafted, is what would typically be considered an 'attempt' to commit fraud contrary to s 2 in fact an instance of the full offence? Consider D, who goes to an elderly person's home and tells her that her roof needs extensive repairs that will cost £5,000. D begins to 'repair' the roof but runs away when

the victim's son is called. Although D never received a deposit for the 'repairs', is he not guilty of the full offence as soon as he made the false representation with the requisite mens rea? For the contrary position, see *Ward* [2011] EWCA Crim 212. Think back to Ashworth, section 16.1.1, p 416.

(2) Does the idea of attempted fraud extend the scope of criminal liability too widely or is it necessary to catch the putative fraudster who inadvertently makes a true representation?

16.2.1.3 Express or implied representations

By s 2(4), a representation may be express or implied. Subsection (4) is included for the avoidance of doubt. The inclusion of the word 'implied' might prove problematic as it adds to the ambiguity of the scope of the offence. One of the acknowledged difficulties with the old law was that it presented problems for the courts in relation to implied representations: see *DPP v Ray* (section 16.2.1.1, p 419).

In *Government of UAE v Allen* [2012] EWHC 1712 (Admin), the Court reviewed the authorities (*Hazelton* (1874) LR 2 CCR 134, *Metropolitan Police Comr v Charles* [1976] 3 All ER 112, [1977] AC 177, HL, *Gilmartin* [1983] 1 All ER 829, [1983] QB 953, CA) and Toulson LJ concluded:

> 39. To summarize, it is easy to see that a person who obtains goods or services by giving a cheque in payment which he knows that he is not going to be in a position to meet, but who does not disclose that fact to the supplier, carries out a form of deception.

16.2.1.4 Credit cards and debit cards

When a person presents his credit or debit card he makes a representation (a) that he has the authority to use that card, and (b) that payment will be made. Under the old law this caused problems. That difficulty is now removed because under the 2006 Act the only requirements are that the representation made is false and that D intends to gain/cause loss by that false representation. Under the old law it had to be shown to be by the false representation that D obtained. However, the difficulty might be said not to be eliminated altogether, but to have shifted from an element of causation in the actus reus to one of mens rea. Whereas under the old law it had to be shown to be by the false representation that D obtained; under the new law it has to be shown that D intends that by his false representation he will gain.

Consider D who proffers a card which he has no authority to use. The fact that payment will be made by the card-issuing company means that D's representation as to payment will in most cases *not* be false. The debit card contains an undertaking by the bank that, if the conditions on the card are satisfied, the payment will be honoured. The position with credit cards is similar. The bank issuing the card enters into contracts with the trader, agreeing to pay the trader the sum shown on a voucher signed by the customer/confirmed by chip and pin when making a purchase, provided that the conditions are satisfied. In the case of credit cards, the contract between the bank and the trader precedes the purchase by the customer, whereas in the case of the debit card the contract is made when the trader accepts the customer's cheque/ debit card, relying on the card which is produced. The trader accepting either type of card will usually do so simply because the conditions on the card are satisfied. He will not know whether the customer is exceeding his authority and using the card in breach of contract with the bank. He will get his money in any event.

Is D making a separate false representation that he is authorized to use the card? Some commentators argue that there is not even a false representation in such circumstances: 'there is no rule of law that the user of a cheque card or credit card is deemed to represent that he has authority to use it' (J. Parry et al, *Arlidge and Parry on Fraud* (5th edn, 2016), para 4.068). The argument is that there can only be a representation as to authority by D if he thinks that it will matter to V, and since the trader, V, will not care whether D is authorized, there is no false representation. It is submitted this interpretation places too much emphasis on the likely significance to V. That issue is no longer of relevance under the 2006 Act because the question is not whether V might be deceived or believe a matter, but rather whether it is a representation to the trader that D has authority to use the card. If he did not, the trader would not accept it because otherwise the trader would be an accomplice to D's fraud on the bank.

The Law Commission in its Report No 276 stated, at para 7.16:

> One of the defects of the present law identified in Part III above, however, is that the concept of deception arguably implies a *belief*, on the part of the victim, in the truth of the proposition falsely represented by the defendant. In general such a requirement would present no more difficulty than the requirement in the pre-1968 law that the property be obtained *by* the false pretence, because if the victim handed over the property despite *not* believing the pretence to be true then the required causal link would not be present. Even where the representation is successful in achieving the desired objective, however, in certain circumstances it is arguably unrealistic to speak of the representee *believing* it. The chief example is the misuse of credit cards and other payment instruments. We now believe that such conduct would be covered in a more convincing and less artificial way if the concept of deception were replaced by that of misrepresentation. Since the merchant who accepts the card in payment does not care whether the defendant has authority to use it, it is debatable whether the merchant can be said to be *deceived*. It is clear from *Charles* and *Lambie*, however, that by tendering the card the defendant is impliedly and falsely *representing* that he or she has authority to use it for the transaction in question. In our view that should suffice, even if the defendant knows that the representee is indifferent whether the representation is true. We have therefore concluded that this form of the new offence should be defined in terms of misrepresentation rather than deception. For most practical purposes, however, the distinction is immaterial.

Is it *by the* false representation as to the authority to use the card that D intends to gain/cause loss/expose to a risk of loss? See *Gilbert* (2012) discussed at section 16.2.5.3, p 428.

16.2.1.5 Representations as to 'fact' or 'law' or opinion

Representations as to present facts will create little difficulty for the courts. If D asserts that he is selling a genuine Rolex watch and it is to his knowledge a fake, he commits the offence. Section 2(3) also expressly provides that 'any representation' as to law will suffice. Representations of law ought to be equally simple: for example, D and V are reading a will and D, V's solicitor, deliberately misrepresents its legal effect.

Section 2(3) also provides that a representation as to a state of mind of any person will suffice. A representation as to a present intention of either the accused or some other person will therefore be sufficient. Representations as to present intentions may be express or implied. In *Allen* (section 16.2.1.1, p 419), the Divisional Court held that a statement that amounts only to a promise of future action may have effect as a contractual promise, but will not come within the legal classification of a representation.

≈ *Questions*

(1) In response to V's demand for payment of his invoice, D sends an email saying he will pay V tomorrow. What is D's liability if:

(a) D had no intention of paying tomorrow and was just fobbing V off?

> (b) D genuinely believed that he would be able to pay tomorrow provided D himself
>   was paid today?
> (2) D advertises his beer as 'probably the best in the world'. Fraud?
> (3) D embellishes the qualifications on his CV in order to gain a succession of higher paying
>   jobs. Fraud?

Problems arise in relation to quotations as to price. Under the old law it was held that it is a misrepresentation of fact for the accused to state 'that they [had] effected necessary repairs to a roof [which repairs were specified], that they had done the work in a proper and workmanlike manner and that [a specified sum] was a fair and reasonable sum to charge for the work involved': *Jeff and Bassett* (1966) 51 Cr App R 28, CA. The evidence showed that nothing needed to be done to the roof, what had been done served no useful purpose and it could have been done for £5, whereas £35 was charged.

Under the old law, in *Silverman* (1987) 86 Cr App R 213, [1987] Crim LR 574, CA, D charged two elderly sisters grossly excessive prices for work done on their flat. The sisters trusted D and assumed that the price was a fair one. D's conviction for deception was quashed for other reasons but the court said, 'In such circumstances of mutual trust, one party depending on the other for fair and reasonable conduct, the criminal law may apply if one party takes dishonest advantage of the other by representing as a fair charge that which he, but not the other, knows is dishonestly excessive.'

Under the new legislation there are numerous cases in which individuals have been found guilty of fraud in circumstances where they have told the victim, only sometimes incorrectly, that remedial work was required on their property and have then gone on to charge excessive prices for it. For example, in *Wenman* [2013] EWCA Crim 340, D was found guilty of fraud for charging an elderly person £25,600 for work to his house that was actually valued at £800. In *Greig* [2010] EWCA Crim 1183, D was paid £6,850 for work that was unnecessary and in any event should only have cost £300. In this case the jury were invited to infer that D must have dishonestly misrepresented the value of the job given the discrepancy between its true value and what D was paid.

> ≋ **Question**
> Suppose a car dealer, aware that the buyer does not know the first thing about cars, sells the buyer a car for £10,000 which he knows to be worth not more than £2,500. Fraud? To what extent does the fraud offence conflict with capitalist ideals of sharp business practice?

16.2.2 False representations and machines

The prevailing opinion under the old law was that it was not possible in law to deceive a machine. The problem of how to criminalize the 'deception' of a machine has become an acute one in recent years, as businesses become increasingly automated with, for example, facilities to pay by credit card via an automated telephone system or via the internet. The offence under s 2 is capable of meeting some of these difficulties and, coupled with the offence in s 11 of the 2006 Act (section 16.5, p 438), should offer adequate protection against electronic frauds across a wide range of circumstances. See also I. Walden, *Computer Crimes and Digital Investigations* (2007), paras 3.50–3.53.

According to the Explanatory Notes, s 2(5) is designed to put beyond doubt that:

fraud can be committed where a person makes a representation to a machine and a response can be produced without any need for human involvement. (An example is where a person enters a number into a 'CHIP and PIN' machine.) The Law Commission had concluded that, although it was not clear whether a representation could be made to a machine, such a provision was unnecessary [see para 8.4 of their report]. But subsection (5) is expressed in fairly general terms because it would be artificial to distinguish situations involving modern technology, where it is doubtful whether there has been a 'representation', because the only recipient of the false statement is a machine or a piece of software, from other situations not involving modern technology where a false statement is submitted to a system for dealing with communications but is not in fact communicated to a human being (e.g., postal or messenger systems).

Under s 2(5) it is sufficient if 'anything implying' a representation is made in any form to any device.

> ∼∼ *Questions*
> (1) Is a document 'submitted' when the defendant saves the typing to his hard drive on his internet-ready computer, or is it only 'submitted' when he sends it via email?
> (2) Suppose D1 intends to circulate his sales brochure with false statements in it by email at 8 am the following day, and he puts this false prospectus in his 'mail waiting to be sent' folder addressed to V. Has he committed the offence?

16.2.3 'False' representation

The representation must be false. This requires not only that it is untrue or misleading, but that D is aware that it is or might be untrue or misleading. The definition has an element of mens rea. It is necessary for the Crown to establish as a matter of actus reus that the representation is false or misleading aside from any issue about D's knowledge as to its truth or otherwise. However, the states of mind of the parties are likely to be important. Whether a representation is false usually depends on the meaning intended or understood by the parties. That will usually be a question for the jury, even where the statement is made in a document. There may, however, be exceptional cases where the issue is about the legal effect of a document. In those circumstances it is for the judge to decide.

What do the words 'untrue' or 'misleading' mean? The Home Office in its *Response to Consultees* (2004, para 19) accepted that misleading meant 'less than wholly true and capable of an interpretation to the detriment of the victim'.

If the representation is untrue or misleading, there is no explicit defence that the representation was made for good reason or with lawful excuse, as where D said he made the false representation in order to recover property which he believed belonged to him. In such a case the defendant must rely on the claim of a lack of dishonesty.

In *Augunas* [2013] EWCA Crim 2046, the Court of Appeal confirmed that the Crown must prove that D knew the representation was false; it is not sufficient that the reasonable person would have known it to be false. The test is subjective, not objective.

16.2.3.1 Untrue

The word is an ordinary English word and no doubt the courts will suggest that juries should be directed to approach it as such. The only potential difficulties in application relate to those representations made by the accused which are not *wholly* untrue. It should be noted that there is no requirement that the falsity relates to a material particular. The fact that D's representation relates to a peripheral matter will not *entitle* him to an acquittal.

〰 *Questions*
(1) Delboy, a market trader selling football shirts, shouts that this is 'The one worn by Beckham in person'. All those assembled laugh at the banter. Victor buys the shirt not believing for one minute that it was worn by Beckham. Is Delboy guilty of fraud?
(2) Don and Delia book into Victor's hotel as Mr and Mrs Smith. They are not married. At the end of their stay they pay the bill in full. Subsequently, Victor, a devoutly religious man, discovers the lie. He wants to bring a private prosecution against Don and Delia for fraud. Would you advise him that he is likely to succeed?

Problems may arise if the proving that D's statement was untrue requires the prosecution to prove a negative. What of D who advertises his goods for sale adding 'You cannot buy this cheaper anywhere'?

16.2.3.2 Misleading

Being 'untrue' and being 'misleading' are distinct. An untrue statement is one which is literally false—'this is a Renoir painting' when it is not a painting by Renoir. A statement can be misleading even though it is literally true. Common examples are where D fails to provide a comprehensive answer to a question.

〰 *Question*
V, a potential purchaser, asks D, a car salesman, 'Have you had many faults reported with this model' and D replies, 'Only one this year'. That is a true statement. D fails to reveal that there were 200 faults reported the previous year. V does not buy the car in any event as he does not like the colour. Has D committed a fraud offence?

16.2.4 Dishonesty

The principal element of mens rea for the offence is that of dishonesty. The Law Commission and the Home Office intended that the *Ghosh* definition should apply, and this is confirmed in the parliamentary debates (Hansard HL, 19 July 2005, col 1424 (Attorney General)). If D is claiming a lack of dishonesty, the *Ghosh* test (taken from *Feely* [1973] QB 530 and *Ghosh* [1982] QB 1053 (section 13.6, p 366)) provides a two-part mixed subjective and objective test.

(1) Was what was done dishonest by the ordinary standards of reasonable and honest people? If no, not guilty; if yes, consider (2).
(2) Must D have realized that what he was doing was dishonest according to these standards? If yes, guilty.

The test of dishonesty is based solely on *Ghosh*; there is no equivalent to s 2 of the Theft Act 1968 and therefore D's claims to be acting under a claim of right are no guarantee of acquittal. If D has a claim of right to the property he should not ordinarily be at risk of criminal liability. What of D who lies in order to recover property that is his and to which he is legally entitled but cannot afford the lawyers' bills to recover in a civil action?

The Law Commission in Report No 276 stated:

> 7.66 We do not therefore recommend that a 'claim of right' should be a complete defence to the offence of fraud, nor do we recommend that 'belief in a claim of right' should be a complete defence. However, we believe that in the vast majority of such cases the requirements of *Ghosh* dishonesty will suffice to ensure that justice is done, and that the civil and criminal law are kept closely in line with each other.
>
> 7.67 The first limb of the *Ghosh* test requires the jury to consider, on an objective basis, whether the defendant's actions were dishonest. If the defendant may have believed that she had a legal right to act as she did, it will usually follow that the jury will be unable to conclude that they are sure that she was dishonest, on an objective basis. In appropriate cases we believe it would be proper for a judge to direct the jury to the effect that if that is the case then an acquittal should follow, without their having to consider the second limb of the *Ghosh* test.
>
> 7.68 In some exceptional cases it may be important for the judge in summing up to emphasise to the jury that the 'belief in a claim of right' should be considered in the context of the first limb of the *Ghosh* test, rather than the second limb. Such cases may arise where a defendant recognises that 'reasonable and honest' people might consider his actions dishonest, despite also believing that he had a legal right to act as he did. For example, D works for V plc as a shop manager, and has accrued many hours of overtime. V plc has failed to pay him for his overtime, despite D's repeated requests and complaints. D feels that he cannot sue the company for the money, because he would risk being sacked, but on the other hand he cannot afford to let the matter drop. Eventually D uses his position as a manager to take cash from V plc's account. Knowing that he is not authorised to take money from the account to pay himself, he falsifies the documentation. D states in evidence that he genuinely believed that he had a legal right to the money, that he was only taking that which he believed was already his by the only means available to him, but he concedes that he also believed that most reasonable, honest people would consider his actions dishonest. Although he would, on his own admission, have fallen foul of the second limb of the *Ghosh* test, if the jury were not satisfied that his actions were *in fact* dishonest, on the ordinary standards of reasonable and honest people, it would be wrong for them to convict D merely on the basis that he *erroneously* believed that reasonable, honest people would find his actions dishonest.

≈≈ *Questions*
Should D in this example be prosecuted for fraud? Is he dishonest?

As noted in section 13.6, p 367, because *Ghosh* leaves a question of law to the jury to define, the *Ghosh* approach to dishonesty may also fall foul of Article 7 of the European Convention on Human Rights (ECHR), which proscribes retrospective criminalization. The Law Commission initially doubted the potential compliance with Article 7 ECHR, of a general fraud offence based wholly on dishonesty (Law Com Consultation Paper No 155, *Legislating the Criminal Code: Fraud and Deception* (1999), paras 5.33–5.53) and repeated that view in its final Report No 276, *Fraud*. The Fraud Act has been confirmed by the Home Secretary and the Attorney General as being ECHR compatible—as is required by s 19 of the Human Rights Act 1998. The Joint Parliamentary Committee on Human Rights, in its Fourteenth Report (2005–6) (at para 2.14) concluded that the new offences were compatible with Article 7 ECHR and common law requirements of certainty:

> the new general offence of fraud *is not* a general dishonesty offence. Rather, it embeds as an element in the definition of the offence some identifiable morally dubious conduct to which the test of dishonesty may be applied, as the Law Commission correctly observed is required by the principle of

legal certainty. We are therefore satisfied that, as defined in the Bill, the new general offence of fraud satisfies the common law and ECHR requirement that criminal offences be defined with sufficient clarity and precision to enable the public to predict with sufficient certainty whether or not they will be liable.

The Committee did, however, confirm that:

a general dishonesty offence would be incompatible with the common law principle of legality. In our view it would also be in breach of the requirement of legal certainty in Articles 5 and 7 ECHR for the same reasons.

〰 *Question*
What 'morally dubious' element over and above dishonesty renders the conduct criminal?

16.2.5 With intent to gain or cause loss or to expose to a risk of loss

Section 5 defines the meaning of 'gain' and 'loss' for the purposes of ss 2 to 4.

(1) The references to gain and loss in sections 2 to 4 are to be read in accordance with this section.

(2) 'Gain' and 'loss'—

  (a) extend only to gain or loss in money or other property;

  (b) include any such gain or loss whether temporary or permanent;

  and 'property' means any property whether real or personal (including things in action and other intangible property).

(3) 'Gain' includes a gain by keeping what one has, as well as a gain by getting what one does not have.

(4) 'Loss' includes a loss by not getting what one might get, as well as a loss by parting with what one has.

The definitions are essentially the same as those in s 34(2)(a) of the Theft Act 1968. Under these definitions, 'gain' and 'loss' are limited to gain and loss in money or other property. 'Property' in this context is defined as in s 4(1) of the Theft Act 1968, section 13.4, p 358. The definition of 'property' covers all forms of property; the Act is coherent with the Theft Act. None of the special exceptions in s 4 of the 1968 Act apply: there can be fraud with intent to gain/cause loss of land, wild animals and flora, but they cannot be stolen. In *Idrees v DPP* [2011] EWHC 624 (Admin), D paid someone to impersonate him in order to ensure that he passed his driving test. The Divisional Court upheld D's conviction, demonstrating that 'gain' is not confined to financial gain, presumably the licence was the property for the purposes of that allegation.

〰 *Question*
There is a separate offence in s 174 of the Road Traffic Act 1988 of knowingly making a false statement for the purpose of obtaining a driving licence. Should D have been charged with that offence rather than fraud?

In addition, there is no requirement that actual loss is caused, nor even that V's economic interests are imperilled. In its Report No 276, the Law Commission stated:

Arguably the full offence should not be committed unless the defendant has succeeded in *actually* causing a loss or making a gain: where the defendant has acted with *intent* to cause loss or make a gain, but that intent has been frustrated, a conviction of attempt would adequately reflect the criminality of the defendant's conduct. It may sometimes be debatable, however, whether a loss has actually been caused or a gain made, whilst it is clear beyond doubt that the defendant *intended* to bring about one or both of those outcomes. We think it would be unfortunate if, in such a case, it had to be determined whether there had in fact been gain or loss within the meaning of the Act, when that question had little bearing on the gravity of the defendant's conduct or the appropriate sentence. We think that, as in the case of those offences under the Theft Act 1968 whose definitions employ the concepts of gain and loss, it should be sufficient if the defendant acts *with intent* to make a gain or to cause a loss.

16.2.5.1 Loss or gain

In most cases 'an intention to gain' and an 'intention to cause loss' will go hand in hand; V's loss will be D's gain. The phrase 'intent to cause loss' is not, however, superfluous. There may be circumstances in which D intends to cause a loss to V without any corresponding gain to D, for example where D lies to V to pay X. Problems arose in some cases under the old law because the deception might cause a gain which did not correspond to a loss.

≈ *Question*

What if D intends to gain the formula to a drug that another pharmaceutical company, his arch rival, makes a lot of money from producing? Can such information constitute 'property' for the purposes of fraud? Think back to *Oxford v Moss* (1979) 68 Cr App R 183 (section 13.4.3 p 360).

16.2.5.2 Intention

Intention should bear its ordinary meaning, and should extend as elsewhere in the criminal law to include the foresight of a virtually certain consequence (see section 5.2.2, p 92). This may be significant in extending the scope of the offences. For example, it is sufficient that D makes a false representation foreseeing that it is virtually certain to cause loss to V although that is not his purpose, and although he hopes that V will not lose.

16.2.5.3 Remoteness

As noted, the causal issue of whether V was deceived to transfer property, etc, was an element of actus reus in the old deception offences. It has become an issue of mens rea in the Fraud Act offences. The question is whether it is '*by the*' false representation that D *intended* to make the gain or cause the loss. This is an important feature of the offence that must be proven in every case and was considered in *Gilbert* [2012] EWCA Crim 2392.

G, S and H were charged with various offences including a count of fraud contrary to s 2 of the Fraud Act 2006. The allegations were that between 1 December 2008 and 30 January 2009 they had dishonestly and with the intent made false representations to Lloyds Bank in that they had supplied false details in support of an application to open a bank account.

When applying to open the bank account for a building company, a meeting with a bank official had taken place and a checklist form had been completed. During the meeting, H dishonestly informed the bank that savings and assets were available to fund property development. G then signed a form confirming the truth of the information they had provided. After the account was opened, the company acquired computers and office equipment by issuing post-dated cheques to the supplier. The company subsequently stopped the cheques, causing a loss to the supplier of approximately £130,000. G was convicted of fraud in relation to the dishonest representations made to the bank. However, it was not suggested that she was party to the fraudulent scheme to acquire the computer equipment. There was disputed evidence about who had written on the form that G had 'savings' that would be available.

The defence argued that without proof the word 'savings' had been written by G, there was no 'misrepresentation' under s 2 and further that the prosecution had never identified any particular loss or gain. The recorder allowed the case to go to the jury on the basis that G might gain from future legitimate property development, rather than a gain arising directly from any representation made at the meeting at the bank or directly from the opening of the bank account. The recorder also directed the jury that it was open to them to find that a gain could be inferred if they concluded that the opening of the bank account was simply to enable development or the sale of the company.

The Court of Appeal quashed the conviction.

> An intention to make a gain (or to cause loss to another or expose another to risk of loss) is not of itself enough to meet the requirements of the section. In order to commit fraud by representation, a defendant must (a) make a false representation as defined in s.2(2)–(5) of the Act, (b) do so dishonestly and (c) intend, *by making the representation*, to make a gain (or to cause loss to another or expose another to a risk of loss). The jury must, therefore, be sure that the defendant intended to make a gain or cause loss or exposure to loss by making the false representation and it is a matter for the jury on the facts of each case whether the causative link between the intention and the making of the false representation, required by the section, is established. (per Roderick Evans J at [29])

In this case, although the word 'savings' might have amounted to a false representation, it was not proved that it was *by use on the form of the falsity* that the defendant intended to cause loss to the bank or make a gain.

~~~ *Questions*
How remote can D's intentions be? Suppose that D makes false representations to induce V, a wealthy lawyer, to marry him. Is he guilty of the s 2 offence if one intention is to enrich himself?

16.2.5.4 Claims of entitlement to the gain

It is not necessarily a good defence that D believes he has a right to the gain or loss he seeks. If he has such a belief, then he might not be dishonest under *Ghosh*, but he still has the intention to gain (and/or to cause loss). D lies to V to get back the money V owes him. What is the 'gain' to D? In the false accounting case of *A-G's Reference (No 1 of 2001)* [2002] Crim LR 844, the Court of Appeal held that the element of intent to gain is satisfied by proof of an intention to 'acquire' property even if it is that property to which D is entitled.

> ≋ *Questions*
>
> (1) D is sick and tired of V who has not returned the lawnmower that D lent him months ago. D tells V falsely that D's mother-in-law is coming and it is crucial that he mows the lawn. Fraud?
>
> (2) D is a generous character and usually lends V money when he asks. On this occasion V asks D for a loan and D denies it to him by saying falsely that he has no money to spare. Is D guilty of fraud?

16.2.5.5 Exposure to temporary loss

Unlike theft, there is no requirement that D acts with intent to deprive V permanently of any property. It would seem to be sufficient under s 2, for example, that D makes a false representation to V with intent to cause V to lend D property which D intends to return in an unaltered form. The offence comes close to criminalizing dishonest deprivation of the value of an item's usefulness. This strains the property-based foundation of the offence. It supports the argument that the offence is one centred on lying. See further, D. Ormerod, 'Criminalising Lying' [2007] Crim LR 193.

16.2.5.6 Intention to expose another to a risk of loss

It is sufficient that D intends that V will be exposed to the risk of loss; there is no need for the Crown to prove that D had a more specific intention that V *will* lose. D, who makes a false representation on his health insurance form, will be liable (under s 2). He intends the insurance company to be exposed to a risk of loss, even though he desperately hopes that he will remain healthy and they will not incur actual loss. How much of a risk must there be though? Should there be a defence of *de minimis* or would this be relevant to the issue of whether D was dishonest?

16.2.6 Knowing that the representation is or might be false

The third element of the mens rea in the s 2 offence is that D must know that the representation he makes is or might be false. The varieties of criminal knowledge that will satisfy this element are: knowledge that it *is untrue*; knowledge that it *might be untrue*; knowledge that it *is misleading*; knowledge that it *might be misleading*.

16.2.6.1 Knowledge

Knowledge is a strict form of mens rea. It is much stricter than 'belief', 'suspicion', 'having reasonable grounds to suspect' and even 'recklessness'. See section 5.5, p 113.

Definitions of knowledge in criminal cases in England were rare until relatively recently. In *Montila* [2004] 1 WLR 3141, the House accepted (at [27]) that:

A person cannot know that something is A when in fact it is B. The proposition that a person knows that something is A is based on the premise that it is true that it is A.

Subsequently, in *Saik* [2006] UKHL 18 the House of Lords concluded:

the word 'know' should be interpreted strictly and not watered down . . . knowledge means true belief.

In the present context, proof of knowledge will often be by inference—D must have known the statement was untrue having regard to the surrounding circumstances—rather than by express admission by D.

> ∼ *Question*
>
> In response to V's demand for payment of his invoice, D sends an email saying he will pay V tomorrow. What is D's liability if D genuinely believed that he would be able to pay tomorrow because he hoped he would receive payment from someone who owes him money today?

It is sufficient that D is shown to have known that his representation *might* be false. Is the offence rendered too wide by this alternative mens rea?

> ∼ *Questions*
>
> D, who sells works of art, tells a customer that he has a Renoir for sale.
>
> (1) D knows that there is a risk, as with all art, that the painting might be a fake. D knows that the statement *might be* misleading. Fraud?
>
> (2) What if D admits that he thought of the possibility of such a risk and dismissed it from his mind? Is that knowledge that the statement might be false?
>
> (3) What of D who simply failed to check the provenance of the painting properly because he was in such a rush to open the gallery?

The Attorney General addressed this example:

> If an art dealer said, 'This is a painting by Renoir', knowing that that statement can have a huge impact on the value of the painting—but not knowing whether it is true and thinking that it might be untrue—it would be for a jury to decide whether he was dishonest. If he was dishonest, I see no difficulty in saying that he is guilty of fraud in those circumstances. (Hansard HL, 19 July 2005, col 1417)

> ∼ *Question*
>
> Do you think it is right that the dealer is exposed to a prosecution for fraud in these circumstances?

16.3 Section 3: fraud by failing to disclose information

Section 3 provides the second form of the general fraud offence introduced by s 1.

> A person is in breach of this section if he—
>
> (a) dishonestly fails to disclose information to another person, which he is under a legal duty to disclose, and
>
> (b) intends, by failing to disclose the information—
>
>   (i) to make a gain for himself or another, or
>
>   (ii) to cause loss to another or to expose another to a risk of loss.

The elements of the offence: failing to disclose information to a person; being under a legal duty to disclose; dishonestly, with an intention to make a gain/cause loss.

R v Razoq
[2012] EWCA Crim 674, Court of Appeal, Criminal Division

(Hallett LJ, Griffith Williams and Singh JJ)

D was a Syrian national who had fled Syria and sought asylum in the UK. D was a doctor and wished to practise in the UK. In addition to his working for an NHS hospital, D also began to work for a number of locum agencies. A few months into practising, D was subject to disciplinary proceedings and suspended from his work at the hospital. The letter notifying D of his suspension warned him not to undertake work for any locum agency during the period of his suspension. This was in addition to the guidelines sent to all doctors by the General Medical Council (GMC) stipulating the same thing. D said that he had not read these documents, as they seemed like common sense. The locum agencies that D had signed up to work for all stated in their terms of employment that they must be notified if D became subject to disciplinary proceedings; D failed to notify them that he had been suspended from work, as he claimed he had never seen these documents. The prosecution alleged that D was under a legal duty within the meaning of the Fraud Act to disclose any exclusion, either as an express term in the contract, as an implied term in the contract or because it was a contract of utmost good faith and it was a material matter to be disclosed. D's case was that he did not believe he was under a legal duty to disclose his exclusion or that it was material to the work from the locum service, because his GMC registration was unaffected. He did not intend to gain as a result and he was not acting dishonestly. He genuinely believed that he could do the work involved properly, he intended to do the work and he did the work. D stated that the failure to disclose had no effect on his qualifications or his capacity and intention to do the work. The judge directed the jury that they could either find that the duty was implied within the terms of the contract or that it existed because the contract was one of utmost good faith.

Hallett LJ:

. . . [Counsel] helpfully summarised the various elements of the offences. The actus reus of an offence contrary to section 2 is making a false, i.e an untrue, or misleading representation.

The mens rea, however, is three-fold. First, it is making a representation that the accused knows is or might be untrue or misleading. The second is the accused intends to make a gain by the representation. The third is the question of dishonesty.

Similarly the actus reus of an offence contrary to section 3 is making a misleading, i.e incomplete, representation when under a legal duty to disclose. The mens rea is the same, save for the fact that a further issue might arise as to whether an accused knows of the existence of a legal duty to disclose.

[Counsel] did not argue that it was necessary to prove that an accused knew of the existence of a legal duty, but he reminded the court properly that lack of knowledge of such legal duty would be relevant to dishonesty. The section 3 offence is, in effect, he submitted a narrower form of the section 2 offence.

As far as the legal duty was concerned, the judge, perhaps influenced by a number of commentaries in the textbooks about the effect of the Fraud Act, took a cautious approach. Having found as a matter of law on a submission of no case that a legal duty to disclose did exist via two routes, (1) as an implied term of the contract and the conditions under which the doctor was registered with the GMC and (2) because the contracts into which he entered were contracts of utmost good faith, having come to those conclusions as a matter of law, however he left the jury three possible routes as to how a legal duty might arise. He did not withdraw the issues of an implied term and contract of utmost good faith from them. He directed them that a legal duty might only be imputed by an express term if the express term had been brought to the doctor's attention. He therefore left to them the question of whether or not the contracts had been received by the doctor and he had been made aware of the express terms to disclose.

As we have indicated, he also left to them the question of whether or not there was an implied term, or whether or not the contracts were of utmost good faith.

The Court of Appeal stated that the question of what constitutes a legal duty is one of law for the judge, who should direct the jury that if they find certain facts proved they could conclude that a duty to disclose existed in all the circumstances. The court accepted that the evidence was overwhelming that D was legally bound to inform the various agencies of his exclusion. Further, the court observed that D must have received the vast majority of all the documents, if not all of them. For this reason, it was held that it was plainly open to the jury to conclude that the express terms were brought to his attention and he was contractually and legally bound to disclose his suspension.

≋ **Questions**
Consider the relationship with s 2 (section 16.2, p 416). Are all cases under s 3 capable of being prosecuted under s 2? Does it matter? Note that neither s 2 nor s 3 creates an offence: both are forms of the s 1 offence. Is it fair to charge D with an offence under s 1 without specifying which form of the offence is being alleged?

16.3.1 Legal duty to disclose

The concept of 'legal duty' is explained in the Law Commission's Report, *Fraud*, which stated:

7.28 Such a duty may derive from statute (such as the provisions governing company prospectuses), from the fact that the transaction in question is one of the utmost good faith (such as a contract of insurance), from the express or implied terms of a contract, from the custom of a particular trade or market, or from the existence of a fiduciary relationship between the parties (such as that of agent and principal).

7.29 For this purpose there is a legal duty to disclose information not only if the defendant's failure to disclose it gives the victim a cause of action for damages, but also if the law gives the victim a right to set aside any change in his or her legal position to which he or she may consent as a result of the non-disclosure. For example, a person in a fiduciary position has a duty to disclose material information when entering into a contract with his or her beneficiary, in the sense that a failure to make such disclosure will entitle the beneficiary to rescind the contract and to reclaim any property transferred under it. For example where a person in a fiduciary position has a duty to disclose material information when contracting with a beneficiary, a failure to make such disclosure will entitle the beneficiary to rescind the contract and to reclaim any property transferred under it.

The statute is much narrower than original proposals which included breaches of moral duties or duties arising from an expectation in the mind of the person with whom D is dealing. Nevertheless, it opens an extremely broad vista of criminal liability. One limitation seems to be implicit: that there is to be no conflict with the civil law. The Attorney General confirmed that:

the Government believe that it would be undesirable to create this disparity between the criminal and the civil law; it should not be criminal to withhold information which you are entitled to withhold under civil law. (Hansard HL, 19 July 2005, col 1426)

A straightforward example of the operation of s 3 will arise where D fails to reveal relevant information on an application form for a loan, a mortgage, life insurance, etc.

~~~ *Questions*

(1) Consider the facts of *Rai* in section 16.2.1.1, p 419. Would Rai be guilty under s 2 or s 3? Does it matter?

(2) Do you think it appropriate that the defendant in *Razoq* was prosecuted for fraud or should this case have been dealt with by the GMC by way of disciplinary proceedings?

(3) Given that there exists uncertainty in civil law about when an implied term will be read into a contract, is this really a suitable basis for criminal liability?

16.3.2 Failing to disclose information

The duty must be one which is to disclose 'information'. That concept is not defined.

Liability appears to be strict as to the existence of a duty. If D claims that he lacked the knowledge or awareness of the duty to disclose that will be subsumed within his plea that he was not dishonest. What of the person who claims that he disclosed the level of information he thought was necessary?

16.3.3 Dishonesty

The *Ghosh* test will apply, as discussed in section 13.6, p 366. The element of dishonesty will be especially important in cases where D claims that he was not aware of his duty and/or that he believed that he had satisfied that duty. This much is borne out by *Razoq*, section 16.3, p 432. Remember that D claimed he had been unaware of the existence of a legal duty to disclose his exclusion from the hospital, having regarded the decision whether to tell the locum agencies as one entirely for himself. The judge directed the jury that D's knowledge as to the existence of a legal duty, or lack of knowledge, went directly to the issue whether he had acted dishonestly.

16.3.4 Intent to gain or cause loss/expose to a risk of loss

This element of the mens rea is discussed at section 16.2.5. There is no requirement that the intention is to cause a loss by which D gains. Nor need there be any intention for the loss to be caused to the person to whom the duty is owed.

16.4 Section 4: fraud by abuse of position

(1) A person is in breach of this section if he—

  (a) occupies a position in which he is expected to safeguard, or not to act against, the financial interests of another person,

  (b) dishonestly abuses that position, and

  (c) intends, by means of the abuse of that position—

    (i) to make a gain for himself or another, or

    (ii) to cause loss to another or to expose another to a risk of loss.

(2) A person may be regarded as having abused his position even though his conduct consisted of an omission rather than an act.

As with ss 2 and 3, the terms of the offence are easy to describe. The actus reus comprises abusing a position in which D is expected to safeguard the interests of another and the mens rea comprises acting dishonestly, an intention by the abuse to make a gain/cause loss. None of the essential terms—'position', 'expected', 'abuse', 'dishonesty'—are defined. Professors Ashworth and Horder state that this is the most controversial of the sections because, 'its key terms crumble into vagueness when scrutinized' (J. Horder, *Ashworth's Principles of Criminal Law* (2016), p 422).

The section is designed to catch the secret profiteers such as the wine waiter who sells his own bottles, passing them off as belonging to the restaurant and pocketing the proceeds of sale: *Doukas* [1978] 1 All ER 1071. It extends much wider than that narrow category of case. The CPS has listed examples of circumstances in which s 4 should be charged to guide prosecutors—see http://www.cps.gov.uk/legal/d_to_g/fraud_act/. These include: an employee of a software company who uses his position to clone software products with the intention of selling the products on his own behalf; a person employed to care for an elderly or disabled person with access to that person's bank account who abuses that position by removing funds for his own personal use; an employee who abuses his position in order to grant contracts or discounts to friends, relatives and associates; a trader who helps an elderly person with odd jobs, gains influence over that person and removes money from their account; the person entrusted to purchase lottery tickets on behalf of others. These demonstrate the reach of the offence. In *Valujevs* [2014] EWCA Crim 2888, the Court of Appeal did confirm that s 4 should not apply in 'the general commercial area where individuals and businesses compete in markets of one kind or another, including labour markets, and are entitled to and expected to look after their own interests' (at [44]). The defendant was liable in that case where he used his position as a gangmaster to withhold monies from labourers.

16.4.1 A 'position'

The Law Commission explained the meaning of 'position':

> 7.38 The necessary relationship will be present between trustee and beneficiary, director and company, professional person and client, agent and principal, employee and employer, or between partners. It may arise otherwise, for example within a family, or in the context of voluntary work, or in any context where the parties are not at arm's length. In nearly all cases where it arises, it will be recognised by the civil law as importing fiduciary duties, and any relationship that is so recognised will suffice. We see no reason, however, why the existence of such duties should be essential. This does not of course mean that it would be entirely a matter for the fact-finders whether the necessary relationship exists. The question whether the particular facts alleged can properly be described as giving rise to that relationship will be an issue capable of being ruled upon by the judge and, if the case goes to the jury, of being the subject of directions.

Despite the Law Commission's explanation, this element of the offence has been derided as having, 'all the rigidity of a hot marshmallow' (J. Horder, *Ashworth's Principles of Criminal Law* (2016), p 422).

≋ *Questions*

(1) Mrs Hinks looks after a vulnerable old man, Mr Dolphin. She ingratiates herself with him. He makes gifts of £60,000 and a plasma screen TV to Hinks. What would the prosecution need to prove to succeed in a prosecution under s 4? Compare *Hinks* [2000] UKHL 53, section 13.3, p 346.

(2) V lends his neighbour, D, a door key to V's house to allow D access to the garden where D is repairing the fence between their properties. Whilst in the property, D answers a phone call on V's phone informing 'the householder' that he has won £25,000 in a prize draw. D accepts the money without telling V. Is D guilty of the offence under s 4?

16.4.2 'Occupies a position'

The section applies only in relation to the positions D 'occupies'. It is clear that the 'abuse' with intent to gain or cause loss must arise while D is in occupation of that position in order for s 4 to apply. According to the Solicitor General in the course of debates in the Standing Committee:

> A person can occupy a position where they owe a duty that goes beyond the performance of a job. A contract that is entered into that obliges a person to have duties of confidentiality, perhaps, can go well beyond the time when that employment ceases. The duty may, however, still arise. The person entered into the duty at the beginning of the employment and it exists indefinitely. Therefore a person may still occupy a position in which there is a legitimate expectation. That may well, by virtue of a contract and the agreement that the employee entered into voluntarily, go beyond redundancy or the point when he leaves the post. (Standing Committee B, 20 June 2006, col 23)

≈ Questions

D is employed by Blue Co. He realizes that one of the deals they are negotiating might involve corrupt payments. He makes secret copies of the negotiation memos, against company policy, and retains them in case it becomes necessary to show that he was not involved in the corruption. Twelve months later D is made redundant for unrelated reasons. He offers to sell the negotiation memos to a tabloid newspaper. Does he commit the s 4 offence? When? Consider also liability under s 6, section 16.6, p 440.

16.4.3 'Expected' to safeguard

The scope of the 'position' is to some extent dependent on the definition of the term 'position in which he is expected to safeguard'. Whose expectation counts? If it is the victim's, this could be a very wide scope of liability subject to the defendant denying liability by way of a lack of dishonesty. If it is a test based on what D thinks his financial duties are, it might be very limited and difficult to prove. The Court of Appeal provided guidance on how this element of the offence ought to be interpreted in *Valujevs* [2014] EWCA Crim 2888. Fulford LJ stated that Parliament must have intended for the 'expectation' in s 4 to be assessed objectively. It is for the judge to assess whether the position held by the individual is capable of being one 'in which he is expected to safeguard, or not to act against, the financial interests of another person'. If it is so capable, it will be for the jury to determine whether or not they are sure that was the case. His lordship held that it would be untenable to suggest that the expectation should be that of either the potential victim or the defendant. The test is therefore based on the position of the reasonable person. For further discussion, see J. Collins, 'Fraud by Abuse of Position and Unlicensed Gangmasters' (2016) 70 MLR 354.

The Government's decision not to limit the offence to cases in which the law imposes a duty of financial responsibility—trustee and beneficiary, employer and employee, etc—was controversial. That limit, if it had been adopted, would have provided a clear boundary to the scope of the offence.

Section 4(2) makes clear that the offence can be committed by omission as well as by positive action.

16.4.4 Dishonesty

The definition is as in *Ghosh* (section 13.6, p 366). In cases in which there is no legal or fiduciary duty on the accused, it is difficult to see what additional element of conduct which is morally dubious prevents the offence being one based solely on dishonesty. As the Joint Parliamentary Committee on Human Rights recognized, such an offence would be likely to infringe Article 7 (section 16.2.4, p 426).

It would appear that liability is strict as to whether D occupies a position in which he is expected to safeguard the financial interests of another. D's lack of awareness that he is in such a position must be subsumed in a plea of lack of dishonesty. There is no explicit mens rea requirement that the defendant must be aware of the existence of any expectation that he must safeguard the financial interests of another.

Like the other forms of the offence, the one in s 4 turns on dishonesty. In *Woods* [2011] EWCA Crim 1305, D appealed her conviction of fraud by abuse of position. D was the deputy manager of a betting shop. D was working alone in the shop when she was approached by a punter wishing to place a £1 bet at 9 to 1 on a horse running in a race in South Africa. Having received the betting slip and money, D altered the stake to £100 and returned the bottom copy to the customer. The appellant rang up the bet on the till as a £100 bet. The horse won. The customer returned to the counter, not realizing that his bet of £1 had been altered to £100; he was happy to receive his original stake of £1 and his £9 winnings. D handed him a £10 note. However, D then went to the safe, counted out £990, placed the money in envelopes and put the envelopes in her bag. When D completed her shift she left with the money in her bag. D knew that such conduct was against her employer's policy, but she contended that she was not guilty of fraud because she was not intending to cause loss or to make dishonest gain because had the horse lost she would have put £90 in the till to cover her personal bet. D's alleged abuse of position was in altering the stake from £1 to £100. D was found guilty and the Court of Appeal upheld her conviction.

> ≈≈ *Questions*
> Why was Woods not charged with theft of the money? Was it because when she appropriated the money from the safe, it in fact belonged to her as it constituted the proceeds of her winning bet? Does the decision in *Hinks* [2000] UKHL 53, section 13.5, p 362 mean that she could still be charged with theft even if the money were lawfully hers, provided that she was dishonest? Does this demonstrate that there is a significant overlap between fraud and theft? Why might a prosecutor decide to charge one rather than the other in a case such as this?

16.4.5 Intent to gain/cause loss

See section 16.2.5, p 427.

16.5 Section 11: obtaining services dishonestly

As the Law Commission explained in Report No 276:

> 8.1 Because it requires proof of deception, the offence under section 1 of the 1978 Act fails to catch a person who succeeds in obtaining a service dishonestly but without deceiving anyone. This may happen in various ways.
>
> (1) The service may be obtained by the defendant's failure to disclose a material fact, rather than by a positive deception.
>
> (2) The service may not be provided for the defendant *personally*, but for anyone who is there to receive it. For example, the defendant climbs over the fence of a football ground and watches the match without paying the admission charge.
>
> (3) The service may not be provided directly by *people* at all, but through a machine. For example, the defendant downloads, via the internet, software or data for which a charge is made, or which is available only to those within a certain category of person who have paid to be included within that category, by giving false credit card or identification details; or receives satellite television transmissions by using an unauthorised validation card in a decoder.
>
> (4) Some cases are a hybrid of types (2) and (3). For example, the defendant gives false credit card details to an automated booking system, or tenders a forged or stolen credit card to an electronic vending machine, and thus obtains a ticket for a journey or entertainment. There is no deception of the booking system (because it is not a person), nor of the staff who check the tickets of the passengers or audience (because the staff are only interested in whether each person has a ticket, not how they got it).

The Law Commission's proposal as endorsed by the Home Office was to remove the troublesome element of deception from the offence and to place the emphasis on dishonesty.

Section 11 now provides:

> (1) A person is guilty of an offence under this section if he obtains services for himself or another—
>
> (a) by a dishonest act, and
>
> (b) in breach of subsection (2).
>
> (2) A person obtains services in breach of this subsection if—
>
> (a) they are made available on the basis that payment has been, is being or will be made for or in respect of them,
>
> (b) he obtains them without any payment having been made for or in respect of them or without payment having been made in full, and
>
> (c) when he obtains them, he knows—
>
>   (i) that they are being made available on the basis described in paragraph (a), or
>
>   (ii) that they might be, but intends that payment will not be made, or will not be made in full.
>
> (3) A person guilty of an offence under this section is liable—
>
> (a) on summary conviction, to imprisonment for a term not exceeding 12 months or to a fine not exceeding the statutory maximum (or to both);
>
> (b) on conviction on indictment, to imprisonment for a term not exceeding 5 years or to a fine (or to both).

According to the Law Commission: 'This offence would be more analogous to theft than to deception, because it could be committed by "helping oneself" to the service rather than dishonestly inducing another person to provide it' (Law Com Report No 276, para 8.8).

The actus reus comprises (a) an act resulting in the obtaining; (b) of services; (c) for which payment is or will become due; and (d) a failure to pay in whole or in part. The mens rea comprises (a) dishonesty; (b) knowing that the services are to be paid for or knowing that they might have to be paid for; (c) with intent to avoid payment in whole or in part.

16.5.1 An act

It is not possible to commit the offence by omission alone.

16.5.2 Obtaining

Unlike ss 2 to 4, this offence is not inchoate; it requires the actual obtaining of the service. The offence is drafted in similar terms in some respects to the offence under s 1 of the 1978 Act. The troublesome issue of whether a 'benefit has been conferred' is not replicated. There is still a causal element in this offence. D's dishonest act must be the cause of the service being obtained. The obtaining may be for D or another.

16.5.3 A service

'Service' is not further defined.

> ≋ **Question**
> By way of an elaborate scheme, D tops up his mobile telephone by charging the cost to unwitting victims, thereby accruing huge costs on their bills. Does D commit an offence under s 11? In *Mariusz Mikolajczak v District Court in Kalisz, Poland* [2013] EWHC 432 (Admin), Keith J held that this would not be an offence under s 11 as D was not obtaining a service, but rather was obtaining credit. Do you agree?

16.5.4 For which payment has been, is being or will be made

The offence is restricted in that it only applies to services for which payment is required. This follows the old s 1 offence under the 1978 Act. Some of the situations in which D obtains a service for free by making a false representation will be caught by s 2 (section 16.2). As under the old law, an application for a bank account or credit card will only be caught by this offence if the service is to be paid for.

Section 11 catches D who climbs over the wall at his local cricket club and watches the game without paying the entrance fee. It also catches D who uses false network cards to enable his television to receive cable/satellite television channels for which he has no intention of paying. It was suggested that it would also catch D illegally downloading music.

16.5.4.1 Without payment

One problem which the s 11 offence was designed to tackle was where D obtains the relevant service by unauthorized use of a credit card or debit card. But does the offence work bearing in mind that even though the use of the card is unauthorized, the payment will be made by the bank/issuing company provided that the PIN is correct and the security number accurate, etc?

> ≋ *Questions*
> (1) D makes a false representation to a machine by using the card when he is not authorized to do so. He obtains a service—say, a theatre ticket. Has he committed the s 11 offence?
> (2) Is D liable under s 2? What has he obtained?

16.5.5 Dishonesty

The *Ghosh* test applies (section 13.6, p 366).

16.5.6 Knowing that the services are to be paid for/might have to be paid for

The additional requirement that D knows that the services are to be paid for or knows that they might have to be paid for is a relatively strict test.

16.5.7 Intention that payment be avoided

The additional requirement that D acts with intent to avoid payment in whole or in part marks a departure from the old s 1 offence and narrows the offence. In many cases where D has made a false representation to obtain services, he will commit the s 2 offence and his claim that he was intending to pay may well be irrelevant unless it is sufficiently plausible to negative his intent to cause loss or dishonesty. The Law Commission were keen to emphasize the limits so that it will not apply, for example, where DD, parents of D, lie about their religion in order to get D into a private school where they will be charged and pay the full fees. The intention to pay precludes liability. This is narrower than the 1978 Act offence.

16.6 Section 6: possession of articles for use in fraud

Section 6 provides a wholly new offence. The Law Commission had proposed simply to replace the form of the s 25 Theft Act offence (see *Smith and Hogan* (14th edn, 2015), p 1036) which covered 'going equipped' with implements for 'deception', with one covering going equipped for 'fraud'. The Home Office in its consultation exercise in 2004 (para 41) proposed much wider reform. The Home Office wanted an offence of mere possession of, for example, computer software for use in 'the course of or in connection with' a fraud. One particular concern of the Home Office was clearly the widespread use of software to read credit cards. Is s 2, section 16.2 (and inchoate versions of it) wide enough to meet these concerns?

Section 6 of the Fraud Act 2006 provides:

> (1) A person is guilty of an offence if he has in his possession or under his control any article for use in the course of or in connection with any fraud.
>
> (2) A person guilty of an offence under this section is liable—
>
>   (a) on summary conviction, to imprisonment for a term not exceeding 12 months or to a fine not exceeding the statutory maximum (or to both);
>
>   (b) on conviction on indictment, to imprisonment for a term not exceeding 5 years or to a fine (or to both).

16.6.1 'Article'

The 2006 Act provides a broad definition of the term in s 8:

> (1) For the purposes of—
>
>   (a) sections 6 and 7, and
>
>   (b) the provisions listed in subsection (2), so far as they relate to articles for use in the course of or in connection with fraud,
>
> 'article' *includes* any program or data held in electronic form.

The Home Office Explanatory Notes on the Act, para 26, state that:

> Examples of cases where electronic programs or data could be used in fraud are: a computer program can generate credit card numbers; computer templates can be used for producing blank utility bills; computer files can contain lists of other peoples' credit card details or draft letters in connection with 'advance fee' frauds.

There is no requirement that the program or data is designed exclusively for fraud. Any word processing or spreadsheet program is capable of being used to produce false invoices or false utility bills. It is difficult to see any restriction on the concept of an 'article' which might limit the offence. A printer and computer, or even a humble pen and paper, are articles and capable of being used in the course of or in connection with fraud and are capable of being possessed.

16.6.2 Has in his possession

There is no requirement that the articles are held in possession in any particular venue. Any article in the possession of the person, whether at home, in public or at work, is capable of satisfying this element of the offence. The term applies to the possession of tangible items such as a deck of marked cards or false die and clearly extends to possessing data on a computer such as software to create false utility bills or for skimming credit cards.

≈ *Questions*

D's son, E, has downloaded onto his laptop software to pirate DVDs. D is unaware of that fact.

(1) Does D commit the offence if (a) the computer remains in E's bedroom? (b) D borrows E's laptop to take to a work conference? What must the prosecution establish that D knew? (c) D sees the software on the laptop but does not know what its function is. Can he be liable under s 6?

(2) D discovers the software on E's computer and realizes what it is, and then deletes it by moving it to the recycle bin on the computer. Does D remain liable under s 6? Cf *Porter* [2006] EWCA Crim 560, [2006] Crim LR 748.

16.6.2.1 Control

Use of the words 'possession' or 'control' must suggest that Parliament intended them to be capable of applying differently. The offence requires possession or control of the *article* that is used in the illicit manner or in connection with the fraud, not control of the illicit use per se. The Court of Appeal has considered this aspect of the s 6 offence in two cases.

In *Tarley* [2012] EWCA Crim 464, D and his co-accused were convicted of being jointly in possession of articles for use in fraud. D's case was that he had no proprietorial right to the property, nor did he exercise or could have exercised control over it. The judge stated that there was little in the Act to assist him in interpreting what was meant by 'possession' or 'control'. Any guidance derived from offences of being in possession of a firearm or drugs would be imperfect. The judge found that on a true construction of the statute D, if he shared a common purpose that the articles be used in the fraud and knew this was why they were carried, and thus exactly the 'scam' intended, was jointly responsible and consequently jointly in possession and had joint control. In upholding D's conviction, Rafferty LJ stated that, 'this is a classic joint enterprise case. We do not accept that an individual cannot be in joint possession and control of items in an application of the doctrine to facts such as these.'

In *Rasoul* [2012] EWCA Crim 3080, one of D's associates was arrested and four envelopes were seized from him. One of the envelopes was addressed to D and contained a National Insurance number, an immigration status document and a residence permit indicating a grant of indefinite leave to remain. The immigration document and residence permit were found to be wholly counterfeit, while the National Insurance number was a valid number issued to a British male last known to be living in Essex. It was never issued to D. D was arrested and pleaded guilty to being in possession of an article for use in fraud. On appeal, D claimed that the National Insurance card was never in his possession. It was in the possession of his associate, who was about to post it to him. The prosecution's contention was that D had control of it. D denied this also and cited the case of *Peaston* (1979) 69 Cr App R 203, [1979] Crim LR 183 in support of his argument:

18. Mr Whelan, counsel for the appellant, in an attractive argument, submitted that as a matter of law he did not even have control. He relied principally on the case of *Peaston* (1979) 69 Cr.App.R 203 which involved a charge under section 5 of the Misuse of Drugs Act 1971. In that case the question was whether the defendant had drugs in his possession. He had ordered the supplier to send drugs to his address and the envelope had arrived and been put through the letter box in the premises where he lived. In those circumstances the court held that he was properly to be regarded as in possession. The goods had been delivered at his invitation. Counsel relies upon the fact that the possession here resulted from the drugs actually having been received by him at his address. Section 37(3) of the Misuse of Drugs Act provides that a person shall be taken to be in possession of anything which is subject to his control, even if it is in the hands of a third party. The submission is that that would have been an easy route to finding possession in this case if the fact that he had ordered these drugs was sufficient, without actual delivery, to constitute possession. So counsel submits that on the authority of that case a mere direction to somebody to send the illicit goods cannot of itself constitute control.

19. We do not accept that submission. We think there are a number of difficulties with it. First, the issue of control and indeed section 37(3) itself was never referred to by the court in *Peaston*. The Court did not need to consider whether there was control, and therefore possession, even without delivery of the goods because that did not arise on the facts. Second, and in any event, as Mr Smith QC (counsel for the prosecution) submits, there may be a different principle in relation to the definition of control under the Fraud Act than there is in the Misuse of Drugs Act The two statutes have different objectives. Third, in this case we do not know precisely what the facts were concerning the relationship between the appellant and his co-accused who were involved in the drugs activity. There never was a trial and so the precise nature of the relationship between them was never explored.

20. We accept that there is a nice question whether or not it could be said that there is control in these circumstances, but we are far from satisfied that such a defence would probably have succeeded so that we can say that there is a clear injustice. In the circumstances, therefore, we reject the appeal against conviction. (per Elias LJ)

> ≋ **Questions**
> (1) D, in England, subscribes to a service offered by a company in Russia which allows him online access to software which can pirate DVDs. Does he commit the s 6 offence?
> (2) Does the Court of Appeal, in the cases analysed previously, expand the scope of the s 6 offence too far by permitting guilt where there is arguably only constructive possession of the article in question? How should 'control' be interpreted?

16.6.2.2 For use in the course of or in connection with

The form of words used is extremely wide. The offences of fraud are so wide that the items which might be used in connection with such activities are endless. D possesses an article which he intends to use if only in the course of covering his tracks after the commission of an offence; would this be enough to found liability under s 6?

16.6.2.3 Any fraud

There is no guidance on the scope of this concept. Is this limited to frauds under the Act? Is conspiracy to defraud caught as well? Is it restricted to the commission of the offence as principal offender or as an accessory or conspirator? Logically, the use must relate to future use. Past illicit use can be evidence of a current intention as to future use.

16.6.2.4 Mens rea

As the Home Office Explanatory Notes, para 25, make clear, a general intention to commit fraud will suffice. The Home Office response to consultation was that the prosecution 'should have to prove a general intention that the article be used by the possessor (or someone else) for a fraudulent purpose, though they should not have to prove intended use in a particular fraud'. Parliament confirmed that the offence was not one of strict liability. The intention is clearly for this offence to follow the mens rea of the s 25 offence. In interpreting that offence in *Ellames* [1974] 3 All ER 130, the court said that:

> In our view, to establish an offence under s 25(1) the prosecution must prove that the defendant was in possession of the article, and intended the article to be used in the course of or in connection with some future burglary, theft or cheat. But it is not necessary to prove that he intended it to be used in the course of or in connection with any specific burglary, theft or cheat; it is enough to prove a general intention to use it for some burglary, theft or cheat; we think that this view is supported by the use of the word 'any' in s 25(1). Nor, in our view, is it necessary to prove that the defendant intended to use it himself; it will be enough to prove that he had it with him with the intention that it should be used by someone else.

In *Sakalouskas* [2013] EWCA Crim 2278, the Court of Appeal confirmed that the interpretation given to s 25 of the Theft Act 1968 in *Ellames* applied in relation to s 6. Mitting J stated:

> 7. In our judgment, the observations of the court in *Ellames* in relation to [section] 25 apply with equal force to an offence charged under section 6. If it were not so, then it is easy to see how an innocent person who knew that an article used by somebody else for the purpose of fraud would commit an offence under section 6 if he knowingly had it in his possession. That cannot have been the intention of Parliament. The intention of Parliament as in the case of section 25 was to prevent the possession of articles that were intended for use then or in the future, not those which had been used in the past.

> ~~ *Questions*
> (1) D opens a drawer in his new office and is horrified to find a machine with the exclusive function of credit card cloning. It is for use in fraud only and has no legitimate function. Is he liable under s 6?
> (2) D opens the drawer in his new office and finds what he thinks is a credit card cloning machine. He is delighted at the prospect of using it. In fact, the machine is a useless piece of machinery which would never produce a plausible copy. Is he liable for any offence?

16.7 Section 7: making, adapting, etc articles for fraud

Section 7 provides for a further broad offence:

> (1) A person is guilty of an offence if he makes, adapts, supplies, or offers to supply any article—
>
> (a) knowing that it is designed or adapted for use in the course of or in connection with fraud, or
>
> (b) intending it to be used to commit, or assist in the commission of, fraud.
>
> (2) A person guilty of an offence under this section is liable—
>
> (a) on summary conviction, to imprisonment for a term not exceeding 12 months or to a fine not exceeding the statutory maximum (or to both);
>
> (b) on conviction on indictment, to imprisonment for a term not exceeding 10 years or to a fine (or to both).

There are in fact several distinct versions of the offence contained in s 7. There are obviously differences between making, adapting, supplying and offering to supply. Section 7(1)(a) is narrower in requiring that the article *is* for use in connection with fraud (otherwise there could be no knowledge that it is for such use: *Montilla* [2004] UKHL 50 and *Saik* [2006] UKHL 18). Under s 7(1)(b) there is no requirement that the article is so designed, etc provided D intends it to be used. Section 7(1)(b) is narrower in a different respect, being restricted to articles for use in the commission of fraud, whereas s 7(1)(a) is wider—encompassing use in connection with fraud.

The only example of its operation provided in the Explanatory Notes to the Act is that where:

> a person makes devices which when attached to electricity meters cause the meter to malfunction. The actual amount of electricity used is concealed from the provider, who thus makes a loss.

16.7.1 Makes or adapts

These narrow forms of the offence seem to be uncontroversial. Interpretation of these terms will rely on similar expressions used, for example, in relation to weapons and elsewhere in the criminal law.

16.7.1.1 Supplies or offers to supply

Given that we are dealing with the supply of articles for illegal purposes, it is unlikely that the courts will take a restrictive or unduly technical approach to the term. The term 'offer to supply' should at least be restricted so as not to extend to cases of mere invitation to treat. A supply clearly does not have to be a commercial supply.

16.7.1.2 Knowing that it is designed or adapted for such use

The requirement is of knowledge. Unlike the offence of handling stolen goods, there is no alternative that D can be convicted on proof of belief alone. This is a relatively strict mens rea requirement. Knowledge involves a state of mind of true belief. Note that the requirement is that D makes, etc any article knowing that it *is* designed for use in the course of or in connection with fraud. The knowledge must exist at the time of the making, adapting, supply or offer to supply. Subsequent knowledge is insufficient.

16.7.2 Intending it to be used to commit or assist in committing

This is an alternative form of mens rea to knowledge. Intention here will presumably include not only direct intention in the sense of purpose, but also an oblique intention (section 5.2, p 83) where the defendant sees the use of the article for fraud as virtually certain. The section does not require an intention that the person who is the maker, adapter or supplier use the item for a fraudulent purpose himself: what is required is that the article will be so used. Who will so use it is immaterial. That intention will therefore embrace the supplier of an item which he knows will be used for, or to assist in, fraud undertaken by the recipient or another person.

As an example of the offence in operation, in *Kirtland* [2012] EWCA Crim 2127, D supplied forged first-class travel passes. A railway company operated a system whereby its contracted staff could travel first class whilst they were on duty. Staff were issued with an annual pass to enable them to do this. These were the passes that D forged and sold to his unwitting customers. D was convicted of an offence under s 7. What frauds were the passes designed or adapted to be of use in?

FURTHER READING

S. P. Green, *Lying Cheating and Stealing: A Moral Theory of White Collar Crime* (2005)

L. Katz, *Ill-Gotten Gains: Evasion, Blackmail, Fraud and Other Kindred Puzzles of the Law* (1996)

D. Ormerod, 'A Bit of A Con: The Law Commission's Proposals on Fraud' [1999] Crim LR 789

D. Ormerod and D. H. Williams, *Smith's Law of Theft* (9th edn, 2007), Ch 3

17
Related offences in the Theft Acts 1968 and 1978

Section 11 of the Theft Act 1968:

It is an offence for D to remove articles from places open to the public without lawful authority.

Section 12 of the Theft Act 1968:

It is an offence for D (a) to take a conveyance (eg a car) without consent of the owner or other lawful authority, or (b) to drive it or allow himself to be carried in or on it knowing that it has been taken without such authority.

Blackmail: s 21 of the Theft Act 1968:

A person commits blackmail if, with a view to gain for himself or another or with intent to cause loss to another, he makes any unwarranted demand with menaces (ie without a belief that he has reasonable grounds for making the demand; and that the use of the menaces is a proper means of reinforcing the demand).

Making off: s 3 of the Theft Act 1978:

It is an offence for a person to make off without payment for goods supplied or a service done knowing that payment on the spot is expected intending to make permanent default.

Some of the controversies that will be examined in this chapter include:

(1) the extent to which it is necessary to have very specific offences based on particular types of property to supplement the general theft offence;

(2) the arguments for offences based on temporary deprivation of a person's property;

(3) in what circumstances demands with threats ought to be criminalized as blackmail;

(4) why it was considered necessary to have an offence of making off without payment.

17.1 Introduction

The Theft Acts 1968 and 1978 contain numerous offences and constraint of space precludes discussion of them all in the current work. This chapter will deal with the following offences:

(1) removing articles from places open to the public—s 11 of the Theft Act 1968;

(2) taking conveyances—s 12 of the Theft Act 1968;

(3) blackmail—s 21 of the Theft Act 1968;

(4) making off—s 3 of the Theft Act 1978.

17.2 Removal of articles from places open to the public

Theft Act 1968, s 11

(1) Subject to sub-sections (2) and (3) below, where the public have access to a building in order to view the building or part of it, or a collection or part of a collection housed in it, any person who without lawful authority removes from the building or its grounds the whole or part of any article displayed or kept for display to the public in the building or that part of it or in its grounds shall be guilty of an offence. For this purpose 'collection' includes a collection got together for a temporary purpose, but references in this section to a collection do not apply to a collection made or exhibited for the purpose of effecting sales or other commercial dealings.

(2) It is immaterial for purposes of sub-section (1) above, that the public's access to a building is limited to a particular period or particular occasion; but where anything removed from a building or its grounds is there otherwise than as forming part of, or being on loan for exhibition with, a collection intended for permanent exhibition to the public, the person removing it does not thereby commit an offence under this section unless he removes it on a day when the public have access to the building as mentioned in sub-section (1) above.

(3) A person does not commit an offence under this section if he believes that he has lawful authority for the removal of the thing in question or that he would have it if the person entitled to give it knew of the removal and the circumstances of it.

(4) A person guilty of an offence under this section shall, on conviction on indictment, be liable to imprisonment for a term not exceeding five years.

The creation of the offence was inspired by a number (there seems to have been barely a handful of them) of 'removals', such as the removal of Goya's portrait of the Duke of Wellington from the National Portrait Gallery and the removal of the Coronation Stone from Westminster Abbey. The thinking behind the creation of the offence appears to be that articles displayed to the public are often irreplaceable and are not as easily protected as articles on private premises. But are they any more vulnerable than books kept on the shelves of a university library, many of which are equally irreplaceable?

∼ Questions

The section provides an excellent opportunity to test your statutory interpretation skills. Consider the following: D enters the grounds of a stately home that is open to the public (on payment of a fee) and, as a prank, he removes a statue from the garden and hides it in a groundsman's shed. Has he committed an offence under s 11? Does it matter whether the stately home is open for business?

17.3 Taking conveyances

Theft Act 1968, s 12

12. Taking motor vehicle or other conveyance without authority

(1) Subject to sub-sections (5) and (6) below, a person shall be guilty of an offence if, without having the consent of the owner or other lawful authority, he takes any conveyance for his own or another's use or, knowing that any conveyance has been taken without such authority, drives it or allows himself to be carried in or on it.

(2) A person guilty of an offence under sub-section (1) above shall be liable on summary conviction to an unlimited fine, to imprisonment for a term not exceeding six months, or to both.

(3) [Repealed.]

(4) If on the trial of an indictment for theft the jury are not satisfied that the accused committed theft, but it is proved that the accused committed an offence under sub-section (1) above, the jury may find him guilty of the offence under sub-section (1) and if he is found guilty of it, he shall be liable as he would have been liable under sub-section (2) above on summary conviction. . . .

(5) Sub-section (1) above shall not apply in relation to pedal cycles; but, subject to sub-section (6) below, a person who, without having the consent of the owner or other lawful authority, takes a pedal cycle for his own or another's use, or rides a pedal cycle knowing it to have been taken without such authority, shall on summary conviction be liable to a fine not exceeding level 3 on the standard scale.

(6) A person does not commit an offence under this section by anything done in the belief that he has lawful authority to do it or that he would have the owner's consent if the owner knew of his doing it and the circumstances of it.

For s 12A, 'Aggravated vehicle-taking', see section 17.4, p 449.

In short, the elements of the offence are (a) the taking for one's own or another's use; (b) of a conveyance; (c) without consent.

17.3.1 Taking for one's own or another's use

Although this element of the offence seems straightforward, there are a number of issues that need to be considered. In *Bow* (1977) 64 Cr App R 54, the Court of Appeal held that 'use' means, and only means, use *as a conveyance*. So although in that case, where D released the handbrake on V's car causing it to roll some 200 yards down a narrow road in order to enable him to remove his own car, the conveyance had been moved, it would not have been *used as a conveyance*. One question that proved problematic was whether D could be guilty of the offence in circumstances where he was already in possession or control of the conveyance, but uses it in an unauthorized way. In *McGill* [1970] RTR 209, D was given permission to use V's car to drive E to the station on condition that he returned it immediately. He subsequently drove it elsewhere and did not return it for some days. D was convicted. In *McKnight v Davies* [1974] RTR 4, the conviction of a lorry driver was upheld when, instead of returning the lorry to the depot at the end of the working day, he used it for his own purposes and did not return it until the early hours of the next morning.

≋ *Question*
Why should a taking of a vehicle not just be treated as theft?

17.3.2 A conveyance

Section 12(7) provides:

For the purposes of this section—

(a) 'conveyance' means any conveyance constructed or adapted for the carriage of a person or persons whether by land, water or air, except that it does not include a conveyance constructed or adapted for use only under the control of a person not carried in or on it, and 'drive' shall be construed accordingly; and

(b) 'owner', in relation to a conveyance which is the subject of a hiring agreement or hire-purchase agreement, means the person in possession of the conveyance under that agreement.

'Conveyance' has been interpreted to mean a mechanical contrivance of some kind. While it obviously includes conveyances such as cars and motorcycles, it does not include horses.

17.3.3 Without the owner's consent or lawful authority

In the vast majority of cases, this will not prove to be an issue. However, what if the owner's consent has been procured by fraud? In *Whitaker v Campbell* [1984] QB 318, it was held that when the owner is induced to part with the conveyance through fraud, it could not be said 'in commonsense terms' that he had not consented to the taking. The position would be different, the court held, if the consent had been procured through force.

17.3.4 Mens rea

The taking must be intentional; it is not enough that the vehicle accidentally moves with D in it. Section 12(6) provides that a person does not commit an offence by anything done in the belief that he has lawful authority to do it or that the owner would have consented. It appears to be the case that the test is a subjective one.

17.3.5 Driving or being carried

An offence under s 12 may be committed not merely by one who takes the conveyance, but also by one who, knowing the conveyance has been taken without authority, drives it or allows himself to be carried in or on it.

17.4 Aggravated vehicle-taking

The taking of motor vehicles (sometimes called 'joyriding' or 'twocking') increased dramatically in the 1990s to an extent where it was described as 'epidemic'. There are significant risks when takers demonstrate their driving 'skills' and high-speed chases ensue in which takers are pursued by police. The Government felt it had to respond to the growing mischief. The Aggravated Vehicle-Taking Act 1992 added a further section, s 12A, to the Theft Act 1968, creating the offence of aggravated vehicle-taking (the offence is confined to the taking of mechanically propelled vehicles). This requires proof:

(1) that D has committed the offence under s 12(1) of the 1968 Act (the 'basic offence'); and

(2) that after the vehicle was taken and before it was recovered, the vehicle was driven or injury or damage was caused in one or more of the aggravating circumstances:

  (a) that the vehicle was driven dangerously;

  (b) that, owing to the driving of a vehicle, an accident occurred by which injury was caused to any person. In *Marsh* [1997] 1 Cr App R 67, the court held that the words 'owing to the driving of the vehicle' were plain and simple and no gloss ought to be provided by referring the jury to the manner of the driving. In *Taylor* [2016] UKSC 5, the Supreme Court disapproved of *Marsh* and held that an individual can only be guilty of aggravated vehicle-taking if there was some act or omission in the control of the car, which involves some element of fault, whether amounting to careless/inconsiderate driving or not, and which contributes in some more than minimal way to the injury or death of the victim;

(c) that, owing to the driving of the vehicle, an accident occurred by which damage was caused to any property, other than the vehicle;

(d) that damage was caused to the vehicle.

There are two offences (one punishable on indictment by imprisonment for two years, and one by imprisonment for 14 years where death is caused). Both offences are draconian. While aggravating circumstance (a) requires a degree of fault, liability is totally strict in relation to the others and the offence is committed though the vehicle taken was driven with due care.

Moreover, liability for the offence extends not only to the driver but to all of the participants in the basic offence. It seems that if D slashes the seats of the taken vehicle, E, who is in the vehicle, is guilty of the offence though he seeks to dissuade D from damaging the seats or even if he seeks to prevent him. See *Dawes v DPP* [1995] 1 Cr App R 65 at 72.

17.5 Blackmail

Blackmail is a crime which conjures up images of secret deals and liaison shrouded in intrigue; hence, its popularity with dramatists and authors. Prosecutions for blackmail tend to involve nasty rather than exotic conduct, with individuals preying on the vulnerable. For example, in *Arshad* [2014] EWCA Crim 2485, D, a bully, was found guilty of blackmail after threatening to distribute topless photographs of a 14-year-old schoolgirl if she did not pay him £50. This is one of the reasons that blackmail is treated so seriously by the courts in sentencing.

Blackmail is also a rather more technical offence than is commonly understood. It raises several interesting issues including some of the more theoretical issues as to the wrongs and harms which the offence of blackmail might be said to involve. There seems to be little consensus about the precise harm the offence of blackmail seeks to guard against.

In summary, blackmail is an offence involving a threat by D, backed by an unwarranted demand by which D intends to gain or cause loss in terms of property.

17.5.1 Definition

Theft Act 1968, s 21

(1) A person is guilty of blackmail if, with a view to gain for himself or another or with intent to cause loss to another, he makes any unwarranted demand with menaces; and for this purpose a demand with menaces is unwarranted unless the person making it does so in the belief:

(a) that he has reasonable grounds for making the demand; and

(b) that the use of the menaces is a proper means of reinforcing the demand.

(2) The nature of the act or omission demanded is immaterial, and it is also immaterial whether the menaces relate to action to be taken by the person making the demand.

(3) A person guilty of blackmail shall on conviction on indictment be liable to imprisonment for a term not exceeding fourteen years.

The elements of blackmail are: (a) a demand; (b) with menaces; (c) the demand must be unwarranted; and (d) a view to gain or intent to cause loss.

17.5.1.1 The demand

A demand may take any form and may be implicit as well as explicit. However, whether it is express or implied, there must actually be a demand. Although it will typically be the case that D will demand money or other property, s 21(2) of the Theft Act 1968 provides that 'the nature of the act or omission demanded is immaterial'. Despite this, the offence can only be committed if D has a view to gain or an intention to cause loss in money or other *property*.

17.5.1.2 Menaces

The word 'menace' is an ordinary English word and as such should not require further elaboration in the majority of cases. The Court of Appeal in *Lawrence and Pomroy* (1973) 57 Cr App R 64 suggested that a jury could easily understand this word and that the judge should not define it for them. In *Clear* [1968] 1 All ER 74, Sellers LJ held that, to constitute menaces, the threats must be 'of such a nature and extent that the mind of an ordinary person of normal stability and courage might be influenced or made apprehensive so as to accede unwillingly to the demand'. The more recent case of *Lambert* [2009] EWCA Crim 2860 emphasized that it is still blackmail if D threatened to do something to V that could not there and then be carried out. See also *Garwood* [1987] Crim LR 476.

17.5.1.3 Unwarranted demand

The demand must be unwarranted or there is no offence. The Theft Act specifies that a demand will be unwarranted unless made in the belief (a) that there are reasonable grounds for making it, *and* (b) that the use of the menaces is a proper means of enforcing the demand. The test is a subjective one: did D believe in the reasonableness of the grounds for making the demand and the propriety of using a menace to enforce the demand? For example, D's belief in the reasonableness might derive from the fact that V owes him money.

Criminal Law Revision Committee, Eighth Report, *Theft and Related Offences*
(1966), Cmnd 2977, paras 121–122

. . .

   At first we proposed to include a requirement that a person's belief that he has reasonable grounds for making the demand or that the use of the menaces is proper should be a reasonable belief. There would be a case for this in policy; for it may be thought that a person who puts pressure on another by menaces of a kind which any reasonable person would think ought to be blackmail should not escape liability merely because his moral standard is too low, or his intelligence too limited, to enable him to appreciate the wrongness of his conduct. The requirement might also make the decision easier for a jury; for if they found that the demand was unwarranted or that the menaces were improper, they would not have to consider whether the accused believed otherwise. But we decided finally not to include the requirement. To require that an honest belief, in order to be a defence, should be reasonable would have the result that the offence of blackmail could be committed by mere negligence (for example, in not consulting a lawyer . . .). The requirement would also be out of keeping with the rest of the Bill, because all the major offences under it depend expressly or by implication on dishonesty. In particular, the provision in clause 2(1) making it a defence to a charge of theft that the defendant believed that he had the right to deprive the owner does not require that the belief should be reasonable.

   . . .

17.5.1.4 View to gain or intent to cause loss
With 'a view to'

The Court of Appeal, in *Dooley* [2005] EWCA Crim 3093, approved the approach to this expression in *Smith and Hogan* (11th edn, 2005) when considering that expression in the context of possession of indecent images 'with a view to' distribution.

D. Ormerod, Case commentary on *Dooley*
[2006] Crim LR 544

The phrase 'with a view to' appears, as the court observes, in many hundreds of statutes and it is surprising that it has not attracted much previous judicial or academic comment. Where it has been discussed, e.g. in the context of false accounting under s.17 of the Theft Act 1968, the focus has tended to be on the consequence D acts towards achieving (in that instance whether he acts with a view to 'gain'): see *Smith and Hogan Criminal Law* (11th edn, 2005), pp.789–790. The courts have acknowledged that the expression does not connote motive: per Chitty L.J. in *J. Lyons and Sons v Wilkins* [1899] 1 Ch. 255 at 269–270, considering the offence under s.7 of the Conspiracy and Protection of Property Act 1875. See also *Bevans* (1988) 87 Cr.App.R. 64: D's unwarranted demand with menaces for pain killer was sufficient for blackmail as he did so with a view to gain even though his motive was to alleviate pain. The academic view of the expression where it appears in offences such as blackmail has been to treat it as simply a form of intention, see, e.g. G. Williams, *Textbook of Criminal Law* (2nd edn, 1983), p.830.

The trial judge [in *Dooley*] regarded it as sufficient for the prosecution to prove that D acted 'with a view to' if D saw it as likely that others might access the files. The Court of Appeal is, with respect, right to reject that as a sufficient form of mens rea. Foresight or awareness of a likelihood of the files being exposed to acquisition by others is not equivalent to an intention that they should be. Nor is proof of foresight of that likelihood sufficient proof that D acted 'with a view to'. The court's conclusion is that it is sufficient that 'one of' D's reasons for possessing the images in that form is so that the files will be accessible to others, drawing on the discussion in *Smith and Hogan*, p.807 in the context of blackmail.

. . . The trial judge sought to distinguish the expression from intention, as did the Court of Appeal. How do the two relate? As far as direct or purposive intent is concerned, it seems obvious that proof of purposive intent satisfies the requirement of acting 'with a view to'. The Court of Appeal also concludes that D acts 'with a view to' a proscribed consequence even if that is not his sole or primary purpose for acting provided it is one of his reasons. How much further does the definition of 'with a view to' extend? The court's discussion implies that 'oblique' intent will not suffice in this context. On an oblique intent approach, D would be liable if in achieving his purpose of downloading images for personal use, he realised that his conduct involved temporary storage of the images in a shared folder, and that it is virtually certain that the files will therefore be available to others. The court considers it unnecessary to engage in the debate on oblique intention, might D be said to have foreseen as virtually certain that the files would be accessible to others without that being 'one of his reasons' for acting in downloading and retaining them in the shared folder?

Gain or loss
Theft Act 1968, s 34(2)

For purposes of this Act—

(a) 'gain' and 'loss' are to be construed as extending only to gain or loss in money or other property but as extending to any such gain or loss whether temporary or permanent; and—

> (i) 'gain' includes a gain by keeping what one has, as well as a gain by getting what one has not: and
>
> (ii) 'loss' includes a loss by not getting what one might get as well as a loss by parting with what one has . . .

Normally the blackmailer intends a gain to himself and a loss to the victim but either will suffice. D may commit blackmail where he secures paid employment by V (view to gain) through menaces even though his intention is to restore the failing fortunes of V's firm (not to cause loss to V). Conversely, D might by menaces cause V to do something—revoke a will, for example—which confers no benefit on D but causes loss to others (or might cause them not to get something which they might have been given).

In *Bevans* (1987) 87 Cr App R 64, [1988] Crim LR 236, CA, D, crippled by osteoarthritis, called a doctor, V, and at gunpoint demanded a painkilling injection which V administered. D was convicted of blackmail and his appeal was dismissed. The drug was property which D had demanded with a view to gain for himself; it was irrelevant that D's ulterior motive was the relief of pain rather than economic gain.

17.6 Making off without payment

The offences in the Theft Act 1968 proved ineffective in dealing with a range of circumstances. Examples included defendants who ate in restaurants and ran off without paying the bill or defendants who filled their cars with petrol at self-service garages before driving off without paying. It was difficult to prosecute for theft if D claimed that he only formed the dishonest intent after the proprietary interest in the property had passed to him (eg when the petrol was in the tank). If his claim as to the timing of dishonest intent was true, he did not dishonestly appropriate property belonging to another; by the time of his dishonest intent forming, it was already his property. Charges of obtaining by deception were sometimes possible, but this required a strained reading of deception to include continuing representations.

It was felt necessary in s 3 of the Theft Act 1978 to provide, exceptionally, for the non-payment of a debt to become criminal. (The other offences in the 1978 Act have been repealed and replaced by the Fraud Act 2006.)

17.6.1 Definition

Theft Act 1978, s 3

> (1) Subject to sub-section (3) below, a person who, knowing that payment on the spot for any goods supplied or service done is required or expected from him, dishonestly makes off without having paid as required or expected and with intent to avoid payment of the amount due shall be guilty of an offence.
>
> (2) For purposes of this section 'payment on the spot' includes payment at the time of collecting goods on which work has been done or in respect of which service has been provided.
>
> (3) Sub-section (1) above shall not apply where the supply of the goods or the doing of the service is contrary to law, or where the service done is such that payment is not legally enforceable.

454 CHAPTER 17. RELATED OFFENCES IN THEFT ACTS 1968 AND 1978

There are five elements of the offence:

(1) D makes off;

(2) without payment;

(3) for goods supplied or a service done;

(4) knowing that payment on the spot is expected;

(5) intending to make permanent default.

On conviction on indictment the offence is punishable with two years' imprisonment.

17.6.2 Elements

17.6.2.1 Makes off

According to the *Oxford English Dictionary* 'makes off' means to depart suddenly 'often with a disparaging implication'. But while making off is usually thought of as carrying the disparaging implication of cowardice, secrecy or stealth, it is not confined to such cases. It simply means to decamp and in *Brooks and Brooks* (1982) 76 Cr App R 66 at 69, CA, the court, with a biblical flourish, said that it 'may be an exercise accompanied by the sound of trumpets or a silent stealing away after a folding of tents'.

The precise legal meaning of the term, however, remains unclear. One interpretation is that D cannot be said to make off when he leaves proof of identity by which V can enforce the debt. J. R. Spencer writes ([1983] Crim LR 573):

Obviously, s 3 is partly concerned to prevent the legitimate expectations of restaurateurs, hoteliers, etc being disappointed by people failing to pay their bills. But equally obviously, the section is aimed at some specific mischief narrower than this. If non-payment had been all that Parliament was concerned with, presumably it would have phrased the offence as 'dishonestly failing to pay'. If mere failure to pay was the true mischief of the offence, there was no need for 'making off' as an ingredient in it at all, whether it means 'leaves' as Professor Smith and others say, or whether it means 'leaves with guilty haste' as Francis Bennion suggests. So we must assume, surely, that 'makes off' points to some additional element of mischief which renders the case significantly worse than simply failing to pay, and to see what 'making off' really is, we ought to consider what conduct is, in practical terms, significantly worse than merely failing to pay. It can hardly be *leaving* without paying, because this, as such, does not worsen the creditor's position. It must surely be *disappearing: leaving in a way that makes it difficult for the debtor to be traced.*

On this view, 'making off' would cover, obviously, the man who runs away. It would also cover the man who tells a lie to get outside, and then runs away. It would also cover a man who leaves a cheque signed in a false name. But it would not cover the person who leaves his correct name and an address at which he may readily be found. Nor would it usually cover the person who leaves behind him a cheque, drawn on his own account, in circumstances where it is likely to be dishonoured. In this case, although D has left, he has not as a rule made it difficult for P to trace him.

Spencer also relied on the fact that s 3(4) created a specific arrest power. That power has now become unnecessary given the general availability of arrest following the reform in the Serious Organised Crime and Police Act 2005; s 3(4) was repealed. Spencer argued:

Years ago the common law set its face against giving hoteliers, restaurateurs and suchlike the power to arrest those who merely fail to pay their bills. Yet if we interpret 'makes off' as synonymous with 'leaves' we give them precisely this. On this view, any customer who sought to leave having failed to pay his bill would—subject to what the jury make of 'dishonestly'—commit the offence of making off without payment, and the hotelier or restaurateur would be able lawfully to detain him. To me, at least, it seems highly undesirable that hoteliers, etc should be given this power, at any rate when they know who the non-paying customer is and where he may later be found. On the other hand, if 'makes off' is limited as I suggest, there is no question of the hotelier having the power to arrest a customer who leaves his name backed with some plausible identification.

〰 *Questions*
(1) D, being well known to V, a restaurateur, decides not to pay his bill and departs via the cloakroom window. Would he be guilty according to Spencer? Is there anything in the section to justify acquittal? (See also Bennion [1980] Crim LR 670.)
(2) Is the effect of the offence to criminalize those who fail to pay a debt? Should the taxi driver or restaurateur not avail themselves of the civil law in order to recover the money owed to them? Why might the offence represent an awkward compromise?

17.6.2.2 Payment on the spot

In *Vincent* [2001] EWCA Crim 295, [2001] 2 Cr App R 150, [2001] Crim LR 488, D stayed at two hotels in Windsor and left without paying his bills. His defence was that he had arranged with the proprietors of the hotels to pay when he could, and payment was not expected on the spot when he left; that he had not acted dishonestly and that he had no intention of avoiding payment. The judge directed that a dishonestly obtained agreement to postpone payment could not be relied on to negate the expectation of payment on the spot and D was convicted. His conviction was quashed: the section did not permit or require an analysis whether the agreement was obtained by deception. The fact that the agreement was dishonestly obtained did not reinstate the expectation of payment on the spot.

Difficulties can arise in identifying the 'spot' at which payment is expected or required. The Court of Appeal considered this issue in *Morris* [2013] EWCA Crim 436. D was a taxi driver who collected four men from a casino. The men had been drinking and were behaving in a rowdy fashion. They told D that there would be two stops. At the first stop, three of the young men got out of the taxi and started walking away at fast speed without paying the fare. D, forgetting that the fourth passenger was still in the back of the taxi and would pay the fare, thought that the men were making off without payment. In order to prevent the passengers from evading the fare, D drove his taxi onto the pavement and in doing so broke V's ankle. D was charged with dangerous (or alternatively careless) driving. D claimed he had a defence under s 3 of the Criminal Law Act 1967 (see Chapter 23), in that he was using force in the prevention of crime. The judge ruled that the offence would have been completed as soon as the men walked away from the taxi. On appeal, one of the issues for the court was whether the offence had already been committed by the time D drove his taxi onto the pavement. After considering the earlier case of *Aziz* (1993) Crim LR 708, Leveson LJ stated:

17. . . . if a passenger were to explain (honestly) to the taxi driver that he had to enter his house in order to obtain the fare, the moment for payment would be deferred for him to do so. A decision not to return to the taxi would mean that, from that moment, the passenger is making off without payment. The taxi driver would never be in a position to know precisely when the passenger decided

not to pay and, in our judgment, must be able to follow the passenger to challenge him in an attempt to prevent the commission of the offence.

18. The same principle can be applied in relation to a restaurant bill. If a diner approached the reception, credit card in hand, was distracted and then walked away, the owner of the restaurant would not know whether (or, if so, when) a decision had been made dishonestly to make off without payment. It would be reasonable for him to follow the diner and stop him on the basis that he was seeking to prevent the commission of the offence of making off or (alternatively) reminding the diner that he had forgotten to pay. He should not thereby risk a complaint of assault. The fact is that a restaurant owner (or a taxi driver) should not be required to make an accurate assumption of the intention of the person who has not, in fact, paid the bill or fare: he needs to be able to find out all the while as the person involved is 'making off'.

≋ **Questions**
Are there any principles governing how the spot at which payment is expected or required is to be determined? Can there be?

17.6.2.3 Goods supplied or service done

Goods may be supplied, or services done, even though many or all of the physical acts to bring about the transfer are done by D and not the provider. All commentators are agreed that fuel is supplied by V at self-service filling stations even though the customer serves himself. Similarly, a service is done by V at a self-service car wash despite the fact that V is not on the premises and the machinery is operated by D.

A more difficult case is the self-service store. Suppose that D takes goods from the shelves which he places in his pocket and leaves the store with them. Obviously this is theft but does he also commit the offence under s 3? A. T. H. Smith ([1981] Crim LR 590) thinks that this case is to be distinguished from the self-service petrol station because in the latter case 'the customer does not just take possession of the petrol, but makes himself owner of it by pouring it into his tank'.

≋ **Question**
D and E visit a 'club' in a disreputable part of town. D uses the services of a prostitute on the premises, and E orders and eats a meal. Subsequently, D and E leave refusing to pay, both claiming that they found the services substandard. Are they liable under s 3?

17.6.2.4 Without having paid

The issue of whether payment is made ordinarily presents no problems. One problem concerns payment by cheque (although in the era of chip and pin instances of payment by cheque are much less common and may eventually die out). If the cheque is supported by a cheque card which the bank must then honour, it would seem clear that V has been paid even though D has exceeded his authority as between himself and the bank. The same would follow where a credit card is used. But what if V accepts a cheque from D which D knows will not be honoured? There is a suggestion in *Hammond* [1982] Crim LR 611 that V has been paid because a cheque taken without a banker's card is always taken at risk by the recipient. The judge in *Hammond* added that he did not see how in such a case it could be said that D made off.

17.6.2.5 Intention to make permanent default

It was settled by *Allen* [1985] 2 All ER 641, [1985] AC 1029, HL, that s 3 requires an intention to make permanent default. Lord Hailsham said, at 643:

> The judgment of the Court of Appeal, with which I agree, was delivered by Boreham J. He said ([1985] 1 All ER 148 at 154, [1985] 1 WLR 50 at 57):
>
>> 'To secure a conviction under s 3 of the 1978 Act the following must be proved: (1) that the defendant in fact made off without making payment on the spot: (2) the following mental elements: (a) knowledge that payment on the spot was required or expected of him: and (b) dishonesty: and (c) intent to avoid payment [sc, 'of the amount due']'.
>
> I agree with this analysis. To this the judge adds the following comment:
>
>> 'If (c) means, or is taken to include, no more than an intention to delay or defer payment of the amount due, it is difficult to see what it adds to the other elements. Anyone who knows that payment on the spot is expected or required of him and who then dishonestly makes off without paying as required or expected must have at least the intention to delay or defer payment. It follows, therefore, that the conjoined phrase "and with intent to avoid payment of the amount due" adds a further ingredient: an intention to do more than delay or defer, an intention to evade payment altogether'.
>
> My own view, for what it is worth, is that the section thus analysed is capable only of this meaning. But counsel for the Crown very properly conceded that, even if it were equivocal and capable of either meaning, in a penal section of this kind any ambiguity must be resolved in favour of the subject and against the Crown. Accordingly, the appeal falls to be dismissed either if on its true construction it means unambiguously that the intention must be permanently to avoid payment, or if the clause is ambiguous and capable of either meaning. Even on the assumption that, in the context, the word 'avoid' without the addition of the word 'permanently' is capable of either meaning, which Boreham J was inclined to concede, I find myself convinced by his final paragraph, which reads:
>
>> 'Finally, we can see no reason why, if the intention of Parliament was to provide, in effect, that an intention to delay or defer payment might suffice, Parliament should not have said so in explicit terms. This *might* have been achieved by the insertion of the word "such" before payment in the phrase in question. It *would* have been achieved by a grammatical reconstruction of the material part of s 3(1) thus, "dishonestly makes off without having paid and with intent to avoid payment of the amount due as required or expected". To accede to the Crown's submission would be to read the section as if it were constructed in that way. That we cannot do. Had it been intended to relate the intention to avoid "payment" to "payment as required or expected" it would have been easy to say so. The section does not say so. At the very least it contains an equivocation which should be resolved in favour of [the respondent]'.
>
> There is really no escape from this argument. . . .

〜〜 *Questions*
Do you agree? Should an intention to delay payment suffice?

FURTHER READING

P. Alldridge, 'Attempted Murder of the Soul: Blackmail, Privacy and Secrets' (1993) 13 OJLS 368

R. Epstein, 'Blackmail, Inc' (1983) 50 U Chicago LR 553

L. Katz, *Ill-Gotten Gains: Evasion, Blackmail, Fraud and Kindred Puzzles of the Law* (1996)

D. Ormerod and D. H. Williams, *Smith's Law of Theft* (9th edn, 2007), Ch 10

J. N. Spencer, 'The Aggravated Vehicle Taking Act 1992' [1992] Crim LR 69

J. R. Spencer, 'The Theft Act 1978' [1979] Crim LR 24

J. R. Spencer, Letter, 'Making Off without Payment' [1983] Crim LR 573

G. Syrota, 'Statutes: Theft Act 1978' (1979) 42 MLR 301

G. Syrota, 'Are Cheque Frauds Covered by Section 3 of the Theft Act 1978?' [1980] Crim LR 413

S. White, 'Taking the Joy out of Joy-Riding' [1980] Crim LR 60

18
Offences of damage to property

Criminal damage:

D commits criminal damage if he, without lawful excuse, destroys or damages any property belonging to another intending to destroy or damage any such property or being reckless as to whether any such property would be destroyed or damaged: s 1 of the Criminal Damage Act 1971.

D commits arson if he causes criminal damage by fire: s 1(3).

D commits aggravated criminal damage if, without lawful excuse, he destroys or damages any property intending to destroy or damage any such property or being reckless as to whether any such property would be destroyed or damaged and intending or being reckless whether a life is endangered by the damage he intended or about which he was reckless: s 1(2) of the Criminal Damage Act 1971.

Some of the controversies that will be examined in this chapter include:

(1) the ability to define damage;

(2) the relationship between the elements of the offence, particularly D's mens rea as to circumstance elements;

(3) the arguments for endangerment offences.

18.1 Introduction

The offences of damage to property are heavily used, with most prosecutions occurring in the magistrates' court. Most of the cases involve relatively minor acts of damage, but the offences also encompass much more serious cases including arson and damaging property intending or being reckless as to whether life is endangered. Some prosecutions for criminal damage also take on an enhanced gravity in constitutional terms because, although the value of the property damaged might be small, the act of damage has been done by way of protest and free expression. All in all, criminal damage offences can involve points of greater legal difficulty than would at first appear.

The principal offences of damage to property are governed by the Criminal Damage Act 1971. This legislation followed from the work of the Law Commission: see the Law Commission Report No 29, *Criminal Law: Report on Offences of Damage to Property* (1970).

18.2 Destroying or damaging property of another

Criminal Damage Act 1971, s 1(1)

A person who without lawful excuse destroys or damages any property belonging to another intending to destroy or damage any such property or being reckless as to whether any such property would be destroyed or damaged shall be guilty of an offence.

Where the damage is caused other than by fire (see section 18.4, p 482) the offence is punishable by imprisonment for up to ten years.

18.2.1 Destroy or damage

The Act does not define 'destroy or damage'. The *Oxford English Dictionary* defines 'damage' as 'injury, harm, *esp* physical injury to a thing such as impairs its value or usefulness'. The courts have used this as a guide to whether damage has occurred in a number of cases.

18.2.1.1 Impairment of usefulness as damage?

The tenor of the cases under the Act indicates that, as under the former law, 'damage' embraces not only physical damage to the property but also any impairment, temporary or permanent, to the value of usefulness of the property: *Morphitis v Salmon* [1990] Crim LR 48, DC.

In *Samuels v Stubbs* [1972] 4 SASR 200 at 203, Walters J said:

It seems to me that it is difficult to lay down any very general and, at the same time, precise and absolute rule as to what constitutes 'damage'. One must be guided in a great degree by the circumstances of each case, the nature of the article and the mode in which it is affected or treated. . . . It is my view, however, that the word . . . is sufficiently wide in its meaning to embrace injury, mischief or harm done to property, and that in order to constitute 'damage' it is unnecessary to establish such definite or actual damage as renders the property useless, or prevents it from serving its normal function . . .

And the judge then held that a 'temporary functional derangement' of a policeman's cap resulting from it being trampled upon constituted damage, even though there was no evidence that the cap might not have been restored to its original shape at no cost and without any real trouble to the owner.

~~~ *Questions*
(1) Is the definition of damage dependent on whether the owner has to spend time and/or money on repair? Should it be?
(2) Can it sensibly be said that the cap in *Samuels v Stubbs* was damaged if it could be pressed back into shape in a matter of moments?

18.2.1.2 Need to pay to repair or restore as evidence of damage?

In some cases, when deciding whether there has been damage, the courts have focused on whether it would cost money to repair or restore the property to its former state. In *Hardman v Chief Constable of Avon and Somerset Constabulary* [1986] Crim LR 330 (Judge Llewellyn Jones and justices), it was held that pavement drawings in water-soluble paint constituted damage when the local authority incurred expense in removing them with high-pressure water jets; and in *Roe v Kingerlee* [1986] Crim LR 735, DC, it was held that where D had smeared mud and graffiti on the wall of a police cell the justices were wrong to conclude that this was incapable of amounting to damage.

≈ *Question*

In *Hardman*, the council clearly incurred expense in washing down the pavement. Would the pavement have been damaged had the council left it to the next downpour to wash away the paint?

In *A (a juvenile) v R* [1978] Crim LR 689, D's conviction for damaging a police officer's raincoat by spitting on it was quashed. 'Spitting at a garment,' Judge Streeter said:

> could be an act capable of causing damage. However, one must consider the specific garment which has been allegedly damaged. If someone spat upon a satin wedding dress, for example, any attempt to remove the spittle might in itself leave a mark or stain. The court would find no difficulty in saying that an article had been rendered 'imperfect' if, after a reasonable attempt at cleaning it, a stain remained. An article might also have been rendered 'inoperative' if, as a result of what happened, it had been taken to dry cleaners. However, in the present case, no attempt had been made, even with soap and water, to clean the raincoat, which was a service raincoat designed to resist the elements. Consequently, there was no likelihood that if wiped with a damp cloth, the first obvious remedy, there would be any trace or mark remaining on the raincoat requiring further cleaning.

≈ *Questions*

(1) Was Judge Streeter right to rule that the raincoat was not damaged because it could be wiped clean with a damp cloth? What if the police officer had insisted (perhaps not unreasonably) that the coat be dry-cleaned before he wore it again?

(2) Is there (should there be) a principle of *de minimis* in relation to criminal damage?

In *Faik* [2005] EWCA Crim 2381, F, in detention in a police cell, placed his blanket down the lavatory and then flushed it repeatedly, causing his cell, and two adjoining cells, to become flooded. Obviously the blanket was wet as a result, although not visibly soiled. The water which caused flooding was clear water from the lavatory falling onto a waterproof cell floor. The blanket was unusable until it was cleaned and dry. The cells themselves had had to be cleaned by a contract cleaner before they were usable. F's conviction for criminal damage was upheld.

18.2.1.3 Damaging by dismantling

Under the former law, it was held that a machine may be damaged by removing an integral part (*Tacey* (1821) Russ & Ry 452); or by tampering with it so that it will not work (*Fisher* (1865) LR 1 CCR 7, DC); or by running it in a manner so as to cause impairment (*Norris* (1840) 9 C & P 241); or by dismantling it (*Getty v Antrim County Council* [1950] NI 114).

To remove the rotor arm or electronic ignition component from a car constitutes damage to the car (though not to the rotor arm or component if this is removed without damaging it) since without the component the car will not go. But a mere denial of use of property does not constitute damage. If a landowner finding a car parked in his courtyard chooses to lock up his premises for the night, there is no damage to the car though its owner will have to wait until the following morning before he can drive it away.

18.2.1.4 Damage undefined?

In *Henderson and Battley* (unreported but noted in *Cox v Riley* (1986) 83 Cr App R 54, [1986] Crim LR 460), the Court of Appeal said that ultimately whether damage was done was a question of fact for the jury; and in *Roe v Kingerlee*, the Divisional Court said that what constitutes damage is 'a matter of fact and degree and it is for the justices to decide whether what occurred was damage or not'. In *Samuels v Stubbs*, counsel for D submitted that the finding 'of fact' by the trial court that the hat had not been damaged ought not to be disturbed. Walters J said that not only was it the practice of Australian courts to distinguish between the determination of the evidence (a matter of fact) and the determination of the inferences to be drawn from those facts (a matter of law) but that this view was based on respected English authorities.

It seems clear that damage can be held to be caused despite the property being enhanced in the view of the defendant or even some other people. For example, if someone were to paint a graffiti mural on a wall that would constitute damage to the wall even if D saw it as a vast improvement. What if the artist was Banksy What if the owner of the wall hated Banksy's work? See also M. Watson, 'Graffiti—Popular Art, Anti Social Behaviour or Criminal Damage?' (2004) 168 JP 668.

> ≋ *Question*
> Does D damage property by improving it (a) in his eyes, (b) in the reasonable person's eyes (eg by painting over offensive slogans: *Fancy* [1980] Crim LR 171)?

18.2.1.5 Computers

The modification of the contents of a computer shall not be regarded as damaging any computer or computer storage for the purposes of the Criminal Damage Act unless its effect on that computer or computer storage medium impairs its physical condition. See the Police and Justice Act 2006, Sch 14, para 2.

18.2.2 Property

Criminal Damage Act 1971, s 10(1)

In this Act 'property' means property of a tangible nature, whether real or personal, including money and:

(a) including wild creatures which have been tamed or are ordinarily kept in captivity, and any other wild creatures or their carcasses if, but only if, they have been reduced into possession which has not been lost or abandoned or are in the course of being reduced into possession; but

(b) not including mushrooms growing wild on any land or flowers, fruit or foliage of a plant growing wild on any land.

For the purposes of this sub-section 'mushroom' includes any fungus and 'plant' includes any shrub or tree.

Law Commission Report No 29, *Criminal Law: Report on Offences of Damage to Property*
(1970), paras 34 and 35

> Offences of criminal damage to property in the context of the present law connote physical damage in their commission, and for that reason we have not included intangible things in the class of property, damage to which should constitute an offence. On the other hand, in the context of damage to property there is no reason to distinguish, as does the Theft Act between land and other property . . . We recommend, therefore, that the property which can be the subject of an offence of criminal damage should be all property of a tangible nature, whether real or personal.

> ≈≈ *Question*
> Why should D be liable for digging up his neighbour's lawn, but not for stealing it?

18.2.2.1 Animals

In *Cresswell v DPP* [2006] EWHC 3379 (Admin), the Divisional Court considered whether badgers which had been enticed into traps set by officials from DEFRA (Department for Environment, Food and Rural Affairs) had become 'property' for the purposes of the Criminal Damage Act 1971. The defendants sought to argue that the badgers were property and that they therefore had a defence to destroying the traps because by destroying the traps they were protecting property—the badgers. Keene LJ, rejecting the argument, stated (at [11]) that:

> merely to entice a wild animal, whether it be a badger or a game bird or a deer, to a particular spot from time to time by providing food there, even with the objective ultimately of killing it in due course, does not form part of the a course normally of reducing it into possession. If the creature were thereby to become the property, say, of the landowner providing the food, it would mean that it could not then be lawfully shot by the adjoining landowner on or over whose land it passed.

Walker J was more hesitant, declining to express a concluded view on what constitutes property. His lordship did express some more general views on the concept of wild animals (at [38]):

> In broad terms, (a) it is a question of law whether an animal is wild or domestic. . . . (b) Once a wild animal is killed or dies, absolute property in the dead animal vests in the owner of the land or, in a case where relevant shooting or sporting rights have been granted, in the owner of those rights. (c) While a wild animal is alive there is no absolute property in that animal. There may, however, be what is known as a qualified property in them in three circumstances. The first is described as a qualified property *per industriam*. Wild animals become the property of a person who takes or tames or reclaims them until they regain their natural liberty and have not the intention to return. Examples of that kind of property include animals such as deer, swans and doves. A second qualified property is described as *ratione impotentiae et loci*. The owner of land has a qualified property in the young of animals born on the land until they can fly or run away. A third type of qualified property is described as *ratione soli* and *ratione privilegii*. An owner of land who has retained the exclusive right to hunt, take and kill wild animals on his land has a qualified property in them for the time being while they are there but if he grants to another the right to hunt, take or kill them then the grantee has a qualified property.

18.2.3 Belonging to another

Criminal Damage Act 1971, s 10

(2) Property shall be treated for the purposes of this Act as belonging to any person:

    (a) having the custody or control of it;

    (b) having in it any proprietary right or interest (not being an equitable interest arising only from an agreement to transfer or grant an interest); or

    (c) having a charge on it.

(3) Where property is subject to a trust, the persons to whom it belongs shall be so treated as including any person having a right to enforce the trust.

(4) Property of a corporation sole shall be so treated as belonging to the corporation notwithstanding a vacancy in the corporation.

The offence under s 1(1) may be committed only where D destroys or damages property 'belonging to another'. Since there are similar policy considerations, s 10(2) of the Criminal Damage Act is similar to, though not identical with, s 5 of the Theft Act 1968 (section 13.5, p 361). It is accordingly enough that V has some proprietary interest in the property which D damages and it does not have to be shown that V is the owner of the property; D may, for example, own a book which he has loaned to V and which V has left in the custody of V2 while he goes for lunch. D may commit an offence against V1 and V2 if they have a proprietary interest in the property and D acts with mens rea. See *Seray-Wurie v DPP* [2012] EWHC 208 (Admin).

But if no party other than D has any interest in the property, D cannot by destroying that property, nor by authorizing its destruction, commit an offence under s 1(1), even if this is done in order to perpetrate a fraud by making a claim against insurers.

~~~ *Questions*

D falls out with his wife and, out of spite, defaces the original Picasso which she bought him as a present. Is D liable for criminal damage? Should he be?

18.2.4 Mens rea: intention or recklessness

It is not enough to prove that D intentionally did the act (threw the stone, fired the gun) which caused damage, nor that D intended to cause damage to the property; it must also be proved that D intended to damage property of *another*. In *Smith (DR)* [1974] 1 All ER 632, D rented a flat. He installed wiring for his music equipment. He also installed new panels and floorboards. As a matter of property law, the boards became part of the property and belonged to the landlord. When D came to leave the property he damaged the panels to gain access to the wiring which he sought to remove. The damage caused was to the value of £130. When interviewed by the police, the appellant said, 'Look, how can I be done for smashing my own property. I put the flooring and that in, so if I want to pull it down, it's a matter for me.' Quashing D's conviction, the court held that D made an error in thinking that the wiring he had installed belonged to him and not to the landlord but as long as he did believe this he could not be convicted of damaging property 'belonging to another'. In the subsequent case of *Appleyard* (1985) 81 Cr App R 319, D and a man called Lawford were charged with arson. It was alleged that they had set fire to premises belonging to Pontefract Tape Ltd. D was the manager of the company and the owner of the premises. D argued that since he was the owner of the premises, he was entitled to set fire to them if he wanted to. The Court of Appeal rejected this argument, however, and upheld D's conviction presumably because the court was not prepared to permit D to escape liability for clearly fraudulent conduct. Compare *Denton* (section 18.2.5.1) where D was claiming that he was entitled to a defence because he believed he had the owner's consent to damage.

In relation to whether the test for recklessness (as to both consequences and whether the property belongs to another) is subjective or objective, it will be recalled from the discussion of *G and another* [2003] UKHL 50 at section 5.3.1, p 98, that this is a subjective inquiry. Lord Bingham confirmed that the definition of recklessness to be applied in criminal damage is now that found in cl 18(c) of the Draft Criminal Code:

> A person acts recklessly within the meaning of section 1 of the Criminal Damage Act 1971 with respect to—
>
> (i)   a circumstance when he is aware of a risk that it exists or will exist;
>
> (ii) a result when he is aware of a risk that it will occur;
>
> and it is, in the circumstances known to him, unreasonable to take the risk.

The courts have applied the new test from *G* unhesitatingly. For example, in *Booth v CPS* (2006) 170 JP 305, the Divisional Court upheld a conviction for criminal damage against D, a pedestrian who had stepped out into the path of a car, causing £517 worth of damage. D was drunk but aware of the risk of a collision and implicitly aware of the risk of damaging the car.

18.2.4.1 Transferred fault

The common law doctrine of 'transferred malice' or, to use a more modern term, 'transferred fault', is considered at section 2.3.1.1, p 24, with particular reference to the law of murder and other offences against the person. The Law Commission assumed that the doctrine would apply to their proposed Criminal Damage Act:

> For the simple offence we think that the necessary mental element should be expressed as an intention to destroy or damage the property of another or as recklessness in that regard. The intention or the recklessness need not be related to the particular property damaged, provided that it is related to another's property. If, for example, a person throws a stone at a passing motor car intending to damage it, but misses and breaks a shop window, he will have the necessary intention in respect of the damage to the window as he intended to damage the property of another. But if in a fit of anger he throws a stone at his own car and breaks a shop window behind the car he will not have the requisite intention. In the latter case the question of whether he has committed an offence will depend upon whether he was reckless as to whether any property belonging to another would be destroyed or damaged. (Law Com Report No 29, *Criminal Law: Report on Offences of Damage to Property* (1970))

Glanville Williams agrees that the doctrine 'almost certainly' applies to the Act: *Textbook of Criminal Law* (2nd edn, 1983), p 907. But, while accepting that it may be right for offences against the person, he has argued that, in principle, it should not apply to criminal damage: (1983) 42 CLJ 85.

He argued that it results in 'unfair labelling' where the property damaged is more valuable than that which D intended to damage or foresaw that he might damage; whereas injury to one person—for example, a broken leg—is presumably as bad as the same injury to any other person. (Cf A. Ashworth, 'Transferred Malice and Punishment for Unforeseen Consequences' in P. Glazebrook (ed), *Reshaping the Criminal Law* (1978), p 92.)

≋ *Questions*

(1) D throws a stone intending to smash V's cheap vase. Unforeseeably, the stone bounces off that cheap, but very solid, vase which is undamaged, and smashes V's priceless Ming vase. *Should* D be guilty of criminally destroying the Ming vase? Is the case materially different from that where D smashes the vase he aims at, believing it to have been bought by V at Poundland, when in fact it is priceless Ming? Assuming D is convicted, should the sentence, in either case, be related to the value of the Ming vase, or the cheap vase—or something in between?

(2) A further interesting question arises as to whether arson is a different offence from criminal damage for the purposes of transferring malice. Though fire is only another means of causing criminal damage, Glanville Williams thinks not ((1983) 42 CLJ 85 at 86) because arson carries a higher maximum punishment. 'The reasonable view,' he says, 'is that arson is a separate offence, so that the intention cannot be transferred.' (Cf *Courtie* [1984] AC 463 which provides that as a general rule if one form of an offence carries a higher penalty than another form of that offence it is to be treated as a separate offence and charged as such. But what if the gas leak caused an explosion, without any attendant fire, which destroyed the premises? Jeremy Horder ('A Critique of the Correspondence Principle in Criminal Law' [1995] Crim LR 759 at 769–770) argues that what really matters is 'the representative label: is it right to label D as an arsonist if he did not intend to start a fire . . . ?' Do you agree? Is this a sufficiently precise concept for the law to operate effectively?

(3) Suppose that D, bent on stealing from a gas meter, knowingly fractures the gas pipe and this leads to a fire in which the premises are destroyed. D is clearly guilty of criminal damage to the pipe but is he guilty of arson? See section 18.4, p 482.

18.2.5 Lawful excuse

Unlike most other statutory offences, the Criminal Damage Act 1971 contains a number of defences. These are found in s 5 of the Act.

Criminal Damage Act 1971, s 5

(1) This section applies to any offence under section 1(1) above and any offence under section 2 or 3 above other than one involving a threat by the person charged to destroy or damage property in a way which he knows is likely to endanger the life of another or involving an intent by the person charged to use or cause or permit the use of something in his custody or under his control so to destroy or damage property.

(2) A person charged with an offence to which this section applies shall, whether or not he would be treated for the purposes of this Act as having a lawful excuse apart from this sub-section, be treated for those purposes as having a lawful excuse—

(a) if at the time of the act or acts alleged to constitute the offence he believed that the person or persons whom he believed to be entitled to consent to the destruction of or damage to the property in question had so consented, or would have so consented to it if he or they had known of the destruction or damage and its circumstances; or

(b) if he destroyed or damaged or threatened to destroy or damage the property in question or, in the case of a charge of an offence under section 3 above, intended to use or cause or permit the use of something to destroy or damage it, in order to protect property belonging to himself or another or a right or interest in property which was or which he believed to be vested in himself or another, and at the time of the act or acts alleged to constitute the offence he believed—

(i) that the property, right or interest was in immediate need of protection; and

(ii) that the means of protection adopted or proposed to be adopted were or would be reasonable having regard to all the circumstances.

(3) For the purposes of this section it is immaterial whether a belief is justified or not if it is honestly held.

(4) For the purposes of sub-section (2) above a right or interest in property includes any right or privilege in or over land, whether created by grant, licence or otherwise.

(5) This section shall not be construed as casting doubt on any defence recognised by law as a defence to criminal charges.

Law Commission Report No 29, *Criminal Law: Report on Offences of Damage to Property* (1970), para 49

In most cases there is a clear distinction between the mental element and the element of unlawfulness, and in the absence of one or the other element no offence will be committed, notwithstanding that damage may have been done to another's property. For example, a police officer who, in order to execute a warrant of arrest, has to force open the door of a house is acting with a lawful excuse although he intends to damage the door or the lock. On the other hand a person playing tennis on a properly fenced court who inadvertently hits a ball on to a greenhouse roof, breaking a pane of glass, acts without lawful excuse, but will escape liability because he has not the requisite intention.

The Law Commission says that in most cases there is a clear distinction between 'the mental element' and 'the element of unlawfulness' and the Act deals separately with these elements. It is not obvious that any such clear distinction can be drawn.

18.2.5.1 Belief in consent

The section permits for a defence where: (a) D correctly believes that X is the owner but mistakenly believes X consented; (b) D erroneously believes that X is the owner and mistakenly believes X consented; (c) D correctly believes X is the owner but wrongly believes X would have consented; (d) D erroneously believes X is the owner and mistakenly believes X would have consented. Is the section too generous to D?

In *Denton* [1982] 1 All ER 65, [1981] 1 WLR 1446, CA, D obviously contemplated a fraudulent claim against insurers and the trial judge ruled that he could not rely on s 5(2) because the section carried a general connotation of lawfulness and it could not be said that the owner was 'entitled' to consent to damage for a fraudulent purpose. Quashing D's conviction, the Court of Appeal pointed out that had T (the owner) been charged, he would (on the admission made in that case) have to be acquitted since it is no crime for a man to set fire to his own property. But if the Crown's contention was right, someone whom the owner directed to set fire to the property could be convicted. The court concluded (at 68):

Quite apart from any other consideration, that is such an anomalous result that it cannot possibly be right. The answer is this: that one has to decide whether or not an offence is committed at the moment that the acts are alleged to be committed. The fact that somebody may have had a dishonest intent which in the end he was going to carry out, namely to claim from the insurance company, cannot turn what was not originally a crime into a crime. There is no unlawfulness under the 1971 Act in burning a house. It does not become unlawful because there may be an inchoate attempt to commit fraud contained in it; that is to say it does not become a crime under the 1971 Act, whatever may be the situation outside of the Act.

Consequently it is apparent to us that the judge, in his ruling in this respect, was wrong. Indeed it seems to us, if it is necessary to go as far as this, that it was probably unnecessary for the defendant to invoke s 5 of the 1971 Act at all, because he probably had a lawful excuse without it, in that T was lawfully entitled to burn the premises down. The defendant believed it. He believed that he was acting under the directions of T and that on its own, it seems to us, may well have provided him with a lawful excuse without having resort to s 5.

≈≈ **Question**
On the face of it, the conduct of Denton falls four-square within s 5(2)(a) but the court thought he probably had a lawful excuse without it. Is s 5(2)(a) therefore superfluous?

Smith (DR) is overtly based on the premise (and *Denton* implicitly so) that the mens rea of criminal damage lies not merely in intentionally or recklessly damaging property but in intentionally or recklessly damaging property of *another*. 'It is not possible,' the court said in *Smith (DR)*, 'to exclude the words "belonging to another" which describe the "property". Applying the ordinary principles of *mens rea*, the intention and recklessness and the absence of lawful excuse required to constitute the offence have reference to property belonging to another.'

In other words, there must be mens rea as to the conduct, the circumstances (property belonging to another) and the consequences (damage or destruction). No doubt D would commit an offence where, not sure whether property which was really V's belonged to himself or V, he nevertheless went ahead and destroyed the property.

Clearly, a belief that the owner *has* consented to the destruction or damage constitutes a lawful excuse within s 5(2)(a). In *Blake v DPP* [1993] Crim LR 586, DC, D, a vicar, protesting against allied action against Iraq in the Gulf War, wrote a biblical quotation on a concrete pillar at the perimeter of the Houses of Parliament. Charged with criminal damage, D claimed that he was carrying out the instructions of God and that he had a lawful excuse because he believed God was 'the person . . . whom he believed to be entitled to consent to the . . . damage to the property in question . . .' Perhaps not surprisingly the court held that a belief, however genuinely held, that D had God's consent was not a defence under 'the domestic law of England'.

18.2.5.2 Protecting property: s 5(2)(b)

Soon after the enactment of the 1971 Act, there was uncertainty over whether the defence in s 5(2)(b) was subjective or objective. In *Hunt* (1977) 66 Cr App R 105, D's wife took up a job as a deputy warden in a block of old people's flats. D helped his wife and his wife's employers by doing jobs at the flats. He discovered that the fire alarm and the emergency alarm did not work. D set fire to a bed in the guest room in a comparatively isolated part of the block of flats. He told his wife he could smell smoke: he then led her past the guest room in their search for the fire so that they 'discovered' the fire and broke the fire alarm in order to show that it was not working. The court made the following observations on how s 5(2)(b) ought to be interpreted.

The question whether or not a particular act of destruction or damage or threat of destruction or damage was done or made in order to protect property belonging to another must be, on the true construction of the statute, an objective test. Therefore we have to ask ourselves whether, whatever the state of this man's mind and assuming an honest belief, that which he admittedly did was done in order to protect this particular property, namely the old people's home in Hertfordshire?

If one formulates the question in that way, in the view of each member of this Court, for the reason Slynn J gave during the argument, it admits of only one answer: this was not done in order to protect property; it was done in order to draw attention to the defective state of the fire alarm. It was not an act which in itself did protect or was capable of protecting property. The learned trial judge, during the argument, mentioned quite correctly, that one, though not necessarily the only, purpose of this sub-section was to make provision whereby a person, in order to protect his own property, might destroy or damage the property of another without being guilty of criminal damage. There are cases of which it is easy to think of examples, in which a person, in order to protect his property in actual or imminent danger of damage, will take steps, maybe drastic steps, legitimately protecting either his property or the property of another. It is that kind of protective action to which this particular sub-section is directed though we do not suggest that that is exhaustive. But the sub-section, on its proper construction, cannot possibly extend to the situation which arose in this present case.

In *Ashford and Smith* [1988] Crim LR 682, CA, D and E were convicted under s 3 of the Act of possessing articles with intent to damage property. They were found in possession of equipment with which as part of a demonstration against nuclear weapons they had tried to cut a wire fence surrounding an RAF base. They claimed they had done this to protect the property of persons abroad and in this country by reducing the risk of nuclear war. The Court of Appeal held the trial judge was right to rule that their conduct did not fall within the definition of lawful excuse since whether an act was done to protect property was to be objectively determined and there was no evidence that any property was in immediate need of protection. *Hill and Hall* (1988) 89 Cr App R 74, [1989] Crim LR 136, CA, were factually similar cases.

In *Kelleher* [2003] EWCA Crim 2486, D decapitated a statue of Baroness Thatcher, and explained his motive as being that he held her responsible for developments in world politics with which he disagreed and that he genuinely feared for the future of his son being brought up in such a world.

∿ Questions
(1) Should the defence under s 5(2)(b) be available to him? What property is he protecting?
(2) Would D have a lawful excuse for burning down a local factory as long as D believed this to be reasonable because he believed that effluent from the factory was ruining his tomatoes? The courts have struggled with how far the subjectivity in s 5 is to be taken.

A question arose relatively recently over whether D's belief in the need to protect property must be reasonable or whether it suffices for it to be genuinely held. The Divisional Court considered this issue in the next case.

Unsworth v Director of Public Prosecutions
[2010] EWHC 3037 (Admin), Divisional Court

(Munby LJ and Lagstaff J)

D was engaged in a dispute with her neighbour over trees which D claimed blocked the light into her property. D wrote a number of letters asking that the trees be reduced in size, but to no avail. Eventually D decided that self-help was her only option and took a saw to the trees, causing substantial damage to them. D was charged with criminal damage and convicted. D sought to plead the defence in s 5(2)(b) of the Act, but this was rejected. D was convicted in the magistrates' court and her appeal against conviction was dismissed by the Crown Court. D appealed to the Divisional Court by way of a case stated.

[Munby LJ, in allowing D's appeal against conviction, stated:]

5. The lawful excuse which can be relied upon by way of defence may of course be a lawful excuse conferred upon the defendant by the civil law, for example if the defendant can demonstrate that in doing what she did she was lawfully exercising a right of abatement conferred upon her by the civil law. Section 5(2), however, provides an extended ambit to the defence of lawful excuse, providing so far as is material for present purposes as follows:

[His lordship set out the relevant provisions of the Act.]

6. It can be seen from an analysis of the language in subsection (2)(b) that there are two elements to the defence. The first element, which for ease of exposition I will refer to as limb (A), is that introduced by the words 'in order to protect property' and so on. The other element, which for ease of exposition I will refer to as limb (B), is the latter part of the subsection beginning with the words 'at the time of the act or acts alleged'. As will be appreciated limb (B) itself has two sub-limbs, those set out in subsection (2)(b) paragraphs (i) and (ii).

7. On a plain reading of the statute the test in relation to limb (B) is and is exclusively a test of the defendant's belief. What on the other hand is the nature of the test in relation to limb (A)? The answer to that question is in my judgment answered definitively by the decisions of the Court of Appeal, Criminal Division, in *R v Hunt* (1977) 66 Crim App Rep 105, followed by and elaborated upon in *R v Hill, R v Hall* (1988) 89 Crim App Rep 74.

8. In *Hunt* the judgment was given by Roskill LJ, who said this at page 108:

'But in our view the question whether he was entitled to the benefit of the defence turns upon the meaning of the words "in order to protect property belonging to another." It was argued that those words were subjective in concept, just like the words in the latter part of section 5(2)(b) which are subjective.

We do not think that is right. The question whether or not a particular act of destruction or damage or threat of destruction or damage was done or made in order to protect property belonging to another must be, on the true construction of the statute, an objective test.'

As I read that, Roskill LJ is clearly distinguishing between what I have referred to as limb (A) and limb (B), is clearly stating that limb (B) is 'subjective' but is accepting that in part at least limb (A) imports 'an objective test'.

9. That reasoning was accepted by Lord Lane LCJ, giving judgment in *Hill and Hall*, as being binding upon the court. However, at page 79 he added these important observations:

'But we add that we think that *Hunt* was correctly decided, for this reason. There are two aspects to this type of question. The first aspect is to decide what it was that the applicant, in this case Valerie Hill, in her own mind thought. The learned judge assumed, and so do we, for the purposes of this decision, that everything she said about her reasoning was true. I have already perhaps given a sufficient outline of what it was she believed to demonstrate what is meant by that. Up to that point the test was subjective. In other words one is examining what is going on in the applicant's mind.

Having done that, the judges in the present cases—and the judge particularly in the case of Valerie Hill—turned to the second aspect of the case, and that is this. He had to decide as a matter of law, which means objectively, whether it could be said that on those facts as believed by the applicant, snipping the strand of the wire, which she intended to do, could amount to something done to protect either the applicant's own home or the homes of her adjacent friends in Pembrokeshire.

He decided, again quite rightly in our view, that that proposed act on her part was far too remote from the eventual aim at which she was targeting her actions to satisfy the test.'

10. Reading that, not merely on its own but in conjunction with the earlier judgment of Roskill LJ, it is clear in my judgment that the discussion by the Lord Chief Justice there was exclusively by reference to limb (A) and not by reference to limb (B). The significance of the principle as there expounded is that limb (A) has, for the reasons explained by the Lord Chief Justice, two aspects: the one subjective, the other objective.

11. From those two judgments, as indeed from the structure and wording of section 5(2)(b) I conclude therefore that limb (A) has both a subjective and an objective aspect, whereas limb (B) has an exclusively subjective aspect. It is also important to bear in mind, not least in the light of certain submissions helpfully put before us by Ms Thomson on behalf of the respondent, the Crown Prosecution Service, that the focus in limb (A) is upon the single question of whether what was done was done 'in order to protect property', whether the property of the defendant or someone else or to protect some interest in property which the defendant believed was vested in himself or somebody else. The matters referred to in paragraphs (i) and (ii) at the end of subsection (2)(b), that is, whether the property was in 'immediate need of protection' and whether the means of protection were or would be 'reasonable having regard to all the circumstances', are to be found within limb (B) and are therefore, for the reasons I have given, subject to an exclusively subjective test.

12. The other authority to which we were referred was the decision of the Divisional Court in *Chamberlain v Lindon* [1998] EWHC Admin 329, [1998] 1 WLR 1252 . . . [His lordship referred to the facts and various parts of the judgment.] Sullivan J said this at paragraph 50 (page 1262C):

> 'In the criminal context the question is not whether the means of protection adopted by the defendant were objectively reasonable, having regard to all the circumstances, but whether the defendant believed them to be so. By virtue of section 5(3) it is immaterial whether his belief was justified, provided it was honestly held.'

18. That in my judgment is an entirely accurate if succinct summary of the statutory provisions set out in limb (B). Limb (B), to repeat, is on the authorities, as in my judgment on the plain reading of statute, entirely subjective. The question and the only question is honest belief. Whether that belief was reasonable or unreasonable is not of itself determinative of the presence or absence of honest belief. It is, as Sullivan J correctly observed, immaterial whether the belief was justified, a reading of the statute which is not merely as it seems to me implicit in the words of section 5(2)(b) but which is made explicit in section 5(3).

19. The final observation to be made on the statute is that although reasonableness as a concept does appear in section 5(2)(b)(ii), what is relevant under the statute is not whether in fact the means of protection adopted or proposed to be adopted by the defendant were or would be reasonable but whether the defendant believed that those means were or would be reasonable. In other words the honest belief which provides the defence includes an honest belief that what is being done is reasonable. If there is honest belief that what is being done is reasonable the fact that, assessed objectively, it is not reasonable is neither here nor there.

[His lordship set out some of the extracts from the Crown Court rulings in the present case and the difficulties posed by the language of the case stated.]

32. Bearing in mind the immediate causal link between the act of lopping off the trees which would *eo instanti* ameliorate the obstruction to Ms Unsworth's light, the present case, as in *Chamberlain*, is as far removed as can be imagined from the tenuous causal chain between action and consequence characterised by *Hill and Hall* and similar such cases. In just the same way as in *Chamberlain*, where the objective element in limb (A) caused no difficulties to the success of the defence, the objective element in limb (A) could not in this case, as it seems to me, be any difficulty in the way of Ms Unsworth establishing the defence.

33. Mr Myers appropriately focussed upon Sullivan J's reference (see paragraph 30) to the question of whether on the facts the steps taken 'could' ameliorate the damage to the property in that case

and, in this case, the obstruction to the easement. Manifestly in the present case as in that case not merely were the steps which Ms Unsworth believed it proper to take steps which *could* ameliorate the problem; they were steps which of their very nature *would* ameliorate the problem and moreover do so immediately

34. Of course it is not for us to find the facts, and we are confined by the facts as set out in the Case, but there is not from beginning to end anything that I can detect in the Case which would indicate that the Crown Court took the view that the objective element in limb (A) was not in fact established, nor indeed anything in the Case which would have entitled the Crown Court to come to that conclusion. In the way in which it formulated the questions which, albeit erroneously, it sought to answer in paragraph 15, the Case demonstrates that the focus of the Crown Court's analysis appears to have been, as inevitably it seems to me it had to be on its approach, not upon the objective element in limb (A), which was taken as satisfied, but impermissibly upon the legally irrelevant question of whether, in the context of limb (B), what Ms Unsworth chose to do was objectively justifiable as being objectively reasonable. In my judgment, with great respect to the judge and his colleagues in the Crown Court, the analysis in paragraph 15 of the Case, which in truth lies at the heart of the decision to dismiss Ms Unsworth's appeal, is both confused and confusing and in any event unsound in law.

. . .

40. There is one final aspect which I should perhaps refer to. As will be apparent, the Crown Court was perturbed as to the possible implications in cases of this kind, if the statutory defence was available in circumstances such as arose in the present case. And, as we have seen, it was concerned about the implications of what Sullivan J had said in particular in paragraph 50 of his judgment in *Chamberlain*. From one perspective, one can perhaps understand such concerns, but it is to be borne in mind, as I have already said, that all that Sullivan J was doing, as all that we are doing, is loyally applying the law as laid down by Parliament.

41. The statutory defence in this particular case is perhaps unusual. The point is well made in Smith and Hogan, *Criminal Law*, ed 12 [2008], para 29.1.5.2:

> 'This provision [that is, I interpolate, section 5(2)(b)] is in line with general principles of defences in so far as it relates to beliefs in facts or circumstances; however, it goes well beyond that in so far as it provides D's *belief* that the means employed *were reasonable* will excuse. This must be contrasted with the position in self-defence and the prevention of crime where D may use such force as *is found by a jury to be reasonable* in the circumstances which D believed to exist. Under the common law defence, the defendant's belief in the trigger for the defence is assessed on a subjective basis but the response to it is assessed objectively.'

In other words, whereas many such defences have a double requirement, a requirement of honest belief coupled with the requirement that that belief be reasonable, this defence is founded exclusively, so far as concerns limb (B) on the honesty of the belief. And although, as we have seen, reasonableness comes into limb (B), it comes in not as an additional criterion to be met but as one of the ingredients of the defendant's honest belief.

42. *Smith and Hogan* goes on to observe that in theory the defence might be relied upon as justification for a defendant 'laying waste an oil refinery because he believes its effluent is damaging his geraniums'. The protection, the safeguard, against such extravagant attempts to rely upon the defence is of course, as the authors point out, that a jury is unlikely in the circumstances postulated to believe that the defendant did think or could possibly have thought that what he was doing was reasonable. In other words the safeguard here is not to be found, as in many such defences, with the super-riding requirement to demonstrate that the belief was reasonable; it is to be found in the pragmatic reality that the fact-finding tribunal, whether in the present case the Magistrates' Court or, in trials on indictment, a jury, is the more unlikely to accept that the defendant's belief was honest the longer the difficulty has been in existence and the more extreme the measures the

defendant takes to remove it. A defendant who has tolerated some obstruction, whether it be an obstruction to a right of way such as in *Chamberlain* or an obstruction to a right of light as in this case, may find it the more difficult to establish the honest belief in the need to take 'immediate steps' the longer that state of affairs has gone on. After all, if you have tolerated something for a very long time how can it be said that you honestly believe that you have to take immediate steps? In just the same way the more extreme the steps taken to ameliorate the perceived damage the more difficult it will be to persuade the fact-finding tribunal that you honestly believed that what you were doing was reasonable.

43. It seems to me that the spectre conjured up and which troubled the mind of the Crown Court is not perhaps as great as it may have feared. The answer in all such cases lies in the good sense and common sense of the fact-finding tribunal in taking a realistic view as to whether the defendant can really honestly have believed that which he or she asserts, in particular if the steps taken are extravagant. It does not take much imagination to imagine what the outcome would be if, in the example given by *Smith and Hogan*, the gentleman who blew up the oil refinery tried to persuade a jury that he honestly believed that was a reasonable step to take to prevent damage to his flowers. In just the same way, although, perhaps unsurprisingly, she was able to establish the defence in the present case, because all that she had done was to lop the upper parts of the trees, Ms Unsworth might have had more difficulty if she had cut the trees down altogether and would, I can confidently assert, have had no prospect whatever of establishing the defence if the remedy of which she availed herself had involved not merely the cutting down of the trees but the demolition of part of the defendant's structure.

44. Be that as it may, the fact is that the defence is perhaps unusual in its width. For the reasons I have given this appeal must in my judgment be allowed.

The Divisional Court in *Unsworth* confirms that for the purposes of the statutory defence in s 5(2)(b) it is sufficient that D honestly believes that he needs to take immediate action to protect his property. It is not necessary to consider whether the belief is objectively justified. The second limb of the defence is exclusively subjective, unlike the first limb which has both an objective and a subjective element.

Immediacy

D must also believe, however, that the property is in 'immediate' need of protection within s 5(2)(b)(i). This suggests that the property must be immediately and not remotely threatened. So in *Hill and Hall*, the trial judge ruled that there was no evidence that D believed that the former Soviet Union was about to declare war or launch a pre-emptive strike. Nor could Hunt believe that a fire would break out next day, next month or even that a fire would ever occur. What Hunt no doubt believed was that *if* a fire ever did occur it might bring with it, in view of the fact that the alarms were not working, disastrous consequences. He had done, in writing to the warden and the council, all that he could do but this had been to no avail. Why could he not claim, within the section, that he believed the property was in *immediate* need of protection albeit the risk was a future one? Had the relevant fire authority been consulted they would surely have insisted on the alarms being repaired immediately and not at any remoter time. So was not the property in immediate need of protection?

In *Johnson v DPP* [1994] Crim LR 673, DC, D, a squatter, chiselled off the lock of the door of the house he was occupying and replaced it with his own lock. Charged with criminal damage, D claimed that the action he had taken was done to protect his property, viz the furniture he had moved into the squat. Upholding his conviction, the court said that D's property was not in 'immediate' need of protection as opposed to a 'speculative future need'. But the risk of theft, like the risk of fire, is always a future risk and neither may ever materialize. But does any reasonable person wait until the burglar calls before securing the door?

18.2.5.3 Relationship with other defences

Section 5(5) makes it clear that the definition of lawful excuse in the section is not exhaustive so that general defences such as self-defence, duress and necessity are available on a charge of criminal damage.

18.2.5.4 European Convention on Human Rights

In *Steele v UK* (1999) 28 EHRR 603, S, with 60 others, attempted to obstruct a grouse shoot. She was arrested for breach of the peace for impeding the progress of a member of the shoot by walking in front of him as he lifted his shotgun. At trial S was convicted of the Public Order Act 1986, s 5 offence and for breach of the peace. Other defendants were convicted for various other unrelated peaceful protest activities. S argued that this infringed her right to freedom of expression under Article 10.

Article 10 reads, so far as relevant, as follows:

> 1. Everyone has the right to freedom of expression. This right shall include freedom to hold opinions and to receive and impart information and ideas without interference by public authority and regardless of frontiers. . . .
>
> 2. The exercise of these freedoms, since it carries with it duties and responsibilities, may be subject to such formalities, conditions, restrictions or penalties as are prescribed by law and are necessary in a democratic society, . . . for the prevention of disorder or crime, . . . [or] for the protection of the reputation or rights of others. . . .

The European Court of Human Rights held:

> 90. The Government submitted that the protest activity . . . was not peaceful, and that Article 10 was not, therefore, applicable.
>
> 91. The Commission found that the measures taken against each of the . . . applicants amounted to interferences with their rights under Article 10.
>
> 92. The Court recalls that the applicants were arrested while protesting against a grouse shoot and the extension of a motorway respectively. It is true that these protests took the form of physically impeding the activities of which the applicants disapproved, but the Court considers nonetheless that they constituted expressions of opinion within the meaning of Article 10. The measures taken against the applicants were, therefore, interferences with their right to freedom of expression.

The Court found that in relation to S, the infringement of her freedom of expression was necessary and proportionate to a legitimate aim under Article 10(2). See [1998] Crim LR 893.

Protestors charged with criminal damage have also sought to rely on a defence that they were acting to prevent illegality in international law. The House of Lords dealt with a number of conjoined appeals in which this plea was raised in the context of s 3 of the Criminal Law Act 1967 but did not address the availability of defences under the Criminal Damage Act 1971. (See *Jones and others* [2006] UKHL 16, [2007] AC 136, section 23.3.2.9, p 634; the criminal damage defence was examined only in the Court of Appeal.)

In *Pritchard and others* [2005] QB 259, [2004] 4 All ER 955, DD had been charged with conspiracy to cause criminal damage and with offences under s 3(b) of the Act. DD had been involved in causing and attempting to cause damage at the military base at RAF Fairford. The defence asserted that the UK's attack on Iraq was an unlawful act and that their acts at the Air Force base were to prevent that illegality. DD sought to rely on the defences of duress of circumstance, necessity, lawful excuse under s 5(2)(b) and the prevention of crime under s 3 of the 1967 Act. The court on a preliminary ruling held that the international crime of aggression could not constitute a crime for the purposes of s 3 of the 1967 Act (see section 23.3.2.9, p 634), and that under s 5(2)(b) the jury was only concerned with the question of DD's honestly held beliefs. Therefore, no issue could arise in relation to the defence under s 5(2)(b) of whether the war in Iraq was illegal. As noted in the commentary in the *Criminal Law Review* ([2005] Crim LR 122):

> ... the court's conclusion that the legality of the war is irrelevant to the *availability* of the section 5(2) defence seems correct. But, is the illegality relevant to its *application*? Surely the circumstances—the immediacy, potency, lawfulness etc—of the action will be important to the jury in its evaluation of D's belief that his conduct is 'reasonable' as the statute requires? The success of the defence on facts such as these nevertheless remains debatable. Is there sufficient immediacy of threat to property, particularly where the charges of conspiracy to damage? Which item of property (the defence does not apply to protect people: *Baker* [1997] Crim LR 497) is D seeking to protect?

In *Hutchinson v Newbury Magistrates' Court* [2000] EWHC 61 (QB), H appealed against her conviction for criminal damage after cutting a perimeter fence at an atomic weapons establishment. H contended that (a) the production of weapons at the establishment was unlawful in customary international law pursuant to an opinion of the International Court of Justice in 1996 on the legality of the threat of use of nuclear weapons; (b) the establishment's activities were therefore also unlawful in English domestic law and, since H's actions had been intended to impede that unlawful activity, they were therefore not a criminal act; (c) by English domestic law the forbidden conduct of the establishment was not only unlawful but also criminal. Buxton LJ observed that:

> It originally seemed to be contended, ... that the fact that Mrs Hutchinson was acting to impede, alternatively to protest about, activities that were unlawful under international law in itself provided her with a lawful excuse in English criminal law. No authority was cited for a claim as broad as that. That is because no authority supports it. It is clear that the claim, when scrutinised, is hopelessly wide. If D commits a crime only to stop X doing an unlawful but not criminal act, he cannot claim the latter unlawfulness alone as an excuse for his own criminal conduct. Quite apart from the lack of authority, the practical implications of such an argument, were it correct, are obvious. What D must do in such a situation is bring his conduct, if he can, under one of the recognised heads of public or private defence, such as the heads that were set out by the judge in the second of her two questions for the opinion of this Court.

18.2.5.5 Section 5(5)

In *Lloyd v DPP* [1992] 1 All ER 982, [1991] Crim LR 904, DC, D, a trespasser, had parked his car on private land aware of notices that said the cars of trespassers would be clamped and that a charge of £25 would be made for their removal. He returned that evening to find his car clamped but refused to pay the £25 for its removal. The following day D returned to remove the clamp using a disc-cutter. D was charged with criminal damage to the clamp. On D's behalf it was argued that he could rely on s 5(5) because at common law the clamping of his car constituted a trespass and he was accordingly entitled to take reasonable steps to recover his property. If this argument was correct, said Nolan LJ:

> ... the only remedy open to a landowner who finds a car parked without authority on his land is to remove the car using as little force as may be required and to place it either on the highway or, if he knows who the owner of the car is, back at the owner's property. The practical difficulties and

dangers which that remedy would involve can readily be imagined: breaking into the car if locked in the first place; propelling it by some means onto the road with or without insurance cover; leaving it where it might cause obstruction at least, if not danger to other road users.

I mention that only to illustrate the problems inherent in this branch of the law and the need to my mind for them to be fully explored in civil proceedings. This court, exercising its criminal jurisdiction, is not concerned with the question whether Mr Lloyd could sue the landowners for trespass to his car and for the inconvenience caused to him or with the precise remedies open in civil law to the landowner. We are solely concerned with the question whether Mr Lloyd had a lawful excuse for damaging the property of South Coast Securities. We are concerned with the civil law only to the extent necessary for determining whether such an excuse existed for the purpose of the criminal law.

For that purpose it is sufficient to decide, as I do, that [the prosecutor's] alternative submission is well founded. It substantially reflects the conclusion of the justices in para 6(d) of the case [In para 6(d) the justices had said: 'The clamping of the appellant's motor vehicle, whether lawful or unlawful, and we considered it to be a trespass, was not such an act that the appellant could not in law consent to it. He consented to the risk of his vehicle being clamped. In this regard the signs erected around the car park were sufficiently clear and unambiguous.'] although that conclusion might more accurately have been expressed by saying that since the applicant had consented to the risk of his car being clamped the clamping was not a trespass. Mr Sharp submits that this conclusion cannot carry the day for the respondent because the appellant's consent to the clamping ceased on his return to the car park at 10.00 pm. Mr Sharp submits that the immobilisation of the car was plainly unlawful thereafter and the appellant was at liberty to exercise his right of recaption using such reasonable force as was necessary to do so.

To my mind, it would be a truly absurd state of affairs if the appellant, having consented to the risk of clamping, was at liberty to withdraw his consent with immediate effect once clamping had occurred and to proceed at once to recover his car by force. I am satisfied that this is not the law. Even assuming in the appellant's favour that the refusal of South Coast Securities to let him remove his car save on payment of £25 was an unlawful restraint, it would by no means follow that there was a lawful excuse for his subsequent action. He had a choice. He could have paid the £25 under protest, removed his car and taken action against South Coast Securities in the county court. Instead he chose to re-enter the car park, once again quite plainly as a trespasser, and to retrieve his car by causing some £50-worth of damage to the property of South Coast Securities.

In my judgment, the suggestion that there was a lawful excuse for his action is wholly untenable. At the worst what he had suffered was a civil wrong. The remedy for such wrongs is available in the civil courts. That is what they are there for. Self-help involving the use of force can only be contemplated where there is no reasonable alternative. . . .

Situations like those which have arisen in the present case are becoming increasingly common. They can cause intense irritation both to the motorist deprived of the use of his car, as he thinks, unreasonably, and to the landowner or other victim of the motorist's unauthorised parking. That makes it all the more necessary for it to be clearly stated that, at any rate as a general rule, if a motorist parks his car without permission on another person's property knowing that by doing so he runs the risk of it being clamped, he has no right to damage or destroy the clamp. If he does so he will be guilty of a criminal offence . . .

There is now a separate offence in s 54 of the Protection of Freedoms Act 2012 of immobilizing a motor vehicle without consent. So although D may be guilty of criminal damage when he damages V's clamp, V may also be guilty of a separate offence for clamping D's vehicle in the first place.

18.3 Destroying, etc property with intent to endanger life

Alongside the 'basic' criminal damage offence, there is an aggravated version. This offence is much more serious and carries a maximum sentence of life imprisonment.

Criminal Damage Act 1971, s 1

(2) A person who without lawful excuse destroys or damages any property, whether belonging to himself or another:

    (a) intending to destroy or damage any property or being reckless as to whether any property would be destroyed or damaged; and

    (b) intending by the destruction or damage to endanger the life of another or being reckless as to whether the life of another would be thereby endangered;

shall be guilty of an offence.

Law Commission Report No 29, *Criminal Law: Report on Offences of Damage to Property* (1970), paras 21–27

This proposed offence gives effect to our view that the policy of the criminal law is, and should continue to be, to select certain offences as attracting exceptionally high maximum penalties, because these offences are accompanied by aggravating factors. There are examples of this approach in ss 8–10 of the Theft Act 1968 dealing with robbery, burglary and aggravated burglary, which may be regarded as theft accompanied by aggravating circumstances . . . None of our commentators suggested that the test should be objective in the sense that one should look only to the consequences or potential consequences of the offender's conduct. All were agreed that the criterion for the aggravated offence was to be found in the offender's state of mind, namely, his intention to endanger the personal safety of another or his recklessness in that regard . . . [I]f no such offence is created, a considerable gap in the law is left, especially where the offender is reckless as to endangering personal safety and yet no injury is caused. In such a case the offender cannot be convicted of an attempt to commit an offence under the Offences against the Person Act 1861, in an attempt to commit an offence, intention and not merely recklessness is necessary . . . We think that the proper criterion should be related to the endangering of life, a concept which appears in s2 of the Explosive Substances Act 1883 and in s16 of the Firearms Act 1968. It is not, therefore, a novel one likely to give rise to difficulties of interpretation, and we think that it correctly expresses the necessary seriousness. It is true that in adopting the criterion of endangering life there may still be some overlapping with offences against the person . . .

> ≋ *Questions*
> Do you agree with the Law Commission that but for the creation of this offence 'a considerable gap is left in the law'? How does the offence differ from attempted murder? See further D. W. Elliott, 'Endangering Life by Destroying or Damaging Property' [1997] Crim LR 382.

The elements of the offence are:

- damage;
- to some property (whether D's or not);

- caused intentionally or recklessly;
- D must intend or be reckless that, *by the* damage that he intended or about which he was reckless, a life would be endangered;
- no life need be endangered in fact.

18.3.1 Damage

In *Meah v Roberts* [1978] 1 All ER 97, [1977] 1 WLR 1187, DC, D, after cleaning pipes in a bar, put some caustic soda 'stronger than that needed to remove paint from woodwork' in a lemonade bottle and left the bottle standing with other lemonade bottles. At this stage, and assuming that D does not intend to kill but is aware of the risk to life, it seems that D commits no offence if the bottle is empty, but commits the offence under s 1(2) if the bottle had contained some lemonade.

18.3.2 Property

The offence under s 1(2) may be committed though the property damaged is D's own property or is damaged with D's permission: *Merrick* [1996] 1 Cr App R 130, [1995] Crim LR 802, CA.

18.3.3 Intention or recklessness as to the damage

See the elements of mens rea in relation to the offence under s 1, section 18.2.4, p 464. The Court of Appeal confirmed in *Cooper* [2004] EWCA Crim 1382 that, as a result of the judgment of the House of Lords in *G*, the risk of danger to life must be obvious and significant to the defendant. In other words, a subjective element is essential before the jury can convict of this offence.

18.3.4 Intending or being reckless as to life endangerment by the damage intended or about which D was reckless

Although this element of the aggravated offence might seem simple, as the next case demonstrates, it gave rise to a difficult point of statutory interpretation.

R v Steer
[1987] 3 WLR 205, House of Lords

(Lords Bridge of Harwich, Griffiths, Ackner, Oliver of Aylmerton and Goff of Chieveley)

D went to the home of his former business partner against whom he bore some grudge and rang the bell waking the occupants who looked out of their bedroom window. D fired a shot aimed at the bedroom window and two further shots, one at another window and one at the front door. No one was hurt. It was never suggested that the first shot had been aimed at any person.

[All their lordships concurred in the speech delivered by Lord Bridge of Harwich:]

Arising from this incident the respondent was arraigned on an indictment containing three counts. He pleaded not guilty to possession of a firearm with intent to endanger life, contrary to section 16 of the Firearms Act 1968 (count 1) and to an offence of damaging property with intent, contrary to section

1(2) of the Criminal Damage Act 1971, which was alleged in the particulars as originally framed as having been committed 'intending by the said damage to endanger the lives of David Gregory and Tina Gregory or being reckless as to whether the lives of David Gregory and Tina Gregory would be thereby endangered' (count 2). He pleaded guilty to a separate offence of damaging property, contrary to section 1(1) of the Act of 1971 (count 3).

[His lordship read s 1 of the Act.]

It is to be observed that the offence created by subsection (2), save that it may be committed by destroying or damaging one's own property, is simply an aggravated form of the offence created by subsection (1), in which the prosecution must prove, in addition to the ingredients of the offence under subsection (1), the further mental element specified by subsection (2)(b). In this case presumably count 2 was intended to relate to the damage done by the shot fired at the bedroom window and count 3 to the damage done by one or other or both the other two shots. It is also significant to note the maximum penalties attaching to the three offences charged. For an offence under section 16 of the Act of 1968 it is 14 years' imprisonment, for an offence under section 1(2) of the Act of 1971 life imprisonment, for an offence under section 1(1) of the Act of 1971 10 years' imprisonment.

At some stage in the trial the particulars of count 2 were amended by deleting the words alleging an intent to endanger life and leaving only recklessness in that regard as the mental element relied on to establish the offence under section 1(2). The prosecution, it appears, presented the case on the footing that counts 1 and 2 were alternatives and, if the case had been left to the jury, the judge would presumably have directed them that, if they found that the respondent intended to endanger the lives of Mr and Mrs Gregory they should convict on count 1, but if they found that he was merely reckless with regard to such danger they should acquit on count 1 and convict on count 2.

At the conclusion of the case for the prosecution, however, counsel for the respondent submitted that there was no case to answer on count 2 on the ground that, in so far as the lives of Mr and Mrs Gregory had been endangered, the danger had not been caused by the damage done to the bungalow, but by the shot fired from the respondent's rifle. Of course, it is obvious that any danger to life in this case was caused by the shot from the rifle itself, not by any trifling damage done to the bedroom window or to any property in the bedroom. But the judge rejected counsel's submission and accepted the submission made for the Crown that the phrase in section 1(2)(b) of the Act of 1971 'by the destruction or damage' refers on its true construction not only to the destruction or damage to property as the cause of the danger to life on which the mental element in the aggravated offence under the subsection depends, but also to the act of the defendant which causes that destruction or damage. On the basis of the judge's ruling the respondent changed his plea to guilty on count 2. He appealed against conviction on the ground that the judge's ruling was erroneous. The Court of Appeal (Criminal Division) (Neill L.J., Peter Pain and Gatehouse JJ) allowed the appeal, but certified that their decision involved a question of law of general public importance in the following terms:

'Whether, upon a true construction of section 1(2)(b) of the Criminal Damage Act 1971, the prosecution are required to prove that the danger to life resulted from the destruction of or damage to the property, or whether it is sufficient for the prosecution to prove that it resulted from the act of the defendant which caused the destruction or damage.'

The Crown now appeals by leave of your Lordships' House.

We must, of course, approach the matter on the footing, implicit in the outcome of the trial, that the respondent, in firing at the bedroom window, had no intent to endanger life, but accepts that he was reckless as to whether life would be endangered.

Under both limbs of section 1 of the Act of 1971 it is the essence of the offence which the section creates that the defendant has destroyed or damaged property. For the purpose of analysis it may be convenient to omit reference to destruction and to concentrate on the references to damage, which was all that was here involved. To be guilty under subsection (1) the defendant must have intended or been reckless as to the damage to property which he caused. To be guilty under subsection (2) he must additionally have intended to endanger life or been reckless as to whether life would be endangered 'by the damage' to property which he caused. This is the context in which the words must be construed and it seems to me impossible to read the words 'by the damage' as meaning 'by the damage or by the act which caused the damage'. Moreover, if the language of the statute has the meaning for which the Crown contends, the words 'by the destruction or damage' and 'thereby' in subsection (2)(b) are mere surplusage. If the Crown's submission is right, the only additional element necessary to convert a subsection (1) offence into a subsection (2) offence is an intent to endanger life or recklessness as to whether life would be endangered simpliciter.

It would suffice as a ground for dismissing this appeal if the statute were ambiguous, since any such ambiguity in a criminal statute should be resolved in favour of the defence. But I can find no ambiguity. It seems to me that the meaning for which the respondent contends is the only meaning which the language can bear.

The contrary construction leads to anomalies which Parliament cannot have intended. If A and B both discharge firearms in a public place, being reckless as to whether life would be endangered, it would be absurd that A, who incidentally causes some trifling damage to property, should be guilty of an offence punishable with life imprisonment, but that B, who causes no damage, should be guilty of no offence. In the same circumstances, if A is merely reckless but B actually intends to endanger life, it is scarcely less absurd that A should be guilty of the graver offence under section 1(2) of the Act of 1971, B of the lesser offence under section 16 of the Firearms Act 1968.

Counsel for the Crown did not shrink from arguing that section 1(2) of the Act of 1971 had created, in effect, a general offence of endangering life with intent or recklessly, however the danger was caused, but had incidentally included as a necessary, albeit insignificant, ingredient of the offence that some damage to property should also be caused. In certain fields of legislation it is sometimes difficult to appreciate the rationale of particular provisions, but in a criminal statute it would need the clearest language to persuade me that the legislature had acted so irrationally, indeed perversely, as acceptance of this argument would imply.

It was further argued that to affirm the construction of section 1(2)(b) adopted by the Court of Appeal would give rise to problems in other cases in which it might be difficult or even impossible to distinguish between the act causing damage to property and the ensuing damage caused as the source of danger to life. In particular, it was suggested that in arson cases the jury would have to be directed that they could only convict if the danger to life arose from falling beams or similar damage caused by the fire, not if the danger arose from the heat, flames or smoke generated by the fire itself. Arson is, of course, the prime example of a form of criminal damage to property which, in the case of an occupied building, necessarily involves serious danger to life and where the gravity of the consequence which may result as well from recklessness as from a specific intent fully justifies the severity of the penalty which the Act of 1971 provides for the offence. But the argument in this case is misconceived. It is not the match and the inflammable materials, the flaming firebrand or any other inflammatory agent which the arsonist uses to start the fire which causes danger to life, it is the ensuing conflagration which occurs as the property which has been set on fire is damaged or destroyed. When the victim in the bedroom is overcome by the smoke or incinerated by the flames as the building burns, it would be absurd to say that this does not result from the damage to the building.

Counsel for the Crown put forward other examples of cases which he suggested ought to be liable to prosecution under section 1(2) of the Act of 1971, including that of the angry mob of striking miners who throw a hail of bricks through the window of the cottage occupied by the working miner and that of people who drop missiles from motorway bridges on passing vehicles. I believe that the criminal law provides adequate sanctions for these cases without the need to resort to section 1(2) of the Act of 1971. But, if my belief is mistaken, this would still be no reason to distort the plain meaning of that subsection.

Some reference was also made to damage caused by explosives. This is the subject of specific provision under the Explosive Substances Act 1883 as amended. The offence created by section 3(1)(a) of that Act, as substituted by section 7(1) of the Criminal Jurisdiction Act 1975, of doing 'any act with intent to cause . . . by an explosive substance an explosion of a nature likely to endanger life, or cause serious injury to property . . .' obviates the need to resort to the Act of 1971 when explosives are used. . . .

I can well understand that the prosecution in this case thought it necessary and appropriate that, even if they could not establish the intent to endanger life necessary to support a conviction under section 16 of the Act of 1968, they should include a count in the indictment to mark in some way the additional gravity of an offence of criminal damage to property in which a firearm is used. But they had no need to resort to section 1(2) of the Act of 1971. A person who, at the time of committing an offence under section 1 of the Act of 1971, has in his possession a firearm commits a distinct offence under section 17(2) of the Act of 1968: see Schedule 1 to the Act of 1968, as amended by section 11(7) of the Act of 1971. If the respondent had been charged with that offence in addition to the offence under section 1(1) of the Act of 1971, he must have pleaded guilty to both and, if the prosecution were content to accept that there was no intent to endanger life, this would have been amply sufficient to mark the gravity of the respondent's criminal conduct in the incident at the Gregory bungalow.

I would accordingly dismiss the appeal. The certified question should be answered as follows: 'Upon the true construction of section 1(2)(b) of the Criminal Damage Act 1971 the prosecution are required to prove that the danger to life resulted from the destruction of or damage to property; it is not sufficient for the prosecution to prove that it resulted from the act of the defendant which caused the destruction or damage.'

Appeal dismissed

Consider *Webster, Warwick* [1995] 2 All ER 168, CA. In *Webster*, defendants and others pushed a coping stone from the parapet of a bridge onto a passenger train passing beneath. The stone penetrated the roof but did not strike anyone; passengers were, however, showered with, though not physically injured by, debris dislodged from the roof by the falling stone. The court said the judge was wrong to direct the jury that the defendants could be convicted of the s 1(2) offence if they intended that life would be endangered *by the falling stone*. The conviction was upheld, however, on the ground that the jury's verdict implied that the defendants must have been reckless as to the lives of the passengers being endangered by falling debris. Would that still be the case now that *G* has overruled *Caldwell*?

In *Warwick*, D, in a stolen car, repeatedly rammed pursuing police vehicles while E, D's passenger, threw bricks at passing police cars, one of which shattered a windscreen and showered the officers therein with broken glass. It was held that D was properly convicted of the s 1(2) offence. D intended that property be damaged and was at least reckless as to the endangering of life since either action—the ramming of the police cars or the breaking of the window—caused damage which in turn might have put the lives of the police officers at risk.

18.3.5 No life need be endangered

The offence under s 1(2) requires that some property be intentionally or recklessly damaged. However, it is not necessary to show that life was in fact endangered if D in fact intended, or was reckless as to, such endangerment. D may be accordingly convicted if he has the relevant mens rea, even though a house in which he starts a fire is unoccupied (*Sangha* [1988] 2 All ER 385, [1988] 1 WLR 519, CA) or the fire which he starts is doused before any endangerment in fact arises (*Dudley* [1989] Crim LR 57, CA). The brick thrown at the police car in *Warwick* might have missed the windscreen and caused only trivial damage to the police car.

D would still be liable if it was thrown with the requisite mens rea; otherwise, said the court in *Warwick*, liability would depend on whether D was a good shot.

18.4 Arson

The Law Commission recommended that there should be no separate offence of damaging property by fire (see Law Com Report No 29, paras 28–33) but this recommendation proved unacceptable to Parliament and s 1(3) of the Act provides 'An offence committed under this section by destroying or damaging property by fire shall be charged as arson.' Since arson is punishable with life imprisonment, arson contrary to s 1(1) must be a separate offence under *Courtie* (which holds that if one form of an offence has a higher penalty it should be treated as separate from other forms of the offence).

A person may therefore be charged with an offence under s 1(1) and (3), to which the definition of lawful excuse in s 5 applies; or with an offence under s 1(2) and (3), to which the definition in s 5 does not apply. In order to constitute arson there must be some damage, however slight, done by fire.

In *Drayton* [2005] EWCA Crim 2013, D was charged under s 1(1) and s 1(3) of the 1971 Act, but the word 'arson' did not appear in the information. The Court of Appeal held that the charge was, in the context of the magistrates' court, a valid charge. The use of the word 'arson' was described as desirable, but the fact that the information alleged 'damage by fire' was sufficient. Since arson was specifically preserved because of the unique stigma attaching to that wrong, and the section is cast in mandatory terms ('shall be charged as arson'), the result is a surprising one.

18.5 Other offences

By s 2 of the Criminal Damage Act it is an offence to threaten to destroy, etc property, and by s 3 it is an offence to possess anything intending to destroy, etc property.

In *Ankerson* [2015] EWCA Crim 432, D was convicted under s 2. He had become estranged from his wife and was in a dispute about contact with his children. He went to social services offices and, according to the officials there, threatened to burn down the family home irrespective of who was in it before committing suicide. D denied threatening anything more than suicide. He claimed that he did not threaten to burn the house down and he did not intend that the officials should fear that such a threat would be carried out. It was clear that under s 2 there must be: words or actions which objectively speaking constitute a threat; the threat must be one which, again objectively considered, amounts to a threat to damage any property though it is not relevant that the particular listener perceived it to be a threat if objectively it would not have been so construed. D must intend that the person hearing the threat would fear that the threat would be carried out. The Court of Appeal held that the judge had not directed adequately on the third limb. Although in some parts of the summing-up the judge repeated the statutory formula that D must have intended that the social worker would fear that the threat *would* be carried out, in other places he said the test was whether D intended her to fear that he *might* carry out the threat. Nevertheless, the conviction was safe. In this case

there is no material difference between a defendant who intends that the listener should fear that the threat will be carried out and one who intends that the listener should fear that it might be carried out. It seems to us that the critical word is 'fear'. To fear that something will happen is not to be equated with a belief that it will happen. It is to be anxious about the possibility it will happen. That anxiety or fear arises where there is a risk that it might happen. So in our view it is enough if the intention is to create in the mind of an objective listener the genuine fear that the threat might be carried out. The listener can have that fear even where he or she is not certain that the threat will be carried out. It is in circumstances where the threat is understood to be serious that the authorities will likely be alerted with all the adverse consequences flowing from that. It will not be enough if the risk, objectively viewed, is merely fanciful because then there would not be a real and genuine fear that the threat would be carried out.

As the court recognized, the purpose of the offence is to ensure that the defendant does not make threats which he intends to be taken seriously even if he does not actually intend to carry them out.

18.6 Racially or religiously aggravated criminal damage

The Crime and Disorder Act 1998 created a new category of racially aggravated crimes. A person commits an offence under s 28 of the 1998 Act if he commits an offence within s 1(1) of the Criminal Damage Act, which is 'racially aggravated' for the purposes of s 29. The offence is punishable summarily by imprisonment for six months or a fine not exceeding the statutory maximum and, on indictment, by imprisonment for 14 years, or a fine, or both.

Section 39 of the Anti-terrorism, Crime and Security Act 2001 extended s 28 to 'religiously aggravated' offences. By s 39(5), 'religious group' means a group of persons defined by reference to religious belief or lack of religious belief. The Law Commission recommended that these offences ought to be extended to include hostility based on gender identity, sexual orientation and disability. See Law Commission Report No 348, *Hate Crime: Should the Current Offences be Extended?* (2014).

FURTHER READING

Criminal damage

D. W. Elliott, 'Criminal Damage' [1988] Crim LR 403

Law Commission Report No 29, *Criminal Law: Report on Offences of Damage to Property* (1970)

19

Parties to offences

Liability as a principal:

D is liable for an offence as a principal (or joint principal) where he performs the actus reus of the offence with the relevant mens rea.

Liability as an accessory:

D is liable for any offence(s) carried out by P (as principal) where D has intentionally assisted or encouraged P with intention that P will commit the offence with knowledge as to the essential elements of P's offence (including any facts as to which the principal bears strict liability).

The controversies that will be examined in this chapter include:

(1) the conceptual basis for secondary liability;

(2) what is meant by 'aiding, abetting, counselling and procuring';

(3) the mens rea necessary to establish secondary liability, with emphasis upon the Supreme Court's recent judgment in *Jogee*;

(4) the rise and fall of so-called 'joint enterprise' liability;

(5) the consequences of the Supreme Court's decision in *Jogee*.

19.1 Introduction

In this chapter we consider the way in which the criminal law applies to those who are responsible for assisting or encouraging crimes. Vast numbers of crimes are carried out by people acting together and it is essential that the criminal law has effective rules in place to deal with the conduct of all who are involved. The way that the law of England and Wales has done so, historically, has been to treat the person who assists as guilty in the same manner and for the same offence as the person who most directly commits the crime. The person who provides the gun to the murderer is prosecuted as a murderer himself and is liable to the same punishment as the person who pulls the trigger.

In this chapter we will consider those who assisted or encouraged the commission of an offence *that was completed or attempted*. In Chapter 22 we consider the responsibility of those who have assisted or encouraged irrespective of whether the crime that they assisted or encouraged was in fact carried out or even attempted.

Suppose that Dawn visits Peter, a 'contract killer', and tells him that she wants him to kill her husband, Victor. Dawn is now liable to conviction for assisting or encouraging Peter to commit murder under s 44 of the Serious Crime Act 2007. That crime is committed as soon as Dawn's words are spoken. It would make no difference if Peter said he would have nothing to do with the proposal (see Chapter 21). If Peter agrees to commit the murder, the pair of them are guilty of conspiracy to murder. Conspiracy to commit a crime is another distinct offence, committed as soon as the agreement is made. It would make no difference to liability for conspiracy (though it would affect the sentence) that, immediately afterwards, they thought better of it and decided to abandon the plan (see Chapter 20).

If Peter goes ahead and kills Victor he is guilty of murder. He is the 'principal offender'. Dawn is also guilty of murder. She is an 'accessory' sometimes also known as a 'secondary party' or 'accomplice'. She may be miles away at the time but she is equally responsible in law with Peter for Peter's act. Suppose that Peter has taken into his confidence two friends, Carl, who lent him a gun with which to shoot Victor, and Eric, who drove him to Peter's house and kept watch outside while Peter did the deed inside. Carl and Eric are also guilty of the murder of Victor. They are also accessories. Dawn, Peter, Carl and Eric are all equally liable to be convicted of murder and liable to the same punishment—which, for murder, must be life imprisonment. In the case of crimes other than murder, where the judge has a discretion in imposing sentence, the permissible maximum is the same for all; but sentences may vary according to the responsibility of each party. The principal is not necessarily the most blameworthy. An accessory such as Dawn may be the 'mastermind' and the dominant personality and her sentence is likely to reflect that.

In this chapter we examine the nature and extent of liability for secondary participation in a crime. As the previous example shows, secondary participation is closely interrelated with assisting and encouraging under the Serious Crime Act 2007 and conspiracy; but as they are distinct crimes they are considered separately, along with the crime of attempt with which they are closely associated, in Chapters 20 to 22.

19.2 The derivative nature of secondary liability

The distinctive feature of secondary liability is that, subject to one exception discussed in section 19.4.1.4, p 492, it is derivative: the liability of Dawn, Carl and Eric 'derives' from that of Peter. It is only when Peter performs the conduct element of the offence of murder that the liability of the others *as accessories* is triggered.

When Peter points the gun at Victor, Dawn, Carl and Eric have done everything necessary to become accessories to murder, but whether they do so depends on whether Peter pulls the trigger. If he changes his mind at the last moment none of them would be guilty of murder, for no murder has been committed. The liability of the secondary party derives from the *guilt* of the principal, not from his *conviction*. If, after killing Victor, Peter kills himself, or goes abroad and is never heard of again, Dawn, Carl and Eric may still be convicted as accessories to the murder Peter committed. If, at their trial, it is proved that Peter (who is absent and not on trial) committed the murder and that they played the parts described, Peter's absence and the fact that he is not convicted are immaterial. We consider later the merits of a scheme based on inchoate liability (where the liability of Dawn, Carl and Eric would arise irrespective of whether Peter committed murder) rather than derivative secondary liability.

Over the centuries a wide variety of verbs were used by the courts and by Parliament to describe the acts which amount to secondary participation. In modern times, however, they have been generally, though not invariably, limited to the following four: 'aid, abet, counsel or procure'. The common law rules of secondary participation apply automatically to every offence unless expressly or impliedly excluded. When Parliament creates a new offence it does not usually provide that anyone who aids, abets, counsels or procures it will be guilty. There is no need to do so. The common law rule is now embodied in statute law.

Accessories and Abettors Act 1861

> **8. Abettors in misdemeanours**
>
> Whosoever shall aid, abet, counsel, or procure the commission of any indictable offence, whether the same be an offence at common law or by virtue of any Act passed or to be passed, shall be liable to be tried, indicted, and punished as a principal offender.

Magistrates' Courts Act 1980

> **44. Aiders and abettors**
>
> (1) A person who aids, abets, counsels or procures the commission by another person of a summary offence shall be guilty of the like offence and may be tried (whether or not he is charged as a principal) either by a court having jurisdiction to try that other person or by a court having by virtue of his own offence jurisdiction to try him.
>
> (2) Any offence consisting in aiding, abetting, counselling or procuring the commission of an offence triable either way (other than an offence Listed in Schedule 1 to this Act) shall by virtue of this sub-section be triable either way.

19.3 Distinguishing principals, innocent agents and accessories

Notwithstanding the provisions of the Accessories and Abettors Act and the Magistrates' Courts Act as set out above, it is sometimes necessary to distinguish between the principal and secondary parties:

(1) in the case of all offences of strict liability because, even in these cases, secondary parties must be proved to have mens rea although the principal need not;

(2) in all cases where the offence is so defined that it can be committed as a principal only by a member of a specified class (eg only a man can commit rape as a principal because the definition of the offence is that a man penetrates *with his penis*);

(3) where vicarious liability is in issue. In some offences vicarious liability may be imposed for the act of another who is a principal or does the act of a principal; but there is no vicarious liability for the act of a secondary party.

19.3.1 Principal

Where there are several participants in a crime we define the principal as the participant 'whose act is the most immediate cause of the actus reus'. With offences in which there is no result or consequence to be proved, the principal offender is perhaps more accurately the person who engages in the conduct element of the actus reus. Thus, in murder for example, he is the person who, with mens rea, fires the gun or administers the poison which causes death; in theft, the person who, with mens rea, appropriates the thing which is stolen, etc.

19.3.2 Joint principal offenders

There may be two or more principal offenders in the same crime. If D1 and D2 make an attack on V intending to murder him and the combined effect of their blows is to kill him, both are guilty of murder as joint principal offenders: *Macklin and Murphy's Case* (1838) 2 Lew CC 225.

The position is different if D causes another person, X (who is fully aware of the circumstances and consequences of what he is being persuaded to do, so is not an *innocent* agent, see section 19.3.4), by persuasion or otherwise, to commit the offence. That does not amount to D causing the actus reus. X's voluntary intervening conduct 'breaks the chain of causation' so that D is not a principal offender. X will be liable as the principal offender. D may be liable (a) under ss 44 to 46 of the Serious Crime Act 2007 (see Chapter 22), depending on his mens rea, or (b) as a secondary party.

19.3.3 Principal or accessory?

It has always been sufficient to secure a conviction that the prosecution can prove that the defendant was either the principal or a secondary party. For example, in *Gianetto* [1997] 1 Cr App R 1, it was sufficient for the prosecution to allege that the defendant killed his wife or that he was an accessory to her death (by contracting a killer to do so). The prosecution could not be sure whether D was the principal offender or a secondary party, but could establish beyond doubt that he was involved in plotting her killing. Provided the defendant knows the allegation he has to meet—in terms of the part he is alleged to have played—in most cases the Crown need not specify whether he was a principal or accessory. This is because he is charged and prosecuted in the same way, and liable to the same penalty, regardless of whether he was in fact the principal or accessory. However, this must be distinguished from the case where there are two defendants and it cannot be proven which defendant committed the principal offence. In *Banfield* [2013] EWCA Crim 1394, the Court of Appeal reaffirmed that if all that can be proven is that the principal offence was committed by either D1 or D2, and it cannot be shown that whichever was not the principal must have been assisting, then both must be acquitted. For example, V is killed and only D and P had access to V at that time. It could have been P alone, D alone, D assisting P or P assisting D, but unless the Crown can establish in relation to each defendant that they were involved in some capacity, they must both be acquitted.

19.3.4 Innocent agents

It may be that the person whose act is the most immediate cause of the actus reus is not a participant in the crime at all. For example, D and E prepare a letter bomb addressed to V and D posts it. The letter passes through several hands in the Post Office and is put through V's letterbox by F, an unsuspecting postman. V opens it and is injured or killed. F's act is the most immediate cause of the killing but F is not a participant in the crime. Obviously D is the principal. F and the other Post Office employees who handled the letter are described as 'innocent agents'.

A person might be an innocent agent because:

(1) he is under 10 years of age and therefore under the age of criminal responsibility; or

(2) he does the act or acts without the fault required for the offence; or

(3) he has a defence.

Our postman falls into category (2). A 9-year-old child who is persuaded to smother a baby would be an example of category (1). A person (X) who is compelled by another (D) by threats of death to wound a third person (Y) would be an example of (3). If charged with wounding, X would have the defence of duress. If Y died of his wounds and D and X were charged with murder, X would now be the alleged principal and D the alleged accessory because duress is not a defence to murder.

The Law Commission proposed replacing the common law innocent agency doctrine with a new statutory offence; see section 19.11, p 533, and R. D. Taylor, 'Procuring, Causation, Innocent Agency and the Law Commission' [2008] Crim LR 32.

See, generally, P. Alldridge, 'The Doctrine of Innocent Agency' (1990) 2 Crim L Forum 45; G. Williams, 'Innocent Agency and Causation' (1992) 3 Crim L Forum 289.

We return to discuss a complexity with innocent agents and procuring at section 19.4.1.4, p 533.

19.4 Liability as an accessory

The accessory is liable for the principal's offence and prosecuted as a principal, but there is no secondary liability in the abstract. D cannot be an accessory per se; he must be an accessory to a specific crime—murder, theft, etc. In approaching the secondary party's liability, it is logical to begin by identifying the principal and the crime the principal is alleged to have committed. It is then necessary to turn to the accomplice's liability. His offence of secondary liability has its own actus reus and mens rea which must be proved before he can be convicted as an accomplice.

19.4.1 Actus reus: aiding, abetting, counselling or procuring

Section 8 of the 1861 Act describes the actus reus of the secondary party as aiding, abetting, counselling or procuring. It is enough that D did one of the four things—aided, abetted, counselled or procured.

One of the disadvantages in having the law relating to accessories based on a statute dating from 1861 and on the common law development since that date is that the principles of liability are not as clearly expressed as they might be. The language is also archaic, adding to the ambiguity and inaccessibility of the law.

Attorney-General's Reference (No 1 of 1975)
[1975] EWCA Crim 1, Court of Appeal, Criminal Division

(Lord Widgery CJ, Bristow and May JJ)

Lord Widgery CJ [delivered the following judgment of the court:]

This case comes before the court on a reference from the Attorney General under s 36 of the Criminal Justice Act 1972, and by his reference he asks the following question:

'Whether an accused who surreptitiously laced a friend's drinks with double measures of spirits when he knew that his friend would shortly be driving his car home, and in consequence his friend drove with an excess quantity of alcohol in his body and was convicted of the offence under the Road Traffic Act 1972, s 6(1) is entitled to a ruling of no case to answer on being later charged as an aider and abettor, counsellor and procurer, on the ground that there was no shared intention between the two, that the accused did not by accompanying him or otherwise positively encourage the friend to drive, or on any other ground.'

The language in the section which determines whether a 'secondary party', as he is sometimes called, is guilty of a criminal offence committed by another embraces the four words 'aid, abet, counsel or procure'. The origin of those words is to be found in s 8 of the Accessories and Abettors Act 1861 which provides:

> 'Whosoever shall aid, abet, counsel, or procure the commission of any misdemeanor, whether the same be a misdemeanor at common law or by virtue of any Act passed or to be passed, shall be liable to be tried, indicted, and punished as a principal offender.'

. . .

Of course it is the fact that in the great majority of instances where a secondary party is sought to be convicted of an offence there has been a contact between the principal offender and the secondary party. Aiding and abetting almost inevitably involves a situation in which the secondary party and the main offender are together at some stage discussing the plans which they may be making in respect of the alleged offence, and are in contact so that each knows what is passing through the mind of the other.

In the same way it seems to us that a person who counsels the commission of a crime by another, almost inevitably comes to a moment when he is in contact with that other, when he is discussing the offence with that other and when, to use the words of the statute, he counsels the other to commit the offence.

The fact that so often the relationship between the secondary party and the principal will be such that there is a meeting of minds between them caused the trial judge in the case from which this reference is derived to think that this was really an essential feature of proving or establishing the guilt of the secondary party and, as we understand his judgment, he took the view that in the absence of some sort of meeting of minds, some sort of mental link between the secondary party and the principal, there could be no aiding, abetting or counselling of the offence within the meaning of the section.

So far as aiding, abetting and counselling is concerned we would go a long way with that conclusion. It may very well be, as I said a moment ago, difficult to think of a case of aiding, abetting or counselling when the parties have not met and have not discussed in some respects the terms of the offence which they have in mind. But we do not see why a similar principle should apply to procuring. We approach s8 of the 1861 Act on the basis that the words should be given their ordinary meaning, if possible. We approach the section on the basis also that if four words are employed here, 'aid, abet, counsel or procure', the probability is that there is a difference between each of those four words and the other three, because, if there were no such difference, then Parliament would be wasting time in using four words where two or three would do. Thus, in deciding whether that which is assumed to be done under our reference was a criminal offence we approach the section on the footing that each word must be given its ordinary meaning.

To procure means to produce by endeavour. You procure a thing by setting out to see that it happens and taking the appropriate steps to produce that happening. We think that there are plenty of instances in which a person may be said to procure the commission of a crime by another even though there is no sort of conspiracy between the two, even though there is no attempt at agreement or discussion as to the form which the offence should take. In our judgment the offence described in this reference is such a case.

If one looks back at the facts of the reference: the accused surreptitiously laced his friend's drink. This is an important element and, although we are not going to decide today anything other than the problem posed to us, it may well be that in similar cases where the lacing of the drink or the introduction of the extra alcohol is known to the driver quite different considerations may apply. We say that because where the driver has no knowledge of what is happening, in most instances he would have no means of preventing the offence from being committed. If the driver is unaware of what has happened, he will not be taking precautions. He will get into his car seat, switch on the ignition and drive home and, consequently, the conception of another procuring the commission of the offence by the driver is very much stronger where the driver is innocent of all knowledge of what is happening, as in the present case where the lacing of the drink was surreptitious.

The second thing which is important in the facts set out in our reference is that following and in consequence of the introduction of the extra alcohol, the friend drove with an excess quantity of alcohol in his blood. Causation here is important. You cannot procure an offence unless there is a causal link between what you do and the commission of the offence, and here we are told that in consequence of the addition of this alcohol the driver, when he drove home, drove with an excess quantity of alcohol in his body.

Giving the words their ordinary meaning in English, and asking oneself whether in those circumstances the offence has been procured, we are in no doubt that the answer is that it has. It has been procured because, unknown to the driver and without his collaboration, he has been put in a position in which in fact he has committed an offence which he never would have committed otherwise. We think that there was a case to answer and that the trial judge should have directed the jury that an offence is committed if it is shown beyond reasonable doubt that the accused knew that his friend was going to drive, and also knew that the ordinary and natural result of the additional alcohol added to the friend's drink would be to bring him above the recognised limit of 80 milligrammes per 100 millilitres of blood.

It was suggested to us that, if we held that there may be a procuring on the facts of the present case, it would be but a short step to a similar finding for the generous host, with somewhat bibulous friends, when at the end of the day his friends leave him to go to their own homes in circumstances in which they are not fit to drive and in circumstances in which an offence under the Road Traffic Act 1972 is committed. The suggestion has been made that the host may in those circumstances be guilty with his guests on the basis that he has either aided, abetted, counselled or procured the offence.

The first point to notice in regard to the generous host is that that is not a case in which the alcohol is being put surreptitiously into the glass of the driver. That is a case in which the driver knows perfectly well how much he has to drink and where to a large extent it is perfectly right and proper to leave him to make his own decision.

Furthermore, we would say that if such a case arises, the basis on which the case will be put against the host is, we think, bound to be on the footing that he has supplied the tool with which the offence is committed. This of course is a reference back to such cases as those where oxyacetylene equipment was bought by a man knowing it was to be used by another for a criminal offence [*Bainbridge*, section 19.6.2, p 514]. There is ample and clear authority as to the extent to which supplying the tools for the commission of an offence may amount to aiding and abetting for present purposes.

Accordingly, so far as the generous host type of case is concerned we are not concerned at the possibility that difficulties will be created, as long as it is borne in mind that in those circumstances the matter must be approached in accordance with well-known authority governing the provision of the tools for the commission of an offence, and never forgetting that the introduction of the alcohol is not there surreptitious, and that consequently the case for saying that the offence was procured by the supplier of the alcohol is very much more difficult.

Our decision on the reference is that the question posed by the Attorney-General should be answered in the negative.

Determination accordingly

The court holds that Parliament must have intended the four words, 'aid, abet, counsel and procure' to have different meanings, but the court did not have the advantage of an exposition of the history of secondary participation and might have arrived at a different conclusion if it had. See J. C. Smith, 'Aid, Abet, Counsel or Procure' in P. R. Glazebrook (ed), *Reshaping the*

Criminal Law: Essays in Honour of Glanville Williams (1978), p 120. The Code Team and the Law Commission thought that the scope of secondary participation as defined in the case law is accurately described by three words, 'procure, assist, or encourage'.

≈ **Questions**

Professor Kadish, with whom Glanville Williams agrees, thinks that only two types of activity are involved—'intentionally influencing the decision of the primary party to commit the crime, and intentionally helping the primary actor to commit the crime': *Blame and Punishment: Essays in Criminal Law* (1987), pp 135, 151.

Does this formula adequately cover a case like the *A-G's Reference*? See discussion at [1991] Crim LR 765 and 930.

Lord Widgery's generous host fills the guest's glass as rapidly as the guest empties it and may be aware that the guest, who has come alone in his car, will drive home with an excess of alcohol. Does the host cause this result? Does he cause it by *endeavour*? Lord Widgery said that 'to procure means to produce by *endeavour*'. What is the significance of the words, 'by endeavour'?

Williams, *Textbook of Criminal Law* (2nd edn, 1983), p 339, writes: 'In so far as *Attorney-General's Reference* purports to decide that merely causing an offence can be said to be a procuring of it, it should be regarded as too incautious a generalisation.'

Despite the decision that all four words have different meanings, they may be used together to charge a person who is alleged to have participated in an offence otherwise than as a principal offender (ie D can be charged with having aided, abetted, counselled or procured, etc). As long as the evidence establishes that D's conduct satisfied one of the words, that is enough. However, where the prosecution chooses only one term—for example, 'procures'—it is necessary to prove that D's conduct fits that term.

19.4.1.1 Aiding

The natural meaning of the word would be to describe someone who helped, perhaps by acting as a lookout while P burgled premises or by supplying the assassin, P, with a gun. It was generally accepted that D could still be liable even though D's aid need not have actually helped P. Perhaps D supplied P with a gun to murder V, but P chose to use a knife instead. D should still be liable for aiding murder. In *Bryce* [2004] EWCA Crim 1231, D was convicted of murder as an aider and abettor. In the course of a drug dealers' dispute D assisted X, who was acting on the orders of another, Black, by transporting X and a gun to a caravan near V's home so that X could carry out the murder. Twelve hours after D had left X at the scene, X shot V with the gun. D assisted in disposing of evidence after the killing. D's appeal was focused on the issue of causation—that what D did was too remote in time and place to the killing and that at the stage when D assisted, X had not yet formed the intention to commit any criminal offence. Upholding D's conviction, the court held that a causal connection, in the strict sense of that term, was not required.

19.4.1.2 Abetting

Where D did not 'procure' the commission of the offence and did not 'aid' the principal, the prosecution may rely on the fact that he encouraged ('abetted') its commission. The natural meaning of 'abet' is 'to incite, instigate or encourage'. It is probably not necessary to prove that P was influenced in any way by D, but he must at least be aware that he has the authority, encouragement or approval of D to do the relevant acts.

19.4.1.3 Counselling

D might also commit the actus reus of being a secondary party by counselling the principal offender. To 'counsel' means to advise or solicit or encourage. In *Calhaem* [1985] 2 All ER 266, the prosecution alleged that Calhaem (C) hired Zajac (Z) to murder Mrs Rendell (R), C's rival for the affections of her solicitor. Z, the principal witness for the prosecution, testified to the hiring and said that he went to R's house, armed but with no intention of killing her; that he intended only to act out a charade so that C and R would think an attempt had been made; but that, when R screamed, he went berserk and killed her. It was argued, *inter alia*, that the judge had misdirected the jury by not telling them that, as in the case of procuring, the counselling by C must have been a 'substantial cause' of the killing. C's appeal was dismissed. The Court of Appeal held that the word 'counsel' should be given its ordinary meaning and that there was no implication in the word itself that there should be any causal connection between the counselling and the offence.

> ⩪ *Question*
> What is the difference between 'connection' and 'cause'?

It is clearly the law that an attempt to counsel does not amount to counselling. Proffered advice or encouragement which has no effect on the mind of the principal offender is not counselling. There is, however, no need for the prosecution to prove that D's counselling was a cause of the commission of the offence by P.

To what extent can D be liable for counselling P if P goes beyond anything D had envisaged or sought to encourage? Note that the secondary liability is derivative (section 19.2, p 485) so the liability of D is only triggered once the full offence is committed by P. By contrast, with inchoate liability, D can be liable for his particular act of encouragement irrespective of what, if anything, P goes on to do.

19.4.1.4 Procuring

The final way in which the defendant can act as an accessory is as a procurer. The Court of Appeal in *A-G's Reference (No 1 of 1975)*, section 19.4.1, p 488, explained that 'To procure means to "produce by endeavour." You cannot procure an offence unless there is a causal link between what you do and the commission of the offence.'

Can D be guilty of procuring P to commit only the conduct element of the offence?

As we saw in section 19.3.4 when discussing innocent agents, if Dawn causes a 9-year-old, or the postman (who acts without the fault required for the offence), or an insane person (who has a defence) to do the act which kills or causes GBH, she causes the harm in law as well as in fact and is liable accordingly as the principal. Once the causation element is satisfied, she fits the definition of the offence. She has herself done what the law forbids.

But it is not every offence which can be committed through an agent. Consider bigamy. D, knowing that P's wife is alive, tells P that she is dead and persuades him to marry V. P has committed the actus reus of bigamy ('being married, marries') but is not guilty of that offence because he lacks mens rea. D has knowingly caused the commission of the actus reus but is it possible to say that he has himself committed it? D may be a bachelor but, whether he is or not, can it be said that he has, by his actions, 'married'? Is bigamy—except in the case of a proxy marriage—a crime which is capable of commission through an innocent agent? *Millward* [1994] Crim LR 527 provides a mechanism for convicting D of procuring an actus reus by P even if P does not commit the full offence. In this case H and M were charged with causing death by reckless driving. H was the driver and M was charged as an aider, abettor, counsellor or procurer. The alleged recklessness was not in the manner of the driving but in taking the vehicle, a tractor with a defective towing mechanism, on the road. The trailer became detached and collided with an oncoming vehicle, causing death. The jury acquitted H and convicted M who appealed, arguing that the actus reus of the offence was never committed. The court disagreed, however, and held that M could be guilty on the basis that he procured the actus reus of the offence.

> In this court's view, the actus reus in the present case was the taking of the vehicle in the defective condition on to the road so as to cause the death of the little boy. It was procured by this appellant. The requisite mens rea was, in our judgment, present on the jury's that is relevant to the decision that we have to make. In this court's view, the actus reus in the present case was the taking of the vehicle ...

The principle in *Millward* can apply only where there has been at least the actus reus performed by P.

It is necessary to invoke the *Millward* principle only where the crime is one which is incapable of being committed by an innocent agent, like rape, bigamy or a driving offence. To be clear, if D has caused P to perform the actus reus with P having an innocent state of mind, D will either be liable as a principal because P is an innocent agent or D will be liable for procuring P's actus reus if the offence is one that P cannot commit as a principal in person.

The question of whether D can be guilty of procuring P's actus reus had been much discussed long before *Millward*. In *Bourne* (1952) 36 Cr App R 125, CCA, a man was held guilty of aiding and abetting his wife to commit buggery with a dog, although she could not have been convicted because she was acting under duress by him. Rupert Cross ((1953) 68 LQR 354) argued that the decision was correct in principle because 'The wife committed the actus reus with the mens rea required by the definition of the crime in question and the husband participated in that mens rea.' The wife had mens rea because she knew exactly what she was doing. That would not explain *Cogan and Leak*, cited in *Millward*, where Cogan may have believed that Mrs Leak was consenting to the sexual intercourse, in which case he committed the actus reus *without* mens rea. Lawton LJ gave two reasons:

(1) that Leak might have been convicted as a principal; but everything that Leak did could have been done by a woman and it would be nonsense to say that a woman could be guilty of rape (which requires penile penetration) as a principal; and

(2) that Leak had procured the *crime of rape* (cf Glanville Williams, *Textbook of Criminal Law* (2nd edn, 1983), pp 371–372)—'no one outside a court of law would say that Mrs Leak had not been [raped]', but Lawton LJ was *in* a court of law.

It would take a bold person to tell Mrs Leak that she had not been raped; but, if Cogan thought she was consenting, she had not been raped by him. A similar argument could be advanced by someone who had had a valuable possession taken: they might think it has been stolen but if the person who took it did so mistaking it for his own similar article there was no theft. However, rightly or wrongly, the second reason given by the court in *Cogan and Leak* was that Leak had procured not merely the actus reus, but the offence, of rape by Cogan.

The theory (advanced in every edition of *Smith and Hogan*), that procuring the actus reus of an offence is sufficient to make D liable for P's conduct, is criticized by S. Kadish (*Blame and Punishment: Essays in Criminal Law* (1987), p 180) saying that it 'at least technically . . . amounts to creating a new crime'. The Law Commission (Consultation Paper No

131, *Assisting and Encouraging Crime* (1993), para 4.207), writing before *Millward*, was also sceptical:

> A prime danger of such a rule is that, in its anxiety to meet cases of the type just discussed (including *Bourne* and *Cogan and Leak*) it will reach too far.

≋ *Questions*

(1) Is the principle in *Millward* limited to procurers, as distinct from aiders, abettors and counsellors—who assist or encourage but do not, by their own acts, *cause*, the commission of the offence by another?

(2) X, a married man, believes on reasonable grounds that his wife, Y, is dead. D knows she is alive. D persuades X to marry Z. E and F also know that Y is alive. E acts as best man at the wedding and F gives the bride away. Are D, E and F guilty of bigamy? Or is only D guilty?

19.4.1.5 Actus reus of secondary parties—further issues

We have now considered all four forms of actus reus of accessories—aiding, abetting, counselling and procuring. We must deal with three other issues.

- Does the accessory's actus reus (aiding, abetting, counselling or procuring) have to cause P's offence?

- Does the accessory's liability only arise from his acts or can the actus reus (aiding, abetting, counselling or procuring) be satisfied by an omission?

- Can the actus reus of the secondary party be satisfied by proof of mere presence when P is committing the offence?

Accessories and causation

Suppose that Dawn hires Peter to beat up Victor and Peter does so. Section 18 of the Offences Against the Person Act 1861 provides that:

> Whosoever shall unlawfully and maliciously . . . cause any grievous bodily harm to any person . . . with intent . . . to do some grievous bodily harm to any person . . . shall be liable to imprisonment for life.

Peter has committed this offence as a principal and Dawn who counselled and procured him to do so is liable as a secondary party. But why is not Dawn a principal? Has she not *caused* grievous bodily harm to Victor with intent—the very thing which the statute forbids? The beating up occurred only because she hired Peter to do it. In a very real sense Dawn did cause GBH to Victor; but in law she is not regarded as having caused the harm. The intervening voluntary act by Peter breaks the chain of causation. If this were not so, the legal distinction between principals and secondary parties would break down because in many, though not all, cases of secondary liability the secondary party, like Dawn in the example, *in fact* is a cause of the actus reus.

In *Kennedy (No 2)* [2007] UKHL 38 (section 3.2.3.2, p 42), the House of Lords reaffirmed this fundamental principle. Lord Bingham stated that:

> 17. . . . Professor Glanville Williams pointed out (at p 398) [in '*Finis* for *Novus Actus*?' (1989) 48 CLJ 391] that the doctrine of secondary liability was developed precisely because an informed voluntary choice was ordinarily regarded as a *novus actus interveniens* breaking the chain of causation:

'Principals cause, accomplices encourage (or otherwise influence) or help. If the instigator were regarded as causing the result he would be a principal, and the conceptual division between principals (or, as I prefer to call them, perpetrators) and accessories would vanish. Indeed, it was because the instigator was not regarded as causing the crime that the notion of accessories had to be developed. This is the irrefragable argument for recognising the *novus actus* principle as one of the bases of our criminal law. The final act is done by the perpetrator, and his guilt pushes the accessories, conceptually speaking, into the background. Accessorial liability is, in the traditional theory, 'derivative' from that of the perpetrator.'

Despite this, judges have sometimes stated that the basis of secondary liability is that D has caused P to commit the principal offence. For example, in *Mendez* [2010] EWCA Crim 516 Toulson LJ stated that:

18. At its most basic level, secondary liability is founded on a principle of causation, that a defendant (D) is liable for an offence committed by a principal actor (P) if by his conduct he has caused or materially contributed to the commission of the offence (with the requisite mental element); and a person who knowingly assists or encourages another to commit an offence is taken to have contributed to its commission.

If this were correct it would have the potential to collapse the distinction between principals and accessories demanded by *Kennedy*. Toulson LJ qualified this *dictum* somewhat in the subsequent case of *Stringer* [2011] EWCA Crim 1396:

48. It is well established that D's conduct need not cause P to commit the offence in the sense that 'but for' D's conduct P would not have committed the offence: see *R v Mendez*, para 23. But it is also established by the authorities referred to in *R v Mendez* that D's conduct must have some relevance to the commission of the principal offence; there must, as it has been said, be some connecting link. The moral justification for holding D responsible for the crime is that he has involved himself in the commission of the crime by assistance or encouragement, and that supposes some form of connection between his conduct and the crime. The Law Commission ~~in~~ ~~Participating~~ *in Crime* [Law Com Report No 305 (2007)], para 2.33:

'However, the precise nature of this sufficient connection
where D's conduct consists of assistance, as meaning t'
to the commission of the offence.'

In 'Sir Michael Foster, Professor Williams and
J. Horder (eds), *The Sanctity of Life and the Crim*
(2013)) Sir Roger Toulson expanded upon what

It is plainly right and just that there should have
repugnant to find a person guilty of murder for
nected with the crime. However, I would rega
that where P commits an offence with D's kno
contributed to the offence, even if his assi
This analysis involves a concept of causatio
alternative foundation on which secondar
a jury that X murdered Y carries with it a
for Y's death.

Although there must be some 'con
offence, that is different from sayir

Webster
which rende
in Webster
ing but knowledg
this . . . approach, we co
by virtue of the speed the veh
was an opportunity to intervene.
his right as owner of the
himself with the dangerous vehicle, which
dangerous driving.'

Accessories and omissions

Can the secondary party be liable for aiding, abetting, counselling or procuring by omission or inactivity?

D can be liable as an accessory to P where the law imposes a *duty* on D to act. Thus, a husband who stands by and watches his wife drown their children is guilty of abetting the homicide.

D can also be liable as an accessory to P's crime if D has a *power or right to control* the actions of another and he deliberately refrains from exercising it, his inactivity *may* be a positive encouragement to the other to perform an illegal act, and, therefore, an aiding and abetting. If a licensee of a public house stands by and watches his customers drinking after hours (principal offence committed by them), he is guilty of aiding and abetting them in doing so: *Tuck v Robson* [1970] 1 All ER 1171.

In *Du Cros v Lambourne* [1907] KB 40, D was charged with driving his Mercedes motor car at a speed dangerous to the public (about 50 mph), contrary to s 8 of the Motor Car Act 1903. A number of witnesses testified that D was driving the car but D and three other persons gave evidence that it was being driven by Miss Victoria Godwin, a 'certified expert motor-car driver'. The Court of Quarter Sessions were satisfied that, whether D or Godwin was driving, he must have known that the speed at which the car was being driven was very dangerous to the public, having regard to the locality and all the circumstances of the case. If Godwin was driving, she was doing so with the consent and approval of D, who was the owner and in control of the car and was sitting by her side, and he could and ought to have prevented her driving at such excessive and dangerous speed, but instead he allowed her to do so and did not interfere in any way. They held that it was therefore unnecessary to decide whether D was himself driving or not. The Divisional Court (Alverstone LCJ, Ridley and Darling JJ) agreed. Alverstone LCJ said:

> It is impossible to come to any other conclusion than that the court was satisfied that the appellant was doing acts which would amount to aiding, abetting, counselling or procuring.

Darling J said, (1906) 21 Cox CC 311 at 316, that allowing Godwin to drive:

> . . . was precisely the same thing as if he did it himself. He had authority and power to interfere but he did not do so although he knew the car was being driven at excessive speed. It seems to me that it is a misuse of language to say that he was not driving the motor-car.

But Darling J evidently had second thoughts because this passage does not appear in his revised judgment in [1907] 1 KB 40 at 46. Were his lordship's second thoughts best?

In *Webster* [2006] EWCA Crim 415, the Court of Appeal approved *Du Cros v Lambourne*, holding that:

> a defendant might be convicted of aiding abetting dangerous driving if the driver drives dangerously
> the owner's presence *and with the owner's consent and approval.*

mphasizes that it must be proved that D knew of those features of P's driving
d it dangerous and failed to take action within a reasonable time. The court
ized the need to establish not only knowledge of the dangerous driv-
time when there was an opportunity to intervene. 'In pursuance of
lude that the prosecution had to prove that [D] knew that [P] was,
le was travelling, driving dangerously at a time when there
was [D's] failure to take that opportunity and, exercise
would lead to the inference that he was associating

If the Crown can prove that it must have been either D or P who was driving but not which, can both D and P be convicted of dangerous driving? What if it was D's car?

Mere presence at the scene as a sufficient actus reus for secondary liability

In most cases, there is some conduct on the part of D which is clearly evidence of his assisting or encouraging P, over and above D's 'mere' presence. In some rare cases, however, the question arises whether D can be held to be aiding and abetting, counselling or procuring simply by being there.

Can mere voluntary presence, without anything more, satisfy the conduct element of secondary liability? Does presence with an intention to encourage satisfy the conduct element of secondary liability? The case law establishes that mere presence at the scene of a crime is *capable* of constituting encouragement or assistance, but a person is not necessarily guilty as a secondary party merely because he is present and does nothing to prevent the crime. In *Robinson* [2011] UKPC 3, the Privy Council made the following comments:

Of course that positive act of assistance may sometimes be constituted by D2 being present, and communicating to D1 not merely that he concurs in what D1 is doing, but that he is ready and willing to help in any way required. The commission of most criminal offences, and certainly most offences of violence, may be assisted by the forbidding presence of another as back-up and support. If D2's presence can properly be held to amount to communicating to D1 (whether expressly or by implication) that he is there to help in any way he can if the opportunity or need arises, that is perfectly capable of amounting to aiding within [the relevant sections of the Bermudan Criminal Code]. It is, however, important to make clear to juries that mere approval of (ie 'assent' to, or 'concurrence' in) the offence by a bystander who gives no assistance, does not without more amount to aiding. It is potentially misleading to formulate aiding according to the second particular without that qualification and without explaining that the communication of willingness to give active assistance is a minimum requirement.

These principles were established earlier by the Court of Appeal in the following cases.

R v Clarkson and Carroll
[1971] 3 All ER 344, Courts-Martial Appeal Court

(Megaw LJ, Geoffrey Lane and Kilner Brown JJ)

The appellants, soldiers, entered a room in their barracks in which a girl was being raped by other soldiers. They were charged with aiding and abetting the rape. There was no evidence that either had done any act or uttered any word which involved direct physical participation or verbal encouragement. They appealed on the ground of misdirection by the judge-advocate.

Megaw LJ [delivered the judgment of the court:]

Coney [(1882) 8 QBD 534] decided that non-accidental presence at the scene of the crime is not conclusive of aiding and abetting. The jury has to be told by the judge, or as in this case the court-martial has to be told by the judge-advocate, in clear terms what it is that has to be proved before they can convict of aiding and abetting; what it is of which the jury or the court-martial, as the case may be, must be sure as matters of inference before they can convict of aiding and abetting in such a case where the evidence adduced by the prosecution is limited to non-accidental presence. [His lordship quoted from *Coney* (1882) 8 QBD 534 at 557, 558.] It is not enough, then, that the presence of the accused has, in fact, given encouragement. It must be proved that he *wilfully* encouraged. In such a case as the present, more than in many other cases where aiding and abetting is alleged, it was essential that that element should be stressed; for there was here at least the possibility that a drunken man with his self-discipline loosened by drink, being aware that a woman was being raped, might be attracted to the scene and might stay on the scene in the capacity of what is known as a voyeur; and, while his presence and the presence of others might in fact encourage the rapers or discourage the victim, he himself, enjoying the scene or at least standing by assenting, might not intend that his presence should offer encouragement to rapers and would-be rapers or discouragement to the victim; he might not realise that he was giving encouragement; so that, while encouragement there might be, it would not be a case in which, to use the words of Hawkins J [(1882) 8 QBD 534 at 558] the accused person wilfully encouraged.

From that it follows that mere intention is not in itself enough. There must be an intention to encourage; and there must also be encouragement in fact, in cases such as the present case.

Appeals allowed

≈≈ **Question**

D, a student, continues to share a room with P whom D knows to be in unlawful possession of drugs. Is D aiding abetting P's drug possession? Consider the next case.

Wilcox v Jeffery

[1951] 1 All ER 464, King's Bench Division

(Lord Goddard CJ, Humphreys and Devlin JJ)

Lord Goddard CJ:

This is a case stated by the metropolitan magistrate at Bow Street Magistrates' Court before whom the appellant, Herbert William Wilcox, the proprietor of a periodical called *Jazz Illustrated*, was charged on an information that 'on 11 December 1949, he did unlawfully aid and abet one Coleman Hawkins in contravening art 1(4) of the Aliens Order 1920, by failing to comply with a condition attached to a grant of leave to land, to wit, that the said Coleman Hawkins should take no employment paid or unpaid while in the United Kingdom, contrary to art 18(2) of the Aliens Order 1920'. Under the Aliens Order, art 1(1), it is provided that

'. . . an alien coming . . . by sea to a place in the United Kingdom—(a) shall not land in the United Kingdom without the leave of an immigration officer . . .'

It is provided by art 1(4) that:

'An immigration officer, in accordance with general or special directions of the Secretary of State, may, by general order or notice or otherwise, attach such conditions as he may think fit to the grant of leave to land, and the Secretary of State may at any time vary such conditions in such manner as he thinks fit, and the alien shall comply with the conditions so attached or varied . . .'

If the alien fails to comply, he is to be in the same position as if he has landed without permission, ie he commits an offence.

The case is concerned with the visit of a celebrated professor of the saxophone, a gentleman by the name of Hawkins who was a citizen of the United States. He came here at the invitation of two gentlemen of the name of Curtis and Hughes, connected with a jazz club which enlivens the neighbourhood of Willesden. They, apparently, had applied for permission for Mr Hawkins to land and it was refused, but, nevertheless, this professor of the saxophone arrived with four French musicians. When they came to the airport, among the people who were there to greet them was the appellant. He had not arranged their visit, but he knew they were coming and he was there to report the arrival of these important musicians for his magazine. So, evidently, he was regarding the visit of Mr Hawkins as a matter which would be of interest to himself and the magazine which he was editing and selling for profit. Messrs Curtis and Hughes arranged a concert at the Princes Theatre, London. The appellant attended that concert as a spectator. He paid for his ticket. Mr Hawkins went on the stage and delighted the audience by playing the saxophone. The appellant did not get up and protest in the name of the musicians of England that Mr Hawkins ought not to be here competing with them and taking the bread out of their mouths or the wind out of their instruments. It is not found that he actually applauded, but he was there having paid to go in, and, no doubt, enjoying the performance, and then, lo and behold, out comes his magazine with a most laudatory description, fully illustrated, of this concert. On those facts the magistrate has found that he aided and abetted.

Reliance is placed by the prosecution on *Coney* [see the previous extract, p 497].

There was not accidental presence in this case. The appellant paid to go to the concert and he went there because he wanted to report it. He must, therefore, be held to have been present, taking part, concurring, or encouraging, whichever word you like to use for expressing this conception. It was an illegal act on the part of Hawkins to play the saxophone or any other instrument at this concert. The appellant clearly knew that it was an unlawful act for him to play. He had gone there to hear him, and his presence and his payment to go there was an encouragement. He went there to make use of the performance, because he went there, as the magistrate finds and was justified in finding, to get 'copy' for his newspaper. It might have been entirely different, as I say, if he had gone there and protested, saying: 'The musicians' union do not like you foreigners coming here and playing and you ought to get off the stage'. If he had booed, it might have been some evidence that he was not aiding and abetting. If he had gone as a member of a *claque* to try to drown the noise of the saxophone, he might very likely be found not guilty of aiding and abetting. In this case it seems clear that he was there, not only to approve and encourage what was done, but to take advantage of it by getting 'copy' for his paper. In those circumstances there was evidence on which the magistrate could find that the appellant aided and abetted, and for these reasons I am of opinion that the appeal fails.

Humphreys J:

I agree that there was evidence sufficient to justify the finding of the magistrate.

Devlin J:

I agree, and I wish to add only a word on the application of *Coney*. Counsel for the appellant sought to distinguish that case on the facts inasmuch as in *Coney* the performance, which was a prize fight, was illegal from beginning to end, whereas in the case we are considering the bulk of the concert was quite legal, the only part of the performance which was illegal being that which involved Mr Hawkins. That, however, is not, in my judgment, a distinction which affects the application to this case of the principle in *Coney*. It may well be that if a spectator goes to a concert he may explain his presence during an illegal item by saying that he hardly felt it necessary to get up and go out and then return when the performance resumed its legality, if I may so call it. It is conceivable that in such circumstances (and I should wish to consider it further if it ever arose) the presence of a person during one item might fall within the accidental or casual class was envisaged by Cave J. Here there was abundant evidence, apart from the mere fact of the appellant's presence, that he was making use of this item in the performance and that his attendance at that item was, therefore, deliberate. In those circumstances I think the principle in *R v Coney* applies, and that the magistrate was justified in drawing the inference which he did draw.

Appeal dismissed with costs

Would liability really depend on whether Wilcox applauded Hawkins?

> ≋ *Question*
>
> Bert and Ernie go to a pub on Saturday night. They know that during the evening an obscene performance lasting half an hour will be given by Vikki on the pole-dancing stage. Bert, who only drinks lemonade, goes because he relishes an obscene show. Ernie, who is not interested in the show, is only there for the beer. The licensee is convicted of keeping a disorderly house. Are Bert and Ernie guilty of abetting him?

19.5 Mens rea of the secondary party

The mens rea requirements of the secondary party are complex, but can be summarized in the following way:

(1) the secondary party must intend to assist or encourage the principal offender's conduct, or in the case of procuring, to bring the offence about;

(2) the secondary party must intend the principal to act with the requisite mens rea for the offence; and

(3) the secondary party must have knowledge as to the essential elements of the principal's offence (including any facts as to which the principal bears strict liability);

(4) if the offence is one of strict liability, then the only mens rea required is that the secondary party intended to assist or encourage the principal to do the prohibited act.

In a joint judgment delivered by the Supreme Court and the Privy Council in *Jogee; Ruddock* [2016] UKSC 8, the court examined the state of mind that must be possessed by the secondary party before he will be guilty. Before proceeding, it is necessary to have an understanding of the law before the judgment in *Jogee; Ruddock*.

The law recognized direct secondary liability—where D assisted or encouraged P to commit one crime. In such a case, so far as mens rea was concerned, D's liability turned on his having intended to assist or encourage, and his knowledge of the essential elements of the offence to be committed by P (eg that it was a crime of dishonesty, etc albeit that D did not need to know the precise details of P's crime in advance).

The law also recognized that D could be an accessory as a 'parasitic accessory' (the term used by the Supreme Court in *Gnango* [2011] UKSC 59; also called 'joint enterprise' liability). For example, where D joined with P with a shared common purpose to commit crime A, and D intentionally participated in the commission of crime A with P or Ps, and P or Ps (whether identified or not) in the course or furtherance of crime A *intentionally* committed crime B with the relevant mens rea for that crime, and D foresaw as a possibility that P or Ps might commit crime B with the relevant mens rea and Ps did commit it in a not fundamentally different manner from that which D foresaw, and D was at the time of the commission of crime B still an active participant with P or Ps in crime A. D could, under this doctrine, be liable for murder if V had been murdered by someone with whom D was engaged in the joint enterprise and D *foresaw* that one member *might* kill with intent to kill or do GBH.

This doctrine of joint enterprise could be traced to at least *Chan Wing-Siu v R* [1985] AC 168. It was unclear what its underlying principled or policy foundation was. Lord Steyn in *Powell; English* [1997] UKHL 45 justified the imposition of liability on this basis in the following terms:

> The foresight of the secondary party must be directed to a real possibility of the commission by the primary offender in the course of the criminal enterprise of the greater offence. The liability is imposed because the secondary party is assisting in and encouraging a criminal enterprise which

he is aware might result in the commission of a greater offence. The liability of an accessory is predicated on his culpability in respect of the greater offence as defined in law. It is undoubtedly a lesser form of mens rea. But it is unrealistic to say that the accessory principle as such imposes constructive criminal liability.

Professor Smith gave the doctrine developed in *Chan Wing-Siu* the name 'parasitic accessory liability' (J. C. Smith, 'Criminal Liability of Accessories: Law and Law Reform' (1997) 113 LQR 453) and it was relied upon to impose liability in numerous cases. The doctrine was the subject of criticism, however, on the basis that it imposed liability on the secondary party for murder even though he might not necessarily have demonstrated the culpability or wrongdoing of the principal.

D. Ormerod and W. Wilson, 'Simply Harsh to Fairly Simple: Joint Enterprise Reform' [2015] Crim LR 3

(iii) Murder liability for mere foresight of a possibility of another's intentional conduct

Particularly in the case of murder, there is a significant injustice arising from the present state of the law founded on the joint enterprise approach. A conviction for being party to a joint enterprise may mean that D suffers all the consequences of a murder conviction, including the offence label and the mandatory sentence (ratcheted up in real terms by the Sch.21 tariffs to the Criminal Justice Act 2003), without necessarily having demonstrated any of the culpability or wrongdoing of the principal offender. Given that the wrong in murder is to kill with malice aforethought, to convict a secondary party of that crime simply upon proof of his contemplation or foresight that this may be what his principal has in mind takes considerable justification.

Simester ['The Mental Element in Complicity' (2006) 122 LQR 578] offers one justification: it is not, in principle, wrong to punish D for the actions of P. By joining with P in a common criminal enterprise which has death as a foreseen outcome D changes his normative position in relation to that outcome. Rough justice it may be, he implies, but justice nevertheless, no less than GBH murder is. We cannot absolve ourselves from responsibility for the consequences of our actions by blaming an unruly fate. That is not how our moral universe is organised. The problem with this argument in the context of PAL [parasitic accessory liability], however, is, as has been explained, that it fails to pay full regard to a central and defining feature underpinning criminal doctrine: that we must take responsibility for our own choices and their outcomes, not the choices of others and their outcomes. Standard accessorial liability accommodates this problem to a degree by basing the liability of secondary parties on their lending (unconditional) support to the criminal projects of the principal. This is why contemplation alone sufficed in *DPP of Northern Ireland v Maxwell* [[1978] 3 All ER 1140]. In *Maxwell* D did not know precisely the crime to be committed, but by assisting P in the knowledge that P might intentionally commit one of a number of crimes, D was deemed, quite fairly, to have lent his support to any of those crimes, if committed. The unknown crime constitutes their common purpose. But in PAL, having lent support to one *crime*, D is also deemed to lend support to another merely because, although it forms no part of their common purpose, he has foreseen, out of the corner of his eye, the possibility that P might commit this further crime. Unconditional support is lent only to crime A and only constructive support, in effect, to crime B, a crime indeed which D may even have counselled his principal *not* to commit or which was at the periphery of his thinking when lending his support to crime A. What moral principle demands that I take responsibility not simply for the consequences of my own choices and those choices of my co-adventurer which I happen to share but also those which I do not share but happen to contemplate that he may, with a following wind, make at some stage in the future? In the specific context of murder, of course, the problem is exacerbated. D is liable despite not having chosen to kill; and not even having chosen to cause serious injury. D's choice, and *pace* Simester admittedly he makes one, is simply not to back out of a criminal enterprise when he realises that P may have more on his mind than what has been agreed. A conviction for murder, rather than manslaughter, is, given the power of the label and the mandatory sentence, not rough justice. It is injustice.

This issue was examined by the Supreme Court/Privy Council in the seminal case of *Jogee*, in which the applicable principles were restated.

R v Jogee
[2016] UKSC 8/[2016] UKPC 7, Supreme Court/Privy Council

(Lords Neuberger, Hughes, Toulson, Thomas and Lady Hale)

D and MH had been together on the evening of the murder. There was animosity between these two and V. MH and D went to a house where they knew V would be spending the night. D, holding a bottle, told MH to 'do something to' V. D waited by the front door, as MH entered V's house. MH took a knife from the kitchen block and stabbed V to death. Both MH and D were convicted of murder. In relation to D, the judge directed the jury that they could only convict him of murder if they were sure that he had encouraged MH in the attack on V with the realization that he might use a knife to cause V at least really serious harm.

Lord Hughes and Lord Toulson (with whom Lord Neuberger, Lady Hale and Lord Thomas agreed):

8. The requisite conduct element is that D2 has encouraged or assisted the commission of the offence by D1.

9. Subject to the question whether a different rule applies to cases of parasitic accessory liability, the mental element in assisting or encouraging is an intention to assist or encourage the commission of the crime and this requires knowledge of any existing facts necessary for it to be criminal: *National Coal Board v Gamble* [1959] 1 QB 11, applied for example in *Attorney General v Able* [1984] QB 795, *Gillick v West Norfolk and Wisbech Area Health Authority* [1986] AC 112 and *Director of Public Prosecutions for Northern Ireland v Maxwell* [1978] 1 WLR 1350 per Lord Lowry at 1374G–1375E, approved in the House of Lords at 1356A; 1358F; 1359E; 1362H and echoed also at 1361D.

10. If the crime requires a particular intent, D2 must intend to assist or encourage D1 to act with such intent. D2's intention to assist D1 to commit the offence, and to act with whatever mental element is required of D1, will often be co-extensive on the facts with an intention by D2 that that offence be committed. Where that is so, it will be seen that many of the cases discuss D2's mental element simply in terms of intention to commit the offence. But there can be cases where D2 gives intentional assistance or encouragement to D1 to commit an offence and to act with the mental element required of him, but without D2 having a positive intent that the particular offence will be committed. That may be so, for example, where at the time that encouragement is given it remains uncertain what D1 might do; an arms supplier might be such a case.

...

14. With regard to the mental element, the intention to assist or encourage will often be specific to a particular offence. But in other cases it may not be. D2 may intentionally assist or encourage D1 to commit one of a range of offences, such as an act of terrorism which might take various forms. If so, D2 does not have to 'know' (or intend) in advance the specific form which the crime will take. It is enough that the offence committed by D1 is within the range of possible offences which D2 intentionally assisted or encouraged him to commit (*Maxwell*).

...

17. Secondary liability does not require the existence of an agreement between the principal and the secondary party to commit the offence. If a person sees an offence being committed, or is aware

that it is going to be committed, and deliberately assists its commission, he will be guilty as an accessory. But where two or more parties agree on an illegal course of conduct (or where one party encourages another to do something illegal), the question has often arisen as to the secondary party's liability where the principal has allegedly gone beyond the scope of what was agreed or encouraged.

Restatement of the principles

...

89. In cases of alleged secondary participation there are likely to be two issues. The first is whether the defendant was in fact a participant, that is, whether he assisted or encouraged the commission of the crime. Such participation may take many forms. It may include providing support by contributing to the force of numbers in a hostile confrontation.

90. The second issue is likely to be whether the accessory intended to encourage or assist D1 to commit the crime, acting with whatever mental element the offence requires of D1 (as stated in para 10 above). If the crime requires a particular intent, D2 must intend (it may be conditionally) to assist D1 to act with such intent. To take a homely example, if D2 encourages D1 to take another's bicycle without permission of the owner and return it after use, but D1 takes it and keeps it, D1 will be guilty of theft but D2 of the lesser offence of unauthorised taking, since he will not have encouraged D1 to act with intent permanently to deprive. In cases of concerted physical attack there may often be no practical distinction to draw between an intention by D2 to assist D1 to act with the intention of causing grievous bodily harm at least and D2 having the intention himself that such harm be caused. In such cases it may be simpler, and will generally be perfectly safe, to direct the jury (as suggested in *Wesley Smith* [[1963] 1 WLR 1200] and *Reid* [(1976) 62 Cr App R 109]) that the Crown must prove that D2 intended that the victim should suffer grievous bodily harm at least. However, as a matter of law, it is enough that D2 intended to assist D1 to act with the requisite intent. That may well be the situation if the assistance or encouragement is rendered some time before the crime is committed and at a time when it is not clear what D1 may or may not decide to do. Another example might be where D2 supplies a weapon to D1, who has no lawful purpose in having it, intending to help D1 by giving him the means to commit a crime (or one of a range of crimes), but having no further interest in what he does, or indeed whether he uses it at all.]

91. It will therefore in some cases be important when directing juries to remind them of the difference between intention and desire.

92. In cases of secondary liability arising out of a prior joint criminal venture, it will also often be necessary to draw the jury's attention to the fact that the intention to assist, and indeed the intention that the crime should be committed, may be conditional. The bank robbers who attack the bank when one or more of them is armed no doubt hope that it will not be necessary to use the guns, but it may be a perfectly proper inference that all were intending that if they met resistance the weapons should be used with the intent to do grievous bodily harm at least. The group of young men which faces down a rival group may hope that the rivals will slink quietly away, but it may well be a perfectly proper inference that all were intending that if resistance were to be met, grievous bodily harm at least should be done.

93. Juries frequently have to decide questions of intent (including conditional intent) by a process of inference from the facts and circumstances proved. The same applies when the question is whether D2, who joined with others in a venture to commit crime A, shared a common purpose or common intent (the two are the same) which included, if things came to it, the commission of crime B, the offence or type of offence with which he is charged, and which was physically committed by D1. A time honoured way of inviting a jury to consider such a question is to ask the jury whether they are sure that D1's act was within the scope of the joint venture, that is, whether D2 expressly or tacitly agreed to a plan which included D1 going as far as he did, and committing crime B, if the occasion arose.

94. If the jury is satisfied that there was an agreed common purpose to commit crime A, and if it is satisfied also that D2 must have foreseen that, in the course of committing crime A, D1 might well commit crime B, it may in appropriate cases be justified in drawing the conclusion that D2 had the necessary conditional intent that crime B should be committed, if the occasion arose; or in other words that it was within the scope of the plan to which D2 gave his assent and intentional support. But that will be a question of fact for the jury in all the circumstances.

95. In cases where there is a more or less spontaneous outbreak of multi-handed violence, the evidence may be too nebulous for the jury to find that there was some form of agreement, express or tacit. But, as we have said, liability as an aider or abettor does not necessarily depend on there being some form of agreement between the defendants; it depends on proof of intentional assistance or encouragement, conditional or otherwise. If D2 joins with a group which he realises is out to cause serious injury, the jury may well infer that he intended to encourage or assist the deliberate infliction of serious bodily injury and/or intended that that should happen if necessary. In that case, if D1 acts with intent to cause serious bodily injury and death results, D1 and D2 will each be guilty of murder.

96. If a person is a party to a violent attack on another, without an intent to assist in the causing of death or really serious harm, but the violence escalates and results in death, he will be not guilty of murder but guilty of manslaughter. So also if he participates by encouragement or assistance in any other unlawful act which all sober and reasonable people would realise carried the risk of some harm (not necessarily serious) to another, and death in fact results: *R v Church* [1965] 1 QB 59, approved in *Director of Public Prosecutions v Newbury* [1977] AC 500 and very recently re-affirmed in *R v F (J) & E (N)* [2015] EWCA Crim 351; [2015] 2 Cr App R 5. The test is objective. As the Court of Appeal held in *Reid*, if a person goes out with armed companions to cause harm to another, any reasonable person would recognise that there is not only a risk of harm, but a risk of the violence escalating to the point at which serious harm or death may result. Cases in which D2 intends some harm falling short of grievous bodily harm are a fortiori, but manslaughter is not limited to these.

97. The qualification to this (recognised in *Wesley Smith, Anderson and Morris* [[1966] 2 QB 110] and *Reid*) is that it is possible for death to be caused by some overwhelming supervening act by the perpetrator which nobody in the defendant's shoes could have contemplated might happen and is of such a character as to relegate his acts to history; in that case the defendant will bear no criminal responsibility for the death.

98. This type of case apart, there will normally be no occasion to consider the concept of 'fundamental departure' as derived from *English*. What matters is whether D2 encouraged or assisted the crime, whether it be murder or some other offence. He need not encourage or assist a particular way of committing it, although he may sometimes do so. In particular, his intention to assist in a crime of violence is not determined only by whether he knows what kind of weapon D1 has in his possession. The tendency which has developed in the application of the rule in *Chan Wing-Siu* to focus on what D2 knew of what weapon D1 was carrying can and should give way to an examination of whether D2 intended to assist in the crime charged. If that crime is murder, then the question is whether he intended to assist the intentional infliction of grievous bodily harm at least, which question will often, as set out above, be answered by asking simply whether he himself intended grievous bodily harm at least. Very often he may intend to assist in violence using whatever weapon may come to hand. In other cases he may think that D1 has an iron bar whereas he turns out to have a knife, but the difference may not at all affect his intention to assist, if necessary, in the causing of grievous bodily harm at least. Knowledge or ignorance that weapons generally, or a particular weapon, is carried by D1 will be evidence going to what the intention of D2 was, and may be irresistible evidence one way or the other, but it is evidence and no more.

99. Where the offence charged does not require mens rea, the only mens rea required of the secondary party is that he intended to encourage or assist the perpetrator to do the prohibited act, with knowledge of any facts and circumstances necessary for it to be a prohibited act: *National Coal Board v Gamble*.

In *Jogee*, the court concluded that the Privy Council in *Chan Wing-Siu* had taken a wrong turn. The court therefore characterized the judgment as merely correcting, rather than substantively reforming, the law of secondary liability. This characterization has been criticized, however. See F. Stark, 'The Demise of "Parasitic Accessorial Liability": Substantive Judicial Law Reform, Not Common Law Housekeeping' (2016) 75 CLJ 550.

As a result of the decision in *Jogee*, the mens rea for the secondary party is as follows: an intention to assist or encourage the principal to commit the offence (which includes the requirement that the secondary party intends the principal to have the necessary mens rea). Whereas the doctrine of parasitic accessory liability mandated guilt for murder when the secondary party *foresaw* that the principal *might* commit intentional GBH or kill, now nothing less than intention as to P's intention will suffice. In the context of murder therefore, D will only be guilty as an accomplice if he intended to assist or encourage the principal to kill and intended the principal to act with an intention to kill or an intention to cause really serious harm. In addition, where the offence requires the existence of particular circumstances, D must have knowledge of any facts necessary to make the act a prohibited one.

Although the law is now easy to state, the judgment in *Jogee* has been the subject of criticism.

A. P. Simester, 'Accessory Liability and Common Unlawful Purposes'
(2017) 133 LQR 73

1. The mishandling of intention

The merits of requiring knowledge when aiding or abetting are all very well, but does *Jogee* commit to them unequivocally? Perhaps not. Doctrinally speaking, the Supreme Court's decision looks at first straightforward. The court asserts that the essence of aiding and abetting is intentional assistance or encouragement. It follows on standard legal principles that S must intend his or her own contribution but need not intend P's conduct. It is the assistance of the crime, not the ultimate crime itself, that must be intended by S. In turn, just as with attempts liability, an 'intention' to do some action requires an intention with respect to the behavioural and consequential components of that action, but is generally satisfied by knowledge or settled belief (with no significant doubt) regarding the action's circumstance elements. The same analysis applies here. It suffices to establish S's intention to assist or encourage P's crime if S intends his or her own contribution, being sure what P will do. From S's perspective, the latter is a circumstance element.

Unfortunately, when the court concludes by restating basic complicity principles, their Lordships' handling of the mens rea requirement becomes insecure. Consider, first, the distinction between S's intending to aid/abet and S's desiring that P's crime be committed. According to the court:

'In cases of concerted physical attack there may often be no practical distinction to draw between an intention by D2 to assist D1 to act with the intention of causing grievous bodily harm at least and D2 having the intention himself that such harm be caused ... However, as a matter of law, it is enough that D2 intended to assist D1 to act with the requisite intent. *That may well be the situation if the assistance or encouragement is rendered some time before the crime is committed and at a time when it is not clear what D1 may or may not decide to do.* Another example might be where D2 supplies a weapon to D1, who has no lawful purpose in having it, intending to help D1 by giving him the means to commit a crime (or one of a range of crimes), but having no further interest in what he does, or indeed whether he uses it at all.'

But it is important to see that the case of joint attack is not analogous to the case of assistance or encouragement rendered 'some time before the crime is committed'.

In establishing this, let us start with the latter type of case, of old-fashioned accessoryship before the fact. Suppose that S, a respectable builder, lends P a jemmy. S realises P that *may* use it to commit a burglary, but is uncertain whether P will, and (as the Supreme Court puts it) has no further interest in what P does. For the reasons summarised earlier, S ought not to be guilty of the burglary that P ultimately commits.

An intention/knowledge test bears this out. On both law and ordinary language, *S lacks the intention to assist P's burglary*. Of course, if S has a further interest, and acts *in order* to assist P should P decide to commit the envisaged crime, that suffices to establish the requisite intention by S. (In accordance with ordinary principles of direct intention, this holds even if S thinks it very unlikely that P will commit the crime.) Similarly, it generally suffices for S to *know*, in the sense of having no significant doubt, that P will commit one of a list of crimes. This is standard law since *R. v Nedrick* and *R. v Woollin*. But it is also where the law stops. In order to intend X, one must either act in order to bring X about or act knowing (i.e. being virtually certain) that one will bring X about. The same applies to aiding and abetting. In order to intend 'to assist P to commit a burglary', S must either act *in order* to assist P to commit a burglary (i.e. because for some reason S has an interest in P's committing it), or act in the practical certainty that his or her conduct *will assist* P to commit a burglary. Will, not may.

Undoubtedly, the stringency of this standard will generate unattractive results. Hard cases often do. But consider the following example:

> S illegally sells handguns. P buys a gun from S. He tells S that he will use the weapon to kill V, his partner, if V (despite being warned) continues to steal from their joint business. P says he is confident that V has given up his defalcations, so the need to kill V may not arise. S could not care less what P does with the gun and is interested only in the money she is paid for it. P later uses the gun to kill V.

There are strong policy arguments in favour of holding S guilty of murdering V and not merely guilty of offences under gun control legislation. Surely, we might propose, it suffices that S knows P will be assisted by S's conduct, if P ultimately does commit crime A? It does not. Many of those policy arguments are specific to the particular example. Once we leave them aside, subject to one important point to be considered below, the example is not significantly different from that of the computer sale, or indeed the laptop theft, both of which would satisfy our proposed test. Much of the normative power in the handgun scenario depends upon the fact that S's conduct is already illegal (and reprehensible). But that feature can no longer make any legal difference to S's liability. The only channel of complicity within which S's liability ever turned on the legality of S's own conduct was common unlawful purpose. Under the core doctrines of assistance/encouragement, it has never been relevant whether S's conduct was independently illegal.

Change the guns, then, to baseball bats. Obviously we don't want to shut down sports goods vendors. Suppose, once more, that P tells S why he is buying the bat ('just in case'). Is it criminal complicity for S to sell P the bat?

As the passage quoted earlier in this section suggests, the Supreme Court thinks it is. The court can only be right about that if we can truly say that S *intends* to assist P's killing of V. Again, however, *Nedrick* and *Woollin* stand in the way. S does not act in order to assist P to kill. Neither does S act in the practical certainty that P will use the bat to kill.

≋ *Question*
Do you agree with Simester's criticisms?

There are a number of aspects of the judgment that are worth considering in more detail.

19.5.1 Inferring intent from foresight

As the extract from *Jogee* demonstrates, the Supreme Court accepted that intention can be inferred from foresight. This is not a novel proposition. In *NCB v Gamble* [1959] 1 QB 11, it was accepted that it need not be the secondary party's purpose to assist or encourage.

In *Woollin* (section 5.2.1, p 89), the House of Lords held that a jury will be entitled to find the necessary intent in a murder case when death or really serious harm was a virtually certain consequence of D's conduct and he appreciated that was the case. Although the Supreme Court held that intention can be inferred from foresight, it did not provide further guidance as to how trial judges ought to direct juries.

D. Ormerod and K. Laird, '*Jogee*: Not the End of a Legal Saga But the Start of One?'
[2016] Crim LR 539 (references omitted)

(ii) What does 'intention' mean in this context?

What the Supreme Court failed to mention is the fact that the common law, in the context of murder at least, imposes a high threshold on the types of foresight from which a jury will be entitled to infer intent. After over 25 years or so of incremental narrowing (i.e. from *Hyam–Woollin*), the House of Lords finally agreed in *Woollin* that: (1) the defendant can be guilty of murder as a principal offender where he intended to kill or cause really serious harm; (2) intention is not limited to purpose or desire; (3) a jury is not entitled to 'find' that the defendant intended to kill or cause really serious harm unless they conclude that death or really serious harm was a virtually certain consequence, barring some unforeseen intervention, and the defendant appreciated that this was the case; (4) there is a threshold on foresight—anything less than foresight of virtual certainty will not be sufficient to entitle the jury to find intention; and (5) foresight is merely evidence and does not equal intention, given that the Court of Appeal subsequently confirmed in *Matthews and Alleyne* that the law has not yet reached a definition of intent in murder in terms of appreciation of a virtual certainty. Therefore the jury retains its 'moral elbow room'.

In *Jogee*, the Supreme Court concluded that: (1) the defendant can be guilty of murder as a secondary offender where he intended to assist or encourage the principal to kill or cause really serious harm with intent; (2) intention is not limited to purpose or desire; and (3) a jury may 'infer' that the defendant possessed the requisite intent if they conclude that he foresaw the principal's intentional conduct. Crucially, however, there is no explicit statement as to what threshold of foresight the defendant must possess before the jury will be entitled to infer the requisite intent—will the defendant's foresight of even the slightest possibility of the principal intentionally acting in the proscribed way be sufficient for a jury to be entitled to infer that he possessed the requisite intention? Alternatively, does there have to be a high level of foresight before the jury will be entitled to infer from this foresight that he possessed the requisite intention? It is the failure to specify what intention means in this context that could lead to difficulty.

To take an example of why this is not merely a theoretical problem, consider *Matthews and Alleyne*. The defendants were convicted of murder after throwing the victim from a bridge and into a river, where he drowned. In light of *Woollin*, the judge directed the jury that in relation to each defendant they could only convict him of murder as a principal if, when he threw the victim from the bridge and into the river, he appreciated that death or really serious harm was a virtually certain consequence, barring some unforeseen intervention. To amend the facts, rather than being joint principals, if P was the principal and D was the secondary party, how should the judge direct the jury in relation to D's liability in light of *Jogee*? What is clear is that the judge should direct the jury that they can convict D of murder as a secondary party if they are sure that he intended to assist or encourage the principal intentionally to kill or do GBH. If D denies having the requisite intent, however, should the judge direct the jury that they can only infer the requisite intent if D foresaw that the principal would intentionally kill or do GBH, so long as D's foresight of that was more than de minimis? Alternatively, should the judge direct the jury that they are only entitled to infer the requisite intent if D foresaw intentional GBH or killing by P as a *virtually certain* consequence of D's act of assistance/encouragement?

The issue becomes particularly striking if the Crown cannot establish the identity of the principal. Can the jury be directed that: (i) they can infer the requisite intent if the defendant they are considering foresaw that the other might intentionally kill or cause GBH so long as this foresight was more than de minimis; but (ii) to be sure D is guilty as a principal he must have foreseen the death or GBH as being virtually certain barring some unforeseen intervention. The jury would then have to be told that there are two different routes to 'finding' intention, depending upon whether the defendant whose guilt they are considering is the principal or accessory. Given that the jury would have to be sure that a murder was committed by one of the defendants, there is potentially no avoiding directing the jury as to the applicability of two different routes. This is surely an undesirable state of affairs in directing a jury on the same word in the gravest of crimes. If there are two different routes, the crucial question is whether the judge would have to leave both. An alternative is for the judge only to leave the route most favourable to the defendant. If the judge were to leave the route most favourable to the prosecution, however, that could reintroduce *Chan Wing-Siu*.

The Supreme Court failed to specify whether the jury are only entitled to infer the necessary intention if they are sure that D possessed a high level of foresight. It is unclear whether it is safe to conclude from this omission that the Supreme Court did not intend for some version of the *Woollin* direction to apply. The House of Lords in *Woollin* did expressly state that its decision applied only to murder and did not state whether it extended to accessorial liability. Indeed, Lord Steyn prefaced his judgment in *Woollin* by remarking that intention does not necessarily have the same meaning in every context of the criminal law. To the extent that the restatement of the law in *Jogee* applies in non-murder cases, a different formulation may therefore be applicable anyway. There will, we suggest, be considerable reluctance to apply the virtual certainty test, because if applied rigorously that test will mean that it will be difficult to secure convictions for murder for any participant.

19.5.2 Conditional intent

The Supreme Court confirmed that the secondary party's intent to assist or encourage the principal may be conditional. It will be recalled that the court held:

92. In cases of secondary liability arising out of a prior joint criminal venture, it will also often be necessary to draw the jury's attention to the fact that the intention to assist, and indeed the intention that the crime should be committed, may be conditional. The bank robbers who attack the bank when one or more of them is armed no doubt hope that it will not be necessary to use the guns, but it may be a perfectly proper inference that all were intending that if they met resistance the weapons should be used with the intent to do grievous bodily harm at least. The group of young men which faces down a rival group may hope that the rivals will slink quietly away, but it may well be a perfectly proper inference that all were intending that if resistance were to be met, grievous bodily harm at least should be done.

This aspect of the judgment has also been subject to criticism by Professor Simester, in the article extracted earlier:

2. The mishandling of conditional intention

The court obscures this difficulty by its repeated assertion that S's intention 'may be conditional'. But in the baseball bat example [in the previous extract], S has no conditional intention. It is P whose intention is conditional. Admittedly, this example presents a special case. S knows that the bat will be used to kill given a certain contingency. This makes it a stronger case for criminalisation than the computer sale or laptop theft examples. Perhaps the normal mens rea requirements for aiding and abetting should be supplemented to accommodate liability for this kind of 'contingent knowledge' case. (Although it is hard to see how to do so without criminalising the computer seller or the lazy laptop leaver, unless we introduce a new set of highly technical and practically unworkable mens rea distinctions.) Either way, however, we should not pretend that this case, special though it be, meets the definition of intending, conditionally or otherwise, to assist a killing.

Crucially, this objection can be generalised to virtually all cases of assistance or encouragement 'rendered some time before the crime is committed and at a time when it is not clear what D1 may or may not decide to do.' Talk of conditional intention in this context is a red herring. Once S's help or encouragement is rendered, *there can be no question of S having a conditional intention*. S's part is done. Any conditional intention to do something requires that the thing to be done lies in the future. For prior aiding and abetting, it is therefore essential that, *at the time of S's own actions*, S already holds the crystallised, unconditional intention to assist or encourage the very crime (perhaps among others) that P ultimately commits.

It may be helpful to elaborate upon this point. A conditional intention is a species of future intention, in the sense that one holds a conditional intention to do X when one holds an intention to do X should the relevant condition be met at some time in the future. Such an intention imports two key constraints. First, X must lie in the future, in that one is not yet actually doing X, although that moment may be close at hand. Secondly, whatever else it relates to, S's intention must also relate to an action *by S*. Someone who opens the back door of a lorry intending to steal the contents should they be valuable still has an action to do (i.e. steal the contents). Hence they can have a conditional intention to steal the contents at the point when they open the door.

But when there is an act of aiding or abetting, S has nothing left to do. What lies in the future is *P's* action. And that action is up to P, not S. Save in special cases of causing or procuring, S cannot intend *that P will do X*. S can of course act *in order* to help or encourage P to do X: S can intend his or her own act of *helping* or *encouraging* P's action. But S can't intend P's action. Neither can S intend P's mens rea. And so S can't conditionally intend them either.

None of this is to deny the possibility of conditionally intending to help another. However, that would be a case where S has not yet rendered help, and means to do so only if some further condition is met (e.g. if P pays the agreed fee, or turns out to be a friend, etc.). In such a case, the actus reus of S's aiding has not yet occurred, so participation cannot be established. By contrast, once the help is rendered—the gun is passed to P—that help is either intended or not. It cannot be conditionally intended: it is done. Of course, there are still conditions to be met before we can say that S did actually aid P to do X. Notably, P must go on to do X. But that is an actus reus condition, not a mens rea one.

Part of the difficulty with the court's restatement is a lack of precision. Aiding or abetting liability requires that, at the time S does the helpful or encouraging act, S intends (either directly or as a foreseen virtual certainty) to help or encourage P *by that act*. Failure to observe this requirement allows the court to state, for example, that:

> 'If [S] joins with a group which he realises is out to cause serious injury, the jury may well infer that he intended to encourage or assist the deliberate infliction of serious bodily injury and/or intended that that should happen if necessary. In that case, if [P] acts with intent to cause serious bodily injury and death results, [P] and [S] will each be guilty of murder.'

Yet this passage succeeds only if S's joining with the group was itself an act of encouraging P to commit GBH and was intended as such at that time. In most of the harder cases, such convenient findings seem unlikely. Moreover, where those findings are unavailable, the act of joining the group drops out of the picture. In terms of aiding and abetting doctrine, it is legally irrelevant. Some later act of intentionally (and actually) encouraging or helping P to commit GBH must be found.

19.5.3 D's liability for manslaughter

The Supreme Court confirmed that even if D did not intend to assist or encourage P to commit murder, that does not mean that he will escape liability altogether. D may still be guilty of manslaughter if he is party to a violent attack on another, without an intent to assist in the causing of death or really serious harm, but the violence escalates and results in death. D will also be guilty of manslaughter if he participates by encouragement or assistance in any other unlawful act which all sober and reasonable people would realize carried the risk of some harm (not necessarily serious) to another, and death in fact results. D can therefore be guilty of manslaughter even though he had no subjective awareness that the unlawful act he encouraged or assisted carried the risk of causing some harm. This is a result of the applicable law on manslaughter, which is discussed in Chapter 9.

19.5.4 Convictions secured under *Chan Wing-Siu*

There were dozens of people found guilty on the basis of the now discredited doctrine of parasitic accessory liability. The Supreme Court was keen to emphasize that correcting the wrong turn taken in *Chan Wing-Siu v R* would not have the effect of rendering every conviction obtained under the old law as unsafe.

> **Past convictions**
>
> 100. The effect of putting the law right is not to render invalid all convictions which were arrived at over many years by faithfully applying the law as laid down in *Chan Wing-Siu* and in *Powell and English*. The error identified, of equating foresight with intent to assist rather than treating the first as evidence of the second, is important as a matter of legal principle, but it does not follow that it will have been important on the facts to the outcome of the trial or to the safety of the conviction. Moreover, where a conviction has been arrived at by faithfully applying the law as it stood at the time, it can be set aside only by seeking exceptional leave to appeal to the Court of Appeal out of time. That court has power to grant such leave, and may do so if substantial injustice be demonstrated, but it will not do so simply because the law applied has now been declared to have been mistaken. This principle has been consistently applied for many years. Nor is refusal of leave limited to cases where the defendant could, if the true position in law had been appreciated, have been charged with a different offence.

> ≈≈ *Question*
> Do you agree, that it is fair for someone to be imprisoned based upon what the Supreme Court has now characterized as a legal wrong turn?

The Court of Appeal in *Johnson* [2016] EWCA Crim 1613 considered the general approach that ought to be taken in cases in which D was convicted upon the basis of the old law and seeks leave to appeal his conviction out of time. In order to be able to appeal his conviction, D must demonstrate a 'substantial injustice'. Relying upon the above passage from *Jogee*, Lord Thomas CJ gave the following guidance:

> In determining whether that high threshold has been met, the court will primarily and ordinarily have regard to the strength of the case advanced that the change in the law would, in fact, have made a difference. If crime A is a crime of violence which the jury concluded must have involved the use of a weapon so that the inference of participation with an intention to cause really serious harm is strong, that is likely to be very difficult. At the other end of the spectrum, if crime A is a different crime, not

involving intended violence or use of force, it may well be easier to demonstrate substantial injustice. The court will also have regard to other matters including whether the defendant was guilty of other, though less serious, criminal conduct. It is not, however, in our view, material to consider the length of time that has elapsed. If there was a substantial injustice, it is irrelevant whether that injustice occurred a short time or a long time ago. It is and remains an injustice.

It is unlikely that many of those whose convictions were based upon the old law will be able to overcome the high threshold mandated by the Court of Appeal. The approach adopted by the Court of Appeal may preclude most of those who were convicted based upon the 'wrong turn' taken in *Chan Wing-Siu* and *Powell and English* from appealing their convictions. Whilst this might satisfy the wider policy considerations that were invoked to justify the imposition of the substantial injustice threshold, it is unlikely to satisfy those who assumed that correcting the 'wrong turn' taken by the law would lead to positive outcomes for those whose convictions were in fact based on an error. For further comment, see K. Laird [2017] Crim LR 216.

19.5.5 The impact of *Jogee* in other jurisdictions

The doctrine propounded in *Chan Wing-Siu v R* also applied in similar guises in a number of other common law jurisdictions. Since the Supreme Court delivered its judgment in *Jogee*, attempts have been made to invite the courts in some of these other jurisdictions to reconsider their law in the light of the Supreme Court's judgment. At the time of writing, this has occurred in both Australia and Hong Kong. The highest courts in both these jurisdictions have rejected the reliance sought to be placed upon *Jogee*. In *HKSAR v Chan Kam Shing* [2016] HKCFA 87, the Court of Final Appeal of Hong Kong rejected the argument that it was anomalous to have different thresholds of mens rea for the principal and accessory.

61. An assessment of the secondary party's culpability is skewed by characterising it as merely the culpability of a person derivatively liable as an accessory and thus somehow less blameworthy than the principal offender. It is on this premise that *Chan Wing Siu* is said to produce an 'anomalous' rule setting a lower threshold for the accessory's, as opposed to the principal's, liability. But even viewed solely in terms of the traditional accessorial liability principles, it is by no means clear that the accessory should necessarily be regarded as having a lesser culpability. The person who procures commission of a murder by a contract killer is at least as culpable as the killer himself. Citing Glanville Williams, Stephen J in *Johns v The Queen* pointed out that Lady Macbeth was surely more blameworthy than was her husband.

62. As the authorities cited above show, the liability of a party to a joint criminal enterprise is not derivative but arises independently by virtue of his or her participation in the joint criminal enterprise. So viewed, there is no *a priori* reason for regarding different *mens rea* requirements considered appropriate to different individuals' participation in the joint enterprise as anomalous.

63. In basic (or 'plain vanilla') cases where the co-adventurers agree to carry out and then implement a planned crime, there can hardly be any doubt as to the culpability of all the participants, whichever one of them actually carried out the *actus reus*. Their culpability is little different from that of joint principals. *Jogee's* holding that where the prosecution cannot prove whether a defendant was principal or accessory, it is 'sufficient to be able to prove that he participated in the crime in one way or another' indicates acceptance of culpability in such cases.

64. In an extended joint criminal enterprise case, the wrongdoing of the participants 'lies in the mutual embarkation on a crime with the awareness that the incidental crime may be committed in executing their agreement.' Such a person agrees to carry out a criminal venture with others, foreseeing that one or more of them might, in certain contingencies, commit some further, more serious offence—where that further offence is murder, that one of them might kill someone with intent to kill

or to cause grievous bodily harm—and proceeds with the venture nonetheless. The foresight required under this rule is not open-ended. It is foresight of the commission of the actual further offence as a possible incident of the execution of their planned enterprise. And it is foresight of a real possibility of the offence being committed and excludes a risk fleetingly foreseen and dismissed as negligible.

In *Miller v The Queen* [2016] HCA 30, the High Court of Australia held that if there was to be change to the rules governing secondary liability, it would have to come from the legislature.

19.6 Knowledge of any facts necessary to make P's act criminal

As the Supreme Court confirmed in *Jogee*, in addition to proof of intention, there is a further, yet more complex, element of the secondary party's mens rea: he must have knowledge of the essential elements of the principal offence. He need not actually know that an offence has been committed, because he may not know that the facts constitute an offence and ignorance of the law is not a defence.

Johnson v Youden
[1950] 1 All ER 300, King's Bench Division

(Lord Goddard CJ, Humphreys and Lynskey JJ)

It was an offence under s 7 of the Building Materials and Housing Act 1945 for a builder to sell a house at a price in excess of that fixed by the local authority in the licence to build the house. The three respondents, partners in a firm of solicitors, were charged with aiding and abetting a builder in an offence under this section and were acquitted. The prosecutor appealed.

Lord Goddard CJ:

. . . In this case the builder had a licence which entitled him to sell the house for £1,025. He induced a railway porter to agree to buy the house for £1,275, ie £250 more than the controlled price, and he instructed a firm of solicitors, in which the three respondents are partners, to act as his solicitors for the sale. The builder was charged with an offence against s 7(1) of the Act of 1945 and was convicted, but the three respondents were acquitted on charges of aiding and abetting him.

In regard to the respondents, the justices found that, until 6 April 1949, none of them knew any-thing about the extra £250 which the builder was receiving, and that the first two respondents, Mr Henry Wallace Youden and Mr George Henry Youden, did not know about it at any time, as the builder deliberately concealed the fact and even refused to give the purchaser a receipt for that £250. The justices, therefore, were right, in our opinion, in dismissing the information against the first two respondents on the ground that they could not be guilty of aiding and abetting the commission of the offence as they did not know of the matter which constituted the offence. If they had known that the builder was receiving the extra £250 and had continued to ask the purchaser to complete, they would have committed an offence by continuing to assist the builder to offer the property for sale, contrary to the provisions of s 7(1) of the Act of 1945, and, as ignorance of the law is no defence, they would have been guilty of the offence even if they had not realised that they were committing an offence, but a person cannot be convicted of aiding and abetting the commission of an offence if he does not know of the essential matters which would constitute the offence.

[The court held that in respect of the third partner the evidence was that correspondence from the builder gave him awareness of the additional £250 which ought not to have been charged. With that awareness he nevertheless arranged for the completion of the sale.]

He was, therefore, clearly aiding and abetting the builder in the offence which the builder was committing.

Humphreys J:

I agree.

Lynskey J:

I also agree.

Appeal dismissed in respect of the first two respondents and allowed in respect of the third respondent. Case remitted to the justices with a direction to convict the third respondent. No order as to costs

19.6.1 'Knowledge'

This is a particularly difficult mens rea to establish. D does not 'know' (ie have true belief) of the circumstances unless he has first-hand knowledge of that fact. In view of the practical difficulties in proving D's knowledge as to future events, the courts have interpreted 'knowledge' as equivalent to D foreseeing (or in some cases turning a blind eye to) the likelihood of the essential matters. In *Bryce*, the court applied a slightly different formula, holding that it was sufficient that D did the act of assistance by transporting P to the scene, and at the time of doing that act 'contemplated a real possibility' of the commission of an offence of the type that P committed. Potter LJ in *Bryce* explained:

46. . . . As was stated by Lord Goddard CJ in *Johnson v Youden* [1950] 1 KB 544, [1950] 1 All ER 300 at 446:

'Before a person can be convicted of aiding and abetting the commission of an offence he must at least know the essential matters which constitute that offence.'

He went on to say:

'He need not actually know that an offence has been committed, because he may not know that the facts constitute an offence and ignorance of the law is not a defence. If a person knows all the facts and is assisting another person to do certain things, and it turns out that the doing of those things constitutes an offence, the person who is assisting is guilty of aiding an [*sic*] abetting that offence.'

This statement was approved by the House of Lords in *Maxwell v DPP for Northern Ireland* [1978] 3 All ER 1140, (1979) 68 Crim App R 128 HL.

47. Sir Robert Lowry CJ in *Maxwell* (supra) at 140–141 stated:

'[The secondary party's] guilt springs from the fact that he contemplates the commission of one (or more) of a number of crimes by the principal and he intentionally lends his assistance in order that such a crime shall be committed. In other words, he knows that the principal is committing or about to commit one of a number of specified illegal acts and with that knowledge helps him to do so.'

48. But does the secondary party actually have to know that the crime will be committed, as this passage suggests, or is something less sufficient? Lord Simon in *Lynch* 698G- 699B cited Devlin J in *National Coalboard v Gamble* [1959] 1 QB 11, [1958] 3 All ER 203, 20 and continued:

'The act of supply must be voluntary (in the sense I tried to define earlier in this speech), and it must be *foreseen* that the instrument or other object or service supplied will *probably (or possibly and desiredly)* be used for the commission of a crime.' (Emphasis added)

49. Those words were uttered in respect of a person participating at the time of the commission of the offence by the actual perpetrator. However, in the context of a person charged as an accessory who

has rendered assistance prior to the commission of the crime by the perpetrator, the circumstances in respect of which knowledge is sufficient for liability may go wider than that of the specific crime actually committed. This is because, as pointed out in *Blackstone's Criminal Practice* (2004) at A6.5 (p.75), it is inappropriate and unworkable to require knowledge of the essential matters constituting the offence in a situation where the offence is yet to be committed in the future or by a person of whose precise intentions the accused cannot be certain in advance. It is thus sufficient for the accused to have knowledge of the type of crime in contemplation. Thus where a person supplies equipment to be used in the course of committing an offence of a particular type, he is guilty of aiding and abetting the commission of any such offence committed by the person to whom he supplies the equipment, providing that he knows the purpose to which the equipment is to be put or realises that there is a real possibility that it will be used for that purpose and the equipment is actually used for that purpose: see *R v Bullock* [1955] 1 All ER 15, 38 Crim App R 151 and *R v Bainbridge* [1960] 1 QB 129, [1959] 3 All ER 200.

19.6.2 Knowledge of the type of crime is sufficient

If D aids, abets, counsels or procures P to commit a crime of a certain 'type', neither party specifying any particular victim, time or place, D may be convicted as a secondary party to any crime of that type which P commits.

R v Bainbridge
[1960] 1 QB 129, Court of Criminal Appeal

(Lord Parker CJ, Byrne and Winn JJ)

B was convicted of being accessory to office-breaking. The Stoke Newington branch of the Midland Bank was broken into by cutting the bars of a window, the doors of the strong room and of a safe inside the strong room. They were opened by means of oxygen cutting equipment and nearly £18,000 was stolen. B had bought the cutting equipment six weeks earlier. The prosecution alleged that he bought it on behalf of one or more of the thieves and that he knew that it was going to be used, if not against that branch, for the purposes of breaking and entering premises.

Lord Parker CJ [delivered the following judgment of the court:]

The appellant's case, as given in his evidence, was this: 'True, I had bought this equipment from two different firms. I had gone there with a man called Shakeshaft to buy it for him. As a result of conversation which I had with him, I was suspicious that he wanted it for something illegal. I thought it was for breaking up stolen goods which Shakeshaft had received, and, as the result, in those purchases I gave false names and addresses; but I had no knowledge that the equipment was going to be used for any such purpose which it was used.'

  The complaint here is that Judge Aarvold, who tried the case, gave the jury a wrong direction in regard to what it was necessary for them to be satisfied of in order to hold the appellant guilty of being an accessory before the fact. The passages in question are these:

'To prove that, the prosecution have to prove these matters; first of all, they have to prove the felony itself was committed. Of that there is no doubt. That is not contested. Secondly, they have to prove that the [appellant] knew that a felony of that kind was intended and was going to be committed, and with that knowledge he did something to help the felons commit the crime. The knowledge that is required to be proved in the mind of [the appellant] is not the knowledge of the precise crime. In other words, it need not be proved he knew the Midland Bank, Stoke Newington branch, was going to be broken and entered, and money stolen from that particular bank, but he must know the type of crime that was in fact committed. In this case it is a breaking and entering of premises and the stealing of property from those premises. It must be proved he knew that sort of crime was intended and was going to be committed. It is not enough to show that he either suspected or knew that some crime was going to be committed, some crime which might have been a breaking and entering or might have been disposing of stolen property or anything of that kind. That is not enough. It must be proved he knew the type of crime which was in fact committed was intended.'

There are other passages to the same effect, in particular, when the jury returned for further directions before they came to their verdict. Later the judge said this:

'If in fact, before it has happened, [the appellant], knowing what is going to happen, with full knowledge that a felony of that kind is going to take place, deliberately and wilfully helps it on its way, he is an accessory . . . If he was not present he would not be guilty as a principal, but then you would have to decide whether he helped in purchasing this equipment for Shakeshaft knowing full well the type of offence for which it was going to be used, and, with that knowledge, buying it and helping in that way.'

Mr. Simpson [counsel for the appellant], who has argued this case very well, contends that that direction is wrong. As he puts it, in order that a man should be convicted of being accessory before the fact, it must be shown that, at the time he bought the equipment in a case such as this, he knew that a particular crime was going to be committed; and by a particular crime Mr. Simpson means that the premises in this case which were going to be broken into were known to the appellant and contemplated by him, and not only the premises in question but the date when the breaking was going to occur; in other words, that he must know that on a particular date the Stoke Newington branch of the Midland Bank is intended to be broken into.

The court fully appreciates that it is not enough that it should be shown that a man knew that some illegal venture is intended. To take this case, it would not be enough if [the appellant] knew—he says he only suspected—that the equipment was going to be used to dispose of stolen property. That would not be enough. Equally, this court is quite satisfied that it is unnecessary that knowledge of the particular crime which was in fact committed should be shown to his knowledge to have been intended, and by 'particular crime' I am using the words in the same way in which Mr Simpson used them, namely, on a particular date and particular premises.

It is not altogether easy to lay down a precise form of words which will cover every case that can be contemplated, but, having considered the cases and the law, this court is quite clear that the direction of Judge Aarvold in this case cannot be criticised. Indeed, it might well have been made with the passage in Foster's *Crown Cases* (3rd ed.) (1809) at p 369, in mind, because there the learned author says:

'If the principal totally and substantially varieth, if being solicited to commit a felony of one kind he *wilfully and knowingly* committeth a felony of another, *he* will stand single in that offence, and the person soliciting will not be involved in his guilt. For on *his* part it was no more than a fruitless ineffectual temptation.'

The converse, of course being that, if the principal does not totally and substantially vary the advice or the help and does not wilfully and knowingly commit a different form of felony altogether, the man who has advised or helped, aided or abetted, will be guilty as an accessory before the fact.

Judge Aarvold in this case, in the passages to which I have referred, makes it clear that there must be not merely suspicion but knowledge that a crime of the type in question was intended, and that the equipment was bought with that in view. In his reference to the felony of the type intended it was, as he stated, the felony of breaking and entering premises and the stealing of property from those premises. The court can see nothing wrong in that direction.

Appeal dismissed

(1) What is a 'type' of crime? Violent? Dishonest? Sexual? How many types of crime are there in English law?

(2) Is this case authority for the proposition that the supplier of equipment for use in committing a particular type of crime is liable for *all* crimes of that type which are committed by the person supplied, using that equipment? Does the fact that the equipment was left behind suggest that it was for use on one occasion only?

19.6.3 Knowledge of one of a number of crimes sufficient

Particular difficulties arise where D is aware that P is going to commit an offence, but is not sure which of a number of offences it will be. The House of Lords added to the principle in *Bainbridge* to meet this problem in the following case.

Director of Public Prosecutions for Northern Ireland v Maxwell
[1978] 3 All ER 1140, House of Lords

(Viscount Dilhorne, Lords Hailsham of St Marylebone, Edmund-Davies, Fraser of Tullybelton and Scarman)

The appellant, a member of the Ulster Volunteer Force, proscribed in Northern Ireland, had guided terrorists to the Crosskeys Inn by leading them there in his car. The trial judge found that the appellant knew there was to be 'an attack on the Crosskeys bar, not a casual or social visit or mere reconnaissance' and that 'the attack would be one of violence in which people would be endangered or premises seriously damaged'. However, the appellant did not know precisely what offence was to be committed. Although the appellant was charged as a principal in the offence of planting a pipe bomb in the Crosskeys Inn, contrary to s 3(1)(a) of the Explosive Substances Act 1883, the true nature of his role was that of an aider and abettor. He appealed against conviction on the ground that he must be shown to have known the type of crime intended to be committed and the kind of means of offence being carried to the scene.

Lowry LCJ [delivering the judgment of the Court of Criminal Appeal in Northern Ireland:]

. . . Suppose the intending principal offender (whom I shall call 'the principal') tells the intended accomplice (whom I shall call 'the accomplice') that he means to shoot A or else leave a bomb at A's house and the accomplice agrees to drive the principal to A's house and keep watch while there, it seems clear that the accomplice would be guilty of aiding and abetting whichever crime the principal committed, because he would know that one of two crimes was to be committed, he would have assisted the principal and he would have intended to assist him. Again, let us suppose that the principal tells the accomplice that the intention is to murder A at one house but, if he cannot be found or the house is guarded, the alternative plan is to go to B's house and leave a bomb there or thirdly to rob a particular bank (or indeed murder somebody, or bomb somebody's house or rob any bank, as to which see *Bainbridge* ([1960] 1 QB 129, [1959] 3 All ER 200)) and requests the accomplice to make a reconnaissance of a number of places and report on the best way of gaining access to the target. The accomplice agrees and makes all the reconnaissances and reports, and the principal then, without further communication, selects a target and commits the crime. It seems clear that, whichever crime the principal commits, all the ingredients of the accomplice's guilt are present. In each of these examples the accomplice knows exactly what is contemplated and the only thing he does not know is to which particular crime he will become an accessory when it is committed. His guilt springs from the fact that he contemplates the commission of one (or more) of a number of crimes by the principal and he intentionally lends his assistance in order that such a crime will be committed. In other words, he knows that the principal is committing or about to commit one of a number of specified illegal acts and with that knowledge he helps him to do so.

The situation has something in common with that of two persons who agree to rob a bank on the understanding, either express or implied from conduct (such as the carrying of a loaded gun by one person with the knowledge of the other), that violence *may* be resorted to. The accomplice knows, not that the principal will shoot the cashier, but that he may do so; and if the principal does shoot him, the accomplice will be guilty of murder. A different case is where the accomplice has only offence A in contemplation and the principal commits offence B. Here the accomplice, although morally culpable (and perhaps guilty of conspiring to commit offence A), is not guilty of aiding and abetting offence B.

The principle with which we are dealing does not seem to us to provide a warrant, on the basis of combating lawlessness generally, for convicting an alleged accomplice of *any* offence which, helped by his preliminary acts, a principal may commit. The relevant crime must be within the contemplation of the accomplice and only exceptionally would evidence be found to support the allegation that the accomplice had given the principal a completely blank cheque. . . .

The facts found here show that the appellant, as a member of an organisation which habitually perpetrates sectarian acts of violence with firearms and explosives, must, as soon as he was briefed for his role, have contemplated the bombing of the Crosskeys Inn as not the only possibility but one of the most obvious possibilities among the jobs which the principals were likely to be undertaking and in the commission of which he was intentionally assisting. He was therefore in just the same situation, so far as guilty knowledge is concerned, as a man who had been given a list of jobs and told that one of them would be carried out. And so he is guilty of the offence alleged against him in count 1 . . .

[The court certified the following point of law of general importance:

> 'If the crime committed by the principal, and actually assisted by the accused, was one of a number of offences, one of which the accused knew the principal would probably commit, is the guilty mind which must be proved against an accomplice thereby proved against the accused?'

The House of Lords dismissed the appeal. All of their lordships approved the judgment of Lowry LCJ. **Lord Edmund-Davies** said that to do more than approve it would be a sleeveless errand; but he agreed with the view (below) of Viscount Dilhorne.]

Viscount Dilhorne:

. . . No objection could be taken to the form of these counts as by statute [Accessories and Abettors Act 1861, s 8; Criminal Law Act 1967, s 1(2)] aiders and abettors can be charged as principals, but the particulars to each count give no indication of the case the prosecution intended to present and which the appellant had to meet. In the particulars to the first count, he is charged with placing the bomb in the Crosskeys Inn; in the particulars to the second with having had it in his possession or under his control. The prosecution did not attempt to prove that he had placed the bomb or that he had been present when the bomb was put in the inn, nor was any attempt made to establish that at any time he had the bomb in his possession or under his control. It is desirable that the particulars of the offence should bear some relation to the realities and where, as here, it is clear that the appellant was alleged to have aided and abetted the placing of the bomb and its possession or control, it would in my opinion have been better if the particulars of offence had made that clear.

Lord Scarman [having quoted from the judgment of Lowry LCJ:]

Lowry LCJ continues:

> 'The relevant crime must be within the contemplation of the accomplice and only exceptionally would evidence be found to support the allegation that the accomplice had given the principal a completely blank cheque.'

The principle thus formulated has great merit. It directs attention to the state of mind of the accused: not what he ought to have in contemplation, but what he did have. It avoids definition and classification, while ensuring that a man will not be convicted of aiding and abetting any offence his principal may commit, but only one which is within his contemplation. He may have in contemplation only one offence, or several; and the several which he contemplates he may see as alternatives. An accessory who leaves it to his principal to choose is liable, provided always the choice is made from the range of offences from which the accessory contemplates the choice will be made. Although the court's formulation of the principle goes further than the earlier cases, it is a sound development of the law and in no way inconsistent with them. I accept it as good judge-made law in a field where there is no statute to offer guidance.

Appeal dismissed

19.6.4 D not liable for P's crime if P makes change of substance

Where D knows that the offence by P that D is assisting or encouraging is to be committed against a particular victim or in respect of a particular item of property, D will be liable provided P does not *deliberately* choose a different victim or item. This is described by Hawkins (*A Treatise of the Pleas of the* Crown (8th edn, 1795), vol II, c 29, s 21):

But if a man command another to commit a felony on a particular person or thing and he do it on another; as to kill A and he kill B or to burn the house of A and he burn the house of B or to steal an ox and he steal an horse; or to steal such an horse and he steal another; or to commit a felony of one kind and he commit another of a quite different nature; as to rob J S of his plate as he is going to market, and he break open his house in the night and there steal the plate; it is said that the commander is not an accessory because the act done varies in substance from that which was commanded.

As the second part of that quotation makes clear, the principle applies where there is a substantial variation from the proposed course of conduct, even if the victim and item are the same.

Hawkins also stated (at s 20):

[I]f the felony committed be the same in substance with that which was intended, and variant only in some circumstance, as in respect of the time or place, at which, or the means whereby it was effected, the abettor of the intent is altogether as much an accessory as if there had been no variance at all between it and the execution of it; as where a man advises another to kill such a one in the night, and he kills him in the day, or to kill him in the fields, and he kills him in the town, or to poison him, and he stabs or shoots him.

This category of case must be distinguished from those in which P's change of plan is not a deliberate one. The doctrine of transferred malice applies to secondary parties as it does to principal offenders (see section 2.3.1.1, p 24). Where P, intending to follow D's advice to kill V, mistakes X for V and kills X, D is guilty as a secondary party, and P as a principal offender, of murder. If D advises P to burn V's house and P does so but the flames spread and burn Y's house, D as well as P is guilty of arson of Y's house: D as accessory and P as principal.

In *Saunders and Archer* (1573) 2 Plowd 473, P intended to murder his wife. Following the advice of D, P gave her a poisoned apple to eat. She ate a little of it and gave the rest to their child. P loved the child, yet he stood by and watched it eat the poison, of which it soon died. It was held that P was guilty of murder of the child, but the judges agreed that D, who, of course, was not present when the child ate the apple, was not an accessory to this murder. If P had been absent when the child ate the apple it is thought that this would have been a case of transferred malice and D would have been liable; but P's presence and failure to act made the killing of the child, in effect, a deliberate, and not an accidental, departure from the agreed plan.

In *Jogee*, the Supreme Court acknowledged that:

> It is possible for death to be caused by some overwhelming supervening act by the perpetrator which nobody in the defendant's shoes could have contemplated might happen and is of such a character as to relegate his acts to history; in that case the defendant will bear no criminal responsibility for the death.

19.6.5 Summary of the 'knowledge' requirement

The case law set out previously establishes that D must know the 'essential matters which constitute P's offence'. D need not know that the essential elements of P's conduct constitute a crime since ignorance of the criminal law is no defence. In summary:

- D must know the conduct element of P's offence, although not all of the details of when, where, etc the commission of the actus reus will occur;

- D must intend that P will act with mens rea. Note that D need not have the same mens rea as P. P must have the mens rea for the principal offence. The difficulties involved in proving one person's intention as to another's state of mind are obvious.

19.7 Legislative reform of parasitic accessorial liability in murder

Prior to the Supreme Court's judgment in *Jogee*, the law in relation to parasitic accessorial liability was one of the most difficult in English criminal law. It has been subjected to scrutiny by law reform agencies on numerous occasions.

The Ministry of Justice published its Consultation Paper on *Murder, Manslaughter and Infanticide: Proposals for Reform of the Law* (2008) including recommendations on complicity (see http://webarchive.nationalarchives.gov.uk/20110218135832/http:/justice.gov.uk/consultations/docs/murder-manslaughter-infanticide-consultation.pdf).

The Consultation Paper represents the most recent publication from government on the homicide law reform project begun by the Law Commission. It draws not only on Law Commission Report No 304, *Murder, Manslaughter and Infanticide* (2006), but also Law Commission Report No 305, *Participating in Crime* (2007). The recommendation is to create a new statutory offence of murder for those who intentionally assist or encourage that offence (cl 1) and a statutory offence of murder where P is guilty of manslaughter owing to a lack of mens rea and D assisted or encouraged intending P to kill or cause serious injury (cl 2). In cases of joint criminal venture, the recommendation adopts the Law Commission proposal to retain a broader offence (cl 3). On the fundamentally different rule, the Government believes that statutory reform is desirable, proposing a more flexible statutory rule based on whether P's act was 'within the scope of the joint criminal venture'. This would be the case where the act did not go 'far beyond that which was planned, agreed to or foreseen by the secondary party' (para 101). The fundamentally different qualification would only be available where D has not foreseen death of V as a possibility, and even when it applies it will result in a manslaughter conviction (cl 4). Do you think these proposals would clarify the law?

In 2012 the Justice Committee of the House of Commons heard evidence on how joint enterprise operated in practice. The Committee concluded that the uncertainty bedevilling this area of law was unacceptable and called for the Government to enshrine the common law in legislation. The Committee recommended that the Government consult on the Law Commission's proposals that were contained in the Report No 305, *Participating in Crime* (see section 19.11, p 533) and to use them as a basis for reform. So far no legislation has been forthcoming. It also recommended that the Director of Public Prosecutions issue guidance on the use of joint enterprise when charging.

Prosecuting offences on the basis of joint enterprise

29. At the evidential stage, a prosecutor must be satisfied that there is sufficient evidence to provide a realistic prospect of conviction. This means that an objective, impartial and reasonable jury (or bench of magistrates or judge sitting alone), properly directed and acting in accordance with the law, is more likely than not to convict. It is an objective test based upon the prosecutor's assessment of the evidence, including any information that he or she has about the defence.

30. A case which does not pass the evidential stage must not proceed, no matter how serious or sensitive it may be.

31. If the evidential stage is satisfied, prosecutors must then go on to consider the second stage: whether a prosecution is required in the public interest.

The evidential stage applied to joint enterprise cases

32. The evidential stage of the Full Code Test applies in the same way to cases involving joint enterprise as it does to all other cases.

33. When assessing the sufficiency of evidence in a joint enterprise case a prosecutor is likely to ask a number of the following questions:

- Is there evidence that the defendants acted as joint principals?
- If not, did D assist or encourage another to commit offence A?
- Or, did D assist or encourage P to commit offence A, intending or merely foreseeing that P might carry out the conduct element of offence B, with the necessary fault element of offence B? Was P's act fundamentally different from what was foreseen by D?
- Does D have a viable claim to have withdrawn from the joint enterprise?

In 2014, the Committee once again called upon the Government to launch an urgent review of the law on parasitic accessory liability.

After the Supreme Court's decision in *Jogee*, the Lord Chancellor wrote to the Chairman of the Justice Committee expressing the view that the judgment went a long way to addressing previous Committee members' concerns. The CPS has yet to amend the above guidance to reflect the impact of the judgment.

19.8 Can an accessory be liable for a more serious offence than the principal?

We have examined the actus reus and mens rea element of the secondary party. Are there any limits of the offences for which D can be liable as an accessory?

R v Burke and Clarkson
[1986] UKHL 4, House of Lords

(Lord Hailsham LC, Lords Bridge, Brandon, Griffiths and Mackay)

The Crown alleged that Burke shot a man (Botton) dead because Clarkson told him to do so to prevent Botton testifying against C at a forthcoming trial. Clarkson denied having any involvement. Burke's defence was that he had agreed to shoot Botton only out of fear of Clarkson; but that in the event the gun went off accidentally and the killing was unintentional and therefore only manslaughter. Both were convicted of murder. The judge directed that if

Burke was guilty only of manslaughter and not murder, then Clarkson could be found guilty at worst of manslaughter. Burke's appeal arguing that this was a misdirection was dismissed by the Court of Appeal. The question certified for the House of Lords was 'can one who incites or procures by duress another to kill or be a party to a killing be convicted of murder if that other is acquitted by reason of duress?'

[Lords Hailsham, Bridge, Brandon and Griffiths dismissed the appeal.]

Lord Mackay:

I am of opinion that the Court of Appeal reached the correct conclusion on [this certified question] as a matter of principle.

Giving the judgment of the Court of Appeal Lord Lane CJ said ([1986] 1 All ER 833 at 839–840, [1986] QB 626 at 641–652):

'The judge based himself on a decision of this court in *R v Richards (Isabelle)* [1973] 3 All ER 1088, [1974] QB 776. The facts in that case were that Mrs Richards paid two men to inflict injuries on her husband which she intended should "put him in hospital for a month". The two men wounded the husband but not seriously. They were acquitted of wounding with intent but convicted of unlawful wounding. Mrs Richards herself was convicted of wounding with intent, the jury plainly, and not surprisingly, believing that she had the necessary intent, though the two men had not. She appealed against her conviction on the ground that she could not properly be convicted as accessory before the fact to a crime more serious than that committed by the principals in the first degree. The appeal was allowed and the conviction for unlawful wounding was substituted. The court followed a passage from *Hawkins's Pleas of the Crown* (2 Hawk PC (8th edn [1795]) p442): "I take it to be an uncontroverted rule that [the offence of the accessory can never rise higher than that of the principal]; it seeming incongruous and absurd that he who is punished only as a partaker of the guilt of another, should be adjudged guilty of a higher crime than the other." James LJ, delivering the judgment in *R v Richards* [1973] 3 All ER 1088 at 1092, [1974] QB 776 at 780, had this to say: "If there is only one offence committed, and that is the offence of unlawful wounding, then the person who has requested that offence to be committed, or advised that that offence be committed, cannot be guilty of a graver offence than that in fact which was committed." The decision in *R v Richards* has been the subject of some criticism (see for example Smith and Hogan *Criminal Law* (5th edn, 1983) p140). Counsel before us posed the situation where A hands a gun to D informing him that it is loaded with blank ammunition only and telling him to go and scare X by discharging it. The ammunition is in fact live (as A knows) and X is killed. D is convicted only of manslaughter, as he might be on those facts. It would seem absurd that A should thereby escape conviction for murder. We take the view that *R v Richards* was incorrectly decided, but it seems to us that it cannot properly be distinguished from the instant case.'

I consider that the reasoning of Lord Lane CJ is entirely correct and I would affirm his view that, where a person has been killed and that result is the result intended by another participant, the mere fact that the actual killer may be convicted only of the reduced charge of manslaughter for some reason special to himself does not, in my opinion, in any way result in a compulsory reduction for the other participant.

The House had decided that duress could never be a defence to murder so the question certified could not arise. If duress were a defence to murder, the supposed killer would be guilty of no offence and it seems perfectly obvious that the duressor would be guilty of murder through an innocent agent.

Question 2 did not raise the question posed by *Richards* and by Burke's defence (above) but Lord Mackay, probably *obiter*, affirmed the Court of Appeal's opinion on that issue. Probably everyone will agree with the court's example of the loaded gun.

≈≈ *Question*

How can the accessory be liable for a more serious offence than the principal if secondary liability is 'derivative' as we explained at the outset?

Academics have struggled to identify a coherent basis for liability being imposed on the accessory for a graver crime than that for which the principal is liable. See Kadish, *Blame and Punishment: Essays in Criminal Law* (1987), p 183 and compare Glanville Williams, *Textbook of Criminal Law* (2nd edn, 1983), p 373.

≈≈ *Questions*

(1) Is it significant that the actions of the two men in *Richards* were 'fully voluntary'? They knew perfectly well what they were doing.

(2) D sends a letter bomb through the post to V. E, the postman, notices wires sticking out of the envelope and is aware that letter bombs have been sent recently by terrorists with fatal results. He thinks, 'This could be a letter bomb—but I'm in a hurry—I'll risk it' and pushes the envelope through V's letterbox. It explodes and kills V. If E is guilty of manslaughter, can D be convicted of murder?

19.8.1 Can D be liable as an accessory to a crime committed on himself?

The traditional approach to this question was found in the case of *Tyrell* [1894] 1 QB 710.

Section 5 of the Criminal Law Amendment Act 1885 made it an offence for a man to have carnal knowledge of a girl over the age of 12 and under the age of 16. The defendant, a girl whose age fell within that bracket, was convicted of (a) aiding, abetting, counselling and procuring the commission of that offence by a man upon herself and (b) of inciting the man to commit the same offence. On appeal these convictions were robustly quashed. Lord Coleridge CJ, giving the leading judgment, said at 712:

> The Criminal Law Amendment Act 1885 was passed for the purpose of protecting women and girls against themselves. At the time it was passed there was a discussion as to what point should be fixed as the age of consent. That discussion ended in a compromise, and the age of consent was fixed at sixteen. With the object of protecting women and girls against themselves the Act of Parliament has made illicit connection with a girl under that age unlawful; if a man wishes to have such illicit connection he must wait until the girl is sixteen, otherwise he breaks the law; but it is impossible to say that the Act, which is absolutely silent about aiding or abetting, or soliciting or inciting, can have intended that the girls for whose protection it was passed should be punishable under it for the offences committed upon themselves. I am of the opinion that this conviction ought to be quashed.

Glanville Williams relied on this case to identify a principle that he described as the 'victim rule':

> . . . where the courts perceive that the legislation is designed for the protection of a class of persons. Such people should not be convicted as accessories to an offence committed in respect of them when they co-operate in it. Nor should they be convicted as conspirators. ('Victims and Other Exempt Parties in Crime' (1990) 10 LS 245 at 245)

The rule was restated in the Supreme Court in *Gnango* [2011] UKSC 59. It was held that the *Tyrell* principle only applies when an offence is intended to protect a particular class of vulnerable people.

> 53. We can see no reason why this court should consider extending the common law so as to protect from conviction any defendant who is, or is intended to be, harmed by the crime that he commits, or

attempts to commit. Such an extension would defeat the intention of Parliament in circumscribing the victim rule in section 51 of the 2007 Act. In *R v Brown (Anthony)* [1994] 1 AC 212 sado-masochists were held to have been rightly convicted of causing injury to others who willingly consented to the injuries that they received. There would have been no bar to conviction of the latter of having aided and abetted the infliction of those injuries upon themselves. It is no doubt appropriate for prosecuting authorities to consider carefully whether there is justification for prosecuting anyone as party to a crime where he is the victim, or intended victim of that crime, but that is not to say that the actual or intended victim of a crime should on that ground alone be absolved from criminal responsibility in relation to it. As Lord Lane CJ observed in *Attorney-General's Reference (No 6 of 1980)* [1981] QB 715, 719: 'it is not in the public interest that people should try to cause, or should cause, each other actual bodily harm for no good reason.'

~~~ *Questions*

A and B are outside a pub one night and get into a fight, with each punching the other on the nose. Could A and B now be guilty not only of assault occasioning actual bodily harm for the blow inflicted on the other, but also of aiding and abetting their own ABH? Do you think this odd?

19.9 Defences available only to secondary parties

A secondary party can rely on the defences that are available generally—duress, infancy, insanity, etc—and in addition there are specific defences made available to secondary parties.

19.9.1 The defence of withdrawal

Recall that liability as a secondary party is derivative on P's liability. Until P's conduct is performed and the crime is attempted or committed, D has no secondary liability. There is an opportunity for withdrawal. This contrasts with inchoate liability where D's liability is complete as soon as he has performed the acts of assistance or encouragement (under the Serious Crime Act 2007, see Chapter 22) or formed the agreement in a conspiracy (Chapter 21) or done the acts more than merely preparatory to the commission of the offence in attempt (Chapter 20). In inchoate offences there is no scope for a plea of withdrawal; it is too late. How, if at all, can a person who is about to become a secondary party to an offence withdraw so as to avoid liability when the crime is committed?

R v Becerra and Cooper
(1975) 62 Cr App R 212, Court of Appeal, Criminal Division

(Roskill and Bridge LJJ and Kilner Brown J)

B, C and G broke into a house with intent to steal from the householder, an old lady, F. While G was holding a pillow over F's face, B cut the telephone wires with a knife with a 3½-inch blade. B then gave the knife to C. The burglars were surprised by the appearance of a man, V, the tenant of a flat in the house. B called out 'Come on, let's go' and, followed by G, climbed out of a window and ran away. C tried the back door but it was locked and, being confronted by V, stabbed and killed him. B and C were convicted of murder and appealed.

Roskill LJ [having held that there was evidence to support the jury's finding of a common design to cause death or serious bodily harm if it was necessary to do so in order to carry out the theft, turned to the argument that B had effectively withdrawn from any common design:]

It is necessary, before dealing with that argument in more detail, to say a word or two about the relevant law. It is a curious fact, considering the number of times in which this point arises where two or more people are charged with criminal offences, particularly murder or manslaughter, how relatively little authority there is in this country upon the point. But the principle is undoubtedly of long standing.

Perhaps it is best first stated in *Saunders and Archer* (1573) 2 Plowd 473 (in the eighteenth year of the first Queen Elizabeth) at p 476, in a note by *Plowden*, thus: '. . . for if I command one to kill JS and before the Fact done I go to him and tell him that I have repented, and expressly charge him not to kill JS and he afterwards kills him, there I shall not be Accessory to this Murder, because I have countermanded my first Command, which in all Reason shall discharge me, for the malicious Mind of the Accessory ought to continue to do ill until the Time of the Act done, or else he shall not be charged; but if he had killed JS before the Time of my Discharge or Countermand given, I should have been Accessory to the Death, notwithstanding my private Repentance'.

The next case to which I may usefully refer is some 250 years later, but over 150 years ago. *Edmeads* (1828) 3 C & P 390, where there is a ruling of Vaughan B at a trial at Berkshire Assizes, upon an indictment charging Edmeads and others with unlawfully shooting at game keepers. At the end of his ruling the learned Baron said on the question of common intent, at p 392, 'that is rather a question for the jury; but still, on this evidence, it is quite clear what the common purpose was. They all draw up in lines, and point their guns at the game keepers, and they are all giving their countenance and assistance to the one of them who actually fires the gun. If it could be shewn that either of them separated himself from the rest, and showed distinctly that he would have no hand in what they were doing, the objection would have much weight in it.'

I can go forward over 100 years. Mr Owen (to whose juniors we are indebted for their research into the relevant Canadian and United States cases) referred us to several Canadian cases, to only one of which it is necessary to refer in detail, a decision of the Court of Appeal in British Columbia in *Whitehouse* (alias *Savage*) [1941] 1 WWR 112. I need not read the headnote. The Court of Appeal held that the trial judge concerned in that case, which was one of murder, had been guilty of misdirection in his direction to the jury on this question of 'withdrawal'. The matter is, if I may most respectfully say so, so well put in the leading judgment of Sloan JA, that I read the whole of the passage at pp 115 and 116:

'Can it be said on the facts of this case that a mere change of mental intention and a quitting of the scene of the crime just immediately prior to the striking of the fatal blow will absolve those who participate in the commission of the crime by overt acts up to that moment from all the consequences of its accomplishment by the one who strikes in ignorance of his companions' change of heart? I think not. After a crime has been committed and before a prior abandonment of the common enterprise may be found by a jury there must be, in my view, in the absence of exceptional circumstances, something more than a mere mental change of intention and physical change of place by those associates who wish to dissociate themselves from the consequences attendant upon their willing assistance up to the moment of the actual commission of that crime. I would not attempt to define too closely what must be done in criminal matters involving participation in a common unlawful purpose to break the chain of causation and responsibility. That must depend upon the circumstances of each case but it seems to me that one essential element ought to be established in a case of this kind: Where practicable and reasonable there must be timely communication of the intention to abandon the common purpose from those who wish to dissociate themselves from the contemplated crime to those who desire to continue in it. What is "timely communication" must be determined by the facts of each case but where practicable and reasonable it ought to be such communication, verbal or otherwise, that will serve unequivocal notice upon the other party to the common unlawful cause that if he proceeds upon it he does so without the further aid and assistance of those who withdraw. The unlawful purpose of him who continues alone is then his own and not one in common with those who are no longer parties to it nor liable to its full and final consequences.'

The learned judge then went on to cite a passage from 1 Hale's *Pleas of the Crown* [1736] 618 and the passage from *Saunders and Archer* (supra) to which I have already referred.

In the view of each member of this court, that passage, if we may respectfully say so, could not be improved upon and we venture to adopt it in its entirety as a correct statement of the law which is to be applied in this case.

The last case, an English one, is *Croft* (1944) 29 Cr App R 169, [1944] 1 KB 295; a well known case of a suicide pact where, under the old law, the survivor of a suicide pact was charged with and convicted of murder. It was sought to argue that he had withdrawn from the pact in time to avoid liability (as the law then was) for conviction for murder.

The Court of Criminal Appeal, comprising Lawrence J (as he then was), Lewis and Wrottesley JJ dismissed the appeal and upheld the direction given by Humphreys J to the jury at the trial. Towards the end of the judgment Lawrence J said, at p 173 (pp 297 and 298): '. . . counsel for the appellant complains—although I do not understand that the point had ever been taken in the court below—that the summing-up does not contain any reference to the possibility of the agreement to commit suicide having been determined or countermanded. It is true that the learned judge does not deal expressly with that matter except in a passage where he says: Even if you accept his statement in the witness-box that the vital and second shot was fired when he had gone through that window, he would still be guilty of murder if she was then committing suicide as the result of an agreement which they had mutually arrived at that should be the fate of both of them, and it is no answer for him that he altered his mind after she was dead and did not commit suicide himself. . . . the authorities, such as they are, show in our opinion, that where a person has acted as an accessory before the fact, in order that he should not be held guilty as an accessory before the fact, he must give express and actual countermand or revocation of the advising, counselling, procuring, or abetting which he had given before.'

It seems to us that those authorities make plain what the law is which has to be applied in the present case.

We therefore turn back to consider the direction which the learned judge gave in the present case to the jury and what was the suggested evidence that Becerra had withdrawn from the common agreement. The suggested evidence is the use by Becerra of the words 'Come on let's go,' coupled, as I said a few moments ago, with his act in going out through the window. The evidence, as the judge pointed out, was that Cooper never heard that nor did the third man. But let it be supposed that that was said and the jury took the view that it was said.

On the facts of this case, in the circumstances then prevailing, the knife having already been used and being contemplated for further use when it was handed over by Becerra to Cooper for the purpose of avoiding (if necessary) by violent means the hazards of identification, if Becerra wanted to withdraw at that stage, he would have to 'countermand', to use the word that is used in some of the cases or 'repent' to use another word so used, in some manner vastly different and vastly more effective than merely to say 'Come on, let's go' and go out through the window.

It is not necessary, on this application, to decide whether the point of time had arrived at which the only way in which he could effectively withdraw, so as to free himself from joint responsibility for any act Cooper thereafter did in furtherance of the common design, would be physically to intervene so as to stop Cooper attacking Lewis, as the judge suggested, by interposing his own body between them or somehow getting in between them or whether some other action might suffice. That does not arise for decision here. Nor is it necessary to decide whether or not the learned judge was right or wrong, on the facts of this case, in that passage which appears at the bottom of p 206, which Mr Owen criticised: 'and at least take all reasonable steps to prevent the commission of the crime which he had agreed the others should commit.' It is enough for the purposes of deciding this application to say that under the law of this country as it stands, and on the facts (taking them at their highest in favour of Becerra), that which was urged as amounting to withdrawal from the common design was not capable of amounting to such withdrawal. Accordingly Becerra remains responsible, in the eyes of the law, for everything that Cooper did and continued to do after Becerra's disappearance through the window as much as if he had done them himself.

Cooper being unquestionably guilty of murder, Becerra is equally guilty of murder. Mr Owen's careful argument must therefore be rejected and the application by Becerra for leave to appeal against conviction fails.

Appeal dismissed

≈≈ *Questions*

What could Becerra have done? To avoid liability, must Becerra:

(1) make clear he is withdrawing;

(2) do all he can to negate the effects of his contribution to the crime; or

(3) do all he reasonably can to stop Cooper?

In *Mitchell and King* [1999] Crim LR 496, an unplanned fight broke out in and around a restaurant. One person was killed. The appellants were convicted of murder, alleged to have been committed in the course of a joint enterprise. M claimed that if there was such an enterprise, he had withdrawn from it before the fatal act. The judge directed the jury by reading the passage from *Whitehouse*, in the previous extract. Quashing M's conviction, Otton LJ said:

The case from which this passage is taken concerned pre-planned violence. It is not necessary when the violence is spontaneous. Although absent any communication, it may, as a matter of evidence, be easier to persuade a jury that a defendant, who had previously participated, had not in fact withdrawn. Such considerations are clearly relevant in such cases, but less so when violence has erupted spontaneously.

Secondary participation consists in assisting or encouraging the principal offender in the commission of the crime. A party who withdraws from an enterprise, spontaneous or not, usually ceases to assist but he does not necessarily cease to encourage. Suppose that P is encouraged in the fight because he knows D is in there with him. If D decides he has had enough and quietly sneaks off without attracting P's attention, the external element of secondary participation still continues. D's encouragement of P is still operative. Does mere withdrawal then relieve D of responsibility? A person who has done an act which makes him potentially liable for a crime cannot relieve himself of responsibility by a mere change of mind. Once the arrow is in the air, it is no use wishing to have never let it go. The archer is guilty of homicide when the arrow gets the victim through the heart. The withdrawer, it is true, does not merely change his mind: he withdraws—but is that relevant if the withdrawal has no more effect on subsequent events than the archer's repentance?

Commenting on *O'Flaherty* [2004] 2 Cr App R 20, Professor Ashworth observes (at [2004] Crim LR 751):

Why should withdrawal be a defence? The main reason must be that a person who aids, abets, counsels or procures at first but then has a voluntary change of mind, before the full offence is completed, is significantly less culpable than an accomplice who continued to support the commission of the offence throughout. The withdrawing accomplice remains liable for what was done up to that point, but not for what was done thereafter. This desert-based rationale must be linked to the nature of the accomplice's contribution to the principal offence, and the requirements of withdrawal should similarly depend on that contribution. In other words, the further D has gone in supporting the commission of the offence, the more it is right to expect by way of withdrawal (cf. K.J.M. Smith, 'Withdrawal in Complicity: A Restatement of Principles' [2001] Crim.L.R. 769). On this approach, then, the law should 'reward' the withdrawing accomplice by providing the possibility of a defence, though strictly circumscribed (mitigation of sentence will provide for those whose purported withdrawal is insufficiently definite). Others prefer to say that the defence is necessary to provide an incentive for accomplices to withdraw, although the language of incentives is really only apposite if people in that situation are aware of the legal rule. But much also depends on whether the rationale for accessorial liability lies primarily in the culpability of the accomplice or in the causal contribution to the principal offence, since withdrawal may negative culpability for subsequent acts but not (in some instances) sever the causal contribution to subsequent acts. Judicial discussion of complicity is suffused with references to 'joint enterprise' and 'common enterprise', and the significance of this decision is to demonstrate the shortcomings of expressing cases of complicity in that way.... [M]any of the cases coming before the courts concern violence erupting outside a pub, club or sporting venue, where some people join in, some stay on the fringes, and others walk away. Thus, in *Mitchell and King* [1999] Crim.L.R. 496, Otton L.J. said (at para.6): 'Communication of withdrawal is a necessary condition for dissociation from preplanned violence. It is not necessary when the violence is spontaneous. Although absent any communication it may, as a matter of evidence, be easier to persuade a jury that a defendant, who had previously participated, had not in fact withdrawn. Such considerations are clearly relevant in such cases, but less so when the violence has erupted spontaneously.' Otton L.J. drew this distinction between planned and spontaneous offences without reliance on any authority. In this case, Mantell L.J. followed the *Mitchell and King* approach ... Thus, the jury must be satisfied 'that the fatal injuries were sustained when the joint enterprise was continuing and that the defendant was still acting within that joint enterprise' (at [64]); and 'in a case of spontaneous violence such as this where there has been no prior agreement, the jury will usually have to make inferences as to the scope of the joint enterprise from the knowledge and actions of individual participants' (at [65]).... Sir John Smith doubted whether the fact that an attack arose spontaneously should lead to an alteration of the requirements for withdrawal: is it right to allow withdrawal without communication, he asked, 'if A was encouraged by B's participation and was unaware that B had withdrawn?' (Smith and Hogan, *Criminal Law* (10th ed., 2002), p.177). The answer depends, surely, on the rationale. If the foundations of complicity and of withdrawal lie chiefly in B's culpability, a definite withdrawal from spontaneous violence (even if not accompanied by communication) should suffice. But if the foundations lie chiefly in B's contribution to A's offence, B's withdrawal in those circumstances may (as Sir John hinted) be no more effective than an uncommunicated withdrawal from a non-spontaneous offence. On the facts of this case, two of the men (R and T) participated in the initial attack but then broke off from the group and did not accompany them into the next street. They did not 'communicate' their withdrawal to anyone. But it was a spontaneous attack, and they had probably not signalled their arrival either, other than by physical participation. Should we speculate on whether the group of attackers who went into the next street were still being encouraged by the belief that the two men were with them, when they were not? Surely the two men's act of leaving should be sufficient to dissociate them from subsequent events, in the absence of any kind of plan to which they had all assented. They were culpable for what they had done up to that point, but not in respect of anything thereafter. The attackers had eyes and ears, and had no reason to believe that the two were still supporting them. But O'Flaherty's position was held to be different because he did follow the attackers into the next street and he was present, holding a cricket bat, when the fatal attack took place. He did not participate actively in the fatal attack, but neither he did he do anything amounting to withdrawal. It is then a question of fact whether his series of actions amounted to aiding and abetting murder, resulting in the mandatory sentence of life imprisonment.

In *Grundy* [1977] Crim LR 543, D had supplied E, a burglar, with information which was presumably valuable to E in committing the burglary in question; but, for two weeks before

E did so, D had been trying to stop him breaking in. It was held that there was evidence of an effective withdrawal which should have been left to the jury. In *Whitefield* (1984) 79 Cr App R 36, [1984] Crim LR 97, there was evidence that D had served unequivocal notice on E that, if he proceeded with a burglary they had planned together, he would do so without D's aid or assistance. It was held that the jury should have been told that, if they accepted this evidence, there was a defence. Cf *McPhillips* (1990) 6 BNIL, section 21.4.6.2, p 582, where an uncommunicated intention to frustrate an agreement to commit murder, to which D was a party, was a defence to a charge of conspiracy to murder and *Rook* [1993] 2 All ER 955, [1993] Crim LR 698.

The principles which apply appear from the case law to be as follows:

- withdrawal will operate only exceptionally: *Mitchell* [1990] Crim LR 496;
- a change of mind by D is insufficient; there must be physical acts demonstrating disengagement: *Bryce* [2004] EWCA Crim 1231;
- the same principles apply whether the offence involves spontaneous or planned violence: *Robinson* [2000] EWCA Crim 8. In *Mitchell* [1990] Crim LR 496, it was emphasized that with spontaneous violence the issue was not whether there had been communication of withdrawal but whether the original joint venture was still continuing at the time of the principal's act. This was followed in *O'Flaherty* [2004] 2 Cr App R 20, where the question was 'whether a particular defendant disengaged before the fatal injury or injuries were caused';
- D must communicate the withdrawal to P unequivocally unless physically impossible in the circumstances: *Robinson*;
- D's withdrawal before P's act must be 'unequivocal': *O'Flaherty*;
- whether D is still a party to the venture is a question of fact and degree for the jury to determine: *O'Flaherty*;
- D throwing down his weapon and walking away *may* be enough: *O'Flaherty*;
- where D is one of the instigators of the attack, more may be needed to demonstrate withdrawal: *Gallant* [2008] EWCA Crim 1111;
- a judge need not direct on withdrawal in every case (eg it is unnecessary where D denies that there was a criminal venture: *Gallant*).

Note that the Supreme Court of Canada in *Gauthier* [2013] 2 SCR 403, [2013] SCC 32 has concluded that withdrawal is best regarded as a defence rather than a denial of the offence of aiding and abetting. There are in Canada two requirements to the defence: (a) there must be conduct, whether words or actions, that demonstrates clearly to others withdrawal from the offending; and (b) the withdrawing party must take reasonable and sufficient steps to undo the effect of his previous participation or to prevent the crime.

≋ *Questions*

Is withdrawal:

(1) a defence that operates only where D brings to an end the actus reus of assisting or encouraging P;

(2) a defence that operates because D's withdrawal negates his mens rea of intention to assist or encourage; or

(3) a defence operating despite the presence of D's continuing actus reus and mens rea as a secondary party?

Which should it be?

R v Bryce

[2004] EWCA Crim 1231, Court of Appeal, Criminal Division

(Potter LJ, Hooper and Astill JJ)

D was convicted of murder as an aider and abettor. D claimed that his assistance 12 hours before P shot V was too remote.

Potter LJ:

75. . . . if the secondary party is to avoid liability for assistance rendered to the perpetrator in respect of steps taken by the perpetrator towards the commission of the crime, only an act taken by him which amounts to countermanding of his earlier assistance and a withdrawal from the common purpose will suffice. Repentance alone, unsupported by action taken to demonstrate withdrawal will be insufficient. Thus, if the secondary party had the necessary mens rea at the time of the act of rendering his advice or assistance, the fact that his mind is 'innocent' at the time when the crime is committed is no defence: see *R v Becerra* (1975) 62 Crim App R 212. In that case it was stated that any communication of withdrawal by the secondary party to the perpetrator must be such as to serve 'unequivocal notice' upon the other party to the common unlawful cause that, if he proceeds upon it, he does so without the further aid and assistance of the withdrawing party: c.f. the position in *R v Whitefield* (1984) 79 Crim App R 36, [1984] Crim LR 97.

See further, D. Lanham, 'Accomplices and Withdrawal' (1981) 97 LQR 575; K. J. M. Smith, 'Withdrawal in Complicity: A Restatement of Principles' [2001] Crim LR 769.

19.9.2 A defence for victims alleged to be parties

Where an offence is created for the protection of a class of persons, a member of the class who is the victim of such an offence cannot be convicted either of inciting or aiding, abetting, counselling or procuring its commission, even though he has done acts which would usually amount to such an offence.

19.9.3 A defence for an accessory who acts under legal duty?

In *Garrett v Arthur Churchill (Glass) Ltd* [1970] 1 QB 92, [1969] 2 All ER 1141, D, who as an agent of P had bought a goblet, was held guilty of being knowingly concerned in the exportation of goods without a licence, when, on P's instructions, he delivered P's own goblet to P's agent who was to take it to the United States. Parker LCJ ([1969] 2 All ER at 1145) said:

albeit there was a legal duty in ordinary circumstances to hand over the goblet to the owners once the agency was determined, I do not think that an action would lie for breach of that duty if the handing over would constitute the offence of being knowingly concerned in its exportation.

In *Lomas* (1913) 9 Cr App R 220, the accused was held to be not guilty of aiding and abetting a burglary by returning to the burglar, King, a jemmy which the accused had borrowed from him.

> ≋ **Question**
> D agrees: (a) to sell, (b) to let on hire, his car to E. D knows that E intends to drive the car himself and—(i) has no licence to drive, or (ii) has no insurance against third party risks, or (iii) is disqualified, or (iv) is subject to epileptic seizures. Is D liable for offences that E commits by driving the car?

19.10 Derivative versus inchoate liability

As we noted at the start of this chapter, the derivative basis for liability is in contrast to the inchoate offences under Part 2 of the 2007 Act and in conspiracy and attempt. See D. Lanham, 'Primary and Derivative Criminal Liability: An Australian Perspective' [2000] Crim LR 707 and Law Commission Report No 300, *Inchoate Liability for Assisting and Encouraging Crime* (2006) and Report No 305, *Participating in Crime* (2007), Ch 3.

Returning to the example at the start, Dawn who hired Peter as a contract killer would be liable for an inchoate offence (ss 44 to 46 of the Serious Crime Act 2007) as soon as she tried to persuade Peter. She would be liable irrespective of whether he went on to commit the offence. Similarly, Carl and Eric would be liable for their acts of assistance or encouragement as soon as those were performed, irrespective of whether Peter went on to commit the offence. The argument for imposing liability at that stage is that the blameworthiness of D, C and E is not affected by what happens later. That is entirely in the hands of Peter.

In its Consultation Paper, *Assisting and Encouraging Crime* (Law Com Consultation Paper No 131) in 1993, the Law Commission proposed to replace all derivative secondary liability with inchoate liability. Would that be a better system?

In its later Report No 300 (*Inchoate Liability for Assisting and Encouraging Crime*) in 2006, the Law Commission rejected its provisional proposals from 1993, citing the arguments of those who responded to the original proposals in 1993:

> 2.7 Those respondents who provided an analysis of whether inchoate liability should supplant secondary liability focused on:
>
> (1) forensic considerations,
>
> (2) public acceptability,
>
> (3) condemnation and labelling,
>
> (4) the connection between D's conduct and the offence committed by P.
>
> **Forensic considerations**
>
> 2.8 By virtue of section 8 of the Accessories and Abettors Act 1861, a person who is an accessory can be charged, indicted and punished as a principal offender. This means that the prosecution can obtain a conviction even if it cannot be proved whether the accused was a principal offender or an accessory provided that he or she must have been one or the other. For example, suppose that D1 and D2 are jointly charged with burglary. It is known that one of them entered the premises while the other kept watch. D1 and D2 can each be convicted of burglary despite the prosecution being unable to prove who entered the premises (the principal offender) and who kept watch (the accessory).
>
> 2.9 This is of considerable assistance to the prosecution in cases where it is difficult or impossible to prove the precise role of the various parties. In addition, the prosecution does not have to specify in advance whether the allegation is that an accused was a principal offender or an accessory. . . .
>
> 2.10 Some respondents felt that these forensic advantages would be jeopardised by adopting a scheme consisting solely of inchoate offences. They felt that such a scheme would adversely affect the law's ability to accurately attribute criminal liability in those cases where it is impossible to be sure who was the principal offender and who was the accessory.
>
> **Public acceptability**
>
> 2.11 Professor Sir John Smith said that the public attaches enormous importance to the consequences that result from a criminal act and that Parliament reacts accordingly. He provided this example:

Example 2C

D gives instructions to P, whom D believes to be a 'contract killer' to kill D's partner, V.

Under the proposals in the [1993 Paper], D would be guilty of the same offence, assisting murder, *irrespective* of whether P decided to kill V or instead to report D to the police.

2.12 Professor Smith doubted whether the public would consider that outcome to be acceptable. He said that society expects an offender to be convicted of and punished for offences that reflect not only his moral culpability but also the harm caused by his or her conduct. Thus, the maximum term of imprisonment for causing dangerous driving is two years but when death is caused the offence becomes causing death by dangerous driving and the maximum term of imprisonment increases to 14 years.

2.13 The Society of Public Teachers of Law agreed. In its view, in a case such as example 2C, should P go on to kill V, it would be unrealistic to attribute responsibility for V's death solely to P given that D would have played a prominent part in bringing about V's death.

Condemnation, culpability and labelling

2.14 There was criticism that the proposals in the CP would not adequately fulfil the condemnatory and labelling function of the law. In particular, they would not adequately connect an accused with the consequences of his or her offence. . . .

2.15 A specific criticism was that to de-couple an accessory's liability from the harmful consequences of the principal's conduct would be particularly anomalous where the culpability of the former exceeds that of the latter. Professor Sir John Smith provided the following example:

Example 2D

D, a gang leader, sends out his subordinate P to detonate a bomb. P does so without warning in a busy shopping centre. The explosion results in the deaths of 20 people.

2.16 Professor Sir John Smith said that, under the proposals in the CP, P would be liable for 20 murders but D merely for one offence of encouraging murder. The anomaly would be even more striking if D had compelled P to carry out the act by holding P's partner, Z, as a hostage and threatening to kill Z because duress is no defence to murder.

2.17 Sometimes, death is an unexpected and unforeseen consequence:

Example 2E

D encourages P to inflict grievous bodily harm on V. P does so. Normally V's injuries would not prove fatal. However, medical complications set in and V dies.

Under the current law, both D and P are guilty of murder. Under the proposals in the CP, P would be guilty of murder but D would be guilty only of encouraging P to cause grievous bodily harm with intent.

2.18 Professor Sir John Smith agreed that it is arguable that in example 1E neither D nor P should be held responsible for the unintended and unforeseen consequences. However, the proposals in the [1993 paper] lead to a conclusion that he thought even less acceptable, namely that P is held responsible for those consequences whereas D, the more culpable party, is not held responsible.

The connection between D's conduct and P's offence

2.19 In the [1993 paper], the Commission said that D's liability for encouraging or assisting P to commit an offence should be inchoate because it was impossible to connect D to P's offence. Professor K J M Smith questioned this assertion: . . .

it has always been implied in the concept of complicity that an accessory's involvement . . . did make some difference to the outcome, and, as a consequence of this, accessories have been implicitly linked to the harm element in the principal offence. No other plausible explanation exists for complicity's tenacious, fundamental requirement of the commission of the principal offence. . . . In sum then, under existing doctrine, the accessory's liability is derivative or parasitic of a principal offence and its harm content. Rather than relying solely on the accessory's mental culpability, unlike inchoate liability, complicity responsibility also implicitly draws on the attributable harm of the principal offence.

CONCLUSION

2.20 We acknowledge that it is possible to preserve some of the forensic benefits of the current law in a scheme consisting solely of inchoate offences. This could be achieved by a statutory provision stating that if the prosecution can prove that D must have been either the principal offender or the encourager/assister, D can be convicted of the inchoate offence.

2.21 However, such a provision would not meet the criticism that the proposals in the [1993] paper would not accurately label and condemn D for his or her conduct:

Example 2F

D gives P chocolates to give to V. V eats them and dies because they are poisoned. D knew the chocolates were poisoned and would kill anyone who ate them.

Under the proposals in the CP, D would be guilty of murder if P was unaware that the chocolates were poisoned because P would be an innocent agent and D would be considered to have perpetrated the offence as a principal offender. However, if P knew that the chocolates were poisoned, P would be guilty of murder but D would be guilty of assisting murder.

2.22 Example 2F illustrates why it would be wrong to abolish secondary liability. It cannot be right that D is guilty of murder if P is unaware that the chocolates are poisoned but only of assisting murder if P is aware that the chocolates are poisoned. D's conduct and state of mind are identical in each case. Further, whereas examples 2D and 2E might be thought to reveal problems with specific aspects of the law of murder that might be better resolved by reforming those aspects, the anomaly in example 2F is not the product of any defects in the law of murder.

2.23 We believe that if P commits an offence that it was D's intention P should commit, account should be taken of D's connection with the harm that results from P committing the offence. D's state of mind in intending that the offence should be committed connects D to the offence and the resulting harm in a morally significant way that can only be properly reflected by convicting D of the offence rather than encouraging or assisting the commission of the offence. In as much as there is a difference in the culpability of P and D, this can be reflected in the nature or severity of the punishment each is to receive for his or her involvement.

. . .

2.25 We acknowledge that the retention of secondary liability may sometimes result in D being liable for unexpected consequences. However, this will usually be the result of anomalies in the substantive law that the doctrine of secondary liability must accommodate. The doctrine of secondary liability is of general application, applying to many different offences whether or not those offences are well structured, well defined or even consistent with one another. Removing D's, but not P's, liability for unforeseen consequences, would simply create a new anomaly.

2.26 One aim of the proposals in the CP was to simplify the law by creating a clear distinction between the liability of the principal offender and the liability of the accessory. We now believe that this simplicity comes at too high a price. If P commits an offence that D either intended should be committed or believed might be committed in the course of a joint venture, there are compelling reasons for convicting D of the offence should P commit it. We now believe that to confine D's liability in such cases to that of encouraging or assisting the offence would be to confine it too narrowly.

≋ **Question**

Do you agree with the consultees' arguments for rejecting the shift to inchoate liability?
See the following section and Chapter 22 for the scheme the Law Commission did recommend, which relies heavily on wide inchoate offences whilst retaining a narrower form of secondary liability.

See also Law Commission Report No 305, *Participating in Crime* (2007), para 3.3.

19.11 Reform

The Law Commission's most recent recommendations on this subject were before the decision in *Jogee*. Since the Law Commission endorsed the *Chan Wing-Siu* approach which was overturned by the Supreme Court, it is unlikely that these recommendations will be adopted.

Law Commission Report No 305, *Participating in Crime* (2007)

AN OUTLINE OF THE SCHEME THAT WE ARE RECOMMENDING IN THIS REPORT

The overall structure

1.46 In place of the common law rules of secondary liability and innocent agency, we are recommending a statutory scheme. . . . The scheme consists of three conceptually distinct forms of liability:

Type 1: secondary liability

1.47 First, D would be liable, provided he or she satisfies the requisite fault element, for an offence that P commits with D's encouragement or assistance (clause 1 of the Bill). Secondly, D would be liable, provided he or she satisfies the requisite fault element, for any offences committed pursuant to a joint criminal venture (clause 2 of the Bill).

CLAUSE 1 OF THE BILL

1.48 Under clause 1 of the Bill, D would be liable for a principal offence committed by P if D assisted or encouraged P to perpetrate the conduct element of the principal offence and *intended* that the conduct element should be perpetrated. This would have the effect of narrowing the scope of secondary liability in cases where D and P are not parties to a joint criminal venture.

1.49 For the purposes of clause 1, D 'intends' only if he or she acts in order that the conduct element of the principal offence is perpetrated. In our use and understanding of the word 'intention', we adopt the common law meaning. This means that if D foresaw as a virtual certainty P engaging in the conduct element of the offence, that would be evidence from which the jury or magistrates could (but would not have to) find that D intended the perpetration of the conduct element.

CLAUSE 2 OF THE BILL

1.50 Clause 2 would govern D's liability where D and P have formed a joint criminal venture. This will cover both agreed offences and collateral offences committed by P in the course of the joint criminal venture.

1.51 In relation to clause 2, D would be liable for any offence committed by P provided that its commission fell within the scope of the joint venture. A joint criminal venture is formed when the parties agree to commit an offence or when they share with each other a common intention to commit an offence. D would be liable for any offence (agreed or collateral) that he or she foresaw might be committed as a possible result of the venture. The mere fact that D was not present when the offence was committed or that he or she would rather that it was not committed would not in itself preclude a jury finding that the offence fell within the scope of the joint venture.

Type 2: innocent agency

1.52 We are recommending that the common law doctrine of innocent agency should be replaced by a statutory regime. D would be liable for an offence as a principal offender if he or she intentionally caused P, an innocent agent, to commit the conduct element of an offence but P does not commit the offence because P:

(1) is under the age of 10 years;

(2) has a defence of insanity; or

(3) acts without the fault required to be convicted of the offence;

Type 3: causing the commission of a no-fault offence

1.54 We are recommending the creation of a new statutory offence of causing another person to commit a no-fault offence. Accordingly, under this form of liability, D would be convicted as a principal offender rather than, as under the current law, a secondary party to the no-fault offence committed by P.

Summary

1.55 Much more so than at common law, the scheme emphasises the derivative nature of secondary liability. Subject to a very limited number of exceptions, D would incur secondary liability only if P commits a principal offence. The exceptions relate to where P does not commit an offence because he or she has a complete defence, for example duress, or a partial defence to murder, for example provocation.

1.56 Our scheme confines secondary liability to cases where D has assisted or encouraged P and/ or has formed a joint criminal venture with P. Under the current law, D can incur secondary liability by 'procuring' P to commit an offence. Under our recommendations, 'procuring' will cease to be a basis of secondary liability. Instead, procuring in the sense of intentionally causing a person to do a criminal act will result in D incurring liability as a principal offender.

Limitations on liability and defences

The Tyrrell exemption

1.57 Under the current law, if an offence is enacted to protect a category of persons and D falls within that category, D cannot be convicted of committing the offence as a secondary party (or of inciting P to commit the offence). This is known as the *Tyrrell* exemption. In *Tyrrell*, P, an adult, had unlawful sexual intercourse with D, a child aged between 13 and 16. It was alleged that D had encouraged P to commit the offence. Despite this, the court held that D could not be liable as a secondary party because the primary offence was intended to protect 'victims from themselves'. Our scheme preserves and refines the common law *Tyrrell* exemption.

1.58 We are recommending that D should not be held liable as a secondary party or as a principal offender by virtue of innocent agency if:

(1) the principal offence is one that exists for the protection of a particular category of person;

(2) D falls within that category; and

(3) D is the victim of the principal offence.

Acting to prevent the commission of an offence or to prevent or limit the occurrence of harm

1.59 We are recommending that if D is charged with committing an offence as a secondary party, it should be a defence if D proves on the balance of probabilities that he or she acted in order to prevent the commission of an offence or the occurrence of harm and that it was reasonable to act as D did.

. . .

AN OVERVIEW OF INCHOATE AND SECONDARY LIABILITY FOR ASSISTING AND ENCOURAGING CRIME

1.60 It is important that the recommendations in this report are read in the light of the recommendations that we made in the first report [now implemented in Part 2 of the Serious Crime Act 2007—see Chapter 22]. In this section, we provide a brief outline of the overall scheme.

D's liability where P does not commit the principal offence

1.61 D's liability would always be inchoate. D would commit an inchoate offence of encouraging or assisting P to commit an offence:

(1) if D does an act capable of encouraging or assisting P to commit an offence:

   (a) intending to assist or encourage P to perpetrate the conduct element of the offence ('the clause 1 inchoate offence'); or

   (b) believing that his or her act will assist or encourage P to perpetrate the conduct element and that P will perpetrate it ('the clause 2 inchoate offence');

AND

(2) if the principal offence requires proof of fault:

   (a) D believes that P will perpetrate the conduct element with the fault element required to be convicted of the offence; or

   (b) D's own state of mind is such that were he to perpetrate the conduct element, he would do so with the requisite fault.

Specific defences

1.62 Where D's liability is grounded on the clause 2 inchoate offence, it would be a defence if D acted reasonably in the circumstances. The burden of proof would be on D to demonstrate that he or she had acted reasonably. The defence would not be available to the clause 1 inchoate offence.

D's liability where P does commit the principal offence

Clause 1

1.63 Beyond inchoate liability, D would be liable for P's offence as a secondary party provided that D intended P to engage in the conduct element of the offence and:

(1) D believed that P would perpetrate the conduct element with the fault required to be convicted of the offence; or

(2) D's state of mind was such that, had he or she perpetrated the conduct element, it would have been with the fault required for conviction of the offence.

1.64 Accordingly, if D indifferently assisted or encouraged P to commit an offence, D would no longer be a secondary party to P's offence. However, if D believed that P would commit the principal offence, D would commit the clause 2 inchoate offence of assisting or encouraging P to commit the principal offence believing D would commit it.

1.65 Accordingly, there is scope for the clause 2 inchoate offence to apply even if P does commit or attempt to commit the principal offence. However, for the clause 2 inchoate offence to apply, D must believe that P *will* commit the principal offence. This means that if D believes that P might commit the principal offence, D will not incur either secondary or inchoate liability in respect of the principal offence.

Clause 2

1.66 D would be liable for any offence committed by P that was within the scope of the joint criminal venture. It would be a question of fact and degree whether the offence committed by P was within the scope of the venture. The fact that D was opposed to the commission of the offence would not in itself prevent the tribunal of fact from finding that the offence was within the scope of the venture.

General defences

1.67 There would be two defences to both inchoate and secondary liability. The first would be where D acted reasonably in order to prevent the commission of an offence or to limit the occurrence of harm. The burden of proof would be on D to establish the defence. The second would be where the principal offence was one which existed for the protection of a particular category of person and D was both a member of that category and the victim of the offence (or would have been had the principal offence been committed).

For critical comment on the proposals, see W. Wilson, 'A Rational Scheme of Liability for Participation in Crime' [2008] Crim LR 3, suggesting the proposals generally 'succeed admirably'; cf G. R. Sullivan, 'Participating in Crime' [2008] Crim LR 19, suggesting the proposals on joint ventures show a disregard for the 'minimum standards of clarity and comprehensibility' and R. D. Taylor, 'Procuring, Causation, Innocent Agency and the Law Commission' [2008] Crim LR 32, who is also critical of the complexity and incoherence of the proposals. See also J. Horder, *Homicide and the Politics of Law Reform* (2012), Ch 6 for a response to Sullivan's criticisms.

> ≈≈≈ *Question*
> Would legislative reform have been preferable to the Supreme Court's judgment in *Jogee*?

FURTHER READING

P. Alldridge, 'The Doctrine of Innocent Agency' (1990) 2 Crim L Forum 45

R. Buxton, '*Jogee*: Upheaval in Secondary Liability for Murder' [2016] Crim LR 324

I. H. Dennis, 'The Mental Element for Accessories' in P. Smith (ed), *Essays in Honour of J. C. Smith* (1987)

I. H. Dennis, 'Intent and Complicity—A Reply' [1988] Crim LR 649

J. Herring, 'Victims as Defendants: When Victims Participate in Crimes against Themselves' in A. Reed and M. Bohlander (eds), *Participation in Crime: Domestic and Comparative Perspectives* (2013)

A. Simester, 'The Mental Element in Complicity' (2006) 122 LQR 578

G. R. Sullivan, 'Intent, Purpose and Complicity' [1988] Crim LR 638

D. Warburton, 'Supreme Court and Judicial Committee of the Privy Council: Secondary Participation in Crime' (2016) 80 J Crim L 160

G. Williams, 'Innocent Agency and Causation' (1992) 3 Crim L Forum 289

20

Attempt

Attempt:

A person commits an offence of attempt if, with intent to commit an offence (eg theft) he does an act which is more than merely preparatory to the commission of that offence: s 1 of the Criminal Attempts Act 1981.

Some of the controversies that will be examined in this chapter include:

(1) the precise mens rea for attempt: whether in addition to intending any result required for the crime, D must also intend the circumstances of the substantive offence in order to be guilty of attempting it;

(2) how far D's acts must go towards committing the substantive offence before he will be guilty of an attempt;

(3) whether the law criminalizes D who attempts to commit an offence even though on the facts it would have been impossible for him to commit the substantive offence;

(4) reasons as to why it is appropriate to criminalize attempts to commit crimes.

20.1 Introduction

As the discussion of earlier issues, particularly actus reus (Chapter 2) and causation (Chapter 3) has highlighted, there are often problems in proving that a defendant is guilty of a particular crime even though he has engaged in blameworthy conduct with a blameworthy state of mind. Take the case of *White* [1910] 2 KB 124 (section 3.2.1, p 37) as an example. D had placed the poison in the drink for his mother to take and he intended her to take it. After he placed the poison, she was found dead. D could not be found guilty of her murder because she had died of natural causes—he had not caused her death. Few people would think that D should escape liability in such circumstances. It is therefore necessary that the criminal law has an appropriate offence to tackle such conduct. The answer lies in the crime of attempts. White was guilty of attempting to murder his mother. The same can be said of people like Deller (1952) 36 Cr App R 184, who when selling his car to V made a statement to V, intending to deceive V. D thought his statement was false but it turned out to be true. D had not deceived V since D told the truth. He had attempted to deceive V (he would now be charged with fraud under the Fraud Act 2006).

For the rationale of a law of attempts, see section 20.7, p 564.

CHAPTER 20. ATTEMPT

20.2 Definition

The common law of attempts was abolished for all purposes by s 6 of the Criminal Attempts Act 1981. The present law of attempts to commit crime is to be found entirely in the 1981 Act. Section 1 provides:

1. Attempting to commit an offence

(1) If, with intent to commit an offence to which this section applies, a person does an act which is more than merely preparatory to the commission of the offence, he is guilty of attempting to commit the offence.

[Subsections (1A) and (1B) which relate to attempts to commit an offence under the Computer Misuse Act 1990 are omitted.]

(2) A person may be guilty of attempting to commit an offence to which this section applies even though the facts are such that the commission of the offence is impossible.

(3) In any case where:

(a) apart from this subsection a person's intention would not be regarded as having amounted to an intent to commit an offence; but

(b) if the facts of the case had been as he believed them to be, his intention would be so regarded,

then, for the purposes of subsection (1) above, he shall be regarded as having had an intent to commit that offence.

(4) This section applies to any offence which, if it were completed, would be triable in England and Wales as an indictable offence, other than:

(a) conspiracy (at common law or under section 1 of the Criminal Law Act 1977 or any other enactment);

(b) aiding, abetting, counselling, procuring or suborning the commission of an offence;

(c) offences under section 4(1) (assisting offenders) or 5(1) (accepting or agreeing to accept consideration for not disclosing information about an offence) of the Criminal Law Act 1967.

Section 1A, which extends jurisdiction to certain attempts to commit offences which, if completed, would not be triable in England and Wales, is omitted here. The method of trial of, and the penalties for, offences of attempt are provided by s 4:

4. Trial and penalties

(1) A person guilty by virtue of section 1 above of attempting to commit an offence shall:

(a) if the offence attempted is murder or any other offence the sentence for which is fixed by law, be liable on conviction on indictment to imprisonment for life; and

(b) if the offence attempted is indictable but does not fall within paragraph (a) above, be liable on conviction on indictment to any penalty to which he would have been liable on conviction on indictment of that offence; and

(c) if the offence attempted is triable either way, be liable on summary conviction to any penalty to which he would have been liable on summary conviction of that offence.

It is submitted that the most logical way of applying the law in relation to attempts is to:

(1) identify the substantive offence that it is alleged D is attempting. There is no attempt in the air—there must be an attempted offence (murder, rape, robbery, burglary, etc);

(2) identify what the elements of the actus reus of that substantive offence are (killing, having non-consensual sex, etc);

(3) assess whether D intended any consequence elements of the substantive offence and intended or was at least reckless as to the relevant circumstances elements if appropriate; and

(4) assess what acts D performed and whether they are more than merely preparatory to the commission of the substantive offence.

The first two steps relate to the elements of the substantive crime. Our analysis in this chapter therefore begins with step (3).

20.3 Mens rea

As with all inchoate offences—that is, those in which the substantive offence has not been committed—the mens rea element assumes an elevated significance because the actus reus may be something relatively innocuous, and in order to ensure that the criminal law does not extend too widely, the offence must only catch those who are truly deserving of criminal punishment. The essence of an attempt to do something is that D is trying to do it and wants it to happen. Taking *White* as an example, D's act of putting poison in V's drink was dangerous, but might have been done accidentally, or negligently, for example if the poison was stored in an old jar similar to that D used for sugar. In those circumstances, most people would agree that it would not be appropriate to convict D of attempted murder.

20.3.1 Defining intention

It will be noted that s 1(1) of the Act begins with the words, 'If, with intent to commit an offence to which this section applies . . .' In *Whybrow* (1951) 35 Cr App R 141, Lord Goddard held that in attempt, the intent is 'the principal ingredient of the crime'. The Act offers no definition of 'intent' but in *Pearman* (1984) 80 Cr App R 259, [1984] Crim LR 675, the Court of Appeal could see no reason why the Act should have altered the common law in this respect and applied *Mohan* [1975] 2 All ER 193. In this case, the Court of Appeal held that for the purposes of a criminal attempt the prosecution must prove, 'a decision to bring about, in so far as it lies within the accused's power, the commission of the offence which it is alleged the accused attempted to commit, no matter whether the accused desired that consequence of his act or not'.

20.3.2 Intention and circumstances

It is clear that, on a charge of attempt, intention is required as to any result/consequence element in the definition of the actus reus of the substantive offence even though intention as to that result is not required on a charge of committing the complete crime. In *Mohan*, it was necessary to prove that the defendant intended to cause bodily harm. The Law Commission in its most recent Report proposed to retain this rule: Law Com No 318, *Conspiracy and Attempts* (2009), para 2.46.

But there has been much controversy over the question whether, on a charge of attempt, intention is required as to a circumstance in the actus reus, where, on a charge of committing the complete crime, recklessness as to that circumstance would suffice.

For example, in criminal damage, the offence comprises elements of actus reus: causing damage (consequence) to property (circumstance) belonging to another (circumstance). The mens rea for the substantive crime requires proof of D's intention or recklessness as to the element of damage and as to the circumstances. On a charge of attempted criminal damage, it is necessary to prove that D intended the consequence (damage), but is it sufficient that he was reckless as to whether the property belonged to another (circumstances)?

The Law Commission, when drafting the report which led to the 1981 Act thought that a distinction between consequences and circumstances would be unworkable and recommended that intention should be required as to all the elements in the definition of the offence. The Criminal Attempts Act 1981 (see section 20.2, p 538) does not deal with the matter expressly. It simply requires 'intent to commit [the] offence'.

The question is therefore as to the proper construction of s 1 of the Criminal Attempts Act 1981. As this section will demonstrate, three different approaches are evident from the case law.

- There must be intention as to the consequence element(s) of the offence, but recklessness as to the circumstance elements will suffice (if that would suffice for the full offence). This was the approach taken in *Khan* [1990] 2 All ER 783.
- There must be intention as to both the consequence element(s) and the circumstance elements. This was the approach taken in *Pace and Rogers* [2014] EWCA Crim 186.
- Having regard to the element of the offence that does not occur (hence, why it is an attempt), did D act with intention as to that element? If D intended that element, he will be guilty of attempt. This was the approach taken in *A-G's Reference (No 3 of 1992)* (1994) 98 Cr App R 383. This is sometimes called the 'missing element' test.

Consider the next case where the offence was attempted rape. The substantive offence of rape requires no proof of any consequence, but does require proof of a circumstance (the lack of V's consent): does attempted rape require proof of intention as to that circumstance—that V is not consenting?

R v Khan
[1990] 1 WLR 813, Court of Appeal, Criminal Division

(Russell LJ, Rose and Morland JJ)

After a disco [a party at which people danced to popular music], a 16-year-old girl accompanied five youths in a car to a house where they were joined by other youths. Three youths succeeded in having sexual intercourse with her. Four others, the appellants, tried to do so but failed. The girl did not consent to any sexual activity. The appellants were convicted of attempted rape and appealed. It was argued that the judge had misdirected the jury by telling them that, even if a defendant did not know the girl was not consenting, he was guilty of attempted rape if he tried unsuccessfully to have sexual intercourse, being reckless whether she consented or not—that is, it was sufficient that he could not care less whether she consented or not. (At that time, D was guilty of rape if he intended to have sex with V without her consent or was reckless (did not care less) whether she consented.)

Russell LJ:

In our judgment an acceptable analysis of the offence of rape [as defined under the 1956 Act, see now the definition in s 1 of the Sexual Offences Act 2003, section 12.2.1, p 302] as is as follows: (1) the intention of the offender is to have sexual intercourse with a woman; (2) the offence is committed if, but only if, the circumstances are that (a) the woman does not consent AND (b) the defendant knows that she is not consenting or is reckless as to whether she consents.

Precisely the same analysis can be made of the offence of attempted rape: (1) the intention of the offender is to have sexual intercourse with a woman; (2) the offence is committed if, but only if, the circumstances are that (a) the woman does not consent AND (b) the defendant knows that she is not consenting or is reckless as to whether she consents.

The only difference between the two offences is that in rape sexual intercourse takes place whereas in attempted rape it does not, although there has to be some act which is more than preparatory to sexual intercourse. Considered in that way, the intent of the defendant is precisely the same in rape and in attempted rape and the mens rea is identical, namely an intention to have intercourse plus a knowledge of or recklessness as to the woman's absence of consent. No question of attempting to achieve a reckless state of mind arises; the attempt relates to the physical activity; the mental state of the defendant is the same. A man does not recklessly have sexual intercourse, nor does he recklessly attempt it. Recklessness in rape and attempted rape arises not in relation to the physical act of the accused but only in his state of mind when engaged in the activity of having or attempting to have sexual intercourse.

If this is the true analysis, as we believe it is, the attempt does not require any different intention on the part of the accused from that for the full offence of rape. We believe this to be a desirable result which in the instant case did not require the jury to be burdened with different directions as to the accused's state of mind, dependent upon whether the individual achieved or failed to achieve sexual intercourse.

We recognise, of course, that our reasoning cannot apply to all offences and all attempts. Where, for example as in causing death by reckless driving or reckless arson, no state of mind other than recklessness is involved in the offence, there can be no attempt to commit it.

In our judgment, however, the words 'with intent to commit an offence' to be found in section 1 of the Act of 1981 mean, when applied to rape, 'with intent to have sexual intercourse with a woman in circumstances where she does not consent and the defendant knows or could not care less about her absence of consent'. The only 'intent', giving that word its natural and ordinary meaning, of the rapist is to have sexual intercourse. He commits the offence because of the circumstances in which he manifests that intent, ie when the woman is not consenting and he either knows it or could not care less about the absence of consent.

Accordingly, we take the view that in relation to the four appellants the judge was right to give the directions that he did when inviting the jury to consider the charges of attempted rape.

Appeals against conviction dismissed

Thus, the court held that *recklessness* as to the circumstance of consent is a sufficient mens rea for the attempt. As a general principle, it seems that recklessness as to a circumstance element of the actus reus of the full offence will be a sufficient mens rea for attempts where recklessness as to that circumstance is a sufficient mens rea for the full offence.

The decision in *Khan* was limited to rape but it was followed in *A-G's Reference (No 3 of 1992)* (1994) 98 Cr App R 383, [1994] Crim LR 348, where the offence charged was attempted arson, being reckless whether life be endangered, contrary to s 1(2) of the Criminal Damage Act 1971. The complainants, V, maintained a night watch over their premises from a motor car. Early one morning, the respondents arrived in a vehicle containing petrol bombs and threw towards V's car a lighted petrol bomb which passed over the car and smashed against a wall. They were charged with attempted aggravated arson, the particulars alleging recklessness whether life would be endangered. The trial judge ruled that, on a charge of attempt, intent to endanger life was required; recklessness was not sufficient. That was the point of law referred by the Attorney General. Before considering the attempts problem, however, the court considered what has to be proved for the completed offences of criminal damage and aggravated criminal damage.

The court stated a general principle, which became known as the 'missing element' test:

> . . . a defendant, in order to be guilty of an attempt, must be in one of the states of mind required for the commission of the full offence, and did [*sic*] his best, so far as he could, to supply what was missing from the completion of the offence. It is the policy of the law that such people should be punished notwithstanding that in fact the intentions of such a defendant have not been fulfilled.

That was a different approach from *Khan*. More recently, in *Pace and Rogers*, the Court of Appeal adopted a third approach, holding that *Khan* was not binding and that there must be intention as to *every* element of the offence in order to be guilty of attempt.

R v Pace and Rogers
[2014] EWCA Crim 186, Court of Appeal, Criminal Division

(Davis LJ, Blake and Lewis JJ)

Thames Valley Police became suspicious that scrap metal yards were handling stolen scrap metal. To ascertain whether this was in fact the case, the police conducted a number of test purchases. This entailed officers pretending to be members of the public seeking to sell scrap metal that was of dubious origin. The metal was not in fact stolen, but was the property of Thames Valley Police. The appellants worked in a scrap metal yard and accepted the metal from the undercover police officers. They were charged with attempting to conceal, disguise or convert criminal property. The reason they were charged with an attempt was because the property was not in fact stolen. The substantive offence was contained in s 327(1)(c) of the Proceeds of Crime Act 2002. To be guilty of the complete offence, it suffices that the defendant had suspicion as to circumstances, namely that the property was the proceeds of criminal conduct. The judge ruled that the appellants could be guilty of attempting the offence in s 327(1)(c) of the Proceeds of Crime Act 2002 if they suspected that the property was the proceeds of criminal conduct. The appellants were convicted and appealed. They argued that the judge was wrong to direct the jury that they could find the appellants guilty if they suspected the metal was the proceeds of criminal conduct.

Davis LJ:

45. The parties sensibly confined their citation of authorities to us. There is a most detailed discussion of the general issues arising contained in the Law Commission's Report on Attempt, and Impossibility in relation to Attempt, Conspiracy and Incitement published in June 1980 helpfully provided to us by the parties who asked us to consider it (as we have done). The Report was, we observe, in general terms somewhat sceptical as to drawing a distinction, in the context of cases of attempt, between 'circumstances' and 'results'. At all events, it was that Report which was the precursor both to the 1981 Act and to the amendment of s.1 of the 1977 Act: albeit the Report and its proposed draft Bill was, it is to be stressed, by no means adopted in all respects in the statutory provisions resulting. In addition, and as is so often the case with topics of difficulty and interest in the criminal law, there is an excellent discussion of the general position in Smith & Hogan's *Criminal Law* (edited by Professor David Ormerod): see 13th edition [2011] at pages 405 ff.

46. A convenient starting point is this. Where the substantive criminal offence specifically requires the consequence of an act, it is well established that an attempt to commit that offence ordinarily requires proof of intent as to that consequence. To take a familiar example, the required intent for murder is either an intent to kill or an intent to cause really serious injury. The required consequence of the act is, of course, death. Accordingly, for a charge of attempted murder to be made out the intent which must be proved is an intent to kill: see *Whybrow* (1951) 35 Cr App R 141. That remains the case

since the 1981 Act. Of course, that is an offence different from the present case. But Mr Stein is at least entitled to make the point that that case is an illustration of the proposition that the mental element required to make a person guilty of an attempted offence may well be different from, and at a higher level than, that applicable to the substantive offence itself.

47. The same point can be made with regard to the case of *Mohan* (1974) 60 Cr App R 272, which also antedated the 1981 Act. In that case the accused was charged with, and convicted of, an offence of attempting, having charge of a vehicle, to cause bodily harm by wanton driving. The trial judge directed the jury that recklessness was capable of being the requisite mental element for the offence and that the prosecution was not required to prove a specific intent to commit the offence. It was argued by counsel for the prosecution on appeal that, because the substantive offence (in that case, under s.35 of the Offences Against the Person Act 1861) did not require proof of an intention on the part of the accused, proof of an attempt to commit the crime likewise did not require proof of an intention. As to that, James LJ in the course of giving the judgment of the court said (at page 274):

'The attraction of this argument is that it presents a situation in relation to attempts to commit crime which is simple and logical, for it requires in proof of the attempt no greater burden in respect of mens rea than is required in proof of the completed offence ...'

Thus, in the context of that particular case, it can be said that counsel's argument (and its attraction) in this respect mirrored that of Mr Farrell's in the present case. But the court in *Mohan* would have none of it. Applying common law principles, it held that intent was an essential ingredient of the offence of attempt. At a later stage in the judgment (at page 278) it further stated that the court 'must not strain to bring within the offence of attempt conduct which does not fall within the well-established bounds of the offence'.

48. We next turn to the decision in *Khan*, which did post-date the 1981 Act and on which Mr Farrell placed great reliance.

49. In that case a group of men set out to rape a girl. Rape under its then statutory definition (since changed by the Sexual Offences Act 2003) was defined as a man having sexual intercourse with a woman who at the time of the intercourse did not consent to the intercourse and at the time the man knew that she did not consent to the intercourse or was reckless as to whether she consented. Three of the men succeeded in having sexual intercourse with the girl without her consent but the appellants, although trying to penetrate her, did not succeed. The jury were directed that the principles of recklessness as to consent were the same in the charges of attempted rape as in the charges of rape. On appeal it was argued by the appellants, in reliance on s.1(1) of the 1981 Act, that recklessness was insufficient to constitute the mens rea of attempted rape.

50. The Court of Appeal rejected that argument. It noted a difference of opinion on the point between academic commentators (which involved Professor Glanville Williams, among others, disagreeing with Professor Griew, among others). It cited passages from the judgment of Mustill LJ in the case of *Millward* v *Vernon* [1987] Crim L.R. 393. That was a case in which it was held that the required mental element was intent, and recklessness would not suffice, where attempted criminal damage was charged. We also observe that, in *Millward* v *Vernon* it was stated that there was no reason why the statutory requirement (viz. under s.1(1) of the 1981 Act) should be 'diluted by reference to the lower standard required by the substantive offence' and that there was 'nothing anomalous' about a situation where, so far as the mental element was concerned, it was easier to prove the substantive offence than the attempt. In addition, however, the judgment in *Millward* v *Vernon* had, by way of proposed example, included in it a discussion of attempted rape. Mustill LJ had in that regard said:

'When one turns to the offence of attempted rape, one thing is obvious, that the result, namely the act of sexual intercourse, must be intended in the full sense. Also obvious is the fact that proof of an intention to have intercourse with a woman, together with an act towards that end, is not enough: the offence must involve proof of something about the woman's consent, and something about the defendant's state of mind in relation to that consent. The problem is to decide precisely what that something is. Must the prosecution prove not only that the defendant intended the act, but also that he intended it to be non-consensual? Or should the jury be directed to consider two different states of mind, intent as to the act and recklessness as to the circumstances?'

51. The court in *Khan* answered the questions so posed by favouring the second version. It held that the intent of a defendant is the same in rape and attempted rape:

'… the intent of the defendant is precisely the same in rape and attempted rape and the mens rea is identical, namely an intention to have intercourse plus a knowledge of or recklessness as to the woman's absence of consent No question of attempting to achieve a reckless state of mind arises: the attempt relates to the physical activity: the mental state of the defendant is the same.' (p.334)

52. One can see the potential support for [counsel for the Crown's] argument that *Khan* affords. He would thus seek to derive from it the proposition that, assuming the acts here were more than preparatory, in the present cases the intention here was to convert the scrap metal (the act) and the required mental state was knowledge or suspicion that the scrap metal was stolen. But the authority of *Khan* is not decisive for present purposes: and indeed, in fairness to [counsel for the Crown], he did not suggest that it was. In *Khan*, the substantive offence admitted of recklessness as the mens rea: which is not the case here. *In.* [*sic*] *Khan*, moreover, the appellants were charged with attempted rape solely because they had not succeeded in penetrating the victim, which is what they had intended to do. Had they succeeded in that act, as they had intended, the full offence of rape would have been made out. But that is not so in the present case. The two appellants here could never have been guilty of the substantive offence of converting criminal property: just because the property in question did not constitute or represent benefit from criminal conduct. Furthermore, the court in *Khan* had been careful to say (at p.35):

'We recognise, of course, that our reasoning cannot apply to all offences and all attempts. Where, for example, as in causing death by reckless driving or reckless arson, no state of mind other than recklessness is involved in the offence, there can be no attempt to commit it.'

53. We were also referred to, and [counsel for the Crown] to some extent relied on, the decision of another constitution of this court in *AG's Reference (No 3 of 1992)* (1994) 98 Cr App R 383, which adopted broadly the same approach as in *Khan*. That too was a decision in a context different from the present case. It related to attempted arson being reckless whether life be endangered, contrary to s.1(2) of the Criminal Damage Act 1971. We have to say that we found, with respect, some of the passages in the judgment somewhat elliptical, if not self-contradictory: and the judgment is in fact subject to some adverse comment in Smith & Hogan's *Criminal Law*. We do not, at all events, *think* that it materially advances the Crown's argument. It is true that, in giving the judgment of the court, Schiemann J said (somewhat tentatively, on one view) at page 390:

'One way of analysing the situation is to say that a defendant, in order to be guilty of an attempt, must be in one of the states of *mind* required for the commission of the full offence and did his best, as far as he could, to supply what was missing from the offence.'

But [counsel for the appellants] himself was in a position to seek to cull from the decision at least some support for his own argument. For at page 390 Schiemann J then went on to say this:

'If the facts are that, although the defendant has one of the appropriate states of mind required for the complete offence, but the physical element required for the commission of the complete offence is missing, the defendant is not to be convicted unless it can be shown that he intended to supply the physical elements.'

And at p.392 he likewise said:

'In order to succeed in a prosecution for attempt, it must be shown that the defendant intended to achieve that which was missing from the full offence.'

Mr Stein's submission was that the 'physical element' in the present case which was missing was conversion of criminal property: and it was the 'supply' of that which had to be shown to be intended.

...

60. Against that citation of authority we turn to the disposal of these two appeals.

61. The starting point has to be s.1(1) of the 1981 Act: indeed, as [counsel for the appellants] pointed out, it is by reference to that statutory provision that the Statement of Offence in the indictment is framed. [Counsel for the Crown] did at one stage of his argument, if we understood it aright, suggest that s.1(3) of the 1981 Act of itself provided a complete answer in favour of the Crown. But that cannot be right. That subsection only applies where 'the facts of the case' had been as the accused had *believed* them to be. But in the present proceedings the Crown's case had been put not on the basis of belief but on the basis of suspicion. Accordingly, one has to revert to s.1(1). That said, we would at least agree with [counsel for the Crown's] acceptance that the 'intention' referred to in s.1(3) must be the same as the intention referred to in s.1(l): that is to say, an intent to commit the offence.

62. Turning, then, to s.1(1) we consider that, as a matter of ordinary language and in accordance with principle, an 'intent to commit an offence' connotes an intent to commit all the elements of the offence. We can see no sufficient basis, whether linguistic or purposive, for construing it otherwise.

63. Once that is appreciated, the fault line in the Crown's argument is revealed. A constituent element of the offence of converting criminal property is, as we have said, that the property in question *is* criminal property. That is an essential part of the offence. Accordingly, an intent to commit the offence involves, in the present case, an intent to convert criminal property: and that connotes an intent that the property should *be* criminal property. But the Crown's argument glosses over that. Its argument connotes that the property in question which it is intended to be converted is *property* known or suspected to constitute or represent benefit from criminal conduct. It ignores the requirement for the substantive offence that the property concerned must be *criminal property* (as defined). The Crown, in effect, thus seeks to make it a criminal offence to intend to convert property suspecting, if not knowing, that it is stolen. But that is not what s.327, read with s.340(3), provides.

64. Reflecting this difficulty in the Crown's argument, there is this further point to be made. For the purpose of the substantive offence, a person may in point of fact convert property intending and believing that it is criminal property: yet he will not be guilty of the substantive offence if, in fact, it is not criminal property *(Montila)*. It is most odd that, on the Crown's case, such a person who cannot on such a scenario be liable for the substantive offence can nevertheless be made liable, where his state of mind is one of suspicion only, if what is charged is, instead, an attempt to commit the offence. We have the greatest difficulty in seeing that the provisions of s.1 of the 1981 Act were designed to bring about such a result.

Convictions quashed

Despite the Court of Appeal in *Khan* accepting that D being reckless as to the circumstance elements in the crime suffices for him to be guilty of an attempt, the court in *Pace and Rogers* held that nothing less than intention will suffice. The judgment in *Pace and Rogers* has been subject to cogent academic criticism:

(1) Findlay Stark argues that the Court of Appeal was wrong to cast doubt upon whether the approach adopted in *Khan* applies to impossible attempts cases. Stark argues that the court failed to have regard to s 1(3)(b) of the Criminal Attempts Act 1981, which provides that the court should assume that facts DD *believed* to exist

actually existed and therefore provides the mens rea in impossible attempts cases. Therefore, although the court was correct to quash the appellants' convictions, because they merely suspected that the metal was stolen rather than believing it was stolen, it should not have cast doubt upon *Khan*. See F. Stark, 'The Mens Rea of a Criminal Attempt' [2014] 3 Arch Rev 7.

(2) Graham Virgo argues that the judgment ought to be treated as *per incuriam* and therefore ignored on the basis that the court failed to apply s 1(3)(b) of the Criminal Attempts Act 1981. Virgo argues that the Court of Appeal has 'destabilised' the offence. See G. Virgo, 'Criminal Attempts—The Law of Unintended Circumstances' (2014) 73 CLJ 244.

(3) Finally, Matthew Dyson argues that, whilst the Court of Appeal's interpretation of s 1(1) is plausible, there are policy reasons for why it should not be followed. For example, in order to convict someone of attempted rape, Dyson argues it must be proven that D intended for the victim not to consent. This, however, would be almost impossible to prove. See M. Dyson, 'Scrapping *Khan*' [2014] Crim LR 445.

The decision does, however, have its supporters. See, for example, J. Child and A. Hunt, '*Pace and Rogers* and the Mens Rea of a Criminal Attempt: *Khan* on the Scrapheap' (2014) 78 J Crim L 220; P. Mirfield, 'Intention and Criminal Attempts' [2015] Crim LR 140; A. Simester, 'The Mens Rea of Criminal Attempts' (2015) 131 LQR 169.

There is disagreement as to whether *Pace and Rogers* now represents the law and *Khan* should be treated as being overruled. Strictly speaking, the Court of Appeal cannot overrule itself, so the decisions are equally authoritative. One way to reconcile the decisions is to say that the decision in *Khan* represents the approach that ought to be taken in cases involving attempted rape and *Pace and Rogers* represents the approach that ought to be taken in cases involving attempting the offence in s 327(1)(c) of the Proceeds of Crime Act 2002. In a prosecution for any other offence the court would be free to choose between the approaches. This is only one view, however. For that reason, in a problem question it would be sensible to apply the approaches set out in *Khan, Pace and Rogers* and *A-G's Reference (No 3 of 1992)* and evaluate whether the defendant is guilty.

≋ *Question*
Which approach ought the Supreme Court to take should the opportunity arise?

20.4 Actus reus

The actus reus of attempt cannot be defined with the same precision as the actus reus of a substantive offence. It can take as many forms as there are substantive offences. It may, moreover, be an objectively innocent act. D puts sugar in V's tea. There is nothing wrong with that—V likes sweet tea. But D believes, mistakenly, that the sugar is arsenic and intends to kill V. He is guilty of attempted murder, the actus reus of the attempt being that objectively innocent act. With *Deller* (see section 20.1), the actus reus was telling the truth!

It will be recalled that Lord Goddard in *Whybrow*, section 20.3.1, p 539, described the intent as the principal ingredient of the offence of attempt. It is not, however, the only ingredient. Something must be done to put the intent into execution. The question is, how much? The law has always distinguished mere acts of preparation from attempts. It was said at common law that the act had to be sufficiently proximate to the complete offence. The doctrine of proximity excluded from liability acts which some thought should entail guilt. The 1981

Act (see section 20.2, p 538), following the recommendations of the Law Commission, makes no attempt to state a test of proximity. It merely requires that the act done by the defendant should be 'more than merely preparatory to the commission of the offence'.

R. A. Duff, *Criminal Attempts* (1996), p 386 observes:

What relates an agent's conduct to the commission of an offence is partly her intention to commit that offence, but it also matters how close she has come to fully actualizing that intent. The conduct of someone who has so far only reconnoitered a building from which he plans to steal, for example, or only obtained a poison with which he intends to kill someone, is still 'remote' from the commission of theft (or burglary) or murder. We could not yet count her actions as essentially larcenous or murderous, or as attacks on property or life; there is still too wide a gap between what she has actually done and the commission, of the intended offence.

This is not to say that we should see her conduct simply as, for instance, 'walking round a building', or 'buying arsenic', which are indeed remote from the commission of the theft or murder that she intends to commit; we understand it, and respond to it, as by her intention, and her commission of the crime has so far only a shadowy existence in the public world: it exists in thought (in her intention), but has yet to acquire any very concrete existence in her actions. As her criminal enterprise advances, and her criminal intention is further actualized in action, her prospective commission of the crime becomes less shadowy, more concrete as an active engagement in the world. Her actions connect her more closely to the commission of the crime, and in the end that crime becomes something she is doing, rather than merely something she is intending or preparing to do.

Why should this matter? Why should we demand not merely conduct undertaken with intent to commit an offence (and perhaps corroborative of that intent), but conduct which comes close to the actual commission of the offence? An initial answer is that the law should leave intending criminals a *locus poenitentiae*: the chance to decide for themselves to abandon their criminal enterprises. This matters, because the law should treat and address its citizens as responsible agents. The central value to which this answer appeals is that of individual freedom to determine one's own actions.

≈ *Questions*

Should it be necessary to prove that:

(1) D had performed the last act short of committing the full offence (crooking the finger round the trigger of the gun and aiming before pulling the trigger)?

(2) D had commenced the final stages of the conduct necessary to complete the commission of the full offence (set out armed on his way to the place where the assassination of V would take place)?

The only well-settled rule of common law was that if D had done the last act which, as he knew, was necessary to achieve the consequence alleged to be attempted, he was guilty. Every act preceding the last one might quite properly be described as 'preparatory'. The assassin crooks his finger round the trigger *preparatory* to pulling it. If every preparatory act were to be regarded as outside the scope of the offence, the effect of the Act would be to narrow the scope of the offence beyond that of the common law position. It was well recognized at common law that some prior acts were sufficiently proximate. Though it has been argued that the word 'merely' does no more than add emphasis (E. Griew, annotations to *Current Law Statutes Annotations* (1981)), it seems that it has a key role. In *Tosti* [1997] Crim LR 746, it was held that the appellant 'had committed acts which were preparatory, but not merely so'. Therefore, not all preparatory acts are excluded; only those that are *merely* preparatory; and it is thought that the assassin's crooking of the finger, though preparatory, would not be regarded as *merely* preparatory.

The reason, it appears, is that he is now engaged in the commission of the offence—as Rowlatt J put it in *Osborn* (1919) 84 JP 63, he is 'on the job'.

Whether the act is more than merely preparatory is a question of fact: s 4(4). In a jury trial it is for the judge to decide whether there is sufficient evidence to support such a finding. In *A-G's Reference (No 1 of 1992)* [1993] 2 All ER 190, [1993] Crim LR 274, the point of law referred was 'Whether, on a charge of attempted rape, it is incumbent on the prosecution, as a matter of law, to prove that the defendant physically attempted to penetrate the woman's vagina with his penis.' The court answered 'no'. It is sufficient that there is evidence of intent to rape and of acts which a jury could properly regard as more than merely preparatory to the commission of the offence—for example, in that case, the respondent's acts of dragging V up some steps, lowering his trousers and interfering with her private parts. (Note that under s 1 of the Sexual Offences Act 2003 the offence is extended to include penile penetration of the vagina, anus or mouth of the complainant.)

〰️ Questions

As rape consists in the physical penetration of a person's vagina, anus or mouth by a man's penis, how can there be an attempt to commit rape if there is no attempt by the man to penetrate an orifice? Is it not a contradiction in terms to say:

(1) he did not attempt to penetrate her, but

(2) he did attempt to rape her?

To take an analogous case, can there be an attempt to commit murder if there is no attempt to kill? Can we properly say:

(1) D did not attempt to kill V, but

(2) he did attempt to murder him?

Is the solution for the courts to give the word 'attempt' a particular meaning for the purposes of the Criminal Attempts Act so that it captures conduct which would not be considered an attempt in the ordinary meaning of the word? Or is it that the ordinary meaning is wider than the court appears to allow? For example, *was* the defendant, lowering his trousers and interfering with V's private parts with intent to penetrate her, 'attempting' to do so in the ordinary meaning of the word? Cf commentary [1993] Crim LR 276.

The Court of Appeal has considered what is meant by 'more than merely preparatory' in numerous cases, but it is difficult to discern how the court determines whether this requirement was made out on the facts of each case. Clarkson argues that most of the cases can be explained on the basis that there is only an attempt if there has been a 'confrontation' between D and the victim, be it an actual person or property. See C. Clarkson, 'Attempt: The Conduct Requirement' (2009) 29 OJLS 25. Examine the following cases and consider the extent to which Clarkson's attempt at (partially) rationalizing the case law is successful.

R v Gullefer

[1990] 1 WLR 1063, Court of Appeal, Criminal Division

(Lord Lane CJ, Kennedy and Owen JJ)

Gullefer jumped on to the track at a greyhound-racing stadium and waved his arms in order to distract the dogs during the running of a race. He later admitted that he hoped that the stewards would declare 'no race' so that he would recover from a bookmaker the stake he had placed on a dog that was losing in the race. He was convicted of attempted theft of his stake from the bookmaker under s 1(1) of the Criminal Attempts Act 1981 and appealed to the Court of Appeal.

[Lord Lane CJ, having cited ss 1(1) and 4(3) of the 1981 Act:]

Thus the judge's task is to decide whether there is evidence upon which a jury could reasonably come to the conclusion that the appellant had gone beyond the realm of mere preparation and had embarked upon the actual commission of the offence. If not, he must withdraw the case from the jury. If there is such evidence, it is then for the jury to decide whether the defendant did in fact go beyond mere preparation. That is the way in which the judge approached this case. He ruled that there was sufficient evidence. [Counsel for the appellant] submits that he was wrong in so ruling.

The first task of the court is to apply the words of the Act of 1981 to the facts of the case. Was the appellant still in the stage of preparation to commit the substantive offence, or was there a basis of fact which would entitle the jury to say that he had embarked on the theft itself? Might it properly be said that when he jumped on to the track he was trying to steal £18 from the bookmaker?

Our view is that it could not properly be said that at that stage he was in the process of committing theft. What he was doing was jumping on to the track in an effort to distract the dogs, which in its turn, he hoped, would have the effect of forcing the stewards to declare 'no race', which would in its turn give him the opportunity to go back to the bookmaker and demand the £18 he had staked. In our view there was insufficient evidence for it to be said that he had, when he jumped onto the track, gone beyond mere preparation.

So far at least as the present case is concerned, we do not think that it is necessary to examine the authorities which preceded the Act of 1981, save to say that the sections we have already quoted in this judgment seem to be a blend of various decisions, some of which were not easy to reconcile with others.

However, in deference to the arguments of counsel, we venture to make the following observations. Since the passing of the Act of 1981, a division of this court in *Reg v Ilyas* (1983) 78 Cr App R 17 has helpfully collated the authorities. As appears from the judgment in that case, there seem to have been two lines of authority. The first was exemplified by the decision in *Reg v Eagleton* (1854) Dears C.C. 515. That was a case where the defendant was alleged to have attempted to obtain money from the guardians of a parish by falsely pretending to the relieving officer that he had delivered loaves of bread of the proper weight to the outdoor poor, when in fact the loaves were deficient in weight.

Park[e] B, delivering the judgment of the court of nine judges, said:

'Acts remotely leading towards the commission of the offence are not to be considered as attempts to commit it, but acts immediately connected with it are; and if, in this case, after the credit with the relieving officer for the fraudulent overcharge, any *further step* on the part of the defendant had been necessary to obtain payment, as the making out a further account or producing the vouchers to the Board, we should have thought that the obtaining credit in account with the relieving officer would not have been sufficiently proximate to the obtaining the money. But, on the statement in this case, no other act on the part of the defendant would have been required. It was the last act, *depending on himself*, towards the payment of the money, and therefore it ought to be considered as an attempt.' (Parke B's emphasis.)

Lord Diplock in *Director of Public Prosecutions v Stonehouse* [1978] A.C. 55, 68, having cited part of that passage from *Reg v Eagleton* (1855), added: 'In other words the offender must have crossed the Rubicon and burnt his boats.'

The other line of authority is based on a passage in *Stephen's Digest of the Criminal Law*, 5th ed. (1894), art 50:

'An attempt to commit a crime is an act done with intent to commit that crime, and forming part of a series of acts which would constitute its actual commission if it were not interrupted.'

As Lord Edmund-Davies points out in *Director of Public Prosecutions v Stonehouse* at p85, that definition has been repeatedly cited with judicial approval: see Byrne J in *Hope v Brown* [1954] 1 WLR 250,

253 and Lord Parker C.J. in *Davey v Lee* [1968] 1 Q.B. 366. However, as Lord Parker C.J. in the latter case points out, *Stephen's* definition falls short of defining the exact point of time at which the series of acts can be said to begin.

It seems to us that the words of the Act of 1981 seek to steer a midway course. They do not provide, as they might have done, that the *Reg v Eagleton* test is to be followed, or that, as Lord Diplock suggested, the defendant must have reached a point from which it was impossible for him to retreat before the actus reus of an attempt is proved. On the other hand the words give perhaps as clear a guidance as is possible in the circumstances on the point of time at which *Stephen's* 'series of acts' begin. It begins when the merely preparatory acts come to an end and the defendant embarks upon the crime proper. When that is will depend of course upon the facts in any particular case.

Appeal allowed

R v Jones (Kenneth)

[1990] 1 WLR 1057, Court of Appeal, Criminal Division

(Taylor LJ, Mars-Jones and Waite JJ)

Jones got into a car driven by his ex-mistress's new lover, Foreman. Jones was wearing overalls and a crash helmet with the visor down and carrying a bag containing a loaded sawn-off shotgun. He had bought the gun and sawn off the barrel a few days earlier. Jones pointed the gun at Foreman at a range of 10 to 12 inches and said, 'You are not going to like this', or similar words. Foreman grabbed the end of the gun and, after a struggle, escaped unharmed. The safety catch on the gun was on and it was unclear whether Jones's finger was ever on the trigger. Jones was charged with attempted murder. It was submitted that there was no case to go to the jury because Jones had at least three acts to do before murder could be committed—(a) to remove the safety catch, (b) to put his finger on the trigger, and (c) to pull it. The judge rejected the submission, the jury convicted of attempted murder and Jones appealed to the Court of Appeal on the ground that the case should have been withdrawn.

[**Taylor LJ**, having cited the last paragraph of the extract from Lord Lane CJ's judgment in *Gullefer*, in the previous extract:]

We respectfully adopt those words. We do not accept counsel's contention that section 1(1) of the Act of 1981 in effect embodies the 'last act' test derived from *Reg v Eagleton*. Had Parliament intended to adopt that test, a quite different form of words could and would have been used.

It is of interest to note that the Act of 1981 followed a report from the Law Commission on *Attempt, and Impossibility in Relation to Attempt, Conspiracy and Incitement* (1980) (Law Com No 102). At paragraph 2.47 the report states:

'The definition of sufficient proximity must be wide enough to cover two varieties of cases; first, those in which a person has taken all the steps towards the commission of a crime which he believes to be necessary as far as he is concerned for that crime to result, such as firing a gun at another and missing. Normally such cases cause no difficulty. Secondly, however, the definition must cover those instances where a person has to take some further step to complete the crime, assuming that there is evidence of the necessary mental element on his part to commit it; for example, when the defendant has raised the gun to take aim at another but has not yet squeezed the trigger. We have reached the conclusion that, in regard to these cases, it is undesirable to recommend anything more complex than a rationalization of the present law.'

In paragraph 2.48 the report states:

'The literal meaning of "proximate" is "nearest, next before or after (in place, order, time, connection of thought, causation, etc)". Thus, were this term part of a statutory description of the actus reus of attempt, it would clearly be capable of being interpreted to exclude all but the "final act"; this would not be in accordance with the policy outlined above.'

Clearly, the draftsman of section 1(1) must be taken to have been aware of the two lines of earlier authority and of the Law Commission's report. The words 'an act which is more than merely preparatory to the commission of the offence' would be inapt if they were intended to mean 'the last act which lay in his power towards the commission of the offence'.

Looking at the plain natural meaning of section 1(1) in the way indicated by the Lord [Lane] Chief Justice, the question for the judge in the present case was whether there was evidence from which a reasonable jury, properly directed, could conclude that the appellant had done acts which were more than merely preparatory. Clearly his actions in obtaining the gun, in shortening it, in loading it, in putting on his disguise and in going to the school could only be regarded as preparatory acts. But, in our judgment, once he had got into the car, taken out the loaded gun and pointed it at the victim with the intention of killing him there was sufficient evidence for the consideration of the jury on the charge of attempted murder. It was a matter for them to decide whether they were sure that those acts were more than merely preparatory. In our judgment, therefore, the judge was right to allow the case to go to the jury, and the appeal against conviction must be dismissed . . .

Appeal dismissed

~~~ *Questions*

In *Jones*, there was an attempt although Jones may have had as many as three more acts to do. How many acts did Gullefer still have to do? Is it helpful to count the acts to be done? Or are *time* and *place* more important? Is it significant that Jones (a) was in the place where the crime was to be committed (see also *Campbell* (1990) 93 Cr App R 350, later in this section) and (b) would have committed it within seconds if the victim had not escaped?

In *Boyle and Boyle* (1986) 84 Cr App R 270, [1987] Crim LR 111, CA, persons who damaged a house door with a view to entering premises were held to have done an act more than merely preparatory to burglary. The court said that in deciding whether an act is more than merely preparatory it was entitled to look at the law before 1981. Was the court right?

In *Campbell* (1990) 93 Cr App R 350, [1991] Crim LR 268, C was arrested within a yard of the door of a post office. He was wearing a crash helmet and gloves and carrying an imitation gun and a threatening note. He admitted that he intended to use the note to frighten the person behind the counter in the post office to hand over money. He claimed he had changed his mind and decided not to carry out the robbery but was arrested before he could leave. His conviction for attempted robbery was quashed: a number of acts remained undone and he had not even gained entry to the place where he could be in a position to perform an act which could properly be said to be an attempt. He was convicted of the offence of carrying an imitation firearm.

~~~ *Questions*

How should the police deal with a man whom they believe to be armed and about to enter and rob a post office? Should they arrest him on the ground that he is, or they have reasonable ground for suspecting that he is, about to commit an offence? Or should they wait until he demands money at the counter of the post office, so that they are sure he has committed attempted robbery?

In *Geddes* [1996] Crim LR 894, D was found in the boys' toilet of a school, equipped in such a way as to suggest strongly that his purpose was kidnapping. His conviction for attempted false imprisonment was quashed. Even clear evidence of what D had in mind 'did not throw light on whether he had begun to carry out the commission of the offence'. The offence would now be one of trespass with intent to commit a sex offence contrary to s 63 of the Sexual Offences Act 2003. *Tosti* [1997] Crim LR 746, where the accused were examining a door to decide how best to break in, was held to fall on the other side of the line: there was sufficient evidence of attempted burglary—that is, of an attempt to enter. In *Bowles and Bowles* [2004] EWCA Crim 1608, the Court of Appeal held that there was no case to answer in respect of a count of attempting to make a false instrument (a last will and testament) with intent, where DDs' acts of drafting the document and placing it in a drawer for safekeeping were no more than preparatory acts within s 1(1) of the Criminal Attempts Act 1981.

In *Mason v DPP* [2009] EWHC 2198 (Admin), D was convicted of attempting to drive while over the limit. D opened the door of his car with the key in his hand, intending to drive off, but was robbed of his keys before he could get into the car. D argued that this was merely a preparatory act and so he was not guilty of attempting to drive while over the limit. The Divisional Court agreed and stated that this case was similar to *Campbell*. It was held that D could not be regarded as embarking on the 'crime proper' until he did something which was part of the actual process of putting the car in motion. Turning on the engine would be such a step, but simply opening the car door was held to be insufficient. In another case involving an attempt to commit a road traffic offence, *Moore v DPP* [2010] EWHC 1822 (Admin), Toulson LJ observed that the law relating to attempts is 'not satisfactory'. His lordship emphasized that the fact an act is preparatory does not mean it cannot constitute an attempt. The act in question must be *merely* preparatory. His lordship went on to question whether use of the phrase 'on the job' is helpful given that it does not elucidate when the 'job' begins. A better exposition of what is meant by 'more than merely preparatory' was said to be the following paragraph taken from the Law Commission's most recent consultation paper (No 183 (2007)).

> To elaborate further, preparatory conduct by D which is sufficiently close to the final act to be properly regarded as part of the execution of D's plan can be an attempt . . . In other words, it covers the steps immediately preceding the final act necessary to effect D's plan and bring about the commission of the intended offence.

As has already been pointed out, it is difficult to discern from the case law what test ought to be applied in order to determine whether what D has done is more than merely preparatory to the commission of the substantive offence. This can lead to cases the outcomes of which are hard to reconcile with each other. For example, in *Ferriter* [2012] EWCA Crim 2211, D was charged with attempted rape. D had been in a bar drinking all night and was the last customer present before it closed. V was the barmaid who was waiting for D to finish his drink so that she could lock up. D went behind the bar to where V was standing and confronted her face to face. A struggle ensued during which V ended up on the floor with D on top of her. It was V's evidence that he attempted to pull down her trousers a number of times. V eventually managed to break free and ran for help. D was charged and convicted of attempted rape. On appeal, D's contention was that there was insufficient evidence from which the jury could have been sure that he intended to commit rape. The Court of Appeal agreed and quashed his conviction. However, the court went on to find that D undoubtedly had a sexual motive and so substituted a conviction for sexual assault. D's actions had gone beyond mere preparation and into the commission of that substantive offence. Hughes LJ asked rhetorically 'was there any evidence or activity which was capable of justifying the conclusion which pointed to an intent to commit rape rather than, for example, an intent to molest her sexually under her clothes in some other way' and concluded not.

In *Bryan* [2015] EWCA Crim 548, B was convicted of attempted rape and outraging public decency. He had seen V asleep on a night bus in London and had taken photos up her skirt while she slept (outraging public decency). He then befriended her when she woke and realized she had missed her stop. He took V to a secluded area of a park and knocked her to the floor and lay on top of her. V struggled and called police. B fled. At no point did he touch her genitals nor had V seen his penis. B was charged with attempted rape. The only interference with V, taken at its highest, was B's hand on her thigh and possibly an attempt to rip her tights at the crotch. There was no evidence he was seeking to remove his clothes or seeking to release his penis. The judge concluded that whilst there was no single feature of the evidence which, taken in isolation, signified or signalled the relevant intent to rape, taking the evidence in the round and looking at the totality of the facts, there was evidence from which a jury could be sure there was an intention to rape. The Court of Appeal upheld the conviction. The court distinguished *Ferriter*. In *Bryan*, the court doubts the value of *Ferriter*.

We should add that we respectfully wonder how helpful the approach suggested in *Ferriter* is. Evidence of an intent to rape will necessarily constitute evidence of some lesser sexual offence. The relevant question is not whether there is any particular piece of evidence which is consistent with the more serious offence of rape but not with a lesser sexual offence. The evidence will often be consistent with both offences. The only question for the judge in the *Galbraith* [1981] 1 WLR 1039 submission is whether the evidence taken at its highest is capable of sustaining a conviction for the offence charged. In answering that essentially straightforward question we think it is an unnecessary, unhelpful and a potentially confusing distraction to focus on distinctions which may be drawn between the evidence necessary to sustain an intent to rape and the evidence necessary to sustain some lesser sexual offence.

But surely not every case in which there is intent to sexually assault is an attempted rape? Attempted rape requires proof of acts more than preparatory to penile penetration.

In *Dagnall* [2003] EWCA Crim 2441, D had been convicted of attempted rape. D and V were waiting at a bus stop. D began to talk to V in a way she found uncomfortable, so she walked to another bus stop. D followed V, walked up beside her and told her that he wanted to 'fuck her'. D told V that he would take her to a dark road where he would remove her trousers. V told D that this was not going to happen and she ran off. However, D grabbed V by the hair and pulled her towards him before pushing her up against a fence, declaring his intention to rape her if she would not have intercourse with him willingly. The ordeal then came to an end when a police car arrived. The Court of Appeal upheld D's conviction as his acts had been more than merely preparatory to the commission of rape. Latham LJ stated that 'In what [D] did he had virtually succeeded in achieving all that he needed. He had overcome [V's] resistance and it was only, it would appear, the arrival of the police car that prevented the ultimate offence from taking place.' This was because D had indicated to V that his intention was to rape her and he had seized her by force.

~~~ *Questions*
(1) Should Dagnall's conviction for attempted rape have been upheld? What test was the court applying to determine whether his actions were more than merely preparatory? Could it be said that the court was swayed more by D's declared intention than what he actually did? If the actus reus of rape is penile penetration of the vagina, anus or mouth

and V's lack of consent, should more not have been necessary before D was found guilty of attempted rape?

(2) Should Ferriter's conviction for attempted rape have been substituted for one of sexual assault? Are the facts of *Ferriter* and *Dagnall* sufficiently distinguishable to justify the different outcomes?

Fletcher (G. Fletcher, *Rethinking Criminal Law* (1978)) breaks down the rationales for criminalizing attempts into objectivist and subjectivist theories. This has implications for what the actus reus of attempts ought to be. Adopting an objectivist approach, D, by intending to commit the crime and committing acts closely connected to it, has crossed a moral threshold. There is thus a similarity between D's moral culpability in having attempted to commit the crime and the moral culpability that would attach if D had succeeded in committing it. D's actions must evince an unequivocal commitment to bringing about the substantive offence. The corollary of this is that the actus reus of an attempt will not be made out until D has come close to committing the offence. In contrast, a subjectivist approach focuses on D's state of mind. All that is required to make D guilty of an attempt on this approach is some action that corroborates D's intention to commit the substantive offence. This means that the law can intervene much earlier than the objectivist approach would permit. The actus reus of an attempt is thus made out much earlier in time.

≈ *Question*

Do the cases examined above evince the adoption by courts in England of an objectivist or subjectivist approach, or an ad hoc mixture of both?

20.4.1 Omission

It is generally thought that s 1(1) of the Criminal Attempts Act 1981, section 20.2, p 538 ('does an act'), rules out attempts by omission, although it was in fact the intention of the Government that in some cases attempt by omission should be an offence.

In *Nevard* [2006] EWCA Crim 2896, D seriously injured his wife by striking her with an axe and a knife. He then forced her to abandon her attempt to dial 999 to call for assistance. The emergency services rang back on the number she had used, but D took the call and told them that his grandchildren must have been fooling around with the phone. The police remained suspicious so attended the scene and found D's wife, whose injuries were not fatal. D was charged with wounding with intent and with attempted murder. He pleaded guilty to the wounding. The jury asked:

Can you clarify whether an attempt to withhold care/emergency services constitutes attempted murder, knowing he has pleaded guilty to wounding with intent?

The trial judge's answer was:

The Crown's case is that he struck the blows with the axe or the axe handle. When that did not work he went and got a knife and stabbed her with that kitchen knife . . . and also that he slashed her arms with a Stanley knife and that when he did those acts, his intention was that she should die. Now, where the withholding of the emergency services may help you is as to what his intention was. . . . In other words, by seeing what he did after the event you may get an insight as to what his intention was.

The judge instructed the jury to regard D's conduct in preventing the emergency services as an element of the overall evidence of D's intention to kill. The Court of Appeal upheld the conviction, but suggested that the judge should have made explicit to the jury that attempting to divert the emergency services could not in itself constitute attempted murder.

> ≋ **Question**
> Was not D's conduct in taking the return call and lying to the emergency services a sufficient 'act'?

20.4.2 Abetting an attempt is an offence, but attempting to abet is not

Section 1(4)(b) of the Criminal Attempts Act is unsatisfactorily worded. As interpreted in *Dunnington* [1984] QB 472 it provides that attempting to commit a crime is itself a crime, so it can be aided and abetted like any other crime; but aiding and abetting is not, as such, an offence, so there can be no attempt to 'commit' it. Bohlander argues that the enactment of the Serious Crime Act 2007 means that this section ought to have been repealed. He argues that under s 44 of the 2007 Act, D can intentionally do an act that would otherwise fall within the ambit of s 1(4)(b). To address this paradox, Bohlander proposes two options. Either the principle that the more recent law implicitly repeals a previous law that regulates the same matter (the *lex posterior* principle) ought to apply, or the legislature expressly repeals or amends s 1(4)(b) to bring it in line with the Serious Crime Act 2007. He prefers the latter option. See M. Bohlander, 'The Conflict Between the Serious Crime Act 2007 and Section 1(4) (b) Criminal Attempts Act 1981—A Missed Repeal?' [2010] Crim LR 483. For the contrary view, see J. Child, 'The Differences Between Attempted Complicity and Inchoate Assisting and Encouraging—A Reply to Professor Bohlander' [2010] Crim LR 924.

20.5 Impossibility and attempts

In attempts we are not concerned with whether the substantive offence has occurred. This leads to some challenging questions: for example, does the English law of attempt criminalize the person who takes his own umbrella believing it is that of another person? The House of Lords addressed this issue in two cases. In the earlier case, *Anderton v Ryan* [1985] AC 560, the House of Lords held that the impossibility of committing the substantive offence was a defence to a charge of attempting to commit it. In that case, there could be no attempt to handle stolen goods if the goods D intended to handle were not in fact stolen. The view was heavily criticized by Glanville Williams. See G. Williams, 'The Lords and Impossible Attempts, or *Quis Custodiet Ipsos Custodes*?' (1986) 45 CLJ 33. The House of Lords soon changed its mind in the following case.

R v Shivpuri
[1986] UKHL 2, House of Lords

(Lord Hailsham LC, Lords Elwyn-Jones, Scarman, Bridge and Mackay)

S was arrested by customs officials while in possession of a suitcase. He admitted that he knew that it contained prohibited drugs. Analysis showed that the material in the suitcase was not a prohibited drug but vegetable matter akin to snuff. S was convicted under s 1(1) of the Criminal Attempts Act 1981 (section 14.2, p 391), of attempting to commit the offence of being knowingly concerned in dealing with and harbouring prohibited drugs contrary to s 170(1)(b) of the Customs and Excise Management Act 1979. He appealed on the ground that because the substance was not a prohibited drug he had not done an act which was 'more than merely preparatory to the commission of the offence' as required by the 1981 Act. The Court of Appeal dismissed his appeal.

[Lord Bridge, having cited s 1 of the Criminal Attempts Act 1981 (section 20.2, p 538), continued:]

Applying this language to the facts of the case, the first question to be asked is whether the appellant intended to commit the offences of being knowingly concerned in dealing with and harbouring drugs of class A or class B with intent to evade the prohibition on their importation. Translated into more homely language the question may be rephrased, without in any way altering its legal significance, in the following terms: did the appellant intend to receive and store (harbour) and in due course pass on to third parties (deal with) packages of heroin or cannabis which he knew had been smuggled into England from India? The answer is plainly Yes, he did. Next, did he, in relation to each offence, do an act which was more than merely preparatory to the commission of the offence? The act relied on in relation to harbouring was the receipt and retention of the packages found in the lining of the suitcase. The act relied on in relation to dealing was the meeting at Southall station with the intended recipient of one of the packages. In each case the act was clearly more than preparatory to the commission of the intended offence; it was not and could not be more than merely preparatory to the commission of the actual offence, because the facts were such that the commission of the actual offence was impossible. Here then is the nub of the matter. Does the 'act which is more than merely preparatory to the commission of the offence' in s 1(1) of the 1981 Act (the *actus reus* of the statutory offence of attempt) require any more than an act which is more than merely preparatory to the commission of the offence which the defendant intended to commit? Section 1(2) must surely indicate a negative answer; if it were otherwise, whenever the facts were such that the commission of the actual offence was impossible, it would be impossible to prove an act more than merely preparatory to the commission of that offence and sub-ss (1) and (2) would contradict each other.

This very simple, perhaps over-simple, analysis leads me to the provisional conclusion that the appellant was rightly convicted of the two offences of attempt with which he was charged. But can this conclusion stand with *Anderton v Ryan*? The appellant in that case was charged with an attempt to handle stolen goods. She bought a video recorder believing it to be stolen. On the facts as they were to be assumed it was not stolen. By a majority the House decided that she was entitled to be acquitted. I have re-examined the case with care. If I could extract from the speech of Lord Roskill or from my own speech a clear and coherent principle distinguishing those cases of attempting the impossible which amount to offences under the statute from those which do not, I should have to consider carefully on which side of the line the instant case fell. But I have to confess that I can find no such principle.

Running through Lord Roskill's speech and my own in *Anderton v Ryan* is the concept of 'objectively innocent' acts which, in my speech certainly, are contrasted with 'guilty acts'. A few citations will make this clear. Lord Roskill said ([1985] 2 All ER 355 at 364, [1985] AC 560 at 580):

'My Lords, it has been strenuously and ably argued for the respondent that these provisions involved that a defendant is liable to conviction for an attempt even where his actions are innocent but he erroneously believes facts which, if true, would make those actions criminal, and further, that he is liable to such a conviction whether or not in the event his intended course of action is completed.'

He proceeded to reject the argument. I referred to the appellant's purchase of the video recorder and said ([1985] 2 All ER 355 at 366, [1985] AC 560 at 582): 'Objectively considered, therefore, her purchase of the recorder was a perfectly proper commercial transaction.'

A further passage from my speech stated ([1985] 2 All ER 355 at 366, [1985] AC 560 at 582–583):

'The question may be stated in abstract terms as follows. Does s 1 of the 1981 Act create a new offence of attempt where a person embarks on and completes a course of conduct, which is objectively innocent, solely on the ground that the person mistakenly believes facts which, if true, would make that course of conduct a complete crime? If the question must be answered affirmatively it requires convictions in a number of surprising cases: the classic case, put by Bramwell B in *R v Collins* (1864) 9 Cox CC 497 at 498, of the man who takes away his own umbrella from a stand, believing it not to be his own and with intent to steal it; the case of the man who has consensual intercourse with a girl over 16 believing her to be under that age; the case of the art dealer who sells a picture which he represents to be and which is in fact a genuine Picasso, but which the dealer mistakenly believes to be a fake. The common feature of all these cases, including that under appeal, is that the mind alone is guilty, the act is innocent.'

I then contrasted the case of the man who attempts to pick the empty pocket, saying ([1985] 2 All ER 355 at 367, [1985] AC 560 at 583):

'Putting the hand in the pocket is the guilty act, the intent to steal is the guilty mind, the offence is appropriately dealt with as an attempt, and the impossibility of committing the full offence for want of anything in the pocket to steal is declared by [sub-s (2)] to be no obstacle to conviction.'

If we fell into error, it is clear that our concern was to avoid convictions in situations which most people, as a matter of common sense, would not regard as involving criminality. In this connection it is to be regretted that we did not take due note of para 2.97 of the Law Commission Report, Criminal Law: Attempt and Impossibility in Relation to Attempt, Conspiracy and Incitement (1980) (Law Com no 102) which preceded the enactment of the 1981 Act, which reads:

'If it is right in principle that an attempt should be chargeable even though the crime which it is sought to commit could not possibly be committed, we do not think that we should be deterred by the consideration that such a change in our law would also cover some extreme and exceptional cases in which a prosecution would be theoretically possible. An example would be where a person is offered goods at such a low price that he believes that they are stolen, when in fact they are not; if he actually purchases them, upon the principles which we have discussed he would be liable for an attempt to handle stolen goods. Another case which has been much debated is that raised in argument by Bramwell B in *Reg v Collins*. If A takes his own umbrella, mistaking it for one belonging to B and intending to steal B's umbrella, is he guilty of attempted theft? Again, on the principles which we have discussed he would in theory be guilty, but in neither case would it be realistic to suppose that a complaint would be made or that a prosecution would ensue.'

The prosecution in *Anderton v Ryan* itself falsified the Commission's prognosis in one of the 'extreme and exceptional cases'. It nevertheless probably holds good for other such cases, particularly that of the young man having sexual intercourse with a girl over 16, mistakenly believing her to be under that age, by which both Lord Roskill and I were much troubled.

However that may be, the distinction between acts which are 'objectively innocent' and those which are not is an essential element in the reasoning in *Anderton v Ryan* and the decision, unless it can be supported on some other ground, must stand or fall by the validity of this distinction. I am satisfied on further consideration that the concept of 'objective innocence' is incapable of sensible application in relation to the law of criminal attempts. The reason for this is that any attempt to commit an offence which involves 'an act which is more than merely preparatory to the commission of the offence' but which for any reason fails, so that in the event no offence is committed, must *ex hypothesi*, from the point view of the criminal law, be 'objectively innocent'. What turns what would otherwise, from the point of view of the criminal law, be an innocent act into a crime is the intent of the actor to commit an offence. I say 'from the point of view of the criminal law' because the law of tort must surely here be quite irrelevant. A puts his hand into B's pocket. Whether or not there is anything in the pocket capable of being stolen, if A intends to steal his act is a criminal attempt; if he does not so intend his act is innocent. A plunges a knife into a bolster in a bed. To avoid the complication of an offence of criminal damage, assume it to be A's bolster. If A believes the bolster to be his enemy B and intends to kill him, his act is an attempt to murder B; if he knows the bolster is only a bolster, his act is innocent. These considerations lead me to the conclusion that the distinction sought to be drawn in *Anderton v Ryan* between innocent and guilty acts considered 'objectively' and independently of the state of mind of the actor cannot be sensibly maintained.

Another conceivable ground of distinction which was to some extent canvassed in argument, both in *Anderton v Ryan* and in the instant case, though no trace of it appears in the speeches in *Anderton v Ryan*, is a distinction which would make guilt or innocence of the crime of attempt in a case of mistaken belief dependent on what, for want of a better phrase, I will call the defendant's dominant intention. According to the theory necessary to sustain this distinction, the appellant's dominant intention in *Anderton v Ryan* was to buy a cheap video recorder; her belief that it was stolen was merely incidental. Likewise in the hypothetical case of attempted unlawful sexual intercourse, the young man's dominant intention was to have intercourse with the particular girl; his mistaken belief that she was under 16 was merely incidental. By contrast, in the instant case the appellant's dominant intention was to receive and distribute illegally imported heroin or cannabis.

While I see the superficial attraction of this suggested ground of distinction, I also see formidable practical difficulties in its application. By what test is a jury to be told that a defendant's dominant intention is to be recognised and distinguished from his incidental but mistaken belief? But there is perhaps a more formidable theoretical difficulty. If this ground of distinction is relied on to support the acquittal of the appellant in *Anderton v Ryan*, it can only do so on the basis that her mistaken belief that the video recorder was stolen played no significant part in her decision to buy it and therefore she may be acquitted of the intent to handle stolen goods. But this line of reasoning runs into head-on collision with s 1(3) of the 1981 Act. The theory produces a situation where, apart from the subsection, her intention would not be regarded as having amounted to any intent to commit an offence. Section 1(3)(b) then requires one to ask whether, if the video recorder had in fact been stolen, her intention would have been regarded as an intent to handle stolen goods. The answer must clearly be Yes, it would. If she had bought the video recorder knowing it to be stolen, when in fact it was, it would have availed her nothing to say that her dominant intention was to buy a video recorder because it was cheap and that her knowledge that it was stolen was merely incidental. This seems to me fatal to the dominant intention theory.

I am thus led to the conclusion that there is no valid ground on which *Anderton v Ryan* can be distinguished. I have made clear my own conviction, which as a party to the decision (and craving the indulgence of my noble and learned friends who agreed in it) I am the readier to express, that the decision was wrong. What then is to be done? If the case is indistinguishable, the application of the strict doctrine of precedent would require that the present appeal be allowed. Is it permissible to depart from precedent under the 1966 *Practice Note* ([1966] 3 All ER 77) notwithstanding the especial need for certainty in the criminal law? The following considerations lead me to answer that question affirmatively. Firstly, I am undeterred by the consideration that the decision in *Anderton v Ryan* was so recent. The 1966 Practice Statement is an effective abandonment of our pretention to infallibility. If a serious error embodied in a decision of this House has distorted the law, the sooner it is corrected the better. Secondly, I cannot see how, in the very nature of the case, anyone could have acted in reliance on the law as propounded in *Anderton v Ryan* in the belief that he was acting innocently and now find that, after all, he is to be held to have committed a criminal offence. Thirdly, to hold the House bound to follow *Anderton v Ryan* because it cannot be distinguished and to allow the appeal in this case would, it seems to me, be tantamount to a declaration that the 1981 Act left the law of criminal attempts unchanged following the decision in *Haughton v Smith* [1975] AC 476. Finally, if, contrary to my present view, there is a valid ground on which it would be proper to distinguish cases similar to that considered in *Anderton v Ryan*, my present opinion on that point would not foreclose the option of making such a distinction in some future case.

I cannot conclude this opinion without disclosing that I have had the advantage, since the conclusion of the argument in this appeal, of reading an article by Professor Glanville Williams entitled 'The Lords and Impossible Attempts, or *Quis Custodiet Ipsos Custodes*?' [1986] CLJ 33. The language in which he criticises the decision in *Anderton v Ryan* is not conspicuous for its moderation, but it would be foolish, on that account, not to recognise the force of the criticism and churlish not to acknowledge the assistance I have derived from it.

I would answer the certified question in the affirmative and dismiss the appeal.

[**Lord Hailsham LC**, having stated that, save for one relatively minor point, he agreed with Lord Bridge, continued:]

I must add, however, that, even had I not been able to follow my noble and learned friend in interring *Anderton v Ryan* [later in this extract] by using the 1966 Practice Statement, I would still have dismissed the instant appeal by distinguishing its facts from that case. Shortly, my reasoning would have been that the appellant was guilty on the clear wording of s 1(1) and (2) of the 1981 Act and that no recourse was therefore necessary to the wording of s 1(3), which if so would be irrelevant.

[His lordship set out the provisions of the Act.]

I would have arrived at this conclusion by asking myself three simple questions to which the answers could only be made in one form. They are: *Question 1.* What was the intention of the appellant throughout? *Answer.* His intention throughout was to evade and defeat the customs authorities of the United Kingdom. He had no other intention. His motive was gain (the bribe of £1,000). But as I pointed out in *Hyam v DPP* [1974] 2 All ER 41 at 5, [1975] AC 55 at 73 motive is not the same thing as intention. *Question 2.* Is the knowing evasion of the United Kingdom customs in the manner envisaged in the appellant's intent an offence to which s 1 of the 1981 Act applies? *Answer.* Yes: see s 1(4). *Question 3.* Did the appellant do an act which was more than preparatory to the commission of the offence? *Answer.* Yes, for the reasons stated in the relevant paragraphs of my noble and learned friend Lord Bridge's speech.

In this connection I do not feel it would have been necessary to invoke the doctrine of dominant and subordinate intention referred to by my noble and learned friend. The sole intent of the instant appellant from start to finish was to defeat the customs prohibition. In *Anderton v Ryan* the only intention of Mrs Ryan was to buy a particular video cassette recorder at a knock-down price, and the fact that she believed it to be stolen formed no part of that intention. It was a belief, assumed to be false and not an intention at all. It was a false belief as to a state of fact, and, if it became an intention, it was only the result of the deeming provisions of s 1(3). Whether or not *Anderton v Ryan* was correctly decided, one has to go to s 1(3) to decide whether Mrs Ryan had committed a criminal attempt under the Act as the result of her belief, assumed to be false, that the video cassette recorder had in fact been stolen.

[**Lord Mackay** agreed with disposal of the appeal proposed by Lord Bridge; but agreed with Lord Hailsham on the 'relatively minor point' referred to by him.]

[**Lord Elwyn-Jones** said that he would have been content to dismiss the appeal by distinguishing *Anderton v Ryan*, as Lord Hailsham had done; but he agreed with Lord Bridge and would dismiss the appeal for the reasons given by him.]

[**Lord Scarman** agreed with Lord Bridge.]

[A second ground of appeal, that is, that the judge was wrong to direct the jury that it was immaterial that the appellant did not know precisely what the prohibited goods were, was also rejected: although s 170(1)(b) created a number of separate offences, the only mens rea necessary was the knowledge that the thing was a controlled drug.]

Appeal dismissed

≋ *Questions*

(1) Does the decision in *Shivpuri* offend the principle of legality (no one shall be convicted of doing something which has not been declared by the law to be an offence)? Cf [1984] Crim LR 584 and [1985] Crim LR 504 at 505 and B. Hogan, 'The Principle of Legality' (1986) 136 NLJ 267. (Note also Article 7 of the European Convention on Human Rights, section 1.5, p 13.)

(2) D and E agree that they will use D's tools to break into V's safe and steal a diamond. D tries to do so. It is quite impossible to break into the safe with those tools. Of what offences are D and E guilty? Does it matter whether the diamond exists? What if D attempts to break open the safe, but it is empty?

(3) D, 16, has sex with V. She consents. He thinks she is only 12, she is in fact 16. Has D attempted to rape a child under 13?

(4) D hates his neighbour, V, and plans to kill him. In order to effectuate his plan, D makes a voodoo doll of V and stabs it through the heart. D believes that this will kill V. Is D guilty of attempted murder? Should he be? If D is not guilty, could the reason be that he has not increased the risk that harm will be caused to V? However, are there not other impossible attempts that only pose a minimal risk of harm but that intuition tells us nevertheless ought to be criminalized?

20.6 Reform

The Law Commission published a Consultation Paper No 183, *Conspiracy and Attempts* (2007) (see also the Law Commission Report No 318, *Conspiracy and Attempts* (2009)).

WHAT IS WRONG WITH ATTEMPTS

Background

12.12 . . . The offence was drafted to cover the sort of conduct associated with 'trying' to commit an intended offence; but it was also designed to encompass earlier preparatory acts—acts sufficiently proximate to a completed attempt to justify the imposition of criminal liability.

12.13 However, as a mechanism for determining the criminal liability of persons who take proximate steps towards trying to commit an offence, we believe this inchoate offence is unsatisfactory. We believe that a change of approach, through legislative intervention, is necessary.

12.14 First of all, in the absence of clear, consistent guidelines the 'more than merely preparatory' test of proximity has proved to be too vague and uncertain a basis for a court to determine whether an attempt has been committed. . . .

12.15 Secondly, because of the absence of any clear, consistent guidance, the Court of Appeal has had to determine where the line between mere preparation and attempt is to be drawn. As a result too much emphasis has on occasion been placed on the offence's label ('attempt')—and therefore on the notion of 'trying' to commit an offence. Too little regard has correspondingly been paid to the underlying rationale for the offence. Under our provisional proposals, clarity would be introduced to the law of attempt in this respect, because the offence of 'attempt' would be confined to the last acts D needs to do to bring about the commission of the offence. The key distinction would become one between 'mere' preparation and 'criminal' preparation, for the purposes of that proposed new offence.

12.16 In that regard, we take the view that there are a number of sound policy reasons for imposing criminal liability for some preparatory conduct occurring before D actually completes or all-but completes an attempt to commit another offence. These are:

(1) the need for effective intervention by the police;

(2) the desirability of imposing criminal liability in relation to conduct associated with a sufficiently vivid danger of intentional harm; and

(3) the high moral culpability associated with preparatory acts closely linked in time with (what would be) the last act towards the commission of an intended offence.

12.17 The case of *Geddes* [explained in section 20.4, p 552] provides perhaps the most worrying example of the Court of Appeal's restrictive approach to the offence of attempt. In our view, it gives rise to the accusation that the criminal law does not adequately protect the public in the way that it interprets that offence. Unfortunately, *Geddes* is not an isolated example.

12.18 Another troubling example is *Campbell* [section 20.4, p 551]. In that case D's conviction for attempted robbery was quashed even though he had been apprehended with an imitation firearm as he came within a metre of the door of a post office he intended to rob, with the aid of a threatening note for the cashier. The Court of Appeal's view was that there was no evidence on which a jury could 'properly and safely' find that D's acts were more than merely preparatory. . . .

12.24 Our third reason for believing section 1(1) of the 1981 Act to be unsatisfactory is that it would appear omissions are currently excluded from the scope of the offence. We take the view that there is no reason in principle, or indeed as a matter of policy, why attempts should be limited to the commission of positive acts, particularly as the Crown must always prove D's intention. If D deliberately starves his or her baby to death, this is murder even though the death is achieved through 'doing nothing' rather than by a positive act of killing. Suppose, however, that someone overhears D admitting that he or she is endeavouring to starve his or her baby to death and has already denied the baby food for a couple of days. We believe it would be wrong if D could avoid liability for attempted murder in such circumstances, but it may well be that this is the present legal position.

12.25 Our fourth reason relates to the current requirement that the jury should be directed to determine whether D's proven or admitted conduct amounts to an 'attempt' for the purposes of the 1981 Act, even when the trial judge has already made a ruling on this issue. This is difficult to reconcile with the general division of roles between judge and jury in criminal proceedings. More worryingly, lay triers of fact may have an insufficient understanding of the scope of the offence, or of the policy considerations underpinning it, to be able to apply it in the way it was intended to be applied. The present test may give rise to inconsistent or perverse verdicts. . . .

12.26 Finally, there is a lack of clarity in relation to the fault element required for circumstance elements of an attempt to commit an offence. It may be that inchoate liability can now arise for attempting an (indictable) offence of strict liability regardless of whether the accused 'intended' to do anything unlawful (and even regardless of whether he or she had any culpable state of mind at all). . . . [This was before the decision in *Pace and Rogers* above, which clearly renders this a more significant problem.]

12.27 We believe it is of crucial importance that the law should properly address the relationship between the various stages in the run up to the commission of an intended offence. There are in effect three such stages:

(1) Stage 1: the preliminary preparatory steps taken by D;

(2) Stage 2: the 'on the job' preparatory steps taken by D (that is, the preparatory acts immediately preceding the (attempted) commission of an intended offence);

(3) Stage 3: conduct beyond what would ordinarily be regarded as 'on the job' preparation, where D is attempting to commit the intended offence.

12.28 For the criminal law to deal properly with this area, a number of questions need to be answered:

(1) Should criminal attempt be restricted, to a specific kind of behaviour prior to the commission of a substantive offence, namely last acts needing to done by D to commit the offence?

(2) If so, should there also be a separate offence of 'preparation' (or additions to the existing battery of offences of preparation) to cover:

   (a) some or all of the types of preparatory conduct which were originally intended to fall within the scope of the present offence of attempt; or

   (b) an even wider band of preparatory conduct?

(3) Alternatively, should section 1(1) of the 1981 Act be retained but remodelled so that its label and/or definition accord more visibly with the true scope of the offence as intended by Parliament that is, an offence extending back beyond the notion of trying or endeavouring to commit an offence?

(4) If so, should there be a further general offence of 'preparation' (or additions to the existing battery of offences of preparation) to cover other preparatory conduct warranting criminal liability?

[The Commission proposed models of the offence.]

Option 1: two offences (without elaboration)

12.35 There would be a narrower general offence of 'attempt' limited in scope to cases of completed or all-but completed attempt where the offender is engaged in the last acts needed to bring about the commission of the offence. However, there would also be a new general offence of 'criminal preparation' (with intent) limited in scope to the narrow band of preparatory acts immediately preceding an attempt (that is, stage 2). This option would expressly declare through the definition given to 'criminal preparation' that the broad interpretation of the present offence of attempt is correct, contrary to the restrictive approach of the Court of Appeal in *Geddes*. However, individuals whose conduct goes no further than stage 2 would no longer be labelled as 'attemptors'.

12.36 The definition of 'criminal preparation' would not be elaborated upon in the relevant legislation. Additional guidance for the courts would, however, be provided in the form of examples set out in our final report. . . .

Option 2: two offences (with statutory examples)

12.38 This approach would follow option 1 in all respects, save for one key difference. Specific examples of 'criminal preparation' would be provided in the legislation to guide the courts in their interpretation of the offence and their understanding of the types of conduct falling within stage 2 (paragraph 12.27 above). No such examples would be provided for the new, narrower offence of 'attempt' because, being limited to last acts needing to be done by D to bring about the commission of the crime, there would be no ambiguity as to its scope.

Examples of criminal preparation

12.39 Irrespective of whether option 1 or option 2 is preferred, we believe that the new general offence of criminal preparation should encompass the following situations:

(1) D gains entry into a building, structure, vehicle or enclosure or (remains therein) with a view to committing the intended offence there and then or as soon as an opportunity presents itself.

(2) D examines or interferes with a door, window, lock or alarm or puts in place a ladder or similar device with a view there and then to gaining unlawful entry into a building, structure or vehicle to commit the intended offence within.

(3) D commits an offence or an act of distraction or deception with a view to committing the intended offence there and then.

(4) D, with a view to committing the intended offence there and then or as soon as an opportunity presents itself:

    (a) approaches the intended victim or the object of the intended offence, or

    (b) lies in wait for an intended victim, or

    (c) follows the intended victim.

Option 3: the minimalist approach

12.40 Under this approach, there would continue to be a single inchoate offence of 'attempt', as currently defined, and its breadth would continue to be controlled by interpretations of section 1(1) of the 1981 Act given by the Court of Appeal.

12.41 However, on the assumption that the courts may come to the definitive conclusion that 'attempt' is to be interpreted narrowly, in line with the Court of Appeal's judgment in *Geddes*, the battery of specific statutory offences of preparation would be carefully reviewed with a view to eliminating anomalies. Our approach would be predicated on the desirability of ensuring that individuals who reach stage 2 (paragraph 12.27 above) in their plan to commit an intended offence do not escape all criminal liability.

≈ *Question*

In its provisional proposals the Law Commission favoured option 1. Do you agree?

Additional proposals

12.43 We also provisionally propose the following:

Proposal 18: Fault

(1) 'Intention' in the two proposed offences should bear its normal meaning, namely that given to it by the House of Lords in *Woollin*, but should also encompass so-called conditional intent;

(2) Intention in the sense just given should be required for the conduct elements and (if any) consequence elements of an offence of attempt or of criminal preparation, but not for the circumstance elements (if any);

(3) If the completed offence requires recklessness, negligence or no fault as to a circumstance element, the fault requirement in relation to an attempt to commit that offence, or in relation to the offence of criminal preparation, should be subjective recklessness;

(4) If the completed offence requires a higher degree of fault in relation to a circumstance element than recklessness (such as knowledge), then that higher degree of fault should also be required in relation to the circumstance element on a charge of attempt or of criminal preparation.

Proposal 19: Omissions

12.44 The two proposed offences should be drafted to cover omissions where, as a matter of law, the intended offence is capable of being committed by an omission.

Proposal 20: The roles of judge and jury

12.45 The procedural rule under the 1981 Act, that it is for the jury to determine not only whether D acted in the way the Crown alleges but also whether that proven conduct amounts to the commission of an attempt, should be abolished in relation to the proposed offences.

Proposal 21: Application to summary offences

12.46 It should be permissible to prosecute D for attempting or preparing to commit a summary offence.

12.47 However, we ask whether the consent of the Director of Public Prosecutions should be required in such cases.

≈≈ *Questions*

Do you think that having crimes of criminal preparation and attempt would be confusing? Would it encourage the courts to extend liability to acts of the accused that are even further remote from the substantive crime and earlier than the current law of attempts?

The Consultation Paper was followed by Report No 318, *Conspiracy and Attempts* (2009). The recommendations made in relation to the law of attempt were far less ambitious:

ATTEMPTS

9.17 We recommend that the Criminal Attempts Act 1981 be amended to provide that, for the purposes of section 1(1), an intent to commit an offence includes a conditional intent to commit it. **(Recommendation 17, paragraph 8.106)**

9.18 We recommend that for substantive offences which have a circumstance requirement but no corresponding fault requirement, or which have a corresponding fault requirement which is objective (such as negligence), it should be possible to convict D of attempting to commit the substantive offence only if D was subjectively reckless as to the circumstance at the relevant time. **(Recommendation 18, paragraph 8.133)**

9.19 We recommend that where a substantive offence has fault requirements not involving mere negligence (or its equivalent) in relation to a fact or circumstance, it should be possible to convict D of attempting to commit the substantive offence if D possessed those fault requirements at the relevant time. **(Recommendation 19, paragraph 8.137)**

9.20 We recommend that the Criminal Attempts Act 1981 be amended so that D may be convicted of attempted *murder* if (with the intent to kill V) D failed to discharge his or her legal duty to V (where that omission, unchecked, could have resulted in V's death).

20.7 Why have a crime of attempt?

Does the criminal law need a crime of attempt:

(1) To allow the investigating agency to intervene before the harm involved in the substantive offence is caused? If so, is the law defined with sufficient clarity to optimize the opportunity for the police to act in a preventative role?

(2) To reflect the moral wrongdoing of one who has tried to commit a crime? Is that moral wrongdoing any less than one who succeeds in the commission of the substantive crime?

Andrew Ashworth, 'Belief and Intent in Criminal Liability' in J. Eekelaar and J. Bell (eds), *Oxford Essays in Jurisprudence* (1987), p 16 asks:

Is A, who shoots at X intending to kill him but misses because X unexpectedly moves, any less culpable than B who shoots at Y intending to kill him and does so? An external description of both sets of events would probably not suggest that they have 'done' the same thing, whereas an account which paid more attention to the actor's point of view and to matters which lay within the actor's control would suggest that they both intended and tried, to the same extent, to do the same thing. The argument here is that, because of the element of uncertainty in the outcome of things which we try to do, it would be wrong for assessments of culpability to depend on the occurrence or non-occurrence of the intended consequences. 'Success or failure . . . makes no difference at all to [an agent's] moral status in relation to his original act. His original act, strictly considered, was simply his trying and that is what moral assessment must concern itself with' (Winch, *Ethics and Action*, 1972, p.139) . . . Moral blame and criminal liability should be based so far as possible on choice and control, on the trying and not what actually happened thereafter. What are the reasons for wishing to reduce the influence of chance upon criminal liability? It cannot be doubted that luck plays a considerable part. Actual results also play a considerable part in judgments of others, and tend to dominate assessments in such fields as business, sport, and education. Those who try hard but are unsuccessful often receive less recognition than those who achieve goals (no matter how little effort they put into it). But these are not moral assessments of the individual and their characters. If one turns to moral and social judgments, it is doubtful whether outcomes should be proper criteria. It may be desirable overall to have fewer bad outcomes and more good outcomes in society, but that does not lead to the conclusion that moral praise and blame should be allocated solely according to result. Indeed, a bad outcome stemming from a good intent may be a better predictor of good outcomes than a good outcome born of a bad intent. From time to time we may praise someone for producing a good result, even though it was not what he was trying to do, but this is more a reflection of our pleasure at the outcome than an assessment of his conduct and character. If we turn to blaming, is it not unacceptable to blame people for causing results irrespective of whether they were caused intentionally, negligently, or purely accidentally? Blaming is a moral activity which is surely only appropriate where the individual had some choice or control over the matter. For this reason the criminal law should seek to minimize the effect of luck upon the incidence and scale of criminal liability.

Compare the view of J. C. Smith, 'The Element of Chance in Criminal Liability' [1971] Crim LR 63:

. . . great significance is still attached to the harm done, as distinct from the harm intended or foreseen. Perhaps the significance of the harm done derives from our emotional reaction to the acts of others. If one of my small boys, not looking what he is doing, throws a stone which just misses the dining room window, I shall be very cross with him; but if the stone breaks the dining room window, I shall be absolutely furious. His behaviour is just as bad and just as dangerous in the one case as in the other; but my indignation is much greater in the case where he has caused the harm than in that where he has not.

It might fairly be answered that the criminal law should be rational and not based on emotional reactions. Is not this naked retribution—and a very crude form of retribution, the degree of punishment being based not on the moral culpability but on the harm done?

On the other hand, it is certain that the legislator cannot afford to ignore altogether the reactions—even the irrational reactions—of ordinary people, in the interests of logic and consistency. Stephen J., the great criminal law judge of the nineteenth century thought that the gratification of public sentiment was a proper purpose of the criminal law . . . He thought there was nothing irrational in basing liability on the harm done:

'If two persons are guilty of the very same act of negligence, and if one of them causes thereby a railway accident, involving the death and mutilation of many persons, whereas the other does no injury to anyone, it seems to me that it would be rather pedantic than rational to say that each had committed the same offence, and should be subjected to the same punishment. In one sense, each has committed an offence, but the one has had the bad luck to cause a horrible misfortune, and to attract public attention to it, and the other the good fortune to do no harm. Both certainly deserve punishment, (*History of the Criminal Law*, Vol. III, pp. 311 et seq.)'

≋ *Question*

Would a crime of endangerment offer a partial solution to this problem?

More recently, Gideon Yaffe has based a complex and detailed theory of attempts upon the 'Transfer Principle'.

G. Yaffe, *Attempts*
(2010), p 21

When the legislature defines a crime—when it specifies a punishment for a person shown beyond reasonable doubt to have acted in a certain way in certain circumstances and with certain results—it succeeds in defining a second crime as well, namely the crime of attempting to commit the crime defined. The legislature could choose specifically not to proscribe the attempt to commit a crime defined, but in the absence of an explicit statement to that effect, by defining the crime the legislature grants the state the power to punish also for the attempt. We seem to accept, that is, the following principle: '*If a particular form of conduct is legitimately criminalized, then the attempt to engage in that form of conduct is also legitimately criminalized.*' Call this 'The Transfer Principle', since, under it, the legitimacy of criminalization transfers from completion to attempt. In accepting the Transfer Principle, the criminal law reflects a deeply entrenched principle of moral thought: if you shouldn't do something, then you shouldn't try to do it either. Moral prohibition, like justifiable criminalization, seems to transfer from completion to attempt.

Generally, it is through appeal to the Transfer Principle that attempts become crimes. The legislature might have a long debate about whether to pass a law making a certain kind of behavior a crime. But it does not then have a separate debate about whether to criminalize attempts to engage in that kind of behavior. Rather, when the law is passed, the attempt, too, has *ipso facto* become a crime. The Transfer Principle, then, is of great practical importance: it serves as a silent premise in the legislature's reasoning about what to criminalize. As such, it is in need of justification. Why do we think that justifiable criminalization transfers automatically from completed crimes to our efforts to engage in them? The principle is in particularly pressing need of justification, given that the first thing (although not necessarily the only thing) that one would cite in defense of criminalizing many completions—think of murder, rape, or robbery—is the harm that such acts cause. But attempts often cause no harm at all. What, then, justifies the Transfer Principle?

Yaffe goes on to consider two rationales that might justify his Transfer Principle, but rejects them both. The first is based on the intuitively appealing notion that when a type of act is wrong, then so is the attempt of it. Yaffe rejects this argument on the basis that for it to be true, completion and attempt must be equally and equivocally wrong. However, since the law criminalizes both 'last act' and non-last act attempts and an individual who engages in a non-last act attempt can be acting while conceiving of the possibility that he will not go through with his plan, non-last act attempts are not as wrong as completed crimes. The second argument rejected by Yaffe is based on the notion that criminalization of attempts is justified on the basis of risk suppression. There are two facets to this argument, both of which are rejected. It could be said that by trying, but failing, to commit the substantive offence, the defendant has demonstrated that he is dangerous and there is therefore a risk that there will be a completed crime on some later occasion. Alternatively, it could be said that the defendant has risked the completion of the crime on the occasion when he failed. The probability that the crime would be committed is higher given the fact that the defendant has attempted it. Both of these arguments are rejected on the basis that the law does not just criminalize those attempts that created a risk, but it also criminalizes attempts to commit a crime even though there was no possibility that the crime could be committed. Of course, Yaffe is here referring to the fact that the law criminalizes impossible attempts.

The justification Yaffe offers for his Transfer Principle is that completed crimes and attempts share features that warrant the criminalization of each. He states that, 'both reflect corruption in the modes of recognition and response to legal reasons employed by the actor, and . . . these modes of recognition and response to reasons play a role in guiding the actor's conduct'. This simply means that D is someone who displays a disregard for the proscriptions of the criminal law. Yaffe assumes that the mens rea elements of a completed crime are indicators of modes of recognition and response to criminal legal reasons of defendants who complete crimes and that the corresponding intention of the person who attempts a crime is an indicator of the same or worse modes.

≈≈≈ *Questions*

(1) Do you find Yaffe's rejection of the risk suppression and moral equivalence justifications compelling?

(2) Husak argues that the Transfer Principle cannot solely be descriptive but must be prescriptive also, in that it also influences what the content of the law is. This is because existing law does recognize exceptions to the Transfer Principle. Some offences should not allow attempt liability because this would constitute double or even triple inchoate liability, for example aiding an attempt. Are all instances of double inchoate liability unjustifiable? See D. Husak, 'Why Punish Attempts at All? Yaffe on "The Transfer Principle"' (2012) 6 Crim L & Philosophy 399.

FURTHER READING

C. Clarkson, 'General Endangerment Offences: The Way Forward?' (2005) 32 Univ Western Aus Law Rev 131

R. A. Duff, *Criminal Attempts* (1996)

P. Glazebrook, 'Should We Have a Law of Attempted Crime?' (1969) 85 LQR 28

J. Horder, 'Varieties of Intention, Criminal Attempts and Endangerment' (1994) 14 LS 335

J. Hornby, 'On What's Intentionally Done' in S. Shute, J. Gardner and J. Horder (eds), *Action and Value in Criminal Law* (1993), p 60

K. J. M. Smith, 'Proximity in Attempt: Lord Lane's Midway Course' [1991] Crim LR 576

J. Stannard, 'Making Up for the Missing Element: A Sideways Look at Attempts' (1987) 7 LS 194

G. R. Sullivan, 'Intent, Subjective Recklessness and Culpability' (1992) 12 OJLS 380

21
Conspiracy

Statutory conspiracy:

A person commits a statutory conspiracy under section 1 of the Criminal Law Act 1977 if he agrees with any other person(s) that a course of conduct will be followed which, if carried out as they agreed, will necessarily involve one or more of the parties committing an offence (or would do so but for the existence of facts which render the commission of the offence or any of the offences impossible).

It is a conspiracy at common law to agree:

(1) to defraud, whether or not the fraud amounts to a crime;

(2) to do an act which tends to corrupt public morals or outrage public decency, whether or not the act amounts to a crime.

Some of the controversies that will be examined in this chapter include:

(1) whether it is necessary and/or desirable to criminalize conspiracies;

(2) the extent to which there can be a conspiracy under the Criminal Law Act 1977 if the parties have only agreed to commit the substantive offence subject to some condition;

(3) what must be agreed and who must intend what to happen for a crime of conspiracy;

(4) the mens rea of statutory conspiracies;

(5) whether common law conspiracies are so vague as to infringe the rule of law.

21.1 Introduction

Conspiracy is a form of inchoate offence based on agreement to commit a crime. It is committed as soon as A and B agree to commit a criminal offence as, for example, where A and B agree to burgle a house next week. The crime is committed and is not undone even if they immediately regret it and abandon the plan. Their repentance would mitigate the sentence but would have no effect on liability to conviction.

At common law, unlike incitement and attempt, conspiracy was not limited to cases where the defendants had in view the commission of a crime. Conspiracy was defined at common law as an agreement to do an unlawful act or to do a lawful act by unlawful means; and the word 'unlawful' included not only all crimes but also some torts, fraud, the corruption of public morals and the outraging of public decency, whether or not the acts in question amounted to crimes when done by an individual. The scope of criminal liability was excessive. The common law of conspiracy has been greatly modified by statute and the law is now found principally in the Criminal Law Act 1977.

21.2 Rationale of offence

Where D1 and D2 agree to graffiti V's house, a conspiracy to commit criminal damage is complete even though they have never been near the house and have taken no further steps to perpetrate that crime. Although no one would doubt that the substantive offence of criminal damage should exist to protect against harm to property, the question is whether the mere agreement to do so ought also to constitute a crime. Some argue that the conduct involved in the agreement represents a different 'wrong' or 'harm' from the commission of the criminal damage itself, but is it a sufficiently serious wrong to warrant criminalization? See the discussion in Law Commission Consultation Paper No 183, *Conspiracy and Attempts* (2007), section 21.4.6.1, p 581, Part 2 and I. Dennis, 'The Rationale of Criminal Conspiracy' (1977) 93 LQR 39. These are not mere 'academic' anxieties: when the Law Commission began its study of the subject in 1970, one of the first questions posed to Glanville Williams was 'Do We Need an Offence of Conspiracy At All?' (D. Hodgson, 'Law Commission No 76: A Case Study in Criminal Law Reform' in P. R. Glazebrook (ed), *Reshaping the Criminal Law: Essays in Honour of Glanville Williams* (1978).)

There are numerous arguments, many of considerable merit, which cannot be dealt with in full here; however, it is possible to give a flavour of the diversity and ingenuity of the objections to what is an offence of considerable pedigree, and significant practical value:

- it criminalizes conduct before it has been confirmed to constitute a harm or real threat of harm—even earlier than an attempt in which an overt act of more than mere preparation is required;

- it allows for the punishment of conduct by two which would not be criminal if performed by a sole actor; and

- procedurally, it allows the Crown to avoid specificity in the case and carries with it the disadvantages inherent in joint trials.

There are equally respectable counter-arguments defending the need for conspiracy:

- the offence allows for the intervention of the police authorities at an early stage of the enterprise and this better protects society against the commission of the substantive crime;

- conspiracy is important in deterring not only the commission of the substantive crime but the planning and collaboration in crime generally. This differs from attempt where no distinct harm, and hence no distinct deterrence, is involved in the performance of an act more than merely preparatory to the offence;

- there is a unique and distinct harm involved in the preparedness to collaborate in criminal activity. As the US Supreme Court has observed:

For two or more to . . . combine together to commit . . . a breach of the criminal laws is an offense of the gravest character, sometimes quite outweighing, in injury to the public, the mere commission of the contemplated crime. It involves deliberate plotting to subvert the laws, educating and preparing the conspirators for further and habitual criminal practices. And it is characterized by secrecy, rendering it difficult of detection, requiring more time for its discovery and adding to the importance of punishing it when discovered. (*US v Rabinowich*, 238 US 78 at 88 (1915))

- collaboration may increase the likelihood of commission of the offence and perhaps even an increased level of harm if committed. (This must surely depend on the type of crime.

Counter-arguments are that the collaboration may also render conspiracies weaker since they are more susceptible to a disclosure of information or one party reneging. On the psychological and economic strengths of conspiracies, see N. Katyal, 'Conspiracy Theory' (2003) 112 Yale LJ 1307);

- conspiracy allows the true nature of the criminality of a group of individuals to be the focus of a prosecution; and
- arguably, conspiracy better respects the principle of fair labelling since the description of D's conduct accurately reflects his personal behaviour.

≈≈ *Questions*

(1) Is a crime of conspiracy necessary bearing in mind that a defendant can be charged with attempt as soon as he goes beyond acts of mere preparation towards the commission of the offence?

(2) To what extent is it desirable and/or possible to have an offence of conspiracy focused on the mere fact of agreement and collaboration?

(3) To what extent must the conspiracy offence depend on the detail of the substantive offence that is the object of the conspiracy?

21.3 Statutory and common law conspiracy

21.3.1 Statutory conspiracy

The Criminal Law Act 1977 created a new offence of statutory conspiracy. Section 1 of that Act (as amended) provides:

1. The offence of conspiracy

(1) Subject to the following provisions of this Part of this Act, if a person agrees with any other person or persons that a course of conduct shall be pursued which, if the agreement is carried out in accordance with their intentions, either:

   (a) will necessarily amount to or involve the commission of any offence or offences by one or more of the parties to the agreement, or

   (b) would do so but for the existence of facts which render the commission of the offence or any of the offences impossible, he is guilty of conspiracy to commit the offence or offences in question.

(2) Where liability for any offence may be incurred without knowledge on the part of the person committing it of any particular fact or circumstance necessary for the commission of the offence, a person shall not be guilty of conspiracy to commit that offence by virtue of subsection (1) above unless he and at least one other party to the agreement intend or know that that fact or circumstance shall or will exist at the time when the conduct constituting the offence is to take place.

(3) [Repealed.]

(4) In this Part of this Act 'offence' means an offence triable in England and Wales.

[Section 1A Conspiracies to commit offences outside the United Kingdom, is omitted.]

Statutory conspiracy is not limited to agreements to commit a statutory crime—agreements to commit the common law offences, such as murder or cheating the Revenue, are charged under this offence—rather, the term 'statutory conspiracy' is used to distinguish it from common law conspiracies. An agreement to commit a crime is a statutory conspiracy, regulated by the 1977 Act instead of the common law.

The penalty for statutory conspiracy is provided by s 3 of the Act—broadly, the conspiracy is punishable in the same manner as the crime the offenders have conspired to commit.

Section 1(1)(b) deals with the issue of 'impossible' conspiracies. The effect of the provision is that the parties to the conspiracy will be judged on the facts as they believed them to be, not what they were in reality. For example, if A and B agree to kill C, but they are unaware that C is already dead, the fact of C's death will not preclude A and B being guilty of conspiracy to commit murder.

21.3.2 Common law conspiracies

It is an offence triable only on indictment to agree:

(1) to defraud, whether or not the fraud amounts to a crime on the defendants' intended plan;

(2) to do an act which tends to corrupt public morals or outrage public decency, whether or not the act amounts to a crime.

The 1977 Act has no part to play in the prosecution of such offences.

The Law Commission expressed its aim to limit conspiracy to agreements to commit crimes. It was thought, however, that the complete abolition of common law conspiracy would leave some unacceptable gaps in the law and that, pending the enactment of some new but undefined substantive offences, it was necessary to ensure that conspiracies to defraud, to corrupt public morals and to outrage public decency continue to be punishable. In the case of conspiracy to defraud, there is an overlap with the statutory conspiracy offence and either can be charged: see s 12 of the Criminal Justice Act 1987.

21.4 The elements of statutory conspiracy

The elements of the offence can be broken down as follows:

(1) an agreement;

(2) to pursue a course of conduct;

(3) necessarily involving the commission of a criminal offence on the defendants' intended plan;

(4) the crime is to be committed by one of the parties to the conspiracy;

(5) intention;

(6) knowledge or intention as to proscribed circumstances.

21.4.1 An agreement

The offence is complete once a concluded agreement (going beyond mere negotiation) exists. In *Saik* [2006] UKHL 18 (extracted in section 21.4.7, p 585), Lord Nicholls stated that, 'The offence therefore lies in making an agreement. Implicitly, the subsection requires also that the parties intend to carry out their agreement. The offence is complete at that stage. The offence is complete even if the parties do not carry out their agreement. The offence is complete even if the substantive offence is not thereafter committed by any of the conspirators or by anyone else.' Once there is an agreement, it (and therefore the criminal conspiracy) subsists until the agreement is performed or abandoned: *DPP v Doot* [1973] AC 807. During this time anyone joining the enterprise, knowing of the criminal purpose, becomes a party to the conspiracy, even if they were not party to the original agreement: *Zezev* [2002] EWHC Admin 589. It is not necessary for all the parties to know each other or even to know what other parties exist: *Meyrick* (1929) 21 Cr App R 94. In that case, the Ds had each been involved in the bribery of a police officer in Soho. Their individual agreements with the police officer enabled them to contravene the licensing laws. A number of the defendants appealed against their conviction on the ground that all those involved in the conspiracy had never even met each other. Their appeals were dismissed.

Lord Hewart CJ:

It seems to us that it was clearly put to the jury that in order to find these persons, or any of them, guilty of the conspiracy charged . . . it was necessary that the prosecution should establish, not indeed that the individuals were in direct communication with each other, or directly consulting together, but that they entered into an agreement with a common design. Such agreements may be made in various ways. There may be one person, to adopt the metaphor of counsel, round whom the rest revolve. The metaphor is the metaphor of the centre of the circle and the circumference. There may be a conspiracy of another kind, where the metaphor would be rather that of a chain; A communicates with B, B with C, C with D, and so on to the end of the list of conspirators. What has to be ascertained is always the same matter: is it true to say, in the words already quoted, that the acts of the accused were done in pursuance of a criminal purpose held in common between them?

But there must be a criminal purpose that the parties to the conspiracy share as their common purpose: *Griffiths* [1966] 1 QB 589: D conspired with each of a number of farmers to defraud the Ministry of Agriculture; but it was not shown to be one conspiracy and therefore was not chargeable as such. In some instances, it is alleged that there are several separate conspiracies: D with A; D with B; D with C, etc. In others, it is alleged that there is a single conspiracy between D, A, B and C. In such a case, it is essential that all members of the conspiracy have a shared common purpose; not a series of separate parallel purposes.

It is clear that in these so-called 'wheel conspiracies', the conspiracy may revolve around some third party, X, who is in touch with each of D1, D2 and D3, though they are not in touch with one another. Provided that the result is that they have a common design—for example, to rob a particular bank—D1, D2 and D3 may properly be charged with conspiring together though they have never been in touch with one another until they meet in the dock. The same is true of a chain conspiracy where D1 communicates with D2, D2 with D3, etc.

The issue of whether there was one conspiracy as opposed to multiple conspiracies arose in *Shillam* [2013] EWCA Crim 160. It was alleged that R was the central character in supplying cocaine and that S and X were regular purchasers from him for onward sale. The evidence showed that R was in regular contact with S, but not with any other alleged conspirator, X. All three were convicted of conspiracy to supply cocaine. The judge directed the jury that they had to be sure that in the case of each defendant he had agreed with at least one other person to supply cocaine to someone else. The jury asked whether the conspiracy had to be between any two of the three defendants or whether it sufficed that it was between one of them and persons unknown. The judge directed the jury that the latter sufficed. S appealed and argued that the judge's direction meant that the jury could convict the defendants without them necessarily being sure that they were all party to the same conspiracy. The Court of Appeal agreed that the judge had misdirected the jury. Toulson LJ stated that:

19. Conspiracy requires a single joint design between the conspirators within the terms of the indictment. . . . the evidence may prove the existence of a conspiracy of narrower scope and involving fewer people than the prosecution originally alleged, in which case it is not intrinsically wrong for the jury to return guilty verdicts accordingly, but it is always necessary that for two or more persons to be convicted of a single conspiracy each of them must be proved to have shared a common purpose or design.

20. In the present case the prosecution's argument was in effect that there was a 'wheel' or 'chain' conspiracy with Robb at its centre or head; but in such a case, although each conspirator need not necessarily know of the identity or even the existence of all the other conspirators, there must be a shared criminal purpose or design in which all have joined, rather than merely similar or parallel ones.

[His lordship then quoted a passage from *Smith and Hogan's Criminal Law* (13th edn, 2011), p 427 before continuing:]

22. The judge's summing up did not address that issue. On the contrary, he directed the jury that for a defendant to be convicted it was sufficient to show that he had agreed with another person, whether identified or unknown, for the supply of cocaine within the period of the indictment. This left it open to the jury to convict all three defendants of the conspiracy charged against them, if satisfied that the appellant and [X] had each made arrangements with Robb to buy cocaine from him, whether or not the appellant or [X] was party to a wider design. This was wrong.

23. Since Robb was put by the prosecution as the head of the alleged conspiracy, and the involvement of the appellant and [X] was with him, the jury should have been directed to consider first the case in relation to Robb. As to that, there was a strong case that he masterminded the acquisition and processing of the drugs for onward distribution, and that this must have involved the knowing participation of others, so rendering him guilty of the conspiracy charged. The jury should next have been told that if they were not sure of Robb's guilt, they should also acquit the other defendants; but that if they were sure of his guilt, they must then consider whether the prosecution had proved as against each of the other defendants that they shared a common purpose or design (as distinct from separate but similar designs) so as to be a party to the *same* conspiracy, i.e. a conspiracy wider than the supply of cocaine to that particular defendant.

In some cases there are question marks around whether some parties have formed an agreement to achieve a more limited purpose and whether they should be liable for the broader conspiracy. How should the law deal with such subplots?

The scope of the plots and subplots has arisen in more recent cases including *Serious Fraud Office v Papachristos* [2014] EWCA Crim 1863. P and K were convicted of conspiracy to corrupt in relation to activities relating to Innospec Ltd. At the outset of the trial, the defendants faced a single count of conspiracy to corrupt, including allegations of conspiring to make corrupt payments in relation to a range of Innospec products as well as specific allegations relating to 'TEL' contracts for Innospec. P and K denied any wrongdoing. At the close of the evidence, the prosecution applied to add a second count alleging an alternative conspiracy separate from the main conspiracy: if the Crown could establish *only* a conspiracy in relation to TEL contracts, the defendants were not guilty of the wider conspiracy alleged without proof that the conspirators were aware of the wider corrupt agreement. The Court of Appeal dismissed the appeal. The allegations, as originally presented to the jury, had not involved more than one conspiracy. The added count involved no more than limiting the scope of the alleged conspiracy to payments relating to one supplier. It was not an allegation that amounted to a different conspiracy; it was the same conspiracy put on a more restricted basis. Fulford LJ stated:

> 57.… 'It is possible […] that the evidence may prove the existence of a conspiracy of narrower scope and involving fewer people than the prosecution originally alleged, in which case it is not intrinsically wrong for the jury to return guilty verdicts accordingly, but it is always necessary that for two or more persons to be convicted of a single conspiracy each of them must be proved to have shared a common purpose or design': *R v Shillam* [2013] EWCA Crim 160, paragraph 19.

The court acknowledges that there will be cases in which it is necessary for conspiracies to be dealt with in different counts to reflect the subplots involved (*Coughlan and Young* (1976) 63 Cr App R 33), but concluded that this was not one of them. 'The question is whether there were distinct agreements or, alternatively, whether the facts concern the same conspiracy in which there may have been greater and lesser levels of knowledge as to the means by which it is to be carried out' per Fulford LJ at [52].

Fulford LJ advanced the following general proposition (at [63]):

> those charged with a conspiracy may have sought to achieve the common aim by different means, and it is not necessary to prove that all of the conspirators were aware of the full range of ways in which the agreement was to be executed. For some, the conspiracy may have had a narrower scope or it may have involved fewer people than the prosecution's case as put at its widest. What matters is that there is a shared common purpose or design in conformity with the charge.

≈≈ Question
How realistic is it to say that D1 and D2 are in agreement on something if they have never met or communicated together?

21.4.2 Course of conduct

The parties must agree 'that a course of conduct shall be pursued which . . . will necessarily amount to or involve the commission of any offence . . . by one or more parties to the agreement'. A 'course of conduct' is an ambiguous phrase. It might mean that A and B need only have agreed on (a) the actual physical acts which they propose shall be done (eg putting poison in V's tea); or (b) that they have agreed on the act and consequences which they intend to follow from their conduct and the relevant circumstances which they know, or believe, or intend, to exist (eg V will die).

'Course of conduct' must include the contemplated result. If A and B agree to kill V by shooting him, this is surely conspiracy to murder even though B knows that he is a rotten shot and may well miss his target. They agree *and* intend to kill. Their objective *is* the intended result, and the agreed course of conduct is merely the means (however flawed) towards that intended end.

As for relevant circumstances, it would again seem absurd not to include these as requirements of the 'course of conduct'. If D1 and D2 agree to have intercourse with a person, V, their liability for conspiracy to rape a child under 13 contrary to s 5 of the Sexual Offences Act 2003 must depend on their agreed course of conduct including the proscribed *circumstance* of the child's age.

21.4.3 'Necessarily amount to or involve the commission of any offence . . . by one or more parties to the agreement'

D1 and D2 agree to marry next Tuesday, knowing that D1's wife is alive. Have they conspired to commit bigamy? Will their agreement necessarily amount to or involve the commission of an offence? Before next Tuesday, D1's wife may die. These events may be unlikely, but they are possible, and therefore it cannot be said that going through the marriage ceremony will *necessarily* amount to, or involve, the offence of bigamy.

≈≈ *Questions*

D1 and D2 agree to receive goods from X. They believe they will be stolen goods. Have D1 and D2 conspired to receive stolen goods? What if the goods are no longer stolen by the time they receive them?

One way the courts tried to get round this difficulty was to take an expansive reading of the mens rea and construe 'course of conduct' to include material circumstances which the parties *believe* will (not may) exist. The main difficulty about this approach is s 1(2) of the Act. This provides that a person is not guilty of conspiracy to commit an offence unless he '*intends or knows*' that circumstances necessary for the commission of the offence shall or will exist at the time when the conduct constituting the offence is to take place. In the examples just given, D cannot 'know' that the circumstances will exist because, as we have seen, they may not do so; this was confirmed in *Saik* [2006] UKHL 18 (extracted in section 21.4.7, p 585) and implicitly in the House of Lords in *Montilla* [2004] UKHL 50 and it seems strange to say that D 'intends' that they shall exist when D has, and knows he has, no control over their existence. D 'believes' they will exist; but s 1(2) does not use that word.

The Law Commission has described the problem in the following terms:

1.26 So far as it relates to the conduct or consequence elements of an offence, the 'necessary involvement' requirement is an important safeguard against overextension of the law of conspiracy. If D1 and D2 agree on a course of conduct that, if carried out in accordance with their intentions, merely 'might' involve criminal conduct or consequences, that agreement should not amount to a criminal conspiracy. D1 and D2 may, for example, agree to drive as fast as possible from London to Manchester, realising that there is a risk of causing death by dangerous driving in so doing. Whatever one may think of their agreement, it is not an agreement to cause death by dangerous driving and is hence not a criminal conspiracy. It is only if causing death by dangerous driving would necessarily be involved in what D1 and D2 plan to do that there is a conspiracy contrary to the 1977 Act.

1.27 If a substantive offence itself requires proof of actual knowledge of particular facts or circumstances, then section 1(1)(a) appears to require proof of such knowledge on a charge of conspiracy to commit that substantive offence. (Law Com Consultation Paper No 183, *Conspiracy and Attempts* (2007))

21.4.3.1 Conditional intentions

It is necessary to consider whether there can be a conspiracy if there is an agreement between D1 and D2 subject to some condition existing before the crime will be committed.

≈≈ *Question*

D1 and D2 agree to rob a bank if the coast is clear. Have they agreed on a course of conduct that will necessarily involve the commission of an offence?

Lord Nicholls in *Saik*, at [18], stated:

An intention to do a prohibited act is within the scope of section 1(1) even if the intention is expressed to be conditional on the happening, or non-happening of some particular event. . . . A conspiracy to rob a bank tomorrow if the coast is clear when the conspirators reach the bank is not, by reason of this qualification, any less a conspiracy to rob. . . . Fanciful cases apart, the conditional nature of the agreement is insufficient to take the conspiracy outside section 1(1).

The problem frequently arises in the context of money laundering. There is commonly an agreement between D1 and D2 to deal with certain quantities of cash if and when they arrive from X, but D1 and D2 do not know of the precise provenance of the cash. It may represent the proceeds of criminal conduct, but it may not. Dealing with criminal property is a money laundering offence under the Proceeds of Crime Act 2002 (see *Smith and Hogan's Criminal Law* (14th edn, 2015), Ch 27). Is agreeing to deal with cash in these circumstances a conspiracy to launder money?

See further, D. Ormerod, 'Making Sense of Statutory Conspiracy' [2006] CLP 185:

. . .

Distinguishing types of 'conditional' intentions

Academic writing has produced a diverse range of classifications and terminology in this area, but three broad categories are accepted.

- We will do 'x' if 'y'.

Kenneth Campbell in his useful analysis of the concepts ['Conditional Intention' [1982] 2 LS 77, 84–85] describes these as 'non-comprehensive conditional intentions.' The defendant's state of mind is declared only in relation to one possible eventuality.

If D1 and D2 declare 'we will transfer the money if it is clean money', there is no declared intention about what course of conduct they would adopt if the money is illicit. This is not, it is submitted, a sufficient state of mind to constitute an intention to launder money. D1 and D2 have, implicitly, seen the risk that the money will be illicit, but have not declared an intention to deal with criminal money. It cannot be said that D1 and D2 have agreed on a course of conduct that will *necessarily* involve them in the commission of an offence if carried out in accordance with their intentions. In fact, acting in accordance with their declared intentions, all we can assert is that they will not commit a money laundering offence.

If the statement is 'we will transfer money if it is criminal', clearly this is a sufficient intention to constitute a conspiracy to launder money. The other eventuality—what they would do if the money is legitimate—is neither here nor there. D1 and D2 have declared an intention to pursue a course of conduct which if carried out in accordance with their intentions (which here must be taken to mean including those circumstances that they anticipate and accept) will necessarily involve a criminal offence. There will be few such cases.

- We will do 'x' only if 'y'

Campbell calls these 'comprehensive conditional intentions.' They differ significantly from the previous category because D1 and D2 have declared intentions as to their course of conduct in both eventualities: where *y* materialises and not.

The money laundering duo might say: 'we will transfer the money *only if* the money is clean, if it is not we will not transfer it'. There is no intention to pursue a course of conduct that will necessarily involve the commission of an offence. There can be no liability for conspiracy. Alternatively, the duo might say 'we will transfer the money only if the money is criminal.' This would obviously constitute an intention to launder. D1 and D2 would have agreed on a course of conduct which if carried out in accordance with their intentions (again, this must include the circumstances they anticipate and accept) will necessarily involve them in the commission of a criminal offence. These will be rare, in the money laundering context at least. It may be that they are more frequent in other examples—the paedophile might say 'I will touch the girl sexually only if she is under 13'; or the thief—'I will steal only if there is something worth stealing'.

. . .

- To do 'x' even if 'y'

Campbell calls these unconditional intentions. They are generally regarded as a form of direct intention. Taking the money laundering duo as an example, let us imagine that D1 and D2 say 'we know that the monies involved in our business might be criminal, we do not know for sure that they will be, but our business is transferring money and we agree that we will pursue such conduct *even though* some of the monies we transfer are criminal.' Their agreement could be reconstructed as one which includes a confirmed intention:

'we intend to pursue a course of conduct (transferring money) which is not criminal money and if certain circumstances transpire (the money is criminal), we intend nevertheless to pursue a course of conduct (transferring money).'

The agreement will, if completed in accordance with one of their intentions, necessarily involve the commission of a crime.

How would this approach work with other problems postulated above:

D1 and D2 agree to pursue a course of conduct (touching a person in a sexual manner) they foresee that the victim might be under 13. They agree to continue if she is under 13. This could be seen as an agreement to touch a person *even if* she is under 13 if that circumstance arises. On that agreement they will necessarily commit an offence: their agreements include one to touch a child sexually if she is under 13.

D1 and D2 agree to pursue a course of conduct (damaging property) they foresee that the property might not belong to D1. They agree to continue *even if* that may be the case. Their agreements include one intentionally to damage property if it belongs to another.

Consider the following two examples provided by the Court of Appeal in *Reed* [1982] Crim LR 819:

In the first, A and B agree to drive from London to Edinburgh in a time which can be achieved without exceeding the speed limits, but only if the traffic they encounter is exceptionally light. Their agreement will not necessarily involve the commission of any offence even if it is carried out in accordance with their intentions, and they do arrive from London to Edinburgh within the agreed time. Accordingly, the agreement does not constitute the offence of statutory conspiracy or indeed of any offence. In the second example, A and B agree to rob a bank, if when they arrive at the bank it seems safe to do so. Their agreement will necessarily involve the commission of an offence of robbery if it is carried out in accordance with their intentions. Accordingly, they are guilty of the statutory offence of conspiracy.

In *Reed*, A and B were held guilty of conspiring to aid and abet suicide where they agreed that A would visit individuals contemplating suicide and either discourage them or actively help them, depending on his assessment of the appropriate course of action. In *Jackson* [1985] Crim LR 442, CA, D and E agreed to shoot their friend V in the leg if he was convicted of the burglary for which he was on trial. (They believed he would thereby receive a lighter sentence.) V was shot and disabled. D and E were convicted of conspiring to pervert the course of justice. They appealed on the ground that their agreement did not necessarily involve the commission of a crime, as everything depended on a contingency—V being convicted. The court held:

> Planning was taking place for a contingency and if that contingency occurred the conspiracy would necessarily involve the commission of an offence. 'Necessarily' is not to be held to mean that there must inevitably be the carrying out of an offence. It means, if the agreement is carried out in accordance with the plan, there must be the commission of the offence referred to in the conspiracy count.

> ≋ *Questions*
> Can these cases be better dealt with as each involving two agreements? In *Reed*, for example: an agreement to drive to Edinburgh and an agreement to speed if traffic is heavy? The latter necessarily involves the commission of a crime subject to a condition, but that does not preclude a conspiracy. Similarly, image D1 and D2 who agree to burgle 20 Acacia Avenue unless there are police outside when they arrive to do so—this is a completed conspiracy, their reservation does not preclude liability.

In *O'Hadhmaill* [1996] Crim LR 509, it was held that an agreement by members of the IRA during the period of the IRA ceasefire to make bombs with a view to causing explosions if, but only if, the ceasefire came to an end, was a conspiracy to cause an explosion. Is this an agreement subject to a reservation, or contingency?

> ≋ *Questions*
> Are burglars guilty of conspiracy to murder if they set out to commit burglary, having agreed that, if it is necessary to do so in order to complete the burglary or to escape, they will shoot to kill? Will their agreement 'necessarily' involve murder?

21.4.3.2 'Either or' conspiracies

It is possible to enter an agreement to commit offence A *or* offence B, but such an agreement in law constitutes a conspiracy to commit offence A *and* offence B. An agreement to rob the first person who comes around the corner if it is a man constitutes a conspiracy to rob. Similarly an agreement to rape the first person to come around the corner if it is a woman constitutes a conspiracy to rape. Thus, an agreement to rob the first person who comes around the corner if it is a man, but to rape if it is a woman, is an agreement to commit only one of two offences, but it is an agreement which in law amounts to a conspiracy to do both. The condition precedent of the one offence excludes the commission of the other, but at the time of the agreement the relevant facts are unknown and it seems that the parties therefore agree to commit robbery or rape as the prevailing circumstances permit.

The courts have concluded that if conspirators agree that they will steal a particular item and that they will, if necessary, either commit burglary or robbery to obtain that item, that will amount to an agreement to commit the offences of theft, burglary *and* robbery: *A-G's Reference (No 4 of 2003)* [2004] EWCA Crim 1944 at [14]; *Suchedina* [2006] EWCA Crim 2543.

21.4.4 Crime to be committed by one or more of the parties to the conspiracy

An agreement will amount to a statutory conspiracy only if carrying it out will necessarily amount to or involve the commission of an offence *by one or more of the parties to the conspiracy.*

In *Hollinshead* [1985] 1 All ER 850 at 857, the defendants had agreed to supply 'black boxes' to a man (in fact an undercover policeman) who was expected to resell them to persons unknown who would use them to defraud electricity boards. (The black box reverses the flow of current so as to make it appear that less electricity has been used. It has no other use.) The Court of Appeal held that there could be no conspiracy where the fraud contemplated was to be carried out, not by any party to the agreement, but by a third party.

21.4.5 'Crime' to be committed by a conspirator must be a substantive crime

The Court of Appeal in *Hollinshead* also held that the offence of conspiracy under s 1 of the Criminal Law Act 1977 requires D1 and D2 to reach an agreement that will involve 'a course of conduct' amounting to or involving 'the commission of an offence'. It was not enough that D1 and D2 had agreed on a course of conduct that would aid and abet X to commit an offence. D1 and D2 had to have agreed on a 'course of conduct' that would amount to a crime. Their agreed course of conduct was selling the equipment. That was not a crime. The prosecution obtained leave to appeal to the House of Lords. The House of Lords allowed the appeal, but declined to answer the question.

In *Kenning* [2008] EWCA Crim 1534, Lord Phillips CJ confirmed the conclusion of the Court of Appeal in *Hollinshead*. The appellants were convicted of 'conspiracy to aid and abet the production of cannabis'. K and F ran a shop selling hydroponic equipment, cannabis seeds and cultivation literature. Undercover officers had gathered evidence of K and F offering advice on cannabis cultivation and anti-detection measures. However, the equipment K and F sold to the officers could have been used for growing legal plants. The judge directed the jury that the offence of aiding, abetting, counselling or procuring the commission of an offence could be made out even if the latter offence was never in fact committed. The appellants submitted that the offence of conspiring to aid and abet was unknown to law. In the Court of Appeal, Lord Phillips CJ quashed the conviction, confirming that there was no such offence as conspiracy to aid and abet:

> We endorse the court's conclusion [in *Hollinshead*] that an agreement to aid and abet an offence is not in law capable of constituting a criminal conspiracy under section 1(1) of the 1977 Act.

If 'course of conduct' is construed more broadly to include P's use of the equipment in growing the cannabis there is still no offence. The agreement must be as to 'the commission of any offence by *one or more of the parties* to the agreement'. P (the grower) is not a party to the agreement. But do the words 'commission of any offence' include *participation* in the offence as a secondary party? Since all the parties to a conspiracy to commit an offence will be guilty of that offence if it is committed, but s 1(1) contemplates that it may be *committed* by only one of them, it is clear that 'commission' means commission by a principal. An agreement to aid and abet an offence is not a conspiracy under the Act. This is desirable, as it ensures that the boundaries of the criminal law are not extended too far and that the law of conspiracy is consistent with that of attempts, as by s 1(4)(b) of the Criminal Attempts Act 1981 it is not an offence to attempt to aid and abet. This interpretation of the offence was confirmed more recently in *Dang* [2014] EWCA Crim 348.

21.4.6 Intention and conspiracy

Part I of the Criminal Law Act 1977 was based on Law Commission Report No 76, *Conspiracy and Criminal Law Reform* (1976), and that includes a full discussion of the mental element to be required for conspiracy (paras 1.25–1.41). The Law Commission's conclusion on the common law was that:

> . . . it is reasonably clear from such authority as there is that what the law requires before a charge of conspiracy can be proved against a defendant is that *he should intend to bring about any consequences prohibited by the offence* and should have full knowledge of all the circumstances or facts which need to be known to enable him to know that the agreed course of conduct will result in a crime. [Emphasis added]

The Commission thought that this was what the law ought to be: 'We think that the law should require full intention and knowledge before a conspiracy can be established.' Their recommendation (5), para 7.2 reads:

> A person should be guilty of conspiracy if he agrees with another person that an offence shall be committed. *Both must intend that any consequence in the definition of the offence will result* and both must *know* of the existence of any state of affairs which it is necessary for them to know in order to be aware that the course of conduct agreed upon will amount to the offence. [Emphasis added]

The Report included a draft Bill, implementing the Commission's intentions. Clause 1, which became s 1 of the 1977 Act, included the phrase, 'in accordance with their intentions', which was discussed by the House of Lords in the next case.

21.4.6.1 Intention to carry out the agreement

A controversy has arisen as to whether there must be an intention to carry out the agreement in order for there to be a criminal conspiracy. It could be argued that s 1 of the Criminal Law Act 1977 assumes the existence of not only an intention of the parties to agree, but also to carry out the agreement. As the next extract demonstrates, however, the House of Lords interpreted the legislation in a different way. In the following case, Lord Bridge held that it sufficed for all the parties to intend to play their part in bringing about the conspiracy, but that it was not necessary for the parties to have an intention that the substantive offence be carried out. In *Anderson* [1985] 2 All ER 961, the appellant was remanded in custody with Ahmed Andaloussi. He confidently expected to be released on bail but Andaloussi was awaiting trial for very serious drug offences. The appellant agreed with Andaloussi's brother Mohamed and Mohamed Assou to participate in a scheme to effect Andaloussi's escape from prison. Anderson agreed to supply diamond wire capable of cutting through metal bars to be smuggled into prison. He received £2,000 on account. Anderson admitted that he intended to supply the wire on payment of a further £10,000 but claimed to the police that he would then have left for Spain and taken no further part in the scheme, which he believed could not possibly succeed. At his trial for conspiracy to commit the crime of escape, Anderson claimed that he lacked the mental element. That plea was rejected by the trial judge and the Court of Appeal. That court held (a) that a person who agrees with two or more others, who do intend to carry out the agreement, but who has a secret intention himself to participate only in part, is guilty of an offence under s 1(1) of the Criminal Law Act 1977; and (b) if he is not guilty as a principal offender, then he may be convicted of aiding and abetting the conspiracy. He appealed to the House of Lords and both points of law were certified for decision. In dismissing the appeal, Lord Bridge held:

> I have said already, but I repeat to emphasise its importance, that an essential ingredient in the crime of conspiring to commit a specific offence or offences under s1(1) of the 1977 Act is that the accused should agree that a course of conduct be pursued which he knows must involve the commission by one or more of the parties to the agreement of that offence or those offences. But, beyond the mere fact of agreement, the necessary mens rea of the crime is, in my opinion, established if, and only if, it is shown that the accused, when he entered into the agreement, intended to play some part in the agreed course of conduct in furtherance of the criminal purpose which the agreed course of conduct was intended to achieve. Nothing less will suffice; nothing more is required.

The Law Commission in its more recent Consultation Paper No 183, *Conspiracy and Attempts* (2007) described the decision in the following terms:

> 1.38 Section 1(1) of the 1977 Act appears unambiguously to require that for a person to be convicted of conspiracy he or she must intend that the conduct element of the principal offence be perpetrated and that the consequence element (if any) of the substantive offence materialise. However, the well-known and much criticised decision of the House of Lords in *Anderson* detracts from the clarity of this position. On the one hand, it requires that D must intend 'to play some part in the agreed course of conduct.' On the other hand, it does not require that D should intend that the agreement be carried through to completion. In both respects, the decision is troublesome.
>   First, there is no reason, in terms of statutory language or policy, for insisting that D must intend to play some part in implementing the agreement. If D1 and D2 agree to murder V, D1 ought to be convicted of conspiracy to murder even if it was not his or her intention to play any part in V's murder. Secondly, an agreement to commit an offence implies an intention that it should be committed, as section 1(1) of the 1977 Act seems to make clear. The idea of a conspiracy that the conspirators agree to take part in but which none intends to see carried out is very unsatisfactory.

In the light of the controversy surrounding the decision in *Anderson*, it is worth pointing out that the decision has been marginalized somewhat. For example, in *Yip Chiu-Ching* [1995] 1 AC 111, Lord Griffiths stated that, 'The crime of conspiracy requires an agreement between two or more persons to commit an unlawful act with the intention of carrying it out. It is the intention to carry out the crime that constitutes the necessary *mens rea* for the offence.' This is contrary to what Lord Bridge had earlier held in *Anderson*. Although the Privy Council was considering common law conspiracy, there is no principled reason why there ought to be a distinction between the two types of conspiracy in relation to this issue.

As will be discussed in section 21.7, the effect of the Law Commission's recommendations would be to overturn the decision in *Anderson*.

21.4.6.2 Can there be a conspiracy without intent to carry out the agreement?

One of the problems with the judgment of the House of Lords in *Anderson* is that it permits liability despite the fact no one intended the substantive offence to be committed. The Court of Appeal has overlooked or distinguished the judgment on a number of occasions. In *Edwards* [1991] Crim LR 45, for example, the court held that it was not sufficient that D agreed to supply the drugs in question unless he also intended to carry out the agreement. *McPhillips* (1990) BNIL provides another example.

R v McPhillips

[1990] 6 BNIL, Court of Appeal of Northern Ireland (unreported)

(Lord Lowry CJ, O'Donnell and Kelly LJJ)

About 11 pm on 10 October 1985 the police stopped a car driven by Drumm, going towards the Seagoe Hotel. McPhillips was in the front passenger seat. Behind the driver's seat was a bomb containing four kilograms of explosive. It was a device of considerable power, capable of causing a significant explosion. In a statement, McPhillips admitted that the bomb was to be placed on the flat roof of the Seagoe Hotel where a disco was taking place. He said that it had been decided by Drumm and other accomplices that the best time for the bomb to go off would be 1 am as the disco was going on until 1.30 am. McPhillips and Drumm were charged with (1) conspiracy to murder, (2) conspiracy to cause an explosion, and (3) offences under the Explosive Substances Act 1883. At the trial, McPhillips accepted that he was a party to the plan to cause the explosion and pleaded guilty to counts (2) and (3). He pleaded not guilty to conspiracy to murder. He said, and the trial judge believed him, that he intended to give a warning to the police in time for the dance hall to be cleared. The judge held that, notwithstanding McPhillips's intention to give a warning, he was guilty as an aider and abettor of conspiracy to murder. He appealed on the ground that this ruling was wrong.

Lord Lowry CJ:

To be guilty at common law of conspiracy to murder the accused must agree with another that murder will be committed and must intend that this will happen. The guilty act is the agreement that the crime contemplated will be committed; the guilty mind is the intention that that crime will be committed. . . . In regard to the offence of statutory conspiracy section 1(1) 'assumes the existence of an intention of the parties to carry out the agreement': Smith and Hogan, *Criminal Law*, 6th edition [1988], p 259. The wording of the identical Article 9(1) [applicable in Northern Ireland] makes this clear: the agreed course of conduct was the planting of a 'no warning' bomb at the Seagoe Hotel and persons who had agreed to that course of conduct intending it to be carried out would be guilty of conspiracy to murder because, if the agreement had been carried out in accordance with their intentions it would (unless all the patrons of the disco had gone home or had a miraculous escape) necessarily involve the commission of murder. But, on the facts found here, this result would not have been in accordance with the intention of the appellant. Therefore he was not guilty of conspiracy to murder. So, although by going to the Seagoe in Drumm's car, the appellant up to a point acted in accordance with the agreed course of conduct (and was thereby guilty of conspiracy to cause an explosion), he was not guilty as an alleged conspirator in respect to count 1. This result is consistent with the doctrine that, if a joint enterprise goes beyond the agreed or authorised act, a party to that enterprise is not guilty beyond the acts which he agreed to or authorised. To put the matter simply, there must be a common criminal design and, in order to be guilty of a conspiracy to carry out that design, the accused must be a party to the design. That condition is not satisfied in this case.

The Crown's alternative proposition is that the appellant was guilty of aiding and abetting a conspiracy to murder on the part of the conspirators and was therefore liable to be tried, indicted and punished (as happened in the instant case) as a principal offender. The need, and the ability, to rely on this proposition must stem from the hypothesis that the appellant was not a party to the conspiracy to murder, and that hypothesis (having regard to the appellant's ostensible acquiescence in the murder plan) must be based on the fact that the appellant did not intend or authorise the commission of murder. But how then, say the appellant's counsel, did he aid and abet a conspiracy to murder? The Crown's answer is that the appellant assisted the conspirators by his presence when the murder plan was devised and by accompanying Drumm in the car which was conveying the bomb to the intended scene of the crime, and counsel relies on the following passage in the judgment of the learned trial judge.

The common law offence of aiding and abetting involves an act of assisting the principal (actus reus) and a guilty intention (mens rea) that the crime will be committed. This intention is not to be confused with purpose, motive or desire (although those elements may be and often are present) but can be inferred from, and has been in the recent past wrongly identified with, the probability, overwhelming probability or certainty (known to the aider and abettor) that the crime will be committed. Conspiracy is a crime which it is possible to aid and abet and thus the ingredients of aiding and abetting a conspiracy remain as we have described them: a person aids and abets a conspiracy to commit a crime when, not being a party to the conspiracy (otherwise he would be a principal offender) and knowing of the agreement and at least its general object, he assists the principal offenders (by an actus reus, such as supplying a vehicle or a weapon) with the guilty intention (mens rea) that the object of the conspiracy should be achieved . . . the decisive point here is that, whether the test is based on *Hyam* or on *Hancock*, the fact that the appellant had the intention, which he could reasonably have expected to implement, that murder would not take place destroys the possibility of finding the necessary mens rea on his part.

[Lord Lowry discussed the decision of the Court of Appeal in *Anderson*, in the previous section, and continued:]

So far as concerns the hearing before the House of Lords, we find it necessary only to recall what Lord Bridge of Harwich, who delivered the leading speech, said in *R v Anderson* [1986] AC 27, [1985] 2 All ER 961, at p 39D of the former report:

'I have said already, but I repeat to emphasise its importance, that an essential ingredient in the crime of conspiring to commit a specific offence or offences under section 1(1) of the Act of 1977 is that the accused should agree that a course of conduct be pursued which he knows must involve the commission by one or more of the parties to the agreement of that offence or those offences.'

It is obvious, for the reasons already given, that, so far as count 1 is concerned, the conduct of the appellant does not satisfy that test. It is equally clear that *R v Anderson* [1986] AC 27, [1985] 2 All ER 961, is not an authority for the proposition that someone who at all times intends to frustrate the commission of the crime 'agreed upon' is guilty of conspiracy to commit that crime or of aiding and abetting such a conspiracy.

[Lord Lowry referred to Lord Bridge's *dictum* in *Anderson* concerning the person who joins a criminal conspiracy with the object of frustrating it and continued:]

In the different circumstances of this case, the same principle applies: the appellant was not guilty of conspiracy to murder either as a principal offender or as an accomplice because his mind did not go with his acts, but on the contrary was directed towards frustrating the conspiracy to murder. The mere fact that the appellant had already committed terrorist offences and was a member of a terrorist organisation does not disable him from relying on the absence of the necessary intent and the principle enunciated in *R v Fitzpatrick* [1977] NI 20, is not in point.

While the conviction on counts 2 and 3 will stand, the conviction appealed against in relation to count 1 must therefore be quashed.

21.4.6.3 Must D play some part in the agreed course of conduct?

In *Anderson*, Lord Bridge held that the mens rea of conspiracy is established, 'if, and only if, it is shown that the accused, when he entered into the agreement, intended to play some part in the agreed course of conduct in furtherance of the criminal purpose which the agreed course of conduct was intended to achieve'. The Court of Appeal in *Siracusa* [1989] Crim LR 712 sought to circumvent *Anderson*. O'Connor LJ held:

> We think it obvious that Lord Bridge cannot have been intending that the organiser of a crime who recruited others to carry it out would not himself be guilty of conspiracy unless it could be proved that he intended to play some active part himself thereafter. Lord Bridge had pointed out that 'in these days of highly organised crime the most serious statutory conspiracies will frequently involve an elaborate and complex agreed course of conduct in which many will consent to play necessary but subordinate roles not involving them in any direct participation in the commission of the offence or offences at the centre of the conspiracy'.

More recently, in *King* [2012] EWCA Crim 805, Pitchford LJ stated that, 'It is a controversial question whether the defendant must harbour an intention to participate in the conduct which constitutes the substantive offence', but declined to settle the issue one way or the other. Should the Court of Appeal now overturn *Siracusa*?

21.4.7 Knowledge or intention as to circumstances

Section 1(2) of the Criminal Law Act 1977 provides:

> Where liability for any offence may be incurred without knowledge on part of the person committing it of any particular fact or circumstance necessary for the commission of the offence, a person shall nevertheless not be guilty of conspiracy to commit that offence by virtue of subsection (1) above unless he and at least one other party to the agreement intend or know that that fact or circumstance shall or will exist at the time when the conduct constituting the offence is to take place.

This deals with the case where the parties are charged with conspiracy to commit an offence which imposes strict liability, or is satisfied by recklessness as to some fact or circumstance. The subsection makes clear that a party to the agreement is not guilty of conspiracy unless he, and at least one other party, 'intend or know that the fact or circumstance shall or will exist'. It appears, then, that the prosecution must prove intention or knowledge as to every fact or circumstance in the actus reus of the crime it is agreed will be committed. This is an exceptionally strict requirement since mens rea at common law was generally satisfied by proof of recklessness.

Consider D1 who agrees to help D2 move out of his flat. D2 is unsure whether the cabling he has installed for his wifi now belongs to him or to his landlord. D1 and D2 confer together and are uncertain, but agree, nevertheless, to remove it knowing their actions will result in damage to the cabling in the process. They therefore have an intention to cause damage, and are reckless as to whether the property belongs to another. The substantive offence of criminal damage requires that D intends or is reckless as to the causing of damage (the result), *and* that D knows or is reckless as to whether the property belongs to another (circumstance). If D1 and D2 went ahead, they would have sufficient mens rea to be convicted of the substantive offence. As for the conspiracy, in the *actual* circumstances that exist, the carrying out of the agreement 'will necessarily amount' to criminal damage; but, on an orthodox reading of s 1(2), it is not a conspiracy to commit criminal damage. It would not be criminal damage in the circumstances which the parties *intend, or know, shall or will exist*. Ds are merely reckless as to the circumstance. Recklessness as to the circumstance of the actus reus (property belonging to another) is not a sufficient mens rea on a charge of conspiracy to commit a crime (criminal damage) even where it is a sufficient mens rea for the crime itself.

The problem became an acute one in prosecutions for money laundering where persons agree to transfer money. This gave rise to a problem: D1 and D2 might agree to transfer money not being certain whether it was criminal property. How can the defendants have the requisite mens rea within s 1(2)? The requirement is that D (and one other party) *knows or intends* the relevant circumstances for the commission of the offence (that the money will be from a criminal source when they transfer it). D1 and D2 may believe or suspect that the money is criminal, but can they know that unless they were involved in generating it by committing the crime themselves? A person who believes that there is a 50/50 chance that something is so can hardly be said to 'know' that it is so; and 'intend' appears to be irrelevant where the parties know they have no control over the existence of the fact or circumstance— as here. See D. Ormerod, 'Making Sense of Statutory Conspiracies' [2006] CLP 185 (section 21.4.3.1, p 576).

A further problem identified was that on a literal reading, intention or knowledge as to all the circumstances of the actus reus is to be required *only* where the agreement is to commit a crime which may be committed with recklessness or strict liability as to a material circumstance. On this reading, intention or knowledge would *not* be required where the substantive offence *does* require knowledge. Section 1(2) would therefore have imposed a more onerous mens rea for conspiracy to commit crimes of strict liability than for conspiracy to commit crimes which in substantive form require proof of knowledge or intention as to circumstances.

These issues were addressed by the House of Lords in the following case.

R v Saik

[2006] UKHL 18, House of Lords

(Lords Nicholls of Birkenhead, Steyn, Hope of Craighead, Baroness Hale of Richmond and Lord Brown of Eaton-under-Heywood)

Saik was charged with conspiracy to launder money. He operated a bureau de change in London. At his trial he pleaded that he did not know the money that he was to transfer in that office was the proceeds of crime. He only suspected this was so. He was convicted (in fact he pleaded because of a misunderstanding about the scope of the offence) of conspiracy and appealed on the basis that he could not know that the money he was agreeing to transfer was criminal property. Although a mens rea of reasonable grounds for suspicion is enough for the substantive offence of laundering money, Saik argued it was not enough for the conspiracy to commit that offence.

The House of Lords accepted that s 1(2) was to be read as applicable even 'where liability for an offence may be incurred without knowledge [etc]'. Section 1(2) applies to all offences and to all ingredients of an offence where the existence of a particular fact or circumstance was at issue. The requirement under s 1(2) is for 'knowledge' which means 'true belief'. It is not enough to show that D suspected the relevant circumstance.

Lord Nicholls of Birkenhead:

The statutory offence of criminal conspiracy

[His lordship referred to s 1 of the 1977 Act.]

3.... The offence therefore lies in making an agreement. Implicitly, the subsection requires also that the parties intend to carry out their agreement. The offence is complete at that stage. The offence is complete even if the parties do not carry out their agreement. The offence is complete even if the substantive offence is not thereafter committed by any of the conspirators or by anyone else.

4. Thus under this subsection the mental element of the offence, apart from the mental element involved in making an agreement, comprises the intention to pursue a course of conduct which will necessarily involve commission of the crime in question by one or more of the conspirators. The conspirators must intend to do the act prohibited by the substantive offence. The conspirators' state of mind must also satisfy the mental ingredients of the substantive offence. If one of the ingredients of the substantive offence is that the act is done with a specific intent, the conspirators must intend to do the prohibited act and must intend to do the prohibited act with the prescribed intent. A conspiracy to wound with intent to do grievous bodily harm contrary to section 18 of the Offences of the Person Act 1861 requires proof of an intention to wound with the intent of doing grievous bodily harm. The position is the same if the prescribed state of mind regarding the consequence of the prohibited act is recklessness. Damaging property, being reckless as to whether life is endangered thereby, is a criminal offence: Criminal Damage Act 1971, section 1(2). Conspiracy to commit this offence requires proof of an intention to damage property, and to do so recklessly indifferent to whether this would endanger life.

5. An intention to do a prohibited act is within the scope of section 1(1) even if the intention is expressed to be conditional on the happening, or non-happening, of some particular event. The question always is whether the agreed course of conduct, if carried out in accordance with the parties' intentions, would necessarily involve an offence. A conspiracy to rob a bank tomorrow if the coast is clear when the conspirators reach the bank is not, by reason of this qualification, any less a conspiracy to rob. In the nature of things, every agreement to do something in the future is hedged about with conditions, implicit if not explicit. In theory if not in practice, the condition could be so far-fetched that it would cast doubt on the genuine[ne]ss of a conspirator's expressed intention to do an unlawful act. If I agree to commit an offence should I succeed in climbing Mount Everest without the use of oxygen, plainly I have no intention to commit the offence at all. Fanciful cases apart, the conditional nature of the agreement is insufficient to take the conspiracy outside section 1(1).

6. Section 1(2) qualifies the scope of the offence created by section 1(1). This subsection is more difficult. Its essential purpose is to ensure that strict liability and recklessness have no place in the offence of conspiracy. [His lordship quoted the section.]

7. Under this subsection conspiracy involves a third mental element: intention or knowledge that a fact or circumstances necessary for the commission of the substantive offence will exist. Take the offence of handling stolen goods. One of its ingredients is that the goods must have been stolen. That is a fact necessary for the commission of the offence. Section 1(2) requires that the conspirator must intend or know that this fact will exist when the conduct constituting the offence takes place.

8. It follows from this requirement of intention or knowledge that proof of the mental element needed for the commission of a substantive offence will not always suffice on a charge of conspiracy to commit that offence. In respect of a material fact or circumstance conspiracy has its own mental element. In conspiracy this mental element is set as high as 'intend or know'. This subsumes any lesser mental element, such as suspicion, required by the substantive offence in respect of a material fact or circumstances. In this respect the mental element of conspiracy is distinct from and supersedes the mental element in the substantive offence. When this is so, the lesser mental element in the substantive offence becomes otiose on a charge of conspiracy. It is an immaterial averment. To include it in the particulars of the offence of conspiracy is potentially confusing and should be avoided.

9. The phrase 'fact or circumstance necessary for the commission of the offence' is opaque. Difficulties have sometimes arisen in its application. The key seems to lie in the distinction apparent in the subsection between 'intend or know' on the one hand and any particular 'fact or circumstance necessary for the commission of the offence' on the other hand. The latter is directed at an element of the actus reus of the offence. A mental element of the offence is not itself a 'fact or circumstance' for the purposes of the subsection. . . .

[His lordship then reviewed the law reform process culminating in the enactment of s 1(2) and continued:]

13. The rationale underlying this approach is that conspiracy imposes criminal liability on the basis of a person's intention. This is a different harm from the commission of the substantive offence. So it is right that the intention which is being criminalised in the offence of conspiracy should itself be blameworthy. This should be so, irrespective of the provisions of the substantive offence in that regard.

14. Against that background I turn to some issues concerning the scope and effect of section 1(2). The starting point is to note that this relieving provision is not confined to substantive offences attracting strict liability. The subsection does not so provide. Nor would such an interpretation of the subsection make sense. It would make no sense for section 1(2) to apply, and require proof of intention or knowledge, where liability for the substantive offence is absolute but not where the substantive offence has built into it a mental ingredient less than knowledge, such as suspicion.

15. So much is clear. A more difficult question arises where an ingredient of the substantive offence is that the defendant must *know* of a material fact or circumstance. On its face section 1(2) does not apply in this case. The opening words of section 1(2), on their face, limit the scope of the subsection to cases where a person may commit an offence *without* knowledge of a material fact or circumstance.

16. Plainly Parliament did not intend that a person would be liable for conspiracy where he lacks the knowledge required to commit the substantive offence. That could not be right. Parliament could not have intended such an absurd result. Rather, the assumption underlying section 1(2) is that, where knowledge of a material fact is an ingredient of a substantive offence, knowledge of that fact is also an ingredient of the crime of conspiring to commit the substantive offence.

17. There are two ways this result might be achieved. One is simply to treat section 1(2) as inapplicable in this type of case. This would mean that the knowledge requirement in the substantive offence would survive as a requirement which must also be satisfied in respect of a conspiracy. In the same way as a conspirator must intend to do the prohibited act with any specific intent required by the substantive offence, so he must intend to do the prohibited act having the knowledge required by the substantive offence. Accordingly, on this analysis, where knowledge of a fact is an ingredient of the substantive offence, section 1(2) is not needed.

18. The other route is to adopt the interpretation of section 1(2) suggested by Sir John Smith. The suggestion is that section 1(2) applies in such a case despite the opening words of the subsection. Section 1(2) is to be read as applicable *even* 'where liability for an offence may be incurred without knowledge [etc]'. It is difficult to see what other function the word 'nevertheless' has in the subsection. This may seem a slender peg on which to hang a conclusion of any substance, but it is enough: see 'Some Answers' [1978] Crim LR 210.

19. The first route accords more easily with the language of section 1(2), but I prefer the second route for the following reason. A conspiracy is looking to the future. It is an agreement about future conduct. When the agreement is made the 'particular fact or circumstance necessary for the commission' of the substantive offence may not have happened. So the conspirator cannot be said to *know* of that fact or circumstance at that time. Nor, if the happening of the fact or circumstance is beyond his control, can it be said that the conspirator *will* know of that fact or circumstance.

20. Section 1(2) expressly caters for this situation. The conspirator must 'intend or know' that this fact or circumstance 'shall or will exist' when the conspiracy is carried into effect. Although not the happiest choice of language, 'intend' is descriptive of a state of mind which is looking to the future. This is to be contrasted with the language of substantive offences. Generally, references to 'knowingly' or the like in substantive offences are references to a past state of affairs. No doubt this language could be moulded appropriately where the offence charged is conspiracy. But the more direct and satisfactory route is to regard section 1(2) as performing in relation to a conspiracy the function which words such as 'knowingly' perform in relation to the substantive offence. That approach accords better with what must be taken to have been the parliamentary intention on how the phrase 'intend

or know' in section 1(2) would operate in this type of case. Thus on a charge of conspiracy to handle stolen property where the property has not been identified when the agreement is made, the prosecution must prove that the conspirator *intended* that the property which was the subject of the conspiracy *would* be stolen property.

21. In my view, therefore, the preferable interpretation of section 1(2) is that the subsection applies to all offences. It applies whenever an ingredient of an offence is the existence of a particular fact or circumstance. The subsection applies to that ingredient . . .

25. Does 'know' in this context have the meaning attributed to it in the *Montila* case when considering the substantive offence? If it does, the identified property to which the conspiracy related must actually be or represent the proceeds of crime, and the conspirator must be aware of this. Or does 'know' in this context mean 'believe', as seems to be suggested in *R v Ali* [2006] 2 WLR 316, 335, para 98? On the ordinary use of language a person cannot 'know' whether property is the proceeds of crime unless he participated in the crime. He can only believe this is so, on the basis of what he has been told. Adopting this approach would mean that, so far as section 93C is concerned, equating knowledge with belief in the case of identified property would achieve a measure of symmetry with the requirement of intention in the case of unidentified property. It would mean that in both cases what matters is the conspirator's state of mind: the actual provenance of the property would not be material.

26. I do not think the latter approach can be accepted. The phrase under consideration ('intend or know') in section 1(2) is a provision of general application to all conspiracies. In this context the word 'know' should be interpreted strictly and not watered down. In this context knowledge means true belief. . . .

Lord Hope [discussed the scope of s 1(2) and continued:]

75. . . . A conspiracy is complete when the agreement to enter into is formed, even if nothing is done to implement it. Implementation gives effect to the conspiracy, but it does not alter its essential elements. The statutory language adopts this approach. It assumes that implementation of the agreement lies in the future. The question whether its requirements are fulfilled is directed to the stage when the agreement is formed, not to the stage when it is implemented.

76. First there is section 1(1). It refers to (i) an agreement, (ii) a course of conduct to be pursued under that agreement and (iii) the fact that, if the agreement is carried out as intended, it 'will necessarily' amount to or involve the commission of an offence by one or more of the parties to the agreement. Let us assume that there are two parties to the agreement: parties X and Y. X is in possession of cash which he knows is the proceeds of crime (A). Y does not know the cash is A, which it is. But he suspects that it is A, and he has reasonable grounds for his suspicion. The agreement is that X will hand over the cash to Y, and that Y will immediately convert it into a different currency. If the agreement is carried out as they intend, the cash will be converted. The conversion of cash which is A by someone who knows that it is A is an offence contrary to section 93C(2). X knows that the cash is A. So the carrying out of the agreement between X and Y in accordance with their intentions will necessarily amount to the commission of an offence by X. This is enough to satisfy section 1(1)(a). But the carrying out of the agreement will also necessarily amount to the commission of an offence by Y. The cash will be A, because that is the fact known to X. And the conversion of cash which is in fact A by someone who has reasonable grounds to suspect that it is A is an offence under section 93C(2). . . .

78. . . . Section 1(2) tells us that a person shall not be guilty of the conspiracy to commit that offence by virtue of subsection (1) unless he and at least one other party to the agreement 'intend or know' that the fact necessary for the commission of the offence—that the cash is A—'shall or will exist' at the time when the cash is converted into a different currency. There is no problem about X, of course. He knows that the cash which he will hand over to Y is A. He knows that it will be A when the conduct takes place—when it is converted into a different currency. But what about Y? He suspects that the

cash is A. But he does not know that it is, or that it will be when it is handed over to him and he converts it. Can it be said that he intends that it should be A, when he does not know what he will be dealing with? Solving this problem is not easy because the word 'intend' in section 1(2) refers to the existence of a fact or a circumstance, not to the consequences of giving effect to the agreement. But the words 'shall or will' indicate that nothing short of intention or knowledge as to its existence will do.

79. I think that the answer to this question will depend on the facts. It could be said of Y that he knows enough about the purpose of the transaction because of the grounds for his suspicion for it not to matter whether he will be able to tell by looking at the cash that it is in fact the proceeds of crime. It may be open to the Crown to prove that Y knew very well what the purpose of the agreement was—that he knew that the cash was to be converted to assist someone to avoid prosecution for an offence or the making or enforcement of a confiscation order, which is what section 93C(2) refers to. It might be going too far to say that he knew that the cash would be A when he came to deal with it. But it could be inferred that he intended that the cash would be A, because he knew that that was the only purpose of the transaction.

80. But in this case all we know is that the appellant suspected that the money 'was' the proceeds of crime. The appellant must be dealt with according to the terms of his plea. We cannot say that he was wilfully blind as to the purpose of the agreement, because that is not what he admits to. He suspected that he was being asked to convert the proceeds of criminal conduct. But he did not know that this was the origin of the money that was actually being given to him. He was prepared to go ahead and convert the money without knowing that it was in fact the proceeds of crime. It would not be quite right to say that he was reckless. All he was to do was simply to convert money from one currency into another—an everyday transaction which involves no risk to anyone. But he was willing to go ahead with this without troubling to find out whether or not what he was proposing to do was criminal. A person who is in that state of mind cannot be said to intend that the fact or circumstance that makes his act criminal should exist. That being the position I would hold that, although he was suspicious, the appellant cannot be said to have intended that the money should be the proceeds of crime when he came to deal with it.

. . .

Baroness Hale:

99. . . . B is not guilty of conspiracy unless both he and A 'intend or know' that the money is the proceeds of crime. A knows that it is. B does not. But does he *intend* that it will be? Is a conditional intent of the 'even if' kind sufficient for the purpose of section 1(2) as many think that it is for the purpose of section 1(1)? My Lords, I cannot see why it should be sufficient for the one but not for the other. The main objection in both cases is that it could be seen as 'a recklessness formula in disguise', a phrase taken from Professor David Ormerod's most helpful Current Legal Problems lecture, 'Making Sense of *Mens Rea* in Statutory Conspiracies' (2006) CLP [185], to which I am much indebted. Even the late Professor JC Smith seems to have regretted that the Law Commission, in their determination to exclude recklessness, might have 'thrown out the baby, conditional intention, with the bathwater, recklessness' (see '*Mens Rea* in Statutory Conspiracy: Some Answers' [1978] Crim LR 210, at 212). My Lords, I do not think that they did. The dividing line between them may be narrow, but it is discernible. Once again, it is important to distinguish between what happens when the substantive offence is committed—when the men have intercourse with the woman whether or not she consents—and what happens when they agree to do so. When they agree, they have thought about the possibility that she may not consent. They have agreed that they will go ahead *even if at the time when they go ahead they know that she is not consenting*. If so, that will not be recklessness; that will be intent to rape. Hence they are guilty of conspiracy to rape.

100. So if, in our example, the conspirator agrees to launder the money even if at the time he does so he is told that it is in fact the proceeds of crime, then he does indeed intend that fact to be the case

when he does the deed. The fact that he is equally happy to convert the money even if it is not the proceeds of crime makes no difference. So perhaps the real question for the jury is, 'what would he have done if, when the money came in, someone had let him know the truth?' Would he have said, 'take it away'? Or would he have said 'hand it over'?

101. In my view, this provides an entirely principled and sensible way of making sense of the language of section 1(1) and (2) of the 1977 Act.

Appeal allowed

≋ *Questions*

Consider the impact of the decision on a prosecution for conspiracy to handle stolen goods in which:

(1) the property which D is to be invited to handle has already been stolen at the time of the offer to D for him to receive it and it is 'identified property' (D1 and D2 agree that they will receive the property which E has stolen and which he shows to them). Is this a knowledge case?

(2) the property has yet to be stolen (D1 and D2 agree that they will receive the property E has suggested to them he will steal later that week). Is the mens rea one of intention or knowledge as to the status of the property?

The majority concluded that knowledge under s 1(2) was not akin to a conditional intention. Baroness Hale dissented on this point. The point did not arise for consideration since the Crown had not shown more than that the defendants had agreed to transfer cash being suspicious as to its criminal provenance. They had not gone further and established that the defendants had agreed that even if the property was criminal, as they suspected, they would launder it nevertheless. It is submitted that it is still open to the courts to accept that such an agreement is a conspiracy to launder.

The House of Lords' decision made it much more difficult to secure prosecutions because the mens rea requirement of intention or knowledge as to circumstances is a demanding one. The Law Commission examined the possibility of reform and published its recommendations in 2009.

Law Commission Report No 318, *Conspiracy and Attempts* (2009)

IS IT NECESSARY TO GO BEYOND WHAT WAS SAID IN *SAIK* ABOUT CONDITIONAL INTENT?

2.110 In our view, the answer to this question is 'no'. The draft Bill makes this explicit.

2.111 In the passage from the speech of Lord Nicholls just cited, Lord Nicholls says that only in 'fanciful' cases will the conditional nature of an intent have a bearing on whether or not proof of that intent will suffice as proof of fault for the purposes of liability for conspiracy. However, the current edition of *Smith and Hogan* [12th edn, 2008] casts some doubt on how 'fanciful' a case may have to be to take it outside section 1(1). In *O'Hadhmaill*, some IRA members agreed to make bombs during a ceasefire period, with the intention of causing explosions if the ceasefire period came to an end. The Court of Appeal found that proof of this 'conditional' intention to cause explosions was enough to satisfy the requirements of a criminal conspiracy. Of this result, *Smith and Hogan* says:

The [decision] may be criticised on the basis that the satisfaction of the condition may be too dependent on DD's own subsequent evaluation of the circumstances to be said to represent a true intention . . . In *O'Hadhmaill*, the question arises whether the ceasefire could be regarded as a fact or circumstance that was clearly determinable without reverting to D's opinion.

2.112 In our view, *O'Hadhmaill* was correctly decided. The triggering of the condition, in D's conditional intention, may often depend on some element of evaluation. To elaborate on Lord Nicholls example, if D1 and D2 decide to go ahead with a robbery only if the coast is clear, whether the coast is 'clear' may depend on an element of evaluation or opinion. For D1, the coast being clear may mean that there must be no security personnel in sight at all, whereas for D2 it may mean only that there is no reason to think that the police are there waiting for them. For D1, the coast may still be clear even if there is someone who has spent the night under cover of the bank entrance way and is causing a slight obstruction, whereas perhaps for D2 the coast would not be 'clear' in such circumstances. Unless such differences of opinion or evaluation prevent D1 and D2 reaching an agreement to rob in the first place (which they clearly do not), then they are, and should be, irrelevant to their liability.

2.113 Deep conceptual waters can be avoided in this context if it is kept in mind that an 'intention' to do something need not involve a high-level commitment, unlike a pledge, vow or oath. In this context, an 'intention' is nothing more than a (possibly, quite weak) provisional conclusion reached in reasoning about action. It is a decision to do something, unless reconsideration (whether or not involving new factors) at some point leads the person who has the intention to abandon or modify it.

2.114 Such considerations or factors may be factually determinable ('will there or will there not be a police officer outside the bank?'), or wholly evaluative ('will I still feel like going through with it when I get to the bank?'). In itself, uncertainty bearing on the fulfilment of conditions need not negate the existence of a conditional intention to do something. This will only happen if the uncertainty prevents the formation of the intention at the relevant time *at all* ('whether I agree to rob the bank depends on how I feel about it when I wake up on the morning in question').

≈≈ **Question**

Consider how wide the conspiracy offence would become.

21.5 Exemptions from liability for conspiracy

Section 2 of the Criminal Law Act 1977 provides:

2. Exemptions from liability for conspiracy

(1) A person shall not by virtue of section 1 above be guilty of conspiracy to commit any offence if he is an intended victim of that offence.

(2) A person shall not by virtue of section 1 above be guilty of conspiracy to commit any offence or offences if the only other person or persons with whom he agrees are (both initially and at all times during the currency of the agreement) persons of any one or more of the following descriptions, that is to say:

   (a) his spouse [or civil partner];

   (b) a person under the age of criminal responsibility; and

   (c) an intended victim of that offence or of each of those offences.

(3) A person is under the age of criminal responsibility for the purposes of subsection (2)(b) above so long as it is conclusively presumed, by virtue of section 50 of the Children and Young Persons Act 1933, that he cannot be guilty of any offence.

In relation to s 2(1) and s 2(2)(c), see *Tyrrell*, discussed in section 22.2.1.3, p 607. Recently, in *Suski* [2016] EWCA Crim 24, D sought to argue that the fact the exemption in s 2(2) only extends to spouses and civil partners was discriminatory and violated Article 14 of the European Convention on Human Rights in conjunction with Article 8. D was not married to his partner, but it was accepted that they cohabited and were living together as husband and wife. The Court of Appeal rejected this argument and held that the boundary Parliament had drawn between spouses and civil partners and others satisfied Article 8(2) of the Convention. McCombe LJ also made the following observation:

> 23. We see no reason to extend any further than statute requires a rule of the common law that has become to be regarded as anomalous today. There are very good grounds why a court trying a charge of conspiracy should not have to inquire closely into the nature of personal relationships of alleged conspirators, infinitely variable as they are likely to be from case to case. Nor, in our judgment, should the criminal law turn upon such vagaries.

≋ *Questions*

(1) Is D guilty of conspiracy if he agrees: (a) with Poppy, a 15-year-old girl, to have sexual intercourse with her, (b) with Poppy to take indecent images of her at her request?

(2) Are any of these exemptions justifiable in the twenty-first century? For proposed reform, see the Law Commission Report in section 21.7, p 597. Do you agree with the reasons given by McCombe LJ in *Suski* for why the marital exemption should not be extended?

21.6 Common law conspiracies

21.6.1 Conspiracy to defraud

It is generally accepted that there are two categories of conspiracy to defraud. The first relates to injury to economic interests, the second to inducing a person to act contrary to his duty. The second category, as well as the first, is relevant to commercial fraud because its most likely application is to inducing acts which will lead to economic gain, such as obtaining an export licence. The nearest approach to a definition of the first category of conspiracy to defraud is the statement by Lord Dilhorne with which all their lordships agreed in *Scott v Metropolitan Police Comr* [1975] AC 819 at 840, HL:

> . . . it is clearly the law that an agreement by two or more by dishonesty to deprive a person of something which is his or to which he is or would be or might be entitled and an agreement by two or more by dishonesty to injure some proprietary right of his, suffices to constitute the offence of conspiracy to defraud.

(Lord Dilhorne put it slightly differently—'might *but for the perpetration of the fraud* be entitled' at p 839 (emphasis added).)

Under the second category, a person is defrauded if he is deceived into acting contrary to his duty. An agreement by deception to induce a public official to issue an export licence (*Board of Trade v Owen* [1957] AC 602, HL) or a National Insurance number to a person not entitled to one (*Moses* [1991] Crim LR 617) is a conspiracy to defraud the official. These examples are all concerned with public officials performing public duties. Lord Diplock, in *Scott*, said that the offence was limited to such cases. In *Wai Yu-tsang v R* [1991] 4 All ER 664 at 670, however, the

Privy Council disapproved of Lord Diplock's *dictum* in *Scott*, pointing out that he alone took this point in that case. But no reference was made in *Wai* to *Withers* [1975] AC 842, HL, where Lords Simon and Kilbrandon seem to have been of the same mind as Lord Diplock. However that may be, the Privy Council considered that:

> . . . the cases concerned with persons performing public duties are not to be regarded as a special category . . . but rather as exemplifying the general principle that conspiracies to defraud are not restricted to cases of intention to cause the victim economic loss. On the contrary they are to be understood in the broad sense described by Lord Radcliffe and Lord Denning in *Welham's* case [1961] AC 103.

Lord Denning said in *Welham*: 'If anyone may be prejudiced in any way by the fraud, that is enough'; and Lord Radcliffe said 'What it [the law] has looked for in considering the effect of cheating on another person and so in defining the criminal intent is the prejudice of that person; what *Blackstone's Commentaries* (4 Bl Com (18th ed) 247) called "to the prejudice of another man's right".'

So it appears that conspiracy to defraud is an agreement dishonestly to do *any* act prejudicial to another. Dishonesty is the concept formulated in *Ghosh* [1982] QB 1053, section 13.6, p 367. In *Withers,* the House of Lords rid the law of an offence of public mischief (an act prejudicial to the public) and conspiracy to effect a public mischief. Nevertheless, we are left with conspiracy to defraud which is extremely broad.

Everything depends on whether the jury consider the agreement to be dishonest.

The Law Commission has been struggling for over 20 years with the problem of replacing common law conspiracy to defraud either with a series of specific offences of dishonesty or a general fraud offence.

Law Commission Report No 276, *Fraud*
(2002) (references omitted)

PART III

DEFECTS OF THE PRESENT LAW

. . .

Conspiracy to defraud

An anomalous crime

3.2 The concept of fraud, for the purposes of conspiracy to defraud, is wider than the range of conduct caught by any of the individual statutory offences involving dishonest behaviour. Thus it can be criminal for two people to agree to do something which it would not be unlawful for one person to do.

3.3 This anomaly has an historical basis. Before the Criminal Law Act 1977, a criminal conspiracy could be based on an agreement to commit an unlawful but non-criminal act, such as a tort or breach of contract. It appears that the justification for this was that there was a greater danger from people acting in concert than alone. As Professor Andrew Ashworth has explained:

> In legal terms, the reasoning seemed to be that acts which were insufficiently antisocial to justify criminal liability when done by one person could become sufficiently antisocial to justify criminal liability when done by two or more people acting in agreement. Such a combination of malefactors might increase the probability of harm resulting, might in some cases increase public alarm, and might in other cases facilitate the perpetration and concealment of the wrong.

3.4 The 1977 Act was the implementation of our Report on Conspiracy and Criminal Law Reform, which 'emphatically' concluded that the object of a conspiracy should be limited to the commission of a substantive offence and that there should be no place in a criminal code for a law of conspiracy extending beyond this ambit. An agreement should not be criminal where that which it was agreed should be done would not amount to a criminal offence if committed by one person.

3.5 This Commission has repeated its adherence to this principle in subsequent reports and we believe it commands very wide support. *Either* conspiracy to defraud is too wide in its scope (in that it catches agreements to do things which are rightly not criminal) *or* the statutory offences are too narrow (in that they fail to catch certain conduct which should be criminal)—*or*, which is our view, the problem is a combination of the two. On any view, the present position is anomalous and has no place in a coherent criminal law.

The definition of 'to defraud'

3.6 As we stated in paragraphs 2.4 to 2.6, the cases on the meaning of 'to defraud' have given it a broad meaning, so that any dishonest agreement to make a gain at another's expense could form the basis of conspiracy to defraud. We take the view that this definition is *too* broad. In a capitalist society, commercial life revolves around the pursuit of gain for oneself and, as a corollary, others may lose out, whether directly or indirectly. Such behaviour is perfectly legitimate. It is only the element of 'dishonesty' which renders it a criminal fraud. In other words, that element 'does all the work' in assessing whether particular facts fall within the definition of the crime.

3.7 In most cases it will be self-evident that the conduct alleged, if proved, would be dishonest, and the question will be whether that conduct has been proved. Nonetheless, in some cases, the defence will argue that the alleged conduct was not dishonest. There is no statutory definition of dishonesty, so the issue is determined with reference to *Ghosh*. In that case it was held that the fact-finders must be satisfied (a) that the defendant's conduct was dishonest according to the ordinary standards of reasonable and honest people, *and* (b) that the defendant must have realised that it was dishonest according to those standards (as opposed to his or her own standards).

3.8 Activities which would otherwise be legitimate can therefore become fraudulent if a jury is prepared to characterise them as dishonest. Not only does this delegate to the jury the responsibility for defining what conduct is to be regarded as fraudulent, but it leaves prosecutors with an uncommonly broad discretion when they are deciding whether to pursue a conspiracy to defraud case. If, for example, the directors of a company enter into 'industrial espionage' in order to gain the edge over a competitor, they could potentially be prosecuted for conspiracy to defraud, despite the absence of any statutory offence governing such activities. As *Smith and Hogan* states, the offence opens 'a very broad vista of potential criminal liability'.

3.9 In effect, conspiracy to defraud is a 'general dishonesty offence', subject only to the irrational requirement of conspiracy.

The Fraud Act failed to follow through the Law Commission's intention of abolition. The Government was concerned that if the common law offence of conspiracy to defraud was abolished, there might be unforeseen lacunae in the protection offered by the criminal law against fraudulent conduct.

The advantages and dangers of the use of conspiracy to defraud are clearly encapsulated in the following statement taken from the inquiry initiated by the Attorney General following the collapse of the Jubilee Line case (a long running conspiracy case which collapsed after 18 months of trial time):

Conspiracy to defraud at common law is an extremely useful weapon for a fraud prosecutor and frequently a course of offending cannot be adequately reflected in an indictment without recourse to it. For example, such a charge avoids the difficulties associated with 'specimen' counts of substantive offences. Not surprisingly, it is frequently used and is the main charge in most SFO prosecutions. However, it can sometimes be resorted to in an attempt to sidestep significant difficulties in the proof of any substantive offence and bridge the gaps in an investigation which has failed to prove more specific offences of dishonesty. Furthermore, as happened in this case, the use of the charge, because of its great breadth, can make potentially relevant a very large body of documentary and other evidence which would not be relevant or admissible in relation to specific statutory offences.

≈≈≈ *Question*

Is an offence which is so vague compatible with Article 7 of the European Convention on Human Rights? See section 1.5, p 13 for an overview of Article 7.

21.6.2 Corruption of public morals and outraging public decency

Shaw v Director of Public Prosecutions
[1961] UKHL 1, House of Lords

(Viscount Simonds, Lords Reid, Tucker, Morris of Borth-y-Gest and Hodson)

The appellant published a booklet entitled 'The Ladies' Directory' with the object of enabling prostitutes to ply their trade. The booklet contained names and addresses and sometimes photographs of prostitutes and in some cases abbreviations indicating the type of conduct in which the woman would indulge. The women paid for the advertisements to be inserted. Shaw was convicted on three counts: (1) conspiracy to corrupt public morals; (2) living wholly or in part on the earnings of prostitution, contrary to s 30(1) of the Sexual Offences Act 1956; and (3) publishing an obscene article contrary to s 2(1) of the Obscene Publications Act 1959. His appeal to the Court of Criminal Appeal was dismissed. That court held that conduct calculated and intended to corrupt public morals was an indictable misdemeanour at common law and that it followed that an agreement to do so was a conspiracy; s 2(4) of the Obscene Publications Act 1959 did not prohibit the prosecution of the appellant for conspiracy because that offence consisted in an agreement to corrupt, and did not 'consist of the publication' of the booklets. The appellant appealed against his conviction on the first and second counts.

The following extracts from the speeches of their lordships relate only to the conspiracy charge.

[**Viscount Simonds**, having asserted that, contrary to the appellant's submission, conspiracy to corrupt public morals is an offence known to the common law, continued:]

Need I say, my Lords, that I am no advocate of the right of the Judges to create new criminal offences? . . .

But I am at a loss to understand how it can be said either that the law does not recognise a conspiracy to corrupt public morals or that, though there may not be an exact precedent for such a conspiracy as this case reveals, it does not fall fairly within the general words by which it is described. I do not propose to examine all the relevant authorities. That will be done by my noble and learned friend. The fallacy in the argument that was addressed to us lay in the attempt to exclude from the scope of general words acts well calculated to corrupt public morals just because they had not been committed or had not been brought to the notice of the Court before. It is not thus that the common law has developed. We are, perhaps, more accustomed to hear this matter discussed upon the question whether such and such a transaction is contrary to public policy. At once the controversy arises. On the one hand it is said that it is not possible in the twentieth century for the Court to create a new head of public policy, on the other it is said that this is but a new example of a well-established head. In the sphere of criminal law, I entertain no doubt that there remains in the Courts of Law a residual power to enforce the supreme and fundamental purpose of the law, to conserve not only the safety and order but also the moral welfare of the State, and that it is their duty to guard it against attacks which may be the more insidious because they are novel and unprepared for. That is the broad head (call it public policy if you wish) within which the present indictment falls. It matters little what label is given to the offending act. To one of your Lordships it may appear an affront to public decency, to another, considering that it may succeed in its obvious intention of provoking libidinous desires, it will seem a corruption of public morals. Yet others may deem it aptly described as the creation of a public mischief or the undermining of moral conduct. The same act will not in all ages be regarded in the same way. The law must be related to the changing standards of life, not yielding to every shifting impulse of the popular will but having regard to fundamental assessments of human values and the purposes of society. Today a denial of the fundamental Christian doctrine, which in past centuries would have been regarded by the Ecclesiastical Courts as heresy and by the common law as blasphemy, will no longer be an offence if the decencies of controversy are observed. When Lord Mansfield, speaking long after the Star Chamber had been abolished, said [in *Delaval* (1763) 3 Burr 1434 at 1438] that the Court of King's Bench was the *custos morum* of the people and had the superintendency of offences *contra bonos mores*, he was asserting, as I now assert, that there is in that Court a residual power, where no statute has yet intervened to supersede the common law, to superintend those offences which are prejudicial to the public welfare. Such occasions will be rare, for Parliament has not been slow to legislate when attention has been sufficiently aroused. But gaps remain and will always remain since no one can foresee every way in which the wickedness of man may disrupt the order of society. Let me take a single instance to which my noble and learned friend, Lord Tucker, refers. Let it be supposed that, at some future, perhaps, early, date homosexual practices between adult consenting males are no longer a crime. Would it not be an offence if, even without obscenity, such practices were publicly advocated and encouraged by pamphlet and advertisement? Or must we wait until Parliament finds time to deal with such conduct? I say, my Lords, that, if the common law is powerless in such an event, then we should no longer do her reverence. But I say that her hand is still powerful and that it is for Her Majesty's Judges to play the part which Lord Mansfield pointed out to them.

The appeal on both counts should, in my opinion, be dismissed.

[**Lord Reid** made a dissenting speech.]

[**Lords Tucker, Morris** and **Hodson** made speeches dismissing the appeal.]

Appeal dismissed

≈≈ *Questions*

Is it appropriate that such vague common law offences are retained? Are they compatible with Article 10 of the European Convention on Human Rights guaranteeing a right to freedom of expression?

In *Knuller v DPP* [1973] AC 435, the House of Lords clarified a number of points in relation to the offence. The appellants published a magazine, the *International Times*, which contained on inner pages columns of advertisements headed 'Males'. Most of these advertisements solicited homosexual acts. In upholding the appellants' convictions, the House of Lords held that it suffices to make out the offence if the material corrupts the morals of such members of the public as may be influenced by the matter published, rather than the public at large. It was also confirmed that it is for the jury to decide whether or not advertisements were, by present-day standards, corrupting of public morals.

Since the Court of Appeal confirmed in *Gibson* [1991] 1 All ER 439 that there is a common law offence of outraging public decency, any conspiracies ought to be charged as statutory conspiracies.

~~~ *Question*
Would these offences withstand challenge in Strasbourg?

21.6.3 Impossibility

There is an important distinction between common law and statutory conspiracies in relation to the issue of impossibility. As has already been pointed out, impossibility is not a defence when considering statutory conspiracies. The same is not true, however, of common law conspiracies. In *DPP v Nock* [1978] AC 979, the House of Lords held that when two or more persons agree upon a course of conduct with the object of committing a criminal offence, but, unknown to them, it is impossible to achieve that object by that course of conduct, they do not commit the crime of conspiracy. However, this principle only applies where the conspiracy could never be achieved. For example, if A and B intend to defraud V, but unbeknownst to them V is already dead, there can be no conspiracy to defraud him.

21.7 Reform of conspiracy

The Law Commission in its Report No 318, *Conspiracy and Attempts* (2009), made the following recommendations:

CONSPIRACY

9.1 We recommend that a conspiracy must involve an agreement by two or more persons to engage in the conduct element of an offence and (where relevant) to bring about any consequence element of the substantive offence.

9.2 We recommend that a conspirator must be shown to have intended that the conduct element of the offence, and (where relevant) the consequence element (or other consequences), should respectively be engaged in or brought about.

9.3 We recommend that an alleged conspirator must be shown at the time of the agreement to have been reckless whether a circumstance element of a substantive offence (or other relevant circumstance) would be present at the relevant time, when the substantive offence requires no proof of fault, or has a requirement for proof only of negligence (or its equivalent), in relation to that circumstance.

9.4 We recommend that where a substantive offence has fault requirements not involving mere negligence (or its equivalent), in relation to a fact or circumstance element, an alleged conspirator may be found guilty if shown to have possessed those fault requirements at the time of his or her agreement to commit the offence.

9.5 We recommend that it should be possible for a defendant to deny that he or she possessed the fault element for conspiracy because of intoxication, whether voluntary or involuntary, even when the fault element in question is recklessness (or its equivalent).

9.6 We recommend that agreements comprising a course of conduct which, if carried out, will amount to more than one offence with different fault as to circumstance elements or to which different penalties apply, should be charged as more than one conspiracy in separate counts on an indictment.

9.7 We recommend that the present requirement for the Director of Public Prosecutions to give consent if proceedings to prosecute a conspiracy to commit a summary offence are to be initiated need not be retained.

9.8 We recommend that the immunity for spouses and civil partners provided for by section 2(2)(a) of the Criminal Law Act 1977 should be abolished.

9.9 We recommend that the present exemption for a non-victim co-conspirator should be abolished but that the present exemption for a victim (D) should be retained if:

(a) The conspiracy is to commit an offence that exists wholly or in part for the protection of a particular category of persons;

(b) D falls within the protected category; and

(c) D is the person in respect of whom the offence agreed upon would have been committed.

9.10 We recommend that the rule that an agreement involving a person of or over the age of criminal responsibility and a child under the age of criminal responsibility gives rise to no criminal liability for conspiracy should be retained.

9.11 We recommend that the defence of acting reasonably provided for by section 50 of the Serious Crime Act 2007 should be applied in its entirety to the offence of conspiracy.

The Commission also made recommendations about liability for conspiracy where the agreement or the commission of the substantive offence did not all take place within England and Wales.

~~~ *Questions*

(1) Consider the recommendation in para 9.1. Does this mean that to be guilty of conspiracy every party to the agreement must intend to play a part in the crime? Will D1, who is the gang boss, escape liability as it is clear that he never intended to play a part personally, he was just agreeing with his gang members what crimes they would commit? Is the offence rendered redundant in relation to the cases in which it is often so useful?

(2) Consider paras 9.3 and 9.4. How would these recommendations work with an offence such as money laundering where the mens rea for the substantive offence requires proof of suspicion as to the circumstance element—that the money is criminal property?

FURTHER READING

L. Alexander and K. Kessler, '*Mens Rea* and Inchoate Crimes' (1997) 87 J Cr L & Cr 1138

I. Dennis, 'The Rationale of Criminal Conspiracy' (1977) 93 LQR 39

D. Hodgson, 'Law Commission No 76: A Case Study in Criminal Law Reform' in P. R. Glazebrook (ed), *Reshaping the Criminal Law: Essays in Honour of Glanville Williams* (1978)

P. E. Johnson, 'The Unnecessary Crime of Conspiracy' (1973) 61 Cal L Rev 1137

N. Katyal, 'Conspiracy Theory' (2003) 112 Yale LJ 1307

P. Marcus, 'Conspiracy: The Criminal Agreement in Theory and in Practice' (1977) 65 Georgetown LJ 925

D. Ormerod, 'Making Sense of Statutory Conspiracies' [2006] CLP 185

A. Reed, 'Conspiracy to Defraud: The Threshold Standardisation' (2012) 76 J Crim L 373

22
Assisting and encouraging: Serious Crime Act 2007, Part 2

Assisting and encouraging crime under the 2007 Act:

- D commits an offence under s 44 if he does an act that is *capable* of encouraging or assisting *intending* to encourage or to assist another, P, to commit an offence;

- D commits an offence under s 45 if he does an act that is *capable* of encouraging or assisting *believing* that the offence by P will be committed and D *believes* that his act will encourage or assist its commission;

- D commits an offence under s 46 if he does an act that is *capable* of encouraging or assisting the commission of one or more of a number of offences and he *believes* (a) that one or more of those offences will be committed (without having any belief as to which particular crime); and (b) that his act will encourage or assist the commission of one or more of them.

Some of the controversies that will be examined in this chapter include:

(1) the difficulties in interpreting the provisions in Part 2 of the Serious Crime Act 2007;

(2) whether the offences violate Article 7 of the European Convention on Human Rights;

(3) the possibility of the offences being reformed so soon after they were enacted.

22.1 Introduction

In this chapter, as in the previous two chapters, we consider inchoate liability. In everyday language, if something is described as being 'inchoate' it has just begun and so is not fully formed. Inchoate liability can thus be contrasted with secondary liability, which was considered in Chapter 19. In secondary liability D has aided, abetted, counselled or procured P to commit an offence that P has in fact committed. In contrast, with inchoate liability D is punished for his conduct that has not in fact led to the commission of a full offence by D or P. The caveat that must be added to this is that there is now an overlap between inchoate liability and secondary liability because of the reforms introduced by the Serious Crime Act 2007, as will be explained in this chapter.

At common law the offence of incitement was a form of inchoate offence. The definition was accepted to be that a person was guilty of an offence if (a) he incited another to do or cause to be done an act or acts which, if done, would involve the commission of the offence or offences by the other; and (b) he intended or believed that the other, if he acted as incited, should or would do so with the fault required for the offence or offences. The offence was commonly used to prosecute those who were instigating others to commit crimes even though the person incited did not go on to commit the offence; for example, where D encouraged P, an undercover police officer, to attack D's wife for a fee to be paid by D.

The common law was said to be problematic. For example, the Law Commission stated that the fault element of the offence had been distorted by decisions of the Court of Appeal that had focused too much on the state of mind of P rather than D. The common law was eventually replaced with the offences contained in Part 2 of the Serious Crime Act 2007.

The offences in Part 2 are extremely complex and care must be taken when examining the Act to ensure that the elements of each offence are understood.

22.2 The Serious Crime Act 2007, Part 2

The Serious Crime Act 2007, Part 2 followed the Law Commission recommendation to abolish the common law offence of incitement (s 59). It is replaced with three new offences under s 44 to 46.

Understanding and applying the provisions is rendered more difficult because they were designed as only part of the package of secondary and inchoate liability which the Law Commission devised. The Law Commission's recommendations in Report No 300, *Inchoate Liability for Assisting and Encouraging Crime* (2006) which have been enacted, were designed to be supplemented with the recommendations in Report No 305, *Participating in Crime* (2007) where the Law Commission advanced a new scheme to deal with all aspects of secondary liability. These have not been enacted. The result is that the law has been left in rather an imbalanced state. The Law Commission deliberately designed the inchoate offences in the 2007 Act to be of wide application because it was also recommending that the offences to replace secondary liability would be much narrower than under present law.

The 2007 Act offences are criticized as being too complex, over broad and impractical: see D. Ormerod and R. Fortson, 'The Serious Crime Act 2007 Part 2' [2009] Crim LR 389.

(iv) Breadth of inchoate liability

Aside from the potential for the offences to overlap significantly with the principal offence and supersede secondary liability, their breadth raises concerns even in terms of the appropriate limits of inchoate liability. We are not seeking here to revisit the academic debate on the appropriateness of inchoate liability generally. Nor on the significance which the law ought to attach to the infliction of harm in the form proscribed in the principal/substantive offence as opposed to the willingness of an offender to try to bring it about by his efforts. Our point is simply this: Pt 2 creates broad offences whereby liability can be imposed for conduct far removed from what might typically be regarded as the offence 'paradigm' of blameworthy wrongdoing resulting in a proscribed harm. As Professor Ashworth has succinctly stated, 'as the form of criminal liability moves further away from the infliction of harm, so the grounds of liability should become more narrow'. We submit that this is certainly not the case with the offences under ss.45–46. Indeed, all the Pt 2 offences focus on D's conduct in acts capable of assisting or encouraging P, but the imposition of criminal responsibility on D for that conduct is twice removed from the principal offence. Inchoate liability can be founded on the actions of the accused alone, far removed from the commission of the principal offence, and in the case of ss.45 and 46 in particular, on proof of mens rea requirements of less than purpose or intent. There is the stark risk of over-criminalisation.

> ≈≈ *Question*
> As you proceed through the chapter, consider whether you agree with the above analysis.

The 2007 Act offences are unduly complex. This is particularly true in respect of the s 46 offence. They necessitate close analysis of the substantive offence which it is alleged D has assisted or encouraged P to commit. D's liability will turn on whether D's conduct was capable of assisting or encouraging P in terms of the conduct, circumstances and consequence elements of P's anticipated substantive offence but, of course, the offence by P need not have been committed. The 2007 Act offences also require that D has mens rea about what mens rea P will have if P carries out the anticipated offence.

22.2.1 Intentional assisting or encouraging

Serious Crime Act 2007, s 44

> (1) A person commits an offence if—
>
>   (a) he does an act capable of encouraging or assisting the commission of an offence; and
>
>   (b) he intends to encourage or assist its commission.
>
> (2) But he is not to be taken to have intended to encourage or assist the commission of an offence merely because such encouragement or assistance was a foreseeable consequence of his act.

Section 44 is triable in the same way (in the Crown Court or magistrates' court) as the 'anticipated offence' (s 55(1)): that offence which D is intentionally assisting or encouraging P to commit but which P does not in fact need to commit. Where the anticipated offence is murder, the sentence on conviction under s 44 is a maximum of life: s 58(1). Where the anticipated offence is any offence other than murder the maximum sentence is that available for the full anticipated offence if it had been committed: s 58(2).

The offence is inchoate. As the Law Commission suggested:

> ... If D sells P a weapon that D intends P will use to murder V, D has done everything that that he or she intends to do. Nothing more turns on D's subsequent conduct whereas P has yet to take the step of attempting to commit the offence. (Law Com Report No 300, para 4.25)

> ≈≈ *Questions*
> D sends an email to P telling him to murder all 'unbelievers'. Consider the following scenarios: (a) P does not receive the email; (b) P receives the email and ignores it because he was going to kill V, an 'unbeliever', in any event; (c) P is so persuaded by the email that he commits murder when previously he had no intention of doing do. In each scenario:
> (1) Is D guilty of an offence under s 44? What is the maximum sentence for his conduct?
> (2) Is D also guilty of aiding and abetting under s 8 of the Accessories and Abettors Act 1861? If so, which offence would you choose to prosecute and why?
> (3) What if P had intended to kill V but had only succeeded in wounding him? For what offences would D be liable (i) under s 44 or (ii) as an accessory?
> (4) Since the offence is committed at the time when D emails P, there is no scope for a defence of withdrawal. Should there be?

The facts of one of the conjoined appeals against sentence in *Blackshaw* [2011] EWCA Crim 2312 provides a stark example of this offence in operation and also demonstrates the forms of behaviour that may now potentially come within the scope of the offences in Part 2 of the 2007 Act. There were a number of conjoined appeals against sentence after convictions arising from the riots that broke out in various British cities in the summer of 2011. D set up a Facebook page entitled 'The Warrington Riots', which was available for public viewing. On this webpage D included a photograph of police officers in riot equipment in a 'stand off position' with a group of rioters. He also included a photograph of himself and others in a pose described by police as 'gangster-like'. D sent messages via Facebook to 400 contacts inviting them to meet at a local venue. Forty-seven people confirmed their intention to attend the meeting. Concerned citizens of Warrington who saw or heard about D's Facebook page contacted the police. Before the police could close the website down, D retracted his invitation and stated online that it was all a joke. D was arrested and pleaded guilty to intentionally encouraging or assisting the commission of an offence contrary to s 44 of the Serious Crime Act 2007. The offence which D pleaded guilty to intentionally assisting or encouraging was riot. D was sentenced to four years' imprisonment and the Court of Appeal upheld D's sentence. In doing so, Lord Judge CJ stated:

> 72. When dealing with these two appeals we are, of course, conscious of the fact that in the end no actual harm in the streets of Northwich and Warrington actually occurred. It is not however accurate to suggest that neither crime had any adverse consequences. We know for a certainty that in each case a number of decent citizens were appalled by what they had read, and given the widespread rioting throughout the country, which at that time was spiralling out of control, we have no doubt that some, at least, of them were put in fear. In any event the fact that no rioting occurred in the streets of Northwich or Warrington owed nothing to either defendant. The reality was that armed with information from members of the public who were disturbed at the prospect, the police were able to interfere and bring the possibility of riot to an end.
>
> 73. We are unimpressed with the suggestion that in each case the defendant did no more than make the appropriate entry in his Facebook. Neither went from door to door looking for friends or like-minded people to join up with him in the riot. All that is true. But modern technology has done away with the need for such direct personal communication. It can all be done through Facebook or other social media. In other words, the abuse of modern technology for criminal purposes extends to and includes incitement of very many people by a single step. Indeed it is a sinister feature of these cases that modern technology almost certainly assisted rioters in other places to organise the rapid movement and congregation of disorderly groups in new and unpoliced areas.

≋ *Questions*

(1) Do you think that D's criminality justified the imposition of a four-year custodial sentence?

(2) Should D have been able to plead a defence of withdrawal?

(3) Could D have argued that his entire course of conduct, including his withdrawal of the invitation to meet, was reasonable and so avoided liability by pleading the defence in s 50? See section 22.2.1.3, p 606 for discussion of this defence.

22.2.1.1 Actus reus

D's conduct must be 'capable' of 'assisting or encouraging'. The focus is on D's conduct, not P's. D's conduct can include a 'course of conduct' (s 67) as where D supplies a number of articles to

P over time. Section 67 provides that 'a reference in this Part to an act includes a reference to a course of conduct, and a reference to doing an act is to be read accordingly'.

There is no requirement that D's act does in fact encourage or assist P or anyone. Perhaps D's email in the earlier example is not received by P. P might ignore D's assistance or encouragement, or find it of no encouragement or assistance at all. It is arguable that there is not even any need for P to be aware of D's acts which were intended to assist or encourage him.

What does capable of encouraging mean?

Under the common law offence of incitement, a very broad view was taken of what might amount to encouragement. For example, in *Invicta Plastics Ltd v Clare* [1976] RTR 251, the defendant company manufactured a device called 'Radatec' which made a noise when approaching a police radar trap. The company advertised the device in a motoring magazine. The advertisement stated, 'You ought to know more about Radatec. Ask at your accessory shop or write for name of nearest stockist . . .' It depicted a view of a road and a speed limit sign through a car windscreen with the device attached. In response to a request by the prosecutor, the company sent him a stockist's name and a leaflet which included the words: 'The majority of [such] transmissions are not intended for public use and therefore their deliberate reception is illegal unless licensed by the Post Office. . . . However, no licence is required to receive [other such] transmissions. It is illegal to employ the Radatec specifically for the reception of, for instance, police radar transmissions.' The defendants were convicted by the justices of inciting readers of the magazine and of the leaflet to contravene s 1(1) of the Wireless Telegraphy Act 1949, which forbade the use of any wireless telegraphy apparatus except under a licence. On appeal, Park J referred to the fact that:

When summing up to the jury on a case of incitement, judges sometimes use such words as 'incitement involves the suggestion to commit the offence' or 'a proposal to commit the offence' or 'persuasion or inducement to commit the offence' which the defendant is alleged to have incited. But Lord Denning MR considered the meaning of 'incitement' in *Race Relations Board v Applin* [1973] QB 815, 825G, where he said:

'Mr Vinelott suggested that to "incite" means to urge or spur on by advice, encouragement, and persuasion, and not otherwise. I do not think the word is so limited, at any rate in this context. A person may "incite" another to do an act by threatening or by pressure, as well as persuasion.'

Accordingly, the justices had to decide whether, in the context, the advertisement amounted to an incitement to the readers of the magazine to commit the offence . . .

I think that it is necessary to look at the advertisement as a whole. Approaching it in this way, I have come to the conclusion that the company did incite a breach of the Act by means of the advertisement. I think, therefore, that the justices were right to convict the company of this offence.

> ≈≈ *Question*
> Would the manufacturers of such a device be liable under s 44 of the 2007 Act?

The scope of the actus reus under s 44 is extended further by s 65.

(1) A reference in this Part to a person's doing an act that is capable of encouraging the commission of an offence includes a reference to his doing so by threatening another person or otherwise putting pressure on another person to commit the offence.

(2) A reference in this Part to a person's doing an act that is capable of encouraging or assisting the commission of an offence includes a reference to his doing so by—

    (a) taking steps to reduce the possibility of criminal proceedings being brought in respect of that offence;

The actus reus extends further still by s 65(2)(b) whereby:

. . . doing an act that is capable of encouraging or assisting the commission of an offence includes a reference to his doing so by—

. . .

    (b) failing to take reasonable steps to discharge a duty.

(3) But a person is not to be regarded as doing an act that is capable of encouraging or assisting the commission of an offence merely because he fails to respond to a constable's request for assistance in preventing a breach of the peace.

∿ *Questions*

D, a night-time security guard at the bank, is so bored with his job that he forgets to set the alarm. P burgles the bank. Is D liable under s 44? For what offence?

The actus reus is extended yet further by s 66 of the 2007 Act:

If a person (D1) arranges for a person (D2) to do an act that is capable of encouraging or assisting the commission of an offence, and D2 does the act, D1 is also to be treated for the purposes of this Part as having done it.

∿ *Questions*

(1) D1 supplies a gun to D2 to supply to P to kill V. P receives the gun and shoots at but misses V. Who is guilty of what?

(2) Don, a police officer, encourages P, a drug dealer, to sell drugs to V. P ignores the request. Is Don guilty of an offence? See s 50 in section 22.2.1.3, p 606.

The offence is extended not only against D who does an act capable of assisting or encouraging, but also to P. The Law Commission gave the following example:

P asks D to supply him or her with an article so that P can commit an offence, P is doing an act capable of encouraging D to do an act capable of assisting P to commit an offence. In other words, if D supplies the article to P, not only is D committing the [s 45] offence but, by encouraging D to commit the [s 45] offence, P is committing the [s 44] offence. (Law Com Report No 300, para 4.26)

If D's act is capable of encouraging or assisting the commission of a number of offences, then by s 49(2), s 44 will apply separately in relation to each offence that he intends to encourage or assist to be committed.

22.2.1.2 Mens rea

There are four elements of mens rea to be proved under s 44 of the 2007 Act.

Intention to do acts capable of assisting or encouraging

There must be an intention to do the act which is *capable* of encouraging or assisting. In the previous example with the email relating to killing the unbeliever, D must intend to do the act by which he intends P to be encouraged or assisted in the murder. This element means that D is not liable if he recklessly leaves open his gun cupboard allowing P to take a gun to shoot V.

Intention to assist or encourage

D must intend to encourage or assist. Section 44(2) makes clear that this is not satisfied by proof that the encouragement was a foreseeable consequence of D's intentional acts; oblique intention has no part to play here.

If D's act is capable of encouraging or assisting the commission of a number of offences then, by s 49(2), s 44 will apply separately in relation to *each* offence that he intends to encourage or assist to be committed.

> ∼ *Question*
>
> D provides P with a gun which he intends P to use in threatening a number of D's debtors. Will D be liable for each offence or robbery, blackmail, etc which P commits or for each one that D intended that he commits?

D's mens rea as to P's mens rea

Where the anticipated crime is one of mens rea, D must believe or be reckless as to whether P *will* (not might) perform the conduct element for the anticipated offence and that P will at that time act with the prescribed mens rea. Section 47(5)(a) provides that it must be proved that:

  (i)   D believed that, were the act to be done, it would be done with that fault;

  (ii) D was reckless as to whether or not it would be done with that fault; or

  (iii) D's state of mind was such that, were he to do it, it would be done with that fault;

> ∼ *Question*
>
> D encourages P to touch V sexually. What would the prosecution have to prove for D to be liable under s 44 for encouraging the offence? (The mens rea of the offence under s 3 of the Sexual Offences Act 2003 is an intention to touch a person sexually, see section 12.2.3, p 332.)

Section 47(5)(a)(iii) deals with the cases where D would have mens rea if *he* committed the anticipated crime even though he does not believe and is not reckless as to whether P would have it.

> ∼ *Questions*
>
> D encourages P to rape V. P has sex with V but lacks mens rea for rape because he reasonably believed V was consenting. Can D be guilty of encouraging rape? See s 47(6)). What if D is a woman?

D's mens rea as to consequences and circumstances of P's offence

D must also have mens rea as to the consequences and circumstances, if any, of the anticipated offence.

By s 47(5)(b) if the offence is one requiring proof of particular circumstances or consequences (or both), it must be proved that:

(i) D believed [or intended] that, were the act to be done, it would be done in those circumstances or with those consequences; or

(ii) D was reckless as to whether or not it would be done in those circumstances or with those consequences.

22.2.1.3 Defences and exemptions to s 44

The standard defences that are discussed in Chapters 23 and 24 will apply. If, when he hands P a weapon, D is insane or acting in self-defence he will be entitled to an acquittal. By s 47(2), 'If it is alleged under section 44(1)(b) that a person (D) intended to encourage or assist the commission of an offence, it is sufficient to prove that he intended to encourage or assist the doing of an act which would amount to the commission of that offence.' It is therefore no defence that D is unaware that the conduct by P that D is intentionally encouraging or assisting would be criminal. It is no defence for D to claim that no offence is actually committed by P: s 49(1).

Reasonable conduct

It is a defence for D to prove on the balance of probabilities that he acted reasonably.

Serious Crime Act 2007, s 50

(1) A person is not guilty of an offence under this Part if he proves—

(a) that he knew certain circumstances existed; and

(b) that it was reasonable for him to act as he did in those circumstances.

(2) A person is not guilty of an offence under this Part if he proves—

(a) that he believed certain circumstances to exist;

(b) that his belief was reasonable; and

(c) that it was reasonable for him to act as he did in the circumstances as he believed them to be.

(3) Factors to be considered in determining whether it was reasonable for a person to act as he did include—

(a) the seriousness of the anticipated offence (or, in the case of an offence under section 46, the offences specified in the indictment);

(b) any purpose for which he claims to have been acting;

(c) any authority by which he claims to have been acting.

It is not enough that D thinks that his conduct is reasonable; it must be found to be reasonable by the jury. Three specific examples of the defence in operation were offered by the Law Commission:

D, a motorist, changes motorway lanes to allow a following motorist (P) to overtake, even though D knows that P is speeding; D, a reclusive householder, bars his front door to a man trying to get into his house to escape from a prospective assailant (P); D, a member of a DIY shop's check-out staff, believes the man (P) purchasing spray paint will use it to cause criminal damage. (Law Com Report No 300, para A.63)

Defences for victims

The *Tyrrell* ([1894] 1 QB 710) principle is put in statutory form. D will have a defence if he is a 'victim'. Section 51 provides that a person does not commit an offence if:

> (1) . . .
>
> > (a) he falls within the protected category; and
> >
> > (b) he is the person in respect of whom the protective offence was committed or would have been if it had been committed.
>
> (2) 'Protective offence' means an offence that exists (wholly or in part) for the protection of a particular category of persons ('the protected category').

〰 *Questions*

(1) D, aged 12, encourages P, aged 15, to have sex with her. Is D guilty of an offence of encouraging P to engage in sexual activity with a child under 13?

(2) D's mother, E, allows D, aged 12, to have her boyfriend P, aged 15, over to stay and to sleep with D in D's room. Is E liable for an offence?

(3) D, an adult, asks P, also an adult, to beat him for his sexual gratification. Is D guilty of an offence under s 44 if the beating takes place?

22.2.1.4 What crimes are capable of being assisted or encouraged?

The 2007 Act describes D's conduct in terms of acts capable of encouraging or assisting the commission of '*an offence*'. Read literally, this is wide enough to mean that D can be liable under s 44 for assisting or encouraging substantive crimes, attempts and conspiracies.

Assisting or encouraging attempts or conspiracies

The Law Commission proposed that D should be liable for the inchoate offence of doing an act, which is capable of encouraging or assisting D2 to *attempt* to commit an offence, but *only if* it was his *direct intention* that P should do so (Law Com Report No 300, para 7.23). Under s 44, D can be convicted of an offence if he performs acts capable of assisting or encouraging P to *attempt* to commit an offence.

Under s 5(7) of the Criminal Law Act 1977 it was no offence to incite a conspiracy but the Law Commission in Report No 300 recommended that D should be liable for acts capable of encouraging or assisting P to *conspire* to commit an offence, but only if it was D's *direct intention* that P should do so. D can be liable under s 44 where he does acts capable of assisting or encouraging P1 and P2 to *conspire* to commit an offence. Section 5(7) of the Criminal Law Act 1977 is repealed (Serious Crime Act 2007, Sch 6, Part 2, para 54). The 2007 Act does not repeal s 1(4)(b) of the Criminal Attempts Act 1981 which precludes there being an offence of attempting to aid, abet, etc. The failure to repeal this provision has been criticized in the following terms (M. Bohlander, 'The Conflict Between the Serious Crime Act 2007 and Section 1(4)(b) Criminal Attempts Act 1981—A Missed Repeal?' [2010] Crim LR 483):

> So, on the one hand, it still is conceptually not possible to attempt to aid, abet, counsel or procure, in other words doing acts capable of encouraging or assisting another's offence under s.1(4)(b) of the Criminal Attempts Act 1981. Even if D were to commit acts that are more than merely preparatory to encouraging and assisting P to commit an offence, liability would be excluded under s.1(4)(b). On the

other hand, however, ss.44 et seq. of the Serious Crime Act 2007 would appear to cover exactly this sort of behaviour. We need to remember that for s.44 to be triggered, it is not even necessary that P himself does any act that is more than merely preparatory. At the very least s.44 clashes conceptually with s.1(4)(b); the latter would now appear to be mostly devoid of substance and creates confusion with the Serious Crime Act 2007.

Assisting or encouraging the act of assisting or encouraging

D can be liable for performing acts capable of encouraging or assisting P1 to encourage or assist P2. If D supplies a weapon to P1 knowing that the weapon will be passed to P2 to perpetrate a murder, D is liable under s 44. As the Law Commission explained (at para 7.15), 'If it is D's intention that P should encourage or assist X, his or her conduct should not be considered too remote from the principal offence merely because, were P to encourage or assist X, P would not intend X to commit the principal offence.' Does this form of 'double' inchoate liability extend the ambit of the criminal law too far?

Attempting or conspiring to commit: s 44

D's acts need only be capable of assisting or encouraging. The possibility of attempting to assist or encourage arises where, for example, D is about to post the letter to P containing details of how to break into V's safe. There seems to be nothing wrong in principle with liability for conspiracy: D1 agreeing with D2 that D1 will perform acts capable of assisting or encouraging P to commit an offence against V. For example, D1 and D2, serious drug villains, agree that D1 should supply a local hoodlum with a weapon so that he will kill V, a competitor in the local drug market.

> ≋ *Question*
> What if D1 cannot get hold of D2: is he attempting to conspire with D2 to assist or encourage P?

22.2.2 Section 45

By s 45 of the Act a person commits an offence if:

(a) he does an act capable of encouraging or assisting the commission of an offence; and
(b) he believes—
   (i) that the offence will be committed; and
   (ii) that his act will encourage or assist its commission.

D supplies a gun to P, *believing* that P would use it to commit a murder. D would not be liable for assisting or encouraging unless P committed the murder. D would not be liable for conspiring with P unless there was a common agreement. Under the law before the Serious Crime Act 2007, D could not have been charged with incitement unless there was encouragement rather than pure assistance. Under s 45, D can now be convicted of the inchoate offence of assisting or encouraging the commission of a crime, even if P does not commit the crime.

The s 45 offence is triable in the same way as the 'anticipated offence' (ie that P would commit if he did as D believed): s 55(1). Where the anticipated offence is murder, the maximum sentence on conviction under s 45 is life: s 58(1). Where the anticipated offence is any offence other than murder the maximum sentence is that available for the full anticipated offence if it had been committed: s 58(2).

By way of an example, in *Woodford* [2013] EWCA Crim 1098, D hired a van for C to use. In addition, D had booked passage on a ferry for C to travel from the continent to Dover. He also provided him with a satnav for use on the trip. C was stopped by the UK Border Agency at Dover and in the back of the van there was found a significant quantity of a powder commonly known to be used as a cutting agent in the supply of heroin. C was arrested. Two months later D contacted police and told them that the van was his and the powder was for use on his mother's lawn. D was also arrested. D was convicted of encouraging or assisting the commission of an offence of supplying a controlled drug of Class A, heroin, believing that the offence would be committed, contrary to s 45 of the 2007 Act.

> ≈ *Questions*
> (1) Could D and C have been guilty of conspiracy? If so, why were they not charged with this offence?
> (2) On these facts, do you believe that there was sufficient evidence to infer that D believed that the offence of supplying heroin would be committed? What if D testified that he had not found anyone to supply heroin and that, as a consequence, he was going to spread the powder on his mother's lawn?

22.2.2.1 Actus reus

D's conduct needs only to be *capable* of assisting or encouraging (as with s 44). There is no requirement that P is actually encouraged or assisted nor that P commits the offence. D's conduct can be a 'course of conduct': s 67. Conduct capable of assisting or encouraging includes threats or putting pressure on another person: s 65(1). The extended definitions from s 65 (see section 22.2.1.1) apply as in s 44 (taking steps to reduce the possibility of criminal proceedings being brought, and failing to fulfil a duty) and failing to assist a police officer preventing a breach of the peace does not. If D arranges for P to do an act capable of encouraging or assisting X and P does that act, D is treated as also having done it: s 66.

22.2.2.2 Mens rea

Serious Crime Act 2007, s 47

(3) If it is alleged under section 45(b) that a person (D) believed that an offence would be committed and that his act would encourage or assist its commission, it is sufficient to prove that he believed—

(a) that an act would be done which would amount to the commission of that offence; and

(b) that his act would encourage or assist the doing of that act.

. . .

(5) In proving for the purposes of this section whether an act is one which, if done, would amount to the commission of an offence—

(a) if the offence is one requiring proof of fault, it must be proved that—

(i) D believed that, were the act to be done, it would be done with that fault;

(ii) D was reckless as to whether or not it would be done with that fault; or

(iii) D's state of mind was such that, were he to do it, it would be done with that fault; and

(b) if the offence is one requiring proof of particular circumstances or consequences (or both), it must be proved that—

    (i) D believed that, were the act to be done, it would be done in those circumstances or with those consequences; or

    (ii) D was reckless as to whether or not it would be done in those circumstances or with those consequences.

Belief that acts will assist or encourage

D must be proved to have *believed* that his act *will* (not might) encourage or assist P in his performance of the conduct element of the offence.

∼∼∼ *Questions*

D supplies P with poison believing that P will use it to kill his wife as he previously threatened. Is D liable under s 45? What for exactly?

Belief that offence will be committed

Under s 45, D must believe that an act will be done which 'would amount to the commission' of the anticipated offence. In the previous example, D must believe that P will use the poison to cause GBH or death.

D's mens rea as to P's mens rea

Where the anticipated crime is one of mens rea, say murder, D must believe or be reckless as to whether P would perform the conduct element of the offence with the prescribed mens rea for that offence with which he, P, would be charged: s 47(5).

∼∼∼ *Question*

D supplies the poison to P believing he will use it to kill V. What more must the prosecution prove about D's mens rea in order to convict him under s 45?

D's mens rea as to circumstances and consequences

D must also have mens rea as to the consequences and circumstances of the offence he anticipates by P: s 47(5)(b).

∼∼∼ *Questions*

D encourages P to touch V sexually. Is D liable if he believes that P will sexually touch V with intent (which is the mens rea required under the Sexual Offences Act 2003, s 3)? If V is 12, what mens rea must D have as to V's age if he is to be prosecuted under the 2007 Act? (Liability as to age is strict under s 7 of the Sexual Offences Act 2003, see section 12.3.1, p 337.)

22.2.2.3 Defences and exemptions to s 45

There is no defence that the anticipated offence did not occur. It is a defence for D to prove that he acted reasonably under s 50. D cannot be liable if he is a 'victim': s 51. These defences are considered in section 22.2.1 when discussing s 44.

22.2.2.4 To which offences does s 45 not apply?

D cannot be convicted under s 45 for:

- assisting or encouraging offences listed in Sch 3 to the 2007 Act (offences listed in Parts 1 to 3 include (*inter alia*) those under the Offences Against the Person Act 1861, s 4; the Criminal Law Act 1977, ss 1(1), 5(2) and (3); the Criminal Attempts Act 1981, s 1(1); and the Public Order Act 1986, ss 12(6), 13(9) and 14(6). Also covered are offences of attempt under special statutory provisions (see the Criminal Attempts Act 1981, s 3);

- doing an act capable of encouraging/assisting P to encourage or assist X;

- encouraging or assisting a conspiracy to commit an offence, on mere belief that the offence (conspiracy) will be committed: Sch 3, para 32;

- doing an act that is capable of encouraging or assisting P to attempt to commit an offence, on a mere belief that the attempt will be committed: Sch 3, para 33; or

- encouraging or assisting P to do an act which is capable of assisting X to commit a crime: s 49(4).

22.2.3 Section 46

By s 46 of the 2007 Act, D is guilty of this offence if:

> . . .
>
>   (a) he does an act capable of encouraging or assisting the commission of one or more of a number of offences; and
>
>   (b) he believes—
>
>   (i) that one or more of those offences will be committed (but has no belief as to which); and
>
>   (ii) that his act will encourage or assist the commission of one or more of them.
>
> (2) It is immaterial for the purposes of subsection (1)(b)(ii) whether the person has any belief as to which offence will be encouraged or assisted.

It is not necessary for the prosecution to specify in the indictment every offence that D potentially might have encouraged or assisted, but the indictment must specify all the offences which the Crown alleges D contemplated might be committed: s 46(3). Note that an offence charged under s 46 is triable only on indictment: s 55(5).

D supplies a knife which is capable of encouraging or assisting the commission of one or more of a number of offences (eg one or more robberies or murders). D is liable under s 46 if:

- D *believes* that one or more such offences *will* be committed (even if it cannot be proved that D had a belief or intent as to which *one* will be committed); and

- D believes that his act of supplying the knife to P *will* encourage or assist the commission of at least one of those offences; and

- D believes, or is reckless as to whether, when P is to perform the conduct element of the offence, P will do so with the mens rea required for that offence (or D's state of mind is sufficient itself as such that, were he to do it, it would be done with the fault required); and

- D believes or is reckless as to whether, were the conduct to be done by P, it would be done in those circumstances or with those consequences, if any, of which the offence requires proof.

≈≈ *Questions*

D is a member of an extreme racist organization. He receives an email inviting him to attend a meeting at which 'radical action' has been promised. He is unsure whether this will involve just the usual speeches and rhetoric or whether the leaders might engage in something more serious as they have been promising. He thinks that they might go through with some of the earlier threatened action to: (a) graffiti the local synagogue, (b) attack the owner of the local curry house who is from Bangladesh, (c) look for local black youths to fight with and possibly kill.

D replies saying that he will be there and that he hopes that this time they mean 'radical *action*' not words. The meeting takes place but D is unable to attend. Has D committed an offence? How is the judge to sentence D (on the basis of the appropriate sentence for (a) criminal damage, (b) assault, (c) murder)?

22.2.3.1 Actus reus

D's conduct needs only to be *capable* of assisting or encouraging. There is no requirement that the conduct does in fact encourage or assist P or anyone. As under s 44 and s 45, D's conduct can be a 'course of conduct'; it can be satisfied by threats or putting pressure on another person (s 65). The extended definitions from s 65 apply so that D is liable if he takes steps to reduce the possibility of criminal proceedings being brought, or fails to fulfil a duty, but failing to assist a police officer preventing a breach of the peace does not. Under s 66, if D arranges for P to do an act capable of encouraging or assisting X and P does that act, D is treated as also having done it.

22.2.3.2 Mens rea

There are no fewer than five elements of mens rea to be proved.

D's belief that he will assist or encourage

D must believe that his act will encourage or assist one or more of the offences. It is not necessary that the Crown establish a belief as to which offence will be committed.

≈≈ *Questions*

D believes that the knife he provides to P will be used to rob V. P uses it to kill V. Can D be liable under s 46? For what exactly?

D's belief as to offences

D must believe that one or more of the offences *will* be committed. It is sufficient that D believes that the offence, or one of the offences, will be committed if certain conditions apply (s 49(7)).

≈≈ *Questions*

D believes that the knife he provides to P will be used to rob V if V refuses to hand over his iPad. P uses it to kill V. Can D be liable under s 46? For what exactly?

D's belief as to one of a number of offences

If the allegation is that D believed one or more of a number of offences would be committed and that his act would encourage or assist the commission of one or more of them, by s 47(4), it is sufficient to prove that D believed:

(a) that one or more of a number of acts would be done which would amount to the commission of one or more of those offences; and

(b) that his act would encourage or assist the doing of one or more of those acts.

The aim of the provision is to allow for a conviction where although it cannot be proved that D had a belief or intent as to which *crime* will be committed, it can be proved that D *believes* that one or more such offences *will* be committed. However, the section refers to the 'act' of P.

~~~ *Questions*

D provides P with a can of petrol believing that P will use it to start a fire. P uses the petrol to burn his own possessions. Has D committed the s 46 offence? Has P committed a crime (if the property is his own)? Does that matter?

D's mens rea as to P's mens rea

Where the anticipated crime is one of mens rea, D must believe or be reckless as to whether P would act with the mens rea for one of the anticipated offences with which he would be charged. Section 47(5) provides:

(5) In proving for the purposes of this section whether an act is one which, if done, would amount to the commission of an offence—

(a) if the offence is one requiring proof of fault, it must be proved that—

(i) D believed that, were the act to be done, it would be done with that fault;

(ii) D was reckless as to whether or not it would be done with that fault; or

(iii) D's state of mind was such that, were he to do it, it would be done with that fault; and

(b) if the offence is one requiring proof of particular circumstances or consequences (or both), it must be proved that—

(i) D believed that, were the act to be done, it would be done in those circumstances or with those consequences; or

(ii) D was reckless as to whether or not it would be done in those circumstances or with those consequences.

(6) For the purposes of subsection (5)(a)(iii), D is to be assumed to be able to do the act in question.

D's mens rea as to circumstances and consequences of P's act

If the offence is one requiring proof of particular circumstances or consequences (or both) D must also have mens rea as to the consequences and circumstances of one of the anticipated offences: s 47(5).

~~~ *Questions*

D, aged 15, encourages his friend P, aged 14, to sexually touch or have sexual intercourse with V, aged 12. Is D liable for an offence under s 46? What mens rea must D have as to the anticipated offences? (Rape of a child under 13 involves proof of an intentional act of penetration but liability is strict as to the child's age. Sexual touching of a child under 13 requires proof of an intentional sexual touching but liability as to the age of the child is strict, see section 12.3.1, p 337.)

There have been two cases examining the proper interpretation of s 46. They are unusual as they concern the same defendant and in the most recent case the Court of Appeal effectively overturned the earlier one. In *S & H* [2011] EWCA Crim 2872, D was convicted of supplying various chemical cutting agents believing that they would assist in the supply of Class A or Class B drugs, contrary to s 46 of the Serious Crime Act 2007. D argued that the offence in s 46 was so vague and uncertain that it rendered it contrary to Article 7 of the European Convention on Human Rights. The Court of Appeal rejected this argument and went on to examine the mens rea of the s 46 offence. The question the Court of Appeal addressed was whether it suffices for D to believe that one of the offences A, B or C may be committed, although he does not know which one, or whether in a case where a single count particularizes offences A, B and C, D must believe that all the particularized offences will be committed. The Court of Appeal considered that the latter interpretation was the most appropriate one. The practical consequence of the judgment was that when D is charged with an offence contrary to s 46, each separate offence, A, B and C, which his act is capable to assisting or encouraging must be charged as a separate count on the indictment. Some commentators were critical of this decision. For example, Graham Virgo in 'Encouraging or Assisting More Than One Offence' [2012] 2 Arch Rev 6 stated as follows:

As a consequence of this ruling, it was held that, when the defendant is charged with an offence contrary to s.46, each offence which the defendant's act is capable of encouraging or assisting (known as the reference offence) must be charged as a separate count. Further, for each count it must be shown that the defendant believed that that particular offence will be committed with the necessary fault. The application of this decision can be tested by considering the facts of *Blackshaw*, modified slightly. A defendant has posted a message on Facebook inviting those who read the message to meet the next day at a designated spot in order to wreak havoc in a named town. Posting such a message is capable of encouraging a variety of crimes, including burglary, riot and criminal damage. It could include many other offences as well, such as affray, violent disorder, theft or robbery, but it was recognised in *S and H* that not every possible reference offence needs to be charged. The defendant is likely, therefore, to be charged with encouraging the commission of offences contrary to s.46 and each count would designate a separate reference offence which was capable of being encouraged by his conduct. So, the first count would identify burglary as the relevant offence. The defendant would only be guilty of encouraging this offence if he believed both that burglary will be committed and that the message on Facebook will encourage the offence to be committed. But such a defendant would be unlikely to believe that burglary will necessarily be committed. Much more likely is the belief that an offence will be committed and that this might be burglary. Similarly, with the separate counts of riot and criminal damage.

It follows that the typical case of a defendant who contemplates a variety of offences being assisted or encouraged by his act and believes that only one of them will be committed, but is unsure which, cannot be guilty of the s.46 offence and so cannot be guilty of any offence under the Serious Crime Act. Further, the conviction of the defendant in *Blackshaw* is now suspect, since it is not apparent that he believed that any of the reference offences of burglary, riot or criminal damage would necessarily be committed. The decision of the Court of Appeal in *S and H* has one further implication. In the modified *Blackshaw* scenario, the defendant would have to be charged with three separate counts, relating to each reference offence which is considered to be capable of being encouraged by the defendant's act. The defendant will only be guilty of each count if he believes that the particular reference offence will be committed and that his act will encourage that offence. But this is also what must be proved for the s.45 offence. It follows that there is no longer any need to charge the defendant under s.46 at all. Section 46 has been rendered effectively redundant by *S and H.* It would still be possible to use s.46 where the act is capable of encouraging or assisting a number of offences and the defendant believes that one particular offence will necessarily be committed, but there is no reason why this cannot be charged under s.45, since the defendant will have done an act which is capable of assisting or encouraging a particular crime, even though it is capable of encouraging or assisting other crimes, and the defendant believes that the particular crime will be committed and that his act will encourage or assist its commission. Indeed, the statute states that, where a person's act is capable of encouraging or assisting a number of offences, the s.45 offence applies separately in respect of each offence which the defendant believes will be encouraged or assisted: s.49(2)(b).

〰 *Questions*

Was the effect of the Court of Appeal's decision to render the offence in s 46 redundant? If so, might this be desirable?

This is not the end of the saga, however. The Court of Appeal considered the safety of D's conviction again in *Sadique* [2013] EWCA Crim 1150. The judgment of Lord Judge CJ differs from that of his brethren in the earlier case.

---

30. As we have already explained, the 2007 Act created three distinct offences. It is not open to the court to set one or other of them aside and the legislation must be interpreted to give effect to the creation by statute of the three offences. It may well be that the common law offence of inciting someone else to commit an offence was less complex. It may equally be that the purpose of the legislation could have been achieved in less tortuous fashion. Nevertheless these three distinct offences were created by the 2007 Act, with none taking priority over the other two. S.46 creates the offence of encouraging or assisting the commission of one or more offences. Its specific ingredients and the subsequent legislative provisions underline that an indictment charging a s.46 offence of encouraging one or more offences is permissible.

31. This has the advantage of reflecting practical reality. A defendant may very well believe that his conduct will assist in the commission of one or more of a variety of different offences by another individual without knowing or being able to identify the precise offence or offences which the person to whom he offers encouragement or assistance intends to commit, or will actually commit. As Professor Virgo explains in his most recent article, the purpose of the s.46 was 'to provide for the relatively common case where a defendant contemplates that one of a variety of offences might be committed as a result of his or her encouragement'. We entirely agree.

32. *DPP v Maxwell* [1978] 1 WLR 1350 provides a clear example of how the s.46 offence should operate. Maxwell was a member of the Ulster Volunteer Force who agreed to drive his own car and lead a second car containing three or four other men to a remote public house. Having guided them to the scene, he drove slowly passed the public house, and then returned home. The car containing the gang of men stopped, one of the occupants got out, and ran towards the public house, where he threw a pipe bomb containing explosives into the hall way. As it happened the attack failed. He was convicted as an accomplice of doing an act with intent to cause an explosion by a bomb, and with possession of a bomb, both offences contrary to the Explosives Substances Act 1883. On appeal to the House of Lords it was submitted that Maxwell could not properly be convicted of aiding and abetting the commission of these crimes because he did not know the form the attack would take, or of the presence of the bomb in the car containing the gang.

33. The appeal was dismissed. Maxwell could properly be convicted of aiding and abetting the commission of these offences provided he contemplated the commission of one of a limited number of crimes by the principals and intentionally lent his assistance in the commission of such crimes. It was irrelevant that when he lent his assistance Maxwell did not know which of those particular crimes the principal intended to commit, or indeed the precise target or weapons which the gang would use. In short, save that the broad purpose of the gang he led to the site was encompassed in the concept of terrorism, Maxwell did not know (or believe) which particular offence that gang was intent on perpetrating.

34. In our judgment the ingredients of the s.46 offence, and the ancillary provisions, and s.58(4)–(7) in particular, underline that an indictment charging a s.46 offence by reference to one or more offences is permissible, and covers the precise situation for which the legislation provides. Before the appellant in the present case could be convicted, the jury had to be satisfied that (a) he was involved in the supply of the relevant chemicals and (b) that, if misused criminally, the chemicals were capable of misuse by others to commit offences of supplying or being concerned in the supply of, or being in possession with intent to supply class A and/or class B drugs. None of this would be criminal unless it was also proved (c) that at the time when the relevant chemicals were being supplied, the appellant believed that what he was doing would encourage or assist the commission of one or more of these drug related offences and (d) that he also believed that this was the purpose, or one of the purposes, for which the chemicals would be used by those to whom he supplied them. If those ingredients were established, as the chemicals could be used for cutting agents for class A drugs or class B drugs, or both, it was not necessary for the Crown to prove that he had a specific belief about the particular drug related offence which those he was encouraging or assisting would or did commit.

35. So far as the defendant in Maxwell's position was concerned, s.46 remains apt to cover the encouragement or assistance he offered, not only when the explosive device was actually thrown (when he might equally have been convicted as an accomplice) but also if the plans were not brought to fruition, because of a sudden change of plan so that the device was hurled at a police officer rather than thrown into the public house, or even if the presence of a large number of police officers at the locality led the terrorist gang to drive away without any explosive being thrown at all.

The Court of Appeal effectively adopted the interpretation of s 46 which had previously been rejected. While some welcome this decision (see Virgo [2013] 7 Arch Rev 4) the outcome is not one that all commentators welcome. See Rudi Fortson QC's case comment at [2014] Crim LR 60.

≈≈≈ *Questions*

D supplied X with a crowbar and is charged with doing an act capable of assisting or encouraging the commission of murder, burglary and criminal damage believing that one or more of those offences will be committed but having no belief as to which. If D is convicted, is there the possibility that four members of the jury were sure that in supplying X with the crowbar D believed that criminal damage would be committed, another four were sure that D believed that burglary would be committed, while the final four jurors were sure that D believed that murder would be committed? Is it fair to convict D? Of what? How is the judge to approach the task of sentencing D? Section 58(4)–(7) states that the maximum sentence when D is found guilty under s 46 is the same as the offence which D believed might be committed that carries the longest sentence. If there is the possibility that not all the jurors were sure that D believed that murder would be committed, do you think it fair that D potentially receives a life sentence?

22.2.3.3 Defences

There is no defence that the anticipated offences did not occur: s 47(4). It is a defence for D to prove that he acted reasonably under s 50. D cannot be liable if he is a 'victim': s 51. These are discussed earlier in the chapter.

22.2.3.4 Which offences are capable of being assisted or encouraged?

In deciding under s 46 whether an act is capable of encouraging or assisting the commission of one or more of a number of offences, listed offences in Sch 3 (see section 22.2.2.4). D cannot be liable for encouraging or assisting:

- P to commit a statutory incitement of X;
- P to attempt to commit an offence;
- P to do an act which is capable of assisting X to commit a crime; or
- conspiracy to commit an offence.

22.3 Impossibility and the Serious Crime Act 2007

What if D believes he is doing an act capable of assisting or encouraging murder, intending to assist or encourage, but in fact the substantive offence in question is impossible to commit because V is already dead? The 2007 Act makes no reference to the position regarding impossibility. The Law Commission believed that impossibility would be no defence and that this has been achieved by its silence. The Law Commission gave the following example.

> if D . . . provides P with a weapon believing that P will use it to attack V1 (intending to kill V1), D is guilty of assisting murder irrespective of whether P uses the weapon to attack anyone. Were P to attack and murder V2, instead of V1, D would be equally guilty of encouraging or assisting murder. If P attacked V2 because V1 was already dead at the time that D provided the weapon, D would still be guilty of encouraging or assisting murder. It may have been impossible for V1 to be murdered but, nonetheless, D had done an act capable of encouraging or assisting the conduct element of murder, namely an attack on any human being. (Law Com Report No 300, para 6.63)

Although this example may seem straightforward, less clear is the case where D's act, which he thinks is capable of assisting or encouraging, is in fact incapable of doing so.

22.4 The possibility of reform?

In addition to the criticisms of Part 2 that have been made by academics and the judiciary, the House of Commons Justice Committee had the following to say.

> 26. We expect the Ministry to consider the effect of the Court of Appeal's 2013 judgment in the case of *Sadique* upon its analysis of Part 2 of the SCA. In the light of this fresh judgment (upon which, at the time of preparing this report, there were no academic articles), we make no conclusions or recommendations in relation to the contents of Part 2, save that we concur with the academics who told us that the sections are complex and difficult to understand for lawyers, let alone for defendants, jurors and other lay-people working in the criminal justice system. We consider that the Court of Appeal's use of the word 'tortuous' in the 2013 *Sadique* judgment is entirely apt to describe the complexity and prolixity of Part 2 of the SCA.

. . .

31. In relation to the SCA, as stated above, we are concerned about the complexity of the provisions, and the difficulties that academics, lawyers and judges have found in interpreting the provisions. At the same time, we accept that there are, as yet, relatively few cases, and that the latest judgment in the case of *Sadique* may allow the legislation to settle into accepted use and interpretation. *We recommend that the Ministry conduct a further and full post-legislative assessment of Part 2 in 2016. If, in the meantime, the number of appeals on Part 2 increases, we expect the Ministry to consider bringing forward legislative proposals for revising, or even replacing, Part 2 to meet the purpose of the legislation in a less tortuous fashion.*

Available in full at http://www.publications.parliament.uk/pa/cm201314/cmselect/cmjust/639/63904.htm.

≋ *Question*
Do you agree that Part 2 ought to be revised, or even completely replaced?

FURTHER READING

D. Baker, 'Complicity, Proportionality and the Serious Crime Act 2007' (2011) 14 New Crim L Rev 403

J. Child, 'Exploring the *Mens Rea* Requirements of the Serious Crime Act 2007: Assisting and Encouraging Offences' (2012) 76 J Crim L 220

J. Child and A. Hunt, 'Mens Rea and the General Inchoate Offences: Another New Culpability Framework' (2012) 63 NILQ 247

R. Fortson and D. Ormerod, 'The Serious Crime Act 2007 Part 2' [2009] Crim LR 389

Law Commission Consultation Paper No 131, *Assisting and Encouraging Crime* (1993)

Law Commission Report No 300, *Inchoate Liability for Assisting and Encouraging* (2005)

F. Stark, 'Encouraging or Assisting Clarity?' (2013) 72 CLJ 497

23
General defences

The controversies that will be examined in this chapter include:

(1) whether the fact of childhood constitutes a defence;

(2) the extent to which duress can negate criminal liability;

(3) whether necessity ought to be a defence;

(4) the impact of legislative attempts to clarify self-defence;

(5) the distinction between justifications and excuses and whether these classifications have any practical import.

23.1 Introduction

In this chapter we are concerned with defences in the strictest sense of the word. The defendant is not denying that he committed the actus reus with mens rea. He is asserting the existence of other facts which, he claims, justify or excuse his doing what would otherwise be a crime. Following *Woolmington* [1935] AC 462 the defendant does not have to prove the existence of those facts. If there is some evidence of them, the onus is on the prosecution to disprove one or more of them. This means that in a criminal trial, although the Crown will bear the legal burden of proving the offence against the defendant (if they fail to do so the defendant is acquitted), the defendant will often bear an evidential burden in relation to defences he wishes to run. The evidential burden does not oblige D to prove the particular defence in order to be acquitted. It is not a legal burden. It obliges the defendant to 'raise evidence' of the defence in order to get it on its feet. Once the defendant has raised the defence it is for the Crown to disprove it; the Crown has the legal burden of proving that the defence was not applicable on the facts. The defence succeeds if, on consideration of the whole of the evidence, the jury think it reasonably possible that all the elements of the defence were present. If so, the prosecution has not proved beyond reasonable doubt that the defendant is guilty. Taking a simple example, if D is charged with murdering V and he pleads self-defence, the Crown must establish that D caused the death of V under the Queen's Peace, intending to kill or cause at least GBH. If D raises his defence of self-defence by identifying evidence in support of that defence, the Crown must then rebut it by proving that D was not acting in self-defence when he killed V.

23.2 The incapacity of children

> 〰 *Question*
> From what age should children be subject to prosecution and punishment for acts which constitute criminal offences under English criminal law?

23.2.1 Children under 10 years

Children and Young Persons Act 1933, s 50

50. Age of criminal responsibility

It shall be conclusively presumed that no child under the age of ten years can be guilty of any offence.

There may be the clearest evidence that a young child satisfied the actus reus and mens rea of the offence but once it is shown that he was, or may have been, under the age of 10 at the time of the act, no criminal proceedings may follow.

23.2.2 Children aged 10–13

At common law there was a rebuttable presumption that these children were *doli incapax*, incapable of forming a criminal state of mind. The presumption was rebutted only if the prosecution proved beyond reasonable doubt not only that the child caused the actus reus, but also that he knew the particular act was 'seriously wrong' (as opposed to merely naughty or mischievous). That presumption was removed by s 34 of the Crime and Disorder Act 1998:

The rebuttable presumption of criminal law that a child aged ten or over is incapable of committing an offence is hereby abolished.

The House of Lords concluded in *T* [2009] UKHL 20 that the clear intention of Parliament was to abolish the concept of *doli incapax*. This means that a child over 10 can be convicted of an offence, provided they have the necessary mens rea.

Although the defence of *doli incapax* is no longer available to 10–13-year-olds, the law has recently begun to recognize the need for a child defendant to be able to participate effectively in proceedings (*T & V v UK* (2000) 30 EHRR 121). Amendments to criminal procedural rules have sought to achieve this.

The age of criminal responsibility in England is set at a remarkably low level, and many have called for it to be raised. The issue of the appropriate age of criminal responsibility is a complex one with political and human rights dimensions.

23.3 Duress by threats or circumstances

It is now established that two forms of duress are recognized by the criminal law. The first, duress by threats, has existed for centuries but, until modern times, made very rare appearances in the law reports. In the last 50 years, the law has developed relatively quickly and is now reasonably well defined. However, several areas of uncertainty remain. Much more recent is the recognition of the existence of the related defence of duress of circumstances, the first case *Willer* (1986) 83 Cr App R 225, appearing in the law reports in 1986, the first use of the phrase by the courts in 1988 (*Conway* [1989] QB 290, section 23.4.1, p 647) and its recognition as a general defence in 1995 (*Pommel* [1995] 2 Cr App R 607).

The typical case of duress by threats is that where D is told, 'Do this (the crime charged) or else . . .' D yields to the threat and does the criminal act he was told to do. Duress of circumstances may arise more widely, when no one is telling the accused to commit the crime. The effect of the threat, however, may be the same. For example, D who is disqualified from driving:

(1) is told by a menacing gang of youths, 'Drive the car or we will kill you';

(2) sees the same gang bearing down on him with shouts of 'Kill him' and the only way he can escape is to drive the car.

In both cases, D intentionally commits the actus reus of the offence of driving while disqualified and in both cases he does so in order to save his life from the same menace. If he has a defence in the one case, he ought to have a defence in the other. The close relationship is illustrated by the fact that in *Willer* the court was concerned with a case of type (1) (circumstances) but it showed no awareness of this and relied on the law relating to duress by threats. In *Martin*, by contrast the court decided the case as one of duress by circumstances, whereas closer inspection would have revealed that it was duress by threats.

The principles applicable to the two types of duress are probably the same and the cases below, though mainly concerned with duress by threats, also state the law for duress of circumstances. They are considered here together with some further discussion of duress of circumstances, section 23.4, p 647.

23.3.1 Overview of the current law

In the following case, the House of Lords restated the constituent elements of duress by threats, in order to clarify what must be present in order for the defence to be successfully pleaded. In doing so, the House of Lords affirmed the limited scope of the defence.

R v Hasan
[2005] UKHL 22, House of Lords

(Lords Bingham of Cornhill, Steyn, Rodger of Earlsferry, Baroness Hale of Richmond and Lord Brown of Eaton-under-Heywood)

H was charged with aggravated burglary and pleaded duress. He claimed that he had been coerced into committing the burglary by S, a drug dealer with a reputation for violence, who had threatened that H and his family would be harmed if H did not commit the crime. H claimed that he had had no chance to escape and go to the police.

Lord Bingham of Cornhill [his lordship dealt with the facts of the case and other unrelated issues]:

17. The common sense starting point of the common law is that adults of sound mind are ordinarily to be held responsible for the crimes which they commit. To this general principle there has, since the 14th century, been a recognised but limited exception in favour of those who commit crimes because they are forced or compelled to do so against their will by the threats of another. Such persons are said, in the language of the criminal law, to act as they do because they are subject to duress.

18. Where duress is established, it does not ordinarily operate to negative any legal ingredient of the crime which the defendant has committed. Nor is it now regarded as justifying the conduct of

the defendant, as has in the past been suggested: *Attorney-General v Whelan* [1934] IR 518, 526; Glanville Williams, *Criminal Law, The General Part* (2nd edn, 1961), p 755. Duress is now properly to be regarded as a defence which, if established, excuses what would otherwise be criminal conduct: *Director of Public Prosecutions for Northern Ireland v Lynch* [1975] AC 653, 671, 680, 710–711; *Hibbert v The Queen* (1995) 99 CCC (3d) 193, paras 21, 38, 47, per Lamer CJC.

19. Duress affords a defence which, if raised and not disproved, exonerates the defendant altogether. It does not, like the defence of provocation to a charge of murder, serve merely to reduce the seriousness of the crime which the defendant has committed. And the victim of a crime committed under duress is not, like a person against whom a defendant uses force to defend himself, a person who has threatened the defendant or been perceived by the defendant as doing so. The victim of a crime committed under duress may be assumed to be morally innocent, having shown no hostility or aggression towards the defendant. The only criminal defences which have any close affinity with duress are necessity, where the force or compulsion is exerted not by human threats but by extraneous circumstances, and, perhaps, marital coercion under section 47 of the Criminal Justice Act 1925.

20. Where the evidence in the proceedings is sufficient to raise an issue of duress, the burden is on the prosecution to establish to the criminal standard that the defendant did not commit the crime with which he is charged under duress: *R v Lynch*, above.

[His lordship referred to Law Commission proposals.]

The prosecution's difficulty is of course the greater when, as is all too often the case, little detail of the alleged compulsion is vouchsafed by the defence until the trial is under way.

21. Having regard to these features of duress, I find it unsurprising that the law in this and other jurisdictions should have been developed so as to confine the defence of duress within narrowly defined limits. Most of these are not in issue in this appeal, but it seems to me important that the issues the House is asked to resolve should be approached with understanding of how the defence has developed, and to that end I shall briefly identify the most important limitations:

(1) Duress does not afford a defence to charges of murder (*R v Howe* [1987] AC 417), attempted murder (*R v Gotts* [1992] 2 AC 412) and, perhaps, some forms of treason (Smith & Hogan, *Criminal Law*, 10th edn, 2002, p 254). The Law Commission has in the past (eg. in 'Criminal Law. Report on Defences of General Application' (Law Com No 83, Cm 556, 1977, paras 2.44–2.46)) recommended that the defence should be available as a defence to all offences, including murder, and the logic of this argument is irresistible. But their recommendation has not been adopted, no doubt because it is felt that in the case of the gravest crimes no threat to the defendant, however extreme, should excuse commission of the crime. . . .

(2) To found a plea of duress the threat relied on must be to cause death or serious injury. In *Alexander MacGrowther's Case* (1746) Fost. 13, 14, 168 ER 8, Lee CJ held:

'The only force that doth excuse, is a force upon the person, and present fear of death.'

But the Criminal Law Commissioners in their Seventh Report of 1843 (p 31, article 6) understood the defence to apply where there was a just and well-grounded fear of death or grievous bodily harm, and it is now accepted that threats of death or serious injury will suffice: *R v Lynch*, above, p 679; *R v Abdul-Hussain* (Court of Appeal (Criminal Division), 17 December 1998, unreported).

(3) The threat must be directed against the defendant or his immediate family or someone close to him: *Smith & Hogan*, above, p 258. In the light of recent Court of Appeal decisions such as *R v Conway* [1989] QB 290 and *R v Wright* [2000] Crim LR 510, the current (April 2003) specimen direction of the Judicial Studies Board suggests that the threat must be directed, if not to the defendant or a member of his immediate family, to a person for whose safety the defendant would reasonably regard himself as responsible. The correctness of such a direction was not, and on the facts could not be, in issue on this appeal, but it appears to me, if strictly applied, to be consistent with the rationale of the duress exception.

(4) The relevant tests pertaining to duress have been largely stated objectively, with reference to the reasonableness of the defendant's perceptions and conduct and not, as is usual in many other areas of the criminal law, with primary reference to his subjective perceptions. It is necessary to return to this aspect, but in passing one may note the general observation of Lord Morris of Borth-y-Gest in *R v Lynch*, above at p 670:

> '. . . it is proper that any rational system of law should take fully into account the standards of honest and reasonable men. By those standards it is fair that actions and reactions may be tested.'

(5) The defence of duress is available only where the criminal conduct which it is sought to excuse has been directly caused by the threats which are relied upon.

(6) The defendant may excuse his criminal conduct on grounds of duress only if, placed as he was, there was no evasive action he could reasonably have been expected to take. It is necessary to return to this aspect also, but this is an important limitation of the duress defence and in recent years it has, as I shall suggest, been unduly weakened.

(7) The defendant may not rely on duress to which he has voluntarily laid himself open. The scope of this limitation raises the most significant issue on this part of this appeal, and I must return to it. [See section 23.3.2.5, p 627.]

22. For many years it was possible to regard the defence of duress as something of an antiquarian curiosity, with little practical application. Sir James Stephen, with his immense experience, never knew or heard of the defence being advanced, save in the case of married women, and could find only two reported cases: *A History of the Criminal Law of England* (1883), vol II, p 106. Edwards, drawing attention to the absence of satisfactory modern authority, inferred that the defence must be very rare: 'Compulsion, Coercion and Criminal Responsibility' (1951) 14 MLR 297. Professor Hart described duress as a defence of which little is heard: *Punishment and Responsibility* (1960), p 16. This has changed. As Dennis correctly observed in 'Duress, Murder and Criminal Responsibility' (1980) 96 LQR 208,

> 'In recent years duress has become a popular plea in answer to a criminal charge.'

This is borne out by the steady flow of cases reaching the appellate courts over the past 30 years or so, and by the daily experience of prosecutors. As already acknowledged, the House is not invited in this appeal to recast the law on duress. It can only address, piecemeal, the issues which fall for decision. That duress is now regularly relied on as a complete defence to serious criminal charges does not alter the essential task which the House must undertake, but does give it additional practical importance. I must acknowledge that the features of duress to which I have referred in paras 18 to 20 above incline me, where policy choices are to be made, towards tightening rather than relaxing the conditions to be met before duress may be successfully relied on. In doing so, I bear in mind in particular two observations of Lord Simon of Glaisdale in *R v Lynch* above. . . .

> '. . . your Lordships should hesitate long lest you may be inscribing a charter for terrorists, gang-leaders and kidnappers.' (p 688).
> 'A sane system of criminal justice does not permit a subject to set up a countervailing system of sanctions or by terrorism to confer criminal immunity on his gang.' (p 696).

The House of Lords in *Hasan* confirmed that duress by threats has the following constituent elements:

(1) a threat of death or really serious harm;

(2) the threat must have been directed towards D, his immediate family or someone for whom D would reasonably regard himself as responsible;

(3) D's belief in the existence of the threat must be reasonable and his decision to commit the offence in question must also be reasonable. This is an objective assessment;

(4) D's decision to commit the criminal offence must be directly attributable to the threat;

(5) there must have been no evasive action D could reasonably have taken;

(6) D cannot rely upon threats to which he has voluntarily laid himself open;

(7) the defence is unavailable to murder, attempted murder or treason.

The following sections will examine each of these elements in turn.

23.3.2 The nature of the threat

There are a number of issues to consider in relation to the nature of the threat and its sufficiency to found the defence of duress or duress of circumstances.

(1) Is there a threat of death or serious injury?

(2) Against whom must the threat be made?

(3) Must the threat emanate from a source external to D?

(4) Must the threat of death or serious injury be the sole cause of D committing the crime?

(5) Can D rely on a threat he has 'courted'?

(6) How immediate must the threat of death or serious injury be?

(7) Need the duressor specify a particular crime that D must commit?

(8) Need there be a threat in fact, or is it sufficient that D believes in one?

(9) Must the threat be criminal?

23.3.2.1 A threat of death or serious injury

In *DPP for Northern Ireland v Lynch* [1975] AC 653, D was charged with helping others to murder a police officer in Northern Ireland. D drove the gunmen to and from the crime. D pleaded duress as he was ordered to drive the car by a gunman known for his ruthlessness. On the issue of what constitutes a sufficient threat, the House of Lords concluded, per Lord Simon, at 686:

> The type of threat which affords a defence must be one of human physical harm, (including possibly, imprisonment) so that threat of injury [*sic*] to property is not enough . . .

Threats of a non-violent nature, no matter how overwhelming, will not suffice. In *Singh* [1973] 1 All ER 122, D was trafficking in illegal immigrants and pleaded duress based on the threats of blackmail against him. The Court of Appeal held, per Lawton LJ, at 126:

> the submission on duress which counsel for the appellant . . . made was old but wrong. He asked us to say that a man who commits a crime at the request of a blackmailer whom he fears can plead duress. He cannot. Duress arises from threats of violence not exposure.

The Court of Appeal has consistently resisted attempts to widen the scope of the defence by permitting it to be pleaded in circumstances where D fears something less than death or serious injury. For example, in *Vinh van Dao* [2012] EWCA Crim 1717 DD were convicted of cultivating cannabis and sought to plead duress. The trial judge rejected the submission that a threat of false imprisonment was sufficient to permit them to raise the defence. The Court of Appeal, relying on Lord Bingham's judgment in *Hasan* accepted, *obiter*, that this approach was the correct one. Gross LJ stated as follows:

44. In our judgment, even if only provisionally, policy considerations point strongly towards confining the defence of duress to threats of death or serious injury and against extending the defence to treat threats of false imprisonment as sufficing. Our reasons follow.

45. First, there are the difficulties of proof alluded to by Lord Bingham in [*Hasan*], at [20]. These should not be underestimated. If once the evidence is sufficient to permit the defence to be raised, the burden is on the prosecution to disprove it to the criminal standard. In practical terms, the defence may consist of little more than assertions, only expanded upon at trial. It would be all too easy to assert a threat of false imprisonment, especially if it is unnecessary for any such assertion to be underpinned by a threat of death or serious injury.

46. Secondly, having regard to Lord Simon of Glaisdale's words of warning as to the ramifications of the defence of duress, highlighted by Lord Bingham in [*Hasan*] at [22] and set out above, it must be right to hesitate before permitting a widening of the defence and thus its more ready availability.

47. Thirdly, with respect to Mr. Unwin, we are not persuaded that the other limitations of the defence would furnish a sufficient safeguard against unwarranted over-reliance on the defence, if once broadened to encompass the threat of false imprisonment without the threat of death or serious injury.

48. Fourthly, confining the defence within its present relatively narrow limits does not preclude doing justice when sentencing, to reflect a defendant's true culpability—even if, on the facts, falling short of the requirements for reliance on duress: see [*Hasan*] at [22].

49. Accordingly, the policy considerations, foreshadowed in authority, point strongly towards confining the threats necessary to establish duress to those of death or serious injury. For completeness, we are not at all persuaded that it would be illogical to draw the line there but, however that may be, we would in this area place the requirements of practical policy ahead of those of strict logic. All that said, as already explained, our view remains provisional rather than final.

In *Ashley* [2012] EWCA Crim 434, A had retracted a complaint of rape made against her husband (H). A then reasserted that she had been raped and issued proceedings for a non-molestation order in the county court. A was charged with perverting the course of justice by falsely retracting a true allegation of rape. The Court of Appeal considered (a) A's argument that she had a duress defence to perverting the course of justice on account of the domestic violence H subjected her to and (b) that the prosecution should not have proceeded. In dismissing her appeal, the Court of Appeal held that the defence was subject to clear limitations. There had to be a threat of death or serious injury, which would include rape, and those threats could not be reasonably evaded. It was emphasized that the limitations of the defence of duress should not be eroded. On the facts, A had never suggested to her legal advisers or to the police that when she falsely retracted her truthful complaints she was acting under the threat of violence from H. See Laura Hoyano's case comment on *Ashley* [2013] Crim LR 242.

If she had been threatened by him with violence if she did not withdraw the complaint, as it seems to us, it is unconceivable that she would not have said so at the time. If she was asserting that he forced a retraction by raping her or threatening to rape her, there was no reason why she should not also have explained her retraction of the rapes by reference to any such threats. (at [64] per Lord Judge CJ)

~~~ *Questions*

Is a threat of damage to property, or of blackmail, sometimes as effective on D's will as a threat of violence? Should the law in each case balance the harm threatened against the seriousness of the crime committed?

23.3.2.2 Against whom must the threat be made?

The Law Commission recommended (Law Com Report No 218, *Legislating the Criminal Code: Offences Against the Person and General Principles* (1993), paras 28.1 et seq) that there should be no formal limitation to any class of persons against whom the threat must be directed. The relationship between D and the person threatened should be only one of the circumstances to be taken into account in determining whether the threat was one which D could reasonably be expected to resist (on which, see section 23.3.5, p 639). In *Shayler* [2001] 1 WLR 2206, the Lord Chief Justice at [49], approving a statement of Rose LJ in *Hussain*, stated that:

> the evil must be directed towards the defendant or a person or persons for whom he has responsibility or, we would add, persons for whom the situation makes him responsible; . . . [this extends], by way of example, [to] the situation where the threat is made to set off a bomb unless the defendant performs the unlawful act. The defendant may have not have had any previous connection with those who would be injured by the bomb but the threat itself creates the defendant's responsibility for those who will be at risk if he does not give way to the threat.

~~~ *Question*

If a bank robber threatens to shoot a customer in the bank unless D, the clerk, hands him the keys, does D have a defence of duress to a charge of being an accessory to the robbery?

23.3.2.3 The threat must be an extraneous one

The threat must have some source extraneous to the defendant himself. In *Rodger and Rose* [1998] 1 Cr App R 143, D who was serving a life sentence was informed that his tariff had been substantially increased. He broke out of prison and raised duress as a defence to the charge of prison-breaking. It was conceded for the purpose of the appeal that he broke out because he had become suicidal and would have committed suicide had he not done so. There was a threat to his life, but since the threat did not come from an extraneous source, it was no defence. To allow it, said the court, 'could amount to a licence to commit crime dependent on the personal characteristics and vulnerability of the offender'.

23.3.2.4 Duress and mixed motives

There may be several threats, one capable of amounting to duress, the others not: 'Do it or you will be made bankrupt, your adultery will be revealed to your wife and you will be maimed'; or there may be a threat capable of amounting to duress coupled with a promise: 'Do it and there is £100,000 for you; don't do it and you will be shot.'

In *Valderrama-Vega* [1985] Crim LR 220, D was charged with importing cocaine from Colombia. His defence was (a) that he and his family had been subjected to threats of death or injury by an organized crime group in Colombia; (b) that he was heavily indebted and under severe financial pressure; and (c) that he had been threatened with disclosure of his homosexual inclinations. Neither (b) nor (c) could amount to duress. The jury were directed that duress was a defence only if D acted *solely* as the result of threats of death or serious injury. Though D's conviction was upheld, it was held that the use of the word 'solely' was wrong: it 'might have led the jury to convict even though they believed that [D] would not have acted as he did in the absence of threats to his life, if there were other motives or reasons for his actions . . .'.

〰 *Questions*

(1) What if D would not have done it for the money alone. He would have resisted the threats but for the offer of the money; but the combination of the money and the threats was irresistible?

(2) What if D would have done it for the money alone but was terrified by the threat and would have yielded to it even if no money had been on offer?

23.3.2.5 The (risk of the) threat must not be one D has 'courted'

This element operates as a further important limitation on the defence, and one that has become increasingly important as the courts have sought to prevent the defence being too readily available to those involved in drug-related and terrorist crime, in particular where their involvement demonstrates a degree of prior culpability. The problem commonly arises where D has joined a criminal organization and, having committed a crime as part of that organization or on behalf of it, D pleads that members of the organization threatened death or serious injury to him/others unless he committed the crime.

〰 *Questions*

What limitations might be placed on the defence to meet these concerns? What if D has not voluntarily joined the organization? Perhaps he was under duress to join? To what type of risk must D be exposing himself? Must D be aware of the risk that he is exposing himself to or is it sufficient that he ought to have been aware? Must D be aware of the type of crime he might be compelled to commit?

This is one of the issues that the House of Lords considered in *Hasan*. Lord Bingham held that D cannot plead duress by threats if he voluntarily associated himself with others engaged in criminal activity and he foresaw or ought reasonably to have foreseen the risk of being subjected to threats of violence. There are important features to note about Lord Bingham's judgment. First, there will be cases when D will be unable to plead duress even though, subjectively speaking, he did not foresee the risk that he would be subjected to threats of violence. Secondly, D must have joined with others *already engaged* in criminal activity. Lord Bingham was heavily influenced by policy considerations in arriving at this conclusion, as the following extract demonstrates.

The policy of the law must be to discourage association with known criminals, and it should be slow to excuse the criminal conduct of those who do so. If a person voluntarily becomes or remains associated with others engaged in criminal activity in a situation where he knows or ought reasonably to know that he may be the subject of compulsion by them or their associates, he cannot rely on the defence of duress to excuse any act which he is thereafter compelled to do by them. It is not necessary in this case to decide whether or to what extent that principle applies if an undercover agent penetrates a criminal gang for bona fide law enforcement purposes and is compelled by the gang to commit criminal acts.

In *Ali* [2008] EWCA Crim 716, the Court of Appeal applied the full rigour of Lord Bingham's objective approach in *Hasan*, and arguably went further, holding that if D has joined with others whom he ought to have realized might subject him to threats of violence, he is denied the defence of duress. The defence is lost irrespective of whether he has joined an existing criminal gang or not. D was convicted of the robbery at knifepoint of a vehicle owner. His plea of duress had been rejected at trial on the basis that D had voluntarily joined with the alleged duressor, BH, a co-accused in the robbery. D knew that BH carried a knife and had been warned not to associate with BH.

≋ *Question*

D is a drug addict. He associates with X, a drug dealer. Will D have any opportunity to rely on a defence of duress if X subsequently threatens D with serious injury or death unless D commits crimes to acquire money to pay his debts for drugs bought?

In her minority speech in *Hasan*, Baroness Hale adopted a more subjective approach, suggesting that the defence is denied only where D has himself foreseen a risk that he will be compelled by threats of violence to commit crime. It is submitted that this is a preferable approach to that in *Ali*.

Baroness Hale [her ladyship referred to the Law Commission's Report, *Legislating the Criminal Code: Offences Against the Person and General Principles* (Law Com No 218, 1993) (published when her Ladyship was a Law Commissioner) in which the Commission had recommended placing the burden on the accused:]

73. . . . I remain attracted by the Law Commission's proposals. The real reasons for the unpopularity of the defence are those given by Lord Lane CJ in *Howe*: that it is readily raised by the least deserving of people but difficult for the prosecution to disprove. We are told by Mr Perry [for the Crown] that, perhaps because of advances in forensic science which have made crimes easier to detect and more difficult to defend, duress is now very frequently raised, often late in the day, by defendants up and down the country.

74. If we are not to have legislation to alter the burden of proof, and I agree that it is not open to us to do it ourselves, then I understand your lordships' desire to maintain the objective standards set by Lord Lane in *Graham*. But it seems to me that the best counter to Lord Lane's concerns is the *Fitzpatrick* doctrine [that a defendant is denied the defence of duress if he courted the risk of being threatened] which is the issue in this case. Logically, if it applies, it comes before all the other questions raised by the defence: irrespective of whether there was a threat which he could not reasonably be expected to resist, had the defendant so exposed himself to the risk of such threats that he cannot now rely on them as an excuse? If even on his own story he had done so, then the defence can be withdrawn from the jury without more ado; if that issue has to be left to the jury, but they resolve it against him, there is no need for them to consider the other questions.

. . .

77. . . . The foreseeable risk should be one of duress: that is, of threats of such severity, plausibility and immediacy that one might be compelled to do that which one would otherwise have chosen not to do. The battered wife knows that she is exposing herself to a risk of unlawful violence if she stays, but she may have no reason to believe that her husband will eventually use her broken will to force her to commit crimes. For the same reason, I would say that it must be foreseeable that duress will be used to compel the person to commit crimes of some sort. I have no difficulty envisaging circumstances in which a person may be coerced to act lawfully. The battered wife knows very well that she may be compelled to cook the dinner, wash the dishes, iron the shirts and submit to sexual intercourse. That

should not deprive her of the defence of duress if she is obliged by the same threats to herself or her children to commit perjury or shoplift for food.

78. But this brings me to a concern which I have had throughout this case. It is one thing to deny the defence to people who choose to become members of illegal organisations, join criminal gangs, or engage with others in drug-related criminality. It is another thing to deny it to someone who has a quite different reason for becoming associated with the duressor and then finds it difficult to escape. I do not believe that this limitation on the defence is aimed at battered wives at all, or at others in close personal or family relationships with their duressors and their associates, such as their mothers, brothers or children. The Law Commission's Bills all refer to a person who exposes himself to the risk 'without reasonable excuse'. The words were there to cater for the police infiltrator (see Law Com No 83 [*Report on Defences of General Application* (1977)], para 2.37) but they are also applicable to the sort of association I have in mind. The other elements of the defence, narrowly construed in accordance with existing authority, are more than adequate to keep it within bounds in such cases.

≈ **Question**

Do you agree with Baroness Hale's approach?

23.3.2.6 How immediate must the threat be?

In *Hasan*, Lord Bingham held that D can only plead duress if 'there was no evasive action he could reasonably have been expected to take' to avoid committing the criminal offence in question. As the cases considered in this section will demonstrate, a question has arisen as to whether D will only be denied the offence if he had no opportunity to avoid the threat, no *reasonable* opportunity or only if he believed he had no opportunity.

R v Hudson and Taylor
[1971] EWCA Crim 2, Court of Appeal, Criminal Division

(Lord Parker CJ, Widgery LJ and Cooke J)

The accused, H and T, were girls aged 17 and 19. They were the main prosecution witnesses at the trial of W, on a charge of wounding. They both failed to identify W and testified that they did not know him. W was acquitted. H and T were tried for perjury and admitted that their evidence was false. H said that she had been approached and warned that she would be 'cut up' if she 'told on' W. H passed this on to T, who had also been warned by other girls. The accused were frightened and decided to tell lies to avoid the consequences. Their decision was confirmed when, on arriving in court, they saw one of the threatening men in the public gallery.

The recorder directed that the defence of duress was not open because there was no present immediate threat capable of being carried out there and then, since the accused were in court in the presence of the judge and the police. On appeal, the Crown argued that the ruling could be upheld on the additional ground that the accused should have neutralized the threat by seeking police protection when they came to court or beforehand.

[Lord Widgery CJ, having stated the facts, continued:]

This appeal raises two main questions; first, as to the nature of the necessary threat and, in particular, whether it must be 'present and immediate'; secondly, as to the extent to which a right to plead duress may be lost if the accused has failed to take steps to remove the threat as, for example, by seeking police protection.

It is essential to the defence of duress that the threat shall be effective at the moment when the crime is committed. The threat must be a 'present' threat in the sense that it is effective to neutralise the will of the accused at that time. Hence an accused who joins a rebellion under the compulsion of threats cannot plead duress if he remains with the rebels after the threats have lost their effect and his own will has had a chance to re-assert itself (*McGrowther's case* [(1746) Fost 13] and *A-G v Whelan* [[1934] IR 518]). Similarly a threat of future violence may be so remote as to be insufficient to over-power the will at the moment when the offence was committed, or the accused may have elected to commit the offence in order to rid himself of a threat hanging over him and not because he was driven to act by immediate and unavoidable pressure. In none of these cases is the defence of duress available because a person cannot justify the commission of a crime merely to secure his own peace of mind.

When, however, there is no opportunity for delaying tactics, and the person threatened must make up his mind whether he is to commit the criminal act or not, the existence at that moment of threats sufficient to destroy his will ought to provide him with a defence even though the threatened injury may not follow instantly, but after an interval. This principle is illustrated by *Subramaniam v Public Prosecutor* [[1956] 1 WLR 965], when the appellant was charged in Malaya with unlawful possession of ammunition and was held by the Privy Council to have a defence of duress, fit to go to the jury, on his plea that he had been compelled by terrorists to accept the ammunition and feared for his safety if the terrorists returned.

In the present case the threats of Farrell were likely to be no less compelling, because their execution could not be effected in the court room, if they could be carried out in the streets of Salford the same night. Insofar, therefore, as the recorder ruled as a matter of law that the threats were not sufficiently present and immediate to support the defence of duress we think that he was in error. He should have left the jury to decide whether the threats had overborne the will of the appellants at the time when they gave the false evidence.

Counsel for the Crown, however, contends that the recorder's ruling can be supported on another ground, namely, that the appellants should have taken steps to neutralise the threats by seeking police protection either when they came to court to give evidence, or beforehand. He submits on grounds of public policy that an accused should not be able to plead duress if he had the opportunity to ask for protection from the police before committing the offence and failed to do so. The argument does not distinguish cases in which the police would be able to provide effective protection, from those when they would not, and it would, in effect, restrict the defence of duress to cases where the person threat-ened had been kept in custody by the maker of the threats, or where the time interval between the making of the threats and the commission of the offence had made recourse to the police impossible. We recognise the need to keep the defence of duress within reasonable bounds but cannot accept so severe a restriction on it. The duty, of the person threatened, to take steps to remove the threat does not seem to have arisen in an English case but in a full review of the defence of duress in the Supreme Court of Victoria (*Hurley and Murray* [[1967] VR 526]), a condition of raising the defence was said to be that the accused 'had no means, with safety to himself, of preventing the execution of the threat'.

In the opinion of this court it is always open to the Crown to prove that the accused failed to avail himself of some opportunity which was reasonably open to him to render the threat ineffective, and that on this being established the threat in question can no longer be relied on by the defence. In deciding whether such an opportunity was reasonably open to the accused the jury should have regard to his age and circumstances, and to any risks to him which may be involved in the course of action relied on.

In our judgment the defence of duress should have been left to the jury in the present case, as should any issue raised by the Crown and arising out of the appellants' failure to seek police protec-tion. The appeals will, therefore, be allowed and the convictions quashed.

Appeals allowed

In *Abdul-Hussain* [1999] Crim LR 570, the appellants were convicted of hijacking, contrary to s 1(1) of the Aviation Security Act 1982. They were Shiite Muslims from Southern Iraq, living in Sudan, and they feared return by the Sudanese authorities to Iraq, followed by torture and probable death. Using imitation hand grenades and plastic knives, they hijacked an aircraft bound for Amman and eventually landed in England. The judge withdrew the defence of duress from the jury.

Following *Hudson and Taylor*, in the previous extract, the Court of Appeal in *Abdul-Hussain* held that the defence should have been left to the jury. While the threat must be 'imminent', it need not be 'immediate'; nor need the reaction be 'spontaneous'. The appellants were in no immediate danger of death or serious bodily harm, but there was evidence that the threat was hanging over them, that it was 'imminent'. In *Abdul-Hussain*, the court gave a vivid and persuasive example to support its decision.

If Anne Frank had stolen a car to escape from Amsterdam and been charged with theft, the tenets of English law would not, in our judgment, have denied her a defence of duress of circumstances, on the ground that she should have waited for the Gestapo's knock on the door.

In *Hasan*, the trial judge had directed the jury that, 'The third question is: Could the defendant have avoided acting as he did without harm coming to his family? . . . If you are sure that he could have avoided acting as he did without harm coming to his family, again the defence fails and he is guilty.' In the House of Lords, Lord Bingham observed that:

24. [T]he Court of Appeal held that the judge had misdirected the jury on question 3 because, it was held, there was no suggestion that the defendant could have taken evasive action. This may, or may not, on the facts, be so, and this suggested misdirection does not feature in the question on duress certified for the opinion of the House the third question put by the judge, and regularly put in such cases, whether or not correctly put on the facts of this case, in my opinion focuses attention on a cardinal feature of the defence of duress, and I would wish to warn against any general notion that question 3 'collapses' into [the question about whether D has responded reasonably to the threat as he reasonably perceives it to be; see section 23.3.4, p 636].

[His lordship referred to the position in other jurisdictions.]

26. The recent English authorities have tended to lay stress on the requirement that a defendant should not have been able, without reasonably fearing execution of the threat, to avoid compliance. Thus Lord Morris of Borth-y-Gest in *R v Lynch*, above, at p 670, emphasised that duress

'must never be allowed to be the easy answer of those who can devise no other explanation of their conduct nor of those who readily could have avoided the dominance of threats nor of those who allow themselves to be at the disposal and under the sway of some gangster-tyrant.'

Lord Simon of Glaisdale gave as his first example of a situation in which a defence of duress should be available (p 687):

'A person, honestly and reasonably believing that a loaded pistol is at his back which will in all probability be used if he disobeys'

In the view of Lord Edmund-Davies (p 708) there had been

'for some years an unquestionable tendency towards progressive latitude in relation to the plea of duress.'

27. In making that observation Lord Edmund-Davies did not directly criticise the reasoning of the Court of Appeal in its then recent judgment in *R v Hudson and Taylor* [1971] 2 QB 202, but that was described by Professor Glanville Williams as 'an indulgent decision' (*Textbook of Criminal Law*, 2nd

edn, 1983, p 636), and it has in my opinion had the unfortunate effect of weakening the requirement that execution of a threat must be reasonably believed to be imminent and immediate if it is to support a plea of duress. [His lordship referred to the decision in *Hudson and Taylor* extracted at the beginning of this section.]

The Court of Appeal placed reliance on the decision of the Privy Council in *Subramaniam v Public Prosecutor* [1956] 1 WLR 965. That case, however, involved a defendant who sought at trial to advance a defence of duress under a section of the Penal Code of the Federated Malay States which provided that, with certain exceptions

> 'nothing is an offence which is done by a person who is compelled to do it by threats, which, at the time of doing it, reasonably cause the apprehension that instant death to that person will otherwise be the consequence'.

The appeal was allowed because evidence relied on by the appellant to show that he had had a reasonable apprehension of instant death was wrongly excluded. It is hard to read that decision as authority for the Court of Appeal's conclusion. I can understand that the Court of Appeal in *R v Hudson and Taylor* had sympathy with the predicament of the young appellants but I cannot, consistently with principle, accept that a witness testifying in the Crown Court at Manchester has no opportunity to avoid complying with a threat incapable of execution then or there. When considering necessity in *R v Cole* [1994] Crim LR 582, 583, Simon Brown LJ, giving the judgment of the court, held that the peril relied on to support the plea of necessity lacked imminence and the degree of directness and immediacy required of the link between the suggested peril and the offence charged, but in *R v Abdul-Hussain*, above, the Court of Appeal declined to follow these observations to the extent that they were inconsistent with *R v Hudson and Taylor*, by which the court regarded itself as bound.

28. The judge's direction on question 3 was modelled on the JSB specimen direction current at the time, and is not in my opinion open to criticism. It should however be made clear to juries that if the retribution threatened against the defendant or his family or a person for whom he reasonably feels responsible is not such as he reasonably expects to follow immediately or almost immediately on his failure to comply with the threat, there may be little if any room for doubt that he could have taken evasive action, whether by going to the police or in some other way, to avoid committing the crime with which he is charged.

More recently, in *Batchelor* [2013] EWCA Crim 2638 the Court of Appeal reiterated the criticisms that were made of *Hudson and Taylor* in *Hasan*. Elias LJ noted that D could have gone to the police at any time over a period of two and a half years. His lordship stated (at [15]):

> The law requires a certain degree of fortitude to be shown by victims in circumstances such as these. The teenaged girls were no doubt in genuine and real fear of their safety in *Hudson*, but that was not a justification for applying the defence of duress because they had the opportunity to avoid complying with the threat. The CACD in that case had allowed its sympathy to distort legal principles. Were we to accede to this appeal, then even assuming that the account of the intimidation was true, we would be doing the same thing.

Although the case has never been formally overturned, developments in the law since it was decided mean that it is highly unlikely a court today would be as generous as the court in *Hudson and Taylor*. Indeed, more recently in *Brandford* [2016] EWCA Crim 1794, the Court of Appeal accepted the trial judge's description of *Hudson and Taylor* as having been 'disapproved' in *Hasan*.

23.3.2.7 Must the threat be backed by a demand to commit a nominated crime?

In the paradigmatic case of duress, the defendant will have been told by the threatening party 'perform this crime or else'. In *Cole* [1994] Crim LR 582, D's defence to robbing two building societies was that moneylenders to whom he owed money had threatened him, his girlfriend and his child. The defence of duress by threats did not apply because the moneylenders did not stipulate that he commit robbery to meet their demands. Simon Brown LJ: 'In our judgment it is plain that the defence of duress by threats can only apply when the offence charged (the offence which the accused asserts he was constrained to commit) is the very offence which was nominated by the person making the threat, ie when the accused was required by the threat to commit the offence charged....' Subsequently, in *Ali* [1995] Crim LR 303, D, a heroin addict, was convicted of robbing a building society and claimed that his supplier, X, who had a reputation for violence, had demanded repayment of money D owed him. Further, that X had provided D with a gun and told D to get the money by the following day from a bank or a building society. The Court of Appeal upheld his conviction but appeared to accept that a threat is capable of amounting to duress when the duressee is charged with robbing a particular building society not specified by the duressor. In view of the strict approach taken to the issue of immediacy in *Hasan*, doubt must be cast on *Ali*.

23.3.2.8 The defendant must believe the reality of the threat; it need not exist in fact

There is no requirement for there to be a threat in fact. It is sufficient that D believes that there is a threat of the relevant gravity. If the defence was only available where the threat was real, D could not plead duress where threatened with an unloaded gun, nor where D escaped from prison erroneously believing it to be on fire. This would be unduly restrictive. If the threat did in fact exist, it would be wholly irrelevant if D was unaware of it. It becomes relevant only if, and to the extent that, D is aware of it.

In *Safi and others* [2003] EWCA Crim 1809, Afghan members of the Organization of Young Intellectuals of Afghanistan (the 'Organization') hijacked a plane which ultimately landed at Stansted. The defence said that the Taliban had discovered that the Organization was its political opponent, and had arrested and tortured four of its members who between them knew the names of the appellants and most of the other members of the Organization. The defendants claimed that their fear of persecution at the hands of the Taliban constituted a defence of duress (of circumstances). The trial judge directed that the defence failed unless there was evidence that there was in fact, or might in fact have been, an imminent peril to the defendants or their families. S appealed on the basis that the defence should be available if he *reasonably* believed that if he had not acted in the way he had, he (and/or the family) would have been killed or seriously injured. Longmore LJ, delivering the judgment of the Court of Appeal, agreed with S and held that it sufficed for D reasonably to believe that he and/or his family would be killed if he had not acted in the way that he had.

The decision clearly does not give carte blanche to hijackers. It decides only that the defence of duress was wrongly explained to the jury. If the defence was left to the jury, they would have had to consider whether the hijacking was a reasonable and proportionate response to the threat—an objective question. The onus would of course have been on the prosecution to prove that it was not; but is not hijacking such a dangerous and terrifying operation that the prosecution might well have succeeded?

23.3.2.9 Need the threats constitute a crime?

In *Jones and others* [2004] EWCA Crim 1981 (affirmed on other grounds in the House of Lords [2006] UKHL 16), Ds were charged with conspiracy to commit criminal damage at an RAF base. Their defences were duress/necessity, lawful excuse under s 5(2)(b) of the Criminal Damage Act 1971 and the prevention of crime under s 3 of the Criminal Law Act 1967. Each of these defences was predicated on the argument that the UK was engaged in an unlawful act of war against Iraq. At a preliminary hearing, Grigson J ruled that the issue of the legality of the war could not be adjudicated on/decided by domestic courts as the UK Government was exercising its prerogative powers relating to foreign policy. His lordship made further rulings in relation to the defences. The Court of Appeal held that the defence of duress of circumstances was potentially a domestic law (ie not international law) defence to a domestic law offence, but no domestic crime was committed by the UK Government. The executive's action in declaring and waging war was, in itself, a lawful exercise of its powers under the prerogative. The trial court would therefore have to consider the extent to which necessity might afford a defence to the defendants in the light of their beliefs on that basis.

23.3.3 Evaluating D's perception of the threat

≈ *Questions*

(1) Must the defendant *reasonably* believe that he or someone for whom he is responsible is under an immediate threat of death or serious injury, etc (and he has not voluntarily exposed himself to a risk of threats)?

(2) Is it enough that D genuinely, though mistakenly, believes he is under threat?

R v Graham

[1981] EWCA Crim 5, Court of Appeal, Criminal Division

(Lord Lane CJ, Taylor and McCullough JJ)

The appellant (G) was a homosexual living in 'a bizarre ménage à trois' with his wife (W) and another homosexual, King (K). G suffered from an anxiety state. He was taking valium which, according to medical evidence, would make him more susceptible to bullying. K was a violent man and had in 1978 tipped G and W off a settee because they were embracing and K was jealous. G knew K had been guilty of other acts of violence. On 27 June 1980 K attacked W with a knife. W then went to G's mother's home. G and K stayed, drinking heavily, while G also took valium. K suggested getting rid of the wife once and for all. G induced her to return by pretending that he had cut his wrists. She knelt beside him as he lay face down on the floor pretending to be seriously hurt. K put a kettle flex round her neck, saying, 'What's it like to know you are going to die?' She put up her hands to the flex. K told G to pull on one end of the flex. He did so, he said, only because he was afraid of K. The plug which he was pulling came off the flex, leaving it in doubt whether his act made any contribution to W's death. G was convicted of murder.

Lord Lane CJ [first dealt with the fact that the Crown at the trial conceded that, on those facts, it was open to the defence to raise the issue of duress to murder. That aspect of the law is now governed by the decision in *Howe* (section 23.3.5, p 639)]:

As a matter of public policy, it seems to us essential to limit the defence of duress by means of an objective criterion formulated in terms of reasonableness. Consistency of approach in defences to criminal liability is obviously desirable. Provocation and duress are analogous. [NB: provocation has since been replaced with a defence of loss of control discussed in Chapter 8.] In provocation the words or actions of one person break the self-control of another. In duress the words or actions of one person break the will of another. The law requires a defendant to have the self-control reasonably to be expected of the ordinary citizen in his situation. It should likewise require him to have the steadfastness reasonably to be expected of the ordinary citizen in his situation. So too with self-defence, in which the law permits the use of no more force than is reasonable in the circumstances. And, in general, if a mistake is to excuse what would otherwise be criminal, the mistake must be a reasonable one.

It follows that we accept Mr Sherrard's [counsel for the Crown] submission that the direction in this case was too favourable to the appellant. The Crown having conceded that the issue of duress was open to the appellant and was raised on the evidence, the correct approach on the facts of this case would have been as follows: (1) Was the defendant, or may he have been, impelled to act as he did because, as a result of what he reasonably believed King had said or done, he had good cause to fear that if he did not so act King would kill him or (if this is to be added) cause him serious physical injury? (2) If so, have the prosecution made the jury sure that a sober person of reasonable firmness, sharing the characteristics of the defendant, would not have responded to whatever he reasonably believed King said or did by taking part in the killing? The fact that a defendant's will to resist has been eroded by the voluntary consumption of drink or drugs or both is not relevant to this test.

Appeal dismissed

D's perception of a threat of death or serious injury must be reasonable.

≈≈≈ **Question**

To what extent do a defendant's personal incapacities affect the requirements that the perception of the threat of death or serious injury and the commission of the crime must be reasonable?

In *Graham*, Lord Lane, equating duress with self-defence in this respect, thought that in self-defence the law permits only force that is reasonable in the circumstances and that only a reasonable mistake would excuse. But less than two years later in *Gladstone Williams* (1987) 78 Cr App R 276, section 23.6.1.1, p 660, Lord Lane himself took a different view regarding self-defence, holding that an unreasonable belief might excuse if it was honestly held. In *Gladstone Williams*, Lord Lane followed *Kimber* [1983] 3 All ER 316, [1983] 1 WLR 1118, a case of indecent assault, where Lawton LJ appreciated the general effect of *DPP v Morgan* [1976] AC 182. Should this have required a change of mind by Lord Lane regarding duress as well? In *DPP v Rogers* [1998] Crim LR 202, DC, the court seems to have mistakenly assumed that the Law Commission recommendation for reform of the law (Law Com No 218, *Legislating the Criminal Code: Offences Against the Person and General Principles* (1993), pp 49–51) had been implemented. *Abdul-Hussain*, however, confirms that it is still the law that a defendant cannot rely on an unreasonable mistake of fact in order to found a defence of duress of either variety. See also *Safi* (section 23.3.2.8).

23.3.4 Evaluating D's response to the perceived threat

As we saw in *Graham*, if the jury think that D may reasonably have held the belief alleged and that that belief may have given him good cause to fear, the next question is whether 'a sober person of reasonable firmness sharing the characteristics of the defendant' would have responded as he did. This objective formulation was approved by Lord Bingham in *Hasan*.

A weak will and irresolution are not relevant. In the leading case of *Bowen* [1996] 2 Cr App R 157, [1996] Crim LR 577, CA, it was held that a low IQ was not a relevant characteristic:

> We do not see how low IQ, short of mental impairment or mental defectiveness, can be said to be a characteristic that makes those who have it less courageous and less able to withstand threats and pressure.

The Court of Appeal in *Bowen* reviewed the cases and confirmed the following principles.

(1) The mere fact that the accused is more pliable, vulnerable, timid or susceptible to threats than a normal person are not characteristics with which it is legitimate to invest the reasonable/ordinary person for the purpose of considering the objective test.

(2) The defendant may be in a category of persons who the jury may think less able to resist pressure than people not within that category. Obvious examples are age, where a young person may well not be so robust as a mature one; possibly sex, though many women would doubtless consider they had as much moral courage to resist pressure as men; pregnancy, where there is added fear for the unborn child; serious physical disability, which may inhibit self-protection; recognized mental illness or psychiatric condition, such as post-traumatic stress disorder leading to learned helplessness. (See the case of *GAC*, later in this section, p 638.)

(3) Characteristics which may be relevant in considering loss of control, because they are a 'circumstance' relevant to something other than D's general capacity for tolerance and self-restraint, will not necessarily be relevant in cases of duress.

(4) Characteristics due to self-induced abuse, such as alcohol, drugs or glue-sniffing, cannot be relevant.

(5) Psychiatric evidence may be admissible to show that the accused is suffering from some mental illness, mental impairment or recognized psychiatric condition, provided persons generally suffering from such conditions may be more susceptible to pressure and threats and thus to assist the jury in deciding whether a reasonable person suffering from such a condition might have been impelled to act as the defendant did. It is not admissible simply to show that in the doctor's opinion an accused, who is not suffering from such illness or condition, is especially timid, suggestible or vulnerable to pressure and threats. Nor is medical opinion admissible to bolster or support the credibility of the accused.

(6) Where counsel wishes to submit that the accused has some characteristic which falls within point (2), this must be made plain to the judge.

(7) In the absence of some direction from the judge as to what characteristics are capable of being regarded as relevant, the direction approved in *Graham* without more will not be as helpful as it might be, since the jury may be tempted, especially if there is evidence, as there was in this case, relating to suggestibility and vulnerability, to think that these are relevant. In most cases, it is probably only the age and sex of the accused that is capable of being relevant. If so, the judge should, as he did in this case, confine the characteristics in question to these (per Stuart Smith LJ at 166–167).

If the defendant with low IQ is no less able to resist pressure than a person with average IQ, there is no need to afford him any special treatment. But the court said that persons suffering from a 'recognised mental illness or psychiatric condition, such as post traumatic stress disorder leading to learned helplessness' (see *Emery* (1992) 14 Cr App R (S) 394, later in this section, p 638) are a category whose condition should be taken into account. Certainly this is so on the subjective issue, that is, whether D's will was in fact 'overborne'; but the question is whether they can be taken into account in applying the objective test. In *Hurst* [1995] 1 Cr App R 82 at 90, Beldam LJ said 'we find it hard to see how the person of reasonable firmness can be invested with the characteristics of a person who lacks reasonable firmness'.

In duress, only characteristics affecting the gravity of the threat would be relevant. Such characteristics, depending on the circumstances, might include age, sex, pregnancy, physical disability—anything which made the threat more frightening. Cf the defence of loss of control in Chapter 8. The divergence between the two defences has been created by s 54(3) of the Coroners and Justice Act 2009. See section 8.2.9. Characteristics which made it harder for D to resist it, making him a person of less than reasonable firmness—and that would seem to include 'recognized psychiatric conditions'—would not be relevant. Though this was not what the Law Commission intended, their recommendation, if enacted, might be construed to reach this result. The threat must be one which:

> in all the circumstances (including any of his personal characteristics *which affect its gravity*) he cannot reasonably be expected to resist. (Law Com Report No 218 (1993), para 29.2, emphasis added)

A further difficulty is that, according to one expert opinion, there are no recognized criteria identifying a group whose ability to withstand threats is reduced and that the test in *Bowen* is unworkable: A. Buchanan and G. Virgo, 'Duress and Mental Abnormality' [1999] Crim LR 517 at 529. However, the courts continue to apply it. In *Rogers* [1999] 9 Arch News 1, CA, it was held that the appellant's history of 'Asperger Syndrome and other co-morbid conditions which would have made him peculiarly amenable [to threats]' should have been taken into account. On the other hand, in *Hegarty* [1994] Crim LR 353 evidence that the defendant was 'emotionally unstable' and 'in a grossly elevated neurotic state' was not to be taken into account in applying the objective test. In *Hurst* (earlier in this section), the judge refused to admit the evidence of a psychiatrist of the effect of sexual abuse upon the defendant as a child. It was held that he was right to do so, even if it indicated that D, due to her experiences, suffered from a personality defect which made her lack the firmness and resolution to be expected of someone of her age and sex.

Horder [1994] Crim LR 334 is also critical of this aspect of the Law Commission's proposal. He puts the case of a practising paedophile who has been threatened with serious injury unless he has intercourse with a child: 'The fact that he is inured to intercourse with children might well be something that made it less reasonable to expect him to resist the threat.' But does the fact that D is a paedophile affect the 'gravity of the threat'? The threat to beat him up might be more terrifying because D is small, or a haemophiliac, or otherwise physically vulnerable; but is it any more terrifying because he happens to be a paedophile? The fact that D is a 'racist' may cause him more readily to succumb to a demand that he assault a person of a different race; but does it affect the gravity of a threat to slash his face if he does not do so? Are not paedophilia and racism irrelevant by any test?

The Law Commission confirmed that in its view:

> in deciding whether a person of reasonable firmness might have acted as the defendant did, the jury should be able to take into account all the circumstances of the defendant, including his or her age but not any other characteristics which bear upon his or her capacity to withstand duress. (Law Com Report No 304, *Murder, Manslaughter and Infanticide* (2006), para 6.86)

> ∿ *Question*
>
> If the threats are sufficient to wear down the will of even a defendant of ordinary fortitude, will they suffice for the defence of duress whoever the defendant is?

A simple threat to twist an arm is one thing. A threat to twist an arm after 24 hours of continuous arm-twisting is quite another. The person of reasonable fortitude who would certainly resist the former may well succumb to the latter. Attention cannot reasonably be confined to the final act which caused the defendant to give way. In *Emery* (1992) 14 Cr App R (S) 394, D relied unsuccessfully on duress to a charge of cruelty to a child. The Court of Appeal held that expert medical evidence admitted at the trial was allowed to go too far but that it would have been properly admitted if it had been confined to 'an expert account of the cause of the condition of dependent helplessness, the circumstances in which it might arise and what level of abuse would be required to produce it'. Lord Taylor CJ said:

> The question for the doctors was whether a woman of reasonable firmness with the characteristics of Miss Emery, if abused in the same manner which she said, would have had her will crushed so that she could not have protected the child.

Obviously a woman of reasonable firmness suffering from a condition of dependent helplessness would be a contradiction in terms.

> ∿ *Questions*
>
> Is the point that the alleged history of violence said to have produced that condition is all part of the duress? Does the jury have to envisage an ordinary woman who is of reasonable firmness before the history of violence begins and consider whether, by the time of the alleged offence, her will would have been so overborne that she would be unable to resist the threat?

In *Emery*, the ill-treatment of the child was an ongoing state of affairs. If the defendant was a person of reasonable firmness when she began to commit the crime she was presumably then liable and continued to be liable for acts done up to the point when it became unreasonable to expect her to escape from or resist the threat. After that point, she had the defence but only in respect of acts done to the child thereafter. If she had a defence to the cruelty offences would she not, once reduced to 'dependent helplessness', also have had a defence to any other crimes committed in response to her oppressor's threats—for example, to rob a bank or to inflict grievous bodily harm? In *GAC* [2013] EWCA Crim 1472, the Court of Appeal dealt with G's claim of duress to a charge of importing drugs. G claimed that she had not been in a position to plead duress at trial as she was a victim of domestic violence at the hands of X who was responsible for making her import the drugs. There was evidence of X's violence to her and expert psychiatric reports that G was suffering from battered woman syndrome (BWS) and was in a state of 'learned helplessness' at the time. The court held that duress by threats may be available in such a case. The court accepted that the approach to the BWS claim for duress was counterintuitive. A woman who was claiming BWS would be relying on her learned helplessness which would itself have produced inconsistencies in her accounts and may result in her withdrawing allegations of violence committed against her. Duress was not available on the evidence in this case because, although G suffered some violence at the hands of X, it was not of the kind that might raise the possibility of duress. The court noted that not every woman who suffered from domestic violence went on to suffer from BWS, and not every woman who suffered from BWS could claim the defence of duress. The question was whether the BWS was so severe that D's will was overborne; in this case, the evidence did not suggest that it was.

23.3.5 To which crimes is duress available?

Duress is not available as a defence to all crimes. As the cases in this section will demonstrate, the courts have held that duress cannot be pleaded as a defence to murder, attempted murder and treason.

In the 1970s, the House of Lords held, in *Lynch v DPP* [1975] 1 All ER 913, that duress could operate as a defence to murder where D acted as a secondary party in the killing. In the Privy Council in *Abbott v The Queen* [1976] 3 All ER 340 a few months later, the Board held that duress was no defence to murder committed as a principal offender. The confusion was resolved and the law settled by the House of Lords in the following case.

R v Howe and Bannister; R v Burke and Clarkson
[1986] UKHL 4, House of Lords

(Lord Hailsham LC, Lords Bridge, Brandon, Griffiths and Mackay)

There were two separate cases conjoined on appeal before the House of Lords.

(1) The appellants, Howe and Bannister, were charged with murder together with Murray and Bailey who pleaded guilty. The four of them drove Elgar, to whom Murray had offered a job, to a remote spot. Murray told the appellants that Elgar was a 'grass' and they were going to kill him. Both appellants kicked and punched Elgar and he was finally strangled by Bailey. The appellants said they attacked Elgar only because they believed they would receive the same treatment if they did not. Very similar events resulted in the death of another man, Pollitt. The appellants appealed against their conviction for murder on the ground, *inter alia*, that the judge had misdirected the jury that the defence of duress was not available to a person charged as a principal in the first degree to murder (ie the killer).

(2) Burke shot a criminal, Botton, on the doorstep of Botton's house. The prosecution alleged that he had done this at the request of Clarkson who was anxious to prevent Botton giving evidence against him. Clarkson's defence was that he had nothing to do with the shooting. Burke's defence was that he had agreed to shoot Botton only out of fear of Clarkson; but that, in the event, the gun went off accidentally and the killing was unintentional and therefore only manslaughter. Burke appealed on the ground, *inter alia*, that the judge had misdirected the jury in not leaving the defence of duress to them on the murder charge. The appeals were dismissed by the Court of Appeal.

One of the questions certified for the House of Lords was:

Is duress available to a person charged with murder as principal in the first degree (the actual killer)?

The House dismissed the appeal, holding that the defence of duress is not available to a person charged with murder whether as principal or as accessory.

[Lord Hailsham and Lord Bridge made speeches dismissing the appeal.]

Lord Brandon [expressed his agreement with Lord Mackay:]

I cannot pretend, however, that I regard the outcome as satisfactory. It is not logical, and I do not think it can be just, that duress should afford a complete defence to charges of all crimes less grave than murder, but not even a partial defence to a charge of that crime. I say nothing as to treason, for that is not here in issue. I am persuaded, nevertheless, to agree with my noble and learned friend by three considerations. First, it seems to me that, so far as the defence of duress is concerned, no valid distinction can be drawn between the commission of murder by one who is a principal in the first degree and one who is a principal in the second degree. Secondly, I am satisfied that the common law of England has developed over several centuries in such a way as to produce the illogical, and as I think unjust, situation to which I have referred. Thirdly, I am convinced that, if there is to be any alteration in the law on such an important and controversial subject, that alteration should be made by legislation and not by judicial decision.

[Lord Griffiths made a speech dismissing the appeal.]

Lord Mackay:

The question whether duress is available as a defence in law to a person charged with murder as a principal in the first degree (actual killer) has not been the subject of a previous decision of this House. The matter received consideration in this House in *Director of Public Prosecutions for Northern Ireland v Lynch* [1975] AC 653. It was accepted by the majority of the House in *Lynch's* case that at that time the balance of such judicial authority as existed was against the admission of the defence of duress in cases of . . . murder [as a principal offender]. The writers were generally agreed in saying that the defence was not available in murder although later writers appear to have said so following Hale. The references are *Hale's Pleas of the Crown* (1736) vol. 1, pp. 51, 434; *East's Pleas of the Crown* (1803) vol. 1, p. 294; *Blackstone Commentaries on the Laws of England* 1809 ed., vol. 4, p. 30; Glanville Williams *Criminal Law*, 2nd ed. (1961) p 759, para 247; *Russell on Crime* 12th ed. (1964) vol. 1, pp. 90–91; Smith and Hogan *Criminal Law* 3rd ed. (1973) pp. 166–167. . . .

Counsel for Burke, Bannister and Howe in his very detailed and careful submission accepted this position as reflecting the law up to the time of *Lynch's* case. Since that time, on this question there has been the decision of the Privy Council in *Abbott v R* [1976] 3 All ER 140, [1977] AC 755, a majority decision in which the minority consisted of Lord Wilberforce and Lord Edmund-Davies, who, along with Lord Morris, had constituted the majority in *Lynch's* case. Counsel for these appellants submitted that your Lordships should hold that the reasoning of the majority in *Lynch's* case should be applied and extended to cover the present cases. . . .

The first question, accordingly, that arises in this appeal is whether any distinction can be made between this case and *Lynch's* case.

[His lordship quoted from the speeches in *Lynch's* case.]

In my opinion, it is plain from these quotations that the majority of this House in *Lynch's* case, and particularly Lord Morris, were reaching a decision without committing themselves to the view that the reasoning which they had used would apply to an actual killer.

While therefore *Lynch* was decided by reasoning which does not extend to the present case, the question remains whether there is a potential distinction between this case and that of *Lynch* case by which to determine whether or not the defence of duress should be available. I consider that *Smith and Hogan* were perfectly right in the passage cited from that work by Lord Edmund-Davies to which I have already referred. ['The difficulty about adopting a distinction between the principal and secondary parties as a rule of law is that the contribution of the secondary party to the death may be no less than that of the principal': 3rd edn, 1973, p 166.] I have not been able to find any writer of authority that is able to give rational support for the view that the distinction between principals in the first degree and those in the second degree is relevant to determine whether or not duress should be available in a particular case of murder. . . .

I believe that the discussions of this matter have shown that at one extreme, namely that of the person who actually kills by a deliberate assault on a person who is then present, there is a fair body of support for the view that the defence of duress should either not be allowed or that the practical result will be, even if it is allowed, that it will never be established, while there is also strong support for the view that at the other extreme minor participation which the law regards as sufficient to impute criminal guilt should be capable of being excused by the defence of duress.

So far, I have not found any satisfactory formulation of a distinction which would be sufficiently precise to be given practical effect in law and at the same time differentiate between levels of culpability so as to produce a satisfactory demarcation between those accused of murder who should be entitled to resort to the defence of duress and those who were not.

The House is therefore, in my opinion, faced with the unenviable decision of either departing altogether from the doctrine that duress is not available in murder or departing from the decision of this House in *Lynch*. While a variety of minor attacks on the reasoning of the majority were mounted by counsel for the Crown in the present case, I do not find any of these sufficiently important to merit departing from *Lynch* on these grounds. I do, however, consider that, having regard to the balance of authority on the question of duress as a defence to murder prior to *Lynch's* case, for this House now to allow the defence of duress generally in response to a charge of murder would be to effect an important and substantial change in the law. In my opinion too, it would involve a departure from the decision in the famous case of *Reg. v Dudley and Stephens* (1884) 14 QBD 273. The justification for allowing a defence of duress to a charge of murder is that a defendant should be excused who killed as the only way of avoiding death himself or preventing the death of some close relation such as his own well-loved child. This essentially was the dilemma which Dudley and Stephens faced and in denying their defence the court refused to allow this consideration to be used in a defence to murder. If that refusal was right in the case of Dudley and Stephens it cannot be wrong in the present appeals. Although the result of recognising the defence advanced in that case would be that no crime was committed and in the case with which we are concerned that a murder was committed and a particular individual was not guilty of it (subject to the consideration of the second certified question) that does not distinguish the two cases from the point of view now being considered.

To change the law in the manner suggested by counsel for the appellants in the present case would, in my opinion, introduce uncertainty over a field of considerable importance.

So far I have referred to the defence of duress as if it were a precisely defined concept, but it is apparent from the decisions that it is not so. [His lordship referred to difficulties with the defence identified by Lord Simon in *Lynch's* case [1975] AC 653 at 686, [1975] 1 All ER 913 at 931.]

To say that a defence in respect of which so many questions remain unsettled should be introduced in respect of the whole field of murder is not to promote certainty in the law.

[His lordship referred to the fact that the Law Commission had made reform recommendations in 1985.]

I notice that in the Law Commission report No. 143, dated 28 March 1985, which contains a report to the Law Commission in respect of the codification of the criminal law by a team from the Society of Public Teachers of Law, doubt is expressed on the soundness of this recommendation in Report No. 83. This particular matter does not arise in the circumstances of the present case, but the great difficulty that has been found in obtaining a consensus of informed opinion upon it is just one illustration of the uncertain nature of what would be introduced into this most important area of the criminal law if the defence of duress were to be available.

Since the decision in *Lynch* the Law Commission have published in their report No. 83, to which I have referred, the result of an extensive survey of the law relating to duress and have made recommendations upon it which have been laid before Parliament. In my opinion the problems which have been evident in relation to the law of murder and the availability of particular defences is not susceptible of what Lord Reid described as a solution by a policy of make do and mend. While I appreciate fully the gradual development that has taken place in the law relating to the defence of duress, I question whether the law has reached a sufficiently precise definition of that defence to make it right for us sitting in our judicial capacity to introduce it as a defence for an actual killer for the first time in the law of England. Parliament, in its legislative capacity, although recommended to do so by the report of the Law Commission, has not taken any steps to make the defence of duress available generally to a charge of murder even where it has the power to define with precision the circumstances in which such a defence would be available.

It has also been suggested for consideration whether, if the defence of duress is to be allowed in relation to murder by the actual killer, the defence should have the effect, if sustained, of reducing the crime to that of manslaughter by analogy with the defence of provocation. Provocation itself was introduced into the law by judicial decision in recognition of human frailty, although it is now the subject of a statutory provision and it was suggested that the same approach might be taken now with regard to duress. . . . [See now loss of control discussed in Chapter 8.]

In my opinion we would not be justified in the present state of the law in introducing for the first time into our law the concept of duress acting to reduce the charge to one of manslaughter even if there were grounds on which it might be right to do so. On that aspect of the matter the Law Commission took the view that where the defence of duress had been made out it would be unjust to stigmatise the person accused with a conviction and there is clearly much force in that view.

The argument for the appellants essentially is that, *Lynch* having been decided as it was and there being no practical distinction available between *Lynch* and the present case, this case should be decided in the same way. The opposite point of view is that, since *Lynch* was concerned not with the actual killer but with a person who was made guilty of his act by the doctrine of accession, the correct starting point for this matter is the case of the actual killer. In my opinion this latter is the correct approach. The law has extended the liability to trial and punishment faced by the actual killer to those who are participants with him in the crime and it seems to me, therefore, that, where a question as important as this is in issue, the correct starting point is the case of the actual killer. It seems to me plain that the reason that it was for so long stated by writers of authority that the defence of duress was not available in a charge of murder was because of the supreme importance that the law afforded to the protection of human life and that it seemed repugnant that the law should recognise in any individual in any circumstance, however extreme, the right to choose that one innocent person should be killed rather than another. In my opinion that is the question which we still must face. Is it right that the law should confer this right in any circumstances, however extreme? While I recognise fully the force of the reasoning which persuaded the majority of this House in *Lynch* to reach the decision to which they came in relation to a person not the actual killer. It does not address directly this question in relation to the actual killer. I am not persuaded that there is good reason to alter the answer which Hale gave to this question. No development of the law or progress in legal thinking which have taken place since his day have, to my mind, demonstrated a reason to change this fundamental answer. In the circumstances which I have narrated of a report to Parliament from the Law Commission concerned, inter alia, with this very question, it would seem particularly inappropriate to make such a change now. For these reasons, in my opinion, the first certified question should be answered in the negative.

It follows that, in my opinion, the House should decline to follow the decision in *Lynch*.

Appeals dismissed

Lord Hailsham criticized what he took to be the view of the majority in *Lynch* and the minority in *Abbott* that 'the ordinary man of reasonable fortitude is not to be supposed to be capable of heroism if he is asked to take an innocent life rather than sacrifice his own'.

See K. J. M. Smith, 'Must Heroes Behave Heroically?' [1989] Crim LR 622 and 'Duress and Steadfastness: In Pursuit of the Unintelligible' [1999] Crim LR 363.

~~~ *Questions*
(1) Should a person be liable to conviction for murder for failing to be a hero?
(2) Are there no circumstances in which a person of reasonable fortitude would submit to threats and kill?
(3) If duress were a defence to murder, would a person have a defence if he submitted to threats which would not prevail upon a person of reasonable fortitude?

Lord Hailsham also thought that a man who takes the life of another to save his own cannot claim that he is choosing the lesser of two evils.

The argument that Parliament had not acted on the recommendation of the Law Commission some years earlier that the defence of duress should be extended to murder is a weak one. In *Hasan*, Lord Bingham referred to the Law Commission's view:

> The Law Commission has in the past (eg. in 'Criminal Law. Report on Defences of General Application' (Law Com No 83, Cm 556, 1977, paras 2.44–2.46)) recommended that the defence should be available as a defence to all offences, including murder, and the logic of this argument is irresistible.

⌇ Question

Is it a good argument against allowing the defence of duress to murder that in 'hard cases' no prosecution will be brought (the 'duressee' may be a prosecution witness on the trial of the duressor) or that, if he is prosecuted and convicted of murder (and sentenced to life imprisonment), he will soon be let out (on licence for the rest of his life, of course)?

Wilson [2007] EWCA Crim 1251 illustrates the now well-established principle that duress cannot be a defence to a charge of murder, even if the person seeking to rely on that defence is a child and even if his alleged role in the murder was that of a secondary party acting out of fear of an adult perpetrator. The 13-year-old defendant in this case was not able to plead duress, but argued instead that he had 'not known what he was doing in that his mind did not go with his actions'. His police interview did not support this defence, but suggested that he acted under duress from his father—the very defence he was precluded from running. The Court of Appeal observed that there 'might be grounds for criticising' a rule that denied a child any defence to a charge of murder on the ground of adult or parental duress, but had no choice but to apply the law as it stood.

⌇ Question

Could D have pleaded simply a lack of intention? Whether a defence of duress would have been accepted had the alleged offence been something other than murder remains a matter for speculation.

The Law Commission has recommended on more than one occasion that duress become a defence to murder—with the burden of proof on the accused. See Law Commission Report No 304, *Murder, Manslaughter and Infanticide* (2006), Ch 6. The Law Commission had provisionally proposed that duress would only be a partial defence to what would in their proposed scheme be first degree murder, reducing the crime to one of second degree murder (Law Com Consultation Paper No 177, *A New Homicide Act for England and Wales* (2006), para 7.32). In its final report, the Commission rejected that option and rejected a number of other options for reform (Law Com Report No 304). The Law Commission preferred the option that duress should be a full defence to first degree murder, second degree murder and attempted murder:

> 6.43 The argument that duress should be a full defence to first degree murder has a moral basis. It is that the law should not stigmatise a person who, on the basis of a genuine and reasonably held belief, intentionally killed in fear of death or life threatening injury in circumstances where a jury is satisfied that an ordinary person of reasonable fortitude might have acted in the same way. If a reasonable person might have acted as D did, then the argument for withholding a complete defence is undermined. In the words of Professor Ormerod, 'if the jury find that the defendant has, within the terms

of the defence, acted reasonably, it seems unfair to treat him as a second degree murderer or even a manslaughterer'.

6.44 Further, the option also accords with the way that duress operates as a complete defence in relation to other offences and it is, therefore, conducive to coherence and consistency as we pointed out above.

6.45 One respondent who favoured duress being a partial defence to first degree murder did so because he thought that this was the best way of accommodating each side in the moral debate. We see the force of this argument. However, we believe that if the arguments of principle and morality point decidedly in one direction, our recommendation should reflect what we believe to be a principled approach rather than one based on a desire to accommodate the different viewpoints.

6.46 An important counter-argument is that the law rightly attaches special sanctity to innocent human life and that this should preclude duress ever being a full defence to first degree murder. We now depart from this view, in so far as we believe that the 'sanctity of life' argument was not meant to deal with examples such as ten year olds or peripheral secondary parties becoming involved in killing under duress. The 'sanctity of life' argument may be more confusing than illuminating in this context.

. . .

6.52 We also think it important to bear in mind the stringent qualifying conditions that attach to the defence. In particular, the majority of the House of Lords in [*Hasan*] were firmly of the view that the defence ought not to be available to D if he or she saw or ought to have foreseen the risk of being subjected to any compulsion by threats of violence. We believe that this will serve to exclude the most unmeritorious cases where the defence should simply not be available. It is true that it will not in itself exclude all undeserving cases but we believe that juries should be trusted not to accept the defence in undeserving cases.

6.53 Above all, we believe that it is essential to recognise and accord proper weight to the fact that for the defence to succeed, a jury must form a judgement that a reasonable person in D's position might have committed first degree murder. If a jury forms that judgement, we believe that D should be completely exonerated despite having intentionally killed. . . .

6.76 We recommend that for duress to be a full defence to [our recommendation for] first degree murder, second degree murder and attempted murder, the threat must be one of death or life-threatening harm. (Footnotes omitted)

The Law Commission also rejected any distinction based on whether or not the defendant acted in response to a threat against his own person. Similarly, the Commission rejected a distinction in application of the defence between principal offenders and secondary parties.

〰 **Question**

Should the burden of proof be reversed where D pleads duress to murder?

Lord Bingham in *Hasan* at [20], section 23.3.1, p 621, expressed reservation as to whether the reverse burden would withstand scrutiny by the House of Lords.

It took many years and many cases to establish the generality of the principle in *Woolmington* [1935] AC 462, that the burden of disproving defences which have been properly raised is, with the anomalous exception of insanity, on the prosecution. The case for shifting the onus of proof of duress (whether by threats or of circumstances) to the defendant was very fully argued by the Law Commission in Law Commission Report No 218, *Legislating the Criminal Code: Offences Against the Person and General Principles* (1993), pp 59–62, and again in Law Commission Report No 304, *Murder, Manslaughter and Infanticide* (2006), Ch 6.

> ≈ *Questions*
>
> Can it be justifiable that a person who is acquitted on grounds of duress of an offence under s 18 of the Offences Against the Person Act 1861 (section 10.4.3, p 265) should become guilty of murder if his victim subsequently dies? How can it be that the act which was excusable as long as the victim lived became inexcusable when he died?

Not all jurisdictions agree that duress should be unavailable as a defence to murder. In *Aravena* [2015] ONCA 250, the Ontario Court of Appeal held that duress could be pleaded as a defence to murder and gave the following reasons for why it disagreed with the English authorities:

75. The English authorities provide two main reasons for denying the duress defence to persons charged with murder. First, these authorities argue that permitting duress as a defence to murder strengthens the hand of terrorists and other criminal organizations. Allowing duress as a defence to murder encourages criminals to use threatened intermediaries as a means of conducting their criminal activity and encourages those putative intermediaries to yield to the threats rather than resist.

76. This is essentially a deterrence-based policy argument. Whatever the merits of the policy argument, it cannot withstand the head-on collision with the principle of moral involuntariness, now entrenched in s. 7 of the *Charter*. Even if punishing morally involuntary conduct would deter criminal organizations from coercing others into criminal acts and deter threatened persons from engaging in criminal acts, punishment of those whose conduct is morally involuntary will still infringe on the individual's right to liberty in a manner that is contrary to the principles of fundamental justice. Unless that infringement can be justified under s. 1 of the *Charter*, criminal policy goals, no matter how legitimate, cannot be pursued at the expense of the constitutional protections afforded by s. 7 of the *Charter*.

77. Furthermore, even if the principles of fundamental justice did not operate as a brake on an unfettered policy of deterrence, the validity of the deterrence argument is dubious. The argument assumes that persons subject to the sorts of threats that would engage the duress defence would take the time to consider their options in light of the manner in which they might be treated by the criminal law were they to be arrested and prosecuted at some point in the future. Surely, a person faced with a true 'kill or be killed' option would have little regard for how the criminal law might react to the choice she makes. Any concern she might have about future punishment would be trumped by a more immediate concern about her own survival.

78. We are also unable to see how excluding murder from the defence of duress would deter terrorists and other criminal organizations from using coercion to conscript others to assist in crime. The terrorist or organized criminal is guilty of the crime regardless of whether the coerced party has a defence. We cannot see how the criminal would have any interest in what the law might eventually do to the coerced party.

79. There is nothing in the Canadian experience to support the contention that accepting duress as a defence to persons charged as parties to murder would encourage criminal organizations to employ duress or would encourage individuals to yield to threats. Duress has been an accepted defence to persons charged as a party to murder in several Canadian provinces, including Ontario, for many years. We are unaware of any data or commentary suggesting that the availability of this defence has created problems in the enforcement or administration of the criminal law. Nor do we know of any such data in various civil jurisdictions in which duress is an accepted defence to murder or in those common law jurisdictions which have expanded duress to murder by statute.

80. The second reason advanced in the English cases and relied on by the trial judge for excluding murder from the duress defence rests on the assertion that the innocent victim's right to life is inherently more valuable than any right of the accused. As the trial judge put it, at para. 99:

[The court quoted from the trial judge's direction.]

81. That position reflects a conception of duress as a justification: see, e.g., *R. v. Dudley and Stephens* (1884), 14 Q.B.D. 273, at pp. 286–88; *Howe*, at pp. 430–33. On that view, duress is not a defence to murder because killing the innocent victim is never justified: it cannot be said that taking one life to save another is the lesser of two evils, or that the harm avoided is greater than the harm caused. Justifying the killing of the innocent victim would require prioritizing the right to life of one over the right to life of another. That kind of evaluation is both unworkable and inconsistent with *Charter* values.

82. Canadian criminal law does not, however, regard duress as a justification. As outlined above, duress is an excuse. The person excused from criminal liability is not said to have accomplished a greater good, but is rather said to have had no realistic choice but to act as she did. The harm caused/harm avoided inquiry in an excuse-based defence, looks not to the promotion of the greater good (the harm avoided is greater than the harm caused), but rather for a level of comparable harm (the harm caused is not out of proportion to the harm avoided).

83. An individual told to 'kill or be killed' cannot make a decision that will fully vindicate the right to life, especially if the choice is between the lives of two equally innocent third parties. Whatever the threatened person decides, an innocent life may well be lost. A *per se* rule which excludes the defence of duress in all murder cases does not give the highest priority to the sanctity of life, but rather, arbitrarily, gives the highest priority to one of the lives placed in jeopardy.

84. The availability of the defence of duress cannot be settled by giving automatic priority to the right to life of the victim over that of an accused. Instead, the right to life of the victim must be factored into the proportionality assessment as part of the broader moral involuntariness inquiry.

≈≈ *Question*

Do you agree with the court's rejection of the justifications that were given in *Howe* for not permitting duress to be pleaded as a defence to murder?

The judges in *Howe* and in *Gotts* and more recently in *Hasan* seem generally to accept that the time is ripe for Parliament to consider the defence of duress and to decide whether it should exist at all and, if so, what its extent should be. Lord Lowry says, 'The real logic would be to grant or withhold the duress defence universally.'

In 2006, the Law Commission recommended that duress becomes a full defence to attempted murder (Law Com Report No 304):

6.70 Since we are recommending that duress should be a full defence to [our recommendation for] first degree murder, it would be anomalous were we to recommend otherwise in relation to second degree murder and attempted murder.

6.71 We recommend that duress, if successfully pleaded, should be a full defence to second degree murder and attempted murder.

6.72 We believe that our recommendations that duress should be a full defence to first degree murder, second degree murder and attempted murder are conducive to achieving clarity and coherence. However, we have rejected other options not merely because we think that they are intellectually untidy. Ultimately, the function of the criminal law is not to produce intellectual tidiness for its own sake but, rather, to do practical justice as it would be seen by ordinary members of the public. We do not believe that the options that we have rejected would achieve that result. We believe that the recommendations we are making would do so.

23.4 Duress of circumstances

The elements of the defence of duress of circumstances are almost identical to those for duress. The significant difference is that with duress of circumstances, it is sufficient that D perceives the threat of death or serious injury, to himself or someone for whom he is responsible, to arise from the circumstances at the time of the crime. There need not be another person whom the defendant believes is threatening such violence.

Curiously, all the early cases on duress of circumstances related to driving offences but *Pommel* [1995] 2 Cr App R 607, acknowledged that the defence of duress of circumstances applies generally (although it is not strictly a duress case at all), and this is confirmed by *Abdul-Hussain*, section 23.3.2.6, p 631. It applies to all offences except murder, attempted murder and some forms of treason. There is a tentative suggestion in *Abdul-Hussain* that it does not apply to conspiracy; but the defence of duress by threats was held applicable (though not made out on the facts) to a charge of conspiracy to defraud in *Verrier* [1965] Crim LR 732.

≈≈ *Questions*

If duress is a defence to doing something, must it not also be a defence to agreeing to do it? Otherwise, might not two duressees find themselves effectively deprived of the defence, whereas, in exactly similar circumstances, one would not?

23.4.1 Relationship with duress by threats

R v Conway
[1988] EWCA Crim 1, Court of Appeal, Criminal Division

(Woolf LJ, McCullough and Auld JJ)

A passenger in the appellant's car, Tonna, had been the target of an attack on another vehicle a few weeks earlier when another man was shot and Tonna was chased and narrowly escaped. On the occasion which was the subject of the present appeal, two young men in civilian clothes came running towards the appellant's parked car and Tonna shouted hysterically, 'Drive off.' The appellant drove off because he said he feared a fatal attack on Tonna. His car was chased by the two men in an unmarked vehicle and he drove in a manner which would undoubtedly be normally regarded as reckless. He was convicted of reckless driving. The two young men were police officers who knew Tonna was the subject of a bench warrant (ie an arrest warrant issued by a judge) but the appellant said he did not know this until after the incident. It was accepted at the trial that the case could not be distinguished from *Denton* (1987) 85 Cr App R 246 where the trial judge refused to leave the defence of necessity to the jury and an appeal was dismissed.

Woolf J:

In *R v Denton* the court went on to comment on another recent decision of this court, *R v Willer* (1986) 83 Cr App Rep 225. In *R v Willer* the appellant had been convicted of reckless driving. As he drove up a narrow road he was confronted with a gang of shouting and bawling youths, 20 to 30 strong. He heard one of them shouting, 'I'll kill you, Willer,' and another threatening to kill his passenger. He stopped and tried to turn the car around. The youths surrounded him. They banged on the car. One of the youths dived on the passenger who was sitting in the back and, in the words of Watkins LJ (at 226):

'The appellant realised that the only conceivable way he could somehow escape from this for-midable gang of youths, who were obviously bent on doing further violence, was to mount the pavement on the right-hand side [of the road] and on the pavement to drive through a small gap into the front of the shopping precinct (which he did at about 10 miles per hour).'

Subsequently he returned, driving back very slowly, because he realised one of his passengers was missing from the car. Throughout this period there was still a youth fighting with one of his rear passengers in the car, so the appellant drove to the local police station and reported the matter. During the course of the trial Willer changed his plea after a ruling that he was not entitled to rely on the defence of necessity. In dealing with this change of plea, Watkins LJ said (at 227):

'Returning to how the appellant came to change his plea, one begins with the reasons advanced by the assistant recorder for declaring that the defence of necessity was not available to the appellant. He seems to have based himself upon the proposition, though saying that necessity was a defence known to English law, that it was not, albeit available to the appellant in respect of the journey through the gap into the car park in front of the shopping precinct, available to him upon the return journey because he was not at that stage being besieged by the gang of youths. We feel bound to say that it would have been for the jury to decide, if necessity could have been a defence at all in those circumstances, whether the whole incident should be regarded as one, or could properly be regarded as two separate incidents so as to enable them to say that necessity applied in one instance but not in the other. For that reason alone the course adopted by the assistant recorder was we think seriously at fault. Beyond that upon the issue of necessity we see no need to go for what we deem to have been appropriate in these circumstances to raise as a defence by the appellant was duress. The appellant in effect said: "I could do no other in the face of this hostility than to take the right turn as I did, to mount the pavement and to drive through the gap out of further harm's way, harm to person and harm to my property." Thus the defence of duress, it seems to us, arose but was not pursued. What ought to have happened therefore was that the assistant recorder upon those facts should have directed that he would leave to the jury the question as to whether or not upon the outward or the return journey, or both, the appellant was wholly driven by force of circumstance into doing what he did and did not drive the car otherwise than under that form of compulsion, ie under duress.'

It will be noted from the passage in Watkins LJ's judgment that in *R v Willer* it was apparently accepted by the assistant recorder and counsel that there could be a defence of necessity to reckless driving. This may explain why the report does not suggest that any authorities were cited to the Court of Appeal, although apparently authorities, including American and Australian authorities, were cited to the assistant recorder.

It is convenient to refer to the 'duress' of which Watkins LJ spoke as 'duress of circumstances'. In *R v Denton* (1987) 85 Cr App Rep 246 at 248, in relation to *R v Willer*, the court said:

'This authority might be taken to suggest that the court assumed that on the facts of the case the defence of necessity could have been raised to a charge of reckless driving. We do not think this authority goes so far. We think it shows that the court doubted whether necessity as a defence could have been raised on the facts of that case but the court saw no need to decide whether such a defence existed as a matter of law. The court said a very different defence was available, which was duress, which should have been left to the jury. It should be observed that where the head-note says ((1986) 83 Cr App Rep 225) "Further the judge erred in ruling that the defence of necessity was not available to the defendant" it is referring to the argument advanced by the appellant and not to the decision of the appellate court.'

The judgment in *R v Denton*, while making this reservation on the decision in *R v Willer* so far as the defence of necessity is concerned, made no similar reservation with regard to what was said in *R v Willer* as to duress. In *R v Willer* there were a number of grounds on which this court disapproved of the way in which the case had been dealt with in the Crown Court. However, in relation to duress we regard the decision as binding on this court.

We have, in addition, had the advantage of having been referred to such other authorities as there are on the subject. In particular, we have been referred to the views of Professor Glanville Williams in his *Textbook of Criminal Law* (2nd edn, 1983) p 517 and Smith and Hogan *Criminal Law* (6th edn, 1988) p 224. We have also been referred to the Law Commission's Report on Defences of General Application (Law Com no 83 (1977)), which recommended that 'there should be no general defence of necessity and if any such general defence exists at common law, it should be abolished'. This conclusion was in striking contrast to the commission's provisional proposals in its Working Paper no 55 (1974), to which we were also referred. We have also seen the Law Commission's report on the Codification of the Criminal Law (Law Com no 143 (1985)), which took the view that necessity should remain as a defence at common law, in so far as it is one already. It appears that it is still not clear whether there is a general defence of necessity or, if there is, what are the circumstances in which it is available.

We conclude that [the defence is only available to] a charge of reckless driving where the facts establish 'duress of circumstances', as in *R v Willer*, ie where the defendant was constrained by circumstances to drive as he did to avoid death or serious bodily harm to himself or some other person.

As the learned editors point out in Smith and Hogan *Criminal Law* (6th edn, 1988) p 225, to admit a defence of 'duress of circumstances' is a logical consequence of the existence of the defence of duress as that term is ordinarily understood, ie 'do this or else'. This approach does no more than recognise that duress is an example of necessity. Whether 'duress of circumstances' is called 'duress' or 'necessity' does not matter. What is important is that, whatever it is called, it is subject to the same limitations as the 'do this or else' species of duress. As Lord Hailsham LC said in his speech in *R v Howe* [1987] AC 417 at 429, [1987] 1 All ER 771 at 777:

'There is, of course, an obvious distinction between duress and necessity as potential defences: duress arises from the wrongful threats or violence of another human being and necessity arises from any other objective dangers threatening the accused. This, however, is, in my view a distinction without a relevant difference, since on this view duress is only that species of the genus of necessity which is caused by wrongful threats. I cannot see that there is any way in which a person of ordinary fortitude can be excused from the one type of pressure on his will rather than the other.'

No wider defence to reckless driving is recognised. Bearing in mind that reckless driving can kill, we cannot accept that Parliament intended otherwise. When Parliament intended a wider defence it made express provision. Section 36(3) of the Road Traffic Act 1972, in relation to the lesser offence of driving motor vehicles elsewhere than on roads, provides:

'A person shall not be convicted of an offence under this section with respect to a vehicle if he proves to the satisfaction of the court that it was driven in contravention of this section for purposes of saving life or extinguishing a fire or meeting any other like emergency.'

It follows that a defence of 'duress of circumstances' is available only if from an objective standpoint the defendant can be said to be acting in order to avoid a threat of death or serious injury. The approach must be that indicated by Lord Lane CJ in *R v Graham* [1982] 1 All ER 801. Lord Lane CJ, in a passage of his judgment approved by the House of Lords in *R v Howe*, said [the passage is set out in section 23.3.5, p 639].

Adopting the approach indicated by Lord Lane CJ, and not that argued by counsel, which involved a subjective element, we ask ourselves whether the judge in the Crown Court should have left the defence of 'duress of circumstances' to the jury, notwithstanding the submission made by his counsel that it was 'impossible to run the defence of necessity . . . or indeed leave it to the jury.'

On the facts alleged by the appellant we are constrained to hold that the judge was obliged to do so, notwithstanding the appellant's counsel's submission at the hearing. The judge was referred to both *R v Denton* and *R v Willer*, and it appears that the explanation for counsel not relying on *R v Willer* is that he was wrongly of the view that the facts of this case are indistinguishable from those in *R v Denton*. However, in fact, as indicated by the judge, his client's defence was that he drove as he did because he was in fear for his life and that of Tonna. Although it is unlikely that the outcome of the jury's deliberations would have been any different, they should have been directed as to the possibility that they could find the appellant not guilty because of duress of circumstances, although they were otherwise satisfied that he had driven recklessly.

The jury not having received this direction, this is not a case in which we can properly apply the proviso. On the facts the non-direction related in reality to the appellant's only conceivable defence, and, although unlikely, it is just possible that the jury, if properly directed, would have found the appellant not guilty because of this defence.

Accordingly, we allow this appeal and quash the conviction.

J. C. Smith, *Justification and Excuse in the Criminal Law*
(The Hamlyn Lectures, 1989), discussing *Conway*

It seems probable, therefore, that duress of circumstances, like duress by threats, is a defence to crimes generally, but not a defence to murder, or perhaps attempted murder. It applies not only to an act done for the preservation of one's own life and safety but also to an act done to protect another— probably any other person who is in peril. It does not appear that there was any relationship between Conway and Tonna, other than that of driver and passenger. The case is therefore of considerable importance. Consider the following hypothetical case put by Lord Denning in *Buckoke v Greater London Council* [1971] 2 All ER 254, CA:

> 'A driver of a fire engine with ladders approaches the traffic lights. He sees 200 yards down the road a blazing house with a man at an upstairs window in extreme peril. The road is clear in all directions. At that moment the lights turn red. Is the driver to wait for 60 seconds or more, for the lights to turn green? If the driver waits for that time, the man's life will be lost.'

Lord Denning accepted the opinion of both counsel in that case that the driver would commit an offence if he crossed the red light. Necessity would be no answer to a charge of breaking the Road Traffic Regulations. But would it be the same now that the courts have discovered the defence of duress of circumstances? The threat to the fictional man at the upstairs window seems to be no less than the threat to the passenger in Conway's car. The necessity for immediate action is no less. If we have to look for some relationship between the defendant and the person rescued, that between a fireman and a person imperilled by a fire is surely enough—the fireman probably has a duty to do all that he lawfully and reasonably can to rescue any member of the public. But it is thought that the better view is that no special relationship is necessary. Suppose that Mr Tonna had leapt into the car of a perfect stranger, screaming that he was about to be shot. Would not the stranger be excused, no less than Mr Conway, for any infringement of the letter of the law which reasonably appeared to him to be necessary to save a man from being murdered? Should a private citizen, driving a van with a long ladder, be less deserving of excuse than a fireman because he crossed the red light to make a rescue? I submit, not.

Perhaps Lord Denning would not be displeased by this result. He was applying the law as he believed it then to be; but he said of his hypothetical fire engine driver who crossed the red light: he 'should not be prosecuted. He should be congratulated.' It has always seemed to me very odd that the great Master of the Rolls should find that this conduct was both a breach of the criminal law and a case for congratulation. Plainly, he thought that, from a moral point of view, the driver's conduct was not only excusable but justifiable.

> ≈ **Questions**
> (1) Is there any good reason to treat the defences of duress by threats and duress of circumstances differently?
> (2) In *Willer*, *Conway* and *Martin* (in the following extract), the threat came from the actions of human beings. In *Buckoke* [1971] Ch 655, it came from a fire. Is that a material difference? Should the result have been any different in *Willer* or *Conway* if the threat had come from a wall of floodwater, a runaway lorry or a herd of charging bulls?

The definition of the defence in terms similar to those for duress by threats was confirmed in *Martin (CM)* [1988] EWCA Crim 2. In that case, the Court of Appeal held that the elements of duress of circumstances are as follows:

(1) The defence arises as a result of objective dangers threatening D or others for whom he reasonably feels responsible.

(2) The defence is available only if, from an objective standpoint, D can be said to be acting reasonably and proportionately in order to avoid a threat of death or serious injury.

(3) Assuming the defence to be open to D on his account of the facts, the issue should be left to the jury, who should be directed to determine these two questions: first, was D, or may he have been, impelled to act as he did because as a result of what he reasonably believed to be the situation he had good cause to fear that otherwise death or serious physical injury would result; secondly, if so, would a sober person of reasonable firmness, sharing the characteristics of D, have responded to that situation by acting as D acted? If the answer to both those questions was Yes, then the jury would acquit; the defence of necessity would have been established.

Martin lays down the clearest definition of the defence of duress of circumstances. It was unclear, however, whether the defence was available only in respect of road traffic offences (where it is frequently pleaded) or of wider application. The subsequent case of *Pommell* [1995] 2 Cr App R 607 was the first to confirm its general application.

23.5 Necessity

Duress of circumstances was treated by the courts in *Conway* and *Martin* as a defence of necessity. As noted previously, the effect, logically, should have been to extend the defence to some cases where it was previously thought not to apply, as in the conduct of Lord Denning's hypothetical fireman in *Buckoke*'s case. It could also have had the effect of limiting the defence by importing the restrictions which seem to have become established on the defence of duress by threats—the limitation to threats of death or GBH and the objective tests of *reasonable* belief in facts creating the necessity, *good* cause for fear and the response of a person of *reasonable* firmness. The courts have limited the duress of circumstances defence by restricting it in the same terms of duress by threats. There is, however, a separate defence of necessity at common law which is not restricted in the same way. It is rarely successful and its limits are not clearly defined in the case law.

It is important to appreciate that the availability of a plea of necessity to a statutory offence will turn on the particular statutory scheme. In *CS* [2012] EWCA Crim 389, it was held that no defence of necessity was available to a parent charged under s 1 of the Child Abduction Act 1984 who believed (without foundation) that the child's father posed a risk of sexually abusing her. The statutory scheme, with the requirement for court orders to sanction one parent taking a child from the other, made it 'impossible to see how, within the legislative scheme, the legislature could have contemplated that a parent could have the defence of necessity available in respect of the offence of removing a child from England and Wales where the whole purpose of making removal an offence was to reinforce the objective of retaining the child within England and Wales so the child could be subject to the protection of the court' (at [13] per Sir John Thomas P). The court left open the question whether the defence of necessity is different from that of duress of circumstances (at [15]).

The defence of necessity has the following elements, which are derived largely from the judgment of Brooke LJ in the following case.

- The act was needed to avoid an irreparable and inevitable evil.
- No more should be done than is reasonably necessary for the purpose to be achieved.
- The evil inflicted must not be disproportionate to the evil avoided.

Re A (children) (conjoined twins: separation)
[2000] EWCA Civ 254, Court of Appeal, Civil Division

(Ward, Brooke and Robert Walker LJJ)

Brooke LJ:

Necessity: modern academic writers

At the coroner's inquest conducted in October 1987 into the Zeebrugge disaster, an army corporal gave evidence that he and dozens of other people were near the foot of a rope ladder. They were all in the water and in danger of drowning. Their route to safety, however, was blocked for at least ten minutes by a young man who was petrified by cold or fear (or both) and was unable to move up or down. Eventually the corporal gave instructions that the man should be pushed off the ladder, and he was never seen again. The corporal and many others were then able to climb up the ladder to safety.

In his third lecture, 'Necessity and Duress', Professor Smith [Hamlyn Lectures (published under the title *Justification and Excuse in the Criminal Law* (1989))] evinced the belief at pp 77–78 that if such a case ever did come to court it would not be too difficult for a judge to distinguish *R v Dudley and Stephens*. He gave two reasons for this belief. The first was that there was no question of choosing who had to die (the problem which Lord Coleridge had found unanswerable in *R v Dudley and Stephens*) because the unfortunate young man on the ladder had chosen himself by his immobility there. The second was that unlike the ship's boy on the Mignonette, the young man, although in no way at fault, was preventing others from going where they had a right, and a most urgent need, to go, and was thereby unwittingly imperilling their lives.

I would add that the same considerations would apply if a pilotless aircraft, out of control and running out of fuel, was heading for a densely populated town. Those inside the aircraft were in any event 'destined to die'. There would be no question of human choice in selecting the candidates for death, and if their inevitable deaths were accelerated by the plane being brought down on waste ground, the lives of countless other innocent people in the town they were approaching would be saved.

It was an argument along these lines that led the rabbinical scholars involved in the 1977 case of conjoined twins to advise the worried parents that the sacrifice of one of their children in order to save the other could be morally justified. George J Annas *Siamese Twins: Killing One to Save the Other* (Hastings Center Report, April 1987) p 27, described how they—

'reportedly relied primarily on two analogies. In the first, two men jump from a burning aeroplane. The parachute of the second man does not open, and as he falls past the first man, he grabs his legs. If the parachute cannot support them both, is the first man morally justified in kicking the second man away to save himself? Yes, said the rabbis, since the man whose parachute didn't open was "designated for death". The second analogy involves a caravan surrounded by bandits. The bandits demand a particular member of the caravan be turned over for execution; the rest will go free. Assuming that the named individual has been "designated for death", the rabbis concluded it was acceptable to surrender him to save everyone else. Accordingly, they concluded that if a twin A was "designated for death" and could not survive in any event, but twin B could, surgery that would kill twin A to help improve the chance of twin B was acceptable.'

There is, however, no indication in the submission we received from the Archbishop of Westminster that such a solution was acceptable as part of the philosophy he espoused. The judge's dilemma in a case where he or she is confronted by a choice between conflicting philosophies was thoughtfully discussed by Simon Gardner in his article 'Necessity's Newest Inventions' (1991) 11 OJLS 125. He explored the possibility of rights-based justifications based on a principle that otherwise unlawful actions might be justified where the infraction was calculated to vindicate a right superior to the interest protected by the rule, but he was perplexed by the idea that judges in a democracy could make their own decisions as to what was right and what was wrong in the face of established law prohibiting the conduct in question. The whole article requires careful study, but its author concluded that in jurisdictions where rights were guaranteed, the judicial vindication of a guaranteed right would be seen as protecting democracy rather than contravening it. This consideration does not, however, assist us in a case where there are conflicting rights of apparently equal status and conflicting philosophies as to the priority, if any, to be given to either.

Before I leave the treatment afforded to the topic of necessity by modern academic writers of great distinction (there is a valuable contemporary summary of the issues in Smith and Hogan's *Criminal Law* (9th edn, 1999) pp 245–252 [14th edn, 2015, pp 412–423]), I must mention the section entitled 'Justifications, Necessity and the Choice of Evils' in *Principles of Criminal Law* (3rd edn, 1999) by Professor Andrew Ashworth. After referring to the facts of the Zeebrugge incident he said at pp 153–154:

'No English court has had to consider this situation, and it is clear that only the strongest prohibition on the taking of an innocent life would prevent a finding of justification here: in an urgent situation involving a decision between n lives and $n + 1$ lives, is there not a strong social interest in preserving the greater number of lives? Any residual principle of this kind must be carefully circumscribed; it involves the sanctity of life, and therefore the highest value with which the criminal law is concerned. Although there is a provision in the Model Penal Code allowing for a defence of "lesser evil", it fails to restrict the application of the defence to cases of imminent threat, opening up the danger of citizens trying to justify all manner of conduct by reference to overall good effects. The moral issues are acute: "not just anything is permissible on the ground that it would yield a net saving of lives". Closely connected with this is the moral problem of "choosing one's victim", a problem which arises when, for example, a lifeboat is in danger of sinking, necessitating the throwing overboard of some passengers, or when two people have to kill and eat another if any of the three is to survive. To countenance a legal justification in such cases would be to regard the victim's rights as morally and politically less worthy than the rights of those protected lives saved and deaths avoided in the aggregate but must somehow attempt to come to grips with the nature of the rights and duties being assessed. This would seem to be consistent with Lord Coleridge's conclusion that necessity can provide no justification for the taking of a life, such an act representing the most extreme form of rights violation. As discussed above, if any defence for such a homicidal act is to succeed, it would have to be framed as an excuse grounded on self-preservation. It could not possibly be declared by the court to be rightful ...'

...

According to Sir James Stephen there are three necessary requirements for the application of the doctrine of necessity: (i) the act is needed to avoid inevitable and irreparable evil; (ii) no more should be done than is reasonably necessary for the purpose to be achieved; (iii) the evil inflicted must not be disproportionate to the evil avoided. Given that the principles of modern family law point irresistibly to the conclusion that the interests of Jodie must be preferred to the conflicting interests of Mary,

I consider that all three of these requirements are satisfied in this case. Finally, the doctrine of the sanctity of life respects the integrity of the human body. The proposed operation would give these children's bodies the integrity which nature denied them.

See Richard Huxtable, 'Separation of Conjoined Twins: What Next for English Law?' [2002] Crim LR 459; J. Rogers, 'Necessity, Private-Defence and the Killing of Mary' [2001] Crim LR 515.

≈ Questions

(1) According to a report in *The Times*, 5 May 1998, the commander of an Australian naval ship 'took the decision to save the rest of his crew by sealing four sailors in the blazing engine room, consigning them to certain death, after rescuers were beaten back by the flames'. Was the officer guilty of murder of the four sailors? If he had refused to seal the engine room and the four had escaped but the ship had been lost with most of the crew, would he have been guilty of any offences? Can it be the law that both of the alternative courses amount to crimes? If the officer's belief that the only way to save the ship and crew was to sacrifice the four men was reasonable, is it conceivable that he would be convicted of murder?—or any crime?

(2) Consider the case of conjoined twins who have only one heart. The heart cannot be divided, as some other organs can. It cannot support both twins and, if nothing is done, both will soon die. Should that be allowed to happen if one can be saved by being given the heart? Will the inevitable death of the other be murder? Should it make any difference that one is (a) slightly stronger, (b) very much stronger, than the other? Or that one is a boy and the other a girl and the parents dearly want a boy and are not interested in a girl (or vice versa)?

(3) Is it lawful for a military aircraft to shoot down a hijacked passenger aircraft, killing all the passengers and crew where the hijackers on board are piloting the plane on a suicide mission towards a skyscraper in the city? See M. Bohlander, 'In Extremis: Hijacked Airplanes, Collateral Damage and the Limits of the Criminal Law' [2006] Crim LR 579, and the letter by D. Ormerod [2006] Crim LR referring to the Sixth Report of the Parliamentary Defence and Security Committee (2002).

23.5.1 Necessity as a defence to murder?

R v Dudley and Stephens
[1881–5] All ER Rep 61, Queen's Bench Division

(Lord Coleridge CJ, Grove and Denman JJ, Pollock and Huddleston BB)

The two accused, with a third man and the deceased, a 17-year-old boy, were cast away in an open boat, 1,600 miles from land. When they had been eight days without food and six days without water, the accused killed the boy, who was weak and unable to resist but did not assent to being killed. The men fed upon his body and blood for four days until they were picked up by a passing vessel. At the trial for murder, the jury found by a special verdict that if the men had not fed upon the boy they would probably not have survived the four days; that the boy was likely to have died first; that at the time of the act there was no reasonable prospect of relief; that it appeared to the accused that there was every probability that they would die of starvation unless one of the castaways was killed; that there was no appreciable chance of saving life except by killing; but that there was no greater necessity for killing the boy than any of the three men. The finding of the jury was referred to the Queen's Bench Division for its decision.

Lord Coleridge CJ [having referred to the special verdict, continued:]

. . . this is clear, that the prisoners put to death a weak and unoffending boy upon the chance of pre-serving their own lives by feeding upon his flesh and blood after he was killed, and with a certainty of depriving him of any possible chance of survival. The verdict finds in terms that: 'if the men had not fed upon the body of the boy, they would probably not have survived . . .' and that 'the boy, being in a much weaker condition, was likely to have died before them'. They might possibly have been picked up next day by a passing ship; they might possibly not have been picked up at all; in either case it is obvious that the killing of the boy would have been an unnecessary and profitless act. It is found by the verdict that the boy was incapable of resistance, and, in fact, made none; and it is not even suggested that his death was due to any violence on his part attempted against, or even so much as feared by, them who killed him. . . .

[His lordship dealt with objections taken by counsel for the prisoners which do not call for report, and continued:]

First, it is said that it follows, from various definitions of murder in books of authority—which defi-nitions imply, if they do not state, the doctrine—that, in order to save your own life you may lawfully take away the life of another, when the other is neither attempting nor threatening yours, nor is guilty of any illegal act whatever towards you or anyone else. But, if these definitions be looked at, they will not be found to sustain the contention. The earliest in point of date is the passage cited to us from Bracton, who wrote in the reign of Henry III . . . But in the very passage as to necessity, on which reli-ance has been placed, it is clear that Bracton is speaking of necessity in the ordinary sense, the repel-ling by violence—violence justified so far as it was necessary for the object—any illegal violence used towards oneself. If, says Bracton (Lib iii, *Art De Corona*, cap 4, fol 120), the necessity be '*evitabilis et evadere posset absque occisione, tunc erit reus homicidii*'—words which show clearly that he is think-ing of physical danger, from which escape may be possible, and that '*inevitabilis necessitas*', of which he speaks as justifying homicide, is a necessity of the same nature.

It is, if possible, yet clearer that the doctrine contended for receives no support from the great authority of Lord Hale. It is plain that in his view the necessity which justifies homicide is that only which has always been, and is now, considered a justification. He says (I Hale, PC 491):

'In all these cases of homicide by necessity, as in pursuit of a felon, in killing him that assaults to rob, or comes to burn or break a house, or the like, which are in themselves no felony.'

Again, he says that the necessity which justifies homicide is of two kinds:

'(1) That necessity which is of private nature; (2) That necessity which relates to the public justice and safety. The former is that necessity which obligeth a man to his own defence and safeguard; and this takes in these inquiries: 1. What may be done for the safeguard of a man's own life;'

and then follow three other heads not necessary to pursue. Lord Hale proceeds (I Hale PC 478):

'1. As touching the first of these, viz, homicide in defence of a man's own life, which is usually styled *se defendendo*.'

It is not possible to use words more clear to show that Lord Hale regarded the private necessity which justified, and alone justified, the taking the life of another for the safeguard of one's own to be what is commonly called self-defence. But if this could be even doubtful upon Lord Hale's words, Lord Hale himself has made it clear, for, in the chapter in which he deals with the exemption created by compul-sion or necessity, he thus expresses himself (I Hale PC 51):

'If a man be desperately assaulted, and in peril of death, and cannot otherwise escape, unless to satisfy his assailant's fury he will kill an innocent person then present, the fear and actual force will not acquit him of the crime and punishment of murder if he commit the fact, for he ought rather to die himself than to kill an innocent; but if he cannot otherwise save his own life, the law permits him in his own defence to kill the assailant, for, by the violence of the assault and the offence committed upon him by the assailant himself, the law of nature and necessity hath made him his own protector *cum debito moderamine inculpatae tutelae*.'

But, further still, Lord Hale, in the following chapter (I Hale PC 54), deals with the position asserted by the casuists, and sanctioned, as he says by Grotius and Puffendorf [*sic*], that in a case of extreme necessity, either of hunger or clothing,

'theft is no theft, or at least not punishable as theft, and some even of our own lawyers have asserted the same; but I take it that here in England that rule, at least by the laws of England, is false, and, therefore, if a person, being under necessity for want of victuals or clothes, shall upon the account clandestinely and *animo furandi* steal another man's goods, it is a felony and a crime by the laws of England punishable with death.'

If, therefore, Lord Hale is clear, as he is, that extreme necessity of hunger does not justify larceny, what would he have said to the doctrine that it justified murder?

It is satisfactory to find that another great authority, second probably only to Lord Hale, speaks with the same unhesitating clearness on this matter. [His lordship referred to *Foster's Discourse on Homicide*, Ch 3, and other authorities.]

There remains the authority of Stephen J who both in his *Digest* (art 32) and in his *History of the Criminal Law* (vol 2, p 108) uses language perhaps wide enough to cover this case. The language is somewhat vague in both places, but it does not in either place cover this case of necessity, and we have the best authority for saying that it was not meant to cover it. If it had been necessary we must with true deference have differed from him; but it is satisfactory to know that we have, probably at least, arrived at no conclusion in which, if he had been a member of the court, he would have been unable to agree. Neither are we in conflict with any opinion expressed upon this subject by the learned persons who formed the commission for preparing the Criminal Code. They say on this subject:

'We are not prepared to suggest that necessity should in every case be a justification; we are equally unprepared to suggest that necessity should in no case be a defence. We judge it better to leave such questions to be dealt with when, if ever, they arise in practice by applying the principles of law to the circumstances of the particular case.'

It would have been satisfactory to us if these eminent persons could have told us whether the received definitions of legal necessity were, in their judgment, correct and exhaustive, and, if not, in what way they should be amended; but as it is we have, as they say, 'to apply the principles of law to the circumstances of this particular case.'

It is admitted that the deliberate killing of this unoffending and unresisting boy was clearly murder, unless the killing can be justified by some well-recognised excuse admitted by the law. It is further admitted that there was in this case no such excuse, unless the killing was justified by what has been called necessity. But the temptation to the act which existed here was not what the law has ever called necessity. Nor is this to be regretted. Though law and morality are not the same, and though many things may be immoral which are not necessarily illegal, yet the absolute divorce of law from morality would be of fatal consequence, and such divorce would follow if the temptation to murder in this case were to be held by law an absolute defence of it. It is not so.

To preserve one's life is generally speaking, a duty, but it may be the plainest and the highest duty to sacrifice it. War is full of instances in which it is a man's duty not to live, but to die. . . . It is not correct, therefore, to say that there is any absolute and unqualified necessity to preserve one's life. . . . It is enough in a Christian country to remind ourselves of the Great Example which we profess to follow.

It is not needful to point out the awful danger of admitting the principle which has been contended for. Who is to be the judge of this sort of necessity? By what measure is the comparative value of lives to be measured? Is it to be strength, or intellect, or what? It is plain that the principle leaves to him who is to profit by it to determine the necessity which will justify him in deliberately taking another's life to save his own. In this case the weakest, the youngest, the most unresisting was chosen. Was it more necessary to kill *him* than one of the grown men? The answer be, No. . . .

There is no path safe for judges to tread but to ascertain the law to the best of their ability, and to declare it according to their judgment, and if in any case the law appears to be too severe on individuals, to leave it to the Sovereign to exercise that prerogative of mercy which the Constitution has entrusted to the hands fittest to dispense it. It must not be supposed that, in refusing to admit temptation to be an excuse for crime, it is forgotten how terrible the temptation was, how awful the suffering, how hard in such trials to keep the judgment straight and the conduct pure. We are often compelled to set up standards we cannot reach ourselves, and to lay down rules which we could not ourselves satisfy. But a man has no right to declare temptation to be an excuse, though he might himself have yielded to it, nor allow compassion for the criminal to change or weaken in any manner the legal definition of the crime. . . .

[The Lord Chief Justice thereupon passed sentence of death in the usual form. The prisoners were afterwards respited and their sentence commuted to one of six months' imprisonment without hard labour.]

Judgment for the Crown

≈≈ *Questions*

(1) Was the corporal in Zeebrugge guilty of murder under the law as stated in *Dudley and Stephens*?

(2) Should it be a defence that many lives would be saved by the sacrifice of one?

(3) The Model Penal Code, §3.02 provides: 'recognizing that the sanctity of life has a supreme place in the hierarchy of values, it is nonetheless true that conduct that results in taking life may promote the very value sought to be protected by the law of homicide.' Is this what the judges should have recognized in *Dudley and Stephens*?

(4) What if, instead of choosing to kill and eat the cabin boy, the crew had drawn lots and it was cabin boy who happened to draw the shortest lot? Would this have impacted upon the court's reasoning? Should it have?

(5) A is injured and needs an immediate blood transfusion to save his life. B is the only person who can be found locally with the same rare blood group. He refuses to give any blood. May B be overpowered and the blood taken without his consent?

(6) Should the criminal law set up standards reasonable people cannot reach?

See further on *Dudley and Stephens*, A. W. B. Simpson, *Cannibalism and the Common Law* (1984).

In *Re A*, the case involving the conjoined twins, Brooke LJ distinguished *Dudley and Stephens*. One of the reasons for doing so was the fact that, unlike in *Dudley and Stephens*, there was no issue of the doctors choosing whose life would be sacrificed: nature had made that choice. This case should not, however, be taken as deciding unequivocally that necessity is a defence to murder. In *R (on the application of Nicklinson) v Ministry of Justice* [2013] EWCA Civ 961, the Court of Appeal stated that *Re A* was 'too slender a thread on which to hang such a far-reaching development of the common law'. The Supreme Court agreed with this assessment, holding that *Re A* was an exceptional case. See *R (on the application of Nicklinson) v Ministry of Justice* [2014] UKSC 38.

23.5.2 The doctrine of double effect

This is a philosophical or theological rather than a legal doctrine which applies where a person knows that his act will inevitably have two immediate consequences, one good and one bad. If he acts with the sole purpose of bringing about the good consequence, he is not to be blamed for bringing about the bad one. According to Glanville Williams, *The Sanctity of Life in the Criminal Law* (1957), p 184, 'it is allowed to be used only when both effects are the immediate result of the act'. The doctrine is not applied if the good effect is the result of the bad one for this would be to admit the unacceptable proposition that the end justifies the means.

Ward LJ in *Re A (children) (conjoined twins: surgical separation)* [2000] EWCA Civ 254 readily accepted that the doctrine could apply to the doctor administering drugs to a patient for the sole purpose of relieving pain, knowing that the effect would be to accelerate the patient's death, but thought it could not apply in the case before him where the good effect was on one patient and the bad effect on another. Brooke LJ also thought that:

> . . . the doctrine of double effect could have no possible application in this case because . . . by no stretch of the imagination it could be said that the surgeons would be acting in Mary's best interests when they prepared an operation which benefit Jodie but kill Mary.

This is difficult to follow since the doctrine presupposes one bad as well as one good consequence. Although Robert Walker LJ thought the operation would be in the best interests of both twins, he recognized that to kill Mary, merely because it was in her best interests to die, would have been murder and, if it was murder, it could hardly be regarded, in law, as other than an evil consequence, albeit an evil consequence which would not be unlawful because it was not 'the purpose or intention of the surgery'.

> ≈≈ *Questions*
> Did not Ward and Brooke LJJ in substance apply the doctrine of double effect (at least as it is described by Glanville Williams) in *Re A*? Was their purpose not to bring about the good result—the healthy survival of Jodie while simultaneously causing the (as they acknowledged) bad result, killing Mary?

23.5.3 Relationship between defences of duress and necessity

In *Shayler*, the Court of Appeal (Woolf LCJ, Wright and Leveson JJ) (reported sub nom *S (D)* in [2001] Crim LR 986) discussed the relationship between duress of circumstances and necessity. The House of Lords ([2002] 2 All ER 477) held that no question of duress or necessity arose and that it was 'a little unfortunate' that these topics had been discussed by the trial judge and the Court of Appeal. Lord Bingham (at [15]) and Lord Hutton (at [117]) made it clear that they did not necessarily agree with all that was said about these defences. The Court of Appeal's remarks are therefore *obiter* but, coming from a strong court, of some weight. Woolf LCJ said that *Abdul-Hussain* (section 23.3.2.6, p 631) reflected other decisions 'which have treated the defences of duress and necessity as being part of the same defence and the extended form of the defence [ie, duress of circumstances] as being different labels for essentially the same thing'. The case is unclear about whether they are separate.

> ≈ **Question**
>
> What are the courts so worried about having a separate defence of necessity?

(1) It seems to be settled that duress cannot be a defence to murder or attempted murder (*Howe and Bannister*, section 23.3.5, p 639, *Gotts*) but is it not now reasonably clear that, following *Re A (children) (conjoined twins)*, necessity may in some circumstances be a defence?

(2) The only occasion for a defence of duress of either variety is imminent threat of death or GBH. But is necessity so limited? Should it not be a defence to a charge of battery that D was pushing a child to save him from some quite minor injury or even damage to his clothing?

(3) Necessity is a defence only if the evil which D seeks to avoid is greater than that which he knows he is causing. But if D yields to torture which no ordinary person could be expected to resist, should he not be excused, however grave the consequences of his capitulation?

(4) It seems that necessity may create a duty to act—cf *Re A*—but can duress ever do so?

If Parliament were to abolish the defence of duress by threats, thereby remedying the present inconsistencies, what would become of duress of circumstances? Since the latter has developed by analogy to the former, it would be logical to decide that they stand or fall together. It would certainly be very strange if the main growth were cut down and the off-shoot left standing. It is not clear what effect this would have on the defence of necessity, which certainly exists though its limits are uncertain. It would be absurd to provide that threats of, or the imminence of, death or serious bodily harm should never be a defence if other less serious threats or dangers might; so the logical implication might be the abolition of any existing defence of necessity as well. This was at one time proposed by the Law Commission but the proposal attracted such powerful criticism that it was soon withdrawn.

23.6 The use of force in public or private defence

Force causing personal injury, damage to property or even death may be justified or excused because the force was reasonably used in the defence of certain public or private interests. Public and private defence is therefore a general defence to any crime of which the use of force is an element or which is alleged to have been committed by the use of force. It is clear that the burden of disproving claims of public or private defence rests on the prosecution.

The common law governing self-defence had evolved to a clear position. Private or 'self'-defence at common law coexisted and often overlapped with the statutory plea under s 3 of the Criminal Law Act 1967 which applies only where D uses force in the prevention of a crime. Parliament has now intervened so that we have a common law defence 'clarified' in the Criminal Justice and Immigration Act 2008 existing alongside s 3 for cases where D is using force to prevent crime and a supposedly different test to be applied where D's use of force was against a trespasser in a dwelling.

All these defences based on use of force can be conveniently described in terms of trigger and response:

- the trigger being D's belief that the circumstances render it reasonable or necessary for him to use force; and

- the response being the objective assessment of the proportionality of the amount of force he uses.

At common law it was clear that for the trigger element of the defence it is sufficient that D genuinely though mistakenly and unreasonably believes that there is a need for force. For the response element of the defence, the degree of force used must, in the opinion of the jury, be reasonable based on the facts as D believed them to be. For example, if D believed that he was being attacked with a deadly weapon and he used only such force as was reasonable to repel such an attack, he has a defence to any charge of an offence arising out of his use of that force. It is immaterial that he was mistaken. Indeed, it is immaterial that he was unreasonably mistaken.

Section 76 of the Criminal Justice and Immigration Act 2008 now confirms this established common law principle.

23.6.1 The belief in the need to use force

23.6.1.1 The common law test of D's belief in the need for some force

At common law, D could rely on self-defence where he had a genuine belief in the need for the use of force. D's belief in the need to use force does not need to be reasonable.

R v Gladstone Williams

(1987) 78 Cr App R 276, Court of Appeal, Criminal Division

(Lord Lane CJ, Skinner and McCowan JJ)

One M saw a youth rob a woman in a street. He caught the youth and held him, but the latter broke from M's grasp. M caught the youth again and knocked him to the ground. The appellant, who had only seen the later stages of the incident was told by M that he, M, was arresting the youth for mugging a woman. M said that he was a police officer, which was untrue, so when asked by the appellant for his warrant card, he could not produce one. A struggle followed and the appellant assaulted M by punching him in the face and was charged with assault occasioning actual bodily harm contrary to section 47 of the Offences against the Person Act 1861. His defence was that he honestly believed that the youth was being unlawfully assaulted by M. The jury was directed that, on the assumption that M was acting lawfully, the appellant's state of mind on the issue of defence of another was to be determined by whether the appellant had an honest belief based on reasonable grounds that reasonable force was necessary to prevent a crime. The appellant was convicted and appealed on the ground that the judge had misdirected the jury. Held, that the jury should have been directed that, first, the prosecution had the burden of proving the unlawfulness of the appellant's actions; secondly, if the appellant might have been labouring under a mistake as to facts, he was to be judged according to his mistaken view of the facts, whether or not the mistake was, on an objective view, reasonable or not. The reasonableness or unreasonableness of the appellant's belief was material to the question whether the belief was held by him at all. If the belief was held, its unreasonableness, so far as guilt or innocence was concerned, was irrelevant. Accordingly, the appeal must be allowed and the conviction quashed.

[In the course of his judgment Lord Lane CJ, discussing the offence of assault, said ([1987] 3 All ER 411 at 414):]

The mental element necessary to constitute guilt is the intent to apply unlawful force to the victim. We do not believe that the mental element can be substantiated by simply showing an intent to apply force and no more.

This decision was approved in the Privy Council in the following case.

Beckford v R
[1987] UKPC 1, Privy Council

(Lords Keith, Elwyn-Jones, Templeman, Griffiths and Oliver)

The appellant, a police officer, while investigating a report that a man was terrorizing his family, shot and killed a man who ran out of the back of the house. There was a conflict of evidence as to the circumstances. At the trial of the appellant for murder, the judge directed the jury that he was entitled to be acquitted on the ground of self-defence if he had a reasonable belief that his life was in danger or that he was in danger of serious bodily harm. He appealed to the Court of Appeal in Jamaica on the ground that the jury should have been told that he had a defence if he had an honest belief in the danger, even if it was unreasonable. The appeal was dismissed. He appealed to the Privy Council.

Lord Griffiths:

The common law recognises that there are many circumstances in which one person may inflict violence upon another without committing a crime, as for instance in sporting contests, surgical operations or, in the most extreme example, judicial execution. The common law has always recognised as one of these circumstances the right of a person to protect himself from attack and to act in the defence of others and if necessary to inflict violence on another in so doing. If no more force is used than is reasonable to repel the attack such force is not unlawful and no crime is committed. Furthermore, a man about to be attacked does not have to wait for his assailant to strike the first blow or fire the first shot: circumstances may justify a pre-emptive strike.

It is because it is an essential element of all crimes of violence that the violence or the threat of violence should be unlawful that self-defence, if raised as an issue in a criminal trial, must be disproved by the prosecution. If the prosecution fail to do so the accused is entitled to be acquitted because the prosecution will have failed to prove an essential element of the crime, namely that the violence used by the accused was unlawful.

If then a genuine belief, albeit without reasonable grounds, is a defence to rape because it negatives the necessary intention, so also must a genuine belief in facts which if true would justify self-defence be a defence to a crime of personal violence because the belief negatives the intent to act unlawfully. Their Lordships therefore approve the following passage from the judgment of Lord Lane in *Gladstone Williams* at p. 218 as correctly stating the law of self-defence:

'The reasonableness or unreasonableness of the defendant's belief is material to the question of whether the belief was held by the defendant at all. If the belief was in fact held, its unreasonableness, so far as guilt or innocence is concerned, is neither here nor there. It is irrelevant. Were it otherwise, the defendant would be convicted because he was negligent in failing to recognise that the victim was not consenting or that a crime was not being committed and so on. In other words the jury should be directed, first of all, that the prosecution have the burden or duty of proving the unlawfulness of the defendant's actions; secondly, that if the defendant may have been labouring under a mistake as to the facts he must be judged according to his mistaken view of the facts; thirdly, that is so whether the mistake was, on an objective view, a reasonable mistake or not. In a case of self-defence, where self-defence or the prevention of crime is concerned, if the jury came to the conclusion that the defendant believed, or may have believed, that he was being attacked or that a crime was being committed, and that force was necessary to protect himself or to prevent the crime, then the prosecution have not proved their case. If, however, the defendant's alleged belief was mistaken and if the mistake was an unreasonable one, that may be a powerful reason for coming to the conclusion that the belief was not honestly held and should be rejected. Even if the jury come to the conclusion that the mistake was an unreasonable one, if the defendant may genuinely have been labouring under it, he is entitled to rely upon it.'

Looking back, *Morgan* can now be seen as a landmark decision in the development of the common law, returning the law to the path upon which it might have developed but for the inability of an accused to give evidence on his own behalf. Their Lordships note that not only has this development the approval of such distinguished criminal lawyers as Professor Glanville Williams and Professor Smith: see *Textbook of Criminal Law* (2nd Ed. [1983] at pp. 137–138 and Smith and Hogan *Criminal Law* (5th Ed.) [1983] at pp. 329–330) but it also has the support of the Criminal Law Revision Committee (see 14th Report on Offences against the Person (1980) Cmnd 7844; and of the Law Commission: see The Law Commission report (1985) No. 143, Codification of the Criminal Law.

There may be a fear that the abandonment of the objective standard demanded by the existence of reasonable grounds for belief will result in the success of too many spurious claims of self-defence. The English experience has not shown this to be the case. The Judicial Studies Board, with the approval of the Lord Chief Justice, has produced a model direction on self-defence which is now widely used by judges when summing up to juries. The direction contains the following guidance:

> 'Whether the plea is self-defence or defence of another, if the defendant may have been labouring under a mistake as to the facts, he must be judged according to his mistaken belief of the facts: that is so whether the mistake was, on an objective view a reasonable mistake or not.'

Their Lordships have heard no suggestion that this form of summing up has resulted in a disquieting number of acquittals. This is hardly surprising, for no jury is going to accept a man's assertion that he believed that he was about to be attacked without testing it against all the surrounding circumstances. In assisting the jury to determine whether or not the accused had a genuine belief the judge will of course direct their attention to those features of the evidence that make such a belief more or less probable. Where there are no reasonable grounds to hold a belief it will surely only be in exceptional circumstances that a jury will conclude that such a belief was or might have been held.

Their Lordships therefore conclude that the summing up in this case contained a material misdirection and they answer question 1(a) by saying that the test to be applied for self-defence is that a person may use such force as is reasonable in the circumstances as he honestly believes them to be in the defence of himself or another.

Appeal allowed. Conviction quashed

23.6.1.2 The statutory 'clarification'

The position that pertained at common law is now reflected in s 76 of the Criminal Justice and Immigration Act 2008.

76. Reasonable force for purposes of self-defence etc.

(1) This section applies where in proceedings for an offence—

    (a) an issue arises as to whether a person charged with the offence ('D') is entitled to rely on a defence within subsection (2), and

    (b) the question arises whether the degree of force used by D against a person ('V') was reasonable in the circumstances.

(2) The defences are—

    (a) the common law defence of self-defence;

   (aa) the common law defence of defence of property; and

    (b) the defences provided by section 3(1) of the Criminal Law Act 1967

(3) The question whether the degree of force used by D was reasonable in the circumstances is to be decided by reference to the circumstances as D believed them to be, and subsections (4) to (8) also apply in connection with deciding that question.

(4) If D claims to have held a particular belief as regards the existence of any circumstances—

  (a) the reasonableness or otherwise of that belief is relevant to the question whether D genuinely held it; but

  (b) if it is determined that D did genuinely hold it, D is entitled to rely on it for the purposes of subsection (3), whether or not—

    (i) it was mistaken, or

    (ii) (if it was mistaken) the mistake was a reasonable one to have made.

(5) But subsection (4)(b) does not enable D to rely on any mistaken belief attributable to intoxication that was voluntarily induced.

In *Keane* [2010] EWCA Crim 2514, Hughes LJ made the following observations on the operation of s 76.

4. The law of self-defence is not complicated. It represents a universally recognised commonsense concept. In our experience juries do not find that commonsense concept at all difficult to understand. The only potential difficulty for a judge is that he needs to remember the potential possibility of what lawyers would call a subjective element at an early stage of the exercise, whilst the critical question of the reasonableness of the response is, in lawyer's expressions, an objective one. In using those lawyer's terms we do not for a moment suggest that it is helpful to use them in a summing-up.

5. It is however very long established law that there are usually two and sometimes three stages into any enquiry into self-defence. There may be more, but these are the basic building blocks of a large proportion of the cases in which it is raised:

1. If there is a dispute about what happened to cause the defendant to use the violence that he did, and there usually is such a dispute, then the jury must decide it, attending of course to the onus and standard of proof.

2. If the defendant claims that he thought that something was happening which the jury may find was not happening, then the second question which arises is what did the defendant genuinely believe was happening to cause him to use the violence that he did? That question does not arise in every case. If it does arise then whether his belief was reasonable or not, providing it is genuinely held, he is to be judged on the facts as he believed them to be unless his erroneous belief is the result of voluntarily taken drink or drugs, in which event it is to be disregarded.

3. Once it has thus been decided on what factual basis the defendant's actions are to be judged, either because they are the things that actually happened and he knew them or because he genuinely believed in them even if they did not occur, then the remaining and critical question for the jury is: was his response reasonable, or proportionate (which means the same thing)? Was it reasonable (or proportionate) in all the circumstances? Unlike the earlier stages which may involve the belief of the defendant being the governing factor, the reasonableness of his response on the assumed basis of fact is a test solely for the jury and not for him. In resolving it the jury must usually take into consideration what are often referred to as the 'agony of the moment' factors. That means that the jury must be reminded when it arises, as it very often does, that there is in a confrontation no opportunity for the kind of hindsight or debate which can take place months afterwards in court. The defendant must act on the instant at any rate in a large number of cases. If he does so, and does no more than seems honestly and instinctively to be necessary, that is itself strong evidence that it was reasonable. It is strong evidence, not conclusive evidence. Whilst the jury's attention must be directed to these factors if they arise,

the jury must also be made to understand that the decision of what is a reasonable response is not made by the defendant, it is made by the jury. We should perhaps add that 'in all the circumstances' means what it says. There can be no exhaustive catalogue of the events, human reactions and other circumstances which may affect the reasonableness or proportionality of what the defendant did. That is explicitly recognised by section 76(8).

6. The single judge invited the court to consider whether the statutory formulation of the law in section 76 might have contributed to any degree of confusion and debate which ensued before the judge in the second of our cases. We do not think in fact that section 76 contributed significantly to the debate in question, nor to such degree of confusion as there was. For the avoidance of doubt, it is perhaps helpful to say of section 76 three things: (a) it does not alter the law as it has been for many years; (b) it does not exhaustively state the law of self-defence but it does state the basic principles; (c) it does not require any summing-up to rehearse the whole of its contents just because they are now contained in statute. The fundamental rule of summing-up remains the same. The jury must be told the law which applies to the facts which it might find; it is not to be troubled by a disquisition on the parts of the law which do not affect the case.

≋ *Question*

How if at all does s 76 of the Criminal Justice and Immigration Act 2008 'clarify' the common law principle as laid down in *Beckford*?

For many years the courts stated that a defendant could rely on a public or private defence only if he believed *on reasonable grounds* in the circumstances which entitled him to take the defensive action—for example, a belief that he faced certain death at the hands of an aggressor unless he took the action in question was no defence to a charge of murder unless the belief was based on reasonable grounds. As we have seen, in *Gladstone Williams*, section 23.6.1.1, p 660, the Court of Appeal held that this was an incorrect statement of the common law and that the only question was whether the belief was honestly held. The view that only reasonable mistakes of fact can excuse has now been comprehensively repudiated by the House of Lords: *B (a minor) v DPP* [2000] UKHL 13 and *K* [2001] UKHL 41.

On the other hand, we have also seen that in the common law of duress the courts still insist that the defence is open only to one who believes on reasonable grounds in the threat of death or grievous bodily harm: *Graham*, approved in *Howe*, section 23.3.5, p 639.

Not everyone agrees with the 'subjective' approach to self-defence. The Australian courts require reasonable grounds for a defence of self-defence, an approach which is defended by S. M. H. Yeo, *Compulsion in the Criminal Law* (1990), pp 200–219. A distinction is made between elements of offences (as to which a subjective test is appropriate) and defence elements, where the test is objective. The distinction is related to the theory of justification and excuse. Yeo puts the case of 'a person who is unnaturally apprehensive or cowardly which leads her to honestly but unreasonably believe that she is being attacked. Without the limitation of reasonable belief, such a person can react violently with impunity. And she can do so time and again if that is her inclination.'

≋ *Questions*

(1) Is this a valid objection to the subjective test?

(2) Will jurors see through spurious claims of self-defence?

(3) Does s 76 of the 2008 Act make it more or less likely that those who take the law into their own hands will be convicted?

23.6.2 Evaluating the reasonableness of the force used

23.6.2.1 The common law test for assessing the amount of force D used

Owino [1996] 2 Cr App R 128, [1995] Crim LR 743 confirms explicitly that, 'a person may use such force as is (objectively) reasonable in the circumstances as he (subjectively) believes them to be'. See also *DPP v Armstrong-Braun* [1999] Crim LR 416.

R v Martin (Anthony)

[2002] 1 Cr App R 323, Court of Appeal, Criminal Division

(Lord Woolf CJ, Wright and Grigson JJ)

M lived alone in an isolated farmhouse ('Bleak House'). Two men, evidently burglars, broke a window and entered the house at night. M shot them both with a pump-action shotgun and one died. M's defence of self-defence was rejected by the jury who convicted him of murder. He appealed on various grounds. It was held that he was not entitled to rely on the evidence of two psychiatrists, not called at the trial, to the effect that he was suffering from an abnormality of mind, a long-standing personality disorder; and that the breaking into his house would be perceived by him as being a greater threat to his safety than it would in the case of a normal person.

Lord Woolf CJ:

Mr Wolkind [for the appellant] relied on the recent decision of the House of Lords in *R v Smith (Morgan)* [2001] 1 Cr App Rep 31 [2001] 1 AC 146. This was also a provocation case that Mr Wolkind contended could be applied to the similar issues which arise when a defendant relies on self-defence. In that case Smith was relying upon evidence that he suffered from clinical depression. There was no dispute that the evidence was admissible and relevant on the issue as to whether he was provoked, the subjective issue. The problem was whether the evidence was admissible as being relevant on the objective issue of loss of self-control. As to this the majority of their Lordships came to the conclusion that the jury were entitled to take into account some characteristic, whether temporary or permanent, which affected the degree of control which society could reasonably expect of a defendant and which it would be unjust not to take into account. [See now Loss of Control in Chapter 8].

Is the same approach appropriate in the case of self-defence? There are policy reasons for distinguishing provocation from self-defence. Provocation only applies to murder, but self-defence applies to all assaults. In addition, provocation does not provide a complete defence; it only reduces the offence from murder to manslaughter. There is also the undoubted fact that self-defence is raised in a great many cases resulting from minor assaults and it would be wholly disproportionate to encourage medical disputes in cases of that sort. Lord Hobhouse in his dissenting speech in *Smith* recognised that in relation to self-defence, too generous an approach as to what is reasonable could result in an 'exorbitant defence' (para. 186). Lord Hoffmann also appeared conscious of this. As a matter of principle we would reject the suggestion that the approach of the majority in *Smith* in relation to provocation should be applied directly to the different issue of self-defence.

We would accept that the jury are entitled to take into account in relation to self-defence the physical characteristics of the defendant. However, we would not agree that it is appropriate, except in exceptional circumstances which would make the evidence especially probative, in deciding whether excessive force has been used to take into account whether the defendant is suffering from some psychiatric condition. . . .

[Having rejected the defence of self-defence, the court quashed the conviction for murder and substituted a conviction for manslaughter on the ground of diminished responsibility. NB: the defence of provocation has been replaced by that of loss of control—see Chapter 8.]

In *Shaw v R* [2002] 1 Cr App R 77, [2002] Crim LR 140, PC, D appealed against his conviction for murder in Belize, having unsuccessfully raised self-defence. It was common ground that the applicable law was as stated in Smith and Hogan, *Criminal Law* (9th edn, 1999), p 253, and as it was put by D's counsel: '. . . you will judge him as he saw it and only as he saw it'. The Board (Lords Bingham, Hoffmann, Cooke and Scott, and Sir Patrick Russell), applying the common law of England and Belize framed the two essential questions for the jury:

(1) Did the appellant honestly believe or may he have believed that it was necessary to defend himself?

(2) If so, and taking the circumstances *and the danger* as the appellant honestly believed them to be, was the amount of force which he used reasonable?

23.6.2.2 The statutory 'clarification'

Criminal Justice and Immigration Act 2008, s 76(3)

The question whether the degree of force used by D was reasonable in the circumstances is to be decided by reference to the circumstances as D believed them to be, and subsections (4) to (8) also apply in connection with deciding that question.

It is important to point out that although the reasonableness of the force used is to be evaluated by reference to the circumstances as D believed them to be, not all circumstances are permitted to be considered. In *Oye* [2013] EWCA Crim 1725 (see section 24.6, p 706), the Court of Appeal held that the reasonableness of D's actions was not to be judged according to what his delusions caused him to believe was necessary, namely that he was repelling an attack by evil spirits (who were in fact police officers). Davis LJ stated that: 'An insane person cannot set the standards of reasonableness as to the degree of force used by reference to his own insanity.' It was held that the statutory 'clarification' did not mandate a wholly subjective test. In the subsequent case of *Press* [2013] EWCA Crim 1849, Pitchford LJ explained the ratio of *Oye* in these terms: 'in the assessment of reasonableness of force used in self defence, an honest and instinctive belief in the necessity for the force used, formed because the defendant was acting under an insane delusion as to the nature of the threat, was to be left out of account'.

By virtue of s 76(6A) of the Criminal Justice and Immigration Act 2008, in deciding whether the force D used was reasonable in the circumstances as he believed them to be, the possibility that D could have retreated is to be considered (so far as relevant) as a factor to be taken into account, rather than as giving rise to a duty to retreat.

≈≈ *Questions*

(1) Would Martin have been any more likely to be acquitted under s 76 of the 2008 Act than at common law?

(2) Does s 76 clarify the law in respect of the characteristics of the accused which may be taken into account in evaluating his plea of self-defence?

23.6.3 'Householder' cases

Section 76 as amended by the Crime and Courts Act 2013 provides:

(5A) In a householder case, the degree of force used by D is not to be regarded as having been reasonable in the circumstances as D believed them to be if it was grossly disproportionate in those circumstances.

(6) In a case other than a householder case, the degree of force used by D is not to be regarded as having been reasonable in the circumstances as D believed them to be if it was disproportionate in those circumstances.

(6A) In deciding the question mentioned in subsection (3), a possibility that D could have retreated is to be considered (so far as relevant) as a factor to be taken into account, rather than as giving rise to a duty to retreat.

(7) In deciding the question mentioned in subsection (3) the following considerations are to be taken into account (so far as relevant in the circumstances of the case)—

  (a) that a person acting for a legitimate purpose may not be able to weigh to a nicety the exact measure of any necessary action; and

  (b) that evidence of a person's having only done what the person honestly and instinctively thought was necessary for a legitimate purpose constitutes strong evidence that only reasonable action was taken by that person for that purpose.

(8) Subsections (6A) and (7) are not to be read as preventing other matters from being taken into account where they are relevant to deciding the question mentioned in subsection (3).

(8A) For the purposes of this section '*a householder* case' is a case where—

  (a) the defence concerned is the common law defence of self defence,

  (b) the force concerned is force used by D while in or partly in a building, or part of a building, that is a dwelling or is forces accommodation (or is both),

  (c) D is not a trespasser at the time the force is used, and

  (d) at that time D believed V to be in, or entering, the building or part as a trespasser.

(8B) Where—

  (a) a part of a building is a dwelling where D dwells,

  (b) another part of the building is a place of work for D or another person who dwells in the first part, and

  (c) that other part is internally accessible from the first part, that other part, and any internal means of access between the two parts, are each treated for the purposes of subsection (8A) as a part of a building that is a dwelling.

(8C) Where—

  (a) a part of a building is forces accommodation that is living or sleeping accommodation for D,

  (b) another part of the building is a place of work for D or another person for whom the first part is living or sleeping accommodation, and

  (c) that other part is internally accessible from the first part, that other part, and any internal means of access between the two parts, are each treated for the purposes of subsection (8A) as a part of a building that is forces accommodation.

(8D) Subsections (4) and (5) apply for the purposes of subsection (8A)(d) as they apply for the purposes of subsection (3).

(8E) The fact that a person derives title from a trespasser, or has the permission of a trespasser, does not prevent the person from being a trespasser for the purposes of subsection (8A).

(8F) In subsections (8A) to (8C)—

  'building' includes a vehicle or vessel, and

  'forces accommodation' means service living accommodation for the purposes of Part 3 of the Armed Forces Act 2006 by virtue of section 96(1)(a) or (b) of that Act.

(9) This section, except so far as making different provision for householder cases, is intended to clarify the operation of the existing defences mentioned in subsection (2).

(10) In this section—

    (a) 'legitimate purpose' means—

        (i) the purpose of self-defence under the common law,

        (ia) the purpose of defence of property under the common law, or

        (ii) the prevention of crime or effecting or assisting in the lawful arrest of persons mentioned in the provisions referred to in subsection (2)(b);

    (b) references to self-defence include acting in defence of another person; and

    (c) references to the degree of force used are to the type and amount of force used.

If the case is 'a householder case', as defined in s 8A of the Act, the degree of force D used is not to be regarded as having been reasonable in the circumstances as D believed them to be if it was grossly disproportionate in those circumstances. This is intended to provide a degree of 'heightened protection' for householders. In a Ministry of Justice circular (Circular No 2013/02), this new element of the defence was explained in the following terms:

8. The provisions in section 43 of the Crime and Courts Act also amend section 76 of the 2008 Act. These changes go further than clarifying existing law; they strengthen the law in relation to householders who are defending themselves from intruders in their homes.

9. Section 43 adds new subsection (5A) to section 76 of the 2008 Act. The effect of subsection (5A) is that householders who use a disproportionate level of force to protect themselves or others in their homes will not automatically be regarded as having acted unlawfully and treated as criminals. The use of grossly disproportionate force will continue to be unlawful however.

10. The provision does *not* give householders free rein to use disproportionate force in every case they are confronted by an intruder. The new provision must be read in conjunction with the other elements of section 76 of the 2008 Act. The level of force used must still be reasonable in the circumstances as the householder believed them to be (section 76(3)). Section 76(7) says if people only do what they honestly and instinctively thought was necessary for a legitimate purpose, this will be strong evidence that only reasonable action was taken for that purpose.

11. The key change introduced by section 43 is that if householders act honestly and instinctively to protect themselves or their loved ones from intruders using force that was reasonable in the circumstances as they saw them, they will not be guilty of an offence if the level of force turns out to have been disproportionate in those circumstances. The provision is designed to give householders greater latitude in terrifying or extreme situations where they may not be thinking clearly about the precise level of force that is necessary to deal with the threat faced.

12. The court will need to consider the individual facts of each case, including the personal circumstances of the householder and the threat (real or perceived) posed by the offender. There are no hard and fast rules about what types of force might be regarded as 'disproportionate' and 'grossly disproportionate'. The following example is included for illustrative purposes only and prosecutors and the court would need to come to its own view, taking into account all of the evidence available and individual circumstances of the cases.

'A householder is woken during the night by the sound of breaking glass downstairs. His wife and children have also woken up and are very frightened. The householder goes downstairs to investigate and meets an intruder armed with a knife in the hallway. The intruder had broken a glass panel in the front door to enter the property. A scuffle ensues and the householder wrestles the knife from the intruder's hand and it drops to the floor. Having dropped his weapon and with

> the mother and children screaming upstairs, the intruder realises he has met his match and turns to flee through the open door. With adrenaline pumping and heart pounding, the householder instinctively punches the intruder on the back of the head as he leaves. He falls awkwardly and is knocked unconscious.'

13. In this case, the householder arguably did not need to strike the intruder again; he had already dropped the knife and was turning to make his escape. The level of force used in that split second was on one view disproportionate to the threat posed by the intruder in that instant. Section 43 of the Crime and Courts Act means that the householder would not be guilty of an offence in these circumstances, providing the court were satisfied that the use of force was reasonable in the circumstances as he saw them.

14. It is important to note, however, that new subsection (5A) adds that the use of grossly disproportionate force will never be lawful. This is to ensure, for example, that violent and/or calculated acts of revenge or retribution do not go unpunished. In the example given above, had the householder kicked and punched the intruder repeatedly or picked up the knife that had been dropped and stabbed him with it knowing full well that he was already unconscious, such an action is more likely to be considered as grossly disproportionate.

≈≈≈ *Questions*

(1) Does this make the defence even more complex? Was this amendment necessary? Will it have any practical effect?

(2) If D confronts V in the garden, is this a 'householder case'? What about in the garden shed?

This provision was considered in detail in the civil case of *R (on the application of Collins) v Secretary of State for Justice* [2016] EWHC 33 (Admin). The claimant entered a house through the unlocked front door. He was confronted by one of the householders, who placed him in a headlock and wrestled him to the floor. As a result of this altercation, the claimant suffered serious injury. The CPS decided not to prosecute the householder. One of the reasons for this decision was the prosecutor's conclusion that the householder test meant that unless the jury found that the use of force was grossly disproportionate D must be acquitted. The claimant sought a declaration that s 76(5A) was incompatible with the right to life, enshrined in Article 2 of the European Convention on Human Rights (ECHR), on the basis that the provision meant that the state had failed to discharge its positive obligation to put in place effective criminal law provisions to deter the commission of offences against the person.

Sir Brian Leveson P rejected the claimant's submission that the householder provision was incompatible with Article 2. In doing so, his lordship provided guidance on how s 76(5A) ought to be interpreted.

(1) The provision does not alter the common law. Rather, it adopts and preserves the second limb of self-defence at common law.

(2) The crucial question for the jury is not whether the force used was proportionate, disproportionate or grossly disproportionate. The question for the jury in each case is whether the force D used was reasonable in the circumstances as he believed them to be.

(3) The operation of s 76(5A) automatically excludes a degree of force which is grossly disproportionate from being reasonable in householder cases. If the degree of force was not grossly disproportionate, s 76(5A) does not prevent that degree of force from being considered reasonable within the meaning of the second self-defence

limb. On the other hand, it does not direct that any degree of force less than grossly disproportionate is reasonable. Whether it was or was not reasonable will depend on the particular facts and circumstances of the case. If, however, the force D used was 'completely over the top', then such actions would be grossly disproportionate and the defence would be unavailable.

Sir Brian Leveson P held that the mistake made by the CPS was in concluding that D would necessarily be acquitted unless the prosecution made the jury sure that the amount of force he used was grossly disproportionate. In addition, his lordship warned against conflating proportionality with reasonableness and stated that it is possible for a jury to find that the force D used was proportionate but not reasonable.

∼∼ *Questions*
(1) Can you think of an example of circumstances where a jury would conclude that the amount of force D used was proportionate but not reasonable?
(2) Does the judgment in *Collins* undermine the heightened protection s 76(5A) was intended to afford householders?
(3) Should D, in a householder case, be entitled to rely on his mistakes as to the amount of force needed even if they are based on his voluntary intoxication?

23.6.4 Use of force in making arrest or preventing crime

Criminal Law Act 1967, s 3

> (1) A person may use such force as is reasonable in the circumstances in the prevention of crime, or in effecting or assisting in the lawful arrest of offenders or suspected offenders or of persons unlawfully at large.
>
> (2) Sub-section (1) above shall replace the rules of the common law on the question when force used for a purpose mentioned in the sub-section is justified by that purpose.

Section 3 operates only where D responds to prevent a 'crime'. In *Jones and others* [2006] UKHL 16, the House of Lords concluded that the concept of 'crime' in this context can only have been intended to mean a 'domestic' crime (ie not a crime only in international law). The Criminal Law Revision Committee (CLRC) explained the proposed s 3 in very broad terms:

> [T]he court, in considering what was reasonable force, would take into account all the circumstances, including in particular the nature and degree of force used, the seriousness of the evil to be prevented and the possibility of preventing it by other means; but there is no need to specify in the clause the criteria for deciding the question. Since the clause is framed in general terms, it is not limited to arrestable or any other class of offences, though in the case of very trivial offences it would very likely be held that it would not be reasonable to use even the slightest force to prevent them. (Seventh Report, *Felonies and Misdemeanours* (1965), Cmnd 2659, para 23)

Section 3 excuses only the use of force. In *Blake v DPP* [1993] Crim LR 586, D, demonstrating against the Iraqi war, wrote with a felt pen on a concrete pillar near the Houses of Parliament. He was charged with criminal damage and argued that his act was justified by, *inter alia*, s 3. The court held that his act was 'insufficient to amount to the use of force within the section'.

The defence is only available if the defendant uses force to prevent crime, or to effect or assist in the lawful arrest of offenders or suspected offenders. It is no defence therefore if D drives dangerously, where he is intent only on ascertaining the registration number of a car D believed had earlier crashed into his. This point was made clear in *Bailey* [2013] EWCA Crim 378.

≈≈≈ **Questions**

(1) If D in *Blake* had used a chisel to inscribe his protest on the pillar, would he have been able to rely on s 3? Would he have been able to rely on the common law defence?

(2) If D is attacked by a child under 10 or an insane person, can he use reasonable force to defend himself and rely on s 3?

One issue that remained uncertain until relatively recently is whether it is necessary for D to have a reasonable belief that force was necessary in the prevention of crime or whether it suffices that D's belief is honest. In *Morris* [2013] EWCA Crim 436, D was a taxi driver who mistakenly thought a passenger, X, was attempting to make off without payment. D mounted the pavement to prevent X from committing the offence and X was injured. The judge ruled that the offence of making off without payment would have been committed as soon as X left the taxi, so by the time D drove onto the pavement he could not have been acting in the prevention of crime as the offence had already been committed. Therefore D could only rely on second limb of s 3(1), that he was using force in effecting or assisting the lawful arrest of an offender. What D had forgotten was that there was another individual in the back of the taxi, Y, who was intending to pay the fare. The judge ruled that D had to have a reasonable belief that the use of force was necessary. D was convicted. In rejecting the approach adopted by the trial judge, Leveson LJ stated:

19. The use of reasonable force in self defence or in defence of another person is lawful. The essence of these defences is the honestly held belief of the defendant as to the facts (but not the law: see *R. v Jones (Margaret)* [2006] UKHL 16; [2006] 2 Cr. App. R. 9 (p.136); [2007] 1 A.C. 136; [2006] 2 W.L.R. 772 per Lord Bingham of Cornhill at [24] and Lord Hoffmann at [72]). In relation to use of force in the prevention of crime (such as to prevent an unlawful attack on another), the defence is afforded by s.3 of the Criminal Justice Act 1967. If honest belief affords a defence under s.3 in those circumstances, it must equally do so for a person who claims to have used reasonable force to prevent the commission of a crime other than a crime of violence against another.

20. Accordingly, if, as the appellant contended in this case, he honestly believed that the men were making off without payment, he was entitled to use reasonable force in order to prevent the commission of that offence; the jury would thus be required to consider whether driving on to the pavement (howsoever that occurred) was the reasonable exercise of the use of force. The difficulty with the way in which the judge put the case was that his direction required the jury to consider whether the appellant had reasonable grounds to believe that it was necessary to arrest [X] to prevent him making off before a constable could assume responsibility for him. If they concluded that he did not have reasonable grounds (perhaps because he should have realised the fourth man was still in the cab), they never get to the question of the use of reasonable force.

21. The judge did not deal with the possibility that the jury could conclude that the appellant was acting to prevent crime because he concluded, as a matter of law, that once the passengers had moved away from the window of the taxi (ie where they should have paid the fare), they had 'made off'. He thereby failed to ensure that the jury focused on what the appellant honestly (i.e. genuinely) believed were the facts before using their conclusions as to that belief to go on to decide whether he may have had reasonable grounds for suspecting that an offence was being committed (or had been committed such that he had a reasonable belief that an arrest was necessary) and crucially, whether

the force used may have been reasonable. This approach is consistent with *R. v Faraj* [2007] EWCA Crim 1033; [2007] 2 Cr. App. R. 25 (p.322).

22. In the circumstances, we accept the submission that there was an error of law in the direction of law that the jury were given. Although we have real reservations about the question whether a jury properly directed could ever have concluded that the use of force in this case was or may have been reasonable and, thus, that the offence of dangerous driving was not made out, in the light of the failure to focus on the honest belief of the appellant, we conclude that the conviction is unsafe.

Private defence and the prevention of crime are sometimes indistinguishable. If D goes to the defence of E whom V is trying to murder, he is exercising the right of private defence but he is also seeking to prevent the commission of a crime. It would be absurd to ask D whether he was acting in defence of E or to prevent murder being committed and preposterous that the law should differ according to his answer.

23.6.5 Defence against attacks on property

23.6.5.1 Common law

R v Hussey
(1924) 18 Cr App R 160, Court of Criminal Appeal

(Lord Hewart CJ, Avory and Salter JJ)

Appeal against conviction and sentence.

H was convicted of unlawful wounding, and was sentenced to 12 months' imprisonment with hard labour. H had rented a room at Brixton from a Mrs West. Mrs West purported to give him oral notice to quit. H contended that was not valid notice. West and two others armed with a hammer, a spanner, a poker and a chisel, tried to force their way into the room. H had barricaded himself in. H fired a gun through a break in the door wounding two of the three. The appeal against conviction was based on the question whether the defence was available that H's use of violence was necessary to protect his life and that of his wife and children. He appealed.

The Lord Chief Justice:

No sufficient notice had been given to appellant to quit his room, and therefore he was in the position of a man defending his house. In *Archbold's Criminal Pleading, Evidence and Practice*, 26th edn, p 887, it appears that:

'In defence of a man's house, the owner or his family may kill a trespasser who would forcibly dispossess him of it, in the same manner as he might, by law, kill in self-defence a man who attacks him personally; with this distinction, however, that in defending his home he need not retreat, as in other cases of self-defence, for that would be giving up his house to his adversary.'

That is still the law, but not one word was said about that distinction in the summing-up, which proceeded on the foundation that the defence was the ordinary one of self-defence. The jury, by their verdict, negatived felonious intent, and with a proper direction they might have come to a different conclusion. This appeal must therefore be allowed.

Conviction quashed

In *Faraj* [2007] EWCA Crim 1033, the Court of Appeal considered the defence of protection of property where D had made a mistake in thinking that a gas repair man, Mr Haq, was a burglar. Faraj detained him and threatened him with a knife. Tuckey LJ stated:

> We can see no reason why a house-holder should not be entitled to detain someone in his house whom he genuinely believes to be a burglar. He would be acting in defence of his property by doing so. Here full effect can be given to the defendant's belief however unreasonable it may be. But this defence, like self defence, has its limits. The householder must honestly believe that he needs to detain the suspect and must do so in a way which is reasonable. So if the appellant believed that Mr Haq was a burglar he would be entitled to be judged on this basis even if his belief was unreasonable. If all that he had done was to detain Mr Haq for the purposes of establishing his identity it is most unlikely that he would be found to have acted unreasonably. Whether his use of a knife to do so was reasonable is another matter which, like everything else, would be for the jury to decide.
>
> Should there be some free standing right to detain which is not subject to the limits which arrest and defence of property are, as [counsel] contends? We do not think so. The law has always jealously guarded the right to freedom of movement. Any restriction of that right has to be justified and confined within established limits. In the event we think that in the circumstances of this case defence of property gave the appellant sufficient protection.

≈ *Questions*

(1) Hussey was acting in the defence of his home. Was he also acting in the prevention of crime? Should it make any difference to the amount of force he might lawfully use? Would it have been different if the assailants had intended not to dispossess Hussey but to gate-crash a party he was giving?

(2) Could it be reasonable to stand and fight in defence of the home when it would be unreasonable to stand and fight if the attack was directed at the defendant's person?

(3) Al and Ben try to burst open the door of Dan's ground-floor room, intending to tar-and-feather him. Dan could easily escape through the window. He fires a shotgun through the door and wounds Al. Is he guilty of unlawful wounding?

23.6.5.2 Statutory impact

The s 76 provisions apply where D was using force to protect property, but the heightened householder test does not.

23.6.6 Defending oneself against non-criminal acts?

23.6.6.1 Common law

In *A (children) (conjoined twins)*, section 23.5, p 652, Ward LJ said:

> The reality here—harsh as it is to state it, and unnatural as it is that it should be happening—is that Mary is killing Jodie. That is the effect of the incontrovertible medical evidence and it is common ground in the case. Mary uses Jodie's heart and lungs to receive and use Jodie's oxygenated blood. This will cause Jodie's heart to fail and cause Jodie's death as surely as a slow drip of poison. How can it be just that Jodie should be required to tolerate that state of affairs? One does not need to label Mary with the American terminology which would paint her to be 'an unjust aggressor', which I feel is wholly inappropriate language for the sad and helpless position in which Mary finds herself.

> I have no difficulty in agreeing that this unique happening cannot be said to be unlawful. But it does not have to be unlawful. The six-year-old boy indiscriminately shooting all and sundry in the school playground is not acting unlawfully for he is too young for his acts to be so classified. But is he 'innocent' within the moral meaning of that word as used by the Archbishop? I am not qualified to answer that moral question because, despite an assertion—or was it an aspersion—by a member of the Bar in a letter to *The Times* that we, the judges, are proclaiming some moral superiority in this case, I for my part would defer any opinion as to a child's innocence to the Archbishop [of Westminster] for that is his territory. If I had to hazard a guess, I would venture the tentative view that the child is not morally innocent. What I am, however, competent to say is that *in law* killing that six-year-old boy in self-defence of others would be fully justified and the killing would not be unlawful. I can see no difference in essence between that resort to legitimate self-defence and the doctors coming to Jodie's defence and removing the threat of fatal harm to her presented by Mary's draining her life-blood. The availability of such a plea of quasi self-defence, modified to meet the quite exceptional circumstances nature has inflicted on the twins, makes intervention by the doctors lawful.

The common law therefore seems to follow the Draft Criminal Code, cl 44 which, having provided that a person does not commit an offence by using necessary and reasonable force to protect himself or another from unlawful force or unlawful personal harm, goes on:

> (3) For the purpose of this section, an act is 'unlawful' although a person charged with an offence in respect of it would be acquitted on the ground only that—
>
> (a) he was under 10 years of age; or
>
> (b) he lacked the fault required for the offence or believed that an exempting circumstance existed; or
>
> (c) he acted in pursuance of a reasonable suspicion; or
>
> (d) he acted under duress, whether by threats or circumstances; or
>
> (e) he was in a state of automatism or suffering from severe mental illness or severe mental handicap.

23.6.7 Availability of defences to initial aggressor

23.6.7.1 What if D is the initial aggressor?

In *Rashford* [2005] EWCA Crim 3377, [2006] Crim LR547, the Court of Appeal made it clear that D does not lose the opportunity to rely on self-defence even if he was the initial aggressor, if the person whom he attacks not only defends himself but goes over to the offensive. This seems right, subject to the restriction that it should not be available where D deliberately provoked the attack with the intention of killing purportedly in self-defence.

In *Hichins* [2011] EWCA Crim 1626, it was recognized that self-defence and the defence under s 3 of the Criminal Law Act 1967 extended to the use of force against an innocent third party where such force was used to prevent a crime from being committed against someone else. Examples of the defence arising included a police constable bundling a person out of the way to get to another person who was about to detonate an explosive device, and where, for example, a person knocked car keys out of the hands of a third party to prevent the keys being given to a drunk person who was attempting to drive. However, facts giving rise to such a defence would be rare and the degrees of likelihood, and the imminence of the commission of a crime, were important factors to be borne in mind.

23.6.7.2 Section 76 and the duty to retreat

As has already been pointed out, the Act now explicitly states that there is no duty to retreat.

> (6A) In deciding the question mentioned in subsection (3), a possibility that D could have retreated is to be considered (so far as relevant) as a factor to be taken into account, rather than as giving rise to a duty to retreat.

23.6.8 The effect of a successful plea

If D pleads the defence successfully it results in an acquittal for all crimes. The Crown must disprove the defence to the criminal standard. Does this mean that the grossly mistaken killer will be completely acquitted? Not necessarily. Gross negligence is now acknowledged to be a sufficient fault for manslaughter (section 9.3, p 228) so why should not the grossly negligent mistake, resulting as it does in death, be a ground of liability in itself? See also *O'Grady* [1987] QB 995, section 25.7, p 740. In the case of non-fatal offences, the grossly negligent mistake would exempt the defendant entirely; but this is consistent with the present law, that causing non-fatal injuries by gross negligence is not an offence.

If D has a belief in force, but has used excessive force even on the facts as he believed them to be, the self-defence plea fails completely and D is convicted.

Many have argued that in such cases, where the charge is murder, D should have a partial defence.

R v Clegg
[1995] UKHL 1, House of Lords

(Lords Keith, Browne-Wilkinson, Slynn, Lloyd and Nicholls)

C was a soldier on patrol in the course of his duties in Northern Ireland in 1990. A car approached the patrol at speed. C fired three shots at the windscreen and a fourth after the car had passed him. The last shot killed the passenger. C was charged with murder. His defence was that he fired in defence of himself and a fellow soldier. C was convicted of murder and his appeal was dismissed by the Court of Appeal of Northern Ireland. He appealed to the House of Lords.

[**Lord Lloyd** said that the first question (whether, when force used in self-defence is excessive, the law allows a verdict of manslaughter instead of murder), did not arise since the danger had passed when C fired the fourth and fatal shot; but that it was convenient to deal with it. Having discussed the Report of the Royal Commission of 1879, he continued:]

There does not appear to have been any development in the law until *R v Howe* (1958) 100 CLR 448, decided by the High Court of Australia in 1958. There was an extensive citation of all the authorities in this corner of the law going back to *Rex v. Cook* (1640) Cro Car 537. The decision of the court is well summarised in the following paragraph of the headnote:

'Where a plea of self-defence to a charge of murder fails only because the death of the deceased was occasioned by the use of force going beyond what was necessary in the circumstances for the protection of the accused or what might reasonably be regarded by him as necessary in the circumstances, it is, in the absence of clear and definite decision, reasonable in principle to regard such a homicide as reduced to manslaughter.'

Twelve years later the same point came before the Privy Council on appeal from the Supreme Court of Jamaica, see: *Palmer v R* [1971] AC 814. Lord Morris of Borth-y-Gest, giving the opinion of the Privy

Council, declined to follow *Howe's* case preferring the decision of the West Indian Federal Supreme Court in *De Freitas v R* (1960) 2 W.I.R 523.

After setting out the elements of the defence of self-defence, he said at 832:

'... if the prosecution have shown that what was done was not done in self-defence then that issue is eliminated from the case. If the jury consider that the accused acted in self-defence or if the jury are in doubt as to this then they will acquit. The defence of self-defence either succeeds so as to result in an acquittal or it is disproved in which case as a defence it is rejected.'

In other words, there is no half-way house. There is no rule that a defendant who has used a greater degree of force than was necessary in the circumstances should be found guilty of manslaughter rather than murder.

In 1971 a Court of Appeal consisting of Edmund Davies L.J. and Lawton and Forbes J.J. approved and followed *Palmer's case: See R v McInnes* [1971] 1 W.L.R. 1600 at p1608:

'But where self-defence fails on the ground that the force used went clearly beyond that which was reasonable in the light of the circumstances as they reasonably appeared to the accused, is it the law that the inevitable result must be that he can be convicted of manslaughter only, and not of murder? It seems that in Australia that question is answered in the affirmative ... but not, we think, in this country. On the contrary, if a plea of self-defence fails for the reason stated, it affords the accused no protection at all.'

Of course, as the court pointed out, the verdict may be reduced from murder to manslaughter on other grounds, for example, if the prosecution fail to negative provocation, where it arises, or fail to prove the requisite intent for murder. But so far as self-defence is concerned, it is all or nothing. The defence either succeeds or it fails. If it succeeds, the defendant is acquitted. If it fails, he is guilty of murder.

In a subsequent case in Australia, *Viro v R* (1978) 141 C.L.R. 88, the High Court decided by a bare majority over a strong dissent by Barwick C.J. to follow *Howe* in preference to *Palmer*. Mason J suggested that in self-defence cases juries should be directed in accordance with six propositions which he formulated at the end of his judgment, and which, in his view, best accorded 'with acceptable standards of culpability'. But the propositions proved to be unworkable in practice. Juries found difficulty in applying, or perhaps even understanding them. As a result, a full court of seven judges was convened to reconsider the position in *Zecevic v D.P.P. (Victoria)* (1987) 162 C.L.R. 645. The High Court decided by a majority of five to two to revert to the law as stated in *Palmer* and *McInnes*, and declined to follow *Howe* and *Viro*. Wilson, Dawson and Toohey JJ said at p. 665:

'Believing, as we do, that the law as we have set it out is dictated by basic principle upon a matter of fundamental importance, it is unthinkable that the court should abdicate its responsibility by declining to declare it accordingly. It has the virtue of being readily understandable by a jury. It restores consistency to the law relating to self-defence whether raised in the case of homicide or otherwise. Finally, it has the effect of expressing the common law in terms which are in accord with the views expressed in *Palmer* (adopted in England in *McInnes)* and which are generally consonant with the law in the code States.'

[Lord Lloyd went on to hold that the degree of permissible force, and the consequence of the use of excessive force, is the same, whether the force be used in self-defence or in the prevention of crime; and in the circumstances of this case, it made no difference that C was a member of the security forces, acting in the course of his duty. There is no defence of superior orders.]

Appeal dismissed

Lord Lloyd said that the question whether the law should be changed to allow a conviction of manslaughter was, in truth, part of the wider question whether the mandatory sentence for murder should still be maintained. But is not that a different question? Members of the CLRC who were in favour of the abolition of the mandatory life sentence nevertheless thought that the defences of diminished responsibility and provocation reducing murder to manslaughter should be maintained: Fourteenth Report, *Offences Against the Person* (1980), Cmnd 7844, para 56. Similarly, the recommendations of the Committee that killing by excessive force in self-defence should be manslaughter and not murder was quite independent of the question of the mandatory life sentence. The Select Committee of the House of Lords on Murder and Life Imprisonment (HL Paper 78-1, session 1988–89, para 83) agreed with the CLRC's opinion; and the Select Committee's own recommendation for a defence to murder of excessive self-defence was coupled with its principal recommendation that the mandatory life sentence should be abolished: 'If murder is to be reserved for those homicides most deserving of stigma this does not seem to be one of them', para 88.

Noting that the House had, by a majority, extended the defence of duress to a charge of aiding and abetting murder in *Lynch v DPP for Northern Ireland*, section 23.3.5, p 639, Lord Lloyd remarked that the difference is that duress is a matter of common law, whereas in the use of force to prevent crime 'Parliament has already taken a hand by enacting section 3 of the 1967 [Criminal Law] Act. Parliament did not, in doing so, see fit to create a qualified defence in cases where the defendant uses excessive force in preventing crime.' Does not this overlook the fact that, notwithstanding the title of the Act, the law stated in s 3 is primarily civil law? It states when force may be used—when its use is lawful, so that it is neither a tort nor a crime. It says nothing at all about defences to crime, which is a different question as is demonstrated by *Gladstone Williams*, section 23.6.1.1, p 660 and its successors.

A person who uses force which is *unreasonable* in the circumstances to prevent crime and who cannot therefore justify his actions under s 3 nevertheless has a defence to a criminal charge if the force would have been reasonable if the circumstances had been as he mistakenly (and even unreasonably) believed them to be. The questions whether the use of force is justified under s 3 and whether the user has a defence to a criminal charge are not the same. See generally, J. C. Smith, 'Using Force in Self-Defence and the Prevention of Crime' (1994) 47 CLP 101.

A holding that the user of excessive force is guilty only of manslaughter and not of murder would have been in no sense inconsistent with s 3. See further, J. Rogers, 'Justifying the Use of Firearms by Policemen and Soldiers: A Response to the Home Office's Review of the Law on the Use of Lethal Force' (1998) 18 LS 486 and S. Skinner, 'Citizens in Uniform: Public Defence, Reasonableness and Human Rights' [2000] PL 266.

The Law Commission (Report No 290, *Partial Defences to Murder* (2004)) concluded that no new partial defence to murder should be created for the defendant who kills by using excessive force. In its more recent proposals in Report No 304, *Murder, Manslaughter and Infanticide* (2006), the Law Commission confirmed this view. A defendant will, in appropriate circumstances, be able to advance a 'pure' self-defence plea and the new broader loss of control-based plea. Under the proposed scheme, if the jury rejects the self-defence plea, they might still return a manslaughter verdict on the application of the new defence.

Note that where D loses self-control and kills because of a fear of serious violence from V, D is entitled to plead the loss of self-control defence under ss 54 to 56 of the Coroners and Justice Act 2009, and if successful will be convicted of manslaughter only. See Chapter 8.

23.6.9 ECHR limits to self defence

The Human Rights Act has prompted many to ask whether the protection English law affords to a victim of a defendant acting in 'self-defence'/'private defence' is compatible with Article 2.

The fact that D is entitled to an acquittal if he held a genuine though unreasonable belief in the need for violence is argued to be too generous to D, and results in the UK providing inadequate protection for its citizens' lives under Article 2. See A. Ashworth, 'Human Rights: Case Commentary on *Andronicou and Constantinou v. Cyprus*' [1998] Crim LR 823. See also A. Ashworth, 'The European Convention and Criminal Law' in J. Beatson (ed), *The Human Rights Act and the Criminal Justice and Regulatory Process* (1999); F. Leverick, *Killing in Self-Defence* (2006); B. Sangero, *Self Defence in Criminal Law* (2006).

Article 2 ECHR provides that:

> (1) Everyone's right to life shall be protected by law. No-one shall be deprived of his life intentionally save in the execution of a sentence of a court following his conviction of a crime for which this penalty is provided by law.
>
> (2) Deprivation of life shall not be regarded as inflicted in contravention of this article when it results from the use of force which is no more than absolutely necessary:
>
>   (a) in defence of any person from unlawful violence;
>
>   (b) in order to effect a lawful arrest or to prevent the escape of a person lawfully detained;
>
>   (c) in action lawfully taken for the purpose of quelling a riot or insurrection.

F. Leverick, 'Is English Self-Defence Law Incompatible with Article 2 of the ECHR?' [2002] Crim LR 347 concludes that:

> English law is contrary to Article 2 of the ECHR. The reason for this claim is that, in allowing the unreasonably mistaken defendant to escape punishment in this way, English law fails to respect the right to life of the person who, through no fault of their own, is mistaken for an attacker. An examination of relevant case law leads to the conclusion that the substance of English law does indeed contravene Article 2. It had been suggested that because killing in self-defence is not an intentional killing, Article 2 does not apply. Regardless of the theoretical merits of this suggestion, it can be dismissed as it has consistently been held that self-defensive killing does fall to be assessed under Article 2. Further, an examination of relevant cases shows that the court has consistently required that a mistaken belief in the need to use self-defensive force be based on good reasons. It is also clear, from cases such as *A v. United Kingdom* and *X and Y v. Netherlands*, that a violation of the Convention can take place when there has been a failure on the part of the State to provide a criminal law sanction that protects its citizens from the violent acts of other individuals, regardless of whether these individuals were State officials or private citizens. This is not to say that the Convention would necessarily require English law to convict the unreasonably mistaken self-defender of murder. It may be that a conviction for a lesser offence, such as manslaughter, is sufficient. Consideration of the degree of punishment appropriate in such circumstances is outside the scope of this paper. The point is that English law as it stands at present contains no sanctions whatsoever for the defendant who deprives another of her life in the unreasonable belief that she was an attacker.

Sir John Smith responded [2002] Crim LR 952:

> The established English law is that, where a person is charged with a crime requiring mens rea and alleged to be committed by the use of force when acting in public or private defence, he is to be judged on the facts as he honestly believed them to be, whether reasonably or not. If, in light of the supposed circumstances, it was reasonable to use that degree of force, he is not guilty of such a criminal offence. It has been suggested by no less an authority than Professor Andrew Ashworth [Commentary on *Andronicou and Constantinou v Cyprus* [1998] Crim L R 823–825] that this may be incompatible with Article 2 (Right to Life) of the ECHR—that the Article requires a criminal sanction where a person kills

on the basis of an erroneous and unreasonable belief. I have argued otherwise and have recently written [[2001] Crim L R 400 at 402–403] that the point appears to be settled for English law by the decision in *Re A (children) (conjoined twins): surgical separation* [section 23.5] . . . Article [2] proscribes only intentional killing, which means by an act done with the purpose of killing. The doctors in that case intended to kill within the meaning of the common law of murder because they knew that death was certain to result from their act but they did not act with the purpose of killing, so the Article was inapplicable.

Fiona Leverick criticises my argument and states that I cite no authority for my view. If that were so, I would indeed be remiss, but I thought, and think, it is obvious that my authority was the very decision for the Court of Appeal on which I was commenting. The judgments of the three Lords Justices, though arriving at the same result, differ in some important respects. But they appear to be unanimously of the opinion that 'intentionally' in the Article means 'with the purpose of' [Brooke LJ at 1050a–e and Robert Walker LJ at 1067–1068]; and this ruling is the ratio decidendi of the court on this issue. For the purposes of the English law of murder, the doctors intended to kill baby Mary but, as their only purpose was to save the life of twin Jodie, they were not killing Mary intentionally within the meaning of the Article.

Ms Leverick states that my argument 'can be fairly easily dismissed' from an examination of the case law on Article 2 and goes on to discuss a series of decisions of the European Court of Human Rights ('ECtHR'). But, while an English court must 'take into account' any judgment of the ECtHR, such a judgment is not binding but only persuasive—as, of course, Ms Leverick knows. I was, and am, discussing English law and, if there is an inconsistency between the interpretation put on the Convention by the English courts and that which appears to be put on it by the ECtHR, it is the English court's ruling which prevails and represents the law of England.

It appears that the court in *Re A* received extensive written and oral argument on the issue of Article 2 and that relevant decisions of the ECtHR were cited. I do not venture into this arena, but, if the court's interpretation of those decisions differs from that of Ms Leverick, it is the court's interpretation which must prevail. She cites some European decisions delivered after *Re A* but, however persuasive they might be, they cannot affect the authority of *Re A* unless and until an English court decides otherwise.

 . . . So I adhere firmly to my view that, until the House of Lords or Parliament decide otherwise, Re A decides that Article 2 has no application to a person acting bona fide in self-defence and that is the law of England.

What if the Article does require a criminal sanction?

Ms Leverick concedes that the Convention would not necessarily require English law to convict the unreasonably mistaken self-defender of murder:

> 'It may be that a conviction for a lesser offence, such as manslaughter, is sufficient . . . The point is that English law as it stands at present contains no sanction whatsoever for the defendant who deprives another of her life in the unreasonable belief that she was an attacker.'

This is an understandable view because there is no direct authority that the unreasonably mistaken killer in self-defence is guilty of a crime. However, I do not believe it is the law and I have so argued long before the question of compatibility with the ECHR arose.

Where the force used was reasonable in the circumstances which the defendant believed to exist. The defendant is not guilty of murder but the question whether he may be guilty of manslaughter at common law does not appear to have been raised in any case.

Where the evidence suggests that the defendant was acting under a mistaken belief, a jury should be directed that, if the force used was reasonable in the circumstances as he honestly believed them to be, then they must acquit him of murder. But, if they do so acquit him, they must go on to consider whether (i) in the actual circumstances, the force used was unreasonable and, if it was, (ii) whether the defendant, in making the mistake, was guilty of gross negligence, so bad as in their judgment to amount to a crime. If they are sure that he was, then they should convict him of manslaughter . . .

Ms Leverick concentrates on private defence but suggests that the incompatibility argument may be 'especially compelling' where force is used in the prevention of crime and section 3 of the Criminal Law Act 1967 is in issue because 'section 3 of the Human Rights Act 1998 requires primary legislation to be read and given effect in a way which is compatible with Convention rights'. But a person who uses more than reasonable force in the prevention of crime is in breach of section 3. He is acting unlawfully, whatever his honest belief. Section 3 can hardly be said to be incompatible with the Convention but, notwithstanding the title of the Act, this section does not say anything about the criminal law. When the defendant is charge with a criminal offence, it is the criminal law which is in issue. The court is not construing section 3. The requirements of mens rea are the same, whether it is public or private defence which is in issue.

See Fiona Leverick's further response at [2002] Crim LR 963.

≈≈ *Question*
Do you find Sir John's argument persuasive?

In the more recent pronouncements from the English court, it has been accepted that the current rules of English law on the use of potentially lethal force by the police are not incompatible with the European Convention. In judicial review proceedings, in *R (Bennett) v HM Coroner for Inner London* [2006] EWHC 196 (Admin), a coroner's decision not to leave unlawful killing as a possible verdict for the jury was challenged. B's son had died as a result of being shot by a police officer. A witness had told the police that the deceased was carrying a gun and two firearms officers attended the scene. In 30 seconds, one officer fired six shots, four of which struck the deceased in the back and side and one of which was fatal. At the inquest, the coroner decided not to leave a verdict of unlawful killing to the jury and the jury returned a verdict of lawful killing. B sought judicial review on the ground that the coroner's direction on self-defence had failed to pay heed to Article 2. In the High Court, Collins J held, having regard to the case law, that:

the European Court of Human Rights has considered what English law requires for self defence, and has not suggested that there is any incompatibility with Article 2. In truth, if any officer reasonably decides that he must use lethal force, it will inevitably be because it is absolutely necessary to do so. To kill when it is not absolutely necessary to do so is surely to act unreasonably. Thus, the reasonableness test does not in truth differ from the Article 2 test as applied in *McCann* [(1995) 21 EHRR 97].

The Court of Appeal upheld that decision ([2007] EWCA Civ 617). The basis of appeal was principally that it had been a misdirection not to direct the jury to consider whether the officer's claim to have acted in self-defence was reasonable in the light of the requirement in the relevant ACPO manual to reassess at all times whether it was 'absolutely necessary' to shoot.

As was discussed above, in *R (on the application of Collins) v Secretary of State for Justice* the claimant argued that the householder provision in s 76(5A) of the Criminal Justice and Immigration Act 2008 was incompatible with the state's positive obligation in Article 2 to put in place effective criminal law provisions to deter the commission of offences against the person. Sir Brian Leveson P rejected this argument for the following reasons.

Article 2 ECHR: application

58. For the present purpose, what results from the above is one simple question: does the criminal law of England and Wales effectively deter offences against the person in householder cases?

59. The starting point must be the deterrent effect of the catalogue of offences against the person for which a householder using force against an intruder may be liable. Murder, manslaughter, and non-fatal offences against the person apply without distinction in terms of the substantive definition of the offence in householder cases.

60. In both householder and non-householder cases, the defendant may seek to establish a defence of self-defence. In both cases, the basic elements of the test are the same: whether the defendant genuinely believed that it was necessary to use force to defend himself; and whether the nature and degree of force used was reasonable in the circumstances as the defendant genuinely, even if mistakenly, believed them to be. In relation to the second limb, in both cases section 76(7) puts on a statutory basis the Palmer direction that (a) a person acting for a legitimate purpose may not be able to weigh to a nicety the exact measure of any necessary action; and (b) evidence of a person's having only done what the person honestly and instinctively thought was necessary for a legitimate purpose constitutes strong evidence that only reasonable action was taken by that person for that purpose.

61. In this context, section 76(5A) serves to exclude a householder's grossly disproportionate use of force from being reasonable. When read with section 76(6), which provides that in non-householder cases all disproportionate force is excluded from being reasonable, section 76(5A) can be seen to offer a discretionary area of judgment to the jury as to whether if the force was disproportionate, it was nevertheless reasonable in the circumstances. The effect of section 76(5A) is not to give householders carte blanche in the degree of force they use against intruders in self-defence. A jury must ultimately determine whether the householder's action was reasonable in the circumstances as he believed them to be.

62. There may be instances when a jury may consider the actions of a householder in self-defence to be more than what might objectively be described as the minimum proportionate response but nevertheless reasonable given the particular and extenuating circumstances of the case. This does not weaken the capacity of the criminal law of England and Wales to deter offences against the person in householder cases. The headline message is and remains clear: a householder will only be able to avail himself of the defence if the degree of force he used was reasonable in the circumstances as he believed them to be. In that context, it is not irrelevant that article 2 and article 8 rights of the householder are also engaged.

63. It is important to note that in this regard, the ECtHR has consistently held that the reasonableness limb of self-defence (in the circumstances as the defendant believed them to be) as applied in state actor cases is compatible with the article 2.2 requirement of 'absolute necessity': see *McCann v United Kingdom* (1995) 21 EHRR 97, paras 134–200, *Bubbins v United Kingdom* (2005) 41 EHRR 24, paras 138–140, *Bennett v United Kingdom* (2010) 52 EHRR SE7, paras 67–83. On any view, therefore, the test of reasonableness in the circumstances in private party householder cases, even after the minor qualification of section 76(5A), would not cause a breach of the article 2.1 positive obligation, which is shorn of strict proportionality.

64. All of this adds up to there being reasonable safeguards against the commission of offences against the person in householder cases. In the circumstances, I conclude that the criminal law of England and Wales on self-defence in householder cases, taken as a whole, fulfils the framework obligation under article 2.1.

...

Conclusion

70. Having regard to the analysis above, I am satisfied that section 76(5A) of the 2008 Act does not extend the ambit in law of the second limb of self-defence but, properly construed, provides emphasis to the requirement to consider all the circumstances permitting a degree of force to be used on an

intruder in householder cases which is reasonable in all the circumstances (whether that degree of force was disproportionate or less than disproportionate). In particular, it does not alter the test to permit, in all circumstances, the use of disproportionate force and, to that extent, the CPS reviewer adopted the wrong test when reconsidering the facts of this case. Neither does the provision offend article 2 of the ECHR.

The compatibility of domestic law with the ECHR was considered recently by the European Court of Human Rights in *Da Silva v UK* (2016) 63 EHRR 12. JM was shot dead by police officers in London after being mistaken for a suicide bomber. The applicants, who were family of the deceased, argued that the test for self-defence in English law was lower than the standard required by Article 2 ECHR. The court rejected this argument in the following terms:

251. It is clear both from the parties' submissions and the domestic decisions in the present case that the focus of the test for self-defence in England and Wales is on whether there existed an honest and genuine belief that the use of force was necessary. The subjective reasonableness of that belief (or the existence of subjective good reasons for it) is principally relevant to the question of whether it was in fact honestly and genuinely held. Once that question has been addressed, the domestic authorities have to ask whether the force used was 'absolutely necessary'. This question is essentially one of proportionality, which requires the authorities to again address the question of reasonableness: that is, whether the degree of force used was reasonable, having regard to what the person honestly and genuinely believed.

  252. So formulated, it cannot be said that the test applied in England and Wales is significantly different from the standard applied by the Court in the *McCann* judgment and in its post-*McCann* case-law. Bearing in mind that the Court has previously declined to find fault with a domestic legal framework purely on account of a difference in wording which can be overcome by the interpretation of the domestic courts, it cannot be said that the definition of self-defence in England and Wales falls short of the standard required by art.2 of the Convention.

23.6.10 Unknown circumstances of justification or excuse

In *Dadson* (1850) 2 Den CC 35, the circumstances which would have justified or excused D's conduct in shooting at V if he had been aware of them were no defence because D was unaware that those circumstances existed. The majority of the CLRC were satisfied that the principle of that case was correct and it was embodied in their recommendation in their Fourteenth Report as to the law of private defence.

  In *Gladstone Williams*, discussed in section 23.6.1.1, the Court of Appeal held that the recommendation was a true statement of the common law and therefore it now is the law. An arrest can be lawful only if the arrestor is in a position to state a valid ground for arrest. Dadson was not in that position. 'I arrest you on the ground that you have stolen wood from the copse' would not satisfy the common law or s 28 of the Police and Criminal Evidence Act. Stealing the wood was not a felony but an offence punishable only on summary conviction by a fine of £5 with no power to arrest the offender.

≋ *Questions*

(1) Does s 76 of the Criminal Justice and Immigration Act 2008 clarify the position in English law on the use of force to a threat of which D is unaware?

(2) D shoots V dead. Unknown to D at the time that he shot V, V was about to take aim to shoot him (D) with intent to kill. What is D's criminal liability? What should it be?

23.7 Judicial development of defences

Glanville Williams, 'Necessity'
[1978] Crim LR 128

[Having pointed out that a purpose of codification is to enable the citizen to know what conduct is penalized, the writer continues:]

It by no means follows that it should be any part of the purpose of a code to get rid of open-ended defences, or to fetter the power of the courts to create new defences in the name of the common law. That the courts have power to enlarge defences is sometimes denied by the judges, just as they deny in terms their power to enlarge offences; but history records some examples of the former activity as well as innumerable examples of the latter.

The Draft Code of 1879 recognised this distinction of policy. It contained two sections (5 and 19), one removing the power of the judges to create new crimes and the other preserving judicial creativity in respect of justifications and excuses. The proposal was immediately criticised by Cockburn LCJ on the ground that the arguments for exhaustive codification of offences applied equally to defences. Stephen, the architect of the code, replied to this criticism in a notable article. [See the *Nineteenth Century* for January 1880, pp 152–157. I am indebted to Sir Rupert Cross for calling my attention to this article.] He first distinguished two meanings of the term 'common law': a body of relatively fixed principles resulting from judicial decisions, and the qualified power of the judges to make new law under the fiction of declaring existing law, or in other words 'not a part of the law actually existing, but law which has only a potential existence—that which, if the case should ever occur, the judges would declare to be the law.' Stephen thought it justifiable to save the common law in the second sense in respect of defences, though not in respect of offences. The central passage of his argument is worth quoting rather fully.

'It appears to me that the two proposed enactments stand on entirely different principles. After the experience of centuries, and with a Parliament sitting every year, and keenly alive to all matters likely to endanger the public interest, we are surely in a position to say the power of declaring new offences shall henceforth be vested in Parliament only. The power which has at times been claimed for the judges of declaring new offences cannot be useful now, whatever may have been its value in earlier times.

On the other hand it is hardly possible to foresee all the circumstances which might possibly justify or excuse acts which might otherwise be crimes. A long series of authorities have settled certain rules which can be put into a distinct and convenient form, and it is of course desirable to take the opportunity of deciding by the way minor points which an examination of the authorities shows to be still open. In this manner rules can be laid down as to the effect of infancy, insanity, compulsion, and ignorance of law, and also as to the cases in which force may lawfully be employed against the person of another; but is it therefore wise or safe to go so far as to say that no other circumstances than those expressly enumerated shall operate by way of excuse or justification for what would otherwise be a crime? To do so would be to run a risk, the extent of which it is difficult to estimate, of producing a conflict between the Code, and the moral feelings of the public. Such a conflict is upon all possible grounds to be avoided. It would, if it occurred, do more to discredit codification than anything which could possibly happen, and it might cause serious evils of another kind. Cases sometimes occur in which public opinion is at once violently excited and greatly divided, so that conduct is regarded as criminal or praiseworthy according to the sympathies of excited partisans. If the Code provided that nothing should amount to an excuse or justification which was not within the express words of the Code, it would, in such a case, be vain to allege that the conduct of the accused person was justifiable; that, but for the Code, it would have been legally justifiable; that every legal analogy was in its favour; and that the omission of an express provision about it was probably an oversight. I think such a result would be eminently unsatisfactory. I think the public would feel that the allegations referred to ought to have been carefully examined and duly decided upon.

To put the whole matter very shortly, the reason why the common law definitions of offences should be taken away, whilst the common law principles as to justification and excuses are kept alive, is like the reason why the benefit of a doubt should be given to a prisoner. The worst result that could arise from the abolition of the common law offences would be the occasional escape of a person morally guilty. The only result which can follow from preserving the common law as to justification and excuse is, that a man morally innocent, not otherwise protected, may avoid punishment. In the one case you remove rusty spring-guns and man-traps from unfrequented plantations, in the other you decline to issue an order for the destruction of every old-fashioned drag or lifebuoy which may be found on the banks of a dangerous river, but is not in the inventory of the Royal Humane Society. This indeed does not put the matter strongly enough. The continued existence of the undefined common law offences is not only dangerous to individuals, but may be dangerous to the administration of justice itself. By allowing them to remain, we run the risk of tempting the judges to express their disapproval of conduct which, upon political, moral, or social grounds, they consider deserving of punishment, by declaring upon slender authority that it constitutes an offence at common law; nothing, I think, could place the bench in a more invidious position, or go further to shake its authority . . .

Besides the well-known matters dealt with by the Code, there are a variety of speculative questions which have been discussed by ingenious persons for centuries, but which could be raised only by such rare occurrences that it may be thought pedantic to legislate for them expressly beforehand, and rash to do so without materials which the course of events has not provided. Such cases are the case of necessity (two shipwrecked men on one plank), the case of a choice of evils (my horses are running away, and I can avoid running over A only by running over B), and some others which might be suggested.

Any ingenious person may divert himself, as Hecato did, by playing with such questions. The Commission acted on the view that in practice the wisest answer to all of them is to say, 'When the case actually happens it shall be decided'; and this is effected by the preservation of such parts of the common law as to justification and excuse as are not embodied in the Code. Fiction apart, there is at present no law at all upon the subject, but the judges shall make one under the fiction of declaring it, if the occasion for doing so should ever arise.'

≈ *Question*
Should we leave it to Parliament to create offences and the courts defences?

In *Kingston* [1995] 2 AC 355, section 25.4, p 733, although counsel was not disposed to argue the point, Lord Mustill considered ([1994] 3 All ER at 370) whether the House might take the 'bold step' of recognizing a new defence of involuntary intoxication. He suspected that no new general defence had been created in modern times (but what about duress of circumstances?), adding:

Nevertheless, the criminal law must not stand still, and if it is both practical and just to take this step, and if judicial decision rather than legislation is the proper medium, then the courts should not be deterred simply by the novelty of it.

Having examined the nature of the proposed defence, Lord Mustill found that it ran into difficulties at every turn. Involuntary intoxication was best left to be taken into account in sentencing; but the question of a new defence was one which the Law Commission might usefully consider.

23.8 Justifications and excuses

It is said by philosophers who take an interest in this particular area of the law that there exists a dichotomy in criminal defences between excuses and justifications. It is sometimes claimed that 'actors are excused; acts are justified'. However, what does this mean and are these distinctions valid? Andrew Simester argues that there are four types of 'exculpatory defence', encompassing three types of excuse. These are distinct from non-exculpatory defences, such as diplomatic immunity, which immunize the defendant from the jurisdiction of the court but do not negate the wrongfulness of his act. Simester states that there exist justifications and three different classes of excuse. First of all, there are 'irresponsibility defences', which are predicated on a denial of the defendant's responsibility for doing the prohibited act. These defences, such as insanity or the incapacity of children, recognize D's inadequacy as an agent capable of moral responsibility. The second type of excuses are 'rationale-based excuses'. These are different from irresponsibility defences, which ask whether D was morally *responsible* for the act, by asking whether D was morally *culpable* for the act. The exculpatory power of these defences depends on the nature and seriousness of D's action, as well as upon the circumstances in which it was committed: they ask *why* D did the act. The final category articulated by Simester is mistake-based. These can be mistakes as to actus reus, for example where D thought he was shooting a deer but it turned out to be a human being. In this case, the mistake as to actus reus would result in D denying that he had the requisite mens rea to make him guilty of homicide. In the following extract, Simester seeks to disaggregate the distinctions between these types of defence.

A. Simester, 'On Justifications and Excuses'
in L. Zedner and J. V. Roberts (eds), *Principles and Values in Criminal Law and Criminal Justice: Essays in Honour of Andrew Ashworth* (2012)

2. Distinguishing Justification and Excuse

A justified action is a morally appropriate response to the circumstances and is, for that reason, permissible. D has a justification when his reasons for [doing the prohibited act] are sufficient to defeat those that militate against [doing the prohibited act], that [doing the prohibited act] is morally permitted. Permitted, not tolerated. Douglas Husak suggests that 'an act is permissible when it is tolerated'. That may be true—legally speaking. Not morally. Something that is morally permissible does not call for toleration, because there is nothing wrong with it. One can only tolerate something that one considers to be wrongful. Justified [wrongdoing] is not like that. It may be harmful is some way. It may generate reasons for regret. But where it is morally justified, [doing the prohibited act] is not, all things considered, wrongful.

Notice that the foregoing definition takes account of D's own reasons. In putting it this way, I am embracing a thesis that, for reasons of space, cannot be defended here: that justification depends upon D's actual or 'subjective' reasons for [doing the prohibited act] and not solely upon any guiding— 'objective' reasons that are in fact available to justify [doing the prohibited act]. Hence it is not sufficient that [the wrongdoing] be justifi*able* in the circumstances. D's own reasons must themselves be valid, and sufficient, for D's act of [wrongdoing] to be justi*fied*.

For convenience, let me call this the motivational thesis. While controversial, its validity will be assumed here. In any case, that debate concerns the scope of reasons eligible to justify D's [wrongdoing]. The important point to start with is that, whatever reasons are treated as eligible, justification requires those reasons to be sufficient. They must pass an evaluative, objective, test of whether, taken as a whole, they supply D with good reasons to [do the prohibited act]. Overall, they must defeat, or at least match, the reasons D has not to [do the prohibited act]. They must make it morally okay—or as Greenawalt puts it, warranted—to [do the prohibited act].

No such requirement exists for excuses. That said, there is a tendency to relegate excuses to a catch-all dustbin. Expressed more generally, D can be said to have an excuse if the reasons why he [does the prohibited act] are such that he is not culpable for doing so. Unfortunately, while that definition is appealingly simple, it can be applied more-or-less to all four kinds of exculpatory defences we identified earlier, and certainly to justifications. No surprise, then, that writers tend to add a proviso that excused conduct is unjustified, or that they sometimes conflate irresponsibility defences with rationale-based excuses.

Excuses differ from irresponsibility defences in that they address D's own reasons for action, not his capacity for reasoning. D's [wrongdoing] is excusable if, in choosing to [do the prohibited act] he exhibits no shortcoming of a kind that grounds blame—no shortfall of the character or moral judgment that we should expect of an ordinary, decent person. D need not be perfect. We all have limitations, even decent folk. Exoneration requires only that the limitations explaining why D [did the prohibited act] be normal ones, ones that do not reflect badly on D. Perhaps supererogation [ie an act going beyond the call of duty] was possible. Perhaps D could have exhibited abnormal levels of altruism, etc, and refrained from [committing the prohibited act]. But blame does not turn on D's failure to merit praise. It requires that he fall short, not of standards of perfection, but of standards of reasonableness. And excuses require only that his failings be, so to speak, understandable or reasonable ones.

Like justifications, and unlike the irresponsibility defences, all rationale-based excuses therefore require that D's reasons for [committing the prohibited act] be subjected to evaluative assessment. Moreover, the assessment is not relativized to any personal limitations of virtue that the defendant might have. The difference lies in the conclusion of that assessment. When justified, there is no moral error—it is morally okay for D to [do the prohibited act]. In the case of excuse, D is not culpable for [wrongdoing] even though [wrongdoing] might not be okay. Any moral error by D is understandable, the kind of error that a decent person might well make.

≈ Questions
Which categories do the defences discussed in this chapter fall into? Do you think it matters?

Glanville Williams ([1982] Crim LR 732) expressed the view that while the distinction between excuses and justifications was of theoretical significance, it was of no practical significance. He stated:

What is the difference between a justification and an excuse? Very little. They are both defenses in the full sense, leading to an acquittal. However, when the act is not justified but only excused it is still regarded as being in some tenuous way wrong, for certain collateral purposes.

This assertion has more recently been challenged by Paul Robinson, who uses the following, vivid examples to illustrate his point.

P. H. Robinson, 'Four Distinctions that Glanville Williams Did Not Make: The Practical Benefits of Examining the Interrelation Among Criminal Law Doctrines'
in D. J. Baker and J. Horder (eds), *The Sanctity of Life and the Criminal Law: The Legacy of Glanville Williams* (2013)

A third example of the practical importance of these general defense distinctions is seen in the problem of ambiguous acquittals that arises when these distinctions are not recognized. Note that justification and excuse defences say directly opposite things about the defendant's conduct: a justification defense announces that the conduct is condoned; an excuse defense announces that the conduct is condemned. Where these two kinds of general defences are not distinguished, as in a general verdict of acquittal, it is easy for an excuse to be mistaken for a justification.

Recall the Rodney King case in which, after a long car chase, officers surrounded Rodney King and continued to beat him. The jury acquitted the officers, and riots in Los Angeles followed. The jury acquittal may well have been on the theory that the adrenaline build-up during the long car chase, the lack of adequate training to deal with the circumstances, as well as the lack of good supervision on the scene, meant that the conduct was not justified—it was excessive—but that the defendants did not deserve to be punished for it. In other words, the striking conduct on the tape is an example of conduct that we would not want repeated in the same circumstances in the future, but it is not to be punished in this instance because the officers were blameless for it. Yet with an ambiguous general verdict of acquittal, people in the community could easily have come to the conclusion that the conduct they saw on the tape was conduct that the criminal law was condoning (as objectively justified), and that could be quite upsetting. It is easy enough to construct a more nuanced verdict system of a 'no violation' verdict and a 'blameless violation' verdict, but such a solution would be ineffective where the doctrine does not distinguish between (objective) justifications and excuses.

A fourth illustration of practical value concerns what one might call post-acquittal collateral consequences. For a justification defense, there ought to be none. What the defendant did was the right thing to do, which others can do in similar situations in the future. For an excuse defense, one might want to at least ask the question whether the cause of the excusing conditions is recurring. We already do this with insanity acquittals, by having a special verdict for 'not guilty by reason of insanity', which is commonly followed by an examination to determine whether civil commitment is appropriate. But there may be any number of situations that give rise to excuse defenses that would benefit from future civil supervision or even just education. Non–exculpatory defenses present an even stronger case for the possible need for collateral consequences. It may well be that we want to give the serial child molester a double jeopardy defense for the case at hand, but that does not mean that we should not be sure that he is denied a license to drive school buses.

≈≈ *Question*

Do you agree with Robinson that there are practical ramifications that follow from whether a defence is classified as an excuse or a justification?

FURTHER READING

P. Alldridge, 'Developing the Defence of Duress' [1986] Crim LR 433

A. Ashworth, 'Criminal Liability in a Medical Context: The Treatment of Good Intentions' in A. Simester and A. T. H. Smith (eds), *Harm and Culpability* (1996)

R. Christopher, 'Unknowing Justification and the Logical Necessity of the *Dadson* Principle in Self Defence' (1995) 15 OJLS 229

C. Clarkson, 'Necessary Action: A New Defence' [2004] Crim LR 81

I. H. Dennis, 'Duress Murder and Criminal Responsibility' (1980) 106 LQR 208

J. Dressler, 'Justifications and Excuses: A Brief Review of the Concepts and the Literature' (1987) 33 Wayne L Rev 1155

J. Dressler, 'Reflections on *Dudley and Stephens* and Killing the Innocent: Taking a Wrong Conceptual Path' in J. Horder and D. Baker (eds), *The Sanctity of Life and the Criminal Law: The Legacy of Glanville Williams* (2013)

D. W. Elliott, 'Necessity, Duress and Self-Defence' [1989] Crim LR 611

S. Gardner, 'Necessity's Newest Invention' (1991) 11 OJLS 125

P. Glazebrook, 'The Necessity Plea in English Criminal Law' (1972) 30 CLJ 87

K. Laird, 'Evaluating the Relationship Between Section 45 of the Modern Slavery Act 2015 and the Defence of Duress: An Opportunity Missed?' [2016] Crim LR 395

J. Loveless, 'Domestic Violence, Coercion and Duress' [2010] Crim LR 93

P. H. Robinson, 'Criminal Law Defenses: A Systematic Analysis' (1982) 82 Columbia L Rev 199

J. Rogers, 'Necessity, Private Defence and the Killing of Mary' [2001] Crim LR 515

W. Wilson, 'The Structure of Defences' [2005] Crim LR 125

24
Mental conditions

Some of the controversies that will be examined in this chapter include:

(1) when an individual can be regarded as mentally incapable of being tried;

(2) the relationship between insane and sane automatism;

(3) the extent to which the insanity defence reflects modern psychiatric practice;

(4) whether the lack of direct correlation between the medical and legal definitions of 'insanity' infringes the European Convention on Human Rights (ECHR);

(5) how the insanity defence ought to be reformed.

24.1 Introduction

The mental condition of a person (D) accused of crime may be relevant at three stages of criminal proceedings:

- pre-trial where D's mental condition is so bad that he cannot be brought to court;
- at trial where D's mental condition is such that he is unfit to be tried; and
- at trial where D is fit to be tried, but pleads that at the time of the offence he was insane or a sane automaton.

In each case, we have to consider in what circumstances it is appropriate, fair and just to subject someone with a mental condition to a criminal trial. We must also consider to what extent it is fair and just to deny a suspect a right to a trial by hospitalizing him or detaining him in some other way without having established his guilt for the crime alleged beyond a reasonable doubt. These issues are difficult enough. In addition, we have to consider the stark differences between the legal understanding of mental disorder and definitions of insanity applied in the criminal courts as compared to the approach of the medical professions. The law's categorization of certain people as being insane would shock and offend the layperson. In fact, the manner in which the criminal law deals with those suffering from a mental disorder is unsatisfactory, archaic and lacking in modern medical foundation. Note that the discussion of diminished responsibility was covered in Chapter 8. Diminished responsibility is only available as a plea to a charge of murder.

24.2 Fitness to plead

When D is brought up for trial, it may then be asserted by D, or the prosecution, or the judge, that D is 'unfit to plead'—that is, incapable, because of a disability, of being properly tried. In *M* [2003] EWCA Crim 3452, the trial judge ruled that the defendant had to have sufficient ability in relation to six things: (a) to understand the charges; (b) to understand the plea; (c) to challenge jurors; (d) to instruct counsel and his solicitor; (e) to understand the course of the trial; and (f) to give evidence if he chooses.

The number of people pleading unfitness continues to rise. See R. D. Mackay, B. Mitchell and L. Howe, 'A Continued Upturn in Unfitness to Plead—More Disability in Relation to the Trial under the 1991 Act' [2007] Crim LR 530, revealing an increase from 50 unfitness findings in 1997 to a peak of 80 in 1999. More recently, the Law Commission asked Professor Mackay to conduct research to ascertain how often D's fitness to plead is called into question. Professor Mackay's research revealed that from 2002–12, there were a total of 725 unfitness to plead findings, giving an annual average of 103.6. This was the first time the average number of unfitness to plead findings had reached over 100.

Since s 22 of the Domestic Violence, Crime and Victims Act 2004 came into force, the issue of whether D is fit to be tried is now to be determined by a court without a jury. The court cannot find that D is unfit to be tried except on the evidence of two medical practitioners. The Court of Appeal in *Leaderman* [2015] EWCA Crim 1308 confirmed that if the medical practitioners disagree, then the court cannot find that D is unfit to be tried. The procedure is set out in the Criminal Procedure (Insanity) Act 1964 as amended:

- if D is found by the trial judge, sitting alone, to be fit to plead the trial proceeds with a jury;
- if he is found unfit to be tried by the trial judge, a jury is empanelled to determine whether he has 'done the act or made the omission charged'. If not, he is simply acquitted; if he is found by the jury to have 'done the act or made the omission charged' he may be dealt with under the powers in s 5 of the 1964 Act (section 24.2.1, p 691).

In *Chinegwundoh* [2015] EWCA Crim 109, the Court of Appeal confirmed that the point of the procedure mandated by the Criminal Procedure (Insanity) Act 1964 is to protect those unfit to be tried from the full process of the criminal law and in particular the stigma of conviction. In *Marcantonio* [2016] EWCA Crim 14, the Court of Appeal observed that a strong case could be made out for a test which drew a distinction between the capacity of a defendant to *plead guilty* in a trial and his capacity to participate effectively in *a trial*. As this issue was not fully argued before the court, however, it was not necessary to decide it.

If D suffers from a disability that renders him unfit to be tried, it is for the jury to determine whether the evidence satisfies them that D 'did the act or made the omission charged against him as the offence'. This is known as a 'trial of the facts' and is determined by a jury. The procedure is now set out in s 4 and s 4A of the Criminal Procedure (Insanity) Act 1964 as amended. Where the court has determined that D is unfit then it must proceed to a trial of the facts. It cannot continue with a normal trial making allowances for D's disability: *Orr* [2016] EWCA Crim 889.

If before the court has begun to decide on whether D did the acts alleged, D is found to have recovered so as to be fit to stand trial, the court should revisit the question of fitness to plead. This reflects the important principle that D should, wherever possible, have an opportunity to contest his guilt in a normal criminal trial: *R (Hasani) v Blackfriars CC* [2005] EWHC 3016 (Admin).

In *Antoine* [2000] UKHL 20, the House of Lords held that when the jury is determining whether D has 'done the act' alleged, they should be directed to consider whether he committed the actus reus of the offence in question. This meant that D could not rely upon the defence of diminished responsibility, as it was held to relate to mens rea. The problem, however, is that this assumes that the elements of a criminal offence can be divided neatly into actus reus and mens rea, which is not necessarily the case. In *Wells* [2015] EWCA Crim 2, Sir Brian Leveson P confirmed that the actus reus of an offence cannot always be separated from all consideration of the mens rea. The next case provides a demonstration of this problem.

In *B* [2012] EWCA Crim 770, a 24-year-old man with Asperger's was convicted of two counts of voyeurism. The mothers of two 6-year-old boys had seen B lying on his back looking under the dividers between cubicles in changing rooms watching their sons while they were naked. At trial, the judge found B to be unfit to be tried. The issue arose as to what the 'act' was in the offence of voyeurism. The judge ruled that it was the physical act of 'observing' the boys in their state of undress in a private place, but that it was not also necessary to establish that B acted 'for the purpose of sexual gratification'. That element would be required to prove the full offence, but not on a s 4A hearing. On appeal, the Court of Appeal quashed the finding. It was held that in determining, under s 4A(2) of the Criminal Procedure (Insanity) Act 1964, whether a defendant who was unfit to stand trial was guilty of voyeurism, the jury had to be satisfied that he had deliberately observed another person doing a private act *for the purpose of his own sexual gratification*. It was not necessary to be sure of the accused's knowledge that the person observed does not consent to being observed for the purposes of the accused's sexual gratification. Having regard to the 'social mischiefs' which the voyeurism offence was created to tackle, the court held (at [65]) that:

> the link between deliberate observation and the purpose of sexual gratification of the observer is central to the statutory offence of voyeurism. To use Lord Hutton's phrase, it is that purpose which turns the deliberate observation of another doing an intimate act (such as undressing) in private into an 'injurious act' . . . If that is so, then we must conclude that, in the case of an offence of voyeurism under section 67(1) of the [Sexual Offences Act 2003], the relevant 'act . . . *charged as the offence*' of the purposes of section 4A(2) is that of deliberate observation of another doing a private act where the observer does so for the specific purpose of the observer obtaining sexual gratification. That omnibus activity is the 'injurious act'. Although the activity has two components, they are indissoluble; together they are the relevant '*act*'.

The court acknowledges the criticism and potential irony that the s 4A procedure, which aims to protect defendants with a disability from a full criminal trial and an inquiry into their mental state which they cannot defend (in the sense that they are unfit to be tried and so cannot give instructions to their lawyers and cannot, save in exceptional circumstances, give evidence) means that the system might place them in a worse position than they would otherwise be (at [57]).

On ECHR concerns with the operation of the procedure, see E. Baker, 'Human Rights and McNaughten and the 1991 Act' [1994] Crim LR 84; R. D. Mackay, 'On Being Insane in Jersey Part Two' [2002] Crim LR 728; 'On Being Insane in Jersey Part Three—The Case of the *Attorney General v O'Driscoll*' [2004] Crim LR 219. For reform options, see the Law Commission Report No 364, *Unfitness to Plead* (2016) which recommends, *inter alia*, a shift to a test based on whether D is capable of participating effectively in his trial, and that the scheme ought to apply in the magistrates' and youth courts.

24.2.1 Disposal

Since the 1991 Act, a person who is found unfit to plead but not to have done the act or made the omission charged simply goes free unless there is a civil power of detention applicable. Where he is found to be unfit *and* to have done the act or made the omission, a wider range of disposals is now generally available. Section 24 of the Domestic Violence, Crime and Victims

Act 2004 inserts a new s 5 into the 1964 Act, so that in any case other than one of a fixed sentence, the court may now make:

(1)   a hospital order (with or without a restriction order);

(2)   a supervision order; or

(3)   an order for absolute discharge.

24.2.2 Reform

The Law Commission recently published a report recommending reform of the test for determining whether an individual accused of a criminal offence is fit to be tried (see Law Com Report No 364, *Unfitness to Plead* (2016)). The Commission concluded that the current test for determining whether someone accused of a crime is fit to be tried places too much emphasis upon his intellectual ability and fails to take into account other conditions which might interfere with the ability to engage in the trial process. For this reason, the Commission recommended that the test be reformulated to focus more on the defendant's capacity to participate effectively in a trial. For analysis, see A Loughnan, 'Between Fairness and "Dangerousness": Reforming the Law on Unfitness to Plead' [2016] Crim LR 451.

24.3 The relationship between automatism and insanity

If at trial D is found fit to plead, or that issue is not raised, he may claim that his mental condition at the time of the alleged offence was such that he was not responsible for his actions. D may plead insanity (one form of which is insane automatism). Alternatively, D may plead that he was in a state of sane automatism.

24.3.1 Distinguishing sane and insane automatism

The law draws a fundamental distinction between pleas of a lack of control which amount to 'insane' and 'non-insane' automatism. It is an unsatisfactory distinction which turns on whether the cause is an 'internal' or an 'external' factor. If the automatism is caused by an internal factor, the plea is, in law, one of not guilty by reason of insanity. If the automatism is caused by an external factor, it is a simple plea of not guilty.

24.3.1.1 Sane automatism

If the defendant's ability to control his movement is impaired because of an external factor such as the taking of medicines, drugs, a blow to the head, etc his plea is one of sane automatism.

(1)   The defendant bears only an evidential burden: he does not have to prove anything, but must introduce such evidence as might leave a reasonable jury in reasonable doubt whether he was in the state alleged.

(2)   If the automatism is self-induced, the defendant's liability will turn on the principles explained in Chapter 25 on intoxication. That will depend on whether the offence is one of specific or basic intent and whether the substance ingested is one commonly known to create states of automatism and whether D was aware of that. See section 25.3, p 717.

(3)   If the automatism is not self-induced, then unless the prosecution can disprove automatism, the verdict will be one of outright acquittal.

24.3.1.2 Insanity/insane automatism

A plea that D was suffering from some mental incapacity caused by some internal malfunctioning of some element his body (diabetes, epilepsy, sleepwalking, etc) is one of insanity—it is a 'disease of the mind' (see section 24.5.1, p 701):

(1) the burden of proof (on the balance of probabilities) is on the defence;

(2) it must be supported by the written or oral evidence of two or more registered medical practitioners at least one of whom is 'duly approved': Criminal Procedure (Insanity and Unfitness to Plead) Act, 1991, s 1 (section 24.5, p 700); and

(3) if the defence succeeds, the defendant will be found not guilty by reason of insanity but will not necessarily walk free. He may be made the subject of a hospital order or other measure authorized by s 5(2) of the Criminal Procedure (Insanity) Act 1964, as amended, see section 24.5.6, p 708).

24.4 Sane automatism

The Law Commission recently identified different categories of sane automatism. See Discussion Paper, *Insanity and Automatism* (2013).

5.16 (3) Automatism arising from the accused ingesting or taking substances (for example, the accused who, having taken insulin, suffers a hypoglycaemic episode). This results in a complete acquittal unless the accused was at fault in inducing or failing to avoid the loss of control. If the accused was at fault, either because he foresaw the likelihood of a loss of control and unreasonably failed to avert it or because he took a drug commonly known to create loss of control, he or she will be liable for any offences of basic intent charged. A recent example of this is the case of C [[2007] EWCA Crim 1862 at [16]] in which it was said that for the automatism defence to succeed, the accused, who claimed a hypoglycaemic attack, would have to show an evidential basis for a conclusion that he was 'totally unable to control the car due to an unforeseen hypoglycaemic attack' and 'that he could not reasonably have avoided the attack, by advance testing, and that there were no advance warnings during the course of his drive'.

This will be the subject of discussion in Chapter 25. This is another aspect of the prior fault doctrine.

5.17 (4) Automatism arising from some external physical factor other than the accused taking substances (for example, the accused has been stung by a wasp while driving, or struck by a stone thrown up from the road surface causing a reflex action). A person suffering a blow to the head causing concussion is another example. If successful, this leads to a not guilty verdict for any offence charged.

This is the subject matter of this section.

24.4.1 Sane automatism defined

Unfortunately, the courts have failed to provide a clear definition of sane automatism. In *Bratty v Attorney-General for Northern Ireland* [1963] AC 386, D was accused of killing a girl whom he was driving in his car by taking off her stocking and strangling her with it. He gave evidence that a 'blackness' came over him and said 'I didn't know what I was doing. I didn't realise anything.' There was evidence that he might have been suffering from psychomotor epilepsy which could cause ignorance of the nature and quality of acts done. At the trial, the defences of automatism and insanity were raised. The trial judge rejected the defence of insanity. The Court of Criminal Appeal in Northern Ireland dismissed an appeal against conviction for murder. On appeal to the House of Lords the House discussed the difference between sane and insane automatism. Viscount Kilmuir LC suggested that automatism is a term connoting the state of a person who, though capable of action, is 'not conscious of what he is doing … it means unconscious voluntary action'. Lord Denning emphasized that an act is not involuntary just because D cannot remember doing it. His lordship also sought to emphasize that if the involuntariness arises from either drunkenness or a disease of the mind, then that does not mean D will escape liability altogether. The rules on intoxication and insanity will apply respectively. According to Lord Denning, the category of cases in which it can be said that D's act was truly involuntary will be very narrow. This begs the question, however, as to what degree of automatism will negate D's liability.

24.4.2 What level of (sane) automatism negates liability?

In *Coley* [2013] EWCA Crim 223, Hughes LJ (at [22]) confirmed that D must have suffered a complete loss of voluntary control in order for his liability to be negated. His lordship did emphasize, however, that this does not require D to be unconscious.

> Automatism, if it occurs, results in a complete acquittal on the grounds that the act was not that of the defendant at all. It has been variously described. The essence of it is that the movements or actions of the defendant at the material time were wholly involuntary. The better expression is complete destruction of voluntary control: *Watmore v Jenkins* [1962] 2 QB 572 and *Attorney-General's Reference (No 2 of 1992)* [1994] QB 91. Examples which have been given in the past include the driver attacked by a swarm of bees or the man under hypnosis. 'Involuntary' is not the same as 'irrational'; indeed it needs sharply to be distinguished from it.

24.4.3 The difficulty in distinguishing external and internal causes

Sane automatism depends on there being an external cause for D's loss of control. The law draws this crucial distinction between insanity and sane automatism on the basis of the internal or external cause of the defendant's loss of control. Can that distinction be drawn in such a way that it applies logically and fairly? Consider the next two cases. Why is one classified as sane automatism and one insanity? Which defendant is more culpable for losing control? Is one defendant more likely than the other to suffer a similar episode and pose a risk of future harm?

R v Quick and Paddison
[1973] EWCA Crim 1, Court of Appeal, Criminal Division

(Lawton LJ, Mocatta and Milmo JJ)

The appellants were nurses employed at a mental hospital. They were convicted of assault occasioning actual bodily harm to a paraplegic patient at the hospital. Quick called medical evidence to show that he was diabetic and that at the time of the alleged assault he was suffering from hypoglycaemia and was unaware of what he was doing. He submitted that the evidence established a defence of automatism. Bridge J ruled that the defence raised was one of insanity, whereupon Quick changed his plea to guilty. Paddison was convicted by the jury on the basis that he had abetted Quick. Quick appealed on the ground that the judge's ruling was wrong and that a diabetic in a temporary and reversible condition of hypoglycaemia was not, while in that condition, suffering from any defect of reason from disease of the mind.

[**Lawton LJ**, delivering the judgment of the court, reviewed the evidence and the decisions in *Bratty, Kemp, Hill v Baxter* [1958] 1 All ER 193, [1958] 1 QB 277 and *Kay v Butterworth* (1945) 173 LT 191, and continued:]

In this quagmire of law seldom entered nowadays save by those in desperate need of some kind of a defence, *Bratty* provides the only firm ground. Is there any discernible path? We think there is—judges should follow in a common sense way their sense of fairness. This seems to have been the approach of the New Zealand Court of Appeal in *Cottle* [[1958] NZLR 999] and of Sholl J in *Carter* [[1959] VR 105]. In our judgment no help can be obtained by speculating (because that is what we would have to do) as to what the judges who answered the House of Lords' questions in 1843 [see section 24.5, p 698] meant by disease of the mind, still less as to what Sir Matthew Hale meant in the second half of the 17th century [(1682) Vol I, Ch IV] . . . Our task has been to decide what the law means now by the words 'disease of the mind'. In our judgment the fundamental concept is of a malfunctioning of the mind of transitory effect caused by disease. A malfunctioning of the mind caused by the application to the body of some external factor such as violence, drugs, including anaesthetics, alcohol and hypnotic influences cannot fairly be said to be due to disease. Such malfunctioning, unlike that caused by a defect of reason from disease of the mind, will not always relieve an accused from criminal responsibility. A self-induced incapacity will not excuse (see *R. v. Lipman* (1970) 1 Queen's Bench 152 [see section 25.4, p 728]) nor will one which could have been reasonably foreseen as a result of either doing, or omitting to do something, as for example, taking alcohol against medical advice after using certain prescribed drugs, or failing to have regular meals whilst taking insulin. From time to time difficult borderline cases are likely to arise. When they do, the test suggested by the New Zealand Court of Appeal in *Cottle* is likely to give the correct result, viz can this mental condition be fairly regarded as amounting to or producing a defect of reason from disease of the mind?

In this case Quick's alleged mental condition, if it ever existed, was not caused by his diabetes but by his use of the insulin prescribed by his doctor. Such malfunctioning of his mind as there was, was caused by an external factor and not by a bodily disorder in the nature of a disease which disturbed the working of his mind. It follows in our judgment that Quick was entitled to have his defence of automatism left to the jury and that Mr. Justice Bridge's ruling as to the effect of the medical evidence called by him was wrong. Had the defence of automatism been left to the jury, a number of questions of fact would have had to be answered. If he was in a confused mental condition, was it due to a hypoglycaemic episode or to too much alcohol? If the former, to what extent had he brought about his condition by not following his doctor's instructions about taking regular meals? Did he know that he was getting into a hypoglycaemic episode? If yes, why did he not use the antidote of eating a lump of sugar as he had been advised to do? On the evidence which was before the jury Quick might have had difficulty in answering these questions in a manner which would have relieved him of responsibility for his acts. We cannot say, however, with the requisite degree of confidence, that the jury would have convicted him. It follows that his conviction must be quashed on the ground that the verdict was unsatisfactory.

Appeals allowed

What would have been the result if the court had found that it was the diabetes and not the insulin which caused the automatism? Compare the next case.

R v Hennessy

[1989] EWCA Crim 1, Court of Appeal, Criminal Division

(Lord Lane CJ, Rose and Pill JJ)

H, a diabetic, was charged with taking a conveyance and driving while disqualified. His defence was that at the relevant time he had failed to take his proper dose of insulin due to stress, anxiety and depression and consequently was suffering from hyperglycaemia (excessive blood sugar) and was in a state of automatism. The trial judge ruled that the condition, if it existed, was caused by diabetes, a disease, so that the defence was one of insanity under the *M'Naghten* Rules. H then pleaded guilty. He appealed, arguing that the judge's ruling was wrong and that his depression and marital troubles were a sufficiently potent external factor to override the effect of the diabetic shortage of insulin. The Court of Appeal held this was an insanity plea.

Lord Lane CJ quoted from the judgment of Devlin J in *Hill v Baxter* [1958] 1 QB 277 at 285:

'I have drawn attention to the fact that the accused did not set up a defence of insanity. For the purposes of the criminal law there are two categories of mental irresponsibility, one where the disorder is due to disease and the other where it is not. The distinction is not an arbitrary one. If disease is not the cause, if there is some temporary loss of consciousness arising accidentally, it is reasonable to hope that it will not be repeated and that it is safe to let an acquitted man go entirely free. But if disease is present the same thing may happen again, and therefore, since 1800, the law has provided that persons acquitted on this ground should be subject to restraint.'

That is the submission made by Mr Owen as a basis for saying the Judge's decision was wrong and that this was a matter which should have [been] decided by the jury.

In our judgment, stress, anxiety and depression can no doubt be the result of the operation of external factors, but they are not, it seems to us, in themselves separately or together external factors of the kind capable in law of causing or contributing to a state of automatism. They constitute a state of mind which is prone to recur. They lack the feature of novelty or accident, which is the basis of the distinction drawn by Lord Diplock in the case of *Sullivan*. It is contrary to the observations of Devlin J, to which we have just referred in the case of *Hill v Baxter*. It does not, in our judgment, come within the scope of the exception 'some external physical factor such as a blow on the head or the administration of an anaesthetic.' . . .

Appeal dismissed

The fact that D's potential liability depends upon whether the source of his involuntary conduct was external or internal has been subject to sustained and cogent criticism. One of the most compelling criticisms is the fact that the courts have wrongly assumed that there is a precise correlation between the source of D's involuntariness and the possibility of recurrence. This is a criticism that has also been remarked upon by the courts. For example, in *Burgess* [1991] WLR 1206 Lord Lane CJ stated that, 'if there is a danger of recurrence that may be an added reason for categorising the condition as a disease of the mind. On the other hand, the absence of the danger of recurrence is not a reason for saying that it cannot be a disease of the mind.' As the following extract demonstrates, the Law Commission has also been critical of the distinction made in the law between internal and external causes.

Law Commission, *Criminal Liability: Insanity and Automatism: Discussion Paper* (2013) (references omitted)

The Commission criticizes the failure to distinguish logically between insanity and sane automatism.

1.41 [The law] has adopted a distinction between whether the cause of the accused's lack of control was due to an 'internal factor' (ie some malfunctioning of the person's body) or an 'external factor' (such as a blow to the head). Involuntary conduct caused by an 'internal factor' is classed as insanity and that leads to the special verdict. Involuntary conduct caused by an 'external factor' is classed as (sane) automatism, leading to a simple acquittal. This leads to illogical results. The 'line drawn between sane and insane automatism can never make medical sense'. It 'makes illogical, hair-splitting distinctions inevitable, allowing some an outright acquittal while condemning others to plead guilty or take the risk of a special verdict' . . .

[The Commission describes the cases of *Hennessy* and *Quick*.]

1.43 The upshot is that a diabetic who, without fault, fails to take insulin and then commits an alleg-edly criminal act would be treated as insane. In contrast, a diabetic who took insulin in accordance with a medical prescription would be acquitted if he or she was an automaton at the time of commit-ting an allegedly criminal act, whether that was because he or she had an unexpected reaction to the insulin or because having taken the insulin he or she failed to eat through no fault of their own. As Professor Ashworth has written:

> There can be no sense in classifying hypoglycaemic states as automatism and hyperglycaemic states as insanity, when both states are so closely associated with such a common condition as diabetes.

1.44 Beyond its application to diabetes, another basis for criticism is that with some conditions, both internal and external factors may operate simultaneously, as in sleepwalking or hypnosis: some people are more susceptible to sleep disorders, but then there may be an external trigger (an interruption to sleep) which also plays a part in loss of capacity.

1.45 A yet further difficulty with this boundary between internal (insanity) and external (automa-tism) has arisen in so-called 'psychological blow' cases where the accused enters into a dissociative state following a traumatic event.

The Commission identified a further situation in which automatism might arise but which would not fall within the insanity plea or easily be described as an external cause case.

5.13 An example might be where an accused, who is driving, experiences a sudden cramp in his leg, causing him to press on the accelerator and crash the car. There is no external factor which triggers the symptom—it has a purely internal cause—yet there has been no impairment of the accused's mental functioning and the effect is purely physical. There is therefore no disease of the mind in the sense adopted in *Sullivan* [section 24.5.1, p 701] which could found a defence of [insanity]. This results in a complete acquittal unless the defendant was at fault in inducing or failing to avoid the loss of control.

5.14 Such a case has never, to our knowledge, been directly considered by the courts. We take the view that if one were to arise, it would be treated as sane automatism. This is supported by a non-binding comment about self-induced automatism in *Quick*, where Lord Justice Lawton says:

> A self-induced incapacity will not excuse . . . nor will one which could reasonably have been fore-seen as a result of either doing something, or omitting to do something, as, for example, taking alcohol against medical advice after taking certain prescribed drugs, or failing to have regular meals while taking insulin.

5.15 We recognise that this departs from the orthodox understanding of the internal/external distinc-tion, but we think that this must be the present state of the law. This is because the defendant in the cramp example above cannot be categorised either as having a disease of the mind (so that he could be included within the insane automatism category), nor as being incapacitated due to any external cause. He must, therefore, fall into the sane automatism category, but with an internal cause.

≋ *Question*
Does this demonstrate simply that the decisions are based on policy about how likely a condi-tion is to recur and affect a defendant?

24.5 Insanity: the *M'Naghten* Rules

If D pleads insanity (including insane automatism), the *M'Naghten* Rules apply. The result of a finding of insanity is a 'special verdict' of not guilty by reason of insanity. Astonishingly, the law governing a plea of insanity is to be found in the opinion of the Law Lords delivered over 170 years ago.

M'Naghten's Case
(1843) 10 Cl & Fin 200

M'Naghten was charged with the murder by shooting of Edward Drummond. He pleaded not guilty. Medical evidence was called on his behalf to prove that he was not, at the time of committing the act, in a sound state of mind. The evidence was to the effect that persons of otherwise sound mind might be affected by morbid delusions and that M was in that condition; that a person labouring under a morbid delusion might have a moral perception of right and wrong, but that in the case of M it was a delusion which carried him away beyond the power of his own control, and left him with no such perception; and that he was not capable of exercising any control over acts which had connection with his delusion: that it was the nature of the disease with which M was affected to go on gradually until it had reached a climax, when it burst forth with irresistible intensity: that a man might go on for years quietly, though at the same time under its influence, but would all at once break out into the most extravagant and violent paroxysms.

 Some of the witnesses who gave this evidence had previously examined M, while others had never seen him until he appeared in court and formed their opinions on hearing the evidence given by other witnesses.

[Tindal CJ directed the jury:]

The question to be determined is whether at the time the act in question was committed, the prisoner had or had not the use of his understanding, so as to know that he was doing a wrong or wicked act. If the jurors should be of opinion that the prisoner was not sensible, at the time he committed it, that he was violating the laws of both God and man, then he would be entitled to a verdict in his favour: but if, on the contrary, they were of opinion that when he committed the act he was in a sound state of mind, then their verdict must be against him.

Verdict, Not guilty, on the ground of insanity

This verdict was made the subject of debate in the House of Lords and it was determined to take the opinion of all the judges on the law governing such cases The judges attended on two occasions and, on the second occasion, five questions were put to them.

[Maule J having referred to the difficulty which he felt about answering hypothetical questions on which he had heard no argument and his fear that the answers might embarrass the administration of criminal justice, stated that he would have been glad if his learned brethren would have joined him in praying their lordships to excuse them from answering the questions. Maule J then offered his own answers.]

Tindal CJ:

The first question proposed by your Lordships is this: 'What is the law respecting alleged crimes committed by persons afflicted with insane delusion in respect of one or more particular subjects or persons: as, for instance, where at the time of the commission of the alleged crime the accused knew he was acting contrary to law, but did the act complained of with a view, under the influence of insane delusion, of redressing or revenging some supposed grievance or injury, or of producing some supposed public benefit?'

In answer to which question, assuming that your Lordships' inquiries are confined to those persons who labour under such partial delusions only, and are not in other respects insane, we are of opinion that, notwithstanding the party accused did the act complained of with a view, under the influence of insane delusion, of redressing or revenging some supposed grievance or injury, or of producing some public benefit, he is nevertheless punishable according to the nature of the crime committed, if he knew at the time of committing such crime that he was acting contrary to law; by which expression we understand your Lordships to mean the law of the land.

Your Lordships are pleased to inquire of us, secondly, 'What are the proper questions to be submitted to the jury, where a person alleged to be afflicted with insane delusion respecting one or more particular subjects or persons, is charged with the commission of a crime (murder, for example), and insanity is set up as a defence?' And, thirdly, 'In what terms ought the question to be left to the jury as to the prisoner's state of mind at the time when the act was committed?' And as these two questions appear to us to be more conveniently answered together, we have to submit our opinion to be, that the jurors ought to be told in all cases that every man is to be presumed to be sane, and to possess a sufficient degree of reason to be responsible for his crimes, until the contrary be proved to their satisfaction; and that *to establish a defence on the ground of insanity, it must be clearly proved that, at the time of the committing of the act, the party accused was labouring under such a defect of reason, from disease of the mind, as not to know the nature and quality of the act he was doing; or, if he did know it, that he did not know he was doing what was wrong.* [Emphasis added.] The mode of putting the latter part of the question to the jury on these occasions has generally been, whether the accused at the time of doing the act knew the difference between right and wrong: which mode, though rarely, if ever, leading to any mistake with the jury, is not, as we conceive, so accurate when put generally and in the abstract, as when put with reference to the party's knowledge of right and wrong in respect to the very act with which he is charged. If the question were to be put as to the knowledge of the accused solely and exclusively with reference to the law of the land, it might tend to confound the jury, by inducing them to believe that an actual knowledge of the law of the land was essential in order to lead to a conviction; whereas the law is administered upon the principle that everyone must be taken conclusively to know it, without proof that he does know it. If the accused was conscious that the act was one which he ought not to do, and if that act was at the same time contrary to the law of the land, he is punishable; and the usual course therefore has been to leave the question to the jury, whether the party accused had a sufficient degree of reason to know that he was doing an act that was wrong: and this course we think is correct, accompanied with such observations and explanations as the circumstances of each particular case may require.

The fourth question which your Lordships have proposed to us is this: 'If a person under an insane delusion as to existing facts, commits an offence in consequence thereof, is he thereby excused?' To which question the answer must of course depend on the nature of the delusion: but, making the same assumption as we did before, namely, that he labours under such partial delusion only, and is not in other respects insane, we think he must be considered in the same situation as to responsibility as if the facts with respect to which the delusion exists were real. For example, if under the influence of his delusion he supposes another man to be in the act of attempting to take away his life, and he kills that man, as he supposes, in self-defence, he would be exempt from punishment. If his delusion was that the deceased had inflicted a serious injury to his character and fortune, and he killed him in revenge for such supposed injury, he would be liable to punishment.

The question lastly proposed by your Lordships is: 'Can a medical man conversant with the disease of insanity, who never saw the prisoner previously to the trial, but who was present during the whole trial and the examination of all the witnesses, be asked his opinion as to the state of the prisoner's mind at the time of the commission of the alleged crime, or his opinion whether the prisoner was conscious at the time of doing the act that he was acting contrary to law, or whether he was labouring under any and what delusion at the time?' In answer thereto, we state to your Lordships, that we think the medical man, under the circumstances supposed, cannot in strictness be asked his opinion in the terms above stated, because each of those questions involves the determination of the truth of the facts deposed to, which it is for the jury to decide, and the questions are not mere questions upon a matter of science, in which such evidence is admissible. But where the facts are admitted or not disputed, and the question becomes substantially one of science only, it may be convenient to allow the question to be put in that general form, though the same cannot be insisted on as a matter of right.

Trial of Lunatics Act 1883, s 2 (as amended)

2. Special verdict where accused found guilty, but insane at date of act or omission charged, and orders thereupon

(1) Where in any indictment or information any act or omission is charged against any person as an offence, and it is given in evidence on the trial of such person for that offence that he was insane, so as not to be responsible, according to law, for his action at the time when the act was done or omission made, then, if it appears to the jury before whom such person is tried that he did the act or made the omission charged, but was insane as aforesaid at the time when he did or made the same, the jury shall return a special verdict that the accused is not guilty by reason of insanity.

(2)–(4) [Repealed.]

Criminal Procedure (Insanity and Unfitness to Plead) Act 1991

1. Acquittals on grounds of insanity

(1) A jury shall not return a special verdict under section 2 of the Trial of Lunatics Act 1883 (acquittal on ground of insanity) except on the written or oral evidence of two or more registered medical practitioners at least one of whom is duly approved.

[Section 1(2) contains provisions respecting proof of an offender's mental condition.]

If D pleads insanity, the prosecution must prove that the accused performed the act alleged. There is then a burden on the accused to prove:

(1) that he suffered from *a disease of the mind*;

(2) that the disease of the mind caused a *defect of reason* such that:

    (a) he did not know the *nature and quality of his act*; or

    (b) he *did not know it was 'wrong'*.

If the defence succeeds (unusually D bears the burden of proof and must prove that it is more likely than not that each element was present), D will be found Not Guilty by Reason of Insanity.

The court will then have 'disposal' options (since D is not guilty, he is not 'sentenced') of either a hospital order with or without restriction, supervision order or absolute discharge.

Each of the elements of the insanity defence will be examined in the following sections.

24.5.1 Disease of the mind

What types of malfunctioning of the mind will amount to a disease of the mind to constitute insanity?

In *Kemp* [1957] 1 QB at 407, [1956] 3 All ER at 253, D made an entirely motiveless and irrational attack on his wife with a hammer. He was charged with causing GBH to her with intent to murder her. It appeared that he suffered from arteriosclerosis which caused a congestion of blood in his brain. As a result, he suffered a temporary lapse of consciousness during which he made the attack. It was conceded that D did not know the nature and quality of his act and that he suffered from a defect of reason but it was argued on his behalf that this arose not from any mental disease, but from a purely physical one. It was argued that if a physical disease caused the brain cells to degenerate (as in time, it might), then it would be a disease of the mind; but until it did so, it was said, this temporary interference with the working of the brain was like a concussion or something of that sort and not a disease of the mind. Devlin J rejected this argument and held that D was suffering from a disease of the mind. He said:

> The law is not concerned with the brain but with the mind, in the sense that 'mind' is ordinarily used, the mental faculties of reason, memory and understanding. If one reads for 'disease of the mind' 'disease of the brain,' it would follow that in many cases pleas of insanity would not be established because it could not be proved that the brain had been affected in any way, either by degeneration of the cells or in any other way. In my judgment the condition of the brain is irrelevant and so is the question of whether the condition of the mind is curable or incurable, transitory or permanent.

The definition encompasses mental conditions suffered by large numbers of the population. For example, in *Sullivan* [1983] 2 All ER 673 D suffered from epilepsy which was controlled by medication. One day when visiting his 86-year-old neighbour he had a seizure and kicked a fellow visitor aged 80 around the head and body. He had no recollection of the incident. He was charged with maliciously inflicting GBH and intentionally causing GBH under ss 20 and 18 of the Offences Against the Person Act 1861. In the House of Lords, Lord Diplock accepted that epilepsy could constitute a disease of the mind for the purposes of the insanity defence. In arriving at this conclusion, his lordship made the following observation:

> My Lords, it is natural to feel reluctant to attach the label of insanity to a sufferer from psychomotor epilepsy of the kind to which the appellant was subject, even though the expression in the context of a special verdict of not guilty by reason of insanity is a technical one which includes a purely temporary and intermittent suspension of the mental faculties of reason, memory and understanding resulting from the occurrence of an epileptic fit. But the label is contained in the current statute, it has appeared in this statute's predecessors ever since 1800. It does not lie within the power of the courts to alter it. Only Parliament can do that. It has done so twice; it could do so once again.

> ≈≈≈ *Questions*
> Would any doctor describe Sullivan as insane? Should the law be permitted to be so out of step with medical understanding and definitions?

The *M'Naghten* Rules extend the definition of insanity to epileptics (*Sullivan* [1984] AC 156), diabetics (*Hennessy* [1989] 2 All ER 9) and pre-menstrual syndrome sufferers (*Smith* [1982] Crim LR 531). In *Burgess* [1991] 2 All ER 769, the Court of Appeal accepted that even someone who has been sleepwalking could be classified in law as insane. Particular emphasis was placed upon the fact that sleepwalking is a condition that can recur. Lord Lane CJ stated:

> It seems to us that if there is a danger of recurrence that may be an added reason for categorising the condition as a disease of the mind. On the other hand, the absence of the danger of recurrence is not a reason for saying that it cannot be a disease of the mind.

It has been argued that the way in which insanity is defined for the criminal law describes forms of 'manifest madness' familiar to the layperson. See A. Loughnan, *Manifest Madness: Mental Incapacity in the Criminal Law* (2012). The Law Commission, in its Discussion Paper on Insanity and Automatism (2013), proposed a new defence of Not Criminally Responsible by Reason of Recognised Medical Condition. The Commission proposal would treat all medical conditions as potentially relevant to that new defence, provided they caused a total loss of control. See section 24.9.

24.5.1.1 Intoxication as a disease of the mind?

R v Coley
[2013] EWCA Crim 223, Court of Appeal, Criminal Division

(Hughes LJ, Hickinbottom and Holroyde JJ)

In a series of three conjoined appeals, the Court of Appeal considered aspects of the insanity defence. D was charged with attempted murder. One evening he dressed up in combat gear and broke into his neighbour's house. He was carrying what was called a 'Rambo knife'. D stabbed the neighbour repeatedly before escaping the house. D then went to his own house where he was calmed by his father and waited for the police. D was heard to say that he thought he had done something very wrong. D's evidence was that he had 'blacked out' and had no recollection of the stabbing. D was a heavy user of cannabis and had been so for some time. Three psychiatrists testified that D was not suffering from an underlying mental illness but that there was a real possibility that he had suffered a 'brief psychotic episode' induced by the cannabis. The judge declined to leave the issues of insanity and automatism to the jury. D was convicted of attempted murder and appealed.

> 13. The judge ruled that insanity was not available on the evidence. He held that this was a case of voluntary intoxication, rather than insanity. The possible abnormality of mind could not be classified as insanity in law because it arose from an external and not an internal cause and was self induced. It was a temporary malfunctioning of the mind caused by the application to the body of illegal drugs, and that did not constitute insanity within the M'Naghten rules He relied upon the principled limitation imposed by the law on the extent to which voluntary intoxication can be a defence to criminal charges He also relied on the decision of this court in *R v Quick* [1973] QB 910.
>
>   14. [Counsel for D] contends that this was not a case of intoxication but rather had passed to a recognised condition of mental illness, namely a psychotic episode, no matter how transient. He contends that insofar as *Quick* holds otherwise, it is wrong and inconsistent with the law's recognition of the difference between intoxication or drunkenness *simpliciter*, on the one hand, and a disease of the mind induced by drunkenness on the other.
>
>   15. We agree that the law has long recognised the distinction which [counsel for D] identifies between intoxication and a disease of the mind induced by intoxicants. That distinction can be found in many cases. [Counsel for D] rightly identifies one of the earliest in the direction of Stephen J to the jury in *R v Davis* (1881) 14 Cox CC 563, which was approved by Lord

Birkenhead LC giving the sole speech in the famous intoxication case of *Beard* (1920) 14 Cr App R 160 at 194:

> 'But drunkenness is one thing and the diseases to which drunkenness leads are different things, and if a man by drunkenness brings on a state of disease which causes such a degree of madness, even for a time, as would have relieved him from responsibility if it had been caused in any other way, then he would not be criminally responsible'.

We also agree that, as Lord Birkenhead also made clear, insanity which is temporary is as much insanity as that which is long-lasting or permanent. *Davis* was a case of a defendant suffering (temporarily) from *delirium tremens*. That, self evidently, is not intoxication. It is, if anything, the opposite. It is a condition brought about by the protest of the brain and nerve receptors against the *removal* of intoxicants to which the body has become accustomed.

16. We do not doubt that the possible state of mind in which this defendant stabbed the man next door can properly be called a mental abnormality (or, in the nineteenth century language of *M'Naghten*, a defect of reason) which is recognised medically by psychiatrists As a matter of fact, some care may need to be exercised in discovering exactly how the expressions 'psychosis' or 'psychotic' are used, which was not much explored in the evidence in this case, save to explain that the doctors were speaking of a state in which the mind becomes detached, to a greater or lesser extent, from reality. Generally, as we understand it, these expressions are more often encountered as descriptions of symptoms than as constituting a mental illness in their own right. The underlying cause of such symptoms may vary. Well understood ones certainly include schizophrenia and bi-polar disorder, which are no doubt mental disorders or illnesses Another well known possible cause of psychotic symptoms is drug abuse, which is not a mental disorder. But with that caveat, we agree that to speak of a psychotic episode is no doubt to speak of a temporary abnormality of the brain or mind and thus of a defect of reason for the purposes of the *M'Naghten* rules.

17. However, the key thing to understand is that whether there is or is not a 'disease of the mind' for the purpose of the *M'Naghten* rules is, and has to be, a question of law and not of medical usage. It makes excellent sense for medical people to classify a great variety of conditions as recognised medically. It enables statistics to be gathered, resources allocated, diagnoses understood with reasonable consistency and treatment to be advised: see the discussion in the slightly different context of diminished responsibility in *R v Dowds* [2012] EWCA Crim 281. But the law has to cope with the synthesising of the law of insanity with the law of voluntary intoxication. The first calls for a special verdict of acquittal and very particular means of disposal. The latter is generally no defence at all, but may be relevant to whether the defendant formed a specific intention, if the offence in question is one which requires such: *DPP v Majewski* [1977] AC 443. In most, but not all, intoxication cases, the intoxication will be possibly relevant to a serious offence allegedly committed but will afford no defence to a lesser offence constituted by the same facts: for example causing grievous bodily harm with intent (s 18) and causing grievous bodily harm without such intent (s20), or of course murder and manslaughter. In the development of the common law, intoxication was historically regarded chiefly as an aggravation of offending, rather than as an excuse for it. For all the reasons explained in *Majewski*, the law refuses as a matter of policy to afford a general defence to an offender on the basis of his own voluntary intoxication. The pressing social reasons for maintaining this general policy of the law are certainly no less present in modern conditions of substance abuse than they were in the past.

18. The precise line between the law of voluntary intoxication and the law of insanity may, we do not doubt, be difficult to identify in some borderline cases. But the present case falls comfortably on the side of the line covered by voluntary intoxication. It matters not that the condition of the defendant as observed in the aftermath of his attack on the neighbour was not that of conventional intoxication, in the sense that he was not, for example, staggering or unable to speak clearly. If the

doctors were right about his state of mind, his mind was to an extent detached from reality by the direct and acute effects on it of the ingestion of cannabis Every intoxicated person has his mind affected, and to an extent disordered, by the direct and acute effects of the ingestion of intoxicants; all intoxication operates through the brain. Not infrequently it would be perfectly legitimate to say of a very drunken man that his mind had become detached from reality by the intoxication; that is obviously true, for example, of the drunken man who suffers delusions as a result of the drink, but the proposition is not limited to that case. In order to engage the law of insanity, it is not enough that there is an effect on the mind, or, in the language of the *M'Naghten* rules, a 'defect of reason'. There must also be what the law classifies as a disease of the mind. Direct acute effects on the mind of intoxicants, voluntarily taken, are not so classified. That is the distinction drawn by Stephen J in *Davis* and maintained ever since. In the slightly different legal context of diminished responsibility a similar distinction is recognised: see *R v Wood* [2008] EWCA Crim 1305. [Counsel for D's] superficially simple argument amounts to treating every 'defect of reason' as a 'disease of the mind', but that is not the law.

The Court of Appeal recognized that in some instances distinguishing between voluntary intoxication and insanity may not be easy. Even if the effect of the intoxication is to induce a state where the mind becomes detached from reality (a defect of reason), this will not necessarily qualify as insanity. In addition to a 'defect of reason' (which the Court of Appeal emphasized is a question of law), there must be what the law classifies as a 'disease of the mind'. If D's defect of reason arises only from his having voluntarily consumed intoxicants, that is not recognized by the law as a disease of the mind. However, if D's chronic substance misuse causes him to have a disease of the mind (eg alcohol dependence syndrome), and that causes a defect of reason, he will have a defence of insanity. In this case, D had suffered from a brief psychotic episode brought on by his voluntary intoxication. That was not insanity; it was not a case of a disease of the mind caused by the prolonged misuse. Much will turn on the evidence of the experts, but remember these are questions of law, not medicine or psychiatry.

Once a disease of the mind is established, the question is whether D falls into one of the two categories of insanity: not knowing the nature of the act or not knowing it was wrong.

24.5.2 Not knowing the nature and quality of the act

This limb of the insanity defence means that the defendant did not know what he was doing in a physical sense. Stephen gave the example of someone who kills another under the delusion that he is breaking a jar. Kenny gave the similarly colourful example of the individual who cuts the victim's throat under the delusion that he is cutting a loaf of bread. In both these examples, the defendant did not know that he was killing another human being and therefore did not know the nature and quality of his act.

24.5.3 Not knowing that the act is 'wrong'

Does the defendant have to prove that he did not know that the act was legally wrong or morally wrong? In *Windle* [1952] 2 All ER 1, D was convicted of murdering his wife. He was described as being of 'weak character' married to a woman 18 years older than himself and in an unhappy marriage. Medical opinion was that his wife was mentally ill and was always talking about committing suicide. D became obsessed with this and discussed it with his workmates until they were tired of hearing him, and on one occasion, just before this crime was committed, one of them said 'Give her a dozen aspirins.' D gave his wife

100 aspirin tablets. She took them and died; D told the police that he 'supposed he would be hanged for it'. At the trial, D pleaded insanity. There was some evidence that D suffered from some defect of reason or disease of the mind. The defence expert said it was a form of communicated insanity known as *folie à deux* which arises when a person is in constant attendance on a person of unsound mind. D was convicted and appealed to the Court of Criminal Appeal. The issue for the court to decide was what was meant by the term 'wrong' in the *M'Naghten* Rules. In deciding that the term 'wrong' means contrary to the law, Lord Goddard CJ stated:

> Courts of law, however, can only distinguish between that which is in accordance with the law and that which is contrary to law ... The law cannot embark on the question and it would be an unfortunate thing if it were left to juries to consider whether some particular act was morally right or wrong. The test must be whether it is contrary to law.

In *Johnson* [2007] EWCA Crim 1978, the Court of Appeal held that whilst there is an argument for extending the scope of the defence of insanity to include acts which the defendant knew to be legally wrong, but thought were morally justified, the law remained as settled in *Windle*.

It appears that Johnson was unfortunate to have had legal and medical practitioners who applied the strict letter of the law. Professor Mackay's research has revealed that in practice the narrow *Windle* definition is often ignored and little distinction is made between a lack of awareness of legal and moral wrong, concluding that: 'in many of the [cases] the "wrongness" limb was interpreted to cover whether the defendant thought his/her actions were legally/morally justified, and/or whether the actions were in perceived self defence of themselves or others, in the sense of protecting their physical or spiritual well-being'. See R. Mackay, B. Mitchell and L. Howe, 'Yet More Facts About the Insanity Plea' [2006] Crim LR 399.

Law reformers and academic commentators have repeatedly suggested that the narrow approach in *Windle* ought to be reconsidered. The Butler Committee, 'The Report of the Committee on Mentally Abnormal Offenders' (1975), Cmnd 6244, observed (at para 18.8) that:

> knowledge of the law is hardly an appropriate test on which to base ascription of responsibility to the mentally disordered. It is a very narrow ground of exemption since even persons who are grossly disturbed generally know that murder and arson are crimes.

The Law Commission also proposes changing this element of the defence in its 2013 Discussion Paper. Similarly, Professor Mackay criticizes *Windle* for its 'extremely narrow cognitive approach towards the rules ensuring that their application would be restricted to fundamental or extreme intellectual defects' in *Mental Condition Defences in the Criminal Law* (1995), p 97.

See R. D. Mackay, B. J. Mitchell and L. Howe, 'Yet More Facts about the Insanity Defence' [2006] Crim LR 399, discussing research which suggests that there continues to be a gradual increase in the use of the defence, with the 'wrongness limb' of *M'Naghten* being used more commonly than the 'nature and quality limb'.

≈≈≈ *Question*

Is the test under-inclusive because it focuses so heavily on the cognitive state of the accused (has he appreciated the nature or wrongness) rather than on whether he had the capacity to be held responsible? See V. Tadros, *Criminal Responsibility* (2005), Ch 12.

24.5.4 Insanity and self-defence

What is the law if D suffers from an insane delusion that he is being attacked by evil spirits and uses the force that he honestly believes is necessary to repel them? Can D plead self-defence when it transpires that the evil spirits are in fact police officers or is insanity his only available defence? The Court of Appeal considered this issue in *Oye* [2013] EWCA Crim 1725. As we explored in the previous chapter, self-defence has two limbs. The first is whether D genuinely believed it was necessary to use force. This is a subjective test. The second limb requires an assessment of the reasonableness of the degree of force used. While the requirement that the use of force be reasonable imports an objective evaluation, it is important to bear in mind that s 76(3) and (4) of the Criminal Justice and Immigration Act 2008 mandates that the assessment of the reasonableness of the force used is to be decided by reference to the circumstances as D believed them to be. The question that arose is whether the reasonableness of D's actions are to be judged by reference to what his insane delusions told him was necessary? The Court of Appeal has rejected this proposition.

R v Oye

[2013] EWCA Crim 1725, Court of Appeal, Criminal Division

(Davis LJ, Keith and Lewis JJ)

Davis LJ:

44. From this background, and from the provisions of s 76(3) in particular, one can now appreciate the nature of the main argument advanced on behalf of the appellant. In essence—although rather masked in the very long and elaborate written grounds—what it comes to is this. Here not only was the agreed psychiatric evidence to the effect that the appellant acted as he did thinking that he had to defend himself by reason of his insane delusions but also it was positively accepted by the Crown at trial that that was so and that he was indeed suffering from an insane delusion that evil spirits were intent on harming him. That was this the basis on which the trial proceeded. As we have said, [counsel for the Crown] also confirmed that the Crown did not dispute that in the circumstances the first limb of self-defence had been made out (or rather, could not be disproved by the prosecution). [Counsel for D] thus submitted that *in the circumstances as the appellant believed them to be* the prosecution could not, on the evidence prove that the degree of force used was unreasonable or disproportionate in those circumstances. That his belief in those circumstances derived from his insane delusion, it was submitted, was immaterial. The point was that it was his genuine, if insanely deluded belief.

45. If this is right, the potential implication for other cases are most disconcerting. It could mean that the more insanely deluded a person may be in using violence in purported self-defence, the more likely that an entire acquittal may result. It could mean that an individual who for his own benefit and protection may require hospital treatment or supervision gets none. It could mean that the public is exposed to possible further violence from an individual with a propensity for suffering insane delusions, without any intervening preventative remedies being available to the courts in the form of hospital or supervision orders. Thus, whatever the purist force in the argument, there are strong policy objections to the approach advocated on behalf of the appellant.

46. In our view it is not right.

47. The position remains, as we think plain from the provisions of s 76 of the 2008 Act, that the second limb of self-defence does include an objective element by reference to reasonableness, even if there may also be a subjective element: see in particular s 76(6) and see also the decision in *R v Keane & McGrath* [2011] EWCA Crim 2514. An insane person cannot set the standards of

reasonableness as to the degree of force used by reference to his own insanity. In truth, it makes little sense to talk of the reasonable lunatic as it did, in the context of cases on provocation, to talk of the reasonable glue-sniffer.

The Court of Appeal observed that the wording of s 76(3) could be interpreted widely so as to bear the meaning contended for by D but that this would entail changing the common law, whereas s 76(9) states that the purpose of the 2008 Act is merely to 'clarify' it. The approach in *Oye* was followed by the Court of Appeal in *Press* [2013] EWCA Crim 1849 where the defence was one of sane automatism brought about by D's PTSD from his military service. Perhaps a sensible approach is to say that if a reasonable person would have used force in the circumstances, and indeed used that amount of force actually used by D, the fact that D based his belief in the need for force on a delusion should not deny him the defence.

24.5.5 Insanity and the ECHR

Most of the modern reported cases concerning the *M'Naghten* Rules have been concerned with the question whether the accused's alleged condition was the result of a 'disease of the mind' or some other cause, see section 24.5.1, p 701.

The focus on the definition *in legal terms* with no direct correlation with medical definitions renders this aspect of the test potentially incompatible with Article 5(1)(e) ECHR where it results in D's loss of liberty.

R. D. Mackay and C. Gearty, 'On Being Insane in Jersey—The Case of *Attorney General v Jason Prior*'
[2001] Crim LR 560

1. The M'Naghten Rules and the Human Rights Act

. . . the way in which the English courts have interpreted 'disease of the mind' to include conditions such as diabetic hyperglycaemia and epilepsy does seem to run counter to the *Winterwerp* [*Winterwerp v Netherlands* (1979) 2 EHRR 387] requirement that there must be objective medical expertise supporting the fact that the accused is of unsound mind. In this connection it is of particular importance to note that the objective medical evidence that is required, relates not to whether the accused suffered from hyperglycaemia or epilepsy, but to the fact of mental disorder. A lack of such objective medical expertise supporting the fact that the accused is suffering from a true mental disorder in these diabetes and epilepsy cases seems to present an insuperable problem from a Convention perspective. Further, in the recent decision of the European Court of Human Rights in *Varbanov v. Bulgaria* [5 October 2000, Application No 31365/96], it was stated in a case dealing with the lawfulness of detention under article 5(1)(e), that 'the medical assessment must be based on the actual state of mental health of the person concerned and not solely on past events. A medical opinion cannot be seen as sufficient to justify deprivation of liberty if a significant period of time has elapsed'. This additional requirement presents a further problem in so far as the defence of insanity relates to the accused's state of mind at the time of the commission of the offence.

As far as English law is concerned there is nothing in the relevant statutory provisions under the 1964 and 1991 Acts to prevent the detention in hospital of a defendant based solely on the fact that the was legally insane at the time of the commission of the offence rather than on his present mental state. It appears that the same is true of the law in Jersey. The fact that English law has introduced flexibility of disposal under the Criminal Procedure (Insanity and Unfitness to Plead) Act 1991 fails to answer this point for two reasons. First, the 1991 Act retains compulsory detention in cases where the sentence is fixed by law, which means a court has no opportunity, but to hospitalise the defendant even in cases where this may not be appropriate. Secondly, in those cases where a court is able to choose how to dispose of a defendant found not guilty by reason of insanity, although in exercising a choice between guardianship, a supervision and treatment order or absolute discharge the court must decide which one 'is most suitable in all the circumstances of the case (see below)' the same requirement does not apply to the making of an admission order to hospital. This means that there is nothing in the statute to prevent a court making such an admission order although by the time of the trial the accused is mentally well and does not require in-patient treatment . . .

See further R. D. Mackay, 'On Being Insane in Jersey Part Two' [2002] Crim LR 728; 'On Being Insane in Jersey Part Three—The Case of the *Attorney General v O'Driscoll*' [2004] Crim LR 219.

24.5.6 Disposal of persons unfit to plead or not guilty by reason of insanity

Until 1991 a person found not guilty by reason of insanity, like a person found unfit to plead, had to be ordered to be detained indefinitely in a mental hospital. Defendants who may in truth have been not guilty by reason of insanity sometimes preferred to plead guilty rather than incur the stigma of the insanity label and indefinite detention. Cf *Sullivan* [1984] AC 156, section 24.5.1, p 701. The stigma remains but indefinite detention is no longer the necessary result of a finding either of unfitness to plead or a verdict of not guilty by reason of insanity, except in a case where the sentence is fixed by law—in practice, murder. Defendants may be more ready to raise the defence of insanity in future.

Criminal Procedure (Insanity) Act 1964
(Sections substituted by the Criminal Procedure (Insanity and Unfitness to Plead) Act 1991)

5. Powers to deal with persons not guilty by reason of insanity or unfit to plead etc

(1) This section applies where—

   (a) a special verdict is returned that the accused is not guilty by reason of insanity; or

   (b) findings have been made that the accused is under a disability and that he did the act or made the omission charged against him.

(2) The court shall make in respect of the accused—

   (a) a hospital order (with or without a restriction order);

   (b) a supervision order; or

   (c) an order for his absolute discharge.

(3) Where—

   (a) the offence to which the special verdict or the findings relate is an offence the sentence for which is fixed by law [ie murder], and

   (b) the court have power to make a hospital order,

   the court shall make a hospital order with a restriction order (whether or not they would have power to make a restriction order apart from this subsection).

24.6 Reform of the law

The Law Commission has recently undertaken a review of this area of the law and made the following proposals (Discussion Paper, *Criminal Liability: Insanity and Automatism* (2013)).

Proposal 1

10.6 We provisionally propose that the common law rules on the defence of insanity be abolished. [4.158]

Proposal 2

10.7 We provisionally propose the creation of a new statutory defence of not criminally responsible by reason of recognised medical condition. [4.159]

Conclusion 1

10.1 We provisionally conclude that there should be a defence which allows for a special verdict where the case is not proved against the accused because of his or her mental disorder as well as where it is proved because of the mental disorder. [2.34]

In short, the new law would involve the following elements:

(1) A total loss of a relevant capacity.

10.8 The party seeking to raise the new defence must adduce expert evidence that at the time of the alleged offence the defendant wholly lacked the capacity:

(i) rationally to form a judgment about the relevant conduct or circumstances;

(ii) to understand the wrongfulness of what he or she is charged with having done; or

(iii) to control his or her physical acts in relation to the relevant conduct or circumstances as a result of a qualifying recognised medical condition. [4.160]

(2) The total loss of a relevant capacity must not arise from the defendant's prior fault—if it does, the rules on intoxication govern liability.

(3) The total loss of capacity must arise from a recognized medical condition—not merely those which are mental illnesses.

(4) The recognized medical condition must be one that is a 'qualifying' recognized medical condition in law. The proposal is that certain medical conditions will not be qualifying ones (that question being one of law):

We provisionally propose that certain conditions would not qualify. These include acute intoxication or any condition which is manifested solely or principally by abnormally aggressive or seriously irresponsible behaviour. [4.161]

(5) The burden of proof would then be on the prosecution:

If sufficient evidence is adduced on which, in the opinion of the court, a properly directed jury could reasonably conclude that the defence might apply, the defence should be left to the tribunal of fact to consider. The prosecution then bears the burden of disproving the defence beyond reasonable doubt. [4.163]

(6) The verdict.

> 10.2 We provisionally conclude that there should be a special verdict in those cases of total lack of criminal capacity resulting from a recognised medical condition (provided the other criteria of the defence are met) without limiting it to mental disorders [2.63]
>
> 10.12 The jury (or magistrates) shall return a special verdict of 'not criminally responsible by reason of recognised medical condition' unless satisfied beyond reasonable doubt that the accused did not suffer a complete loss of capacity by reason of a qualifying recognised medical condition. [4.164]
>
> 10.13 We provisionally propose that the special verdict of 'not criminally responsible' may only be returned where evidence on the accused's medical condition has been received from two or more experts, one of whom is a registered medical practitioner. [4.165]

(7) Disposal.

> **Proposal 10**
>
> 10.15 We provisionally propose that the following disposals should be available following a special verdict of 'not criminally responsible by reason of recognised medical condition': a hospital order (with or without a restriction), supervision order, or an absolute discharge. [4.167]

In addition to its proposals for reform of the insanity defence, the Law Commission also made proposals as to how the defence of automatism could also be improved. The two new defences would be mutually exclusive.

THE REFORMED AUTOMATISM DEFENCE

General features

5.108 As with the defence of recognised medical condition, the reformed automatism defence would be available in respect of all offences. No distinction would be drawn between charges of basic and specific intent.

5.109 The reformed automatism defence would not lead to a special verdict. If successful, this defence would result in a simple acquittal.

5.110 It would not be available where the loss of capacity was due to a recognised medical condition. In practice, therefore, the defence of automatism is likely to be applicable in relation to automatic reflex reactions, or to transient states or circumstances; if a person's condition persists and worsens it might then qualify as a recognised medical condition.

No prior fault

5.111 If the accused's loss of capacity to control his or her actions is due to something he or she culpably did or failed to do (as provided for by the common law), then the defence of automatism should not be available to him or her. In this respect we are not proposing any change to the law.

Denial of actus reus or of mens rea?

5.112 As we have seen above, commentators do not agree as to whether the defence of automatism is a denial of the actus reus or of the mens rea, and at least one commentator would see it as a denial that there has been any voluntary act. Our proposed defence allows that there is an act but provides that D is not guilty if that act occurs in particular circumstances.

Total loss of control or loss of effective control?

5.113 As we discuss above, the essence of the defence of automatism lies in a lack of capacity to control one's actions (or inactions). The loss of ability to control the body may be accompanied by loss of consciousness, but that is not an essential feature. The next question is what degree of lack of control should be required for a defence of automatism.

5.114 We note in Appendix A that there is potential for confusion about the precise meaning of 'voluntary' and 'involuntary', so we do not propose to put the defence in terms of loss of voluntary control. (In the draft Criminal Code we thought the word 'involuntary' was best avoided, because of 'the variable use to which it tends to be put'.)

5.115 As noted, the case law on the current defence of (sane) automatism requires there to be a 'total destruction of voluntary control' on the part of the accused, even if only for a short time, in order for a plea of automatism to succeed. The draft Code referred instead to a person being deprived of 'effective control'. It did so because the authors believed that a person in the position of the defendant in *Broome v Perkins* should not be convicted. In *Broome v Perkins* the accused had suffered an episode of hypoglycaemia and had driven five or six miles in that state, driving erratically and causing a collision. The Divisional Court held that the defence of automatism was not open to him because on the evidence he must have had control for at least some of the journey. Under our proposals someone in this position would rely on the defence of not criminally responsible by reason of recognised medical condition.

5.116 Was the draft Criminal Code right to shift the requirement from total loss of control to loss of effective control? Ashworth has written that in this respect the draft Code 'rightly recognizes that total absence of control should not be required, but it therefore leaves us with a test dependent on a judgment of degree and value ("effective"), and does so without identifying the relevance of the defendant's capacity rather than awareness and "choice"'. We noted above that the cases seemed to set a higher standard where the offence was a driving offence, and that this might be for reasons of policy, namely, the need to avoid the risk of dangerous drivers being acquitted. That risk was mitigated by requiring the driver to show total loss of control. If, however, the requirement were only for loss of the capacity for effective control, then it would be a more flexible standard for the courts to define, one which could accommodate a greater variety of situations We suspect the courts would interpret the notion of loss of effective control as amounting to something close to total loss of control in driving cases, but the more flexible standard would not require them to do so in every case.

5.117 There is, however, a risk that a defence in terms where the accused says he or she was deprived of 'effective control' will lead to litigation about what amounts to 'effective control'. That will have significant implications in cost and delay at trial.

Conclusion

5.118 Our provisional conclusion is that the defence of automatism should require the accused to have a total loss of capacity to control his or her physical actions We are not limiting the new defence to cases of unconsciousness.

The Commission's new scheme for the defences is represented in Figure 24.1.

≈≈ **Question**
Would these proposals represent an improvement on the current law?

Figure 24.1 Steps a court would take where a defendant enters a plea by reason of a recognized medical condition

24.7 Diminished responsibility

For the purposes of the law of murder only, a much broader category of mental abnormality may, since the Homicide Act 1957, afford a defence. See section 8.3, p 192.

FURTHER READING

A. Duff, 'Fitness to Plead and Fair Trials' [1994] Crim LR 419

P. Fennell, 'The Criminal Procedure (Insanity and Unfitness to Plead) Act 1991' (1992) 55 MLR 547

D. Grubin, 'What Constitutes Unfitness to Plead' [1993] Crim LR 748

A. Loughnan, 'Of Blurred Boundaries and Prior Fault: Insanity, Automatism, and Intoxication' in A. Reed and M. Bohlander, *General Defences in Criminal Law* (2014)

R. D. Mackay, *Mental Condition Defences in Criminal Law* (1998)

R. D. Mackay, 'The Insanity Defence in Operation' (2014) 65 NILQ 153

R. D. Mackay and W. Brookbanks, 'Protecting the Unfit to Plead' [2005] JR 173

R. D. Mackay and G. Kearns, 'The Trial of the Facts and Unfitness to Plead' [1997] Crim LR 644

R. D. Mackay and G. Kearns, 'More Facts(s) about the Insanity Defence' [1999] Crim LR 714

R. D. Mackay and M. Reuber, 'Epilepsy and the Defence of Insanity—Time for a Change' [2007] Crim LR 782

R. D. Mackay, B. Mitchell and L. Howe, 'A Continued Upturn in Unfitness to Plead—More Disability in Relation to the Trial under the 1991 Act' [2007] Crim LR 530

S White, 'The Criminal Procedure (Insanity and Unfitness to Plead) Act 1991' [1992] Crim LR 4

W. Wilson et al, 'Violence, Sleepwalking and the Criminal Law' [2005] Crim LR 601 and 614

25

Intoxication

Intoxication:

Involuntary intoxication:

If D pleads that he was involuntarily intoxicated at the time of the offence and that led to a lack of mens rea at the time of the actus reus, then unless the prosecution disprove that, D should be acquitted of the crime if it is one of mens rea.

Voluntary intoxication:

If D pleads that he was voluntarily intoxicated:

(1) and that he lacked mens rea because of that intoxication, then unless the prosecution can disprove that he should be acquitted of any crime of 'specific intent';

(2) he should be convicted of any 'basic intent' crime if the *drug* which led to his intoxication was one *of a dangerous nature* (ie one known to create states of unpredictability or aggression) even if he lacked mens rea when committing the offence.

Some of the controversies that will be examined in this chapter include:

(1) the extent to which intoxication can negate criminal liability;

(2) the difference between crimes of basic and specific intent;

(3) the relevance of a substance being one that is considered by the law to be dangerous.

25.1 Introduction

Many offences are committed by people who are intoxicated by alcohol or other drugs. Many of these offences would not have been committed if the offender had not been intoxicated. Alcohol weakens the restraints and inhibitions which normally govern a person's conduct. It also impairs perception and judgement so that a drunken person is liable to be involved in incidents which would not happen if he were sober. See, generally, G. Dingwall, *Alcohol and Crime* (2005) and J. Herring and C. Regan, *Intoxication and Society: Problematic Pleasures of Drugs and Alcohol* (2012).

It has never been a defence for a person simply to say, however truthfully, that he would not have committed the offence if he had not been drunk—that 'it was the drink that did it'. If that is all, his intoxicated condition is, at most, a matter to be taken into account in imposing sentence. The fact that he had been drinking may sometimes mitigate the gravity of the offence, and sometimes—as in dangerous driving—it may aggravate it.

Special rules of substantive law are generally accepted to be necessary to deal with those cases in which the definition of the offence includes a subjective mental element and the defendant claims that he lacked that mental element because he was intoxicated—that is, he failed to foresee a result which he would have foreseen had he been sober or he made a mistake of fact which he would not have made when sober. In such cases if he is, or may be, telling the truth and the mistake or failure to foresee negatives the mens rea of the offence, the prosecution has not proved its case. However, the inquiry into the defendant's blameworthiness must proceed further in such cases. If the intoxication is 'involuntary'—for example, the defendant was unaware that his lemonade had been heavily laced with vodka—he will be acquitted. Where the intoxication is voluntary, the law has never allowed this defence in all cases. With voluntary intoxication a distinction is made between:

- offences requiring 'specific intent'. Intoxication is an answer to these charges if because of the intoxication D lacked mens rea;

- offences of basic intent. The defendant will be convicted of the offence of basic intent even though the mental element, which must be proved in the case of all sober defendants, has not been proved against him. This is known, after the leading case, as 'the *Majewski* approach';

- offences requiring only negligence as a fault element. Mistakes caused by D's voluntary intoxication are not an answer to offences requiring negligence because they amount to a failure to comply with the standard of conduct which the law requires. The reasonable, prudent person is not voluntarily intoxicated. *A fortiori*, such mistakes and failures are not an answer to offences of strict liability, not requiring fault.

25.1.1 Structured approach to the issues

As the very basic outline in Figure 25.1 demonstrates, cases involving intoxication may usefully be approached by considering several questions in sequence.

(1) Is the intoxication *voluntary or involuntary*? If involuntary, and D lacks mens rea at the time of the actus reus, D is to be acquitted of any mens rea crime. But a drunken intent is still an intent, so the negation of mens rea must be total.

(2) If the intoxication is voluntary, the next issue is whether the crime charged is one of '*specific*' intent or '*basic*' intent. The courts have failed to distinguish these with any principled precision, but as a working rule, crimes with mens rea of intent are specific intent and those of recklessness or negligence are basic intent. If the crime is one of specific intent and D was voluntarily intoxicated so that he lacked the mens rea for the crime, he should be acquitted of that crime.

(3) If the intoxication is voluntary and the crime is one of basic intent, the next question is whether the *drug* involved is one *of a dangerous nature* (ie one known to create states of unpredictability or aggression). If so, in assessing D's guilt, the jury or magistrates should ignore his intoxication in considering whether he was reckless as to the harm caused/whether he was negligent as to the harm caused. If the drug is one of a non-dangerous form (eg a soporific drug such as valium) D will be guilty of the crime charged if he was reckless as to becoming unpredictable or aggressive by taking that drug.

The operation of these questions which focus on the three key distinctions drawn in the law may be illustrated by a hypothetical case. D stabbed his friend, V, believing, because he was intoxicated, that he was stabbing a theatrical dummy. Suppose that V had survived and D had been charged with wounding with intent to cause GBH, contrary to s 18 of the Offences Against the Person Act 1861 (OAPA). The intoxication was voluntary—it was not a case of D's drink being laced or of D taking prescribed medicines in accordance with the medical instructions. The crime under s 18 involves an 'intent to cause GBH' and is a specific intent

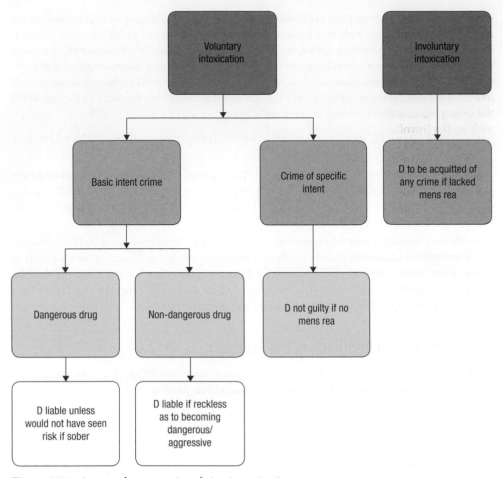

Figure 25.1 Approach to cases involving intoxication

crime and, as D obviously had no such intent, he must be acquitted. If D, however, is charged instead with unlawful and malicious wounding, contrary to s 20 OAPA, his voluntary intoxication is no excuse to s 20 which is a basic intent crime. Section 20 requires proof that the accused was aware that his act might cause physical harm to a person but that requirement is not a specific intent. D, believing that he was stabbing a dummy, was not aware that his act might cause physical harm to any person: but, since his lack of awareness arose from voluntary intoxication, he may be liable to conviction. The final question is whether the intoxicant D took was one commonly known to create states of unpredictability or aggression. If so (eg if the drug was alcohol, LSD, etc), D will be liable for the s 20 offence. This approach follows from the decision in *Majewski*, section 25.3, p 718.

25.2 Voluntary and involuntary intoxication

In most cases the intoxication will be entirely voluntary. Kenny gives a vivid illustration (also referred to by Lord Denning in *Gallagher* [1961] 3 All ER 299, section 25.6, p 738) of a nurse who got so drunk at a christening that she put the baby on the fire in mistake for a log of wood. She was clearly capable of forming an intent to make up the fire so she must have been *capable* of forming an intent to kill, however improbable it was that she would do so. Equally clearly, she did not form that intention and so must be acquitted of murder. Being voluntarily intoxicated, she would have no defence to a charge of manslaughter or any other offence of basic intent. If she had merely dropped the supposed log, causing the baby a slight injury, she would have had no defence to a charge of assault occasioning actual bodily harm (also basic intent). Suppose, however, that her intoxication was due, not to her too liberal indulgence in the champagne, but to her orange juice having been heavily laced, without her knowledge, with vodka (involuntary intoxication). Even if she was *capable* of committing an assault, is there any ground for convicting her of that offence? Or of manslaughter, if the baby died as a result of being dropped, or put on the fire?

Hughes LJ in *Coley* [2013] EWCA Crim 223 held that where D knew of the effects of mixing prescription medication with alcohol, this would constitute voluntary intoxication despite the fact that the drug had been medically prescribed.

> ∿ **Questions**
> Should D's intoxication be regarded as involuntary where he knew he was drinking alcohol, but underestimated the strength of the alcohol? In *Allen* [1988] Crim LR 698, the Court of Appeal held that ignorance of the precise strength of the alcohol being consumed does not make drinking involuntary so long as D knew he was consuming alcohol. Do you agree with this approach?

See J. Horder, 'Pleading Involuntary Lack of Capacity' (1993) 52 CLJ 298; R. Smith and L. Clements, 'Involuntary Intoxication, the Threshold of Inhibition and the Instigation of Crime' (1995) 46 NILQ 210.

25.3 'Specific' and 'basic' intent

The distinction between the two categories has a profound importance and yet has never been adequately explained by the courts.

The distinction drawn by the courts could be interpreted as meaning:

(1) that all offences for which the mens rea is predominantly that of intention or knowledge are to be treated as specific intent crimes, and all offences for which the predominant fault element is of recklessness, or negligence or in which liability is strict, are basic intent offences; or

(2) that specific intent offences are those for which the mens rea goes beyond the immediate actus reus. For example, in a crime such as causing criminal damage with intent or recklessness to endanger life, the mens rea goes beyond the immediate act of causing criminal damage. There is an ulterior intent, and the offence is therefore one of specific intent. This approach means that offences for which the mens rea involves nothing more than recklessness can still be categorized as ones of specific intent. For example, reckless criminal damage being reckless as to whether life is endangered; or

(3) that crimes of specific intent are those for which the defendant must act 'purposively'.

The leading authority on the distinction between specific and basic intent is *Majewski*. As the following extract will demonstrate, it is not entirely clear which of the approaches outlined above was favoured by a majority of the House of Lords.

Director of Public Prosecutions v Majewski
[1976] UKHL 2, House of Lords

(Lord Elwyn-Jones LC, Lords Diplock, Simon of Glaisdale, Kilbrandon, Salmon, Edmund-Davies and Russell of Killowen)

The appellant was convicted on three counts of assault occasioning actual bodily harm and on three counts of assault on a police constable in the execution of his duty. The evidence which was largely undisputed showed that the offences were committed in the Bull public house in Basildon and that during a fierce struggle Majewski shouted at the police: 'You pigs, I'll kill you all, you fucking pigs, you bastards.' He had consumed large quantities of drugs and alcohol shortly before the offences. He was a drug addict, and admitted that he had previously 'gone paranoid' but said that this was the first time he had 'completely blanked out'. He claimed not to have known what he was doing. The medical evidence suggested that such a state, called 'pathological intoxication', was possible but unlikely: it was quite possible for an intoxicated person to know what he was doing at the time and to suffer an 'amnesic patch' later. Judge Petre directed the jury to 'ignore the subject of drink and drugs as being in any way a defence' to the assaults. An appeal to the House of Lords was unanimously dismissed.

Lord Elwyn-Jones LC:

. . . If a man consciously and deliberately takes alcohol and drugs not on medical prescription, but in order to escape from reality, to go 'on a trip', to become hallucinated, whatever the description may be, and thereby disables himself from taking the care he might otherwise take and as a result by his subsequent actions causes injury to another—does our criminal law enable him to say that because he did not know what he was doing he lacked both intention and recklessness and accordingly is entitled to an acquittal?

Originally the common law would not and did not recognise self-induced intoxication as an excuse. Lawton LJ [[1975] 3 All ER 296 at 305, 306] spoke of the 'merciful relaxation' to that rule which was introduced by the judges during the 19th century, and he added:

'Although there was much reforming zeal and activity in the 19th century Parliament never once considered whether self-induced intoxication should be a defence generally to a criminal charge. It would have been a strange result if the merciful relaxation of a strict rule of law had ended, without any Parliamentary intervention, by whittling it away to such an extent that the more drunk a man became, provided he stopped short of making himself insane, the better chance he had of an acquittal . . . The common law rule still applied but there were exceptions to it which Lord Birkenhead LC [DPP v Beard] tried to define by reference to specific intent.'

There are, however, decisions of eminent judges in a number of Commonwealth cases in Australia and New Zealand (but generally not in Canada nor in the United States), as well as impressive academic comment in this country, to which we have been referred, supporting the view that it is illogical and inconsistent with legal principle to treat a person who of his own choice and volition has taken drugs and drink, even though he thereby creates a state in which he is not conscious of what he is doing, any differently from a person suffering from the various medical conditions like epilepsy or diabetic coma and who is regarded by the law as free from fault. However, our courts have for a very long time regarded in quite another light the state of self-induced intoxication. The authority which for the last half century has been relied on in this context has been the speech of Lord Birkenhead LC in *DPP v Beard* [[1920] AC 479 at 494, [1920] All ER Rep 21 at 25]:

'Under the law of England as it prevailed until early in the nineteenth century voluntary drunkenness was never an excuse for criminal misconduct; and indeed the classic authorities broadly assert that voluntary drunkenness must be considered rather an aggravation than a defence. This view was in terms based upon the principle that a man who by his own voluntary act debauches and destroys his will power shall be no better situated in regard to criminal acts than a sober man.'

Lord Birkenhead LC made an historical survey of the way the common law from the 16th century on dealt with the effect of self-induced intoxication on criminal responsibility. This indicates how, from 1819 on, the judges began to mitigate the severity of the attitude of the common law in such cases as murder and serious violent crime when the penalties of death or transportation applied or where there was likely to be sympathy for the accused, as in attempted suicide. Lord Birkenhead LC [[1920] AC 479 at 499, 500, [1920] All ER Rep 21 at 27, 28] concluded that (except in cases where insanity was pleaded) the decisions he cited:

> 'establish that where a specific intent is an essential element in the offence, evidence of a state of drunkenness rendering the accused incapable of forming such an intent should be taken into consideration in order to determine whether he had in fact formed the intent necessary to consti- tute the particular crime. If he was so drunk that he was incapable of forming the intent required he could not be convicted of a crime which was committed only if the intent was proved. . . . In a charge of murder based upon intention to kill or to do grievous bodily harm, if the jury are satis- fied that the accused was, by reason of his drunken condition, incapable of forming the intent to kill or to do grievous bodily harm . . . he cannot be convicted of murder. But nevertheless unlawful homicide has been committed by the accused, and consequently he is guilty of unlawful homicide without malice aforethought, and that is manslaughter: per Stephen J in *Doherty's* case [(1887) 16 Cox CC 306 at 307]. [He concluded the passage:] the law is plain beyond all question that in cases falling short of insanity a condition of drunkenness at the time of committing an offence causing death can only, when it is available at all, have the effect of reducing the crime from murder to manslaughter.'

From this it seemed clear—and this is the interpretation which the judges have placed on the decision during the ensuing half-century—that it is only in the limited class of cases requiring proof of specific intent that drunkenness can exculpate. Otherwise in no case can it exempt completely from criminal liability . . .

[His lordship discussed *A-G for Northern Ireland v Gallagher* (section 25.6, p 738) and *Bratty v A-G for Northern Ireland* (section 24.4.1, p 693).]

The seal of approval is clearly set on the passage of the *Beard* decision. In no case has the general principle of English law as described by Lord Denning in *Gallagher's* case and exposed again in *Bratty's* case [[1963] AC 386, [1961] 3 All ER 523] been overruled in this House and the question now to be determined is whether it should be.

I do not for my part regard that general principle as either unethical or contrary to the principles of natural justice. If a man of his own volition takes a substance which causes him to cast off the restraints of reason and conscience, no wrong is done to him by holding him answerable criminally for any injury he may do while in that condition. His course of conduct in reducing himself by drugs and drink to that condition in my view supplies the evidence of mens rea, of guilty mind certainly sufficient for crimes of basic intent. It is a reckless course of conduct and recklessness is enough to constitute the necessary mens rea in assault cases: see *Venna* [[1975] 3 All ER 788 at 793] per James LJ. The drunkenness is itself an intrinsic, an integral part of the crime, the other part being the evidence of the unlawful use of force against the victim. Together they add up to criminal recklessness. On this I adopt the conclusion of Stroud [(1920) 36 LQR at 273] that:

> 'It would be contrary to all principle and authority to suppose that drunkenness (and what is true of drunkenness is equally true of intoxication by drugs) can be a defence for crime in general on the ground that "a person cannot be convicted of a crime unless the *mens was rea*". By allowing himself to get drunk and thereby putting himself in such a condition as to be no longer amenable to the law's commands, a man shows such regardlessness as amounts to mens rea for the pur- pose of all ordinary crimes.'

This approach is in line with the American Model Code [s 2.08(2)]:

> 'When recklessness establishes an element of the offence, if the actor, due to self-induced intoxi-cation, is unaware of a risk of which he would have been aware had he been sober, such unaware-ness is immaterial.'

Acceptance generally of intoxication as a defence (as distinct from the exceptional cases where some additional mental element above that of ordinary mens rea has to be proved) would in my view under-mine the criminal law and I do not think that it is enough to say, as did counsel for the appellant, that we can rely on the good sense of the jury or of magistrates to ensure that the guilty are convicted. It may well be that Parliament will at some future time consider, as I think it should, the recommenda-tion in the Butler Committee Report on Mentally Abnormal Offenders [(1975) Cmnd 6244] that a new offence of 'dangerous intoxication' should be created. But in the meantime it would be irresponsible to abandon the common law rule, as 'mercifully relaxed', which the courts have followed for a century and a half . . .

The final question that arises is whether s 8 of the Criminal Justice Act 1967 has had the result of abrogating or qualifying the common law rule. That section emanated from the consideration the Law Commission gave to the decision of the House in *DPP v Smith* [[1961] AC 290, [1960] 3 All ER 161]. Its purpose and effect was to alter the law of evidence about the presumption of intention to produce the reasonable and probable consequences of one's acts. It was not intended to change the common law rule. In referring to 'all the evidence' it meant all the *relevant* evidence. But if there is a substantive rule of law that in crimes of basic intent, the factor of intoxication is irrelevant (and such I hold to be the substantive law), evidence with regard to it is quite irrelevant. Section 8 does not abrogate the substantive rule and it cannot properly be said that the continued application of that rule contravenes the section. For these reasons, my conclusion is that the certified question should be answered Yes, that there was no misdirection in this case and that the appeal should be dismissed.

My noble and learned friends and I think it may be helpful if we give the following indication of the general lines on which in our view the jury should be directed as to the effect on the criminal respon-sibility of the accused of drink or drugs or both, whenever death or physical injury to another person results from something done by the accused for which there is no legal justification and the offence with which the accused is charged is manslaughter or assault at common law or the statutory offence of unlawful wounding under s 20, or of assault occasioning actual bodily harm under s 47 of the Offences against the Person Act 1861.

In the case of these offences it is no excuse in law that, because of drink or drugs which the accused himself had taken knowingly and willingly, he had deprived himself of the ability to exercise self-control, to realise the possible consequences of what he was doing or even to be conscious that he was doing it. As in the instant case, the jury may be properly instructed that they 'can ignore the sub-ject of drink or drugs as being in any way a defence to' charges of this character.

[**Lord Diplock** said that he agreed with the speech of Lord Elwyn-Jones LC.]

Lord Simon:

. . . The best description of 'specific intent' in this sense that I know is contained in the judgment of Fauteux J in *George* [(1960) 128 CCC 289 at 301]:

> 'In considering the question of mens rea, a distinction is to be made between (i) intention as applied to acts considered in relation to their purposes and (ii) intention as applied to acts apart from their purposes. A general intent attending the commission of an act is, in some cases, the only intent required to constitute the crime while, in others, there must be, in addition to that general intent, a specific intent attending the purpose for the commission of the act.'

In short, where the crime is one of 'specific intent' the prosecution must in general prove that the purpose for the commission of the act extends to the intent expressed or implied in the definition of the crime . . .

As I have ventured to suggest, there is nothing unreasonable or illogical in the law holding that a mind rendered self-inducedly insensible (short of *M'Naghten* [*M'Naghten's case* (1843) 10 Cl & Fin 200, [1843–60] All ER Rep 229 [section 24.5, p 698] insanity), through drink or drugs, to the nature of a prohibited act or to its probable consequences is as wrongful a mind as one which consciously contemplates the prohibited act and foresees its probable consequences (or is reckless whether they ensue). The latter is all that is required by way of mens rea in a crime of basic intent. But a crime of specific intent requires something more than contemplation of the prohibited act and foresight of its probable consequences. The mens rea in a crime of specific intent requires proof of a purposive element. This purposive element either exists or not; it cannot be supplied by saying that the impairment of mental powers by self-induced intoxication is its equivalent, for it is not. So that the 19th century development of the law as to the effect of self-induced intoxication on criminal responsibility is juristically entirely acceptable; and it need be a matter of no surprise that Stephen stated it without demur or question.

[**Lord Kilbrandon** said that he agreed with the speech of Lord Elwyn-Jones.]

Lord Salmon:

. . . [A]n assault committed accidentally is not a criminal offence. A man may, eg, thoughtlessly throw out his hand to stop a taxi, or open the door of his car and accidentally hit a passer-by and perhaps unhappily cause him quite serious bodily harm. In such circumstances, the man who caused the injury would be liable civilly for damages but clearly he would have committed no crime. It is, I agree, possible to commit assault and other crimes of violence recklessly, not caring whether or not what you do causes injury. There are no doubt some contexts, eg, commercial contracts in which the words 'very carelessly' and 'recklessly' are synonymous, but I do not think that this is usually true in the context of the criminal law, except perhaps in the case of manslaughter. I do not, however, wish to take up your Lordships' time in discussing this topic further for it is hardly relevant to the question before this House.

There are many cases in which injuries are caused by pure accident. I have already given examples of such cases: to these could be added injuries inflicted during an epileptic fit, or whilst sleep-walking, and in many other ways. No one, I think, would suggest that any such case could give rise to criminal liability.

It is argued on behalf of the appellant that a man who makes a vicious assault may at the material time have been so intoxicated by drink or drugs that he no more knew what he was doing than did any of the persons in the examples I have given and that therefore he too cannot be found guilty of a criminal offence.

To my mind there is a very real distinction between such a case and the examples I have given. A man who by voluntarily taking drink and drugs gets himself into an aggressive state in which he does not know what he is doing and then makes a vicious assault can hardly say with any plausibility that what he did was a pure accident which should render him immune from any criminal liability. Yet this in effect is precisely what counsel for the appellant contends that the learned judge should have told the jury.

A number of distinguished academic writers support this contention on the ground of logic. As I understand it, the argument runs like this. Intention, whether special or basic (or whatever fancy name you choose to give it), is still intention. If voluntary intoxication by drink or drugs can, as it admittedly can, negative the special or specific intention necessary for the commission of crimes such as murder and theft, how can you justify in strict logic the view that it cannot negative a basic intention, eg, the intention to commit offences such as assault and unlawful wounding? The answer is that in strict logic this view cannot be justified. But this is the view that has been adopted by the common law of England, which is founded on common sense and experience rather than strict logic. There is no case in the 19th century when the courts were relaxing the harshness of the law in relation to the effect of drunkenness on criminal liability in which the courts ever went so far as to suggest that drunkenness, short of drunkenness producing insanity, could ever exculpate a man from any offence other than one which required some special or specific intent to be proved . . .

[**Lord Edmund-Davies** and **Lord Russell of Killowen** made speeches dismissing the appeal.]

Appeal dismissed

Although there is no doubt that *Majewski* is the leading case on the distinction between crimes of basic and specific intent, it is not entirely clear what the House of Lords decided. A number of different approaches were posited in the judgments of the various Law Lords. In his judgment, for example, Lord Simon suggested that the distinction between specific and basic intent crimes is that, 'the mens rea in a crime of specific intent requires proof of a purposive element'. Lord Elwyn-Jones LC, however, stated that specific intent crimes are those crimes that cannot be committed recklessly. Under this approach, what is determinative is whether the predominant mens rea of the offence in question is intention, knowledge or dishonesty. If so, the offence is one of specific intent. If some lesser mens rea, such as recklessness, suffices, then the offence is one of basic liability. This latter approach, the 'predominant mens rea approach', was generally considered to represent the applicable test until an important decision of the Court of Appeal entitled *Heard*, in which the court offered a fundamental reinterpretation of *Majewski* based on Lord Simon's speech in that case.

R v Heard
[2007] EWCA Crim 125, Court of Appeal, Criminal Division

(Hughes LJ, Henriques and Field JJ)

D, while drunk, exposed his penis and rubbed it against the thigh of a police officer. D had no recollection of the incident. D relied on his voluntary intoxication as negating his mens rea of an intention to touch for the purposes of s 3(1)(a) of the Sexual Offences Act 2003. The trial judge ruled that the intentional touching element of the offence required proof of a basic intent, and that it followed that voluntary intoxication was not a defence. The offence is defined as follows:

3. Sexual assault

   (1) A person (A) commits an offence if—

      (a) he intentionally touches another person (B),

      (b) he touching is sexual,

      (c) does not consent to the touching, and

      (d) does not reasonably believe that B consents.

   (2) Whether a belief is reasonable is to be determined having regard to all the circumstances, including any steps A has taken to ascertain whether B consents.

   (3) Sections 75 and 76 apply to an offence under this section.

Applying the established interpretation of *Majewski*, on a charge such as that under s 3 with the requirement of an 'intentional' touching, it was arguable at least that the crime would be one of specific intent. The effect of that categorization would be that if D sought to rely on his voluntary intoxication to deny that he had the mens rea for the offence, the Crown would be obliged to prove that he formed the intent, despite his intoxication. The circumstances where a sufficient degree of intoxication would arise to negative mens rea, certainly in cases of intoxication by alcohol, would be limited in practice.

[Hughes LJ set out the facts and the judge's direction to the jury:]

9. The appellant contends that . . . the offence is . . . one requiring proof of a specific intent and the jury should have been directed to consider whether the drink which the appellant had taken meant that he did not have the intention to touch. The Crown on the other hand contends that the offence is one of basic intent and that evidence of self-induced intoxication is simply irrelevant. . . .

11. In a little more detail, Mr Stern's argument for the appellant runs like this:

i) The correct reading of *DPP v Majewski* and subsequent cases is that voluntary intoxication is incapable of being a defence only where recklessness suffices as the mens rea of the offence; it is such offences which are properly described as those of 'basic intent'.

ii) The present offence is one for which reckless touching will not suffice; only intentional touching will do.

iii) Therefore this is an offence of specific and not of basic intent. Voluntary intoxication is a relevant factor to consider when asking whether the appellant did or did not have the intention to touch required by the section.

12. For the Crown, Mr Perry's argument, similarly summarised, runs as follows:

iv) The *Majewski* concept of crimes of basic intent, in which voluntary intoxication cannot be advanced as a defence, is not limited to those where recklessness suffices; the correct distinction is between crimes requiring ordinary intent (where voluntary intoxication cannot be relied upon), and those requiring specific or purposive intent (where it can).

v) There is however no universally logical test for distinguishing between crimes in which voluntary intoxication can be advanced as a defence and those in which it cannot; there is a large element of policy; categorisation is achieved on an offence by offence basis.

vi) Before the Sexual Offences Act 2003, indecent assault could only be committed by intentional touching; yet voluntary intoxication was not a defence, as it was also not to rape. The decisions of *Woods* (1982) 74 Cr App R 312 and *R v C* [1992] Crim LR 642 are relied upon. The new Act was not intended to change the law in this respect; on the contrary its object was to improve the protection of potential victims of sexual interference. To treat sexual assault as a crime of specific intent would mean treating similarly the very many other sexual offences created by the 2003 Act which are structured in the same way, including rape (section 1), assault by penetration (section 2) and most of the child sex offences. In sexual assault (and in rape and other similar offences) a defendant's belief in consent is said by the statute to provide a defence only if it is reasonable, and that must mean that a drunken belief cannot be relied upon.

vii) Where it applies, the rule that voluntary intoxication cannot be relied upon is a rule of substantive law; accordingly in sexual assault and other similarly structured sexual offences under the 2003 Act voluntarily taken intoxicants are simply to be ignored for all purposes when considering whether the offence has been committed.

viii) Although the requirement that the touching be intentional means that it must be deliberate, if accident is suggested the question whether what happened was accidental or not must be answered as if the defendant had been sober, even though he was not.

Discussion

. . .

14. The first thing to say is that it should not be supposed that every offence can be categorised simply as either one of specific intent or of basic intent. So to categorise an offence may conceal the truth that different elements of it may require proof of different states of mind. In the law of rape, as it stood immediately before the passing of the Sexual Offences Act 2003, rape was sexual intercourse with a woman who did not in fact consent, by a man who either knew she did not or was reckless as to whether she did. No-one doubted that the act of intercourse could only be committed intentionally. But when it came to the defendant's state of mind as to the woman's lack of consent, either knowledge or recklessness sufficed for guilt: section 1 Sexual Offences (Amendment) Act 1976. Many other examples of the point could be cited. The current legislative practice of itemising separately different elements of offences created by statute, which is much exhibited in the Sexual Offences Act 2003, may occasionally have the potential to complicate matters for a jury, but it demonstrates the impossibility of fitting an offence into a single pigeon-hole, whether it be labelled 'basic intent' or 'specific intent'.

15. The offence of sexual assault, with which this case is concerned, is an example. The different elements of the offence, identified in paragraphs (a) to (d) of section 3, do not call for proof of the same state of mind. Element (a), the touching, must by the statute be intentional. Element (b), the sexual nature of the touching, takes one to section 78. By that section the primary question is a purely objective one, as set out in s 78(a). If, however, the act itself is objectively equivocal, the *purpose* of the Defendant may be a relevant consideration, as provided by s 78(b), and that must be a reference to his own (subjective) purpose. The state of mind in a defendant which must be proved in relation to element (c), the absence of consent, is expressly stipulated by element (d) and by s 3(2), and the stipulation is in terms which make it clear that the test is substantially objective; a belief in consent which was induced largely by drink would be most unlikely to be reasonable. It is accordingly of very limited help to attempt to label the offence of sexual assault, as a whole, one of either basic or specific intent, because the state of mind which must be proved varies with the issue. For this reason also, it is unsafe to reason (as at one point the Crown does) directly from the state of mind required in relation to consent to the solution to the present question.

16. Since it is only the touching which must be intentional, whilst the sexual character of the touching is, unless equivocal, to be judged objectively, and a belief in consent must be objectively reasonable, we think that it will only be in cases of some rarity that the question which we are posed in this appeal will in the end be determinative of the outcome.

17. We do not think that it determines this appeal. On the evidence the Appellant plainly did intend to touch the policeman with his penis. That he was drunk may have meant either:

ix) That he was disinhibited and did something which he would not have done if sober; and/or

 x) That he did not remember it afterwards.

But neither of those matters (if true) would destroy the intentional character of his touching. In the homely language employed daily in directions to juries in cases of violence and sexual misbehaviour, 'a drunken intent is still an intent.' And for the memory to blot out what was intentionally done is common, if not perhaps quite as common as is the assertion by offenders that it has done so. In the present case, what the appellant did and said at the time, and said in interview afterwards, made it perfectly clear that this was a case of drunken intentional touching. Although the Judge directed the jury that drink was no defence, he also directed the jury that it must be sure that the touching was deliberate. That amounted to a direction that for conviction the appellant's mind (drunken or otherwise) had to have gone with his physical action of touching. Mr Stern realistically conceded that he could not hope to improve upon that direction.

18. We do not attempt the notoriously unrealistic task of foreseeing every possible permutation of human behaviour which the future may reveal. But it nevertheless seems to us that in the great majority of cases of alleged sexual assault, or of comparable sexual crimes, as in the present case, the mind will have gone with the touching, penetration or other prohibited act, albeit in some cases a drunken mind.

19. It is, however, possible to envisage the exceptional case in which there is a real possibility that the intoxication was such that the mind did not go with the physical act. In *R v Lipman* (1969) 55 Cr App R 600 the defendant contended that when he killed his victim by stuffing bedclothes down her throat he was under the illusion, induced by hallucinatory drugs voluntarily taken, that he was fighting for his life against snakes. If an equivalent state of mind were (assumedly genuinely) to exist in some-one who committed an act of sexual touching or penetration, the question which arises in this appeal would be directly in point.

20. A different situation was also put to us in the course of argument. Its formulation probably owes much to Professor Ormerod's current edition of *Smith and Hogan's Criminal Law* (11th edition [2005], page 624). It is that of the intoxicated person whose control of his limbs is unco-ordinated or impaired, so that in consequence he stumbles or flails about against another person, touching him or her in a way which, objectively viewed, is sexual—for example because he touches a woman on her private parts. Can such a person be heard to say that what happened was other than deliberate when, if he had been sober, it would not have happened?

21. In the present case the Judge directed the jury that drunkenness was not a defence, although coupling with it the direction that the touching must be deliberate. Whether or not the jury's deci-sion was likely to be that the appellant had acted intentionally (albeit drunkenly), the Judge had to determine whether or not it was necessary for the jury to investigate the suggestion that the appellant was so drunk that his mind did not go with his act. That question may also face judges and juries, as it seems to us, in many cases where a defendant wishes to contend that he was thus intoxicated, and scientific or medical evidence can say no more than that in an extreme case drink or drugs are capable of inducing a state of mind in which a person believes that what he is doing is something different to what he in fact does. In those circumstances, and in deference to the full argument which we have heard, we have concluded that we should address the issue, rather than confine ourselves to saying that this conviction is safe.

22. We are in the present case concerned with element (a), the touching. The Act says that it must be intentional. We regard it as clear that a reckless touching will not do. The Act plainly proceeds upon the basis that there is a difference between 'intentionally' and 'recklessly'. Where it wishes to speak in terms of recklessness, the Act does so: see for example sections 63(1), 69(1)(c) & (2)(c) and 70(1)(c). It is not necessary to decide whether or not it is possible to conceive of a reckless, but unintentional, sexual touching. Like their Lordships in *R v Court* [1989] 1 AC 28, we think that such a possibility is a remote one, but we are unable wholly to rule it out. One theoretical possible example might be a Defendant who intends to avoid (just) actual physical contact, but realises that he may touch and is reckless whether he will.

23. Because the offence is committed only by intentional touching, we agree that the Judge's direction that the touching must be deliberate was correct. To flail about, stumble or barge around in an unco-ordinated manner which results in an unintended touching, objectively sexual, is not this offence. If to do so when sober is not this offence, then nor is it this offence to do so when intoxi-cated. It is also possible that such an action would not be judged by the jury to be objectively sexual, on the basis that it was clearly accidental, but whether that is so or not, we are satisfied that in such a case this offence is not committed. The intoxication, in such a situation, has not impacted on inten-tion. Intention is simply not in question. What is in question is impairment of control of the limbs. Accordingly we reject Mr Perry's submission number (v). . . . We would expect that in some cases where this was in issue the Judge might well find it useful to add to the previously-mentioned direction

that 'a drunken intent is still an intent', the corollary that 'a drunken accident is still an accident'. To the limited, and largely theoretical, extent that a reckless sexual touching is possible the same would apply to that case also. Whether, when a defendant claims accident, he is doing so truthfully, or as a means of disguising the reality that he intended to touch, will be what the jury has to decide on the facts of each such case.

24. The remaining question is whether the Judge was also correct to direct the jury that drunkenness was not a defence.

25. We do not agree with Mr Stern's submission for the appellant that the fact that reckless touching will not suffice means that voluntary intoxication can be relied upon as defeating intentional touching. We do not read the cases, including *DPP v Majewski*, as establishing any such rule. As we shall show, we would hold that it is not open to a defendant charged with sexual assault to contend that his voluntary intoxication prevented him from intending to touch. The Judge was accordingly correct, not only to direct the jury that the touching must be deliberate, but also to direct it that the defence that voluntary drunkenness rendered him unable to form the intent to touch was not open to him. Our reasons are as follows.

26. In *Majewski* the rival contentions before the House of Lords were these. For the appellant it was contended that if intoxication affected the mind of the defendant it was illogical and unethical to distinguish between its effect on one state of mind and on another; it was capable of destroying any state of mind which is required as a component of a criminal offence. There was thus, it was argued, no permissible distinction between offences of basic intent and those of specific intent. The Crown contended that that distinction had nevertheless represented the law of England for many years. The House upheld the Crown's contention. It did so in the full knowledge that it was not perfectly logical. It so held, in large measure, on grounds of policy. As was observed by several of their Lordships, historically the law of England regarded voluntary intoxication as an aggravation rather than a potential excuse and the development of the law had been by way of a partial, but only a partial, relaxation of that common law rule where a specific intent was required. Both Lord Elwyn-Jones LC (at 471H) and Lord Edmund-Davies (at 494F) approved what Lawton LJ had said in the Court of Appeal: [His lordship referred to the speeches in *Majewski* (section 25.3, p 718).]

27. Mr Stern's proposition that *Majewski* decides that it is only where recklessness suffices that voluntary intoxication cannot be relied upon derives from a part of the speech of Lord Elwyn-Jones LC in *Majewski* and some observations, *obiter*, of Lord Diplock in the subsequent case of *R v Caldwell* [1982] AC 341.

[His lordship referred to the passage in Lord Elwyn-Jones's speech (section 25.3, p 718).]

28. In *Caldwell*, Lord Diplock added this, at page 355F

'The speech of Lord Elwyn-Jones LC in *Reg v Majewski* . . . is authority that self-induced intoxication is no defence to a crime in which recklessness is enough to constitute the necessary mens rea . . . Reducing oneself by drink or drugs to a condition in which the restraints of reason and conscience are cast off was held to be a reckless course of conduct and an integral part of the crime.'

[His lordship described the facts of *Caldwell*.]

. . .

30. There are a number of difficulties about extracting Mr Stern's proposition [for the defence] from the passages cited.

xi) Lord Elwyn-Jones was addressing the submission made on behalf of the appellant in *Majewski* that it was unprincipled or unethical to distinguish between the effect of drink upon the mind in some crimes and its effect upon the mind in others. In rejecting that submission, and upholding the distinction between crimes of basic and of specific intent, he was drawing attention to the fact that a man who has got himself into a state of voluntary intoxication is not, by ordinary standards, blameless. Both the Lord Chancellor and others of their Lordships made clear their view that to get oneself into such a state is, viewed broadly, as culpable as is any sober defendant convicted of a crime of basic intent, whether because he has the basic intent or because he is reckless as to the relevant consequence or circumstance. Throughout *Majewski* it is clear that their Lordships regarded those latter two states of mind as equivalent to one another for these purposes. It therefore does not follow from the references to recklessness that the same rule (that voluntary intoxication cannot be relied upon) does not apply also to basic intent; on the contrary, it seems to us clear that their Lordships were treating the two the same.

xii) The new analysis of recklessness in *Caldwell* may have led readily to the proposition that voluntary intoxication is broadly equivalent to recklessness, thus defined. But that analysis and definition of recklessness have now been reversed by the House of Lords in *R v G* [2004] 1 AC 1034. As now understood, recklessness requires actual foresight of the risk.

xiii) Since the majority in *Caldwell* held that it was enough for recklessness that the risk was obvious objectively (thus, to the sober man) no question of drink providing a defence could arise; it follows that the explanation of *Majewski* which was advanced was plainly *obiter*.

xiv) Lord Diplock's proposition in *Caldwell* attracted a vigorous dissent from Lord Edmund-Davies, who, like Lord Diplock, had been a party to *Majewski*, and with whom Lord Wilberforce agreed. They dissented not only from the new definition of recklessness, but also from the analysis of *Majewski*. Their view was that arson being reckless as to the endangering of life is an offence of specific, not of basic, intent; that would seem to have been because the state of mind went to an ulterior or purposive element of the offence, rather than to the basic element of causing damage by fire.

xv) There were, moreover, many difficulties in the proposition that voluntary intoxication actually supplies the mens rea, whether on the basis of recklessness as re-defined in *Caldwell* or on the basis of recklessness as now understood; if that were so the drunken man might be guilty simply by becoming drunk and whether or not the risk would be obvious to a sober person, himself or anyone else. That reinforces our opinion that the proposition being advanced was one of broadly equivalent culpability, rather than of drink by itself supplying the mens rea.

31. It is necessary to go back to *Majewski* in order to see the basis for the distinction there upheld between crimes of basic and of specific intent. It is to be found most clearly in the speech of Lord Simon, at pages 478B to 479B. Lord Simon's analysis had been foreshadowed in his speech in *DPP v Morgan* [1976] AC 182, 216 (dissenting in the result), which analysis was cited and approved in *Majewski* by Lord Elwyn-Jones (at 471). It was that crimes of specific intent are those where the offence requires proof of purpose or consequence, which are not confined to, but amongst which are included, those where the purpose goes beyond the actus reus (sometimes referred to as cases of 'ulterior intent').

[His lordship referred to Lord Simon's quotation from Fauteux J in *Reg v George* (1960) 128 Can CC 289 at 301 (section 25.3, p 720).]

That explanation of the difference is consistent with the view of Lord Edmund-Davies that an offence contrary to s 1(2)(b) Criminal Damage Act is one of specific intent in this sense, even though it involves no more than recklessness as to the endangering of life; the offence requires proof of a state of mind addressing something beyond the prohibited act itself, namely its consequences. We regard this as the best explanation of the sometimes elusive distinction between specific and basic intent in the sense used in *Majewski*, and it seems to us that this is the distinction which the Judge in the present case was applying when he referred to the concept of a 'bolted-on' intent. By that test, element (a) (the touching) in sexual assault contrary to s 3 Sexual Offences Act 2003 is an element requiring no more than basic intent. It follows that voluntary intoxication cannot be relied upon to negate that intent.

32. We therefore accept Mr Perry's submission number (i). We also, however, recognise the accuracy of submission number (ii). There is a great deal of policy in the decision whether voluntary intoxication can or cannot be relied upon. We have already referred to one of several passages in *Majewski* where the rule is firmly grounded upon common sense, whether purely logical or not. We agree that it is unlikely that it was the intention of Parliament in enacting the Sexual Offences Act 2003 to change the law by permitting reliance upon voluntary intoxication where previously it was not permitted. *R v Woods*, relied upon by the Crown, does not entirely resolve the question which we are now addressing. What was there decided was that a defendant charged with rape could not rely on voluntary drunkenness when the question was whether he was reckless as to whether the woman consented. By the statute then in force, the presence or absence of reasonable grounds for belief in consent was made a factor to be taken into account. There are now separate, and differently expressed, statutory provisions as to belief in consent, which make it clear that belief must not only be held in fact but be objectively reasonable.

Appeal dismissed

≈ **Question**

If not every offence could be categorized simply as either one of 'specific intent' or of 'basic intent', what is this other category that exists?

The court's reinterpretation of *Majewski* aligning specific intent with an ulterior mens rea produces difficulties, as illustrated by two examples each producing unsatisfactory results. Consider a character who, like *Lipman* (1969) 55 Cr App R 600, CA (section 25.3, p 735), becomes so heavily intoxicated on LSD that he genuinely has no appreciation of the circumstances or consequences surrounding his physical actions. D might be so intoxicated that he thinks he is stroking an animal at the centre of the earth when in fact he is stroking a woman's breast. On the court's approach, since the offence is one of 'basic' intent this actor will be guilty. But it is submitted that in such a case it would be difficult in any ordinary sense of the word to say that D 'intended' to touch V sexually as s 3 requires. Nor can his conduct properly be described as 'accidental'.

In contrast, consider someone who is heavily intoxicated, fooling around with his mates in a pub and who pretends to strike the bottom of a woman who is bending over to reach to the bar and who cannot see him. He aims to avoid contact by stopping his hand short, thereby amusing his mates in the process. His intoxication causes him to misjudge the distance and he ends up patting her on the bottom. It is submitted that it would be a misuse of the word 'intention' to say that he had intended to touch her sexually. He intends to move his arm and intends to come close to touching her, but specifically does not intend to in fact touch her. He is reckless about that consequence: he has seen the risk and gone on to take it. But recklessness will not do under s 3, as the court acknowledges. Hughes LJ concludes that D must in these circumstances be acquitted, but does so (at [23]) by describing D's conduct as 'accidental'.

≈ **Question**

Does this broad application of the word 'accidental' which results in acquittal undermine the whole protective purpose of the law's approach to intoxication and basic intent?

Will the court's *obiter* rejection of the orthodox interpretation of *Majewski* be applied throughout the criminal law? There are several reasons why it is respectfully submitted that this would be undesirable. First, it is more difficult to apply: looking for the 'bolt on' element of additional mens rea in a crime in order to categorize it appropriately is less straightforward than asking simply whether it was one for which recklessness suffices. Secondly, looking for this ulterior mens rea creates no fewer anomalies than the established interpretation of *Majewski*: murder should be a specific intent offence but where is the 'bolt on' intent beyond that to kill? Indeed, this was one of the principal bases on which *Majewski* was criticized; cf G. Williams, *Textbook of Criminal Law* (1978), p 429. Thirdly, the complexity will be exacerbated by the fact that an offence can be one of specific intent even if it contains no element of intent at all—provided there is an ulterior mens rea: reckless criminal damage being reckless as to whether life is endangered thereby would be a crime of specific intention. Finally, despite its obscure exposition in the House of Lords, and its unsatisfactory theoretical underpinnings, the *Majewski* approach had subsequently been knocked into pragmatic shape: it was an established and universally applied test. Those virtues ought not to be undervalued.

The courts do not seem to have produced the greatest clarity in distinguishing between basic and specific intention. Have the academics done any better?

S. Gough, 'Intoxication and Criminal Liability: The Law Commission's Proposed Reforms'
(1996) 112 LQR 335 at 342 (references omitted)

. . .

The Specific-Basic Distinction

The origins of the terminology of 'specific intent'

The distinction between offences of specific and basic intent has been a persistent headache for criminal lawyers, especially over the last two or three decades. The terminology of 'specific' intent is traceable to the mid nineteenth century. Patterson J. spoke in *Cruse* (1838) [8 C & P 541] of intoxication's ability to defeat the 'positive intention' required by murder, while in *Monkhouse* (1849) [4 Cox CC 55] Coleridge J. noted that drunkenness would not lead to an acquittal unless, inter alia, it deprived the defendant of 'the power of forming any specific intention.' Most importantly, Lord Birkenhead L.C. referred to specific intent in *D.P.P. v. Beard* (1920):

'Where a specific intent is an essential element in the offence, evidence of a state of drunkenness rendering the accused incapable of forming such an intent should be taken into consideration in order to determine whether he had in fact formed the intent necessary to constitute the particular crime.' [[1920] AC 479 at 499]

Yet these cases gave no indication that a 'specific intent' was different from an ordinary intent. Indeed, other intoxication cases of the period omit any reference to 'specific' intent and speak simply of intoxication's ability to negate intent [*Meakin* (1836) 7 C & P 297]. *Beard* is particularly confusing in that, having used the language of 'specific intent' in the first half of his opinion, Lord Birkenhead switches to the language of intent simpliciter in the second half [[1920] AC 479 at 504–505]. In short, the terms 'intent' and 'specific intent' seem to have been used interchangeably.

Why, then, did some judges use the term 'specific intent' instead of just 'intent'? In answering this question we must bear in mind the 19th and early 20th century approach to mens rea. Stephen, writing in the late 19th century, points to 'malice' as a sufficient mental element for most offences. The word carried its common meaning of moral depravity or 'wickedness' [*General View of the Criminal Law of England* (1863), p 82], and there is no indication that any subjective mental state was required. This is confirmed by Harris who, writing around the same time, noted that

'Malice is found not only in cases: i) Where the mind is actively or positively in fault, as where there is a deliberate design to defraud, but also: ii) Where the mind is passively or negatively to blame, that is, where there is culpable or criminal inattention or negligence.' [S. F. Harris, *Principles of the Criminal Law* (1st edn, 1877), p 14.]

In any event, as Harris pointed out, many offences would have been satisfied even in the absence of malice:

> 'When the law expressly declares an act to be criminal, the question of intention or malice need not be considered; at least, except by the judge in estimating the amount of punishment.' [ibid]

Early 20th century criminal lawyers paint a similar picture [C. S. Kenny, *Outlines of Criminal Law* (1st edn, 1902)].

Intoxicatedly inadvertent behaviour would have been perfectly consistent with liability for an offence with a mental element of malice or less. As Kenny noted around the turn of the century, '[D's] mens rea in allowing himself to become intoxicated is sufficient to supply the ordinary mental element of guilt to any criminal act which may ensue from it.' [p 60] The key words here are 'ordinary mental element'. Some offences, as Kenny later points out, required mental elements that were out of the ordinary. In these cases intoxication might, depending on the nature of the mental element required, operate to negate liability for that offence:

> '[Intoxication] may disprove the presence of some additional mens rea that is essential to the definition of some particular crime. It may, for instance, disprove the presence of murderous malice, or of an intent to do grievous bodily harm, or of an intent to commit a felony.' [p 61]

Here, then, is an explanation for the occasional use of words like 'specific' or 'positive' in the early cases. The ordinary mental element required by offences at this time was 'malice', a form of negligence that intoxication would obviously not negate. There were, though, a few offences that specifically (or positively or explicitly) required specific (or particular or positive) mental states. Depending on their exact nature, these extra mental requirements might be incompatible with extreme intoxication. In other words, 'specificity' was not a characteristic of the intent required by an offence, although 'specifically requiring intent' might be a characteristic of offences themselves.

The specific-basic distinction in modern law

The casually used terminology of specific intent has been pressed into service in modern law to ensure that the kinds of offences that would have allowed liability for (objective) intoxicated wrongdoing in the past can continue to do so despite their more recent subjectivist overhaul. In simple terms, where the offence is one of 'specific intent', the defendant cannot be liable unless he acted with the necessary mental state. It makes no difference that his lack of mens rea was the result of intoxication. On the other hand, where, apart from his mental state, the defendant satisfies the conditions of liability for an offence that is not one of 'specific intent' (that is, of a 'basic intent' offence), he will (effectively) be held liable irrespective of his lack of mens rea. However, this explanation leaves at least two questions unanswered. How can modern offences that ostensibly require a subjective mens rea be satisfied by inadvertent intoxicated wrongdoing? And why is it that only some (ostensibly) subjective offences can be treated in this way while other (actually) subjective offences cannot?

There have been several attempts to explain the mechanism by which intoxicated wrongdoing satisfies the requirements of subjective offences. The Law Commission [Law Com No 229, *Legislating the Criminal Code: Intoxication and Criminal Liability* (1995)] considered two approaches, one that treats intoxicated wrongdoing as a substitute for subjectively reckless wrongdoing and another that presumes that there is subjectively reckless wrongdoing where intoxicated wrongdoing is shown to be present. Neither approach is particularly attractive. Intoxicated wrongdoing is not a direct alternative to subjectively reckless wrongdoing, and that is a good reason for not presuming it to be. Rather, there are differences between the two types of wrongdoing that may need to be reflected in different sentences or—and this is the important point—in different offence headings.

Considerations of fair labelling, the set of principles governing the assimilation of particular types of wrongdoing under particular offence headings, have driven the specific-basic distinction into the law. Intoxicated wrongdoing is not equivalent to subjective wrongdoing, but where it is perceived to share the salient characteristics of the wrong or family of wrongs associated with a particular offence heading, including any characteristics given salience by being specified in the offence heading itself, there will be little objection to assimilating it under that heading. Any remaining differences between the two types of wrongdoing will be minor enough to be taken into account at the sentencing stage. There are, on the other hand, some offence headings that do not exhibit this degree of flexibility. Killing in drunken inadvertence, for example, while it is a very serious form of wrongdoing, could hardly be considered equivalent to the specific and serious wrongs normally associated with murder. Or, at least, to treat it as murder would so broaden the types of wrongdoing associated with that offence as to risk diluting the special opprobrium attaching to it. Similarly, where a heading gives salience to particular characteristics of the wrongs prohibited by explicitly specifying them—wounding with intent to do grievous bodily harm, for example—it would be paradoxical to use it to convict the unthinking drunken wounder whose wrongdoing exhibits no such characteristic.

This is not to say that the specific-basic distinction can be explained solely in terms of fair labelling. The common law judges have had to work with existing offence headings and there are certain types of intoxicated wrongdoing that do not fit particularly neatly under any of these. Where such wrongdoing is considered relatively venial, the temptation may be to sacrifice the conviction of deserving offenders in order to preserve the coherence of the law's labelling scheme. Perhaps thoughtless drunken trespass or appropriation ought to be criminal, but it would seem wrong to deal with such offenders under the ancient and emotive headings of burglary and theft, and in the absence of appropriate existing offence headings they go free. Where the intoxicated wrongdoing is considered more serious, by contrast, the temptation may be to sacrifice the principles of fair labelling in order to secure the conviction of deserving offenders. The classification of rape as a basic intent offence may be an example of this type of compromise. There are serious doubts whether the rapist who drunkenly believes his victim to be consenting should be dealt with under the same opprobrious heading as the advertent rapist who knowingly risks that they are not. Since there is no other appropriate offence heading, though, it is better to convict the intoxicated individual under the rape heading than to acquit completely.

Objections to the specific-basic distinction

I should mention three objections that might be raised against this approach to the specific-basic distinction.

(1) It may be objected that the process of tacitly extending offences to cover closely related but not explicitly prohibited wrongs is contrary to the rule of law (in that it involves retrospective criminalisation and judicial legislation) or that it is impractical (in that its role in securing the conviction of a handful of admittedly deserving individuals does not justify the complexity and difficulty that it introduces). Such objections are not particularly persuasive. Judicial extension of offences to cover closely related types of wrongdoing is not confined to the intoxication rules: it is a common technique used to give flexibility to offence headings, to circumvent the letter of the law and give effect to its spirit. . . . Consider also the non-contemporaneity cases like *Church* [[1966] 1 QB 59]. *Thabo Meli* [[1954] 1 WLR 228] (and, it may be added, *Gallagher* [[1963] AC 349]). The defendants had all committed wrongs similar to the central wrong prohibited by murder save only that their behaviour did not satisfy the contemporaneity requirements of that offence. That is, while they had intended to kill and had caused death, the acts causing death had not involved an intent to kill. The instinct of the courts in each case was to ignore the minor difference between the actual and the required wrongdoing and convict under the murder heading. To the extent that it would be undesirable to rewrite the law in these various respects and allow plainly culpable individuals to get off scot-free, perhaps it is not the

specific-basic distinction that we should be rethinking but our assumptions about the practical and constitutional difficulties presented by the current intoxication rules.

(2) A second objection rejects the specific-basic distinction as unprincipled because it cannot be reduced to a neat general formula. Many people have attempted to find such a formula—some have tried to identify specific intent with ulterior intent, others with purpose, others with subjective reck-lessness. All of these enterprises make the mistake, identified above, of assuming 'specificity' to be a quality of the mental elements required by certain offences and, as a result, they all fail to capture the common law distinction. Some of them require counterintuitive amendments to the accepted cat-egorisations of offences as specific or basic—under the 'purpose' of 'ulterior intent' approaches, for example. Murder would have to be reclassified as a basic intent offence because neither of those men-tal states is necessary for its commission. Others overconfidently classify as specific or basic offences like rape over which the common law has understandably dithered.

In fact, to search for a neat reduction of the specific-basic distinction is to misunderstand its nature. 'Specific intent offence' is an (inapt) label given to offences which, for the kinds of reasons already discussed, cannot appropriately be extended to cover inadvertent intoxicated wrongdoing. We do not expect a general formula to tell us whether a certain offence heading should cover a certain objectively reckless wrong, subjectively reckless wrong, intentional wrong, or wrong characterised by a special quality like dishonesty or indecency. It is similarly misguided to expect a general theory to tell us whether a particular offence heading should cover a given intoxicated wrong.

. . .

(3) Finally, many have wanted to deal with intoxicated wrongdoing under a special heading ('dan-gerous intoxication', for example) rather than, as at present, under ordinary offences. While there may be an argument to be made along these lines, it is difficult to imagine that it would be very persuasive. In particular, it seems implausible to claim, as advocates of a new offence must be claiming, that the reasons against grouping intoxicated vandals alongside advertent vandals under the existing criminal damage heading are more powerful than the reasons against grouping intoxicated vandals alongside intoxicated killers under some new offence. The underlying mistake is the assumption that wrongs should be grouped primarily according to their mental components and with little reference to their other characteristics. Not only have offence labels always reflected the non-mental characteristics of the wrongs they prohibit, but in many cases such characteristics are the only basis for a labelling distinction—consider the separate classification of murder as opposed to section 18 wounding, or of common assault as opposed to section 47 actual bodily harm, or of attempted offences as opposed to completed offences. Why should we apologise for distinguishing between intoxicated killers and intoxicated vandals on the same grounds? All this being said, it is doubtful how many of the advocates of a new offence realise they are making this implausible argument. Most of them are, I suspect, motivated by a vague and unfocused objection to objective liability per se. The attempt to reconcile such extreme subjectivist views with an uneasy acceptance that it would not be right or, at least, not politically acceptable for intoxicated offenders to get off leads to the rather sloppy conclusion that there should be a special offence—a criminal law ghetto in which the slightly fishy intoxicated wrongs are kept separate from 'proper' (subjective) criminal wrongdoing.

The introduction of one bland offence heading to cover all criminal intoxicated wrongdoing may well be undesirable, but we should not rule out the possibility that a range of narrowly circumscribed new offences should be introduced to cover forms of intoxicated wrongdoing that are difficult to cat-egorise at present. On the other hand, there are dozens of other considerations bearing on whether such reforms should be introduced. Should the law be made even more complex? How far would the new offences be open to abuse? How, for example, would deterrence and respect for the law be affected if enough real rapists were able to bluff themselves into a new 'forcible intercourse' category designed to catch inadvertent offenders? Even leaving these difficulties aside, though, it is hard to accept that very many intoxicated wrongs sit uncomfortably under their existing basic intent offence headings. Even if we were given carte blanche to rewrite the specific-basic distinction and to introduce new offences where necessary, I doubt that we would want to change very much. Certainly, it seems unlikely that we would want to bring intoxicated killers under any other category than manslaughter, or intoxicated vandals under any other category than criminal damage or intoxicated wounders under any other categories than unlawful wounding or assault occasioning actual bodily harm.

See also J. Horder, 'Crimes of Ulterior Intent' in A. Simester and A. T. H. Smith (eds), *Harm and Culpability* (1996) and J. Horder, 'The Classifications of Crimes and the Special Part' in R. A. Duff and S. P. Green (eds), *Defining Crimes: Essays on the Special Part of the Criminal Law* (2005).

≋ **Question**

Would it be better to have an offence of 'committing [the actus reus of offence X] while intoxicated'? See R. Williams, 'Voluntary Intoxication—A Lost Cause?' (2013) 129 LQR 264.

25.4 Prior fault

The approach taken in *Majewski* can be explained in terms of 'prior fault'. There is a degree of fault in the accused's decision to become so heavily intoxicated, and that fault, albeit well before he commits any criminal acts, is sufficient to provide the necessary blameworthiness for the offence, even though at the time of the criminal conduct the accused does not have the relevant mens rea for the offence because he is too intoxicated to form it. For example, in a case of wounding contrary to s 20 OAPA where at the time D stabs V he is so intoxicated that he thinks he is stabbing a theatrical dummy, D has no intention to stab a human being at the time nor can he be said to be reckless about that since he has not foreseen the risk that his action will result in a wounding of a human being. The reason for that lack of mens rea required is that he is too intoxicated to form it. Following *Majewski*, D's decision to take the intoxicating substances to the extent that he becomes dangerous in his actions involves an element of fault on D's part. That prior fault compensates for the lack of fault at the time of the stabbing and justifies D's conviction.

≋ **Questions**

(1) Is it justifiable to convict on the ground that D was reckless at the time he took the intoxicant? See S. Gough, section 25.3, p 729.

(2) What was D reckless about at that time of becoming intoxicated? Is that the same type of fault as the fault required for the offence of wounding? Over how long a period can we transfer the prior fault in intoxication to the subsequent criminal acts?

R v Kingston
[1994] UKHL 9, House of Lords

(Lords Keith, Goff, Browne-Wilkinson, Mustill and Slynn)

D was a man with a sexual interest in under-age boys, but had never before committed any offences against children. D was engaged in a business dispute with X who knew of D's sexual interest in children. X invited D round to his flat and laced his drink with a drug that he knew would lower D's inhibitions. Also present at the flat was a 15-year-old boy who was uncon-scious due to his having taken a drink which X laced with a soporific drug. Once D's inhibi-tions were lowered, he committed indecent assault on the boy. X video-recorded the offences for the purposes of blackmailing D. Having rejected D's argument that he lacked the neces-sary mens rea on the general principle that an intoxicated mens rea is still a mens rea, Lord Mustill thought it necessary to consider the law laid down in *Majewski*. He concluded that, as in other common law jurisdictions, evidence of voluntary intoxication is excluded, except in 'specific intent' cases, as a matter of policy. He continued:

> There remains the question by what reasoning the House [in *Majewski*] put this policy into effect. As I understand it two different rationalisations were adopted. First that the absence of the neces-sary consent is cured by treating the intentional drunkenness (or more accurately, since it is only in the minority of cases that the drinker sets out to make himself drunk, the intentional taking of drink without regard to its possible effects) as a substitute for the mental element ordinarily required by the offence. The intent is transferred from the taking of drink to the commission of the prohibited act. The second rationalisation is that the defendant cannot be heard to rely on the absence of the mental ele-ment when it is absent because of his own voluntary acts. Borrowing an expression from a far distant field it may be said that the defendant is estopped from relying on his self-induced incapacity.
>
>   Your Lordships are not required to decide how these two explanations stand up to attack, for they are not attacked here. The task is only to place them in the context of an intoxication which is not voluntary. Taking first the concept of transferred intent, if the intoxication was not the result of an act done with an informed will there is no intent which can be transferred to the prohibited act, so as to fill the gap in the offence. As regards the 'estoppel' there is no reason why the law should preclude the defendant from relying on a mental condition which he had not deliberately brought about. Thus, once the involuntary nature of the intoxication is added the two theories of *Majewski* fall away, and the position reverts to what it would have been if *Majewski* had not been decided, namely that the offence is not made out if the defendant was so intoxicated that he could not form an intent. Thus, where the intoxication is involuntary *Majewski* does not *subtract* the defence of absence of intent; but there is nothing in *Majewski* to suggest that where intent is proved involuntary intoxication *adds* a further defence.

Lord Mustill considered authorities in other jurisdictions. In particular, he discussed a num-ber of Scottish decisions involving involuntary intoxication. These make it clear that, in Scotland, a defence is made out if it is 'based . . . on an inability to form mens rea due to some factor which was outwith the accused's control and which he was not bound to foresee'; or if he was 'suffering from a total alienation of reason rendering him incapable of controlling or appreciating what he was doing'. These and the other *dicta* all require an inability to form the intent.

≋ **Question**
Should excuse be limited to situations of inability, or should it extend to the case where a per-son capable of forming an intent fails to do so because he is involuntarily intoxicated?

25.5 Voluntary intoxication leading to a loss of mens rea

The rules are clear: if the case is one of voluntary intoxication, the defendant can rely on his intoxication as an excuse only to a crime of specific intent (eg murder), but not one of basic intent (eg manslaughter). In some instances, D's voluntary intoxication is so great that he becomes an automaton. However. D cannot plead automatism to a crime of basic intent if he induced that state through his voluntary consumption of alcohol or drugs (for confirmation see *Coley* [2013] EWCA Crim 223).

R v Lipman
[1970] 1 QB 152, Court of Appeal, Criminal Division

(Widgery and Fenton Atkinson LJJ, James J)

Both the applicant, L, and the victim, V, were drug addicts and both took a quantity of LSD in V's room. The next morning L (who was a US citizen) hurriedly left the country. V's land-lord found her dead in her room the following day. She had suffered two blows on the head causing haemorrhage of the brain, but she died of asphyxia as a result of some eight inches of sheet having been crammed into her mouth. L was eventually tracked down and arrested. He explained how after taking LSD with V he had the illusion of descending to the centre of the earth and being attacked by snakes, with which he had fought. He killed the victim in the course of this experience, but he said he had no knowledge of what he was doing and no intention to harm her. He was charged with murder, but the jury evidently accepted that he lacked the necessary intention to kill or to do grievous bodily harm, as to manslaughter. Milmo J directed the jury that L 'would be guilty of manslaughter if the jury were to find either—(1) that he must have realized before he got himself into the condition he did by taking the drugs, that acts such as those he subsequently performed and which resulted in the death, were dangerous; or (2) that the taking of the drugs which the defendant took that night was dangerous and that the [defendant] must have realized that by taking them he was incurring a risk of some harm, not necessarily serious harm, to some other person or persons; or (3) that in taking these drugs in the circumstances in which he took them, the [defendant] was grossly negligent and reckless and this involves the jury considering whether or not he thought that what he was doing was safe so far as other people were concerned.' (See [1970] 1 QB 152.)

The jury found the defendant not guilty of murder but guilty of manslaughter by reason of grounds (1) and (3) above. The defendant appealed.

[**Widgery LJ** delivered the judgment of the court:]

In this court counsel for the applicant contends that . . . the jury should have been directed further that it was necessary for the Crown to prove that the applicant had intended to do acts likely to result in harm, or foresaw that harm would result from what he was doing.

For the purposes of criminal responsibility we see no reason to distinguish between the effect of drugs voluntarily taken and drunkenness voluntarily induced. As to the latter there is a great deal of authority. [His lordship quoted from the speeches of Lord Birkenhead in *Beard*'s case and Lord Denning in *Bratty*'s case (see section 24.4.1, p 693) and *Gallagher*'s case (see section 25.6, p 739)].

These authorities show quite clearly, in our opinion, that it was well established that no specific intent was necessary to support a conviction for manslaughter based on killing in the course of an unlawful act and that, accordingly, self-induced drunkenness was no defence to such a charge.

[His lordship cited the facts and a passage from the judgment of Edmund Davies J, noting that the appellant was arguing that some intention or foresight was an essential element of manslaughter as defined in *Church*.]

In our judgment, there is a flaw in the applicant's argument; and the flaw lies in the assumption that *Church* introduced a new element of intent or foreseeability into this type of manslaughter. All that the judgment in *Church* says in terms is that whereas, formerly, a killing by any unlawful act amounted to manslaughter, this consequence does not now inexorably follow unless the unlawful act is one in which ordinary sober and responsible people would recognise the existence of risk. The development recognised by *Church* relates to the type of act from which a charge of manslaughter may result, not in the intention (real or assumed) of the prisoner. It is perhaps unfortunate that a reference to mens rea, which had been found unhelpful by Lord Atkin, was repeated in *Church*, and to give it the effect now contended for would be contrary to *DPP v Beard* and the other authorities which we have cited. The decision in *Church* was referred to in this court later in *Lamb* [see section 9.2.1.1, p 210] where the accused had pointed a revolver at the victim in the belief, as he said, that there was no round in the chamber, but the revolver had fired and the victim was killed. It was pointed out in this court that no unlawful act on the part of the prisoner had been proved in the absence of the necessary intent to constitute an assault. But this is intention of a different kind. Even if intent has to be proved to constitute the unlawful act, no specific further intent is required to turn that act into manslaughter. Manslaughter remains a most difficult offence to define because it arises in so many different ways and, as the mental element (if any) required to establish it varies so widely, any general reference to mens rea is apt to mislead.

We can dispose of the present application by reiterating that when the killing results from an unlawful act of the accused no specific intent has to be proved to convict of manslaughter, and self-induced intoxication is accordingly no defence. Since in the present case the acts complained of were obviously likely to cause harm to the victim (and did, in fact, kill her) no acquittal was possible and the verdict of manslaughter, at the least, was inevitable.

Appeal dismissed

≈≈ **Questions**
(1) Why is it relevant whether a person knows it is dangerous to cram eight inches of bedsheet into a woman's mouth if he has no idea that he is going to do, or is doing, such an act?
(2) According to (a) Milmo J's summing-up and (b) the Court of Appeal, was the act for which Lipman was responsible (i) the taking of the drugs or (ii) the acts done?
(3) The court concedes, 'even if intent has to be proved to constitute the unlawful act . . .' Was any intent proved with respect to the unlawful acts done?

In *Coley* [2013] EWCA Crim 223, Hughes LJ stated that the line between voluntary intoxication and insanity may in some cases be difficult to draw with precision. His lordship stated that, 'it would be perfectly legitimate to say of a very drunken man that his mind had become detached from reality by the intoxication'. Some such extreme cases will turn on whether there was a disease of the mind, see section 24.5.1, p 710.

25.5.1 Voluntary intoxication by dangerous drugs

In the case where D has become voluntarily intoxicated and the offence with which he is charged is one of basic intent, there remains one important issue to consider—whether the substance ingested is dangerous, that is, commonly known to create states of unpredictability or aggression. Even if the drug is not one that is commonly known to create such states, D may nevertheless be liable if he mixes it with alcohol and has been warned against doing so. This was confirmed recently in *Coley* [2013] EWCA Crim 223, and the leading authority on this remains *Hardie* which we now consider.

R v Hardie

[1984] EWCA Crim 2, Court of Appeal, Criminal Division

(Parker LJ, Stuart-Smith and McCowan JJ)

The defendant's relationship with the woman with whom he was living broke down and she left him. He became upset and took several tablets of valium, a sedative drug, belonging to the woman. Later he started a fire in the bedroom of the flat while the woman and her daughter were in the sitting room. Charged with an offence under s 1(2) of the Criminal Damage Act 1971, he argued that the effect of the drug was to prevent him having the mens rea. The judge directed the jury that this could be no defence because the drug was self-administered. The defendant appealed on grounds of misdirection.

Parker LJ:

In *R v Bailey* (1983) 2 All E.R. 503 this court had to consider a case where a diabetic had failed to take sufficient food after taking a normal dose of insulin and struck the victim over the head with an iron bar. The judge directed the jury that the defence of automatism, i.e. that the mind did not go with the act, was not available because the incapacity was self-induced. It was held that this was wrong on two grounds: (a) because on the basis of *DPP v Majewski* it was clearly available to the offence embodying specific intent and (b) because although self-induced by the omission to take food it was also available to negative the other offence which was of basic intent only.

Having referred to *DPP v Majewski* and *Lipman* Lord Justice Griffiths, giving the considered judgment of the court, said:

'It was submitted on behalf of the Crown that a similar rule should be applied as a matter of public policy to all cases of self-induced automatism. But it seems to us that there may be material distinctions between a man who consumes alcohol or takes dangerous drugs and one who fails to take sufficient food after insulin to avert hypo-glycaemia. It is common knowledge that those who take alcohol to excess or certain sorts of drugs may become aggressive or do dangerous or unpredictable things; they may be able to foresee the risks of causing harm to others, but nevertheless persist in their conduct. But the same cannot be said, without more, of a man who fails to take food after an insulin injection. If he does appreciate the risk that such a failure may lead to aggressive, unpredictable and uncontrollable conduct and he nevertheless deliberately runs the risk or otherwise disregards it, this will amount to recklessness. But we certainly do not think that it is common knowledge, even among diabetics, that such is a consequence of a failure to take food; and there is no evidence that it was known to this appellant. Doubtless he knew that if he failed to take his insulin or proper food after it he might lose consciousness, but as such he would only be a danger to himself unless he put himself in charge of some machine such as a motor car, which required his continued conscious control. In our judgment, self-induced automatism, other than that due to intoxication from alcohol or drugs, may provide a defence to crimes of basic intent. The question in each case will be whether the prosecution has proved the necessary element of recklessness. In cases of assault, if the accused knows that his actions or inaction are likely to make him aggressive, unpredictable or uncontrolled with the result that he may cause some injury to others and he persists in the action or takes no remedial action when he knows it is required, it will be open to the jury to find that he was reckless.'

In the present instance the defence was that the Valium was taken for the purpose of calming the nerves only, that it was old stock and that the Appellant was told it would do him no harm. There was no evidence that it was known to the Appellant or even generally known that the taking of Valium in the quantity taken would be liable to render a person aggressive or incapable of appreciating risks to others or have other side effects such that its self-administration would itself have an element of recklessness. It is true that Valium is a drug and it is true that it was taken deliberately and not taken on medical prescription, but the drug is, in our view, wholly different in kind from drugs which are liable to cause unpredictability or aggressiveness. It may well be that the taking of a sedative or soporific drug will, in certain circumstances, be no answer, for example in a case of reckless driving, but if the effect of a drug is merely soporific or sedative the taking of it, even in some excessive quantity, cannot in the ordinary way raise a conclusive presumption against the admission of proof of intoxication for the purpose of disproving mens rea in ordinary crimes, such as would be the case with alcoholic intoxication or incapacity or automatism resulting from the self-administration of dangerous drugs.

In the present case the jury should not, in our judgment, have been directed to disregard any incapacity which resulted or might have resulted from the taking of Valium. They should have been directed that if they came to the conclusion that, as a result of the Valium, the Appellant was, at the time, unable to appreciate the risks to property and persons from his actions they should then consider whether the taking of the valium was itself reckless. We are unable to say what would have been the appropriate direction with regard to the elements of recklessness in this case for we have not seen all the relevant evidence, nor are we able to suggest a model direction, for circumstances will vary infinitely and model directions can sometimes lead to more rather than less confusion. It is sufficient to say that the direction that the effects of Valium were necessarily irrelevant was wrong.

Appeal allowed

≋ *Questions*

(1) Are drugs to be divided into two categories—(a) alcohol and 'dangerous' drugs which attract the operation of *Majewski* and (b) other drugs which do not?

(2) In *Chaulk* (2008) 223 CCC (3d) 174, the Nova Scotia Court of Appeal held that the test for self-induced intoxication is that D voluntarily consumed a substance, which he knew *or ought to* have known was an intoxicant, and the risk of becoming intoxicated was *or should have been* within his contemplation. There was held to be no need to prove that the substance was illegal or that D knew precisely what the substance was. Do you agree with that approach?

25.6 Drinking 'with intent': Dutch courage

In some cases, D forms the intention to commit the crime and then intoxicates himself to strengthen his resolve to go through with it. Should it be a defence if he lacked mens rea at the time of the offence?

Attorney-General for Northern Ireland v Gallagher
[1961] UKHL 2, House of Lords

(Lords Reid, Goddard, Tucker, Denning and Morris of Borth-y-Gest)

G had a grievance against his wife because she had been instrumental in getting him detained in a mental hospital. He had made up his mind to kill her and bought a knife for that purpose. He also drank most of a bottle of whisky—'either to give himself Dutch courage to do the deed or to drown his conscience after it'—and killed her. He raised pleas of insanity and intoxication. The Court of Criminal Appeal in Northern Ireland quashed the conviction for murder because the trial judge, in their view, had directed the jury to apply the *M'Naghten* test (section 24.5, p 698) not to the time when the accused killed his wife but to the morning of that day, before he opened the bottle of whisky.

[Lord Tucker, with whom **Lords Goddard** and **Reid** agreed, held that the jury had not been misdirected.]

Lord Denning:

. . . My Lords, this case differs from all others in the books in that the accused man, whilst sane and sober, before he took to the drink, had already made up his mind to kill his wife. This seems to me to be far worse—and far more deserving of condemnation—than the case of a man who, before getting drunk, has no intention to kill, but afterwards in his cups, whilst drunk, kills another by an act which he would not dream of doing when sober. Yet, by the law of England, in this latter case his drunkenness is no defence even though it has distorted his reason and his will-power. So why should it be a defence in the present case? And is it made any better by saying that the man is a psychopath? The answer to the question is, I think, that the case falls to be decided by the general principle of English law that, subject to very limited exceptions, drunkenness is no defence to a criminal charge nor is a defect of reason produced by drunkenness. This principle was stated by Sir Matthew Hale in his *Pleas of the Crown* [1736], Vol I, p 32, in words which I would repeat here:

> 'This vice "(drunkenness)" doth deprive men of the use of reason, and puts many men into a perfect, but temporary frenzy . . . by the laws of England such a person shall have no privilege by this voluntary contracted madness, but shall have the same judgment as if he were in his right senses.'

This general principle can be illustrated by looking at the various ways in which drunkenness may produce a defect of reason: A. It may impair a man's powers of perception so that he may not be able to foresee or measure the consequences of his actions as he would if he were sober. Nevertheless, he is not allowed to set up his self-induced want of perception as a defence. Even if he did not himself appreciate that what he was doing was dangerous, nevertheless, if a reasonable man in his place, who was not befuddled with drink, would have appreciated it, he is guilty; see *Rex v. Meade* [1909] 1 K.B. 895, as explained in *Director of Public Prosecutions v Beard* [1920] A.C 479 at pp. 502–4 [see section 25.3, p 718]. B. It may impair a man's power to judge between right or wrong, so that he may do a thing when drunk which he would not dream of doing while sober. He does not realise he is doing wrong. Nevertheless, he is not allowed to set up his self-induced want of moral sense as a defence. In *Beard's* case [1920] A.C. 479 at p. 506 Lord Birkenhead L.C. distinctly ruled that it was not a defence for a drunken man to say he did not know he was doing wrong. C. It may impair a man's power of self-control so that he may more readily give way to provocation than if he were sober. Nevertheless, he is not allowed to set up his self-induced want of control as a defence. The acts of provocation are to be assessed, not according to their effect on him personally, but according to the effect they would have on a reasonable man in his place. [His lordship referred to the old law on provocation—see now section 8.2, p 167.]

. . .

I would allow this appeal and restore the conviction of murder.

Appeal allowed

25.7 Intoxication and defences

Just as a state of mind is a necessary element in the definition of an offence, so also it is a necessary element in some defences—eg D must *believe* in the need for force before he can rely on self-defence to justify his use of force. Just as intoxication may cause a person to *lack* the mens rea of an *offence*, so it may cause him to *have* the necessary mental element of a *defence*. It is necessary for a defendant who relies on self-defence to offer evidence that he believed he was being attacked in such a way as to justify or excuse the force which he used to defend himself.

What if that belief was mistaken—he was not under attack at all—and the mistake was made because he was drunk at the time? The issue is whether intoxication is always to be ignored when explaining the seemingly incredible mistake which the accused is relying on. The position can be summarized as follows:

- as a matter of policy the courts have taken the approach of treating as irrelevant a defendant's mistaken beliefs in facts that would, if true, provide grounds for a defence where the basis for the mistake is one of self-induced intoxication. However, while this is true of some defences, for example self-defence, it is questionable whether it is true of others, such as loss of control or necessity;

- if D is pleading self-defence, he is to be treated as being aware of anything which he would have been aware of had he not been intoxicated.

These principles are derived from the following cases and are now enshrined in s 76 of the Criminal Justice and Immigration Act 2008 in relation to self-defence.

R v O'Grady
[1987] EWCA Crim 2, Court of Appeal, Criminal Division

(Lord Lane CJ, Boreham and McCowan JJ)

The defendant (O) and his friend, the deceased (M), had been drinking heavily and fell asleep in O's flat. O said that he awoke to find M hitting him, that M had a piece of glass in one hand and that he, O, picked up a piece of glass and hit M. M died of the injury caused. At the invitation of counsel for the prosecution, Judge Underhill gave the following additional direction to the jury:

> It might be a view that you might take, I know not, that this defendant thought he was under attack from the other man mistakenly and made a mistake in thinking that he was under attack because of the drink that was in him. If he made such a mistake in drink he would nevertheless be entitled to defend himself even though he mistakenly believed that he was under attack. He would be entitled in those circumstances to defend himself. But if in taking defensive measures, then he went beyond what is reasonable either because of his mind being affected by drink or for any other reason, then the defence of self-defence would not avail him because, as I told you earlier on, you are entitled to defend yourself if it is necessary to do so, but the defensive measures that you take must be reasonable ones and not go beyond what is reasonable.

O was convicted of manslaughter and appealed on the grounds, *inter alia*, that the judge was wrong to limit the reference to mistake as to the *existence* of an attack and should have included a reference to the possibility of a mistake as to the *severity* of it; and that the judge had 'in effect divorced the reasonableness of the appellant's reaction from the appellant's state of mind at the time'.

Lord Lane CJ [having said that the court had found no case directly in point which was binding:]

As the learned single Judge pointed out [McCullough] helpfully in his observations for the benefit of the Court:

> 'Given that a man who *mistakenly* believes he is under attack is entitled to use reasonable force to defend himself, it would seem to follow that, if he is under attack and mistakenly believes the attack to be more serious than it is, he is entitled to use reasonable force to defend himself against an attack of the severity he believed it to have. If one allows a mistaken belief induced by drink to bring this principle into operation, an act of gross negligence (viewed objectively) may become

lawful even though it results in the death of the innocent victim. The drunken man would be guilty of neither murder nor manslaughter.'

How should the Jury be invited to approach the problem? One starts with the decision of this Court in *R v Gladstone Williams* (1984) 78 Cr App R 276, namely that where the defendant might have been labouring under a mistake as to the facts he must be Judged according to that mistaken view, whether the mistake was reasonable or not. It is then for the Jury to decide whether the defendant's reaction to the threat (real or imaginary) was a reasonable one. The Court was not in that case considering what the situation might be where the mistake was due to voluntary intoxication by alcohol or some other drug.

We have come to the conclusion that, where the Jury are satisfied that the defendant was mistaken in his belief that any force or the force which he in fact used was necessary to defend himself and are further satisfied that the mistake was caused by voluntarily induced intoxication, the defence must fail. We do not consider that any distinction should be drawn on this aspect of the matter between offences involving what is called specific intent, such as murder, and offences of so called basic intent, such as manslaughter. Quite apart from the problem of directing a Jury in a case such as the present where manslaughter is an alternative verdict to murder, the question of mistake can and ought to be considered separately from the question of intent. A sober man who mistakenly believes he is in danger of immediate death at the hands of an attacker is entitled to be acquitted of both murder and manslaughter if his reaction in killing his supposed assailant was a reasonable one. What his intent may have been seems to us to be irrelevant to the problem of self-defence or no. Secondly, we respectfully adopt the reasoning of Mr Justice McCullough already set out.

This brings us to the question of public order. There are two competing interests. On the one hand the interest of the defendant who has only acted according to what he believed to be necessary to protect himself, and on the other hand that of the public in general and the victim in particular who, probably through no fault of his own, has been injured or perhaps killed because of the defendant's drunken mistake. Reason recoils from the conclusion that in such circumstances a defendant is entitled to leave the Court without a stain on his character. . . .

We have therefore come to the conclusion that a defendant is not entitled to rely, so far as self-defence is concerned, upon a mistake of fact which has been induced by voluntary intoxication.

As already indicated, the Judge's addendum to his summing up, which he made at the suggestion of prosecuting counsel, was unnecessary and erred in favour of the appellant.

The appeal against conviction is accordingly dismissed.

Appeal dismissed

The proposition in *O'Grady* that a drunken mistake could not found a defence of self-defence on a murder charge was subjected to heavy criticism.

The Law Commission, in declining to follow that proposition in the Draft Code said (Law Com Report No 177 (1989), para 8.42):

. . . it would, we believe, be unthinkable to convict of murder a person who thought, for whatever reason, that he was acting to save his life and who would have been acting reasonably if he had been right.

The Court of Appeal, however, continued to think the unthinkable in *O'Connor* [1991] Crim LR 135. They were aware of the heavy criticism of *O'Grady* but declared that the case was binding on them. This too appears to be *obiter*, being unnecessary to the decision because O'Connor's conviction of murder was quashed on the ground that the judge omitted to direct the jury that voluntary intoxication could have prevented the appellant from forming the specific intent to kill or cause GBH.

In *Hatton* [2005] EWCA Crim 2951, the Court of Appeal confirmed that the decision in *O'Grady* applied equally to cases of manslaughter and murder: a defendant seeking to rely on self-defence could not rely on a mistake induced by voluntary intoxication. H, who had drunk more than 20 pints of beer, killed V, who was found with at least seven blows from a sledgehammer. H stated that he could not recall V's death but that he had a vague recollection that a stick fashioned in the shape of a Samurai sword had been involved. H said that he believed that V had hit him with the stick and that he must have believed that V was attacking him. H wished to raise self-defence based on his own mistaken belief that he thought he was being attacked by an SAS officer (as V had earlier pretended to be) with a sword. The judge ruled, following *O'Grady*, that it was not open to H to rely on a mistake induced by drunkenness. H argued that if he had mistaken the nature of the attack because of intoxication, he was entitled in law to have defended himself in a manner that was reasonable having regard to his drunken perception of the danger he faced and the jury should have been directed accordingly. H argued that the discussion of the matter in *O'Grady* was *obiter dicta* because it related to manslaughter only and not murder. The Court of Appeal held that *O'Grady* was applicable to both murder and manslaughter.

Section 76 of the Criminal Justice and Immigration Act 2008 now confirms this approach:

> (4) If D claims to have held a particular belief as regards the existence of any circumstances—
>
>   (a) the reasonableness or otherwise of that belief is relevant to the question whether D genuinely held it; but
>
>   (b) if it is determined that D did genuinely hold it, D is entitled to rely on it for the purposes of subsection (3), whether or not—
>
>   (i) it was mistaken, or
>
>   (ii) (if it was mistaken) the mistake was a reasonable one to have made.
>
> (5) But subsection (4)(b) does not enable D to rely on any mistaken belief attributable to intoxication that was voluntarily induced.

As this section has demonstrated, the general rule is that D cannot plead a defence if it is necessary for him to rely upon a belief induced by intoxication in order to satisfy all the elements of that defence. The offence of criminal damage, however, constitutes an exception to this rule. In *Jaggard v Dickinson* [1981] QB 527, the defendant lived in a house belonging to her friend. Making her way home drunk, she went by mistake to the wrong house, found it locked and did damage by breaking in. She was charged with an offence under s 1(1) of the Criminal Damage Act 1971. She relied on s 5(2) of the Act, section 18.2.5, p 466, saying that she believed that her friend would have consented to her doing the damage in the circumstances. The magistrates held that this drunken belief could not be a defence. The Divisional Court held that D could rely upon her voluntary intoxication to substantiate all the elements of the defence. What mattered was whether D's belief was honestly held, irrespective of whether it was reasonable or induced by alcohol.

The courts have recognized that the decision in *Jaggard v Dickinson* represents an exception to the general rule that D's voluntary intoxication must be disregarded when deciding whether he can plead a defence. In *Magee v CPS* [2014] EWHC 4089 (Admin), D was charged with failing to stop after an accident, contrary to s 170(4) of the Road Traffic Act 1988. The district judge accepted that D's intoxicated state meant that she had a genuine belief that no accident had occurred, but nevertheless found her guilty. D argued that she should have been able to plead as a defence the fact that she had a genuine belief that no accident had occurred. Relying upon *Jaggard v Dickinson*, D submitted that it was irrelevant that this belief was induced by intoxication. Elias LJ rejected this approach and gave the following reasons:

7. The well established rule is that intoxication cannot be asserted as a defence in crimes of basic intent as this one surely is: see *DPP v Majewski* [1977] AC 447. The appellant submits that is too sweeping an approach. She relies on the case of *Jaggard v Dickinson* [1980] 3 All ER 716 for the proposition that a mistaken view of the circumstances, even if induced by drink, will constitute a defence as long as the defendant genuinely did not believe an accident had occurred. The fact that the genuine belief was formed as a result of drink is irrelevant.

[His lordship then set out the facts of *Jaggard v Dickinson* and what the court decided.]

31. [Counsel for D] submits that that is precisely the position here; we are concerned only with genuine belief. In those circumstances whether that belief is the result of drink or not, the only question is whether it is genuine.

32. I do not agree. In my judgment, the principle enunciated in *Jaggard* does not apply in the circumstances of this case. First, there is considerable doubt whether *Jaggard* is still good law in the light of such cases as *O'Connor* [1991] CLR 135 and *R v Hatton* [2005] EWCA Crim 2951. In the latter case, the Court of Appeal Criminal Division held in a murder case that an honest but mistaken belief by the defendant that he was being attacked and was entitled to use self defence was not a defence where that belief was attributable to his voluntarily being drunk.

33. That principle is now found in the Criminal Justice and Immigration Act 2008 section 76, whenever an issue arises as to whether a defendant can rely on self defence.

34. Second, in any event I am satisfied that *Jaggard* could, and should, be narrowly rather than widely construed. *Jaggard* turned on the construction of the specific defence in section 5 of the 1971 Act, as the passages I have quoted demonstrate.

35. Here, the onus is on the defendant to negate the natural inference that once the accident has occurred she will have been aware of it. It seems to me that there is no reason why the common law should be construed so as to allow her to pray in aid her own state of drunkenness as the reason for the mistake, and there is every reason of policy why it should not be extended in that way.

36. Accordingly, in my judgment, even if the court could properly find that the appellant was unaware of the accident because of her drunken state, she could not rely upon that as a defence. She would have been able to rely on it had she been sober, but not where she is voluntarily intoxicated. It follows that the answer to Question D is that a distinction is to be drawn between a sober and intoxicated driver in so far as the latter does not perceive that an accident has occurred because of her drunken state.

≈≈ **Questions**
(1) Do you think *Jaggard* remains good law in the light of *O'Connor* and *Hatton*? Should it be overturned?
(2) What is the difference between D who claims that his intoxication led him to make a mistake about whether his action would cause damage to property ('I did not think the stone I threw would get close to V's window') and D2 who claims his intoxication led him mistakenly to believe he had the consent of V to smash his window?

25.8 Reform of the law

The Law Commission published its latest recommendations in Report No 314, *Intoxication and Criminal Liability* (2009).

In relation to voluntary intoxication, the Law Commission recommended that a statutory form of the *Majewski* rule be enacted:

> There should be a general rule that
>
> (1) if D is charged with having committed an offence as a perpetrator;
> (2) the fault element of the offence is not an integral fault element (for example, because it merely requires proof of recklessness); and
> (3) D was voluntarily intoxicated at the material time;
>
> then, in determining whether or not D is liable for the offence, D should be treated as having been aware at the material time of anything which D would then have been aware of but for the intoxication. (para 3.35)

In addition, it proposed that:

> If the subjective fault element in the definition of the offence, as alleged, is one to which the justification for the *Majewski* rule cannot apply, then the prosecution should have to prove that D acted with that relevant state of mind. (para 3.42)

'Specific intent'-type offences are excluded from this rule:

> The following subjective fault elements should be excluded from the application of the general rule and should, therefore, always be proved:
>
> (1) intention as to a consequence;
> (2) knowledge as to something;
> (3) belief as to something (where the belief is equivalent to knowledge as to something);
> (4) fraud; and
> (5) dishonesty. (para 3.46)

> ### ≈ Questions
> (1) Does this replicate the *Majewski* rule as you understand it?
> (2) Would this clarify the law?

In relation to mistakes, the Law Commission recommended that:

> D should not be able to rely on a genuine mistake of fact arising from self-induced intoxication in support of a defence to which D's state of mind is relevant, regardless of the nature of the fault alleged. D's mistaken belief should be taken into account only if D would have held the same belief if D had not been intoxicated. (para 3.53)

But if the offence charged:

> requires proof of a fault element of failure to comply with an objective standard of care, or requires no fault at all, D should be permitted to rely on a genuine but mistaken belief as to the existence of a fact, where D's state of mind is relevant to a defence, only if D would have made that mistake if he or she had not been voluntarily intoxicated.

In relation to involuntary intoxication, the Law Commission proposed as a general rule that:

D's state of involuntary intoxication should be taken into consideration:

(1) in determining whether D acted with the subjective fault required for liability, regardless of the nature of the fault element; and

(2) in any case where D relies on a mistake of fact in support of a defence to which his or her state of mind is relevant. (para 3.121)

Significantly, the Commission sought to provide a non-exhaustive list of situations which would count as involuntary intoxication:

(1) the situation where an intoxicant was administered to D without D's consent;

(2) the situation where D took an intoxicant under duress;

(3) the situation where D took an intoxicant which he or she reasonably believed was not an intoxicant;

(4) the situation where D took an intoxicant for a proper medical purpose.

D's state of intoxication should also be regarded as involuntary if, though not entirely involuntary, it was *almost* entirely involuntary. (paras 3.125–3.126)

≋ **Question**
Would this clarify the law on involuntary intoxication?

FURTHER READING

T. Brooks, 'Involuntary Intoxication: A New Six-Step Procedure' (2015) 79 J Crim L 138

S. Gough, 'Surviving without *Majewski*' [2000] Crim LR 719

P. Handler, 'Intoxication and Criminal Responsibility in England, 1819–1920' (2013) 33 OJLS 243

J. Horder, 'Pleading Involuntary Lack of Capacity' (1993) 52 CLJ 298

A. C. E. Lynch, 'The Scope of Intoxication' [1982] Crim LR 139

G. Orchard, 'Surviving without *Majewski*' [1993] Crim LR 426

R. Smith and L. Clements, 'Involuntary Intoxication, the Threshold of Inhibition and the Instigation of Crime' (1995) 46 NILQ 210

26

Liability of corporations

> **Corporate liability:**
>
> The principal way in which corporations are held criminally liable in English law is by the identification doctrine: if, in the course of the corporation's business, an officer of sufficient seniority to control the corporation's affairs fulfils the actus reus and mens rea of an offence, a corporation will be liable for that officer's conduct.
>
> **Some of the controversies that will be examined in chapter include the variety of ways a corporation might be liable:**
>
> (1) personal liability of individuals within an organization;
>
> (2) vicarious liability;
>
> (3) corporate liability:
>
> - by breaching a statutory duty imposed on the organization;
> - by committing strict liability offences;
> - by being liable for the acts of individuals under the identification doctrine;
> - the specific statutory liability of organizations for homicide under the Corporate Manslaughter and Corporate Homicide Act 2007;
> - by failing to prevent a person associated with the company from committing an offence.
>
> (4) liability of unincorporated associations.

26.1 Introduction

This chapter deals with the potential criminal liability of organizations. The main focus is on corporations, which include public limited companies (plc) and private limited companies (Ltd) as well as limited liability partnerships (LLP). The criminal law has developed special rules and procedures to deal with the fact that corporations have a separate legal identity. They are treated in law as having a legal personality distinct from the natural persons—members, directors, employees, etc—who make up the corporation. That presents the opportunity, in theory, of imposing liability on the corporation separately from any criminal liability which might be imposed on the individual members for any wrongdoing.

26.2 Personal liability

Individuals who are directors, managers, employers, etc can be prosecuted for their personal wrongdoing just like any other human being. For example, the managing director of a film company who makes films which involve indecent images of children or extreme pornography (contrary to the Criminal Justice and Immigration Act 2008, s 63 as amended) will be at risk of personal prosecution. An employee salesperson who commits offences of driving carelessly while on company business, or frauds etc will be personally liable. The general principles of criminal liability which are described throughout this book will apply.

If a corporation is found criminally liable, an individual employee or director, etc can also be liable as a secondary party to the corporation's wrongdoing under s 8 of the Accessories and Abettors Act 1861 (see Chapter 19). Occasionally Parliament precludes such liability, as for example with the corporate manslaughter offence (see section 26.6). Sometimes a provision will create an offence that a corporation can be guilty of committing and simultaneously creates an additional form of liability for which an officer of the company can be liable. An example of such a provision is the Regulatory Reform (Fire Safety) Order 2005 which imposes liability on a director for conniving or being party to the company's neglect. It was confirmed in *Wilson* [2013] EWCA Crim 170 that provisions such as these are not discrete offences but forms of secondary liability.

Many statutes, particularly those dealing with regulatory offences, create offences that can be committed by the specified person (eg the employer) in person. If the specified person is in breach of that duty, he commits the actus reus of the offence and, if it imposes strict liability, he is personally guilty of the offence. A good example is the Health and Safety at Work etc Act 1974. By s 3(1) the Act imposes on every employer a duty 'to conduct his undertaking in such a way as to ensure, so far as is reasonably practicable' that persons not in his employment are not exposed to risk. In *British Steel plc* [1995] 1 WLR 1356, [1995] Crim LR 654, D's subcontractor, negligently conducting D's undertaking, caused V's death. D had not ensured as far as was, in the opinion of the court, reasonably practicable, that persons were not exposed to risk and D was therefore guilty. D was liable for his own failure to ensure that there was no risk of such a thing happening. This was a case of personal liability being imposed by the statute. D was not being held liable for the acts of the independent contractor who caused death but for the breach of his own personal duty to protect against the harm.

26.3 Vicarious liability

Vicarious liability is a mechanism commonly used in the civil law to impose liability on employers for the acts of their employees. Employers are generally liable for the tortious acts of their employees committed in the course of their employment. In tort law, this makes good sense because an employee will rarely have the means adequately to compensate a person he has caused to suffer a serious injury, so the loss will lie with the innocent victim unless the employer can be required to pay. As between the victim and the employer, it is thought right in tort that the employer should bear the loss, even though he may personally be blameless. The primary function of the criminal law, however, is not the compensation of the victim but the punishment of the wrongdoer—and the grounds for punishing the blameless employer are tenuous at best. The employee's wrongful act is sometimes a crime as well as a tort. It may be theft, fraud, assault or even manslaughter and the employee is of course liable to conviction of the crime. The employer, even though responsible for the act in the civil law and liable to pay compensation, is not criminally liable. Criminal liability is of a personal nature. That is the general rule and, with the exception of the anomalous offence of public nuisance, now the universal rule at common law; but in statutory offences there are exceptions, or apparent exceptions, to it. These tend to arise in areas of law regulating sales or licensing. It is easy to see how this might be useful where, for example, a major store has sold an 18-rated DVD to a child, *Tesco Stores Ltd v Brent London Borough Council* [1993] 2 All ER 718, [1993] Crim LR

624, DC, or a waiter in a restaurant (in breach of the licence) serves alcohol to someone who is not dining but merely on the premises, *Vane v Yiannopoullos* [1964] 3 All ER 820, HL. We do not discuss the forms of vicarious liability further here. See *Smith and Hogan's Criminal Law* (14th edn, 2015), p 310.

26.4 Liability of a corporation

A corporation is a legal person, for example a limited company, a person distinct from the persons who are members of it. The corporation, as distinct from its members, has no physical existence. It exists only in law. It cannot therefore act or form an intention except through its members. But a corporation can incur legal liabilities, both civil and criminal.

26.4.1 Crimes a corporation cannot commit

A corporation cannot commit a crime for which it cannot be sentenced. So it cannot commit murder, as a principal or an accessory, because the mandatory sentence is life imprisonment and a corporation is incapable of being imprisoned. Nearly all crimes can be punishable by a fine so this is not a serious limitation on the scope of criminal liability. There are other offences which it is extremely unlikely that an official of a corporation could commit within the scope of his business; for example, bigamy, rape, incest and perjury (cf *Re Odyssey (London) Ltd v OIC Run Off Ltd* (2000) The Times, 3 March, CA (Civ Div)).

The fact that a corporation cannot commit the offence as a principal does not mean, however, that it is incapable of committing it as an accessory. It is difficult to imagine a case in which a company could be held liable as a principal for dangerous driving but it may certainly be convicted as a secondary party: *Robert Millar (Contractors) Ltd* [1970] 1 All ER 577, [1970] 2 QB 54.

≈≈≈ ***Question***

The manager of ABC Dating Co, a marriage advisory bureau, arranged a marriage which he knew to be bigamous. Is the company guilty?

26.4.2 The liability of corporations for statutory offences

When Parliament creates an offence the statute usually provides that it is an offence for 'a person' to do or omit to do the act in question; and s 5 of the Interpretation Act 1978 provides: 'In any Act, unless the contrary intention appears, words and expressions listed in Schedule 1 to this Act are to be construed according to that Schedule.'

Schedule 1 provides: ' "Person" includes a body of persons corporate or unincorporate. [1889].'

By Sch 2, para 4(1)(a), the date, '[1889]', means that the definition of 'person' applies to Acts passed after 1889. Schedule 2, para 4(5) provides: 'The definition of "person", so far as it includes bodies corporate, applies to any provision of an Act whenever passed relating to an offence punishable on indictment or on summary conviction.'

The effect of these complex provisions is that, where it is a statutory offence for 'a person' to do or not do something, that offence may (unless the 'contrary intention' appears) be committed by a corporation, whatever the date of the statute, and be committed by an unincorporate body if the statute was passed after 1889. A contrary intention may appear because, for example, the actus reus is incapable of being committed by a corporation.

26.4.2.1 Breach of statutory duty

A corporation, as distinct from its employees or managers etc, can be criminally liable for offences laid down by Parliament as applying specifically to corporations. As a legal entity, a corporation may be placed under a duty by Parliament to comply with a particular regulation and the failure to do so may result in criminal liability.

26.4.2.2 Strict liability offences

Offences of strict liability can be committed by a corporation. Since there is no need for proof of mens rea, there is no difficulty in establishing any fault on the part of the corporation. Corporate liability for strict liability offences is in theory no different from strict liability imposed on human actors. No more need be said about this form of liability. It was considered in full in Chapter 6.

26.4.3 The identification doctrine?

In criminal law the corporation can be held to be *personally* liable because the acts in the course of the corporation's business of those officers who control its affairs (in the Draft Code called 'controlling officers'), and the intentions with which those acts are done, are deemed to be the acts and intentions of the corporation. This is so in respect of common law as well as statutory offences (a corporation may therefore be a party to a common law conspiracy and could commit manslaughter). A corporation is *not* criminally liable for the acts of its members or employees who are not controlling officers, unless it is an offence to which the rules of vicarious liability considered previously apply—for example, it is a case of selling in breach of a statutory provision. In the case of offences where the identification doctrine is relied on, the question is often whether the status of the individual perpetrator is that of a controlling officer.

In *H. L. Bolton (Engineering) Co Ltd v T. J. Graham & Sons Ltd* [1956] 3 All ER 624, [1957] 1 QB 159, Denning LJ likened a company to a human body: 'It has a brain and nerve centre which controls what it does. It also has hands which hold the tools and act in accordance with directions from the centre.'

Where a corporation is charged with an offence which can be committed only personally and not vicariously, a crucial question is whether the person who did the relevant acts was 'the directing mind and will of the company'. If he is, the company has done those acts. If he is not, there may be a question whether the company should nevertheless be held liable for them. In *Meridian Global Funds Management Asia Ltd v Securities Commission* [1995] 3 WLR 413, PC, the Board recognized that the liability of a company under the identification doctrine turns on the rules by which the corporation operates, its structure, the language of the offence, etc. Contrast was made between the two previous leading cases. Lord Hoffmann described them.

Tesco v Nattrass [1972] AC 153:

Tesco were prosecuted for displaying a notice that goods were being 'offered at a price less than that at which they were in fact being offered . . .'. Its supermarket in Northwich had advertised that it was selling certain packets of washing powder at the reduced price of 2s 11d [21p], but a customer who asked for one was told he would have to pay the normal price of 3s 11d [26p] . This happened because the shop manager had negligently failed to notice that he had run out of the specially marked low-price packets. Section 24(1) provided a defence for a shopowner who could prove that the commission of the offence was caused by 'another person' and that: 'He took all reasonable precautions and exercised all due diligence to avoid the commission of such an offence by himself or any person under his control.' The company was able to show that it owned hundreds of shops and that the board had instituted systems of supervision and training which amounted, on its part, to taking reasonable precautions and exercising all due diligence to avoid the commission of such offences in its shops. The question was: whose precautions counted as those of the company? If it was the board, then the defence was made out. If they had to include those of the manager, then it failed. The House of Lords held that the precautions taken by the board were sufficient for the purposes of section 24(1) to count as precautions taken by the company and that the manager's negligence was not attributable to the company. It did so by examining the purpose of section 24(1) in providing a defence to what would otherwise have been an absolute offence: it was intended to give effect to 'a policy of consumer protection which does have a rational and moral justification': per Lord Diplock, at pp194–195. This led to the conclusion that the acts and defaults of the manager were not intended to be attributed to the company. . . .

Re Supply of Ready Mixed Concrete (No 2) [1995] 1 AC 456:

A restrictive arrangement in breach of an undertaking by a company to the Restrictive Practices Court was made by executives of the company acting within the scope of their employment. The board knew nothing of the arrangement; it had in fact given instructions to the company's employees that they were not to make such arrangements. But the House of Lords held that for the purposes of deciding whether the company was in contempt, the act and state of mind of an employee who entered into an arrangement in the course of his employment should be attributed to the company. This attribution rule was derived from a construction of the undertaking against the background of the Restrictive Trade Practices Act 1976: such undertakings by corporations would be worth little if the company could avoid liability for what its employees had actually done on the ground that the board did not know about it.

In *Great Western Trains Co* (30 June 1999, unreported), Scott Baker J ruled that the only basis on which a corporation might be liable under the directing mind and will doctrine was by identifying some *one* person within the company whose gross negligence was that of the company itself. As no such person was identified, he directed a verdict of not guilty. The Attorney General referred the case to the Court of Appeal. In *Attorney-General's Reference (No 2 of 1999)* [2000] 2 Cr App R 207, the Court of Appeal agreed with the trial judge.

Unless an identified individual's conduct, . . . can be attributed to the company the company is not, in the present state of the common law, liable.

The identification doctrine has been relied upon to hold companies liable for criminal offences for a wide range of conduct but the doctrine has been subject to criticism. The Law Commission in its Consultation Paper No 195, *Criminal Liability in Regulatory Contexts* (2010), set out the weaknesses with the identification doctrine in the following terms (references omitted).

THE WEAKNESSES OF THE IDENTIFICATION DOCTRINE

Interpreting directing mind and will

5.81 First, it is important to note that directing mind and will is a phrase that has been interpreted in various ways. As Pinto and Evans have suggested, it, 'appears to be less a term of art than a matter of construction depending on the context and the meaning of the section under consideration'.

5.82 Further recognition of this uncertainty can be seen in the current editions of practitioner texts. For example, Blackstone's Criminal Practice states that:

> Precisely which employees or officers are identified with the company for these purposes is a matter of some debate . . . it seems that it will normally only be senior persons at or close to board level who will normally be identified with the company.

5.83 From an examination of the case law on the issue, it seems that the uncertainty over directing mind and will extends beyond merely differences of approach depending on context. *Nattrass* is often seen as the case which unequivocally applied the directing mind and will theory; yet even in that case three of their Lordships described the test in significantly different terms, capable of leading to different results if applied to a different set of facts than the one they faced.

Inappropriate method

5.84 Perhaps of greater concern regarding the identification doctrine is that, quite apart from the difficulties apparent in its application, it may simply be an inappropriate and ineffective method of establishing criminal liability of corporations. This wider concern may be particularly evident when the identification doctrine is applied in its strictest sense, in which case Smith & Hogan [12th edn, 2008, p 249] note that:

> Only the very senior managers will be likely to fit the description as the directing mind and will of the company. This illustrates one of the major shortcomings of the identification doctrine—that it fails to reflect the reality of the modern day large multinational corporation . . . it produces what many regard as an unsatisfactorily narrow scope for criminal liability.

5.85 This concern that the doctrine is inappropriate for modern corporations has been widely expressed, Professor Gobert has stated that the doctrine, 'fails to capture the complexity of the modern company' [*Rethinking Corporate Crime* (2003)]. By focusing on attributing the acts and state of minds of a limited range of senior people to the corporation, the identification doctrine fails to reflect the fact that, in modern corporations, a good deal of important policy or strategic decision-making may be de-centralised, or regional rather than national.

5.86 Further, Professor Clarkson notes that, 'the doctrine ignores the reality of modern corporate decision-making which is often the product of corporate policies and procedures rather than individual decisions'. This may be one of the reasons that the courts have in recent cases sought to avoid an application of the identification doctrine, undermining any status it might have had as a general principle. In that regard, one commentator, drawing on an analysis of recent cases, reaches the conclusion that 'courts are beginning to recognise the "corporateness" of corporate conduct, thus acknowledging the limitations inherent in the controlling officer, directing mind, conception of liability'. Similarly, another commentator sees the confusion apparent in the latest authorities as indicating that, 'a fundamental shift of direction has occurred'.

5.87 A related difficulty with the identification doctrine, as a method of establishing corporate liability, is that it necessarily involves applying the same test to corporations of very different sizes, from one-man-bands to multinational corporations. This may create unfairness, as between the two groups. It is more likely that in small companies Directors (or equivalent persons) will have a direct hand in the running of the business at the front line, and hence will have the knowledge required to impute their individual fault to the company itself because they embody the directing mind and will of the company. In a large or multinational corporation, Directors are much less likely to take such an active front line role, and the policies that they set for those at the front line to follow may intentionally give considerable decision-making latitude to employees further down the line.

5.88 Accordingly, large or multinational corporations with complex multi-level organisational structures will find it easier to deny that individuals who took decisions that led to the commission of fault-based offences had a truly directing mind and will. The result is the company itself avoids liability for what was, in fact, the devolved decision of an employee, even though that employee might have been quite a senior employee. Professor Gobert [*Rethinking Corporate Crime* (2003), p 63] recognised this weakness when he noted that:

> The identification doctrine propounds a test of corporate liability that works best in cases where it is needed least [small businesses] and works worst in cases where it is needed most [big business].

5.89 This situation can be contrasted with that generated in law by the extended vicarious liability approach adopted by the court in *Pioneer* [[1995] 1 AC 456, 475], where Lord Nolan noted that:

> Liability can only be escaped by completely effective preventative measures. How great a burden the devising of such measures will cast upon individual employers will depend upon the size and nature of a particular organisation.

Conclusion

5.90 It is clear from the examination of the main authorities dealing with the application of the identification doctrine that the law in this area suffers from considerable uncertainty. Professor Cartwright [*Consumer Protection and the Criminal Law* (2001), p 105] notes that 'it is troubling that we are left with a series of cases which do not provide a definite answer to important issues of corporate and vicarious liability'. Certainly, it would have been a considerable improvement if Parliament had stepped in long ago to define the nature and scope of the identification doctrine.

5.91 However, it is unlikely that having only one basis on which companies can be found criminally liable, however broadly stated, will prove to be workable or desirable across the board. Recent legislation in fact points in the opposite direction, namely in the direction of specially tailored solutions to fit different contexts in which crimes may come to be committed by, or on behalf of, companies.

The limitations of the identification doctrine were recognized more recently when the Government was considering how best to draft a new criminal offence that would criminalize care providers whose employees ill-treat or wilfully neglect residents in their care. The Government explicitly rejected reliance on the identification doctrine on the basis that it could prove difficult to determine who the directing mind and will of the organisation was and even more difficult to attribute mens rea to that person. Instead, the Government chose to rely upon and adapt the approach adopted in the Corporate Manslaughter and Corporate Homicide Act 2007, which is discussed in the next section. For further discussion, see K. Laird, 'Filling a Lacuna: The Care Worker and Care Provider Offences in the Criminal Justice and Courts Act 2015' (2016) 37 Statute L Rev 1.

26.5 Failure to prevent offences

There is an additional way a corporation may be held liable for a criminal offence, distinct from those analysed in the previous sections. Section 7 of the Bribery Act 2010 makes it an offence for a commercial organization to fail to have adequate procedures in place to prevent a person associated with it from committing bribery. Set out in full, s 7 provides:

7. Failure of commercial organisations to prevent bribery

(1) A relevant commercial organisation ('C') is guilty of an offence under this section if a person ('A') associated with C bribes another person intending—

   (a) to obtain or retain business for C, or

(b) to obtain or retain an advantage in the conduct of business for C.

(2) But it is a defence for C to prove that C had in place adequate procedures designed to prevent persons associated with C from undertaking such conduct.

(3) For the purposes of this section, A bribes another person if, and only if, A—

    (a) is, or would be, guilty of an offence under section 1 or 6 (whether or not A has been prosecuted for such an offence), or

    (b) would be guilty of such an offence if section 12(2)(c) and (4) were omitted.

(4) See section 8 for the meaning of a person associated with C and see section 9 for a duty on the Secretary of State to publish guidance.

(5) In this section—'partnership' means—

    (a) a partnership within the Partnership Act 1890, or

    (b) a limited partnership registered under the Limited Partnerships Act 1907,

or a firm or entity of a similar character formed under the law of a country or territory outside the United Kingdom,'relevant commercial organisation' means—

    (a) a body which is incorporated under the law of any part of the United Kingdom and which carries on a business (whether there or elsewhere),

    (b) any other body corporate (wherever incorporated) which carries on a business, or part of a business, in any part of the United Kingdom,

    (c) a partnership which is formed under the law of any part of the United Kingdom and which carries on a business (whether there or elsewhere), or

    (d) any other partnership (wherever formed) which carries on a business, or part of a business, in any part of the United Kingdom.

The Bribery Act 2010 was the result of work undertaken by the Law Commission (see Law Com Consultation Paper No 185, *Reforming Bribery* (2007) and Law Com Report No 313, *Reforming Bribery* (2008)). The first conviction for the s 7 offence was obtained in February 2016 against the Sweett Group plc.

G. R. Sullivan, 'The Bribery Act 2010: Part 1: An Overview'
[2011] Crim LR 87

Failure of Commercial Organisations to Prevent Bribery

Section 7 creates a broad and innovatory offence that can be committed by a commercial organisation that fails to prevent bribery carried out on its behalf. It should be noted at the outset that this is a crime of unrestrained extra-territorial jurisdiction, a matter returned to in the next section. The principal offender must be the commercial organisation. But unlike the offence of corporate manslaughter where liability is confined to the company (complicity on the part of individuals associated with the company's offence is closed off), the Bribery Act 2010 does not contain any provision insulating persons employed by or associated with the organisation from secondary liability derived from any primary liability on the part of the organisation for the failure of prevention offence. Under the Act, commercial organisations include but are not limited to companies and partnerships incorporated or registered under the law of any part of the United Kingdom. A company or partnership wherever incorporated or registered will be a commercial organisation within the purview of the Act if it carries on a business or part of a business in any part of the United Kingdom. A commercial organisation (C) will potentially commit the failure offence if a person (A) associated with C bribes another person to obtain or retain business for C or to obtain or retain a business advantage for C. The payment of the bribe must amount to an offence by A under s.1 or s.6 of the Bribery Act 2010. In deciding that question, the fact that A may lack a 'close connection' with the United Kingdom (a condition that otherwise must be met to give ss.1 and 6 extra-territorial effect) is to be disregarded.

An associated person is a person who 'performs services for or on behalf of C.' If A is an employee of C, it is to be presumed until the contrary is proved that A performs services on behalf of C. In other cases the prosecution must prove that A is a service provider for C. That question must be resolved 'disregarding any bribe under consideration.' So if the only evidence of service provision on the part of A are the bribes he is charged with paying for C, the case must fail. Bribes that are the basis of charges must be 'under consideration.' But what if the prosecution wish to introduce evidence of bribes that are not the subject of charges to establish A as a service provider for C? (Clearly as a matter of fact bribing on behalf of another is a service). However any bribe relevant to establishing the prosecution's case is presumably a bribe under consideration. And even if a different view were to be taken, to introduce evidence of bribes paid by A for C in addition to those bribes which are the subject of charges would be highly prejudicial and very likely inadmissible unless adduced to show a distinctive method or system for the paying of bribes. As a practical matter it would seem that the prosecution must have evidence that A does things for C in addition to paying bribes on its behalf. This seems an unnecessary restriction on the offence. It would have been better to allow proof of payment of a bribe by A made ostensibly on behalf of C to raise an inference that by that act alone C must be taken to be a service provider for A unless A can show that the bribe was not act done on its behalf.

If a failure of prevention offence is proved against C, liability can be avoided if C can prove that it had in place adequate procedures designed to prevent persons associated with C from undertaking such conduct. On the face this defence is based on an evaluation of the company's procedures. Any failure on the part of the procedures to improve the actual practices of the organisation would not as such entail the failure of the defence. Indeed the defence comes into play on proof that a bribe has been paid on behalf of the company to gain or retain business. But in forensic contexts one would anticipate a thorough testing of the adequacy of the organisation's procedures against what can be proved about the company's practices.

≋ **Question**

Should the failure to prevent model be expanded beyond bribery to include, for example, fraud?

See also the recent expansion in the Criminal Finances Act 2017 to a case where an organisation can be liable for the conduct of its associate in providing tax evasion advice to X. The organisation will be liable for the failure to prevent, even though (unlike s 7 Bribery Act), the tax evasion is not carried out on behalf of the organisation. The model is extended significantly.

26.6 Corporate manslaughter

Various disasters each with large loss of life—in particular the *Herald of Free Enterprise* ferry disaster (*P & O European Ferries (Dover) Ltd* (1990) 93 Cr App R 72), and various rail crashes (Southall, Ladbroke Grove, Paddington, Hatfield)—all reinforced the public desire for legislation fixing the corporation with liability.

The Law Commission Report No 237, *Legislation the Criminal Code: Involuntary Manslaughter* (1996) made recommendations for a corporate manslaughter offence. See H. Keating, 'The Law Commission Report on Involuntary Manslaughter: (1) The Restoration of a Serious Crime' [1998] Crim LR 535; A. McColgan, 'Heralding Corporate Liability' [1994] Crim LR 547. See also S. Field and N. Jorg, 'Corporate Liability and Manslaughter: Should We

Be Going Dutch?' [1991] Crim LR 156 and C. Wells, 'The Corporate Manslaughter Proposals: Pragmatism, Paradox and Peninsularity' [1996] Crim LR 545 at 553.

The Law Commission Report was followed by a Home Office Consultation Paper, *Reforming the Law on Involuntary Manslaughter: The Government's Proposals* (2000). After considerable delay a Bill appeared in 2005 as a commitment to a manifesto promise of the Labour Government. Following a Report of the Home Affairs and Work and Pensions Committees in 2005, the Government finally responded in March 2006 with another Bill which, after much controversy in Parliament, became the present Act.

26.6.1 The Corporate Manslaughter and Corporate Homicide Act 2007

The Act abolishes gross negligence manslaughter as far as it applies to corporations and other bodies to which the 2007 Act applies (s 20). An organization can, although this is much less likely, be convicted of unlawful act manslaughter in appropriate circumstances (eg where D is the manager of a company who encourages employee X to set fire to the company premises in an insurance scam which leads to the death of V on the premises). The corporation may also be liable as an accessory to the principal individual offender in other homicide offences such as causing death by dangerous driving.

26.6.1.1 The offence

The offence of corporate manslaughter is triable only on indictment (s 1(6)). The offence is defined in s 1.

> (1) An organisation to which this section applies is guilty of an offence if the way in which its activities are managed or organised—
>
>   (a) causes a person's death, and
>
>   (b) amounts to a gross breach of a relevant duty of care owed by the organisation to the deceased.
>
> . . .
>
> (3) An organisation is guilty of an offence under this section only if the way in which its activities are managed or organised by its senior management is a substantial element in the breach referred to in subsection (1).
>
> (4) For the purposes of this Act—
>
>   (a) 'relevant duty of care' has the meaning given by section 2, read with sections 3 to 7;
>
>   (b) a breach of a duty of care by an organisation is a 'gross' breach if the conduct alleged to amount to a breach of that duty falls far below what can reasonably be expected of the organisation in the circumstances;
>
>   (c) 'senior management', in relation to an organisation, means the persons who play significant roles in—
>
>   (i) the making of decisions about how the whole or a substantial part of its activities are to be managed or organised, or
>
>   (ii) the actual managing or organising of the whole or a substantial part of those activities.
>
> (5) The offence under this section is called—
>
>   (a) corporate manslaughter, in so far as it is an offence under the law of England and Wales or Northern Ireland; . . .
>
>   (6) An organisation that is guilty of corporate manslaughter or corporate homicide is liable on conviction on indictment to a fine.

The offence mirrors many of the core aspects of gross negligence manslaughter. The crucial difference is that 'rather than being contingent on the guilt of one or more individuals, liability for the new offence depends on a finding of gross negligence in the way in which the activities of the organisation are run'.

Determining whether liability arises under the Act is best approached by asking:

- Is the organization one to which the Act applies?
- Is a relevant duty owed to the victim?
- Was the breach of the duty by the organization as a result of the way the activities are managed or organized?
- Was a substantial element of the breach of the duty due to the way the senior management managed or organized activities?
- Was the breach of the duty a gross one?
- Was V's death caused by the breach of the duty?

26.6.1.2 Who can be liable?

The Act provides that individuals cannot be liable as a secondary party to an offence of corporate manslaughter (s 18(1)). Individuals within companies can, of course, still be prosecuted for manslaughter as principal offenders subject to what has been said previously.

The Act extends to 'organizations' rather than merely corporations. Section 1(2) defines the organizations to which the new offence applies:

> (2) The organisations to which this section applies are—
>   (a) a corporation;
>   (b) a department or other body listed in Schedule 1;
>   (c) a police force;
>   (d) a partnership, or a trade union or employers' association, that is an employer.

The list of organizations to which the offence applies can be further extended by secondary legislation, for example to further types of unincorporated association, subject to the affirmative resolution procedure (s 21). Schedule 1 lists the Government departments to which the offence applies.

By s 11:

> (1) An organisation that is a servant or agent of the Crown is not immune from prosecution under this Act for that reason.
> (2) For the purposes of this Act—
>   (a) a department or other body listed in Schedule 1, or
>   (b) a corporation that is a servant or agent of the Crown,
>   is to be treated as owing whatever duties of care it would owe if it were a corporation that was not a servant or agent of the Crown.

In the course of debates in the House of Lords it was emphasized how important the extension of the offence to public bodies is:

> there is no reason why the death of an individual in one situation should be considered less of a death, or less deserving of justice, merely because that situation was presided over by government officials

as opposed to privately employed foremen. Indeed, it is all the more of a tragedy and contravention of the natural principle of justice where the state itself acts with such gross negligence that the very lives of its own citizens are forfeit. (Hansard HL, 15 January 2007, col GC189 (Lord Hunt))

26.6.1.3 Is there a duty on the organization?

By s 2:

(1) A 'relevant duty of care', in relation to an organisation, means any of the following duties owed by it under the law of negligence—

  (a) a duty owed to its employees or to other persons working for the organisation or performing services for it;

  (b) a duty owed as occupier of premises;

  (c) a duty owed in connection with—

    (i) the supply by the organisation of goods or services (whether for consideration or not),

    (ii) the carrying on by the organisation of any construction or maintenance operations,

    (iii) the carrying on by the organisation of any other activity on a commercial basis, or

    (iv) the use or keeping by the organisation of any plant, vehicle or other thing;

  (d) a duty owed to a person who, by reason of being a person within subsection (2), is someone for whose safety the organisation is responsible.

[Subsection (2) lists the organizations referred to in (d) above, and is discussed in full below.]

(3) Subsection (1) is subject to sections 3 to 7.. . .

(7) In this section—

'construction or maintenance operations' means operations of any of the following descriptions—

  (a) construction, installation, alteration, extension, improvement, repair, maintenance, decoration, cleaning, demolition or dismantling of—

    (i) any building or structure,

    (ii) anything else that forms, or is to form, part of the land, or

    (iii) any plant, vehicle or other thing;

  (b) operations that form an integral part of, or are preparatory to, or are for rendering complete, any operations within paragraph (a);

The duties reflect the duties of care arising at common law. The duty is that owed in the common law of negligence or, where applicable, the statutory duty which has superseded the common law duty. This is made clear by s 2(4):

A reference in subsection (1) to a duty owed under the law of negligence includes a reference to a duty that would be owed under the law of negligence but for any statutory provision under which liability is imposed in place of liability under that law.

Some common law duties which have been superseded by statute are expressly incorporated within s 2(1) by s 2(7), for example the Occupiers' Liability Act 1957. Section 2(4) does not therefore apply to occupiers' liability since the statutory duty of care is already included as part of 'the law of negligence' by virtue of s 2(7) and thus can be a relevant duty of care under the Act. Section 2(4) is, however, applicable to preserve a (fault-based) duty of care for these purposes in cases where the law of negligence has been superseded by a statutory provision imposing strict liability. The Explanatory Notes give the example of the Carriage by Air Act 1961.

Who decides on the duty question?

Given the potential breadth of the categories of duty and examination of the common law which might be necessary to determine whether a duty does exist, it is reassuring to see that the question whether a duty of care is owed is a question of law. It is for the judge to decide: s 2(5). Moreover, 'the judge must make any findings of fact necessary to decide that question'. This latter provision about the judge finding facts is highly unusual.

The scope of the duty

(6) For the purposes of this Act there is to be disregarded—

(a) any rule of the common law that has the effect of preventing a duty of care from being owed by one person to another by reason of the fact that they are jointly engaged in unlawful conduct;

(b) any such rule that has the effect of preventing a duty of care from being owed to a person by reason of his acceptance of a risk of harm.

Section 2(6) makes it clear that the duty of care will not be excluded by *ex turpi causa* and *volenti* doctrines. This is potentially very important. The scope of liability at common law is restricted in practice by the operation of these doctrines. However, the reason that they are excluded as defences or limits on criminal liability in this context is easy enough to deduce.

The duty in relation to detained individuals

The most controversial category is that relating to duties arising from detention.

Section 2(2) contains the list of people for whom a duty is owed on the basis that they comprise those for whose safety the organization is responsible, as referred to in s 2(1)(d). It provides:

(2) A person is within this subsection if—

(a) he is detained at a custodial institution or in a custody area at a court, a police station or customs premises;

(aa) he is detained in service custody premises;

(b) he is detained at a removal centre or short–term holding facility;

(c) he is being transported in a vehicle, or being held in any premises, in pursuance of prison escort arrangements or immigration escort arrangements;

(d) he is living in secure accommodation in which he has been placed;

(e) he is a detained patient.

Lord Ramsbotham, former Chief Inspector of Prisons, was successful in the House of Lords in amending the Bill to include what is now s 2(1)(d). There was considerable Government opposition and the Bill almost lapsed. Several powerful speeches were made arguing for the extension of liability to cover deaths in custody. The final compromise was that commencement of s 2(1)(d) would require the further approval of both Houses of Parliament, by way of the affirmative resolution procedure. This approval was subsequently given and the provisions have been in force since 1 September 2011.

≈≈ **Questions**

(1) McKay, a prison governor, allows the state of his prison to fall into disrepair. Fletcher, an inmate, is killed when a brick falls on his head in the exercise yard. Godber is distraught at the loss of his cellmate. His mental condition is acknowledged by the prison doctor to be serious and there is concern that he may be suicidal. The prison warder, Mr Barraclough, fails to keep regular watch on Godber and he commits suicide in his cell. Does the prison authority have any criminal liability for these deaths?

(2) Would it make any difference if Mr McKay were unable to perform the repairs owing to budget cuts imposed on him by central government? See later, s 3 in section 26.6.5.1.

26.6.2 The breach of the duty by the organization must be as a result of the way the activities are managed or organized

The second element of the offence is designed to ensure that the focus is on the management failure. The old limitations of the identification doctrine are gone. This test is not linked to a particular level of management but considers how an activity was managed within the organization as a whole. It will now be possible to aggregate the shortcomings of a wide variety of individuals within the organization to prove a failure of management *by the organization*. The language is designed to reflect the concentration of things done consistently with the organization's culture and policies more generally.

≈≈ **Question**

What difficulties might there be in proving this?

26.6.2.1 Senior managers

Under s 1(3), the offence is committed by an organization *only* if:

the way in which its activities are managed and organised *by its senior management* is a substantial element in the breach referred to in subsection (1).

By s 1(4)(c) the senior managers are:

(c) 'senior management', in relation to an organisation, means the persons who play significant roles in—

(i) the making of decisions about how the whole or a substantial part of its activities are to be managed or organised, or

(ii) the actual managing or organising of the whole or a substantial part of those activities.

This extends beyond the narrow category of senior individuals who would be caught at common law by the identification doctrine being the directing mind and will.

≈≈ **Questions**

(1) Is the test too restrictive? Will companies seek to avoid this by nominating people in less senior positions to take responsibility for all health and safety policies?

(2) Is this a clearer test than that of the controlling officer in *Meridian*?

26.6.2.2 Senior managers were a substantial element in the breach

The senior managers' management and organization must be a 'substantial element' in the breach of duty leading to death. Two important consequences flow from this aspect of the offence. First, since the senior managers' involvement need only be a substantial element in the organization etc, the involvement and conduct of others—'non-senior managers' who are involved in the management and organization of activities—is also relevant. Secondly, when assessing the management failure the contribution of these individuals who are not senior management can be taken into account even if their involvement is 'substantial' provided it is not so great as to render the senior managers' involvement something less than substantial.

> ≈≈ *Questions*
> Can there be more than one substantial element causing a result? If so, will this not be a relatively easy element for the prosecution to establish?

26.6.3 A 'gross' breach of duty?

This element of the offence is clearly designed to echo the gross negligence manslaughter offence at common law. Section 1(4)(b) provides a more detailed explanation of the concept:

> (b) a breach of a duty of care by an organisation is a 'gross' breach if the conduct alleged to amount to a breach of that duty falls far below what can reasonably be expected of the organisation in the circumstances.

The language chosen is similar to that proposed by the Law Commission as a suitable form of words to replace gross negligence. The test retains a degree of circularity, although not to the extent of that in the common law offence of gross negligence manslaughter (see section 9.3.3, p 238).

26.6.3.1 Determining the grossness of the breach

The question is one for the jury. By s 8:

> (1) This section applies where—
>   (a) it is established that an organisation owed a relevant duty of care to a person, and
>   (b) it falls to the jury to decide whether there was a gross breach of that duty.
> (2) The jury must consider whether the evidence shows that the organisation failed to comply with any health and safety legislation that relates to the alleged breach, and if so—
>   (a) how serious that failure was;
>   (b) how much of a risk of death it posed.
> (3) The jury may also—
>   (a) consider the extent to which the evidence shows that there were attitudes, policies, systems or accepted practices within the organisation that were likely to have encouraged any such failure as is mentioned in subsection (2), or to have produced tolerance of it;
>   (b) have regard to any health and safety guidance that relates to the alleged breach.
> (4) This section does not prevent the jury from having regard to any other matters they consider relevant.

(5) In this section 'health and safety guidance' means any code, guidance, manual or similar publication that is concerned with health and safety matters and is made or issued (under a statutory provision or otherwise) by an authority responsible for the enforcement of any health and safety legislation.

Note that the jury 'must' consider these issues. Note also that the jury is obliged to consider whether the 'organization' complied, not just whether its senior management complied. Section 8(3) emphasizes that the jury may have reference to general organizational and systems failures. This section has been influenced, as has much of this Act, by the Australian legislation and academic comment in Australia. See B. Fisse and J. Braithwaite, *Corporations, Crime and Accountability* (1993). The inability to consider the corporation's policies under the old law was a source of common complaint. How the 'attitudes etc' are proved is a different matter. There is the potential for lengthy arguments and evidence comparing practices across the particular sector or industry. Imagine a prosecution of a rail company and the potential for it to adduce evidence of safety procedures and policies across the sector to demonstrate the quality of its own.

> ≈≈ *Questions*
> In the Zeebrugge case, should the jury have heard about the practices of other cross-channel ferry companies? Would that help to determine liability? Does it matter that the other companies also operated negligently?

26.6.4 Causing death

There must be a death of a person. Causation must be established in accordance with orthodox principles, see Chapter 3.

26.6.5 Excluded liability

The most important aspect of the legislation is not the scope of the relevant duty and of potential liability under s 1 and s 2, but rather what the Government excluded from the scope of liability under ss 3 to 7. The excluded categories of duty are considerable. The different categories and sub-categories of duty also make the interpretation of whether a duty is owed rather more complex.

26.6.5.1 Public policy

The broadest exclusion comes in s 3(1) and deals with decisions of public policy taken by public authorities.

Any duty of care owed by a public authority in respect of a decision as to matters of public policy (including in particular the allocation of public resources or the weighing of competing public interests) is not a 'relevant duty of care'.

> ≈≈ *Question*
> To what extent will the criminal courts be willing to engage in detailed evaluations of the common law on this issue?

Section 3(2) provides a less extensive exclusion in relation to things done 'in the exercise of an exclusively public function':

> (2) Any duty of care owed in respect of things done in the exercise of an exclusively public function is not a 'relevant duty of care' unless it falls within section 2(1)(a), (b) or (d).. . .
>
> (4) In this section—'exclusively public function' means a function that falls within the prerogative of the Crown or is, by its nature, exercisable only with authority conferred—
>
>   (a) by the exercise of that prerogative, or
>
>   (b) by or under a statutory provision;
>
> 'statutory function' means a function conferred by or under a statutory provision.

The duty of care owed as employer or occupier or custodian under s 2(1)(a), (b) or (d) still applies in these circumstances. This exclusion relates only to the public functions involved in s (2)(1)(c), such as the supply of goods or services, construction work or the use of vehicles, etc.

26.6.5.2 Military activities: s 4

Many of the activities performed by the armed forces will be excluded by virtue of s 3(2) (see the previous extract). Section 3(2) does not prevent liability arising as an employer or occupier. Section 4 goes further by providing a total exclusion for some active service-type activities.

26.6.5.3 The police: s 5

The exemptions provided for police activities are also complex. Two categories exist. Section 5(1) and (2) create a total exemption, that is, no relevant duty arises for some types of policing activity. In short, these are where there are operations in relation to terrorism or civil unrest.

In other circumstances, by s 5(3) a 'relevant duty of care' is owed where the organization is acting as employer, occupier or custodian (ie s 2(1)(a), (b) or (d)). This exemption will exclude circumstances where a member of the public has been killed in the pursuit of law enforcement activities.

26.6.5.4 Emergency services: s 6

In the law of tort, considerable difficulties have arisen in identifying the scope of the duty of care owed by the emergency and rescue services in the course of performing rescue activity. Section 6 puts beyond doubt that the corporate manslaughter offence does not apply generally to these agencies when responding to emergencies. The emergency services may still be liable for a death arising from their status as employer or occupier even where the death arises in the course of an emergency. The emergency services may also be liable for breaches of duties that do not relate to *the way in which* a body responds to an emergency. For example duties to maintain vehicles in a safe condition will be capable of engaging the offence. The exemption does not extend to medical treatment itself, or to decisions about this (other than decisions that establish the priority for treating patients). Matters relating to the organization and management of medical services will therefore be within the ambit of the offence (s 6(4)).

26.6.5.5 Child protection and probation: s 7

Section 7 applies in relation to the duty of care that a local authority or other public authority owes in respect of the exercise of its functions under Parts 4 and 5 of the Children Act 1989 and in relation to probation.

26.6.6 Penalty

An organization guilty of the offence is liable to an unlimited fine (s 1(6)). In *Cotswold Geotechnical Holdings Ltd* [2011] EWCA Crim 1337, the Court of Appeal upheld the imposition of a fine that had the effect of putting the defendant company into liquidation. Such a situation was 'unavoidable and inevitable'. In addition to a fine, the court has power on the application of the prosecution to impose a remedial order against an organization convicted of corporate manslaughter requiring it to take specified steps to remedy: the breach; any matter appearing to have resulted from it and to have been a cause of the death; or any health and safety deficiency in the 'organisation's policies, systems or practices' appearing to be indicated by the breach (s 9(1) and (2)). This provision is also heavily influenced by Australian experience.

Any such order must be on 'such terms (whether those proposed or others) as the court considers appropriate having regard to any representations made, and any evidence adduced, in relation to that matter by the prosecution or on behalf of the organisation' (s 9(2)).

Section 9(4) provides for the form of a remedial order. It must specify a period within which the remedial steps are to be taken and may require the organization to supply evidence of compliance. Periods specified may be extended or further extended by order of the court on an application made before the end of that period or extended period.

An organization which fails to comply with a remedial order commits an offence triable only on indictment and punishable with an unlimited fine (s 9(5)). There appears to be nothing to prevent the conviction of a director as an accessory to this offence.

≈≈ *Questions*

What basis should be used for determining the level of fine to be imposed? Annual profits? If a global corporation, say a petrochemical company, with a turnover of billions of pounds is fined say £100m for causing a number of deaths on one of its oil rigs, who will bear the cost? Is it worth imposing the fine on the company if it is to be borne by thousands of innocent motorists who pay the additional cost for fuel?

The Sentencing Council has published a definitive guideline on sentencing for corporate manslaughter and health and safety offences causing death. It applies to sentences imposed on or after 15 February 2010.

In addition, the court has power to impose a 'publicity order' under s 10 'requiring the organisation to publicise in a specified manner' its conviction, specified particulars, the amount of any fine and the terms of any remedial order. The Corporate Manslaughter and Corporate Homicide Act 2007 (Commencement No 2) Order 2010 (SI 2010/276) brought s 10 of the Act into force on 15 February 2010. Before imposing such an order, the court must ascertain the views of any relevant enforcement authority as it considers appropriate, and have regard to any representations made by the prosecution or the organization. Section 10(3) provides for the form of a remedial order. It must specify a period within which the publicity order must be complied with and may require the organization to supply evidence of compliance. An organization which fails to comply with an order commits an offence triable only on indictment and punishable with an unlimited fine (s 10(4)).

Section 10 was added to the Bill during its passage in the House of Lords. It is clearly predicated on the assumption (probably correct) that large organizations are more concerned about adverse publicity than a fine.

> ≈≈ *Question*
> What type of publicity order would be appropriate in a case such as the Zeebrugge ferry disaster if that had led to prosecutions under the 2007 Act?

26.6.7 Evaluating the effectiveness of the Corporate Manslaughter and Corporate Homicide Act 2007

The 2007 Act has been on the statute book for a decade, which makes this an opportune time to assess the effectiveness of the legislation. As the following extract demonstrates, not only has the substance of the legislation been subject to sustained criticism, so has its enforcement.

C. Wells, 'Corporate Criminal Liability: A Ten Year Review'
[2014] Crim LR 849 (references omitted)

Who are or what is 'senior management'?

The offence is only committed if the way senior management have managed or organised activities has played a substantial role in the breach of a relevant duty. This in turn means we need to know to whom or what 'senior management' refers. 'Senior management' means the persons who play '*significant roles*' in making decisions about, or in actually managing, the '*whole or a substantial part*' of the organisation's activities. It might appear that the more definitions we are given the better except that the adjectives 'significant' and 'substantial' leave much room for debate. What does 'substantial' mean? It is used both to define the extent to which senior management is involved in the breach and to define those within an organisation who might be regarded as 'senior' management. Often in criminal law the word 'substantial' has a broad meaning, something more than de minimis. In common usage it can mean something much more restrictive, more like 'a large part of'. In relation to its use to define those within an organisation who might be regarded as part of the *senior* management, it could well be interpreted as including only a narrow range of people whose responsibilities are central to the organisation's decision-making. The reasoning here is that 'substantial' supplements 'the whole', suggesting that it means something close to the whole if not the whole itself. And this still leaves the question of 'significant' role. Far from addressing the difficulties in capturing organisational fault, the CMCH Act slips between two grammatical uses of the word management. 'Management' can mean either 'the action or manner of managing', or the 'power of managing', or it could function as a collective noun for 'a governing body'. Again the Explanatory Notes do not shed much light: '... [senior management] covers both those in the direct chain of management as well as those in, for example, strategic or regulatory compliance roles'. The CPS also hedges its bets: senior management is 'likely to be limited to those whose involvement is influential and will not include those who simply carry out the activity' and recommends prosecutors to obtain an organogram to determine whether the breach is at senior management level.

> '... [the test] is wider than the former "controlling mind" which effectively restricted the offence to actions of directors. A regional manager would probably count but this may itself depend on the number of regions, the number of higher tiers of management, the diversity of the organisation's activities and his own job description.'

Field and Jones speculate on how this test might apply to police forces:

> '[Senior management] will undoubtedly include the chief constable, and the deputy or assistant chief constable. In addition, a police superintendent responsible for the management of a specific

police station would appear to fall within its remit. What is less clear is how far the definition will go—whether for example for the purposes of the CMCHA it will extend to custody officers.'

By requiring the 'substantial' involvement of 'senior management' and then defining this body as 'those persons who play significant roles' the Act gives the lie to the Government's claimed commitment to an organisational version of fault that is not dependent on the actions of specified individuals.

The gross breach

Suppose, then, that a death has occurred and that it can be said to have been caused by the way that the organisation's activities were managed or organised. In addition, it must be shown that there was *a gross* breach of a relevant duty. A departure from a standard of care is 'gross' if the 'conduct … falls far below what can reasonably be expected of the organisation in the circumstances'. This builds on the common law definition of gross negligence but avoids the circularity of saying that the *criminal* standard for negligence is met when the jury thinks the breach was *criminal*. The CMCH Act goes further, providing some factors for the jury to take into account. Again, these seem to complicate rather than clarify.

To begin with, the 'the jury must consider whether the evidence shows that the organisation failed to comply with any health and safety legislation that relates to the alleged breach …' and, if so, how serious the failure was and how much of a risk it posed. Section 8 continues that a jury *may* also consider the extent to which the evidence shows that there were 'attitudes, policies, systems or accepted practices within the organisation' that were likely to have encouraged, or produced tolerance of, the failure to comply with such legislation. They may also have regard to any health and safety guidance relating to the breach. These are effectively instructions to the trial judge. She must instruct the jury to take into account breaches of health and safety legislation. But how that is taken into account will be left to the mysteries of the jury room. She must instruct the jury that they may take into account company culture, and/or breaches of guidance. It is also explicitly stated that none of this prevents the jury from having regard to other matters they consider relevant. This is odd. In one sense, s.8 states the obvious for it must be reasonable to expect an organisation to have regard to health and safety legislation and guidance. The rest is not mandatory. And none of this actually helps the jury decide whether the failure is 'gross,' or falls 'far below' what can be reasonably expected. Furthermore, the wording has opened a Pandora's box inviting defendants to play off the CMCHA and the HSWA against each other (with their different burdens of proof) and to use plea bargaining to shift blame on to the company and away from individual directors. This is discussed further in the section entitled 'Enforcement policies and patterns' below.

The exemptions

The Act circumscribes when a public authority, as opposed to a commercial organisation, may be liable. Section 3(1) states that a 'duty of care owed by a public authority in respect of a decision as to matters of public policy (including in particular the allocation of public resources or the weighing of competing public interests) is not a "relevant duty of care"[']. An exclusively public function is one that either falls within the Crown prerogative or is 'by its nature, exercisable only with authority conferred by or under a statutory provision'. In other words, 'the *nature* of the activity involved must be one that requires a statutory or prerogative basis, for example licensing drugs or conducting international diplomacy'. It would not cover an activity 'simply because it was one that required a licence or took place on a statutory basis'. Merely because a function is carried out by a public body or free of charge to the public does not make it 'exclusively public'. Indeed, were the CMCH Act to be interpreted to mean anything else it would render almost nugatory any role in relation to public authorities acting in any capacity other than as employers or occupiers. Emergencies provide a further set of (complicated) exceptions that would be relevant in the health care context.

Territorial extent

Murder and common law manslaughter committed anywhere in the world by a British subject can be prosecuted in England or Ireland. But corporate manslaughter is confined to deaths (or the harm that led to the death) occurring in the United Kingdom. This is not only in stark contrast with the extra territorial application of the corporate bribery offence discussed in Pt II of this article, it also makes little sense when corporate activities are increasingly globalised. British companies used the Rana Plaza clothing factory which collapsed in 2013 killing more than 1,100 workers. Most of those companies have joined in a compensation fund—but should they not also be subject to UK corporate manslaughter jurisdiction?

Penalties

The CMCH Act provides for three types of penalty: a fine, a publicity order, and/or a remedial order. The maximum fine is unlimited as it is for offences under the HSW Act when sentenced in the Crown Court. Combined sentencing guidelines for corporate manslaughter *and* health and safety offences causing death were published in January 2010. The factors that courts should consider in assessing the financial consequences of a fine include: the effect on the employment of the innocent; the effect upon the provision of services to the public. Although the Guidelines suggest that the starting point should be £500,000, as discussed below, none of the concluded cases has yet reached or exceeded that figure.

A *publicity order* requires an organisation convicted of corporate manslaughter to advertise the fact of its conviction, specify particulars of the offence, the amount of any fine imposed, and the terms of any remedial order that has been made. The imposition of a publicity order on Princes Sporting Club at a point when it was no longer trading was, on the face of it, a little pointless other than as a warning to future corporate defendants. The purpose of the *remedial order* under which an organisation may be ordered to take steps to remedy the breach is unclear. This is another example of confusing the underlying aims of an offence of corporate manslaughter. Rather than minimising risk directly, which is the main function of health and safety regulation, the aim of this offence is to punish in a retributive sense. It may secondarily act as a general deterrent or encouragement to take safety compliance more seriously but the time lag between the event and the trial renders the idea of relevant remedial action impractical. A manslaughter trial would not, in any case, be the most effective forum in which to decide on appropriate remedial action. The penalty for failing to comply with any remedial order, a fine, would again only be enforceable against the organisation itself. The government has rejected the suggestion that company directors should be liable for failing to take the specified steps.

Enforcement policies and patterns

The CPS Guidance draws attention to many of the points of uncertainty in the CMCH Act. It also deals explicitly with the relationship between investigations and prosecutions for the offence and those under health and safety legislation which are prosecuted by the Health and Safety Executive. Any organisation which is an employer could be liable for HSWA offences as well as for manslaughter. The guidance refers to the existing protocol for liaison agreed between the CPS, the HSE, and other regulatory agencies under which each agency will investigate within its own area of operation (the police will conduct the investigation into any possible manslaughter, the HSE for health and safety breaches) but any prosecution arising should be managed jointly. The CMCH Act states that where an organisation is charged both under the CMCH Act and HSW Act, the jury may return a verdict on both charges. The guidance comments that:

> 'As a jury may take into account whether, and the extent to which, the organisation has breached health and safety, it is unlikely that the defence will plead guilty to HSWA unless the prosecution agrees not to pursue the corporate manslaughter charge.'

Instead, companies (via their directors) have chosen to plead guilty to corporate manslaughter to save directors from gross negligence or HSW charges.

On average there are 150 fatalities from accidents at work each year and 13,000 deaths from work related diseases. In the period 2008–2013 there were at least 104 prosecutions as a result of fatalities at work mostly for breaches under the Health and Safety at Work etc Act. The CPS opened 141 corporate manslaughter cases between 2009 and 2012. But there have been few trials and fewer convictions for corporate manslaughter.

The Table summarises the cases that have been or are about to be concluded. Some patterns have emerged, though with prosecutions running at about one a year, conclusions should be treated with caution:

- All have been small companies, which has left the 'senior management' test unchallenged. Many ceased trading before the case came to court.
- Thus far the fines have not reached the £500,000 starting point in the Sentencing Guidelines. Lion Steel was fined £487,000 despite being one of the larger companies to be prosecuted, with a turnover of £10 million per annum and gross profits of between £187,000 and £317,000. The judge considered it would be regrettable if the effect of an order of the court was to put any of the 142 jobs at risk and gave the company four years to pay. There was tougher talk, however, when Princes Sporting Club was fined the totality of its remaining assets. The judge commented had the company been trading at the time, he would have imposed a fine which would have put it out of business.
- There has been a clear trade off between guilty pleas for the CMCH charge and dropping those against individual directors (whether for manslaughter or health and safety offences). Lion Steel, for example, was originally charged with corporate manslaughter but at the preliminary hearing that charge was severed from gross negligence manslaughter and HSWA charges against three of its directors. During the trial of the directors, the judge ruled that there was insufficient evidence on which the jury could convict two of the directors of gross negligence manslaughter and one of those two directors of the s.37 Health and Safety at Work Act charge. Only the director charged with manslaughter faced a custodial sentence if convicted (the case predated the Health and Safety (Offences) Act 2008 which introduced the possibility of a custodial penalty). The negotiations that followed resulted in agreement that Lion Steel would enter a plea to corporate manslaughter with all remaining charges against the individual directors being withdrawn.
- Where employers have been charged under the HSW Act the sentences have been relatively low or they have been given time to pay. The most stringent individual sentence was in Mobile Roadsweepers. This may be a sign that prosecutors recognise the danger that the CMCH Act will be a shield behind which negligent directors can hide.
- Of the few cases which have gone to trial, juries have acquitted in two (PS and JE Ward, and MNS Mining). In the latter case, this may indicate jury sympathy for the mine manager who was tried for common law manslaughter at the same time. The case against both hinged on whether the manager had inspected the coal face earlier. The prosecution did not convince the jury that he had not.
- Prosecution policies seem to be varied. So for example there appear to have been no health and safety charges in MNS Mining.

These first prosecutions underline the limitations of the CMCH Act. The number of convictions is low, and as most concerned very small firms, might well have been successfully convicted under the common law had the deaths occurred pre-2008. The plethora of potential charges arising from the same fatality (CMCHA, individual common law manslaughter, HSWA corporate or individual charges) allows plea bargains. On the plus side, the very fact of the corporate manslaughter investigation often serves to put the case in to the headlines. With hefty fines for health and safety offences in some of these cases and with reporting often confusing corporate and director liability, it can be concluded that the Act has achieved some of its purpose, as one mechanism for flagging some of the worst examples of poor workplace safety practices. The Belfast Recorder summed up the case against JMW Farms, incidentally a company with pig farms/factories throughout Ireland, following the death of an employee when an unsecured metal bin fell on him from a forklift truck: 'Yet again, the court is faced with an incident where common sense would have shown that a simple, reasonable and effective solution would have been available to prevent this tragedy …'.

~~~ *Question*

Do you think the 2007 Act has been a success?

26.7 Unincorporated associations

Criminal liability of unincorporated associations involves quite separate principles from those relating to corporations. Subject to important exceptions, unincorporated associations are not regarded as having legal personality. There are numerous statutory offences which are expressly applicable to associations. In relation to all other statutes creating criminal offences (since 1889), the question whether the unincorporated association is subject to prosecution turns on s 5 of and Sch 1 to the Interpretation Act 1978: 'In any Act, unless the contrary intention appears, . . . "Person" includes a body of persons corporate or unincorporate.'

In *L* [2008] EWCA Crim 1970, the chairman and treasurer of a golf club with 900 members were prosecuted for polluting a watercourse by an escape of heating oil from the premises caused directly by an independent contractor. The question arose as to whether it was correct to prosecute the individuals rather than the association. The trial judge ruled that the club should itself have been charged. The prosecution conceded that this would have been a better approach. The Court of Appeal disagreed.

Hughes LJ explained that in determining whether 'person' includes a body of persons corporate or unincorporate or whether 'a contrary intention appears', there is no form of words applied universally:

there is no doubt that several statutes do make specific provision for the criminal liability of unincorporated associations. However, on inspection, these provisions vary so greatly that there is no settled policy which can be discerned from them, and we find it impossible to draw from them any general proposition that there is a form of enactment which is to be expected if an unincorporated association is to be criminally liable, and of which the absence signals a contrary intention for the purposes of section 5 of the Interpretation Act. (at [22])

Different considerations apply in mens rea offences and those at common law. Where individual members of an unincorporated association are prosecuted, it is not on the basis of some form of vicarious liability.

Vicarious liability, when it exists, arises out of the employment by the defendant of another person to act for him. There is no sense in which the chairman, treasurer, or any other member of this club employed the club to do anything for them. The criminal liability of the members of the club, including the chairman and the treasurer, is primary liability, not vicarious liability. (at [34])

> ≋ **Questions**
> Which of the 900 golf club members could be prosecuted for the leakage from the oil pipe caused directly by the act of the independent contractor? Those who hired him? The committee? All members? The richest, that is, those most likely to be able to pay the fine?

26.8 Why convict corporations at all?

What is the purpose of imposing criminal liability upon a corporation? It is a creature of the law with no physical existence. It cannot suffer imprisonment or any kind of physical punishment. It can be fined but the fine does not have the effects it does upon a human being. The corporation cannot go cold or hungry or feel the loss of the luxuries of life. It cannot feel shame, remorse or repentance. It is as devoid of moral as of physical sensations. Of course, its officers can suffer like other persons, but the penalties of the criminal law can be imposed on them without making the corporation liable. The imposition of a fine may affect a company's shareholders by reducing their dividends, but in the case of large companies this is likely to be imperceptible, except in the case of a quite exceptionally large fine. (See for a full discussion of fines: M. Jefferson, 'Corporate Criminal Liability: The Problem of Sanctions' (2001) 65 J Crim L 235.) In any case, the shareholders rarely have any effective control over the day-to-day operation of the company's business and so, morally, may well be thought to have no responsibility for the company's transgressions. Moreover, many corporations do not have shareholders. A heavy fine on the University of Poppleton could adversely affect only the staff and students and the research and other activities of the university.

On the other hand, it is clear that the officers of corporations do care about a criminal conviction of the corporation. It is something they are anxious to avoid. Sometimes directors go to expensive efforts to get the company's conviction quashed. Obviously, directors are worried not about the trivial amount of the fine, but about the effect of the conviction on the standing and reputation of the company. The conviction of the company has an effect on the public mind that the conviction of individual officers does not. If directors are so very concerned about the effect of a conviction, is it not likely that they will make strenuous efforts to avoid contravention of the criminal law? And if they do, has not the law achieved its purpose? Do we need to look for any further justification?

But there is another aspect. The victims of corporate wrongdoing may have a powerful urge to punish the corporation. Press reports suggest that the indignation of many of those bereaved by the Zeebrugge ferry disaster was directed not so much at individual officers as at the shipping company itself. It is perhaps significant that the corporation was prosecuted not merely for regulatory offences but for the common law crime of manslaughter, punishable in the case of a human being with life imprisonment. When the prosecution of the company failed, the prosecution of individual officers was discontinued—though the grounds for dismissal of the charge against the company did not necessarily remove the basis of the case against some of the officers. Similar reactions against corporations have been observed in other disasters, such as the Southall rail crash. Although Great Western Trains was fined as much for its offence under the Health and Safety at Work etc Act as it would have been on conviction for manslaughter, public disquiet at its acquittal of homicide was unabated. The satisfaction of the demand for retribution by those injured by crime has long been recognized as a proper ground for the imposition of punishment.

~~~ *Questions*

(1) Is it a sufficient ground for the imposition of criminal liability on a corporation that strong public feeling demands that corporate wrongdoing should be publicly condemned by the courts? If that feeling exists, does it matter whether it is rational or irrational?

(2) To what extent is our decision whether to criminalize corporate wrongs conditioned by how that can be done within the existing legal framework?

J. Gobert, 'A Corporate Criminality: New Crimes for the Times'
[1994] Crim LR 722

The subject of corporate criminality is ripe for systematic review by Parliament. Liability should not depend upon the identification of those persons responsible for the crime in question, a task which is difficult at best; let alone on the determination of the perpetrators' status within the company, as required under *Nattrass*. Instead, a model of 'corporate fault' should be adopted [J. Gobert, 'Corporate Criminality: Four Models of Fault' (1994) 14 LS 393]. A company should be criminally liable where a crime is authorised, permitted or tolerated as a matter of company policy or de facto practice. In this situation liability should be for the substantive offence which has occurred.

The difficulty with formulating liability in these terms is one of proof. A prosecutor may search in vain for a company policy which authorises, permits, or tolerates criminal behaviour. Far more likely to be found is a pro forma resolution which prohibits crimes by company personnel or which exhorts employees to conduct themselves in accord with the highest ethical standards. To pierce this different type of corporate veil, another form of criminal liability is needed. The focus would be on the creation of risks likely to lead to the occurrence of serious harm. If the harm in fact materialised, the company's liability would be for the failure to prevent the harm rather than for the substantive crime itself. Penalties would not necessarily be identical to those for the substantive offence, although some overlap might be desirable to cover cases where it was both foreseeable and virtually inevitable that the corporate failure would lead to the actual harm which occurred.

. . . The crux of the liability proposed in this article . . . is a failing on the company's part, but it is that failing in and of itself which would constitute the offence. That the risk created did not eventuate would not necessarily be fatal to a prosecution, although it might be of evidentiary significance as to whether there actually was a danger. The proposed liability is predicated on an implied duty on the part of a company to prevent crime. From where might such a duty arise? The state allows companies to carry on a business for profit under the protective umbrella of its laws. Its courts provide relief from the unfair practices of competitors, and a mechanism for securing debts owed to the company. In exchange for being able to operate within this legal structure, created and enforced by the state, comes a corresponding duty not to conduct its business in a way which exposes innocent individuals to the dangers of harms proscribed by that same state's criminal laws [L. Leigh, 'The Criminal Liability of Corporations and Other Groups' (1977) 9 Ottawa L Rev 247 at 287].

Furthermore, a company is free to choose the business which it enters into, and the methods by which it conducts that business. From these choices it derives its profit. Often the nature of a company's activities engenders risks to the public. A company that creates a situation of danger, or places an employee in a better position to perpetrate a crime than he or she would otherwise have been in, has an obligation to take steps to prevent criminal harm from occurring. What this means in practical terms is that companies have a duty to promulgate and adopt policies directed towards the prevention of crime and, more intangibly but no less importantly, to establish a corporate ethos which gives appropriate place to protecting the public from crimes which might occur in the course of the company's business.

As for mens rea in the corporate context, this construct may confound rather than promote reasoned analysis. Again it may prove helpful to return to basics, and ask what function mens rea is designed to serve. In instrumental terms mens rea provides a useful tool for identifying defendants who have acted in a blameworthy manner and for assessing the degree of their culpability. Without a concept of mens rea, it might be argued, companies that have done their best to prevent harm might be convicted of crime. Not so. Mens rea is one way, but not the only way, of getting at the issue of blameworthiness.

An alternative, arguably more apropos in the corporate context, is to ask whether the company could have taken steps to identify and avoid the occurrence of harm, whether it was reasonable for it to do so, and whether it in fact did so. In other words, instead of requiring the Crown to prove mens rea, it should be a defence for the company to prove due diligence. Such a defence is not unknown in English law. On occasion Parliament has incorporated it into a statute (Weights and Measures Act 1985, s. 34). What is envisaged here, however, is more broadly conceived, across-the-board defence which would protect a corporate defendant from liability where the company has made a conscientious and reasonable effort to prevent the substantive crime which has occurred (American Law Institute, Model Penal Code, s. 2.07(5). [See also Note, 'Developments in the Law—Corporate Crime: Regulating Corporate Behaviour Through Criminal Sanctions' (1979) 92 Harv L Rev 1127 at 1257–1259.]

As the company is in the best position to know what it has done to protect against the commission of a crime, the burden of establishing due diligence should be on it. The burden should not be simply that of presenting evidence in the first instance but should extend to convincing the trier of fact by a balance of probabilities that it acted with due diligence. More severe a burden would be too onerous, and any less a burden would put the Crown in the position of having to disprove due diligence when records and other relevant evidence lay buried within a mountain of files controlled by the defendant. The burden should not be subject to discharge by mere proof of an unawareness of the dangers on the part of management without also a showing that it was not reasonable to expect the company to have been aware of the risks [C. Wells, 'Corporations: Culture, Risk and Criminal Liability' [1993] Crim LR 551.] Nor should it be enough for the company to establish that its mode of operation conformed to that which was prevalent in the industry. Although compliance with an industry wide standard may be evidence of due diligence, the possibility must nonetheless be entertained that the entire industry has acted in a culpable manner.

How much must a company do in order to satisfy the demands of due diligence? No simple answer is possible or even desirable. The likelihood of harm and the extent of harm, should the risk which has been created eventuate, will need to be balanced against the social utility of the activity in question and the practicability and cost of eliminating risk. A company will have to demonstrate that it took reasonable and appropriate steps under the circumstances to prevent harm from occurring. . . .

At some point the question of corporate criminality becomes one of political will. There is an understandable legislative ambivalence about addressing corporate crime that is not present when the offender is an individual. The typical murder or theft has no social redeeming value, and there are few compunctions about imprisoning the perpetrator of such a crime. A company, on the other hand, often contributes to the public welfare through the products it manufactures. Through the taxes it pays and its employment of workers it promotes the economic well-being of the nation. It is not so obviously in the government's interest to jeopardise its own financial position by discouraging corporate activity that might border on the criminal. . . .

A fair yet firm approach to corporate crime is called for. Regulatory offences lack the muscle to provide a sufficient disincentive from activities which are profitable but which may entail the commission of criminal offences, and the *Nattrass* approach to conventional criminal law may simply encourage devolved decision-making as a means of avoiding liability. The role of corporate policy (or absence thereof) in the bringing about of the crime warrants close examination, and the Crown should not be satisfied with the scapegoat prosecutions of individuals. The law needs to be restructured so that companies that do not take seriously their responsibilities to society are sanctioned, and those which do are not inadvertently drawn into the net of the criminal law. Much more than it has to date, the law must grapple with the questions of when it can be said that a company has acted in a blameworthy manner and what consequences attach to a showing of such blameworthiness.

<hr>

≋ *Question*

To what extent does the 2007 Act allow the jury to take account of corporate attitudes and policies in determining guilt for manslaughter?

<hr>

There is a recent development in the law that makes corporate criminal liability procedurally distinct from the liability of individuals, namely deferred prosecution agreements. Deferred prosecution agreements were introduced by s 45 of the Crime and Courts Act 2013. A deferred prosecution agreement is an agreement between the prosecuting authority, for example the Serious Fraud Office, and a person, P, whom the agency is considering prosecuting for a specified offence. Under a deferred prosecution agreement (DPA), P agrees to comply with the requirements imposed upon P by the agreement. Upon approval by a court, the prosecuting agency prefers a bill of indictment against P but suspends the proceedings. The suspension cannot be lifted during the time when the deferred prosecution agreement is in force. The driving force behind the introduction of deferred prosecution agreements was the difficulty in achieving convictions for economic crime.

M. Bisgrove and M. Weekes, 'Deferred Prosecution Agreements: A Practical Consideration' [2014] Crim LR 416

Principles

Corporate economic crime is undoubtedly a serious problem, costing the taxpayer billions of pounds every year as well as causing harm to those directly and indirectly affected by it. It causes an unfair distortion of the market for businesses that act lawfully, and damages the global reputation and perception of the UK economy.

The foreword to the initial consultation on DPAs illustrates the driving force behind their introduction: the difficulty in achieving successful investigations and prosecutions of corporate offenders. This has long been a problem in the field of economic crime, and key areas of difficulty are well known to practitioners. It is worth repeating those concerns in order to assess whether DPAs as created by the Act will be successful in improving the detection and prosecution of economic crime.

Traditional methods of dealing with the problem by means of a criminal investigation and prosecution are generally slow and costly. The criminal law in relation to companies is a comparatively recent development. The impetus behind the early decisions holding that companies could be liable for misfeasance was one of pragmatism, not principle: criminal liability was the only effective deterrent. In *The Great North of England Railway Co* Denman C.J. stated:

> 'There can be no effective means of deterring from an oppressive exercise of power, for the purpose of gain, except the remedy by an indictment against those who truly commit it, that is, the corporation acting by its majority.'

The trend throughout the 19th and 20th century has been to attempt to fit corporate liability into the existing criminal justice structure. This is not always straightforward, not least because of the cumbersome nature of the 'guiding mind' principle, which can cause enormous difficulties in prosecuting large corporations. The introduction of DPAs can therefore be seen as a further pragmatic step to try to obviate some of the hurdles in regulating the behaviour of corporate entities. Although an important aspect of corporate liability is the ability to hold companies accountable for their actions, influencing the culture of the company can be as important as punishing the wrongdoing. Where the object of a company is to make money, deterrence by way of financial punishment and reputational sanction may be particularly effective.

The detection of economic crime is also often difficult. Prosecuting agencies rely heavily on whistle-blowers, referrals by interested third parties, and on self-reporting. Self-reporting can be an unattractive option for a company. While, for example, the guidelines on the prosecution of bribery offences make clear that the fact that an offence is self-reported weighs against prosecution, it is equally clear that self-reporting is no guarantee of non-prosecution. In the event of reporting an offence with a view to entering a guilty plea, although significant credit would be given for the admission, the penalties are uncertain and the court have spoken strongly against any attempt between the Crown and Defence to agree an appropriate sentence. In his sentencing remarks in the prosecution of Innospec Ltd by the Serious Fraud Office in 2010, Thomas L.J. stated:

> '... it is for the Court ultimately to determine the sanction to be imposed for the criminal conduct, and agreement between prosecutors as to the division, even if it had been within the power of the Director of the SFO (which as I have explained it was not) cannot be in accordance with basic constitutional principles ...
>
> ... it is for the Court to decide on the sentence and to explain that to the public, as I have endeavoured to do, in a manner that is both open and transparent, as that is what justice requires.'

Likewise, attempts by prosecution and defence to limit the courts' role in dealing with the consequences of self-reported economic crime by means of charging only minor offences (and the promise to cease further investigations) in return for voluntary reparation in respect of the greater uncharged criminality have met with judicial disapproval. Bean J.'s sentencing remarks in *BAE Systems Plc (2010)* make for unattractive reading for any party considering such a step.

Unwillingness to offer to the prosecution evidence of wrongdoing not only impacts on the detection of corporate criminality, but also individual criminality. In many instances, where the prosecution of a body corporate may not be in the public interest or where the evidence of corporate criminality is insufficient, it may still be appropriate to charge individual directors or employees. Thus, any hesitation by a company as to whether or not to self-report harms the effective detection of the crimes of individuals.

From the point of view of the state, where a company self-reports and a decision is taken not to prosecute, the opportunities to recover the proceeds of any wrongdoing, to influence the governance of the company, or to compensate those affected are limited. Even when a prosecution is successful, it can often take many years from the start of the investigation to the conclusion of such proceedings. Investigating and then prosecuting a case which results in a late guilty plea has been estimated to cost the Serious Fraud Office £1.6 million and take 8 years to conclude. This lengthy delay is undesirable, not only to the prosecution and to the defendant company, but also to those trying to do business with the defendant company. It has been suggested that the disclosure regime is the most important factor explaining the low number of cases prosecuted by the SFO. Rather than adopting a 'keys to the warehouse' approach and allowing the defendant company to go through the material to find those parts of it which assist its defence, the duty of examining the unused material falls on the prosecuting agency who must decide which parts of it are capable of assisting the defendant. Where the volumes of material seized are large, the review of that material takes up disproportionate resources. Any failings in disclosure can be exploited by defendants who may seek to exclude relevant evidence or to stay proceedings.

In summarising the difficulties faced by prosecuting agencies, the initial consultation paper concluded:

'The current system does not allow for swifter alternatives to prosecution which can deal with wrongdoing effectively, proportionately and with a greater degree of certainty. We need to look afresh at prosecutorial and other enforcement options for dealing with offending by commercial organisations.'

Alternatives to prosecution are not unknown to the criminal law. Fixed penalty notices are the clearest example. By payment of a financial penalty, it is possible to discharge the relevant criminal liability. Initially fixed penalty notices were introduced in respect of minor motoring offences. More recently, Penalty Notices for Disorder (PNDs) have been introduced to cover anti-social behaviour. The stated aim of such notices is to offer a quick and effective alternative for dealing with low level anti-social or nuisance offending. Similar concepts exist in respect of unpaid taxes, which can be settled by negotiation with HMRC or pursued through the tax tribunal without recourse to criminal investigation and prosecution.

The rationale, then, in creating a novel prosecutorial tool is to provide a more efficient and effective means of combating economic crime. Introduction of the alternatives is clearly not supposed to be a gold standard for prosecution but a compromise, allowing for effective punishment and regulation within a reasonable timeframe where, in their absence, there might be none.

It may be argued that DPAs are unfair in that they allow corporate defendants to avoid prosecution in exchange for payment—that there are different rules for different types of defendants. However, companies are by their nature very different from natural persons and it is only to be expected that different considerations arise. The company itself has no mind and no morals—those are provided by individuals who control it. The individuals can change while the company itself stays the same. So when considering, for example, the public interest in pursuing a prosecution, it would be wrong to ignore the fundamental circumstances of whether the defendant is an individual or a company.

While they are a novel device, the concept of a DPA and the pragmatic approach to combating economic crime is not such a radical step as it may at first seem. Such a tool may, in time, not only encourage cooperation by defendant companies, but may be used to encourage and enforce changes in corporate culture.

At the time of writing there have been three DPA agreements approved by the courts. Two of those have involved the corporate body self reporting its offence.

≈ Question
Are deferred prosecution agreements unfair because they allow corporate defendants to avoid prosecution in exchange for payment?

FURTHER READING

Corporate liability
D. Bergman, *The Case for Corporate Responsibility* (2000)

N. Cavanagh, 'Corporate Criminal Liability: An Assessment of the Models of Fault' (2011) 75 J Crim L 414

C. Clarkson, 'Kicking Corporate Bodies and Damning their Souls' (1996) 59 MLR 557

J. Gobert, 'Corporate Criminality: Four Models of Fault' (1994) 14 LS 393

J. Gobert and M. Punch, *Rethinking Corporate Crime* (2003)

R. Grantham, 'Corporate Knowledge: Identification or Attribution?' (1996) 59 MLR 732

L. Price, 'Finding Fault in Organisations—Reconceptualising the Role of Senior Managers in Corporate Manslaughter' (2015) 35 LS 385

G. R. Sullivan, 'Expressing Corporate Guilt' (1995) 15 OJLS 281

C. Wells, *Corporations and Criminal Responsibility* (2nd edn, 2001)

Corporate manslaughter

S. Field and L. Jones, 'Five Years On: The Impact of the Corporate Manslaughter and Corporate Homicide Act 2007: Plus ça change?' [2013] ICCLR 239

P. R. Glazebrook, 'A Better Way of Convicting Businesses of Avoidable Deaths and Injuries' (2002) 61 CLJ 405

J. Gobert, 'Corporate Killing at Home and Abroad: Reflections on the Government Proposals' (2002) 118 LQR 72

J. Horder, 'Corporate Manslaughter and Public Authorities' in *Homicide and the Politics of Law Reform* (2012)

H. Keating, 'The Law Commission Report on Involuntary Manslaughter: (1) The Restoration of a Serious Crime' [1998] Crim LR 535

D. Ormerod and R. Taylor, 'The Corporate Manslaughter and Corporate Homicide Act 2007' [2008] Crim LR 589

Index